T0180728

Lecture Notes in Computer Science 12426

More information about this series at http://www.springer.com/series/7409

Constantine Stephanidis ·
Margherita Antona · Qin Gao ·
Jia Zhou (Eds.)

HCI International 2020 – Late Breaking Papers

Universal Access and Inclusive Design

22nd HCI International Conference, HCII 2020
Copenhagen, Denmark, July 19–24, 2020
Proceedings

Editors
Constantine Stephanidis
University of Crete and Foundation for Research and Technology – Hellas (FORTH)
Heraklion, Crete, Greece

Margherita Antona
Foundation for Research and Technology – Hellas (FORTH)
Heraklion, Crete, Greece

Qin Gao
Tsinghua University
Beijing, China

Jia Zhou
Chongqing University
Chongqing, China

ISSN 0302-9743 ISSN 1611-3349 (electronic)
Lecture Notes in Computer Science
ISBN 978-3-030-60148-5 ISBN 978-3-030-60149-2 (eBook)
https://doi.org/10.1007/978-3-030-60149-2

LNCS Sublibrary: SL3 – Information Systems and Applications, incl. Internet/Web, and HCI

This Springer imprint is published by the registered company Springer Nature Switzerland AG
The registered company address is: Gewerbestrasse 11, 6330 Cham, Switzerland

Foreword

The 22nd International Conference on Human-Computer Interaction, HCI International 2020 (HCII 2020), was planned to be held at the AC Bella Sky Hotel and Bella Center, Copenhagen, Denmark, during July 19–24, 2020. Due to the COVID-19 pandemic and the resolution of the Danish government not to allow events larger than 500 people to be hosted until September 1, 2020, HCII 2020 had to be held virtually. It incorporated the 21 thematic areas and affiliated conferences listed on the following page.

A total of 6,326 individuals from academia, research institutes, industry, and governmental agencies from 97 countries submitted contributions, and 1,439 papers and 238 posters were included in the volumes of the proceedings published before the conference. Additionally, 333 papers and 144 posters are included in the volumes of the proceedings published after the conference, as "Late Breaking Work" (papers and posters). These contributions address the latest research and development efforts in the field and highlight the human aspects of design and use of computing systems.

The volumes comprising the full set of the HCII 2020 conference proceedings are listed in the following pages and together they broadly cover the entire field of human-computer interaction, addressing major advances in knowledge and effective use of computers in a variety of application areas.

I would like to thank the Program Board Chairs and the members of the Program Boards of all Thematic Areas and Affiliated Conferences for their valuable contributions towards the highest scientific quality and the overall success of the HCI International 2020 conference.

This conference would not have been possible without the continuous and unwavering support and advice of the founder, conference general chair emeritus and conference scientific advisor, Prof. Gavriel Salvendy. For his outstanding efforts, I would like to express my appreciation to the communications chair and editor of HCI International News, Dr. Abbas Moallem.

July 2020 Constantine Stephanidis

HCI International 2020 Thematic Areas and Affiliated Conferences

Thematic Areas:

- HCI 2020: Human-Computer Interaction
- HIMI 2020: Human Interface and the Management of Information

Affiliated Conferences:

- EPCE: 17th International Conference on Engineering Psychology and Cognitive Ergonomics
- UAHCI: 14th International Conference on Universal Access in Human-Computer Interaction
- VAMR: 12th International Conference on Virtual, Augmented and Mixed Reality
- CCD: 12th International Conference on Cross-Cultural Design
- SCSM: 12th International Conference on Social Computing and Social Media
- AC: 14th International Conference on Augmented Cognition
- DHM: 11th International Conference on Digital Human Modeling & Applications in Health, Safety, Ergonomics & Risk Management
- DUXU: 9th International Conference on Design, User Experience and Usability
- DAPI: 8th International Conference on Distributed, Ambient and Pervasive Interactions
- HCIBGO: 7th International Conference on HCI in Business, Government and Organizations
- LCT: 7th International Conference on Learning and Collaboration Technologies
- ITAP: 6th International Conference on Human Aspects of IT for the Aged Population
- HCI-CPT: Second International Conference on HCI for Cybersecurity, Privacy and Trust
- HCI-Games: Second International Conference on HCI in Games
- MobiTAS: Second International Conference on HCI in Mobility, Transport and Automotive Systems
- AIS: Second International Conference on Adaptive Instructional Systems
- C&C: 8th International Conference on Culture and Computing
- MOBILE: First International Conference on Design, Operation and Evaluation of Mobile Communications
- AI-HCI: First International Conference on Artificial Intelligence in HCI

Conference Proceedings – Full List of Volumes

1. LNCS 12181, Human-Computer Interaction: Design and User Experience (Part I), edited by Masaaki Kurosu
2. LNCS 12182, Human-Computer Interaction: Multimodal and Natural Interaction (Part II), edited by Masaaki Kurosu
3. LNCS 12183, Human-Computer Interaction: Human Values and Quality of Life (Part III), edited by Masaaki Kurosu
4. LNCS 12184, Human Interface and the Management of Information: Designing Information (Part I), edited by Sakae Yamamoto and Hirohiko Mori
5. LNCS 12185, Human Interface and the Management of Information: Interacting with Information (Part II), edited by Sakae Yamamoto and Hirohiko Mori
6. LNAI 12186, Engineering Psychology and Cognitive Ergonomics: Mental Workload, Human Physiology, and Human Energy (Part I), edited by Don Harris and Wen-Chin Li
7. LNAI 12187, Engineering Psychology and Cognitive Ergonomics: Cognition and Design (Part II), edited by Don Harris and Wen-Chin Li
8. LNCS 12188, Universal Access in Human-Computer Interaction: Design Approaches and Supporting Technologies (Part I), edited by Margherita Antona and Constantine Stephanidis
9. LNCS 12189, Universal Access in Human-Computer Interaction: Applications and Practice (Part II), edited by Margherita Antona and Constantine Stephanidis
10. LNCS 12190, Virtual, Augmented and Mixed Reality: Design and Interaction (Part I), edited by Jessie Y.C. Chen and Gino Fragomeni
11. LNCS 12191, Virtual, Augmented and Mixed Reality: Industrial and Everyday Life Applications (Part II), edited by Jessie Y.C. Chen and Gino Fragomeni
12. LNCS 12192, Cross-Cultural Design: User Experience of Products, Services, and Intelligent Environments (Part I), edited by P.L. Patrick Rau
13. LNCS 12193, Cross-Cultural Design: Applications in Health, Learning, Communication, and Creativity (Part II), edited by P.L. Patrick Rau
14. LNCS 12194, Social Computing and Social Media: Design, Ethics, User Behavior, and Social Network Analysis (Part I), edited by Gabriele Meiselwitz
15. LNCS 12195, Social Computing and Social Media: Participation, User Experience, Consumer Experience, and Applications of Social Computing (Part II), edited by Gabriele Meiselwitz
16. LNAI 12196, Augmented Cognition: Theoretical and Technological Approaches (Part I), edited by Dylan D. Schmorrow and Cali M. Fidopiastis
17. LNAI 12197, Augmented Cognition: Human Cognition and Behaviour (Part II), edited by Dylan D. Schmorrow and Cali M. Fidopiastis

18. LNCS 12198, Digital Human Modeling & Applications in Health, Safety, Ergonomics & Risk Management: Posture, Motion and Health (Part I), edited by Vincent G. Duffy
19. LNCS 12199, Digital Human Modeling & Applications in Health, Safety, Ergonomics & Risk Management: Human Communication, Organization and Work (Part II), edited by Vincent G. Duffy
20. LNCS 12200, Design, User Experience, and Usability: Interaction Design (Part I), edited by Aaron Marcus and Elizabeth Rosenzweig
21. LNCS 12201, Design, User Experience, and Usability: Design for Contemporary Interactive Environments (Part II), edited by Aaron Marcus and Elizabeth Rosenzweig
22. LNCS 12202, Design, User Experience, and Usability: Case Studies in Public and Personal Interactive Systems (Part III), edited by Aaron Marcus and Elizabeth Rosenzweig
23. LNCS 12203, Distributed, Ambient and Pervasive Interactions, edited by Norbert Streitz and Shin'ichi Konomi
24. LNCS 12204, HCI in Business, Government and Organizations, edited by Fiona Fui-Hoon Nah and Keng Siau
25. LNCS 12205, Learning and Collaboration Technologies: Designing, Developing and Deploying Learning Experiences (Part I), edited by Panayiotis Zaphiris and Andri Ioannou
26. LNCS 12206, Learning and Collaboration Technologies: Human and Technology Ecosystems (Part II), edited by Panayiotis Zaphiris and Andri Ioannou
27. LNCS 12207, Human Aspects of IT for the Aged Population: Technologies, Design and User experience (Part I), edited by Qin Gao and Jia Zhou
28. LNCS 12208, Human Aspects of IT for the Aged Population: Healthy and Active Aging (Part II), edited by Qin Gao and Jia Zhou
29. LNCS 12209, Human Aspects of IT for the Aged Population: Technology and Society (Part III), edited by Qin Gao and Jia Zhou
30. LNCS 12210, HCI for Cybersecurity Privacy and Trust, edited by Abbas Moallem
31. LNCS 12211, HCI in Games, edited by Xiaowen Fang
32. LNCS 12212, HCI in Mobility, Transport and Automotive Systems: Automated Driving and In-Vehicle Experience Design (Part I), edited by Heidi Krömker
33. LNCS 12213, HCI in Mobility, Transport and Automotive Systems: Driving Behavior, Urban and Smart Mobility (Part II), edited by Heidi Krömker
34. LNCS 12214, Adaptive Instructional Systems, edited by Robert A. Sottilare and Jessica Schwarz
35. LNCS 12215, Culture and Computing, edited by Matthias Rauterberg
36. LNCS 12216, Design, Operation and Evaluation of Mobile Communications, edited by Gavriel Salvendy and June Wei
37. LNCS 12217, Artificial Intelligence in HCI, edited by Helmut Degen and Lauren Reinerman-Jones
38. CCIS 1224, HCI International 2020 Posters (Part I), edited by Constantine Stephanidis and Margherita Antona
39. CCIS 1225, HCI International 2020 Posters (Part II), edited by Constantine Stephanidis and Margherita Antona

40. CCIS 1226, HCI International 2020 Posters (Part III), edited by Constantine Stephanidis and Margherita Antona
41. LNCS 12423, HCI International 2020 – Late Breaking Papers: User Experience Design and Case Studies, edited by Constantine Stephanidis, Aaron Marcus, Elizabeth Rosenzweig, P.L. Patrick Rau, Abbas Moallem, and Matthias Rauterberg
42. LNCS 12424, HCI International 2020 – Late Breaking Papers: Multimodality and Intelligence, edited by Constantine Stephanidis, Masaaki Kurosu, Helmut Degen, and Lauren Reinerman-Jones
43. LNCS 12425, HCI International 2020 – Late Breaking Papers: Cognition, Learning and Games, edited by Constantine Stephanidis, Don Harris, Wen-Chin Li, Dylan D. Schmorrow, Cali M. Fidopiastis, Panayiotis Zaphiris, Andri Ioannou, Xiaowen Fang, Robert Sottilare, and Jessica Schwarz
44. LNCS 12426, HCI International 2020 – Late Breaking Papers: Universal Access and Inclusive Design, edited by Constantine Stephanidis, Margherita Antona, Qin Gao, and Jia Zhou
45. LNCS 12427, HCI International 2020 – Late Breaking Papers: Interaction, Knowledge and Social Media, edited by Constantine Stephanidis, Sakae Yamamoto, Hirohiko Mori, Gabriele Meiselwitz, Fiona Fui-Hoon Nah, and Keng Siau
46. LNCS 12428, HCI International 2020 – Late Breaking Papers: Virtual and Augmented Reality, edited by Constantine Stephanidis, Jessie Y.C. Chen, and Gino Fragomeni
47. LNCS 12429, HCI International 2020 – Late Breaking Papers: Digital Human Modeling and Ergonomics, Mobility and Intelligent Environments, edited by Constantine Stephanidis, Vincent G. Duffy, Norbert Streitz, Shin'ichi Konomi, and Heidi Krömker
48. CCIS 1293, HCI International 2020 – Late Breaking Posters (Part I), edited by Constantine Stephanidis, Margherita Antona, and Stavroula Ntoa
49. CCIS 1294, HCI International 2020 – Late Breaking Posters (Part II), edited by Constantine Stephanidis, Margherita Antona, and Stavroula Ntoa

HCI International 2020 (HCII 2020)

The full list with the Program Board Chairs and the members of the Program Boards of all thematic areas and affiliated conferences is available online at:

http://www.hci.international/board-members-2020.php

HCI International 2021

The 23rd International Conference on Human-Computer Interaction, HCI International 2021 (HCII 2021), will be held jointly with the affiliated conferences in Washington DC, USA, at the Washington Hilton Hotel, July 24–29, 2021. It will cover a broad spectrum of themes related to human-computer interaction (HCI), including theoretical issues, methods, tools, processes, and case studies in HCI design, as well as novel interaction techniques, interfaces, and applications. The proceedings will be published by Springer. More information will be available on the conference website: http://2021.hci.international/

General Chair
Prof. Constantine Stephanidis
University of Crete and ICS-FORTH
Heraklion, Crete, Greece
Email: general_chair@hcii2021.org

http://2021.hci.international/

Contents

Design for All Methods, Techniques and Tools

Design for All Methods, Techniques and Tools

Co-design of Augmented Reality Storybooks for Children with Autism Spectrum Disorder

Bushra Alkadhi[1,2(✉)], Ghadah Alnafisi[1], Layan Aljowair[1], Leena Alotaibi[1], Nouf Alduaifi[1], and Raghad Alhumood[1]

[1] Software Engineering Department, King Saud University, Riyadh, Saudi Arabia
balkadhi@ksu.edu.sa

[2] Human-Computer Interaction (HCI) Design Lab, Riyadh, Saudi Arabia

Abstract. Spectrum of autism is one of the most serious disorders that negatively affect the normal development of the brain. Children with autism usually face different levels of difficulties in communication and practicing essential life skills such as reading due to language delays and intellectual disability. The limitations in manipulating written text as well as understanding it make it challenging for them to read and enjoy storybooks, and here where technology-based interventions can take place. Yohka is an Arabic augmented reality storybook application designed for children with Autism Spectrum Disorder (ASD) and their caregivers to enhance their reading experience and communication. It shows a more interactive and animated version of the story that helps the child to understand the story and the interactions between its characters, which make it enjoyable and therapeutic at the same time. The design of reading companions is rapidly growing in the interaction design domains. While the promise of interactive learning technologies has widely been demonstrated and relevant research is proliferating, little is known about how augmented reality applications might play a positive role in this development and the effective design process is not necessarily recognized. This paper describes the collective creative co-design process that was followed in Yohka as a user-centered design project for developing augmented reality application for - and with - children on the autism spectrum and its consequences on the finished application. It discusses the design innovation modules for ASD technologies and the effective role of relevant stakeholders and expert evaluation in achieving high standards while designing such technologies. Children, parents, specialists, and caregivers have been actively involved since early stages of the project as co-designers and have contributed hugely through different ways and mediums that are covered in this paper. Designing with the users through several iterations helps in promoting usability especially for this kind of educational and therapeutic technologies. Design implications and future directions for this work are also discussed.

Keywords: User centered design · Augmented reality · Autism Spectrum Disorder · Co-design · Co-create · Children

C. Stephanidis et al. (Eds.): HCII 2020, LNCS 12426, pp. 3–13, 2020.
https://doi.org/10.1007/978-3-030-60149-2_1

1 Introduction

Reading books is a crucial element of every child's development. It stimulates imagination and improves their understanding of the world around them. Moreover, it is considered as a useful practice to develop focus and concentration, and boosts the memory of the child and learning process. Children with autism, one of the fastest growing developmental disabilities, face difficulties in reading comprehension and communication and hence find it challenging to engage in the context while reading a book. Autism Spectrum Disorder (ASD) is a developmental disorder that affects an individual's communication and behavior. It causes delays and difficulties in many different skills that are necessary to carry out basic tasks and in developing self-reliance. Autism encompasses a spectrum of symptoms that vary in severity among individuals. The limitations in manipulating language bring a unique set of challenges for a child as well as for parents and teachers. It has been established that children with autism learn better through visual and interactive approach. Therefore, reading a story or a book may not be as enjoyable as it should be if it was not supported with a suitable learning environment [1, 2].

As technology has a profound effect on different aspects of life, it has advanced so much that its use has been made more significant by assisting people with special needs. Interactive learning technologies can help compensate for verbal and interaction problems and facilitate exchanges between people with ASD and others [3]. The promise of interactive learning technologies has widely been demonstrated and relevant research is proliferating; yet little is known about how Augmented Reality (AR) applications might play a positive role in this development and the effective design process is not necessarily recognized.

Yohka is an Arabic augmented reality storybook application designed to assist children with ASD to adapt written storybooks into a format that is easier for them to understand using AR technology. It aims to enhance their overall reading experience and engagement by enabling them to read and understand storybooks without assistance, which reduces the risk of social exclusion that may come with autism. Additionally and to promote emotion recognition, the child goes through a set of exercises at the end of the story to measure his/her understanding of the story and the involved emotions of its characters, which may enable parents and caregivers to monitor the progress of the child development.

With the increasing complexity of today's technologies, collaboration is a key to success. It is not only about the individual knowledge that stakeholders may have, but also about discovering their unique and creative perspectives on the system being developed, which makes it vital to create together. While user-centered design approaches focus on designing for the user, in our collaborative co-design process that was followed in designing Yohka (see Fig. 1), we put a major emphasis on designing for - and with - the user [4]. This paper describes that collective innovative co-design process that was followed and discusses the design innovation modules for ASD technologies. Children with autism, clinicians, parents, and experts played an effective role as co-designers in Yohka project, which took the quality and accessibility of the system to the next level.

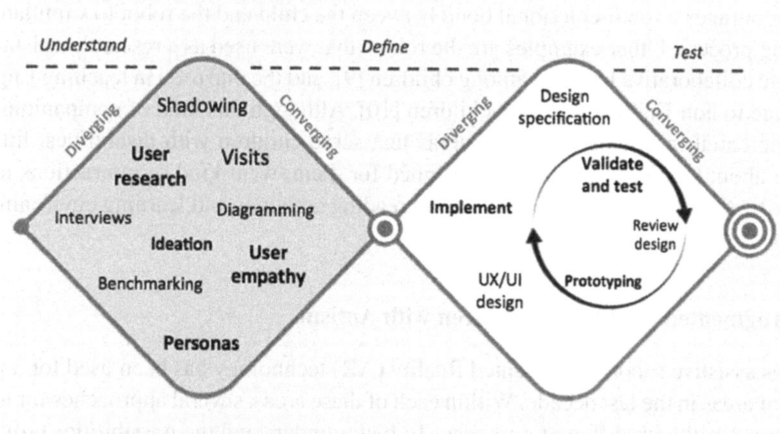

Fig. 1. General design process model adopted in the project.

The remainder of this paper is structured as follows: Sect. 2 describes the background research on reading companions and augmented reality technology for autism. Section 3 describes the humanistic co-design process in the Yohka project, followed by a discussion on design innovation modules for ASD technologies in Sect. 4. We conclude in Sect. 5 with a summary of contributions and future directions for this research.

2 Background and Motivation

In this section, we describe the body of work in the field of reading companions and augmented reality with a specific focus on children with autism. The aim is to shed light on the prior state-of-the-art in this domain and to highlight gaps in research and areas for further development.

2.1 Reading Companions

The concept of using reading companions as an aide to improve reading literacy skills has been around for a decade; however not all of the earlier solutions were powerful and easily accessible [5]. As technology evolves, reading companions become more effective and hold a great promise as companions and peer learners for children. Learning companion robots have the potential to enhance learning by supplementing its activities and there is wide evidence in literature about the benefits of using robot-assisted learning [6]. Prior work in this field demonstrates their potential as supplemental tools to enhance learning. Social robots have been used to transform the reading experience into a collaborative activity where sharing knowledge and ideas promotes reading comprehension and social interaction as cognitive activities are being distributed among the peers [7]. Michaelis and Mutlu [6] designed a social learning companion robot named Minnie to support guided reading activity for children and studied its impact on an in-home reading experience. Moreover, Jones et al. [8] designed empathetic robotic tutors for personalized learning that encourages a socio-emotional bond between the child and the robot to stimulate the learning process. Other examples are the robots that were used as a research assistant to promote collaborative learning among children [9], and the one used in teaching English language to non-English speaking children [10]. Although this kind of companions has great potential in a wide variety of areas that serve children with disabilities, little is known about how they can be best designed for them, what kind of interactions make them effective, and how they might fit into reading activities and learning environments for those children.

2.2 Augmented Reality for Children with Autism

Besides assistive robots, Augmented Reality (AR) technology has been used for a wide range of areas in the last decade. Within each of these areas, several approaches for using AR are noticed with different purposes. To better understand the possibilities provided by AR, it is necessary to understand it first. While people in Virtual Reality (VR) are totally immersed in a virtual environment, AR technology mixes virtual elements with reality. That is why it has been sparking the interest to be used in the autism community. AR technology was found to be effective in overcoming, or at least mitigating, some of the limitations that might be caused by autism [11]. One of the applications in this area is using AR to promote social interactions for children with autism given the difficulty they have in recognizing facial expressions and the underlying emotions [12]. Similarly, Kerdvibulvech et al. [13] have built a three-dimensional AR application for assisting children with special needs in communicating interactively. Lumbreras et al. [14] have also designed a mobile AR application with the purpose of helping them in their learning process. As mentioned earlier, while these contributions demonstrate the promise for AR based technologies for ASD, there is an important gap in the research literature regarding how to effectively design such systems for children with autism and the best practices to take user experience to the next level. In this paper, we address this gap in the literature by presenting the co-design process that we followed while developing Yohka application and how it would affect the overall experience with this kind of technology.

3 Humanistic Co-design for the Yohka

The design and development of Yohka was aligned with the Design Innovation modules for co-designing technology with users and stakeholders [15].

3.1 Co-design Process

The Yohka project archetypally progressed through 4 phases, from Discover, to Define, to Develop to Deliver and iterating through that. The sequence of activities is depicted in Fig. 2 for the first iteration of the system's design process. In this diagram, we plot chronologically the design methods used and the time spent in each phase throughout the project.

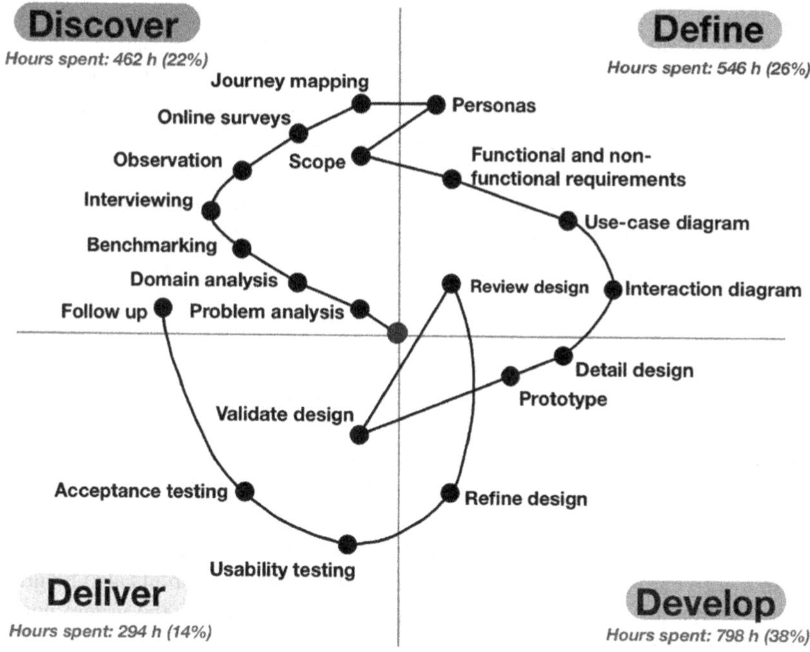

Fig. 2. Chronological plot of HCI methods used in the co-design process for Yohka project. The plot describes the method, sequence of activities along with corresponding time spent for each activity.

4 Reflections on Design Innovation Modules: Design Signatures

4.1 Discover

The main goal of the discovery phase is to understand the users and their needs. It involved several activities, which ranged from analyzing the problem to drawing journey maps. Each activity was selected with a clear goal in mind to collectively develop a full picture of the system.

After defining the problem, the team carried out a domain analysis and benchmarking where they looked at and analyzed related software systems and technologies being used in this domain. This would promote design and creativity and ensure high quality standards as it can shed light on new opportunities for developing the system.

Designing a usable system for people with disability is critical and it may surface challenges and tensions in finding solutions to satisfy them and encourage them to adopt the system. Therefore and in addressing these tensions, including people with disabilities and related stakeholders in the design process is considered an essential part of addressing the user experience and it is an important complement to both functional and non-functional aspects of the system. In building Yohka application, the team worked side by side with children with autism, specialists, and parents as co-designers since early stages of the project. Two autism specialists who work in a center for rehabilitation and learning disabilities were interviewed to understand the needs and challenges of children with autism and to gather requirements. Moreover, the team had spent some time observing four children with autism in the classroom to get insight into their way of communication and learning. Naturalistic observation is a method of behavior observation in the natural setting that is not initiated or manipulated by the investigator and without any attempt to intervene. It allows multiple ways of data collection and requires time commitment since it may take longer time for specific behaviors to appear [14].

Parents also played an effective role in this journey through online survey by sharing information about their children and ideas on how to help them use technology to facilitate their life. The survey was filled by 68 parents who have a child with autism, and it focuses on:

- The way their children interact with people.
- How technology affects them in a positive or negative way.
- Similar tools that their children use.
- How much progress their children have made from using this kind of applications.
- The ability of their children to read and understand written text.

Among all the received responses, around 70% are having children with autism in the age group 6–17 year old and 73.5% cannot read books. 80% of parents also mentioned that their children are having reading difficulties, which indicates the urgent need for such technologies that enhance their reading.

4.2 Define

This phase involved several analysis and design activities, which started with the creation of personas, fictitious but realistic representations of target users of augmented reality storytelling applications for children with ASD. The purpose of creating personas in this phase was to make the users seem more real, and to help designers keep realistic ideas of children with ASD throughout the design process of Yohka. Sample of personas that were created during this phase is shown in Fig. 3 below.

The focus on the co-designers in the previous phase gave rise to both functional and non-functional issues that need to be taken in consideration by the team while designing the system. Keeping that in mind, the team spent time carefully defining the functional and non-functional requirements of the system. Functional requirements define the main system and its components while the non-functional requirements are the quality and accessibility constraints that the system must satisfy according to the user needs. Following that and part of the design process, the team drew use-case and interaction diagrams to clearly represent the system and the interactions between its components. Interaction diagram focuses on describing the interactive behavior among different elements and actors in the model based on system architecture.

4.3 Develop

With a clear understanding of the users, tasks and environments from the Discover and Define phases, this phase involved the detailed design of the user interfaces (UI) with several iterations of rapid prototyping. The UI defines the user experience. Satisfying

	Abeer is an 11-years-old girl who was diagnosed with autism. She likes to read books but faces some difficulties in understanding the content besides that she does not use technology that much. She does not know any language other than Arabic.

	Ahmed is a 6-years-old boy with autism disorder. He likes to use the iPad to view comics and he is familiar with technology. However, due to his young age, he is not able to read yet.

Fig. 3. Samples of the personas created in Yohka.

user experience would definitely make users like the tool and would create the desire to use it again, while bad experience can negatively affect their attitude towards the tool despite its other benefits.

A lot of research has been done and many standards and guidelines are available in regard to accessibility. Although they give a solid foundation for building accessible user interfaces, they are not sufficient for creating good user experience for users with ASD as most of these guidelines are targeted towards users with other disabilities such as visual and hearing impairments. However, there are recent efforts in establishing general guidelines for designing UI for children with autism such as using simple graphics with few elements on screen, large and clear buttons, soft colors, and easy navigation [16]. Moreover and because autism symptoms may vary in severity among individuals, co-designers including clinicians, caregivers, and parents played a vital role in recommending best practices based on their experience with ASD.

The low fidelity prototype, Fig. 4(a), was created to check and test functionality rather than the visual appearance of the system where only key elements of the content are included with minimal visual attributes of the final system. This kind of prototypes allows both the team and stakeholders to have a much clearer expectation about the upcoming system and provide a fast way to iterate design ideas. In contrast and to validate the interaction concept in the application, medium fidelity prototype, Fig. 4(b), was built upon storyboards and user scenarios in the second design iteration. It provides clickable areas with limited functionality, which presents the interactions and navigation options available to the user through the application.

Validating these designs is a key element in the co-design process that we adopted in developing Yohka application. Therefore, the team revisited the center for rehabilitation and learning disabilities where two autism specialists evaluated the prototype considering the users' abilities and modified the design as necessary. Their overall feedback was positive and they suggested some design enhancements that would promote the child's experience when using the application. At this level, re-examination occurs several times

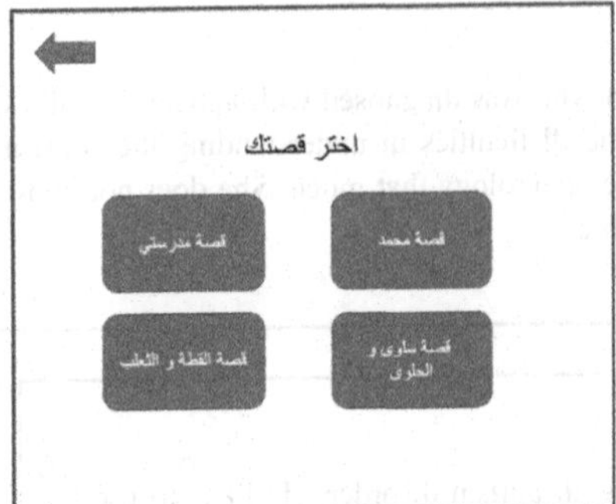

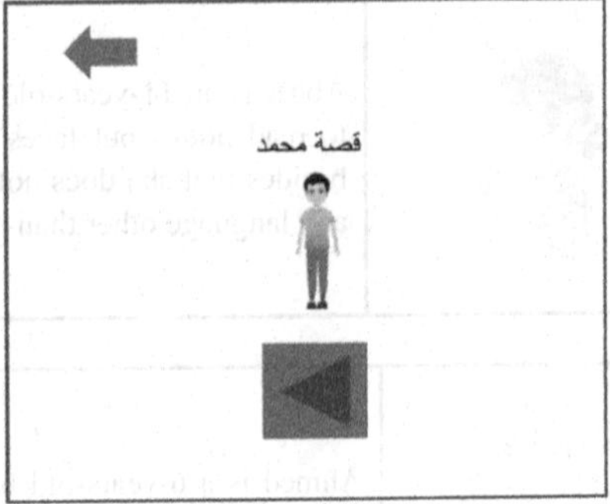

a. Low-fidelity prototype

b. Medium- fidelity prototype

Fig. 4. Low-fidelity prototype in the first iteration of interface design (a) and a Medium- fidelity prototype in the second iteration.

before the final design may be built. The specialists' recommendations were crucial in designing the interfaces for children with autism to suit their cognitive ability and needs. One of the specialists emphasized the importance of these design constraints:

> *"The design has a great influence on how the child perceives the concept behind the application and accepting it. From my experience with children with autism, they feel more comfortable with simple designs that have few elements and they perform poorly with complex tasks. Loud sounds would definitely make them anxious. Pictures and words must be easy to understand."*

4.4 Deliver

This phase focuses on validation and testing with co-designers. The design went through several validation cycles before the UI design was generated and deployed (see Fig. 5). Previous preliminary phases resulted in good feedback and more improvements could be made in terms of the design flow and the user interface design after testing it on a large group of users.

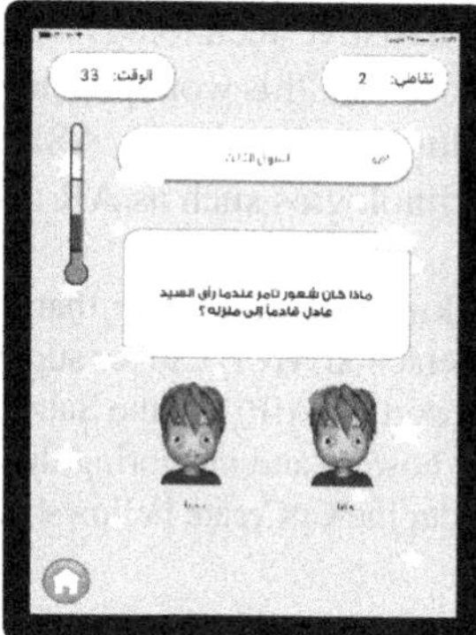

Fig. 5. Frontend designs for Yohka's interfaces on mobile devices

Beside the continual experts' validation, the application will be tested on children with and without autism as both could use the application. Usability and user acceptance tests are crucially important in ensuring high quality standards. What a usability test is really testing is that, given the users' expectations based on their experiences, they will be able to accomplish tasks easily and successfully. On the other hand, user acceptance test is used to validate the output of the system and verify that it is performing correctly as intended. Morae software is being used to monitor overall user experience. As an initial step and until the team get access to children with autism, the application was tested on two typically developing children, 5 and 7 year old. They were asked to read the story using Yohka application. Both of them were able to use the tool with minimum number of errors and were able to answer the end-of-story exercises. Although children were co-designers throughout the project development, these testing sessions have so far helped the team to recognize some minor issues that were unnoticeable in earlier stages such as adding audio to the exercises section in case the child cannot read at all.

5 Conclusion

This paper presented a preliminary work that tries to outline a new effective collaborative participatory design approach for people with autism, with the aim to close a gap in the literature, through co-designing and co-creation of an augmented reality storybook application for children with autism to properly support and enhance the user experience in such assistive technologies. The project, Yohka, archetypally progressed through 4 phases, from Discover, to Define, to Develop to Deliver and iterating through that. Children with autism, clinicians, parents, and experts played the role of co-designers throughout the project and made an effective contribution to the design of this tool with their expertise and feedback. Although more testing is needed, this design process had a positive impact on the quality and the level of confidence towards the system's outcomes from all stakeholders being part of the design journey. It helps to cultivate the team's design thinking when users design their own system.

Future directions of work include further evaluation and testing of this design process and its effect on the overall user experience. It might also be applied on a wider range of assistive technology to improve its accessibility besides the one targeting autism. Moreover, this work provides a valuable base to build upon, with further ideas and design solutions to enhance ASD children wellbeing with the usage of interactive learning technologies such as AR and VR.

Acknowledgment. We thank the Humanistic Co-Design Initiative and the Human-Computer Interaction (HCI) Lab for supporting this work. We also thank the Saudi Authority for Intellectual Property (SAIP) and the Saudi Health Council's National Lab for Emerging Health Technologies for hosting and mentoring this work. This work is part of the authors' project that is carried out under the CoCreate Fellowship for Humanistic Co-Design of Access Technologies.

References

1. Suliman, S.: Autistic child between compassion mastery understanding and care. Al Manual. Egypt (2014)
2. Amaral, D., Geschwind, D., Dawson, G.: Autism Spectrum Disorders. Oxford University Press, Oxford (2011)
3. Bölte, S., Golan, O., Matthew, S., Goodwin, S., Zwaigenbaum, L.: What can innovative technologies do for autism spectrum disorders? Autism **14**(3), 155–159 (2010). https://doi.org/10.1177/1362361310365028
4. British Design Council: Eleven lessons. A study of the design process. www.designcouncil.org.uk. Accessed 10 June 2020
5. Grueneberg, K., Katriel, A., Lai, J., Feng, J.: Reading companion: a interactive web-based tutor for increasing literacy skills. In: Baranauskas, C., Palanque, P., Abascal, J., Barbosa, S.D.J. (eds.) INTERACT 2007. LNCS, vol. 4663, pp. 345–348. Springer, Heidelberg (2007). https://doi.org/10.1007/978-3-540-74800-7_28
6. Michaelis, J., Mutlu, B.: Reading socially: transforming the in-home reading experience with a learning-companion robot. Sci. Robot. **3** (2018). https://doi.org/10.1126/scirobotics.aat5999
7. Sweet, E., Snow, C.: Rethinking Reading Comprehension. Solving Problems in the Teaching of Literacy, pp. 1–12. Guilford Publications (2003)
8. Jones, A., et al.: Empathic robotic tutors for personalised learning: a multidisciplinary approach. In: Tapus, A., André, E., Martin, J.C., Ferland, F., Ammi, M. (eds.) ICSR 2015. LNCS (LNAI), vol. 9388, pp. 285–295. Springer, Cham (2015). https://doi.org/10.1007/978-3-319-25554-5_29
9. Miyake, N., Oshima, J., Shirouzu, H.: Robots as a research partner for promoting young children's collaborative learning. In: IEEE/ACM Human-Robot Interaction Conference (Robots with Children Workshop) Proceedings, Hong Kong (2011)
10. Funakoshi, K., Mizumoto, T., Nagata, R., Nakano, M.: The chanty bear: toward a robot teaching english to children. In: IEEE/ACM Human-Robot Interaction 2011 Conference (Robots with Children Workshop) Proceedings, Hong Kong (2011). https://doi.org/10.1145/1957656.1957701
11. Bai, Z.: Augmenting imagination for children with autism. In: ACM International Conference Proceeding Series, pp. 327–330 (2012). https://doi.org/10.1145/2307096.2307159
12. Cunha, P., Brandão, J., Vasconcelos, J., Soares, F., Carvalho, V.: Augmented reality for cognitive and social skills improvement in children with ASD. In: Proceedings of 13th International Conference on Remote Engineering and Virtual Instrumentation, REV 2016, pp. 334–335 (2016). https://doi.org/10.1109/rev.2016.7444495

13. Kerdvibulvech, C., Wang, C.-C.: A new 3D augmented reality application for educational games to help children in communication interactively. In: Gervasi, O., et al. (eds.) ICCSA 2016. LNCS, vol. 9787, pp. 465–473. Springer, Cham (2016). https://doi.org/10.1007/978-3-319-42108-7_35
14. Lumbreras, M.A.M., de Lourdes, M.T.M., Ariel, S.R.: Aura: augmented reality in mobile devices for the learning of children with ASD-augmented reality in the learning of children with autism. In: Augmented Reality for Enhanced Learning Environments, pp. 142–169 (2018). https://doi.org/10.4018/978-1-5225-5243-7.ch006
15. Michaelis, J.E., Mutlu, B.: Someone to read with: design of and experiences with an in-home learning companion robot for reading. In: Proceedings of the 2017 CHI Conference on Human Factors in Computing Systems (CHI 2017), pp. 301–312. Association for Computing Machinery, New York 2017. https://doi.org/10.1145/3025453.3025499
16. Pavlov, N.: User interface for people with autism spectrum disorders. J. Softw. Eng. Appl. **07**(02), 128–134 (2014). https://doi.org/10.4236/jsea.2014.72014
17. Camburn, B.A., et al.: Design innovation: a study of integrated practice. In: ASME 2017 International Design Engineering Technical Conferences and Computers and Information in Engineering Conference. American Society of Mechanical Engineers Digital Collection (2017). https://doi.org/10.1115/detc2017-68382
18. Sng, K.H.E., Raviselvam, S., Anderson, D., Blessing, L., Camburn, B.A., Wood, K.: A design case study: transferring design processes and prototyping principles into industry for rapid response and user impact. In: DS 87-1 Proceedings of the 21st International Conference on Engineering Design (ICED 2017), vol. 1: Resource Sensitive Design, Design Research Applications and Case Studies, Vancouver, Canada, pp. 349–358 (2017)
19. Khowaja, K., et al.: Augmented reality for learning of children and adolescents with autism spectrum disorder (ASD): a systematic review. IEEE Access (2020). https://doi.org/10.1109/ACCESS.2020.2986608
20. Mesa-Gresa, P., Gil-Gómez, H., Lozano-Quilis, J.-A., Gil-Gómez, J.-A.: Effectiveness of virtual reality for children and adolescents with autism spectrum disorder: an evidence based systematic review. Sensors **18**(8), 2486 (2018). https://www.mdpi.com/1424-8220/18/8/2486

Empowering Assistive Technology Communities to Make Strategic Use of Intellectual Property: Three Case Studies from the CoCreate Program

Sarah Almoaiqel[1(✉)], Shiroq Al-Megren[2,3], Mark Oleksak[3,4], Ghadeer Alfajhan[5], and Areej Al-Wabil[3]

[1] King Saud University, Riyadh 11451, Saudi Arabia
salmoaiqel@ksu.edu.sa
[2] Ideation Lab, Massachusetts Institute of Technology, Cambridge, MA 02139, USA
shiroq@mit.edu
[3] Human-Computer Interaction (HCI) Design Lab, Riyadh, Saudi Arabia
marko@nemsmed.com, areej@mit.edu
[4] STEM Pioneers Group, Inc. Research Division, Boca Raton, FL 33431, USA
[5] Saudi Authority for Intellectual Property (SAIP), Riyadh, Saudi Arabia
gfjhan@saip.gov.sa

Abstract. This paper explores good practices as exemplified by emerging strategies for co-design of assistive technology (AT) for persons with disabilities (PWDs). Designed not as a thorough study, but as a small set of grassroots exemplars that can inspire and instruct designers, developers, caregivers, service providers, and policy makers, the study examines three co-design projects. The three projects utilize the Humanistic Co-Design approach to designing assistive devices tailored to the needs of those with visual, mobility, and speech and language impairments. Implications for the design of AT in open innovation models are discussed, as well as potential real-world implementations.

Keywords: Persons with disabilities (PWDs) · Intellectual property (IP) · Assistive technology (AT) · Co-design · Accessibility

1 Introduction

Persons with disabilities (PWDs) are often viewed as helpless, dependent, and passive [1, 2]. Assistive Technologies (ATs) have made a great impact on the disabled community through empowering individuals by enabling independence. Unfortunately, 35% or more AT devices that are purchased become unused or abandoned [3–5], as they are not aligned with their needs. The main reason for this is not engaging PWDs in the design of AT, which not only results in poor acceptance rates but also encourages continued dependence. These issues mainly arise due to the fact that PWDs are often on the receiving end of help and they are not viewed as contributors of help and support [2].

There is a need for culturally sensitive, user-centered design models for assistive devices and services that empower PWDs, thus transitioning them from victims and

C. Stephanidis et al. (Eds.): HCII 2020, LNCS 12426, pp. 14–23, 2020.
https://doi.org/10.1007/978-3-030-60149-2_2

receivers of help to drivers and subjects of rights. In order to fulfil this need, it is first necessary to understand what users, caregivers and stakeholders conceptualize as the goal for the person with a disability. Caregivers often cite dignity, independence and purpose. When the questions related to AT design and service provision are addressed and ideas are more definitively understood, service providers and policy makers are better able to translate these concepts into the sustainable provision of AT devices, products and services for people with disabilities.

2 Background and Motivation

In this section, we summarize how co-design models have been applied in HCI research and practice. We then describe the Design Innovation (DI) approach. This is followed by prior work in Humanistic Co-Design and its alignment with open innovation and policy regulating the ownership and use of intellectual property (IP) rights for the different stakeholders in the CoCreate program (e.g. researchers, technicians, students, co-designers) and commercialization partners such as industrial sponsors, consultants, non-profit organizations, and SMEs. Finally, we describe the gap in knowledge that Humanistic Co-Design can begin to fill in HCI, open innovation and IP utilization.

2.1 Studies of Co-design

Assistive technology companies are often composed of teams with either clinical or engineering backgrounds [6]. The main goals of those teams are problem-solving, and cost-cutting. They follow a linear, top-down approach, starting from the problem towards the solution. Although these linear processes work for problems that are well defined [7], they do not apply well to problems built around assistive technology for PWDs. Problems concerning disabled people are complex. It would be inadvisable to rely on traditional data gathering and analysis techniques. These problems require iterative trial and error in order to better understand the social, emotional, physical, and cognitive needs of PWDs. Co-design builds on the methods and underlying principles of User Centered Design (UCD), which assumes PWDs to be experts in their own domain, and that they should, therefore, be actively involved in the design of assistive and accessible technologies [8]. Therefore, co-design aims at collaboratively validating solutions with users, putting the user at the center of the iterative process and working on understanding their perspective, and engaging latent perceptions and emotional response. The iterative approach aims at better understanding 'what is needed?' and 'what can be built?' [6]. During every cycle, more insight is gained. Co-design has been used as a methodology to design ATs for PWDs, such as serious gaming technologies for children with hearing impairments [9] and the technologies described in [10].

2.2 IDC Design Process

The Design Innovation (DI) process is a human-centred and interdisciplinary approach for innovation that was developed by the International Design Centre (IDC) in Singapore [11]. The process integrates creative, technical, and analytical methods from well-established schools of thought: Design Thinking, Business Design, Design Engineering and Systems Engineering. The DI process begins with the execution of design methods that advocate for user-centredness. The choice of methods and the transitions between them is governed by a series of processes known as the 4D process. The DI process aims to promote the culture of design with ubiquitous best practices, mindsets, and principles that guide the execution of design methods throughout the design process.

The IDC's DI Process progresses iteratively through four phases, i.e. the 4D process: Discover, Define, Develop, and deliver. In the discovery phase, designers utilise research methods, such as interviews and journey maps, to identify and understand the needs of their users by collaborating and co-creating with stakeholders. During the discovery phases, designers are encouraged to adopt an empathetic lens to encourage the understanding of others and their feelings free of judgement, as well as support divergent thinking within the opportunity space. The define phase follows next to converge and narrows downs the ideas into an 'opportunity statement' by mapping user needs into activities, functions, and representations mindfully and without judgement. Several research methods are used in the 'define' phases, including personas, activity diagrams, hierarchy of purpose, and affinity diagrams. In the next phase, develop phase, designers divergently ideate and model concepts that are based on the identified opportunity statement. Designers are encouraged to adopt a joyful mindset when applying research methods (e.g. collaborative sketching, mind-mapping, or design by analogy) for the 'develop' phase of the DI process. Concepts developed in the develop phase are iteratively delivered to the stakeholder in the 'deliver' phase as prototypes for the purpose of evaluating and refining them. While the 4D process sequence is archetypal, in practice the design projects will grow iteratively between the phases.

2.3 The Humanistic Co-design Program

The Humanistic Co-Design Program, CoCreate, adopts the DI process in its co-design practices by focusing on what the user and the organisation really need and want to support strategic impact and digital transformation. The program started in January of 2020, when MIT's Humanistic Co-Design team introduced the program to Saudi Arabia with a three-day workshop ending with the formation of teams, focused on designing and developing AT. What makes the Humanistic Co-Design approach different from the traditional co-design approach is its focus on human values of PWDs, such as dignity, independence, and purpose, that can only be understood through various empathy exercises. According to Dr. Kyle Keane, head of the Humanistic Co-Design Initiative, "Humanistic Co-Design is an extension of contemporary design approaches, such as design thinking and human-centered design, that emphasizes the emergent inspiration that comes from the dissolution of the designer-client relationship in favor of a mutual engagement of peers with complementary experiences and expertise" [12].

The program aims at helping designers, makers, and engineers apply their skills in collaboration with PWDs, placing PWDs in the driver's seat as contributors to design solutions. In addition, the program worked in collaboration with individuals, organizations, and institutions to increase awareness about how to empower PWDs, allowing them to become subjects of rights by enabling advocacy and ownership through the potential publications and commercialization of assistive technologies through entrepreneurship or licensing agreements. The central goal of the program is to develop solutions to real-world problems in this community, empower PWDs, bring awareness of disability, and promote cooperation within this field.

CoCreate Roadmap. MIT's Humanistic Co-Design team used the DI process and Humanistic Co-Design approach to design the CoCreate roadmap (Fig. 1 below). The main participants involved in the program were the designers and co-designers. MIT's Humanistic Co-Design mentors served as supporting figures for the design process, while the Saudi Arabian IP Authority and the Saudi Health Council's National Health Lab for Emerging Technology served as local supporting figures. There are six main steps in the roadmap: empathize, identify opportunity, gather information, ideate, prototype, and test and refine.

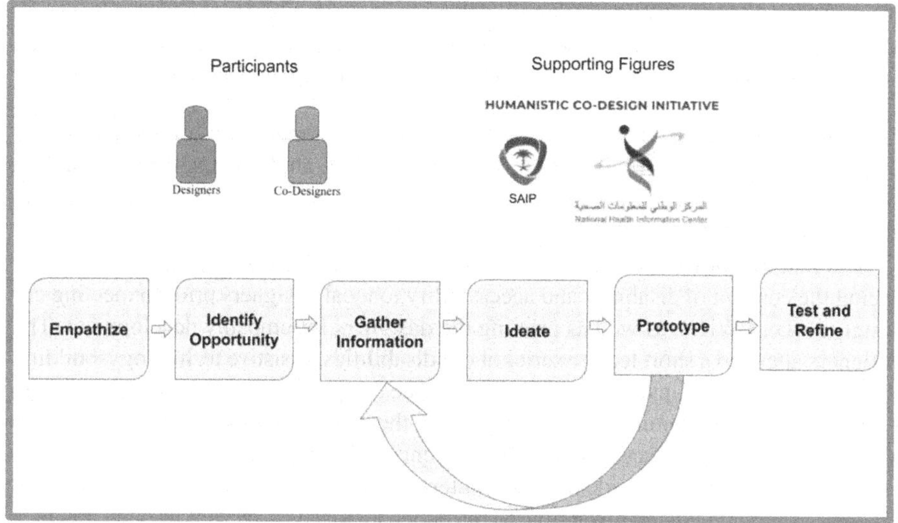

Fig. 1. CoCreate roadmap

Roles of Designers and Co-designers. The designers are the engineers and clinical specialists who act as supporters of PWDs in finding an opportunity space and solution. Their role is to first better understand the disability community, then engage PWDs in order to answer the question of 'what is needed' and 'what can be built'. After this, they must go through iterative trial and error with the help of the PWDs, in order to better define the problem and better design the solution.

In this program, the label Co-Designer was given to the PWDs, as they are empowered to make design decisions. The co-designer is involved from the inception of the project, in identifying a design opportunity, and throughout the iterative design process. As the development of the project continues, more co-designers are recruited to gain more feedback.

Roles of MIT's Humanistic Co-design Mentors, SAIP, and NHLET. Humanistic Co-Design Initiative team actively coached the designers and co-designers throughout their design process and provided resources. Meanwhile, the role of the Saudi Authority for Intellectual Property (SAIP) comes into play to empower innovators through the process of creation and utilization of IP, as Intellectual property (IP) is a key factor in fostering innovation and value-creation. SAIP offers on-site consultations and other related services through IP Clinics on Intellectual Property Rights (IPR), which include patents, copyright, industrial design, and trademarks. SAIP also provides IP and business advice, resulting in turning strong innovative ideas into businesses and directing creativity while generally contributing to raising the awareness of intellectual property. The Saudi Health Council's National Health Lab for Emerging Technologies (NHLET) also offered to mentor by connecting teams to local organizations, advocate groups, institutions, and policymakers. These supporting figures were vital in creating awareness about how to empower PWDs by allowing them to become subjects of rights by enabling advocacy and ownership through the potential publications and commercialization of assistive technologies through entrepreneurship or licensing agreements.

Three Day Workshop. The inception of the program started with a three-day workshop. The aim of the workshop was to kickstart the program by going through the first phases of the CoCreate roadmap: empathize, identify opportunity, gather information, ideate, and prototype.

The first day of the workshop was structured to help designers empathize by introducing the concept of disability and accessibility to local designers prior to meeting co-designers (i.e. PWDs), as well as priming the designers for empathy development. The designers attended a short lecture series about disabilities, assistive technology, building co-designer relationships, and product design. The designers were then brought through a series of disability simulation activities where they try to accomplish a series of tasks while using props to induce artificial impairments and limitations.

The second day of the workshop was centered around identifying an opportunity. Co-designers were invited and given time to introduce themselves, as well as pitch any idea they presently have. After which, designers were broken up into arbitrary groups in order to circulate among co-designers to learn more about their daily lives, interests, strengths, and challenges. After all groups have met each co-designers, designers were allowed to organically form into project teams centered around a particular co-designer. Teams were encouraged to develop an interview protocol to identify an activity the co-designer could use a piece of technology to engage in more independently. Throughout the day, designers are given mini-lectures to introduce them to research methods popularly adopted within the DI process, such as scenarios and journey mapping. These techniques often followed interviews with co-designers to uncover users' intentions, motivations, and emotions.

On the last day of the workshop, teams worked on gathering information, ideating, and prototyping. They completed a template to specify the project plan with an initial idea that will serve as their first prototype. This report included a visual mockup of the idea, market research, potential production materials/technologies, and a detailed description of the device and what problem it solves. The team then pitched their completed project plan to a panel composed of professionals with expertise within the field of assistive technology. The panel provided constructive feedback to each team, and a select number of teams were invited to join the year-long fellowship (Fig. 2).

Fig. 2. Sessions with co-designers, ideation and mentoring, and showcasing creations

Continuous Iteration through a Year-Long Fellowship. After the three day workshop, more co-designers were recruited to gather feedback on the initial prototype. After going through the loop of gathering information, ideating, and prototyping several times, the final step is to test and refine the final prototype. Throughout the process, designers and co-designers are involved in all steps, and supporting figures helped mentor the teams. Opportunities for publishing and filing for IP became clearer as the solution space became more well defined. The ultimate goal of the program was to develop solutions to real-world problems, empower PWDs, bring awareness of disability, and promote cooperation within this field.

3 Methods

This study focuses on three case studies that utilize the Humanistic Co-design approach during the CoCreate program. The three case studies were among the 2020 Fellowship cohort in Saudi Arabia. The case studies analyze and identify the opportunities for advancing ideas from concepts to products and the major barriers facing each team in the co-creation process; document the theory of change for each AT product cycle; and assess the implications for the future Humanistic Co-Design programs in the local socio-technical context. The sample is small and highly selective and so the findings are advanced here as a set of rich insights into a range of co-design frameworks with an HCI focus.

Our analysis documents the vision, challenges, hurdles, knowledge, and good practices undertaken to develop each AT product. As families, caregivers, designers and communities - regardless of where they are geographically - ultimately shoulder the responsibility of identifying and appropriating AT for this population, these case studies also highlight ways in which those with this responsibility can be supported, taking into account existing policy, local conditions, sociocultural norms, and resources.

4 Case Studies

Our analysis documents the vision, challenges, hurdles, knowledge, and good practices undertaken to develop each AT product. As families, caregivers, designers and communities - regardless of where they are geographically - ultimately shoulder the responsibility of identifying and appropriating AT for this population, these case studies also highlight ways in which those with this responsibility can be supported, taking into account existing policy, local conditions, sociocultural norms, and resources. The three projects utilize the Humanistic Co-Design approach to designing assistive devices tailored to the needs of those with visual, mobility and speech and language impairments.

4.1 AT for People with Visual Impairments

The co-creation of assistive and accessible technology empowers people of all abilities and creates the right environment to collaborate, communicate, and produce. The project involved the co-designer, a person with visual impairments, with the team of developers in the requirements elicitation phase of the project and maintained engagement in the multiple iterations for the product development process as a partner in the creation of intellectual property being filed for indoor navigation aids. The co-designer was interviewed and discussed how she walks every day from her home to her office, with the help of her assistant. The individual wanted to be more independent but felt hesitant to walk alone, as there were many objects along the way. The same thing happens in new indoor environments for her. She needs a solution that can help navigate indoor areas without a cane, so she can feel better about doing tasks on her own. Based on this the team focused on a solution with glasses with a camera attachment that can be worn and be able to "see" objects through a software program. The goal is that this product will warn the user of where objects are and allow them to walk freely in a new environment.

4.2 Co-design of Wheelchair Tray Table for People with Physical Disabilities

The Humanistic Co-Design program set the tone for facilitating the partnership between the designers and a wheelchair-bound PWD through the ideation, planning and design of a bespoke wheelchair tray table. The co-ownership of intellectual property that is filed, ranging from the industrial designs of the tray tables and patents to the co-authorship of publications related to the design process, have linked a sense of empowerment for the PWD to better outcomes in the scope of product design and portfolios of the designers and co-designers in this project. The co-design for this project uses a table often and wants something easier to set up and put away. Many problems exist with current solutions, such as a table being too high or too low, or if it doesn't extend over the front portion of the wheelchair. These issues are compounded by the presence of the control elements, such as the joystick, above the armrests, which may require tables to be placed higher than is comfortable for the user. The potential product is an automated table that can be attached to an existing wheelchair model. The current evaluation shows that this can use a stepper motor to rotate a lead screw which lifts the up and over the armrest of the wheelchair where it will then rotate downwards in front of the user. The main design consideration is that the area beside the armrest, and by extension the armrest itself, should remain unconstrained so it can be moved up and down as not to impede the normal function of the wheelchair.

4.3 Augmentative and Alternative Communication (AAC) Co-design for Autism

The Humanistic Co-Design program facilitated the commercialization of augmentative and alternative communication applications that were designed in partnership with speech and language pathologists (SLPs) in local disability service centers. Being cross-institutional in the composition of its team of contributors, the project emphasized shared ownership of the licensing of the software that was developed in partnership with practitioners and co-designers. Moreover, the project facilitated shared IP filing for the copyright of designs in picture-based communication content that was designed and developed with co-designers.

5 Discussion

A number of themes emerge from these three case studies. And while any theme can be advanced only as an informed observation – given the methods used to identify these projects from within the Humanistic Co-Design community projects – it can inform the AT development of new and replicative co-design processes for PWDs.

The Humanistic Co-Design program, CoCreate, served as an important structure between individual causes and proposals and social impact. The program offered a turning point in which PWDs are pushed towards increasing involvement in movements for social change. This turning point includes interacting with familiar individuals expressing challenges, and discussing painful experiences (medical errors or discrimination) with the community of PWDs and designers, makers, and developers, and inspiring design solutions.

The Humanistic Co-Design model followed in this paper demonstrated ways in which empowerment can be achieved by encouraging advocacy and ownership through publications, licensing agreements, and entrepreneurial roles. Socialization of PWDs into empowered co-designer roles occurred through three main avenues, first, engaging them in intensive interactions with new PWDs who have already internalized struggles, goals, and design solutions, to encourage commitment to advocate. Second, providing them with resources, surrounding them with designers, makers, and developers, and connecting them to policy makers in order to empower them and make a direct impact in the community. Finally, giving them ownership through publication rights and entrepeneurialship and licensing agreements, thus creating a future business model, allowing them to participate in the financial remuneration benefits.

This work has formidable implications for the co-design of assistive technology through the future Humanistic Co-Design programs in the local socio-technical context. designers, makers and developers must examine their work practices with PWDs and strive to treat them as drivers and rights bearers rather than victims and receivers of help. The designers, makers, and developers must act as consultants and helpers rather than dictators of decisions. It may be difficult for designers, makers, and developers to take a back seat in the decision making, as they often expect to be in control. Thus, they need to educate themselves to prepare for their new role. They may need to redefine disability for themselves by becoming involved with local disability rights groups and developing friendships with PWDs. Finally, they may contribute to redefining disability by facilitating interaction between PWDs, the general public, and public policy makers through avenues such as publications and licensing agreements. Through this new paradigm, PWDs not only become self-advocates, but they are given ownership of their ideas through publications and IP and thus move to systems advocacy, potentially affecting public policy decisions.

6 Conclusion

This work aims to raise awareness of disability and promote cooperation within this field. The outcomes show potential into the future implementation in AT development of novel and reproducible co-design processes for PWDs. The solutions presented are representative of the products and services that can be utilized by these persons in order to improve their overall quality of life. This paper also addresses the current deficit in evidence-based knowledge on designing technology solutions for PWDs, and significance as a component of the increasingly pressing global sustainable development and health challenges for well being and inclusion.

Acknowledgement. We thank the Humanistic Co-Design Initiative and the Human-Computer Interaction (HCI) Lab for supporting this work. We also thank the Saudi Authority for Intellectual Property (SAIP) and the Saudi Health Council's National Health Lab for Emerging Technologies for hosting and mentoring this work. Finally, we thank the participants of the CoCreate program for their dedication and hard work.

References

1. Maybee, J.E.: Making and Unmaking Disability: The Three-Body Approach. Rowman & Littlefield, Lanham (2019)
2. Schlaff, C.: From dependency to self-advocacy: redefining disability. Am. J. Occup. Ther. **47**(10), 943–948 (1993)
3. Hurst, A., Tobias, J.: Empowering individuals with do-it-yourself assistive technology. In: The Proceedings of the 13th International ACM SIGACCESS Conference on Computers and Accessibility, pp. 11–18, October 2011
4. Phillips, B., Zhao, H.: Predictors of assistive technology abandonment. Assist. Technol. **5**(1), 36–45 (1993)
5. Scherer, M.J.: Outcomes of assistive technology use on quality of life. Disabil. Rehabil. **18**(9), 439–448 (1996)
6. De Couvreur, L., Goossens, R.: Design for (every) one: co-creation as a bridge between universal design and rehabilitation engineering. CoDesign **7**(2), 107–121 (2011)
7. Conklin, J.: Dialogue Mapping: Building Shared Understanding of Wicked Problems. Wiley, Chichester (2005)
8. Law, C.M., Yi, J.S., Choi, Y.S., Jacko, J.A.: Are disability-access guidelines designed for designers? Do they need to be? In: Proceedings of the 18th Australia Conference on Computer-Human Interaction: Design: Activities, Artefacts and Environments (OZCHI 2006), pp. 357–360. Association for Computing Machinery, New York (2006). https://doi.org/10.1145/1228175.1228244

9. Peñeñory, V.M., Fardoun, H.M., Bacca, Á.F., Collazos, C.A., Alghazzawi, D.M., Cano, S.P.: Towards the design of user experiences for psychomotor rehabilitation for hearing impaired children. In: Proceedings of the 5th Workshop on ICTs for improving Patients Rehabilitation Research Techniques (REHAB 2019), pp. 118–121. Association for Computing Machinery, New York (2019). https://doi.org/10.1145/3364138.3364163
10. Aflatoony, L., Jin Lee, S.: AT makers: a multidisciplinary approach to co-designing assistive technologies by co-optimizing expert knowledge. In: Proceedings of the 16th Participatory Design Conference 2020 - Participation(s) Otherwise - vol. 2 (PDC 2020), pp. 128–132. Association for Computing Machinery, New York (2020). https://doi.org/10.1145/3384772.3385158
11. Design Innovation. https://www.dimodules.com/
12. Humanistic Co-Design Initiative. https://www.humanistic.app/

Humanistic Co-design for Specific Learning Difficulties Using Scenario-Based Personas: Tangible Arabic Alphabet Blocks for Dyslexia

Mawaddah AlSabban[1,3](✉), Sundus Alorij[1], Ghadeer Alshamrani[2], and Ohoud Alharbi[4]

[1] Saudi Authority for Intellectual Property (SAIP), Riyadh, Saudi Arabia
{msabban,soraij}@saip.gov.sa
[2] King Abdulaziz University, Jeddah, Saudi Arabia
ghadeer.alshamrani@acm.org
[3] Human-Computer Interaction (HCI) Design Lab, Riyadh, Saudi Arabia
[4] Simon Fraser University, Burnaby, Canada
Oalharbi@sfu.ca

Abstract. In this paper, we describe the design rationale and iterative development process of a scenario-based technique for conveying the results of user analysis studies for children with dyslexia, and the first evaluation results for our scenario-based personas. Personas are well established in the user-centered design (UCD) and co-design communities, however, they are inadequately understood by practitioners not familiar with user experience (UX) design. We developed scenario-based personas for specific learning difficulties based on the main contexts of reading difficulties such as dyslexia. The method combines personas and scenarios in the artefacts for designing interactive learning products. Personas are depicted in silhouettes of children, educators or caregivers, which are overlaid in scenario contexts of learning and leisure. Scenarios were designed to describe the stories and context behind why learners and educators would consider using tangible blocks for developing phonological skills in literacy education. Methodological considerations for using scenario-based personas in user research will be discussed.

Keywords: Dyslexia · SpLD · Learning difficulty · LD · Literacy · Phonology

1 Introduction

Using personas and scenarios in co-design contexts have generated a rapidly growing interest in the user experience (UX) design community [1, 2]. However, the method of combining personas with scenarios is relatively new in the assistive technology (AT) and inclusive design communities [e.g. 3–5]. AT for Specific Learning Difficulties (SpLDs) are often considered as niche products because they address special needs in a highly-segmented market [6]. SPLDs are neurodevelopmental disorders that are characterized

C. Stephanidis et al. (Eds.): HCII 2020, LNCS 12426, pp. 24–33, 2020.
https://doi.org/10.1007/978-3-030-60149-2_3

by severe and persistent difficulties in learning to efficiently read, and they impact literacy development in children [7]. According to the World Health Organization (WHO), up to 20% of the world's population could be struggling with specific learning difficulties (SpLDs) such as dyslexia, dyscalculia and dyspraxia [7]. Yet when it comes to creating accessible products and platforms, SpLDs are often overlooked when processing the Arabic language and designers are often ill-equipped to create accessible digital products or online experiences for users with SpLDs in Arabic speaking populations [8]. In designing learning aids and applications for children with SpLDs, research suggests that co-design is effective in eliciting requirements for diverse users, different contexts and scenarios of use [9]. The study's research questions was: When we create a persona, how do we balance making an accurate portrayal of persons with disabilities (PwD) and facilitating effective usage of the persona by the designers and co-designers?

This paper is structured as follows: Sect. 2 describes the background and motivation for using personas and scenarios in user-centered design projects in the scope of assistive technology for SpLDs. Following that, we describe the design process and artefacts in Sect. 3 followed by the design implications in Sect. 4. We conclude in Sect. 5 with a summary of contributions and directions for future research.

2 Personas and Scenarios in Designing Technology for SpLDs

Acquiring and improving literacy skills throughout life is an intrinsic part of the right to education. In recent years, AT has been developed for the early identification and remediation of SpLDs, and specifically for people with Dyslexia [10]. The ways in which people with SpLDs cope with difficulties in reading are accompanied by a broad array of social conditions influencing how technology, language and literacy interact in learning contexts. In this section, we describe the background research and motivation for designing literacy aids for children with SpLDs.

2.1 Co-design of Assistive Technology for Literacy Aids

Language, literacy and technology are products of design. Language is a social and cognitive system that helps individuals create and express meanings, as rightly noted by Kern in [11]. In designing literacy aids, the design process is aligned with the notion that language's meaning potential and 'is only actualized in contexts of use such as in speech, writing, thought or gesture' [11]. Evidence suggests that co-design methods contribute toward more effective AT for people with SPLDS in general [12, 13], and Dyslexia in particular [e.g. 14]. Personas and scenarios are well-established in user-centered design [1–4], yet they are often not effectively utilized by non-experts such as the use cases highlighted in [1] or by developers in later stages of AT as noted in [5, 13]. Moreover, personas depicting fictional characters with photos are often perceived differently when the selected characters do not reflect the diversity of a population [e.g. 14, 15]. Different variations of personas and scenarios have been reported in the HCI literature and explored in practice [16, 18, 20]. The research on personas and scenarios in the design of AT is less explored and inadequately understood as noted in [2].

2.2 Insights from Personas and Scenarios in AT Design for Dyslexia

Many people who have SpLDs depend on technology to augment their cognitive and sensory abilities [4, 6, 10, 14]. In recent years, technologies have been designed for children who have SpLDs to develop their reading and phonological processing skills [e.g. 15–17]. The design process for innovative products in the context of learning is often more effective when learners and educators are involved as co-designers [15]. Towards this model of co-design, personas and scenarios emerge as important tools for communicating the needs and requirements that would be considered in the product designs [18, 19].

In the field of user-centered design (UCD), scenarios are considered important both for designing assistive technologies and for usability testing with persons with disabilities [19]. Personas have been used in the design process of learning aids for children with dyslexia. The aids ranged from tangible objects [15, 17] to digital programs [e.g. 20–24]. Research with personas suggests that designers develop more empathy with target user populations and stronger alignment with contexts of use for the technologies [16, 18]. Different approaches have been used to generate personas in these projects. Approaches include ethnographic research studies [e.g. 16], focus groups [e.g. 24, 25], interviews as described in [20] and observation studies [e.g. 14, 15]. In these studies, personas were perceived by developers to be useful in building empathy in early stages of design and aligning features with user needs and user-acceptance testing in later stages of development, yet they were not perceived as helpful in describing diverse perceptions of context without scenarios as noted in [16].

3 Method

In co-design models, scenarios are often used to "extract and understand needs that arise specifically to the context of use of the product, service or system" [19]. The work on personas in this study stemmed from the need to find ways to bring co-designers, engineers, clinicians, educators and developers together into a single, cohesive team. Motivated by addressing the lack of literacy aids for the Arabic language, the co-design model of [19] as aligned with methodological considerations for involving SpLD practitioners and learners, described in [14, 15]. The goal of the scenario-based personas was to allow the development team to live and breathe the user's world in the context of co-designing tangible digital blocks for the Arabic alphabet.

3.1 Designing Scenario-Based Personas

The process of designing the scenario-based personas started with user research involving educators, technologists and learners in the local context of Saudi Arabia [i.e. 14–16, 20]. From our ethnographic research on children with SpLDs, we chose to focus our personas less on the user type and more on the user mode – we focused on their actions rather than their essence as depicted in Fig. 1.

Designing scenarios involved identifying the different contexts of use in which we envisioned literacy teaching and learning would take place, such as a classroom (individual or peer learning activities) or home environment (remote learning with teachers

Fig. 1. Tangible Scenario-based Persona Artefacts for Designers and Co-Designers *persona box designed by personabox.design*

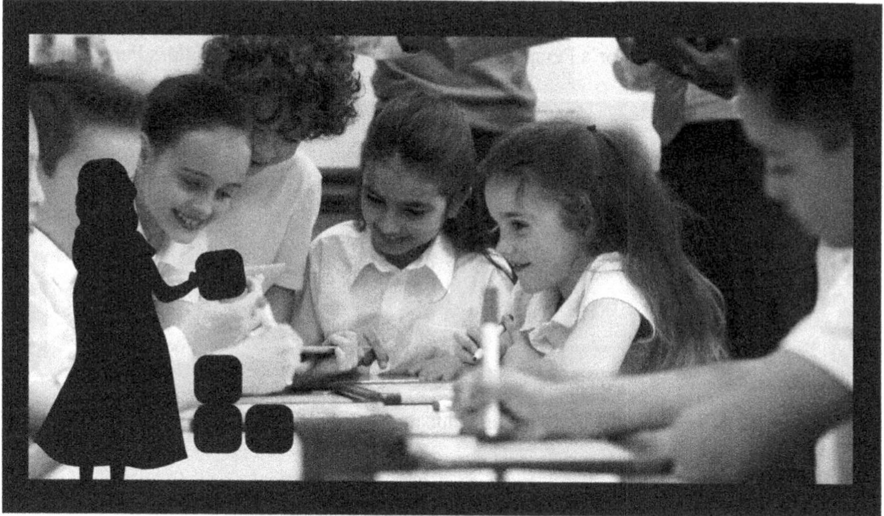

Fig. 2. Silhouette of an educator (teacher or teaching assistant) overlaid in a classroom setting.

and peers, or playful learning with parent or caregiver). Following that, silhouettes are overlaid on the backdrop image as in Fig. 2.

We needed a tool to guide strategic decisions about the alphabet blocks' focus, enable better tactical-level design decisions, and assist co-designers in making inevitable design trade-offs. Scenarios which involved co-location of the learner and caregiver or teacher and remote-learning contexts needed to go beyond task-oriented personas to include information-oriented and immersion-oriented aspects of the context of use as depicted in Fig. 3.

The concept of two-level personas [26] was considered, as these artefacts were also designed for designer users. For example, co-designers included teachers of children with SpLDs who were taking part in the design team. The scenarios were also created to allow the team of co-designers to filter out personal quirks of personas representing PwDs (or their caregivers/teachers) and focus on motivations and behaviors typical of a broad range of children with SpLDs, while still relating to users as individuals (Fig. 4).

Remote Scenario via Educator's Perspective

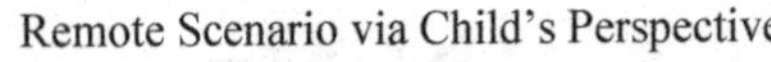

Fig. 3. Silhouette of a child and an educator overlaid in a remote-learning setting.

School Scenario via Educator's Perspective

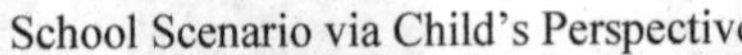

Fig. 4. Silhouette of a child and an educator overlaid in a classroom setting.

3.2 Synthesis of User Research Data in Scenario-Based Personas

In a sense, trying to build scenario-based personas with sufficient actionable detail was similar to data storytelling in educational technology contexts. Information about people in scenario-based personas included biographic, geographic, demographic, and psychographic background information about the people as well as the persona's specific goals, needs, attitudes, knowledge and proficiencies.

Information about the context of use involved the emotional aspects of the UX, accessibility issues and relationships among personas. Examples include remote-learning contexts being described from the educator's perspective as well as the learner's perspective (Fig. 5).

Table 1 lists the personas that depict a summary of a specific type of student, educator, parent or caregiver. These personas represent archetypes rather than stereotypes of a broader segment or group of learners and educators. As in all persona creations, user research was conducted and the collected data was used in order to ensure accurate representations of the tangible alphabet blocks' users [14, 15, 20–23]. Each persona was created to summarize who the users are (i.e. learners, educators, caregivers) and why they are using the learning artefacts for developing literacy skills, as well as what behaviors, assumptions, and expectations determine their view of the learning artefacts.

Home Scenario via Caregiver's Perspective

Home Scenario via Child's Perspective

Fig. 5. Silhouette of a child overlaid a scenario depicting a home setting.

Table 1. Persona Descriptions in Different Scenarios

Scenario's Context	Persona	Description
School	Educator	Nora is a 34 year old teacher in a gender-segregated school, teaching first grade students literacy skills and often uses artefacts depicting the Arabic alphabet in the daily literacy hour with her students. In this scenario, students work in groups of 3 to 5 students in a shared table setting
	Learner	Sara is a 7 year old student with SpLD in reading. She struggles to recognize Arabic letters and link them to their sound in reading. Sara practices her phonological skills in the classroom setting with her peers (typically developing children) with learning aids such as software on tablets or alphabet blocks
Home with parent or caregiver	Educator	Lana is a 29 year old mother of three children, ages 7 and 3 years old. Her son, Sami has dyslexia and an attention deficit disorder. Lana helps Sami develop his literacy skills at home in a daily 1 h session of play using alphabet artefacts (e.g. blocks and puzzles) which are recommended by his teachers. Sami often explores these gamified assignments with his younger sister, Mona in their daily play sessions at home
	Learner	Sami is a 7 year old boy diagnosed with dyslexia and an attention deficit disorder by an educational psychologist. Sami struggles to keep up with his peers at school in literacy lessons (reading and writing). Sami's teacher worked with his mother, Lana to arrange a daily home-assignment of exercises that Sami conducts in a playful context at home with his parents' assistance

(*continued*)

Table 1. (*continued*)

Scenario's Context	Persona	Description
Remote-learning with peers and educator	Educator	Ali is a 35 year old teacher in a remote-learning setting due to temporary social distancing restrictions in his school district. Ali teaches first grade students reading and writing in the Arabic language. In his class of 20 students, Ali often has 2 to 4 students enrolled who have SpLDs
	Learner	Yasir is a 13 year old boy studying in the first grade. Yasir's school implemented remote classes during a social distancing timeframe during which Yasir connects daily for 30 min with his teacher, Ali to learn reading in the Arabic language. Yasir struggles to catch up with his peers in the synchronous session when his teacher Ali presents letters and asks students to identify them and work with these letters during in-session assignments

4 Discussion and Design Implications

Creating abstract representations of assistive technology (AT) users (i.e. persons with disabilities and their caregivers) can be a powerful tool for improving users' experiences with AT products and services. In this study, we were particularly interested in identifying and creating methods that help organizations and co-design teams put personas to use once the personas are created. The focus was on a tool for humanistic co-design rather than a tool for persuasion.

In the humanistic co-design model for AT in the CoCreate program, designers had to study the persona artifacts to determine what questions they could ask co-designers (i.e. person with SpLD) or their teachers, which gave them a head start in internalizing the scenario-based personas. In addition, the artefact provided an enjoyable context for co-designers and engineers to cross social barriers and begin interacting with each other. In eliciting feedback from co-designer teams, the scenario-based personas were perceived as effective in enabling assistive technology developers to focus on a manageable and memorable group of user groups. Findings also suggest that the artefacts also helped them ideate different designs of tangible objects for developing literacy skills for different kinds of students and context of use, and to tailor the design to meet the needs of the diverse groups of student and educator user groups.

5 Conclusion and Future Work

In this study, we described the methods we have developed to put personas to work in the humanistic co-design model for developing assistive and accessible technologies for persons with disabilities. We also shed light on how the use of personas has impacted the product design lifecycle in a participatory design community. The effectiveness of the scenario-based persona approach was investigated in an exploratory study and the results suggest that scenario-based personas add value when designing AT for PwDs. Through the use of methodologies like scenario-based personas, co-designers were able to identify design opportunities and create innovative solutions to better serve children with SpLDs, their caregivers, and educators. Findings addressed the how of creating effective personas and using them to design accessible technology products that are aligned with the needs of persons with SpLDs and the people who support them in developing their literacy skills. Future work involves exploring effective methods through which users, designers and developers can co-create, co-interpret, communicate, and coordinate through shared representations of PwDs, AT and contexts of use for AT. Directions for future work also explore how co-design of AT for SpLDs is accompanied by co-deployment in learning contexts, and investigating how co-deployment contributes towards managing the reception and eventual acceptance of novel aT solutions in a particular learning environment.

Acknowledgement. Authors would like to thank all participants in the user studies, as well as the Humanistic Co-Design Initiative at MIT and the Human-Computer Interaction (HCI) Lab for supporting this work. We also thank the Saudi Authority for Intellectual Property (SAIP) and the Saudi Health Council's National Lab for Emerging Health Technologies for supporting the local CoCreate program in Saudi Arabia. This work is part of the authors' project that is carried out under the CoCreate Fellowship for Humanistic Co-Design of Access Technologies. Our thanks go to Dr. Shiroq Almegren and Dr. Areej Al-Wabil for their insightful comments and valuable suggestions on the drafts of this paper.

References

1. Saez, A.V., Domingo, M.G.G.: Scenario-based persona: introducing personas through their main contexts. In CHI 2011 Extended Abstracts on Human Factors in Computing Systems (CHI EA 2011), p. 505. Association for Computing Machinery, New York (2011). https://doi.org/10.1145/1979742.1979563
2. Chang, Y., Lim, Y., Stolterman, E.: Personas: from theory to practices. In Proceedings of the 5th Nordic Conference on Human-computer Interaction: Building Bridges (NordiCHI 2008), pp. 439–442. Association for Computing Machinery, New York (2008). https://doi.org/10.1145/1463160.1463214
3. Moser, C., Fuchsberger, V., Neureiter, K., Sellner, W., Tscheligi, M.: Revisiting personas: the making-of for special user groups. In CHI 2012 Extended Abstracts on Human Factors in Computing Systems (CHI EA 2012), pp. 453–468. Association for Computing Machinery, New York (2012). https://doi.org/10.1145/2212776.2212822
4. Sulmon, N., Slegers, K., Van Isacker, K., Gemou, M., Bekiaris, E.: Using personas to capture assistive technology needs of people with disabilities. In: Persons with Disabilities Conference (CSUN), 22 January 2010–27 January 2010, San Diego. CSUN (2010)
5. Herriott, R.: Are inclusive designers designing inclusively? An analysis of 66 design cases. Design J. **16**(2), 138–158 (2013)
6. Benton, L., Johnson, H.: Widening participation in technology design: a review of the involvement of children with special educational needs and disabilities. Int. J. Child Comput. Interact. **3**, 23–40 (2015)
7. Karande, S., D'souza, S., Gogtay, N., Shiledar, M., Sholapurwala, R.: Economic burden of specific learning disability: a prevalence-based cost of illness study of its direct indirect and intangible costs. J. Postgrad. Med. **65**(3), 152 (2019)

8. Farghaly, A., Shaalan, K.: Arabic natural language processing: challenges and solutions. ACM Trans. Asian Lang. Inf. Process. (TALIP) **8**(4), 1–22 (2009)
9. Roschelle, J., Penuel, W.R.: Co-design of innovations with teachers: definition and dynamics. In Proceedings of the 7th International Conference on Learning Sciences, pp. 606–612, June 2006
10. Reid, G., Strnadová, I., Cumming, T.: Expanding horizons for students with dyslexia in the 21st century: universal design and mobile technology. J. Res. Spec. Educ. Needs **13**(3), 175–181 (2013)
11. Kern, R.: Language, Literacy, and Technology. Cambridge University Press, Cambridge (2015)
12. Garzotto, F., Gonella, R.: Children's co-design and inclusive education. In: Proceedings of the 10th International Conference on Interaction Design and Children, pp. 260–263, June 2011
13. How, T.V., Hwang, A.S., Green, R.E., Mihailidis, A.: Envisioning future cognitive telerehabilitation technologies: a co-design process with clinicians. Disabil. Rehabil. Assistive Technol. **12**(3), 244–261 (2017)
14. Al-Wabil, A., Meldah, E., Al-Suwaidan, A., AlZahrani, A.: Designing educational games for children with specific learning difficulties: insights from involving children and practitioners. In: 2010 Fifth International Multi-Conference on Computing in Global Information Technology, pp. 195–198, September 2010
15. Al-Abdulkarim, L., Al-Wabil, A., Al-Yahya, M., Al-Humaimeedy, A., Al-Khudair, S.: Methodological considerations for involving SpLD practitioners and specialists in designing interactive learning systems. In: Miesenberger, K., Klaus, J., Zagler, W., Karshmer, A. (eds.) ICCHP 2010. LNCS, vol. 6180, pp. 1–4. Springer, Heidelberg (2010). https://doi.org/10.1007/978-3-642-14100-3_1
16. Al-Wabil, A., Drine, S., Alkoblan, S., Alamoudi, A., Almozaini, M., Al-Abdulrahman, R.: The use of personas in the design of an arabic auditory training system for children. In: Proceedings of the Conference Universal Learning Design, Linz, pp. 199–205 (2012)
17. Pandey, S., Srivastava, S.: Tiblo: a tangible learning aid for children with dyslexia. In: Proceedings of the Second Conference on Creativity and Innovation in Design (DESIRE 2011), pp. 211–220. Association for Computing Machinery, New York (2011). https://doi.org/10.1145/2079216.2079247
18. Salminen, J., Jung, S., Santos, J.M., Chowdhury, S., Jansen, B.J.: The effect of experience on persona perceptions. In: Extended Abstracts of the 2020 CHI Conference on Human Factors in Computing Systems (CHI EA 2020), pp. 1–9. Association for Computing Machinery, New York (2020). https://doi.org/10.1145/3334480.3382786
19. Camburn, B.A., et al.: Design innovation: a study of integrated practice. In: International Design Engineering Technical Conferences and Computers and Information in Engineering Conference (IDETC), ASME 2017, pp. V007T06A031–V007T06A031. American Society of Mechanical Engineers (2017)
20. Asma, A., Alsuwaidan, A.: A framework for designing multimedia remedial programs for children with specific learning difficulties. In: EdMedia + Innovate Learning, pp. 2002–2006. Association for the Advancement of Computing in Education (AACE), June 2011. https://www.learntechlib.org/p/38137/
21. Al-Wabil, A., Al-Sheaha, M.: Towards an interactive screening program for developmental dyslexia: eye movement analysis in reading arabic texts. In: Miesenberger, K., Klaus, J., Zagler, W., Karshmer, A. (eds.) ICCHP 2010. LNCS, vol. 6180, pp. 25–32. Springer, Heidelberg (2010). https://doi.org/10.1007/978-3-642-14100-3_5
22. Al-Edaily, A., Al-Wabil, A., Al-Ohali, Y.: Dyslexia explorer: a screening system for learning difficulties in the Arabic language using eye tracking. In: Holzinger, A., Ziefle, M., Hitz, M., Debevc, M. (eds.) SouthCHI 2013. LNCS, vol. 7946, pp. 831–834. Springer, Heidelberg (2013). https://doi.org/10.1007/978-3-642-39062-3_63

23. Al-Edaily, A., Al-Wabil, A., Al-Ohali, Y.: Interactive screening for learning difficulties: analyzing visual patterns of reading Arabic scripts with eye tracking. In: Stephanidis, C. (ed.) HCI 2013. CCIS, vol. 374, pp. 3–7. Springer, Heidelberg (2013). https://doi.org/10.1007/978-3-642-39476-8_1
24. Al-Shareef, L.: A study of provision for specific learning difficulties (dyslexia) in primary education in the Kingdom of Saudi Arabia, Doctoral dissertation, University of Birmingham (2017). https://etheses.bham.ac.uk/id/eprint/7279/
25. Alkhashrami, S., Alghamdi, H., Al-Wabil, A.: Human factors in the design of arabic-language interfaces in assistive technologies for learning difficulties. In: Kurosu, M. (ed.) HCI 2014. LNCS, vol. 8511, pp. 362–369. Springer, Cham (2014). https://doi.org/10.1007/978-3-319-07230-2_35
26. Dittmar, A., Hensch, M.: Two-Level personas for nested design spaces. In: Proceedings of the 33rd Annual ACM Conference on Human Factors in Computing Systems (CHI 2015), pp. 3265–3274. Association for Computing Machinery, New York (2015). https://doi.org/10.1145/2702123.2702168

Heuristic Evaluation for the Assessment of Inclusive Tools in the Autism Treatment

Gustavo Eduardo Constain Moreno[1(✉)], César A. Collazos[2(✉)], Habib M. Fardoun[3(✉)], and Daniyal M. Alghazzawi[3(✉)]

[1] University of Cauca, National Open and Distance University, Cauca, Colombia
gconsta@unicauca.edu.co, gustavo.constain@unad.edu.co

[2] University of Cauca, Cauca, Colombia
ccollazo@unicauca.edu.co

[3] Abdulaziz King University Jeddah, Jeddah, Saudi Arabia
{hfardoun,dghazzawi}@kau.edu.sa

Abstract. This article seeks to present the previous experience made and the definition of inclusive application design criteria taken into account within a heuristic assessment process applied to validate the relevance of these tools in the treatment of Autism Spectrum Disorder -ASD. The article presents the procedure performed, as well as the formation of the team of experts who participated in this study and finally the results obtained.

What is expressed in this letter is part of an investigation that, from the systematic review of literature and the conduct of a case study, obtains the identification of the most relevant - functional and non-functional - characteristics that the software used in the treatment of Autism Spectrum Disorder -TEA should have. The study is based on the use of computer applications focused on strengthening social and motivation skills, as well as the characteristics linked to the training processes of autistic children.

The project includes the exploration of state of the art and technique on Emotional Intelligence, children with disabilities such as autism and architecture models for the design of inclusive software applications. All this is validated by qualitative and quantitative metrics and analyses with indicators of assessment on appropriation or strengthening of emotional skills in autistic children. The tools considered are tools for collecting non-invasive information, filming activities and analyzing emotions through recognition of facial expressions.

Keywords: Inclusive applications · Autism Spectrum Disorder (ASD) · Heuristic assessment

1 Introduction

The experience presented is part of the PhD project "Framework for the Design of Inclusive Computational Applications Related to The Achievement of Emotional Intelligence Skills in Children with Autism Spectrum Disorder -ASD" which contemplates

C. Stephanidis et al. (Eds.): HCII 2020, LNCS 12426, pp. 34–51, 2020.
https://doi.org/10.1007/978-3-030-60149-2_4

the design of methodological and technological models for psycho-educational intervention that allows the increase of levels of emotional intelligence expected in children with such disability.

The U.S. Center for Disease Control and Prevention (CDC) recognizes many ways to maximize an autistic child's ability so that he or she can grow and learn new skills. Generally, these treatments are divided into several categories, such as the Behavioral and Communication Approach, as a principle for the development of behavioral and communication skills [1]. However, these treatments include behavioral and communication therapies, skills development, or medications to control symptoms, but there are few cases where you have deepened the design of models for the use of inclusive technologies that enhance your skills and competencies.

One of the current drawbacks in the treatment of children with ASD is the traditional management of emotions by their therapists with training in aspects such as collaborative learning, social adaptation, decision-making, the ability to face conflicts, i.e. the management of emotional intelligence; but linked to this practice it is necessary to explore other alternatives related to strengthening skills without applying instruments in an invasive way or the use of computational tools that stimulate those competencies in a more natural way. One of these aspects to explore is the characteristic of how most children with ASD show interest in images (pictograms), from the notion of physical representation that is then configured as an idea in the work of these people.

That is why thinking about the design of inclusive computational applications that allow the integration of some pictographic elements into the work processes of children with ASD, can result in a significant improvement in the way they acquire skills for emotional intelligence [2], and therefore the question to be solved is to what extent can the use of inclusive computational applications facilitate the implementation of therapeutic activities that facilitate the strengthening of the levels of emotional and social intelligence in children with ASD and how this would allow to propose a framework for the development of inclusive applications aimed at the treatment of this disorder?

This is why article relates to the heuristic assessment performed on a group of computational tools made for mobile devices (APPs) included in the Apple Store and Play Store databases mainly; all this framed in a case study with children suffering from low levels of autism and with which the positive variation of their emotional states was required through the use of these tools.

People with Autism have Special Educational Needs (SEN) who until recently were only worked by a traditional methodology, but at present Information and Communication Technologies (ICT) make more and more resources adapted to people with ASD with the aim of improving virtually any area of development and their basic competences [3]. Thus, it is necessary to validate its relevance and levels of usability based on its purpose within a formal treatment for the afore mentioned disorder.

2 About Autism Spectrum Disorder

The Autism is part of permanent neurodevelopmental disorders, in which areas related to social interaction, communication, behavior and interest among others deteriorate.

According to [4] the educational environment the affective dimension of learning processes is given importance, however, the emotional aspects in education remain a complex challenge today. The emotion consists of three components: Neurophysiological, Behavioral and Cognitive. The neurophysiological component manifests itself in aspects such as breathing, sweating and hypertension, which, while involuntary responses that the individual cannot control, clarifies that if they can be prevented by appropriate techniques. The behavioral component is related to facial expressions, nonverbal language, tone of voice and body movements, among others. Unlike the neurophysiological component, these expressions are controllable and provide quite precise signals about the emotional state of the person. The cognitive component is the one that relates to feelings, because fear, anguish and anger, among other emotions are expressed in this component.

The diversity of hypotheses about the nature of autism disorder over the past few decades, all of which are more rooted in the cause than on the underlying mental processes, has greatly limited the effectiveness of the different treatments applied to "rehabilitation" [5].

Advances in this type of research, relate three (3) types of autism according to the affectation of your neurological system:

1. TEA Level 1: No intellectual developmental disorder and requiring assistance.
2. TEA Level 2: With affectation of verbal and nonverbal social communication or abnormal response to the social approaches of others. Requires essential support.
3. TEA Level 3: Severe deficit in verbal and nonverbal social communication skills that cause severe functioning disabilities; very limited initiation of social interactions and minimal response to the social approaches of others. It requires support in an especially important and constant way.

The use of technologies to particularly improve and stimulate children's communication with ASD has increased exponentially in recent times. These tools in therapeutic contexts enable a generalization of the behavior towards natural contexts of the child [6]. Therefore, it is intended to verify in this case study whether the use of specialized software and mobile devices allows children diagnosed with level 1 ASD to advance with their treatment, outside the clinical field, being able to use it at home/school to communicate with their close social links; therefore, this study will be designed using human-computer interaction models.

Any type of treatment that is used, analyzes the behavior of the child with ASD and according to the results the program of integral educational intervention is elaborated. It should be borne in mind that a person with ASD generally manifests deep and complex alterations in the area of communication, both verbal and non-verbal, presenting absence of communicative intent or alterations in the use of language. Therefore, within non-verbal communication, it is necessary to distinguish between instrumental acts, natural gestures and Alternative Communication Systems (SACs). For this project, we focus exclusively on alternative systems of communication, which are the skills of emotional and social intelligence that is intended to be analyzed and for which a later solution with a focus on interaction would be developed human-computer [1].

3 The Research Problem

Having understood that emotional and social management is very complex in cases of children with Autism Spectrum Disorder, where each case is different from the others, the developments and implementations of computational solutions to support treatments of this type of condition have been experienced in isolation to specialized clinical treatments [8].

Generally, these treatments are divided into several categories including the Focus on Behavior and Communication as the primary framework for behavioral and communication skills development. However, these treatments include behavioral and communication therapies, skills development, or medications to control symptoms, but there are few cases where you have deepened the design of technology use models inclusive to enhance their skills and competencies.

That is why thinking about the design of inclusive computational applications that allow the integration of some pictographic elements into the work processes of children with ASD, can result in a significant improvement in the way they acquire skills for emotional intelligence, and therefore the question is to what extent the use of inclusive computational applications can facilitate the implementation of therapeutic activities that facilitate the strengthening of intelligence levels emotional and social in children with ASD and how does this allow us to propose a framework for the development of inclusive applications aimed at the treatment of this disorder?

4 Precedent

The heuristic evaluation is based on a case study conducted with girls approximately 7 years old, which have been diagnosed with levels one of Autism, which are part of treatments based on behavioral and recreational therapies that did not include the use of computational tools. This explores and determines the characteristics of computational applications that allow the management of pictograms as an emotional and behavioral management alternative, taking as a reference the user-centered design models (DCU).

At this stage, you get a group of approximately fifty mobile apps that meet the expected functionality:

1. To be a communicative-linguistic tool. These applications favor body language development and self-recognition.
2. Be social and emotional tools. Designed for users to enjoy and learn when interacting and playing autonomously with the specific browser or application.
3. Be cognitive tools. They are tools with which you can design personalized and adapted educational activities that can be used anywhere, in addition to favoring the social integration of the user.

For the development of this aspect, it uses the exploration of the state of the art related to the existence of computational applications focused on supporting ASD treatments, discriminating between various factors such as: Manufacturer, Application Description, Type of Licensing, Technological Characteristics, Application Context. Finally, 12 of these tools are defined according to criteria of ease of use, ease of access and download, documentation and aesthetics.

Table 1. Computational applications for study

APP	Developer	License	Context
APP1. José Learns	Visual Apprentices - Orange Foundation www.aprendicesvisuales.com	Free	iPad and iPhone platforms
APP2. PictoTEA	Velociteam	Free	Android platform
APP3. Proyect@ Emotions	University of Valparaiso - Chile	Free	Android platform
APP4. Day by Day	Orange Foundation	Free	Android 6 platform
APP5. TEA Asperger	Proyecto-TIC.es	Free	Android platform
APP6. Pict One: TEA - Communication with pictograms	B1A Studio	Free	Android platform
APP7. SpeaksEasy Autism DiegoDice	Green Bubble Labs	Free	Android platform
APP8. Proyect@ Portraits - Autism	University of Valparaiso - Chile	Free	Android platform
APP9. Autism Languaje and Cognitive Therapy with MITA	ImagiRation LLC	Free	Android platform
APP10. Impressively Autistic	Android in London	Free	Android platform
APP11. EmoPLAY	Orange Foundation	Free	Android platform
APP12. e-Motion	University of Illinois (USA) and University of Amsterdam (Netherlands) www.visual-recognition.nl	Free	Desktop app for Windows

It is emphasized that the purpose of the case study was to verify by applying models of human-computer interaction whether the use of specialized software, and through mobile devices, allows progress in the results of treatment of children with Autism Spectrum Disorder –ASD developing some emotional and social skills such as self-recognition and social performance of children. Con this purpose, the case study is carried out in the context of the City of Popayán (Colombia), where autism is the seventh type of disability most found in early childhood educational institutions, as reported in the last decade by the National Administrative Department of Statistics of Colombia –DANE [10].

In this case, two test units were used, corresponding to two nine-year-old girls who have previously been diagnosed with Autism Level 1 and who currently develop their treatment with expert people, a physiotherapist, or a psychologist. The first girl is part of the Leonardo Davinci Pedagogical Center, which is a private educational institution, which provides mixed school education at the levels of preschool, elementary, secondary school, cyclic baccalaureate for adults and technical work by competencies. This center is in the municipality of Popayán (Cauca-Colombia), and aims to generate a new pedagogical and social approach through educational innovation. The second case identified is a person who also has the professional accompaniment requirements that are required for research.

4.1 Data and Evidence Collection

For the implementation of the sessions of application of computational tools within the treatment of children with ASD, the documentary preparation of permits and consents should have been carried out aimed at parents of autistic children, the design of didactic activities that made use of the collected applications and the organization and enlistment of both physical spaces and tools for the taking of evidence and results to be collected.

For the collection of analytical information, the adaptation and application of conceptual tools already designed by professionals' experts in the identification and study of autism spectrum disorder –ASD is used. In this sense, the following formats are defined to be applied to each of the selected analysis units:

1. Instrument 1 – Informed consent model for parents.
2. Instrument 2 – Clinical-therapeutic approach.
3. Instrument 3 – Technological approach -study usability of inclusive applications for ASD.

Similarly, the most appropriate space for the conduct of the case study is defined by applying the TEACCH Model ("Treatment and Education of Autistic and related Communication Handicapped Children"), through the application of the prepared activities, the identification in the child of the levels of autonomy for carrying out activities involving the use of emotional skills, while recognizing the difficulties of communication and understanding of the language [11].

Tasks for children with ASD who begin working with this methodology are considered complementary to established therapies where they must follow instructions, use materials and everything defined for emotional or skills management Social (Fig. 1).

An alternative to TEACH has been the use of NFC ("Near Field Communication") software applications for children with functional diversity that, through their use on mobile devices, use animated pictograms for the representation of a person's day-to-day activities, which seek to promote communication, allow to plan, organize and anticipate certain activities.

It is hoped to validate whether these tools contribute to conventional therapies and promote better social interaction. The activities of the applications are intended to be developed in a tripartite way, i.e. the interaction between the child, new technologies and the professional or tutor will be encouraged and is sought to be transferable to different areas of reference of the child, mainly family and the educational center in which he/she is located [12]. For this purpose, it is considered the need to analyze what characteristics

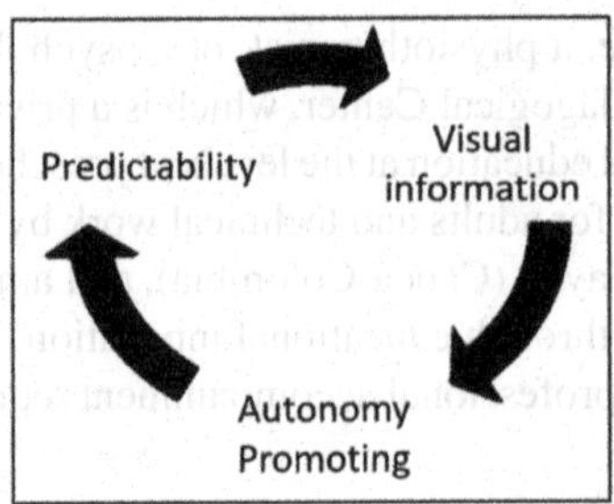

Fig. 1. Model TEACCH

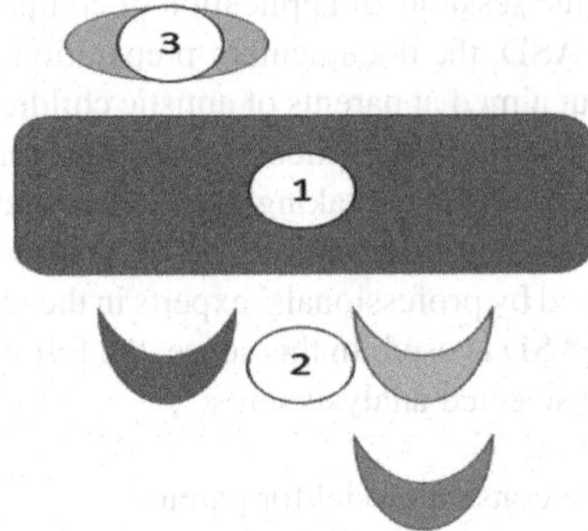

Fig. 2. Distribution of artifacts in physical space

should be, functional and non-functional, which should have an inclusive computational application that is effectively used in the treatment of autism.

The purpose of the case study is to verify by applying human-computer interaction models whether the use of specialized software, and through mobile devices, allows progress in the results of treatment of children with Autism Spectrum Disorder –ASD developing some emotional and social skills such as self-recognition and social performance of children.

In this step, the case study was designed for two (2) analysis units, which correspond to seven-year-old girls who have been previously diagnosed with level 1 of autism and who are accompanied by professionals in phono-audiology and physiotherapy. During this activity, the best physical distribution of the technological elements and equipment to be used during the study should be designed, so that during experimental activities with autistic girls they could use the inclusive applications while we could record their emotional changes through facial recognition.

The selected distribution of the elements was:

1. Workbench: On which is located a digital or mobile tablet where the applications selected for the study have been loaded in advance.

2. Chairs: Where the child with ASD is located and the person who runs the activity. An additional chair may also be available for the person collecting the information (observation sheets).
3. Filming Camera: For the capture of facial expressions of the child during the development of activity and the identification of expressed emotional changes.

5 Methodology

The word heuristic comes etymologically from the Greek word "euriskein" that comes from "eureka", a word that means find or find. Based on the above definition, the Computer Person Interaction (IPO, in Spanish) presents the Heuristic Evaluation (HE) as a method of evaluating usability by inspection that must be carried out by expert evaluators based on principles (called "heuristics") previously established. As a usability evaluation technique, the EH aims to measure the quality of the interface of any interactive system in relation to its ease to be learned and used by a certain group of users in a given context of use [ISO98, UNET06].

The Heuristic, also called the Heuristic Principle or heuristic criterion, tries to apply conversational norms to the interaction between a person and a system: its objective is to try to create a "communicational bridge" in which both the person and the system understand and work together in pursuit of a goal to achieve. These general empirical rules are used within the planning of an HE as a starting point for the creation of an item checklist that will later be used by the expert evaluator within the implementation of the evaluation. In this way, these general rules are appropriate to each specific case of evaluation to reflect in the items to be evaluated the nature and type of interface to be evaluated and the context of its use.

The usefulness of the heuristic evaluation for the applications used in this part of the project seeks to identify the most relevant functional and design characteristics of these applications and that should be taken into account for a possible improvement within the future construction of a new inclusive application that is adapted to the treatment of autism spectrum disorder (Fig. 3).

5.1 Pre-assessment Activities Carried Out

In general, activities were oriented as follows:

Theoretical Support and Systematic Review of Literature. The concepts of emotional intelligence skills, especially Self-Knowledge and Social Skills, were explored; the most relevant features of Autism Spectrum Disorder; what treatment and education programs exist and their level of effectiveness; Notions of User-Centered Design (DCU) and Accessibility; Typology of existing mobile applications for the treatment of autism; and finally metrics and heuristics that may exist to assess the usability of inclusive applications.

This phase included searching, exploring functional features and selecting inclusive app with authoritative child pictogram handling, defining usability standards in software engineering, and finding a measurement tool (no invasive) of emotional changes and software usability.

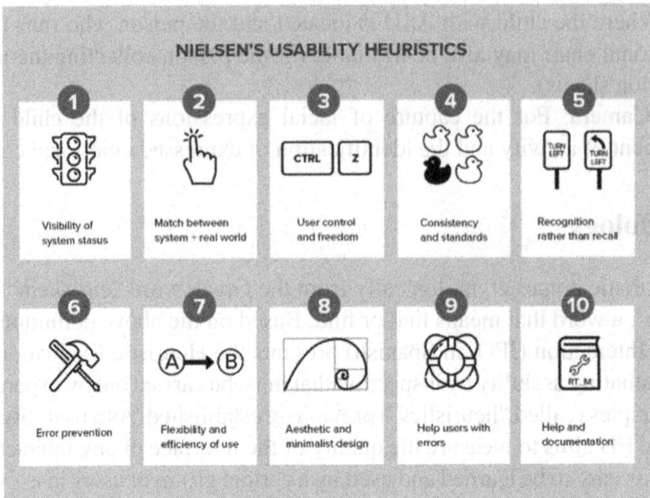

Fig. 3. Nielsen's usability heuristics

Exploring Inclusive Applications for ASD. For this, an app search was performed on the Apple Store and Play Store (Table 1) databases about software that was based on autism knowledge and also presented treatment alternatives based on the management of pictograms for the construction of communication structures. Post-this collection had information relevant to each app such as the type of license, a description of the app's functionality, and an explanation of why it was selected.

Definition of Heuristic Assessment Metrics. At this stage, the usability criteria that inclusive applications that are applied within autism treatment should be defined. These criteria were:

1. Ease of use
2. Documentation included for the app
3. Aesthetic
4. Operation
5. Ease of access to the tool

With the criteria already defined, an instrument was built that would allow heuristic evaluation, based on expert criteria, to be applied to the list of apps selected in the previous activity (Table 2).

The instrument built in MS Excel for heuristic evaluation applies a formula to calculate the usability percentage (UP) of each of the applications analyzed.

5.2 Development of Heuristic of Inclusive App for ASD

This application evaluation was done from the look of two profiles in the project: Expert and User. The first consisted of expert evaluation in User-Centered Design and Mobile

Table 2. Heuristic evaluation format

Usability criteria for inclusive applications for ASD	
1. Easy to use	Value
1.1. The representations in the interface are analogous to real-world aspects 1.2. Words, phrases and concepts are familiar and appropriate for the child with ASD 1.3. The information appears in a logical and natural order 1.4. The use of images that do not generate correspondence with the real world and do not contribute to learning (development of emotional or social skills) is avoided 1.5. Consistent and intuitive handling is evident in all phases of the application	
2. App Documentation	
2.1. The application presents its own documentation or consultation links aimed at facilitators, therapists, teachers or parents and relatives of children with ASD 2.2. Contact information for application developers is presented	
3. Esthetic	
3.1. The colors of the application have good contrast and are pleasing to the view of different users 3.2. The quality of the figures and graphic representations presented are similar to real-world homologous objects	
4. Operability	
4.1. The application is easy to use by children with ASD according to their motor skills (use of buttons, links, navigation arrows, etc.)	
5. Access to the tool	
5.1. The software tool is easily accessible through application repositories for mobile devices 5.2. The application has no cost to download, at least in its basic version that allows low-cost work in homes and educational institutions	

Table 3. Expert groups in heuristic assessment

Mobile app heuristic assessment team for TEA		
Date	Expert level	Number
16/02/2019	User-centered design and HCI	Evaluator 1: Phd. Gabriel Elias Chanchí
23/04/2019	Developer of web and mobile applications	Evaluator 2: Andrés Arias
23/04/2019	Graphic designer	Evaluator 3: Rúmel Correa Vargas

App Developers. The second type of evaluator consisted of the evaluation of the app according to the operation of the application by the user, i.e. the autistic child (Table 3).

Each of the experts had a mobile device (Tablet or Smart Phone) that had the previous installation of the applications to be evaluated and a personal computer with the heuristic review instrument for inclusive App designed for the project.

Each expert analyzed the mobile applications and delivered the following ratings (Table 4, Figs. 4 and 5):

Table 4. Heuristic evaluation results

Eval	Percentage (%) inclusive APP usability									
	APP4	APP7	APP3	APP11	APP10	APP9	APP2	APP6	APP8	APP5
Eval 1	58	84.2	96.11	97.7	94.4	88	97.7	97.7	80.8	94
Eval 2	59	89.2	96.11	97.7	96.1	88	100	100	80.8	92.3
Eval 3	58	84.2	96.11	97.7	94.4	90	97.7	100	80.8	94

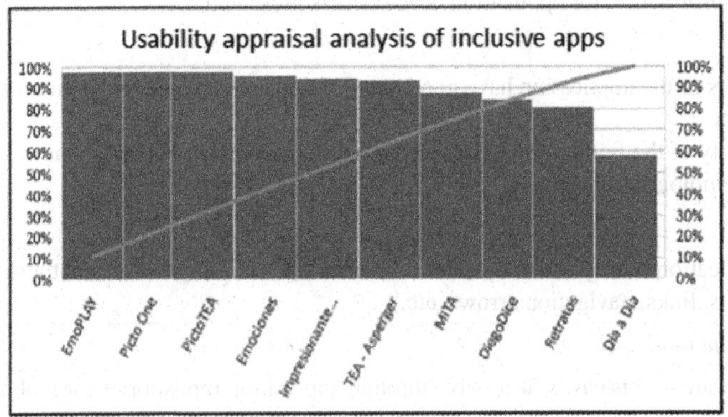

Fig. 4. Inclusive app valuation analysis

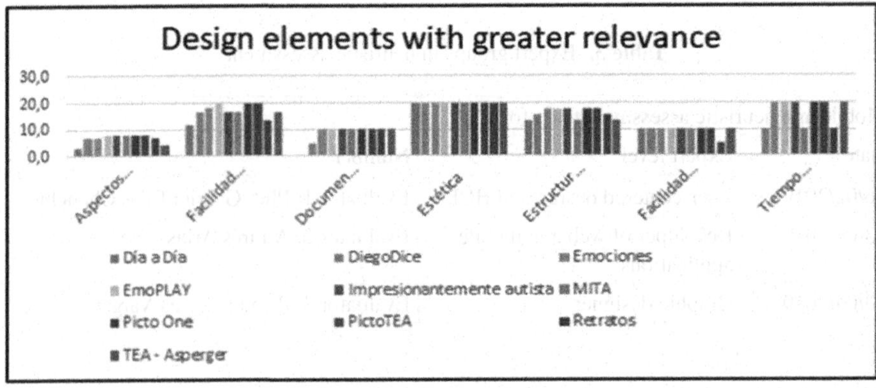

Fig. 5. Major design elements

This heuristic evaluation of inclusive applications was based on the definition of usability metrics of selected applications based on the most relevant standards that refer to software usability, such as ISO/IEC 9241-11, 9126-1, ISO 13407, 14598-1, 14915-1, ISO/TR 18529, 16982.

Also, usability heuristics for child learning applications are defined by classifying the set of heuristics into three categories:

1. Nielsen usability.
2. Usability for children.
3. Usability for learning.

Subsequently, for the evaluation of mobile applications, a usability assessment instrument is designed for the selected applications, which collects the results of their use during working sessions with the analysis units and selects those that best perform from the approach of usability and user-centered design, which in our case are children with the degree 1 of autism.

The formula for the calculation of the usability percentage achieved by each APP is as follows:

$$PU = \frac{\sum_{i=1}^{i=ncc}(vc * re)}{\sum_{i=1}^{i=ncc}(cc * rc)} * 100$$

Where:

- vc: Criterion value
- re: Relevance of evaluation
- rc: Relevance of criterion
- cc: Number of criteria evaluated

The selection criteria for the most relevant apps were: Ease of use, Documentation, Aesthetics, Operability and Ease of Access.

The state of the art made it possible to identify design models of inclusive applications that could be applied or adapted for the development of applications focused on the treatment of autism. In this sense, there are some generic models that can be used in this purpose and another that was created exclusively for inclusive developments. The methods explored were:

1. MDA Method: Containing the necessary steps to define the Mechanics, Dynamics and Aesthetics of a user-centered development.
2. 6D Method: Organized in generic design stages of computational applications that can be adapted to inclusive development through the stages of: Problem Description, Solution Definition, Solution Design, Solution Development, Debugging and testing and finally the Documentation.
3. MPIu+a method: This is the only method contemplated that was created for the design of inclusive applications. Its stages are: Requirements Analysis, Design, Prototype Implementation, Launch and Evaluation.

4. Gamification Method: Great value for adding playful features to inclusive development. In this case you can use Gamification Canvas or Octalisys models and instruments for the design of activities.

5.3 Recognition of Emotional Changes

The arrangement of a controlled environment was considered for the performance of this activity. In this case, for each of the analysis units selected in the project, the physical space was organized and prepared so that all the required elements were available, as expressed in the physical distribution alternatives presented in Fig. 2.

In this case, the distribution in which the person conducting the study observes from a non-participatory perspective and less visible to the unit of analysis, i.e. from the back of the child with ASD, is preferred. This option has less control over the development of the tasks requested by the software and promotes independence in the child, while allowing direct observation of the reactions achieved during each prepared activity. It also highlights the realization of monitoring and collection of emotional responses from a non-invasive and limited approach to capturing facial expressions while performing the proposed activities on the mobile device.

It should highlight the location of a camera on the front of the child interacting with each mobile app, this in order to identify and document the emotional states that the child goes through during their interaction with each application used. In our case, it should have been tested on several occasions with cameras located on tripods or the use of a good quality webcam for the closest identification of facial movements generated by emotional diagnostic images in application users Computer.

With the above in mind, 2 working days were carried out with each unit of analysis, in which it was sought to observe the emotional state at the time of use of the selected Apps and the weighting of the time spent on each occasion. In these sessions a mobile device (Tablet HP Slate 7) was arranged with the selected applications installed and in front a pc with webcam activated with the e-Motion application for capturing emotions under the technique of facial recognition (Fig. 6).

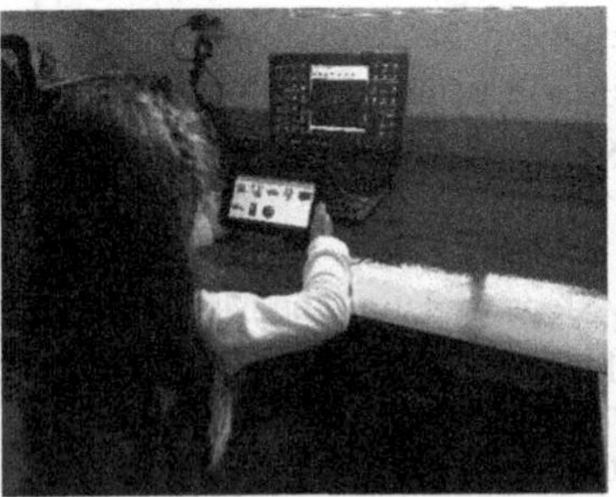

Fig. 6. Usability assessment development

The algorithm contained in E-motion allows to recognize the type of emotion expressed by validating the movements in the muscles of the face. In our case, the emotion expressed by autistic girls during each type of activity carried out with the inclusive apps that were selected for the case study was validated (Fig. 7).

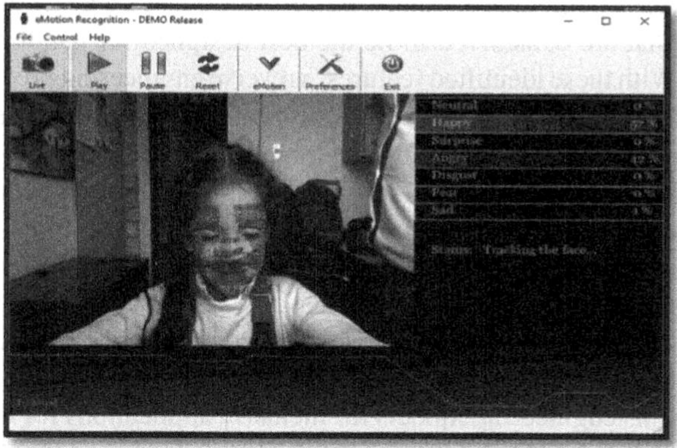

Fig. 7. Facial recognition technique

Identifying Prevailing Emotions During the Case Study. After several experimentation sessions with autistic girls where the inclusive applications selected for this stage of the project were used in the context of pictogram management-based treatment, a relationship was obtained between the Activity performed and the predominant Emotion that this originated (See Table 5 below).

Table 5. Expressions generated in case study

Activity	Predominant emotion
Display pictograms and listen pronunciation	Surprise
Organize sentences based on pictograms	Sad
Recognize parts of your body expressed graphically	Surprise
Possibility of expressing feelings, desires and activities to perform	Happy
Play with characters and complete task	Happy

6 Results

Through this procedure, expert evaluation results are collected, in addition to their use during working sessions with the analysis units for the identification of those computational tools that best perform from the approach of usability and user-centered design.

The results obtained are the formula for calculating the percentage of usability achieved by each APP and establishing the best characteristics that an inclusive application suitable for use in the treatment of autism in the development of emotional skills.

From the point of view of the design elements of the evaluated applications, the average values of each heuristically valued aspect are analyzed leaving at the end a base of ten (10) tools that are considered to be the best designed for handling emotions in autistic children. With these identified features, a reverse engineering process is expected to obtain a framework of technical software infrastructure features suitable for the design of inclusive applications that are valid for the treatment of Autism.

The project obtains as more relevant results a list of validated computational tools for formal linking to clinical treatment processes of autism spectrum disorder; A base of user-centric design recommendations for inclusive applications is also achieved, including the design process, a gamification model, and a software architecture proposal. Finally, the project facilitated the generation of new knowledge related to the area of human-computer interaction applied in clinical contexts.

The requirements engineering models for inclusive applications for the treatment of autism add new factors to take into account, which should ensure the development of applications with a much better degree from the point of view functional, that is, from its usability and accessibility for children with ASD.

During the development of a computational application, once the functionalities that the system must cover together with the rest of its features derived from the context of the interaction are resolved, the activity design and design of the as the main activities that make up the overall process of designing such an interaction. In addition to this, the quality attributes mentioned by ISO 25010 and the gameplay characteristics required for gamified applications should be considered, therefore a cycle of evaluation (or improvement) of the application must be included develop within its architectural definition. This is where the MPIu+a models and the MDA or 6D design frameworks mentioned to ensure that functional and non-functional requirements are achieved from the start of application design and not to the end of testing with children who are immersed in ASD treatment.

To define usability criteria, the cognitive skills of children are mainly taken into account, the same as those specified in each of the development phases of the Agile Extreme Programming (XP) methodology, where each of them yields a product which is used as input for the following definition, thus generating specific and different criteria.

Software development may be framed in the use of Facade, Usability and Feedback design patterns that ensure stability and use of the final application.

The study of the characteristics (functional and non-functional) of computational tools focused on the specific use of children with autism, if allowed the determination of user-centered design alternatives for inclusive applications to support the development of emotional and social skills within the current therapeutic conditions of ASD intervention. The above validates the hypothesis raised at the beginning of the investigation.

It is also clear that the design of computer applications focused on clinical treatments such as ASD must be in line with existing quality standards. It could also be experimented with the use of gambling techniques (Gamification) that can result in a motivating factor for the interactivity between the autistic child and software applications that are used as therapeutic support.

7 Conclusions

It is possible to formulate a framework that seeks the parameterization of the design of computer applications that support the treatment of children with ASD, especially for the development of some specific predefined skills. A framework for the design of inclusive computational applications for TEA treatment can be based on the use of established software architecture patterns; however, these should be adjusted to the extent that therapeutic and technical conditions require it. The MPIu+a Model remains a guide to the engineering process of usability and accessibility par excellence, however, cases of disability it may require some methodological adjustment for the achievement of objectives desired.

The design models of computer applications, such as MDA, 6D and MPIu+a, that provide help for autism, but these have generally been used autonomously and without rigorous monitoring by the clinical specialist or without the involvement of the family of the child in the treatment follow-up.

These same models, especially MDA and 6D, facilitate the development of computer applications for contexts of application of gamified elements, but taking into account the end user for whom they must be designed, that is, children with autistic disorder. Regarding the design of these specialized software applications, there are generalized models, patterns and recommendations for inclusive software design, but these lack some particular elements for the treatment of syndromes such as ASD.

The state of the art and state of the technique finds the existence of inclusive application design models (such as MPIu+a) from which the proposal to create a specific framework based on human interaction can be initiated. computer, for the adaptation of inclusive computer applications, suitable to support the treatment of autism. This model of integration of inclusive computer applications and elements specific to the treatment of autism must be elaborated step by step and with a consequent validation of results from the most relevant usability and accessibility heuristics.

In any case, the lessons learned from the first part of the project determine that the appropriate heuristics must be defined for the evaluation of the computational tools studied and the design of workspaces adapted for children with autism. This facilitates the preparation of children with ASD, which is essential for the development of practices and tests of use of computer applications.

Likewise, the design of computer applications focused on clinical treatments such as ASD, must be adjusted to existing quality standards. Likewise, one could experiment with the use of game techniques (Gamification) that can result in a motivating factor for interactivity between the autistic child and the software applications that are used as therapeutic support.

It is possible to formulate a framework that seeks to parameterize the design of computer applications that support the treatment of children with ASD, especially for the development of some specific predefined skills. A framework for the design of inclusive computational applications for the treatment of ASD can start from the use of established software architecture patterns; however, these must be adjusted to the extent that the therapeutic and technical conditions require. The MPIu+a Model continues to be a guide for the usability and accessibility engineering process par excellence, however, cases of disability, it may require some methodological adjustment to achieve the desired particular objectives.

References

1. Gonzalez, R.M.M., Ibarra, N.A.: Emotional intelligence in education. Complut. J. Educ. **27**(2), 887–888 (2016)
2. Marquez Street, M.G., Remolina De Claves, N.: Incidence of emotional intelligence in the learning process, p. 112. NOVA - Scientific Publication in biomedicas sciences (2011)
3. Villalta, R., Sánchez Cabaco, A., Villa Estevez, J.: Design of digital applications for people with ASD. Int. J. Dev. Educ. Psycol. **4**(1), 291–297 (2012)
4. Petersen, M.M., Feldt, F.R., Mujtaba, S.: Systematic mapping studies in software engineering (2008)
5. Kitchenham, B., Charters, S.: Guidelines for performing systematic literature reviews in software engineering. Engineering **2**, 1051 (2007)
6. Núñez Cubero, L.: Emotional education as a model of intervention to prevent gender-based violence. Education, gender and equality policies. In: XI National Congress of Education Theory, pp. 171–183 (2008)
7. Bisquerra, R.: Emotional education and basic life skills. J. Educ. Res. **21**(1), 7–43 (2013)
8. Repeto Gutierrez, S.: Nature of autistic spectrum disorders. General developmental disorders: an approach from practice, vol. 1. Education counseling. Junta de Andalucía (2010)
9. Molina Montes, A.: How to promote communication in students with autism spectrum disorder. General developmental disorders: an approach from practice, vol. 1. Education counseling. Junta de Andalucía (2010)
10. Gortázar, P.: The educational response to difficulties in the field of communication and language. Educational intervention in autism. Autism days. Tenerife (2001)
11. Rodríguez, M, Ma Del, C.: The TEACCH response in the classroom for students within the autistic spectrum. Educational intervention in autism. Jornadas de autismo. Tenerife (2001)
12. Muñoz, R., Kreisel, S.: Proyect@Emociones: software to stimulate the development of empathy in children with autism spectrum disorders (2012). Conference Paper recovered from www.researchgate.net/publication/234166847
13. University Conference on Educational Technology (JUTE 2011), University of Seville, Spain. Information and Communication Technologies (ICT) in the Process of Teaching and Learning students with Autism Spectrum Disorder (ASD) (2011). http://congreso.us.es/jute2011/es/comunicaciones.php
14. Liddy, E., Paik, W., McKenna, M.: User interface and other improvements to the system and method of retrieving information in natural language (2016)
15. Liu, W.: Natural user interface- Next main product user interface. In: 2010 IEEE 11th International Conference on Computer-Aided Industrial Design & Conceptual Design (CAIDCD) (2011)
16. Cawood, S., Fiala, M.: Augmented Reality, a practical guide. The pragmatic bookshelf (2008). ISBN 978-1-93435-603-6
17. Contreras, V., Fernandez, D.: Gestial interfaces for children suffering from autism spectrum disorder. Department of Systems and Communications, National University of José C. Paz, Leandro N. Alem 4731, José C. Paz, Province of Buenos Aires, Argentina (2016)

18. Lara Cruz, R., Fernandez, H., Olvera, A.: Kinect interactive platform applied to the treatment of autistic children. Final report of thesis in communications engineering and electronics. National Polytechnic Institute. Mexico City (2013)
19. Renilla, M., Sanchez, A., Estévez, J.: Designing digital applications for people with ASD. Scientific Journals of Latin America, the Caribbean, Spain and Portugal. Scientific Information System. (2012). http://www.redalyc.org/articulo.oa?id=349832337031
20. Granollers, T.: MPIu+a methodology that integrates software engineering, human-computer interaction and accessibility in the context of multidisciplinary development teams (2007)
21. Constain, M.G.E.: Model of architectural proposal for inclusive computational applications, in the treatment of autism spectrum disorder. Universidad del Cauca -Colombia (2018)
22. Schopler, E., Mesibov, G.: Behavioral Problems in Autism. Plenium Press Editorial, New York (1994)
23. Schopler, E., Van Bourgondien, M.E.: Preschool Problems in Autism. Plenium Editorial, New York (1993)
24. Schopler, E., Mesibov, G.: Learning and Cognition in Autism. Plenium Press Editorial, New York (1995)
25. Koegel, R., Kern, L.: Teach children with autism. Paul H. Brokers (2015)
26. Ruggieri, V.L., Alberas, C.L.: Therapeutic approaches to autism spectrum disorders. J. Neurol. **60**(Supplement 1), S45–S49 (2015)
27. Mules, F., Ros-Cervera, G., Millá, M.G., Etchepareborda, M.C., Abad, L., Tellez de Meneses, M.: Intervention models in children with autism. Neurol. J. **50** (3), S77–S84 (2010)
28. Mesivob, G., Howley, M.: Access to the curriculum for students with autism spectrum disorders: use of the TEACCH program to promote inclusion (2010)
29. Lang, P.J.: Emotional excitement and activation of the visual cortex: an fRMI analysis. Psychophysiology **35**(2), 199–210 (2010)
30. Adams, D., Oliver, C.: Expression and evaluation of emotions and internal states in people with severe or profound intellectual disabilities. Clinical Psychology Review **31**(3), 293–306 (2011)
31. Petry, K., Maes, B.: Identification of expressions of pleasure and displeasure for people with profound and multiple disabilities. J. Intell. Dev. Disabil. **31**(1), 28–38 (2006)

Persona Design in Participatory Agile Software Development

Susanne Dirks(✉)

TU Dortmund University, Emil-Figge-Str. 50, 44227 Dortmund, Germany
susanne.dirks@tu-dortmund.de

Abstract. Personas are a popular method of user centered design (UCD) in technical product development and have become indispensable in software development. In agile software development, which is nowadays predominantly used in modern projects, personas do not have a role of their own. User needs are usually introduced into development via the Product Owner role by means of user stories. Especially when software is developed for user groups with special needs, it is often difficult for developers to understand the needs of the users based on common user stories.

The study presented in this paper was conducted as part of the EU-funded research and development project *Easy Reading*. It demonstrates how personas for users with learning difficulties can be designed in inclusive research teams and how they can be successfully embedded into the agile development process.

Keywords: Software development · Agile development · UCD · Persona · User story · Accessible software · Digital participation · Usability · Easy Reading

1 Introduction

Introduced in 1999 by Alan Cooper [1] personas are a widely used interaction design tool in user centred design. Personas are used for a better understanding of the user group's goals and behaviors. Personas are usually fictional, but are derived from data of real users collected in surveys, interviews and observations. They are of great value in any development project because they provide a comprehensive insight into the relevant user characteristics [2]. Although the persona method is controversial, it offers great potential for the development of user friendly products – as long as the personas are developed based on data of real users and are considerately used throughout the development process.

In modern software development projects, agile development methods are increasingly used. Unlike the classical methods, these approaches do not foresee a clearly defined phase for the analysis of user requirements. They are iteratively introduced into the development cycle as user stories. Although user stories are a suitable method to define user requirements, many developers still find it difficult to capture the concrete needs of the users based on these stories. This is especially true when users have specific requirements, such as people with disabilities. To meet the needs of these user groups,

C. Stephanidis et al. (Eds.): HCII 2020, LNCS 12426, pp. 52–64, 2020.
https://doi.org/10.1007/978-3-030-60149-2_5

it is indispensable that user requirements are specifically addressed in the development process.

The study presented here demonstrates how to design personas with disabilities and persona based user stories for the agile development of cognitively accessible software. The persona descriptions were created in inclusive research teams together with people with learning disabilities. They provide the basis for the user stories used for the iterative agile development of accessible software.

1.1 Benefits of Personas

A persona is represented by a fictitious individual who represents a group of real consumers with similar characteristics [3]. Even though a persona is not a real person, usually an abstract or real name is given and a compatible picture is selected. The description of the persona is mostly written in a narrative form. This makes it possible to capture the needs of the persona in the context of the intended product. A persona description also includes a description of the individual's personality type, likes and dislikes and general life story. This brings the persona to life and enables developers to relate to it [1, 4]. In the next phase, the specific needs and personal goals of the persona are put into the context of the solution to be developed. This way, user-oriented decisions about functional and non-functional characteristics can be made. Ideally, the requirements derived from the persona descriptions correspond to the contents of the formal requirements documents. Figure 1 shows an example of a persona description as it is usually used in software development projects.

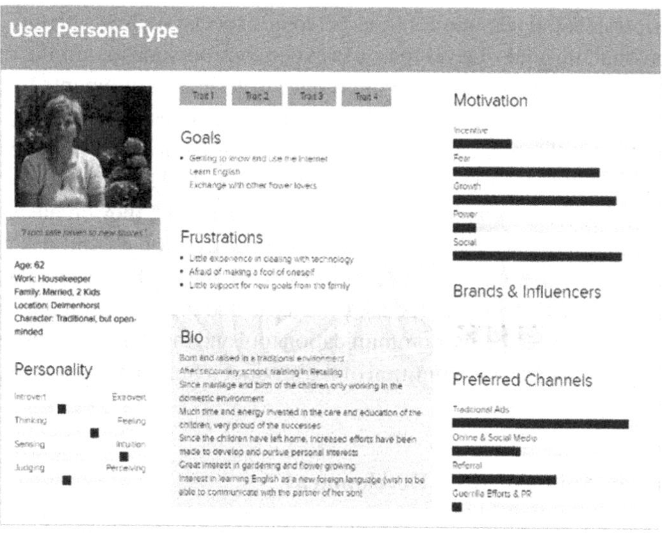

Fig. 1. Persona Example, created with Xtensio [21]

Various studies have shown that the use of personas in software development projects offers many advantages over other traditional methods. According to Prudin and Gruitt [4] personas offer the following benefits:

- Personas create a strong focus on users and work contexts.
- The act of creating personas makes the assumptions about the target audience explicit.
- Personas are a medium for communication.
- Personas focus attention on a specific target audience.

In a Delphi online study with usability experts, Miaskiewicz and Kozar [5] investigated the advantages of personas for product design. From a total of 22 potential benefits, which the authors compiled on the basis of a literature study, the following five benefits were rated as most important by the experts:

- Audience focus
- Product requirements prioritization
- Audience prioritization
- Challenge assumptions
- Prevention of self-referential design

Marsden and Haag [6] also describe personas as a tool for creating empathy for the users within the developer community. In User Centered Design, the exploration of empathy in design processes is of particular importance in order to overcome egocentric perspectives. With the help of personas, it is easier for developers to adopt the user's perspective because they can convey an emotional connection. Therefore, it is crucial that the description of the persona contains personal aspects, such as a picture, hobbies or important personal life goals. Developers can experience personas as similar or dissimilar to themselves. The experience that personas have different requirements for the system than the developers themselves can lead to a conscious focus on these differences [7]. However, there are still too few results to allow a final assessment of the role of empathy and its influence on the design and development of technical systems.

In summary, there are two main benefits of personas. First, they create an awareness that end users are different and more diverse than the developers and designers might imagine. Second, personas enable the developers to understand the real needs and wishes of the end users. Thus, they help to focus on the users and their needs in the development process. Personas are an effective communication tool and their use leads to better design decisions and to a more precise definition of the product's functional scope in accordance with the users' needs [4–10].

1.2 Personas in Agile Software Development

In recent years, agile management methods have become the methods of choice in software development. In agile projects, the software is developed in iterative and incremental steps in cross-functional teams. The focus is on the development itself and not on specification or documentation. These modern approaches correspond much more to the modern, constantly changing technological environment that the classical approaches [3].

From the set of possible agile methods, Scrum is the most frequently used process today. The Scrum method involves the development of software components and functions in successive iterations of about 10–20 days in multidisciplinary teams of 8–10 members.

As with all agile methods, the Scrum method does not provide a separate role for the user. The product owner as the main person responsible for the product vision must act as an advocate for the user. The product owner works in close contact with the various stakeholders and describes the functions to be developed in the product backlog. The product backlog is gradually filled with additional functions in the course of iterative development. The individual functions are then implemented and evaluated during the development sprints.

In Scrum projects, epics and user stories are used to represent the user perspective and the use of the product in different contexts. An epic is a rather abstract requirement description from which different user stories can be derived. User stories describe the product requirements from the user's perspective. They are used in both the product backlog and the sprint backlog, whereas epics are only used in the product backlog.

User stories move within the requirements space without switching to the solution space [11]. They do not provide technical solutions. Depending on the project, user stories may be written by various stakeholders such as clients, users, managers or development team members.

According to Cohn [11] the most common format for describing a user story is (Fig. 2):

As a < type of user >, I want < some goal > so that < some reason >.

Fig. 2. User story template [11]

Including the user perspective in agile development seems to be rather complex. Several approaches have been proposed, but no final method has been found yet [3].

As one possible solution to this problem, several authors have suggested using personas as a basis for writing user stories [11, 12]. Empirical studies show, however, that these stories are rarely used by IT experts in Scrum projects, even if IT experts find the method useful for involving the user perspective in software development [13, 14].

Nevertheless, it can be assumed that the use of person-based user stories facilitates both the development and the evaluation of software products [3].

1.3 Personas with Disabilities

By focusing on the needs of the users, personas can also be used to raise the awareness for the needs of people with disabilities. Moreover, the use of personas with disabilities helps to meet accessibility requirements [15].

The accessibility of a technical system is often equated with usability or understood as a component of usability. In practice, however, accessibility goes beyond usability in various aspects, e.g. in terms of interoperability with individually used support technologies.

According to Zimmermann and Vanderheiden, one of the most common obstacles to user centered design is that the designers of a product have little knowledge of how the actual users will use the product. This is especially true when the designers are young and technically perceptive and have to design a product to be used by elderly or people with disabilities [15].

Descriptions of personas with disabilities should include, in addition to general information, information on the use of assistive technologies and descriptions of situations and contexts that are particularly challenging. The AEGIS research project [16], for example, has developed exemplary personas with different types of disabilities [17]. Although the descriptions are somewhat outdated, especially with regard to the technologies used, the examples demonstrate the basic structure and content of a persona description very well. Figure 3 shows an example of a description of a persona with disabilities from the AEGIS project.

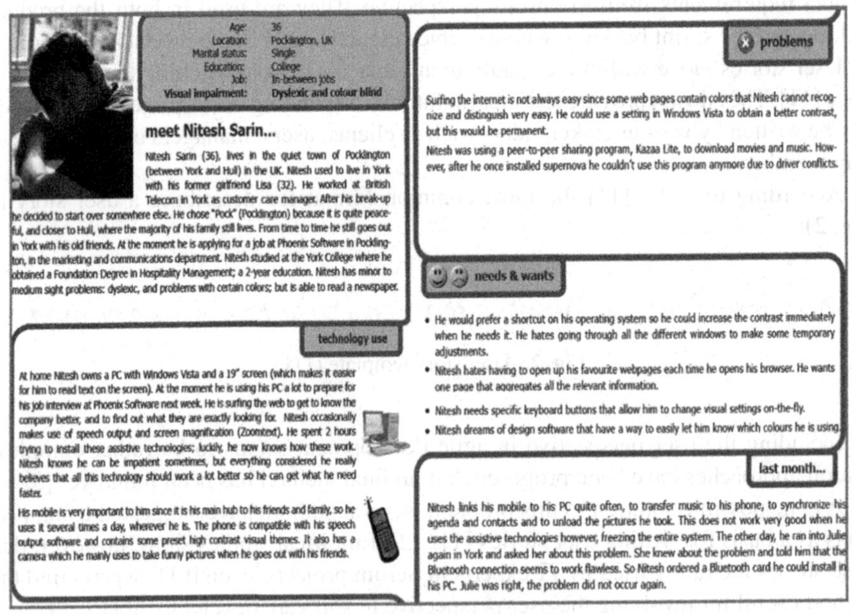

Fig. 3. Example of a persona with disability [17]

People with disabilities, like all users, are a heterogeneous user group and therefore have very individual support needs, goals and personal traits.

Users with learning difficulties are particularly dependent on accessible software products and technical systems, as there are very few technical aids tailored to their support needs that they could use. Moreover, the support needs of people with learning difficulties differ significantly from person to person.

On the one hand, there are many different manifestations of learning difficulties of varying degrees of severity and therefore people have developed different compensation strategies. On the other hand, the abilities of people with disabilities are particularly dependent on secondary factors, like mood, anxiety, fatigue or stress. Many things that can be done on a good day or in the mornings without any difficulty can be major obstacles on other days or later in the afternoon. Emotional stress or pressure to succeed can also lead to a situation where skills that are generally available cannot be used temporarily. As a result of all these factors, the development of personas with disabilities is very complex.

Given the fact that the number of users with learning difficulties and other cognitive impairments will rise in the coming years due to demographic changes in society, this user group should receive special attention in the development of technical systems.

Therefore, the use of personas with disabilities and user stories based on these persona descriptions should be an integral part of every software development project.

2 Study

In recent years, various national and international research projects have been launched to improve the digital participation of people with learning difficulties and to provide them with equal access to digital information and communication services. The EU funded research project Easy Reading [18] aims at the participatory development of a software framework that enables people with learning difficulties to adapt the content and layout of existing websites to their needs. Together with people with learning difficulties, tools have been developed that allow the view of any internet page to be adapted to the current support needs of the user by reducing, simplifying or enriching its content and layout.

The Easy Reading framework is designed as an open source project. A simple interface allows the integration of tools developed within the framework of the project as well as third party services. Even if the target group directly involved in the conception and development were people with learning difficulties, the Easy Reading tools can also bring benefits to other user groups, e.g. senior citizens, people with migration background or users with low reading skills. Figure 4 shows the Easy Reading function 'Symbol support' in use. In this function, symbols from a general symbol collection or a personal image collection are displayed above the words to facilitate text comprehension.

Corresponding to the participatory approach of the Easy Reading project user requirements were gathered by the inclusive teams using different methods suitable for people with learning difficulties. Due to the heterogeneity of the target group many different and sometimes contradicting requirements were collected, which could not be transformed into concise user stories. Even though the inclusive research teams were intensively involved in the requirements analysis, in testing during development and in the evaluation of the Easy Reading system, it became clear that the developers at the different locations needed additional information and methods to be able to focus on the needs of the target users.

To solve this problem, user group related personas were developed to make the user's wishes and requirements better comprehensible. This was especially helpful for the developers who were not directly working in inclusive research teams.

Under the guidance of usability and accessibility experts of TU Dortmund University, the personas were developed by the German speaking inclusive research team of the project partner PIKSL (In der Gemeinde leben gGmbH) in close cooperation with the Austrian inclusive research team of the project partner KI-I (JKU Linz).

Fig. 4. Symbol support function of the Easy Reading Framework

Within the inclusive research team at PIKSL, five colleagues with learning difficulties work together with three coaches and supervisors. The team at KI-I has around 10 participants and includes team members who are not directly involved in the Easy Reading project.

The development of the persona descriptions was carried out in four different stages. The phasing was based on the description of the Living Lab research cycle by Pierson and Lievens [19, 20], but was used in a modified context. In each stage, the most appropriate research methods were applied to meet the needs of the inclusive research team.

In the *conceptualization phase*, first, a common understanding of the role of persona descriptions in software development was established through group discussions. Furthermore, existing persona templates were analyzed in focus groups and evaluated for their suitability for use in the Easy Reading project.

In the *concretization phase* a template for descriptions of people with learning difficulties was developed. The contents and format of the template were worked out in group discussions.

In the *implementation phase*, descriptions for different personas with different types of learning difficulties were developed based on the template created in the concretization phase. Interviews and group discussions were used as research methods in this phase.

The fourth and last phase of the persona development, the *feedback phase*, is still ongoing. In the feedback phase, in a first step, the developed personas are evaluated through group discussions with the other inclusive research teams and, if necessary, adapted and expanded. In a second step, the personas and the persona related user stories are made available to the developers. In this step, the methods survey and participating observation are applied.

Finally, the results of the persona development, the process description and a description of the adapted research methods for the inclusive research teams will be published in a handbook for participatory software development.

3 Results

After introducing the inclusive research teams to persona design, it became obvious, that the commonly used methods are not suitable in the participatory setting of the Easy Reading project. In order to enable the inclusive research team to work successfully the approach for participatory persona design needed to be different from the common approaches.

The conceptualization phase showed that the participants in the teams had very different ideas about personas. Although all team members had a good basic knowledge of Internet technologies and their application through their previous work in the Easy Reading project or other projects, they were not familiar with many common concepts and terms of software development and user centered design.

After a mutual basic understanding of the role of personas in software development was established in various group discussions, different examples of standard persona descriptions were analyzed. The team realized that a lot of information that was considered relevant for persona development was missing. In particular, the team members wished for more personal information on skills, self-image and life goals as well as more specific information about difficulties and challenges in using digital resources.

In the concretization phase, in focus groups and group discussions a template for a description of a person with learning difficulties was developed. Different templates were created in the focus groups. While one group focused primarily on personal characteristics, uses and goals in life, another group focused on the challenges that the Internet offers for people with learning difficulties. The developed templates were elaborated and complex and it was difficult for the members of the other teams to understand and remember the content of the template. In several steps of guided group discussions, the various templates were shortened and harmonized. Finally, a template was developed that all team members agreed on.

There were further challenges in the implementation of the persona descriptions. Since the persona descriptions should be prototypical descriptions of different user groups, certain abstractions had to be carried out during implementation. In order to simplify the process, the personas were developed in the first step as very individualized descriptions of real team members. These descriptions should then be generalized and additional persona descriptions for users with different support needs should be developed. The difficulties in achieving these tasks were the reduced understanding of the need for a more generalized persona description and the limited ability to imagine users with support needs other than their own. The necessity of a generalization was communicated and clarified in joint discussions. The development of personas with additional support needs was realized in small groups with the help of specific case descriptions developed by the supervisors. Figure 5 shows an example of a persona with disabilities as developed in the Easy Reading project.

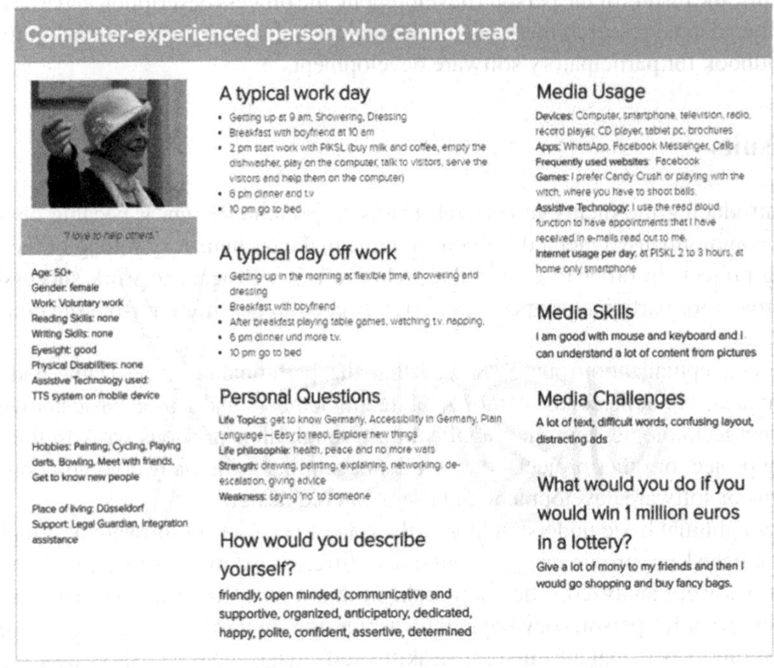

Fig. 5. Easy Reading Persona with disabilities, created with Xtensio [21]

As already noted, the feedback phase is not completed yet. In the first step, the developed persona descriptions have been reviewed and evaluated by the other inclusive research teams. It became apparent that the other teams could understand and relate well to the developed persona descriptions, but from their point of view, there were still gaps in the coverage of the respective user groups. The Austrian team pointed out that there are also user groups with learning difficulties and additional motor and sensory impairments that were not included in the portfolio of existing personas. The Swedish team consists primarily of members who, in addition to a cognitive limitation, also have a communication disorder. Although this team did not consider it necessary to develop additional persona descriptions, it was pointed out that the use of symbol-based communication or the enrichment of existing websites with individualized symbols is an important function for certain target groups of people with learning difficulties.

In the further course of the feedback phase, the persona descriptions and the resulting user stories are submitted to the development team. Figure 6 shows some examples of a persona based user story used in the Easy Reading project.

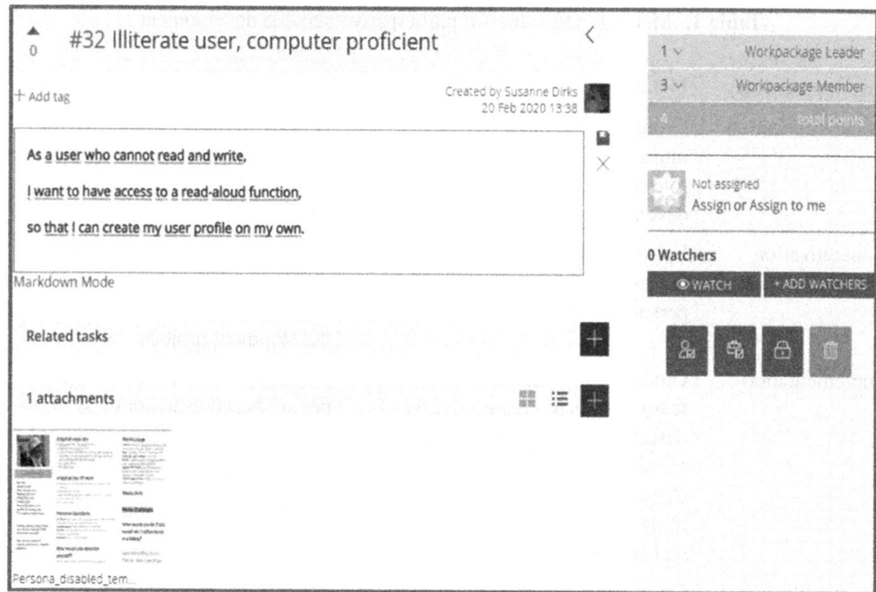

Fig. 6. Easy Reading User Story, created in Taiga.io [22]

As the Easy Reading project also aims to create a comprehensive methodology for the participatory development of accessible software products, the methods used in persona development were systematically documented and evaluated. An overview of the methods applied in the different steps of the persona development process and their value for software development project is given in Table 1.

The feedback process is still ongoing and the process of persona development is not yet completed, further results are expected. All research and development outcomes of the Easy Reading project will be used to build a comprehensive methodology for the participatory development of cognitively accessible software systems.

4 Discussion

In software development, as in all other product development projects, it is of central importance that potential users and their needs are taken into account [23]. When developing accessible software products, it is important that the developers also consider user needs that differ from their own preferences and world of experience.

The ideal approach is to design and develop software products in participative and diverse teams. However, development teams still predominantly consist of young and highly specialized male programmers and engineers. If users are brought into the development process, they are often only involved in requirements analysis and user tests. And all too often it happens that the errors and usability problems found in the user tests are not fixed due to budget and time constraints. In order to develop accessible software products in these teams, easy-to-use and comprehensible methods must be provided.

Table 1. Methods and values of participative persona development

Development step	Methods	Project value
Contextualization	Group discussions to develop a mutual basic understanding of the role of personas in software development	Design of target group-oriented training material for inclusive research teams in software development
Concretization	Focus groups and group discussions for creation of a template of a persona with learning difficulties	Creation of a general template for the description of personas with learning difficulties for software development projects
Implementation	Guided group discussions and small focus groups to create persona descriptions for different user groups of people with learning disabilities Creation of user stories on the basis of the developed personas in small inclusive workshops	Development of personas and person-based user stories as resources for the development of cognitively accessible software systems
Feedback	Group discussions and questionnaires for assessment and evaluation of the developed personas and user stories by others inclusive research teams and the development teams	Evaluation, improvement and enhancement of existing resources for the development of cognitively accessible software systems

Personas and user stories are common methods in software development to integrate the requirements and support needs of users into the development process.

The Easy Reading project, in which the presented research was conducted, is a participatory research and development project [24]. Researchers and developers work together in inclusive teams and engage in an intensive exchange of ideas in all project phases. However, it became apparent that developers who do not work directly with team members with learning difficulties require additional methods to be able to focus on the needs of diverse user groups. Therefore, the inclusive research teams created persona descriptions that represent different user groups within the group of people with learning disabilities. These persona descriptions were used as a basis for the development of user stories, which are used in agile software development as a method to describe software functions and user needs.

As has already been shown for other aspects of software development [25], this study also revealed that the cooperation with user groups with special needs implies particular challenges. Standard research methods need to be adapted and team members need to have a lot of patience and mutual respect to be able to cooperate successfully. Furthermore, it is essential that project planning is adapted to the additional time and personnel requirements of the participatory development processes.

To improve the digital participation of people with disabilities and special needs, more efforts need to be invested in the development of accessible software products.

In an ideal situation, software products and other technical systems are designed and developed in a participatory approach in close cooperation with the end users. However, since software products are still often developed in homogeneous and non-inclusive engineering teams, suitable methods have to be provided to bring the needs of special user groups into the development process. Persona descriptions and user stories that focus on the needs of people with disabilities can help to develop software products, which are accessible and can be used by all people.

Acknowledgements. The work presented in this paper is part of the Easy Reading project and has received funding from the European Union's Horizon 2020 Research and Innovation Programme under Grant Agreement No 780529. Without the support of the colleagues at PIKSL, Proqualis and DART this research would not have been possible. Special appreciation is owed to the colleagues with learning difficulties, who have always proven the importance and value of their contributions to participatory research and development of the Easy Reading framework.

References

1. Cooper, A.: The Inmates are Running the Asylum. Macmillan Publishing Co., Inc., Indianapolis (1999)
2. Pruitt, J., Grudin, J.: Personas: practice and theory. In: DUX 2003, pp. 1–15 (2003)
3. Nielsen, L.: Personas – User Focused Design. Springer, London (2019). https://doi.org/10.1007/978-1-4471-4084-9
4. Grudin, J., Pruitt, J.: Personas, participatory design and product development: an infrastructure for engagement. In: Paper Presented at the Meeting of the Proceedings of Participation and Design Conference (PDC2002), Sweden (2002)
5. Miaskiewicz, T., Kozar, K.A.: Personas and user-centered design: how can personas benefit product design processes? Des. Stud. **32**(5), 417–430 (2011)
6. Marsden, N., Haag, M.: Stereotypes and politics: reflections on personas. In: Proceedings of the SIGCHI Conference on Human Factors in Computing Systems (CHI 2016), pp. 4017–4031 (2016)
7. Haag, M., Marsden, N.: Exploring personas as a method to foster empathy in student IT design teams. Int. J. Technol. Des. Educ. **29**(3), 565–582 (2018). https://doi.org/10.1007/s10798-018-9452-5
8. Pröbster, M., Herrmann, J., Marsden, N.: Personas and persons - an empirical study on stereotyping of personas. In: Proceedings of Mensch und Computer 2019, MuC 2019, pp. 137–145 (2019)
9. Singh, V.: Personas and scenarios as a methodology for information science. Qual. Quant. Methods Libraries **7**(1), 123–134 (2019)
10. Billestrup, J., Stage, J., Bruun, A., Nielsen, L., Nielsen, K.: Creating and using personas in software development: experiences from practice. In: 5th International Conference on Human-Centred Software Engineering (HCSE), Paderborn, Germany, pp. 251–258 (2014)
11. Cohn, M.: User Stories Applied for Agile Software Development. Addison-Wesley, Boston (2004)
12. DeMarco Brown, D.: Agile User Experience Design. Morgan Kaufman Publishers, San Francisco (2012)
13. Jia, Y., Larusdottir, M.K., Cajander, Å.: The usage of usability techniques in scrum projects. In: Winckler, M., Forbrig, P., Bernhaupt, R. (eds.) HCSE 2012. LNCS, vol. 7623, pp. 331–341. Springer, Heidelberg (2012). https://doi.org/10.1007/978-3-642-34347-6_25

14. Lárusdóttir, M.K., Gulliksen, J., Cajander, Å.: A license to kill - improving UCSD in agile development. J. Syst. Softw. **123**, 214–222 (2017)
15. Zimmermann, G., Vanderheiden, G.: Accessible design and testing in the application development process: considerations for an integrated approach. Univ. Access Inf. Soc. **7**, 117–128 (2008). https://doi.org/10.1007/s10209-007-0108-6
16. AEGIS project. http://www.aegis-project.eu. Accessed 19 Feb 2020
17. AEGIS project – Personas. http://www.aegis-project.eu/index.php?option=com_content&view=article&id=63&Itemid=53. Accessed 20 Feb 2020
18. Easy Reading – Keeping the user at the digital original. https://www.easyreading.eu. Accessed 20 Feb 2020
19. Pierson, J., Lievens, B.: Configuring living labs for a 'Thick' understanding of innovation. In: Ethnographic Praxis in Industry Conference, vol. 1, pp. 114–127 (2005)
20. Coorevits, L., Schuurman, D., Oelbrandt, K., Logghe, S.: Bringing personas to life: user experience design through interactive coupled open innovation. Persona Stud. **2**(1), 97–114 (2016)
21. Xtensio Business Communication Platform. https://xtensio.com. Accessed 21 Feb 2020
22. Taiga Project Management Platform. https://taiga.io. Accessed 20 Feb 2020
23. Heumader, P., Miesenberger, K., Koutny, R.: The easy reading framework - keep the user at the digital original. In: 33rd Annual International Technology and Persons with Disabilities Conference Scientific/Research Proceedings, San Diego, pp. 1–13 (2019)
24. Dirks, S.: Empowering instead of hindering – challenges in participatory development of cognitively accessible software. In: Antona, M., Stephanidis, C. (eds.) HCII 2019. LNCS, vol. 11572, pp. 28–38. Springer, Cham (2019). https://doi.org/10.1007/978-3-030-23560-4_3
25. Dirks, S., Bühler, C.: Assistive technologies for people with cognitive impairments – which factors influence technology acceptance? In: Antona, M., Stephanidis, C. (eds.) UAHCI 2018. LNCS, vol. 10907, pp. 503–516. Springer, Cham (2018). https://doi.org/10.1007/978-3-319-92049-8_36

A Web Authoring Tool for the Generation of Adventure Educational Games for Deaf Children

Rafael dos Passos Canteri[1](✉), Laura Sánchez García[2], and Tanya Amara Felipe[3]

[1] UFMS - Federal University of Mato Grosso do Sul, Pantanal Campus, Corumbá, Brazil
rafael.canteri@ufms.br

[2] Department of Informatics, UFPR - Federal University of Paraná, Curitiba, Brazil
laura@inf.ufpr.br

[3] Department of Higher Education, INES - National Institute of Deaf Education, Rio de Janeiro, Brazil
tfelipe@ines.gov.br

Abstract. Video games have been widely used in the teaching-learning process for the most diverse educational contents. There is an increasing amount of study and development of educational games with positive results, however these games are almost always developed focusing on hearing people. If the Deaf teachers themselves, who know the curriculum and the teaching methodologies, have the facility to create educational games for their students, this scenario of scarcity can be overcome. This paper presents an authoring tool, based on a conceptual framework, which enables the construction of educational games for Deaf children in early childhood, a crucial phase in the linguistic development of the person. The games that can be generated through the tool present educational content relevant to the age range of the target audience. The instructional content to be included are of the author's choice and are presented in the Brazilian Sign Language (Libras) and in Portuguese. In order to demonstrate the functionality of the tool, an educational adventure video game is generated from it and evaluated by specialists in an experiment.

Keywords: Authoring tools · Educational video games · Deaf education

1 Introduction

Educational games can provide a more immersive environment that enables more contextual education, using elements such as interactive scenarios, challenge mechanisms, artifacts, and people interactions (i.e. collaboration). Active learning and problem solving are inherent features of educational games [15].

C. Stephanidis et al. (Eds.): HCII 2020, LNCS 12426, pp. 65–75, 2020.
https://doi.org/10.1007/978-3-030-60149-2_6

Students learn better in an interactive and dynamic learning experience [13]. In addition, games can simulate real-world situations [6].

The design of educational games is a complex task that requires a very good relationship between the instructional process and the game design in order for the game to be effective [7]. The literature provides good examples of game design applicable to educational and learning games [14,17]. However, the development is complex and the design is an intricate activity, not allowing knowledge holders and experts in teaching methods to produce an educational game in a simple way. Thus, the work described in this paper aims to facilitate the process of making educational video games by teachers of Deaf[1] children, through a web application based on game design processes and educational methodologies.

Adaptation is a fundamental concern in the development of educational digital games, particularly for people with specific needs [8]. Therefore, it is important to allow teachers and educators (people without experience in game design) to build a game in a semi-automatic way, through a system that adapts elements such as learning scenarios, dynamics and domain elements to meet the individual's unique characteristics, like the need of sign language use.

This paper is structured in five main sections. Section 2 addresses the authoring tools related to this research. Section 3 describes the characterization, architecture and the interface-interaction environment of the web authoring tool. Section 4, in turn, shows the games created from the authoring environment. Section 5 presents the evaluation experiment, along with the results obtained. Section 6 presents the final considerations of the research and possible future works.

2 Authoring Tools

Authoring, in Education, is the process of organizing or producing a sequence of information in order to compose software for teaching and learning [1], such as, for example, intelligent tutoring systems (ITS), which enable user interaction with a specific domain. Authoring tools have been used to build tutors across multiple domains. An authoring tool can be defined as a software which a human tutor can manipulate to create, alter or delete teaching sessions [9].

The main goals of authoring tools are [10]:

- The reduction of the effort required to build educational software;
- The decrease in the minimum skill required to deal with content outside the author's specific domain;
- The easiness of rapid prototyping.

Together, these objectives should provide a more effective way of teaching and learning. The authoring tools allow the inclusion of the teacher as an active subject in the construction of teaching-learning materials with a computer.

[1] This convention is used to refer to Deaf people as part of a community, not as disabled individuals [5].

Regarding related software for the generation of video games, the equivalent of game authoring tools, there are some known tools. Some examples are "Construct", "RPG Maker" and "GameMaker Studio".

Construct [18] is a game editor focused mainly on non-developers. It has a proprietary license and several versions for different platforms. It is based on direct manipulation, that is, it allows dragging and dropping game elements on the screen. Programming is carried out from an event system. It works by default with 2D graphics, and can be used to create games of multiple genres.

GameMaker Studio [16], a platform based on the C Language, with resources for building games from the graphical interface. It has a proprietary license and a high acquisition cost. It requires basic knowledge of Computer Programming, which prevents its use by inexperienced users. This tool allows the creation of games with advanced 3D graphics.

RPG Maker [11] is a series of game creation simplification tools focused specifically on the Role Playing Games (RPG) genre. It has a proprietary license and is available on dozens of platforms, whether on PC or video game consoles. Over time, with the evolution of the new versions, online multiplayer capabilities, 3D graphics, and the possibility of creating massive games have been added.

It is important to note that none of the mentioned tools are specialized on educational games. Moreover, all of them require a certain knowledge in event-driven programming, and this differentiates them from the tool built during the research and development processes of the tool described in this paper, which requires only basic computer skills to create a digital game.

3 The JEIS Tool

The authoring tool is based on the conceptual framework Games for the Early Childhood Education for the Deaf (JEIS) [2,3]. The conceptual framework for the design of educational games for Deaf children, was built upon extensive study in the specific literature of Game Design, Informatics in Education, Educational Games, Early Childhood Education and methodologies for Early Childhood Education for the Deaf. Figure 1 shows the overview of the framework structure.

Thus, a game generated from the tool will be organized according to the modular structure of the framework, that is, with each of its four modules - Gameplay and Tutoring, Teaching-Learning, Player or Student and Graphics and Interface. In addition, the essential characteristics in an educational game for Deaf children will be present in the created game. Therefore, the generated game will have clear objectives; a form of evaluation and support to the player during his playing time; relevant content for the target age group, as well as have appropriate interface and graphics to the specific characteristics of Deaf children.

The purpose of the authoring tool created was to enable the generation of educational digital games for Deaf children without the need of computer programming or game development skills by the author. Thus, the tool's target audience and main user is the teacher of Early Childhood Education for the

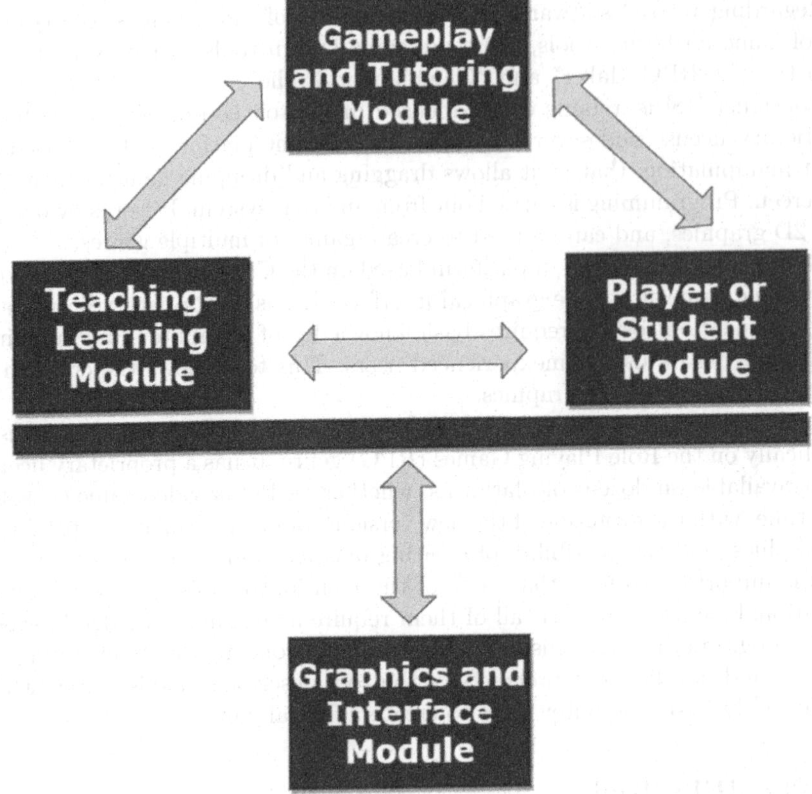

Fig. 1. Conceptual framework for educational games design

Deaf, a professional who has the knowledge to be taught, and that understands the specific characteristics of the public of his classes, his Deaf students. Through the tool, teachers have the possibility to use educational games in their classes, applying active methodologies and playful activities. With this, it is expected to increase the stimulation and motivation of Deaf children of preschool age in the study of the fundamental subjects for this stage of education.

The tool works as described below: it allows access to a database of images and their respective themes for use within games. In addition to accessing the database, the tool allows the teacher to include new Libras' signs and illustrations for later access by other users who may use the tool to create their own games.

The software architecture of the authoring tool is made up of three fundamental modules: the **Web Platform Module**, the **Generator Module** and the **Database Module**. The software architecture can be seen in Fig. 2.

The Web Platform Module is the one with which the user interacts. All visual features of the tool are in this module. It communicates with both the Generator

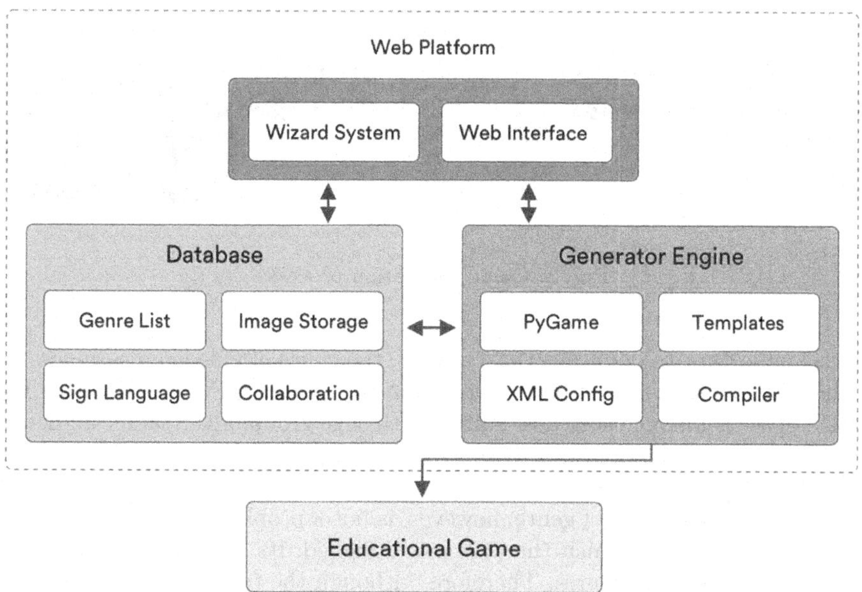

Fig. 2. Authoring tool architecture

Module and the Database Module, as the user can either start a game generation or view/store new media resources in the database.

The Generator Module is responsible for automatically generating a new educational electronic game from the input parameters received from the user by the Web Platform Module. All computer game programming logics, such as input manipulation and graphics engine, are implemented in this module. In addition, this module requests the Database Module to provide the images chosen for a given game.

Finally, the Database Module has a set of images that can be used in different games. The database is responsible for storing the resources associated with the concepts to be taught. Each concept is classified into three groups: object illustration, sign in Libras (Brazilian Sign Language) and word in Portuguese, thus enabling the use of a bilingual methodology by the teacher.

The game generation process involves getting all user-defined data during the interaction with the tool. All parameters are used to generate an eXtensible Markup Language (XML) file format, using the PHP language. The XML feeds the variables and data structures of the Generator Module, this allows different games to be generated. This XML file is read and processed by the game core, which was developed in the Python programming language. This reading happens at the moment of the execution of the game. Therefore, it is possible to run different games with a plug-and-play level of flexibility, as all games share the same programming core. The generation process is shown in Fig. 3.

Fig. 3. Game generation process

It is important to point out that, at first, the genre of video games generated by the tool was specified as Adventure, from the subgenre Point and Click. The defined genre is among those best suited to the age group of the target audience, as it allows working with storytelling, a teaching strategy used effectively in Early Childhood Education [4].

This initial definition of genre, however, is not a problem, because due to the comprehensive way in which the tool was designed, its functionality can meet the most diverse game genres. Therefore, although the tool available is initially linked to a specific genre, it will be possible to extend it with the ability to build games from other genres. When this functionality is implemented, there will be no need for much new learning by the user to create games of different genres, since the only interface environment that will change from one genre to another is that of Gameplay and Tutoring.

The "Create Game" environment holds the end capacity of the tool. In it, the teacher who wants to create a game has the possibility to create a name and choose the attributes and representations that will be part of the game in question. In Fig. 4, it is possible to check the initial tasks that the user has at his disposal in the authoring tool - the first steps to generate an educational video game.

The teacher can also define the match maximum time and the number of objectives needed to complete the levels. From these options, one can then make a game more difficult or easier, depending on the intended goal, the ages and the skills of the students. The author of the game must choose one of the themes offered by the tool such as Hygiene, Transportation, Food, Nature, Emotions, among others. All of them are contents that are part of the curriculum of Early Childhood Education. The game creation process fully follows the modular structure built on the JEIS framework, that is, Teaching-Learning Module, Gameplay and Tutoring Module, Player or Student Module and Graphics and Interface Module.

To author a game, it is necessary to interact and enter data in the following sub-environments:

- Home;
- Teaching - Learning: defines the content to be taught;
- Gameplay and Tutoring: determines the gameplay mechanics with which the player will interact;

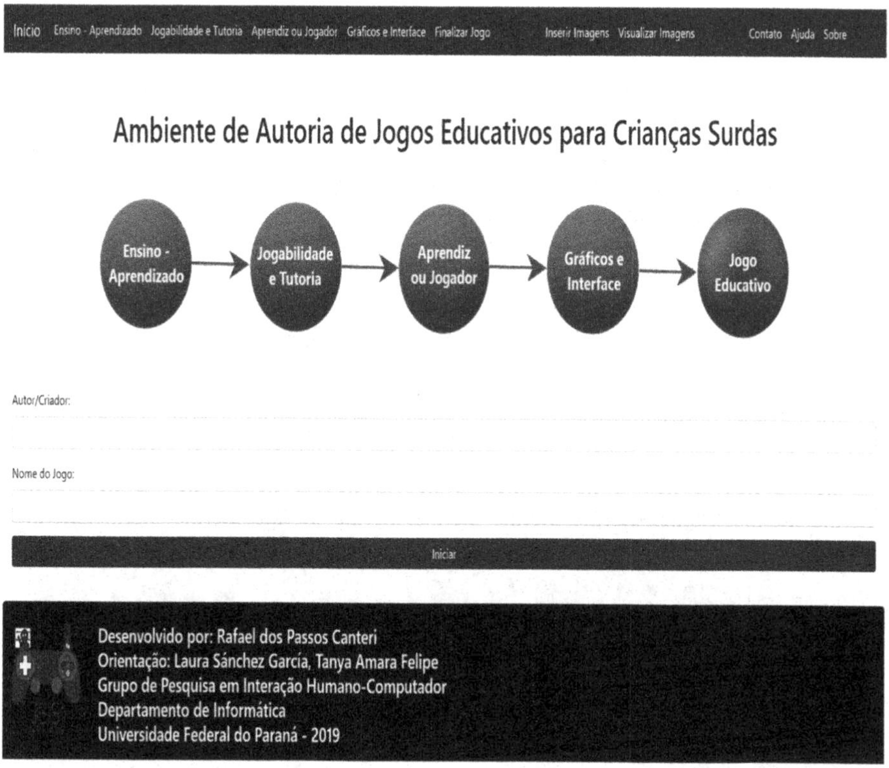

Fig. 4. System's home screen

- Player or Student: configures the hint system, the player evaluation process and the difficulty level;
- Graphics and Interface: allows the choice of visual elements that will be part of the game such as illustrations of objectives, backgrounds and avatar;
- Finish Game: displays the final report of the generated game and allows the download of the respective game or the return for desired changes.

After setting the game up and confirming the choices, the Generator Module compiles the game with the associated images, programming libraries and the XML configuration file. Then, the tool performs the process of compressing all files, folders and subfolders of the generated game. This way, the user can easily access the game, since all files are encapsulated within only one compressed file.

At the end of the process, the author can download the generated software for Windows or Linux operating systems. With this, the author has the possibility to copy the game to computers that students will use in class, as well as to distribute it to other classes, teachers and schools. The generated games do not require installation to be played and are independent of the operating system, the user just needs to unzip the downloaded file and double-click the executable file in the main game folder.

4 The Generated Game

A game was developed as a proof of concept of the authoring tool. The game presented below was entirely generated from the authoring tool. The process of creating the game shown leads to the expectation that users with basic computer skills will be able to produce a similar game using the tool.

In this example, the player needs to find all the animals that are present throughout the stage. When the player successfully finds an animal, he receives positive feedback and a balloon with the corresponding sign in Libras is displayed. This feedback with the sign in Libras is shown in Fig. 5. In this case, the player guided the character using the mouse until he touched one of the objectives of the level, the figure of a duck. This causes the image of a boy to appear, signaling the Duck sign in Libras, which remains on the screen for a few seconds so that the player can memorize the concept.

Fig. 5. Generated educational adventure game

In the upper right corner there is the button that activates the tips feature. The other interface elements present are: the red hearts that represent the amount of the character's remaining lives; the targets, which represent the number of errors allowed; a numerical value that controls the player's current score; a numerical timer counting down time in seconds; there is also the representation of the special power available for the character, which grants temporary invincibility to the player, symbolized by the icon of a flute.

In addition to the interface aspects, the game consists of the background together with the gameplay items. Such elements are: the player's avatar, in this case an Indigenous girl; the objectives to be found - the animals in this domain;

the distractors, who increase the challenge of gameplay by displaying elements that are not part of the objectives; and the opponents, represented by green little monsters, which the player must avoid in order not to waste the character's lives, this increases the player's challenge.

5 Experts Evaluation

The educational video game was evaluated by a group of seven experts. Participants were selected according to their familiarity and experience in the Human-Computer Interaction (HCI) area. Each participant was asked to play and experience all the features present in the game, with no time limit. After that, each participant was asked to answer an evaluative questionnaire of 28 closed-ended questions about the quality of the examined software, containing answers on the Likert Scale: Strongly disagree, Disagree, Neither agree nor disagree, Agree, Strongly agree. There is also one last question with an open-ended answer, with possible suggestions for improvement on the game experience.

The evaluation methodology chosen for the game was based on an extensive research, which resulted in a Doctoral Thesis [12] focused specifically on the evaluation of educational digital games. The work cited analyzed the main methodologies for evaluating educational games, and proposed, built and validated a new method in 62 case studies performed by specialists. One of the tools proposed and used in the evaluation of the games is a questionnaire with 31 questions and 5 possible answers for each one.

The evaluation questionnaire proposed by [12] has undergone some modifications in order to meet the particularities of the educational game generated by the proposed authoring tool. Aspects that took into account multiplayer modes have been removed, since the game presented in this paper is single player only. Moreover, as the educational game in question is aimed at Deaf children, three questions were added regarding the Brazilian Sign Language: "Is the game a Libras teaching method?", "Do I prefer to learn Libras with this game rather than with another form?" and "Could a Deaf child easily play this game?".

5.1 Evaluation Results

From the 28 questions presented, 26 of them received positive responses from the evaluators - Agree and Totally Agree. The analysis of the research results shows the quality of the educational game generated from the authoring tool, which in turn was guided by the conceptual framework JEIS.

The questions that received mostly negative responses were only two. The question that asked whether the game was challenging for the evaluator (question number 13), which was expected not to be, since the game challenge is designed for children aged from 2 to 6 years. The other question that received negative answers was about the video tutorial (question number 24), because at the time of the evaluations, the video tutorial faced compatibility problems with the Linux operating systems. This has already been resolved, as the technology responsible for displaying the tutorial has been changed.

6 Conclusions and Future Work

The developed web authoring tool allows Early Childhood Education teachers without any programming skills or advanced computer knowledge to create their own educational games for their students. The construction of the tool was a project that involved six different languages, front-end, back-end and game development technologies, in addition to integration and testing in web, mobile, Linux and Windows platforms. The web tool created will be presented, together with awareness of the potential of using educational games, in workshops to be held in schools that work with bilingual education for Deaf children, through the research and education partnership with the Brazilian National Institute of Deaf Education (INES). The developed artifacts are also going to be delivered and presented to inclusive regular schools. Likewise, the aim is to train teachers of Early Childhood Education so they can be able to use the artifacts, as well as encouraging their contribution with new illustrations in the media database.

The first future work to be performed on the authoring tool is recording videos in Libras for all topics in the application's Help sub-environment. These videos will be recorded by interpreters or Deaf teachers. Thus, it is intended to ensure greater accessibility to end users. The inclusion of other forms of representation of Libras signs in the authoring tool and, consequently, in the generated games, such as SignWriting, 3D avatar and video is also a possibility for future work. All of these forms of representation involve additional costs in research and development, such as the production costs of recording and editing videos for each Libras sign to be used. Another future work to be pointed out is the functionality of allowing authors to further customize the appearance of educational games generated through the authoring tool; this will be based on the study of graphic design researches specialized in Deaf children. Such customization would take place through the possibility of choosing visual themes (light, dark and neutral), in addition to the customization of colors and animations of the games.

Finally, there is an opportunity to allow the authoring tool to generate educational video games of other genres. To make this possible, the Gameplay and Tutoring module should certainly be adapted for this purpose, but a deeper analysis should be carried out to verify that the other environments do not contain genre-dependent elements. The next potential genres to be included are Platform, Puzzle and RPG, as they are genres that appeal to children and are consistent with the purpose of supporting education for the target audience.

References

1. Aroyo, L., Mizoguchi, R.: Process-aware authoring of web-based educational systems. In: Conference: The 15th Conference on Advanced Information Systems Engineering (CAiSE 2003), January 2003
2. Canteri, R.D.P.: JEIS - Framework Conceitual e Ferramenta de Autoria para a Construção de Jogos Digitais para Educação Infantil de Surdos. Ph.D. thesis, Pós-Graduação em Informática, Curitiba - PR (2019)

3. Canteri, R.D.P., Garcıa, L.S., Felipe, T.A., Galvao, L.F.O., Antunes, D.R.: Conceptual framework to support a web authoring tool of educational games for deaf children, pp. 226–235 (2019)
4. Delmar, A.S.M.: Conto e reconto de histórias na educação infantil: o uso de estratégias visuais no letramento de crianças surdas. Instituto Nacional de Educação de Surdos, vol. 1 (2016)
5. Golos, D.B., Moses, A.M., Wolbers, K.A.: Culture or disability? Examining deaf characters in children's book illustrations. Early Childhood Educ. J. **40**(4), 239–249 (2012). https://doi.org/10.1007/s10643-012-0506-0
6. Guigon, G., Humeau, J., Vermeulen, M.: A model to design learning escape games: SEGAM. In: Proceedings of the 10th International Conference on Computer Supported Education - Volume 2: CSEDU, pp. 191–197. INSTICC, SciTePress (2018). https://doi.org/10.5220/0006665501910197
7. Hotte, R., Ferreira, S.M., Abdessettar, S., Gouin-Vallerand, C.: Digital learning game scenario - a pedagogical pattern applied to serious game design. In: Proceedings of the 9th International Conference on Computer Supported Education - Volume 2: CSEDU, pp. 87–94. INSTICC, SciTePress (2017). https://doi.org/10.5220/0006260300870094
8. Laforcade, P., Loiseau, E., Kacem, R.: A model-driven engineering process to support the adaptive generation of learning game scenarios. In: Proceedings of the 10th International Conference on Computer Supported Education - Volume 2: CSEDU. pp. 67–77. INSTICC, SciTePress (2018). https://doi.org/10.5220/0006686100670077
9. Marczal, D., Direne, A.: FARMA: Uma ferramenta de autoria para objetos de aprendizagem de conceitos matemáticos. In: Simpósio Brasileiro de Informática na Educação. Rio de Janeiro - RJ (2012)
10. Murray, T.: An overview of intelligent tutoring system authoring tools: updated analysis of the state of the art. In: Murray, T., Blessing, S.B., Ainsworth, S. (eds.) Authoring Tools for Advanced Technology Learning Environments. Springer, Dordrecht (2003). https://doi.org/10.1007/978940170819717
11. Perez, D.: Beginning RPG Maker MV. Apress, Berkeley (2016). https://doi.org/10.1007/978-1-4842-1967-6
12. Petri, G.: A method for the evaluation of the quality of games for computing education. Ph.D. thesis, Programa de Pós-Graduação em Ciência da Computação, November 2018
13. Pivec, M.: Play and learn: potentials of game-based learning. Br. J. Educ. Technol. **38**(3), 387–393 (2007)
14. Randel, J.M., Morris, B.A., Wetzel, C.D., Whitehall, B.: The effectiveness of games for educational purposes: a review of recent research. Simul. Gaming **23**(3), 261–276 (1992)
15. Ritzko, J.M., Robinson, S.: Using games to increase active learning. J. Coll. Teach. Learn. **3**(6), 45–50 (2006)
16. Rohde, M.: GameMaker: Studio For Dummies. Wiley, Hoboken (2014)
17. Squire, K., Jenkins, H.: Harnessing the power of games in education. Insight **3**, 5–33 (2003)
18. Subagio, A.: Learning Construct 2. Packt Publishing, Birmingham (2014). Community experience distilled

Toward a Disability-Centric Model of User Participation in Accessibility Efforts: Lessons from a Case Study of School Children

Alison Gavine and Frank Spillers(✉)

Experience Dynamics, Portland, OR 97213, USA
{alison,frank}@experiencedynamics.com

Abstract. Designing for users with disabilities presents challenges to designers that stem from methodological as well as social origins. Designing accessible technology experiences for children with disabilities presents even greater challenges. The lack of focus on user research in accessibility efforts has created a disadvantage for designers and developers in gaining adherence and compliance to accessibility standards and best practices.

Keywords: Accessibility · Ethnography · Accessibility testing · Stigma · Disability

1 Introduction

While accessibility has come a long way [9] it also has a long way to go [10]. The public sector seems to embrace accessibility more easily as a requirement, perhaps driven by stricter regulations and inclusion requirements. However, both government and business continue to struggle to adopt accessibility guidelines, best practice and compliance. Educational institutions are required to provide accessibility in software, especially non-voluntary use of software as in the case of educational performance evaluation ("testing"). Almost all schools in the United States rely on software created by private corporations. Accessibility guideline and standard adherence varies greatly between software providers.

As with all efforts to enable participation of disadvantaged or disparate user groups, including the actual end-users or recipients of a design solution [15] in the design process continues to be a key challenge. The problem of ignoring user needs during the creation of design solutions is particularly problematic when designing for accessibility, with designers considering themselves the end-users, not the actual users [22].

Exclusion from the software creation process is especially impactful to marginalized or disadvantaged populations, where access to critical software features defines educational attainment itself. Including users with disabilities in accessibility efforts for product or service experiences suffers the same problem: inclusion of the target audience [23].

C. Stephanidis et al. (Eds.): HCII 2020, LNCS 12426, pp. 76–86, 2020.
https://doi.org/10.1007/978-3-030-60149-2_7

1.1 Adopting a Different Model to Accessibility

Accessibility efforts typically take a technology-centric model to improving access to content, which is understandable because Assistive Technology, such as a screen reader, interacts with actual code such as properly tagged digital content: e.g. Alternative text (ALT text) for images will allow the screen reader to detect and describe the image. However, this narrow approach to improving accessibility solely by following guidelines and optimizing code reduces the task to a model that inadvertently excludes users as part of the process.

Most approaches to accessibility follow a guideline, checklist or algorithmic approach to compliance checking. Software tools for testing accessibility continue to be developed to meet the demand. The problem with this technology-centric approach, is that users are rarely included in the testing process. As a result, assessing software defects with users with disabilities (Accessibility Testing) is rarely done.

Worse, trying to understand and design to user needs before beginning the design or optimization of accessibility, is even less frequently performed. User needs analysis, or ethnographic study, offers an opportunity for designers and developers to develop an advocacy approach to disability requirements. Field studies provide the ability to *empathize* as well as understand the *context-of-use* of a feature while using, for example a screen reader or magnifier. Understanding context-of-use in the accessibility user experience is rarely seen as a worthwhile effort. Official guidelines (e.g. W3C's WCAG) fail to suggest its value and instead promote the technology-centric model to accessibility.

Case Study with Schoolchildren. In this paper we will describe how a disability-centric model provided marked improvement in overall outcomes for the users but also for the developers and designers. In this paper, we discuss key lessons learned from an ethnography of school children with disabilities ages 5–18 years old. The study was conducted for a not-for-profit organization that develops software for 9,500 schools, districts, and education agencies in 145 countries. We will describe an inclusive design approach that included Ethnography followed by Interaction design and Accessibility Testing for school children with disabilities. The goal of the project was to update non-accessible software (web application) used in educational performance assessment. We aimed to ground the software improvement project by including target users (schoolchildren with disabilities) throughout the project. This included an early needs analysis (Ethnographic field study) that informed how features were designed, followed by Accessibility Testing of the new features.

Disability-Centric Model. Because the use of technology by users with disabilities is so nuanced, a new approach is required. Relying on guidelines and algorithmic tools that check accessibility alone is too risky and prone to user exclusion. Taking a disability-centric approach to accessibility puts disability at the center of the optimization effort—with an understanding of user needs and observed performance—as core to designer decision-making and developer fact-checking.

1.2 Role of Empathy in Disability User Research

For designers and developers, accessibility offers a critical opportunity to develop empathy [3]. Social neuroscience considers empathy a defining characteristic of social intelligence [6]. This seems to imply that designers and developers can improve their decision-making toward others by increasing their empathy. The popular human-centered design methodology, *Design Thinking*, specifically points to empathy as a vital tool for gaining direction into designing for others [7]. Brown notes empathy is a means to an end or vehicle for understanding user needs, not the solution itself [8].

However, the issue of empathy as a design tool has been questioned for its overall validity in the design process [5]. Studies have even shown that empathy can unintentionally distance designers from users with disabilities [4]. Norman [5] points to this fix for distorted empathy: "So we're proposing to combine experts and community workers. Instead of recommending solutions, experts should be facilitators, guides, and mentors. We need an approach that's top-down, the expert knowledge, and bottom-up, the community people". Activating the empathy process in design seems to require careful intent, that according to research, can be greatly aided with *a learning and reciprocity approach* when studying the needs of disparate groups [16].

Empathy arises from including users in the design process. The more contact you have with users the more you are likely to understand their needs [28]. User research (Ethnography and user testing) are critical for improving or gaining insight into disability issues and understanding the disability experience. For example, in our consulting practice at Experience Dynamics we have seen qualitative leaps in understanding from observing users with disabilities using Assistive Technology (AT) in their native environment (device, home etc.). We have found that observing the precise set-up of AT in context-of-use can have marked impact on fixing accessibility issues [28]. Nind [19] points to the need for a strong ethics grounding to avoid compromising, for example, children with learning difficulties, communication difficulties or users on the autism spectrum. Other researchers emphasize the need for ethnographers to give *agency* or control back to users, particularly children, regarding the content and comfort of their contributions with researchers [26, 27].

Empathy plays a critical role in the motivation to do user research. This is especially true with understanding the experience of children with disabilities adapting to digital technology, in particular in a school context where it is mandatory, not voluntarily accessed. Researchers have found that understanding the social consequences of AT in context, for example, can greatly improve design approaches in particular with error handling by blind users [11].

1.3 Stigma in Conducting Research with Users with Disabilities

Gaining access to stigmatized populations such as users with disabilities is a challenge to conducting vital user research [13]. This is due largely to the varying disability types and the lack of understanding of which types of disabilities require priority over others as well as the varying configurations, versions and AT devices types, not to mention individual user proficiency with AT. Dawe [24] found challenges in generalizing accessibility issues when conducting accessibility testing: "The types of AT devices in use for different disabilities vary widely. A single abandonment rate for all AT does not provide a very useful picture for anyone, given the large differences among the devices and the populations that use them".

Designing for children with disabilities is even more problematic, as noted in several studies with young adults [25]. Further, Dawe [24] found "teachers and parents played prominent roles at different stages of the adoption process, which also created unintended challenges to adoption". Worse, research among young children with learning disabilities "has not always been considered a valid focus of inquiry" [27].

Researchers [17] point to key challenges with how *designers frame disability design challenges* for children by taking an "enabling" of the disabled approach that "repairs" or rescues users with design (the medical model of disability) instead of imagining solutions that empower and enhance the quality of their experience.

A meta-analysis of research examining visibility of disability shows that many disabilities go undetected and therefore ignored from the design process [12] as an issue, while "advocacy is stigmatized" with legal action as a primary motivator [29].

Those unfamiliar with disability (user) research can quickly get discouraged and move away from embracing a disability-centric model to digital accessibility and inadvertently remove users from the process: focusing solely on 'testing' with a technology-centric model; assuming they can perceive issues like a user with disabilities [22]; or by solely checking WCAG guidelines—again sans users with disabilities.

2 Methodology

Before beginning the optimization of an existing web application developed by a not-for-profit organization, used to evaluate U.S. Department of Education standards for learning proficiency, we conducted an ethnography of students with disabilities. The purpose was to first understand user needs in the context of AT and school software use, before beginning the feature-optimization process and/or adherence to accessibility standards. The research was conducted using user observations and interviews across a range of disabilities and age ranges. The aim of the ethnographic field study was to understand current experiences with AT and *accommodations* in the context of the 'test' taking and assessment experience. The key question we sought to answer was: What obstacles and barriers did children with disabilities experience, especially compared with children without disabilities?

The field data was used to inform new features and interface improvements including new accessibility tools that would be required to interact with the proficiency evaluation software. The software code was then created, and we conducted several rounds of accessibility testing with children with disabilities (observing AT use with the target newly optimized accessible interfaces), in order to assess the quality of the code improvements and updates.

Children were observed using AT in their natural environment, and then informally interviewed for between 30–60 min. AT use, in classroom context, was observed. We focused on understanding the disability school experience across grade ranges. Under what conditions were students taking 'tests'? What obstacles or barriers did they confront as part of their disabilities? How did technology or current (competitor) software respond to accessibility challenges? We wanted to know what was working for students, and what AT software features were frustrating or difficult to use. Interviews were conducted with teachers or assistants present. Parents were invited to attend the interviews.

2.1 Participant Selection

A total of 22 students in K-12 (ages 5–18) at Austin Public Schools (Austin, Minnesota USA) from a sampling of disabilities represented in the school district, as well as the major areas of disability were included in the research. The school was currently using a different educational performance assessment software, similar to but not the same as that of our client. This competitor software had been optimized already for accessibility, and this allowed us an opportunity to see how well a complete 'product' performed in the field.

Students with the following disabilities were included in the user needs analysis (Table 1):

Table 1. Students recruited for the accessibility study.

Disability	Grade level: Middle school (ages 11–13)
Specific Learning Disability (SLD)	4
Visually Impaired (VI)	1
Other Health Disability (OHD)–due to Attention Deficit Hyperactivity Disorder (ADHD) and Dyslexia	3
Disability	Grade level: Elementary (ages 5–10)
Deaf Hard of Hearing (DHH)	1
Physically Impaired (PI)	1
Specific Learning Disability (SLD)	1
Autism Spectrum Disorder (ASD)	1
Speech/Language Impaired (SLI)	1
Other Health Disability (OHD)–due to Attention Deficit Hyperactivity Disorder (ADHD)	1
Disability	Grade level: High School (ages 13–18)
Specific Learning Disability (SLD)	4
Severely Multiply Impaired (SMI)–due to Deaf Hard of Hearing (DHH) and Visually Impaired (VI)	2
Other Health Disability (OHD)–due to Attention Deficit Hyperactivity Disorder (ADHD)	1

Once the user needs analysis was complete, the insights were used in the interaction design process. Developers created proof-of-concept features that could be tested with actual users with disabilities. For the follow-on Accessibility testing, we recruited a further 20 children (in the Portland area), from the major disability groups, across the K-12 age range: Visual (blind, low vision, color blindness), Deaf/hard of hearing, Motor (inability to use a mouse, slow response time, limited fine motor control), Cognitive (Learning Disabilities, distractibility, inability to remember or focus on large amounts of information or complex steps). These students helped accessibility test the educational performance assessment software with new or improved (access-optimized) features.

3 Results

The field study provided evidence of the current adoption, use and support students were receiving from AT and tools available at school. This helped us specify inclusive design solutions such as the design of digital Highlighter pens, Rulers, magnifiers etc. It showed us where children were at and what issues and obstacles they were facing in their physical, social and digital environments.

An illustration of the value of conducting the Ethnography and spending time with users with disabilities, was found in the Special Education (SPED) room- a dedicated space where children with disabilities can relax, study or take computer-based tests. We observed a blue filter over ceiling lights in the Special Education (SPED) room. This teacher-created filter allowed students to stay calm and manage stress caused by the typical classroom social environment. This *mood-enhancing* solution, we then observed being leveraged by the competitor (educational performance assessment) software being used by the children–see Fig. 1 below. We interviewed these SPED teacher advocates, who confirmed that students liked the 'mood light' and used the blue filter on the software frequently. This example illustrates the value of direct observation in a user's environment and how such an insight translates to the prioritization and value (to users) of a proposed feature.

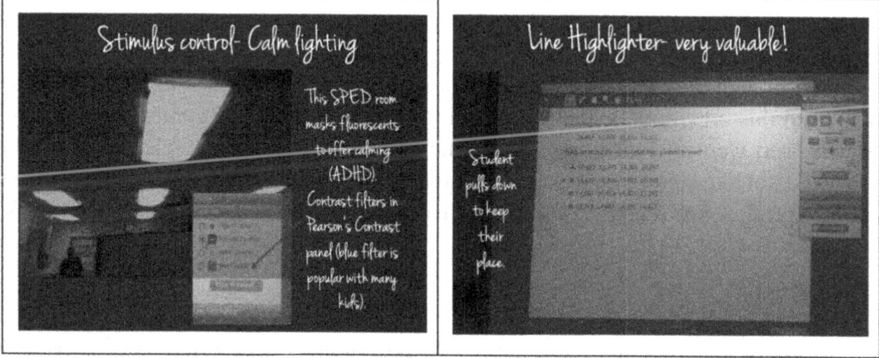

Fig. 1. Blue light filter over classroom lights (left); accessibility tool (blue filter feature-right) observed in use in curriculum assessment software. (Color figure online)

Further findings gave us specific insights into the AT toolbar that would be introduced into the software. In the schools, we noticed that physical calculators were more popular than digital ones, and that physical AT rulers and protractors were missing. We noticed physical magnifiers in use but an absence of AT screen magnifiers (ZoomText and MaGic, for example). Screen magnifiers help low vision users perceive text and details on a screen and are built into Apple's iOS, for example. Several middle school students with low vision who might benefit, did not realize their iPads had a Magnifier feature available. Formally activating the feature on her iPad (Settings > Accessibility etc.). at school was too embarrassing for a high school student, meaning AT tools should be 'just-in-time' to bypass schoolroom stigma—especially at older grade levels where social scrutiny from peers is high. This example illustrates how understanding *social* context-of-use can increase the priority or placement of a feature (Fig. 2).

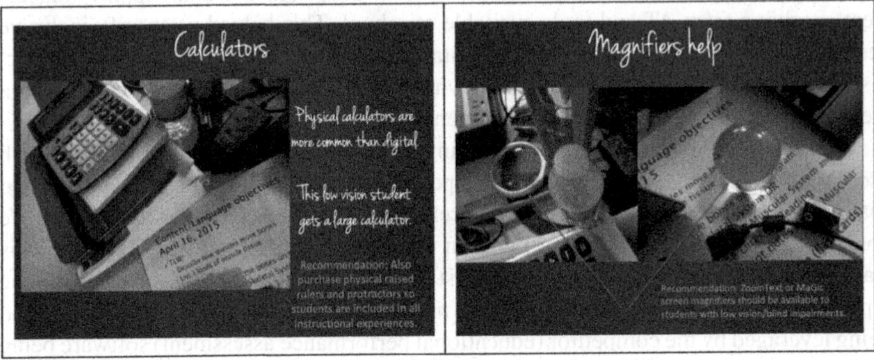

Fig. 2. Physical calculators were more prevalent (left); which magnifiers were very common (right) they were not always available in software used by the students.

Later in the process, during accessibility testing of proof-of-concept features, we observed users struggling with online protractors seemingly due to their physics behaviors on screen, but also novelty or lack of familiarity—findings we had observed in context, during the field study. Students had not seen a physical protractor and physical versions with AT features, e.g. *Braille rulers* or *Tactile protractors*, were not available at school, though they can be easily purchased online. The user testing allowed us to understand this important context-of-use of the tool within the AT context specifically, and why users were uncomfortable with certain technologies. For example, students told us they did not like laptops because they required more eye-hand coordination as well as keyboard proficiency. iPads or tablets were easier to interact with, they said. See Fig. 3.

4 Analysis

The process of including users throughout the design process centered gave us critical direction and guidance that would have otherwise been theoretical or guess-work. The ability to use the 'empathy insights' from the user research was invaluable in providing strategic direction as well as tactical guidance throughout the project lifecycle. Instead

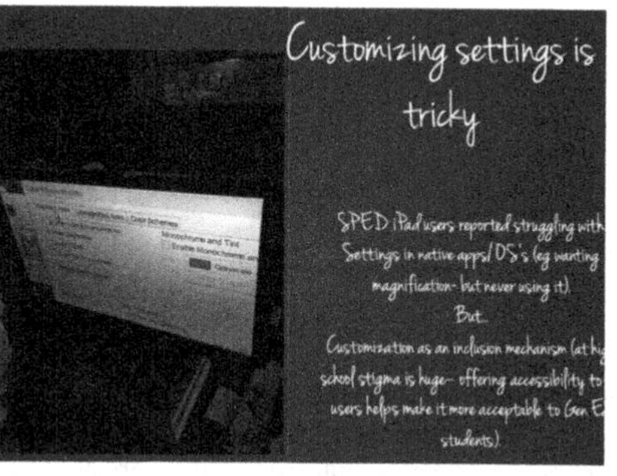

Fig. 3. Students struggled with keyboard use and found tablet interaction easier. We observed that games that provide keyboard mapping tips on-screen, the students found helpful (left). Customizing settings was challenging for users (right) and at the high school level contributed to social stigma within the peer community—if a setting was not apparent, having to go configure it showed a 'special' need. High school students do not want to feel singled-out, or 'special'.

of defining UI features and design ideas on *internal design decisions* and then matching accessibility guidelines to the "new AT tools", the way many organizations conduct accessibility efforts, we instead had evidence-based validation and insights that designers and developers used to better interpret and comply with government and W3 WCAG guidelines.

The key findings emerging from our disability-centric model of user participation, clustered around the following themes:

- Observing pain points and context-of-use allowed for greater empathy and understanding about what might work or not work in interaction design. For example, users seemed to need direct access to AT tools or configuration options. We evidenced this from observing students with visual impairments (low vision in particular), not using standard Screen Magnifier AT. We observed students with cognitive impairments not enjoying school-issued laptops due to inefficiency and added effort of use. We noted the preference for iPads due to direct, rapid interaction for students with cognitive and mobility impairments.
- Understanding how users work-around cumbersome or absent AT solutions provided clear direction for possible design solutions. For example, it appeared that the absence of physical protractors meant a steeper learning curve for students when discovering a digital tool modeled after a real-world tool. Even calculators seem to be a newer concept for the digital generation and the literacy of using a calculator seems to require some exposure—it was not an immediate use experience for primary and elementary students, unlike most adults (teachers) who have grown up with the familiar mental model. In both calculator and protractor examples, user testing showed us that we had to design the tools with not only accessibility guidelines (see Fig. 4) but also with a simplified interaction model.

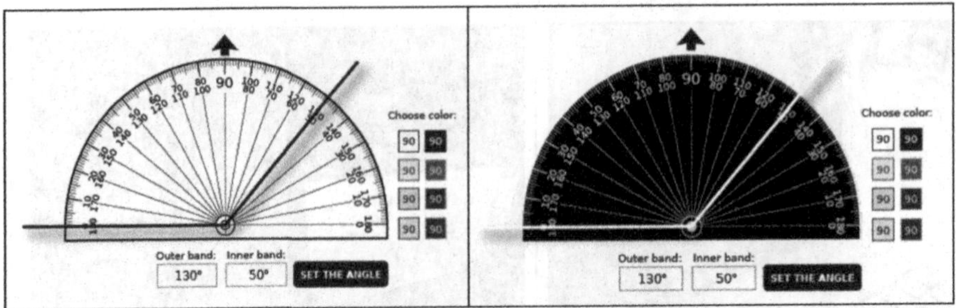

Fig. 4. Standard contrast protractor (left) and high-contrast protractor (right). The high-contrast design is accessibility compliant for low vision users. In addition, the interaction (usage of) the protractor has been simplified to allow greater access to children unfamiliar with the physical manipulation of a protractor.

- Checking accessibility enhancements and new accessible UI concepts with children with disabilities against WCAG guidelines, allowed us to identify accessibility 'bugs' and report them to the developers for investigation. By conducting Accessibility Testing, we were able to directly observe children struggling with the proposed tools and access features in the educational performance assessment software experience. We believe a standard machine-level accessibility tool check, or review against the W3 WCAG guidelines, would not have identified these issues. For example, much of the UI feedback related to icon intuitiveness, leading us to redraw icons several times to allow them to be more perceivable by the students. This reinforces the need to include users with disabilities in accessibility quality improvement efforts, instead of assuming designers or developers can interpret the guidelines sufficiently [22].
- Being mindful of inclusion in design, early-on, enables an 'accessibility first' approach (disability-centric model) that will likely reduce the common 'build, then make accessible later' approach. It seems that such a bolt-on accessibility approach creates the need for *excessive iterative testing* as we learned with placement of our toolbar AT. The new toolbar interface was created based on software requirements: e.g. Test question + toolbar: "Read this problem and use the tools to solve the equation". Our findings indicated that users did not explore the tool bar unless the precise problem-solving tools were offered for that particular test question. A persistent generic toolbar with "all tools" was all too often ignored by the students. Instead, we had to be mindful of the ordering of tool bar icon/buttons—a trade-off in maintaining consistency of the toolbar UI, vs providing contextually-supported tools. Thinking of our users with disabilities, knowing the struggle they have to endure—even with the right AT—we were able to make more carefully calculated interaction design decisions.

5 Conclusions and Recommendations

By including users with disabilities throughout the accessibility enhancement or improvement process, we were aided by practical insights and strategic findings that helped not only improve the immediate software but also helped the designer and developer team apply learnings to avoid future mistakes. The process of developing a disability-centric model of interaction design helped us include users with disabilities and optimize around their real needs, not merely relying on official accessibility guidelines or automated checking tools. We found that enabling participation of users with disabilities not only kept the project grounded but forced us to reality-check guidelines and gain observed evidence as to their practicality and performance.

References

1. Huck, J.: Supporting empathy through embodiment in the design of interactive systems. In: Proceedings of the Ninth International Conference on Tangible, Embedded, and Embodied Interaction (TEI 2015), pp. 523–528. ACM, New York (2015)
2. Coulton, P.: Designing interactive systems to encourage empathy between users. In: Proceedings of the 2014 companion publication on Designing interactive systems (DIS Companion 2014), pp. 13–16. ACM, New York (2014)
3. Putnam, C. Dahman, M., Rose, E., Cheng, J., Bradford, G.: Teaching accessibility, learning empathy. In: Proceedings of the 17th International ACM SIGACCESS Conference on Computers & Accessibility (ASSETS 2015), pp. 333–334. ACM, New York (2015)
4. Bennet, C.L., Rosner, D.K.: The promise of empathy: design, disability, and knowing the "Other". In: Proceedings of the 2019 CHI Conference on Human Factors in Computing Systems (CHI 2019), vol. 298, pp. 1–13. ACM, New York (2019)
5. Norman, D.: Why I don't believe in empathic design (2019). https://xd.adobe.com/ideas/perspectives/leadership-insights/why-i-dont-believe-in-empathic-design-don-norman/. Accessed 1 Jun 2019
6. Herzig, A., Lorini, E., Pearce, D.: Social intelligence. AI & Soc. **34**(4), 689 (2017). https://doi.org/10.1007/s00146-017-0782-8
7. Brown, T.: Change by Design. HarperCollins, New York City (2019)
8. Nusca, A.: IDEO CEO Tim Brown: For design, 'empathy is not the end, it's the means (2019). https://fortune.com/2019/03/05/ideo-ceo-tim-brown/. Accessed 14 Aug 2019
9. Ladner, R.E. Accessibility is becoming mainstream. In: Proceedings of the 18th International ACM SIGACCESS Conference on Computers and Accessibility (ASSETS 2016), p. 1. ACM, New York (2016)
10. Rode, J., et al.: SIG on the state of accessibility at CHI. In: Proceedings of the 2016 CHI Conference Extended Abstracts on Human Factors in Computing Systems (CHI EA 2016), pp. 1100–1103. ACM, New York (2016)
11. Easley, W., et al.: Let's get lost: exploring social norms in predominately blind environments. In: Proceedings of the 2016 CHI Conference Extended Abstracts on Human Factors in Computing Systems (CHI EA 2016), pp. 2034–2040. ACM, New York (2016)
12. Faucett, H., Ringland, K., Cullen, A., Hayes. G.: (In)Visibility in disability and assistive technology. ACM Trans. Accessible Comput. **10**(4), 1–17 (2017)
13. Maestre, J., et al.: Conducting research with stigmatized populations: practices, challenges, and lessons learned. In: Companion of the 2018 ACM Conference on Computer Supported Cooperative Work and Social Computing (CSCW 2018), pp. 385–392. ACM, New York (2018)
14. Moore, J.E., Love, M.S.: An examination of prestigious stigma: the case of the technology geek. In: Proceedings of the 2004 SIGMIS Conference on Computer Personnel Research: Careers, Culture, and Ethics in a Networked Environment (SIGMIS CPR 2004), pp. 103–103. ACM, New York (2004)
15. McGarvey, D.: Poverty Safari: Understanding the Anger of Britain's Underclass. Luath Press Ltd, Edinburgh (2017)

16. Brereton, M., Roe, P., Schroeter, R., Hong, A.: Beyond ethnography: engagement and reciprocity as foundations for design research out here. In: Proceedings of the SIGCHI Conference on Human Factors in Computing Systems (CHI 2014), pp. 1183–1186. ACM, New York (2014)
17. Frauenberger, C., Good, J., Alcorn, A.: Challenges, opportunities and future perspectives in including children with disabilities in the design of interactive technology. In: Proceedings of the 11th International Conference on Interaction Design and Children (IDC 2012), pp. 367–370. ACM, New York (2012)
18. Abdolrahmani, A., Easley, W., Williams, M., Branham, S., Hurst, A.: Embracing errors: examining how context of use impacts blind individuals' acceptance of navigation aid errors. In: Proceedings of the 2017 CHI Conference on Human Factors in Computing Systems (CHI 2017), pp. 4158–4169. ACM, New York (2017)
19. Nind. M.: Conducting qualitative research with people with learning, communication and other disabilities: Methodological challenges. Project Report. National Centre for Research Methods (2008)
20. Disability rights commission report, the web: access and inclusion for disabled people (2004). https://www.city.ac.uk/__data/assets/pdf_file/0004/72670/DRC_Report.pdf. Accessed 1 Jan 2018
21. Hartblay, C. Inaccessible accessibility: an ethnographic account of disability and globalization in contemporary Russia (2019). https://cdr.lib.unc.edu/concern/dissertations/2v23vv61m. Accessed 25 Oct 2019
22. Law, C.M., Yi, J.S., Choi, Y.S., Jacko, J.A.: Are disability-access guidelines designed for designers?: Do they need to be?. In: Kjeldskov, J., Paay, J. (eds.) Proceedings of the 18th Australia conference on Computer-Human Interaction: Design: Activities, Artefacts and Environments (OZCHI 2006), pp. 357–360. ACM, New York (2006). http://dx.doi.org/10.1145/1228175.1228244
23. Farmer, M., Macleod, F.: Involving disabled people in social research. Office for Disability Issues. HM Government, UK (2011). https://assets.publishing.service.gov.uk/government/uploads/system/uploads/attachment_data/file/321254/involving-disabled-people-in-social-research.pdf. Accessed 11 Nov 2019
24. Dawe, M.: Desperately seeking simplicity: how young adults with cognitive disabilities and their families adopt assistive technologies. In: Grinter, R., Rodden, T., Aoki, P., Cutrell, E., Jeffries, R., Olson, G. (eds.) Proceedings of the SIGCHI Conference on Human Factors in Computing Systems (CHI 2006), pp. 1143–1152. ACM, New York (2006)
25. Dawe, M.: Understanding mobile phone requirements for young adults with cognitive disabilities. In: Proceedings of the 9th international ACM SIGACCESS conference on Computers and accessibility (Assets 2007), pp. 179–186. ACM, New York, NY (2007)
26. Davis, J., Watson, N., Cunningham-Burley, S.: Learning the lives of disabled children. In: Christensen, P., James, A. (eds.) Research with Children: Perspectives and practices. Routledge, London (2000)
27. Nind, M., Flewitt, R., Payler, J.: The experiences of young children with learning disabilities attending both special and inclusive preschools (2010). https://eprints.soton.ac.uk/162713/1/Social_experience_for_eprints.doc. Accessed 21 May 2019
28. Spillers, F.: What exactly is the benefit of Ethnographic interviews for accessibility? (2018). https://www.experiencedynamics.com/blog/2018/07/what-exactly-benefit-ethnographic-interviews-accessibility. Accessed 2 May 2019
29. Pulrang, A.: Why is accessibility still a problem? What can we do about it? forbes (2019). https://www.forbes.com/sites/andrewpulrang/2019/11/21/why-is-accessibility-still-a-problem-what-can-we-do-about-it/#4fa18e97f23a. Accessed 22 Nov 2019

Institutionalizing Universal Design: How Organizational Practices Can Promote Web Accessibility

G. Anthony Giannoumis(✉) and Lars Henrik Nordli

Oslo Metropolitan University, Oslo, Norway
gagian@oslomet.no

Abstract. This article examines organizational practices for ensuring that web content is designed to be usable by everyone – i.e., universal design – and accessible for persons with disabilities. Qualitative data from a case study of the Norwegian Broadcasting Corporation (NRK) demonstrates that barriers exist, which prevent persons with disabilities from using the web content produced by NRK. The results further demonstrate that although editorial employees at NRK have some awareness and knowledge of universal design and web accessibility principles, requirements and techniques, organizational practices including reporting, communication and training constrain opportunities for promoting and ensuring universal design and web accessibility.

Keywords: Web accessibility · Universal design · Institutional change · Organizational processes

1 Introduction

The United Nations (UN) Convention on the Rights of Persons with Disabilities (CRPD) obligates State Parties to ensure access for persons with disabilities to information and communication technology (ICT), including the web, on an equal basis with others. The UN also obligates State Parties to "undertake or promote research and development of universally designed goods, services, equipment and facilities". According to the UN, universal design refers to "the design of products, environments, programmes and services to be usable by all people, to the greatest extent possible".

Research on universal design and web accessibility demonstrates that persons with disabilities experience barriers accessing and using web content, which has resulted in a digital divide [1–4]. This article refers to the digital divide as the social inequality that results when service providers design ICT that is not usable by one or more groups of people, e.g., persons with disabilities.

However, despite efforts by the UN and national governments to eliminate the digital divide, barriers to ensuring universal design and web accessibility remain [5–11]. Countries such as the United States, United Kingdom, Norway and Australia have enacted legislation aimed at eliminating discrimination against persons with disabilities, which

C. Stephanidis et al. (Eds.): HCII 2020, LNCS 12426, pp. 87–102, 2020.
https://doi.org/10.1007/978-3-030-60149-2_8

State and non-State actors concerned with disability rights have used to promote web accessibility [6, 12, 13]. Research demonstrates that ensuring web accessibility requires organizations to adapt existing and adopt new practices [5, 6]. Essentially, research suggests that in order to remove barriers for persons with disabilities in accessing and using web content, service providers must change organizational norms, values and procedures.

Research has examined organizational norms values and procedures as social institutions [14]. Research has adopted different analytic perspectives for examining how social institutions structure and constrain organizational practices [14–16]. Hall and Taylor [16] argue that, from an historical perspective, social institutions generate preferences over time, which become part of the taken-for-granted assumptions of organizational practice. However, the authors also argue that from a sociological perspective, social institutions structure organizational expectations and opportunities for action and change. Research on social institutions provides a useful basis for examining the institutional constraints for ensuring web accessibility in practice.

While research has examined how social institutions structure and constrain organizational practices, research has also examined the mechanisms for institutional change [17–20]. Research on institutional change suggests that the implementation of web accessibility law and policy can influence organizational practices [12, 21, 22]. Research has attempted to characterize the mechanisms and types of institutional change, and provides a useful perspective for examining the how and to what extent social norms may be integrated with organizational practices [18, 23, 24].

However, research has yet to fully examine web accessibility from an institutional perspective and as a process of institutional change. In addition, research in business communication has only recently begun to investigate topics related to disability and accessibility [25]. This cutting-edge research has shown that social justice issues, including those related to disability, can form an essential part of ensuring access to information for persons with disabilities in business and professional communication pedagogy and practice [26–31]. This article, in particular, builds on research by [29], which has investigated the mechanisms that influence whether and to what extent accessibility barriers are constructed within an organization. This article aims to fill these gaps by using institutional theory to examine the constraints and opportunities for ensuring universal design and web accessibility in practice. This article asks, "How do social institutions influence organizational practices for ensuring web accessibility?"

2 Analytic Framework

This article uses theory and models of social institutions and institutional change to examine the potential relationship between organizational practices and social norms, values and procedures for promoting and ensuring universal design and web accessibility.

2.1 Institutions

Dacin, Goodstein [23] state that "Institutional theory has risen to prominence as a popular and powerful explanation for both individual and organizational action". Institutional theory highlights how cultural influences affect decision-making and formal structures in the institution. Institutions also represent the constraints and barriers in organizations, and these barriers tend to lead the people towards a certain type of behaviour [32].

An institution is defined as a collection of established rules and organized activities and practices that perpetuates and changes over time [33]. March and Olsen [33] states that "[i]nstitutionalism connotes a general approach to the study of political institutions, a set of theoretical ideas and hypothesis concerning the relations between institutional characteristics and political agency, performance and change" [33]. In other words, the authors argue that investigating institutions requires an examination of the relationship between features of the institution and opportunities for action. Barley and Tolbert [32] have additionally argued that "... institutions are socially constructed templates for action, generated and maintained through ongoing interactions" [32]. In other words, institutions are not static but in a constant state of renewal based on the behaviours of institutional actors.

Institutional theory provides a useful basis for examining organizational norms, values and procedures. This article uses institutional theory to examine the relationship between the norms, values and procedures at NRK and universal design principles and practices.

2.2 Institutional Change

Although institutions are typically defined as relatively enduring, and are therefore perpetual and difficult to change, March and Olsen [33] argue that institutionalized "[r]ules, routines, norms and identities are both instruments of stability and arenas for change". Research suggests that although institutions are difficult to change, institutions may change incrementally and over time [18]. As Barley and Tolbert [32] state, "[i]nstitutions, therefore, represent constraints on the options that individuals and collectives are likely to exercise, albeit constraints that are open to modification over time" [32]. In other words, while institutions may structure and constrain actor behaviour over the long-term, institutional characteristics may shift and adjust over time in response to internal or external pressures for change.

Research has examined the paradox of institutions as stable features of society and as arenas for change by investigating self-reinforcing processes [34, 35]. While Greif and Laitin [34] view institutions as self-enforcing, the authors argue that two mechanisms underlie institutional change. First, the authors reason that the validity and soundness of the values, rules and practices in an institution may be too weak to be self-enforced, and will therefore change. This can be viewed as an internal stressor for institutional change. Second, the authors argue that external shocks, or stressors, may affect institutional values, rules and practices, and will therefore change. Examples of external shocks are customer complaints or new or altered legislation that applies to the institution, and therefore forces it to change. Dacin, Goodstein [23] characterize the scope of institutional change stating that "[i]nstitutional change can proceed from the most micro interpersonal and suborganizational levels to the most macro societal and global levels".

Scott [36] refers to the process of institutional change as deinstitutionalization. Deinstitutionalization explains how institutions, including its rules and practices, can weaken and disappear, and by doing so make institutions receptive for new ideas and practices, that may ultimately create new institutions.

Research has also attempted to characterize the mechanisms behind institutional change [24]. Oliver [24] poses three mechanisms that can effect change in institutions including functional, political and social sources. Functional pressures are those that evolve from perceived problems or efficiencies in existing practices. Political pressures are those that evolve from shifts in the underlying power distributions, which cause an organization to question the legitimacy of the institution. Social pressures are those that evolve from a lack of consensus on the purpose of organizational practices [24].

Research has also attempted to create a typology of institutional changes [18]. Mahoney and Thelen [18] presented four types of institutional change including, displacement, layering, drift and conversion. The authors describe displacement as "the removal of existing rules, and the introduction to new ones". Layering is described as "the introduction of new rules on top of or alongside existing ones" [18]. Drift is described as "the changed impact of existing rules due to the shifts in the environment" [18]. Conversion is described as "the changed enactment of existing rules due to their strategic redeployment" [18].

Models of institutional change provide a useful basis for examining the mechanisms for and categories of change in organizational norms, values and procedures. This article uses institutional change theory to assess the mechanisms for and types of changes that promote and ensure web accessibility and universal design in practice.

3 Methods, Data and Analysis

This article uses qualitative data from an in-depth case study to examine the institutional constraints and opportunities for ensuring universal design in practice. According to Lazar, Feng [37], a case study is an "in-depth study of a specific instance … within a real life context" [37, p. 144]. Further, they explain that case studies work well to "build understanding, generate theories … present evidence for the existence of certain behaviour, or to provide insight that would otherwise be difficult to gather" [37, p. 144]. According to Berg, Lune [38, p. 251], "Case study methods involve systematically gathering enough information about a particular person, social setting, event, or group to permit the researcher to effectively understand how the subject operates or functions". Case studies are effective at investigating entities such as phenomena, communities, or institutions, in addition to uncover characteristics of the entities [38, p. 251]. The rich data that case study methods provide enable researchers to identify nuances, patterns, and deviations that other research methods may overlook [38, p. 251].

NRK provides a useful case for examining the drivers for creation and perpetuation of social institutions that constrain the promotion of web accessibility and universal design in practice. In addition, this case study of NRK attempts to gain insights on the potentially causal relationships between social institutions and the institutional changes that would ensure universal design in practice.

This case study utilizes three forms of data. All data collection was approved by the Norwegian Centre for Research Data and the authors have obtained permission to use the data in publication. Data was first collected using on-site observations, which were performed at the NRK offices and aimed to document relevant practices and procedures. Second, this article uses interview data from a purposive sample of seven participants including journalists, editors, editors in-chief and shift leaders involved in publishing textual, image, or video content to NRK's website. The interviews aimed to capture the roles and responsibilities of content creators at NRK, software and systems used at NRK, and knowledge and awareness of universal design practices. Third, this article uses internal and external document data including national and international law and policy and organizational policies and practices. Investigators compared the data from the on-site observations, semi-structured interviews and documents to confirm or clarify the results.

In order to examine the relationship between universal design and web accessibility norms, values and procedures and organizational practices at NRK, this article uses different forms of analysis. First this article uses thematic analysis to identify common patters and themes present in the data [38, p. 200, 39]. Thematic analysis uses open coding, which focuses on categorizing the data into concepts and categories informed by the analytic framework and previous research [40]. The data was therefore used to probe and interrogate the assumptions embedded in a mix of different models and theories for institutions and institutional change. Second, after the observational, interview and document data was coded, it was recursively abstracted to summarize and contextualize the data [41]. The abstracted summaries were cross-checked with the coded data, which ensured that the summaries stayed consistent with the interviews.

4 Universal Design and Digital Media in Norway

Norway has ratified the CRPD, which obligates the Norwegian government to take all appropriate legislative, administrative or other measures to ensure ICT accessibility. In 2009, the Norwegian government enacted legislation, which, among other things, obligates service providers to ensure the universal design of ICT. The law refers to universal design as "designing or accommodating the main solution with respect to the physical conditions, including ICT, such that the general function of the undertaking can be used by as many people as possible" [44]. Subsequently, the Norwegian government published regulations pursuant to the obligation for universal design, which require service providers to comply with a web accessibility standard called the Web Content Accessibility Guidelines (WCAG).

In Norway, like many other countries, journalism and the news media has undergone a paradigm shift in response to the introduction of digital and social media [45]. McNair [45] explains that the traditional objective model of journalism changes towards a model where journalism is increasingly "networked, globalized and participatory". This shift has occurred as a result of more users consuming and producing digital media. Consumers have drastically changed the way they consume news due to the increase in news sources and the availability of the news sources. This creates a need for more frequent updates of the news sources, which in turn may undermine the more time-consuming investigative and analytical reporting. As Weaver [46] states, "… news websites demand frequent updating throughout the 24-h news cycle, restricting time for fact checking and independent reporting, especially the investigative and analytical reporting that often takes weeks or months to do".

The developments and consequences of the paradigm shift, in how news is created and consumed, suggests that the editorial employees at NRK are likely to work on multiple smaller tasks at once, in a fast paced and quickly moving environment, with less room for time-consuming and investigative reporting [45, 46]. Therefore, editorial employees may not always consider universal design as a priority due, in part, to the cognitive effort of ensuring accessible content [47].

NRK is Norway's largest media organization and public broadcaster, delivering news articles online, television and radio content. NRK aims to, among other things, "be accessible to the public … and … take into consideration people with disabilities" [48]. All of NRK's products are available on NRK's website. NRK is a governmentally-owned, non-commercial organization that relies on yearly fees from the population on Norway. This article argues that the size and role of the organization, nationally, makes NRK a relevant case for examining the organizational challenges that the editorial employees face, the responsibilities that editorial employees have in promoting accessibility and universal design.

While NRK has a legal obligation to comply with WCAG, persons with disabilities still experience barriers accessing content on NRK's website [49]. The Norwegian government's "Action Plan for Universal Design" specifically targets "universal design of all of NRK's public broadcasting media" [50]. However, this measure does not cover NRK's digital services, but rather focuses on broadcast television programmes.

Journalists, editors and domain experts, collectively referred to as editorial employees, are continuously creating and revising digital print and multimedia content for NRK's website. This makes the web content subject to constant change depending on different work practices and product views from both internal and external sources. For example, a change in an article can occur because an editor in-chief disagrees or wishes to add additional important content to the article. As another example, where articles are based on collaborations with external actors, e.g., experts or journalists, articles may change if the external source notices that something is wrongly reported.

All textual and multimedia content on NRK's website is published through NRK's in-house Content Management System (CMS) called Polopoly (PP). CMS typically act as a collaborative platform as well as a low-threshold alternative for the creation and modification of web content. The employees at NRK have frequent daily interactions with PP, which, together with a system called Panorama, renders the text content and metadata for NRK's website. Most of Polopoly's functionality is developed in-house at NRK. Polopoly stores both textual content and metadata, over which the editorial employees have access and control. However, editorial employees do not control the rendering process.

NRK has issued an internal policy called the "Blue Book", which contains rules and guidelines regarding how editorial employees should prepare, compose, and publish textual and multimedia content. It also contains grammar and punctuation rules. The Blue Book was created by and is periodically reviewed and edited by the NRK's board of directors. The Blue Book does not contain any reference or mention of usability, accessibility or universal design. However, all of the participants explained that they periodically receive a group e-mail regarding NRK's practices for ensuring image accessibility. All of the participants explained that this e-mail required and reminded them to enter text descriptions for images that relate to the contents and the context of the image.

5 Institutionalizing Universal Design

The results of this research suggest that the norms, values and procedures associated with web accessibility and universal design have yet to be fully integrated into the organizational practices at NRK.

5.1 Knowledge and Awareness of Universal Design Norms, Values and Procedures

The data suggests that the majority of the editorial employees are unfamiliar with universal design principles, requirements and techniques.

Universal Design Principles. Six out of seven participants claimed to be familiar with the term universal design. However, the participants' definitions differed from definitions used by the UN and the Norwegian government. One participant defined universal design as "a system that is usable by everyone, independent of previous technical experience and knowledge". This definition conceptualizes universal design in reference to an individual's experience using computers and technical tools, and reflects other statements made by the same participant, which demonstrated a lack of awareness regarding accessibility and usability criteria.

Another participant defined universal design, as "it should be understandable and available for those with visual impairments or hearing impairments". The participation did not clarify to what "it" referred. However, this definition more closely relates to accessibility than universal design. Yet another participant defined universal design as "that all services in the society should be adapted to be usable independent of challenges … What comes to mind first for me, is universal design in buildings". This definition conceptualizes universal design in relation to the built environment and does not address ICT or websites. The participant further expressed familiarity with the use of screen readers – i.e., a type of assistive technology that uses a speech synthesizer to read text.

The last participant defined universal design as "that all of our systems should be able to communicate and work in the same way, so that the people who know one system, knows them all". This definition also focuses on usability of the technical system, maybe at NRK. This definition also does not mention users, but focuses on "systems", i.e. products.

Collectively, the results demonstrate that some of the participants are familiar with conceptualizations of universal design although none of their definitions reflect the scope of conceptualizations used by the Norwegian government and the UN.

Requirements for Universal Design. One participant stated that "universal design means that we are obligated, required by the law to retrofit/adjust our content so that everyone can enjoy content, no matter if they are for example blind". This definition addresses universal design as a legal requirement instead of based on usability or accessibility. Only two of the seven participants reported to know that a national requirement for universal design of ICT existed, which covered web accessibility. One participant was somewhat familiar with the wording of the requirements, and another participant reported that, although never having read the requirements, they were reminded of the requirement through e-mails.

The remaining participants reported some mixed responses. For instance, one participant reported to be familiar with accessibility guidelines for the built environment, referring specifically to wheel-chair accessibility, and not to ICTs. The remaining five participants were not familiar with the national requirement for universal design of ICT. One participant, frustratingly, stated that "I have heard of no such thing! … I have no idea what tools we have to improve our articles for people with disabilities. … I think it is discouraging – we [NRK] are a governmental organization".

None of the participants reported that they were familiar with any external or internal guidelines regarding usability, accessibility or universal design. For example, none of the participants reported to be familiar with the WCAG standard, which are referred to in the national regulations for universal design of ICT.

Techniques for Ensuring Universal Design. This section outlines what the participants reported regarding particular techniques related to universal design and web accessibility. Four of the seven participants reported to actively take measures towards improving usability, accessibility or universal design for the user. However, the participants did not use those terms. The participants may not relate these measures with usability, accessibility or universal design. The measures that the participants discussed focused on image accessibility and text readability.

Image Accessibility. Generally, the participants demonstrated knowledge of what and how image descriptions should be used to benefit blind or visually impaired users. However, one participant expressed uncertainty about what the image descriptions should be, and where this became visible and verifiable in the published article. The participant clearly recognized the use of the term "alternative text" and that an image needed one neutral descriptive description, and one context specific description. The participant asked "shouldn't the neutral description and context-specific description be a sufficient alternative text?". This suggests that the participant was familiar with the concept of alternative text, but rather unfamiliar on how it was generated and how it worked for the end users. In addition to this, the participant also asked if "this [alternative text] is something that is solved technically, right?", which may suggest that the participant does not feel responsible for how the alternative text was created in the final article. The participant further stated that "journalists will never enter any extra content to images or articles", presumably because the journalists are in a high-paced and dynamic environment where the work must be finished quickly.

Five of the seven participants reported that image descriptions were something that they have been told to do through e-mails, and that this is something they actively consider when adding images to news articles. However, one participant seemed to be unsure of what alternative text should be, and whether their colleagues in fact provided descriptive and contextualized image descriptions in practice.

One participant raised concerns about the extra time it took to enter such a description to images, stating that "It is more work to enter this description, and if something urgent happening, the solution is to make a short version of this".

Another participant raised concerns over Search Engine Optimization (SEO) and reflected on the use of image descriptions to improve SEO. SEO typically refers to the process of designing a website to improve the ranking or visibility in search results.

Readability and Comprehension. While one participant did not report conducting any particular language or readability adjustments, the majority of the participants take readability, length of text, and text comprehension seriously. More specifically, three participants explicitly underlined the importance of language simplicity, readability and comprehensibility when writing articles for NRK's website. Two other participants explicitly reported that writing clearly is something on which all journalists in the organization are required to focus, and something that is actively reinforced and maintained through courses and constant reminders. Another participant also mentioned that they are very aware on how to make content easy to read, both in terms of how to write content, and to always have "weaker-readers" in mind, given that most journalists are usually strong readers.

One participant explained that NRK recently established restrictions on article length, in an effort to further stress readability. This restriction had been introduced because of "statistics made from NRK, showing that users do not read more than 450 words of an article before closing or moving on to another article". Another participant reported to have previously used a tool called LIX to calculate the readability of an article based on "repeating words and long words among others". The participant reported that editorial employees soon started to question the validity of the tool, and how it actually helped the language in an article. Therefore, the participant, and many other editorial employees, stopped using the tool.

One participant reported that the journalists are encouraged to include fact boxes or info boxes on topics that require backstory, context or further explanation. Specifically, the participant stated, "We [the editorial employees] make sure that all articles contain sources and fact boxes where more context is needed". The participant further revealed that these fact boxes are, technically, elements in PP that can be re-used, changed, added or removed. This can be interpreted as a consideration that the journalists, at least the one participant, makes to provide the user with an explanation to terms, jargon or context of an article.

5.2 Organizational Practices

This section addresses the participants' reports on the current practices at NRK and focuses on delegation and reporting, communication and training procedures. The participants additionally reported on a variety of design and feature limitations of the technological tools used at NRK, which may constrain efforts to ensure accessibility and universal design. However, as this article focuses on the relationship between the norms, values and procedures of universal design and web accessibility and organizational practices, it is beyond the scope of this article to analyse system specific usability features.

Delegation and Reporting. All the participants reported confusion regarding how the editorial employees relate to NRK's hierarchy, both internally and externally. According to the participants, the lack of clarity and understanding of the roles and responsibilities of NRK's decision-making personnel resulted in news articles being published late, frustration and demotivation among the editorial employees, and misunderstandings in the chain of command.

One participant explained that editorial offices in the same department have different leaders, and that this is confusing and illogical when the two editorial office report on the same matters. Two other participants reported that, on several occasions, competitor news agencies had been noticeably quicker on publishing breaking matters than NRK, due to disagreements between leaders at different departments. One of the participants stated that "there has to be a clearer chain of command … there are a lot of comments from above [the leaders] with messages and counter messages that forces us [journalists] to check with everyone again on the new decision – this steals a lot of time for us". The other participant reported "… none of the leaders or chains of command seem to have any more power than the others".

Four of the participants attributed delays, frustrations and demotivation to the lack of clarity regarding decision-makers' roles and responsibilities. However, the participants do not propose to centralize decision-making processes. Rather the participants suggested, "they [leaders] should figure out who has the last say on distinct matters and situations" on a last-say-basis, considering that disagreements and discussions cause unnecessary delays and frustration. This is further supported by another participant, who stated, "it is difficult to know who to ask when I have a question about an article". The findings suggest that the efficiency of the editorial employees is reduced due to lack of coordination among the editorial employees and decision-makers.

The lack of clarity regarding decision-makers' roles and responsibilities also demotes collaboration between the editorial employees. One participant reported that "one has to make sure that one does not step on other editorial offices' feet [interfere or report on same cases] if one is writing about the same case or a similar matter … this requires coordination". The participant further reported that because it is unclear who has responsibility of coordination, coordination takes a lot of time from the editorial work and thus demotes collaboration between editorial employees.

The lack of coordination relates to whether and to what extent editorial employees have the time to promote and ensure universal design and web accessibility. One participant explained that the editorial employees do not have the time to spend time on improving the usability and accessibility of articles. According to the participant "we must get allocated the time to further process our articles [for improved usability and universal design]". The participant suggests that "all journalists may not necessarily have to be forced to process articles for usability or universal design, this might be delegated to a particular employee or a group of employees in the editorial offices, like we have with social media … Someone has to do it, and they must get this time allocated".

Thus, the results suggest that a lack of clear reporting structures and opportunities for delegation may constrain efforts to ensure universal design and web accessibility at NRK.

Communication. Most of the participants reported that the physical and organizational structure of NRK produces barriers to effective communication. For instance, the physical distance between editorial offices results in a "complicated information flow". One participant reported to have more or less lost overview and contact with other editorial employees in other editorial offices. The participant further explained that a close relationship with other employees "creates a relationship of trust" and helps ensure priorities and quality of the articles.

Another participant reported that the physical placement of editorial offices and responsibilities are on different floors in NRK's office in Oslo. For an article, it is not uncommon to have the following structure of resources: the reporter is on one floor, the front-page team in a different floor, and the editorial office and the shift leader who oversees the article is on another floor. This creates disturbances in the workflow and makes it difficult for everyone to be updated on the articles progress. Compounded over the number of articles published each day, the effects are even more substantial. This is evident by one participant's statement, that "this [difficulties with communication] is time consuming and demotivating".

Communication problems also affect the efficiency of the workflow. The participants reported that they had experienced that the same article had been developed by two different departments, district offices, or journalists. For instance, one participant reported that one of the district offices had created an article without the responsible editorial office being aware. Another participant reported that articles would not be developed by anyone, because "everyone thinks that someone else is on the case". Another participant also reported that there is no formal policy to notify other departments of district offices that may be interested in a topic or case. This has created several situations where the party has not been notified.

One participant explained that there are no routines for external proof reading of articles, and that this is problematic for the editorial employees as well as the end-user. The participant states that "This creates more responsibility for the editorial employees … it is a shame. Someone should really read through the articles before they are published". The participant expresses that this is problematic because other employees are highly likely to give valuable input and to read the articles with an "independent set of eyes", giving the article a more nuanced and objective viewpoint. This suggests that collaboration with other editorial employees is not prioritized, even though the editorial employees express that it is something that would assist and relieve their work. Another participant explained that article content is verified and quality assured, from time to time, by the editorial office leader or shift leader for bigger, more in-depth articles.

Thus, the results suggest that the structure of the physical space and the lack of clear communication regarding workflow and a lack of consistent quality assurance may constrain efforts for ensuring universal design and web accessibility in practice.

Training. All of the participants reported to have been a part of a mandatory course in the content management system PP. According to the participants, these courses had not informed the journalists on matters regarding accessibility or universal design. However, there is one exception to this, as one participant was informed during the course that image descriptions were important for visually impaired users that utilize screen readers. The participant stated, "I'm unsure if this was a part of the course or just that the instructor thought this was important".

Another participant reported to have had several writing courses that focused on comprehension and understanding. A second participant reported to have attended several journalist's writing courses, organized and provided by NRK. It is, however, not evident if this is the case for all journalists or just something in which this participant had taken. It is, regardless, a finding of a type of course/training that the journalists have gotten from the organization. Finally, a third participant reported that NRK recently hired two new reporters, where accessibility and universal design was not mentioned in the PP course, nor in other training.

Thus, the results suggest that although universal design and web accessibility have yet to be fully integrated in mandatory trainings for existing employees or new hires, some editorial employees have had training in writing and others have had training in accessibility techniques due to the interests of the course instructors.

6 Discussion

This article asked, "How do social institutions influence organizational practices for ensuring web accessibility?" The results broadly demonstrate that although NRK has a legal obligation for ensuring universal design and web accessibility, the norms, values and procedures relevant for promoting universal design and web accessibility have yet to be fully integrated into their organizational practices. In addition, the results demonstrate that institutionalized procedures including delegation and reporting, communication and training may simultaneously constrain opportunities for ensuring universal design and web accessibility and provide an arena for change.

Specifically, the results demonstrate that the editorial employees at NRK show some knowledge and awareness of accessibility and universal design principles, requirements and techniques. However, their knowledge and understanding at times differs from generally accepted conceptualizations of universal design and web accessibility. In addition, their knowledge of universal design and web accessibility requirements and techniques is incomplete.

The results also demonstrated that organizational practices at NRK may constrain opportunities for ensuring universal design and web accessibility in three ways. First, the results demonstrate that unclear roles and responsibilities, reporting structures and delegation have negatively affected editorial employees' working life and abilities to ensure universal design and web accessibility. Second, the results demonstrate that the physical environment, workflow and quality assurance procedures have also negatively impacted editorial employees' working life and may act to constrain their ability to ensure universal design and web accessibility. Third, the results demonstrate that although training is mandatory for new editorial employees, training curricula has yet to incorporate fully, universal design and web accessibility principles, requirements and techniques.

6.1 Political Mechanisms for Institutional Change

Research on institutional change demonstrates that political pressures evolving from shifts in power can undermine existing institutions and provide an opportunity for gradual institutional change [24]. This article provides evidence that although NRK has a legal obligation to ensure universal design and web accessibility, universal design and accessibility principles and practices have yet to be fully integrated in practice – i.e., signifying a shift in power, editorial employee's awareness towards universal design and web accessibility is incomplete, and existing training procedures have yet to fully integrate universal design and web accessibility principles, requirements and techniques. However, the results suggest that efforts to further promote awareness of and training in universal design and web accessibility may provide a basis for institutional change. For example, NRK strategically redeploying the mandatory training program to include universal design and web accessibility principles, requirements and techniques could provide a basis for institutional conversion. Alternatively, institutional layering may provide an opportunity to promote universal design and web accessibility knowledge and awareness by adding principles, requirements and techniques onto existing training procedures.

6.2 Social Mechanisms for Institutional Change

Research on institutional change demonstrates that social pressures evolving from a lack of consensus on the purpose of organizational practices can undermine existing institutions and provide an opportunity for gradual institutional change [24]. This article provides evidence that although editorial employees' lack a clear understanding of decision-makers' roles and responsibilities, this has yet to provide a basis for institutional change. However, the results suggest that efforts to ensure clarity in delegation and reporting may provide an opportunity for promoting universal design and web accessibility. For example, reorganizing decision-makers at NRK may provide an opportunity for institutional displacement – i.e., replacing existing rules. Reorganizing decision-makers by replacing existing roles and responsibilities with new roles and responsibilities may provide an opportunity to clarify reporting structures and incorporate specific mechanisms for accountability in universal design and web accessibility. Alternatively, institutional layering may provide an opportunity to introduce universal design and web accessibility as a new responsibility for editorial employees.

6.3 Functional Mechanisms for Institutional Change

Research on institutional change demonstrates that functional pressures evolving from inefficient organizational practices can undermine existing institutions and provide a basis for institutional change [24]. This article provides evidence that the lack of clarity regarding delegation and reporting and the physical and organizational barriers to communication produce workflow inefficiencies. However, these organizational inefficiencies have yet to provide a basis for institutional change. Nonetheless, the results suggest that efforts to reduce organizational inefficiencies may provide an opportunity for ensuring universal design and web accessibility. For example, restructuring the physical environment may provide a basis for institutional drift. Essentially, restructuring the office environment may provide an opportunity to ensure that employees with some knowledge and understanding of universal design and web accessibility principles, requirements and techniques can share that knowledge and understanding with other editorial employees. Alternatively, institutional layering may provide an opportunity to introduce and support quality assurance procedures that verify the universal design and accessibility of web content.

7 Conclusion

Data collected from semi-structured interviews, policy documents and participant observations suggest that social institutions have constrained the behaviours of actors within NRK. The analysis suggests that the editorial employees are involved with producing web content, yet they are typically unaware of universal design and web accessibility policies and feel unaccountable for producing inaccessible web content. This article argues that social institutions, in the form of social, organizational and technological barriers, structure whether and to what extent editorial employees can act to ensure web accessibility in practice. However, this article further argues that social institutions can also act as a locus of change for ensuring web accessibility. The article argues that mechanisms for institutional change provide a useful basis for promoting web accessibility where organizations respond to demands for web accessibility by replacing, augmenting or recreating existing practices.

In conclusion, the results provide a useful basis for future research and practice. First, the results suggest that future research could usefully examine the universal design and web accessibility institutional constraints and opportunities change in comparable cases from other countries and industries. Second, the results suggest that future advocacy efforts could usefully include proposals for processes that aim to strategically replace, augment or recreate existing organizational practices in a way that ensures universal design and web accessibility. Third, educators in a variety of fields including business, technology and disability studies could usefully evaluate whether and to what extent existing pedagogical approaches provide students with an understanding of and an ability to examine the potential constraints of social institutions and mechanisms for institutional change in ensuring universal design and web accessibility in practice.

References

1. Wolk, L.: Equal access in cyberspace: on bridging the digital divide in public accommodations coverage through amendment to the Americans with Disabilities Act. Notre Dame L. Rev. **91**, 447–447 (2015)
2. Macdonald, S.J., Clayton, J.: Back to the future, disability and the digital divide. Disab. Soc. **28**(5), 702–718 (2013)
3. Vicente, M.R., Lopez, A.J.: A multidimensional analysis of the disability digital divide: some evidence for internet use. Inf. Soc. **26**(1), 48–64 (2010)
4. Muir, A., Oppenheim, C.: National information policy developments worldwide II: universal access - addressing the digital divide. J. Inf. Sci. **28**(4), 263–273 (2002)
5. Velleman, E.M., Nahuis, I., van der Geest, T.: Factors explaining adoption and implementation processes for web accessibility standards within eGovernment systems and organizations. Univ. Access Inf. Soc. **16**(1), 173–190 (2015). https://doi.org/10.1007/s10209-015-0449-5
6. Giannoumis, G.A.: Auditing Web accessibility: The role of interest organizations in promoting compliance through certification. First Monday **20**(9), 1–15 (2015)

7. Brown, J., Hollier, S.: The challenges of web accessibility: the technical and social aspects of a truly universal web. First Monday **20**(9), 1–16 (2015)
8. Thatcher, J., et al.: Web Accessibility Web Standards and Regulatory Compliance. Springer, New York (2006). https://doi.org/10.1007/978-1-4302-0188-5
9. Kelly, B., et al.: Accessibility 2.0: next steps for web accessibility. J. Access Serv. **6**(1–2), 265–294 (2009)
10. De Andrés, J., Lorca, P., Martínez, A.B.: Factors influencing web accessibility of big listed firms: an international study. Online Inf. Rev. **34**(1), 75–97 (2010)
11. Blanck, P.: eQuality: The Struggle for Web Accessibility by Persons with Cognitive Disabilities. Cambridge University Press, New York (2014)
12. Giannoumis, G.A.: Regulating web content: the nexus of legislation and performance standards in the United Kingdom and Norway. Behav. Sci. Law **32**(1), 52–75 (2014)
13. Shi, Y.: E-government web site accessibility in Australia and China a longitudinal study. Soc. Sci. Comput. Rev. **24**(3), 378–385 (2006)
14. Powell, W.W., DiMaggio, P.: The New Institutionalism in Organizational Analysis. University of Chicago Press, Chicago (1991)
15. Hall, P.A.: Historical institutionalism in rationalist and sociological perspective. In: Mahoney, J., Thelen, K.A. (eds.) Explaining Institutional Change: Ambiguity, Agency, and Power, pp. 204–223. Cambridge University Press: Cambridge, New York (2010)
16. Hall, P.A., Taylor, R.C.R.: Political science and the three new institutionalisms. Polit. Stud. **44**(5), 936–957 (1996)
17. Rixen, T., Viola, L.A.: Putting path dependence in its place: toward a taxonomy of institutional change. J. Theor. Polit. **27**, 301–323 (2014)
18. Mahoney, J., Thelen, K.A.: A theory of gradual institutional change. In: Mahoney, J., Thelen, K.A. (eds.) Explaining Institutional Change: Ambiguity, Agency, and Power, pp. 1–37. Cambridge University Press, Cambridge, New York (2010)
19. Streeck, W., Thelen, K.A.: Beyond Continuity: Institutional Change in Advanced Political Economies. Oxford University Press, Oxford, New York (2005)
20. Hall, P.A., Thelen, K.: Institutional change in varieties of capitalism. Socio-Econ. Rev. **7**(1), 7–34 (2009)
21. Giannoumis, G.A.: Transatlantic learning: from Washington to London and beyond. Inclusion **3**(2), 92–107 (2015)
22. Giannoumis, G.A.: Self-regulation and the legitimacy of voluntary procedural standards. Adm. Soc. **49**(7), 1–23 (2014)
23. Dacin, M.T., Goodstein, J., Scott, W.R.: Institutional theory and institutional change: introduction to the special research forum. Acad. Manag. J. **45**(1), 45–56 (2002)
24. Oliver, C.: The antecedents of deinstitutionalization. Organ. Stud. **13**(4), 563–588 (1992)
25. Knight, M.: Accessibility and disability: absent keywords in business and professional communication. Bus. Prof. Commun. Q. **81**, 20–33 (2018)
26. Hitt, A.: Foregrounding accessibility through (inclusive) universal design in professional communication curricula. Bus. Prof. Commun. Q. **81**, 52–65 (2018)
27. Meloncon, L.: Orienting access in our business and professional communication classrooms. Bus. Prof. Commun. Q. **81**, 34–51 (2018)
28. Clegg, G.M.: Unheard complaints: integrating captioning into business and professional communication presentations. Bus. Prof. Commun. Q. **81**, 100–122 (2018)
29. Konrad, A.: Reimagining work: normative commonplaces and their effects on accessibility in workplaces. Bus. Prof. Commun. Q. **81**, 123–141 (2018)
30. Oswal, S.K.: Can workplaces, classrooms, and pedagogies be disabling? Bus. Prof. Commun. Q. **81**, 3–19 (2018)

31. Wheeler, S.K.: Harry Potter and the first order of business: using simulation to teach social justice and disability ethics in business communication. Bus. Prof. Commun. Q. **81**, 85–99 (2018)
32. Barley, S.R., Tolbert, P.S.: Institutionalization and structuration: studying the links between action and institution. Organ. Stud. **18**(1), 93–117 (1997)
33. March, J.G., Olsen, J.P.: Elaborating the "new institutionalism". In: The Oxford Handbook of Political Institutions, vol. 5, pp. 3–20 (2006)
34. Greif, A., Laitin, D.D.: A theory of endogenous institutional change. Am. Polit. Sci. Rev. **98**(04), 633–652 (2004)
35. David, P.A.: Clio and the economics of QWERTY. Am. Econ. Rev. **75**(2), 332–337 (1985)
36. Scott, W.R.: Institutions and Organizations. Sage, Thousand Oaks (2001)
37. Lazar, J., Feng, J.H., Hochheiser, H.: Research Methods in Human-Computer Interaction. Wiley, New York (2010)
38. Berg, B.L., Lune, H., Lune, H.: Qualitative Research Methods for the Social Sciences, vol. 5. Pearson, Boston (2004)
39. Glaser, B., Strauss, A.: The Discovery Grounded Theory: Strategies for Qualitative Inquiry. Aldin, Chicago (1967)
40. Oun, M.A., Bach, C.: Qualitative research method summary. J. Multi. Eng. Sci. Technol. **1**(5), 252–258 (2014)
41. Polkinghorne, M., Arnold, A.: A Six Step Guide to Using Recursive Abstraction Applied to the Qualitative Analysis of Interview Data. Bournemouth University, Poole (2014)
42. Collier, D.: Understanding process tracing. PS Polit. Sci. Polit. **44**(4), 823 (2011)
43. Ford, J.K., et al.: Process tracing methods: contributions, problems, and neglected research questions. Organ. Behav. Hum. Decis. Process. **43**(1), 75–117 (1989)
44. BLID, Act June 20 2008 No 42 relating to a prohibition against discrimination on the basis of disability (Equality and Anti-Discrimination Act) Unofficial translation (2008)
45. McNair, B.: Journalism in the 21st century—evolution, not extinction. Journalism **10**(3), 347–349 (2009)
46. Weaver, D.H.: US journalism in the 21st century—what future? Journalism **10**(3), 396–397 (2009)
47. Law, C.M., et al.: Are disability-access guidelines designed for designers?: do they need to be? In: Proceedings of the 18th Australia conference on Computer-Human Interaction: Design: Activities, Artefacts and Environments, pp. 357–360. ACM, Sydney (2006)
48. Vedtekter for Norsk rikskringkasting AS (1996)
49. Sanderson, N.C., Chen, W., Kessel, S.: The accessibility of web-based media services – an evaluation. In: Antona, M., Stephanidis, C. (eds.) UAHCI 2015. LNCS, vol. 9175, pp. 242–252. Springer, Cham (2015). https://doi.org/10.1007/978-3-319-20678-3_24
50. Norwegian Ministry of Children Equality and Social Inclusion. The Government's Action Plan for Universal Design (2015)

Development of a Multilingual Questionnaire for the Deaf Community – Guidelines and Challenges

Astrid Oehme(✉), Vaishnavi Upadrasta, and Philipp Kotsch

HFC Human-Factors-Consult GmbH, Köpenicker Str. 325, 12555 Berlin, Germany
{oehme,upadrasta,kotsch}@human-factors-consult.de

Abstract. To understand user requirements and needs of deaf TV consumers in the project CONTENT4ALL, and in order to set specifications and standardizations for an acceptable TV layout design, an online survey was conducted during the project's user research. The paper describes the development of a four-stage online questionnaire accessible for deaf participants, which includes demographic data, assessments of single layout questions as well as a layout do-it-yourself-puzzle. The insights gathered during the survey's development have been solidified into a draft guideline for similar user-research approaches, which will be briefly described. The survey was implemented using vue.js framework in conjunction with the associated state management vuex, and realized in five European sign languages and spoken languages in accordance with the consortium composition. Participants were asked to rate 36 possible layout combinations based on their preferences of the position and size of the different objects and subjects that are depicted, and then were given the opportunity to create their own layout as per their liking. The paper concludes with a report of first findings and highlights the challenges faced during the preparation process.

Keywords: Media accessibility · User research · Online questionnaire for deaf users · TV layout · Sign language interpreter

1 Introduction

1.1 Background

CONTENT4ALL, a project funded by the European Commission under agreement N°762021, aims to make more content accessible to the deaf community. Broadcasting companies are continuously seeking for solutions to increase the number of programs that can be translated into sign language, while the deaf community is carefully looking at these solutions to guarantee the quality of interpretation and language purity. The CONTENT4ALL project positions itself in between the needs of the broadcasters and of the deaf community: The objective of the project is to help broadcasters in reducing the cost of personalized sign-interpreted content creation and to increase the accessibility to these media content for deaf users.

C. Stephanidis et al. (Eds.): HCII 2020, LNCS 12426, pp. 103–113, 2020.
https://doi.org/10.1007/978-3-030-60149-2_9

For this purpose, a television studio is being developed that is not based at the TV station but can be used remotely (remote studio). This installation will facilitate the work of sign language interpreters, not requiring them to travel to the TV station but instead to use the remote studio facilities, even at their own premise. It will also make it easier and cheaper for television stations to produce sign language programs in the future. As a result, more programs in sign language can be offered.

In CONTENT4ALL the necessary technologies and algorithms to capture the sign interpreter in the remote studio, to process these data and render them via broadcast are being developed in such a way that the sign language interpreter is represented by a photorealistic 3D human avatar. Thus, deaf viewers will see the television content as enriched with a virtual 3D representation of the captured sign language interpreter.

1.2 User-Centered Design Process

The project follows a user-centered design process, during which different methods of user research are applied [1]. The user research started with workshops and interviews as a base for deriving high level user requirements (see [2] for an overview). The system is planned to be designed in a way that it is the most effective and good-looking for the television viewers. Thus, one of our research questions focused on the deaf consumers' opinion on how such a content should be designed and spatially arranged in the best possible way on the TV screen. The lack of available literature on the topic and the expectation of media consumption-related cultural differences induced the research team to aim for a large, multinational sample. Therefore, an online questionnaire accessible for deaf participants was developed to explore preferences for the general layout of sign-translated TV.

The following chapters describe how the questionnaire was designed, prepared, implemented, and received by the participants and which insights thus were gained.

2 The Questionnaire

2.1 Content and Layout

After completing the above-mentioned requirement analysis, several relevant features that should be taken into account when designing an accessible TV interface were identified and a metric was formed to calculate the number of possible design variations. This process underwent a number of iterations before the final variables were established. Based on the established variables, several possible layout design variations for accessible TV were generated, which relate to the four main categories *background*, *size and position* of the (virtual) sign language interpreter, *appearance* (completeness of the image/image detail), and *tilt* of the TV picture. These categories and the general layout on the TV-screen are depicted in Fig. 1.

The survey consists of four parts: In the first part, respondents received a brief overview about the C4A-project and the purpose of the survey. This was followed by general demographics questions concerning gender, age, mother tongue, level of deafness, and media usage. In terms of the latter, frequency of usage of media devices such

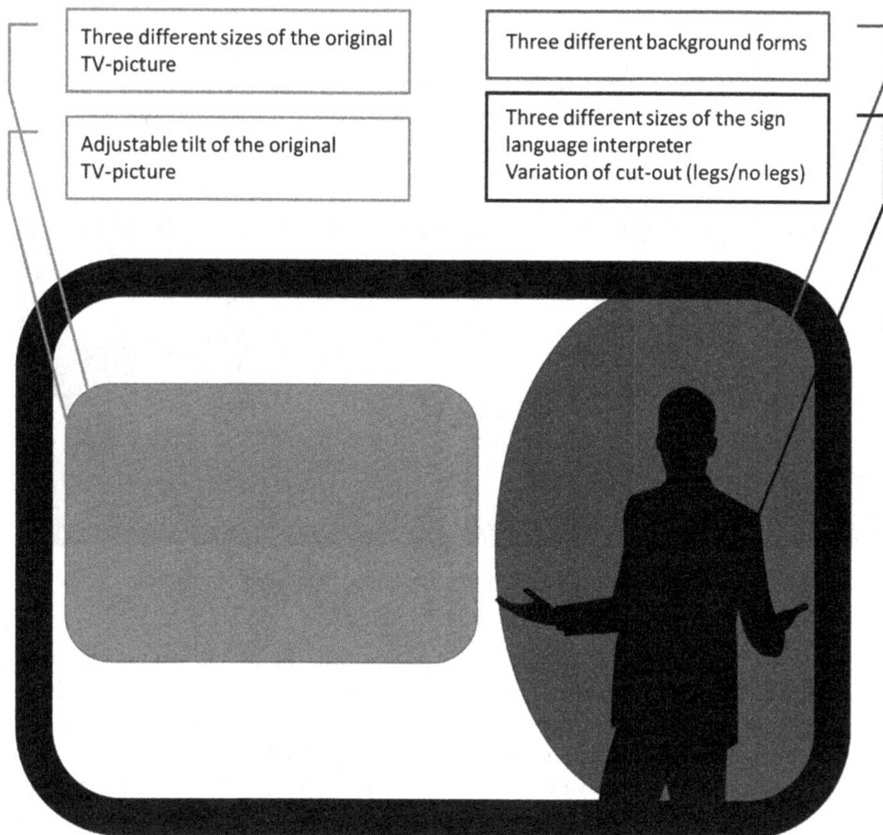

Fig. 1. Established variables for designing an accessible TV interface.

as TV, smartphone, tablet as well as participants' preferred media providers/apps such as Facebook, YouTube, Netflix, etc. were inquired. In the second part, the different TV layouts were presented to the respondents. The 36 pictures resulted from different combinations of the three variables *size of the original TV picture* (50%, 75%, 100%), the *size of the sign language interpreter* (without legs: 50%, 75%, 100%, with legs: 75%), and the *form of the cutout/background behind* (square, circle and transparent/none). The TV picture and sizes of the sign language interpreter refer to volumes in relation to the overall TV-layout, which always featured all components depicted in Fig. 1. These combinations were presented to the participants in randomized order to avoid sequence effects.

Respondents were expected to rate each picture on a 5-point Likert-scale, implemented as a five-star rating, with one star being the worst rating and five stars being the best. They were asked to rate the picture with regards to the layout and size of the depicted objects. Figure 2 displays two different layouts and the star-based rating format as an example. Following the main application scenario of the project, the questionnaire depicted a weather forecast image for this research. Part three aimed at collecting qualitative data regarding the preferred layout design of the respondent. Open questions were asked concerning respondents' personal opinion on how the TV interface should look. These included: 'What made a good TV screen for you?' 'What made a bad layout/segmentation for you?' 'What would you do completely different?' 'What had been lacking?' and 'What else do you want to tell us?'

Fig. 2. Layout and rating examples displaying the possible variables.

The fourth part of the study featured a puzzle task, in which respondents were able to design their own preferred TV layout with a sign language interpreter. Here, respondents could adjust all of the features/objects of the TV screen, i.e. all variables in Fig. 1, freely by themselves. The individual elements (background, TV picture, sign language interpreter) could be varied with corresponding buttons. The position and size in the overall image could be individually adjusted interactively by dragging and resizing. For this part of the online survey, two versions were designed, one optimized for the smartphone as shown in Fig. 3, and the other for larger displays (Fig. 4).

For the display on a large monitor at a convention, the same puzzle was designed in a visually more elaborate way. To increase immersion, the puzzle was integrated into a TV set in a living room scene and the interaction elements floated next to it like a virtual remote control (Fig. 4). The adaption of the layout and input elements to the possible devices used by the participants (e.g. different screen sizes and different situations) increases usability and user experience. Design principles of Gestalt psychology, e.g. [3], like the laws of similarity, proximity, and closure were applied when structuring the general layout and the set-up of the input elements of both versions.

2.2 Preparation and Set-Up

Online questionnaires usually consist of standardized HTML elements derived from or similarly structured like paper-and-pencil forms. These comprise different types of text input fields (short and long text, numeric input, date input), selects, single-choice questions (radio buttons) or multiple-choice questions (checkboxes).

Surveys that exclusively cover these formats can nowadays be created quickly and free of charge even without own development using different provider platforms (e.g. LimeSurvey, Survey Monkey or Survio). However, the formats of questions and answers

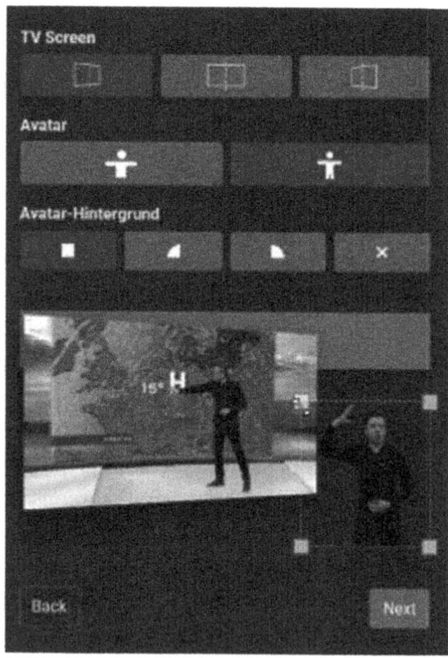

Fig. 3. Implementation of the puzzle task for smartphone. Interaction elements are depicted on the upper part of the image.

Fig. 4. Implementation of the puzzle task for PC/laptop monitor. Interaction elements to manipulate TV layout are depicted as a remote control (left).

are then limited to the existing service and there is only limited control over the collected data. In order to have exclusive access to the data and consider GDPR requirements, it was decided to host the questionnaire software in-house and not to collect the data via an external provider. Furthermore, as an in-house project HFC developed its own online survey framework in order to take advantage of the many possibilities to interactively collect data with creative question formats that go beyond the previously mentioned form elements.

The back end, i.e. the routing and database administration, was realized with the php framework Laravel. The front end, i.e. the questionnaire per itself, was implemented as a single-page application in the javascript framework vue.js with the state management library vuex. Single-page application means that the entire interaction takes place after the initial request on the client side in the browser. The website is not reloaded every time the user clicks "Next". This ensures faster transitions, and the interaction and procedure feel smooth at all times for the user.

Since users are very likely to fill out the questionnaire on a mobile device, the design also placed great emphasis on a high usability on smartphones. In this mobile first approach, the design was optimized initially for small screens and touch operation and then adapted for larger screens and desktop use.

The architecture of the questionnaire is modular and component-based. This allows the individual question types to be parameterized as components that can be reused as required. In this way, the already established form inputs were provided first and then new question formats were added as required. In addition to the question formats, there are also components for structuring the page, which do not collect any data. These are, for example, headings and text blocks but also images, animations and videos for instructions. Especially the integration of videos for instructions was very important for the target group of CONTENT4ALL.

For deaf consumers, a spoken language is naturally not a mother tongue, but sign language is. Written language such as media subtitles is equivalent to a foreign language. However, written communication and digital formats like WhatsApp, SMS and Email are frequently used, the latter especially if video chat is not applicable. In order to create an accessible online-survey, care was taken to produce short and comprehensible instructions for the four questionnaire parts. All instructional text passages were translated into sign language videos. In accordance with the project partner nationalities and the Deaf associations involved in the project, the survey was implemented in the sign languages DGS (German Sign Language), DSGS (German Swiss Sign Language), VGT (Flemish Sign Language), BSL (British Sign Language) and LSF (French Sign Language) and the spoken languages German, Dutch, English and French. As a default setting, instructions were provided in sign language video formats. Written instructions were also made available and could be accessed by just one click on the respective option. The texts as well as the videos were checked regarding comprehensibility and instructional flow with regard to the questionnaire procedure.

Due to the modular structure, the five different language versions could be integrated quickly after finalizing the base version of the questionnaire. The collected data retains the same structure across the board and can be analyzed collectively without time-consuming fusion.

In addition, the inputs were written to the database asynchronously in the background for each intermediate step in the questionnaire. Therefore, none of the data already entered was lost even if the participants chose to leave the survey before full completion.

Alongside user responses, the online questionnaire also collected metadata, which facilitates evaluation, and informs about the necessity of additional acquisition impulses. For example, the times when the questionnaire was first opened and the last update of user input were stored. An average time to complete the questionnaire could thus be determined and it could be estimated when the distribution of the link needed a new acquisition impulse because the response rate was decreasing.

2.3 Response Rate and Feedback

The survey was online from mid-January 2020 until end of March 2020. Participants were recruited via members of the Swiss and Flanders Deaf associations, who are in advisory contact with the project, as well as the project partners' contacts with the national Deaf associations. By the end of the survey period, the survey link had been used more than 1,000 times, out of which 213 participants completed or nearly completed the survey. The sample consists of 115 German, 50 Swiss, 27 Belgian and 6 British respondents, with additional 15 respondents from other countries or unknown locations. Data analysis is currently being prepared.

As a first result, the free comments in the questionnaire were explored to receive an overall feedback on the survey's reception. Remarkably, these comments not only included many positive statements on the topic of the survey but also about the interactive study design and the involvement of the deaf community. Additionally, the researchers received several feedback emails from different participants stressing the necessity of this research and acknowledging the usability of the questionnaire.

3 Lessons Learned: Challenges and Guidelines

As a result of the user research and during questionnaire preparation and conduct several challenges were faced and insights were gained by the research group, which led to the aggregation of guidelines. These guidelines will inform our further research and may be of help to a wider research community. The following paragraphs briefly discuss these guidelines.

3.1 Know Your User Group

In user research, it is clear that each user group has its own special requirements regarding a respective system or service. Thus, oftentimes it is not sufficient to just address well-known usability aspects, such as task adequacy or self-descriptiveness [4], but thrive for accessibility and user experience as well. This consideration renders a user-centered design process mandatory. Such a process has to start with a thorough requirements analysis and cannot just rely on technological possibilities. In Böhm [2], our colleague describes why it is so important to put a user-requirement analysis on a broad database, in order to take the different topics of this group and its needs towards a product or service into consideration.

An example: For the deaf community, communication is quite different from that of hearing people. Sign language is their mother tongue. Most of the information intake relies on visual cues from the face, the hands, the posture and movements of a signing person. This leads to special requirements regarding the signing quality, the clothes, and the emotions conveyed by a sign language interpreter (see [1] and [2] for more details). These requirements have to be considered when developing the virtual sign-language interpreter representation in the project. However, the requirements analysis carried out in CONTENT4ALL also helped us to build the questionnaire in a way that was comprehensible and easy to use for our target group. The instructional text passages were as short as possible, in as easy a language as possible, and more importantly, all instructions were implemented as sign-language videos in the above-mentioned five different sign languages. Furthermore, the survey addressed a useful and valuable aspect for the target group, i.e. the layout of sign-language enriched media provision for TV programs.

For a different target group, these factors might be irrelevant. Visually impaired TV consumers, for instance, rely on a good audio quality and meaningful audio-descriptions of a scene. The latter, however, should not distract from the direct speech of presenters, moderators or movie actors. An online questionnaire useful for this group has to facilitate screen-reader software. For all user groups it is preferable to provide clear and comprehensible text (instructions, items, explanations) made of easy language.

To know your user group helps to prioritize the content of your survey and facilitates user-centered information provision and interaction and media format choices.

3.2 Try to Compose a Usable and Fun Survey

Besides basic implementations for a better survey usability, such as the sign-language videos, other more general features can be very helpful to facilitate usability and user experience. One of these features is hiding irrelevant questions. In analogue paper-and-pencil forms, optional questions are often introduced with 'if yes, then…'. In the online version, the relevant preconditions can be checked while filling out the form and the additional questions are only shown if the relevant criteria are met. This shortens the questionnaire and saves the user unnecessary effort.

There are no restrictions for the user in paper-and-pencil questionnaires when entering data: additional comments and free notes on paper can be added at any time. This freedom to allow open comments can be offered in the online version as well. For example, a question for final conclusions, recommendations or simply any feedback can be placed at the end of the survey.

To provide a means of perceived controllability [4], bars should inform the participant about the progress during task completion. Additionally, encouraging statements on the progress can be presented.

For the fun aspect of the survey, the puzzle task was introduced, which enabled free design of the TV interface. Care was taken to implement the interaction interface in a natural (remote control) and intuitive way. Most users of digital media are used to being able to manipulate interactive elements directly on the screen. Both, positioning and scaling could therefore be changed in the survey in direct interaction with the respective element. The variables, which were not freely adjustable, but were only intended to have predefined values, were set using simple buttons. These settings were the tilt of the TV picture in three versions (tilt left, none and tilt right), the visible parts of the virtual sign language interpreter (visible legs or not) and the type of background for the interpreter (a box, an ellipse or none).

A usable and fun survey facilitates participant acquisition, increases response rates and number of completed data sets.

3.3 Consider Different Media for Presentation and Processing

Closely related to the fun aspect of a questionnaire is the use of different media for presentation and processing. While a rapid change of item and answering schema formats might confuse users, an occasional switch might help to keep up the interest, especially if the survey comprises many items. A switch of formats should always be introduced by some sort of short instruction and an example of the new format. This is most often conveyed by a text passage, but could also be achieved by a video or gif explaining how to use the respective item. In accordance with the user group and the topic addressed in a survey, different media and presentation formats can be chosen, e.g. traditional text passages, images, graphs or pictures, gifs, short video clips or audio samples. Similarly, processing formats may also be provided rich in variety. Besides classic closed-question items or free text formats, tasks that are more creative can be prepared, such as ranking order tasks, design tasks or puzzles with pre-defined shapes, buttons or other graphical items. Precondition for an enriched survey is a definition of the topic and targeted user group, so it can be carefully crafted to their needs and not to the manifold technical possibilities. To be able to provide these possibilities, on the other hand, the necessary survey framework has to be in place.

A carefully crafted and media-enriched survey keeps up the participants' interest, increases the number of completed data sets, and facilitates re-acquisition of sample members for subsequent (online) research.

3.4 Take Time for Quality Checks

The questionnaire described in this paper was complex in terms of its components (4 different tasks), but also in terms of its content, which had to be translated into four different spoken and five different sign languages. The set-up of the framework and the implementation of the different tasks as well as the translation and production of the text passages and the videos took about six months, not including iterations to improve the survey content (items, basic instructions, selection of puzzle items, etc.). In order to receive the correct number of short videos for the different introduction parts of the questionnaire, text with video cutting instructions was prepared. During the production process at the different partners' premises, these numbers of videos changed however for different reasons, resulting in slightly different set-ups for the five survey versions. These changes, however, did not comprise the instructions as such but only involved the number of instructional videos, leading to a range of three to 15 single videos per survey. Videos were combined when possible and if necessary, to maintain some level of consistency. Then, a careful placement of these videos within the questionnaire was needed to accommodate for this disparity.

The translations, text and video as implemented in the survey, were submitted to a quality check regarding their translation quality and suitability of placement. The quality check had to be performed under time pressure due to the envisaged launch deadline. While some improvements especially regarding the text passages could still be implemented, some issues went unnoticed or could not be changed due to time constrictions. Given the time used for implementation, a lesson learned here is that there should be ample time reserved for quality checks. In the worst case, launch deadlines should be rather postponed than risking compromising on survey content quality. Fortunately, the respective survey only carried minor issues, which presumably did not affect the participants' user experience.

A thorough quality check needs ample time and is necessary to ensure high user experience and valid data output. Ideally, it is carried out together with a pre-sample study. Subsequently, time has to be provided for implementing all required improvements.

3.5 Be Available for Questions and Feedback

A very basic service feature for participants is that a contact for questions and feedback is provided in the survey. This is also a requirement of GDPR regulations, in case of personal-data related questions of participants. Regarding the research reported here, valuable feedback was received not only in the questionnaire's open comments fields but also directly via email to the survey contact person.

Being available for questions and feedback is mandatory for survey conduct and any other user research. It empowers the participants and facilitates their acceptance to take part in the study.

4 Outlook

The questionnaire data is currently being analyzed with regard to overall and cultural-based TV layout preferences of deaf media consumers. The results will inform further implementations in the project CONTENT4ALL, but will also be made available in respective publications.

Regarding the online survey framework, the next step is to implement an admin front end for test managers to enable a direct setup of a survey by user researchers, and thus reduce the amount of support by the developer. Required features include creating and editing new questionnaires with the already available components as well as monitoring, exporting and evaluating the collected data. This involves a multiuser setup with authentication and a database structure that supports multiple surveys running at the same time.

A further focus lies on the component library. The library grows with each study implemented and is to be extended by established psychological scales (e.g. SUS [5] and SAM [6]). Due to the high demand for voice interfaces at present, new input modalities are also being tested. Answers via voice message can, for example, help in the design of conversational dialogues or can be requested for training of speech recognition. In connection with a speech output, online questionnaires with a good user experience for a target group with visual impairments could also be realized.

Acknowledgements. The research presented was conducted in the project CONTENT4ALL, which received funding from the European Commission within the Horizon 2020 Program (H2020-ICT-2016-2, call ICT-19-2017) under the grant agreement no.° 762021. This publication reflects only the authors' view and the European Commission is not responsible for any use that may be made of the information it contains. A big thank you goes to all participants for taking part in this research and to all project partners and associates who strongly supported these studies.

References

1. Upadrasta, V., Oehme, A., Böhm, S.: User centered design for accessibility in media content – sign language and virtual signer. In: Human-Computer Interaction International 2020. Springer, Heidelberg (2020)
2. Böhm, S.: Do you know your user group? Why it is essential to put your user-requirementanalysis on a broad data base. [Manuscript submitted for publication]. HFC Human-Factors-Consult GmbH
3. Katz, D., Metzger, W.: Gestaltspsychologie. Schwabe & Co., Basel (1969)
4. Ergonomics of human-system interaction - Part 110: Dialogue principles (ISO 9241-110:2006); German version EN ISO 9241-110:2006. DIN Deutsches Institut für Normung e.V. Beuth, Berlin (2006)
5. Brooke, J.: SUS: a "quick and dirty" usability scale. In: Jordan, P.W., Thomas, B., Weerdmeester, B.A., McClelland, A.L. (eds.) Usability Evaluation in Industry. Taylor and Francis, London (1996)
6. Bradley, M.M., Lang, P.J.: Measuring emotion: the self-assessment manikin and the semantic differential. J. Behav. Ther. Exper. Psychiatry **25**(1), 49–59 (1994). https://doi.org/10.1016/0005-7916(94)90063-9. Accessed 31 Mar 2020

MOOC Accessibility from the Educator Perspective

Dimitris Spiliotopoulos[1(✉)], Vassilis Poulopoulos[2], Dionisis Margaris[3], Eleni Makri[1], and Costas Vassilakis[1]

[1] Department of Informatics and Telecommunications, University of the Peloponnese, Tripoli, Greece
{dspiliot,costas}@uop.gr, eleni.g.makri@gmail.com

[2] Knowledge and Uncertainty Research Lab, University of the Peloponnese, Tripoli, Greece
vacilos@uop.gr

[3] Department of Informatics and Telecommunications, University of Athens, Athens, Greece
margaris@di.uoa.gr

Abstract. This work presents the universal access design principles and methods for natural language communication design in e-learning for the disabled. It unfolds a theoretical perspective to the design-for-all methodology and provides a framework description for technologies for creating accessible content for educational content communication. Main concerns include the problem identification of design issues for universal accessibility of spoken material, the primary pedagogical aspects that such content implementation should follow upon, as well as look into the state of the most popular e-learning platforms for which educators create and communicate educational content in an e-learning environment. References to massive open online course platform types of content that exist at the moment are examined in order to understand the challenges of bridging the gap between the modern design of rich courses and universal accessibility. The paper looks into the existing technologies for accessibility and a frame for analysis, including methodological and design issues, available resources and implementation using the existing technologies for accessibility and the perception of the designer as well as the user standpoint. Finally, a study to inform and access how potential educators may perceive the accessibility factor shows that accessible content is a major requirement toward a successful path to universally accessible e-learning.

Keywords: MOOC · Universal accessibility · Design-for-all · Speech processing · Interactive e-learning · Technologies for accessibility

1 Introduction

Accessibility and design-for-all apply to extended groups of people seeking knowledge and information from a distance such as the visually impaired, the mobile user, the elderly, etc. These users require special technology in order to access information, collectively

C. Stephanidis et al. (Eds.): HCII 2020, LNCS 12426, pp. 114–125, 2020.
https://doi.org/10.1007/978-3-030-60149-2_10

called Technologies for Accessibility, ranging from underlying design (web accessibility) to specific implementation (voice browsing) and applied technology (screen readers, adaptive interfaces). Educational material in e-learning environments includes textbooks and technical documents that may contain a mixture of textual information, as well as originally designed visual information such as mathematics, line diagrams, pictures, spatial information and navigational parameters. Furthermore, such material includes format-independent pedagogical elements such as instructional (learning) design, cognitive standpoint, behavioural and contextual perspective; all elements contained in the underlying structure of the formatted material and manifested by visual elements [1].

E-learning, from the stakeholders' perspective, is required to address teacher-learner-content interactivity to satisfy the three-dimensional interaction that most contemporary learning theories emphasise upon [2]. The Open University in the UK estimated that about one out of seven learners are disabled [3]. Massive Open Online Course (MOOC) applications and other e-learning platforms are a step forward, towards accessibility through e-learning, by addressing the mobility aspects of disability as well as the social and personal aspects, such as gender, segregation, language, culture, social status and learner age. For the first time, learners may study from home without the need for physical presence at an education institute (mobility), watch lectures at their own time (working students) and with support for their native language (language barriers).

Facing the issue of accessibility in education is not a novel problem, more specifically in e-learning, a domain directly related to computer and technology. Research work is done in order to analyse and access the criteria that should be met in order to achieve universal accessible e-learning environment that can fulfil their pedagogical scopes. Focusing furthermore to e-learning material, several factors may occur that make it difficult to achieve a universally accessible learning environment. In particular, e-learning material differentiates from traditional educational documents by the concepts and educational notions that need to be relayed to students and the respective feedback to the educators. In most cases, the content is much richer, including multimedia, rich text and interactive elements for quizzes, exams and peer grading. While, in many cases, metadata can be omitted or otherwise tacked by screen readers, in the case of e-learning metadata is a crucial, desirable and indispensable component of the learning procedure to provide high-level meta-information to all learners as well as feedback to educators.

This work overviews the state of the art in e-learning methods and applications, examines technologies for accessibility that are or can be utilised and then examines the level of accessibility of major MOOC platforms, such as Udacity and Coursera for reference to the needs and requirements for universal accessibility for educational information communication.

The following sections present the theoretical background to accessibility and human-computer interaction for e-learning, the technologies for accessibility available for the design-for-all approach, the MOOC accessibility status and the conclusion.

2 Accessibility in HCI – The E-learning Paradigm

E-learning deploys multiple information and communication technologies. Most of the current major e-learning platforms utilise Web 2.0 aspects and technologies. Web 3.0

describes how the semantic web, linked data, ontologies and internet of things transform the web from social web to web of data [4]. Accessibility and e-learning are also transforming as the e-learning systems evolve in complexity [5]. The existing accessibility frameworks for e-learning utilise information technologies to the fullest and are expected to adopt the semantic web technologies as well [6].

MOOC platforms made higher education reachable to students all over the world in the recent years [7]. As MOOCs diversify to include new functionalities and technologies, so do the educational resources and delivery methods for the content to the students [8]. Al-Mouh et al. studied the accessibility issues that visually impaired students faced using an earlier version of the Coursera platform [9]. They found that the version of that time failed to comply with all priority levels (A-AA-AAA) of the WCAG 2.0. Similarly, Sanchez-Gordon researched how the EdX platform could conform to the accessibility guidelines, providing prospective course content authors with recommendations on how to achieve accessibility for web and mobile web access [10].

Recent studies show that accessibility is one of the major factors for the adoption of MOOCs [11]. In fact, accessibility has a significant impact on the learner motivation to take a MOOC course [12]. That is a reason that, recently, several works studied MOOC accessibility for specific disability groups that make up a significant percentage of the learner body in the recent years, such as older adults [13] and the elderly [14].

Educational resources are not in abundance and that is also the case for special education resources, where it is especially apparent that the educators do not have many at their disposal [15]. Therefore, researchers argue that if accessibility is considered from the designers and educators during the design process, it would be much easier for them to create accessible content afterwards. In that respect, MOOC accessibility guidelines for the design process is a step towards universal accessibility for both educational technologies, platforms and content [16].

Universal Design for Learning (UDL) is a framework that was conceptualized and elaborated for universal Access through Accommodations and Modifications [17]. UDL provides the framework for creating more robust learning opportunities for all students. It is an inclusive approach to course development and instruction that underlines the access and participation of all students. Rather than waiting to learn that a specific student needs additional or specialized support, the UDL approach encourages educators to plan their curriculum and pedagogy to anticipate broad diversity in student learning needs and proclivities [18]. Recent works have attempted a UDL Implementation for online courses [19]. In conjunction to that, accessibility recommendations for educational games [20] constitute an approach that may be used to handle the type of interaction that educational exam quizzes and other grading tasks require.

3 Technologies for Accessibility

Technologies for Accessibility are used in the broad spectrum of information communication, designed to relay complex information to specific user groups [21]. Such technologies can be applied during the design, implementation or application of specialized systems as well as for the creation or analysis of the actual educational content, in the form of documents, webpages, talking books, etc. An abridged list includes:

- *Web.* Specific web accessibility guidelines are provided by the W3C including recommendations for creating accessible web documents, guidelines and priorities for accessing and manipulating information from existing pages and templates [22]. Moreover, accessibility support is provided by VoiceXML as a means for implementing the above recommendation to the acoustic modality [23].
- *Speech synthesis.* Used widely for the rendition of electronic documents to the acoustic modality. The text-to-speech systems utilize prosodic modelling in order to provide natural rendition of textual information [24].
- *Document-to-audio.* While text-to-speech systems are usually applied to simple text documents, a document-to-audio platform may be used to process visual documents of great complexity and render the visual properties (colours, complex visual structures, spatial information, etc.) to audio [25]. Apart from synthetic speech, there are certain auditory features that are used for proper acoustic representation. Earcons are abstract musical melodies which are symbolic of tasks or objects contained in a document. Auditory icons are real-world sounds used for the interaction of a user with specific objects. Spatial information may be conveyed using specific models that extract the logical representation between sections of text or from visual data structures and rendered to speech using synthetic speech, sometimes assisted by earcons or auditory icons [26].
- *Screen readers* are used for accessing information from a display, supported by screen navigation, synthetic speech or specialized interfaces [27].
- *Adaptive interfaces* offer customization and personalization services for reducing complexity, user modelling and flexible environment for increased efficiency of human-machine communication [28–30]. Such parameters can be used to assist the main rendering modality (e.g. speech) to relay the educational content in a precise and speedy manner [31].
- *Document analysis* is a technology tightly related universal accessibility especially in e-learning environments where the educational material is user specific. The educational material is designed to be presented to specific users or students in a particular way according to the target group social, behavioural and contextual perspective [32]. Therefore, certain content extraction and categorization techniques as well as rendition parameters need to be modelled to accommodate such information provision [33, 34].
- Similarly, *natural language processing*, is utilized during the stages between document analysis and document-to-audio in order to retain meta-information on the semantics of the rendered information [35, 36].
- *Computer vision* methods for the disabled, especially the visually impaired, aim to process the visual world and present the information to the human user or an assistive system or application [37]. Such methods include obstacle detection and scene recognition as well as distance and object size calculation. They can be coupled with voice user interfaces for guidance.
- For user interaction, *spoken dialogue systems* can be used for human-machine communication and several navigation, summarization and accessibility parameters can be implemented in order to increase the place, manner and effectiveness of the accessible data [38].

- *Voice agents.* With the popular adoption of smart mobile devices, intelligent interaction is implemented using interactive agents that communicate mostly via voice but also involve multimodal content such as text, images, videos maps and others. Voice agents are mainly used for personal assistance [39] but also for training and learning [40].

E-learning accessibility initiative guidelines should be followed in all stages of creation and implementation of e-learning content and respective voice interfaces in order to provide means for quality assessment.

4 Accessibility and MOOCs

An aspect that is of interest for this work is the actual perception of educators on the accessibility features for online learning [41]. This translates to a diverse set of features and accommodations that, in essence, describe universal accessibility for both learners and teachers. The educators have the perspective that e-learning platforms as technologies and content providers should strive to create accessible courses that would address the needs of the disabled learners [3, 42].

Tools for automatic accessibility evaluation have been extensively used in the literature [43]. AChecker and WAVE are among the most popular for website accessibility evaluation [19]. For the purpose of this work, we have selected to use WAVE to create reports on accessibility issues for Udacity and Coursera course pages. The webpages that were examined were the following course pages, accessed in January 2020:

- Udacity: Web Accessibility by Google (free course)
- Coursera: An Introduction to Accessibility and Inclusive Design

For starters, it is quite hopeful that specialised accessibility courses are offered by the two e-learning platforms, especially since those are offered by non-other than a top university and the largest web company in the world today.

Figure 1 shows the Udacity course main page as rendered by WAVE. The main course page was reported to contain 17 errors and 24 contract errors. The errors mostly included missing alternative text, missing language and empty headings and links. The contrast errors were all about very low contrast in for several page items. Upon entering the course, for lesson one, only 3 errors and 6 contrast errors were reported. The errors were the missing language and two instances of empty buttons. That is a positive outcome, since the specific errors can be easily corrected. Moreover, standard screen readers may be successful in controlling them. The same number or errors was reported for the quiz section of the lesson.

The same testing was followed for the accessibility evaluation of the Coursera course main page. Figure 2 shows the visualized distribution of issues for the webpage, as reported by WAVE. A total of 69 errors and 3 contrast errors were reported. All errors were broken ARIA references. Visiting lesson one, 38 errors and 5 contrast errors were identified. Four errors were empty buttons and the rest were broken ARIA references. Low contrast issues are important to people with low sight, travelers that access a page from small and mobile screens and other learners with visual disabilities.

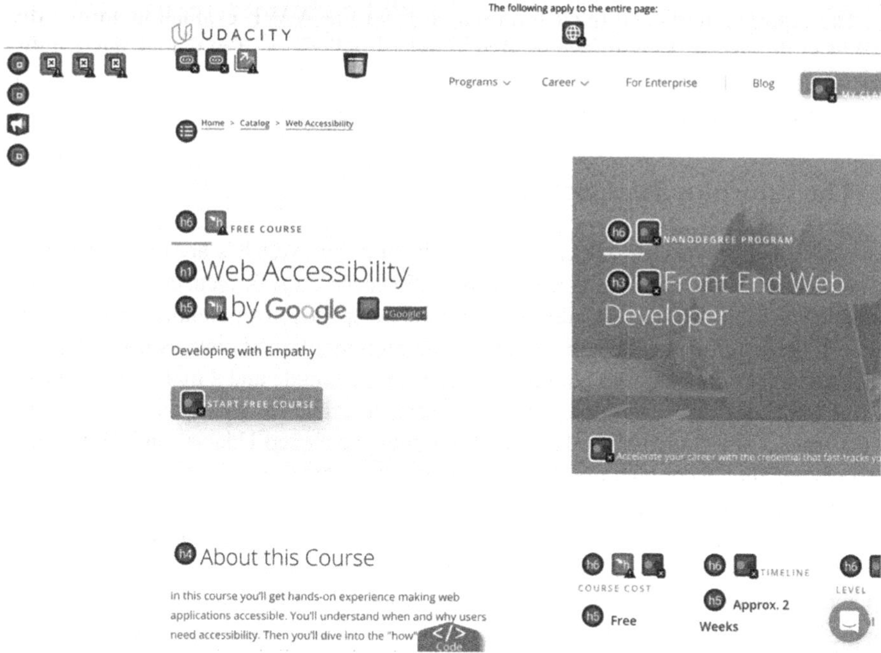

Fig. 1. A Udacity course accessibility test report visualization

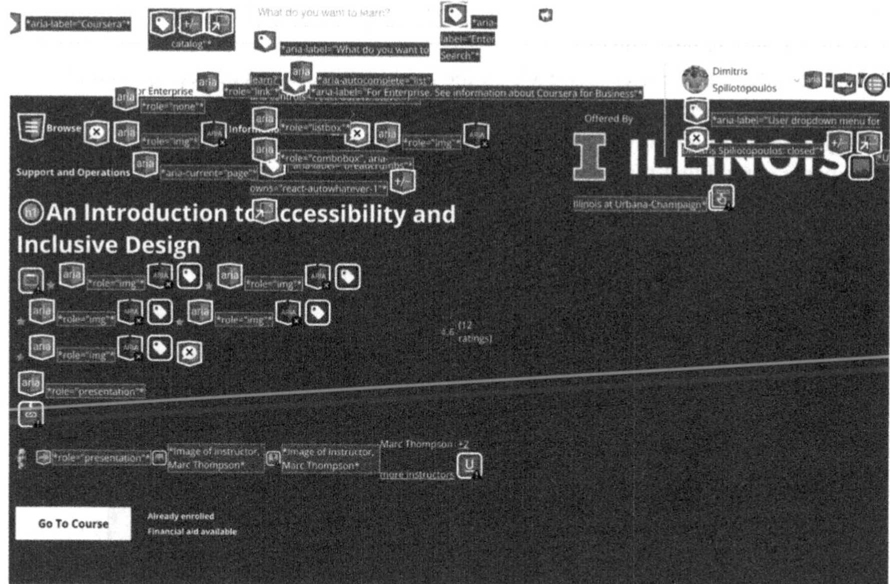

Fig. 2. A Coursera course accessibility test report visualization

The reported alerts and other information from the WAVE evaluation are not discussed in this paper. Reports are used as standard indicators of potential accessibility issues. However, reports cannot fully identify all accessibility issues as successfully as human users can when interacting and accessing the content.

5 The Educator Perspective

Educators and prospective educators generally find that MOOCs are one of the most prominent methods for teaching and learning. However, most of them consider the fully abled teacher and learner. In order to assess the perspective of potential educators, we asked four postgraduate students to access the aforementioned courses using a screen reader. The participants were between 23–29 years, 2 female and 2 male. They all have postgraduate degrees in computer science or equivalent and were pursuing a PhD degree at the time of the study. All had reported that they have used Udacity and Coursera as learners and they were planning to use them as educators, too.

The study setup had all four participants use Safari on a MacBook Pro 15" mid 2019, accessing the two courses in random order, using the MacOS built in Voice Over reader. The purpose was to provide the participants – prospective educators and users of the MOOC platforms – with the experience of the disabled learner. The formal justification for the introduction to the study was that, in real life, any abled person may be temporarily disabled due to situation or health related factors.

During the recruitment, about three months before the study took place, the participants filled in very short questionnaires on their opinion and feedback form the use of the MOOC platforms in the past. After the experience with the screen reader, they reported again on the same questionnaire.

Figure 3 depicts the user feedback on the accessibility impact as comprised of their perceived acceptance, friendliness, motivation to use and social morality (is universal accessibility the moral thing to do?). Before the experience with the screen reader, all participants agreed that the two MOOCs were very friendly and acceptable (usability),

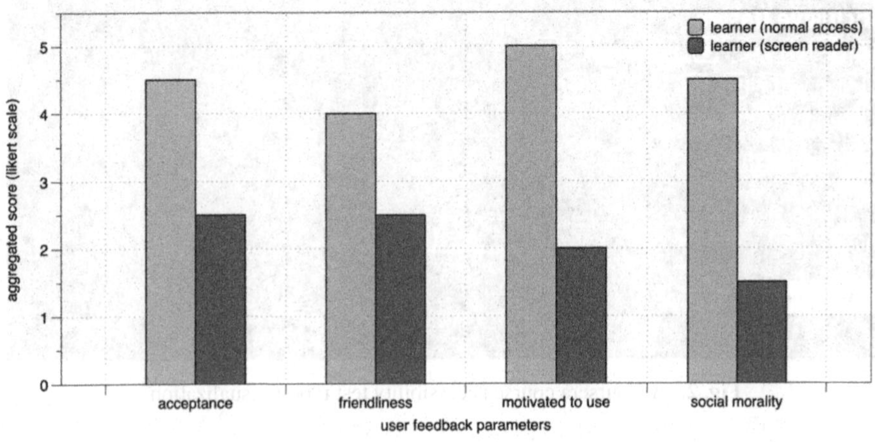

Fig. 3. Educators as learners, user feedback on accessibility impact

they were very motivated to use and that is was suitable for everyone. After the experience, being in the position to appreciate the difficulties that accessibility non-compliance or partial compliance presents to the disabled learners, the users responded that the platforms and the courses were not acceptable since they are still not fully accessible to all students and that it is a societal issue for everyone.

6 Conclusion and Future Work

An e-learning-for-all approach requires that all content should be accessible to all user groups with a firm and loyal devotion to the educational perspective. In this context, design parameters of conversational agents for accessibility are modelled according to specific needs. The methods used for creating and rendering universally accessible information are formed according to design parameters and associated resources. The resource management includes exclusive analyses stages of the information source content, structure and target modality. Each analysis stage is performed by applying specific models for document browsing, section identification, navigation hierarchy, contextual analysis and categorization.

This paper presented the theoretical framework for accessible online e-learning, the current state of the research in accessibility and the technologies for accessibility that may be applied to ensure accessibility. The state of research on the content created for e-learning was analysed. Then, two typical course pages from Udacity and Coursera were evaluated for accessibility using the WAVE voice renderer. Finally, human participants experienced the websites using a screen reader and reported how their perspective on the use of the MOOC platforms has been affected.

Given the fact that even the special education online websites struggle to meet the accessibility compliance levels and directives [44], content should be a top priority for universal accessibility for e-learning. Future work includes the use of the proposed methodology with recommender systems [45–47] and especially combination with collaborative filtering techniques [48–53]. Finally, we are planning the proposed approach to be incorporated in social related recommendation applications [54–58].

References

1. Schefbeck, G., Spiliotopoulos, D., Risse, T.: The recent challenge in web archiving: archiving the social web. In: Proceedings of the International Council on Archives Congress, pp. 1–5 (2012)
2. Choudhury, S., Pattnaik, S.: Emerging themes in e-learning: a review from the stakeholders' perspective. Comput. Educ. **144** (2020). https://doi.org/10.1016/j.compedu.2019.103657
3. Iniesto, F., McAndrew, P., Minocha, S., Coughlan, T.: Accessibility of MOOCs: understanding the provider perspective. J. Interact. Media Educ. **20**, 1–10 (2016). https://doi.org/10.5334/jime.430
4. Berners-Lee, T., Hendler, J., Lassila, O.: The semantic web. Sci. Am. **248**, 34–43 (2001). https://doi.org/10.1038/scientificamerican0501-34
5. Al-Fraihat, D., Joy, M., Masa'deh, R., Sinclair, J.: Evaluating e-learning systems success: an empirical study. Comput. Hum. Behav. (2020). https://doi.org/10.1016/j.chb.2019.08.004

6. Burgstahler, S., Havel, A., Seale, J., Olenik-Shemesh, D.: Accessibility frameworks and models: exploring the potential for a paradigm shift. In: Seale, J. (ed.) Improving Accessible Digital Practices in Higher Education, pp. 45–72. Springer, Cham (2020). https://doi.org/10.1007/978-3-030-37125-8_3
7. El Ahrache, S.I., Badir, H., Tabaa, Y., Medouri, A.: Massive open online courses: a new dawn for higher education? Int. J. Comput. Sci. Eng. **5**, 323–327 (2013)
8. Iniesto, F., Rodrigo, C.: A preliminary study for developing accessible MOOC services. J. Access. Des. All **6**, 125–149 (2016). https://doi.org/10.17411/jacces.v6i1.117
9. Al-Mouh, N.A., Al-Khalifa, A.S., Al-Khalifa, H.S.: A first look into MOOCs accessibility. In: Miesenberger, K., Fels, D., Archambault, D., Peňáz, P., Zagler, W. (eds.) ICCHP 2014. LNCS, vol. 8547, pp. 145–152. Springer, Cham (2014). https://doi.org/10.1007/978-3-319-08596-8_22
10. Sanchez-Gordon, S., Luján-Mora, S.: How could MOOCs become accessible? The case of edX and the future of inclusive online learning. J. Univers. Comput. Sci. **22**, 55–81 (2016). https://doi.org/10.3217/jucs-022-01-0055
11. Ma, L., Lee, C.S.: Investigating the adoption of MOOCs: a technology–user–environment perspective. J. Comput. Assist. Learn. **35**, 89–98 (2019). https://doi.org/10.1111/jcal.12314
12. Deshpande, A., Chukhlomin, V.: What makes a good MOOC: a field study of factors impacting student motivation to learn. Am. J. Distance Educ. 275–293 (2017). https://doi.org/10.1080/08923647.2017.1377513
13. Harrington, C.N., Koon, L.M., Rogers, W.A.: Design of health information and communication technologies for older adults. In: Sethumadhavan, A., Sasangohar, F. (eds.) Design for Health, pp. 341–363. Academic Press (2020). https://doi.org/10.1016/B978-0-12-816427-3.00017-8
14. Sanchez-Gordon, S., Luján-Mora, S.: Web accessibility of MOOCs for elderly students. In: 2013 12th International Conference on Information Technology Based Higher Education and Training, ITHET 2013 (2013). https://doi.org/10.1109/ITHET.2013.6671024
15. Bayly, M., Morgan, D., Froehlich Chow, A., Kosteniuk, J., Elliot, V.: Dementia-related education and support service availability, accessibility, and use in rural areas: barriers and solutions. Can. J. Aging (2020). https://doi.org/10.1017/S0714980819000564
16. Robles, T.D.J.Á., González, A.M., Gaona, A.R.G., Rodríguez, F.A.: Addressing accessibility of MOOCs for blind users. In: Accessibility and Diversity in Education (2019). https://doi.org/10.4018/978-1-7998-1213-5.ch027
17. Rose, D.: Universal design for learning. J. Spec. Educ. Technol. **16**, 66–67 (2001). https://doi.org/10.1177/016264340101600208
18. Sanger, C.S.: Inclusive pedagogy and universal design approaches for diverse learning environments. In: Sanger, C.S., Gleason, N.W. (eds.) Diversity and Inclusion in Global Higher Education. LNCS, pp. 31–71. Springer, Singapore (2020). https://doi.org/10.1007/978-981-15-1628-3_2
19. Ladonlahti, T., Laamanen, M., Uotinen, S.: Ensuring diverse user experiences and accessibility while developing the TeSLA e-assessment system. In: Baneres, D., Rodríguez, M.E., Guerrero-Roldán, A.E. (eds.) Engineering Data-Driven Adaptive Trust-based e-Assessment Systems. LNDECT, vol. 34, pp. 213–238. Springer, Cham (2020). https://doi.org/10.1007/978-3-030-29326-0_10
20. Neto, L.V., Fontoura Junior, P.H., Bordini, R.A., Otsuka, J.L., Beder, D.M.: Design and implementation of an educational game considering issues for visually impaired people inclusion. Smart Learn. Environ. **7**(1), 1–16 (2019). https://doi.org/10.1186/s40561-019-0103-4
21. Pino, A., Kouroupetroglou, G., Kacorri, H., Sarantidou, A., Spiliotopoulos, D.: An open source/freeware assistive technology software inventory. In: Miesenberger, K., Klaus, J., Zagler, W., Karshmer, A. (eds.) ICCHP 2010. LNCS, vol. 6179, pp. 178–185. Springer, Heidelberg (2010). https://doi.org/10.1007/978-3-642-14097-6_29

22. Spiliotopoulos, D., Tzoannos, E., Stavropoulou, P., Kouroupetroglou, G., Pino, A.: Designing user interfaces for social media driven digital preservation and information retrieval. In: Miesenberger, K., Karshmer, A., Penaz, P., Zagler, W. (eds.) ICCHP 2012. LNCS, vol. 7382, pp. 581–584. Springer, Heidelberg (2012). https://doi.org/10.1007/978-3-642-31522-0_87
23. Xydas, G., Spiliotopoulos, D., Kouroupetroglou, G.: Modeling emphatic events from non-speech aware documents in speech based user interfaces. In: Proceedings of Human Computer Interaction, pp. 806–810 (2003)
24. Xydas, G., Spiliotopoulos, D., Kouroupetroglou, G.: Modeling improved prosody generation from high-level linguistically annotated corpora. IEICE Trans. Inf. Syst. **E88-D**, 510–518 (2005). https://doi.org/10.1093/ietisy/e88-d.3.510
25. Spiliotopoulos, D., Xydas, G., Kouroupetroglou, G.: Diction based prosody modeling in table-to-speech synthesis. In: Matoušek, V., Mautner, P., Pavelka, T. (eds.) TSD 2005. LNCS (LNAI), vol. 3658, pp. 294–301. Springer, Heidelberg (2005). https://doi.org/10.1007/11551874_38
26. Spiliotopoulos, D., Stavropoulou, P., Kouroupetroglou, G.: Acoustic rendering of data tables using earcons and prosody for document accessibility. In: Stephanidis, C. (ed.) UAHCI 2009. LNCS, vol. 5616, pp. 587–596. Springer, Heidelberg (2009). https://doi.org/10.1007/978-3-642-02713-0_62
27. Spiliotopoulos, D., Xydas, G., Kouroupetroglou, G., Argyropoulos, V., Ikospentaki, K.: Auditory universal accessibility of data tables using naturally derived prosody specification. Univers. Access Inf. Soc. **9** (2010). https://doi.org/10.1007/s10209-009-0165-0
28. Margaris, D., Georgiadis, P., Vassilakis, C.: A collaborative filtering algorithm with clustering for personalized web service selection in business processes. In: 2015 IEEE 9th International Conference on Research Challenges in Information Science (RCIS), pp. 169–180 (2015). https://doi.org/10.1109/RCIS.2015.7128877
29. Margaris, D., Georgiadis, P., Vassilakis, C.: On replacement service selection in WS-BPEL scenario adaptation. In: Proceedings - 2015 IEEE 8th International Conference on Service-Oriented Computing and Applications, SOCA 2015, pp. 10–17 (2015). https://doi.org/10.1109/SOCA.2015.11
30. Margaris, D., Vassilakis, C., Georgiadis, P.: Improving QoS delivered by WS-BPEL scenario adaptation through service execution parallelization. In: Proceedings of the 31st Annual ACM Symposium on Applied Computing, pp. 1590–1596. Association for Computing Machinery, New York (2016). https://doi.org/10.1145/2851613.2851805
31. Kouroupetroglou, G., Spiliotopoulos, D.: Usability methodologies for real-life voice user interfaces. Int. J. Inf. Technol. Web. Eng. **4**, 78–94 (2009). https://doi.org/10.4018/jitwe.2009100105
32. Antonakaki, D., Spiliotopoulos, D., Samaras, C.V., Ioannidis, S., Fragopoulou, P.: Investigating the complete corpus of referendum and elections tweets. In: Proceedings of the 2016 IEEE/ACM International Conference on Advances in Social Networks Analysis and Mining, ASONAM 2016, pp. 100–105 (2016). https://doi.org/10.1109/ASONAM.2016.7752220
33. Demidova, E., et al.: Analysing and enriching focused semantic web archives for parliament applications. Futur. Internet **6**, 433–456 (2014). https://doi.org/10.3390/fi6030433
34. Risse, T., et al.: The ARCOMEM architecture for social- and semantic-driven web archiving. Futur. Internet **6**, 688–716 (2014). https://doi.org/10.3390/fi6040688
35. Xydas, G., Spiliotopoulos, D., Kouroupetroglou, G.: Modeling prosodic structures in linguistically enriched environments. In: Sojka, P., Kopeček, I., Pala, K. (eds.) TSD 2004. LNCS (LNAI), vol. 3206, pp. 521–528. Springer, Heidelberg (2004). https://doi.org/10.1007/978-3-540-30120-2_66

36. Androutsopoulos, I., Spiliotopoulos, D., Stamatakis, K., Dimitromanolaki, A., Karkaletsis, V., Spyropoulos, C.D.: Symbolic authoring for multilingual natural language generation. In: Vlahavas, I.P., Spyropoulos, C.D. (eds.) SETN 2002. LNCS (LNAI), vol. 2308, pp. 131–142. Springer, Heidelberg (2002). https://doi.org/10.1007/3-540-46014-4_13
37. Iakovidis, D.K., Diamantis, D., Dimas, G., Ntakolia, C., Spyrou, E.: Digital enhancement of cultural experience and accessibility for the visually impaired. In: Paiva, S. (ed.) Technological Trends in Improved Mobility of the Visually Impaired. EICC, pp. 237–271. Springer, Cham (2020). https://doi.org/10.1007/978-3-030-16450-8_10
38. Spiliotopoulos, D., Xydas, G., Kouroupetroglou, G., Argyropoulos, V.: Experimentation on spoken format of tables in auditory user interfaces. In: 11th International Conference in Human-Computer Interaction, Las Vegas, Nevada, USA, pp. 361–370. Lawrence Erlbaum Associates, Inc. (2005)
39. Abdolrahmani, A., Storer, K.M., Roy, A.R.M., Kuber, R., Branham, S.M.: Blind leading the sighted: drawing design insights from blind users towards more productivity-oriented voice interfaces. ACM Trans. Access. Comput. **12**, 18 (2020). https://doi.org/10.1145/3368426
40. Alexandersson, J., et al.: Metalogue: a multiperspective multimodal dialogue system with metacognitive abilities for highly adaptive and flexible dialogue management. In: Proceedings - 2014 International Conference on Intelligent Environments, IE 2014, pp. 365–368 (2014). https://doi.org/10.1109/IE.2014.67
41. Kim, A.A., Monroe, M., Lee, S.: Examining K-12 educators' perception and instruction of online accessibility features. Comput. Assist. Lang. Learn. 1–32 (2020). https://doi.org/10.1080/09588221.2019.1705353
42. Iniesto, F., McAndrew, P., Minocha, S., Coughlan, T.: An investigation into the perspectives of providers and learners on MOOC accessibility. In: 5th International Conference on Technological Ecosystems for Enhancing Multiculturality, pp. 1–8 (2017). https://doi.org/10.1145/3144826.3145442
43. Zhang, X., et al.: Accessibility within open educational resources and practices for disabled learners: a systematic literature review. Smart Learn. Environ. **7**(1), 1–19 (2019). https://doi.org/10.1186/s40561-019-0113-2
44. Baule, S.M.: Evaluating the accessibility of special education cooperative websites for individuals with disabilities. TechTrends **64**(1), 50–56 (2019). https://doi.org/10.1007/s11528-019-00421-2
45. Margaris, D., Vassilakis, C.: Exploiting rating abstention intervals for addressing concept drift in social network recommender systems. Informatics **5**, 21 (2018). https://doi.org/10.3390/informatics5020021
46. Margaris, D., Vassilakis, C.: Exploiting internet of things information to enhance venues' recommendation accuracy. SOCA **11**(4), 393–409 (2017). https://doi.org/10.1007/s11761-017-0216-y
47. Margaris, D., Vassilakis, C., Georgiadis, P.: Recommendation information diffusion in social networks considering user influence and semantics. Soc. Netw. Anal. Mining **6**(1), 1–22 (2016). https://doi.org/10.1007/s13278-016-0416-z
48. Margaris, D., Georgiadis, P., Vassilakis, C.: Adapting WS-BPEL scenario execution using collaborative filtering techniques. In: Proceedings - International Conference on Research Challenges in Information Science (2013). https://doi.org/10.1109/RCIS.2013.6577691
49. Margaris, D., Vassilakis, C.: Improving collaborative filtering's rating prediction accuracy by considering users' rating variability. In: Proceedings - IEEE 16th International Conference on Dependable, Autonomic and Secure Computing, IEEE 16th International Conference on Pervasive Intelligence and Computing, IEEE 4th International Conference on Big Data Intelligence and Computing and IEEE 3 (2018). https://doi.org/10.1109/DASC/PiCom/DataCom/CyberSciTec.2018.00145

50. Margaris, D., Vassilakis, C., Georgiadis, P.: An integrated framework for adapting WS-BPEL scenario execution using QoS and collaborative filtering techniques. Sci. Comput. Program. **98**, 707–734 (2015). https://doi.org/10.1016/j.scico.2014.10.007
51. Margaris, D., Vassilakis, C.: Improving collaborative filtering's rating prediction quality by considering shifts in rating practices. In: 2017 IEEE 19th Conference on Business Informatics (CBI), pp. 158–166 (2017). https://doi.org/10.1109/CBI.2017.24
52. Margaris, D., Vasilopoulos, D., Vassilakis, C., Spiliotopoulos, D.: Improving collaborative filtering's rating prediction accuracy by introducing the common item rating past criterion. In: 10th International Conference on Information, Intelligence, Systems and Applications, IISA 2019, pp. 1022–1027 (2019). https://doi.org/10.1109/IISA.2019.8900758
53. Margaris, D., Kobusinska, A., Spiliotopoulos, D., Vassilakis, C.: An adaptive social network-aware collaborative filtering algorithm for improved rating prediction accuracy. IEEE Access **8**, 68301–68310 (2020). https://doi.org/10.1109/ACCESS.2020.2981567
54. Margaris, D., Spiliotopoulos, D., Vassilakis, C.: Social relations versus near neighbours: reliable recommenders in limited information social network collaborative filtering for online advertising. In: Proceedings of the 2019 IEEE/ACM International Conference on Advances in Social Networks Analysis and Mining (ASONAM 2019), Vancouver, BC, Canada, pp. 1160–1167. ACM (2019). https://doi.org/10.1145/3341161.3345620
55. Margaris, D., Vassilakis, C., Spiliotopoulos, D.: Handling uncertainty in social media textual information for improving venue recommendation formulation quality in social networks. Soc. Netw. Anal. Mining **9**(1), 1–19 (2019). https://doi.org/10.1007/s13278-019-0610-x
56. Margaris, D., Vassilakis, C., Georgiadis, P.: Knowledge-based leisure time recommendations in social networks. In: Alor-Hernández, G., Valencia-García, R. (eds.) Current Trends on Knowledge-Based Systems. ISRL, vol. 120, pp. 23–48. Springer, Cham (2017). https://doi.org/10.1007/978-3-319-51905-0_2
57. Aivazoglou, M., et al.: A fine-grained social network recommender system. Soc. Netw. Anal. Mining **10**(1), 1–18 (2019). https://doi.org/10.1007/s13278-019-0621-7
58. Margaris, D., Vassilakis, C., Spiliotopoulos, D.: What makes a review a reliable rating in recommender systems? Inf. Process. Manag. **57**, 102304 (2020). https://doi.org/10.1016/j.ipm.2020.102304

User-Centred Design for Accessibility in Media Content – Sign Language and Virtual Signer

Vaishnavi Upadrasta(✉), Astrid Oehme, and Sandra Böhm

HFC Human-Factors-Consult GmbH, Köpenicker Str. 325, 12555 Berlin, Germany
{Upadrasta,oehme,boehm}@human-factors-consult.de

Abstract. Even though User-Centred Design (UCD) is widely accepted and employed in the design and development of interactive systems, there are limited guiding procedures on how such approaches can be translated to the development of products, systems, and services that are focusing primarily on accessibility. This paper reports on the application of UCD for such a system within an EU project CONTENT4ALL under the domain accessibility for the Deaf. Each step in the UCD process and the respective activities within each step are described in detail with a focus on the methods and techniques adopted for assisting in the development of the novel technology. The insights gained during the entirety of the user-centred design and evaluation process have led to a compilation of important factors for creating sign-translated media content. This possible guideline comprises a list of useful and necessary components pertaining to sign language delivery in media, particularly sign television. The objective of this paper is to highlight lessons learned presented in the form of recommendations for human factors researchers on key UCD procedures for the development of accessibility products, systems and services based on the performed user activities within the project. An attempt has been made to reduce the gap in literature and add to a possible UCD guiding process exclusively for accessibility.

Keywords: User-centred design in accessible systems · Sign language and virtual signer · Accessibility in media · User-centred design · Sign language delivery guidelines · Sign-translated TV

1 Introduction

1.1 Project Overview

The Deaf community for years has been discriminated against and are oftentimes excluded from partaking in information exchange and communication, for example by not having media access available in their mother tongue, i.e. in sign language. As per the UN Convention on the Rights of Persons with Disabilities from 2008 [1], the Deaf are entitled to full and equal enjoyment to access information and communications, including information and communications technologies and systems. Consequently, the UN Convention has made it obligatory for national government and broadcast industry regulators to make television content accessible to the Deaf. Broadcasting companies

C. Stephanidis et al. (Eds.): HCII 2020, LNCS 12426, pp. 126–143, 2020.
https://doi.org/10.1007/978-3-030-60149-2_11

are continuously seeking for solutions to increase the number of programs that can be translated into sign language, however the cost of producing sign language content and the negative impact of having a sign-interpreter appearing on the content for hearing counterparts has resulted in very little progress to provide accessible media content to the Deaf community.

To address this issue, a network of six European partners (including national broadcasters and sign language experts) is currently conducting the research and innovation project CONTENT4ALL (C4A), with the aim to make more content accessible to the Deaf community. In the project, a remote signing apparatus (located off-premises of the broadcaster) is developed to capture a human sign-interpreter's signs, poses, and facial expressions. The captured information is processed and rendered in real-time via broadcast into a photo-realistic 3D representation, i.e. a virtual signer. This will make the work of sign language interpreters easier, as they are not required to travel to the TV station but instead are able to use the remote studio facilities, even feasible at their own premises. Such a remote apparatus will directly contribute to reducing the production costs that would have been incurred if the sign language interpreter had to be present in the broadcaster's studio in order to translate. This would allow for a low-cost personalization of content for Deaf viewers and thus will facilitate content production in sign language. This goal of the project would encourage broadcasters to increase accessibility practices and support the production of sign-translated television.

1.2 Purpose

Within the development of a new system, and to reach acceptance by the users, it is important to involve future users from the beginning and include them during the whole design process to make sure that the technical solutions fit the users' needs. This applies even more for products that are aimed at supporting people with disabilities. Thus, all user-related activities within the C4A project are conducted applying a user-centred design (UCD) approach according to [2, 3], i.e. users are involved during requirements collection, prototyping and testing.

There is less information available on how to best adapt the UCD process when designing products, systems, and services that focus solely on accessibility. The available UCD guidelines only specify the need of considering users' needs that encompass a wide range of user groups. The ISO 9241 [3] additionally emphasizes the legal requirement in many countries to achieve accessibility when developing such products, systems, and services. What the literature is lacking at the moment are key aspects of UCD activities when developing accessible products, systems, and services.

Within the C4A project, we adapted the UCD model described by [4] to the projects' demands. The model focusses not only on reaching a high usability of systems but also on improving User Experience. We report on the UCD activities revised for C4A project, with a focus on the methods and techniques performed during the different development stages. As the project is currently ongoing, user evaluations conducted up to this point are described. During the UCD process, it soon became evident that this particular process not only helps in the development of the novel technology but provides valuable insights into the domain of sign language delivery of media content, which is beneficial to broadcasters and media providers. These insights were analyzed, and a possible guide is established for European sign television, which is reported in this paper.

Additional, due to low information in the literature on how to adapt the UCD process to the development of accessibility systems, we share our lessons learned up to now, which we derived from the user-related activities within the C4A project development. We suggest recommendations for human factors researchers that would be valuable when conducting user-centred evaluations with user groups with disabilities.

2 User-Centred Design (UCD)

2.1 UCD, UX and Relations Between Key Concepts

During the C4A project, all user-related features are developed on the basis of the UCD approach according to [2, 3]. The guideline defines UCD or human-centred design (HCD) as an "approach to systems design and development that aims to make interactive systems more usable by focusing on the use of the system and applying human factors/ergonomics and usability knowledge and techniques". The basic principles of UCD incorporate 1) the involvement of users throughout the design and development, 2) a design refinement using iterative user-centred evaluation, and 3) working with a design team with multidisciplinary skills and perspectives. For decades now general UCD activities within a development life cycle outline four key iterative and interlinked procedures: understanding and specifying the context of use, specifying the user requirements, producing design solutions, and evaluating the design [2]. A great deal of planning is required in order to integrate UCD into all development phases of a product, system, or service lifecycle. Moreover, the planning should correspond with the overall project plan and its goals. The ultimate goals of applying UCD is to create a product or a service, which is easy to use or apply and tailored to the needs of the specific user group.

Related to these goals, some crucial concepts have to be considered. Usability is defined as the "extent to which a product can be used by specified users to achieve specified goals with effectiveness, efficiency, and satisfaction in a specified context of use" [5]. General classes of usability measures address the key criteria effectiveness, efficiency and satisfaction. Specifications of these classes however vary with respect to the product, system, or service [6]. Usability is one key aspect in describing user experience (UX), along with emotional and aesthetic aspects. UX comprises the entire set of affects that result from the interaction between a user and a product.

The UX of a system consists of at least two qualities: pragmatic or instrumental qualities and hedonic or non-instrumental qualities (i.e. [7–10]). Pragmatic or instrumental qualities refer to product qualities such as its usefulness and usability. Hedonic or non-instrumental qualities focus on aspects such as the product's aesthetics and its haptic quality, i.e. the feel of the product. These components result in the user's overall appraisal of the product or system which in turn characterizes their opinion, attitude towards or behavior towards the product, such as the decision to use the product or not, if yes then how often, intentions towards the product, etc.

Aspects such as quality of service (QoS), quality of experience (QoE), and UX are closely linked with each other. The user-oriented model developed by [11] describes the relationship between the three variables QoS, UX, and QoE. QoS refers to the technical characteristics that are related to the overall technical performance of a system. On the other hand, QoE refers to the user's perception of the performance of a system or service [12] and UX helps in exploring how users feel about using a product, system, or service [13]. QoE and UX focus on the perception of the user and thus build a base for user evaluation requirements and planning. A variety of UX, usability, and related concept methods could be used during the UCD activities, with the exact selection always depending on the issues in question and/or the respective project design and development goals. The approach should be geared to a user-centred design process according to [2] and its conversion.

2.2 UCD Activities for CONTENT4ALL

The UCD framework for the C4A project was established as an internal guidance to the consortium. Adapting to the UCD model described by [4], the UCD process implemented by C4A was segregated into four main blocks: ideation, concept and planning, iterative implementation, and UX-testing (see Fig. 1). The first two were part of early-stages of development while the latter two belong within the mid-stages and post-stages of development. The four blocks were used as guidelines in integrating the user activities with the project plan, its goals, period of development, and available resources. Accordingly, user evaluation goals for the C4A system were set for every phase of the development process. Depending on the evaluation stage, different qualitative and/or quantitative methods were used. The information acquired was then evaluated, processed, and improvements were implemented in an iterative nature. As the C4A project is still in progress, only the completed user evaluations are reported in this paper.

Identifying Initial User Requirements. Defining the context of use and identifying the initial user requirements was the starting point of the UCD activities in the C4A project. The very first activity was to understand the characteristics, needs, goals, and values of the identified users. Two types of users were identified: end-users (people who can sign which includes deaf, hard of hearing and hearing signers such as family and friends of deaf people, professional sign language interpreters, students of Deaf studies, etc.) and organizational users[1] (broadcasters and other stakeholders). The information was collected using several analysis techniques: in-depth user-interviews with deaf and hearing signers, in-depth interviews with stakeholders, an online questionnaire inquiry for signers, and a workshop with young signers.

Based on the input received during the interviews, online questionnaire, and workshop with the young, it was clear that the users' expectations encompassed a broad range of categories (e.g. from system features to appearance of the interpreter). A detailed description of the findings of the initial user requirements analysis can be found in [14].

All the acquired data were analyzed individually, classified into distinct outcomes, and reported in an aggregated way. All repetitions were removed, and the expectations were paraphrased when required. The analysis revealed a long list of users' expectations

[1] In [5] it has been emphasized that users may not only refer to only those who are typically considered as users i.e. end-users but may include all recognized stakeholders.

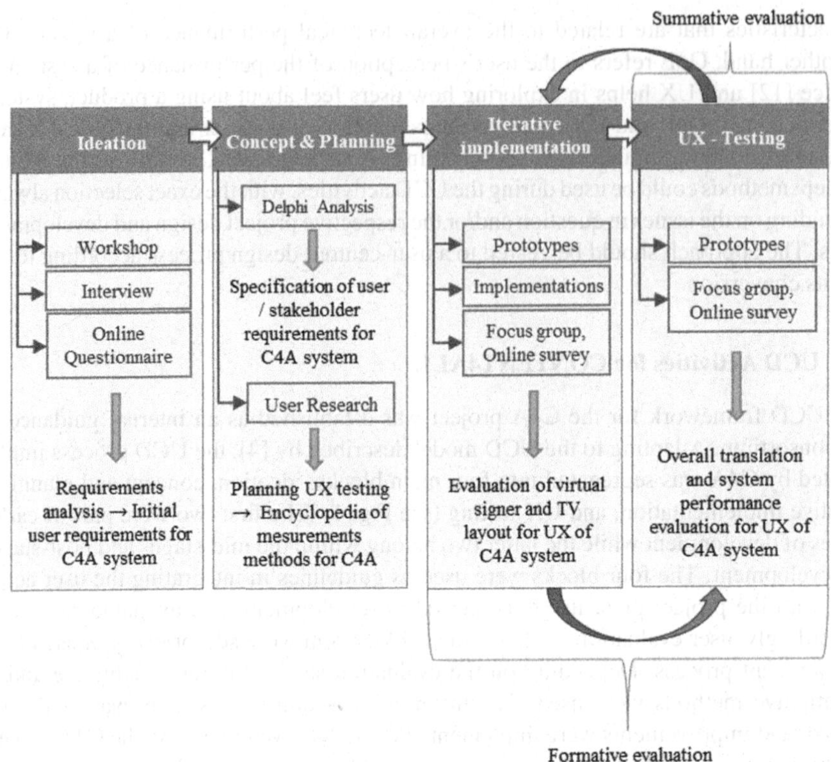

Fig. 1. User-centred design process for C4A (adapted from [4]).

for the future C4A system. This comprehensive, high-level list cannot constitute a compilation of final 'requirements' for the system. Users (and other stakeholders) are not able to generate requirements in the narrower sense of the word, for systems which are novel and so far have no comparable equal available on the market. Thus, ideas of possible users are often much more idealistic and do not take into account technical feasibilities available at the time of development. It is the task of human factors specialists and the project's technical specialists to translate user expectations into systems requirements. At a first stage, we labeled preliminary expectations as 'initial user requirements'. This multidisciplinary approach is a key factor of the UCD.

Specifying Final User Requirements. The initial user requirements have to be further refined with regards to the intended context of use, technical feasibility, the scope of the projects, and exploitation objectives of the system. Specifying the final requirements should be done in a careful and systematic manner, as the defined user requirements form a guideline to early prototyping and evaluation plans of a product or system.

In C4A, a conformance process was accomplished with the help of the Delphi method (i.e. [15–17]. The aim of using this method was to determine which user requirements were achievable within the project and which were out of scope for the project. A total of three rounds were performed with representatives of all project partners in order to maintain internal consistency and determine the final set of high-level requirements for the C4A system. The method helped in resolving potential conflicts and trade-offs and establishing final consensus within the consortium in a systematic fashion.

Even though the user requirements are determined in the early-stages of development, due to the iterative nature of the UCD process, the final specifications may require to be altered due to identification of new requirements and/or rejection or refinement of the established ones during the development lifecycle. Furthermore, new technologies may become available, which enables an even better consideration of high-level requirements and their translation into a new system.

Planning User-Centred Evaluation. One important step during the development of the user evaluation plan is to incorporate scales and measurements relevant to the UX of C4A in a way that is as faithful as possible to the empirically tested sources while adhering to the requirements of efficiency and validity. For this purpose, an encyclopedia of measurement methods was compiled with the aim of planning the user tests (both formative and summative testing). Formative evaluation "aims to provide feedback which can be used to improve the design and to generate new ideas", whereas summative evaluation "aims to assess whether user and organizational usability objectives have been achieved" [18].

A wide range of evaluation tools, methods, and benchmarks that cover aspects of UX, usability, QoE and the other above-presented concepts were collected, categorized, and assessed regarding their suitability in the context of C4A UX testing. The encyclopedia of methods was created by defining categories, according to which the methods were classified: type of UX aspect addressed (pragmatic, hedonic, social), the type of collected data (qualitative or quantitative), the study type (laboratory, field, online), collection method (questionnaires, physiological measurements, self-reports, user observations, expert evaluations, etc.), time of evaluation (before, in situ, after) as well as the methods' strengths and weaknesses, and their estimated costs. Each method was then given a relevance-rating (low medium, high) based on important UX aspects that were identified as more significant for user-testing of the C4A system: overall UX, usefulness, aesthetics, stressful/demanding and acceptance. Twelve 'high relevance' methods (see Table 1) were selected as potentially serving the purpose of testing prototypes of components (formative testing) or the final demonstrator (summative testing) of the C4A system.

Developing Design Solutions and Prototypes. According to [2] "a prototype may be as simple as a sketch or static mock-up or as complicated as a fully functioning interactive system with more or less complete functionality". The documented context of use, results of requirements analysis and early user-centred evaluations, feedback of users, available guidelines and standards, and expertise of the multidisciplinary team contribute to producing initial design solutions and prototypes of a product, system, or service. The established final user requirements for C4A system formed the foundation for the first attempt of the virtual signer and first concepts of the sign TV interface.

The developed prototypes should be assessed using user-centred evaluation methods and the analyzed results then communicated to those responsible for implementing improvements, so that new and better versions can be realized. When developing prototypes, it is important to consider the whole UX of the system.

Table 1. Selected methods for UX testing of C4A prototypes

Sr. no	Selected methods	UX/QoE	Type	Focus on...
1	SAM	QoE	Questionnaire, quantitative	Social qualities
2	3E expressing, experience & emotion	QoE	Collage/drawing, qualitative	Social qualities
3	AXE	QoE	Self-report, qualitative	Social qualities
4	Affect grid	UX	Self-report, quantitative	Hedonic qualities
5	AttrakDiff	QoE	Questionnaire, quantitative	Hedonic qualities
6	Hedonic utility scale	UX	Questionnaire, quantitative	Hedonic qualities
7	Aesthetics	QoE	Questionnaire, quantitative	Hedonic qualities
8	Co-discovery	UX	Self-report, qualitative	Pragmatic qualities
9	Pluralistic walkthrough	UX	Self-report, qualitative	Pragmatic qualities
10	Workshops	UX	Self-report/interview, qualitative	Pragmatic qualities
11	User experience questionnaire	UX	Questionnaire, quantitative	Pragmatic qualities
12	meCUE	UX	Questionnaire, quantitative	Pragmatic and hedonic qualities,

Evaluating Design Solutions and Prototypes. Evaluating the design solutions and prototypes is an essential step of a product's or system's development life cycle, and the UCD approach in general. The most important purpose of evaluating design solutions is to validate if user and stakeholder objectives have been achieved, i.e. if the final requirements and specifications of the users and other stakeholders are met [19]. Various UX methods can be selected for this purpose. According to [3], methods can be generically classified into empirical user-based testing methods and inspection-based evaluation methods. In contrast to user-based testing methods, inspection methods do not necessarily involve users directly, but make use of guidelines, standards, or heuristics.

As per the goals of the C4A project two user evaluation aspects are crucial: the first one regards interface design and virtual signer (early and mid-stage design concepts), while the second one focuses on the overall translation and system performance of the C4A system (finalized prototypes). Due to the project's innovative nature, specific guidelines and standards were not available, necessitating a sole focus on the use of user-based testing methods. Suitable assessment methods were chosen with the help of the created encyclopedia of methods. However, certain UX and usability paradigms of interaction were identified to have low application in evaluating the C4A system. As a result, even most of the preselected 12 methods of standardized UX and usability tests proved to be unsuitable for the specifics of the project after further consideration. New procedures and evaluation criteria were hence developed based on the user requirements analysis. Subsequently, tasks, activities, and questionnaires had to be created.

In accordance with the UCD approach, future users were integrated into this developmental stage by evaluating first concepts in two different focus groups. The participants were selected with regards to variation in age group and gender for a holistic range of inputs. This formative evaluation allows understanding which aspects of the current prototype status are sufficient and what errors or misunderstandings exist, even with a small user group. This user-centred evaluation led to essential insights and the basis for improvements of the first prototype. Two improved versions of the C4A system were then developed. To evaluate this iterative implementation, two further focus groups were conducted with the same participants. The subsequent focus group sessions were structured similarly and the tasks majorly based on the same evaluation criteria. The aim was to make comparisons between the different versions. Repertory Grid Technique [20, 21] was used to assist in the assessment.

When conducting user-centred evaluations, sufficient and comprehensive testing should be carried out in order to achieve meaningful results for the system as a whole [3]. Therefore, in addition to focus groups, a quantitative multi-lingual online questionnaire was conducted with deaf, hard of hearing, and hearing signers. Also, as the second group of future users of the C4A system, feedback was collected from broadcasters and similar media-related companies via a face-to-face survey.

Later Versions. Based on the iterative findings of the user-centred evaluations, new and final versions of the C4A virtual signer will be developed. As per C4A goals, final summative user-tests (within the project time frame) will be conducted to evaluate the overall translation and system performance. With the help of the encyclopedia of methods, an appropriate method will be chosen to complete the user research. This final user test is currently being planned and is thus not reported in this paper.

3 Guide for Sign Language Delivery in Sign Translated Media

The UCD process that was adhered to, as well as the implementation of the UUX methods and techniques, benefit the development of the best possible C4A solution. Many challenges could be identified upfront in the early to mid-stages of the development process, especially unforeseen complexities in areas such as sign language translation, sign language delivery, sign language presentation etc. During the UCD process, we realized that many findings essential for the C4A system could also be applicable to a broader picture beyond the project specifications. They can be generalized to the domain of sign language delivery for media content and sign translated television as a whole. Even with improved attempts from broadcasters to make television and media content more accessible to the Deaf community, little information in the form of standardizations exists on how to present sign translated content best in order to maximize comprehensibility. Currently, broadcasters follow their own set of personalized parameters for a specific country or region. Projects like C4A that aim at providing more media content in possibly multiple sign-translated languages than ever before, will require standardized regulations. The developed guidelines attempt to address the need for a standardized sign translated television on a European level.

Within the UCD process of the project, the human factors team iteratively evaluated and analyzed the data collected via the several methods and techniques conducted. The following sub-sections present the key findings of the initial user requirements, and of the focus groups and its second iteration that contributed to the identification of the guidelines. The findings of the initial requirements analysis built a foundation in establishing evaluation criteria. The analysis of the focus groups provided a comprehensive assessment of positive factors as well as room for improvement of the various versions, which was essential for the technical team. Due to the limited scope of this paper, only major findings relevant to the guidelines on sign translated television are compiled below under the three major categories that we consider most important: 'quality of sign language', 'quality of the presentation of the sign translated content in a TV picture' and 'appearance of the sign language interpreter'.

As the gathered data from the focus groups were based on 3D representations (virtual signing models), i.e. virtual signers, some guidelines may not be completely suitable for a recording of a human sign language interpreter. However, most derived key aspects apply for both sign language interpreters and virtual signers. For the purpose of this chapter, the two terms can be interchangeable unless mentioned.

3.1 Quality of Sign Language

The initial requirements analysis started, among others, with gathering data on basic understanding of how the Deaf community communicates, principally in sign language. Deaf users understand their surroundings largely through visual input. "Sign language is a complex combination of facial expressions, mouth/lip shapes, hand and body movements, and fingerspelling" [22]. To achieve the best possible overall quality of sign language, three benchmarks were discovered: 1) correctness of vocabulary and grammar, 2) reasonable signing speed and 3) communication of emotions and mood. Table 2 summarizes key aspects regarding the quality of the presented sign language.

Correctness of Vocabulary and Grammar. Signs (that include hand movements, hand positions, hand orientation, and hand forms), finger movements, facial expressions (that include mouth, cheeks, eyes, eyebrows), body movements, position, orientation (that include head, shoulder, upper torso), and attitude, etc. are all part of sign language. Each component is required to be accurate, clear, and in sync for the language/content to be understandable. Precise hand and body movements and positions define the correctness of the vocabulary and grammar in sign language. Hand forms or handshapes that are used to form words, and hand orientation (i.e. the rotation of the hand when signing) to a large extent contribute to achieving precise hand movements. These aspects are applicable to recordings of human sign language interpreters as well as to virtual signers.

The following aspect, on the other hand, was more relevant to a virtual signer than a direct recording of a human sign interpreter. The 'flow' of a virtual signer is extremely

Table 2. Key aspects pertaining to quality of sign language in sign-translated media content

GUIDL01	Precise hand movements, hand positions, hand forms, and hand orientation to ensure accurate signs for correctness of grammar and vocabulary
GUIDL02	Reasonable signing speed by the signer to enable clear visuals and level of understanding
GUIDL03	Signer should communicate emotions and mood → animated facial expressions + expressive signing are prerequisites for conveying mood and emotions, and necessary for avoidance of monotonous signing
GUIDL04	Display clear and accurate facial expressions – includes mouth, cheek, eyes, and eyebrow movement that are in sync with signs and body movement
GUIDL05	'In flow' signing – includes clear points of transition between sentences, fluency in body movements that match facial expressions, and insertion of appropriate pauses between sentences

vital for the quality of sign language. The flow in sign language includes points of transitions between sentences, e.g. clear beginnings and ends, effects of the body, i.e. fluency in movements, and appropriate pauses in-between sentences. A virtual representation of a signer can be compared to an electronic audio signal. Just as it is difficult for a hearing person to listen and comprehend electronic audio with inadequate pauses or poor 'flow', for the Deaf signs and gestures which are not fluent hinder their understanding, making it difficult to watch. Besides, the facial expressions and body should complement each other, i.e. movements have to be smooth, with no disruptions, while matching with facial expressions. For example, in a question vs. a statement, the whole face code is different. Difficulties in recognizing facial movements (mouth, eyes, eyebrows) could lead to misinterpretation of the content.

Reasonable Signing Speed. Being a visual language, sign language can be perceived differently when seen on devices like television and smartphones as compared to when seen/signed in person. Hence, appropriate measures should be taken to minimize this gap to maintain the same understanding level. One factor contributing to this is the speed of signing. Sign language is a detailed combination of rapid hand (especially fingers) and body movements, which may be seen as a blur via digital representation [22]. Appropriate resolution quality must be ensured to avoid this.

Communication of Emotions and Mood. Moreover, with regards to the level of understanding, it is necessary that the sign language interpreter/virtual signer communicates emotions and mood along with visually clear signs. To achieve this, animated facial expressions (mouth, cheeks, eyes, and eyebrow movements) that are clear and accurate are required. It is also necessary to avoid monotonous signing.

3.2 Technical Presentation and Motion of Sign Language Interpreter/Virtual Signer

It was found that the manner in which a sign language interpreter/virtual signer is implemented on a screen within a TV picture layout can greatly influence the level of understanding of the signed content. These technical concerns include how well the signer is presented, i.e. depicted in the layout space, and how effective or successful the depicted motions are with regards to comprehensibility.

The aim should be to optimize visual clarity. The visual clarity of the sign language interpreter/virtual signer's movements can be enhanced by applying a 15° depth shift, i.e. the signer should be shifted to a 15° angle instead of front-facing. Also, the signer should not be a mirror image/mirror reflection. This would cause difficulties in apprehending the hand movements, especially the hand orientation, thereby reducing the visual clarity. Moreover, in the context of layout, adequate space around the sign language interpreter must be allotted to permit larger gestures. This is also necessary for correctness of grammar. Finally, motor activities must look natural in particular for virtual signing models, wherein detailed attention should be given to body, hand, and face to ensure that they are well combined and integrated. Guidelines regarding the presentation of sign language can be found in Table 3.

Table 3. Key aspects pertaining to technical implementation and motion of sign language interpreter/virtual signer

GUIDL06	Appropriate resolution quality should be set to avoid blur → especially for clear visuals of hand and finger movements
GUIDL07	Appropriate optimization of signing space around the signer (in particular overhead signing and elbow sideward signing space) to permit larger gestures → space is important for correctness of grammar
GUIDL08	Apply depth shift – shift signer to 15° angle → for better visual and understanding
GUIDL09	Do not use mirror image/mirror reflection of signer → to avoid difficulty in apprehending hand movements especially hand orientation and reducing visual clarity
GUIDL10	Natural motor movements with no disruptions, i.e. natural, smooth and fluent motor movements with no 'stuttering' – body, shoulder, head, face, and hand should be well-combined, integrated, and complementing each other

3.3 Appearance of the Sign Language Interpreter/Virtual Signer

The findings of the in-depth interviews and online questionnaire indicated how aesthetics of the sign language interpreter/virtual signer impact the visual clarity as well as level of understanding of the signed content. Various pre-requisites concerning the color of clothing (should be plain), background-color (should be contrasting), hairstyle (should be off the face for clear visuals of eye and eyebrow movements), facial features (such as beard should not hinder the visual clarity of mouth movements), gender (unimportant), etc. were discovered. Participants unanimously agreed that the visual appearance of a signer should incorporate appropriate color contrasts. The face/skin tone and clothing should be contrasting with each other to enhance visual clarity of the signer's motions, and to avoid an overall appearance that is too uniform. The interpreter's clothes should be monochrome, i.e. plain colored without design or texture, and with three-quarter sleeve length. This would make the signer's hand and finger movements more visible and well-defined. Furthermore, questions regarding a signer's features like facial hair such as beard and jewelry/accessories including wedding rings were met with neutral responses. However, it is essential that such features do not obstruct the visual clarity of the signs and facial expressions, especially mouth movements. For example, scarfs were perceived as visually obstructing. Lastly, it was found that characteristics like gender and figure of the signer were insignificant, but the signer's looks or style should be suitable, i.e. match the program. For example, a signer with tattoos and face piercings is not acceptable for a news broadcast but may be tolerable for music/concert related broadcasts. Table 4 summarizes the respective recommendations.

Table 4. Key aspects pertaining to visual impression and appearance of sign language interpreter/virtual signer

GUIDL11	Color contrast – face/skin tone and clothing should contrast each other, not too uniform → enhances visual clarity of signer's motions
GUIDL12	Clothes - plain colored without design or texture with three-quarter sleeve length → enhances visual clarity of hand and finger movements
GUIDL13	Non-obstructing hairstyle that is clear from the face → increases visibility of facial expressions - very relevant for better visibility of eye and eyebrow movements
GUIDL14	Facial hair e.g. beard or jewelry/accessory, e.g. wedding ring should not obstruct visual clearness of signs and facial expression (particularly mouth movements), e.g. scarf could be obstructive
GUIDL15	Gender and figure are unimportant, but appearance should suit/match the program

3.4 Other Factors for Sign Language Media Production

The insights gained during the entire UCD process so far highlighted additional aspects that should be considered for achieving good quality sign language. The need for sign language interpreters who are not only experts in sign language translation but also skilled and fluent in the specific topic was established. Unfamiliarity with the content may result in the wrong choice of signs/words. This could lead to a lack of understanding or misinterpretations. One also has to consider regional variations and differences that can impact the comprehensibility of the translated content. Hence, it is always recommended to conduct quality checks with Deaf experts (i.e. deaf people or professional signers), in order to avoid or at least minimize larger deviations from what may be considered as mainstream. Broadcasters and media regulators should also incorporate periodic quality controls as part of their procedures.

Another broad finding was that younger Deaf as compared to their older counterparts are familiar using spoken languages as much as their mother tongue sign language. It is common practice for them to view media and television content using subtitles (when available). Even though they expressed that sign translated content would be beneficial, they emphasized the need for good quality subtitles for all audio-visual media. The inclusion of subtitles was not the focus of the C4A project and thus was rendered to be out of scope during the Delphi prioritization procedure conducted within the UCD process. In subsequent projects, however, it should be considered that the younger Deaf generation is more accustomed to using subtitles. Thus, this should be a key feature alongside sign translated content in sign translated media programs.

In the case of virtual signers as in C4A, possible trendy system features were expressed. Different virtual signers may be used for different people or characters in a program. For example, in the case of a panel discussion, one virtual signer per person could be allotted. Also, the option of choosing a preferred signer from a selection according to one's preference may result in higher acceptance of such a system. Importantly, the availability of subtitles with sign translated content and the ability of turning each on and off separately as per demand was desired. The findings are summarized in Table 5.

Table 5. Key aspects pertaining to Sign language media production

GUIDL16	Use signers who are experts or skilled in the topic (trained in translating and fluent in the topic) → avoidance of wrong choices of signs, unfamiliarity with a certain content could lead to lack of understanding or/and misinterpretations
GUIDL17	Conduct quality checks with Deaf experts, perform quality controls of the virtual signer in shorter frequency/regularly
GUIDL18	Provide good quality subtitles along with sign translated content – best scenario: ability to choose either one or both upon demand

4 Recommendations for UCD in Designing and Developing Systems for Accessibility

A literature review showed that UCD has often been employed in the development of assistive technologies for people with a range of disabilities. By placing the needs of users with disabilities in the center of development, this approach has proven itself to be quite resourceful. However, there are very limited guiding procedures for the UCD activities that human factors researchers could adhere to when developing such specific accessibility products, systems, and services. Most available guidelines inform about achieving accessibility when designing products, systems, and services that are used by people with a wide range of capabilities, or they focus on how to integrate accessibility throughout the UCD process. However, what necessary steps must researchers pay attention to when accessibility is not a part of the design solution, but the core idea and concept like in the C4A project? When conducting various UCD activities in different developmental stages within the C4A project, we were able to identify certain key aspects/actions that were necessary or proved to be significant in addition to the UCD guidelines as per [2]. Those lessons learned about the implementation of UCD in the development of an accessibility-focused systems are detailed in the form of recommendations below. They have proven to be beneficial in the development of the C4A system so far and will continue to inform us up to the end of the project.

4.1 Include Relevant Stakeholders and Experts in Internal Team

The most basic principle of UCD is to involve users throughout the design and development lifecycle. This is even more necessary in developing assistive technology systems and services for people with specific necessities like in the C4A project. Deaf and hard of hearing people have certain requirements to understand audiovisual media. This early stage of understanding the users' goals, tasks, and needs regarding the system and its context of use is a very important starting point in the development lifecycle. Therefore, in addition to just 'involving' users at singular points during the development cycle, including them and other relevant stakeholders in the internal team would be highly beneficial. These project partners and advisors could not only be able to provide insight into the community's characteristics, environment, and problems they face in a much more highly frequent, immediate and rapid fashion than regular user surveys, but also advise on how the human factor team should conduct user-centred evaluations with this specific user group. They could also able to provide quality checks of the prepared materials for user-centred evaluation. Moreover, including the users and stakeholders in the project team truly fulfills the UCD principle of founding an internal team that collectively features multidisciplinary skills and perspectives.

4.2 Try Using a Multi-method Approach

In projects with a high degree of innovation that comprise novel interfaces that are developed for a specific user group, intensive user research encompassing several methods and techniques is advantageous, as it is possible to cross-validate the data and results. Early analysis using various investigation techniques in C4A allowed us to attain stronger results and a more holistic understanding of the topic. We put emphasis on reflecting the communities' heterogeneity on key characteristics (such as age, level and history of impairment), experiences, and resulting individual requirements to the system. Moreover, grounded knowledge about the community by professionals in the area of sign language (professional signers, researchers) added additional value. For the iterative implementation phase, a combination of UX testing evaluation methods was chosen to showcase various prototype versions and their variants. Such combinations of evaluation tools and methods also allow the transition from formative to summative evaluation. The carefully planned multi-method approach used in C4A allowed us to gather representative findings in a sufficient way, which would not have been possible when using singular methods.

4.3 Incorporate Interactive Settings and Techniques

Another important aspect is the inclusion of suitable interactive methods for collecting user-based information and assessment in the user-centred evaluation activities. It is essential when getting familiar with the user group(s) as well as in later evaluation stages to make sure that their needs and feedbacks are considered carefully. This enables valid and reliable testing and discussions, and is a prerequisite for the UCD. Ultimately, higher user acceptance is only achieved, if the addressed user group is involved from the beginning and in a proper manner. In C4A, most of the applied methods consist of interactive settings like the interviews, workshops, or focus groups. Tasks were designed in a way that encouraged activities, collaborations, and open discussions.

4.4 Conduct Early User-Centred Evaluation

Even though this perspective is applicable for UCD of all products, systems, and services, it is especially valid when developing novel systems or services for a specific user group. The UCD aim should be to perform multiple evaluations, starting right from preliminary design concepts up until the finalized prototype. This would not only ensure early examination of individual concepts and its evaluation on how effectively it was implemented [23]. but also provide valuable feedback on the acceptability of the proposed design [3]. Such early user feedback enables iterative improvements that can be relatively inexpensive compared to having to implement drastic changes in later development stages.

4.5 Overcome Communication Barriers

When facilitating face to face sessions and eliciting feedback from users with disabilities, human factors researchers have to consider the user group's communication requirements. Consequently, traditional evaluation procedures may require to be altered or new and suitable procedures need to be developed and applied. Likewise, researchers should be prepared for using alternative facilitating techniques or a combination of different techniques. When evaluating the C4A system with deaf users, we experienced the communication barriers that the deaf are facing regularly. Face-to-face contacts between deaf/hard of hearing and hearing people have to rely on the help of third parties like (professional) sign language interpreters. To avoid procedural and task misunderstandings, we communicated information such as plans, procedures, and materials before-hand with the third parties. Sending materials and a rough script to the interpreters ahead of time, allowed them to better prepare translations and focus on reducing communication gaps. This required timely planning and organizing as well as a state of constant mindfulness of the users' needs not only regarding the system in development, but also regarding their involvement and inclusion in the UCD process, permitting adequate preparations to overcome barriers. Naturally, working with other user groups with disabilities would entail other needs and barriers; however, the need to overcome possible communication barriers should always be accounted for, no matter which specific peculiarities those barriers have.

4.6 Integrate Accessibility in Evaluation Methods

The chosen UX-testing methods should incorporate accessibility, especially when directed towards people with disabilities. Test materials like information, tasks, questions etc. should be provided in the participants' preferred format. In C4A, for example, digital investigations and evaluations with the signing user group required the use of sign language. As much information, tasks, and questions as possible were provided in multiple sign languages. Moreover, in terms of the two-senses principle, everything was additionally provided in easy written language. Designing user research, therefore, requires awareness for the interests of the users as well as a high degree of methodical sensitivity and flexibility.

4.7 Plan for Flexibility

UCD is planned in a way that it is well integrated into all stages of the development lifecycle as well as corresponds with the project plan and goals. Two essential elements in planning UCD activities are identifying appropriate methods and developing effective evaluation strategies. Within the C4A project, a structured approach was applied in the form of an encyclopedia of measurement methods. It facilitates planning the respective evaluations and allows to adapt them flexibly and promptly to the analysis required. Such flexibility might be required in case of any constraints such as technical delays, organizational impacts, social, political, or environmental influences, etc. For example, the upcoming and last few user-centred evaluations in C4A were planned in detail in the form of face-to-face evaluation settings. Due to current Covid-19 regulations, we cannot proceed in the same way and are currently re-planning by switching to digital procedures. The created encyclopedia will be very helpful along with our experiences in preparing and conducting online surveys that we gained within the project. For detailed information on these gained experiences, check [24] that is part of the same proceedings.

5 Conclusion

With projects like C4A that aim at increasing the amount of sign language content for media productions, there is a growing need for standardizations that can be used by broadcasters to produce and present media content with high-quality, comprehensible sign-translated language. With this paper, we hope to have provided some essential guidelines for this purpose, in aggregating the data collected in a UCD approach. Key findings were gained for quality parameters of sign language, the technical presentation of a (virtual) sign language interpreter, its appearance, and factors relating to sign language media production.

The UCD approach once more proved to be valuable for the development of an innovative product. Especially a creative and encouraging user involvement is key for a valid requirements analysis and subsequent test phases. Our lessons learned were presented as recommendations, which might foster similar procedures in accessibility design projects. Ultimately, with the accepted and wide use of UCD for products, systems, and services for accessibility, it is necessary to establish additional UCD principles and procedures concerning this domain. The provided recommendations based on the undergone UCD process stemmed from the lessons learned and the human-factor researchers' experiences gained during the course of the project. These key aspects or actions proved to be beneficial in the development of the C4A system until this point and will continue to be until the end of the project. These recommendations attempt to contribute to the establishment of a possible UCD standardized guide for accessible products, systems, and services. There is a call for further input from other related projects and studies.

Acknowledgements. The research presented was conducted in the project CONTENT4ALL, which received funding from the European Commission within the Horizon 2020 Program (H2020-ICT-2016-2, call ICT-19-2017) under the grant agreement no.° 762021. This publication reflects only the authors' view and the European Commission is not responsible for any use that may be made of the information it contains. A big thank you goes to all participants for taking part in this research and to all project partners and associates who strongly supported these studies.

References

1. United Nations Convention on the Rights of Persons with Disabilities. https://www.un.org/disabilities/documents/convention/convention_accessible_pdf.pdf. Accessed 04 May 2020
2. ISO 9241: Ergonomics of human-system interaction—Part 210: Human-centred design for interactive systems (2019)
3. ISO 9241: Ergonomics of human-system interaction—Part 210: Human-centred design for interactive systems (2010)
4. Moser, C.: User Experience Design. Springer, Heidelberg (2012). https://doi.org/10.1007/978-3-642-13363-3
5. ISO 9241: Ergonomics of human-system interaction—Part 11: Usability: Definitions and Concepts (2018)
6. Brooke, J.: SUS-A quick and dirty usability scale. Usability Eval. Ind. **189**(194), 4–7 (1996)
7. Hassenzahl, M.: User experience (UX) towards an experiential perspective on product quality. In: Proceedings of the 20th International Conference of the Association Francophone d'Interaction Homme-Machine, pp. 11–15 (2008)
8. Hassenzahl, M., Tractinsky, N.: User experience – a research agenda. Behav. Inf. Technol. **25**(2), 91–97 (2006)
9. Thüring, M., Mahlke, S.: Usability, aesthetics and emotions in human–technology interaction. Int. J. Psychol. **42**(4), 253–264 (2007)
10. Schrepp, M., Hinderks, A., Thomaschewski, J.: Applying the user experience questionnaire (UEQ) in different evaluation scenarios. In: Marcus, A. (ed.) DUXU 2014. LNCS, vol. 8517, pp. 383–392. Springer, Cham (2014). https://doi.org/10.1007/978-3-319-07668-3_37
11. Oehme, A., Horn, H.-P., Wieser, M., Waizenegger, W., Fernando, W.A.C.: User experience in immersive TV – a research agenda. In: Proceedings of IEEE International Conference on Image Processing (ICIP), Phoenix, USA, 25–28 September 2016 (2016)
12. Diepold, K.: The quest for a definition of quality of experience. Qualinet Newslet **2**(5), 2–8 (2012)
13. Vermeeren, A.P., Law, E.L.C., Roto, V., Obrist, M., Hoonhout, J., Väänänen-Vainio-Mattila, K.: User experience evaluation methods: current state and development needs. In: Proceedings of the 6th Nordic Conference on Human-Computer Interaction: Extending Boundaries, pp. 521–530. ACM (2010)

14. Böhm, S.: Do you know your user group? Why it is essential to put your user-requirement analysis on a broad data base. In: Universal Access in the Information Society (under review)
15. Dalkey, N., Helmer, O.: An experimental application of the delphi method to the use of experts. Manag. Sci. **9**(3), 458–467 (1963). https://doi.org/10.1287/mnsc.9.3.458
16. Brown, B.: Delphi Process: A Methodology Used for the Elicitation of Opinions of Experts. Paper published by RAND, Document No: P-3925 (1968)
17. Sackman, H.: Delphi Assessment: Expert Opinion, Forecasting and Group Process. R-1283-PR (1974)
18. ISO/IEC 13407: Human-Centred Design Processes for Interactive Systems. International Organization for Standardization, Genéve, Switzerland (1999)
19. Heinilä, J., et al.: NOMADIC MEDIA: User-Centred Design: Guidelines for Methods and Tools (2005)
20. Kelly, G.A.: The Psychology of Personal Constructs. Volume One. A Theory of Personality. Norton & Company, New York (1955)
21. Hassenzahl, M., Wessler, R.: Capturing design space from a user perspective: the repertory grid technique revisited. Int. J. Hum.-Comput. Interact. **12**(3&4), 441–459 (2000)
22. Muir, L.J., Richardson, I.E.: Perception of sign language and its application to visual communications for deaf people. J. Deaf Stud. Deaf Educ. **10**(4), 390–401 (2005)
23. Rubin, J., Chisnell, D.: Handbook of Usability Testing: How to Plan. Design and Conduct Effective Tests. Wiley, Hoboken (2008)
24. Oehme, A., Upadrasta, V., Kotsch, P.: Development of a multilingual questionnaire for the deaf community – guidelines and challenges. In: Human-Computer Interaction International 2020. Springer, Heidelberg (2020)

Contribution of Clinical Data to the Design of Assistive Systems

Frédéric Vella[1(✉)], Nadine Vigouroux[1], Rozenn Baudet[1], Antonio Serpa[1], Philippe Truillet[1], Xavier Carrau[1], Jean-François Camps[2], Caroline Mercardier[3], Charline Calmels[3], Karine Gigaud[4], Victoria Fourgous[4], and Mélodie Blanchard[5]

[1] IRIT, CNRS, UPS, 118 Route de Narbonne, 31062 Toulouse CEDEX 9, France
{Frederic.Vella,Nadine.Vigouroux}@irit.fr

[2] URI Octogone-Lordat, UT2J, 5, allée Antonio Machado, 31058 Toulouse CEDEX 9, France

[3] Fondation OPTEO, MAS La Boraldette, 12500 St Côme d'Olt, France

[4] IEM «Les Babissous», Saint Mayme, 12850 Onet Le Château, France

[5] MAS la Valette, 12780 St-Léon, France

Abstract. The objective of our work is to adapt a new user-centered design (UCD) methodology in the field of design of assistive systems for multiple disabilities people who live in specialized care homes. We have adopted a specific approach by integrating clinical data interpreted on these people with multiple disabilities by medical and social staff. This is a new approach to remedy their difficulty in identifying and/or expressing their needs for assistive technologies. We will show through a case study how these clinical data have enabled us to design high-fidelity prototypes for communication and environmental control devices.

Keywords: User centered design · Interaction technique, multiple disabilities · Medical data interaction technique

1 Introduction

User-centered design (UCD) is a design approach where the specific needs, expectations and characteristics of end users are taken into account at each step of the product design process. The standard ISO 9241-210 [1] (See Fig. 1) has defined the steps for implementing this approach. It is based on the hypothesis that end-users are best placed to express their needs, participate in the design, evaluate and use the interactive system, until the needs and requirements expressed by users are met. The relevance of the UCD is well established [2]. However, expressing needs is quite impossible for end user with communication difficulties. In addition, there is an emerging stream of consideration of deficiency characteristics in the design process. Several approaches have been studied to involve people with disabilities in the design process and to consider disabilities data. These approaches are reported in the related work section of this article.

The aim of this article is to illustrate how clinical data and the profile of the person with a multiple disability impact the prototyping phases of the user-centered design

C. Stephanidis et al. (Eds.): HCII 2020, LNCS 12426, pp. 144–157, 2020.
https://doi.org/10.1007/978-3-030-60149-2_12

method. To answer this question, we will describe the implementation of the user-centered approach, focusing on the clinical data acquisition scales and how we used them in the prototyping phases. We will illustrate this approach with a case study for a person with multiple disabilities. We will end our article with a discussion on the consideration of clinical data in the UCD process.

2 Related Works

In the context of the design of assistive technology systems, User Centered Design (UCD) tools and methods may not be appropriate [3] for the participation of people with multiple disabilities. The team of Antona et al. [3] evaluated a set of methods and techniques according to two main criteria: (disability and age) and a set of .sub criteria (sensory, motor and/or cognitive impairments). Each of the methods is then qualified as " ✓Appropriate", " ■Needs modifications and adjustments", and " ☒Not recommended" (See Table 1). Ritter et al. [4] proposed a human-centered approach based on how human capacities are affected during direct interaction with the interactive system itself.

Several research studies have proposed adaptations of the implementation of the UCD method. The works [5–7] and [8] showed that the participation of people (family, medical and social workers, etc.) close to the end users was beneficial in the design of prototypes meeting their needs. Guffroy et al. [8] defined the concept of ecosystem, which represents this whole human environment (professional and sometimes family caregivers). Roche et al. [9] proposed AMICAS (Innovative Methodological Approach to Adapted Systemic Design), which aims to take into account the analysis grids (context, profiles, and characteristic action situations) of people with multiple disabilities

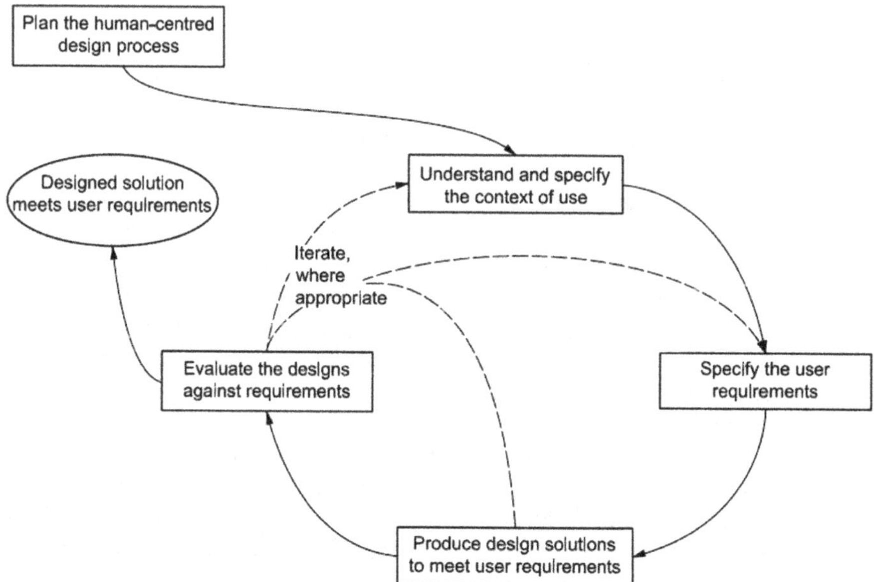

Fig. 1. Interdependence of user-centered design activities according to ISO [1].

Table 1. Summary of user requirements elicitation methods [3].

User Requirements Elicitation	Disability				Age	
Methods and Techniques	Motion	Vision	Hearing	Cognitive/ Communication	Children	Elderly
Brainstorming	✓	✓	■	■	■	■
Direct observation	✓	✓	✓	✓	✓	✓
Activity diaries and cultural probes	■	■	✓	■	■	✓
Survey and questionnaires	■	■	■	☒	■	■
Interviews	✓	✓	■	☒	■	■
Group discussions	✓	✓	■	☒	■	■
Empathic modelling	✓	✓	✓	☒	☒	☒
User trials	■	■	■	■	■	■
Scenarios and personas	✓	✓	✓	✓	✓	✓
Prototyping	✓	✓	✓	✓	✓	✓
Cooperative and participatory design	✓	✓	✓	■	■	■
Art-based approaches					✓	✓

by matching them with the situations of use in order to identify which tasks users can perform and describe the difficulties encountered.

Other work shows the importance of disability [10] or health [11] data to develop ontologies. These are used to design, for example, adapted systems for generating therapeutic programs [10] or for the adaptation of assistive technologies [11]. It is in this trend towards taking clinical data into account that our approach to the design of communication assistive devices for people with multiple disabilities is based, for whom the evaluation and characterization of their capacities can be difficult and can evolve over time. We are planning to implement this methodology for the design of OUPSCECI assistive technologies (AT) for communication and environmental control. The OUPSCECI AT consists of a virtual interface (see Fig. 6, Fig. 7) and a control box for the interaction devices (see Fig. 5).

3 Implementation of the UCD Approach

The study population concerns adults and children with motor and severe mental impairment, associated with various disease (behavioral disorders, sensory disorders, (no or little written and/or oral language), hosted by a specialized care homes (SCH) or by an institute for motor skills development (IMS). According to the professionals involved, these residents suffer from social isolation and loneliness, a sense of powerlessness and a reduced self-image. They need assistive technologies to communicate with their ecosystem. In addition, this population is composed of people who have difficulty expressing their needs due to the nature of their disability. The abilities of the residents in the sense of ICF (International Classification of Functioning) [12] are constantly evolving (worsening of disabilities, appearance of associated disorders, etc.). This potential change in capabilities confronts us with two challenges: the adaptation of user requirements and the adaptation of assistive technology to meet the changing needs. To address these challenges, we have implemented the UCD approach of ISO 9241-210 [1] in which we will demonstrate the importance of observational methods, including the contribution of both clinical scales and ecosystem expertise in all stages of UCD (see Fig. 2) for people with multiple disabilities.

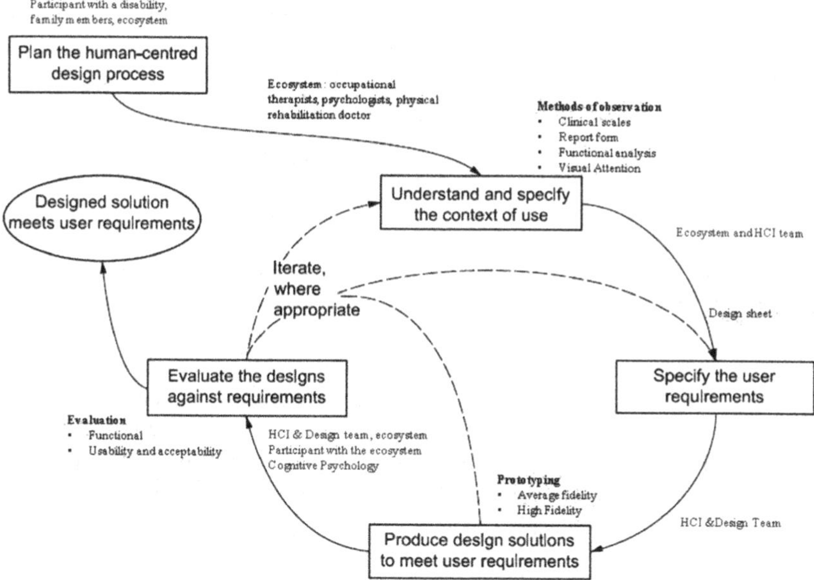

Fig. 2. Interdependence of user-centered design activities according to ISO with the role of the ecosystem (in blue) and the role of the data used (clinical data) or produced (design sheet) (in red). (Color figure online)

3.1 Understanding and Specificity of the Usability' Context

For this study population, a set of observational tools was used by occupational therapists, psychologists and a psychology student with the objectives of assessing motor, communication, memory span, visual attention, reasoning and learning skills. This set of tools is composed of:

- The Corsi's test [13]; It measures the person's visual-spatial memory span; this will allow us to define the level of depth (sub-menu of the virtual interface) of the assistance system;
- The ComVoor tool [14]; It allows us to evaluate the perception and representation of stable mode of communication (objects, images, pictograms and written). For our design issue, the ComVoor tool makes it possible to define which form of communication is most suitable and at which level of meaning attribution the communication can be implemented;
- The ECP (Polyhandicap Cognitive Skills Rating Scale) [15]; It measures cognitive abilities (attentional, communicative, learning, reasoning and spatio-temporal) as well as social, emotional and autonomy abilities for people with multiple disabilities. For design purposes, the ECP scale makes it possible to define the complexity of the interface (e.g. number of items per menu level, which mode of communication, etc.) according to the learning and reasoning abilities of the person with multiple disabilities. During the evaluation phase, the ECP will also aim to qualify the evolution of social and emotional skills during the appropriation phase of the assistive technologies;

- A clinical rating scale for the flexion-extension of long fingers using the Kapandji scale [16]; this scale gives recommendations for the choice of the interaction device according to the flexion and extension skills. This measurement is supplemented by an indication of the grip force estimated by an occupational therapist as well as recommendations (type of switch recommended, body parts allowing interaction, ergonomics of tablet setting on the wheelchair and so on).

A functional analysis grid completes these measures. This grid is an adaptation of the ABC (Immediate Antecedents, Behavior, and Consequent Context) behavior functional analysis grid [17]. It aims to describe the modalities of communication behavior, to understand the context, in which the participant's communication and/or interaction behavior appears, as well as its nature and modality, and then the responses provided by his ecosystem. Moreover, the grid allows the identification of daily activities and interests and will eventually allow the specification of the functionalities of the CECI (Environmental Control and Integrated Communication) high-fidelity prototype that will be designed with the SoKeyTo design platform [18]. The Fig. 3 illustrates how the clinical data are used to provide the design sheet.

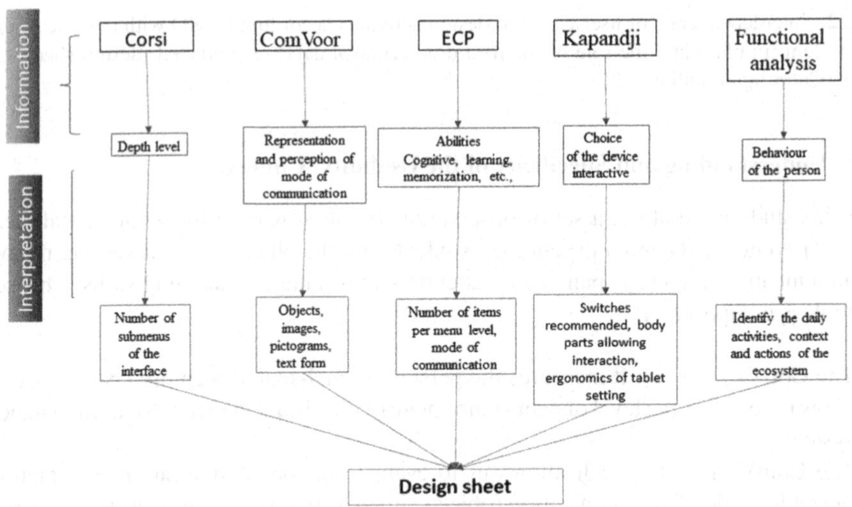

Fig. 3. Clinical data and their use in providing specifications.

3.2 Specifying the User' Requirements

For the 9 study's participants, three focus groups were set up. Each of them determines the needs for 3 participants living respectively in 2 SCH and one IMS The objective of these Focus Groups was to be able to interpret the information provided by the evaluation scales and translate them into needs and interface features. These Focus Groups consisted of a psychologist, an occupational therapist, two Master 1 students (psychology and Human Computer Interaction) and three senior HCI researchers. The medico-social staff previously interpreted the scale information to present their functional recommendations and the HCI researchers proposed interaction specifications (interaction modes, interaction techniques, user feedback, interface layout, etc.). Arbitration were made on the proposals between the two fields of expertise in order to arrive at a needs sheet for the specification of assistive technologies that is best suited to the needs and abilities of the person with multiple disabilities.

3.3 Prototyping of OUPSCECI Virtual Interfaces

From the requirements sheet established, high-fidelity prototypes have been made using the SoKeyTo platform [18], which allows to define the features of the virtual interfaces. These are the size, shape, icon returns and interaction techniques, the number of items and the number of levels in the interface. The versions of the first and second level of the virtual interfaces are submitted to the occupational therapist for testing and feedback to the design team until approval. A videoconference between the psychologist and occupational therapist and the three HCI designers takes place every two weeks. The various design specifications are arbitrated during these progresses of the discussion. The HCI and designers and the medical-social team meet in focus groups on request within the establishments. We propose to illustrate the steps of the UCD of participant P1.

3.4 Prototyping of the Control Box of Interaction Devices

The diversity of people with motor disabilities means that they need access to a computer with several types of devices. In relation to this diversity and the results of the assessment scales, occupational therapists were asked to have the option of using either a joystick, touch and/or ON/OFF switches for validation. Based on this, we developed a prototype circuit board (see Fig. 4) in order to be able to connect these three types of interaction devices. The interest of this control box is to allow the occupational therapist to refine these device choices and their settings for the person with a disability. That is to say, to be able to test other interaction devices and to configure them by means of software. This device is composed of a Teensy 3.2[1] microcontroller because it implements touch input pins that allows touch interaction for people with little strength.

On this microcontroller we have connected a joystick and four jack type connections. These allow up to four switches to be connected. This option makes it possible to connect a maximum of four contactors depending on the residual movements of the person (palm of the hand, finger, head movement, etc.). Our device has been developed with the open-source Arduino language.

[1] https://www.prjc.com/teensy.

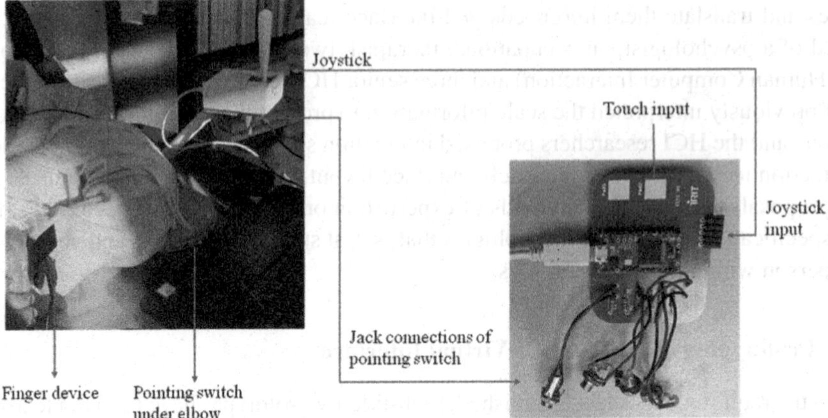

Fig. 4. Control device system architecture.

4 P1 Case Study

4.1 Profile of P1

P1 is an adult person with cerebral palsy, without written and oral expression. P1 uses a foot control device, with five switches, to control his electric wheelchair (see Fig. 5). He has athetotic movements in his upper limbs but there are fewer of them at foot level. The movements that P1 can control are:

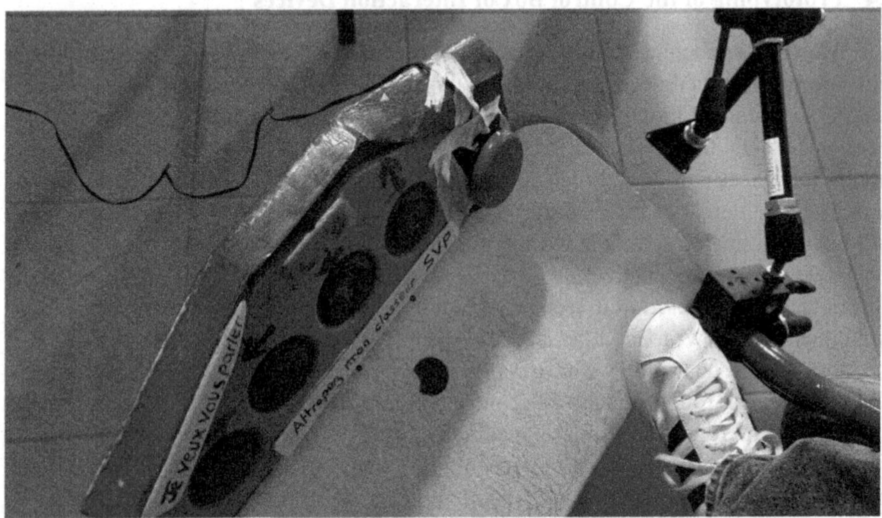

Fig. 5. Control device for the P1 chair and the OUPSCECI interface. The four grey buttons are used to control the wheelchair and the two yellow markers for "*I want to talk to you*" and "*Please grab my communication notebook*". The last red ON/OFF switch on the right end will be used for the virtual OUPSCECI interface of P1.

- On the right with switch above the buttons of movement of the wheelchair: 30 press of the button per minute;
- On the left with switch on the footrest on the left of his left foot: press of the button per minute.

Currently, he communicates using a paper's notebook, designed by the medico-social staff of his place of live. It is used with a third person who slides his finger over the various pictograms in the communication notebook to help him express his needs. The choice of the pictogram is validated by the nodding of your head. These pictograms are listed according to eleven categories: feelings, body, grooming, clothing, family, questions, activities, objects, colors, SCH personnel and life events.

4.2 Needs Sheet

The request of P1's ecosystem is that his paper's communication notebook should be integrated into the digital interface, in which there will also be a home automation part (music management, television control, access to his calendar), functionalities identified in the functional analysis grid.

Table 2 illustrates how the information from the various clinical scales impacts the specifications for prototyping. For example, the ComVoor tool informs us about the categorization capacity and the ECP about its learning capacity: this translates into the fact that a given screen will be composed of a maximum of twelve pictograms relating to a topic and seven navigation pictograms in the OUPSCECI virtual interface (see Fig. 6, Fig. 7). Similarly, the value of the Corsi test indicates that we should not go beyond five screen pages (submenus), but this should be confirmed during the interface appropriation phase for P1. The ComVor and Corsi tests advocate highlighting the contours of the pictograms (of the line, column or only pictogram of the line, column) in order to distinguish them from the others. On the other hand, validation tests carried out by the occupational therapist have shown that it is preferable to validate the selection when releasing the switch.

4.3 High-Fidelity Prototypes

We have designed two versions of the high-fidelity prototype (V0 and V1) of OUPSCECI's virtual interface with the platform SoKeyTo. The first prototype was composed of only three rows and three columns (See Fig. 6 as illustration) for each interface level. The selected pictograms were those of its paper's communication notebook. The last line was made up of navigation pictograms (previous , next  and return to topic selection ). The scanning strategy was a line/column scanning strategy with a scanning speed of 3,5 s. Validation was effective when the button was pressed with the right foot of P1. However, the choice of the foot to be used for navigation and pictogram selection is not yet defined. This choice will require pressure and release tests in real situations during the appropriation phases of OUPSCECI. Table 3 reports advantages and disadvantages depending on the pressure foot after preliminary trials carried out by

Table 2. Specification sheet.

Scales	Interaction components	Features	Choice made
Kapandji	Device	Control device	Foot pedals
Kapandji, functional analysis	Interaction techniques	Physical selection 1 to 1	Yes
		Scanning strategies	Yes, Read direction
		Pointing technique (finger, stylus, mouse)	No, none
		Validation principle	Yes, button push
ComVor, Corsi, ECP, eye tracking	Visual representation	Layout	Line/column (affordance of the paper communication notebook)
		Item number	6 or 9 per screen
		Icon Shape	Rectangular with Highlighting edge
		Icon size	5 cm × 5 cm
		Color preference	Primary
		Object characterization capability	Yes
		Maximum number of levels	5
ComVor, ECP	Feedback	Visual	Ye
		Textual	No, no mastery of language
		Sound	Yes
		Multimodal	Yes
Functional Analysis, eye tracking	Device setting	Tablet under windows	Anywhere, preferentially in the visual field, at a distance

the occupational therapist. In addition, tests to determine the foot for which movements are best controlled should also be carried out real conditions. The first trials conducted by the occupational therapist led to discussions and modifications to take into account his cognitive and motor abilities in next versions of the OUPSCECI virtual interface.

In version 1, the interface displayed currently consists of three blocks:

- 1st line (in yellow), navigation pictograms (previous: return to the previous interface of the same pictogram topic; next: move to the next interface of the same topic and back: return to the screen of the 11 pictogram categories;

Fig. 6. Example of the OUPSCECI virtual interface of P1 (version 0).

- 4th column (in yellow), pictogram of choice of the communication theme; pictogram signifying a choice error; return to the first level of the interface with a choice between three pictograms ("I want to talk to you" which is intended to indicate to the interlocutor that P1 wants to talk; "communication" pictograms" and "home automation" pictogram).
- The central block composed of 4 lines/3 columns is made up of communication pictograms. Table 4 gives the meaning of the pictograms. To facilitate communication between P1 and her caregivers (family and professional) a textual description was added. The navigation pictograms have been moved to the first line for easier access (time saving).

Real-world trials will be required to define whether pressure or release is used as a validation technique to select a pictogram. The muscles involved in each movement (pressure or release) are not the same, so each action does not mobilize the same muscles:

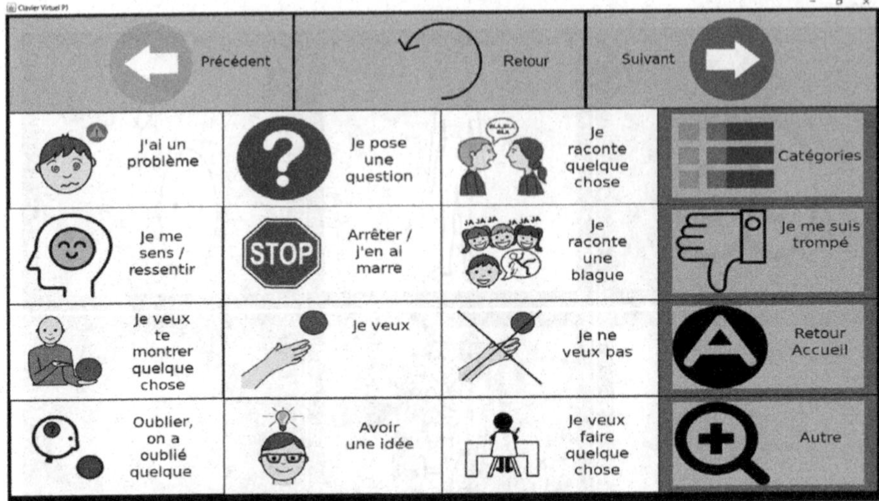

Fig. 7. Example of the OUPSCECI virtual interface of P1 (version 1).

Table 3. Advantages and disadvantages depending on the pressure foot.

Switch on the left foot	Switch on the right foot
Advantages - Better control in movement repetition - Fewer unrestrained movements **Disadvantages** - Limit the positioning by the wheelchair's switches - Risk of two presses of the button (wheelchair switch and OUPSCECI application switch)	**Advantages** - More possibilities for positioning the switch - P1 prefers the right side because he feels more precise **Disadvantages** - Less control in the repetition of movements - More unrestrained movements

- Validation by release essentially involves the levator muscles of the foot;
- Validation by support requires the mobilization of several muscles and more coordination.

These three blocks were chosen because they allow the pictograms to be categorized (navigation, central communication or environment control block, change of topic or mention of an error). This layout has been retained because P1 has characterization capabilities under development. Ongoing tests carried out by the occupational therapist show that the representation of the interface is suitable even if the number of items is greater than initially envisaged by the ECP scale (from 9 to 12 for the central block).

A feedback (red, primary color suggested by ComVor scale) mentions that the pictogram block or the current pictogram depending on the scanning strategy chosen for P1. The text description of the pictogram by means of text-to-speech can be activated. Several scanning strategies (block by block, or row/column) and several selection modes

Table 4. Pictograms and signification.

	Previous		I'm felling
	Back		I m tired something
	Next		I'm telling a joke.
	Topics		I want to show something
	I was mistaken		I want
	Home		I don't want
	Others		To forget, to have forgotten something
	I have a problem		Have an idea
	I'm asking a question		I want to show something
	I'm telling something		

(row by row and then block by block or block by block) are being evaluated. All these configurations can be modified in the profile file of P1.

5 Discussion/Conclusion

Designing assistive technologies for the benefit of a population of multi-disabled users living in institutions involves the implementation of a UCD. Our approach is to integrate clinical data in addition to the needs. Considering the lack of oral or written language, our approach integrates needs expressed by the ecosystem and when possible by end-users himself or herself The case study presented here has allowed us, through a concrete case, to validate the relevance of this approach and to better understand the contribution of clinical data in the two design phases (*understand and specify the context of use* and *prototyping* phases). These clinical data will also be used by occupational therapists to adapt the assistive technology to daily life. They will be supplemented by data from the log analysis of the use of the technical aid and ecosystem interviews. The real contribution of these data sources will be measured during the phase of appropriation of the assistive technology and its adaptation to the requirements of the person with a disability. Moreover, each participant in our study, depending on his or her degree of autonomy and the evolution of his or her pathological profile, will have specific needs that are likely to evolve over time. This is why, when scaling up (all nine residents), in addition to using clinical data to express needs, we also wish to adopt an agile approach [19] in the development of these technical aids. The next step will be to validate the contribution of clinical data in the design stage by analyzing the phases of appropriation of the technical aids and to write recommendations for the design and configuration for occupational therapists and psychologists.

Acknowledgement. This project is partially supported by "Region Occitanie" and OPTEO Foundation (France).

References

1. ISO 9241-11: Ergonomic requirements for office work with visual display terminals-Part 11: Guidance on usability. ISO, Geneva (1998)
2. Marti, P., Bannon, L.J.: Exploring user-centred design in practice: some caveats. Knowl. Technol. Policy **22**(1), 7–15 (2009)
3. Antona, M., Ntoa, S., Adami, I., Stephanidis, C.: User requirements elicitation for universal access (chapter 15). In: Universal Access Handbook, pp. 15-1–15-14. CRC Press (2009)
4. Ritter, F.E., Baxter, G.D., Churchill, E.F.: Foundations for Designing User-Centered Systems: What System Designers Need to Know about People. Springer, London (2014). https://doi.org/10.1007/978-1-4471-5134-0
5. Sauzin, D., et al.: MATT, un dispositif de domotique et d'aide à la communication: un cas d'étude de co-conception. In: Congrès de la SOFMER (SOFMER 2015), Société Française de Médecine Physique et de Réadaptation (2015)
6. Augusto, J., Kramer, D., Alegre, U., Covaci, A., Santokhee, A.: The user-centred intelligent environments development process as a guide to co-create smart technology for people with special needs. Univ. Access Inf. Soc. **17**(1), 115–130 (2017). https://doi.org/10.1007/s10209-016-0514-8
7. Branco, R.M., Quental, J., Ribeiro, Ó.: Playing with personalisation and openness in a codesign project involving people with dementia. In: Proceedings of the 14th Participatory Design Conference: Full papers, vol. 1, pp. 61–70. ACM (2016)
8. Guffroy, M., Vigouroux, N., Kolski, C., Vella, F., Teutsch, P.: From human-centered design to disabled user & ecosystem centered design in case of assistive interactive systems. Int. J. Sociotechnology Knowl. Dev. (IJSKD) **9**(4), 28–42 (2017)
9. Roche, A., Lespinet-Najib, V., André, J.M.: Development of a pedagogical aid tool for pupils with multiple disabilities: setting up a systemic design method. In: Congress of Applied Psychology. UCAP 2014 (2014)
10. Robles-Bykbaev, V.E., Guamán-Murillo, W., Quisi-Peralta, D., López-Nores, M., Pazos-Arias, J.J., García-Duque, J.: An ontology-based expert system to generate therapy plans for children with disabilities and communication disorders. In: 2016 IEEE Ecuador Technical Chapters Meeting (ETCM), pp. 1–6. IEEE (2016)
11. Skillen, K.L., Chen, L., Nugent, C.D., Donnelly, M.P., Solheim, I.: A user profile ontology based approach for assisting people with dementia in mobile environments. In: 2012 Annual International Conference of the IEEE Engineering in Medicine and Biology Society, pp. 6390–6393. IEEE (2012)
12. http://apps.who.int/classifications/icfbrowser/
13. Berch, D.B., Krikorian, R., Huha, E.M.: The Corsi block-tapping task: methodological and theoretical considerations. Brain Cogn. **38**(3), 317–338 (1998)

14. Noens, I., Van Berckelaer-Onnes, I., Verpoorten, R., Van Duijn, G.: The ComVor: an instrument for the indication of augmentative communication in people with autism and intellectual disability. J. Intell. Disabil. Res. **50**(9), 621–632 (2006)
15. Scelles, R.: Evaluation – Cognition – Polyhandicap (ECP), Rapport de recherche, November 2014 – November 2017
16. Kapandji, A.: Proposition pour une cotation clinique de la flexion-extension des doigts longs. Annales de Chirurgie de la Main **6**(4), 288–294 (1987)
17. Willaye, E.: Analyse fonctionnelle du comportement. In: 11e Université d'automne, le Bulletin scientifique de l'arapi - numéro 29, pp. 35–43 (2012)
18. Sauzin, D., Vella, F., Vigouroux, N.: SoKeyTo: a tool to design universal accessible interfaces. In: International Conference on Applied Human Factors and Ergonomics - AHFE 2014 (2014)
19. Garcia, A., Silva da Silva, T., Selbach Silveira, M.: Artifacts for agile user-centered design: a systematic mapping. In: Proceedings of the 50th Hawaii International Conference on System Sciences (HICSS-50), 10 p. IEEE (2017). http://doi.org/10.24251/HICSS.2017.706

Accessibility Solutions and User Experience

Designing SignSpeak, an Arabic Sign Language Recognition System

Abeer Al-Nafjan[1,2(✉)], Layan Al-Abdullatef[1], Mayar Al-Ghamdi[1], Nada Al-Khalaf[1], and Wejdan Al-Zahrani[1]

[1] Computer Sciences Department, College of Computer and Information Sciences, Al-Imam Muhammad Ibn Saud Islamic University, Riyadh, Saudi Arabia
annafjan@imamu.edu.sa, {lsalabdullatef,mnsalghamdi,namalkhalaf, weaalzahrani}@sm.imamu.edu.sa

[2] Human-Computer Interaction (HCI) Design Lab, Riyadh, Saudi Arabia

Abstract. Deaf and hearing-impaired individuals who communicate using sign language face several communication difficulties. Because the vast majority of people do not know sign language, the need for a sign language translator is growing significantly, especially for Arabic sign language (ArSL). Today, technology plays a significant role in people's lives. Leap Motion technology can be used to address the aforementioned issues and improve communication between Saudi Arabia's deaf and hearing individuals. In this study, we investigated the possibility of using a Leap Motion system to provide continuous ArSL recognition for two-way communication to improve communication between deaf and hearing individuals in terms of speed and independence. The system translates ArSL into spoken words for hearing individuals and transcribes spoken Arabic language into text for deaf individuals.

Keywords: Arabic sign language (ArSL) · Deaf · Hearing impairment · Assistive technology · Sign recognition · Translation

1 Introduction

Hearing other people's voices during communication enables a person to communicate easily through listening and responding. However, people with hearing impairments cannot communicate with others in this manner. Therefore, they rely on sign language. Unfortunately, sign language is incomprehensible to most people. Because this creates a considerable communication barrier, deaf individuals face many difficulties in their daily lives.

According to the World Health Organization, 466 million people worldwide have hearing loss [1]. In addition, the results of the 2017 disability survey conducted by the General Authority for Statistics in Saudi Arabia indicated that 1.4% of the Saudi Arabian population have been diagnosed with a hearing impairment or hearing loss [2]. This percentage, when applied to the Saudi Arabian population estimates for 2017, reveals that an estimated 456,576 people suffer from hearing impairment or hearing loss [3].

C. Stephanidis et al. (Eds.): HCII 2020, LNCS 12426, pp. 161–170, 2020.
https://doi.org/10.1007/978-3-030-60149-2_13

Deaf individuals worldwide face daily challenges in meeting their daily needs. They need to communicate with hearing people to function in society. To assist them, some sign language recognition systems have been developed. In recent years, the sign language recognition and translation fields have attracted numerous researchers and developers, and many systems have been presented for translating sign language into text or voice and translating text or voice into sign language to facilitate two-way communication. Some researchers, such as those in [4–6], have had the educational goal of helping people learn sign language, whereas others, such as [7], have advocated for translation.

In general, sign language recognition systems are aligned with one of three approaches: a vision-based approach, a sensor-based approach, and a hybrid approach that combines the first two. The vision-based approach requires a camera to capture hand gestures and facial expressions. Many systems, such as [8, 9], have been developed using this approach. The sensor-based approach is used mostly with gloves embedded with various sensors, but it can also be used with a wearable device [7]. The hybrid approach requires both a camera and sensors. One such example is the Leap Motion Controller (LMC), which was proposed in [10, 11].

Hand gesture recognition is the process behind identifying the correct meaning of a gesture. The mechanism of recognizing sign language depends on three steps [12]: (1) detecting the hand gesture, (2) analyzing this gesture to map its correct meaning, and (3) interpreting the results.

Furthermore, sign language is used in three ways [12, 13]: (1) fingerspelling, the most basic approach, which uses sign language alphabets and numbers only; (2) isolated words; and (3) continuous gesturing, which is the most beneficial approach because it translates sentences formed by gesturing.

Our project's primary aim was to develop and construct a system that facilitates two-way communication between hearing and deaf or hearing-impaired individuals. Thus, in this paper, we propose SignSpeak, an Arabic sign language (ArSL) recognition system that uses the LMC, a system capable of recognizing signs for the 28 letters of the Arabic alphabet. The contribution of this study is a framework that categorizes two-way communication to provide deaf and hearing-impaired individuals with an alternative communication method.

This remainder of this paper is organized into four sections. In Sect. 2, we review related works; in Sect. 3, we present our system design; in Sect. 4, we review the challenges we anticipated encountering during and after implementation; and finally, in Sect. 5 we conclude with a summary of our findings, future work, and design considerations.

2 Related Work

Motion sensors such as the LMC and Microsoft Kinect are widely used in sign language recognition for their known accuracy and closeness in a relatively natural and comfortable environment. Virtual reality (VR) applications depend on tracking of the body and hands. Thus, by using existing tools and technology to develop the proposed system, we could focus on hand gesture recognition rather than the development of a new tracking device.

In 2014, Marin et al. [14] proposed two hand gesture recognition algorithms using the Microsoft Kinect and LMC. In [11], the gestures were extracted using both devices.

The LMC provided the position of the fingertips, center of the palm, and orientation of the hand, and the Kinect provided a complete depth map and 3D distance. Gesture classification was performed using a support vector machine (SVM). The experiment results showed that the Kinect features resulted in higher accuracy compared with the LMC features. Still, the combination of features from both devices yielded an accuracy of 91.28%. A more recent study in 2016 [15] also used the Kinect and LMC to recognize ArSL gestures in real time. However, there remains room for improvement in terms of the interference of both sensors.

Similarly, in 2015, Sun et al. [16] presented a vision-based latent SVM model for sign language word and sentence recognition. A dataset that included American Sign Language (ASL) words and sentences was created using a Microsoft Kinect sensor. The presented model depended on two types of features: Kinect features and ordinary features (a histogram of oriented gradients and optical flow). Ultimately, the latent SVM model resulted in accuracies of 86.0% for words and 84.1% for sign language sentences.

In 2016, Deepali and Milind [17] proposed an ASL recognition system capable of recognizing the 26 letters of the ASL alphabet, all of which are one-handed signs. The database contained 20 samples of each alphabet, or 520 samples in total. A palm features set and a finger features set were normalized and fed to a multi-layer perceptron (MLP) neural network (NN) to be classified. An accuracy of 96.15% was achieved.

In 2016, Clark and Moodley [18] proposed a hand gesture recognition system that utilizes an Oculus Rift headset for visualization with an LMC mounted on it to detect hand gestures. The VR visualization application was created in the Unreal Engine 4 using the Unreal LMC plug-in. The k-nearest neighbor (KNN) algorithm performed hand gesture classification in real time with static hand gestures and predefined dynamic gestures. The static hand gestures resulted in an accuracy of 82.5%. The system focused on hand gesture recognition in VR using an LMC; however, it can be modified to recognize sign language hand gestures.

In 2019, Vaitkevicius et al. [17] proposed a VR based ASL gesture recognition system that used the LMC. For classification, a hidden Markov model (HMM) algorithm was used. The LMC is used in many fields for various purposes, including VR. The text input experiment used 18 pangrams (i.e., sentences that use every letter of a given alphabet at least once). The results (mean $\pm$ SD) revealed a gesture recognition accuracy of $86.1 \pm 8.2\%$ and a gesture typing speed of 3.09 ± 0.53 words per minute.

In 2019, Guzsvinecz et al. [13] published a literature review regarding the suitability of the Kinect sensor and LMC for investigating whether they can replace other, more expensive sensors. Two versions of the Kinect device were compared with the LMC. The comparison was centered on the state of the art, device type, accuracy, precision, algorithms for gesture recognition, and device price. Notably, the LMC suffered from a tracking problem when fingers were too close to each other. The Kinect and LMC are both considered low-cost visual sensors.

Several studies have concentrated on the suitability of Kinect sensors in certain fields, including virtual laboratories for education, the establishment of a gesture-controlled interface for people with disabilities, and VR therapies. Likewise, LMCs are used in several fields, especially in studies related to gesture recognition. The authors concluded the following: First, all three devices are popular, but the Kinect V1 is more popular than the Kinect V2 because the environment requires more attention with the Kinect V2. Second, by comparing the three devices with various sensors, the researchers found that the LMC is one of the most accurate, low-cost hand tracking sensors, and the Kinect V1 and V2 are two of the most accurate low-cost sensors for whole-body motion tracking. Finally, the results of the comparison indicated that these sensors can replace expensive sensors, and when the LMC is used with the Kinect, higher accuracy can be achieved.

In 2014, Mohandes et al. [10] proposed an ArSL recognition system using the LMC. The system translates all 28 Arabic letters. The work stages were as follows: data acquisition, preprocessing, and feature extraction classification. For classification, two classifiers were used: MLP NNs, which had an accuracy of 98%, and the Naïve Bayes classifier, which had an accuracy of 99.1%.

In 2016, Khelil and Amiri [19] presented an ArSL hand gesture recognition system using the LMC along with an SVM algorithm as a classifier. The system resulted in an accuracy of 91.3% for static hand gestures. However, system limitations concerning the LMC included a limited detection range, the inability to detect the hands in the presence of obstacles, and the limitation to one hand at a time.

In 2017, Hisham and Hamouda [11] proposed a model for ArSL recognition that is capable of recognizing static and dynamic gestures using an LMC. Their proposed model includes five phases: preprocessing, tracking, feature extraction, classification, and sign recognition. Two feature sets, namely a palm features set and a bone features set, were used along with four classifiers: SVM, KNN, NN, and dynamic time wrapping (DTW). SVM, KNN, and NN were used to classify static gestures, but the KNN classifier dominated the others and achieved accuracies of 99% and 98% for the palm features set and bone features set, respectively. On the other hand, two methods were suggested for classifying dynamic gestures. In the first method, each frame was classified individually—because dynamic gestures consist of a sequence of frames—using the SVM, KNN, and NN classifiers, after which the result was selected using a simple majority. In the second method, DTW was used. The second method dominated the first and achieved accuracies of 97.45% and 96.97% for the palm features set and bone features set, respectively. In addition, a simple segmentation method that depends on palm speed was proposed.

In 2019, Deriche et al. [20] proposed a framework for ArSL recognition using dual LMCs. A front LMC and a side LMC were used to address hand occlusion and missing data problems. The database contained 100 dynamic signs used in daily conversations. A total of 16 features obtained from both LMCs were selected, and two scenarios were considered. The first was when a gesture had been detected by one LMC, and the second was when a gesture had been detected by both LMCs. In the first scenario, only the obtained data from the detected LMC was fed to the classifier. In the second scenario, the obtained data from both LMCs were fused using the Dempster–Shafer (DS) evidence-based fusion approach and then fed to the classifier. For classification, a Bayesian classifier based on Gaussian mixture model GMM and linear discriminant analysis were used, achieving an accuracy of 92%.

3 System Description

SignSpeak is aimed at serving users with or without hearing impairments. Therefore, the system has two subsystems intended for translation and transcription. The translation subsystem, which converts ArSL into speech by converting sign language to spoken Arabic language, can be used by hearing-impaired users, whereas the transcription subsystem can be used by hearing users. It transcribes spoken language by converting speech to text, as shown in Fig. 1.

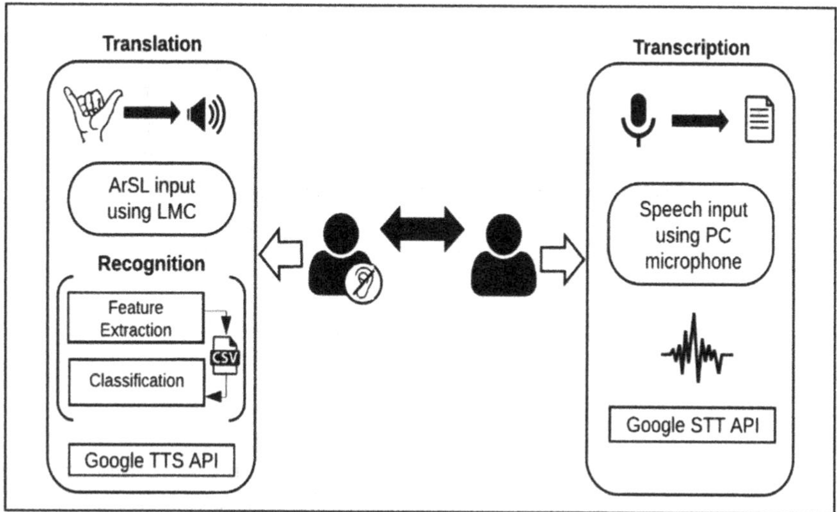

Fig. 1. SignSpeak system framework

Translation. The translation subsystem works as follows: a deaf or hearing-impaired user performs signs, which the LMC captures. Then, the sign language recognition system receives the data from the LMC and generates a file of the gesture features, which it sends to the classifier. The sign is then assigned to a class, which in this version of SignSpeak is the related Arabic letter. The output is produced as spoken language for a hearing user through sending the results of the classifier to the Google Text-To-Speech (TTS) application program interface (API).

Transcription. The transcription subsystem works as follows: a hearing individual speaks, and the speech recognition system receives the data, codes them, and sends the code of the speech to the Google Speech-To-Text (STT) API. Finally, the text equivalent of the speech is presented to the deaf or hearing-impaired user.

3.1 Materials

Leap Motion Controller. The LMC is a specialized sensor developed by Leap Motion. Recently, Leap Motion and Ultrahapitic merged to become Ultraleap [21]. The LMC device combines two near-infrared cameras and three LEDs to prevent overlaps. Figure 2 depicts the LMC's components. It is capable of detecting hand movements and other hand elements, including fingers, joints, and bones within an interaction zone of 60 cm extending from the device in a 120 × 150° field of view. Furthermore, the detection range is an arm's length, which is up to 80 cm, although it may differ depending on hand conditions.

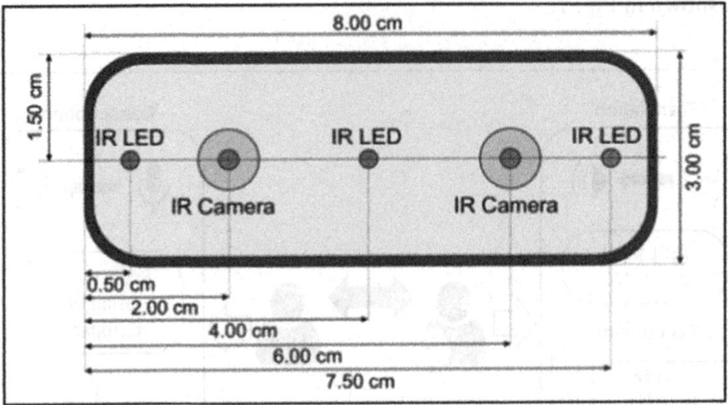

Fig. 2. Leap Motion Controller

Dataset. SignSpeak's system uses a flat-file database. The file stores the 28 Arabic letters and the sign language features for each letter. The data were collected from two signers who repeated each letter 10 times. Thus, the file includes 560 samples. The file also contains the following features: hand direction, palm position, finger direction, fingertip position, bone direction, base of the bone, and end of the bone. It should be noted that all the features are given as vectors (i.e., with respect to x, y, and z).

SignSpeak Prototype. We developed an application to interface with the users and collected data from them. In brief, we developed a graphical user interface (GUI) that presents two options: signing and speaking.

If the user chooses the signing option, as shown in Fig. 3, the system records his or her hand movements. The user can re-enter the hand movement in case of a mistake, and the system records the new movement. After that, the system checks whether the sign can be detected. If the sign cannot be detected, the system asks the user to re-enter the hand movement. Otherwise, the system translates the sign into audio and plays the audio. If the user chooses the speech option, the system records his or her speech. The user can re-record the speech in case of a mistake, and the system records the new speech. Next, the system checks whether the speech can be detected. If the speech cannot be detected, the system asks the user to repeat the recording process. Otherwise, the system transcribes the speech to text and outputs this text to the users.

The SignSpeak system uses two machine learning classifiers. Both are supervised learners that start by acquiring data from a CSV file. They then split the data into training

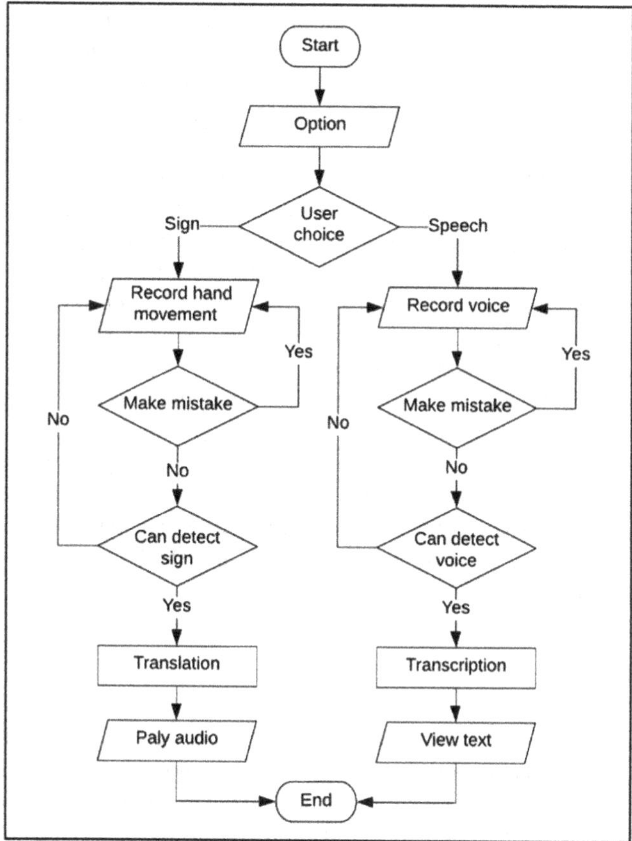

Fig. 3. Flowchart of the system's graphical user interface

and testing sets. Notably, the classifier splits the data into 80% for the training set and 20% for the testing set. Therefore, when a hearing-impaired individual moves his or her hand, the system directly records that movement and extracts the features.

Then, the recognition subsystem's classifiers (SVM/KNN) output the equivalent text. Subsequently, the system sends the text to Google's TTS API to output the audio. Finally, the system plays the audio to the hearing individual. Moreover, when the hearing individual speaks, the system records his or her voice and sends the recording to Google's STT API to transfer it to text. Finally, the system outputs the text to the deaf or hearing-impaired individual.

4 Discussion

Deployment of the system and testing phases indicated that the system is well-aligned with user and system requirements. Deaf individuals can record hand gestures to be translated and read the text equivalent of hearing individuals' responses or speech. Likewise, a hearing individual can acquire a spoken translation of ArSL and record their spoken response or speech. Furthermore, the system has a clear interface with the proposed functionalities, asks the user to repeat the input, and produces an output in an average of 4 s. However, the system has some limitations, which are mainly related to the LMC's performance. Problems include a limited range of motion and lag between movements.

As for the LMC, common issues include its limited range of motion, small number of features, and the inability to detect both hands [19]. However, a few studies have used both the LMC and Kinect [13], [14] to minimize these issues and increase overall accuracy. In addition, in [20], the proposed ArSL recognition system used two LMCs to address the issue of a limited tracking range and increase the number of features. Future work in VR and motion tracking sensors requires enhanced hand gesture recognition, an easily deployable system, and a wider tracking range.

For classification, we used the SVM/KNN algorithm. In the gesture recognition field, the algorithm used depends on the type of gesture (i.e., static or dynamic). In our case, we aimed to recognize the 28 Arabic letters, which involves static gesturing. Various methods can be used to execute gesture classification, such as NN, HMM, MLP, and Naïve Bayes. All have acceptable accuracy, but based on our literature review and the nature of our system, the most suitable algorithms are SVM and KNN. We end with SVM classification method.

5 Conclusion

In the SignSpeak system, we use an LMC to recognize sign language. Moreover, the translation process is performed immediately and does not require special "start" and "end" gestures from the user. When translating ArSL to speech and speech to ArSL, recognizing ArSL in itself is a challenge. Because the Arabic language is rich, ArSL uses many gestures to convey words, and the physical distinctions differentiating one gesture from another are subtle. These gestures also involve different parts of the body, which makes ArSL difficult for a system to interpret.

As for the system decomposition, the SignSpeak system has two main functions: translation and transcription. For transcription, we used the Google API with no further decomposition, and for translation, the decomposition was roughly unchangeable. We decomposed it further into three tasks: data acquisition, a recognition task that includes feature extraction and classification, and output production. The data acquisition was related to the LMC input. In the recognition task, we identified the features of the performed sign and classified it according to the related letter. As for the output, text was received from the classification component and converted to speech using the Google API.

Although SignSpeak provides a feasible starting point for building a motion-based ArSL translation tool, many more features and directions could be considered. In this section, we lay out some relatively immediately accessible avenues for future work.

- New gestures: SignSpeak currently includes only ArSL letters. We intend to add static words to enhance SignSpeak's effectiveness for both ArSL learning purposes and translation.

- Facial expressions: Although we neglected facial expressions in this version of SignSpeak, facial expressions are crucial in ArSL. Thus, we intend to recognize facial features in future versions by adding additional sensors to track facial expressions.
- Dynamic gestures: The addition of dynamic gesture recognition will allow deaf individuals to communicate more naturally.
- 3D animations: Animations should further improve the GUI experience for the user. As our meeting with an ArSL expert revealed, most deaf individuals cannot read Arabic due to a lack of proper education. Thus, animations will improve the application and make it more appealing to various user demographics.

Acknowledgment. We thank the Humanistic Co-Design Initiative and the Human-Computer Interaction (HCI) Lab for supporting this work. We also acknowledge the contribution of the Saudi Authority for Intellectual Property (SAIP) and the Saudi Health Council's National Lab for Emerging Health Technologies in hosting and mentoring this work. This work is part of the authors' project that is carried out under the CoCreate Fellowship for Humanistic Co-Design of Access Technologies.

References

1. Deafness and hearing loss. https://www.who.int/news-room/fact-sheets/detail/deafness-and-hearing-loss. Accessed 16 May 2020
2. Disability Survey 2017 | General Authority for Statistics. https://www.stats.gov.sa/en/5669. Accessed 16 May 2020
3. Population Estimates | General Authority for Statistics. https://www.stats.gov.sa/en/43. Accessed 16 May 2020
4. Alnafjan, A., Aljumaah, A., Alaskar, H., Alshraihi, R.: Designing 'Najeeb': technology-enhanced learning for children with impaired hearing using arabic sign-language ArSL applications. In: International Conference on Computer and Applications (ICCA), pp. 238–243 (2017)
5. Al-Nafjan, A., Al-Arifi, B., Al-Wabil, A.: Design and development of an educational arabic sign language mobile application: collective impact with tawasol. In: Antona, M., Stephanidis, C. (eds.) UAHCI 2015. LNCS, vol. 9176, pp. 319–326. Springer, Cham (2015). https://doi.org/10.1007/978-3-319-20681-3_30
6. Joy, J., Balakrishnan, K., Sreeraj, M.: SignQuiz: a quiz based tool for learning fingerspelled signs in indian sign language using ASLR. IEEE Access **7**, 28363–28371 (2019)
7. Lee, B.G., Lee, S.M.: Smart wearable hand device for sign language interpretation system with sensors fusion. IEEE Sens. J. **18**(3), 1224–1232 (2018)
8. Mohandes, M., Aliyu, S., Deriche, M.: Prototype arabic sign language recognition using multi-sensor data fusion of two leap motion controllers. In: 12th International Multi-Conference on Systems, Signals and Devices (2015)
9. Elbadawy, M., Elons, A.S., Shedeed, H.A., Tolba, M.F.: Arabic sign language recognition with 3D convolutional neural networks. In: IEEE 8th International Conference on Intelligent Computing and Information Systems (ICICIS), vol. 2018-Janua, pp. 66–71 (2018)
10. Mohandes, M., Aliyu, S., Deriche, M.: Arabic sign language recognition using the leap motion controller. In: IEEE International Symposium on Industrial Electronics, pp. 960–965 (2014)
11. Hisham, B., Hamouda, A.: Arabic static and dynamic gestures recognition using leap motion. J. Comput. Sci. **13**(8), 337–354 (2017)

12. Suarez, J., Murphy, R.R.: Hand gesture recognition with depth images: a review. In: IEEE International Workshop on Robot and Human Interactive Communication, pp. 411–417 (2012)
13. Guzsvinecz, T., Szucs, V., Sik-Lanyi, C.: Suitability of the kinect sensor and leap motion controller—a literature review. Sensors **19**(5), 1072 (2019)
14. Marin, G., Dominio, F., Zanuttigh, P.: Hand gesture recognition with leap motion and kinect devices. In: IEEE International Conference on Image Processing, pp. 1565–1569 (2014)
15. Almasre, M.A., Al-Nuaim, H.: A real-time letter recognition model for arabic sign language using kinect and leap motion controller v2. Int. J. Adv. Eng. Manag. Sci. (IJAEMS) **2**(5), 239469 (2016)
16. Sun, C., Zhang, T., Xu, C.: Latent support vector machine modeling for sign language recognition with kinect. ACM Trans. Intell. Syst. Technol. (TIST) **6**(2), 1–20 (2015)
17. Naglot, D., Kulkarni, M.: Real time sign language recognition using the leap motion controller. In: International Conference on Inventive Computation Technologies (ICICT), vol. 2016 (2016)
18. Clark, A., Moodley, D.: A system for a hand gesture-manipulated virtual reality environment. In: Proceedings of the Annual Conference of the South African Institute of Computer Scientists and Information Technologists, vol. 26-28-Sept, pp. 1–10 (2016)
19. Khelil, B., Amiri, H.: Hand gesture recognition using leap motion controller for recognition of arabic sign language. In: 3rd International Conference on Automation, Control Engineering and Computer Science (ACECS), pp. 233–238 (2016)
20. Deriche, M., Aliyu, S., Mohandes, M.: An intelligent arabic sign language recognition system using a pair of LMCs with GMM based classification. IEEE Sens. J. **19**(18), 1–12 (2019)
21. Digital worlds that feel human | Ultraleap. https://www.ultraleap.com/. Accessed: 16 May 2020

Co-design of Color Identification Applications Using Scenario-Based Personas for People with Impaired Color Vision

Mawaddah AlSabban[1(✉)], Arwa Karim[2], Virginia H. Sun[3], Jood Hashim[4], and Osama AlSayed[4]

[1] Saudi Authority for Intellectual Property, Riyadh, Saudi Arabia
Msabban@saip.gov.sa

[2] King Abdullah University of Science and Technology, Thuwal, Saudi Arabia
arw2.ak.23@gmail.com

[3] Massachusetts Institute of Technology, Cambridge, MA, USA
gsun@mit.edu

[4] CoCreate Fellowship for the Humanistic Co-design of Access Technology, Riyadh, Saudi Arabia
joodayh@gmail.com, osamab.alsayed@gmail.com

Abstract. Designers and system analysts have long struggled to extract and repurpose data from user research by laboriously presenting content in the form of storyboards, behavioral-type personas, or journey maps. An alternative is to convey insights from user research through scenario-based personas that represent user research data through storytelling. This provides a more streamlined way to convey data rather than character-based personas; however, scenarios are effortful for developers to articulate and envision. In this work, we empower assistive technology development teams to access authentic user experiences with scenario-based personas through tangible and digital artifacts. Scenario-based personas were used for conveying the results of a user analysis study for color identification mobile applications for people with visual impairments. We developed scenario-based personas for persons with impaired color vision based on the main contexts identified in user research studies. The method combines personas depicted in silhouettes of people with impaired color vision and scenario contexts that capture the place and activities. Silhouettes were used in the artifacts to reduce the bias that a face often generates in persona-based scenarios. Preliminary findings suggest that scenario-based persona tools were effective in describing the stories and context behind why a person with a visual disability would consider a color identification application. Through this method, scenario-based personas were able to foster understanding of the application's target user population by showing their main contexts of using these mobile applications and create playful and tangible artifacts to capture and convey such user information to designers and developers in the Humanistic Co-Design community. Methodological considerations for using scenario-based personas in user research will be discussed.

Keywords: Participatory design · Mobile applications · Co-design · Co-creation · Color identification · Scenarios · Visually impaired

C. Stephanidis et al. (Eds.): HCII 2020, LNCS 12426, pp. 171–183, 2020.
https://doi.org/10.1007/978-3-030-60149-2_14

1 Introduction

Personas are well established in the user-centered design (UCD) and co-design contexts; however, they are often not utilized by developers of assistive technology [1–3]. Scenarios are critical both for designing assistive technologies and for usability testing with persons with disabilities. Moreover, personas depicting fictional characters with photos are often perceived differently when the selected characters do not reflect the diversity of a population. Different variations of personas and scenarios have been reported in the HCI literature and explored in practice [1, 2]. The research on personas and scenarios in the design of assistive technology is less explored and inadequately understood [2].

Many people who have visual disabilities worldwide depend on mobile applications to augment their sensory abilities [4–8]. A large part of them are unable to detect colors. In recent years, color identification technologies have been designed for people who have visual disabilities [6, 7]. Techniques range from color detection based on image processing (e.g. Seeing AI [9]) to fiducial marker-based methods [10, 11].

The design process for innovative products is often more effective when users are involved as co-designers. Towards this model of co-design, personas and scenarios emerge as important tools for communicating the needs and requirements that would be considered in the product designs [3]. While current applications can partially assist the visually impaired, they lack features that could prove useful to the user. Not using personas as a foundation for building an application could be considered a reason and factor for the lack of helpful features. Personas are an essential part of the design phase for an application, as they represent the needs of users and how they plan to use an application [12].

In designing color identification applications, it is important for developers to focus on the requirements of users who seek mobile applications to translate images captured by the camera into spoken words to aid them in identifying the color. The spoken words are extracted from a color dictionary which is often accessible for mainstream languages, yet is not available for some languages, such as Arabic. Understanding the diverse users, different contexts, and scenarios of usage requires collective efforts of users and designers.

This paper is structured as follows: Sect. 2 describes the background and motivation for using personas and scenarios in user-centered design for assistive technology. Following that, we describe the method in Sect. 3 followed by the design implications in Sect. 4. We conclude in Sect. 5 with a summary of contributions and directions for future research.

2 Personas and Scenarios in Designing Assistive Technology for People with Visual Impairments

Although mobile devices include accessibility features, individuals who have visual impairments still face a variety of challenges such as small form factors, small or undifferentiated keys, and tiny on-screen text [13]. Personas and scenarios arise as important tools for communicating the needs and requirements that would be considered in the design of the product. Towards the overarching goal of accessible mobile application design, we discuss here existing scenario-based personas and applications for individuals with visual impairments.

2.1 Scenarios in Assistive Technology Design

Designers of assistive technologies often inadvertently propose solutions based on assumptions that are not grounded in user-research [14]. Some assistive technologies require far too much scrolling or directional swipes to produce actions on a mobile screen. Furthermore, people who have lost some sensitivity in their fingers or those who have visual impairments would benefit from better-designed buttons and switches [15].

Mobile accessibility has plagued the assistive technology field for many years [16]. In order to solve this issue, designers have utilized personas and scenarios to give life and substance to user research findings.

Personas have been employed in assistive technology in various ways, one of them being the AEGIS project (Accessibility Everywhere: Groundwork, Infrastructure, Standards). "The AEGIS project attempts to establish whether 3rd generation access techniques would provide a more accessible, more exploitable, and deeply embeddable approach to mainstream information and communication technology (ICT)" [17]. AEGIS identifies user needs and interaction models for several user groups and develops open source-based generalized accessibility support for mainstream ICT devices/applications [17]. Within the AEGIS project, a variety of methods were used to identify users' needs. A total of seventeen personas were made and were presented across five sections. Each persona is introduced with a name, a photo, and a short description of his personal situation. Furthermore, an overview of the problems of a persona in using the technology in itself or in using the assistive technology is provided. Based on these problems, the next section of each persona gives an overview of their needs and wants [18].

As a result of their approach, the researchers ensured that the needs of a number of user groups were considered in all cycles of design and development of accessible applications. The user groups include users with visual, hearing, movement, speech, and cognitive impairments, in addition to the application developers themselves.

In another context, personas were also used to exemplify the process of using mobile applications by an aging patient population. The resultant personas improved the design, development, and implementation plans of a smartphone application to assist chronically ill aging Chinese diabetic population capable of disease self-management [19].

2.2 Personas in Assistive Technology Design for the Blind and/or Low-Vision

The utilization of personas has become an essential tool that assists designers, developers, and the assistive technology industry. Using personas that simulate the needs of persons who are blind and/or low-visioned can help with understanding the needs of the visually impaired which in-turn leads to the development of assistive technologies.

To better understand the needs of persons who are blind and/or low-visioned, in 2018, designers E. Brule and C. Jouffrais have used scenario-based personas to include children living with visual impairments in the design process. They used activities aimed at raising empathy through storytelling, persona cards, and role-playing. Their study aimed at better understanding the educational context and the experiences of visually impaired children [20].

The field study helped to better describe children living with visual impairment and how they interact with assistive technologies. It also demonstrated how those interactions are shaped by a larger context (e.g. policy, culture, etc.). These observations guided the development of a set of design cards and workshop activities, which aimed to improve the representation of users and increase empathy [20].

3 Method

In co-design models, scenarios are often used to understand the needs of the user for the product, service, and/or system in a specific context [7]. The work on personas in this study stemmed from the need to find ways to bring co-designers, engineers, and developers together into a single, cohesive team. The goal of the scenario-based personas was to allow the development team to live and breathe the target user population's world in the context of color identification scenarios.

3.1 Designing Scenario-Based Personas

The process of designing the scenario-based personas started with semi-structured interviews as part of the user research in a Humanistic Co-design for assistive technology workshop. From our ethnographic research on people with visual impairments and impaired color vision, we focused our personas in the first iteration of design on the user mode of action rather than the user demographics (such as age, gender, abilities) or their essence (e.g. attitudes) as depicted in Fig. 1.

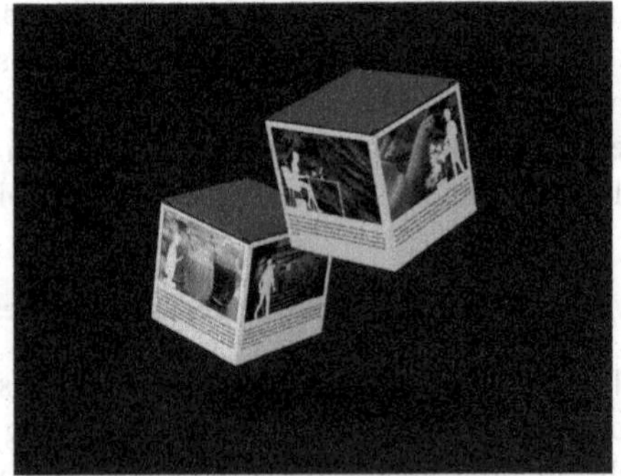

Fig. 1. Tangible scenario-based persona artefacts for designers and co-designers

Designing scenarios involved identifying the different contexts of use in which we envisioned color identification would take place, such as in the context of grocery shopping, clothing shopping, paint color selection, or vehicle showroom. Following that, silhouettes are overlaid on the backdrop image as in Fig. 2.

The scenario depicted in Fig. 2 could apply to fruits that are relatively similar in shape and form such as apples, grapes, and pears but vary in color, flavor, and nutrition. Color identification is important for shoppers when buying apples, to facilitate choosing those without any bruises or soft, mushy spots and to look for fruit with shiny skin—dull skin

Fig. 2. Silhouette of a shopper would be overlaid on a "selecting fruit based on color" activity in a grocery store setting.

Visual scene depicting objects in a restaurant	Description of people, place, and issue(s)
 A server places the drinks on the table for a group of diners then returns to the kitchen to serve other diners The drinks were served in identical glasses and had no differentiating garnish and can only be identified by color. Ali is a person with impaired color vision, and he was alone at the table, and needed to select his/her drink but was not able to differentiate between the drinks.	***Scenario in a restaurant*** A server places the drinks on the table for a group of diners then returns to the kitchen to serve other diners. The drinks were served in identical glasses and had no differentiating garnish and can only be identified by color. Ali is a person with impaired color vision, and he was alone at the table waiting for his friends to join, and he wanted to select his drink but was not able to differentiate between the drinks.

Fig. 3. Silhouette of a diner overlaid on a 'restaurant table' scene

hints at a lack of crispness and flavor. Independent detection of these subtle variations in color empower users in the activity of shopping for these items and in daily living when these items are selected for meals or during cooking (Figs. 3, 4, 5, 6, 7, 8, 9, 10, 11, 12 and 13).

Visual scene of shopping in a clothing store

Description of people, place, and issue(s)

Scenario in a clothing store

Sumaya is a 30-year-old teacher with impaired color vision. She is shopping for clothing items in a store and finds it difficult to differentiate between the colors of similar items of clothing on the rack.

Sumaya prefers to browse independently rather than ask for a shop attendant for assistance because the assistants often shadow her during the shopping experience which makes her feel uncomfortable.

Fig. 4. Silhouette of a shopper overlaid on a clothing shop scene with a shopper browsing items

Visual scene of a customer in a paint store

Description of people, place, and issue(s)

Scenario in a paint store

Lana is a 40-year-old homeowner and is renovating two rooms in her house. She is shopping for paint at her local hardware store. Lana has impaired color vision and needs assistance in differentiating between the slight variations of colors in paint samples and making sure that her paint-selection is aligned with her home's interior design scheme (furniture, flooring, curtains)

Fig. 5. Silhouette of a shopper overlaid over wall displays of a paint shop

Visual scene of a car showroom	Description of people, place, and issue(s)
	***Scenario in a car showroom*** Yousef is a 65-year-old retired accountant and is shopping for a new vehicle in a local car dealer. Yousef has impaired color vision and needs assistance in differentiating between the slight variations of colors in car paint colors.

Fig. 6. Silhouette of a shopper overlaid on a crowded scene in a showroom or exhibit

Visual scene of an art studio	Description of people, place, and issue(s)
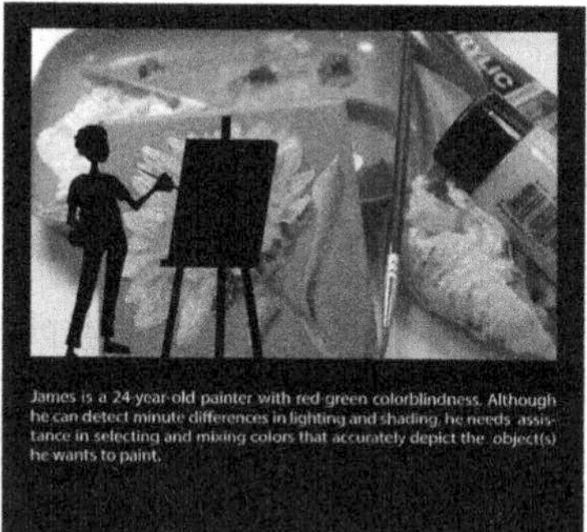	***Scenario in an art studio*** James is a 24-year-old painter with red-green colorblindness. Although he can detect minute differences in lighting and shading, he needs assistance in selecting and mixing colors that accurately depict the object(s) he wants to paint.

Fig. 7. Silhouette of a painter overlaid in an art studio

Visual scene of gift-wrapping station	Description of people, place, and issue(s)
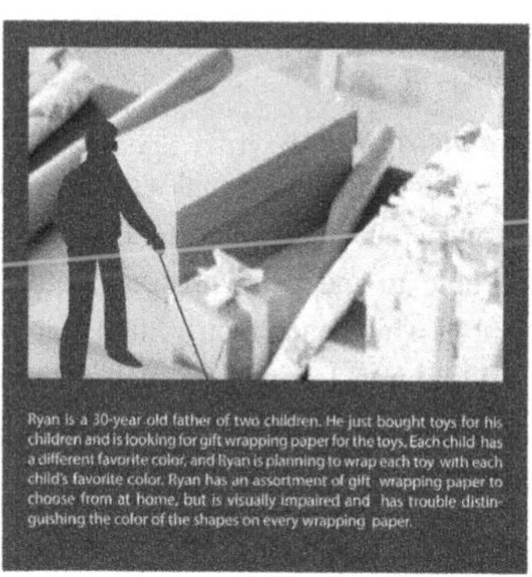	***Scenario in a gift-wrapping station*** Ryan is a 30-year old father of two children. He just bought toys for his children and is looking for gift wrapping paper for the toys. Each child has a different favorite color, and Ryan is planning to wrap each toy with each child's favorite color. Ryan has an assortment of gift-wrapping paper to choose from at home, but has a visual impairment and has trouble distinguishing the color of the shapes on every wrapping paper.

Fig. 8. Silhouette of a shopper overlaid in a gift-wrapping station

Visual scene of taking photos in a studio	Description of people, place, and issue(s)

Scenario in a photography studio

Ahmad is a 20-year-old freelance photographer with impaired color vision. His customer owns a watch company and gave him five of the same watch but with different strap colors. While photographing, Ahmad had difficulty differentiating the watch straps' colors which made the process of choosing harmonic backgrounds harder.

Fig. 9. Silhouette of a photographer overlaid on a photography studio scene with a photographer browsing different backgrounds

Visual scene of a student in a finance class	Description of people, place, and issue(s)

Scenario in a university class

Sarah is a 20-year-old finance student at university with impaired color vision. Her professor displays a pie chart that shows an example of an expense analysis. However, Sarah is having trouble differentiating which color represents each section.

Fig. 10. Silhouette of a student overlaid on a finance class with a pie chart

Visual scene of an adult in a metro station.	Description of people, place, and issue(s)

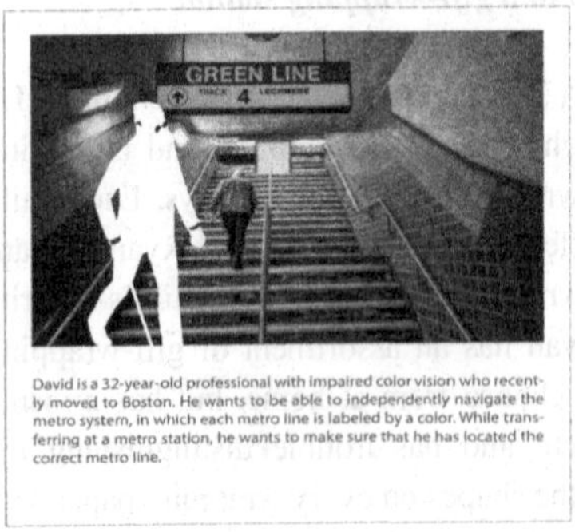

Scenario in a metro station

David is a 32-year-old professional with impaired color vision who recently moved to Boston. He wants to be able to independently navigate the metro system, in which each metro line is labeled by a color. While transferring at a metro station, he wants to make sure that he has located the correct metro line.

Fig. 11. Silhouette of an adult overlaid on a metro station

Visual scene of a researcher analyzing an image	Description of people, place, and issue(s)
 Vanessa is a 36-year-old biological researcher with red-green color blindness. She is tasked with analyzing a stained image of a plant expressing both red and green-fluorescent proteins. She has difficulty distinguishing red from green and black, and is therefore uncertain if her results are accurate.	***Scenario in research lab*** Vanessa is a 36-year-old biological researcher with red-green color blindness. She is tasked with analyzing a stained image of a tissue sample expressing both red and green-fluorescent proteins. She has difficulty distinguishing red from green and black, and is therefore uncertain if her results are accurate.

Fig. 12. Silhouette of a researcher analyzing a fluorescent-stained image

Visual scene of an adult in a garden	Description of people, place, and issue(s)
 Maya is a 22-year-old woman with deuteranopes which is a color blindness that can confuse bright greens with yellow. A shop asked to partner with her to take the flowers she gardens once they are bright yellow. However, she is unable to tell if the flowers turned bright and yellow yet.	***Scenario in a garden*** Maya is a 22-year-old woman with deuteranopes, a color blindness that can confuse bright greens with yellow. A shop asked to partner with her to take the flowers she gardens once they are bright yellow. However, she is unable to tell if the flowers turned bright and yellow yet.

Fig. 13. Silhouette of a gardener tending to yellow flowers in a garden. (Color figure online)

4 Discussion and Design Implications

While senses such as sound, taste, smell, and touch can be used to either substitute or supplement low vision in certain scenarios, color is one of the unique properties that can only be identified through vision. The above personas were created through user discussions and case studies of individuals with various vision impairments, including color-blindness, low vision, and complete blindness. Depending on each individual's unique interests and abilities, the user may present different scenarios in which they would use a color-identification application. Additional user-scenarios can be created by recruiting more co-designers and/or exploring situations in which they would need accurate color detection and identification to perform a task. In this section, we describe the design implications of such scenario-based personas by outlining its use cases and impact.

4.1 Use Cases of Scenario-Based Personas for People with Impaired Color Vision

In designing assistive technology, it is important for the designer to understand the situation in which such technology would be used. Although it is recommended to have people with visual impairments to play an active role in designing assistive technology as a co-designer [21], scenario-based personas can be used in place of a co-designer if unavailable. Assistive technology hackathons, for example, have recently grown in popularity and draws in both students and professionals around the world [22–24]. These user-centered hackathons require the designers to understand the context and perspective surrounding the individual and his/her problems [25]. One or more of the scenarios outlined in Sect. 3 may be used as a problem statement, or launching board, for a hackathon project. The resulting solution may then be adopted by people with impaired color vision and applied in real-world situations.

The aforementioned scenario-based personas may also be used in educational settings, such as design classes and assistive-technology workshops. In an example use-case scenario, a student in a design class may choose a persona to expand on. While conducting research on the selected scenario, the designer may assess whether existing color-identification applications adequately address the needs of the individual described in the persona. After uncovering issues with the existing solutions, the designer can then create a prototype that will allow the individual to independently navigate through the described scenario. If time permits, further designing, testing, and iterating can lead to a fully-functional product. Through this activity, the designer will have conducted research, defined a problem, generated ideas, developed designs, and evaluated designs—all principal components of the user-centered design process [26].

Even when co-designers are available, the scenario-based personas we described can help supplement their input when designing a color-identification tool. By designing an application based on multiple users and personas, the designer can ensure that the end-result is scalable and applicable across a wider range of scenarios.

4.2 Impact of Scenario-Based Personas for People with Impaired Color Vision

By encouraging the use of scenario-based personas when developing assistive technology for people with impaired color vision, the designer approaches the project by considering the individual, activity, and context for which the technology is to be applied to. This framework, known as the human activity assistive technology (HAAT) model, is necessary to consider when designing and implementing assistive technology [27].

Through these scenarios, the designer may also adopt an *interactional* model of color vision impairment, rather than a *functional-limitation* model. That is, rather than attributing a person's disabilities for any disadvantages, the *interactional* model states that the interaction between the environment and the individual determines if a disability exists [28]. In these scenarios, a properly designed color-identification application will prevent people with impaired color vision from being disadvantaged at all. Adopting an *interactional* model may allow individuals to approach disability with a more positive perception by acknowledging that disadvantages may stem from society's treatment of people with disabilities, rather than the disability itself.

These scenario-based personas may introduce individuals to personal stories that are outside of their own experience. Recognizing the unique characteristics, abilities, and interests associated with the scenario-based personas may help designers develop greater empathy towards people with impaired color vision. The personas may also help inspire designers by providing a glimpse into what users they want to interview and recruit in developing a product. With the development of an application that fits the co-designer's specific needs, the co-designer would feel more empowered as they can navigate through these situations without the assistance of another individual.

5 Conclusion and Future Work

5.1 Conclusion

Although developers and designers try to keep the needs of users in mind, the design of the application suggests that the development process may be driven by assumptions of the user [2]. We found that scenario-based personas present as a valid option for designers in identifying a user's specific needs. Scenario-based personas introduce individuals to personal stories that are outside of their own experience, which in-turn helps the designers develop more efficient assistive technologies. We believe that the scenario-based personas we developed through user interviews and case studies will be able to foster understanding of the application's target user population by offering various contexts for using color-identification applications.

5.2 Future Work

To develop a more accurate understanding of the various use-cases for color-identification applications, more persona-based scenarios should be collected. Additional scenarios may be discovered via interviews of individuals with color vision impairments and their caregivers (i.e. family, personal care assistants, ophthalmologists).

As demonstrated in Fig. 1, the scenario-based personas can be developed into tangible objects that can be used for additional research (e.g. via persona box design). We hope to further study how such objects can be integrated into design settings to increase empathy for people with visual impairments and encourage principles of universal design. An example experimental design could consist of several groups of design students, each given a subset of persona-based scenarios displayed on a tangible object, with a control group given no personas. After assigning each group with an identical design task, the final design could be evaluated based on accessibility. Similarly, we hope to further analyze where and when persona-based scenarios can be used to substitute and/or supplement co-designers with visual impairments, and if one result leads to better design outcomes and greater empathy over the other.

Acknowledgment. We thank the Humanistic Co-Design Initiative and the Human-Computer Interaction (HCI) Lab for supporting this work. We also thank the Saudi Authority for Intellectual Property (SAIP) and the Saudi Health Council's National Lab for Emerging Health Technologies for hosting and mentoring. This work is part of the authors' project that is carried out under the CoCreate Fellowship for Humanistic Co-Design of Access Technologies. We would also like to thank the participants in the user study, as well as Dr. Areej Al-Wabil, Dr. Shiroq Al-Megren, Dr. Kyle Keane, and Anna Musser, for their mentorship and support.

References

1. Saez, A.V., Domingo, M.G.G.: Scenario-based persona: introducing personas through their main contexts. In: Extended Abstracts on Human Factors in Computing Systems (CHI EA 2011), p. 505. Association for Computing Machinery, New York (2011). https://doi.org/10.1145/1979742.1979563
2. Moser, C., Fuchsberger, V., Neureiter, K., Sellner, W., Tscheligi, M.: Revisiting personas: the making-of for special user groups. In: CHI '12 Extended Abstracts on Human Factors in Computing Systems (CHI EA 2012), pp. 453–468. Association for Computing Machinery, New York (2012). https://doi.org/10.1145/2212776.2212822
3. Chang, Y.N., Lim, Y.K., Stolterman, E.: Personas: from theory to practices. In: Proceedings of the 5th Nordic conference on Human-computer interaction: building bridges (NordiCHI 2008), pp. 439–442. Association for Computing Machinery, New York (2008). https://doi.org/10.1145/1463160.1463214
4. Medeiros, A.J., Stearns, L., Findlater, L., Chen, C., Froehlich, J.E.: Recognizing clothing colors and visual textures using a finger-mounted camera: an initial investigation. In: Proceedings of the 19th International ACM SIGACCESS Conference on Computers and Accessibility (ASSETS 2017), pp. 393–394. Association for Computing Machinery, New York (2017). https://doi.org/10.1145/3132525.3134805
5. Nguyen, R., Geddes, C.: Exploring haptic colour identification aids. In: The 21st International ACM SIGACCESS Conference on Computers and Accessibility (ASSETS 2019), pp. 709–711. Association for Computing Machinery, New York (2019). https://doi.org/10.1145/3308561.3356111
6. Flatla, D.R., Andrade, A.R., Teviotdale, R.D., Knowles, D.L., Steward, C.: ColourID: improving colour identification for people with impaired colour vision. In: Proceedings of the 33rd Annual ACM Conference on Human Factors in Computing Systems (CHI 2015), pp. 3543–3552. Association for Computing Machinery, New York (2015). https://doi.org/10.1145/2702123.2702578
7. Li, W., Flatla, D.R.: 30 years later: has CVD research changed the world? In: The 21st International ACM SIGACCESS Conference on Computers and Accessibility (ASSETS 2019), pp. 584–590. Association for Computing Machinery, New York (2019). https://doi.org/10.1145/3308561.3354612
8. Popleteev, A., Louveton, N., McCall, R.: Colorizer: smart glasses aid for the colorblind. In: Proceedings of the 2015 workshop on Wearable Systems and Applications (WearSys 2015), pp. 7–8. Association for Computing Machinery, New York (2015). https://doi.org/10.1145/2753509.2753516
9. Seeing AI App from Microsoft. https://www.microsoft.com/en-us/ai/seeing-ai. Accessed 18 June 2020
10. Mattos, A.B., Cardonha, C., Gallo, D., Avegliano, P., Herrmann, R., Borger, S.: Marker-based image recognition of dynamic content for the visually impaired. In: Proceedings of the 11th Web for All Conference, pp. 1–4. Association for Computing Machinery, New York (2014). https://doi.org/10.1145/2596695.2596707
11. Prasanna, S., Priyadharshini, N., Pugazhendhi, M.A.: Textile robot for matching and pick up clothes based on color recognition. Asian J. Appl. Sci. Technol. (AJAST) **1**(3), 62–65 (2017)

12. Miaskiewicz, T., Kozar, K.A.: Personas and user-centered design: how can personas benefit product design processes? Des. Stud. **32**(5), 417–430 (2011). https://doi.org/10.1016/j.destud.2011.03.003
13. Kane, S.K., Jayant, C., Wobbrock, J.O., Ladner, R.E.: Freedom to roam: a study of mobile device adoption and accessibility for people with visual and motor disabilities. In: Proceedings of the 11th International ACM SIGACCESS Conference on Computers and Accessibility, pp. 115–122. Association for Computing Machinery, New York (2009). https://doi.org/10.1145/1639642.1639663
14. Law, C.M., Yi, J.S., Choi, Y.S., Jacko, J.A.: Are disability-access guidelines designed for designers? Do they need to be? In: Proceedings of the 18th Australia Conference on Computer-Human Interaction: Design: Activities, Artefacts and Environments (OZCHI 2006), pp. 357–360. Association for Computing Machinery, New York (2006). https://doi.org/10.1145/1228175.1228244
15. Rainger, P.: Usability and accessibility of personal digital assistants as assistive technologies in education. Learning with mobile devices: research and development. Learning and Skills Development Agency, London, UK, pp. 131–137 (2004)
16. El-Glaly, Y.N., Peruma, A., Krutz, D.E., Hawker, J.S.: Apps for everyone: mobile accessibility learning modules. ACM Inroads **9**(2), 30–33 (2018). https://doi.org/10.1145/3182184
17. About AEGIS. http://www.aegis-project.eu. Accessed 13 June 2020
18. Sulmon, N., Slegers, K., Van Isacker, K., Gemou, M., Bekiaris, E.: Using personas to capture assistive technology needs of people with disabilities (2010)
19. LeRouge, C., Ma, J., Sneha, S., Tolle, K.: User profiles and personas in the design and development of consumer health technologies. Int. J. Med. Informatics **82**(11), 251–268 (2013). https://doi.org/10.1016/j.ijmedinf.2011.03.006
20. Brulé, E., Jouffrais, C.: Representing children living with visual impairments in the design process: a case study with personae. In: Langdon, P., Lazar, J., Heylighen, A., Dong, H. (eds.) Designing Around People, pp. 23–32. Springer, Cham (2016). https://doi.org/10.1007/978-3-319-29498-8_3
21. Kane, S., Hurst, A., Buehler, E., Carrington, P., Williams, M.: Collaboratively designing assistive technology. Interactions **21**(2), 78–92 (2014)
22. ATHack. http://assistivetech.mit.edu/events. Accessed 14 June 2020
23. Boston Grand Hack 2019. https://grandhack.mit.edu/boston-2019. Accessed 14 June 2020
24. #include <girl>'s Assistive Technology Hackathon. https://code.likeagirl.io/include-s-assistive-technology-hackathon-1ff7d1caf83a. Accessed 14 June 2020
25. Gubin, T.A., et al.: A systems approach to healthcare innovation using the MIT hacking medicine model. Cell Syst. **5**(1), 6–10 (2017). https://doi.org/10.1016/j.cels.2017.02.012
26. Watkins, S.M., Dunne, L.E.: Functional Clothing Design: From Sportswear to Spacesuits, 1st edn, pp. 2–29. Fairchild Books, New York (2015)
27. Cook, A.M., Polgar, J.M.: Cook & Hussey's Assistive Technologies: Principles and Practice, 3rd edn, pp. 34–53. Mosby Elsevier, Maryland Heights (2008)
28. Burgstahler, S., Doe, T.: Disability-related simulations: if, when, and how to use them. Rev. Disabil. Stud. **1**(2), 4–17 (2004)

Proposal for an Interactive Software System Design for Learning Mexican Sign Language with Leap Motion

Teresita Alvarez-Robles[1(✉)], Francisco Álvarez[2], and Mónica Carreño-León[1]

[1] Universidad Autónoma de Baja California Sur, Sur KM5.5, 23080 La Paz, Mexico
{tj.alvarez,mcarreno}@uabcs.mx

[2] Universidad Autónoma de Aguascalientes, Av. Universidad 940, 20131 Aguascalientes, Mexico
fjalvar@correo.uaa.mx

Abstract. The main objective of this work is to carry out a proposal of an interactive software system (ISS) design that makes use a Hardware device (Hw) "Leap Motion" and is centered average users as an interactive solution for communication with deaf people is feasible.

With this proposal we hoped to achieve a natural recognition of hand movements, in this way will be obtained a support system for the average user in the learning of Mexican Sign Language (MSL) and, through gamification techniques applied to the ISS, the user can learn and communicate with a person with hearing impairment.

To carry out this proposal we review the literature, in general we can observed that several of the papers consider another type of sign language or another technique for the recognition of signs, therefore, the number of papers that specifically focus on the "Mexican Sign Language" learning and that use the Hw of "Leap Motion" is considerably reduced.

Which allows us to conclude that the proposal for the design of an ISS for training in the learning of Mexican Sign Language for average people is feasible not only by using an Hw tool that allows communication and interpretation of MSL and gamification techniques, It also has the support of related papers which guarantee that the "Leap Motion" is a tool that can be used for such action.

Keywords: Access to education and learning · Design for all education and training · Design for quality of life technologies · Evaluation of accessibility · Usability · User experience

1 Introduction

Mexico's National Survey of Demographic Dynamics (ENADID) reported in 2014 that there are 7,184,054 persons with disabilities in Mexico – or 6% of the population - 2,405,855 of whom have hearing disabilities [1].

C. Stephanidis et al. (Eds.): HCII 2020, LNCS 12426, pp. 184–196, 2020.
https://doi.org/10.1007/978-3-030-60149-2_15

People with disabilities face daily and routine barriers to full social participation. Deaf people face a particular barrier when they are invited to an event (of any kind) as communication with others present is difficult. The presence of sign language interpreters is rare in any part of the world, but in Mexico, it is particularly endemic as the most recent date suggests that there are approximately 40 certified MSL interpreters [2].

Providing the necessary tools so that an average person can learn MSL could therefore go a long way to overcoming the problems associated with so few certified interpreters with such a large number of hearing-impaired persons.

There have been studies on the use of hardware tools as support in the field of computer science. Our literature review revealed that there are little to no published works specifically related to Mexican Sign Language and the use of a hardware device, including the "Leap Motion" device, for learning it.

This paper proposes the following:

- Leap Motion (and other hardware) can be used to learn, and to support learning, of MSL (Based on the literature review).
- This can be done by average, or non-professional persons.
- Supporting the average user also provides the convenience to collaterally support and enhance communication between and the hearing impaired and the non-hearing impaired.

2 Mexican Sign Language and Related Works

Mexican sign language – which originates from the French sign language family – is used and "spoken" by an estimated 130,000 people [3].

As with any language, it has its own syntax, grammar, lexicon [4]; Mexicans express themselves and communicate with visual within a Mexican linguistic structure. Hand gestures and movement are very important as it represents a large percentage of communication. The movement of hands, body, and arms, the forms that are made, the orientation, as well as the facial gestures all allow the interlocutor to better understand meanings, emotions, emphasis, along with the content of communication that is conveyed [4].

A sign language consists of three main parts:

1. Manual features.
2. Non-manual features.
3. Finger spelling.

Hence, a sign language involves several features which have, as main component, the hands [5].

The Mexican Sign Language consists of a series of articulated gestures signs with a linguistic function that is part of the linguistic heritage of the community and is as complex in grammar and vocabulary as any oral language.

Although sign languages are very useful, there is still a barrier between speakers and deaf people because the recipient of the message must know the symbols in order to understand it. As a consequence, the communication, and the process of communicating, can either break down or be non-existant.

Taking into account the above, we consider it important that a hearing person has access to learning Mexican Sign Language naturally (using a non-invasive Hw device) through an interactive software system (ISS). As a consequence, we expect an increase in the number of people who know and can use MSL which will in turn promote and facilitate the inclusion of Mexico's hearing-impaired population.

2.1 Hand Alphabet

MSL studies can be grouped into two categories: static sign recognition and dynamic sign recognition [6]. Static signs include most of the letters of the hand alphabet that are made with a specific fixed posture of the hand. Dynamic signs involve the movement of one or both hands to perform a letter of the manual alphabet, a word or a statement.

MSL is composed of more than 1000 different signs which have regional variations, MSL hand alphabet has 29 signs (see Fig. 1) corresponding to letters: A, B, C, D, E, F, G, H, I, J, K, L, LL, M, N, Ñ, O, P, Q, R, S, T, U, V, W, X, Y, Z.

This work focuses on a first phase of learning the alphabet and greetings. Therefore, the aim is an ISS that focuses on the recognition of static signs, as is the case of [5,7–11].

Much of the existing literature focuses on artificial intelligence (AI), fuzzy logic and various sensors, including the Kinect. Others focus on aspects such as number learning [13], medical issues [14–16], videogames [17,18], or another type of sign language [19–22], who perform hand gesture recognition with a sensor known as "Leap Motion", which has a very good response to the development of systems that involve hand gestures.

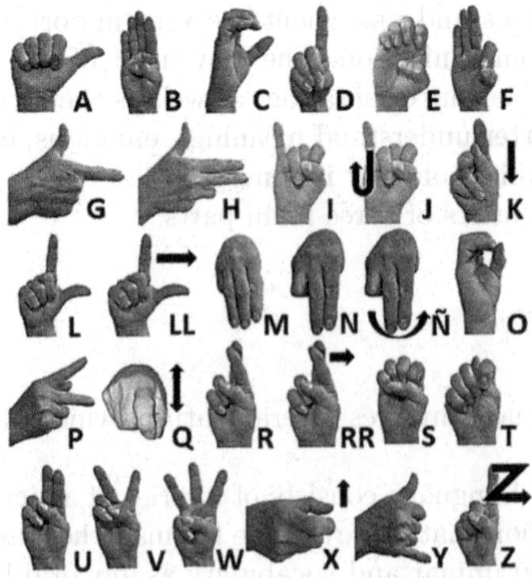

Fig. 1. MSL alphabet. Source: [6]

2.2 Leap Motion

The Leap Motion Controller (LM) is an optical hand tracking module that captures the movements of the hands with unparalleled accuracy and use a simple sensor that detects the hands (see Fig. 2) [23].

The Leap Motion Controller in conjunction with the hand tracking software captures all the subtlety and complexity of natural hand movements [23]. The LEDs of the Leap Motion Controller illuminate the hands with infrared light (see Fig. 3).

According to the manufacturer, the Leap Motion Controller is designed to provide real-time tracking of hands and fingers in a tridimensional space with 0.01-mm accuracy, according to the manufactured.

The positions of the hands and fingertips are detected in coordinates relative to the center of the controller, taking as reference the right-handed coordinate system and millimeters as the unit. Several gestures can be natively identified by the LM such us swipe gesture, circle gesture, key tap gesture and screen tap gesture [24].

The characteristics of the LM have resulted in a number of studies and papers on the recognition of hand gestures [13,25,26] to name a few. These studies, among others, highlight current interest in the recognition of hand gestures regarding Human-Computer Interaction (HCI) [27].

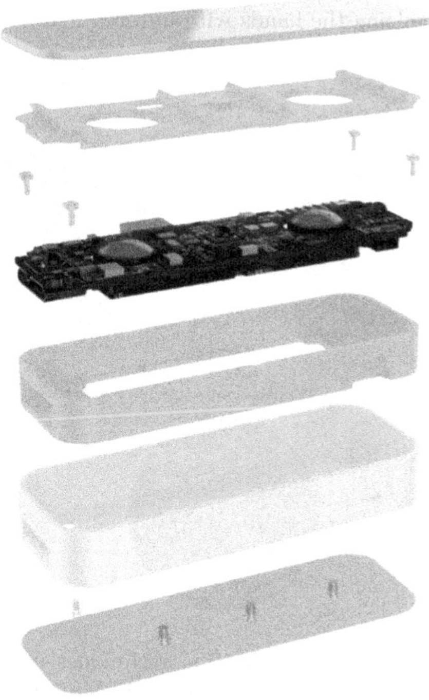

Fig. 2. Sensors of Leap Motion Controller that recognize the hands Source: [23]

Although there are works that specifically focus on the recognition of hand gestures using Leap Motion or Microsoft Kinect in different areas, none of them focuses on the recognition of the Mexican sign language alphabet using Leap Motion. The majority of papers in Mexican Sign Language has been performed using Kinect (67%) followed by camera (33%), (see Fig. 4) [3].

Further, works on MSL have been done for static signs (67%) followed by dynamic signs (33%). Therefore, 100% of the research has been performed on isolated signs only. Finally, it has been observed that 67% of work in MSL has been performed on single handed signs and followed by 33% using both single and double handed signs as shown in Fig. 4 [3].

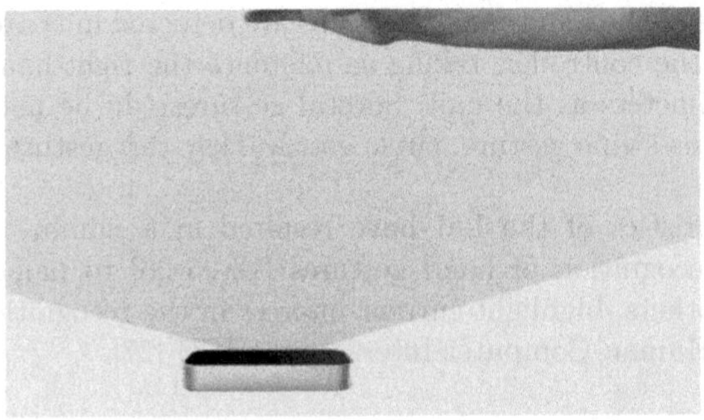

Fig. 3. Recognizing the hands with infrared light. Source: [23]

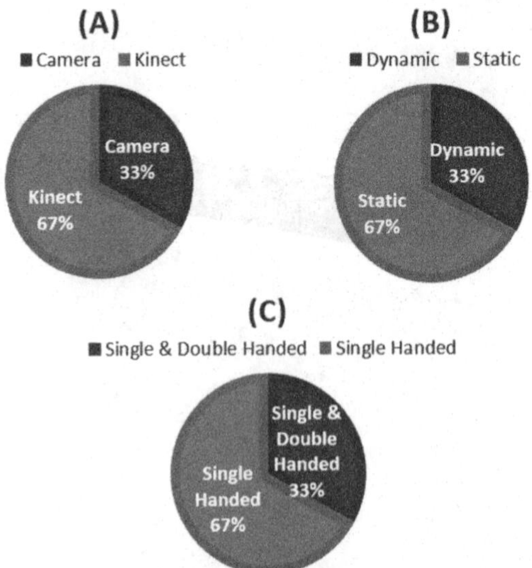

Fig. 4. A) Usage of different data acquisition techniques used in MSL systems. B) Research work carried out on static/dynamic signs in MSL. C) Percentage of research work carried out on the basis of singledouble handed signs in MSL. Source: [3]

Based on this, and the features of Leap Motion, we propose the design of an ISS that supports the learning of Mexican Sign Language among the non-hearing impaired.

3 Proposal of an Interactive Software System Design for Learning the MSL

Key to this proposal is the basis of its design. The ISS will be designed for the non-hearing impaired, who will make use of a Natural User Interface (NUI). Using Ben Schneiderman's 8 Golden Rules of Interface Design will help guarantee that the interface will be intuitive for the user.

Shneiderman's collection of principles are derived heuristically from experience and applicable in most interactive systems after being refined, extended, and interpreted [28]:

- Strive for consistency.
- Enable frequent users to use shortcuts.
- Offer informative feedback.
- Design dialog to yield closure.
- Offer simple error handling.
- Permit easy reversal of actions.
- Support internal locus of control.
- Reduce short-term memory load.

This research will adopt the eight Golden Rules of Interface design for the design. For example, to comply with the first rule, consistency, the system's icons, menu, color, among other things, will be consistent.

3.1 Proposal of Design for the ISS

This ISS design proposal will use the Leap Motion sensor and workstation (PC) (see Fig. 5). The function of the LM sensor is to recognize the hand gestures corresponding to the MSL, in turn, the PC will process the ISS with which the user will have a natural interaction.

The main idea is to manage levels within the ISS by applying gamification techniques to promote learning in users who are interested in learning MSL. In this way the user will gradually learn different aspects of the MSL by interacting with the system through the Hw Leap Motion device.

To follow Schneiderman's design rules we propose the use of an intuitive main (see Fig. 6) where the user will can select a "basic" level or to undertake and exam for a more "advanced" level (see Fig. 7).

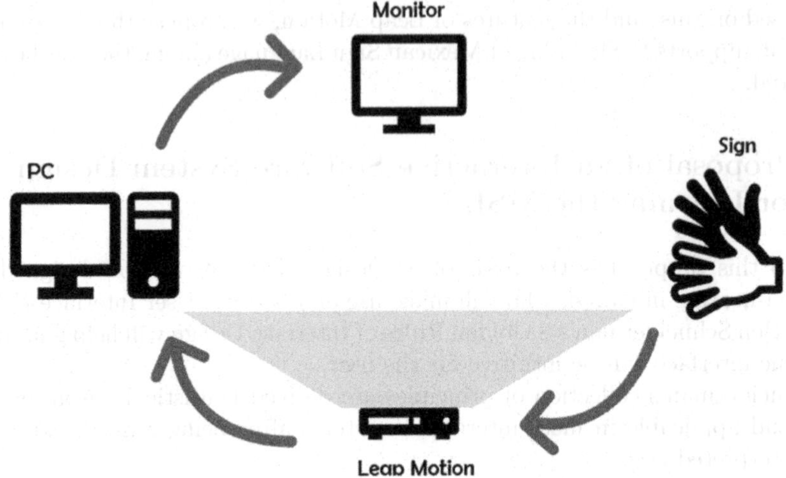

Fig. 5. System architecture. Source: Own creation

Fig. 6. MainScreen of the proposal ISS "DoubleHands". Source: Own creation

After the user enters a level, a series of exercises will be shown that must be performed until the necessary points are obtained to continue with the next lesson and so on until the next level is unlocked (see Fig. 8).

Each time the user finishes a lesson or level, the user will be informed with a message (see Fig. 9).

If you make a mistake somewhere in the lesson, you will be given the option to see the solution and do a practice exercise (see Fig. 10).

Regarding the operation of the ISS with Leap Motion, when the user is in a lesson and is asked to make a particular signal, the LM will obtain a representation of the hand gesture which will compare with that stored in the system database (DB) and if they are equal, the exercise will be marked as correct, otherwise a life will be subtracted and you can continue with the lesson. The representation of the skeleton of the hand created with LM is shown in Fig. 11

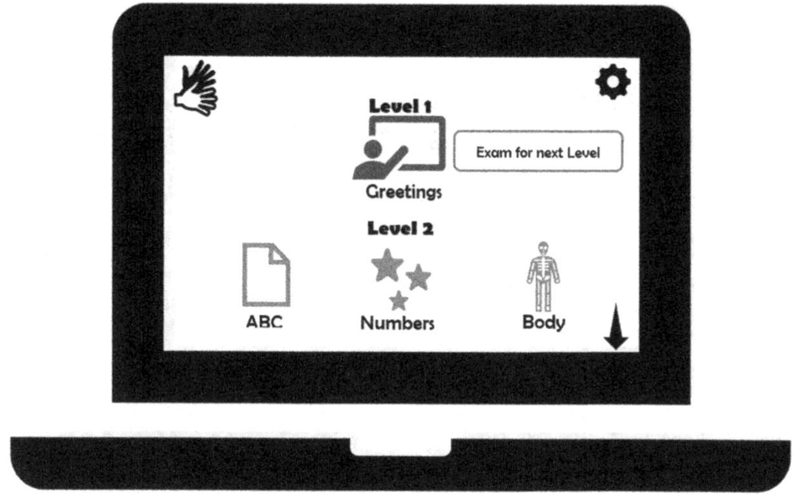

Fig. 7. Level selection. Source: Own creation

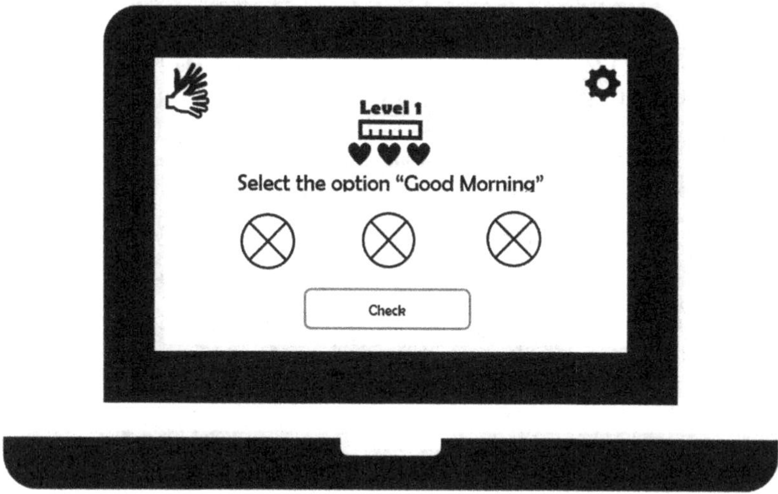

Fig. 8. Exercise example Source: Own creation

and 12. This representation of the hand gesture is analyzed in the ISS to compare and validate the exercise.

As it can be observed, the intention is that the ISS complies with the bases of the design rules for interfaces recommended by Schneiderman and that at the same time the interaction is naturally for the hearing user.

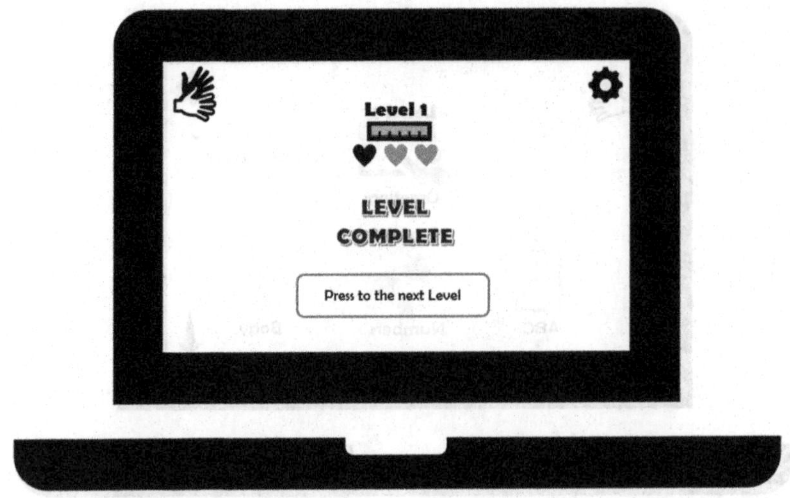

Fig. 9. Screen that will be displayed at the end of a level. Source: Own creation

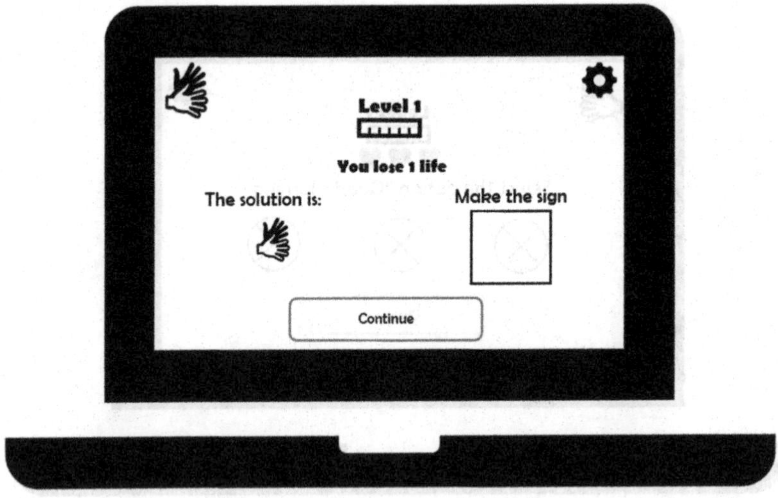

Fig. 10. When the user makes a mistake, the correct sign is displayed and must be imitated with the use of LM. Source: Own creation

Points to Evaluate from the ISS Design Proposal. The expectation is that the ISS design proposal and Shneiderman's interface design rules will ensure a user-friendly interface.

Therefore, in the proposal the first golden rule "Strive for consistency" can be observed in the use of familiar icons to the user, in the colors and in the hierarchy of the elements on the screen (see Fig. 7, 8, 9 and 10).

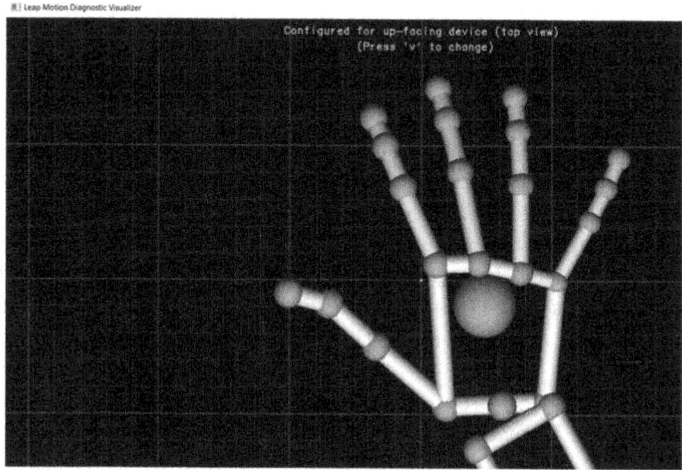

Fig. 11. Hand representation in Leap Motion. Source: Own creation

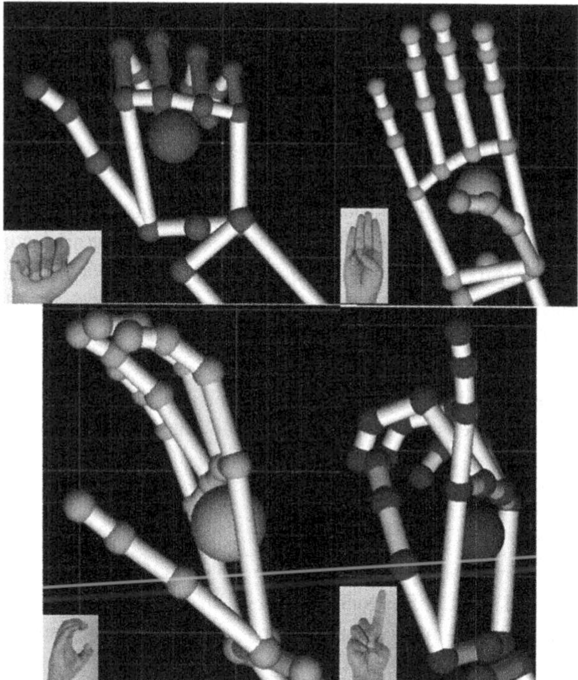

Fig. 12. Recognition of hand movement with Leap Motion. Source: Own creation

Figure 7 demonstrates the second rule - enable frequent users to use shortcuts - in the form a button that allows one to jump a level and another that returns to the beginning.

Figures 8 and 9 illustrate the third rule - information feedbacks - via an information bar highlighting the user's progress.

Ensuring messages are visible to the user will ensure compliance with the fourth rule - "Design dialog to yeld closure" - (see Fig. 9).

The user will have the opportunity to learn and review the element which will in turn give him or her a sense of control over the ISS. This will permit easy reversal of actions (both the fifth and sixth rules).

In order to comply with the seventh rule, the minimum of icons is used in the interface design using the spaces in the appropriate manner, thus trying to make the interface as simple as possible for the user, thus avoiding that it is difficult to remember a way to reach the option you are looking for within the ISS.

At first glance, the ISS proposal will therefore comply with the 8 Schneiderman rules. This will be evaluated by using the "Thinking Aloud" method, this method evaluates a set of tasks the user must perform to verify that all of the elements in the system design proposal are intuitive and can solve any situation.

4 Conclusions and Future Works

The Leap Motion Controller is an effective hardware tool in recognizing hand gestures in different areas. We propose that this tool, when used in tandem with a natural user interface, will allow an average user to learn Mexican Sign Language.

Phase 1 and Phase 2 (which is pending) would involve the "interface" and the "DB of Mexican Sign Language" respectively. Phase 3 would correspond with the analysis and design validation of the ISS. It may be that the design rules can be achieved and seen with the naked eye, however, corresponding validation tests must be performed for greater certainty.

Acknowledgement. I want to thank E. Girard for support in the revision/correction of this paper and in the case of A. Cruz for making all the convenient reviews to improve it.

References

1. SEDESOL-CONADIS La Sordoceguera en México: datos por el 27 de junio, día internacional de la sordoceguera. https://www.gob.mx/conadis/es/articulos/la-sordoceguera-en-mexico-datos-por-el-27-de-junio-dia-internacional-de-la-sordoceguera?idiom=es. Accessed 6 Jan 2020
2. SIPSE En México se hacen ciegos ante los sordos. https://sipse.com/mexico/sordos-discapacidad-gobierno-mexico-224324.html. Accessed 6 Jan 2020
3. Wadhawan, A., Kumar, P.: Sign language recognition systems: a decade systematic literature review. Arch. Comput. Methods Eng. 1–29 (2019)
4. Gobierno de México. https://www.gob.mx/conadis/articulos/lengua-de-senas-mexicana-lsm?idiom=es. Accessed 6 Jan 2020

5. Trujillo-Romero, F., Caballero-Morales, S.-O.: 3D data sensing for hand pose recognition. In: CONIELECOMP 2013, 23rd International Conference on Electronics, Communications and Computing, pp. 109–113. IEEE (2013)
6. Sosa-Jímenez, C., Ríos-Figueroa, H., Rechy-Ramírez, E., Marin-Hernandez, A., González-Cosío, A.: Real-time Mexican Sign Language recognition. In: 2017 IEEE International Autumn Meeting on Power, Electronics and Computing (ROPEC), pp. 1–6. IEEE (2017)
7. Luis-Pérez, F.E., Trujillo-Romero, F., Martínez-Velazco, W.: Control of a service robot using the Mexican sign language. In: Batyrshin, I., Sidorov, G. (eds.) MICAI 2011. LNCS (LNAI), vol. 7095, pp. 419–430. Springer, Heidelberg (2011). https://doi.org/10.1007/978-3-642-25330-0_37
8. Solís, J.-F., Toxqui-Quitl, C., Martínez-Martínez, D., Margarita, H.-G.: Mexican sign language recognition using normalized moments and artificial neural networks. In: Optics and Photonics for Information Processing VIII, pp. 92161A. ISOP (2014)
9. Galicia, R., Carranza, O., Jiménez, E.-D., Rivera, G.-E.: Mexican sign language recognition using movement sensor. In: 2015 IEEE 24th International Symposium on Industrial Electronics (ISIE), pp. 573–578. IEEE (2015)
10. López, E., Velásquez, J., Eleuterio, R., Gil, L.: Interfaz de reconocimiento de movimientos para el lenguaje de señas mexicano implementando el Kinect. Revista Aristas: Investigación Básica y Aplicada **4**(7), 130–133 (2015)
11. Solís, F., Martínez, D., Espinoza, O.: Automatic Mexican sign language recognition using normalized moments and artificial neural networks. Engineering **8**(10), 733–740 (2016)
12. Jimenez, J., Martin, A., Uc, V., Espinosa, A.: Mexican sign language alphanumerical gestures recognition using 3D Haar-like features. IEEE Latin Am. Trans. **15**(10), 2000–2005 (2017)
13. Wang, Q., Wang, Y., Liu, F., Zeng, W.: Hand gesture recognition of Arabic numbers using leap motion via deterministic learning. In: 2017 36th Chinese Control Conference (CCC), pp. 10873–10828. IEEE (2017)
14. Li, W.-J., Hsieh, C.-Y., Lin, L.-F., Chu, W.-C.: Hand gesture recognition for post-stroke rehabilitation using leap motion. In: 2017 International Conference on Applied System Innovation (ICASI), pp. 386–388. IEEE (2017)
15. Morando, M., Ponte, S., Ferrara, E., Dellepiane, S.: Biophysical and motion features extraction for an effective home-based rehabilitation. In: Proceedings of the International Conference on Bioinformatics Research and Applications 2017, pp. 79–85. ACM (2017)
16. Nicola, S., Stoicu-Tivadar, L., Virag, I., Crişan-Vida, M.: Leap motion supporting medical education. In: 2016 12th IEEE International Symposium on Electronics and Telecommunications (ISETC), pp. 153–156. IEEE (2016)
17. Dzikri, A., Kurniawan, D.-E.: Hand gesture recognition for game 3D object using the leap motion controller with backpropagation method. In: 2018 International Conference on Applied Engineering (ICAE), pp. 1–5. IEEE (2018)
18. Zhi, D., de Oliveira, T.-E.-A., da Fonseca, V.-P., Petriu, E.-M.: Teaching a robot sign language using vision-based hand gesture recognition. In: 2018 IEEE International Conference on Computational Intelligence and Virtual Environments for Measurement Systems and Applications (CIVEMSA), pp. 1–6. IEEE (2018)
19. Mapari, R., Kharat, G.: American static signs recognition using leap motion sensor. In: Proceedings of the Second International Conference on Information and Communication Technology for Competitive Strategies, p. 67. ACM (2016)

20. Kotsidou, D., Angelis, C., Dragoumanos, S., Kakarountas, A.: Computer assisted gesture recognition for the Greek sign language/fingerspelling. In: Proceedings of the 19th Panhellenic Conference on Informatics, pp. 241–242. ACM (2015)
21. Chavan, P., Ghorpade, T., Padiya, P.: Indian sign language to forecast text using leap motion sensor and RF classifier. In: 2016 Symposium on Colossal Data Analysis and Networking (CDAN), pp. 1–5. IEEE (2016)
22. Anwar, A., Basuki, A., Sigit, R., Rahagiyanto, A., Zikky, M.: Feature extraction for Indonesian sign language (SIBI) using leap motion controller. In: 2017 21st International Computer Science and Engineering Conference (ICSEC), pp. 1–5. IEEE (2017)
23. Ultraleap. https://www.ultraleap.com/product/leap-motion-controller/. Accessed 13 Jan 2020
24. Ameur, S., Khalifa, A.-B., Bouhlel, M.-S.: A comprehensive leap motion database for hand gesture recognition. In: 2016 7th International Conference on Sciences of Electronics, Technologies of Information and Telecommunications (SETIT), pp. 514–519. IEEE (2016)
25. Sharma, A., Yadav, A., Srivastava, S., Gupta, R.: Analysis of movement and gesture recognition using leap motion controller. Procedia Comput. Sci. **132**, 551–556 (2018)
26. Zeng, W., Wang, C., Wang, Q.: Hand gesture recognition using leap motion via deterministic learning. Multimedia Tools Appl. **77**(21), 28185–28206 (2018). https://doi.org/10.1007/s11042-018-5998-1
27. Chaudhary, A., Raheja, J.-L., Das, K., Raheja, S.: Intelligent approaches to interact with machines using hand gesture recognition in natural way: a survey. arXiv preprint arXiv:1303.2292 (2013)
28. Yamakami, T.: A four-stage gate-keeper model of social service engineering: lessons from golden rules of mobile social game design. In: 2012 9th International Conference on Ubiquitous Intelligence and Computing and 9th International Conference on Autonomic and Trusted Computing, pp. 159–163. IEEE (2012)

Designing a Tangible User Interface for Braille Teaching

Mónica Carreño-León(✉), J. Andrés Sandoval-Bringas(✉), Teresita Alvarez-Robles, Rafael Cosio-Castro, Italia Estrada Cota, and Alejandro Leyva Carrillo

Universidad Autónoma de Baja California Sur, La Paz, B.C.S., Mexico
{mcarreno,sandoval,tj.alvarez,iestrada,aleyva}@uabcs.mx, r.cosiocastro@gmail.com

Abstract. Nowadays, technology is present in all aspects of daily life. In many schools children use computers as part of their learning process. Attention to people with different abilities has been a topic of interest to different areas of science and technology. The development of new technologies focused on this issue is of vital importance as it allows improving the quality of life and incorporation into society.

Special education needs new applications that allow teaching in an innovative way helping to improve the education of its students according to their specific needs. Attention to people with special needs is a growing area in society. This paper presents the development of a support tool for learning the Braille system. The design of an interactive concept with the integration of tangible elements and software applications is proposed. The proposed user interface is an RFID reader board and a set of objects with RFID tags so that they can be recognized by the software. Each of the objects represents the letters in the Braille system, which were made with a 3D printer and the RFID code was inserted through a card in a slot next to the object. The proposal was evaluated at first by special education teachers and at second by a child, obtaining favorable results in both case studies.

Keywords: Tangible UI · Braille teaching · Blindness

1 Introduction

The vision represents a central role in the autonomy and development of any person and, especially, during child development. Visual impairment limits the work, intellectual and social development of people who suffer from it. Nowadays, technology is present in all aspects of daily life. Attention to people with different abilities has been a topic of interest to different areas of science and technology. The development of new technologies focused on this issue is of vital importance as it allows improving the quality of life and incorporation into society.

C. Stephanidis et al. (Eds.): HCII 2020, LNCS 12426, pp. 197–207, 2020.
https://doi.org/10.1007/978-3-030-60149-2_16

1.1 Blindness and Vision Impairment

Disability is the life condition of a person, acquired during pregnancy, birth or childhood, which is manifested by significant limitations in intellectual, motor, sensory (vision and hearing) and adaptive behavior [1].

Visual impairment is defined based on visual acuity and the field of vision. There is talk of visual impairment when there is a significant decrease in visual acuity even with the use of lenses, or a significant decrease in the visual field. Visual acuity is the ability of a subject to perceive clearly and clearly the shape and shape of objects at a certain distance. The visual field refers to the portion of space that an individual can see without moving his head or eyes. A person with normal vision has a visual field of 150° horizontally and 140° vertically.

The WHO (World Health Organization) classifies visual function into four levels: normal vision, moderate vision impairment, severe visual impairment and blindness. Where moderate vision disability and severe visual impairment are structured as low vision, low vision together with blindness as a whole are the general cases of visual impairment [2].

In Mexico, according to data from INEGI (for its acronym in Spanish) 7 million 650 thousand people reported having some disability, which represents 6.4% of the total population, of which 1 million 561 thousand people have visual impairment. Within the group of visually impaired people, 63.5% do not use some kind of technical help, and only 4.6% use the Braille system [3].

1.2 Braille System

The braille or language system for the blind is used by people with visual impairment or blindness to write and read. The blind read by touch, by sliding their fingers over an alphabet specially designed for them [4].

The Braille method is a reading system for people with visual impairment, it consists of six points in relief (generating sign), whose combination produces all the letters of the alphabet, the mathematical signs and musical notes. The different combinations of these six points allow obtaining seventy-three signs or characters [4, 5]. Despite its effectiveness in the access of blind people to information, reading and study, the Braille method is rarely used.

Braille is a tool of great help to blind people to acquire all the information they need and develop at a cognitive and intellectual level, in addition to providing great autonomy. It is their usual form of contact with culture and written media and their main learning channel. A blind child can, through Braille, access the same degree of knowledge as students of the same age and with a similar learning pace.

In order to learn to read in Braille, three things are basically needed: Developing touch, Learning the code and Reading animation [4]. To be able to read and write Braille, children need to learn not only each letter of the Braille alphabet, but also its image in the mirror. Also, it is only known if they have written it correctly when the page is turned. The entire process represents a great challenge for young children who are learning to read and write. Figure 1 shows the Braille alphabet.

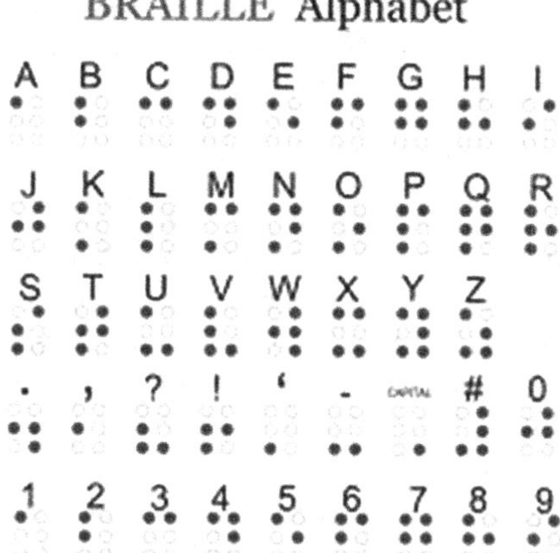

Fig. 1. Braille alphabet, punctuation and numbers

Learning and familiarization with the Braille method is done progressively. Children initially work exercising sensory development and especially touch, handling sheets and puzzles that help them distinguish textures and simple shapes. Little by little, children begin to learn the sequence of reading from left to right, to handle basic numerical concepts and to coordinate both hands to distinguish three-dimensional shapes. The first contacts are in the form of a game.

1.3 Tangible User Interfaces

Attention to the disabled has been an issue of interest to the different areas of science and technology. The development of new technologies focused on disability is of vital importance as it allows improving the quality of life and incorporation into society.

Tangible user interfaces (TUI) are user interfaces in which people interact with digital information through physical environments. Various studies show that tangible interfaces are useful because they promote active participation, which helps in the learning process. These interfaces do not intimidate the inexperienced user and encourage exploratory, expressive and experimental activities.

TUIs have been shown to enhance learning for children by enriching their experience, play and development [6, 7]. The use of tangible interaction in educational settings has gained importance, and has been the focus of study through different investigations [8–14].

Some authors mention the need for TUIs for people with physical or cognitive disabilities [15, 16], other authors express their importance for older adults [17], as well as in early childhood [6, 18–20]. In other words, these interfaces can have great potential for all people, which is why some authors also consider their use in a general way, independent of physical and cognitive abilities, simply because of their practicality and improvement in the concretion of certain tasks [21, 22].

Taking into account the above, the design of an interactive system with the integration of tangible elements and application software is proposed, in order to support the learning process of the Braille system mainly of blind children.

2 Methodology

For the construction of the tool, the life cycle model called the evolutionary prototype was adopted. The evolutionary prototype is based on the idea of developing an initial implementation by exposing it to the user's comments and refining it through the different versions until an adequate system is developed, allowing responding quickly to the changes that may occur.

For the design of the interactive system of tangible interfaces, work meetings were held with experts in the area of special education, as well as basic education teachers. The meetings analyzed the strategies for learning the Braille system, as well as the fundamental requirements and characteristics of the system elements.

Figure 2 shows the scheme of the components of the interactive system of tangible user interfaces and software applications: a) The tangible user interface, b) The RFID reader board and c) The software that allows interaction with the RFID reader board and the tangible user interface.

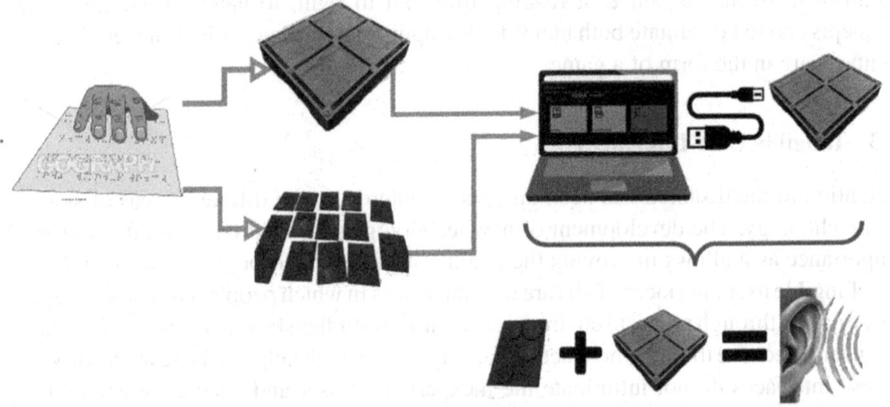

Fig. 2. Scheme of the interactive system of tangible user interfaces and software applications

In the meetings that were held, the following requirements could be identified:

- Design tangible objects for each of the braille system symbols.
- Consider that the size of tangible objects is appropriate for the handling of children aged 4–10 years.
- Design a board that allows the reading of each of the tangible objects and allows communication with the software.
- Design the software that generates the audio of the corresponding symbol in the Braille system.
- Design the software that allows the configuration of the tangible objects that will be used.
- That the software allows interaction with the user in game mode.

2.1 Tangible User Interface

Historically, children have played with physical objects to learn a variety of skills, a tangible interface (TUI), therefore, it would seem like a natural way for them [23].

During the first phase for the development of the tool, the TUIs were designed and created with a 3D printer, for each of the braille system symbols. Figure 3 shows the TUI design of both the front and rear. The distribution of the 6 points that form the braille system generator sign is shown in relief on the front. On the back of the object an RFID card associated with the braille symbol is inserted, which allows communication with the RFID reader board.

Fig. 3. Physical design of the tangible user interface on both sides

2.2 RFID Reader Board

During the second phase of the development of the tool, the RFID reader board was designed, which allows the communication of each of the tangible objects with the developed software. RFID (Radio Frequency Identification) technology allows the use of real objects to interact with the computer, reducing the symbolic load of the interface, simplifying it by making it more natural and improving accessibility. Unlike other tags, RFID tags are immersed in objects without altering their attributes or interfering with user perception.

The basic components that were used for the construction of the RFID reader board are:

1) **Arduino mega board.** A mega Arduino board was used, which consists of an electronic board that is based on an ATmega2560 microcontroller. It has 54 digital pins that function as input/output, 16 analog inputs, a 16 MHz oscillator crystal, a USB connection, a reset button and an input for the board power [24].
2) **RFID-RC522 chip reader.** Four chip readers were used. RFID readers are mainly used in identification systems. Its principle of operation is to pass a tag near the RFID reader, and the tag has the ability to send information to the reader. The information can be from a simple code or a whole package of information stored in the tag's memory.

Figure 4 shows the connection diagram of the components used in the RFID reader board.

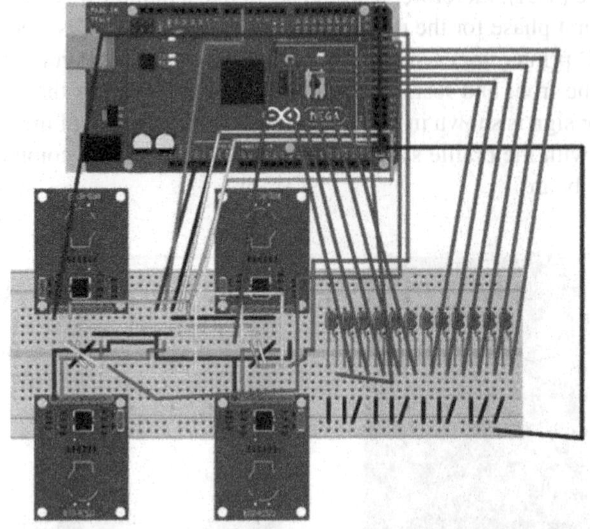

Fig. 4. Electronic components connection diagram of the RFID reader board

Figure 5 shows the design of the container that groups the electronic components used for the operation of the RFID reader board. The module connects to a computer through a USB port.

Fig. 5. Physical design of the electronic components container of the RFID reader board

2.3 Software to Interact with Tangible Interfaces

During the third phase the software was developed that allows the interaction of the TUI with the RFID reader board and the user. The main user of the software is the facilitator who is in charge of the teaching-learning process of the Braille system. The software allows interactive system setting.

Figure 6 shows the initial interface of the interactive system, where the main setting options are shown: library, card registration and learning braille.

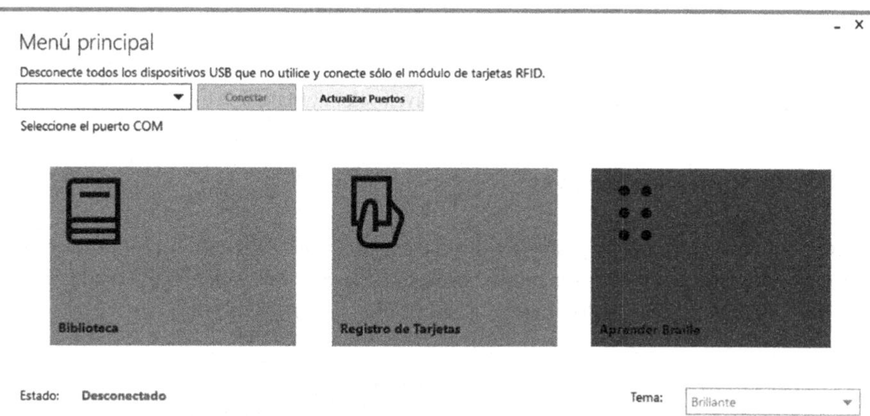

Fig. 6. Initial interface of the interactive system of tangible user interfaces

1) **History option.** This option allows you to check previously stored records.
2) **Card registration option.** This option allows you to register new RFID codes to be recognized by the system.
3) **Learn braille option.** This option allows you to select the modes available for the child's interaction with the system.

The software allows the user to interact in two ways:

1) **Learn mode.** This mode allows knowing each of the braille system symbols represented in the TUI. The user can bring each of the TUIs to the RFID reader board, and once he identifies the RFID card code, the corresponding audio is emitted by the speaker.
2) **Play mode.** This mode allows the user to demonstrate that he knows each of the braille system symbols. Randomly, the user is requested to bring the corresponding TUI to the RFID reader board. During the game, a feedback is included, so that the user knows if his selection was correct or incorrect. If the choice was incorrect, the user is asked to try again.

Figure 7 shows the play mode interface, which serves as a guide for the facilitator during the teaching-learning process.

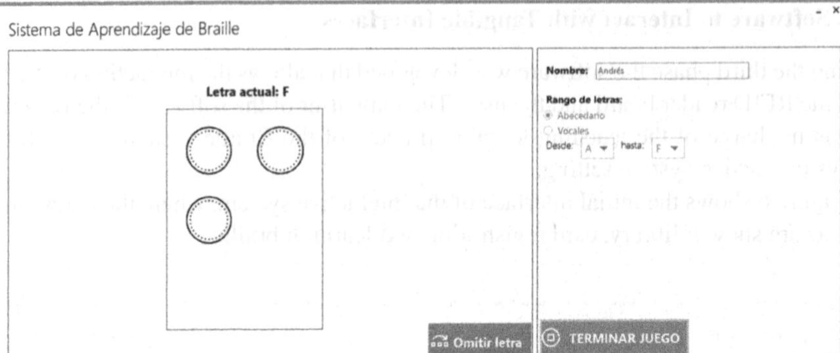

Fig. 7. Play mode interface of the interactive system of tangible user interfaces.

3 Results and Conclusions

The interactive system developed provides a technological environment to facilitate the learning of the Braille system for blind children. Figure 8 shows the RFID reader board as well as some of the tangible objects of the braille system symbols.

Fig. 8. RFID reader board and tangible interfaces

Two case studies allowed knowing the level of acceptance of the proposal of the interactive system of tangible user interfaces. In the first case study, the tool was presented to four teachers in the special education area, who reviewed each of the aspects of the tool. Additionally, they were given a questionnaire that was used to quantify the assessment of the tool. The questions were based on usability criteria of the interactive system, and whose objective was to know if the tool met the requirements of the interactive system operation. The results obtained were favorable, experts agree that the tool meets the requirements, and that its use is viable in children with visual impairment. It is important to mention that one of the experts who evaluated the tool is blind from birth.

For the second case study, an educational institution was visited where the test was conducted with a child, who used the tool with the help of a special education teacher. During the test phase it was observed that the child did not present problems when using the interactive system, on the contrary, he showed quite interest. The results obtained in the evaluation of the tool with the user are considered favorable. In Fig. 9 the child can be seen interacting with the system of tangible interfaces.

Fig. 9. Test session of the interactive system of tangible interfaces.

There is a diverse society, with different ways of thinking, learning and acting. The educational system must know how to include this diversity, value it and offer answers in each situation. The development of ICT has positively benefited many sectors of society, including education. The integration of ICT facilitates the possibility of integration of students who have special educational needs.

References

1. CONAFE: Discapacidad visual. Guía didáctica para la inclusión en educación inicial y básica, México (2010)
2. WHO. https://www.who.int/news-room/fact-sheets/detail/blindness-and-visual-impairment. Accessed 21 Dec 2019

3. INEGI: Discapacidad: La discapacidad en México datos al 2014 (2014)
4. Martínez-Liébana, I., Polo-Chacón, D.: Guía didáctica para la lectoescritura Braille. ONCE, Madrid (2004)
5. Jawasreh, Z., Ashaari, N., Dahnil, D.: Braille tutorial model using braille fingers puller. In: 6th International Conference Electrical Engineering and Informatics (ICEEI) (2017)
6. Xie, L., Antle, A., Motamedi, N.: Are tangibles more fun? Comparing children's enjoyment and engagement using physical, graphical and tangible user interfaces. In: 2nd International Conference on Tangible and Embedded Interaction, Bonn, Germany (2008)
7. Zaman, B., Abeele, V.: How to measure the likeability of tangible interactin with preschoolers, de CHI Nederland (2007)
8. O'Malley, C.: Literature Review in Learning with Tangible Technologies. NESTA Futurelab (2004)
9. Price, S.: A representation approach to conceptualizing tangible learning environments. In: TEI 2008, Bonn, Alemania (2008)
10. Marshall, P.: Do tangible interfaces enhance learning?. In: TEI 2007, Baton Rouge, LA, USA (2007)
11. Manches, A., O'Malley, C., Benford, S.: The role of physical representations in solving number problems: a comparison of young children's use of physical and virtual materials. Comput. Educ. **54**, 622–640 (2009)
12. Zufferey, G., Jermann, P.L.A., Dillenbourg, P.: TinkerSheets: Using Paper Forms to Control and Visualize Tangible Simulations (2009)
13. Guisen, A., Baldasarri, S., Sanz, C., Marco, J., De Giusti, A., Cerezo, E.: Herramienta de apoyo basada en Interacción Tangible para el desarrollo de competencias comunicacionales en usuarios de CAA. In: VI Congreso Iberoamericano de Tecnologías de Apoyo a la Discapacidad (IBERDISCAP 2011), Palma de Mallorca, España (2011)
14. Sanz, C., Baldassarri, S., Guisen, A., Marco, J., Cerezo, E., De Giusti, A.: ACoTI: herramienta de interacción tangible para el desarrollo de competencias comunicacionales en usuarios de comunicación alternativa. Primeros resultados de su evaluación. In: VII Congreso de Tecnología en Educación y Educación en Tecnología., Buenos Aires, Argentina (2012)
15. Muro Haro, B.P., Santana Mancilla, P.C., García Ruiz, M.A.: Uso de interfaces tangibles en la enseñanza de lectura a niños con síndrome de Down. El hombre y la máquina, no **39**, 19–25 (2012)
16. Avila-Soto, M., Valderrama-Bahamóndez, E., Schmidt, A.: TanMath: a tangible math application to support children with visual impairment to learn basic arithmetic. In: 10th International Conference on Pervasive Technologies Related to Assistive Environments, ACM (2017)
17. Galiev, R., Rupprecht, D., Bomsdorf, B.: Towards tangible and distributed UI for cognitively impaired people. In: Antona, M., Stephanidis, C. (eds.) UAHCI 2017. LNCS, vol. 10278, pp. 283–300. Springer, Cham (2017). https://doi.org/10.1007/978-3-319-58703-5_21
18. González González, C.S.: Revisión de la literatura sobre interfaces naturales para el aprendizaje en la etapa infantil (2017)
19. Devi, S., Deb, S.: Augmenting non-verbal communication using a tangible user interface. In: Satapathy, S.C., Bhateja, V., Das, S. (eds.) Smart Computing and Informatics. SIST, vol. 77, pp. 613–620. Springer, Singapore (2018). https://doi.org/10.1007/978-981-10-5544-7_60
20. Bouabid, A., Lepreux, S., Kolski, C.: Design and evaluation of distributed user interfaces between tangible tabletops. Univ. Access Inf. Soc. **18**(4), 801–819 (2017). https://doi.org/10.1007/s10209-017-0602-4
21. De Raffaele, C., Serengul, S., Orhan, G.: Explaining multi-threaded task scheduling using tangible user interfaces in higuer educational contexts. In: Global Engineering Education Conference (2017)

22. Dimitra, A., Ras, E.: A questionnaire-based case study on feedback by a tangible interface. In: Proceedings of the 2017 ACM Workshop on Intelligent Interfaces for Ubiquitous and Smart Learning (2017)
23. Xu, D.: Tangible user interface for children an overview. In: Proceedings of the UCLAN Department of Computing Conference (2005)
24. Arduino, Getting Started with Arduino MEGA2560, (2017). [En línea]. https://www.arduino.cc/en/Guide/ArduinoMega2560

Understanding Pattern Recognition Through Sound with Considerations for Developing Accessible Technologies

Nicole Darmawaskita and Troy McDaniel(✉)

Arizona State University, Mesa, AZ 85212, USA
{ndarmawa,troy.mcdaniel}@asu.edu

Abstract. This work explores whether audio feedback style and user ability influences user techniques, performance, and preference in the interpretation of node graph data among sighted individuals and those who are blind or visually impaired. This study utilized a posttest-only basic randomized design comparing two treatments, in which participants listened to short audio clips describing a sequence of transitions occurring in a node graph. The results found that participants tend to use certain techniques and have corresponding preferences based on their ability. A correlation was also found between equivalently high feedback design performance and lack of overall feedback design preference. These results imply that universal technologies should consider avoiding utilizing design constraints that allow for only one optimal usage technique, especially if that technique is dependent on a user's ability.

Keywords: Assistive technology · Accessible education · Sonification

1 Introduction

In the U.S., educators are required to adapt their lessons to national accessible learning standards [1], but many students who are blind or visually impaired are unable to complete their education, with 22.3% not completing high school and only 15.7% earning a bachelor's degree in 2016 [2]. Accessible education, therefore, has much room for improvement to ensure those with visual impairments have equal opportunity. Node graphs are a commonly used educational aid that have yet to see a popular, modern, and accessible counterpart. In response, this research aims to develop effective accessible node graphs to improve the educational environment for these students.

Prior research found the use of nonspeech feedback, compared to the use of speech-only, in an accessible table, reduced a user's workload, but both feedback methods provided the same effectiveness in performance [3]. Additional research exploring the usage of multimodal feedback in the presentation of graphical information found most participants implemented the same generic technique in their interactions with accessible graphics [4]. A study comparing the usage of various feedback methods to present graph

C. Stephanidis et al. (Eds.): HCII 2020, LNCS 12426, pp. 208–219, 2020.
https://doi.org/10.1007/978-3-030-60149-2_17

concepts found no significant difference in preference nor effectiveness between feedback methods [5], demonstrating a correlation in which participants equally preferred all feedback methods that performed comparably and highly effectively. Additionally, all the highest performing participants used the same generic technique to interpret feedback, while the majority of lower performing participants used a different, albeit less performance-optimized, generic technique [5]. These observations suggest that certain design constraints encourage the usage of certain generic techniques in individuals based on their ability. When considering the wide variety of user ability, the correlation between performance and preference can be explained through individuals performing better and/or finding additional value—such as reduced workload—when interacting with certain design constraints, leading an overall userbase to equally prefer a variety of designs.

The current study explored whether audio feedback style and user ability influenced user techniques, performance, and preference in the interpretation of node graph data among sighted individuals and those who are blind or visually impaired. Specifically, this research seeks to find if relationships exist between feedback style, user techniques, performance, feedback preference, and user ability.

2 Method

2.1 Participants

47 participants were recruited for this IRB-approved study through email lists and referrals by colleagues and friends. Of the participants, 8 individuals were blind or visually impaired, and 39 were sighted. Most of the participants were local Arizona residents, with most of the sighted participants Arizona State University students. Sighted participants received $10 cash compensation, while those who were blind or visually impaired received $25.

2.2 Materials

Node Graph Structure. Participants listened to audio clips describing a sequence of transitions occurring in a unique node graph. For consistency, each node graph contained at most three nodes named 1, 2, and 3, respectively. Each sequence began at node 1 and contained four transitions. Each node in a node graph could transition by either taking a "Left" or a "Right."

Patterns. Each sequence contained either a "Dead End" pattern, "Alternating" pattern, or "No Pattern."

The "Dead End" pattern occurred in a sequence that contained a self-looping node on both "Left" and "Right." Since the "Dead End" pattern could occur in any node, participants were provided with three sub-patterns to clarify which of the three nodes was the "Dead End": "Dead End at 1", "Dead End at 2", and "Dead End at 3" (Fig. 1).

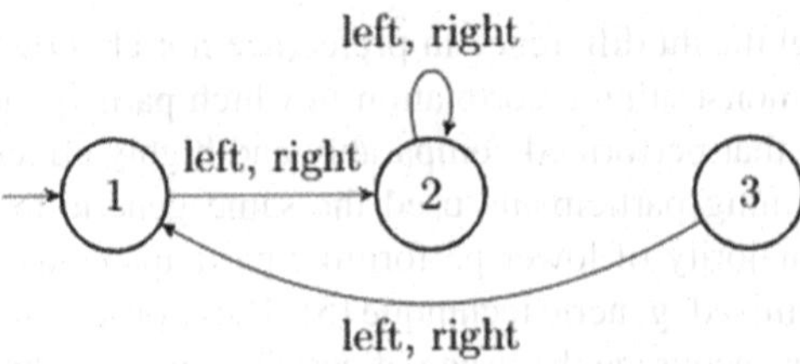

Fig. 1. A sample visualization of a node graph containing the "Dead End at 2" sub-pattern.

The "Alternating" pattern occurred in a sequence that contained the alternation between two nodes in succession through repetitions of either "Left" or "Right." Since the "Alternating" pattern could occur with either transition direction, participants were provided with two sub-patterns to clarify which of the transition directions the sequence was alternating on: "Alternating Left" and "Alternating Right" (Fig. 2).

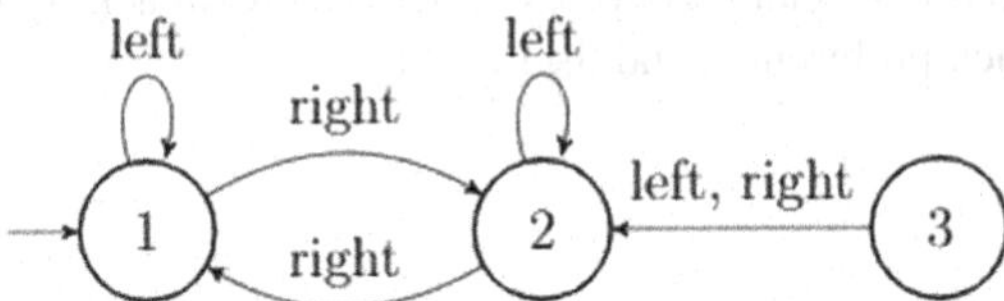

Fig. 2. A sample visualization of a node graph containing the "Alternating Right" sub-pattern.

"No Pattern" occurred in a sequence that contained neither the "Dead End" nor "Alternating" pattern (Fig. 3).

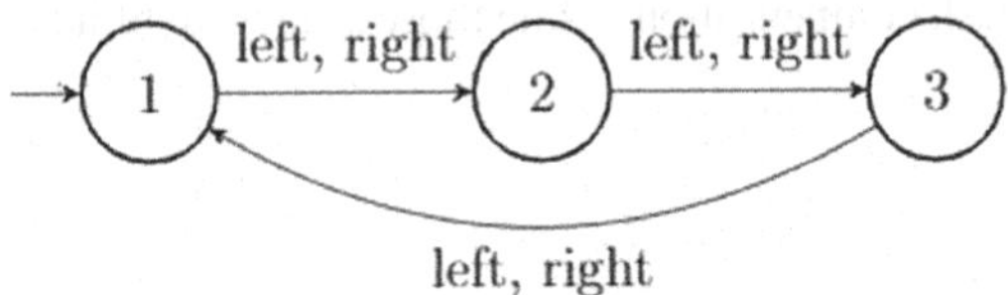

Fig. 3. A sample visualization of a node graph containing "No Pattern."

Audio Feedback Styles. The sequences were presented in two audio styles: Speech-Only and Speech-And-Nonspeech-Sounds. The Speech-Only clips were presented in the form of: "Start at 1. <"Left" or "Right"> <"1", "2", or "3">. <"Left" or "Right"> <"1", "2", or "3">. <"Left" or "Right"> <"1", "2", or "3">. <"Left" or "Right"> <"1", "2", or "3" >." The phrase "Start at 1" indicated the sequence starts at node 1. The use of either a "Left" or "Right" indicated the direction of transition, and the number following indicated the destination node of the transition. The Speech-And-Nonspeech-Sounds clips were presented in a similar form, but "Left" was replaced with a piano tone of High C, and "Right" was replaced with a piano tone of High F#. The audio clips were generated through the combination of the Panopreter Basic text-to-speech software, recordings of piano tones, and the Audacity audio software editor.

For example, the Speech-Only phrase "Start at 1. Left 2. Right 2. Left 2. Right 2." would indicate the "Dead End at 2" pattern as the graph self-loops on node 2 on both transition directions. The Speech-And-Nonspeech-Sounds phrase "Start at 1. <High C> 2. <High C> 3. <High F#> 1. <High F#> 2." would indicate a "No Pattern" sequence as the graph contains neither a self-loop nor successive alternations between nodes.

Audio Feedback Style Training. Participants were introduced to each audio feedback style through respective training phases. Each training phase described its respective audio style structure, how the three patterns would be represented through the audio style and provided three sample audio clips showcasing each pattern for the participant to listen to.

Audio Feedback Style Testing. Participants tested each audio feedback style through respective testing phases. This phase contained nine multiple choice questions displayed in randomized order. Each question contained a unique audio clip of its condition's respective audio style and asked, "Which of the following patterns did you recognize from the audio clip?" The response options were "No pattern (or I don't know)," "Alternating Left," "Alternating Right," "Dead End at 1," "Dead End at 2," and "Dead End at 3."

Post-experiment Survey. A seven-question post-experiment survey was given to participants. Participants were asked to rate on a 5-point scale, from 1 very unintuitive to 5 very intuitive, how intuitive they found each audio feedback style to be in enabling them to identify patterns. Participants were also asked to rate on a 5-point scale, from 1 very difficult to 5 very easy, how easily they were able to identify the nonspeech sounds in the Speech-And-Nonspeech-Sounds audio style. Participants were asked to elaborate on any techniques they used in detecting patterns, which audio style they preferred, and to elaborate on their preference. These responses were used to analyze the participants' spatial hearing abilities, the intuitiveness of the audio styles, common techniques used, design preferences, and the relationship between these components.

2.3 Procedure

Design. This study utilized a posttest-only basic randomized design comparing two treatments. The treatments were the audio feedback styles of Speech-Only and Speech-And-Nonspeech-Sounds. The dependent variables were audio feedback preference and intuitiveness, techniques used, relative pitch ability, and accuracy in the identification of node graph data. Accuracy was used to determine participant and audio feedback performance level. Since the participant pool of individuals who are blind or visually impaired tends to be small, the study utilized a repeated measures design to maximize the sample size for each treatment level. Participants were randomly placed into groups through a trickle process to determine the completion order of the two audio feedback conditions, compensating for any order effects.

Procedure. At the beginning of the study, the participant digitally signed the consent form after reading through it with the study facilitator. The participant then received their cash compensation for the study, and the study began with a short demographic survey.

The participant then listened to short audio clips describing a sequence of transitions occurring in a node graph. Each of these audio clips presented a certain pattern. These transition sequences were presented in two conditions, each with a unique audio feedback style as mentioned above.

The start of each condition included a training phase providing an overview of the condition's audio feedback style, patterns, and sample audio clips of patterns in the condition's audio style. Once the participant understood the information conveyed through the audio style and was able to identify the patterns, they continued onto the testing phase of the study, in which they listened to a total of nine audio clips. Upon listening to each clip, participants were asked to identify, to the best of their ability, the pattern they heard through the audio. Within each condition, the order of the audio clips was also presented in a randomized order to counterbalance any order effects within the conditions. The participant was able to ask for the clips to be repeated as many times as they requested. The participant was scored on their accuracy in identifying patterns but remained unaware of their scores.

Once the two conditions were completed, the participant was asked to complete the post-experiment survey. The participant was then informed that the study had been completed, had the opportunity to ask any further questions, and was thanked for their participation.

3 Results

In analyzing these results, all instances of F-tests were F-tests for equality of variance, all instances of t-tests were 2-tailed paired t-tests, and the significance level of all tests was 0.01.

To verify the order of the study conditions were randomized, a Sign Test (2-tailed 1-Sample Binomial Test with a probability of 0.5) was performed (Table 1). Out of the 47 total participants, 29 completed the Speech-Only condition first, while 18 completed the Speech-And-Nonspeech-Sounds condition first. Out of the 39 sighted participants, 24 completed the Speech-Only condition first, while 15 completed the Speech-And-Nonspeech-Sounds condition first. Out of the 8 participants who are blind or visually impaired, 5 completed the Speech-Only condition first, while 3 completed the Speech-And-Nonspeech-Sounds condition first. Performing a Sign Test determined the order of the study conditions were randomized with a p-value of 0.14, 0.72, and 0.19, respectively.

Table 1. Sign test to determine if condition order was randomized.

Sign test for order ($\alpha = 0.01$)	
Sighted	$p = 0.1996$
Blind or visually impaired	$p = 0.7266$
Total	$p = 0.1439$

3.1 Preference

Of the 47 total participants, 24 preferred the Speech-Only audio style, 20 preferred the Speech-And-Nonspeech-Sounds audio style, and 3 had no preference. Of the 39 sighted participants, 20 preferred the Speech-Only audio style, 16 preferred the Speech-And-Nonspeech-Sounds audio style, and 3 had no preference. Of the 8 participants who are blind or visually impaired, 4 preferred the Speech-Only audio style, 4 preferred the Speech-And-Nonspeech-Sounds audio style, and 0 had no preference (Table 2).

Performing a Sign Test determined a significant difference for having no preference, but no significant difference in preference for Speech-Only or Speech-And-Nonspeech-Sounds audio (Table 3). Since the p-value for no preference was extremely low (<0.0000001) for the total and sighted participants, the choice of No Preference was considered to be an outlier, making the appropriate probability of the Binomial Test to be 0.5 rather than 0.33. Although the p-value for no preference was significant but not extremely low for the participants who were blind or visually impaired, the choice of No Preference may still be considered an outlier due to the small sample size and the tendency of this study's results for this group of participants to reflect the same as those for sighted participants.

Table 2. Participant preference for audio feedback style.

Audio feedback preference			
Participants	Speech-Only	Speech-And-Nonspeech-Sounds	No preference
Sighted	20	16	3
Blind or visually impaired	4	4	0
Total	24	20	3

Table 3. Sign test for audio feedback style preference.

Sign test for audio feedback style preference ($\alpha = 0.01$)			
Participants	Speech-Only	Speech-And-Nonspeech-Sounds	No preference
Sighted	$p \approx 1$	$p = 0.3368$	$p < 0.0001$
Blind or visually impaired	$p = 1$	$p = 1$	$p = 0.0078$
Total	$p \approx 1$	$p = 0.3817$	$p < 0.0001$

3.2 Intuitiveness

The intuitiveness of each audio feedback style was ranked on a scale of 1–5, with 1 indicating very unintuitive and 5 indicating very intuitive. Of the total participants, the average rank for the Speech-Only audio style was 3.06 with a median of 3 and a variance of 1.23. The average rank for the Speech-And-Nonspeech-Sounds audio style was 2.87 with a median of 3 and a variance of 1.72 (Table 4). An F-test determined no significant difference between the variances with a p-value of 0.26. A t-test determined no significant difference between the two rankings with a p-value of 0.31 (Table 5).

Of the sighted participants, the average rank for the Speech-Only audio style was 3 with a median of 3 and a variance of 1.42. The average rank for the Speech-And-Nonspeech-Sounds audio style was 2.84 with a median of 3 and a variance of 1.65 (Table 4). An F-test determined no significant difference between the variances with a p-value of 0.63. A t-test determined no significant difference between the two rankings with a p-value of 0.42 (Table 5).

Of the participants who are blind or visually impaired, the average rank for the Speech-Only audio style was 3.37 with a median of 3 and a variance of 0.26. The average rank for the Speech-And-Nonspeech-Sounds audio style was 3 with a median of 3.5 and a variance of 2.28 (Table 4). An F-test determined a potentially marginal significance between the variances with a p-value of 0.011. However, this marginal significance may be due to the small sample size of 8 and can be considered as not significant when considering the tendency of similar results between both groups of participants. A t-test determined no significant difference between the two rankings with a p-value of 0.58 (Table 5).

Table 4. Average, median, and variance of audio feedback style intuitiveness rankings.

Intuitiveness ranking of audio feedback styles						
	Speech-Only			Speech-And-Nonspeech-Sounds		
Participants	Average	Median	Variance	Average	Median	Variance
Sighted	3	3	1.4210	2.8461	3	1.6599
Blind or visually impaired	3.375	3	0.2678	3	3.5	2.2857
Total	3.0638	3	1.2349	2.8723	3	1.7224

Table 5. F-test and t-test results comparing audio feedback style intuitiveness rankings.

Comparison of intuitiveness rankings (α = 0.01)		
Participants	F-test	t-test
Sighted	p = 0.6344	p = 0.4213
Blind or visually impaired	p = 0.0112	p = 0.5837
Total	p = 0.2628	p = 0.3164

3.3 Accuracy

The total average accuracy of the Speech-Only audio style condition was 78.01% with a standard deviation of 25.64, and that of the Speech-And-Nonspeech-Sounds audio style condition was 74.23% with a standard deviation of 26.12. Of the sighted participants, the average accuracy of the Speech-Only condition was 77.20% with a standard deviation of 27.44, and that of the Speech-And-Nonspeech-Sounds condition was 73.50% with a standard deviation of 28.22. Of the participants who are blind or visually impaired, the average accuracy of the Speech-Only condition was 81.94% with a standard deviation of 14.47, and that of the Speech-And-Nonspeech-Sounds condition was 77.77% with a standard deviation of 11.87 (Table 6).

Performing F-tests and t-tests determined no significant difference between the variance and accuracy of each condition in total and based on participant group (Table 7).

Table 6. Average participant accuracy and standard deviation by audio feedback style.

Average accuracy statistics by audio feedback style				
Participants	Speech-Only		Speech-And-Nonspeech-Sounds	
	Accuracy	Stdev.	Accuracy	Stdev.
Sighted	77.20%	27.44	73.50%	28.22
Blind or visually impaired	81.94%	14.47	77.77%	11.87
Total	78.01%	25.64	74.23%	26.12

Table 7. F-test and t-test results comparing accuracy between audio feedback style conditions.

Comparison of condition accuracy ($\alpha = 0.01$)		
Participants	F-test	T-test
Sighted	$p = 0.8640$	$p = 0.2382$
Blind or visually impaired	$p = 0.6813$	$p = 0.1970$
Total	$p = 0.9006$	$p = 0.1528$

3.4 Relative Pitch vs. Nonspeech Sound Interpretation Technique vs. Feedback Preference

Participant relative pitch ability was determined by their responses in the post-experiment survey. Participants considered to have weaker relative pitch provided responses indicating they had difficulty distinguishing the nonspeech sounds, needed to concentrate more on the nonspeech sounds, and/or found the nonspeech sounds confusing or distracting. Participants considered to have stronger relative pitch provided responses indicating they found the nonspeech sounds instinctively "clicked" in their minds, acted as an easily identifiable label, and/or required less concentration.

30 of the 39 sighted participants provided sufficient responses to determine their relative pitch ability. Of the total participants who provided sufficient responses, 18 had weaker relative pitch, and 20 had stronger relative pitch. Of the sighted participants, 14 had weaker relative pitch, and 16 had stronger relative pitch. Of the participants who are blind or visually impaired, 4 had weaker relative pitch, and 4 had stronger relative pitch (Table 8).

A Sign Test was performed to determine if participant relative pitch ability was disproportionate. The Sign Test found the number of participants with weaker and stronger relative pitch were equivalent in total and for both participant groups (Table 9).

Table 8. Participant relative pitch ability.

Participant relative pitch ability		
Participants	Weaker relative pitch	Stronger relative pitch
Sighted	14	16
Blind or visually impaired	4	4
Total	18	20

Table 9. Sign test to determine if participant relative pitch ability was disproportionate.

Sign test for relative pitch ability proportions ($\alpha = 0.01$)	
Sighted	$p = 0.8555$
Blind or visually impaired	$p = 1$
Total	$p = 0.8714$

Participants uniquely utilized a combination of techniques to interpret each audio feedback style. Some commonly used techniques included visualization, memorization, repeated listening of audio clips to focus on different information, and associating aspects of the audio with a body part and/or movement. In particular, the "translation" technique was unique only to the interpretation of nonspeech sounds. The "translation" technique was used when a user translated nonspeech sounds into language, while its counterpart, the "no translation" technique, was used when a user directly comprehended the nonspeech sounds. Participant usage of the "translation" or "no translation" technique was determined by their responses in the post-experiment survey. All the participants utilizing the "translation" technique had weaker relative pitch, while all the participants utilizing the "no translation" technique had stronger relative pitch (Table 10).

Similarly, all the participants utilizing the "translation" technique also preferred the Speech-Only audio style. Most of the participants utilizing the "no translation" technique preferred the Speech-And-Nonspeech-Sounds audio style, with only 2 having no preference (Table 11). Since having no preference was considered an outlier, the results could be interpreted as essentially all participants utilizing the "no translation" technique preferred the Speech-And-Nonspeech-Sounds audio style.

Table 10. Comparison of participant relative pitch ability to nonspeech sound interpretation technique.

Relative pitch vs. Nonspeech sound interpretation technique			
Participants	Relative pitch	Translation	No translation
Sighted	Stronger	0	16
	Weaker	14	0
Blind or visually impaired	Stronger	0	4
	Weaker	4	0
Total	Stronger	0	20
	Weaker	18	0

Table 11. Comparison of participant nonspeech sound interpretation technique to audio feedback style preference.

Nonspeech interpretation technique vs. Audio feedback style preference				
Participants	Technique	Speech-Only	Speech-And-Nonspeech-Sounds	No preference
Sighted	Translation	14	0	0
	No translation	0	14	2
Blind or visually impaired	Translation	4	0	0
	No translation	0	4	0
Total	Translation	18	0	0
	No translation	0	18	2

4 Conclusion

The study found no significant difference between overall preference for, intuitiveness when using, or accuracy in identifying patterns through either audio feedback method. Both audio feedback methods allowed users to perform equally well with high accuracy, suggesting that both feedback methods are viable avenues for information presentation. The study found "translation" and "no translation" to be generic techniques participants often used when listening to nonspeech audio feedback. The following relationships were found between performance, feedback style, user techniques, participant preference of feedback style, and strength of participant relative pitch:

1. When interacting with the Speech-And-Nonspeech-Sounds audio style, individuals with strong relative pitch utilized the "no translation" technique and found this style more intuitive than the other due to reduced cognitive workload, preferring this style to the other.
2. When interacting with the Speech-And-Nonspeech-Sounds audio style, individuals with weak relative pitch utilized a "translation" technique and found this style less intuitive than the other due to increased cognitive workload, preferring the alternative style.
3. Participants grouped by relative pitch strength utilized the same generic technique, but uniquely employed specific techniques.
4. A correlation was found between equivalently high design performance and lack of overall design preference.

These relationships support the results of prior research [3–5] and imply that:

1. Certain design constraints encourage the usage of certain generic techniques in individuals based on their ability.
2. Users will uniquely adapt to the constraints of their context to find their own ideal strategy.
3. Technology should not be developed with design constraints that allow for only one optimal generic technique. Varying user ability can explain the correlation between equivalently high design performance and lack of overall design preference. Users will perform better when interacting with a design constraint that is conducive to an optimal generic technique that they are able to harness. As such, users will prefer certain design constraints based on their ability. Significant proportions of users have varying ability, which will counterbalance any differences in design performance and preference.

Acknowledgments. The authors would like to thank the National Science Foundation and Arizona State University for their funding support. This material is partially based upon work supported by the NSF under Grant No. 1828010.

References

1. U.S. Government Printing Office: Individuals with disabilities education improvement act of 2004: conference report (to accompany H.R. 1350). U.S. Government Printing Office, Washington, D.C. (2004)

2. Statistics January 2019. https://www.nfb.org/resources/blindness-statistics. Accessed 6 February 2020
3. Ramloll, R., Brewster, S., Yu, W., Riedel, B.: Using non-speech sounds to improve access to 2D tabular numerical information for visually impaired users. In: Blandford, A., Vanderdonckt, J., Gray, P. (eds.) People and Computers XV—Interaction Without Frontiers, pp. 515–529. Springer, London (2001). https://doi.org/10.1007/978-1-4471-0353-0_32
4. Goncu, C., Marriott, K.: GraVVITAS: generic multi-touch presentation of accessible graphics. In: Campos, P., Graham, N., Jorge, J., Nunes, N., Palanque, P., Winckler, M. (eds.) INTERACT 2011. LNCS, vol. 6946, pp. 30–48. Springer, Heidelberg (2011). https://doi.org/10.1007/978-3-642-23774-4_5
5. Toennies, J.L., Burgner, J., Withrow, T.J., Webster, R.J.: Toward haptic/aural touchscreen display of graphical mathematics for the education of blind students. In: 2011 IEEE World Haptics Conference, pp. 373–378. IEEE (2011). https://doi.org/10.1109/whc.2011.5945515

Method for Synchronized Driving of Sign Language Avatar Using a Digital TV Signal

Rodrigo Ribeiro de Oliveira(✉), João Guilherme Reiser de Melo, Leandro Paes, and Davi Frossard

SIDIA Institute of Science and Technology, Manaus, AM 69055-035, Brazil
{rodrigo.oliveira,joao.melo,leandro.paes,davi.frossard}@sidia.com
http://www.sidia.com

Abstract. There are several people around the world with some kind of disability requiring more accessibility on multimedia devices. In this work the main focus is the use of a sign language Avatar to help the deaf or people with hearing loss to have more access to the video content transmitted by digital TV channels. This method aiming to allow the broadcaster to add glosses(Representation of a sign language sign), as a binary file, synchronized with DTV content, as audio and video (A/V), directly on the signal. Glosses represents the signs/gestures (words) that will be reproduced by the Avatar on the receiver side. The synchronization is guaranteed by timestamps multiplexed together to the transmitted stream. Having a DTV signal with this information, on receiver side, an embedded system extracts each gloss-binary file, together with the synchronization data to run the Avatar in a continuous process. This method presents several advantages when compared with usual broadcast methods and web based methods. Among these advantages are: it can be disabled by user, on receiver side, due the sign language interpreter is not attached directly on video media, as is normally used by broadcasters; the receiver does not need to access the internet to translate or get glosses, avoiding problems related to delays or overheads when performing constant communications with external servers to translate the content into sign language, in addition to making the system less prone to intrusion, the translation step is not necessary due the final glosses are added on DTV signal to be showed synchronized with video; and finally, it can also be used on premium content, such as movies, TV shows and documentaries, that normally do not have sign language content, further increasing the possibility of accessibility by the deaf audience.

Keywords: Sign language · Digital TV · Avatar · DTV receivers

1 Introduction

Sign language and spoken language have a very different grammar and syntax. As a result, most people with deafness or hearing loss have difficulty using written

Supported by SIDIA Institute of Science and Technology, Manaus, Brazil.

C. Stephanidis et al. (Eds.): HCII 2020, LNCS 12426, pp. 220–232, 2020.
https://doi.org/10.1007/978-3-030-60149-2_18

language, because the grammar/syntax is very confusing for them [1,2]. Sign languages are composed by visual representation of words or meanings, done by hands, face and body movements to perform communication. Nowadays, there are at least three hundred different sign languages in use around the world [3]. Brazil, for example, uses the Brazilian Sign Language (BSL) or LIBRAS [4], popularly known by Brazilians natives. The United States uses American Sign Language (ASL) [5], South Korea uses KSL (Korean Sign Language) [6], so on. For each idiom, there is a subset of different visual images represented by hands, face and body movements that should be illustrated by a 2D/3D gloss-based animation Avatar, such as widely used in games area.

Avatars can be developed through advanced computer graphics techniques involving, but not limited to, computer vision, deep learning, virtual reality (VR), augmented reality (AR), etc. Game engine are systems that incorporate all of these tools in an environment that assist in the development of games and similar applications. Among the most popular game engines are: "Unity" – supports 2D and 3D development with resources and functionalities across genres, "Unreal Engine" – is a complete suite of creation tools design to meat ambitious artistic visions, etc. These engines generate model files which may include definitions for meshes, bones, animation, materials and textures of the graphic object (e.g. avatar). There are several web systems translating text of browsers and programs interfaces into glosses to be used on gloss-based animation Avatars systems [7–9]. This work uses similar idea of web based systems, where each gloss represents a word of spoken language. Thus, each gloss is represented by a binary file that animates the Avatar with sign language gesture meaning. Nowadays, 3D graphical engines allowed to have sign language avatars very near to human signers [10]. The main advantage of Avatars use is the possibility of automatic data insertion on broadcaster side.

On broadcaster side occurs the gloss packages insertion into DTV signal. These packages are multiplexed with audio and video flow, and with any other kind of data needed to be transmitted, such as files, tables and so on. All Digital TV standards use the MPEG2-TS[1] standard to deliver service information to the receivers. MPEG2-TS (or TS) [11] is a well-defined technology for transmission or recording video data. It can be used with many different video compression standards such as MPEG-2, MPEG-4, and H.264.

Multiple video, audio and data elementary streams can be multiplexed in a single TS. In this work, TS packages are used to carry gloss file from broadcasters to DTV receivers. For this, it is necessary to use data broadcast techniques provided on TS standard to perform data insertion on broadcaster side, further discussed throughout this work. After the multiplexing and modulation steps, the signal is transmitted through an open terrestrial TV channel, each channel using a predefined range of frequencies to broadcast, and reaching the receivers that are within the achieving area of the broadcasted signal. Figure 1 shows the process of DTV signal transmitting previously mentioned. To perform synchronization between elementary streams, the use of timestamps, to guide receiver to keep

[1] Abbreviation for Moving Picture Experts Group - Transport Stream.

synchronization during decodification of elementary streams, is done. Therefore, the TS provides the presentation time stamps (PTS) that is given in units related to a program's overall clock reference, the program clock reference (PCR), which is also transmitted on the TS. The receiver uses timestamps to perform inter-media and intra-media synchronization.

In this work, the PTS values are used as reference data to synchronize Avatar animation with main video elementary stream. It is the same technique used to synchronize subtitles (closed-caption channel) with main video elementary stream. On receiver side the signal is demodulated giving the transport stream as output, which is demultiplexed into different stream flows. Each flow is sent to a specific decoder of audio and video (A/V), where they are decoded and showed to end user as image and sound. In case of data glosses, it must be filtered by a dedicated developed software (SW) filter and used to feed the sign language Avatar engine.

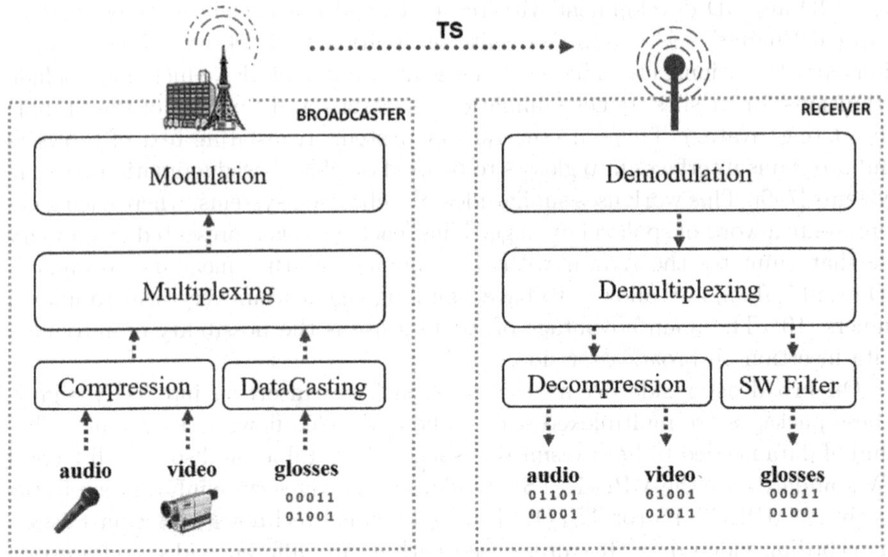

Fig. 1. Shows the insertion of glosses as regular data based on a data-casting mechanism and shows the reception steps to filter glosses on receiver side.

The main focus of this work is to present a method for synchronized driving of sign language Avatar glosses using a digital TV signal. The process of generation of the sent glosses are not the concern of this paper, the broadcaster being in charge of such a task. For validation, this work uses a previously defined glosses dictionary called VLibras [21], being VLibras is a set of open source computational tools that translate digital content (text, audio and video) into brazilian sign language (LIBRAS), allowing computers, cell phones, Web platforms or any other compatible device or platform, accessible to deaf or any person with limited hearing.

2 Related Work

There are several other published projects involving the use of Avatars in sign language that have some similarities with this work, the most notable ones: VLibras [21], which uses a Unity engine based Avatar running in a web browser that translates captured text from web platforms into glosses. VLibras is a solution containing a brazilian sign language glosses dictionary on a web database, and an Avatar, for web applications use, capable of manage the glosses.

SiMAX [22] is a software that translates spoken or written text into sign language. The translation is signed by a digital, 3D-animated avatar. SiMAX presents a translation method where the software uses a learning database in which all previous translations are stored.

[23] presents a telecommunication system for sign language applying VR technology where a person interacts with his/her party's sign language avatar instead of the party's live video.

A system and method for providing sign language video data in a broadcasting-communication convergence system is shown at [24]. All this projects and systems uses the an Avatar model to provide more accessibility on devices helping deaf or hearing loss people to have access to information and dialogues. Most parts of this system is web based, depending exclusively of internet access to perform translation of text into glosses needed to animate a web Avatar based engine.

This paper shows a method that do not uses the internet to perform translation or keep glosses database in the TV devices, due all those data are part of the DTV signal being transmitted and decoded as a regular elementary stream, as already done with main A/V media streams in a digital TV linear content.

3 Background

In this section some relevant background information related with this work are presented. The following subsections presents a overview about data broadcast techniques, graphical engines and sign language.

3.1 Data Broadcast Techniques

This section aims to give an overview about data broadcasting techniques available on MPEG2-TS standard. The transport stream (TS) is basically composed by packages that may encapsulate a number of other sub-streams. Each package, in turn, is composed by a header of 4 bytes and a payload area of 184 bytes, as shown in Fig. 2.

The header is composed by 8 fields with data info used to guide receiver during signal decoding. Among the most relevant fields are the sync byte (0x47) and the packet identifier (PID). The Sync byte is used to synchronize the packet decoding of the transport stream, avoiding loss of timing during the signal reception.

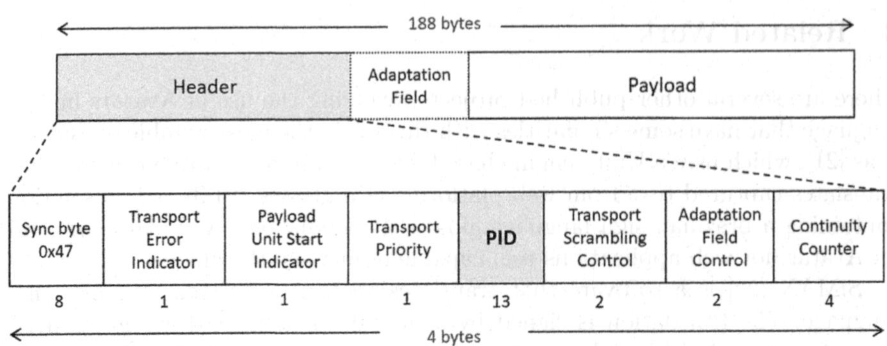

Fig. 2. Shows transport stream package structure

The PID is a 13-bit field used as a unique package identifier, identifying the data content of the payload (audio, video, other data contents). This field is fundamental during the demultiplexing task, since it is used by the demultiplexer to address each package payloads data to the correct decoding process (audio or video) or even to data files remounting into high-level abstraction layers, such as Sections and PES structures.

Finally the payload area is composed by 184 bytes used to carry on the information. This area is shared with the "adaptation field", that is an optional variable length field intended to convey clock references, timing and synchronization information. In this work this field will be very important due it will carry on the timestamps (PTS) data info used to perform inter-media or intra-media synchronization [25]. The presence of adaptation field is given by the 2-bit adaptation field control located on header of TS package. It is important notice that during data filtering is necessary to discount adaptation field size from payload of the package.

Compared to other communication systems, transport stream (TS) is a very trustworthy to high data transfer, due it is less susceptible to interference caused by noisy. This consistency is given, partly, due the small size of TS packages. To be even more robust to error or interference, the DTV standards use redundancy info aiming the error control, and also algorithms as Reed Solomon and Low-Density Parity-Check (LDPC). On the other hand, the TS package size makes it difficult for tasks as data filtering on receiver side.

MPEG2-TS provides other structures to encapsulates data such as Packetized Elementary Stream (PES) and Sections, as a layer abstracting on the transport stream structure, as shown on Fig. 3. The elementary streams, as audio and video, are encapsulated on PES packages to broadcasting. This encapsulation is more indicated to perform data streaming, such as A/V elementary stream and data stream. Normally, Sections are used to encapsulate complex data transfer structures. They are used to broadcast files or even complete file-systems used by data services (e.g. middleware[2] applications).

[2] DASE, MHP, ARIB, Ginga.

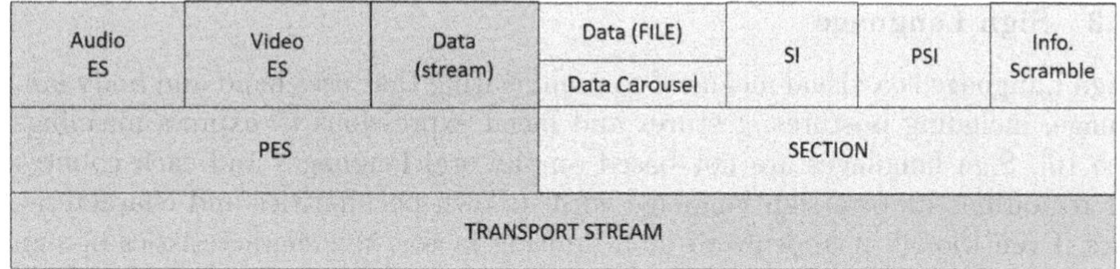

Fig. 3. Shows transport stream hierarchy used to perform data broadcast

Sections are also used to broadcast Program Specific Information (PSI) and System Information (SI) tables, required to provide information about the signal content to the receivers. There are several kinds of tables and descriptors (subsections of tables) that are used to describe the transport stream content. The broadcast of some of those tables are mandatory while others are optional. PSI tables are mandatory for any DTV signal, due they are standardized by the MPEG2 standard bringing programs/services identifiers info needed to have access to the DTV signal [12]. PSI tables are divided in Program Association Table (PAT), Program Mapping Table (PMT), Network Information Table (NIT) and Conditional Access Table (CAT). The SI tables are specific tables containing the characteristics of each digital TV system (e.g. DVB, ISDB, ATSC, DMB-T/H and SBTVD) and their use is optional.

3.2 Graphical Engines

A graphical engine, also known as game engine, game architecture, game framework or gameframe, is a software environment designed to allow the development of video games, movies or any other kind of artificial visual content. Developers use graphical engines to build applications for consoles, mobile devices, personal computers, or any other supported device. The main functionalities provided by this kind of engine includes the rendering engine ("renderer") for 2D or 3D graphics, audio, networking, the physics engine, scripting [13], animation, artificial intelligence, streaming, memory management, threading, and can also include video support for cinematics.

The graphical engines are tools designed to reduce the complexity, cost, and time required in to develop a video games or similar. These tools supply a layer of abstraction on top of the most common development tasks. With the increasing complexity of games over the years, engines have become a mandatory part of the development process [14].

Some of the most remarkable engines used on the market are: *Unreal Engine*, used on the games Gears of War, Borderlands, Bioshock, Batman Arkham City; *Unity*, whose notable games are Cities: Skylines, Hearthstone, Assassin's Creed: Identity; *CryEngine*, used on Crisis, Far Cry, Sniper: Ghost Warrior 3, Hunt: Showdown. For the purposes of this paper, a sign language interpreter Avatar application developed using Unity was adopted.

3.3 Sign Language

Sign Language is a visual means of communicating that uses hand and body language, including postures, gestures and facial expressions to express meanings [15,16]. Sign languages are not based on the oral languages and each country or region has its own sign language with its own peculiarities and characteristics. Even though it appears to be a limiting factor, the characteristics of sign languages allow them to express even the most subtle and complex meanings as well as oral languages [17].

Just like oral languages, sign languages can have different dialects, with variations depending on gender, age, social group, so on [17]. This increases the complexity of the language making it very hard to, to a non human, to simulate the behaviour of a real person using sign language.

[18–20] show some attempts to develop a virtual sign language interpreter. Such attempts are praiseworthy, but are still not very well regarded by the deaf publisher, who complains about the lack of expressiveness of the virtual interpreters. However, with advances in gaming and similar technologies, the quality of these applications tends to improve considerably.

4 Study and Analysis of Different Approach

This section will present a study performed using the sign language Avatar in a different approach than the method proposed on this paper. Before the elaboration of any method or any work proposal, it was necessary to verify if there was any sign language Avatar that was compatible with the television system. The one chosen to be used was VLibras, because it uses the brazilian sign language and for being a web application, easily integrated into the television environment. After the integration of VLibras into the television system, tests were performed to validate its operation with the device.

The first strategy tested during the development of this project was using closed caption data as a data source for the sign language Avatar. Closed caption has the facility to be transmitted, by default, integrated with the digital TV signal, in addition to the vast majority of the broadcasters normally inserting this content in all program schedule. This first approach was tested, however, the results were not at all satisfactory.

Once the closed caption is acquired, the Avatar system, which operates with an online database that performs the translation for glosses, requires an online request to be made for the translation of the content. The implementation of this step was performed, sending the textual content and receiving the glosses as a response. Running the whole system together, two main problems were identified. First, the solution had a considerable delay in relation to the displayed video content. And second, the closed caption + translation presented an unsuitable result.

Regarding the first problem, normally, when transmitting a TV signal, the closed captioning content usually arrives with a certain delay, regarding the video content. With the addition of the translation stage, the delay becomes unacceptable. About the second problem, the content received on the closed caption usually comes with several misspellings, lack of words, etc. Inserting this kind of data into the sign language translator generates unexpected results. The fluency on communication becomes totally impaired, when the translator receives words that are not recognized (misspelling words), the translator will spell them, so on.

After several tests, this approach was disregarded because it did not provide an acceptable result for the target audience. Anyway, it was a first step towards developing a more suitable approach to the problem. In the next section, the proposed method will be explained.

5 Methodology

To better explain the proposed method, this section is divided into two parts: Broadcaster data Insertion and Receiver data Filtering. The first will explain the broadcaster side of the system, how to insert the sign language avatar data on the transport stream. The second will show the steps to filter and use the inserted data inside the TV device.

5.1 Broadcaster Data Insertion

The broadcaster must include sign language information on PES packages following the same approach of subtitles inclusion and other elementary streams as A/V. The glosses need be added during the content edition step, together with other streams, such as A/V ES and subtitles. Threrefore, is necessary to have a glosses dictionary (database) to feed packetizer and generate *gloss.pes* files, as shown in Fig. 4. Following the same way, audio and video are encoded and added into PES packages through Packetizer module. This procedure outputs an *audio.pes* and *video.pes* files. Subtitles are also added into PES files, through packetizer module, generating *subtitle.pes* files as output. Finally all PES files containing distinct elementary streams are multiplexed and interleaved into a single transport stream through MUX module. Worth remembering that on the multiplexing step, beyound the PES elementary streams, the sections are also multiplexed and interleaved in transport packages, creating a single binary stream.

For validation purposes, a VLibras [21] database was used to feed packetizer module and to generate the *gloss.pes* files to be included on TS. To perform the multiplexing steps of the MPEG transport streams, a tool called Opencaster was used. OpenCaster is a free and open source MPEG2-TS data generator and packet manipulator. The timestamps data (PTS) are added automatically by the multiplexer tool during PES files generation. To modulate the DTV signal, a VHF/UHF modulator named DekTec DTU-215 was used, together with the Stream Player software tool DekTec StreamXpress version 3.15.1. The signal was modulated in a ISDB-T standard, that is the base standard used on Brazil.

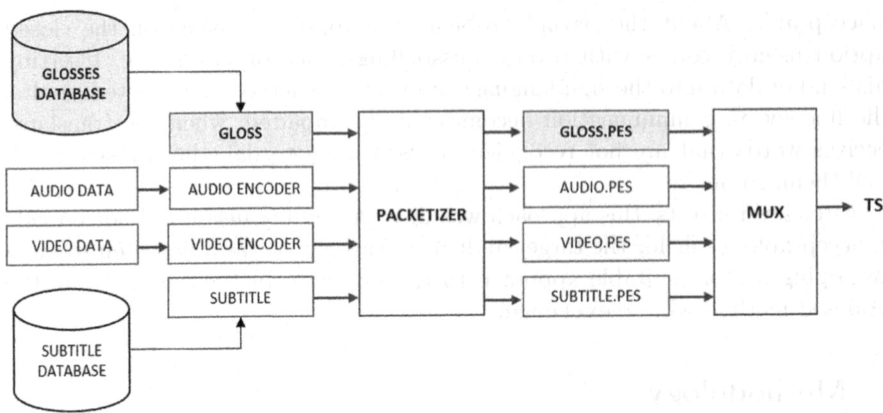

Fig. 4. Shows the insertion of glosses as regular data into PES packages

5.2 Receiver Data Filtering

DTV receivers allow TV viewers navigate through a huge number of channels. This is possible due that receivers cover digital TV frequency spectrum. Once tuned on a specific channel, the receiver starts to receive information (e.g. audio, video and data packages) from this channel as a pipeline. The data that comes from the broadcaster is organized into a hierarchical structure, transported as continuous bit stream. This structure has identifiers in order that the receiver use them to access/filter the information they demand.

The demodulation step, shown on Fig. 1, outputs a TS stream containing all information added on the broadcaster side. Among these data are the sign language binary glosses. During this subsection, will be explained, based on Fig. 5, the method developed for the extraction and displaying of glosses using the sign language Avatar. To facilitate the explanation, each step of the flowchart was numbered and during the description, each step will be referenced by its number.

The flow starts by the system having access to the TS (bit stream). The receiver software starts a continuous filtering process to access the PES packages payload content carrying on glosses data (1). If there are no sign language data content on transport stream (2), the execution line keep filtering the transport stream in search of this data. Otherwise, when the presence of the sign language data info is detected, the execution line reaches statement 3.

On statement 3, a PES filter hardware available on any DTV receiver is used to retrieve the payload information of a given stream ID. To do that, the embedded software configures the PES filter hardware with the stream ID, retrieving (downloading) the gloss data on the receiver memory. If the gloss uses multiple PES packages, this process continuous until the complete gloss data file is retrieved.

On statement 4, the execution line extracts the PTS values located on the extended header of PES packages, to be able to synchronize the Avatar animation

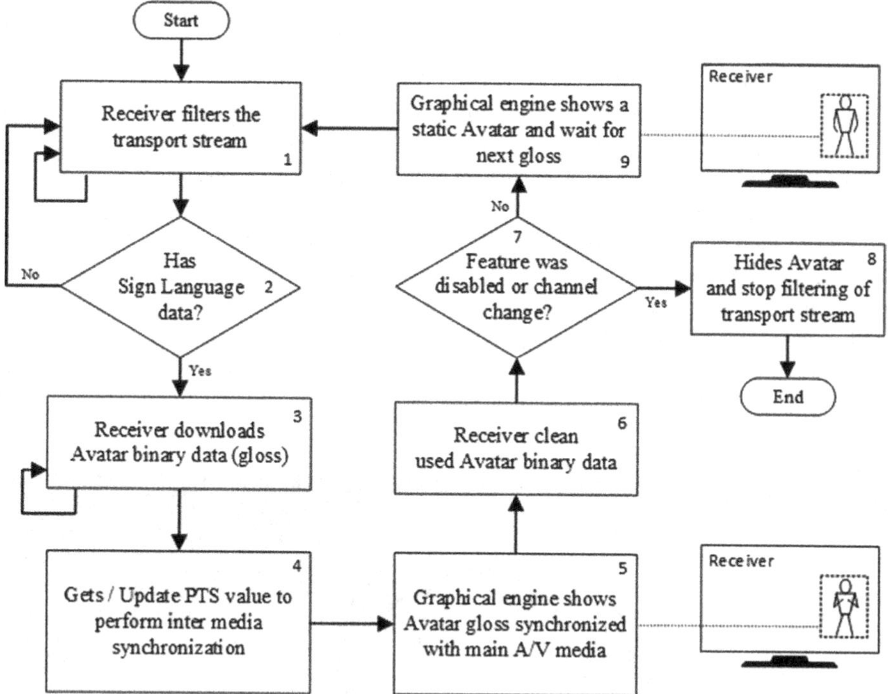

Fig. 5. Flowchart for the embedded system that performs the filtering of glosses raw data sent by broadcaster and the animation cycle performed on Avatar

with A/V media playback. On statement 5, the synchronization is done and the animation is executed on the Avatar, in parallel with the A/V decodification. The binary gloss is used as a input file of a Unit based engine that by our turn animates the Avatar.

Execution line reaches statement 6, where the avatar gloss binary file is erased, in order to not increase the memory consumption of the embedded system. On statement 7 the system checks if the feature keeps enabled/disabled or if a channel change occurs. If the feature was disabled or had the occurrence of a channel change, the execution line is redirected to statement 8, where the system hides the Avatar and the TS filtering process is conclude. Otherwise, the execution line follow through statement 9, where the graphical engine shows a default position, or static Avatar, to wait for the next gloss, on statement 1, restarting the execution of the whole process.

To validate the proposed method, a DTV Receiver platform, based on OS Tizen, was used, to develop a native application to perform the PES package filtering, in order to retrieve the gloss binary files, as shown on Fig. 5. The main purpose of the application is to download and reassemble the gloss, extract the PTS value from the PES extended header packages, calculate the presentation time through PTS value + PCR of the Service, and finally input the gloss file into the Avatar engine.

After all these steps, the gloss is erased from the memory to avoid memory overflow, due that embedded systems usually have limited resources.

The native application is an OS Tizen based application developed in C++ programming language. The Avatar used to validate the methodology was based on VLibras [21] project. This Avatar uses a Unity engine, supported by web browsers, such as Chromium. To operate the Avatar, the native application instantiates a Chromium window that is kept always on top while the feature is active. The TV screen working with the Avatar is shown on Fig. 6. The Avatar can be positioned on any position of the screen, but, for the purposes of this work and keeping the most commonly used pattern of positioning of sign language interpreters, it was fixed in the bottom right of the screen.

Fig. 6. Shows the execution of Avatar on bottom right corner of TV screen

6 Conclusion

There are several people around the world with some kind of disability requiring more accessibility on multimedia devices. This work aimed to present a methodology to control a sign language Avatar through a DTV signal in a way that could be simply integrated to any DTV standard based on MPEG2-TS. The method uses the mechanisms provided by MPEG2-TS to add sign language glosses packages multiplexed with A/V elementary stream, such as any other data present on signal. The most suitable method for this purpose, was the packetized elementary stream (PES), which disposes of synchronization data, essential to integrate the Avatar with the main video stream. Besides that, MPEG2-TS offers other mechanisms to broadcast glosses data. In this case, it is necessary to add synchronization support, what may require some amendments on DTV standards. This method presents some advantages when compared to web based methods, due it bypass the translation step and avoid the overhead caused by glosses translation and download. Here the glosses are transmitted and filtered together with the content to which they refer to, avoiding delays in the process of inserting the sign language interpreter and providing an experience far superior to the end user. Concerning to the inserting of the glosses in the transmitted stream, it is up to the broadcaster to add the glosses information during content editing, a situation similar to what happens with the use of closed caption. In case of live content the broadcaster can use data insert adapted to sign language.

Acknowledgments. We express our gratitude to SIDIA Instituto de Ciência e Tecnologia, for all the given support during the development of this work, and manly to the Visual Display (VD) - Accessibility team by the dedication and effort to complete this work.

References

1. Swisher, M.V.: Similarities and differences between spoken languages and natural sign languages. J. Appl. Linguist. **9**, 343–356 (2016). https://doi.org/10.1093/applin/9.4.343. Oxford Academi
2. Bellugi, U., Fischer, S.D.: A comparison of sign language and spoken language. Cognition **1**, 173–200 (1972). https://doi.org/10.1016/0010-027790018-2. Oxford Academi
3. A guide to the different types of sign language around the world. https://k-international.com/blog/different-types-of-sign-language-around-the-world. Accessed 11 Jun 2020
4. Guimaraes, C., Antunes, D.R., de Trindade, D.F.G., da Silva, R.A.L., Garcia, L.S.: Structure of the Brazilian sign language (Libras) for computational tools: citizenship and social inclusion. In: Lytras, M.D., Ordonez de Pablos, P., Ziderman, A., Roulstone, A., Maurer, H., Imber, J.B. (eds.) WSKS 2010. CCIS, vol. 112, pp. 365–370. Springer, Heidelberg (2010). https://doi.org/10.1007/978-3-642-16324-1_41
5. National institute on deafness and other communication disorders. https://www.nidcd.nih.gov/health/american-sign-language. Accessed 11 Jun 2020
6. National institute of Korean language. https://www.korean.go.kr/front-eng/edu/edu-01.do. Accessed 11 Jun 2020
7. Grigório, F., et al.: VLibras-BOX: flexible Portuguese-LIBRAS translation server encapsulation for distributed, centralized or hybrid scenarios. In: ACM DL, Proceedings of the 21st Brazilian Symposium on Multimedia and the Web, Manaus, Brazil, pp. 173–176 (2015). https://doi.org/10.1145/2820426.2820460
8. The American sign language avatar project at DePaul University. http://asl.cs.depaul.edu/. Accessed 11 Jun 2020

9. Tomuro, N., et al.: An alternative method for building a database for American sign language. Technology and Persons with Disabilities Conference 2000. California State University at Northridge, Los Angeles, CA, 20–25 March 2000
10. Kipp, M., Heloir, A., Nguyen, Q.: Sign language avatars: animation and comprehensibility. In: Vilhjálmsson, H.H., Kopp, S., Marsella, S., Thórisson, K.R. (eds.) IVA 2011. LNCS (LNAI), vol. 6895, pp. 113–126. Springer, Heidelberg (2011). https://doi.org/10.1007/978-3-642-23974-8_13
11. Digital Video Broadcasting (DVB) specification for the use of video and audio coding in broadcasting applications based on the MPEG-2 transport stream (ETSI TS 101 154 V1.9.1). https://www.etsi.org/deliver/etsi_ts/101100_101199/101154/01.09.01_60/ts_101154v010901p.pdf. Accessed 11 Jun 2020
12. ARIB STD-B10. https://www.arib.or.jp/english/html/overview/doc/6-STD-B10v4_6-E2.pdf. Accessed 11 Jun 2020
13. Unity. https://unity3d.com/what-is-a-game-engine. Accessed 11 Jun 2020
14. Halpern, J.: Developing 2D Games with Unity. Apress, New York City (2019)
15. MedicineNet. https://www.medicinenet.com/script/main/art.asp?articlekey=39158. Accessed 11 May 2020
16. Cambridge dictionary. https://dictionary.cambridge.org/dictionary/english/sign-language. Accessed 11 May 2020
17. Emmorey, K.: Language, Cognition, and the Brain: Insights from Sign Language Research. Psychology Press, East Sussex (2001)
18. Elliott, R., Glauert, J.R., Kennaway, J.R., Marshall, I., Safar, E.: Linguistic modelling and language-processing technologies for Avatar-based sign language presentation. Univ. Access Inf. Soc. **6**(4), 375–391 (2008). https://doi.org/10.1007/s10209-007-0102-z
19. Elghoul, M.J.O.: An avatar based approach for automatic interpretation of text to Sign language. Challenges for Assistive Technology, AAATE 07, vol. 20, p. 266 (2007)
20. Lombardo, V., Battaglino, C., Damiano, R., Nunnari, F.: An avatar-based interface for the Italian sign language. In: 2011 International Conference on Complex, Intelligent, and Software Intensive Systems, pp. 589–594 (2011)
21. VLibras. https://www.vlibras.gov.br/. Accessed 11 Jun 2020
22. Simax. https://simax.media/?lang=en. Accessed 12 Jun 2020
23. Kuroda, T., Sato, K., Chihara, K.: An avatar based sign language telecommunication system. Int. J. Virtual Reality **3**(4), 20–26 (1998). International Proceedings IJ VR
24. System and method for providing sign language video data in a broadcasting-communication convergence system. https://patents.google.com/patent/US20060174315A1/en. Accessed 12 Jun 2020
25. Fischer, W.: Digital Video and Audio Broadcasting Technology - A Practical Engineering Guide. Springer, Heidelberg (2008). https://doi.org/10.1007/978-3-540-76358-1

Care4MyHeart-PSG: A Personalized Serious Game Platform to Empower Phase III Cardiac Rehabilitation of Cardiovascular Disease Patients in UAE

Sofia B. Dias[1], Sofia J. Hadjileontiadou[2], José A. Diniz[1], Ahsan H. Khandoker[3], and Leontios J. Hadjileontiadis[3,4,5(✉)]

[1] CIPER, Faculdade de Motricidade Humana, Universidade de Lisboa, 1499-002 Cruz Quebrada, Lisbon, Portugal
{sbalula,Jadiniz}@fmh.ulisboa.pt

[2] Department of Primary Education, Democritus University of Thrace, Alexandroupolis, Greece
shadjil@eled.duth.gr

[3] Department of Biomedical Engineering, Healthcare Engineering Innovation Center (HEIC), Khalifa University of Science and Technology, PO BOX 127788, Abu Dhabi, United Arab Emirates
ahsan.khandoker@kuac.ae, leontios.hajileontiadis@kustar.ac.ae

[4] Department of Electrical and Computer Engineering, Healthcare Engineering Innovation Center (HEIC), Khalifa University of Science and Technology, PO BOX 127788, Abu Dhabi, United Arab Emirates

[5] Department of Electrical and Computer Engineering, Aristotle University of Thessaloniki, 54124 Thessaloniki, Greece
leontios@auth.gr

Abstract. Cardiovascular disease (CVD) is the major cause of death in the UAE, causing one in every five deaths. Effective Cardiac Rehabilitation (CR) can significantly improve mortality and morbidity rates, leading to longer independent living and a reduced use of healthcare resources. The proposed project, namely Care4MyHeart, sets as an overall goal to introduce a personalized home-based CR program, enabling lifestyle behavioral change towards increased quality of life, surpassing the currently unsustainable provision of healthcare for CVD. In particular, the Care4MyHeart-Pesronalized Serious Game (C4MH-PSG) platform targets CVD patients entering Phase III, as this is where large numbers of patients, who would benefit significantly from exercise and CR, drop out. C4MH-PSG supports the key predictors for attendance to CR Phase III programs, including high program availability, ease of access to program location, high social connectivity, peer support (when peers share similar problems or/and can become peer mentors), and high self-efficacy. Within C4MH-PSG, advanced machine learning and modelling techniques are employed to propose gender- and age-specific CVD exercise programs and an autonomous helper-agent, providing informed feedback to the patient and the related physician/carer, establishing a collaborative patient-professional partnership. C4MH-PSG is realized via motion capture, exercise evaluation, physiological and lifestyle monitoring, exercise gaming, home-based human-computer interfacing, multi-parametric data modelling and advanced decision support systems. Finally, the overall concept and system are easily transferable to address

C. Stephanidis et al. (Eds.): HCII 2020, LNCS 12426, pp. 233–250, 2020.
https://doi.org/10.1007/978-3-030-60149-2_19

other diseases/conditions (e.g., diabetes, osteoporosis, obesity), providing market opportunities for the commercialization of C4MH-PSG beyond CVD.

Keywords: Older adults · Healthy ageing · Cardiovascular disease · Phase III cardiac rehabilitation · Personalized serious game platform · Care4myheart

1 Introduction

Cardiovascular diseases (CVD) collectively refers to diseases of the heart and circulatory system including coronary artery disease (CAD) and congenital heart disease (CHD). It is the leading cause of premature death (30% of all deaths) and disability worldwide (WHO) [1]. It is one of the leading causes of long-term sickness and loss to the labor market with a huge economic cost (CVD global cost of US$863b, in EU economy almost EUR 196 billion a year [2]). With changing demographics and deteriorating lifestyle this situation will worsen considerably [1], which is neither economically or socially sustainable. In the UAE, 30% of deaths are due to CVD; a recent (2015) report by the Dubai Health Authority (DHA) shows that CVD is one of the leading causes of death in the Emirates, causing one in every five deaths, as diabetes is a major risk factor for heart attacks and more than 20% of UAE's population is diabetic. Effective Cardiac Rehabilitation (CR) can significantly improve mortality and morbidity rates, leading to longer independent living and a reduced use of health care resources. Despite the high burden of CVDs in Arab countries, little is known about CR delivery [3]. Key reasons for this include: severe lack of programs, travel time, scheduling issues, lack of peer mentoring, and low self-efficacy associated with poor exercise technique and perceived poor 'body image' (not wanting to exercise with large groups of 'strangers'). In fact, CR is "a secondary prevention program, with exercise as the cornerstone of a comprehensive intervention" (European Association for Cardiovascular Prevention & Rehabilitation), which includes an educational program on healthy lifestyle (dietary habits, smoking cessation, substance consumption and learning to manage stress). There are generally three phases of CR, namely: Phase I: in-hospital education; Phase II: a very structured education that begins after leaving hospital with out-patient return visits 2–3 times/week for supervised exercise training and education sessions; and Phase III: it requires the patient to self-manage his/her rehabilitation.

CR results in a significant reduction in cardiovascular mortality of 26% (Odds Ratio 0.74, 95% Confidence Interval, 0.57–0.96) [5] and all-cause hospital readmission rates [2]. Increased exercise/physical activity (PA) alone reduces all-cause mortality by 24% and provides considerable protection from cardiovascular risk factors and co-morbidities, leading to longer independent living and a lower use of health care resources. Nevertheless, patient CR uptake and adherence are very low in Europe [6] and in Arab countries [3], especially for Phase III; therefore, approximately 11% of eligible patients begin a long-term Phase III community-based CR program, which is further diminished by low adherence rates [6].

Care4MyHeart targets patients with CVD entering Phase III, as this is where large numbers of patients, who would benefit significantly from exercise and CR, drop out. Current, traditional methods for home-based behavioral change interventions are limited by a 'one size fits all' phenomenon, i.e., everyone receives similar print or video-based information, failing to consider individuality. Without tailoring, interventions do not adapt to the evolving immediate, short or long-term needs of their patients and feedback on specific elements of information is not delivered at optimal times. Additionally, coordinated social interaction or peer support is difficult to provide [7]. Care4MyHeart will support the key predictors for attendance to CR Phase III programs [8], including high program availability, ease of access to program location, high social connectivity, peer support (when peers share similar problems or/and can become peer mentors), and high self-efficacy.

Moreover, Care4MyHeart presents an end-to-end modular technology platform that will allow CVD patients to better self-manage their illness through a supportive, dynamic, holistic, home-based CR program, which has increased uptake and long-term adherence to exercise as its core aim, transforming completely the way the CR is perceived so far. At the same time, Care4MyHeart allows CR use at any time in a comfortable and personal environment, providing clear benefits to all members of the health ecosystem to move away from a healthcare provider-centric system to a co-production model, which empowers patients to self-manage their health; a home-based system facilitates this.

2 The Care4MyHeart Paradigm

2.1 Overall Concept

The overarching aim of Care4MyHeart is to introduce a radically novel approach to CR that will ensure a paradigm shift towards empowering patients to more effectively self-manage their CVD, set within a collaborative care context with health professionals. It has the potential to deliver significant cost savings to the healthcare system, and direct more appropriate utilization of healthcare resources. This is achieved via a patient-centric holistic approach that specifically addresses the above barriers. To realize the aforementioned aim, Care4MyHeart has set the following concrete objectives:

- Develop Care4MyHeart to empower ordinary people to become 'expert patients', their own primary caregiver, with the know-how to self-manage their CVD. Care4MyHeart, using modules on self-management education will augment traditional patient education by providing remote, direct monitoring, training and feedback to patients, enabling them to gain an understanding of their own health and its challenges and to develop confidence and action plans to accomplish new behaviors.
- Design Care4MyHeart to specifically reduce patients' CVD risk Systematic COronary Risk Evaluation (SCORE) [4] through: (1) enhancing their participation in daily physical activity; (2) monitoring and reducing their time spent sitting; (3) improved patient adherence to standard CVD prevention and treatment guidelines, including their medication regimen, the quality in their dietary behavior and stopping smoking (if a smoker).

- Develop gender and age specific CVD exercise programs (an 'Exerclass' and 'Exergame') and an autonomous agent, manifested as a virtual coach, to deliver the exercise programs and associated behavioral change methodologies.
- Create an information-driven Care4MyHeart platform where Cloud-stored data, analyzed via big data analytics machine learning (e.g., deep learning), are transformed to knowledge that can be used to develop a collaborative patient-professional partnership, a co-production of health, with the aim of optimizing the patient's quality of life.
- Develop a 'co-production of health' business model from a multi-stakeholder ecosystem (patient, healthcare professionals, public healthcare regulators, health data managers, insurers and assurers, and commercial entities) that will maximize the likelihood of integrating Care4MyHeart into healthcare systems across Arab countries and internationally.

Care4MyHeart advances in the state of the art across multiple fields of study that clearly align with Khalifa University mission, strategic goals, and research priorities along with the Abu Dhabi 2030 plan regarding the health sector policy. In particular:

1. Unlike the traditional m-Health and e-Health systems for providing exercise information and monitoring, Care4MyHeart provides an exercise intervention and includes a sensing-intelligent analysis. Beyond the potential for a system specifically targeting CVD rehabilitation the use of serious game type systems as proposed by Care4MyHeart in other diseases of inactivity (e.g., diabetes (severe percentages in UAE), obesity, some form of cancers, osteoporosis) or general health (physical/emotional), would be very straightforward and relatively cheap.
2. High social connectivity is predictive of good health and wellbeing, decreased overall mortality, as well as reducing the incidence of CVD and its progression [9]. However, the generation of socially supportive environment for many technology platforms is associated with significant time, resources (training) and financial burden. Care4MyHeart will become a viable, cost-effective dynamic, interactive, socially connected medium. Its social connectivity module will encourage remote participants (of up to 4 people) to continue exercising together post-hospital discharge in a virtual space from the comfort of their own home, overcoming the challenge of social isolation found in traditional home-based interventions. Care4MyHeart will develop a peer mentor pro-gram, using a combination of group and dyad approaches [9]. In this way, opportunities for problem-solving skill development are evolving as part of the Care4MyHeart program, as patients discuss issues pertinent to living with CVD, not just treating the disease.
3. Care4MyHeart provides to healthcare professionals with extremely relevant, aggregated information (directly sensed and manually input) on their patient's health that they previously did not have access to, which supports their decision-making. This information helps to develop a collaborative patient-professional partnership, a co-production of health [10], with the aim of supporting patients to live the best possible quality of life with their chronic condition.
4. In Care4MyHeart, exercise goes beyond the classic methods of treadmill or bicycle training, where medical knowledge and guidelines coexist with a "steady" activity,

as, by using deep learning [11] and fuzzy logic modeling [12], will: (i) automatically modify elements of the class/game to increase enjoyment and adherence based on the modelled relationship between exercise adherence, enjoyment, and sensed motion, physiological response and social interaction, (ii) use the Avatar coach (in a smart TV, tablet, PC, Virtual Reality headset) within the Exergame/Exerclass to encourage social interaction (based on system sensing of social interaction) and to encourage users to engage in physical activity outside of the home (which could be rewarded with extra 'life-points' in the next gaming session), and (iii) include a standardized exercise (stress-) test to be completed every month as part of an exercise class/game. This also holds for the rest of the games included in the Care4MyHeart Personalized Serious Games (C4MH-PSG) suite (see Sect. 3).

5. Care4MyHeart introduces a new exercise evaluation protocol based on joints' position, orientation, velocity and 3D gesture flow, providing instantaneous local and global level indications/scores. These is combined with signal processing algorithms (e.g., dynamic time warping [13]) for accurate movement comparison.
6. Novel features, such as facial features, head movements, body postures and gestures, are used in Care4MyHeart to provide activity recognition, which will be extended to emotion and intensity recognition within an exercise environment, for measuring affect and engagement [15, 16].

2.2 Structural Characteristics

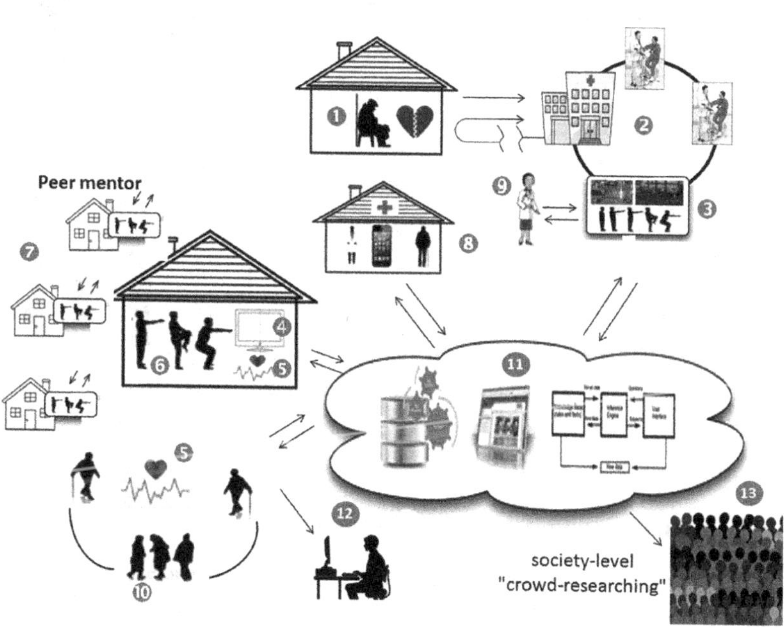

Fig. 1. Schematic representation of the Care4MyHeart project with a sequence of interconnections (1–13).

Care4MyHeart is methodologically deployed (follow Fig. 1, No 1–13) via a collaborative platform [16] that contains an autonomous avatar as a virtual coach (e.g., on smart TV/PC/Tablet or Virtual Reality headset), supporting the C4MH-PSG suite, to be completed individually or by a small number of remote participants, who are at a similar stage of CR. In addition, the platform supports real-time analysis and positive feedback on coping with each game rules, along with day-long monitoring of participants' physiological responses before, during and after interaction with the games. Sensed biosignals, captured by a smartwatch/smartphone and stored in the Cloud (e.g., Microsoft Azure), are combined with patient's supplied information on other lifestyle factors. In this way, all data is accessible anytime-anywhere by the researchers and the related physicians for classification and evaluation purposes. The data archiving follows the rigorous HIPAA (Health Insurance Portability & Accountability Act) compliance requirement [14] to ensure data privacy and security. This process involves guest operational system (OS) and the virtual machines (VMs) in the Cloud, when necessary, for models' updating, retraining and enhancing their predictions/classifications. An epitomized description of the information and data flow within Care4MyHeart is depicted in Fig. 2.

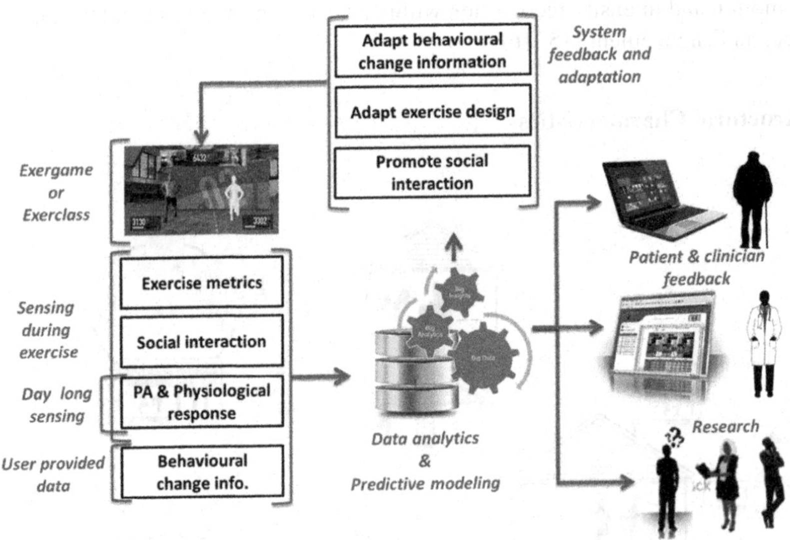

Fig. 2. Information and data flow in the Care4MyHeart platform.

2.3 Big Data Analysis and Behavioral Modelling

Both the sensed and user-provided data will be continuously aggregated and analyzed via big data analytics machine learning (using deep learning [11] and fuzzy logic modeling [12]) and used as the basis for analysis to adapt and personalize the patient's rehabilitation program over time, with abstracted summaries provided as feedback to both the patient and his/her clinician. The structure of human behavior deep learning modeling includes three layers (see Fig. 3): visible layer **v**, hidden layer **h**, and historical layer $\mathcal{H}$ [17]. In this deep learning model, self-motivation, implicit and explicit social influences, and environmental events are naturally incorporated together, so not only to accurately predict human behaviors, but also, for each predicted behavior, to generate explanations. In a graphical representation (see Fig. 3), given a user, each visible variable v_i in the visible layer **v** corresponds to an individual feature f_i at time t. All the visible variables of all the users in the previous N time intervals $\{t-N, \ldots, t-1\}$ are included in a historical layer, denoted by $\mathcal{H}_{t<}$. In addition, the variables in the historical layer are called *historical variables.* Obviously, we will have $|\mathcal{F}| \times |U| \times N$ (see Fig. 3) historical variables. The hidden layer **h** consists of $|\mathbf{h}|$ hidden variables. The process includes connection of the three layers together and modeling of the variables, in order to capture human behavior determinants and provide explanations for the predicted behaviors [17].

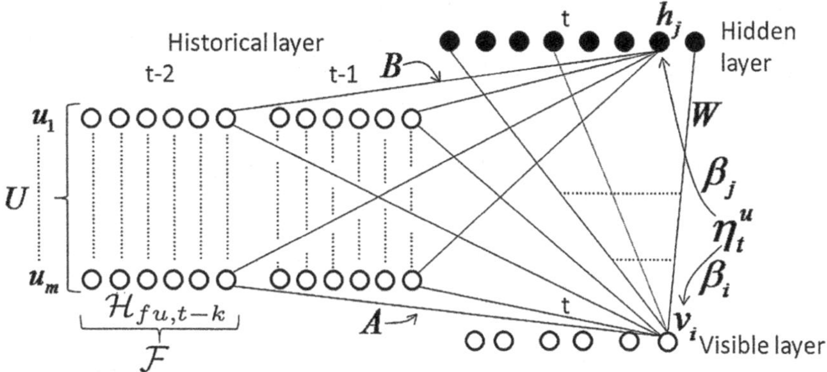

Fig. 3. The structure of the adopted human behavior modeling [17].

3 The Care4MyHeart Personalized Serious Games (C4MH-PSG)

3.1 Driving Knowledge Behind C4MH-PSG Design

The C4MH-PSG design is driven by the crucial factors that are considered by the CVD risk SCORE [4], i.e., High & Low cardiovascular Risk Charts based on gender, age, total cholesterol, systolic blood pressure and smoking status, with relative risk chart, qualifiers and instructions. This information is used to define the target protocols for the patients when using the C4MH platform, the organization of the C4MH-PSG development framework, along with the main categories of the games included.

The protocols that relate with the SCORE parameters target:

- Staying active and controlling blood pressure: Mild to moderate amounts of physical activity can have a big impact on heart health; even the smallest changes make a difference. Hypertension, or high blood pressure, is the most common risk factor for CVD. Reducing stress, eating healthy, and exercising will help keep blood pressure in check.

- Diet changing for cholesterol and saturated fat reduction: Choosing vitamin-rich foods low in cholesterol and fat, benefits heart and whole body.
- Healthy weight maintenance: Carrying excess weight puts significant strain on heart, and can make other cardiovascular disease risk factors worse, such as diabetes. Eating right and exercising regularly can help shed extra kilos.
- Breath control-Stress reduction-Smoking quitting (if applicable): Consistent stress and anger can have damaging effects that could lead to heart attack and stroke. Managing stress by learning relaxation-breathing techniques when feeling overwhelmed would contribute the most. A smoker's risk of developing cardiovascular disease is two to four times greater than non-smokers.

3.2 C4MH-PSG Design Framework

A common framework was adopted to be followed for each game design in C4MH-PSG. The four categories of the aforementioned SCORE-related parameters led to the four categories of the C4MH-PSG, i.e., ExerGames, DietaryGames, EmoGames and Breathing/Stress-SmokeFreeGames (B/SSFGames). Figure 4 illustrates the dynamics and interdependences of the different serious games adopted in the Care4MyHeart, based on five key transversal aspects that are considered to all games, namely:

Fig. 4. The dynamics and interdependences of the different serious games within the Care4MyHeart platform.

- *Data Types and Acquisition Devices.* The Care4MyHeart platform supports certain acquisition devices/controllers. MentorAge® is the main device for the body posture/movement, Apple iWatch monitors the heart rate (unusually low/high rates), noise level, activity, while touch screens and cameras (tablets' built-in) devices are utilized by the Care4MyHeart in a common and transparent way. The output of these devices follows a standard data format.
- *Data Exchange, Storing and Analysis.* The PSG data storage is provided through a database and a common API exposing all the data exchange functionality storying and analysis. As for the analysis, general functions analyze in-game metrics in a common way (average value, deviation, how many times a game was played, values forecasting, etc.) while more complex analysis takes place for each game separately and when this is needed.
- *Safety and Feasibility Issues.* The Care4MyHeart constantly provides instructions and hints to the patient on how the game should be played. When deviation from the proper game play is detected, the game informs the user in order to avoid injuries or other issues.
- *Personalization and Socialization Issues.* The games make the patients reaching their goals progressively in order to keep them in the flow zone which represents the feeling of being complete and energized focus in an activity with a high level of enjoyment and fulfilment towards increased adherence. The game tracks the patients' performance (e.g., maximum angle) and will set an intermediate goal just above the patients' average performance. For instance, the physician had configured the exergaming session to make the patient reach a certain level of leg stretching (i.e., 40°); however, acknowledging the patient's limitations (i.e., history in game measurements show a limit of 25°) the game encourages the patient to reach the preset level, progressively. In other words, the game sets the goal of 30° and when this is well accomplished, it further increases the target to 35° until it reaches the physiotherapists configuration. Moreover, socialization aspects, like participating in groups with others (sharing a common gaming goal) and leader boards will be used at the next level of the games realization as tools for promoting either collaboration or competition among the patients.
- *Reward System and Output Parameters.* The Care4MyHeart rewarding systems runs throughout all the games and activities of the platform. The patients are rewarded ranging from a patient's personal achievement to team achievements, increasing the adherence levels.

The design of the plot of each game within the four categories of the C4MH-PSG (see Fig. 4), is based on the construction of storyboards, that provide an abstract, yet with an embedded dramaturgy, that can be communicated to the users (e.g., CVD patients and physicians), in order to achieve the highest user acceptability, in a co-creation context. Some characteristic examples of such storyboards are described in the proceeding subsections.

3.3 ExerGames

Table 1 summarizes the characteristics of an ExerGame scenario, in terms of the task, its description, except from the storyboard, the various game levels and the game objectives.

Table 1. An example of the ExerGame characteristics.

ExerGame Scenario	
Title	**Picking Citrus Fruit**
Task	To march on a pleasure-environment. During the walking, the users are asked to pick Citrus Fruit (lemons and oranges) from different trees.
Description	Users move to the right to pick lemons (using the upper limb) and to the left to pick oranges (using upper/lower limb) from the trees for the corresponding baskets, following the screen instructions. To simulate the climbing (on the left) users should march and pick the oranges simultaneously.
Storyboard	Picking Citrus Fruit 1: Users move to the right to pick lemons (using the upper limb) and to the left to pick oranges (using upper/lower limb) from the trees for the corresponding baskets, following the screen instructions. Picking Citrus Fruit 2: To simulate the climbing (on the left) users should march and pick the oranges simultaneously. Picking Citrus Fruit 3: Users should follow the doctor recommendations, when pick the highlighted fruits (since the fruits will appear in low, medium or high positions). The time-duration of the highlighted fruits will change according to the level of difficulty. Picking Citrus Fruit 4: To simulate real world, each fruit to be picked will be highlighted and then disappear from the screen. Picking Citrus Fruit 5: The motivational message will change according to the total score reached.
Game-levels	Users should follow the doctors' recommendations, when they pick the highlighted fruits (since the fruits will appear in low, medium or high positions). The time-duration of the highlighted fruits will change according to the level of difficulty.
Game-objectives	Practicing the walk movement; Improving gait mechanisms, balance and coordination aspects.

3.4 DietaryGames

Similarly to Table 1, Table 2 summarizes the characteristics of a DietaryGame scenario, in terms of the task, its description, excerpt from the storyboard, the various game levels and the game objectives.

Table 2. An example of the DietaryGames characteristics.

DietaryGame Scenario	
Title	**The Eatwell Plate**
Task	The user should match each food in the corresponding food group division, based on the Eatwell Plate recommendations that divides the foods and drinks into five main groups, by using the left/right hand for the foods that are presented in the left/right side of the screen.
Description	The users just have to move the hand over the different parts of the food groups shown on the plate to hear what the Chef C4MH-PSG has to say. They can also read the information at the bottom of the plate (e.g., "Water is a healthy/cheap choice; To avoid constipation issues drink at least 6-8 glasses of fluid per day!").
	The Eatwell Plate 1; The Eatwell Plate 2; The Eatwell Plate 3; The Eatwell Plate 4; The Eatwell Plate 5; The Eatwell Plate 6; The Eatwell Plate 7; The Eatwell Plate 8

3.5 EmoGames

Table 3 summarizes the characteristics of an EmoGame scenario, in terms of the task, its description, excerpt from the storyboard, the various game levels and the game objectives.

Table 3. An example of the EmoGame characteristics.

EmoGame Scenario	
Title	**Rhapsody of Faces**
Task	To identify the happy and positive faces.
Description	The user has to identify the happy and positive faces. For every correct selection, more time to continue will be given. In case of wrong selection, the count-down watch will run faster. A wrong choice is when the user selects the wrong one or misses to select a correct one. After selecting the correct photos, a new frame with 4-8 photos is brought up. The final stage presents the correctly identified faces as well as the last wrong one. At the end, motivational messages appear (e.g., "You found 2 happy faces in less than 1 minute. Great work! Try to reach higher level next time!!").

Rhapsody of Faces 1	Rhapsody of Faces 2	Rhapsody of Faces 3	Rhapsody of Faces 4
The faces that will be shown up to the user will be so many, selected randomly based on the difficulty level, that will avoid familiarization.	When the user selects a photo, the game informs her/him about the result. The remaining time in the countdown clock is updated accordingly	A wrong choice is when the user selects the wrong onw or misses to select a correct one. After selecting the correct photos, a new frame with 4-8 photos is brought up.	The final stage presents the correctly identified faces as well as the last worng one.

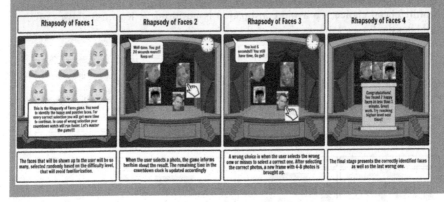

3.6 Breathing/Stress-SmokeFreeGames (B/SSFGames)

As in the previous cases (Tables 1, 2 and 3), Tables 4 and 5 summarize the characteristics of an B/SSFGames scenario, in terms of the task, its description, excerpt from the storyboard, the various game levels and the game objectives.

Table 4. An example of the Breathing/Stress-FreeGame characteristics.

Breathing/Stress-FreeGame Scenario	
Title	**BreathWithMe**
Task	Understand how we breath and practicing it!

Description The mechanisms of breathing are explained in the form of simulating a visit to the doctor, where different levels of information are given as the game proceeds. The user should follow the inhale/exhale process via the microphone of his/her mobile phone via the app, under guided timing and scenarios.

BreathWithMe 1	BreathWithMe 2	BreathWithMe 3
Different mechanisms of breathing are explained in the form of simulating a visit to the doctor.	Then, different levels of information are given as the game proceeds, according to the needs of the user.	Then, different levels of information are given as the game proceeds, according to the needs of the user.

BreathWithMe 4	BreathWithMe 5	BreathWithMe 6
The user should follow the inhale/exhale process via the microphone of his/her mobilephone via the app, under guided timing and scenarios.	The user should follow the inhale/exhale process via the microphone of his/her mobilephone via the app, under guided timing and scenarios.	The user should follow the inhale/exhale process via the microphone of his/her mobilephone via the app, under guided timing and scenarios.

Table 5. An example of the SmokeFreeGames characteristics.

SmokeFreeGame Scenario	
Title	**QuitMe**
Task	Understand the harm of smoking and practicing quitting it!
Description The effects of smoking are explained in a gaming dialogue with a cigarette as a protagonist. This game will be expanded to predict the addition times and evoke supporting messages to avoid smoking and monitor the impact on your health and expenses.	

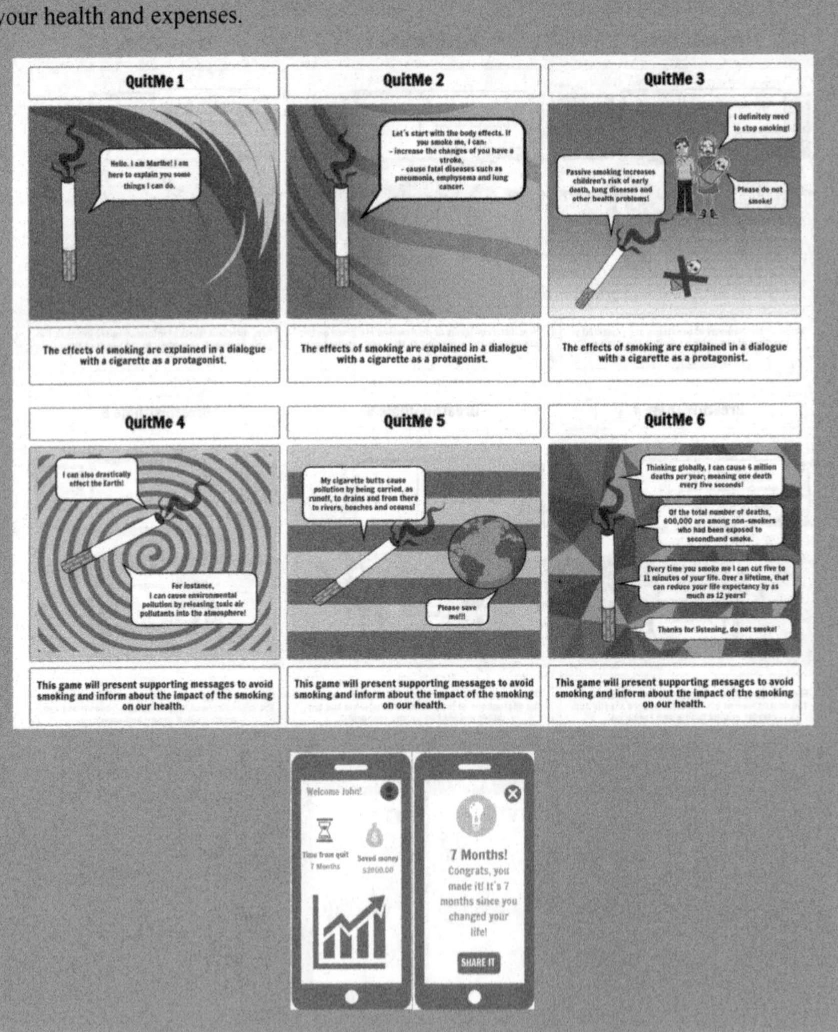

4 Targeted Population and Experiments

4.1 Patients' Characteristics and Sample Size

The sample size for Care4MyHeart is based on the assumption of a mean 10% higher increase (SD 25%) in energy expenditure (METs) in the intervention group compared to the control group during a 6-month period [18]. For this effect size with a power of 0.90 at alpha 0.05 (two-sided), a sample size of 22 participants is required (per treatment group) for the intention-to-treat (ITT) analysis. An estimated drop-out rate of 25% would require minimum 30 participants per group. We aim to recruit cost-wise 60 CVD participants suffering from Coronary Artery Disease (CAD), randomly assigned to participate in groups with intervention (30) and without (30), accordingly. Men and women between the age of 40–80 years with documented CVD, eligible for cardiac rehabilitation and have access to the Internet at home will be targeted, whereas individuals with untreated ventricular tachycardia, life threatening co-existing disease with life expectancy <1 year, significant exercise limitations other than CVD, and intellectual disability that may compromise their ability to use a computer will be excluded from participating in Care4MyHeart.

4.2 Provisional Experimental Protocol

Participants in both groups will make a single visit to the Cleveland Clinic Abu Dhabi (CCAD) rehabilitation laboratory at baseline repeated at 3 and 6 months. During each visit, fasting 5 ml blood sample (for total cholesterol, LDL and HDL, triglycerides, C-reactive protein), DEXA scan, blood pressure and a VO2max with a 12 lead ECG (focusing at ST segment depression/elevation, Q-T morphology) will be measured. In addition, the Care4MyHeart questionnaire will be completed. The experimental group will participate in ≥30 min of moderate to vigorous aerobic-based exercise (MVPA) ≥5 days each week. Exercise will be self-regulated and will be monitored through the combination of sensor monitoring and participant responses to questions asked by the Care4MyHeart Avatar. Participants will self-report a rating of perceived exertion (Borg 20-point category scale) following each exercise session. Daily heart rate and physical activity/inactivity levels will also be monitored via a smartwatch (Apple iWatch) and MentorAge. A unique hardware/software home exercise system will be used to allow exercise to be performed in small social groups of remote participants. A 4-week hospital familiarization phase will embed the Care4MyHeart platform as a normal station within CCAD CR in Phase II program. During the intervention period, there will be no direct human contact between the study participants and the research team. However, the participant's data will be remotely monitored by the research team and the Care4MyHeart Avatar will be designed to remind the participant to engage with Care4MyHeart via their mobile phone or via the Care4MyHeart system. No contact will be made with the control group. To the latter, a lifestyle advice relating to daily physical activity, smoking cessation, moderate substance consumption and healthy eating will be provided [19].

4.3 Ethics

The home-based lifestyle intervention study has been submitted for ethical approval by the research ethics committee of CCAD and all ethical principles for medical research involving human subjects will be followed (Declaration of Helsinki (2008), Directive 2004/23/EC), along with data security and privacy (Directive 95/46/EC, Directive 2002/58/EC). A written consent to participate will be asked in an entirely voluntary manner and will be signed by the participants based on full disclosure of information.

5 Care4MyHeart Impact

With populations that are increasingly older, more sedentary, with more unhealthy lifestyles, combined with growing costs of healthcare and less finances; healthcare service commissioners, employers, insurance and assurance providers are eager to explore new cost-effective and cost-efficient solutions. Care4MyHeart will be attractive because it reduces the time required by healthcare professionals to directly manage patient interaction and health, increases the health outcomes of the Cardiac Rehabilitation (CR) program and provides inbuilt monitoring systems to identify more (cost-) effective and personalized interventions. In addition, it can potentially return patients to work earlier. So far there is not any unified CR program across the UAE; just isolated polices, mainly driven by the CCAD, exist. To this end, the Care4MyHeart intends to integrate the existing policy at the CCAD and further expand it, incorporating novel technology-based approaches towards patients' behavioral change.

Care4MyHeart is an important research and innovation contributor, providing the basis for significant opportunities to demonstrate the creation of new personalized behavioral health interventions fit for global scale up, to facilitate adoption within healthcare systems, to strengthen the research of our academic community, and most importantly, to benefit society and our citizens through improved health. A significant benefit of Care4MyHeart in this regard is the direct (sensed) capture of large amounts of important data (exercise, physical activity, social interaction and behavioral change information access, physiological response).

Moreover, the demand for migration from a highly constrained and regulated structure provides Care4MyHeart with significant and tangible opportunities for commercialization. The Care4MyHeart Cloud-based platform, the behavioral models, the motion capture, analysis and evaluation tools provide new generated Intellectual Property (IP). IP management will be considered and addressed within an ongoing IP Agreement (IPA). An ancillary Exploitation Committee (chaired by the PI) will be formed, to co-ordinate IP-related issues and pursue dissemination and commercialization, especially via the Abu Dhabi's Technology Development Company (TDC) and its partner Mubadala, an R&D technology investment company.

In addition, a research collaboration has been established between the KU and KAIST in South Korea that would leverage on the output of the Care4MyHeart and combine the results with their ongoing research project BeActive in the period of the next two years. Moreover, Care4MyHeart will inform Abu Dhabi 2030 healthcare plan initiatives and UAE organizations, such as Mubadala Healthcare, activated in the areas of personalized medicine, preventative medicine and health awareness, lifestyle adjustment, and treatment, via targeted dissemination activities/events (with the collaboration of CCAD). These activities are expected to be realized at the second year of the project, when the patients will be involved and tangible and quantitative metrics will be uses as proof-of-concept for the success of the Care4MyHeart.

6 Conclusions

The Care4MyHeart-PSG is an end-to-end modular technology platform that allows CVD patients to better self-manage their illness through a supportive, dynamic, holistic, home-based CR program, was presented here. C4MH-PSG allows CR use at any time in a comfortable and personalized environment, capable to provide benefits to all members of the health eco-system to move away from a healthcare provider-centric system to a co-production model, empowering patients to self-manage their health based on a home-based monitoring intelligent system solving the drop out problems in the existing CR programs.

Acknowledgements. This work is funded by the Abu Dhabi Department of Education and Knowledge (ADEK), UAE, under the Award for Research Excellence (AARE) 2018, ref. no: 29934 and partially supported by HEIC fund from Khalifa University.

References

1. World Health Organization, CVD Factsheet, March 2013
2. Nichols, M., et al.: European Cardiovascular Disease Statistics 2012, European Heart Network, Brussels, European Society of Cardiology, Sophia Antipolis (2012)
3. Turk-Adawi, K.I., Terzic, C., Bjarnason-Wehrens, B., Grace, S.L.: Cardiac rehabilitation in Cana-da and Arab countries: comparing availability and program characteristics. BMC Health Serv. Res. **15**, 521–531 (2015). https://doi.org/10.1186/s12913-015-1183-7
4. Piepoli, M.F., Hoes, A.W., Agewall, S., Albus, C., Brotons, C., Catapano, A.L.: European guidelines on CVD prevention in clinical practice, "Systematic Coronary Risk Evaluation (SCORE)" Eur. Heart J. **33**, 1635–1701 (2012). http://doi.org/10.1093/eurheartj/ehs092
5. Jolliffe, J., Rees, K., Taylor, R.R.S., Thompson, D.R., Oldridge, N., Ebrahim, S.: Exercise-based re-habilitation for coronary heart disease. Cochrane Database Syst. Rev. **1**, CD001800 (2009)
6. Jennings, S., Carey, D.: Capacity and equity in cardiac rehabilitation in the eastern region: good and bad news. Ir. J. Med. Sci. **173**(3), 151–154 (2004). https://doi.org/10.1007/BF03167930
7. Ashworth, N., Chad, K., et al.: Home versus centre based physical activity interventions in older adults. Cochrane Database Syst. Rev. **1**, CD004017 (2005)
8. Hughes, A.R., Mutrie, N., MacIntyre, P.D.: Effect of an exercise consultation on maintenance of physical activity after completion of phase III exercise-based cardiac rehabilitation. Eur. J. Cardiovasc. Prev. Rehabil. **14**(1), 114–121 (2007)
9. Sniehotta, F.F., Scholz, U., et al.: Long-term effects of two psychological interventions on physical exercise and self-regulation following coronary rehabilitation. Int. J. Behav. Med. **12**(4), 244–255 (2005). https://doi.org/10.1207/s15327558ijbm1204_5
10. Bodenheimer, T., et al.: Patient self-management of chronic disease in primary care. JAMA **288**(19), 2469–2475 (2002)

11. Goodfellow, I., Bengio, Y., Courville, A.: Deep Learning (Adaptive Computation and Machine Learning series) Hardcover – 11 November 2016. (http://www.deeplearningbook.org/)
12. Douali, N., Csaba, H., De Roo, J., Papageorgiou, E.I., Jaulent, M.-C.: Diagnosis support system based on clinical guidelines: comparison between case-based fuzzy cognitive maps and bayesian networks. Comput. Methods Programs Biomed. **113**(1), 133–143 (2014)
13. Al-Naymat, G., Chawla, S., Taheri, J.: SparseDTW: a novel approach to speed up dynamic time warping. In: Proceedings of the Eighth Australasian Data Mining Conference, Australian Computer Society, Inc., vol. 101, pp. 117–127 (2009)
14. Anderson, S.: Health Insurance Portability and Accountability Act of 1996 (HIPAA). www.healthInsurance.org
15. Broekhuizen, K., et al.: A systematic review of randomized controlled trials on the effectiveness of computer-tailored physical activity and dietary behavior promotion programs: an update. Annals Behav. Med. **44**(2), 259–286 (2012)
16. Bandura, A.: Human agency in social cognitive theory. Am. Psychol. **44**, 1175–1184 (1989)
17. Phan, N., Dou, D., Piniewski, B., Kil, D.: A deep learning approach for human behavior prediction with explanations in health social networks: social restricted Boltzmann machine (SRBM^{+}). Soc. Netw. Anal. Min. **6**(1), 1–14 (2016). https://doi.org/10.1007/s13278-016-0379-0
18. Kodama, S., et al.: Cardiorespiratory fitness as a qualitative predictor of all-cause mortality and cardiovascular events in healthy men and women: a meta-analysis. JAMA **301**(19), 2024–2035 (2009)
19. Neubeck, L., et al.: Telehealth interventions for the secondary prevention of coronary heart dis-ease: a systematic review. Eur. J. Cardiovasc. Prevent. Rehabil. **16**, 281–289 (2009)

The HapBack: Evaluation of Absolute and Relative Distance Encoding to Enhance Spatial Awareness in a Wearable Tactile Device

Bryan Duarte, Troy McDaniel(✉), Ramin Tadayon, Abhik Chowdhury, Allison Low, and Sethuraman Panchanathan

Arizona State University, Tempe, AZ 85281, USA
{bjduarte,troy.mcdaniel}@asu.edu

Abstract. For the significant global population of individuals who are blind or visually impaired, spatial awareness during navigation remains a challenge. Tactile Electronic Travel Aids have been designed to assist with the provision of spatiotemporal information, but an intuitive method for mapping this information to patterns on a vibrotactile display remains to be determined. This paper explores the encoding of distance from a navigator to an object using two strategies: absolute and relative. A wearable prototype, the HapBack, is presented with two straps of vertically aligned vibrotactile motors mapped to five distances, with each distance mapped to a row on the display. Absolute patterns emit a single vibration at the row corresponding to a distance, while relative patterns emit a sequence of vibrations starting from the bottom row and ending at the row mapped to that distance. These two encoding strategies are comparatively evaluated for identification accuracy and perceived intuitiveness of mapping among ten adult participants who are blind or visually impaired. No significant difference was found between the intuitiveness of the two encodings based on these metrics, with each showing promising results for application during navigation tasks.

Keywords: Wearable tactile display · Nonvisual navigation · Spatial awareness

1 Introduction

Navigation in the absence or impairment of visual information is a fairly common task. For the estimated one third of the global population who are blind or visually impaired [27,41], nonvisual navigation is a daily challenge. Even for sighted individuals, characteristics of the environment may obscure vision, making information about obstacles, landmarks, other objects and people very difficult to access through this sensory modality. This spatiotemporal information plays a crucial role in the formation of spatial awareness, a necessity for safe

C. Stephanidis et al. (Eds.): HCII 2020, LNCS 12426, pp. 251–266, 2020.
https://doi.org/10.1007/978-3-030-60149-2_20

and efficient navigation especially through dynamic environments [12]. For individuals who live or work in nonvisual conditions, mobility and an independent lifestyle therefore require the use of sensory substitution using audio, touch or other senses for building spatial awareness during navigation.

Traditional methods for navigation include the cane, guide dog, and human guide. However, these methods each have significant limitations: a cane while walking can only alert the navigator to objects of interest (OI) up to roughly 4–5 ft in front, and only up to waist level; a guide dog and human guide both direct the navigator, signaling him or her on which actions to take, rather than providing the navigator with information to allow him/her to maintain autonomy and control over path planning and movement decisions while navigating. These challenges have resulted in the development of technological solutions designed to assist travel, called Electronic Travel Aids (ETAs). Yet, despite decades of research and development in this field, the adoption rate of ETAs remain quite low relative to traditional approaches.

To determine the reasons for these shortcomings, we conducted a survey of 80 individuals who are blind or visually impaired on the topic of nonvisual travel. This preliminary survey had revealed that, indeed, the cane (63%), guide dog (30%), and sighted human aid (5%) were overwhelmingly popular as the three primary forms of assistance used during travel. Where technological solutions were used, often they were abandoned within five or fewer uses due to the several limitations, which we represent as requirements for an effective ETA:

- *Intuitive*: Information was difficult to understand or took too long to interpret.
- *Non-Audio*: The ETA used audio which served as a distraction or overload to the navigator's sense of hearing, the primary modality used to sense and interact with the environment in the absence of vision.
- *Hands-Free*: The ETA (primarly a smartphone app) required constant usage of the hand, which was non-ideal as the hands were needed to hold a cane or open doors.
- *Discreet*: The device or its interaction violated the navigator's sense of privacy in public spaces.

The latter three requirements relate to the design of the interface, while the former relates to the language of communication. To address these limitations in existing ETAs and the limitations of traditional tools for navigation, this study explores the design of an intuitive tactile language and hands-free, wearable and discreet tactile display (the HapBack) for the delivery of spatiotemporal data to enhance spatial awareness. As a first step in achieving this complex task, we focus this study on evaluating the intuitiveness of a novel tactile language communicating the location of an OI during navigation. In previous work [9], we explored the representation of this information in three dimensions: direction, height, and distance of an OI. While our previous language design delivered highly intuitive direction and height encodings, the intuitive encoding of distance remains a challenge. In the current work, two strategies for encoding an OI's distance from the navigator are explored: absolute patterns, which represent an immediate pulse of the object's distance, and relative patterns, which utilize a series of pulses from a consistent baseline in an attempt to better represent relative distances.

In Sect.. 2, several categories of ETAs and the limitations of current work in each on achieving the above requirements are discussed. In Sect. 3, we detail the design of the HapBack prototype and absolute/relative tactile patterns with examples of each. Section 4 describes the evaluation performed in this study on 10 subjects who are blind or visually impaired, wherein the absolute and relative mappings were evaluated using objective (response accuracy for absolute identification tasks) and subjective (self-reported naturalness of mapping) metrics of intuitiveness. We conclude in Sect. 5 with directions for future development.

2 Related Work

2.1 Nonvisual Navigation

Two frames for the representation of object locations exist: allocentric, wherein an object's location is described relative to that of another object in the environment, or egocentric, wherein an object's location is described relative to the subject [21]. It has been shown in studies of spatial representation that while individuals with vision utilize both for spatial awareness, those who do not have access to vision generally rely on the latter (egocentric) representation for spatial awareness [25,33]. A growing body of evidence supports that access to spatial information is a modal, in that it does not necessarily require the use of a specific modality such as vision and can be abstracted from this sensory mechanism, allowing for sensory substitution strategies to be employed [37]. In fact, with proper sensory substitution, it has been shown that individuals who are congenitally blind can reach equivalent spatial representation to their sighted peers [5].

2.2 Electronic Travel Aids

Cane Augmentation. Perhaps the first and one of the most commonly used sensory substitution device for nonvisual acquisition of spatial awareness is the cane, which demonstrated the effect of neuroplasticity on spatial learning [23]. Many ETA research approaches thus attempt to augment the cane with additional spatiotemporal information in order to overcome its limited range and height of detection. These approaches generally augment the white cane with technology such as sonar, cameras or other sensors and additional real-time feedback [1,6,18,34,43]. For example, one recent approach by Rahman et al. [30] utilizes a laser and camera mounted on the cane for the purpose of detection of obstacles, holes, stairs and other OIs while the individual navigates. Once an OI is detected such as an obstacle, a vibrotactile signal is emitted from the cane and felt by the individual. The closer an individual moves to that obstacle, the greater the frequency of vibration. In this case, the laser and camera mechanism improve the sensing range while a simple tactile signal is used to augment spacial awareness.

Generally, however, smart canes do not provide significantly higher performance at the detection of most obstacles over traditional canes [35]. Several factors may contribute to this observation. One is that when using the cane to send tactile feedback, the interface is limited to the contact between the hand and cane, which is a rather small surface area with relatively low resolution for a tactile display. Hence, sensitivity to distinct signals may be reduced, and many smart cane approaches instead turn to audio for feedback, the limitations of which are discussed below. Another is that the design and usage of a cane make it difficult to implement technology directly within or on the cane for this purpose as the weight of the cane must be kept to a minimum [2] and the cane is constantly being moved left and right while walking, making it difficult to use a camera or other sensing mechanism on the device.

Audio Devices. Alternative solutions have utilized audio or audio-haptic cues for the delivery of real-time feedback on spatiotemporal data [14,22,29]. The advantage of audio as a target modality is that it is highly attuned to distance recognition. Echolocation, for example, is the act of bouncing audio signals off of objects in the environment and using the acoustic properties of the sound's echo to determine size, distance and other attributes of these objects. Echolocation is a commonly used mechanism for audio-based distance detection [39]. Some recent approaches [38,42] have even chosen to leverage echolocation with audio feedback as an ETA, in an attempt to build upon an existing skillset for navigators.

Unfortunately, all interfaces which use audio as a modality for feedback and cueing in the context of nonvisual and navigation share one massive drawback: individuals who are blind or visually impaired utilize hearing as the main sensory channel by which to interact in their environment in the absence of vision, making audio a less ideal modality for guidance [3]. For example, while navigating outdoors, an individual may listen for audio cues at pedestrian crossings or be engaged in a telephone conversation. In each of these cases, audio cues from the ETA may conflict with the interactions already present in this channel or induce unnecessarily high cognitive load [19].

Tactile Devices. As a more effective alternative, tactile ETAs outside of cane augmentation have emerged to assist with the task of nonvisual navigation [11, 17,26,36,40]. These interfaces, often implemented as wearables, are designed to leverage the spatial acuity of the body's surface at various sites toward touch stimuli [7] to deliver information discreetly. A majority of these implementations either implement static spatial representations such as room layouts as tactile maps on a display (for example, the refreshable top-down display style of [26]) or calculate the optimal path for the navigator to take and then utilize tactile signals to direct the navigator past obstacles (for example, the *turn left*, *turn right*, and *go straight* metaphors in approaches such as [40]).

However, many of these methods each have significant challenges for adoption. Tactile map views utilize survey-style (allocentric) reference frames which contradict the egocentric preference of spatial mapping [28], such that when used in conjunction with the traditionally egocentric cane, guide dog or human aid, these devices require simultaneous use of both reference frames for navigation. Furthermore, they require that a reliable and sufficiently informed sensing infrastructure is in place for retrieving the entire spatial layout of the environment prior to and during navigation [31], which may be impractical when used to navigate outdoors in dynamic environments including traffic, people and other moving parts. Tactile interfaces which provide directions for navigation focus on directing, rather than informing the navigator. In this case, the locus of navigational decision making is on the device rather than the user. These interfaces may be undesirable in that they reduce the autonomy of the navigator [4,24,32], reducing the ability to independently form a cognitive map.

Perhaps the most promising method, based on the requirements for ETA use outlined in the nonvisual navigation survey feedback above, is that of van Erp et al. [11], who focused on the provision of spatiotemporal information exhibiting the location of OIs in multiple dimensions: horizontal direction (simply referred to here as direction), distance from the navigator (simply referred to as distance), height (a reference of the height of the OI relative to the navigator) and ID (classification of the OI among several commonly encountered objects during navigation such as stairs). A two-dimensional wearable vibrotactile display on a belt was implemented and utilized to evaluate a tactile language wherein rows, columns, temporal patterns and frequencies were utilized to encode each dimension of this information. It was found that an intuitive depiction of this information requires the design of dimensional encodings that are not only intuitive on their own, but also maintain distinctiveness when combined into multidimensional representations. The implementation had satisfied three of the four requirements above for ETA design (*non-audio*, *hands-free*, *discreet*), with the last requirement (*intuitive*) left for further exploration.

To address these findings, we had previously explored the interplay between body surface, tactor locations, display resolution and spatiotemporal encoding in the design of a vibrotactile display on a wearable belt, the HaptWrap [9], for spatial awareness during nonvisual navigation. In this study, the dimensions of ID and height from above were found to be useful when combined to leverage their redundancies (objects could be classified in major categories based on height when considered as obstacles) which resulted in three dimensions of information: direction, height, and distance. These dimensions were mapped to the columns, rows and rhythmic frequency of vibrotactile cues, respectively. During evaluation it was found that while the encodings of direction and height were highly intuitive in multidimensional patterns, distances were more difficult to distinguish when different rhythmic frequencies were assigned to each. This is consistent with the findings in [11].

Based on the above, the current study focuses on the design and evaluation of intuitiveness of two different implementations of spatial mappings to encode the dimension of distance.

3 Methodology

3.1 HapBack Device Design

As an initial note, the full design of an ETA consists of several components, including a sensing mechanism by which raw visual information is gathered (such as a mounted camera), a processing mechanism by which this information is processed and converted to a multidimensional spatiotemporal representation (such as an image processing mechanism which identifies an OI and estimates the direction, distance and height of the OI based on features of the image/video), and finally, communication (the processed spatiotemporal data is communicated to the navigator). In this work, we are primarily concerned with the communication component. Therefore, for the sake of simplicity, we assume, for now, that at any point, a single OI has been sensed and identified, and its egocentric distance from the navigator is known and readily available; the addition of sensing and processing components to our design will be the focus of future work.

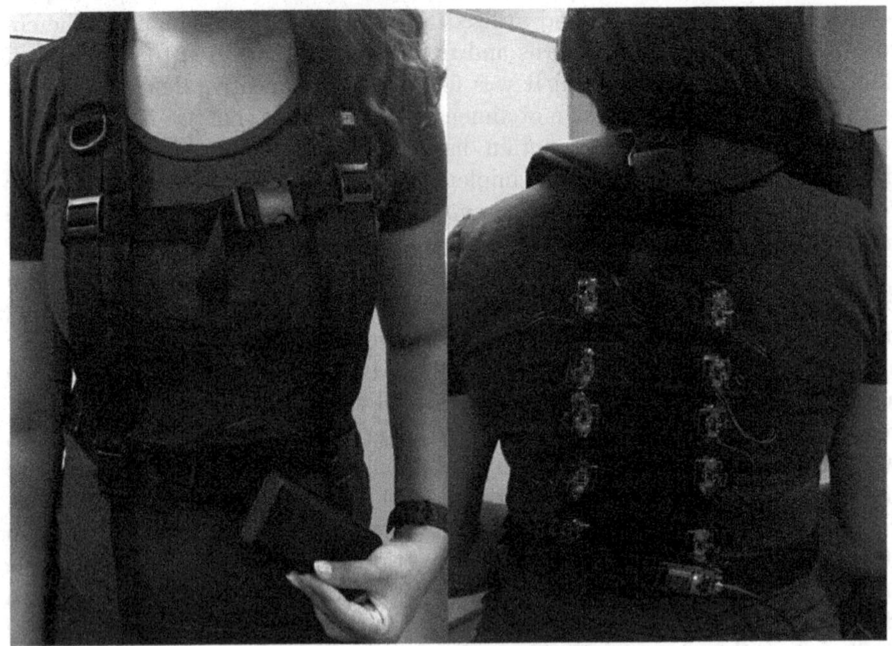

Fig. 1. Prototype of the HapBack device shown from the front (left) and back (right).

In accordance with the aforementioned requirements for ETA design, a wearable tactile interface was chosen as the design for the current prototype. Named the Hapback, this prototype consists of two back-worn vertical straps each embedded with a single column of five vertically distributed vibrotactile motors as shown in Fig. 1. Whereas in the previous HaptWrap implementation, the waist was chosen as the contact site for the haptic display, the back was chosen in this iteration due to the relatively high spatial resolution and stability during motion of the back compared to the waist, forearms and other areas in use while walking [8,15,16].

The motors are connected in pairs by elastic bands along the spine, and the vertical straps are connected at the top and bottom through horizontal straps secured around the top of the chest and the torso to ensure that the device maintains contact with the back of the user. An ESP-WROOM-32 microcontroller allows for real-time automated control of the motors and the delivery of vibrotactile cues in real-time through a partner app installed on a laptop. The entire system is powered by a portable USB rechargeable battery and can be worn above or underneath clothing to use on-the-go, ensuring discreetness and hands-free portable use of tactile feedback.

3.2 Distance Encoding Strategy

Distance in this study refers to egocentric distance, measured in feet, from the navigator to an OI. As a continuous measure, this would require an infinite amount of distinct vibrotactile patterns to represent all possible distances. Fortunately, the context of navigation, the length of the cane, and the intuitions of proxemics [13], a study of the regions of interpersonal distance, together form a set of parameters by which this continuous range can be subdivided into discrete categories. Given that the cane can detect at a range of roughly 4–5 ft, the first distance category represented in this language is 5 ft from the navigator. From there, intervals of 5 ft are used, each representing one full cane length, to reach ranges of the personal, social, public, and beyond public spaces, respectively, as adjustments to the interaction regions defined in American cultural context through proxemics. Therefore, five total distance categories are represented in this approach: 5, 10, 15, 20, and 25 ft. An object's precise location is approximated to the nearest of these five categories. For example, an object at 17.6 ft would be assigned to the 20 ft distance category. Objects outside of the 5–25 foot range are considered not of interest within the walking context, as anything below 5 ft would be detected by a cane and anything above 25 ft would require less immediate attention (with the exception of fast-moving objects, which would be moving too quickly for most detection mechanisms to sufficiently warn the navigator). Note that the value of these categories is not itself significant; when applied to a different context, they can be rescaled as necessary.

Each of these five distance categories corresponds to row of motors on the HapBack device. 5 ft is assigned to the top row, followed by 10 ft in the second row, 15 ft in the third, 20 ft in the fourth, and finally, 25 ft in the bottom row. As the two straps on the hapback are aligned by connecting the motors pairwise on each row, each distance category is therefore mapped to the pair of motors in the corresponding row of the HapBack prototype. When a signal is sent to a particular row, the pair of vibrotactile motors on that row vibrate at the same frequency and amplitude and for the same duration in this implementation. Therefore, the two straps forming the display can effectively be treated as a single column for the sake of mapping.

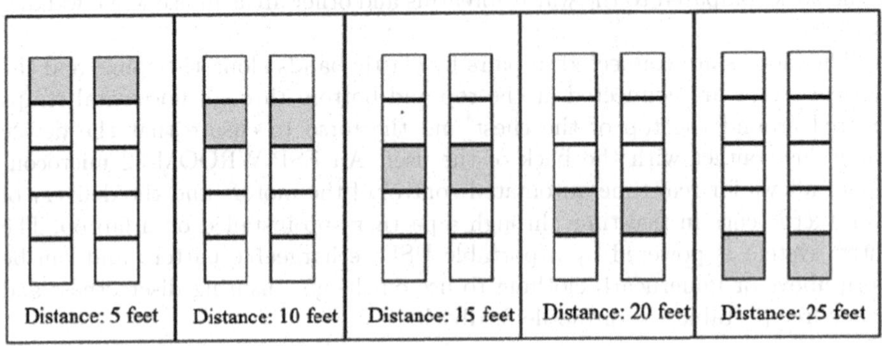

Fig. 2. Illustration of five absolute feedback patterns.

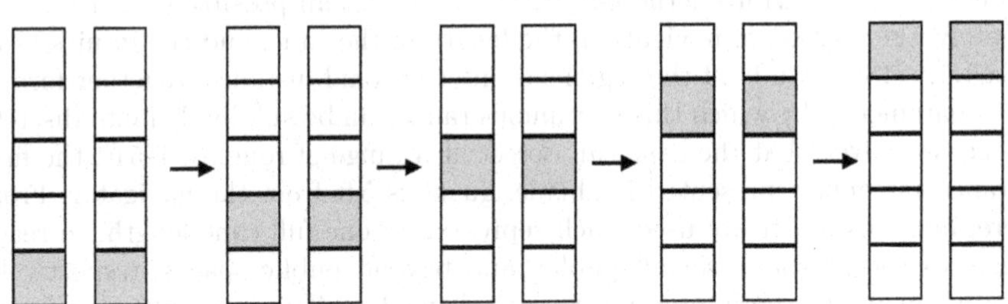

Fig. 3. Illustration of pattern sequence for 5 ft relative feedback pattern.

Two representations are presented in this work to encode a distance in one of the five assigned distance categories: absolute and relative. In the absolute encoding strategy, to communicate a particular distance, the HapBack display pulses its corresponding row once for a preset length of time (roughly 100 ms). For example, to communicate that an object is currently roughly 10 ft away, the second from the top row of the HapBack vibrates a single time. This mapping is shown in Fig. 2. This representation has the advantage of being rapid as only a single vibration is used in every case, allowing for quick capture of an object's location. However, as the only element distinguishing the five patterns in this case is their vertical location along the spine, it is hypothesized that distinguishing between these patterns, particularly those adjacent to one another, may not be as easy as an implementation in which they were also distinct temporally.

To address this hypothesis, a relative representation was developed as an alternative. The relative representation uses the same mapping of rows to distances, but instead of vibrating only the row corresponding to the communicated distance once, the rows of the HapBack are vibrated in a sequence starting from the bottom row and stopping at the row corresponding to that distance. For example, as shown in Fig. 3, to communicate that an object is currently roughly 5 ft away, the fifth row is vibrated, followed by the fourth, the third, the second, and finally the top row which is mapped to 5 ft. These vibrations are spaced evenly apart with 0 ms time delay between them (one vibration starts as soon as the previous one stops). In the case of 25 ft, only the bottom row is vibrated, making it equivalent in its absolute and relative representations. The relative encoding therefore allows us to comparatively evaluate the addition of a temporal sequencing element on an individual's ability to distinguish between one distance and another. It should be noted, however, that with the addition of the temporal element in the relative encoding comes a major drawback: patterns take longer to present, particularly for 5 ft which is a sequence of five vibrations. This makes the communication of distance significantly slower and may even be impractical when the navigator or OI is in motion. Therefore, a tradeoff of time consumption for distinctive clarity is hypothesized.

4 Evaluation

For this study, the goal of evaluation is to comparatively determine how intuitively the relative and absolute modes encode the five categories of distance in the proposed tactile mapping. This is measured objectively through absolute identification accuracy over the range of distances in the language, and subjectively through questionnaire results, as has been shown in previous work [10,11,20].

4.1 Procedure

The evaluation was conducted at the Center for Cognitive Ubiquitous Computing laboratory (CUbiC) at Arizona State University along with a private room at SAAVI Services for the Blind in Phoenix. Ten adults (18 years of age or older) who are blind or visually impaired (19 recruited, with 9 dropped due to issues in the experimental setup) participated in the study. All participation was voluntary and each subject signed a consent form prior to participation. The study was approved by Arizona State University Institutional Review Board prior to initiation.

After giving consent, each subject was asked to wear the HapBack device while seated. The experimenter could then transmit tactile patterns directly to the subject through a laptop interface visible only to the experimenter. Each subject was then evaluated on his or her response to two conditions: absolute (in which the absolute pattern mechanism described above was used) and relative (using the relative patterns described above). The ordering of these two conditions were counterbalanced between the subjects to control for ordering effects.

Each condition consisted of a familiarization phase followed by a testing phase. In the familiarization phase, the experimenter presented each of the five patterns in the current condition (corresponding to the five distances) to the subject in an ordered fashion (smallest to largest or largest to smallest). For each pattern, the experimenter first stated the distance that the pattern corresponded to, and then activated the pattern on the subject's HapBack. Once the subject had felt the pattern, he or she could ask for any number of repetitions. For each repetition, the experimenter would once again state the distance of the pattern and then activate it for the subject to feel. No data was recorded during the familiarization phase.

Once all the distances were presented in the familiarization phase, the testing phase would begin. In this phase, a randomized sequence of 15 patterns in the current condition would be presented to the subject, in which each of the five patterns was included exactly three times. Each time a pattern was presented, the subject was asked to identify the distance to which that pattern corresponded. The correct response and subject's response were both recorded. No feedback was given to the subject in this phase, including whether or not the subject's response was correct. A response was scored correct if it matched the intended distance in the mapping, and incorrect if it did not.

Once each subject had completed all four of these phases (a familiarization and testing phase with relative patterns, followed by a familiarization and testing phase with absolute patterns, or vice versa), he or she was then asked to complete a post-experiment questionnaire with four questions, two for each of the testing conditions (absolute and relative). For each condition, the first question asked the subject to rate, on a Likert scale from 1 to 5, with 1 being *Very Hard* and 5 being *Very Easy*, how natural (intuitive) the mapping was between the vibration patterns for that condition. This was followed by a second question for each condition that asked the subject to explain the ranking he or she chose. This gave each subject a chance to elaborate on why he or she felt a particular mapping was more or less intuitive.

4.2 Results and Discussion

The identification accuracy for each subject in each of the two distance encodings, represented as the number of correct distances identified out of fifteen patterns given in each encoding, is shown in Fig. 4. The average accuracy over all subjects was then collected for each condition and used to determine the intuitiveness of that encoding. Results indicated that both absolute and relative encodings were quite intuitive, with 73% response accuracy (st. dev. 0.182) for absolute patterns and 87% accuracy (st. dev. 0.122) for relative patterns. These are impressive response accuracies given that the subjects did not receive any prior training other than the brief familiarization phase to learn the mappings.

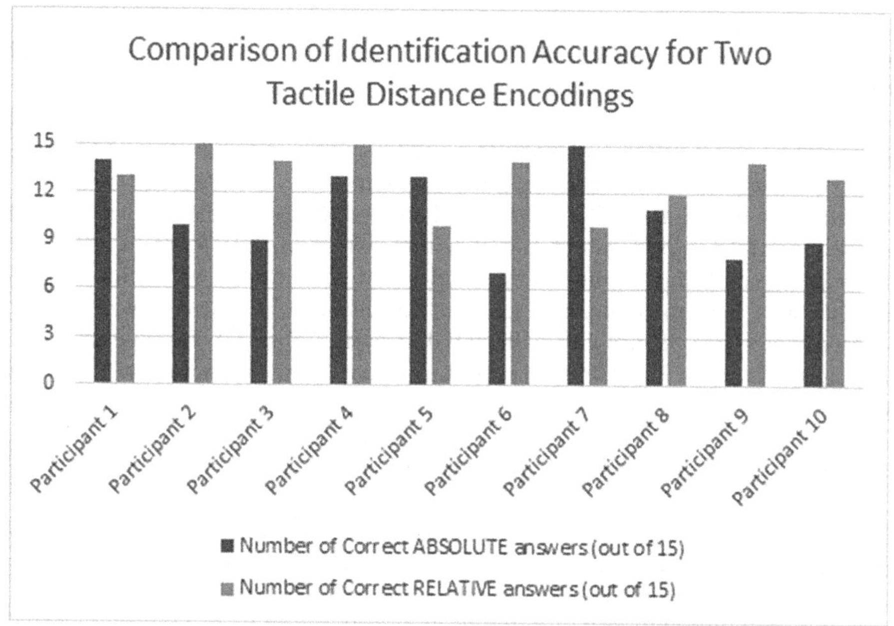

Fig. 4. Identification accuracy for 10 subjects in absolute and relative distance encoding.

Table 1. Post-experiment questionnaire responses on perceived intuitiveness of mapping

Subject	Absolute	Relative
1	4	5
2	3	5
3	2	5
4	5	5
5	3	5
6	4	5
7	4	3
8	4	1
9	4	4
10	4	4

No statistically significant difference was found in response accuracy between the two modes based on a paired two-sample t-test ($P = 0.135$ two-tail, $\alpha = 0.01$), suggesting that both approaches were equally viable for the subject sample.

Post-experiment questionnaire responses (out of 5) for perceived intuitiveness of mapping are shown in Table 1. Subjects reported an average intuitiveness score of 3.7 (st. dev. 0.823) for absolute patterns and 4.2 (st. dev. 1.317) for relative patterns. No statistically significant difference was found in perceived intuitiveness of mapping between the two modes based on a paired two-sample t-test ($P = 0.380$ two-tail, $\alpha = 0.01$), supporting the findings from the experimental phases. However, subject explanations for their questionnaire scores in the open-ended questions provided some further insight into the differences between how the two were felt. Some subjects reported some difficulty in discerning between adjacent patterns/distances in the absolute condition, but found it easier in the relative condition because they could count the number of vibrations and use that as a backup strategy to identify the distance in that condition. Many reported that this difficulty was alleviated over the course of the experiment as they found it easier to identify the patterns that were presented later in each phase.

5 Conclusions and Future Work

Based on the results shown during evaluation, the HapBack prototype and tactile language presented serve as an intuitive method by which distance can be communicated in real-time as a part of a novel ETA for spatial awareness. Furthermore, the wearable, discreet, hands-free and non-audio nature of the HapBack prototype, as well as the provision of spatiotemporal information rather than predetermined path directions, afford the navigator a greater sense of control, privacy and usability. Given that no significant difference could be found between absolute and relative encodings, and both were considered highly intuitive on first use by subjects, it is proposed that the absolute encoding be utilized in most cases as it has the advantage of utilizing only a single tactile pulse for each distance, ensuring speed of delivery and allowing for more practical use in dynamic environments.

The evaluation performed here serves a preliminary purpose in the intuitive encoding of a single dimension of spatiotemporal information. However, to achieve spatial awareness, this dimension of tactile patterns must be integrated with other dimensions of information (direction, height) to form complete, multidimensional representations of OI location. Integration of this mapping with the effective components of the previous mapping used in the HaptWrap require careful consideration of the role of rows in the tactile display, as both distance in the HapBack and height in the HaptWrap are mapped to rows in their corresponding tactile language. Future work will evaluate how it might be possible to combine these elements while maintaining intuitiveness without the use of a temporal element on a two-dimensional display. The integration of multiple wearables (the HapBack in combination with the HaptWrap) is also under consideration, with careful attention toward the effect of multiple displays on cognitive load during a navigation task.

Acknowledgments. The authors would like to thank the National Science Foundation and Arizona State University for their funding support. This material is partially based upon work supported by the NSF under Grant No. 1828010.

References

1. Abeysiriwardhana, W.A.S.P., Maheshi Ruwanthika, R.M., Abeykoon, A.M.H.S.: Vibro-haptic white cane with enhanced vibro sensitivity. In: 2018 2nd International Conference On Electrical Engineering (EECon), pp. 156–161, September 2018. https://doi.org/10.1109/EECon.2018.8540997
2. Arefin, P., Habib, M.S., Arefin, A., Arefin, M.S.: A review on current mechanical and electronic design aspects and future prospects of smart canes for individuals with lower limb difficulties. Mater. Sci. Res. India **17**(1), 25–33 (2020). http://www.materialsciencejournal.org/vol17no1/a-review-on-current-mechanical-and-electronic-design-aspects-and-future-prospects-of-smart-canes-for-individuals-with-lower-limb-difficulties/
3. Bharadwaj, A., Shaw, S.B., Goldreich, D.: Comparing tactile to auditory guidance for blind individuals. Front. Hum. Neurosci. **13** (2019). https://doi.org/10.3389/fnhum.2019.00443. Publisher: Frontiers
4. Brunyé, T.T., Gardony, A.L., Holmes, A., Taylor, H.A.: Spatial decision dynamics during wayfinding: intersections prompt the decision-making process. Cogn. Res. Princ. Impl. **3**(1), 13 (2018). https://doi.org/10.1186/s41235-018-0098-3
5. Chebat, D.-R., Harrar, V., Kupers, R., Maidenbaum, S., Amedi, A., Ptito, M.: Sensory substitution and the neural correlates of navigation in blindness. In: Pissaloux, E., Velázquez, R. (eds.) Mobility of Visually Impaired People, pp. 167–200. Springer, Cham (2018). https://doi.org/10.1007/978-3-319-54446-5_6
6. Chen, Q., et al.: CCNY smart cane. In: 2017 IEEE 7th Annual International Conference on CYBER Technology in Automation, Control, and Intelligent Systems (CYBER), pp. 1246–1251, July 2017. https://doi.org/10.1109/CYBER.2017.8446303
7. Collins, A.A., Brill, J.C., Cholewiak, R.W.: Spatial factors in vibrotactile pattern perception. In: EUROHAPTICS 2001, p. 41 (2001)
8. Dim, N.K., Ren, X.: Investigation of suitable body parts for wearable vibration feedback in walking navigation. Int. J. Hum. Comput. Stud. **97**, 34–44 (2017). https://doi.org/10.1016/j.ijhcs.2016.08.002. http://www.sciencedirect.com/science/article/pii/S107158191630088X
9. Duarte, B., McDaniel, T., Chowdhury, A., Gill, S., Panchanathan, S.: HaptWrap: augmenting non-visual travel via visual-to-tactile mapping of objects in motion. In: Proceedings of the 2nd Workshop on Multimedia for Accessible Human Computer Interfaces, MAHCI 2019, Nice, France, pp. 17–24. Association for Computing Machinery, October 2019. https://doi.org/10.1145/3347319.3356835
10. Duarte, B., et al.: Haptic vision: augmenting non-visual travel and accessing environmental information at a distance. In: Basu, A., Berretti, S. (eds.) ICSM 2018. LNCS, vol. 11010, pp. 90–101. Springer, Cham (2018). https://doi.org/10.1007/978-3-030-04375-9_8
11. van Erp, J.B.F., Kroon, L.C.M., Mioch, T., Paul, K.I.: Obstacle detection display for visually impaired: coding of direction, distance, and height on a vibrotactile waist band. Front. ICT **4** (2017). https://doi.org/10.3389/fict.2017.00023. https://www.frontiersin.org/articles/10.3389/fict.2017.00023/full. Publisher: Frontiers
12. Giudice, N.A.: Navigating without vision: principles of blind spatial cognition. In: Montello, D.R. (ed.) Handbook of Behavioral and Cognitive Geography. Edward Elgar Publishing, Northampton (2018)
13. Hall, E.T.: Proxemics: The study of man's spatial relations (1962)

14. Hoffmann, R., Spagnol, S., Kristjánsson, A., Unnthorsson, R.: Evaluation of an audio-haptic sensory substitution device for enhancing spatial awareness for the visually impaired. Optom. Vis. Sci. **95**(9), 757–765 (2018). https://doi.org/10.1097/OPX.0000000000001284. https://www.ncbi.nlm.nih.gov/pmc/articles/PMC6133230/
15. Jones, L.A., Kunkel, J., Piateski, E.: Vibrotactile pattern recognition on the arm and back. Perception **38**(1), 52–68 (2009). https://doi.org/10.1068/p5914. Publisher: SAGE Publications Ltd STM
16. Karuei, I., MacLean, K.E., Foley-Fisher, Z., MacKenzie, R., Koch, S., El-Zohairy, M.: Detecting vibrations across the body in mobile contexts. In: Proceedings of the SIGCHI Conference on Human Factors in Computing Systems, pp. 3267–3276 (2011)
17. Lisini Baldi, T., Scheggi, S., Aggravi, M., Prattichizzo, D.: Haptic guidance in dynamic environments using optimal reciprocal collision avoidance. IEEE Robot. Autom. Lett. **3**(1), 265–272 (2018). https://doi.org/10.1109/LRA.2017.2738328. conference Name: IEEE Robotics andConference Name: IEEE Robotics and Automation Letters
18. Maidenbaum, S., et al.: The "EyeCane', a new electronic travel aid for the blind: Technology, behavior & swift learning. Restor. Neurol. Neurosci. **32**(6), 813–824 (2014). https://doi.org/10.3233/RNN-130351. https://content.iospress.com/articles/restorative-neurology-and-neuroscience/rnn130351. Publisher: IOS Press
19. Martinez, M., Constantinescu, A., Schauerte, B., Koester, D., Stiefelhagen, R.: Cognitive evaluation of haptic and audio feedback in short range navigation tasks. In: Miesenberger, K., Fels, D., Archambault, D., Peňáz, P., Zagler, W. (eds.) ICCHP 2014. LNCS, vol. 8548, pp. 128–135. Springer, Cham (2014). https://doi.org/10.1007/978-3-319-08599-9_20
20. McDaniel, T.L., Krishna, S., Colbry, D., Panchanathan, S.: Using tactile rhythm to convey interpersonal distances to individuals who are blind. In: CHI 2009 Extended Abstracts on Human Factors in Computing Systems, CHI EA 2009, Boston, MA, USA pp. 4669–4674. Association for Computing Machinery, April 2009. https://doi.org/10.1145/1520340.1520718
21. McNamara, T.P.: How are the locations of objects in the environment represented in memory? In: Freksa, C., Brauer, W., Habel, C., Wender, K.F. (eds.) Spatial Cognition 2002. LNCS, vol. 2685, pp. 174–191. Springer, Heidelberg (2003). https://doi.org/10.1007/3-540-45004-1_11
22. Metsiritrakul, K., Suchato, A., Punyabukkana, P.: Obstacle avoidance feedback system for the blind using stereo sound. In: Proceedings of the 11th International Convention on Rehabilitation Engineering and Assistive Technology, i-CREATe 2017, Singapore Therapeutic, Assistive & Rehabilitative Technologies (START) Centre, Midview City, SGP, pp. 1–4, July 2017
23. Nau, A.C., Murphy, M.C., Chan, K.C.: Use of sensory substitution devices as a model system for investigating cross-modal neuroplasticity in humans. Neural Regen. Res. **10**(11), 1717–1719 (2015). https://doi.org/10.4103/1673-5374.169612. https://www.ncbi.nlm.nih.gov/pmc/articles/PMC4705765/
24. Parasuraman, R., Molloy, R., Singh, I.L.: Performance consequences of automation-induced 'complacency'. Int. J. Aviat. Psychol. **3**(1), 1–23 (1993). ISBN 1050-8414, Publisher: Taylor & Francis
25. Patla, A.E., Prentice, S.D., Robinson, C., Neufeld, J.: Visual control of locomotion: strategies for changing direction and for going over obstacles. J. Exp. Psychol. Hum. Percept. Perform. **17**(3), 603 (1991). ISBN 1939-1277, Publisher: American Psychological Association

26. Pissaloux, E.E., Velázquez, R., Maingreaud, F.: A new framework for cognitive mobility of visually impaired users in using tactile device. IEEE Trans. Hum. Mach. Syst. **47**(6), 1040–1051 (2017). https://doi.org/10.1109/THMS.2017.2736888. Conference Name: IEEE Transactions on Human-Machine Systems
27. Population Reference Bureau: 2019 World Population Data Sheet. https://www.prb.org/worldpopdata/
28. Postma, A., Zuidhoek, S., Noordzij, M.L., Kappers, A.M.: Differences between early-blind, late-blind, and blindfolded-sighted people in haptic spatial-configuration learning and resulting memory traces. Perception **36**(8), 1253–1265 (2007). ISBN 0301-0066, Publisher: SAGE Publications Sage UK: London, England
29. Presti, G., et al.: WatchOut: obstacle sonification for people with visual impairment or blindness. In: The 21st International ACM SIGACCESS Conference on Computers and Accessibility, ASSETS 2019, Pittsburgh, PA, USA, pp. 402–413. Association for Computing Machinery, October 2019. https://doi.org/10.1145/3308561.3353779
30. Rahman, A., Nur Malia, K.F., Milan Mia, M., Hasan Shuvo, A.M., Hasan Nahid, M., Zayeem, A.M.: An efficient smart cane based navigation system for visually impaired people. In: 2019 International Symposium on Advanced Electrical and Communication Technologies (ISAECT), pp. 1–6, November 2019. https://doi.org/10.1109/ISAECT47714.2019.9069737
31. Real, S., Araujo, A.: Navigation systems for the blind and visually impaired: past work, challenges, and open problems. Sensors **19**(15), 3404 (2019). https://doi.org/10.3390/s19153404. https://www.mdpi.com/1424-8220/19/15/3404. Number: 15 Publisher: Multidisciplinary Digital Publishing Institute
32. Risko, E.F., Gilbert, S.J.: Cognitive offloading. Trends Cogn. Sci. **20**(9), 676–688 (2016). ISBN 1364-6613, Publisher: Elsevier
33. Ruggiero, G., Ruotolo, F., Iachini, T.: The role of vision in egocentric and allocentric spatial frames of reference. Cogn. Process. **10**(2), 283–285 (2009). ISBN 1612-4782, Publisher: Springer-Verlag
34. Salat, S., Habib, M.A.: Smart electronic cane for the assistance of visually impaired people. In: 2019 IEEE International WIE Conference on Electrical and Computer Engineering (WIECON-ECE), pp. 1–4, November 2019. https://doi.org/10.1109/WIECON-ECE48653.2019.9019932
35. dos Santos, A.D.P., Medola, F.O., Cinelli, M.J., Garcia Ramirez, A.R., Sandnes, F.E.: Are electronic white canes better than traditional canes? A comparative study with blind and blindfolded participants. Univ. Access. Inf. Soc. (2020). https://doi.org/10.1007/s10209-020-00712-z. http://link.springer.com/10.1007/s10209-020-00712-z
36. Scheggi, S., Talarico, A., Prattichizzo, D.: A remote guidance system for blind and visually impaired people via vibrotactile haptic feedback. In: 22nd Mediterranean Conference on Control and Automation, pp. 20–23, June 2014. https://doi.org/10.1109/MED.2014.6961320
37. Schinazi, V.R., Thrash, T., Chebat, D.R.: Spatial navigation by congenitally blind individuals. WIREs Cogn. Sci. **7**(1), 37–58 (2016). https://doi.org/10.1002/wcs.1375. http://onlinelibrary.wiley.com/doi/abs/10.1002/wcs.1375
38. Syed, S.A., Shaikh, T.M., Aijaz, F., Mehmood, N., Ahmed, S.: Blind echolocation device with smart object detection. Quaid-E-Awam Univ. Res. J. Eng. Sci. Technol. Nawabshah **17**(2), 66–70 (2019). ISBN 2523-0379

39. Thaler, L., De Vos, H.P.J.C., Kish, D., Antoniou, M., Baker, C.J., Hornikx, M.C.J.: Human click-based echolocation of distance: superfine acuity and dynamic clicking behaviour. J. Assoc. Res. Otolaryngol. **20**(5), 499–510 (2019). https://doi.org/10.1007/s10162-019-00728-0
40. Wang, H.C., Katzschmann, R.K., Teng, S., Araki, B., Giarré, L., Rus, D.: Enabling independent navigation for visually impaired people through a wearable vision-based feedback system. In: 2017 IEEE International Conference on Robotics and Automation (ICRA), pp. 6533–6540, May 2017. https://doi.org/10.1109/ICRA.2017.7989772
41. World Health Organization: Blindness and vision impairment (2018). https://www.who.int/news-room/fact-sheets/detail/blindness-and-visual-impairment
42. Ye, Y., et al.: A wearable vision-to-audio sensory substitution device for blind assistance and the correlated neural substrates. J. Phys. Conf. Ser. **1229**, 012026 (2019). https://doi.org/10.1088/1742-6596/1229/1/012026. Publisher: IOP Publishing
43. Zeng, L., Prescher, D., Weber, G.: Exploration and avoidance of surrounding obstacles for the visually impaired. In: Proceedings of the 14th International ACM SIGACCESS Conference on Computers and Accessibility, ASSETS 2012, Boulder, Colorado, USA, pp. 111–118. Association for Computing Machinery, October 2012. https://doi.org/10.1145/2384916.2384936

Automatic Contrast Evaluation for Android Themes

Adriano Gil, Juliana Postal, Adélia Ferreira, Daydlene Gonçalves, Bianca Hayek Bianco, and Mikhail R. Gadelha(✉)

Sidia Instituto de Ciência e Tecnologia, Manaus, Brazil
{adriano.gil,juliana.postal,adelia.ferreira,daydlene.goncalves, bianca.bianco,mikhail.gadelha}@sidia.com

Abstract. Several smartphone vendors now offer theme stores where one can submit themes that change the appearance of the OS. Theme designer must follow policies and guidelines to have their themes accepted. One common issue is the low contrast of elements in system applications, that can cause rework and delay to publish submitted themes. To prevent such problems, these devices need to manually check hundred of different screens. In this paper, we describe an automatic tool that walks in several application screens of a device running Android OS, analyzes them and generates detailed reports about low contrast issues. We use a shallow neural network that was trained with more than 10000 elements extracted from screenshots of several different Android applications. We show that our approach present high recall and precision when analyzing Android screen elements, and higher recall and precision when compared to low contrast check in the Google Accessibility Framework.

1 Introduction

Due to the popularization of smartphones, system and application developers must offer a consistent experience across any given platform. Inconsistency becomes more evident now that system vendors (e.g., Samsung[1] and Huawei[2]) include theme stores in their devices that sell the overall appearance of the system.

Theme stores function similarly to application stores: users design and create themes that are submitted for approval by the system vendor. These themes are then evaluated by human operators and, if approved, they are allowed to be sold in the theme stores. The theme designer, however, is not allowed to submit any content: the theme stores define policies and offer guidelines so that the themes sold at the store are of the highest quality. The rules defined in these documents describe not only simple design choices that must be avoided (e.g., not to submit several themes which only differ by the color of their background), but also less intuitive ones (e.g., no image of alcoholic beverages).

[1] https://www.samsung.com/hk_en/apps/galaxy-themes/.
[2] https://huaweimobileservices.com/huaweithemes/.

C. Stephanidis et al. (Eds.): HCII 2020, LNCS 12426, pp. 267–278, 2020.
https://doi.org/10.1007/978-3-030-60149-2_21

In this paper, we focus on the **automatic detection of low contrast issues in themes for the Android system**. The issue of low contrast in screens is a well-known problem and has been studied since the CRT-era [7]; in 2018 the World Wide Web Consortium (W3C) published the "Web Content Accessibility Guidelines" (WCAG) 2.1 [21], which covers a wide range of suggestions to make Web content more accessible. In particular, item 1.4.3 defines the recommended contrast ratio between back- and foreground elements for both images and text, so that it can be perceived by people with visual impairments.

To avoid low contrast issues is a simple rule but it can be easily violated, causing the themes to be rejected until the issue is fixed. The main challenge of ensuring no low contrast issue is to reliably check all screens and applications changed by the theme: a herculean task if you consider that there are system applications with hundred of screens (e.g., the system settings application).

As an illustrative example of the issue, consider the screenshots in Fig. 1. Both screenshots show vanilla (i.e., with the default system theme) of the same screen in the system settings application. Figure 1a shows the "Trusted credentials" screen in a Motorola G^5 Plus running Android 8.1.0, accessed by following *Settings > Encryption & credentials > Trusted Credentials*, while Fig. 1b shows the "View security credentials" screen in a Samsung Galaxy S9+ running Android 9, accessed by following *Settings > Biometrics and security > Other security settings > View security certificates*. These screens are deep in the system menu and yet a theme design must ensure that changing the color scheme will not cause low contrast issues in such screens[3].

In this context, we propose and evaluate a tool that automatically walks a number of screens and applications in device running an Android OS, captures screenshots and searches for low contrast issues in the screen. We extracted more than 700 screenshots from several applications in the systems (including the home screen with different wallpapers) with a diverse set of themes, which resulted in more the 14000 different screen elements (e.g., text, images, sliders, check-boxes, etc.). We used this data to train a neural network and measured its precision, recall and F1 score. Finally, we compared our results against the Google Accessibility Framework [11], which can take screenshots of Android screens and check for accessibility issues, including low contrast issues. We show that our approach presents higher precision, recall and F1 score than the Google Accessibility Framework.

2 Background

In this section we start by describing the Web Content Accessibility Guidelines (WCAG, described in Sect. 2.1). The WCAG defines the acceptance criteria used by the Google Accessibility Framework, which is later described in Sect. 3.1. Furthermore, in Sect. 2.2 we briefly describe shallow neural networks, which is

[3] As a side note, the word "USER" (top right in Fig. 1a and bottom right in Fig. 1b) in both screens violates the WCAG 2.1 guideline for having a low contrast.

the type of neural network we used to find low contrast issues in our dataset (described in Sect. 3.1).

2.1 Web Content Accessibility Guidelines (WCAG) 2.1

The WCAG 2.1 was created to help the design of UIs for people with visual impairment; it defines a formula to calculate a contrast ratio *cr* between two colors. The guideline defines an acceptance criteria for normal accessibility (level AA) and better accessibility (level AAA):

- **AA**: *cr* must be greater than 4.5 for normal text, and greater than 3 for large text and Graphical Objects and User Interface Components.
- **AAA**: *cr* must be greater than 7 for normal text, and greater than 4.5 for large text and Graphical Objects and User Interface Components.

The guidelines define large text if its font size is at least 18 points or 14 points if bolded. The contrast ratio *cr* is calculated as follows:

$$cr = \frac{L1 + 0.05}{L2 + 0.05} \tag{1}$$

where $L1$ is the relative luminance of the lighter color and $L2$ is the relative luminance of the darker color. The luminance of a RGB color is calculated by:

$$L = 0.2126 \times R + 0.7152 \times G + 0.0722 \times B \tag{2}$$

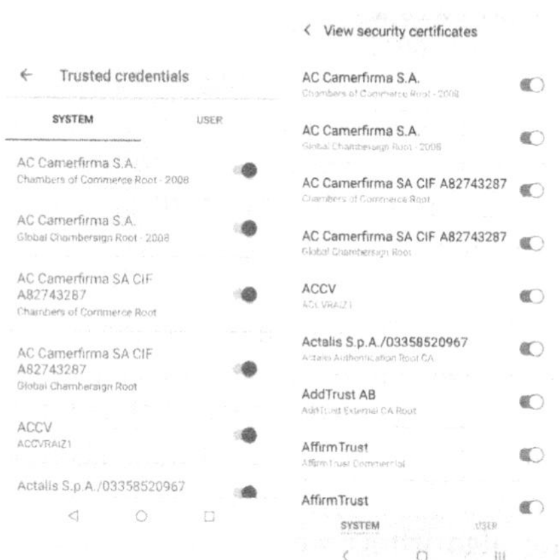

(a) Vanilla Trusted credentials screen in Motorola G5 Plus, Android 8.1.0.

(b) Vanilla View security certificates screen in Samsung S9+, Android 9.

Fig. 1. Vanilla screens of the settings applications from two different vendors. The images have different sizes because the devices have different resolutions.

where R, G, B are:

$$R = \begin{cases} \dfrac{R_{sRGB}}{12.92} & \text{, if } R_{sRGB} \leq 0.03928, \\ \left(\dfrac{R_{sRGB} + 0.055}{1.055}\right)^{2.4} & \text{, otherwise} \end{cases} \tag{3}$$

$$G = \begin{cases} \dfrac{G_{sRGB}}{12.92} & \text{, if } G_{sRGB} \leq 0.03928, \\ \left(\dfrac{G_{sRGB} + 0.055}{1.055}\right)^{2.4} & \text{, otherwise} \end{cases} \tag{4}$$

$$B = \begin{cases} \dfrac{B_{sRGB}}{12.92} & \text{, if } B_{sRGB} \leq 0.03928, \\ \left(\dfrac{B_{sRGB} + 0.055}{1.055}\right)^{2.4} & \text{, otherwise} \end{cases} \tag{5}$$

where R_{sRGB}, G_{sRGB}, B_{sRGB} are the colors in the standard RGB color model [8], defined as follows:

$$R_{sRGB} = \frac{R_{8bit}}{255}, G_{sRGB} = \frac{G_{8bit}}{255}, B_{sRGB} = \frac{B_{8bit}}{255}.$$

where R_{8bit}, G_{8bit}, B_{8bit} are the red, green and blue pixel color in a digital image using 8-bit per channel.

2.2 Shallow Neural Networks

Neural network is a set of parallel processing units that can be used for classification purposes [5]. Each individual unit is a mapping function between input and output values, i.e., neurons. Training algorithms are specifically designed to achieved desired outputs given predetermined inputs, i.e., they work as a supervised approach that consumes a labeled dataset in order to produce a neural model [5].

Deep learning is a keyword in machine learning literature; it is defined as a neural network with a very large number of layers [4]. In contrast, neural architecture with 2 to 4 layers can be characterized as "shallow". We use shallow neural networks for contrast classification because the generated model size is greatly reduced compared to its deep version.

In machine learning algorithms we usually must find hyperparameters to configure the learning phase of our models. For our experiments we decided to employ RMSprop algorithm [20] for training our neural network models, and its update function is given by Eq. 6. The learning rate n is a example of a parameter that can be configured to improve the velocity in which the weights are updated.

$$w_t = w_{t-1} - \frac{n}{\sqrt{E[g^2]_t}} \frac{\partial C}{\partial w} \tag{6}$$

3 Evaluating Android Screens

The development of the project described in this paper started because of a limitation we often faced: as theme designers, we would submit a theme to a theme store only to have it rejected a few weeks later because of a low contrast issue in a screen deep in the system. The main goal of the project is to reduce the costs by reducing rework and increase the overall quality of the themes.

In this section we describe our solution and its core technology: a neural network specially trained to identify low contrast issues (described in Sect. 3.1). Our solution reduces rework by automatically evaluating several screens in an Android OS system and searching for contrast issues. It also generates detailed reports in a fraction of the time taken to receive feedback from a theme store. Our current approach can generate a report for over 700 screens in roughly 30 min.

The main challenge of the project is how to automatically analyze screens of the Android system? To address this challenge, our solution is divided into two modules:

- **Desktop module**: a desktop application for Linux, Windows, and macOS that extracts screenshots from the Android device, analyzes them and generates a detailed report of any low contrast issues it found.
- **Mobile module**: a mobile application for Android that walks into several screens, takes screenshots and extracts UI information [16]. It is installed in the user's device by the desktop module as the first step of the theme analysis.

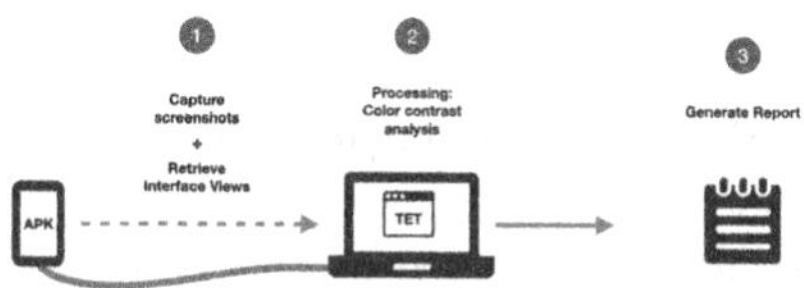

Fig. 2. Theme evaluation process.

Figure 2 shows the evaluation process of our solution; it works as follows:

- The desktop module installs the mobile module in the device.
- The mobile module captures the screenshot (PNG format) and the UI information (XML format) from screens in the system that are affected by themes.
- The desktop module extracts the screenshots and XMLs from the Android device.
- The desktop module analyzes all the screenshots, using the information in the XMLs to identify the elements in the screenshot.
- A report showing the detected issues in the screens is presented in HTML format.

The mobile module is a custom APK that builds on top of two native android frameworks: the UIAutomator [17] and the Accessibility service [11]. The UIAutomator is used to simulate user inputs to reach the screens affected by themes and the Accessibility service is used to extract the XML of the view in the applications. The XML massively simplifies our solution as our neural network does not have to identify elements on the screenshot [15], only to classify them.

The information presented in the XML is vital to the execution of our solution: it contains not only the exact bounding boxes of the elements in the screen but also some of its properties, including if it's enabled, if it has any text, if it holds the current focus, among several others. The algorithms in the desktop module extract the elements from the screenshot and send them to the neural network for classification.

Finally, the report was developed based on the reports generated by the theme stores and focus on showing the error, how the correct screen looks like and how to get to the screen.

The mobile module is written in Android Java [10], while the desktop module is written in Python 3 [19] and makes uses of OpenCV [2] to segment the images.

3.1 Low Contrast Issue Classification Approaches

The core of our solution is the correct classification of low contrast issues in the various elements present in an Android screen. Initially, we relied on the Google Accessibility Framework to classify the elements but it yielded less than optimal results. We then developed our solution based on shallow neural networks. In this section we describe the Google Accessibility Framework in Sect. 3.1 and our neural network-based approach in Sect. 3.1.

Google Accessibility Framework Approach. The algorithm in the Google Accessibility Frameworks works by estimating the foreground and background colors, then applying the formula defined by the WCAG (described in Sect. 2.1). The algorithm is quite simple: given an element in the screen, it selects the highest and lowest relative luminance values that contribute to the most number of pixels in the image – the background and foreground colors.

This naive approach is well-suited for texts, where that are usually two colors: the text color and the background color. However, when a more complex element is analyzed (e.g., an icon), the algorithm tends to estimate the wrong colors for background and foreground.

Fig. 3. Google's "Keep note" application icon. (Color figure online)

As an illustrative example, consider the icon of the Google's "Keep Note" application shown in Fig. 3. The icon was extracted from an Android home screen where the background color is a light blue (RGB(#06A3E2)). The region of the icon that contrasts with the light blue background is a light yellow (RGB(#F7B818)).

In this element, the background color is the light blue and the foreground color is the light yellow, however, when analyzing it using the algorithm in the Google Accessibility Frameworks, it estimates that the background color is a yellow (RGB(#F7B818)) and the foreground is light grey (RGB(#F5F5F5), the color of the bulb. The mismatch is due to the algorithm always searching for the lightest and darker relative colors in the image, which happens to be the colors in the icon itself; this is the major source of misclassification of the algorithm.

Neural Network Approach. To avoid the limitations of the Google Accessibility Framework algorithm, we decided to focus on using machine learning to classify elements with low contrast issues. The idea is simple: our design team creates several themes with a wide range of low contrast issues (e.g., in texts, backgrounds, check-boxes, etc.), we extract the screenshots of these and of other themes with no low contrast issue (to avoid having an unbalanced dataset for training), and we train a neural network using the elements extracted from the screenshots.

However, one question remains: *what should be the input of the neural network?* Neural networks were already used to classify contrast issues in the literature. In particular, Everlandio et al. [6] uses a Faster-RCNN [12] to evaluate a dataset of 1500 artificially generated Android home screens (we describe the authors approach in more details in Sect. 5). The neural network is trained using whole images, however, with an average precision of 79.91% we decided to follow other training strategies.

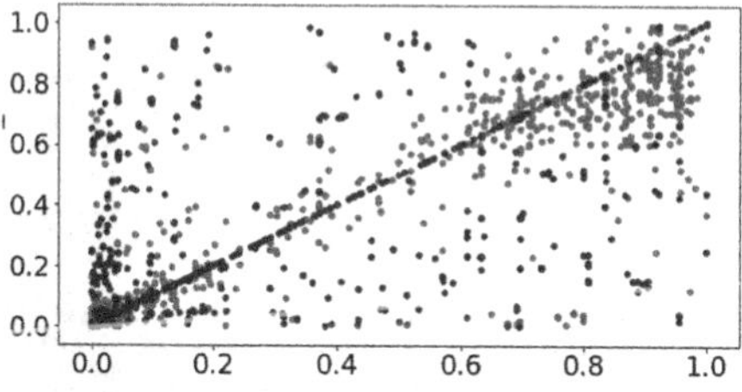

Fig. 4. Normalized background luminance by foreground luminance. Red dots represent low contrast between background and foreground, and blue dots represent good contrast.

Our first approach was to stay close to the previous Google Accessibility Approach and to use luminance to train the neural network. Figure 4 shows the normalized ratio between background and foreground luminance of 14866 elements (extracted using classical image segmentation algorithms [22]) in our training dataset. The red dots represent elements with low contrast and blue dots represents elements with good contrast (according to WCAG formula). Note that, although there are two clusters of elements with low contrast, the elements are evenly spread. Furthermore, note that diagonal "line" in the middle of the graph: it represents elements nearly or identical luminance, and it consists of elements with both low and good contrast. With no clear distinction between good and low contrast, the neural network trained with this approach performed poorly.

The poor results, however, gave us an insight: there is no need to reduce the information retrieved from the element to train the neural networks, i.e., convert back- and foreground colors to luminance value. We used the same dataset used to train the first approach, but instead, we trained the neural network using the RGB channels of back- and foreground colors. Unfortunately, we cannot show a ratio figure similar to Fig. 3, because it requires to show the intersection of two three dimensional objects, for every element.

In our second approach, we used a 6-sized input vector in a 0–255 range for a shallow neural network (described in Sect. 2.2) using two hidden layers. The output of the network is a two-sized vector that is interpreted as one of two classes: regular or irregular. We defined a neural architecture with 40, 10 and 2 neurons in each layer.

We implemented a Keras-based neural network [4] with two hidden layers using relu [1] and softmax [3] as neural functions running for 20 epochs with a batch size equal to 16. Our dataset of 14866 elements is split in 70% for training and 30% for testing. Our python implementation uses OpenCV [2] and Pandas [14] modules to load images and manipulate data.

4 Experimental Evaluation

Fig. 5. Example of screens with low contrast issues in our dataset. Left-to-right: create new event (calendar), set backup password (settings), set touch-and-hold delay timer (settings), schedule message (messages), view security certificates (settings), dialer (phone).

Our experimental evaluation compares the algorithm in the Google Accessibility Framework against the neural network described in Sect. 3.1. First, we describe the dataset in Sect. 4.1, followed by the comparison between the two approaches in Sect. 4.2.

4.1 Dataset

To have a diversified dataset of low and good contrast elements (according to the WCAG 2.1 criteria), our team decided to create 200 themes with a wide range of low contrast issues, which resulted in more than 8000 elements. The dataset, however, was not balanced, i.e., it had more elements with low contrast issue than elements with good contrast. To balance our dataset we used approved themes from the Samsung theme store, which resulted in a total of 14866 elements. Every element in the dataset was manually labeled with either low contrast and good contrast. We picked a resolution of 2280×1080, which is used in the last flagship smartphones Samsung S10.

The 14866 elements were extracted from 718 screens of several applications, including the calculator, calendar, clock, contacts, messages, phone, settings, and from the home screen with different icon arrangements and different wallpapers. Figure 5 shows some examples of screens with low contrast issues in our dataset. Note that the screens have elements with both low contrast issues and with good contrast, e.g., in the dialer screen of the phone application (rightmost screen in Fig. 5), the word "Phone" and the dialed number are visible, but not the numbers on the dial pad.

4.2 Comparison of Low Contrast Evaluation Approaches

In this section, we present the precision, recall and F1 score of two approaches described in Sect. 3.1: the Google Accessibility Framework algorithm, and our approach using a neural network trained with the back- and foreground colors. We do not show the results of the neural network trained using the luminance from the back- and foreground colors because the results are below standard.

Our neural network approach was trained using 10406 randomly selected elements from our dataset and it took approximately 15.488 s in an NVIDIA DGX Station. If we consider the time taken to develop the theme with issues, and the time to train our neural network, the Google Accessibility Framework algorithm is better: it requires no training at all (Fig. 6).

However, despite the high initial cost of our neural network, the results are better. Compared to the Google Accessibility Framework algorithm, our neural network presents higher recall, precision, and F1 score. A deep analysis of the Google Accessibility Framework results shows that it is exceptionally good when analyzing elements with solid back- and foreground colors, but presents bad results for more complex images. This is easily explained by the estimation of back- and foreground color performed by the algorithm. In particular, the Google Accessibility Framework algorithm presents a small recall, i.e., it does not report issues in several elements with low contrast.

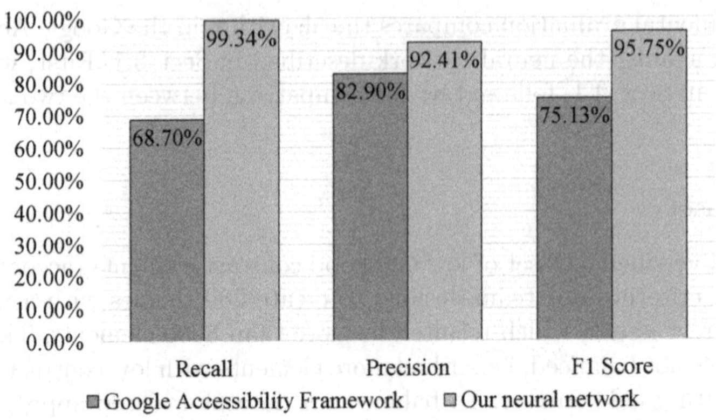

Fig. 6. Comparative results of the analysis of 4461 elements.

Our neural network presents a high recall, meaning it misses very few elements with contrast issues. This behavior is extremely important for our theme designers: it is much more desirable to erroneously report issues in elements with good contrast than to miss reporting elements with contrast issues. To miss reporting elements with contrast issues means that the theme will likely to be rejected, incurring in extra development costs. The erroneous report of elements with good contrast can be manually checked and ignored by the theme designer.

5 Related Works

The closest work we found in the literature was authored by Everlandio et al. [6], where they analyzed 300 artificially generated Android OS home screens, using a Faster-RCNN [18]. They generated all the screens with at least ten elements (icons), with four different levels of contrast: very low, low, regular, and high. To train the neural network they used 1500 screens that were also automatically labeled with the four contrast levels. The authors claim a mean Average Precision (mAP) [12] of 79.91% across the four contrast levels. Compared to the work presented in this paper, our solution is similar but it is extended to a much larger scope: we both use neural networks to identify contrast issues in Android OS screens (we used shallow neural networks while they used Faster-RCNN), and we used a dataset for training that contains generated screens with issues (differently from their automatic generation method, however, ours is manual). The solution proposed in this paper, however, was trained with a much larger dataset and applied to a wider variety of screens, which also included the Android OS home screen. Furthermore, our neural network was also trained with real-world themes and can automatically capture screens from devices. We do not compare their results against ours because of the different datasets used for testing.

Other works explore color contrast issues using WCAG 2.0 criteria. Young Gun et al. [9] links color contrast and readability and compares the WCAG 2.0 guideline with an algorithm based on color temperature. To measure the contrast between back- and foreground they use the luminosity contrast ratio, defined by the WCAG 2.0. The authors are interested in validating that the contrast ratio proposed by the WCAG is sufficiently high for people with learning disabilities or color blindness. They concluded that the minimum level of color contrast between text and background is necessary to avoid readability degradation for people with color blindness, but a higher level of contrast is needed for people with learning disabilities.

Finally, our neural network requires that back- and foreground colors are first extracted from the image. This process is usually simple for texts, where there are two solid colors, but becomes more complicated for images. Liyuan Li et al. [13] proposes a Bayesian model approach that considers spectral, spatial and temporal characteristics of the pixel to define the background. The experimental evaluation showed that combining the spectral, temporal and spatial characteristics of the pixel is an effective strategy and provided a performance increase in complex background detection.

6 Conclusions

In this paper, we presented a solution to automatically walk in several screens of an Android smartphone, take screenshots and UI information, and check for low contrast issues. Our main contribution is the evaluation of several elements extracted from the screenshots using a neural network, with an F1 score of 95%, higher than a solution provided by the Google Accessibility Framework.

Our solution, however, is far from finished. We are currently investigating a hybrid approach, that takes under consideration not only the element type (e.g., text, image, check-box, etc.) but also its properties (e.g., if it is enabled, if it has focus, etc.) to more precisely classify the elements. Furthermore, although our solution should work for any Android version, newer releases of the Android OS will most likely have new screens that need to be analyzed, and our algorithm will need to be updated to reach them, and to collect their screenshot and UI information.

References

1. Agarap, A.F.: Deep learning using rectified linear units (relu). arXiv preprint arXiv:1803.08375 (2018)
2. Bradski, G.: The OpenCV library. Dr. Dobb's J. Softw. Tools **120**, 122–125 (2000)
3. Bridle, J.S.: Training stochastic model recognition algorithms as networks can lead to maximum mutual information estimation of parameters. In: Advances in Neural Information Processing Systems, pp. 211–217 (1990)
4. Chollet, F.: Deep learning with python (2018)
5. Demuth, H.B., Beale, M.H., De Jess, O., Hagan, M.T.: Neural Network Design. Martin Hagan, Boston (2014)

6. Fernandes, E., Correia, R., Gil, A., Postal, J., Gadelha, M.R.: Themes validation tool. In: Stephanidis, C. (ed.) HCI International 2019 - Late Breaking Posters (2019)
7. HFES: Human factors engineering of computer workstations (1988). ANSI-HFES-100-1988
8. Hirsch, R.: Exploring Colour Photography : A Complete Guide, 1st edn. Laurence King Pub., London (2004)
9. Jang, Y.G., Kim, H.Y., Yi, M.: A color contrast algorithm for e-learning standard. Int. J. Comput. Sci. Netw. Secur. **7**(4), 195–201 (2007)
10. Kocakoyun, S.: Developing of android mobile application using java and eclipse: an application. Int. J. Electron. Mech. Mech. Eng. **7**, 1335–1354 (2017)
11. Kraunelis, J., Chen, Y., Ling, Z., Fu, X., Zhao, W.: On malware leveraging the android accessibility framework. In: Stojmenovic, I., Cheng, Z., Guo, S. (eds.) MindCare 2014. LNICST, vol. 131, pp. 512–523. Springer, Cham (2014). https://doi.org/10.1007/978-3-319-11569-6_40
12. Liu, L., Özsu, M.T. (eds.): Mean Average Precision, p. 1703. Springer, Boston (2009)
13. Li, L., Huang, W., Gu, I.Y.-H., Tian, Q.: Statistical modeling of complex backgrounds for foreground object detection. IEEE Trans. Image Process. **13**(11), 1459–1472 (2004)
14. McKinney, W.: Pandas: a foundational python library for data analysis and statistics. Python High Perform. Sci. Comput. **14**, 1–9 (2011)
15. Mozgovoy, M., Pyshkin, E.: Using image recognition for testing hand-drawn graphic user interfaces. In: 11th International Conference on Mobile Ubiquitous Computing, Systems, Services and Technologies (UBICOMM 2017) (2017)
16. Nguyen, T.A., Csallner, C.: Reverse engineering mobile application user interfaces with REMAUI (t). In: 2015 30th IEEE/ACM International Conference on Automated Software Engineering (ASE), pp. 248–259 (2015)
17. Patil, N., Bhole, D., Shete, P.: Enhanced UI automator viewer with improved android accessibility evaluation features, pp. 977–983 (2016)
18. Ren, S., He, K., Girshick, R.B., Sun, J.: Faster r-CNN: towards real-time object detection with region proposal networks. In: NIPS, pp. 91–99 (2015)
19. Solem, J.E.: Programming Computer Vision with Python. O'Reilly, Sebastopol (2012)
20. Tieleman, T., Hinton, G.: Lecture 6.5-rmsprop, coursera: Neural networks for machine learning. Technical Report, University of Toronto (2012)
21. W3C: Web Content Accessibility Guidelines (WCAG) 2.1 (2018)
22. Zhu, Y.P., Li, P.: Survey on the image segmentation algorithms. In: Qu, Z., Lin, J. (eds.) Proceedings of the International Field Exploration and Development Conference 2017, pp. 475–488 (2019)

A Low-Cost Gaze-Based Arabic Augmentative and Alternative Communication System for People with Severe Speech and Motor Impairments

Rabia Jafri(✉), Ameera Masoud Almasoud, Reema Mohammed Taj Alshammari, Shahad Eid Mohammed Alosaimi, Raghad Talal Mohammed Alhamad, and Amzan Abdullah Saleh Aldowighri

Department of Information Technology, King Saud University, Riyadh, Saudi Arabia
rabia.ksu@gmail.com, ammalmasoud@ksu.edu.sa, ReemaMTaj@gmail.com, shahad.alosimi@gmail.com, Raghad025@gmail.com, amzan.1418@gmail.com

Abstract. Interpersonal communication poses a major challenge for individuals with severe speech and motor impairments (SSMI); however, since eye muscle movement control is typically retained, such individuals can alternatively communicate with others by using their gaze to select symbols on electronic communication boards (CBs). Unfortunately, most of the existing systems offering electronic CBs require the purchase of high-cost eye tracking hardware and software components and do not support Arabic language. We have, therefore, developed a low-cost gaze interaction-based Arabic language application to assist pre-literate and early literate individuals with SSMI whose primary language is Arabic to communicate with people in their vicinity. The system utilizes a webcam and open source software for eye tracking, thus, avoiding the need for expensive proprietary eye tracking components. It offers several CBs from which the user can select items to form sentences that are output as speech. The CBs have been carefully designed taking the users' cognitive and motor capabilities into consideration and several features to facilitate and expedite the communication process have been included. An interface has also been provided for caregivers to customize the application according to the users' unique needs by adding and editing items, and setting the user's profile, the background color and the gender for the speech output. The system has been developed in consultation with a speech-language pathologist to ensure that it is compatible with current therapy practices and the actual needs of the targeted users.

Keywords: Assistive technologies · Augmentative and alternative communication · Gaze tracking · Eye tracking · Motor impairments · Speech impairments · Neuromuscular diseases · Arabic communication

C. Stephanidis et al. (Eds.): HCII 2020, LNCS 12426, pp. 279–290, 2020.
https://doi.org/10.1007/978-3-030-60149-2_22

1 Introduction

Communicating with others is essential for one's emotional well-being and for accomplishing several everyday tasks. However, interpersonal communication poses a major challenge for people suffering from severe speech and motor impairments caused by traumatic injuries or by neurological conditions like locked-in syndrome, cerebral palsy, and stroke as these disorders frequently lead to a loss of muscle control hindering the ability to produce articulate speech or to gesticulate [1]; this rules out oral as well as standard non-verbal methods, such as sign language, for conversing. Nevertheless, since eye muscle movement control is typically retained [2–5], such individuals can alternatively communicate by directing their eye gaze to select items on a communication board (CB) - a physical board with symbols representing letters, actions, objects, places, etc., printed on it [4]. Their communication partners (CP) follow their gaze direction to identify the selected symbols and construe their message. Though CBs offer a low-cost, low-tech communication solution, they have several limitations: they entail a steep learning curve and place a high cognitive load on the CPs requiring them to remember the symbols selected so far while closely observing the gaze patterns of the person with severe speech and motor impairments (PSSMI) [2, 5, 6], do not enable the PSSMI to indicate or correct an error [2], do not provide any automated feedback about which symbol has been selected [4], and curtail the privacy and independence of the PSSMI since an interpreter is required if the PSSMI needs to communicate with someone who is not trained to use these boards [3, 5, 7]; moreover, some of these CBs, such as e-tran boards [8], are fairly large and heavy and have to be physically held up by the CPs which may cause them discomfort and fatigue [2].

To attempt to overcome these limitations, a few high-tech solutions have emerged in recent years which provide electronic versions of CBs on various devices, automatically track the PSSMI's gaze to determine which symbols on the CBs have been selected and generate speech and/or visual output based on the selected symbols, thus, easing the burden on the CP and allowing the PSSMI to communicate with any nearby person without an interpreter. However, most of these require the purchase of high-cost commercial eye tracking hardware and software components making them prohibitively expensive for several of the target users [2, 4, 5]; also, some of these employ head-mounted eye trackers which are bulky and heavy – especially for people suffering from motor disabilities – and may impede eye contact and the ability to discern the environment making them uncomfortable and impractical for extended usage [2]. Moreover, the majority of such solutions do not provide support for Arabic language precluding their use for Arabic speaking populations.

We have, therefore, developed a relatively low-cost gaze interaction-based Arabic language application to assist individuals with severe speech and motor impairments to communicate with people in their vicinity. The system is geared towards pre-literate and early literate users whose primary language is Arabic. It captures the user's eye movements via the personal computer (PC)'s built-in webcam and utilizes open source eye tracking software [9] to determine the gaze direction, thereby avoiding the necessity of purchasing costly commercial eye tracking components. The user can select items from several pre-defined CBs by fixating his/her gaze upon them to form sentences which are then output as speech using the Google text-to-speech (TTS) API [10]. The visual and speech interfaces have been carefully designed taking the users' cognitive and motor capabilities into consideration and several features have been included to facilitate and expedite the communication process such as a "Quick" board containing frequently used word/phrases, a mistake button to indicate that an item has been erroneously selected and an alarm button to summon immediate help. The system also offers an interface for the PSSMIs' caregivers enabling them to customize the application according to the users' unique needs by adding and editing new items and CBs, and setting the user's profile, the background color, and the gender for the speech output.

The application has been designed and developed in consultation with the Head of the Speech Department at the Disabled Children's Association in Riyadh, Saudi Arabia to ensure that it is compatible with current therapy practices and the actual needs of the targeted users; her advice has informed many of our design choices such as the organization of the CBs, the frequently used words/phrases, and the option for changing the background color.

We hope that this project will facilitate the social interaction and, thus, improve the autonomy and overall quality of life of pre-literate and early literate PSSMIs whose primary language is Arabic by providing them with a low cost, customizable, user-friendly gaze-based Arabic language solution that enables them to directly, easily and efficiently communicate with other people around them.

The rest of the paper is organized as follows: Sect. 2 provides an overview of existing systems and research solutions for gaze-based communication using electronic CBs for PSSMIs. Section 3 reports details of the interview conducted with a speech language pathologist to gather the requirements for the system. Section 4 describes the system's design and implementation while Sect. 5 explains how it was evaluated. Section 6 concludes the paper and specifies some directions for future work.

2 Related Work

Currently, only a few augmentative and alternative communication (AAC) solutions for electronic CBs exist that have been explicitly designed to provide support for gaze-based interaction. Most of these require proprietary hardware and software components for eye tracking and gaze-based selection (e.g., Tobii's Snap Core First [11], EyeWorld 3.0 [12], Grid 3 [13], IntelliGaze [14] and Gazespeaker [15]). Though some solutions for gaze-based text entry do exist that utilize standard webcams/built-in phone cameras for capturing the eye movements and open source software for tracking the eye gaze [2, 16], these systems only display text symbols (letters, digits, punctuation marks, etc.) and, therefore, are not amenable to pre-literate and early literate users.

We found only one Android application called Livox [17] offering CBs that provides gaze-based interaction utilizing the Android device's built-in camera and also supports Arabic language. The pathologist whom we interviewed brought this application to our attention but mentioned some major usability issues with it (please refer to Sect. 3 for details).

It should be noted that there are also several other AAC applications which provide electronic CBs for speech impaired individuals but offer only touch-based interaction (e.g., Avaz [18], MyTalkTools Mobile [19], Voice4u [20]) precluding their use by people with severe motor impairments who are unable to control their hands. Though some of these might be rendered accessible via eye gaze by exploiting commercial systems that allow a computer to be controlled using the eyes [21, 22] but this would require a substantial financial investment to purchase the requisite components as well as a significant expenditure of time and effort for setup and configuration to attain reasonably accurate performance.

In recent years, some research efforts have also been directed towards developing gaze-based AAC solutions involving CBs: Galante and Menzes [4] developed a desktop application for people with cerebral palsy that utilizes a head-mounted eye tracker to track their gaze direction and allows them to select words from CBs displayed on a computer monitor by pressing an adapted push-button to form simple phrases in Portuguese, which appear as text at the bottom of the screen (there is no audio output); the system compensates for involuntary head movements using binary markers displayed on the screen. Vörös et al. [7] presented a prototype wearable tool comprised of a see-through head-mounted display (HMD), eye tracking glasses and a motion sensor connected to a backend processing unit that allows users to select symbols from CBs displayed on the HMD as well as texts in the environment, converts them into sentence fragments in Hungarian using a natural language processing algorithm and outputs them as speech using TTS software. Lupu et al. [3]'s solution allows patients with neuro-locomotor disabilities to select keywords in English on CBs displayed on a laptop screen by blinking their eyes which are then sent via a server to a caretaker's mobile device; the caretaker can send a response back to the patient; the system utilizes a webcam for image acquisition and open source software to track the eyes.

Our review of the related work, therefore, demonstrates that only a limited number of gaze-based AAC systems exist which provide CBs for pre-literate and early literate users, most of them require the purchase of high-cost components placing them beyond the financial reach of several of the target users, several of them employ head-mounted eye trackers whose bulk and weight may make them uncomfortable for users with motor problems, and almost all of them – with the exception of the Livox app [17] – do not provide explicit support for Arabic language.

3 Requirements Gathering

In order to gain some insight into the use of physical and electronic CBs in the local context, the challenges encountered in using such devices and the desired features to include in these, we conducted a semi-structured interview with the Head of the Speech Department at the Disabled Children's Association in Riyadh, Saudia Arabia who is a senior speech-language pathologist (SLP) with a master's degree in speech and language assessment and has been active in this field for sixteen years. When asked about the use of CBs for patients with speech impairments as well as those suffering from both speech and motor impairments, she explained that their center utilizes several low-tech paper-based solutions which require a user to select an item on the board by pointing to it. In terms of high-tech devices, some simple electronic gadgets, such as QuickTalker [23] and GoTalk [24], are employed which allow the user to press down on an item causing its name to be spoken by the system – however, these are not accessible for patients with severe motor impairments since they necessitate using the hands. She mentioned that only one computer-based solution has been used by them so far, an Android application called Livox [17] which allows the user to select one among several items displayed on the tablet screen by either tapping it or fixing his/her gaze on it and blinking. In response to our inquiries about the usefulness of these devices, she asserted that they were very effective in facilitating communication for the patients and aided them in better expressing their needs. However, she was dissatisfied with the Livox app because it displays a screen for just a few seconds before automatically replacing it with the next one; since many of her patients suffer from involuntary hand and head movements, the display time is not sufficient for them to focus their hand or eyes on the desired image; unfortunately, there is no option to modify the display time rendering the app unusable for many of her patients. When questioned about how best to organize the CBs and what words and categories to include, she answered that this actually depends on the patient's needs and interests; however, the usual organization is subject nouns/pronouns followed by action verbs and then objects represented as categories while words like "yes", "no" and "thank you" are required by all individuals.

When we described our application to her, she expressed enthusiasm for using it with her patients, especially if it solved the display time issue encountered in the Livox app. In response to our requests for any suggestions and design recommendations, she mentioned that the background color should be customizable since many of her patients have trouble distinguishing images on a white background while others get distracted if there are too many colors. She was eager to see the final product and agreed to let us test it out with her patients once it had been completed.

The interview established that CBs are being used in the local context and are proving to be effective for improving the communication skills of individuals with speech and motor impairments. It also highlighted the limited utilization of high-tech solutions for this purpose; the center used only one Android tablet application but the SLP was dissatisfied with it since it had major usability issues with its interaction design. Moreover, the interview yielded several valuable insights for the desired information structure and features for electronic CBs which have informed the design of our system.

4 System Design and Implementation

We have developed "Esmaany" (an Arabic phrase meaning "Listen to Me"), a relatively low-cost gaze interaction-based Arabic language application that assists pre-literate and early literate PSSMIs to communicate with people in their vicinity. The application has been developed for Microsoft Windows [25] PCs. It uses the PC's built-in webcam for capturing the user's eye movements and the built-in speakers for the speech output and, therefore, does not require any external hardware components. It also utilizes the Gaze Tracking Library [9], a framework for open source eye tracking using off-the-shelf components, to determine the gaze direction and the Google Cloud TTS API [10] for generating the speech output and thus, does not require any proprietary software, either. The application software has been written in the C# programming language [26] on the .NET platform [27].

The system comprises of two main components: 1) CBs for the PSSMI along with some related functions and 2) an interface for the PSSMI's caregiver to customize the system according to the user's unique needs. A detailed description of these components is provided below.

4.1 CBs for the PSSMI Along with Some Related Functions

The application provides several CBs for the PSSMI, each containing many items. Each item on the CB represents either a word/phrase or a category (a group of related items, e.g., food, people, etc.); since the targeted users are pre-literate and early literate, each item consists of a simple picture with accompanying text to make it easier to discern.

Four kinds of CBs are provided:

1. A "main" board containing some pronouns, verbs, commonly used words (e.g., "yes", "no") and categories (shown in Fig. 1)
2. A "Quick" board for fast access to frequently needed terms (e.g., "hello", "thank you", I don't know", "I love you", "I am sorry") (shown in Fig. 2)
3. An "About Me" board containing phrases conveying the user's personal information (e.g., his/her name, age, phone number) (shown in Fig. 3)

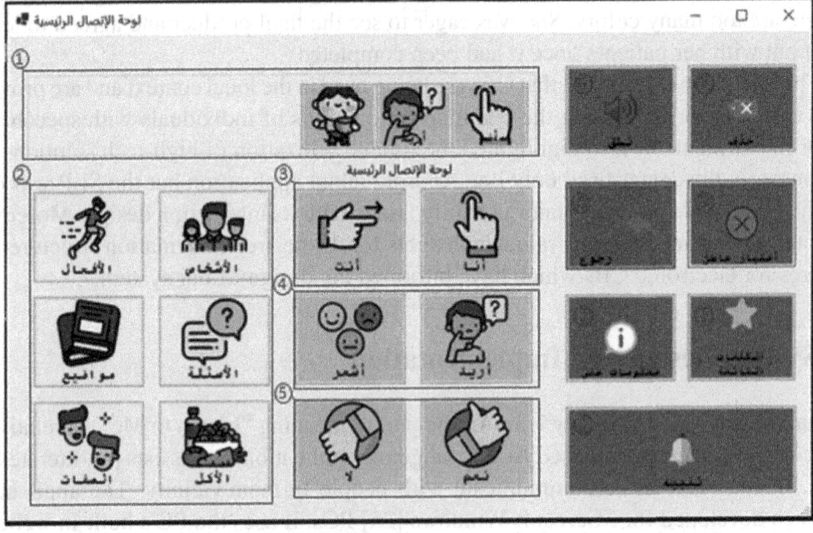

Fig. 1. "Main" board containing (sub-items listed from right to left and top to bottom): (1) Field to display sentence formed so far (e.g., currently displays "I want to drink…"); (2) Categories (people, actions, question words, topics, food, characteristics); (3) Pronouns ("I", "you"); (4) Verbs ("want", "feel") (5) Commonly used words ("yes", "no"). Control panel on the right containing: (6) "Say sentence" button; (7) "Delete previous word" button; (8) "Back" button; (9) "Mistake" button; (10) Button to access "About Me" board; (11) Button to access "Quick" board; (12) "Alert" button.

4. "Category" boards containing items in that category. The first item is always a word/phrase item containing the name of that category in case the user wants to say the category's name or add it to a sentence. Additional items can be words/phrases or sub-categories related to that category. For instance, as shown in Fig. 4, the "food" category board contains a "food" word item, category items like "drinks", "fruits, etc., and some word items for common foods like "chicken", "meat", "bread", etc.

When the application is started, a calibration process is performed during which the user is asked to look at several targets at fixed positions on the screen in order to calculate the coefficients that map the center of the pupil to the gaze coordinates on the screen [28].

Once the calibration is completed, the user can control the mouse pointer using his/her eyes. When the pointer is over a clickable interface element like an item or a menu button, the element gets highlighted and the user can then select it by fixating his/her gaze on it for a few seconds. Selecting a word/phrase causes it to be spoken by the system (via the Google TTS API [10]) while selecting a category displays its CB. Each selected word/phrase is added to a sentence displayed at the top of the screen (see Fig. 1). A "delete" button is also provided if the user wants to delete the previous word/phrase. Once the sentence is complete, the user can press on a "say sentence" button to have the whole sentence spoken; a new sentence can be started after this.

A simple control panel is also provided on the right side of the screen (see Fig. 1). It contains the "say sentence" and "delete" buttons, a "back" button to return to the previous CB as well as buttons to access the "About Me" and "Quick" boards. Moreover, a "mistake" button is provided in case the user erroneously selects an item and wants to immediately apprise the CP of this; pressing this button plays a "I made a mistake" message. Lastly, an "alert" button is given which activates a loud alarm sound allowing the user to grab the attention of a nearby person/caregiver in case the user needs immediate assistance.

All the visual and speech interfaces of the system are in Arabic. Since Arabic is read and written from right to left, the flow of the visual interfaces is also in this direction. The visual interfaces have been carefully designed keeping the cognitive and motor capabilities of the target users in mind. The interface elements have been color-coded to allow them to be easily distinguished from each other: accordingly, control panel buttons are grey, category items are green, word/phrase items are peach, "Quick" board items are pink, while personal information phrase items on the "About Me" board are blue. Since it is challenging to select small targets using the gaze [29], the buttons and items have been rendered reasonably large and only a limited number of items – no more than twelve - have been added to each predefined CB – this compensates for the low spatial resolution handled by our webcam-based eye tracker and also reduces the visual accuracy and physical effort required by the user [5]. Furthermore, the SLP's recommendations have been followed in structuring the information content by providing subjects, action verbs and objects on the main board to form basic sentences, the selection of commonly used words and giving the users control over moving from one CB to the other (rather than having the system replace one CB by the next one automatically which was the key frustrating factor in the Livox app [17]). For the speech interface, we initially considered

Fig. 2. "Quick" board containing frequently used terms (from right to left and top to bottom): "Hello", "Goodbye", "I don't know", "Fine", "Thank you", Good morning", "What's your name?", "Like", "Sorry", "Good night", "I love you", "I don't like it".

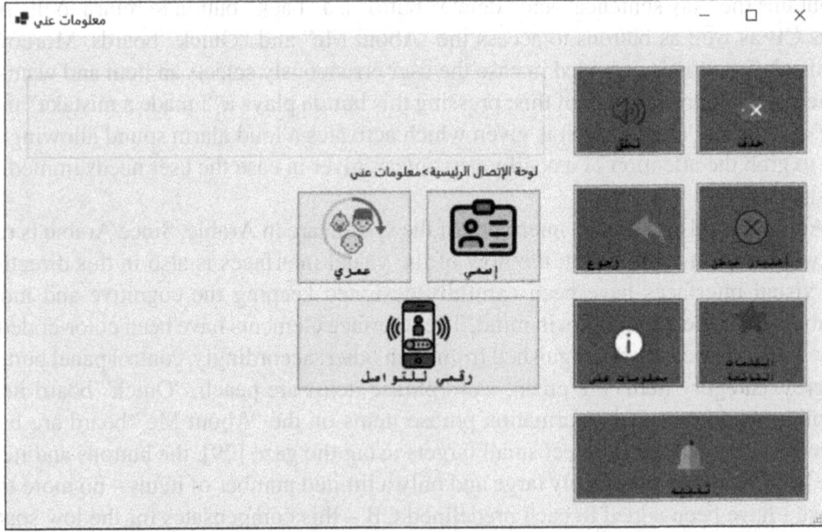

Fig. 3. "About Me" board containing the user's personal information (from right to left and top to bottom): "My name is __", "My age is __", "My phone number is __".

using recorded human voices based on the reasoning that these would be more natural and would convey warmth and friendliness. However, since the system provides options for caregivers to add items (as explained in the next subsection), they would have to

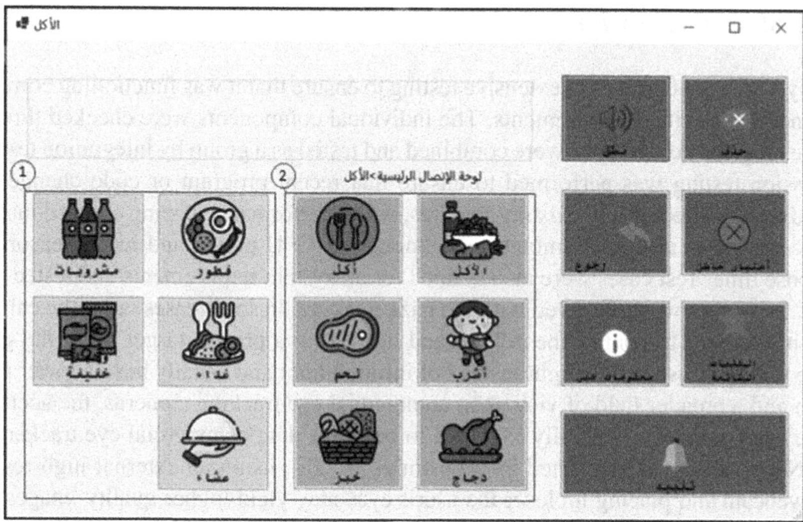

Fig. 4. Category board for "Food" category containing items related to food (sub-items listed from right to left and top to bottom): (1) subcategories for food ("breakfast", "drinks", "lunch", "snacks", "dinner"); (2) Frequently used words for food ("food", "eat", "drink", "meat", "chicken", "bread").

record their own voices for the newly added items causing different words in a sentence to be spoken in different voices which would have been confusing and irritating for the users; therefore, to maintain consistency, we decided to use synthetic voices (a male and a female one) generated using Google TTS [10] so that even when a new word/phrase is added, it is spoken in the same voices.

4.2 Interface for the PSSMI's Caregiver

Since CBs are traditionally customized for each user depending on their cognitive capabilities [4], an interface has been provided for the caregivers to enable them to accomplish this. Through this interface, the caregivers can add new items to the predefined CBs and can also create new categories and add items to them; To create a new item, caregivers are required to specify the type of the item (word/phrase or category), upload an image, and enter the corresponding text. They can also edit and delete any items that they have added – however they are not allowed to edit any of the predefined items. They can also enter the user's personal profile information which is added automatically by the system to the "About Me" board; this information can be edited later and the edits are reflected in the "About Me" board. Furthermore, they can select a male or female voice for the speech output according to the user's gender. Following the SLP's recommendation, an option for changing the background color has also been provided.

Though the application is primarily meant to support gaze-based interaction, to extend its use to a broader range of users including those who suffer only from speech impairments but retain control of their hand movements, an option for switching to mouse-based interaction is also offered.

5 System Evaluation

The system was subjected to extensive testing to ensure that it was functioning correctly and met the specified requirements. The individual components were checked through unit testing, the components were combined and tested as a group by integration testing, regression testing was performed to ensure that recent program or code change had not adversely affected any existing features, while performance testing showed that the application used a limited amount of memory and CPU power and had a reasonable response time. Test cases were also defined for all system requirements and tested out.

A few issues were observed with the gaze tracking. In some cases, after the calibration, it was hard to control the pointer and move it to a precise target using the gaze. Since webcams use visible light instead of infrared light and usually have a lower resolution and a broader field of view than commercial eye tracking cameras, the accuracy of the eye tracking is generally expected to be lower than commercial eye trackers [2, 28]. Nevertheless, as suggested by Agustin et al. [28], using an external high resolution webcam and placing it closer the user's eyes may yield higher quality images and improve the tracking accuracy. Another issue was that the eye tracker required the head to remain in the same position and was not invariant to changes in the head orientation. Though this is not a concern for users who are completely immobile (such as those with locked-in syndrome), for PSSMIs who have involuntary head movements (such as those mentioned by the SLP), the eye tracker would require recalibration every time the head is displaced significantly. To accommodate such users, strategies for compensating for head movements for webcam-based eye tracking [30–33] would be incorporated in future iterations of the system. Furthermore, the dwell time for selecting a target was set by default to 10 s; we believe that it would be challenging and tiring for the users to keep their gaze fixed at one spot for so long. On the other hand, users with severely limited cognitive and motor skills may need to focus on targets for longer periods of time. We will, therefore, determine an appropriate default dwell time based on usability testing conducted with the actual users and will also add an option for the caregiver to customize this time according to the user's capabilities. One final concern was that the users have to go through the calibration process every time the application is started which is inconvenient for them; this is actually a general challenge for gaze tracking systems [30] and various approaches, such as reusing the calibration information for subsequent sessions of the same user [30] or pre-training on a large scale eye tracking database containing data from many users [2, 33], can be exploited to resolve this.

We had obtained permission from the Disabled Children's Association, Riyadh, Saudi Arabia to conduct usability testing for the system with the target users to identify any usability issues and to develop design recommendations for AAC systems that provide gaze interaction via webcams for PSSMIs. Unfortunately, the tests had to be postponed indefinitely following the lockdown due to the Covid-19 pandemic which is still in effect to date. Given the vital importance of testing assistive technologies with the actual users, we do intend to proceed with the usability tests once the lockdown has been lifted and hope that these will yield valuable insights into how the system can be better adapted to the users' needs; this would not only help us improve our system but would also benefit other researchers developing similar systems.

6 Conclusion and Future Work

We hope that our low-cost customizable gaze-based interaction solution in Arabic would make electronic CBs more accessible to PSSMIs whose primary language is Arabic and would enable them to communicate more effectively with people around them, thus, decreasing their social isolation and bolstering their independence. We plan to test the system with actual users to identify any usability issues and better adapt it to their needs. Future work directions include porting the system to a mobile platform, adding more content, including a keyboard to support higher literacy skills, making word predictions based on previously typed in words to improve entry speed and reduce cognitive load, allowing the number of items per board and the item size to be customized by caregivers according to the user's cognitive and motor capabilities and offering alternative selection methods for users with more advanced eye and hand muscle control (such as blinking the eye or pressing a manual switch) to select a target which may be less fatiguing and require less concentration than fixing the gaze upon it for a protracted period of time [29]. The application can also be adapted for remote communication by providing the capability to send the generated text and voice messages to distant CPs via email and social networking services such as WhatsApp [34]. Moreover, various strategies will be employed in future iterations of the system to improve the accuracy of the eye tracking and to reduce the inconvenience to the user, such as using an external high resolution webcam placed closer to the user's eyes, utilizing methods for making the eye tracking head pose invariant, adding an option to customize the dwell time for target selection and exploiting approaches for reducing the need for recalibration every time the application is used.

Acknowledgements. We would like to extend our sincere thanks to Ms. Sameera Alzuaabi, Head of the Speech Department at the Disabled Children's Association, Riyadh, Saudi Arabia, for her invaluable advice and suggestions that have informed the design of our system.

References

1. Motor Impairment. International Neuromodulation Society. https://www.neuromodulation.com/motor-impairment. Accessed 24 May 2020
2. Zhang, X., Kulkarni, H., Morris, M.R.: Smartphone-based gaze gesture communication for people with motor disabilities. In: 2017 CHI Conference on Human Factors in Computing Systems, Denver, Colorado, USA, pp. 2878–2889. Association for Computing Machinery (2017)
3. Lupu, R.G., Bozomitu, R.G., Ungureanu, F., Cehan, V.: Eye tracking based communication system for patient with major neuro-locomotor disabilites. In: 15th International Conference on System Theory, Control and Computing, pp. 1–5. IEEE (2011)
4. Galante, A., Menezes, P.: A gaze-based interaction system for people with cerebral palsy. Procedia Technol. **5**, 895–902 (2012)
5. Bates, R., Donegan, M., Istance, H.O., Hansen, J.P., Räihä, K.-J.: Introducing COGAIN: communication by gaze interaction. Univ. Access Inf. Soc. **6**, 159–166 (2007)
6. Vessoyan, K., Steckle, G., Easton, B., Nichols, M., Mok Siu, V., McDougall, J.: Using eye-tracking technology for communication in Rett syndrome: perceptions of impact. Augment. Alter. Commun. **34**, 230–241 (2018)

7. Vörös, G., et al.: Towards a smart wearable tool to enable people with SSPI to communicate by sentence fragments. In: Cipresso, P., Matic, A., Lopez, G. (eds.) MindCare 2014. LNICST, vol. 100, pp. 90–99. Springer, Cham (2014). https://doi.org/10.1007/978-3-319-11564-1_10
8. Bornman, J.: Low technology. Assistive technology: Principles and applications for communication disorders and special education, pp. 175–220. BRILL (2011)
9. Gaze Tracking Library. Sourceforge. https://sourceforge.net/projects/gazetrackinglib/. Accessed 10 Apr 2020
10. Cloud Text-to-Speech. Google, Inc. https://cloud.google.com/text-to-speech. Accessed 12 Apr 2020
11. Snap Core First. Tobii Dynavox. https://www.mytobiidynavox.com/Store/SnapCoreFirst. Accessed 29 May 2020
12. Eyeworld 3.0. Eyegaze, Inc. https://eyegaze.com/products/eyeworld3/. Accessed 28 May 2020
13. Grid 3. Smartbox Assistive Technology. https://thinksmartbox.com/product/grid-3/. Accessed 17 Apr 2020
14. IntelliGaze. Alea Technologies. https://intelligaze.com/en/. Accessed 29 May 2020
15. Gazespeaker app. Gazespeaker. https://www.gazespeaker.org/. Accessed 29 May 2020
16. GazeBoard. GazeRecorder. https://gazerecorder.com/gazeboard/. Accessed 29 May 2020
17. Livox app. Livox. https://livox.com.br/en. Accessed 30 May 2020
18. Avaz app. Avaz, Inc. https://www.avazapp.com/. Accessed 28 May 2020
19. MyTalkTools Mobile. MyTalk LLC. http://www.mytalktools.com/dnn/2/Products.aspx. Accessed 28 May 2020
20. Voice4u. Voice4u, Inc. https://voice4uaac.com/. Accessed 28 May 2020
21. The Eyegaze Edge. Eyegaze, Inc. https://eyegaze.com/products/eyegaze-edge/. Accessed 10 Apr 2020
22. Classic Tobii Gaze Interaction Software. Tobii Dynavox. https://www.tobiidynavox.com/software/windows-software/windows-control/. Accessed 29 May 2020
23. QuickTalker-23. Ablenet, Inc. https://www.ablenetinc.com/quicktalker-23
24. GoTalk 9+. The Attainment Company. https://www.attainmentcompany.com/gotalk-9
25. Microsoft Windows. Microsoft Corporation. https://www.microsoft.com/en-us/windows. Accessed 5 June 2020
26. C# Documentation. Microsoft Docs. https://docs.microsoft.com/en-us/dotnet/csharp/. Accessed 4 June 2020
27. .Net Documentation. Microsoft Docs. https://docs.microsoft.com/en-us/dotnet/. Accessed 4 June 2020
28. San Agustin, J., et al.: Evaluation of a low-cost open-source gaze tracker. In: 2010 Symposium on Eye-Tracking Research & Applications, New York, NY, United States, Austin, TX, USA, pp. 77–80. Association for Computing Machinery (2010)
29. Biswas, P., Langdon, P.: A new input system for disabled users involving eye gaze tracker and scanning interface. J. Assist. Technol. **5**, 58–66 (2011)
30. Ferhat, O., Vilariño, F.: Low cost eye tracking: the current panorama. In: Wei, Y. (ed.) Computational Intelligence and Neuroscience. Hindawi Publishing Corporation (2016)
31. Valenti, R., Sebe, N., Gevers, T.: Combining head pose and eye location information for gaze estimation. IEEE Trans. Image Process. **21**, 802–815 (2012)
32. Lu, F., Okabe, T., Sugano, Y., Sato, Y.: Learning gaze biases with head motion for head pose-free gaze estimation. Image Vis. Comput. **32**, 169–179 (2014)
33. Zhang, X., Sugano, Y., Fritz, M., Bulling, A.: Appearance-based gaze estimation in the wild. In: 2015 IEEE Conference on Computer Vision and Pattern Recognition (CVPR), pp. 4511–4520 (2015)
34. WhatsApp. WhatsApp Inc. https://www.whatsapp.com/. Accessed 01 June 2020

Rotate-and-Press: A Non-visual Alternative to Point-and-Click?

Hae-Na Lee[1(✉)], Vikas Ashok[2], and I. V. Ramakrishnan[1]

[1] Stony Brook University, Stony Brook, NY 11794, USA
{haenalee,ram}@cs.stonybrook.edu
[2] Old Dominion University, Norfolk, VA 23529, USA
vganjigu@odu.edu

Abstract. Most computer applications manifest visually rich and dense graphical user interfaces (GUIs) that are primarily tailored for an easy-and-efficient sighted interaction using a combination of two default input modalities, namely the keyboard and the mouse/touchpad. However, blind screen-reader users predominantly rely only on keyboard, and therefore struggle to interact with these applications, since it is both arduous and tedious to perform the visual 'point-and-click' tasks such as accessing the various application commands/features using just keyboard shortcuts supported by screen readers.

In this paper, we investigate the suitability of a 'rotate-and-press' input modality as an effective non-visual substitute for the visual mouse to easily interact with computer applications, with specific focus on word processing applications serving as the representative case study. In this regard, we designed and developed bTunes, an add-on for Microsoft Word that customizes an off-the-shelf Dial input device such that it serves as a *surrogate* mouse for blind screen-reader users to quickly access various application commands and features using a set of simple rotate and press gestures supported by the Dial. Therefore, with bTunes, blind users too can now enjoy the benefits of two input modalities, as their sighted counterparts. A user study with 15 blind participants revealed that bTunes significantly reduced both the time and number of user actions for doing representative tasks in a word processing application, by as much as 65.1% and 36.09% respectively. The participants also stated that they did not face any issues switching between keyboard and Dial, and furthermore gave a high usability rating (84.66 avg. SUS score) for bTunes.

Keywords: Screen reader · Word processor · Accessibility

1 Introduction

People who are blind generally rely on special-purpose assistive technology, namely screen readers (e.g., JAWS [10], VoiceOver [2], NVDA [18]), for interacting with computing applications. A screen reader linearly narrates contents of the screen, and also enables blind users to navigate the application GUI using

C. Stephanidis et al. (Eds.): HCII 2020, LNCS 12426, pp. 291–305, 2020.
https://doi.org/10.1007/978-3-030-60149-2_23

predefined keyboard hotkeys or shortcuts. The primary input device for blind users to interact with computer applications using screen readers, is a keyboard. However, most applications manifest visually dense GUIs that are more suited for interaction with a visual pointing device such as a mouse or touchpad. For example, in Microsoft Word, as shown in Fig. 1, to apply a command (e.g., Styles) while editing a document, sighted users can simply move the mouse cursor to that command in the ribbon and click on it. On the contrary, to do the same task, blind users have to either memorize the corresponding shortcut or serially move their screen-reader focus to the command by pressing a multitude of basic navigational keyboard shortcuts. Therefore, tasks that the sighted users can perform almost instantaneously with a simple point-and-click mouse operation, are tedious and cumbersome for blind users using just the keyboard.

Prior approaches [1,5,6,14,25] devised to mitigate this usability divide have primarily focused on passive content navigation or 'consumption', especially in web browsing, accessing maps and graph charts. However, interaction with most general computer applications, especially productivity tools, goes much beyond just content navigation; users also need to frequently access various application commands and features (e.g., formatting, insertions, review, comments, etc., in Microsoft Word) while they navigate or edit the main content. To fill this gap, in this paper, we investigate the suitability and potential of a 'rotate-and-press' input modality as an effective non-visual substitute or 'surrogate' for the visual mouse to enable blind screen-reader users to easily and efficiently access application commands and features while they interact with the main content.

With the additional tangible rotary input modality, blind screen-reader users too will be able to benefit from having two input modalities akin to their sighted peers. For instance, in productivity applications, sighted users can effectively distribute their interaction load over both keyboard and mouse, e.g., using the keyboard for typing and pressing some hotkeys, and using the mouse for instantly accessing application commands. Blind users on the other hand, have to rely solely on the keyboard to do all the tasks. Given the linear content-navigation supported by screen readers, blind users find it tedious and cumbersome to perform even simple tasks such as accessing application commands. However, with the auxiliary 'rotate-and-press' input device, blind users too will be able to effectively split their workload over two input modalities and complete their tasks quickly and easily.

As an investigation tool, we developed bTunes. We chose Microsoft Word as a use scenario due to its popularity among blind users [23] and also its sophisticated GUI containing a variety of application commands. bTunes adapts an off-the-shelf rotary input device, namely Microsoft Surface Dial (see Fig. 1) to serve as a "surrogate mouse", thereby providing an auxiliary tangible interface in addition to keyboard for blind users. As shown in Fig. 1, via simple rotate and press gestures supported by the Dial, bTunes enables a user to easily access all the ribbon commands, without losing their current keyboard context in the main content area of the document. Results from a user study with 15 blind participants were very encouraging in that the time and number of user actions

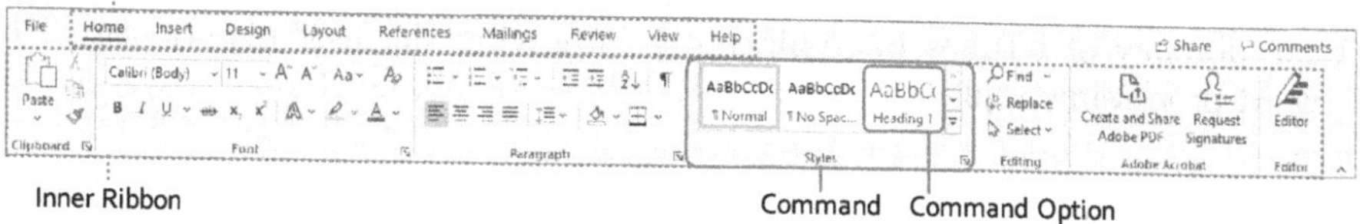

(a) Ribbons in Microsoft Word.

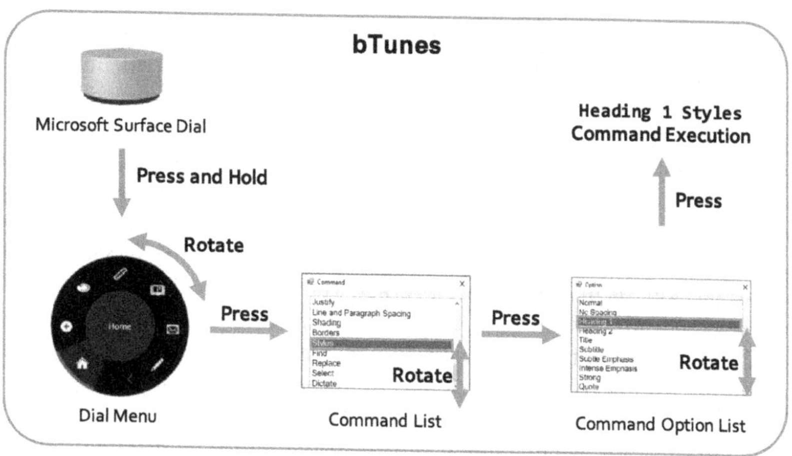

(b) Interaction workflow of bTunes.

Fig. 1. Illustration of bTunes for Microsoft Word: (a) application ribbons containing multitude of commands that can easily accessed with a point-and-click mouse, but harder to access with a keyboard-based screen reader; (b) alternative rotate-and-press bTunes interface for non-visually accessing ribbon commands. Instead of shifting screen-reader focus from main edit area to the ribbon and then sequentially navigating the ribbons, the screen-reader user can simply press-and-hold the Dial to bring up a menu dashboard containing the outer ribbons (i.e., Home, Insert, etc.). The user can then rotate the Dial to focus on the desired ribbon, and then press to shift focus to the corresponding inner ribbon, specifically, bTunes opens up a dialog box with the corresponding inner ribbon commands. The user can repeat the same rotate and press gestures to select commands and command options (if any).

the participants needed for accessing commands with bTunes were significantly reduced by as much as 65.1% and 36.09%, respectively, when compared to their current status quo.

We summarize our contributions as follows:

- The design and implementation of bTunes – an add-on for word processing applications, specifically Microsoft Word, which enables blind users to easily and efficiently access application commands and features using a 'rotate-and-press' interaction modality, thereby enhancing the productivity of blind users with these applications.

– Results from a user study with 15 blind screen-reader users that demonstrated the potency of bTunes in significantly improving the user experience with word processing applications.

2 Related Work

To overcome the limitations of keyboard-based screen-reader interaction, several non-visual input modalities for blind users have been previously explored [1,3, 5,6,14,19–21,24,25]. Broadly, these approaches can be grouped into keyboard adaptation [3,15], audio-tactile devices [6,14,21,25], and assistant interfaces [4, 5,11,16].

Keyboard adaptation approaches repurpose the keyboard to improve interaction experience for blind users. In the IBM Home Page Reader (HPR) [3], the numeric keypad was adapted to serve as an auxiliary input interface for navigating web pages. Khurana et al. [15], on the other hand, propose spatially region interaction techniques that leverage the keyboard surface to facilitate easily non-visual interaction with 2D structures. Besides the need to remember new shortcuts on top of the multiple existing screen-reader shortcuts, both these approaches are exclusive to web browsing, and therefore do not readily generalize to arbitrary computer applications, such as Word supported by bTunes.

Audio-haptic approaches enable screen-reader users to leverage additional tangible audio-tactile input devices to interact with applications. For example, the multimodal audio-haptic interface proposed by Doush et al. [1] enables screen-reader users to navigate and access content in Excel charts. Perhaps the closest related work is the Speed-Dial [6], which supports easy hierarchical navigation of webpage content via its external Microsoft Surface Dial input interface. Also, Soviak et al. [21] present an audio-haptic glove that helps blind users to feel the borders of various webpage segments on the page, thereby giving the users a sense of page layout and content arrangement. A common aspect of all these approaches is that they are designed exclusively for passive content navigation, which is different from interaction with general applications such as Word, where the users not only navigate content, but also frequently accessing the various spatially-distributed application commands and features (e.g., formatting, insertions, review, comments, etc.).

Assistants let blind users interact with applications using spoken commands. For example, the assistant proposed by Gadde et al. [11] lets blind users to rely on a few speech commands to get a quick overview of current webpage and also to navigate to a section of interest. On the other hand, Ashok et al. [5] support a richer set of voice commands that lets blind users also query the webpage content. While speech assistants are known to significantly improve usability for blind users, they have to be custom-designed for each application. The general-purpose assistants like Apple's Siri, Microsoft's Cortana, etc. primarily focus on OS-level commands (e.g., open an application, simulate mouse and keyboard actions, open windows menu, set up alarms, etc.), factoid queries (e.g., time, weather, etc.), and dictation (e.g., insert paragraph, edit word, delete line, etc.). They are presently incapable of providing speech access to the various commands supported within arbitrary applications. Lastly, speech assistants including commercial ones only support a limited set of languages.

Proficiency with word processing applications has been recognized as an important skill for employment of blind individuals [8,22]. Despite the importance of these applications and in contrast to the large body of work on the accessibility of the Web and mobile devices as noted above, there is a dearth of studies on usability of desktop applications, in particular the Office suite [1,17]. Furthermore, none of them focus on understanding user behavior and interaction strategies that blind people employ to create and edit documents. Apple's MacBook Pro Touch Bar [24] is a generic solution that provides contextual menus and navigation shortcuts for arbitrary computer applications. However, the Touch Bar can only contain a few commands, and moreover it is primarily designed for visual consumption, thereby requiring screen-reader users to spend significant time exploring and orienting themselves each time they want to access the features on it. Like Touch Bar, Apple's built-in screen reader, VoiceOver, also provides access to commands via its rotor feature. However, these commands mainly assist in navigating content.

Perhaps the closest work related to this paper is [17], where the authors suggest guidelines for a support tool in Microsoft Word that can assist blind people format their documents independently. However, these guidelines were developed based only on subjective feedback obtained from a preliminary survey with 15 blind users, and therefore did not incorporate objective details regarding user-interaction behavior and strategies. Evans et al. [9] also proposed a technique to assist blind users format documents properly in Word. They first checked the post-interaction documents produced by blind users to figure out common layout and formatting errors, and then based on their observations, built two prototypes to help the blind users detect and rectify errors.

3 bTunes Design

Figure 2 presents an architectural overview of bTunes designed for Microsoft Word application. As shown in the figure, with bTunes, blind screen-reader users have an additional input modality, namely Dial, to access various application commands anytime without having to manually move the keyboard focus away from their current context in the main work-area of the application. These commands correspond to the non-edit word-processing actions such as formatting, commenting, proof-reading, inserting objects, changing design, and so on. bTunes replicates the command structure of Word (i.e., ribbons) in the Dial's radial menu (see Fig. 1) and establishes one-to-one programmatic hooks between the commands in the bTunes interface and the corresponding commands in the application GUI. This way, selecting a command with bTunes emulates selecting the corresponding one in the application GUI, thereby producing the same intended outcome. For commands with options (e.g., font names for the Font command), bTunes refreshes its dialog box to show these options in place of commands (see Fig. 1). The users can access, navigate, and select ribbons and commands in the radial menu and the dialog box using simple rotate and press gestures, as explained later in this section.

3.1 Dial Input Device

The off-the-shelf Surface Dial input device (shown in Fig. 1) is a small rotary puck that supports three simple gestures: *press*, *rotate*, and *press-and-hold*. We also implemented a *double press* gesture, which is triggered when the Dial is pressed twice in quick succession (less than 400 ms). On every gesture, the Dial also provides tactile feedback in the form of vibrations. The Surface Dial is usable with a PC running Windows 10 Anniversary Update or later, and it gets connected to the PC via Bluetooth 4.0 LE.

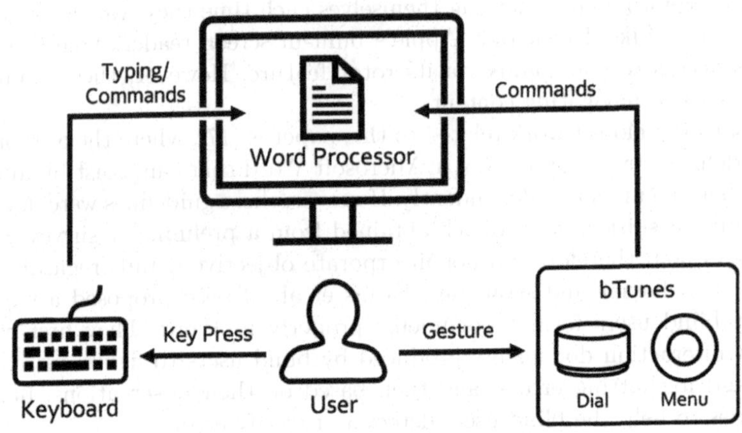

Fig. 2. An architectural overview of bTunes.

3.2 bTunes Interaction Using Gestures

A simple press-and-hold gesture brings up the radial dashboard containing outer command ribbons (i.e., Home, Insert, Design, etc.). A user can perform rotate gestures to access the desired command ribbon, and then execute a single press to shift focus to the inner ribbon containing commands, which is shown in a separate dialog box. In this dialog box, the user can do rotate gestures to access different commands, followed by a press gesture to execute the desired command. If the command has options, the press gesture will refresh the dialog box with the corresponding list of options, and the user can repeat the process of using the rotate gestures to navigate to desired option and then the press gesture to select the desired option (e.g., Font Size). At any instant, a double press gesture shifts focus back one level, i.e., from options list to inner ribbon commands, or from inner ribbon to outer ribbon group. A double press at outer ribbon will automatically close the bTunes interface and the focus will shift back to the main work area. The user can also press a shortcut or simply type at anytime to instantly close the bTunes interface.

3.3 Implementation Details

We implemented bTunes as a Microsoft Word add-in, by utilizing the services of the Office Word Primary Interop Assembly (PIA)[1]. Specifically, we developed bTunes with the Visual C# under Visual Studio .NET Framework 4.6.1. We utilized Visual Studio Tools for Office (VSTO) Add-in[2] to build custom Dial operations and radial menu for the bTunes components.

Table 1. Participant demographics. All information shown were self-reported by the participants in the study.

ID	Age/Gender	Screen reader	Word processor	Proficiency	Frequency
P1	39/M	JAWS, VoiceOver	Word, Pages	Expert	Daily
P2	54/M	JAWS	Word	Beginner	2 days a week
P3	46/F	JAWS, NVDA	Word, WordPad	Expert	Daily
P4	31/F	JAWS, NVDA	Word, Google Docs, WordPad	Expert	Daily
P5	60/M	JAWS	Word	Beginner	3 days a week
P6	61/F	JAWS	Word	Beginner	2 days a week
P7	44/M	JAWS, VoiceOver	Word, Pages	Expert	5 days a week
P8	45/M	JAWS, NVDA, System access	Word	Expert	5 days a week
P9	35/M	JAWS	Word	Beginner	2 days a week
P10	54/M	JAWS, VoiceOver	Word, Pages	Beginner	1 day a week
P11	63/F	JAWS	Word	Expert	Daily
P12	32/F	JAWS, System access	Word, Google Docs	Expert	Daily
P13	56/M	JAWS	Word	Beginner	1 day a week
P14	62/M	JAWS	Word	Beginner	2 days a week
P15	36/F	JAWS, NVDA	Word, WordPad	Expert	Daily

1 https://docs.microsoft.com/en-us/visualstudio/vsto/office-primary-interop-assemblies?view=vs-2019.

2 https://docs.microsoft.com/en-us/visualstudio/vsto/office-solutions-development-overview-vsto?view=vs-2017.

The current bTunes prototype can be easily adapted for any Office productivity application using the corresponding PIA. For arbitrary applications, bTunes can be adapted to leverage the UI Automation accessibility framework [13] instead of Interop services, to obtain the UI composition of any application in the form of a tree, and then automatically identify and enable users to easily and hierarchically navigate the application command 'tree' using Dial gestures.

4 Evaluation

4.1 Participants

For the study, we recruited 15 fully blind participants (6 female, 9 male) through local mailing lists and word-of-mouth. The participants varied in age between 31 and 63 (Mean = 47.86, Median = 46, SD = 11.06). All participants stated that they were either blind by birth or lost eyesight at a very young age (less than 10 years old). None of the participants had any motor impairments that affected their physical interaction with the Dial input device. The inclusion criteria required the participants to be proficient with Microsoft Word and JAWS screen reader. All participants stated that they frequently used Office productivity applications, file explorer, web browsers, communication software, and control panel settings. A few participants also frequently used Integrated Development Environments (IDEs), statistical tools, media players, and music software. Table 1 presents the participant demographics.

4.2 Apparatus

The study was performed using ASUS ROG GU501 laptop with Windows 10, Microsoft Word, and JAWS screen reader installed. Also, an external standard keyboard and Microsoft Surface Dial were connected to the laptop.

4.3 Design

The study required the participants to do the following two tasks:

- **Task 1:** Find and apply a command in the Microsoft Word application.
- **Task 2:** Create an article with a title, a heading, and two paragraphs.

The participants were asked to perform these representative tasks under the following two study conditions:

- **Screen Reader:** Participants used only the JAWS keyboard shortcuts to do the tasks.
- **bTunes:** Participants used both the JAWS keyboard shortcuts and the bTunes's Dial interface (e.g., press, rotate, and double press gestures) to do the tasks.

Task 1 was controlled as it was designed to compare the command-access efficiencies of screen reader and bTunes, whereas Task 2 was think-aloud free-form editing as it was intended to measure perceived overall usability of screen reader and bTunes in a reasonably realistic setting. For Task 1, we chose the following six commands: (a) Set *Text Highlight Color* to 'Dark Blue' in Home ribbon; (b) Insert *Star: 5 Points* shape in Insert ribbon; (c) Set *Page Color* to 'Light Blue' in Design ribbon; (d) Set *Position Object* to 'Bottom Right' in Layout ribbon; (e) Select *Bibliography Style* to 'MLA' in Bibliography ribbon; and (f) Configure *Markup options* to 'Show All Revisions Inline' in Review ribbon. For Task 2, we chose the following two topics: (a) school; and (b) their neighborhood.

In each condition, the participants accessed three commands for Task 1, and created one article for Task 2. To minimize learning effects, the assignment of commands and articles to tasks was randomized, and the ordering of tasks and conditions were counterbalanced. Also, to avoid confounds, for Task 1, we selected commands that are equidistant from the beginning of their corresponding ribbons (i.e., 23rd command considering the linear screen-reading navigation order in each ribbon), and hence would require the same number of basic <Tab> shortcuts or rotate gestures to navigate to them.

4.4 Procedure

The experimenter began the study by demonstrating the bTunes's Dial interface to the participants and letting them practice for 10 min to get comfortable with bTunes. The experimenter then let the participants practice with JAWS screen reader for 10 min and refresh their memory about the various available shortcuts. After the practice session, the participant performed the tasks according to a predetermined counterbalanced order. Post study, the experimenter surveyed the participant with the System Usability Scale (SUS), NASA Task Load Index (NASA-TLX), and custom questionnaires. Each study lasted for 1–1.5 h, and all conversations were in English.

Measurements. During the study, the experimenter measured task completion times, and logged all screen-reader keystrokes and Dial gestures. Audio and computer-screen activities were recorded using the *Open Broadcaster Software.* The experimenter also took notes while the participants were doing the tasks. At the end of the study, the experimenter administered the System Usability Scale (SUS), NASA Task Load Index (NASA-TLX), and a custom open-ended questionnaire to collect subjective feedback.

4.5 Results

Completion Times and User Effort for Task 1. Figure 3 presents the task completion times and number of user actions for Task 1 under both conditions. As shown in the figure, overall, the participants spent an average of 171.44 s (Median = 159, Max = 600, Min = 10) with screen reader, whereas they only needed an average of 59.97 s (Median = 53, Max = 144, Min = 25)

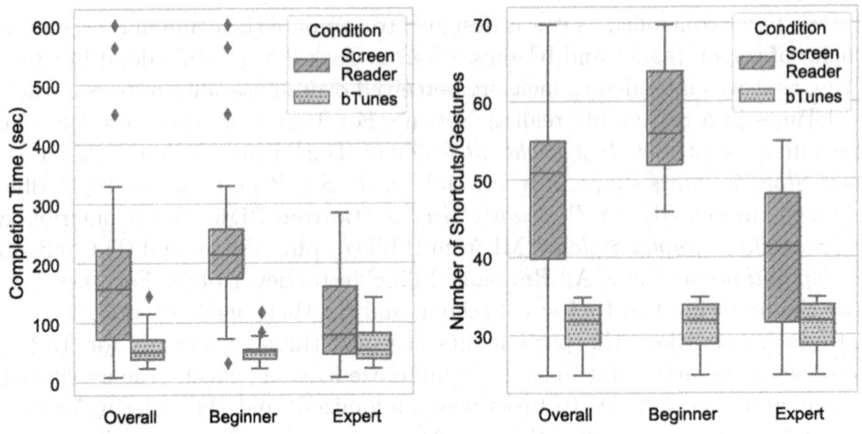

Fig. 3. Completion times and number of shortcuts/gestures for Task 1 under two study conditions, i.e., screen reader and bTunes.

with bTunes. A Wilcoxon signed rank test showed a significant difference in the command-access times between the two study conditions ($z = -5.197$, $n = 45$, $p < 0.00001$). Similar observations were made while analyzing the completion times for individual participant groups, i.e., beginner (Mean = 242.76, Median = 216, Max = 600, Min = 32) and expert (Mean = 109.04, Median = 81.5, Max = 287, Min = 10). We found significant effect of study conditions on completion times for both beginner ($W = 1 < 58$, $n = 21$) and expert ($W = 47 < 84$, $n = 24$) groups. However, between the two groups, the experts were significantly faster than beginners in accessing commands with screen reader (Mann Whitney U test, $U_1 = 88.5$, $U_2 = 415.5$, $p = 0.0001$), but no such significant difference was found while accessing commands with bTunes ($U_1 = 289.5$, $U_2 = 214.5$, $p = 0.393$).

Also, with screen reader, overall, the participants spent an average of 48.57 shortcuts (Median = 51, Max = 70, Min = 25), whereas with bTunes, they only used an average of 31.04 gestures (Median = 32, Max = 35, Min = 25). This difference in input effort was found to be statistically significant (Wilcoxon signed rank test, $|z| = 5.48 < z_c(1.96)$, $n = 45$). We also found significant effect of study conditions on number of shortcuts/gestures for both beginner ($W = 0 < 58$, $n = 21$) and expert ($W = 0 < 81$, $n = 24$) groups. As in case of task completion times, with screen reader, the experts needed significantly fewer shortcuts (Mann Whitney U test, $U_1 = 36.5$, $U_2 = 467.5$, $p < 0.0001$) than beginners to access commands; however, no such significant difference was observed with bTunes ($U_1 = 246$, $U_2 = 258$, $p = 0.89$).

We did not measure the task completion times for Task 2, as it involved uncontrolled think-aloud free-form editing, thereby making the task completion times incomparable between conditions.

Subjective Feedback. At the end of each study session, every participant was administered the standard System Usability Scale (SUS) questionnaire [7] where they rated positive and negative statements about each study condition on a Likert scale from 1 for strongly disagree to 5 for strongly agree, with 3 being neutral. Overall, we found a significant difference in the SUS scores between bTunes ($\mu = 84.66$, $\sigma = 5.07$) and screen reader ($\mu = 57.5$, $\sigma = 17.46$) conditions (paired t-test, $|t| = 6.741 > 2.145$, $df = 14$). The difference in average SUS scores was also statistically significant within both beginner (screen reader: $\mu = 46.07$, $\sigma = 12.94$, bTunes: $\mu = 82.5$, $\sigma = 4.62$), and expert (screen reader: $\mu = 67.5$, $\sigma = 14.52$, bTunes: $\mu = 86.56$, $\sigma = 4.66$) groups ($|t| = 7.47 > 2.447$, $df = 6$ for beginners, and $|t| = 3.977 > 2.365$, $df = 7$ for experts). However, between experts and beginners, the experts rated the screen reader significantly higher than beginners (t-test unequal variances, $|t| = 3.021 > 2.161$, $df = 12.98$, $p = 0.0098$); however, no such difference in ratings was observed for bTunes ($|t| = 1.692 < 2.164$, $df = 12.76$, $p = 0.1149$).

We also administered the widely used NASA-TLX [12] subjective questionnaire for assessing perceived task workload (expressed as a value between 0 and 100, with lower values indicating better results). Overall, we found a significant difference in the TLX scores between screen reader ($\mu = 59.97$, $\sigma = 14.11$) and bTunes ($\mu = 17.35$, $\sigma = 2.55$) conditions (paired t-test, $|t| = 11.92 > 2.145$, $df = 14$). The difference in average TLX scores was also statistically significant within both beginner (screen reader: $\mu = 73.95$, $\sigma = 3.15$, bTunes: $\mu = 18.42$, $\sigma = 2.72$), and expert (screen reader: $\mu = 47.75$, $\sigma = 6.66$, bTunes: $\mu = 16.41$, $\sigma = 1.96$) participant groups (t-test, $|t| = 28.71 > 2.447$, $df = 6$ for beginners, and $|t| = 12.7 > 2.365$, $df = 7$ for experts). However, between experts and beginners, the perceived workload of beginners with screen readers was significantly higher than that of experts (t-test unequal variances, $|t| = 9.931 > 2.221$, $df = 10.255$, $p < 0.001$), however, no such difference was observed in case of bTunes ($|t| = 1.622 < 2.206$, $df = 10.794$, $p = 0.133$).

Qualitative Feedback for Task 2. All participants indicated that they did not have any problems switching between the keyboard and the Dial in bTunes while doing the tasks. On the contrary, they stated they preferred this clear separation of interaction activities, i.e., using the keyboard for typing and pressing few hotkeys, and using the Dial for the accessing the application command and features. They also agreed that bTunes gestures were much simpler, natural, and easier to memorize compared to the screen-reader keyboard shortcuts. Eight participants (P2, P5, P6, P8, P9, P10, P13, and P15) stated that they frequently mix-up the screen-reader's shortcuts for different applications, and therefore waste valuable time due to these recurrent mistakes. However, they indicated that they would never run into such an issue with bTunes, as they don't have to rely on keyboard for doing actions.

Five participants (P2, P6, P9, P12, and P13) also stated that they preferred the small size of Dial input device compared to the large size of keyboard. These participants expressed that they especially liked the Dial interface because it allowed them to easily perform input actions with one hand, in contrast to keyboard where they often have to rely on both their hands to execute complex hotkeys (e.g., ALT + NUMPAD 5 in JAWS). They also indicated that with keyboard, there was a good chance of unintentionally pressing the wrong hotkeys especially when the keyboard buttons involved were far apart from each other; such problems will not occur with the Dial interface of bTunes.

Twelve participants (except P1, P4, and P7) noted that the bTunes interface is 'smooth' and straightforward when accessing the ribbon commands. In contrast, they stated that ribbon access is confusing with keyboard as there are multiple ways in which one can navigate the ribbon using a wide array of hotkeys. They also specified that with keyboard, it is easy to miss certain commands that cannot be accessed through generic shortcuts. For example, while doing Task 1, four participants (P2, P5, P10, and P13) navigated through the ribbon using the LEFT/RIGHT arrow keys, and therefore missed several commands that were only accessible by pressing TAB shortcut. Similarly, while accessing a grid of commands such as *Text Highlight Color*, 5 participants (P2, P5, P6, P10, and P14) initially pressed only the UP/DOWN arrow keys several times before realizing that they could access other colors by pressing the LEFT/RIGHT arrow keys. Furthermore, accidental key presses moved the screen-reader focus away from the ribbon, and therefore the participants had to repeat the tedious process of sequentially navigating a ribbon to find the task command. No such issues were observed with the Dial interface during the study.

5 Discussion

Our results clearly demonstrate the potential of bTunes in serving as an effective non-visual surrogate for visual pointing devices such as mouse and touchpad. The participants also gave higher usability rating for bTunes compared to their preferred keyboard-only screen reader. However, the study also revealed limitations and important avenues for future research, and we discuss a couple of the important ones next.

Command Prediction. Analysis of the study data revealed that further improvements in command access times and user effort can be achieved by predicting the commands that the user will most likely access next given their current application context, and then accordingly reordering the command list in the radial menu and the bTunes's dialog box dynamically such that the most probable commands are placed at the beginning of this list. For example, in Word, commands such as *Alignment*, *Styles*, and *Font* are more likely to be applied on entire paragraphs or collections of paragraphs, compared to commands such as *Bold*, *Italic*, and *Underline* that are more likely to be used on small portions of text within a paragraph. Therefore, if the user highlights a paragraph, dynamically placing the former commands before the latter commands in the dialog box can potentially reduce the time and number of actions to access the desired command.

Content Navigation. While we focused only on accessing application commands and features in this paper, the rotate-and-press interaction modality can also be leveraged to support content navigation. For example, in Word, hierarchical navigation of content tree (i.e., section, subsection, and so on) can easily be supported using the rotate-and-press gestures; rotate to navigate nodes at the same level, single press to one level down the tree, and double press to go one level up. In 2D spreadsheets such as Microsoft Excel, the Dial interface can be used to go through the rows one-by-one using rotate gestures, and the Dial's radial menu can be used to access content in individual columns (e.g., age, date of birth, address, etc.). However, contrary to command access, content navigation requires semantic knowledge of the content layout and arrangement in order to provide an effective navigational interface. Automatically gleaning the semantics is a topic of future research.

Generalizability of Implementation. bTunes implementation can also be easily adapted for other Office productivity tools notably Excel, PowerPoint, Google Sheets, and Google Slides, as these tools too support interoperability services to access their metadata. For general desktop applications beyond office productivity tools, bTunes can leverage OS accessibility APIs (e.g., the UI Automation accessibility framework [13] for Windows) to obtain the UI composition of any application in the form of a tree, and then enable users to easily and hierarchically navigate this application 'tree' using Dial gestures. However, automatically gleaning the application semantics, and then accordingly customizing the bTunes interface for optimal user interaction, is a topic of future research.

6 Conclusion

This paper introduces a non-visual alternative to pointing devices, namely a 'rotate-and-press' Dial interface, to enhance blind users' interaction experience with computers. The paper also provides experimental evidence of the potential of bTunes in improving user satisfaction and experience while interacting with productivity applications, specifically word processors. It is anticipated that further research on this novel interaction paradigm will usher similar productivity and usability gains for all computing applications.

Acknowledgments. The work in this paper was supported by NSF Awards: 1805076, 1936027; NIH Awards: R01EY026621, R01EY030085, R01HD097188; and NIDILRR Award: 90IF0117-01-00.

References

1. Abu Doush, I., Pontelli, E., Simon, D., Son, T.C., Ma, O.: Making microsoft excel^{TM}: multimodal presentation of charts. In: Proceedings of the 11th International ACM SIGACCESS Conference on Computers and Accessibility, Assets 2009, New York, NY, USA, pp. 147–154. Association for Computing Machinery (2009). https://doi.org/10.1145/1639642.1639669

2. Apple Inc.: Vision accessibility - mac - apple (2020). https://www.apple.com/accessibility/mac/vision/
3. Asakawa, C., Itoh, T.: User interface of a home page reader. In: Proceedings of the Third International ACM Conference on Assistive Technologies, Assets 1998, New York, NY, USA, pp. 149–156. ACM (1998). https://doi.org/10.1145/274497.274526
4. Ashok, V., Borodin, Y., Puzis, Y., Ramakrishnan, I.V.: Capti-speak: a speech-enabled web screen reader. In: Proceedings of the 12th Web for All Conference, W4A 2015, New York, NY, USA. Association for Computing Machinery (2015). https://doi.org/10.1145/2745555.2746660
5. Ashok, V., Puzis, Y., Borodin, Y., Ramakrishnan, I.: Web screen reading automation assistance using semantic abstraction. In: Proceedings of the 22nd International Conference on Intelligent User Interfaces, IUI 2017, New York, NY, USA, pp. 407–418. Association for Computing Machinery (2017). https://doi.org/10.1145/3025171.3025229
6. Billah, S.M., Ashok, V., Porter, D.E., Ramakrishnan, I.: Speed-dial: a surrogate mouse for non-visual web browsing. In: Proceedings of the 19th International ACM SIGACCESS Conference on Computers and Accessibility, ASSETS 2017, New York, NY, USA, pp. 110–119. Association for Computing Machinery (2017). https://doi.org/10.1145/3132525.3132531
7. Brooke, J., et al.: SUS-a quick and dirty usability scale. Usab. Eval. Ind. **189**(194), 4–7 (1996)
8. C. Bell, E., M. Mino, N.: Employment outcomes for blind and visually impaired adults. J. Blind. Innov. Res. **5** (2015). https://doi.org/10.5241/5-85
9. Evans, D.G., Diggle, T., Kurniawan, S.H., Blenkhorn, P.: An investigation into formatting and layout errors produced by blind word-processor users and an evaluation of prototype error prevention and correction techniques. IEEE Trans. Neural Syst. Rehabil. Eng. **11**(3), 257–268 (2003). https://doi.org/10.1109/TNSRE.2003.816868
10. Freedom Scientific: Jaws ® - freedom scientific (2020). http://www.freedomscientific.com/products/software/jaws/
11. Gadde, P., Bolchini, D.: From screen reading to aural glancing: towards instant access to key page sections. In: Proceedings of the 16th International ACM SIGACCESS Conference on Computers & Accessibility, ASSETS 2014, New York, NY, USA, pp. 67–74. Association for Computing Machinery (2014). https://doi.org/10.1145/2661334.2661363
12. Hart, S.G., Staveland, L.E.: Development of NASA-TLX (task load index): results of empirical and theoretical research. In: Advances in Psychology, vol. 52, pp. 139–183. Elsevier (1988)
13. Haverty, R.: New accessibility model for microsoft windows and cross platform development. SIGACCESS Access. Comput. **82**, 11–17 (2005). https://doi.org/10.1145/1077238.1077240
14. Jaijongrak, V.r., Kumazawa, I., Thiemjarus, S.: A haptic and auditory assistive user interface: helping the blinds on their computer operations. In: 2011 IEEE International Conference on Rehabilitation Robotics, pp. 1–6. IEEE (2011)
15. Khurana, R., McIsaac, D., Lockerman, E., Mankoff, J.: Nonvisual interaction techniques at the keyboard surface. In: Proceedings of the 2018 CHI Conference on Human Factors in Computing Systems, CHI 2018, New York, NY, USA. Association for Computing Machinery (2018). https://doi.org/10.1145/3173574.3173585

16. Melnyk, V., et al.: Look ma, no aria: generic accessible interfaces for web widgets. In: Proceedings of the 12th Web for All Conference, W4A 2015, New York, NY, USA. Association for Computing Machinery (2015). https://doi.org/10.1145/2745555.2746666
17. Morales, L., Arteaga, S.M., Kurniawan, S.: Design guidelines of a tool to help blind authors independently format their word documents. In: CHI 2013 Extended Abstracts on Human Factors in Computing Systems, CHI EA 2013, New York, NY, USA, pp. 31–36. ACM (2013). https://doi.org/10.1145/2468356.2468363
18. NV Access: Nv access (2020). https://www.nvaccess.org/
19. Owen, J.M., Petro, J.A., D'Souza, S.M., Rastogi, R., Pawluk, D.T.: An improved, low-cost tactile "mouse" for use by individuals who are blind and visually impaired. In: Proceedings of the 11th International ACM SIGACCESS Conference on Computers and Accessibility, Assets 2009, New York, NY, USA, pp. 223–224. Association for Computing Machinery (2009). https://doi.org/10.1145/1639642.1639686
20. Rastogi, R., Pawluk, D.T., Ketchum, J.M.: Issues of using tactile mice by individuals who are blind and visually impaired. IEEE Trans. Neural Syst. Rehabil. Eng. **18**(3), 311–318 (2010)
21. Soviak, A., Borodin, A., Ashok, V., Borodin, Y., Puzis, Y., Ramakrishnan, I.: Tactile accessibility: does anyone need a haptic glove? In: Proceedings of the 18th International ACM SIGACCESS Conference on Computers and Accessibility, ASSETS 2016, New York, NY, USA, pp. 101–109. Association for Computing Machinery (2016). https://doi.org/10.1145/2982142.2982175
22. Wang, K., Barron, L.G., Hebl, M.R.: Making those who cannot see look best: effects of visual resume formatting on ratings of job applicants with blindness. Rehabil. Psychol. **55**(1), 68 (2010)
23. WebAIM: Screen reader user survey #8 results - webaim (2020). https://webaim.org/projects/screenreadersurvey8/
24. Więcek-Janka, E., Papierz, M., Kornecka, M., Nitka, M.: Apple products: a discussion of the product life cycle. In: 4th International Conference on Management Science and Management Innovation, vol. 31, pp. 159–164 (2017)
25. Zeng, L., Miao, M., Weber, G.: Interactive audio-haptic map explorer on a tactile display. Interact. Comput. **27**(4), 413–429 (2015)

Augmented Reality as a Tool to Support the Inclusion of Colorblind People

Julio Cesar Ponce Gallegos[1(✉)], Martin Montes Rivera[2], Francisco Javier Ornelas Zapata[1], and Alejandro Padilla Díaz[1]

[1] Universidad Autónoma de Aguascalientes, Av. Universidad 940, 20131 Aguascalientes, Mexico
{jcponce,fjornel,apadilla}@correo.uaa.mx

[2] Universidad Politecnica de Aguascalientes, Aguascalientes, Mexico
martin.montes@upa.edu.mx

Abstract. Color blindness is a condition that affects the cones in the eyes, it can be congenital or acquired and is considered a medium disability that affects about 8.5% of the world population and it occurs in children, who have special difficulties to the newly enter an educational environment with materials developed for people with normal vision, this work focuses on the development one technology, to allow people with a visual disability known as color blindness, to improve their daily activities which in turn leads to a better inclusion in the social and educational environment.

To help the inclusion of these people an application was made that allows an identification of the type of condition of the user through the Ishihara test, which worked with two versions, the traditional and a variation to work with children, and subsequently the result It is taken into account to work with another Augmented Reality application which first uses an identification of the colors of an image through a color classification system, for this different algorithms were implemented one with automatic programming and another with a particle swarm optimization (PSO), once the algorithm identifies the colors it modifies them in real time to a spectrum of colors that if distinguishable by the student but at the same time identifies the centroids of the objects and labels them in real time with the real color, two forms were used for labeling, the word with the color and a color code ColorADD proposed or by Neiva in 2008.

Keywords: Inclusion · Augmented reality · Colorblind · Code ColorADD

1 Introduction

1.1 A Subsection Sample

The inclusion of people in areas such as social, work, educational, among others, is a topic of great interest and relevance at the international level. Organizations such as the Organization for Economic Co-operation and Development (OECD) that drives the inclusion of people as an important part for the economic development of a city [1], and

C. Stephanidis et al. (Eds.): HCII 2020, LNCS 12426, pp. 306–317, 2020.
https://doi.org/10.1007/978-3-030-60149-2_24

the United Nations (UN) that strive for the realization of inclusion as established by the Universal Declaration of Human Rights, which indicates that this is a right that must be applied regardless of gender, race, nationality, socioeconomic status, far from a physical or mental faculty [2]. In recent years, the countries have opted for public policies that seek to guarantee the inclusion, above all, of the most vulnerable, so they have proposed, generated and applied, laws and programs that seek the inclusion of women and people with some disability or who belong to a vulnerable group.

On the other hand, technology has evolved by leaps and bounds and today is not conceived of daily life without the use of it. From appliances to autonomous vehicles or smart phones and devices. Many research projects have focused on the use technologies not only to facilitate tasks, but to improve the lives of people living some kind of inequality, focusing on the use of information and communication technologies to facilitate and improve the teaching and learning process we have for example, learning objects, open educational resources or intelligent tutors, some works made have been focused to support the teaching-learning process in people with Dawn syndrome, autism or Asperger, but also laboratories virtual chemistry or physics that allow schools with lack of facilities and/or equipment, so that their students can do virtual practices.

One of the most used technologies in recent years is Augmented Reality that allows virtual environments to be mixed with reality.

This paper show the development one technology, to allow people with a visual disability known as color blindness, to improve their daily activities which in turn leads to a better inclusion in the social and educational environment. Color blindness is an unfavorable situation, it occurs in people who have a diminished perception of color compared to the average, this condition was described in a scientific work for the first time in 1793 by John Dalton, it is difficult for them to interact with activities that imply a correct perception of color, some examples of these are recreational activities with games, discussion about objects and their identification, interpretation of signs or driving signs, educational activities with color material, among others.

Such difficulties make color blindness a disability. This affectation occurs since in the retina there are two types of cells that detect light, these cells are the rods and cones. The sticks only detect light and darkness and are very sensitive to low light levels, while the cones detect the colors and are concentrated near the center of vision. There are three types of cones each of which detects a color (red, green and blue) and the brain interprets the information they send to determine the color we perceive. Color blindness occurs when one or more types of cones are absent, do not work, or detect a different color than normal. Within the disease levels the serious occurs when all three types of cones are absent, while the mild occurs when all three types of cones are present, but one of them does not work well. Color blindness can be classified, according to the cone with which one has problems and their severity. In the first instance, color blindness is classified according to its severity in: anomalous trichromacy, dichromacy, monochromacy or acromatopsia and its affectation is 8.5% of the world population, being 8% men and only. 5 women with a distribution in the types of color blindness that can be seen in the Table 1 [3].

Table 1. People distribution with color blindness according to the type of affectation [3].

Type	Denomination	Prevalence	
		Men	Women
Monochromacy	Achromatopsia	0.00003%	
Dichromacy	Protanopia	1.01%	0.02%
	Deuteranopia	1.27%	0.01%
	Tritanopia	0.0001%	
Anomalous trichromacy	Protanomaly	1.08%	0.03%
	Deuteranomaly	4.63%	0.36%
	Tritanomaly	0.0002%	

As part of the tests it is shown how the images look to blindness people and how they look through the application in different types of color blindness.

At present, inclusion is a social problem, but it is important to combat it especially in areas such as educational, economic and social, to ensure equal opportunities for all.

Nowadays there is a great interest on promoting the use of technology in the classroom, because of this we can see a lot of tools such as LMS, Learning Objects, Open Educational Resources, Tangible Interfaces, among others. In this sense, some research projects focused on inclusion in the educational area can be seen using these tools to support teaching and learning processes such as: Learning objects for the inclusion of indigenous people [4], open educational resources for people with visual disabilities [5], design of mobile applications for people with visual disabilities [6], use of augmented reality in learning objects for teaching people with visual disabilities [7, 8], among other.

2 Related Works

2.1 Ishihara Test

The most commonly used pseudochromatic plates are Ishihara plates and their popularity is such that they have become a reference icon for color blindness [3].

The diagnosis is made by presenting the patient with a series of plaques, which are marked with colors that people with color blindness often confuse, so they are based on the theory of copunctual points, the plates are discs with numbers that are confused with the background, and its misidentification serves as a reference to diagnose the variant of color blindness that occurs, however, the severity of the condition cannot be detected [9].

Ishihara Plates are designed for the detection of protanopia, protanomaly, deuteranopia and deuteranomaly, however, other variants cannot be detected by the original Ishihara designs.

2.2 Augmented Reality

As for augmented reality, it is a technology that integrates real-world objects with the virtual. Basogain et al. [10] referred to Augmented Reality as a technology that complements the interaction with the real world and allows the user to be in an augmented real environment with additional information generated by the computer. In this regard Fabregat [11] mentioned that the applications of RA "It uses information and computer-generated images that are superimposed on the user's field of vision." Some of the characteristics of augmented reality are:

1. Mix the real and the virtual. Digital information (text, 2d and 3d images, audio, multimedia) is combined with real world images.
2. It works in real time. The mix of the real and the virtual is done in real time.

The AR is part to a mixed reality can see in Fig. 1, it is made up of the monitor of the computer or mobile device, where the combination of real and virtual elements is reflected; the webcam that takes real-world information and transmits it to augmented reality software; software, which takes the real data and transforms it into augmented reality; and the markers, printed symbols that the camera captures and the software interprets to respond specifically [11].

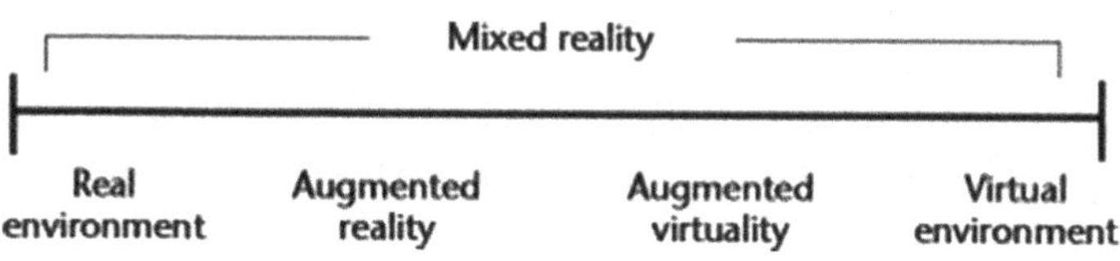

Fig. 1. Type of Mixed reality [12].

Currently, this technology has been used in various fields such as health, entertainment (games), training, marketing, education, among others. Focusing on the educational part we can see different applications in areas of knowledge and specific topics such as mathematics [13], biology [14], chemistry [15], anatomy [16], among others.

2.3 Color Identification System ColorADD

The ColorADDTM color code to assist the colorblind is proposed by Miguel Neiva in a master thesis dissertation made in 2008 [17, 18]. The symbology created by Miguel Neiva, has been widely accepted and has been recognized by associations such as "Color Blind Awareness", "Non-Anonymous Daltonics", "GALILEU" magazine, the "ICOGRADA" organization, and the UN recognizes it as the best 2014 alternative, in the Inclusion and Empowerment category. Company B, which evaluates the concept of business success, has certified it and also has already been presented at a conference within the well-known TEDx program [18]. ColorADDTM allows colors to be identified by symbols. A scheme with the representation of these codes is shown in Fig. 2.

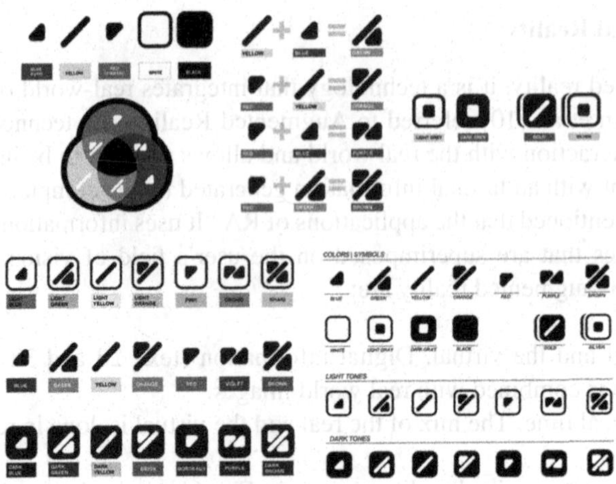

Fig. 2. ColorADDTM color code [18].

2.4 Related Works

Some projects and research papers can see in Table 2.

Table 2. Projects a research papers related to colorblind.

1. Augmented Reality Solution for Color Vision Deficiency CHROMA [19]	Researchers from the Department of Computer Science and Engineering at the University of California in San Diego, CA have developed an augmented reality solution call CHROMA: a wearable, real-time AR app that utilizes the Google Glass to address the real-life issues that people with color blindness face. CHROMA is a digital aid for patients, and can deliver information about shades of colors that the user cannot determine
2. Wearable Improved Vision System for Color Vision Deficiency Correction [20]	Color vision deficiency (CVD) is an extremely frequent vision impairment that compromises the ability to recognize colors. In order to improve color vision in a subject with CVD, they designed and developed a wearable improved vision system based on an augmented reality device. The system was validated in a clinical pilot study on 24 subjects with CVD. The primary outcome was the improvement in the Ishihara Vision Test score with the correction proposed by their system

(continued)

Table 2. (*continued*)

3. An Adaptive Fuzzy-Based System to Simulate, Quantify and Compensate Color Blindness [21]	This paper presents a software tool based on Fuzzy Logic to evaluate the type and the degree of color blindness a person suffer from. In order to model several degrees of color blindness, herein this work they modified the classical linear transform-based simulation method by the use of fuzzy parameters. They also proposed four new methods to correct color blindness based on a fuzzy approach: Methods A and B, with and without histogram equalization. All the methods are based on combinations of linear transforms and histogram operations
4. Image Content Enhancement Through Salient Regions Segmentation for People With Color Vision Deficiencies [22]	The contributions of this work is to detect the main differences between the aforementioned human visual systems related to color vision deficiencies by analyzing real fixation maps among people with and without color vision deficiencies. Another contribution is to provide a method to enhance color regions of the image by using a detailed color mapping of the segmented salient regions of the given image. The segmentation is performed by using the difference between the original input image and the corresponding color blind altered image. A second eye-tracking of color blind people with the images enhanced by using recoloring of segmented salient regions reveals that the real fixation points are then more coherent (up to 10%) with the normal visual system. The eye-tracking data collected during our experiments are in a publicly available dataset called Eye-Tracking of Color Vision Deficiencies
5. Color Blindness Correction using Augmented Reality [23]	Introduction Augmented Reality provides a real-time world environment and allows the viewers to interact with game live. This happens with the help of various augmented factors such as audio, visual, computer graphics and even global positioning input. Augmented reality synchronizes the environment with the graphical structure to provide an ultimate virtual reality gaming experience. Using the same technology, we can alter the saturation of an image in real time to print the correct color that can be perceived as it is by a colorblind person

(*continued*)

Table 2. (*continued*)

6. An Efficient Naturalness Preserving Image Recoloring Method for Dichromats [24]	They present an automatic image-recoloring technique for dichromats that highlights important visual details that would otherwise be unnoticed by these individuals. Their approach preserves, as much as possible, the image's original colors. The results of a paired-comparison evaluation carried out with fourteen color-vision deficients (CVDs) indicated the preference of our technique over the state-of-the-art automatic recoloring technique for dichromats. When considering information visualization examples, the subjects tend to prefer they results over the original images. An extension of our technique that exaggerates color contrast tends to be preferred when CVDs compared pairs of scientific visualization images. These results provide valuable information for guiding the design of visualizations for color-vision deficients

3 Developed Applications

As part of the development of the application of augmented reality as support for people with color blindness, we worked on the development of the Ishihara test for the detection of this condition in users for this the traditional test was automated and a modification was made for children small plates in which plates like those shown in Fig. 3 were used.

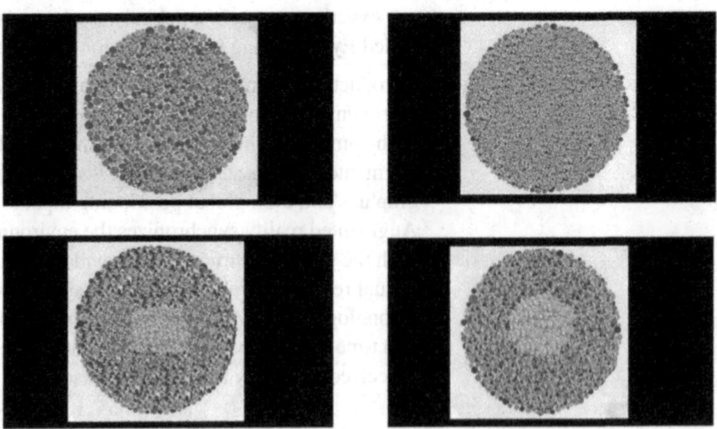

Fig. 3. Plates used to Ishihara test for children.

Another important point is the inclusion since this type of applications can help the user to perform tasks that he cannot do in a normal way since he has to identify objects or parts of the environment where he is located, a common problem in educational institutions is that most of the educational resources are designed for normal students, so it makes it difficult to integrate people with disabilities, to help in this problem the application recolors the image so that the user with color blindness sees it with other distinguishable colors by him facilitating thus user interaction by providing an accessible interface, see Fig. 4.

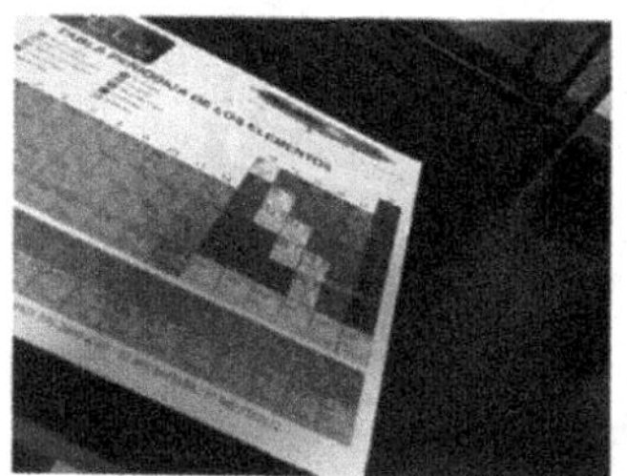
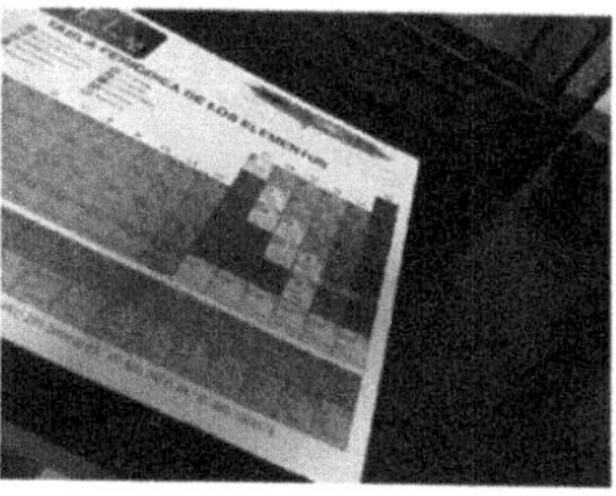

Fig. 4. Recoloring image in real time with the Augmented Reality application [25].

In order to achieve this in the Augmented Reality application it is important to perform several tasks, the first is that the system is able to automatically identify the colors of the original image and then transform the color gamut into based on the type of color blindness of the user, for this task several evolutionary algorithms were identified that identify and classify colors, such as the particle swarm optimization algorithm (PSO) and the genetic algorithms (GA) [26], see Fig. 5.

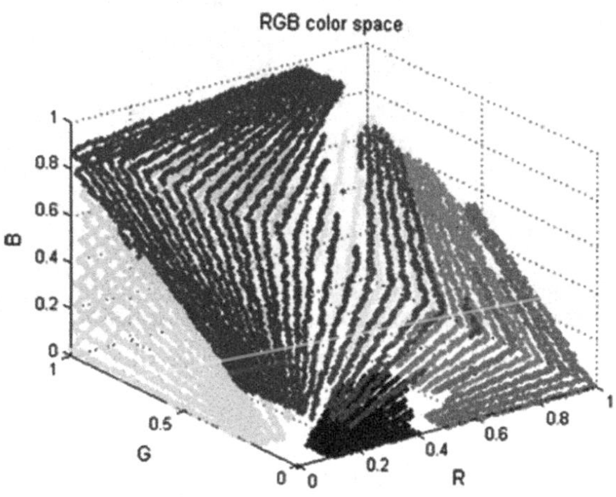

Fig. 5. RGB representation of red, orange, yellow, green, blue, purple and brown colors in RGB [26]. (Color figure online)

Another important application of this system is in the use of safety signs, which is important for the institutions (industries, schools, …) within their security systems to have the appropriate signals, however, some of these are just for they find in colors that are not perceived by colorblind people see Fig. 6, which is a problem, and this application can help save the lives of colorblind people [27].

Fig. 6. Security signals.

Finally other characteristics of the application is that the user is able to identify the colors, for this the image can be maintained with its original colors and use a label on each section that belongs to the same color, this labeling is done in two ways, one is through labels where the original color is written with text and the second type of labels using the ColorADDTM code see Fig. 7.

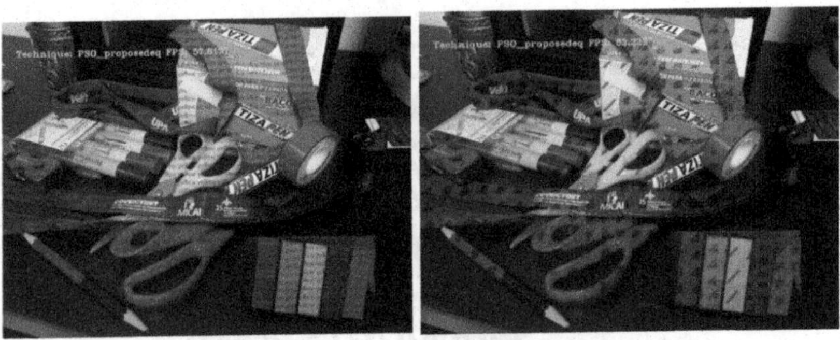

Fig. 7. On the left image with text labels, on the right image with labels using ColorADDTM code.

Color Enhancement Tool Tested with four People with Colorblindness. In this test, four patients with color blindness are subjected to the Ishihara test with and without the assistant color enhancement system. Table 3 shows a comparison between the results obtained. In the LP record it means that a line path is seen and N means that it sees nothing, according to the parameters accepted by the Ishihara test.

Table 3. Results when presenting Ishihara's plaques with and without the proposed system to four patients.

Plate number	Plate to be displayed	View plate without enhancement tool				View plate with enhancement tool			
		P1	P2	P3	P4	P1	P2	P3	P4
1	12	12	12	12	12	12	12	12	12
2	8	3	N	3	N	8	8	8	8
3	29	29	N	N	N	29	29	29	29
4	5	N	N	N	N	5	5	5	5
5	3	N	8	N	N	3	3	3	3
6	15	N	15	15	N	15	15	15	15
7	74	N	21	84	N	74	74	74	74
8	6	N	N	N	N	6	6	6	6
9	45	N	N	N	N	45	45	45	45
10	5	N	8	11	N	5	5	5	5
11	7	N	7	7	N	7	7	7	7
12	16	N	N	16	N	16	16	16	16
13	73	N	N	N	N	73	73	73	73
14	LP	N	N	N	LP	LP	LP	LP	LP
15	LP	N	N	N	LP	LP	LP	LP	LP
16	26	N	26	26	26	26	26	26	26
17	42	N	42	42	4	42	42	42	42
18	LP	N	LP	LP	LP	LP	LP	LP	LP
19	LP	N	N	N	LP	LP	LP	LP	LP
20	LP	N	N	N	N	LP	LP	LP	LP
21	LP	N	N	N	N	LP	LP	LP	LP
22	LP	N	N	N	N	LP	LP	LP	LP
23	LP	N	N	N	N	LP	LP	LP	LP
24	LP	LP	LP	N	LP	LP	LP	LP	LP
Efficiency		8.33%	29.16%	29.16%	25%	100%	100%	100%	100%

4 Conclusions

As it could be seen in several real-life situations to which a color blind person is exposed in his daily life in different social, family, industrial, school environments, etc. This can have problems constantly compared to a normal person, however the use of technology such as the use of augmented reality through a mobile device (smart phone) of medium or high range is possible to reduce or eliminate some of these problems. This is achieved through an interaction through the device with the real world with a friendly interface that guarantees the use of it.

As you can see the inclusion is a problem that must be addressed by society in different areas including education, and to achieve this we can make use of technology as is in this case the use of augmented reality, you can see in the experiment that on controlled cases this type of applications can have an efficiency of 100% by supporting colorblind people to identify objects and their real colors, however there are problems in real situations where the main objects are mixed with the environment and if this has the same colors, there are problems with the identification of the objects and their efficiency can be affected considerably. It can also be seen that the use of technology in computer science can provide tools that support inclusion in different fields, including education.

References

1. OECD. https://www.oecd.org/dev/inclusivesocietiesanddevelopment/acerca-proyecto-inclusion-juvenil.htm
2. UN. https://www.un.org/en/universal-declaration-human-rights/
3. COLORBLINDOR. Color Blind Essentials (2020). Dostupné z. https://www.color-blindness.com/color-blind-essentials
4. Silva, A., Muñoz, J., Ponce, J., Hernández, Y.: Desarrollo de Objetos de Aprendizaje Etnoculturales Lúdicos para la Preservación de la Lenguas, Costumbres y Tradiciones Indígenas. In: Latin American Conference on Learning Objects and Technology (LACLO) (2012)
5. Silva, A., Ponce, J., Silva, A., Ponce, J.: RbraiLe: OER based on intelligent rules for reading Braille. Vínculos: Ciencia, Tecnología y Sociedad **11**(2), 18 (2014)
6. Esparza, A., et al.: Application mobile design for blind people: history memorama. In: User-Centered Software Development for the Blind and Visually Impaired: Emerging Research and Opportunities, pp. 79–95. IGI Global (2020). https://doi.org/10.4018/978-1-5225-8539-8.ch006
7. Sprock, A., Ponce, J.: BER2: Recurso Educativo de Braille con Realidad Aumentada. Anais temporários do LACLO 2015 **10**(1), 207. (2015)
8. Robles, T., Rodríguez, F., Benítez, E.: Apoyo Móvil Haciendo Uso De Realidad Aumentada Para Personas Con Discapacidad Visual: Aplicación Y Resultados. In: Anais do Seminário Nacional de Educação Especial e do Seminário Capixaba de Educação Inclusiva, vol. 1, pp. 368–386 (2016)
9. Ishihara, S.: Test for Colour-Blindness, 24 Plates Edition, Kanehara Shuppan Co. Ltd., Tokyo (1973)
10. Basogain, X., Olabe, M., Espinosa, K., Rouèche, C., Olabe, J.: Realidad Aumentada en la Educación: Una Tecnología Emergente. In: Online Educa Madrid - 2007 7° Conferencia Internacional de la Educación y la Formación Basada en las Tecnologías, pp. 24–29 (2007)
11. Fabregat, R.: Combinando la Realidad con las Plataformas de E-learning Adaptativas, pp. 69–78. Revista Venezolana de Información, Venezuela (2012)
12. Azuma, R.T.: A survey of augmented reality. Pres. Teleoper. Virt. Environ. **6**(4), 355–385 (1997)
13. Ponce, J., Oronia, Z., Silva, A., Muñoz, J., Ornelas, F., Alvarez, F.: Incremento del Interés de Alumnos en Educación Básica en los Objetos de Aprendizaje Usando Realidad Aumentada en las Matemáticas. In: Latin American Conference on Learning Objects and Technology (LACLO) (2014)
14. Garcia, M., Jensen, M., Katona, G.: A practical guide to developing virtual and augmented reality exercises for teaching structural biology. Biochem. Mol. Biol. Educ. **47**(1), 16–24 (2019)
15. Hou, H., Lin, Y.: The development and evaluation of an educational game integrated with augmented reality and virtual laboratory for chemistry experiment learning. In: 6th International Congress on Advanced Applied Informatics, pp. 1005–1006. IEEE (2017)
16. Jamali, S., Shiratuddin, M., Wong, K., Oskam, C.: Utilising mobile-augmented reality for learning human anatomy. Procedia Soc. Behav. Sci. **197**, 659–668 (2015)
17. Neiva, M.: Sistema de identificação de cor para daltônicos: código monocromático (2008)

18. Neiva, M.: ColorADD, color identification system. http://www.coloradd.net/imgs/ColorADDAboutUs_2015V1.pdf
19. Taylor, M.: Augmented Reality Solution for Color Vision Deficiency (2017). http://arinmed.com/augmented-reality-solution-for-color-vision-deficiency/
20. Melillo, P., et al.: Wearable improved vision system for color vision deficiency correction. IEEE J. Trans. Eng. Health Med. **5**, 1–7 (2017)
21. Dos Santos, W., Lee, J.: An adaptive fuzzy-based system to simulate, quantify and compensate color blindness. Integr. Comput. Aided Eng. **18**, 29–40 (2011)
22. Bruno, A., Gugliuzza, F., Ardizzone, E., Giunta, C., Pirrone, R.: Image content enhancement through salient regions segmentation for people with color vision deficiencies. I-Perception **10**, 2041669519841073 (2019)
23. Gurumurthy, S., Rajagopal, R., AjayAshar, A.: Color blindness correction using augmented reality. Madridge J. Bioinform. Syst. Biol. **1**(2), 31–33 (2019)
24. Kuhn, G., Oliveira, M., Fernandes, L.: An efficient naturalness-preserving image-recoloring method for dichromats. IEEE Trans. Vis. Comput. Graph. **14**, 1747–1754 (2008)
25. Montes Rivera, M., Padilla, A., Canul, J., Ponce, J., Ochoa Zezzatti, A.: Realtime recoloring objects using artificial neural networks through a cellphone. Res. Comput. Sci. **148**, 229–238 (2019)
26. Montes, M., Padilla, A., Canul, J., Ponce, J., Ochoa, A.: Comparative of effectiveness when classifying colors using RGB image representation with PSO with time decreasing inertial coefficient and GA algorithms as classifiers. In: Castillo, O., Melin, P., Kacprzyk, J. (eds.) Fuzzy Logic Augmentation of Neural and Optimization Algorithms: Theoretical Aspects and Real Applications. SCI, vol. 749, pp. 527–546. Springer, Cham (2018). https://doi.org/10.1007/978-3-319-71008-2_38
27. Rivera, M., Padilla, A., Canul, J., Ponce, J., Ochoa, A.: Augmented reality labels for security signs based on color segmentation with PSO for assisting colorblind people. Int. J. Comb. Optim. Prob. Inf. **10**(3), 7–20 (2019)

Sign Language Interpreter Detection Method for Live TV Broadcast Content

João Guilherme Reiser de Melo(✉), Leandro Paes de Souza(✉), Davi Frossard(✉), and Rodrigo Ribeiro de Oliveira(✉)

Sidia Institute of Science and Technology, Manaus, AM 69055-035, Brazil
{joao.melo,leandro.paes,davi.frossard,rodrigo.oliveira}@sidia.com
http://www.sidia.com

Abstract. Recent technological improvements in computing and embedded systems have enabled the development and improvement of systems and applications in a way that makes people's lives simpler, safer and more accessible. The development of small and powerful hardware devices for signal processing, together with the use of techniques of artificial intelligence and machine learning can assist people with all kinds of limitations in the use of multimedia content on a TV broadcast video. Some broadcasters insert sign language interpreters on the transmitted content. The size and the position of the interpreter on the screen are not always the more appropriate for the best use of such tool. The use of artificial intelligence techniques make it possible to identify such elements on an image with high accuracy, reliability and repeatability, when compared to traditional systems. On this paper, a machine learning based method was developed with the aim of identify the presence and the position of a sign language interpreter on the screen, take an instance of its content and make it available for magnification, providing greater accessibility and experience improvement on watching TV for people with special needs. The developed system achieved final accuracy greater than 80% with inference time between 2 to 3 s, depending on the used hardware, running on a live broadcast environment.

Keywords: Digital TV · Sign language · Machine learning

1 Introduction

In an increasingly connected world, the search for information by the people and the concern to reach all audiences by the content generators is greater every day. In a world like this the need to make information and content accessible to everyone is growing. For a long time, people have sought to conduct research, develop methods and applications that make the lives of people with some type of disability simpler and more integrated with the rest of the society.

J. Melo, L. Paes, D. Frossard and R. Ribeiro are with Sidia: Institute of Science and Technology, Manaus - Amazonas, Brazil.

C. Stephanidis et al. (Eds.): HCII 2020, LNCS 12426, pp. 318–332, 2020.
https://doi.org/10.1007/978-3-030-60149-2_25

A research of 2018 showed that even today, the main source of news in the US is the television [1]. The Fig. 1 shows the statistics of the main source of news for the US viewers, where he television is the main source, followed by the news on internet. Even with people using the internet more and more in their day-to-day lives, for the purposes of keeping up with the news people still choose television stations as their main source. This shows that the virtual sources of information still need to acquire the trust of a large part of the public that consume content, and in the meantime, television broadcasters and the television sets themselves need to evolve to become increasingly accessible to all audiences.

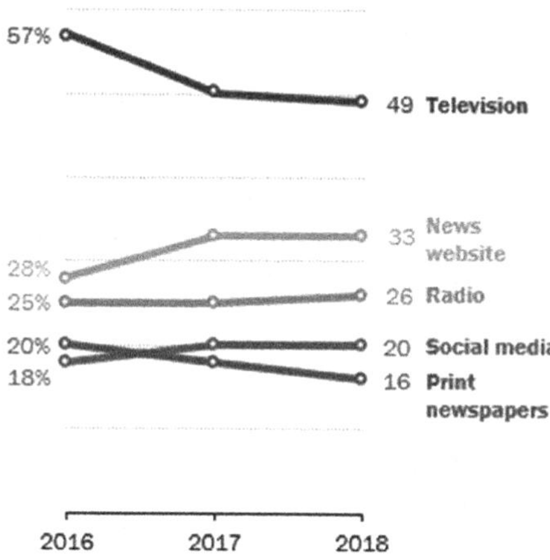

Fig. 1. Statistics of the main source of news for the US viewers [1]

Nowadays, several TV broadcasters are transmitting content containing sign language interpreter attached on the main video. The benefit of this approach is that the interpreter already comes synchronized with the video, not begin necessary to use any synchronization tool on the receptor side. On the other hand, as the interpreter is already attach on the media content, the user doesn't have the option to enable or disable such element. Besides that, there is no regulation about the position and size of the interpreter to be used, at last in Brazil. Thereby, each broadcaster uses its own standards, which compromises the experience of the viewer, and in some cases, when the interpreter is too small, prevents the access to content.

The TV manufactures, together with the broadcasters, are working on different approaches which often impact on the difficulty of adding content on the broadcaster side and, in other cases, the difficulty of the receiver manufacturer providing more memory to store the set of images needed for each sign language gesture. In addition, it is worth remembering that each language has its own sign language version, so, storing the gestures for several languages looks to be impracticable.

One of the technologies that has evolved the most and has shown the most promise for solving problems in the most diverse areas is machine learning. The ability of certain algorithms to extract knowledge from data in a way unimaginable for us humans has made possible its use in several areas of knowledge and its use to solve problems previously extremely difficult to handle. Practically all sectors of the industry have been trying to insert concepts/solutions that use artificial intelligence/machine learning in their products in order to add value and bring a better experience to users.

With that in mind, this paper presents a machine learning based solution for detection, segmentation and magnification of a sign language interpreter in a live broadcast content. This article seeks to encourage the scientific community to research and develop solutions that improve the lives of people with disabilities. In addition, an attempt is made to present a solution of simple integration with TV equipment that can be applied to the most diverse models.

The paper here presented is organized as follows. Section 3 the most relevant related works are presented. Section 4 presents the proposal itself, explaining how it works. Section 5 shows the results achieved. Section 6 concludes this paper and propose some new topics for development.

2 Background

In this section some relevant background information for this paper will be presented. The following subsections will present some aspects about the digital television, sign languages and machine learning.

2.1 Digital TV

The digital television is a broadcasting system capable of transmitting digital signals, which provide a better signal reception, higher resolution and better sound quality, when compared to the previous analogue signal. Furthermore, the digital TV has tools that allow the integration between the broadcast signal and data transmission and internet access [2].

In the old days, the televisions were dedicated devices developed exclusively for the reception and treatment of broadcast signals. Nowadays, televisions have become real computers, with processors, operating system, input and output interfaces, so on. This change allows today's televisions to perform tasks never before imagined, like internet access, real-time interactive systems [3–6], access to stream platforms, and at the same time, it allows that applications aimed at the disabled can be developed [4,7].

There are three major digital TV standards in the world, namely: ATSC, DVB, ISDB. Others were developed based on these three. A standard defines some fundamental characteristics for the functioning of the TV system [8]. Some of these characteristics are: the transmission mode, the transportation mode, the compression system and the middleware (interactive software) features [3].

The Fig. 2 shows the schematic of a digital TV broadcasting system.

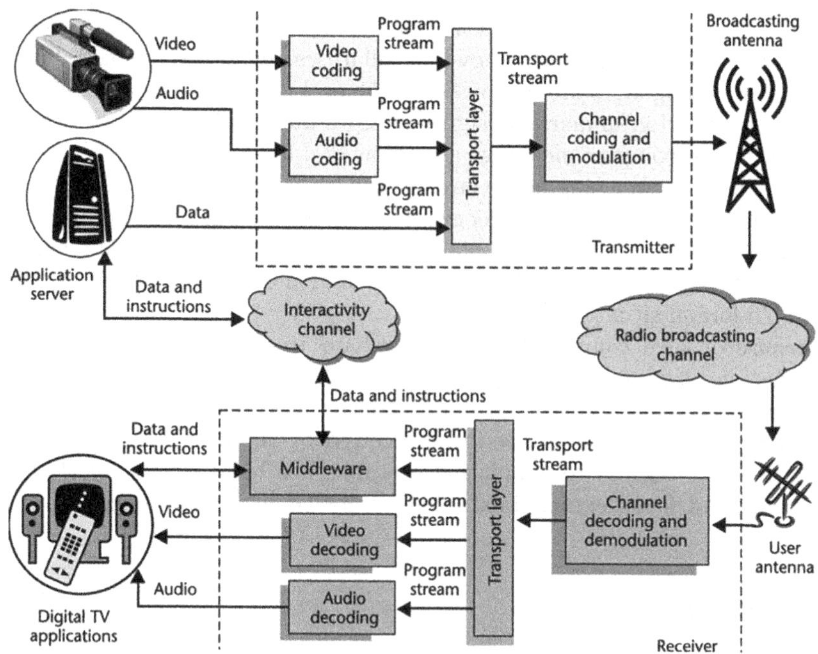

Fig. 2. Schematic of a digital TV broadcast system [9]

The multimedia content to be transmitted is divide into video and audio packages. Both of them are than encoded using the method defined by the standard (some MPEG2 or MPEG4 variant). After that, these packages are broken into pieces and multiplexed with some data packages into a single transport stream, where each part is identified and some synchronization data is also inserted. The next step is the modulation of the signal, where the transport stream is converted into the electrical signal, with the frequency respecting the range intended for the broadcaster that will be transmitted. In this steps some error correction codes are used to improve information reliability.

On the viewer side, the signal is received by the antenna and demodulated back to the transport stream. Each data package is analysed and separated by its type, reassembling the audio, video and data content. The audio and video are decoded and displayed on the TV according to the synchronization data. Some of the data content can be part of the interactive system and will be processed by the middleware. The same system can also receive or send additional data through the internet, in a process called broadband.

2.2 Sign Language

Sign language is a non-verbal language that uses hand and body movements, including postures and facial expressions, used by and to people who are deaf or that cannot talk [10,11]. Contrary to what many people think, there is no universal sign language. As well as the spoken languages, each country or region has its own sign language with its own peculiarities and characteristics. Furthermore, the sign languages are not based on the oral languages. Besides having its own structure and grammar, the sign languages are capable of convey even the most subtle and complex meanings as well as oral languages [12].

Just like the spoken language, the sign languages have different dialects inside the same language, based on the geographic region, social groups and even genre. In addiction to that, situational dialects are also found on sign language, for example, the signing style used in a formal occasion differs from the one used in a causal/informal situation [12].

Because of such complexity, it is very hard to interpret the behaviour of a real person using sign language. Several works have already been done [13–16] trying to develop an artificial sign language interpreter. Such proposals are valid, however, none has yet been well received by the deaf public, since most applications are limited to simulating gestures, not being able to perform the movements and facial expressions necessary for correct communication by the deaf people.

2.3 Machine Learning

Machine learning consists of using computational models that have the ability to learn to identify and classify certain characteristics or scenarios using great amount of data or a specific environment. There are three main categories of learning algorithms: supervised, unsupervised and reinforcement learning. In supervised learning, the main objective is to learn a mapping between the input and output data given a pair input-output [17]. After execute the model with the inserted data, the internal weights are updated to correct its error of judgment. In unsupervised training, only the input information is provided to the model and it must be grouped as having similar characteristics, in a process known as clustering. The main goal here is to identify interesting patterns in the provided data [17]. In reinforcement learning algorithms, the system freely interact with the environment, using some predefined moves and, receiving some results evaluation, through awards or punishments [17], adjusts its internal weights and learns how to behave on each situation.

The solution here proposed works with image and video content with the objective of detecting and performing the segmentation of an area on the image. Thereby, the best fitting algorithm category is the supervised. Next, some algorithms on this scope will be presented.

Haar Cascades. The Haar Cascade algorithm is a supervised machine learning model that uses classical computer vision concepts for its operation. Several small image filters, called haar features, must be defined by the developer in order to detect the desired forms and shapes on an image, such as lines, contours and so for. Once these features are defined, the classifier section of the model is trained using positive and negative samples of the desired element. Figure 3 shows some examples of haar features and its use on a real image.

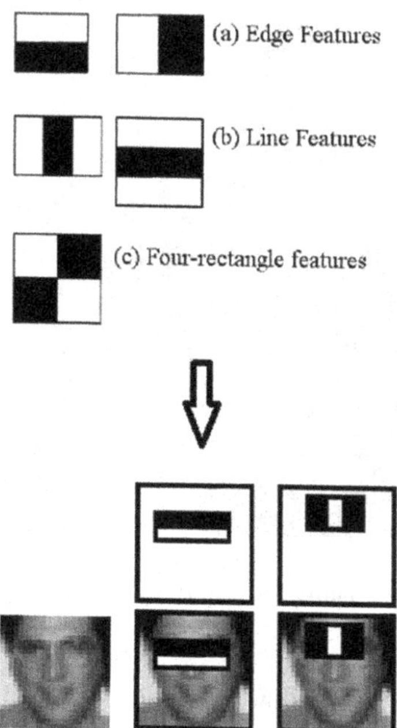

Fig. 3. Examples of haar features and its use on images

A Haar Cascade algorithm is composed of hundreds or thousands of this haar features. If all these features are applied to an image, it will be highly time consuming. To save some time, the algorithm was implemented on a cascade way, where in each step only a few of these features are tested. If the image fail to pass a step, it is immediately discarded and will not run through all the remaining steps. If an image pass all the steps, a match was found [18]. Figure 4 shows an image which a face detected and an eyes detector haar cascade algorithms were used.

The main advantage of this algorithm it is capability of perform the training process with few data samples. As the features extraction is performed manually, only the classifier is trained, so, less data is needed. Beyond that, after trained, haar cascade algorithm generates a lightweight xml file containing all the needed data to run. On the other hand, as the extraction of characteristics is limited, its ability to generalize is compromised.

For a long time, this was the main algorithm for computer vision systems. With the improvement of the processing technology and the availability of huge amounts of data, the deep learning models took its place as the state of the art in the vision computing scenario.

Deep Learning. Deep learning algorithms are currently the state of the art when it comes to systems of vision, classification and detection of characteristics in images or videos. Deep learning is a sub-area of machine learning, which in

Fig. 4. Example using Face and Eye Haar Cascade detector

turn is a branch of artificial intelligence. These computational models are characterized by the ability to extract the necessary attributes for the classification and detection of the objects to be identified, unlike traditional machine learning systems, where the classifiable properties need to be extracted and presented to the classifying model by the developer himself.

The techniques that allow deep learning models to function are not new [19,20], however, due to several impediments, among them computational capacity and amount of data, they only became popular and became viable from 2012, when the AlexNET network [21] was champion ILSVRC, a famous computer vision tournament. Since then, increasingly sophisticated models have been developed that have allowed these systems to surpass the human capacity for image classification.

The models of deep learning used in computer vision are mostly convolutional neural networks (CNN), networks basically composed of trainable filters, also known as kernels, layers of condensation of characteristics (pooling), in addition to one or more layers of classification in output (dense), composed by artificial neurons fully connected [22,23]. Figure 5 shows the described structure for a basic CNN. Among the models that employ deep learning for computer vision solutions, four major areas of application can be identified, namely: recognition/classification, detection, semantic segmentation and detection with segmentation. All of them supervised learning models.

The deep learning algorithms demand an immense amount of data for satisfactory results to be obtained in their training, since both the steps of extracting characteristics and the classification will be trained. In addition, this process requires a lot of time and computational processing power. Beyond that, the trained CNN model is normally a very heavyweight file, somethings achieving

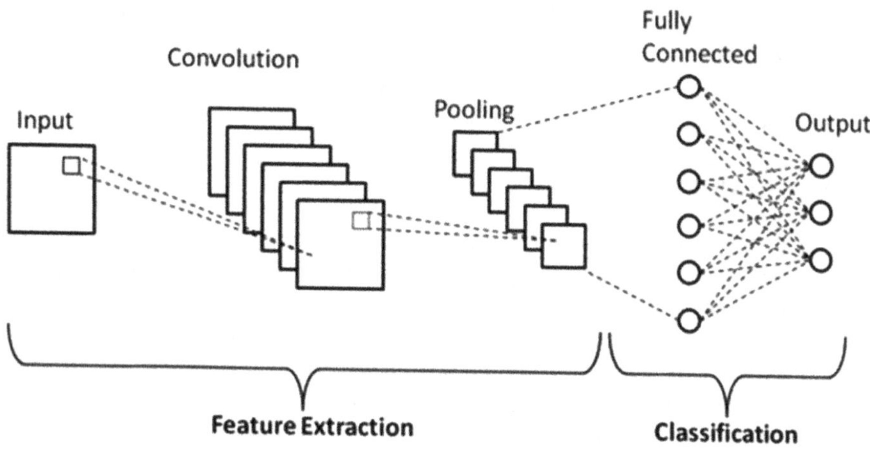

Fig. 5. Convolutional neural network model [22]

hundreds of megabytes. On the other hand, this type of solution achieves high accuracy and capacity for generalization.

3 Related Works

This section will present some works related to the presented paper. Table 1 shows an overview of the indicated related works.

The paper [24] presents a solution using the Microsoft Kinect, CNNs and GPU acceleration to recognize 20 italian sign language gestures. The dataset used was *ChaLearn Looking at People 2014: Gesture Spotting*. The system achieved 91.7% accuracy. [25] is a work where a Faster R-CNN model was used to perform the segmentation and identification of bangladeshi sign language gestures on real time. The average accuracy was 98.2%. The work presented on [26] shows an approach based on Principal Component Analysis (PCA) and KNearest Neighbors (KNN) to recognize pakistan sign language on images, achieving an accuracy of 85%. The paper [27] proposed a deep learning CNN + RNN

Table 1. Related works table

Related papers list		
Paper	Used technology	Accuracy
1	CNN	91.7%
2	Faster R-CNN	98.2%
3	PCA + KNN	85%
4	CNN + RNN	89.9%
5	CNN	99.90%

model to recognize chinese sign language gestures on videos. The results showed an accuracy between 86.9% and 89.9%. Finally, [28] presents a CNN based approach to identify 100 different indian sign language static signs on images. The approach achieved accuracies up to 99%.

4 Methodology

Based on the aforementioned background and discussions, this section will present our proposal for sign language interpreter detection and segmentation for live broadcast content. The parts that make up this work will be presented and explained and some of the choices made will be justified.

First of all, it is necessary to define the technique used to detect the sign language interpreter on the screen. The presented techniques on the previous section were the Haar Cascade algorithm or a Convolutional Neural Network model. The CNN achieves higher accuracy and generalization capability, on the other hand, it needs a dedicated dataset to be trained and a great amount of space on the device data storage. Firstly, no dataset that met the application's needs was found and secondly, the TV devices have very limited flash memory available, making it difficult to add content that requires a large volume of space. Because of that, in a first approach, the Haar Cascade algorithm was chosen for this system.

The modern television set, whose internal structure and functioning is practically identical to that of a computer, has support for most of the available multi-platform libraries. For this reason, the availability of some haar cascade face detector was verified within the OpenCV library. The library has a frontal face haar cascade detector, able to return the position of all frontal face matches on an image.

The frontal face detector itself is not enough to identify a sign language interpreter on the image, since it will get al.l the frontal faces on it. This result needs to be refined in order to identify the correct matching face. For this, a more in-depth research on the pattern of use of interpreters needed to be carried out.

After analyzing a large amount of television content, the most common patterns of use of sign language interpreters in the transmitted content were identified. Figure 6 shows these patterns. The vast majority insert the interpreter in some of the corners, with the bottom right corner being the most used. An interesting detail perceived in this analysis was the use, by some broadcasters, of the interpreter on the left side, in a more central position on the screen, as shown on Fig. 6, in the bottom right image.

Beyond the most common used patterns, some interpreters that are quite different from the standard normally used have been identified. Figure 7 shows an example of such pattern. This pattern uses a more prominent interpreter, occupying a considerable part of the image and having the height of the television screen. As this type of interpreter already has considerable size and prominence and a much greater visibility than the others, the treatment of this type of interpreter was disregarded in the development of the explained system.

Fig. 6. Most common sign language interpreter positioning on screen

Having identified the most used positioning patterns for sign language interpreters, these positions were mapped in order to enable the identification of the frontal faces in an image with the greatest potential to effectively being an interpreter.

Having knowledge of all this information, the flowchart for processing the method was prepared. Figure 8 shows the flowchart with all the steps needed to execute the solution.

The processing begins when the system receives a new video content stream. This content is the after decoding data, see Fig. 2, where the video content is ready to be displayed. At this point, a sample of the video is taken for analysis. With this screenshot image the frontal face detector is executed. A matrix containing all the identified frontal faces on the image is returned. As previously explained, identify a frontal face is not the guarantee of the presence of a sign language interpreter. Because of that, each area identified in the face detector is confronted with the mapped areas most probable to have an interpreter.

After that, only the matches are taken. Each mapped area received a probability value, being the bottom right area the greatest. So, the remaining areas are verified and the one with the greatest probability is chosen. At this point, if no area is remaining, it is considered that no interpreter is present in the image. If that is not the case, the selected area is taken and will be passed to the image controller system of the television, together with the desired zoom for the interpreter.

Fig. 7. Out of standard sign language interpreter

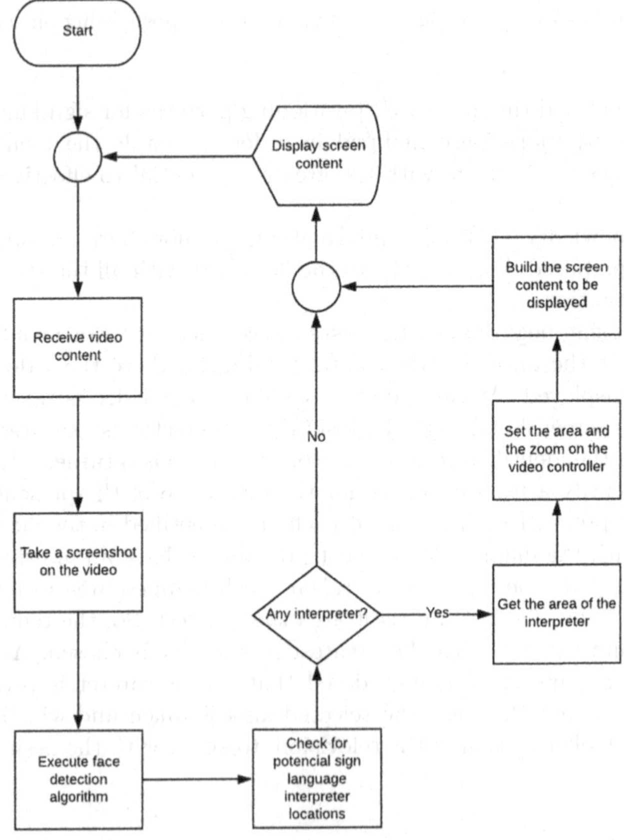

Fig. 8. Flowchart for the proposed solution

The image controller is the software on the TV that controls everything that is displayed on the screen. Each manufacturer has its own solution for it, and it is not the purpose of this paper to detail it. After that, the content to be display is built, positioning the original content with the magnified interpreter. Such step is also not the focus on this paper, because each manufacturer can solve it its own way, and with its own desired layout. The final step is show the content on the screen, containing or not the magnified sign language interpreter, depending on the result of the processing.

5 Results

This section will present the results achieved on the development of this work.

The system described on the previous section was implemented on a Linux based operation system running on a dedicated hardware platform. A platform native C++ application was developed to implement the described method. Figure 9 shows an example of the video content analysed, where the sign language interpreter was identified and later magnified.

After implemented, the system was tested using live broadcast content from different parts of the world, to verify its ability to detect the most diverse sign language interpreters. The system had a requirement to achieve a detection success rate of at least 80%. The tests showed that the proposed method achieved the required accuracy.

Regarding the execution time, the method was tested on several hardware platform models, models with lesser or greater computational capacity. The tests showed that the system took 2 to 3 s, depending on the platform used, to perform the verification and extraction of the sign language interpreter. As the developed application does not demand real-time verification and updates of the interpreter position, the time obtained was within the required limits.

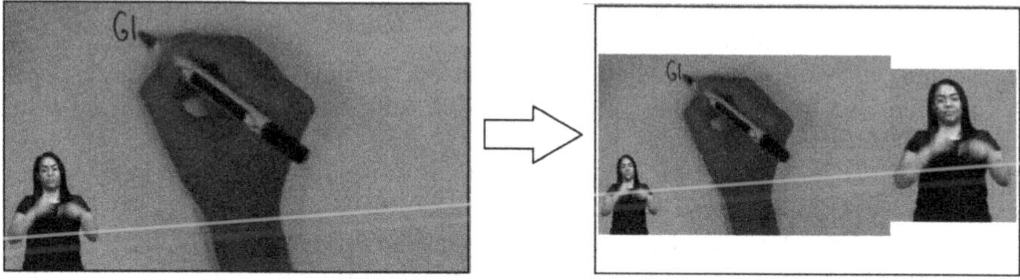

Fig. 9. Resulting video content generated by the method

The method proved to be easy to integrate and adapt regardless of the platform used. In all the tested platforms the system behaved in a similar way and with good repeatability.

6 Conclusion

The search for information by the people and the concern to reach all audiences by the content generators is greater every day. In a world like this the need to make information and content accessible to everyone is growing. The sign language interpreters available on some TV content sometimes are not the best for a better appreciation of the displayed content.

This article sought to present a machine learning based method intended to identify the presence and the position of a sign language interpreter on the screen, take an instance of it and make it available for magnification, providing greater accessibility and experience improvement on watching TV for people with special needs.

The obtained results show that the method achieved the sought accuracy, which was greater than 80%, with an execution time between 2 to 3 s. As previously stated, for the application in question the execution time was not a critical factor. However, for future improvements, an upgrade on the performance of the system in relation to the execution time would be interesting, since time and processing demand are directly linked.

Future works could include the creation of a dedicated sign language interpreters database and the development of a deep learning convolutional neural network based solution for improvement on accuracy and time consumption.

Acknowledgments. This work was partially supported by Samsung Eletrônica da Amazônia Ltda, under the auspice of the informatics law No 8.387/91, and for that, we would like to express our gratitude for the support and the opportunity to develop this work.

References

1. Pew Research Center Homepage. https://www.pewresearch.org/fact-tank/2018/12/10/social-media-outpaces-print-newspapers-in-the-u-s-as-a-news-source/. Accessed 10 May 2020
2. Bolano, C., Vieira, V.: TV digital no Brasil e no mundo: estado da arte. Revista de Economía Política de las Tecnologías de la Información y Comunicación **6**(2), 109 (2004)
3. Montez, C., Becker, V.: TV Digital Interativa: Conceitos, Desafios e Perspectivas para o Brasil. 2ed. Ed. da UFSC, Florianópolis (2005)
4. Piccolo, L.S.G., Baranauskas, M.C.C.: Desafios de design para a TV digital interativa. In: Proceedings of VII Brazilian Symposium on Human Factors in Computing Systems, pp. 1–10 (2006)
5. Dos Santos, D.T., Do Vale, D.T., Meloni, L.G.P.: Digital TV and distance learning: potentials and limitations. In: Proceedings of Frontiers in Education. 36th Annual Conference, pp. 1–6 (2006)
6. Atzori, L., De Natale, F.G.B., Di Gregorio, M., Giusto, D.D.: Multimedia information broadcasting using digital TV channels. IEEE Trans. Broadcast. **43**(3), 242–251 (1997)

7. Gill, J., Perera, S.: Accessible universal design of interactive digital television. In: Proceedings of the 1st European Conference on Interactive Television: From Viewers to Actors, pp. 83–89 (2003)
8. Teleco Homepage. https://www.teleco.com.br/tutoriais/tutorialtvdconsis1/pagina_3.asp. Accessed 11 May 2020
9. ResearchGate Homepage. https://www.researchgate.net/figure/Digital-television-system_fig4_3339060. Accessed 11 May 2020
10. MedicineNet Homepage. https://www.medicinenet.com/script/main/art.asp?articlekey=39158. Accessed 11 May 2020
11. Cambridge Dictionary Homepage. https://dictionary.cambridge.org/dictionary/english/sign-language. Accessed 11 May 2020
12. Emmorey, K.: Language, Cognition, and the Brain: Insights from Sign Language Research. Psychology Press, New York (2001)
13. Elliott, R., Glauert, J.R., Kennaway, J.R., Marshall, I., Safar, E.: Linguistic modelling and language-processing technologies for Avatar-based sign language presentation. Univ. Access Inf. Soc. **6**(4), 375–391 (2008)
14. Elghoul, M.J.O.: An avatar based approach for automatic interpretation of text to Sign language. In: Challenges for Assistive Technology, AAATE 2007, vol. 20, p. 266 (2007)
15. Kipp, M., Heloir, A., Nguyen, Q.: Sign language avatars: animation and comprehensibility. In: Vilhjálmsson, H.H., Kopp, S., Marsella, S., Thórisson, K.R. (eds.) IVA 2011. LNCS (LNAI), vol. 6895, pp. 113–126. Springer, Heidelberg (2011). https://doi.org/10.1007/978-3-642-23974-8_13
16. Lombardo, V., Battaglino, C., Damiano, R., Nunnari, F.: An avatar-based interface for the Italian sign language. In: 2011 International Conference on Complex, Intelligent, and Software Intensive Systems, pp. 589–594 (2011)
17. Murphy, K.P.: Machine Learning: A Probabilistic Perspective. MIT Press, London (2012)
18. OpenCV Homepage. http://opencv-python-tutroals.readthedocs.io/en/latest/. Accessed 10 May 2020
19. Fukushima, K.: A self-organizing neural network model for a mechanism of pattern recognition unaffected by shift in position. Biol. Cybern. **36**, 193–202 (1980)
20. LeCun, Y., Bottou, L., Bengio, Y., Haffner, P.: Gradient-based learning applied to document recognition. Proc. IEEE **86**, 2278–2324 (1998)
21. Krizhevsky, A., Ilya S., Geoffrey, E.H.: ImageNet classification with deep convolutional neural networks. In: Advances in Neural Information Processing Systems, pp. 1097–1105 (2012)
22. Rhee, E., et al.: A deep learning approach for classification of cloud image patches on small datasets. J. Inf. Commun. Converg. Eng. **16**(3), 173–178 (2018)
23. Hertel, L., et al.: Deep convolutional neural networks as generic feature extractors. In: 2015 International Joint Conference on Neural Networks (IJCNN), pp. 1–4 (2015)
24. Priyadharsini, N., Rajeswari, N.: Sign language recognition using convolutional neural networks. Int. J. Recent Innov. Trends Comput. Commun. **5**(6), 625–628 (2017)
25. Hoque, O.B., Jubair, M.I., Islam, M.S., Akash, A.F., Paulson, A.S.: Real time Bangladeshi sign language detection using faster R-CNN. In: 2018 International Conference on Innovation in Engineering and Technology (ICIET), pp. 1–6 (2018)
26. Malik, M.S.A., Kousar, N., Abdullah, T., Ahmed, M., Rasheed, F., Awais, M.: Pakistan sign language detection using PCA and KNN. Int. J. Adv. Comput. Sci. Appl. **9**(54), 78–81 (2018)

27. Liao, Y., Xiong, P., Min, W., Min, W., Lu, J.: Dynamic sign language recognition based on video sequence with BLSTM-3D residual networks. IEEE Access **7**, 38044–38054 (2019)
28. Wadhawan, A., Kumar, P.: Deep learning-based sign language recognition system for static signs. Neural Comput. Appl. **32**(12), 7957–7968 (2020). https://doi.org/10.1007/s00521-019-04691-y

Tech-Inclusion Research: An Iconographic Browser Extension Solution

Tânia Rocha(✉), Hugo Paredes, Paulo Martins, and João Barroso

INESC TEC, University of Trás-os-Montes e Alto Douro, Vila Real, Portugal
{trocha,hparedes,pmartins,jbarroso}@utad.pt

Abstract. In this paper, we aimed at exploring the use of iconographic navigation to support inclusive and accessible search for Web content through an extension for Google Chrome browser, entitled Extension Icon. Despite Extension Icon was developed to be a solution that allows people with intellectual disabilities to search autonomously using an iconographic navigation, supported by platforms as Vimeo and YouTube, it intends to be an accessible solution for ALL users. Through participatory design, the solution was iteratively developed and with the outcomes it was obtained two versions of this solution.

Therefore, in this paper we described the design, implementation and assessment of two Extension Icon versions. Specifically, twenty-eight participants were invited - 18 people with intellectual disabilities and 10 people without of disability - in order to evaluate and participated in the iterative development of the solution. The user preliminary feedbacks showed a major concern regarding the graphical interface therefore it was redesigned to improve and present a more appealing interface. Overall, user tests carried out with the two versions showed and effective, efficient and satisfactory user interaction.

Keywords: Digital inclusion · Usability · Chrome browser extension · Intellectual disabilities

1 Introduction

The Web must be accessible and usable for ALL users. Still, there are groups of users with their access limited, particularly: the group of people with intellectual disabilities.

In previously research, we presented several studies aiming at guarantee an inclusive access and usable interfaces for this specific group of users [2, 8–12]. Specifically, in this paper, an iconographic navigation solution to support web content search through a Google Chrome browser extension is explored. It was intended to present a solution more independent from the Web platform than those formerly presented.

Therefore, an add-on of Google Chrome browser called Extension Icon is presented. The Extension Icon allowed interaction in SAMi interface (a previous tested user interface) and users can search video content on YouTube and Vimeo through the iconographic navigation system.

This paper is structured as follows: the background, where a brief presentation of the thematic is made; then it is described the solution development process - the methods

C. Stephanidis et al. (Eds.): HCII 2020, LNCS 12426, pp. 333–344, 2020.
https://doi.org/10.1007/978-3-030-60149-2_26

trailed, participants involved, experimental design and procedures followed, apparatus used and results obtained. With the feedback and outcomes of this first stage development, a second version is presented with a first user assessment. Finally, we present our conclusions and future work.

2 Background

The number of Web users is increasing, allowing a pronounced Web development. This Web environment - platforms, contents and tools - must be accessible for ALL users (despite individual differences and abilities) [1] as it provides "just a click away" access to countless resources.

In the Web development process, accessibility guidelines and usability factors are keys to improve User Experience and ultimately, increase digital inclusion of people with disabilities [2].

The World Health Organization (WHO) states there are about one billion people with some type of disability, corresponding to approximately 15% of the population. Furthermore, according to a report published by WHO, the probability that people with some kind of disability will increase. Aging (and its consequences) is an important factor for this statistic increase [3, 4].

This states the importance of an accessible and usable Web development.

However, as literature shows there are users with many restrictions in Web access, the group of people with intellectual disabilities are one of the eminent excluded groups [4, 5]. Within the group, each person with intellectual disability can have different characteristics (own disabilities) and different severity levels [6, 7]. They are daily challenged in the Web access because it is difficult (but possible!) to develop accessible content for such a heterogeneous group, with their own disability individualities [4].

Specific tasks, such as: Web content search and navigation can be extremely difficult to perform because the interaction metaphor is based mainly on text input and output and they can have many difficulties in the writing and reading activities.

A number of studies already provide information on how to create accessible and usable contents and platforms for this group [5, 8, 13–15]. For instance, accessibility is directly related to the simplification of the information that is transmitted to the user, i.e., content to be understood must be adapted and textual information must be simplified, do not use extended lines of text [5]. Likewise, using icons or images to navigate and interact is a proven usable metaphor that gives autonomous user interaction [11, 12, 16]. Therefore, to use images instead of text, images should be as objective as possible to convey to its function [8].

3 Extension Icon Solution Development

In this iconographic context, we explore a navigation solution to support Web content search through a Google Chrome browser extension. The iconographic navigation metaphor was developed (designed, implemented and assessed) in previous research [9, 10]. First, we developed with a Web application called SAMi [5]. With this solution, users used an iconographic user interface that allowed Web navigation and search using images (icons) instead of inserting keywords (text). Then, a database allowing to create and add icons to the SAMi user interface was developed. This feature abled parents, tutors or teacher to create icons to enter in the user interface and worked specific video contents [10].

Despite, was rated high in user experience and usability, contributing greatly for autonomous Web interaction of people with intellectual disabilities, the solution was dependent of the YouTube video platform for the video results presentation. Therefore, we needed to developed a video platform more independent solution.

3.1 Extension Icon 1.0: Design and Implementation Descriptions

In this context, a new solution is presented – the Extension Icon. This solution is a Google Chrome extension and allows users to view video content on YouTube and Vimeo.

Specifically, users can start the iconographic navigation and access eight videos, displayed randomly, in two horizontal lines: four from YouTube and the others from Vimeo. Users can choose one of the videos of this first search or can access others by clicking on the arrow navigation icon.

Regarding the design, accessibility and usability guidelines were followed in order to ensure that people with intellectual disabilities can view the desired content and interact through the icon navigation system, allowing access to a wide range of video contents [4, 5, 8, 9, 11–15].

In the first version, a simple and intuitive interface was implemented, capable of providing all information necessary to search video content and facilitating user interaction. Thus, the first user interaction step is to click on the extension available in the Google Chrome extension area and then choose the platform to be use. In this first version, users have two video platform options: YouTube or Vimeo (see Fig. 1).

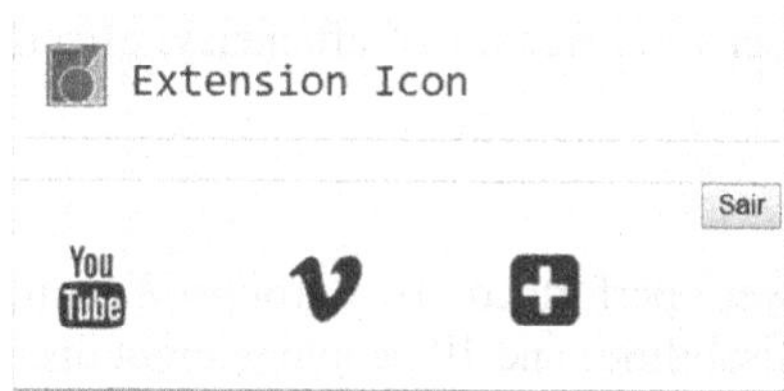

Fig. 1. Extension Icon: main interface

Then, users can use the navigation and search icons presented in the interface. Can find icons created within different categories, for example: Football is in the Sports category. After each click, eight videos will be searched.

These eight videos are presented according the icon selected by the user in the previous step. The APIs of YouTube or Vimeo were used to obtain these videos results. Also, users can interact with navigation icons, allowing to access more videos. The shown videos depend on what the API provides to the user, but only what the user selected is shown.

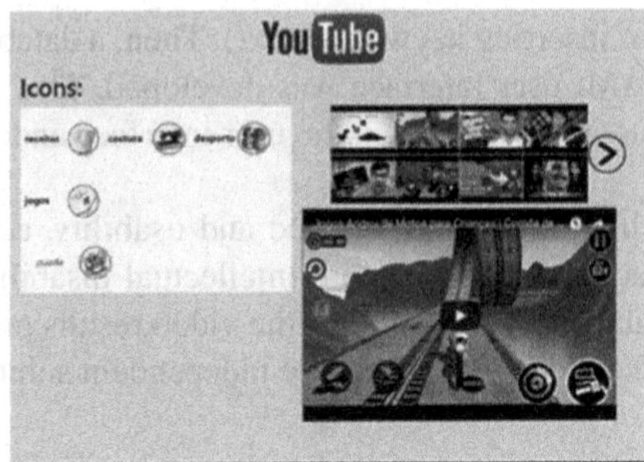

Fig. 2. Extension Icons: example of user interaction steps.

In a last step, after selecting the video, users can use the video player to interact with it. Users are able to view the entire video or if prefer choose another video (see Fig. 2).

For the implementation of this solution, it was used Visual Studio, JavaScript and HyperText Markup Language (HTML). As for the web pages it was used NetBeans and Hypertext Preprocessor (PHP).

3.2 Extension Icon 1.0: User Assessment Description

In order to assess the first developed version, usability tests were carried out.

Next, the user assessment process is described.

Methods

In this study, a participatory design philosophy and a usability evaluation (user tests) was followed. The methods of data collection used are directly related to the research methods adopted and include: logbooks; document analysis, interviews, a Likert questionnaire, direct observation and user tests (record of efficiency, effectiveness, and satisfaction variables).

Participants

Twenty-eight user tests were performed. Two groups of participants were invited: 18 people with intellectual disabilities and 10 people without disabilities.

Specifically, the first group with intellectual disabilities: nine women and nine men, whose ages ranged from 18 to 43 years old. These participants were selected by a special education teacher and a psychologist, according to the average rate of literacy and primary education (coincident with the fourth grade). Regarding their intellectual disabilities and according to DSM–V can be classified according to severity levels, between mild to moderate [6]. Also within the group, ten participants had normal vision and eight have corrected to normal vision.

Regarding the second group without disabilities, six women and four men, whose ages ranged from 18 to 23 years old and were university students. Only one have corrected to normal vision. These participants were invited because we need to observe the user interaction with other group without disabilities to register the accessibility of the solution presented as the main objective is to present a truly accessible and inclusive solution.

All participants were volunteers and give or had permission of their parents or tutors to perform the tests. No participant had used the solution presented before however had previous experience with other digital and Web technologies.

Experimental Design

Each user must perform a natural and complete user interaction with the solution presented. First, need to open the Extension Icon extension in Google Chrome (clicking on the icon). Then, to select the video platform (one click) and choose a general category to search a video of his/her choice (user choice). Afterwards, to select a specific video (selected by the observer) from the eight videos provided (using the navigation icon developed for this proposed) and to view the chosen video in full screen (using the navigation icon developed for this purposed).

For user assessment, it was designed four specific assessed tasks:

1. To find and click in the Sports category icon.
2. To find, click and see the video of the Football Player (Gaitán).
3. To find and click in the Music category icon.
4. To choose and see a Music video.

Regarding the assessment criteria, we followed the variables of usability evaluation (effectiveness, efficiency and satisfaction) to assess user performance and experience. As for effectiveness, we registered how many participants conclude the tasks without giving up. In efficiency, we registered resources spent to achieve effectiveness: time to perform the task and difficulties observed. To record satisfaction, with the two groups, we observed if the participants showed comfort when performing the tasks or if they accepted the task, and if they asked to repeat the tasks.

Also, to measure user satisfaction a Likert questionnaire was used with users without any disabilities. This questionnaire, by James Lewis measures the users' satisfaction, proving to be an important tool to better understand this variable. The questionnaire consists of 19 questions, with a 7-point Likert scale for each of the answers - point 1 corresponding to "Strongly disagree" and 7 corresponding to "Strongly agree". As for users with intellectual disabilities, questions were asked to find out how much they liked the solution developed.

Procedures

Participants were seated correctly in front of the screen in a controlled environment. After we explained the aim of the assessment and global application's functionality and showed them main features of the solution, they started the activity. After explaining the task (main features), the evaluator/observer did not further help the participant.

Apparatus

The following material resources were used: a portable computer with touch screen (15″ display), and a Logitech M100 optical mouse. Note that the user was seated at a distance not superior to one meter of the computer.

Results

With the user assessment stage, it was possible to obtain an analysis of the developed solution, in which the main focus was to evaluate the usability of the Extension Icon solution. Therefore, in this section, the results regarding effectiveness, efficiency and satisfaction are presented and analyzed accordingly.

Regarding effectiveness (conclude successfully tasks without giving up) all participants, with intellectual and without disabilities, completed successfully all assessment tasks. Secondly, we analyzed efficiency (resources spent: time to conclude the task and difficulties observed).

In Table 1, the results (mean and standard deviation) of the time to conclude tasks per people without disabilities (P.W.D.) are presented.

Table 1. Mean and standard deviation results of time to conclude tasks per P.W.D.

Assessment task	Mean	Standard deviation
1. To find and click in the Sports category icon	11.6	2.17
2. To find, click and watch the video of the Football Player (Gaitán)	15.3	1.7
3. To find and click in the Music category icon	16.6	1.71
4. To choose and watch a Music video	13.7	2.87

Table 1 represents the tests carried out with 10 users without disabilities. Users were asked to find and click in the Sports category icon (Task 1), and to find, click and watch a specific video in the Sports Category - The Gaitán video (Task 2). In the Sports category, the average time used was approximately 11.6 s in Task 1 (T1) and 15.3 s in Task 2 (T2). The standard deviation for each of the requested tasks is also shown: in T1, 2.17; and T2, 1.7.

Furthermore, in Table 1, Tasks 3 and 4 concerning the Music category are described. In Task 3 (T3), users must find and click in the Music category icon; and, in Task 4 (T4) to choose and watch a music video (user choice). T3 average time was 16.6 s, and T4, 13.7 s. The T3 standard deviation was 1.71 and 2.87 in T4.

In Table 2, mean and standard deviation results concerning the time took tasks per people with intellectual disabilities (P.I.D.) is displayed.

In the previous Table 2, it is shown the results carried out per 18 users with intellectual disabilities. Users were asked to find and click the Music category icon (Task 1 – T1), and to choose and watch a music video (Task 2 – T2). In the Music category, the average time in T1 was 57.3 s and T2, 28.2 s. The standard deviation of T1 was 40.6 and T2, 24.7.

Table 2. Mean and standard deviation results of time to conclude tasks per P.I.D.

Assessment task	Mean	Standard deviation
1. To find and click in the Music category icon	57.3	40.6
2. To choose and watch a Music video	28.2	24.7
3. To find and click in the Sports category icon	78.3	49.6
4. To find, click and watch the video of the Football Player (Gaitán)	48.8	22.9

The tasks regarding Sports category are described. In Task 3 (T3), users must find and click in the Sports category icon and in Task 4 (T4) find, click and watch a specific Football player video- Gaitán. The T3 average time was 78.3 s in T4, 48.8 s. The T3 standard deviation was 49.6 and T4, 22.9.

Furthermore, it was not observed any major difficulty in user interaction. However, the group with intellectual disabilities showed some confusing with the navigation arrows in the first interaction, after that understood that more videos were chosen if clicking on it. Another important comment made by the group without disabilities was the solution was ease to use but the graphical interface was not very appealing.

Regarding satisfaction (comfort and acceptance of the work within the system) we observed that users liked to interact with the solution presented. The group with intellectual disabilities frequently smiled during interaction and no one asked to stop the interaction in the middle of the assessment tasks. At the end of the experiment, users asked if they could repeat the search and watch other videos of their choice (other categories).

As mentioned before, to measure user' satisfaction a Likert questionnaire was used with users without disabilities, in which it has used a Likert scale from 1 to 7 to classify each questions. Results presented include mean and standard deviation.

In Table 3, it is registered the mean and standard deviation results obtained with 10 users without disability. Overall, the results showed users satisfied with the solution presented. The results obtained to most questions was up to 6 points in a 1 to 7 points Likert scale.

3.3 Extension Icon 2.0: First User Assessment

With the knowledge acquired in the first user assessment, we developed a second version to improve user interface. Consequently, we linked the extension icon and the usable and accessible user interface former developed - SAMi.

Therefore, users can access the SAMi user interface options with only one click. In Fig. 3, it is shown the adaptation made, the user interface of the Extension Icon solution with connection to SAMi running with customized features, in particular: users can select an animated and audio helper – a male or female voice and image – and audio also can choose the background color and icon categories to start the iconographic navigation.

In Fig. 4, it is presented the main interface, can be seen different icon categories chosen displayed and available to search.

Table 3. Likert questionnaire results per users without disabilities.

Questions	Mean	Standard deviation
1. Overall, I am satisfied with how easy it is to use this system	6.1	0.74
2. It was simple to use this system	6.3	0.67
3. I could effectively complete the tasks and scenarios using this system	5.9	0.99
4. I am able to complete my work quickly using this system	6.0	0.94
5. I am able to complete my work efficiently using this system	6.1	0.88
6. I feel comfortable using this system	6.2	0.92
7. It was easy to learn to use this system	5.9	0.99
8. I believe that I become productive quickly using this system	5.9	0.74
9. The system gives error messages that clearly tell me how to fix the problem	3.0	1.33
10. Whenever I make a mistake using the system, I recover easily and quickly	6.1	0.74
11. The information (such as online help, on-screen messages, and other documentation) provided with the system is clear	6.1	0.88
12. It is easy to find the information I need	6.5	0.85
13. The information provided by the system is easy to understand	6.3	0.67
14. Information is effective in helping me complete tasks and scenarios	5.9	0.74
15. The organization of information on the system screens is clear	6.3	0.67
16. The interface of this system is pleasant	6.1	0.74
17. I like to use the system interface	6.1	0.74
18. This system has all the functions and capabilities that I expected it to have	6.2	0.63
19. Overall, I am satisfied with this system	6.1	0.74

Fig. 3. Image and audio helper and colour background features.

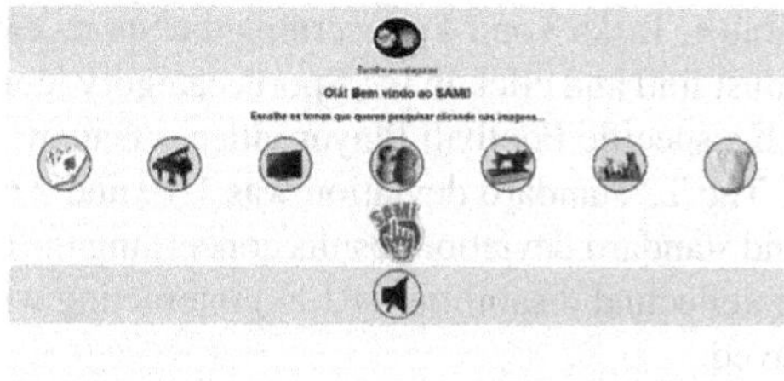

Fig. 4. Main interface with icons search categories chosen.

In order to assess this new adaptation, we carried out a new phase of usability tests. Methods, experimental design, procedures and apparatus were the same of the first user assessment phase. Next, we described this second user assessment results.

User Assessment Results

With the second user assessment phase, it was possible to obtain an analysis of the adaptation developed, in which the main focus was to evaluate the usability of SAMi user interface within the Extension Icon solution.

Therefore, in this section, the results regarding effectiveness, efficiency and satisfaction are presented and analyzed accordingly.

Regarding effectiveness (conclude successfully tasks without giving up), again all participants, with intellectual and without disabilities, completed successfully all assessment tasks and no one give up.

Secondly, we analyzed efficiency (resources spent: time to conclude the task and difficulties observed).

In Table 4, the results (mean and standard deviation) of the time to conclude the tasks per people without disabilities (P.W.D.) interacting with the extension icon new version are presented.

Table 4. Mean and standard deviation results of time to conclude tasks per P.W.D.

Assessment task	Mean	Standard deviation
1. To find and click in the Music category icon	16.2	1.55
2. To choose and watch a Music video	15.1	0.99
3. To find and click in the Sports category icon	19.1	1.19
4. To find, click and watch the video of the Football Player (Gaitán)	28.6	2.6

Table 4 represents the tests carried out with 10 users without disabilities. Users were asked to find and click in the Music category icon (Task 1), and to find and click a Music video (Task 2). In the Music category, the average time used was approximately 16.2 s in Task 1 (T1) and 15.1 s in Task 2 (T2). The standard deviation for each of the requested tasks is also shown: in T1, 1.55; and T2, 0.99.

Furthermore, in Table 4, Tasks 3 and 4 concerning the Sports category are described. In Task 3 (T3), users must find and click in the Sports category icon; and, in Task 4 (T4) to find, click and watch a specific Football Player video – Gaitán. T3 average time was 19.1 s, and T4, 28.6 s. The T3 standard deviation was 1.19 and 2.6 in T4.

In Table 5, mean and standard deviation results concerning the time took to conclude tasks per people with intellectual disabilities (P.I.D.) interacting with the extension icon new version are displayed.

Table 5. Mean and standard deviation results of time to conclude tasks per P.I.D.

Assessment task	Mean	Standard deviation
1. To find and click in the Sports category icon	86.7	56.4
2. To find, click and watch the video of the Football Player (Gaitán)	53.2	23.6
3. To find and click in the Music category icon	64.8	45.6
4. To choose and watch a Music video	30.2	25.2

In the previous Table 5, it is shown the results carried out per 18 users with intellectual disabilities. Users were asked to find and click the Sports category icon (Task 1-T1), and to find, click and watch a specific Football player video - Gaitán (Task 2 – T2). In the Sports category, the average time in T1 was 86.7 s and T2, 53.2 s. The standard deviation of T1 was 56.4 and T2 was 23.6.

Furthermore, the tasks regarding Music category are described. In Task 3 (T3), users must find and click in the Music category icon and in Task 4 (T4), choose and watch a Music video (user choice). The T3 average time was 64.8 s and in T4, 30.2 s. The T3 standard deviation was 45.6 and T4, 25.2.

There were no difficulties observed in user interaction in the two groups.

Regarding satisfaction, users seems to be comfortable and accepted to performed all assessment tasks. Within the group of participants with intellectual disabilities, users frequently asked to performed more video search tasks. They seemed comfortable and were observed smiling and having fun the interaction. Regarding, participants without disabilities, they agree the interface was well structured and easy to follow when using this second version with SAMi.

4 Conclusion and Future Work

People with intellectual disabilities are daily challenged in the Web access. The research and development of solutions that provide Web access to these group previous excluded are extremely important to guarantee digital inclusion and equal opportunities.

In this context, we explored an iconographic navigation solution to support Web content search through a Google Chrome browser extension.

Overall, the results were promising as users considered the solution efficient, effective and acceptable, giving preference to the solution with SAMI interface connection, because they considered that provided greater interactivity and engagement.

Therefore, the Extension Icon solution combined with SAMi interface (plus database) had enabled an autonomous Web interaction for people with intellectual disabilities, as it overcome the need for writing and reading comprehension skills for Web content search. We strongly believe this icon search approach can be replicated in other digital platforms and systems to be a tool for inclusion of previously excluded groups, by improving the effectiveness and efficiency of the search and navigation tasks and offering autonomy on the Web access.

Regarding future work, it is intended to improve the interface design of Extension Icon and to add more platforms and content options in addition to YouTube and Vimeo.

Acknowledgements. This work is financed by National Funds through the Portuguese funding agency, FCT - Fundação para a Ciência e a Tecnologia within project UIDB/50014/2020. Furthermore, the authors would like to thank all participants that help in different phases of the iterative inclusive development of the solution presented, in particular to: Eng. Jorge Santos and Professor Eng. António Marques.

References

1. Lazar, J., Dudley-Sponaugle, A., Greenidge, K.-D.: Improving web accessibility: a study of webmaster perceptions. Comput. Hum. Behav. 269–288. http://citeseerx.ist.psu.edu/viewdoc/download?doi=10.1.1.100.743&rep=rep1&type=pdf. Accessed 28 Nov 2019
2. Rocha, T., Martins, J., Branco, F., Gonçalves, R.: Evaluating youtube platform usability by people with intellectual disabilities (a user experience case study performed in a six-month period). J. Inf. Syst. Eng. Manag. **2**, 1 (2007). https://doi.org/10.20897/jisem.201705. Article 5. ISSN 2468–4376
3. World Health Organization (WHO). Disability and Health. Homepage. https://www.who.int/news-room/fact-sheets/detail/disability-and-health. Accessed 28 Nov 2019
4. Friedman, M.G., Bryen, D.N.: Web accessibility design recommendations for people with cognitive disabilities. Technol. Disabil. **19**(4), 205–212 (2007)
5. Bohman, P.: Cognitive Disabilities, Part I: We still Know Too Little and We Do Even Less (2004). https://webaim.org/articles/cognitive/cognitive_too_little/. Accessed 28 Nov 2019
6. American Psychological Association (APA). DSM-V-The Diagnostic and Statistical Manual of Mental Disorders (5) (2013). http://www.dsm5.org/Pages/Default.aspx. Accessed 14 Nov 2019
7. International Classification of Functioning. Disability and Health (ICFDH). https://catalogo.inr.pt/documents/11257/0/CIF+2004/4cdfad93-81d0-42de-b319-5b6b7a806eb2. Accessed 14 Nov 2019
8. Rocha, T.: Interaction metaphor for Access to Digital Information an autonomous form for People with Intellectual Disabilities. Ph.D Thesis, University of Trás-os-Montes e Alto Douro, Vila Real (2014)
9. Rocha, T., Paredes, H., Barroso, J., Bessa, M.: SAMi: an accessible web application solution for video search for people with intellectual disabilities. In: Miesenberger, K., Bühler, C., Penaz, P. (eds.) ICCHP 2016. LNCS, vol. 9759, pp. 310–316. Springer, Cham (2016). https://doi.org/10.1007/978-3-319-41267-2_43
10. Rocha, T., Pinheiro, P., Santos, J., Marques, A., Paredes, H., Barroso, J.: MyAutoIconPlat: an automatic platform for icons creation. In: Antona, M., Stephanidis, C. (eds.) UAHCI 2017. LNCS, vol. 10277, pp. 423–432. Springer, Cham (2017). https://doi.org/10.1007/978-3-319-58706-6_34

11. Rocha, T.: Accessibility and Usability for people with intellectual disabilities. Master Thesis, University of Trás-os-Montes and Alto Douro (2009)
12. Rocha, T., et al.: The recognition of web pages' hyperlinks by people with intellectual disabilities: an evaluation study. J. Appl. Res. Intellect. Disabil. **25**(6), 542–552 (2012). https://doi.org/10.1111/j.1468-3148.2012.00700.x
13. Freeman, E., Clare, L., Savitch, N., Royan, L., Literhland, R., Lindsay, M.: Improving website accessibility for people with early-stage dementia: a preliminary investigation. Aging Mental Health **9**(5), 442–448 (2005)
14. Roh, S.: Designing accessible Web-based instruction for all learners: perspectives of students with disabilities and Web-based instructional personnel in higher education. Doctoral dissertation, Indiana University, USA (2004)
15. Small, J., Schallau, P., Brown, K., Ettinger, D., Blanchard, S., Krahn, G.: Web accessibility for people with cognitive disabilities. In: Resna Proceedings (2004)
16. Zarin, R.: Mejla Pictogram 2.0. Institute of Design in Umea, Sweden and Swedish Institute for Special Needs Education (2009). http://216.46.8.72/tmp/v2/images/pictoCom/Final_report_Pictogram2.pdf. Accessed 14 Nov 2019

Development of Night Time Calling System by Eye Movement Using Wearable Camera

Kazuki Sakamoto[1], Takeshi Saitoh[1(✉)], and Kazuyuki Itoh[2]

[1] Kyushu Institute of Technology, 680–4 Kawazu, Iizuka, Fukuoka 820–8502, Japan
saitoh@ces.kyutech.ac.jp

[2] National Rehabilitation Center for Persons with Disabilities, 4–1 Namiki, Tokorozawa, Saitama 359–8555, Japan
itoh-kazuyuki-0923@rehab.go.jp

Abstract. This paper proposes a night time call system using a wearable camera for patients. The proposed system consists of a wearable camera, computer, relay controller, and nurse call. The user wears the wearable camera. All captured eye images are fed to the convolutional neural network to detect the pupil center. When the detected pupil center exceeds a preset threshold value, the computer sends the signal to operate the nurse call via each relay controller. Two experiments were conducted to evaluate the proposed system: verification of the accuracy of pupil center detection and quantitative evaluation of call success. In the former experiment, we collected 2,800 eye images from seven people and conducted a pupil center detection experiment on several training conditions. As a result, an average error of 1.17 pixels was obtained. In the latter experiment, a call experiment was conducted on five healthy people. The experiment time for each subject was about five minutes. The subject experimented while lying on the bed. Twelve audio stimuli were given in one experiment, after getting the stimuli, the subject moved his eye. The correct call in response to the audio stimulus was considered successful, and the precision, recall, and F-measure were calculated. As a result, we obtained the precision, recall, and F-measure of 0.83, 1.00, and 0.91, respectively. These experimental results show the effectiveness of the proposed system.

Keywords: Calling system · Eye image · Pupil center detection · Convolutional neural network.

1 Introduction

In amyotrophic lateral sclerosis (ALS) patients with speech and motor dysfunction, multiple system atrophy (MSA) patients, and muscular dystrophy patients, it becomes difficult to communicate their intentions due to severe motor dysfunction. Since eye movements often function until the end-stage, our research project

C. Stephanidis et al. (Eds.): HCII 2020, LNCS 12426, pp. 345–357, 2020.
https://doi.org/10.1007/978-3-030-60149-2_27

focuses on developing an eye movement-based communication support system. In this paper, we develop a system that can be used, especially at night, using a wearable camera.

A (nurse) calling system is a tool for calling a nurse or a caregiver at a hospital or a nursing care insurance facility, and a family at home. It is an indispensable tool for patients to use when a physical abnormality occurs or if they have questions about their life. The patient pushes a call sensor or button, and calls a remote nurse or family member. However, for patients with ALS patients who have difficulty moving their muscles, an input device must be prepared according to the residual function. The eyeSwitch [1] is an operation support switch that can be operated (ON/OFF) by eye movements. The user can make calls, operate home appliances, and communicate through call devices, environmental control devices, and communication devices. The eyeSwitch can be used at night, but it requires large eye movements, it is difficult to detect slight eye movements. The eyeSwitch needs to be fixed near the bed with an arm, but the position needs to be corrected each time the patient's position moves.

In this paper, we introduced an image-based method for detecting the pupil center with a wearable camera with high accuracy at night for a calling system. We also develop a prototype of a calling system that can be used at night time and evaluate the effectiveness of its performance through subject experiments.

2 Related Research

This section briefly introduces the nurse call and eye movement analysis related to this paper.

Ongenae et al. developed an ontology-based Nurse Call System [11], which assesses the priority of a call based on the current context and assigns the most appropriate caregiver to a call. Traditional push button-flashing lamp call systems are not integrated with other hospital automation systems. Unluturk et al. developed an integrated system of Nurse Call System Software, the Wireless Phone System Software, the Location System Software, and the communication protocol [13]. By using this system, both the nurse and the patient know that the system will dedicate the next available nurse if the primary nurse is not available. Klemets and Toussaint proposed a nurse call system [8] that allows nurses to discern the reason behind a nurse call allows them to make a more accurate decision and relieves stress. Regarding the nurse call system, there are many studies on improving the whole system, not individual devices such as switches.

Images and electromyography are available as means for analyzing eye movements. Since the latter uses contact sensors, this paper targets the former, which is a non-contact sensor. As for the image-based eye movement analysis, some products have already released that can estimate the gaze point rather than the movement of the eyes. The devices used can be roughly classified into two types; non-wearable and wearable devices. The former is a screen-based eye tracker that attaches to a display, for example, Tobii Pro Nano [5] and Tobii Pro Fusion [3].

The latter is the type with a small camera mounted on the eyeglass frame, for example, Tobii Pro Glass 3 [4] and Gazo GPE3 [2]. The research target related to eye movement analysis is divided into two types; it uses the existing eye tracker to analyze the gaze [10,14] and proposes a method for detecting the eye or the pupil center point [6,7,15].

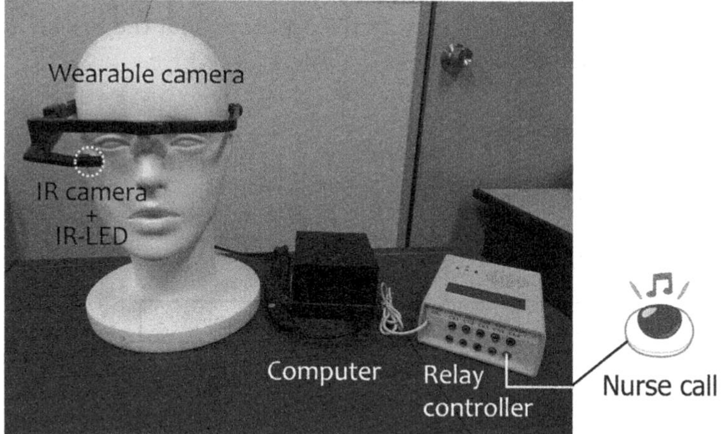

Fig. 1. Overview of the proposed system.

3 Night Time Calling System

3.1 Overview

The proposed system consists of a wearable camera, computer, relay controller, and nurse call, as shown in Fig. 1.

Our system is assumed to use at night. Therefore, a standard color camera is not suitable for shooting at night. Of course, the visible light illumination is not used because the user is too drowsy to sleep. Thus, a near-infrared LED (IR-LED) and near-infrared camera (IR camera) are used. Wearable cameras are not affected by the movement of the user's head, and can always capture stable eye images. Although wearing a wearable camera during sleep puts a burden on the user, we decided to use a wearable camera after discussing it with a physical therapist. The wearable camera attached to the mannequin on the right in Fig. 1 is the device used in our system.

The computer processes all eye images taken by the wearable camera. A large-scale and high-performance computer is desired. However, our system is assumed to install near the bed of the user. At the facility's request, our system avoids the use of both wired and wireless networks. For the above reasons, we adopted a small computer with a GPU for our system.

If our system sends a continuous signal directly from the user's computer to a nurse call, the nurse call will ring every time the nurse call receives the signal.

This system uses a relay controller to prevent a nurse call from being made due to a malfunction.

3.2 Pupil Center Detection

Our system uses the CNN-based pupil center detection method proposed by Chinsatit and Saitoh [6]. The method uses two CNN models, as shown in Fig. 2. The first CNN model is used to classify the eye state, and the second is used to estimate the pupil center position.

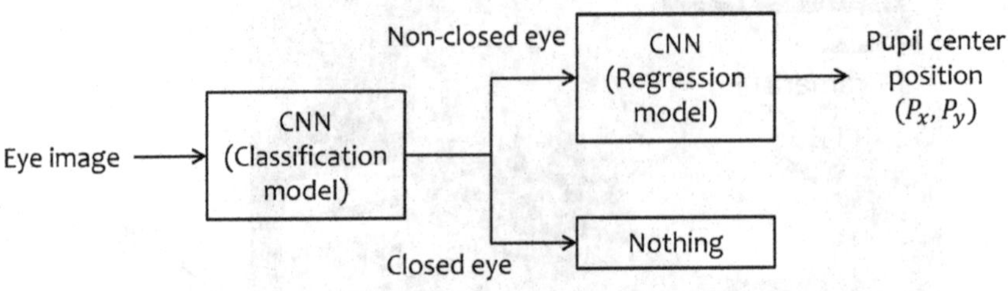

Fig. 2. Two-part CNN model.

The architecture of the classification model is based on AlexNet [9]. The output of this model is two; the closed eye or the non-closed eye. Since the pupil's center cannot be detected from the closed eye, unnecessary processing is skipped.

The second CNN model is based on the pose regression ConvNet [12]. The output of this model is the pupil center position (P_x, P_y).

3.3 ROI Extraction

The eye image is taken with a wearable camera. However, the background sometimes appears in the eye image. In this case, since the pupil detection accuracy may decrease, the region of interest (ROI) is first extracted instead of directly inputting the captured image to the CNN.

An ROI is extracted based on an intensity difference value between two consecutive frames. When accumulates pixels of difference value equal to or larger than a threshold value. The maximum region in the accumulated image within a fixed time is extracted. Next, two types of ROI extracted from this region. The first is to extract without considering the aspect ratio (named ROI1), and the other is to extract a rectangle with a fixed aspect ratio of 3:2 (named ROI2).

Our system uses a wearable camera. Therefore, a pixel having no motion, such as background, has a low difference value. On the other hand, the difference in the pixels of the eyes and the skin around them becomes large due to blinking and eye movements. This makes it possible to crop the ROI around the eyes.

3.4 Calling Mechanism

In our system, the user's intention is read from the detected pupil center, and a signal is outputted from the computer to the relay controller for calling. The target users in this study are patients with intractable neurological diseases. However, the progression of symptoms varies in individuals. For example, the direction and amount of movement of the eye are different. Therefore, it is desirable that the parameters can adjust for each user, and our system adopts a policy of manual adjustment.

In our system, when the user wants to call a person, he or she moves his/her eyes by a certain amount in the up, down, left, or right directions. In other words, four thresholds (upper, lower, left, and right) for the eye position are set in advance, and when the eye position exceeds any of the thresholds, it is determined that the user intends to call. Upon detecting this movement, the system sends a signal to the relay controller.

Figure 3 shows four eye images in which the eye image and four thresholds are drawn. Here, the green circle is the detected pupil center point, and the rectangle around the pupil is four thresholds. In the figure, the left side has the eye facing the front, and the pupil's center is inside the rectangle. The second and third from the left are examples of exceeding the right and lower thresholds, respectively. In the figures, red bands on the right side and the lower side of the image are drawn to visually display the direction in which the threshold value is exceeded. The rightmost one is an example with an eye closed.

Fig. 3. Eye images with thresholds.

3.5 Implementation

As described in Sect. 3.1, our system needs to operate standalone without using the network. Therefore, in our system, we constructed a CNN server by Flask, a web application framework, in the computer, and sent the eye image of the wearable camera acquired by the client software to the server, and received the pupil center position which is the output of CNN. Figure 4 shows the process flow of our system.

Some users can move their eyes quickly, while others can move their eyes only slowly. In the former case, the signal of the relay controller is transmitted from the computer immediately after the eye position exceeds the threshold

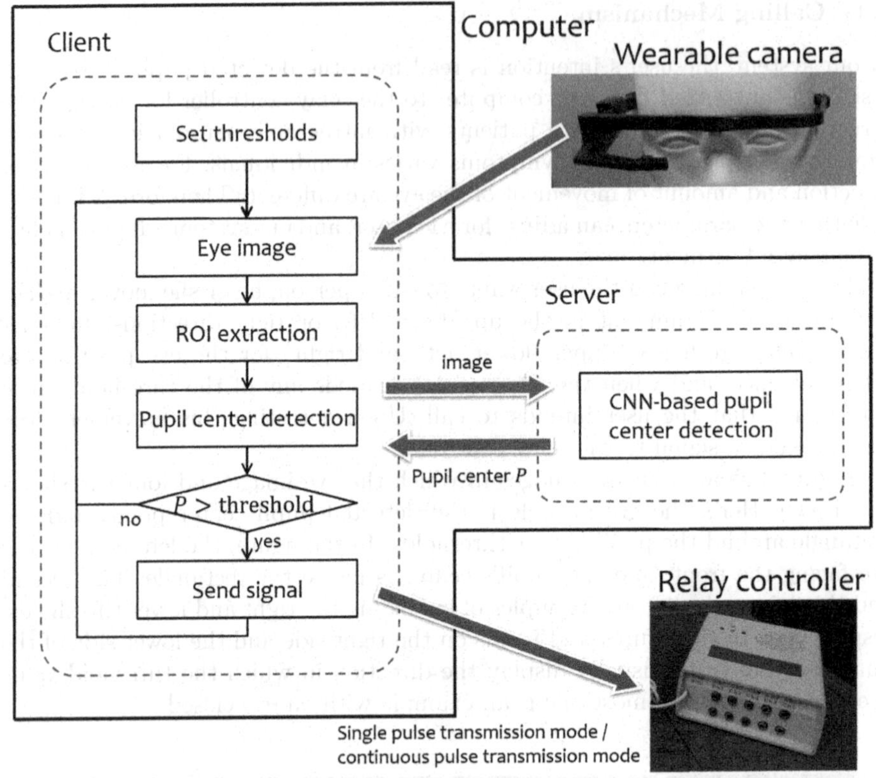

Fig. 4. Process flow of our system.

value. Even if the eye cannot be transmitted because the detection error at the center of the pupil does not exceed the threshold value, it can be moved again to take measures against false detection. Therefore, in this case, the single pulse transmission mode is performed in which a signal is transmitted once each time the threshold value is exceeded. On the other hand, in the latter case, the continuous pulse transmission mode in which signals are continuously transmitted while the threshold value is exceeded is adopted. Switching between these two modes allows the setting to be changed by the user.

Our system requires manual settings such as thresholds and transmission modes, which allows people with various symptoms to respond.

Figure 5 is an image captured on the computer monitor during the experiment. In the figure, the upper left is an eye image overlaid with information. The upper right is the temporal transition of the pupil center's vertical position, and the lower left is the horizontal transition of the pupil center, which is visualized in real-time.

4 Evaluation Experiments

In this research, two experiments were conducted to evaluate the proposed system: verification of the accuracy of pupil center detection and quantitative evaluation of call success.

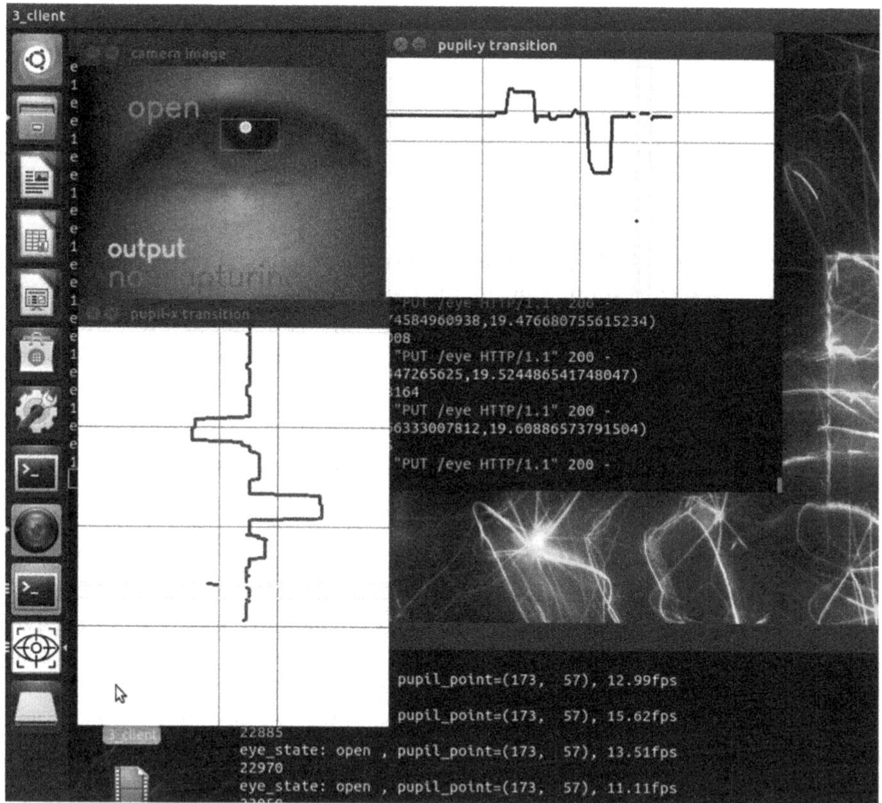

Fig. 5. Main windows of our system.

4.1 Pupil Center Detection

Dataset. We collected eye images from seven people; four healthy staff and three patients, using the proposed system. Table 1 shows the subject information and the number of collected images. At the time of collection, subjects had their eyes moved in five directions: front, up, down, left, and right. Since the number of collected images differs depending on the subjects from Table 1, it was decided to use 400 eye images from each subject, for a total of 2,800 eye images in this experiment.

The size of the eye image taken by the wearable camera is 1280×720 [pixels]. However, it was resized to 120×80 [pixels] to reduce the processing time. It is

Table 1. Subject information and the number of collected images.

ID	Type	Sex	# of collected images
s1	Healthy staff	Male	464
s2		Male	419
s3		Male	480
s4		Male	1,087
s5	Patient	Male	561
s6		Female	1,767
s7		Male	1,859
Total			6,637

necessary to give the ground truth to the eye state and the center of the pupil for each eye image to train and evaluate the CNN models. This work was done visually. Regarding the eye condition, a label of "Non-closed eye" was given when 50% or more of the pupil was visible, and a label of "Closed eye" was given otherwise.

Experimental Conditions. In this paper, we propose two types of ROI extraction methods of ROI1 and ROI2. Therefore, as for ROI, two extraction methods were compared.

It is desirable to prepare a lot of data for training the CNN model. However, in this experiment, we have not collected enough data, so we introduce two approaches, data augmentation (DA) and fine-tuning (FT). Regarding DA, we generated four images for each eye image, which was a combination of scaling, translation, rotation, and brightness value correction. Concerning FT, 1,980 images were collected from six healthy males, three females, nine healthy persons, using a different wearable camera, for a total of 17,820 images. The weight of the CNN models learned by using this is used as the initial value of FT.

Eye-state recognition and pupil center detection were performed under eight conditions that combined the application of two types of ROI, DA, and FT.

A person-independent task was conducted. That is, the test data was one patient, and the training data was six (the remaining two patients and four healthy staff). The experiment was conducted by the one-patient-leave-out method.

Result and Discussion. Experimental results are shown in Table 2. In the table, E_p means the error between the ground truth and the detection result of the pupil center.

Regarding the eye-state recognition, the non-closed eye's recognition accuracy is higher than that of the closed eye. This is presumed to be due to the small number of closed eye training data. The highest recognition accuracy of 82.1% was obtained when ROI1 was used without applying DA and FT.

Regarding the pupil center detection task, the average error was at most 2.3 pixels, although the error varied depending on the conditions. The minimum average error of 1.17 pixels was obtained when DA and FT were applied using ROI1. Figure 6 shows the eye images in which the ground truth (green point) and the detection result (red point) are plotted. The errors of Figs. 6(a), (b), (c) and (d) were 2.63, 2.90, 8.73 and 8.82, respectively. Based on the plot results, it is judged that Figs. 6(a)(b) have been detected successfully. On the contrary, Figs. 6(c)(d) judges that the detection has failed.

Table 2. Eye state recognition and pupil center detection results.

Condition	Eye state recognition accuracy			E_p
	Non-closed [%]	Closed [%]	Total [%]	[pixel]
ROI1	96.8	67.5	**82.1**	1.54
ROI2	96.8	59.6	78.2	1.52
ROI1+DA	96.9	38.0	67.5	1.36
ROI2+DA	93.2	57.2	75.2	2.14
ROI1+FT	96.6	52.7	74.7	1.36
ROI2+FT	97.4	45.2	71.3	1.48
ROI1+DA+FT	95.9	39.7	67.8	**1.17**
ROI2+DA+FT	96.1	37.0	66.6	2.27

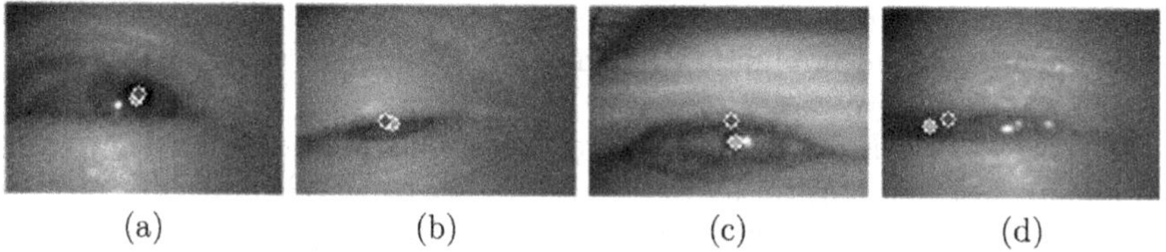

(a) (b) (c) (d)

Fig. 6. Pupil center detection results.

4.2 Calling Experiment

Experimental Protocols. A call experiment was conducted on five healthy people. The experiment time for each subject was about five minutes. The subject experimented while lying on the bed, as shown on the left side of Fig. 7. In order to avoid moving the eyes other than calling, the subject gazed at the image on the monitor mounted on the wall to look at the front, as shown on the right side of Fig. 7.

To reproduce an open call, we prepared a voice stimulus pointing in any direction up, down, left, or right. During the experiment, the subject instructed to perform eye movement after this voice stimulus. The time and direction of voice stimulation are random. Twelve audio stimuli were given in one experiment; that is, the subject was called 12 times by eye movement.

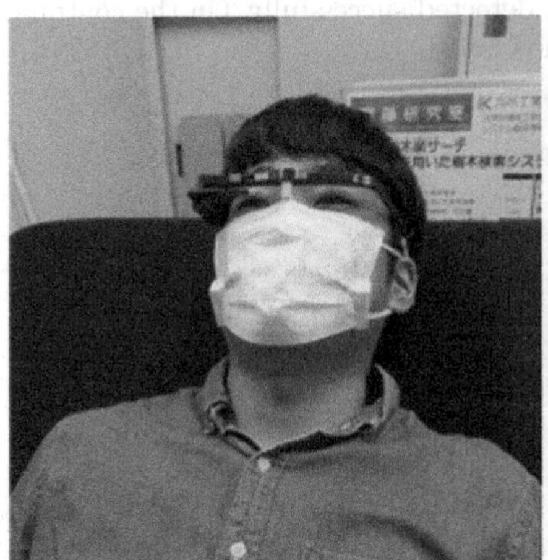
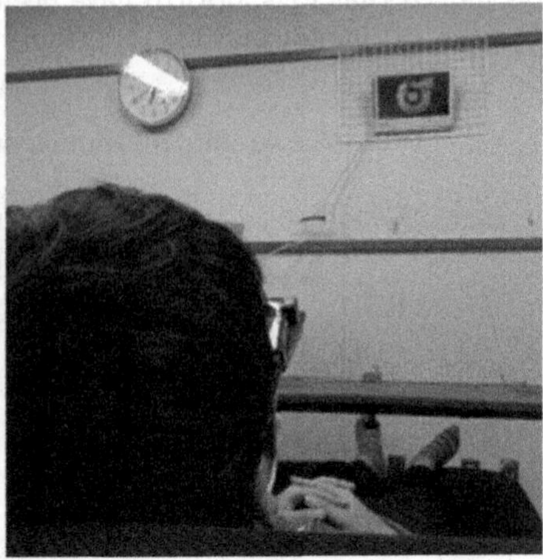

Fig. 7. Experimental scenes of calling experiment.

Result and Discussion. The experiment was conducted by turning off the lights at night. When the brightness during the experiment was measured with an illuminometer, the minimum, maximum, and average were 3.92 lx, 16.7 lx, and 9.9 lx, respectively.

The correct call in response to the voice stimulus was considered successful. The numbers of true positives (TP), false negatives (FN), and false positives (FP) were counted in all experiments. We also calculated precision P, recall R, and F-measure F by the following equations: $P = TP/(TP + FP)$, $R = TP/(TP + FN)$, $F = 2PR/(P + R)$.

Table 3 shows the result. The precision, recall, and F-measure of all subjects were 0.833, 1.000, and 0.909, respectively. The recall is 1.000, which means that the call succeeded without missing. On the other hand, the precision was 0.833. This is because the wrong pupil position was detected when the eyes closed with blinking by S2 and S5.

Figure 8 is a graph showing the temporal transition of the pupil center coordinates in the subject experiment of S4. The horizontal axis is the number of frames, which corresponds to time. The vertical axis is the x or y coordinate. The red curves are the coordinate of the detected pupil center. The horizontal lines of green and blue mean the left and right or upper and lower thresholds. The vertical pink strip indicates that the eyes are closed. From these graphs,

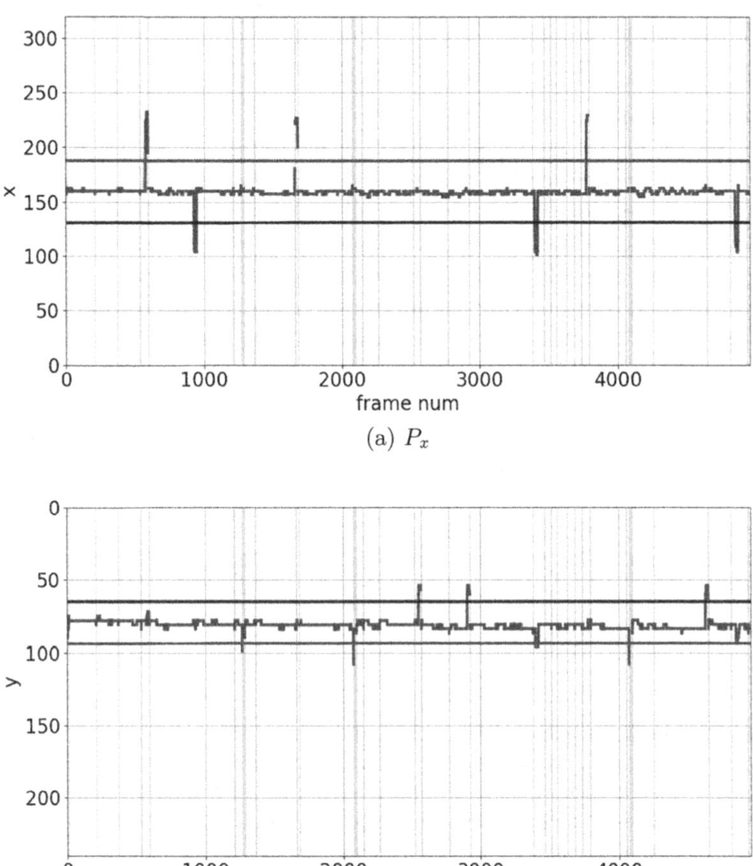

(a) P_x

(b) P_y

Fig. 8. Transition of pupil center (Subject S4).

Table 3. Experimental result of calling experiment.

Subject	S1	S2	S3	S4	S5	Total
TP	12	12	12	12	12	60
FN	0	10	0	0	2	12
FP	0	0	0	0	0	0
P	1.000	0.545	1.000	1.000	0.857	0.833
R	1.000	1.000	1.000	1.000	1.000	1.000
F	1.000	0.706	1.000	1.000	0.923	0.909

it can be confirmed that the pupil position exceeds the upper threshold or the lower threshold for 12 calls.

5 Conclusion

In this research, we developed a system that allows patients to call without stress at night using eye movements. Two experiments of pupil center detection and calling experiments were conducted to evaluate the effectiveness of the development system. As a result, a high detection accuracy with an average error of 1.17 was obtained for detecting the pupil center. In the subject experiment, the experiment was conducted not for the patient but the healthy person, and a high call success rate was obtained.

The user of our system is a patient. We have not been able to perform a call experiment with patient cooperation. We will work on this experiment in the future. In the pupil center detection, there is a failure due to blinking so that we address this problem.

Acknowledgment. This work was supported by JSPS KAKENHI Grant Numbers 19KT0029.

References

1. eyeSwitch. http://www.emfasys.co.jp/index8f.html
2. Gazo GPE3. https://www.gazo.co.jp/gaze_point_estimation
3. Tobii Pro Fusion. https://www.tobiipro.com/product-listing/fusion/
4. Tobii Pro Glasses 3. https://www.tobiipro.com/product-listing/tobii-pro-glasses-3/
5. Tobii Pro Nano. https://www.tobiipro.com/product-listing/nano/
6. Chinsatit, W., Saitoh, T.: CNN-based pupil center detection for wearable gaze estimation system. Applied Computational Intelligence and Soft Computin **2017** (2017). https://doi.org/10.1155/2017/8718956
7. Gou, C., Zhang, H., Wang, K., Wang, F.Y., Ji, Q.: Cascade learning from adversarial synthetic images for accurate pupil detection. Pattern Recogn. **88**, 584–594 (2019). https://doi.org/10.1016/j.patcog.2018.12.014
8. Klemets, J., Toussaint, P.: Does revealing contextual knowledge of the patient fs intention help nurses' handling of nurse calls? Int. J. Med. Inform. **86**, 1–9 (2016). https://doi.org/10.1016/j.ijmedinf.2015.11.010
9. Krizhevsky, A., Sutskever, I., Hinton, G.E.: ImageNet classification with deep convolutional neural networks. In: 26th Annual Conference on Neural Information Processing Systems (NIPS2012), pp. 1097–1105 (2012)
10. Ohya, T., Morita, K., Yamashita, Y., Egami, C., Ishii, Y., Nagamitsu, S., Matsuishi, T.: Impaired exploratory eye movements in children with Asperger fs syndrome. Brain Dev. **36**(3), 241–247 (2014). https://doi.org/10.1016/j.braindev.2013.04.005
11. Ongenae, F., Claeys, M., Kerckhove, W., Dupont, T., Verhoeve, P., Turck, F.: A self-learning nurse call system. Comput. Biol. Med. **44**, 110–123 (2014). https://doi.org/10.1016/j.compbiomed.2013.10.014

12. Pfister, T., Simonyan, K., Charles, J., Zisserman, A.: Deep convolutional neural networks for efficient pose estimation in gesture videos. In: Cremers, D., Reid, I., Saito, H., Yang, M.-H. (eds.) ACCV 2014. LNCS, vol. 9003, pp. 538–552. Springer, Cham (2015). https://doi.org/10.1007/978-3-319-16865-4_35
13. Unluturk, M.S., Ozcanhan, M.H., Dalkilic, G.: Improving communication among nurses and patients. Comput. Methods Programs Biomed. **120**(2), 102–12 (2015). https://doi.org/10.1016/j.cmpb.2015.04.004
14. Wang, C.C., Hung, J.C.: Comparative analysis of advertising attention to Facebook social network: evidence from eye-movement data. Comput. Hum. Behav. **100**, 192–208 (2019). https://doi.org/10.1016/j.chb.2018.08.007
15. Yiu, Y.H., et al.: DeepVOG: open-source pupil segmentation and gaze estimation in neuroscience using deep learning. J. Neurosci. Methods **324**, 108307 (2019). https://doi.org/10.1016/j.jneumeth.2019.05.016

EyeHear: Smart Glasses for the Hearing Impaired

Ishaan Sinha(✉) and Owen Caverly

Glencoe High School, Hillsboro, OR 97124, USA
ishaansinha155@gmail.com, caverlyo@gmail.com

Abstract. The hearing-impaired experience the sound localization problem, defined as the insufficient ability to estimate the direction of sounds. This problem reduces spatial awareness and amplifies social difficulties such as communicating in adverse listening conditions. Current solutions, such as hearing aids and cochlear implants, fail to solve the problem for a multitude of reasons, but recent work in head-computer interfaces can be applied to deliver a robust solution. Thus, this paper develops a smart glass, named EyeHear, that shows the direction of a speech source and its transcription, all in real-time thanks to a modified speech recognition algorithm and speech recognition system. Algorithm testing proved that the device was accurate enough to be feasible in real-world talking situations. User testing affirms that the target audience favors head-mounted displays and indicates that solving the sound localization problem is beneficial. This device paves the way for future work to extend the device to non-speech sounds. EyeHear has the potential to become an assistive technology for the hearing impaired.

Keywords: Interface for disabled and senior people · Hearing loss · Visual display

1 Introduction

1.1 Sound Localization

Sound localization is the ability to estimate the relative location of a sound source, granting basic spatial awareness [1]. Humans enjoy a robust 3D sound localization ability due to use binaural and monoaural cues [2, 3].

Evidence shows that hearing loss drastically impairs sound localization ability [4–6]. This produces the *sound localization problem,* defined as the insufficient ability to localize where sounds are coming from. The consequence of the *sound localization problem* is a lack of spatial awareness [7], amplifying hazards such as avoiding oncoming traffic or worsening social difficulties such as communicating in adverse listening conditions (Fig. 1).

Preexisting Solutions. The two most widely used auditory assistive technologies are hearing aids and cochlear implants. The hearing-impaired population also utilize alternative practices such as sign language. However, there is no solution that effectively solves the sound localization problem.

C. Stephanidis et al. (Eds.): HCII 2020, LNCS 12426, pp. 358–370, 2020.
https://doi.org/10.1007/978-3-030-60149-2_28

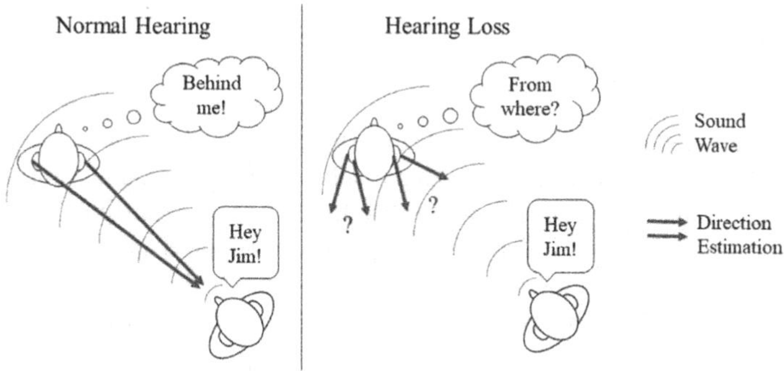

Fig. 1. Depiction of the social difficulties produced by sound localization problem.

Hearing Aids. Hearing aids are electronic devices that amplify certain signals for its user [8], forcing them to localize sound by themselves. However, according to [9], "hearings aids are ultimately insufficient because they fail to compensate for distortions in the specific patterns of neural activity that encode acoustic information." In addition, they disrupt the wearers' compensatory techniques, and do not recoup the loss of natural interaural cues [7].

Cochlear Implants. Cochlear implants (CIs) are surgically embedded devices, usually in the cochlea, that electronically stimulate the auditory nerve [10]. Bilateral cochlear implant users demonstrate a poor ability to localize sounds as well, compared to people with robust hearing [11, 12]. Cochlear implants are also expensive ($30,000–$50,000) [13] and "unaffordable to the developing world" [14].

Deaf Culture. Many of the hearing-impaired population choose not to use invasive technologies such as hearing aids and cochlear implants due to deaf culture. According to [16], deaf culture is the "conviction that deafness is not a disorder, but rather a biological and cultural characteristic." Proponents of deaf culture strongly oppose invasive technologies, especially cochlear implants [15, 16].

Alternative Solutions. One alternative solution is using a visual language system such as American Sign Language (ASL), which consists of a set of movements and facial expressions to communicate language [17]. However, ASL requires that both parties are well-versed in ASL, and not many people know the ASL language [18], indicating that ASL would not be viable in most social situations. In addition, there is no universal sign language [17], which means that people with knowledge of ASL may not understand different variants. Another alternative solution is FM systems, which are essentially transmitter and receiver systems for communication between a hearing-impaired person and another person [19]. However, once again, it requires the participation of other people, which may not be accessible in many social situations.

1.2 Research Focus

Recently, the use of computer interfaces has been extended to hearing related problems. The authors of [20] designed data glasses to help hearing impaired peoples in the workforce. Head-mounted displays have also been extended to support sound localization. In [21], researchers designed peripheral sound displays to support sound awareness.

The authors of [22] created a prototype head-mounted visual display that supported sound localization capabilities. However, the prototype required an in-room multi-array system of microphones to function. This means that the device will not work in most social environments, as most environments do not have microphones in them.

Objective. [22] 's work demonstrated the possibility of applying head-mounted computer interfaces to the sound localization problem, but it required in-room apparatus. The objective of this paper is to design a new smart glass that solves the sound localization problem and is also self-contained to increase the potential usability of these new devices.

2 Materials and Methods

2.1 Design

This paper proposes the implementation of a novel device to solve the sound localization problem, named EyeHear. The device consists of a head-mounted visual display (HMVD) with a rectangular microphone system mounted above the device. The visual display shows the direction and transcription of one speech source, in real-time.

Hardware. The authors use a Google Glass Explorer Edition as an HMVD because the specific Google Glass model supports the development and implementation of new applications. Two microphone arrays, each with two microphones, are mounted on each arm of the Google Glass. A 3D mold was designed to support mounting capabilities. Microphones are wired to a USB Audio Interface, which is connected to a microprocessor, namely the Raspberry Pi Model 4B, due to its powerful computational abilities and small form factor (Figs. 2 and 3).

Fig. 2. CAD model of HDVM and real-life hardware prototype. Microphones are mounted on a 3D plastic mold using adhesive. The 3D mold slides into each arm of the Google Glass.

Fig. 3. CAD model of microprocessor and real-life hardware prototype. The Raspberry Pi is protected by a case. The microphone connects to a USB Audio Interface, which is connected to the microprocessor. This subsection is powered by a portable battery pack.

The HDVM is positioned on the user's head. To avoid physical strain, the microprocessor, audio interface, and battery are positioned in a storage compartment below the user's head, such as in a pocket or backpack.

Software. In order to estimate the direction of a speech source, a combination of sound localization and speech recognition algorithms must be used. The authors applied a modified form of the Generalized Cross Correlation Phase Transform (GCC-PHAT) algorithm to localize sounds and the IBM Speech-To-Text Transcription service to estimate speech.

Sound Localization. The GCC-PHAT algorithm compares the time differences between the amplitudes of two audio chunks (100 ms chunks) in order to estimate direction. Let *x(i)* and *y(i)* represent two microphones, with *i* being the amplitude at a specific frame. Let *d* represent delay and *mx* and *my* represent the mean amplitude of both microphones. The algorithm can be mathematically represented as:

$$r(d) = \frac{\sum_i [(x(i) - mx) * y(i - d) - my)]}{\sqrt{\sum_i (y(i - d) - my)^2}\sqrt{\sum_i (y(i - d) - my)^2}} \quad (1)$$

The algorithm frame shifts one signal and calculates how similar the modified signal is to the other signal. Once all delays are tested, it results in an array of cross-correlation values. The algorithm indexes the delay where the two audio signals are most similar, representing the time difference between two audio signals (τ).

$$\tau = \text{argmax}(r(d)) \quad (2)$$

Then, the direction can be calculated, by utilizing the speed of sound (c) and the distance between the two microphones (D).

$$\theta = \arcsin\left(\frac{\tau c}{D}\right) \quad (3)$$

The same steps are applied to the other microphone array. Finally, the two-direction estimations can be compared to estimate source position and direction. The entire process is repeated for every incoming audio chunk to support real-time sound localization.

Interface. The HMVD shows the calculated direction and speech. An arrow on a circle indicates the direction of the speech source and the transcription is shown in the middle (Fig. 4).

Fig. 4. User's perspective of the HMVD. User sees an arrow pointing towards the speaker and shows their speech. Image simulated.

2.2 Testing

Testing aimed to evaluate the robustness of the sound localization algorithm and gather feedback from the hearing-impaired population. Sound localization testing evaluated whether the device could be technically feasible as a self-contained device, and user feedback was conducted to affirm that the device would be favored by the target audience.

Algorithmic Testing. Noise and reverberation can interfere with sound localization accuracies. As the sound localization algorithm was the most critical element of the design, as well as the deciding factor for the design feasibility, the first experiment aimed to test the robustness of direction and speech conditions under a variety of noise conditions.

The microphone pairs were tested in two conditions: an 18' × 14' × 8' anechoic chamber, devoid of interfering variables such as noise and reverberation, and a noisy room, with a background generator creating artificial noise. The anechoic chamber served as the "control group" where the authors could verify that the design is feasible under optimal conditions and compared that to the experimental group, the noisy room, so that the authors could verify that the design was robust in real-world talking situations (Fig. 5).

In the experiment, a human speaker was positioned such that they were within 1 m to 4 m from the loudspeaker. Six trials of this experiment were run. A computer program ensured that the trials were spread out in 360°. Due to the size constraints of the two rooms, the microphones were turned around in order to simulate a 360-degree range of testing. In each trial, the human speaker orated a random 10 s speech sample previously

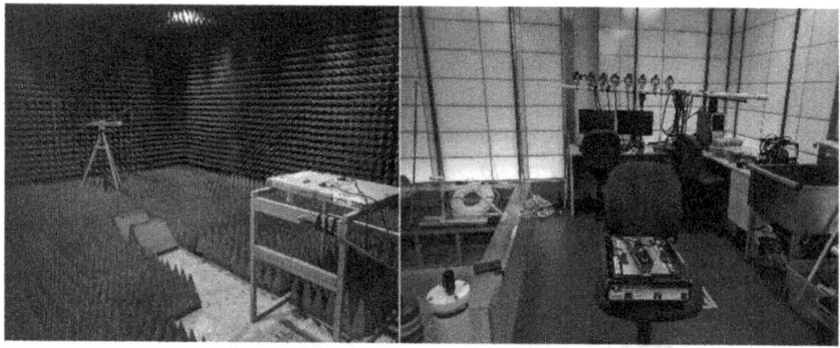

Fig. 5. Images of both testing conditions. Anechoic chamber is on the left and the noisy room is on the right.

determined by the authors. The purpose of random speech was to put the algorithm under a variety of speech frequencies and modulations. This process was used for both conditions (Fig. 6).

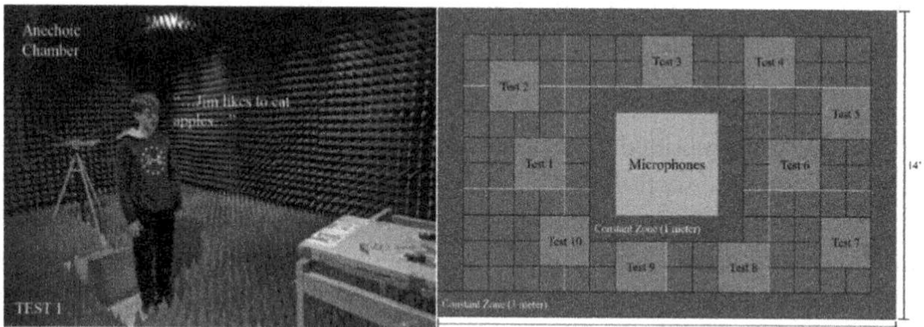

Fig. 6. Image of one test case where a human speaker is talking next to a map of all the trials. A computer randomization program ensures that there is a 360 spread of the trials.

When the human speaker begins orating, the microphones are tasked with estimating the direction of the speech source as well as transcribe the speech of the source, in real-time. Each trial results in a predicted direction and speech transcription, which will be analyzed.

User Testing. While the authors did work with the hearing impaired to construct the ideal design, it was important to reconsult with the target audience to receive opinions, gain insights on future design, and evaluate the future commercialization of the design.

Twelve hearing impaired volunteers, with no previous knowledge or bias of the project, participated in the user testing experiment. Participants were on average 62.6 years old (SD = 13.7, range 44–88) and had varying degrees of hearing loss, ranging from marginal to profound (range 15–91 + dB HL). The demographic of our sample population is representative of the older hearing-impaired population; however, future work should also receive feedback from young adults and children.

The authors met with each volunteer individually to avoid group bias. Each participant experienced the device, by either wearing it or receiving an informatory presentation, whichever one they preferred. Afterwards, the participants completed an anonymous online survey privately. The purpose of this user testing design was to achieve the most ethical and honest results (Fig. 7).

Fig. 7. A conversation with a hearing-impaired person (left). Participant agreed to be photographed.

First, participants inputted their demographic ranges (age, income, hearing loss level). The demographic section was optional but strongly encouraged. Next, the survey entailed a design rubric for the prototype, prompting participants to complete the rubric based on the design dimensions (intuitiveness, sound localization, future commercial success) set by the initial volunteers. The use of a metric was to make the survey as objective as possible. Finally, participants were given a chance to add final thoughts on the design and its implications for the hearing-impaired community (Fig. 8).

Question 9. On a scale of 1 to 5, how beneficial would our sound localization feature be for you? Will it assist you in adverse listening conditions? Will it open up new situations to communicate in? Will it be an added convenience? (Select one.)

O 1 – Useless. Sound localization feature offers no benefit to me. It will not increase the accuracy I localize and will not help me communicate in new environments.	O 2 – Insignificant. Sound localization feature offers little benefit to me. It will insignificantly increase accuracy I localize and will not assist me that much in communicating	O 3 – Mediocre. Sound localization feature offers moderate benefit to me. It increases my sound localization ability and will assist me in communicating, but I will be fine without it.	O 4 – Significant. Sound localization feature offers significant benefit to me. It increases my sound localization ability so much that I would prefer having it when communicating.	O 5 – Great. Sound localization feature offers immense benefit to me. It increases my sound localization ability such that it is essential in communicating in adverse listening conditions.

Fig. 8. Example rubric-type question on the survey. Question asks participant to rate a design dimension (sound localization feature) using a metric.

Surveys resulted in objective ratings of the design, which will be discussed later.

Ethics. Due to the interactive nature of user testing, participants were informed of their ability to withdraw from the experiment at any time. Prior to introduction of the device, subjects completed a consent form, permitting the use of their data. Finally, private demographic information (age, income, hearing loss) corresponding to participants was not released to maintain confidentiality for volunteers.

3 Results and Discussion

Sound localization testing and user testing were both successful, confirming that a self-contained device would be technically feasible and indicates that solving the sound localization problem will make a very positive impact on the hearing impaired.

3.1 Algorithmic Testing

Results. Due to the nature of experimentation, the researchers know the actual direction and speech prior to the sound localization algorithm predictions. To calculate the speech recognition accuracy, researchers used a standard Word Error Rate formula. To calculate direction accuracy, the authors used a percent error formula.

Average direction estimation and speech recognition accuracies in the anechoic chamber were approximately 91% and 90%, respectively. In the noisy environment, average direction estimation and speech recognition accuracies were about 75% and 85%, respectively (Fig. 9).

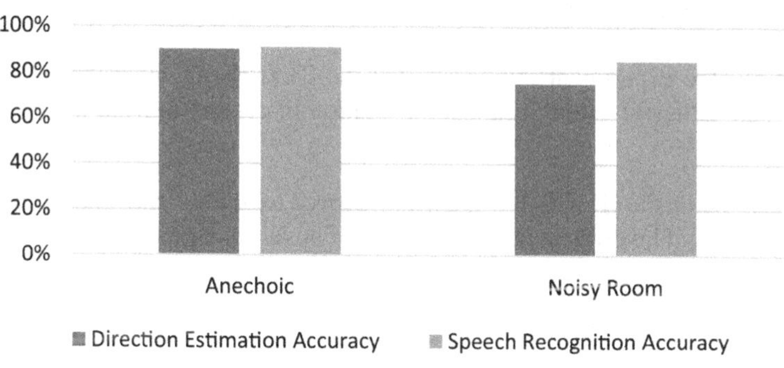

Fig. 9. Direction and speech recognition accuracies in a noiseless and noisy environment.

Discussion. There was a substantial reduction in direction estimate accuracy in the noisy environment but minimal reduction in speech recognition accuracy. Some reduction was expected for both variables, as noise interferes with the algorithm, however, the substantial reduction in direction estimation was surprising.

As noise reaches the audio frames, the GCC-PHAT may produce incorrect cross correlation values, leading to inaccuracies. However, 75% is still relatively accurate in context to direction estimation. It is not imperative to know the exact degree, knowing the general direction is still beneficial. Considering this, the direction estimation accuracy proves that it is feasible in real-world noisy talking situations. The results make it apparent that this device would be optimal in quiet situations, with few persons in the environment.

Another pattern noticed in the data was that noises to the extreme left or right of microphones were drastically inaccurate (Fig. 10).

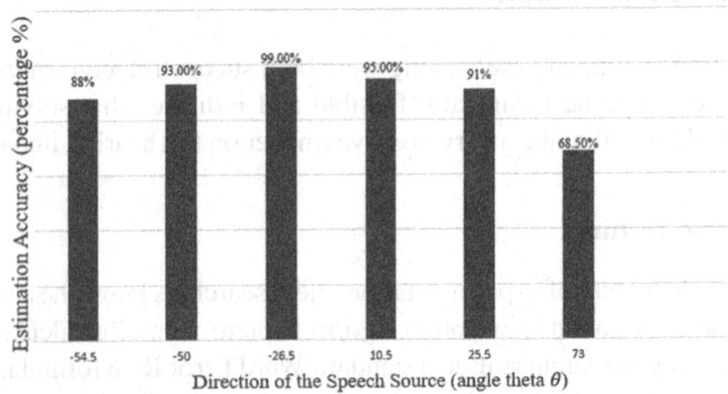

Fig. 10. Estimation accuracy based on the direction of the speech source. The 73 angle, which is to the direct right of the microphones is drastically less accurate than the other values.

When the audio source is to the extreme left or right, the frame differences between the two captured audio signals is so minimal that the algorithm may not be able to identify the difference and produce an accurate cross correlation value. This problem is exacerbated in the noisy environment, as noise also interferes with frame differences calculations.

All in all, the experiment implicates that the GCC-PHAT algorithm is a simple, effective, and sufficient sound localization solution in context to head-mounted visual displays.

Limitations. While the GCC-PHAT algorithm proved to be efficient, it has its problems. Future work should investigate the applications of novel sound localizations algorithms for head-mounted devices.

3.2 User Testing

Results. Participants rated the device on 3 design dimensions (sound localization feature, intuitiveness, future commercial success). The sound localization feature received an average score of 4.6. Participants rated the design a 4.16 on intuitiveness (Figs. 11 and 12).

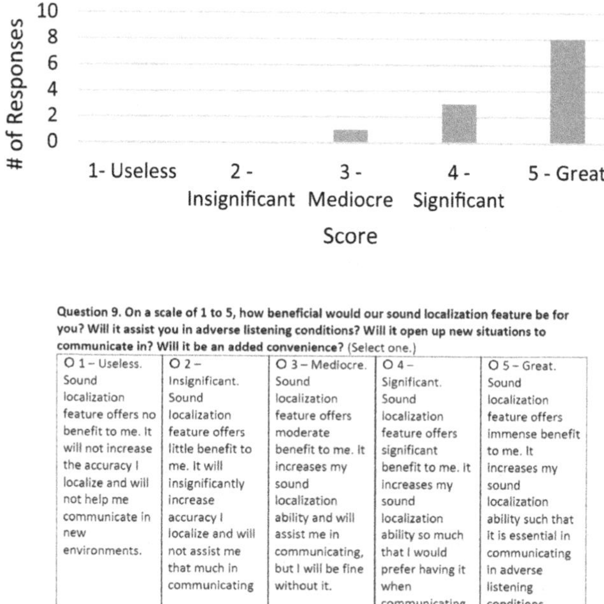

Question 9. On a scale of 1 to 5, how beneficial would our sound localization feature be for you? Will it assist you in adverse listening conditions? Will it open up new situations to communicate in? Will it be an added convenience? (Select one.)

O 1 – Useless. Sound localization feature offers no benefit to me. It will not increase the accuracy I localize and will not help me communicate in new environments.	O 2 – Insignificant. Sound localization feature offers little benefit to me. It will insignificantly increase accuracy I localize and will not assist me that much in communicating	O 3 – Mediocre. Sound localization feature offers moderate benefit to me. It increases my sound localization ability and will assist me in communicating, but I will be fine without it.	O 4 – Significant. Sound localization feature offers significant benefit to me. It increases my sound localization ability so much that I would prefer having it when communicating.	O 5 – Great. Sound localization feature offers immense benefit to me. It increases my sound localization ability such that it is essential in communicating in adverse listening conditions.

Fig. 11. Responses for on sound localization feature and the actual question from the survey. The question is designed to elicit a quantitative response, while still being objective in process.

When evaluating future commercial success, the authors chose to use open-ended questions to gain insight on the device's future, as it is very difficult to objectively evaluate this. Thus, the survey consisted of open-ended questions where participants shared their thoughts (Fig. 13).

Discussion. At a score of 4.6, the sound localization feature received an overwhelmingly positive response. This implicates that solving the sound localization problem is something very important to the hearing impaired, suggesting the production of more solutions like this one. The Graphical User Interface received a less enthusiastic but still positive response, getting a rating of 4.16. Finally, when interpreting the comments, it is noticed that the volunteers immediately saw applications of the device in their personal lives. This suggests possible commercial success.

Limitations. The rating for the Graphical User Interface indicates that while the interface design is sufficient, improvements should be made. Future work can investigate specific interfaces for the hearing impaired.

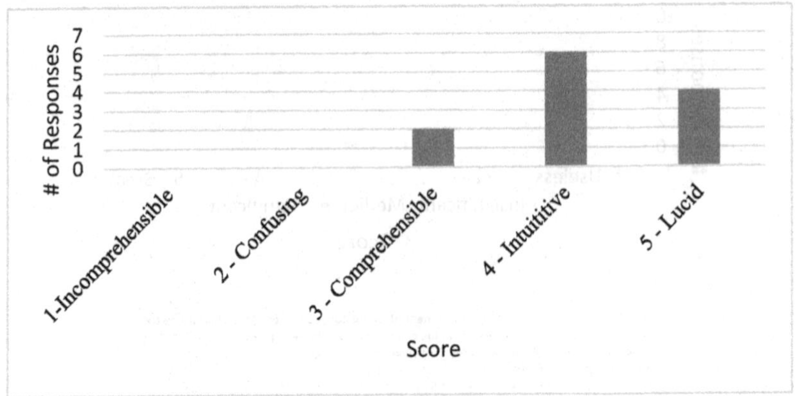

Question 10. On a scale of 1 to 5, how easy is it to use our intuitive Graphical User Interface? If you were to put it on for the first time, how much of it would you understand? How long would it take you to understand the system? (Select one.)

O 1 – Incomprehensible. GUI does not make any sense at all. I do not understand it.	O 2 – Confusing. Most of the GUI does not make sense. Some of it makes sense after thinking about, but overall, it's confusing.	O 3 – Comprehensible. It takes me some time to get used to it, but I understand all elements of the GUI, I wouldn't have displayed the way that it is.	O 4 – Intuitive. GUI make innate sense. It takes some time, but I understand all elements of the GUI. GUI makes logical sense. I would have also displayed in the same way.	O 5 – Lucid. GUI immediately makes sense. It is clear, logical, and exactly the way I would have displayed it.

Fig. 12. Responses for Intuitiveness design dimensions and the actual question from the survey. The question is designed to elicit a quantitative response, while still being objective in process.

"[Sound localization] distinguishes [it] from other technology."
"Normal hearing aids don't help you know where it is."
"Clearly has the potential to increase safety for the severely hearing impaired. Where did that sound come from? Is it a threat? Now, I know where to look."
"It's neat that I would be looking at the person with their words appearing on the glasses. I wouldn't have to guess at what they are saying."

Fig. 13. Some responses from the open-ended section. The purpose of the open-ended survey was to gain insight on the potential for commercialization.

4 Conclusion

Device presents a possible solution for the sound localization problem. Unfortunately, the device encountered few drawbacks not previously shown by past work. Future work should aim to eliminate those drawbacks (discussed below).

Contributions. We have designed a solution that effectively solves the sound localization problem. Sound localization testing proves that the microphone system, even with the design constraints, can sufficiently estimate the direction of speech sources in real-world noisy and non-noisy talking situations. User testing expresses that this device is favored by the hearing-impaired community, and that sound localization features should be investigated in future work.

Shortcomings. Currently, the device can only localize speech-related sounds. It would be a bonus if the device could directionalize important non-speech sounds, such as cars, to increase spatial awareness for the user. Second, the device can only localize one speech source. In many environments, more than one person is talking, and it would be nice to know the direction and speech of multiple talkers. Third, user testing indicates that the Graphical User Interface can be more intuitive.

Future Work. Future work should extend the device's capabilities to non-speech sounds. That could entail applying or modifying preexisting algorithms to even creating novel sound localization algorithms for the specific purpose of smart glass use. Moreover, new sound localization algorithms could feature the ability to showcase multiple speakers in real-time. Lastly, future work should also investigate new interface designs and seek the feedback of the hearing impaired.

Final Remarks. We hope that this device could someday be used by the hearing impaired to help them gain more spatial awareness, improving their quality of life. In the future, it would be amazing if commercial entities produce devices based on this research to bring this prototype to life. We hope that this research helps the hearing impaired.

Acknowledgements. The authors thank Dr. Sam Sennott, Dr. Martin Siderius, and Darcy Kramer for their support and advice. The authors thank the THINK science research program at the Massachusetts Institute of Technology for their funding and mentorship. The authors thank faculty at the Oregon School for the Deaf, and hearing-impaired residents of the Hillsboro community. The authors thank Benjamin Marquez. Lastly, the authors thank the dear friends and family who are members of the hearing-impaired population, who inspired the authors to pursue this work.

References

1. Middlebrooks, J., Green, D.: Sound localization by human listeners. Ann. Rev. Psychol. **42**, 135–159 (1991)
2. Jeffress, L.: A place theory on sound localization. J. Comp. Physiol. Psychol. **41**(1), 35–39 (1948)
3. Musicant, A., Butler, R.: The influence of pinnae-based spectral cues on sound localization. J. Acoust. Soc. Am. **75**(4), 1195–1200 (1984)
4. Abel, S., Hay, V.: Sound localization the interaction of aging, hearing loss and hearing protection. Scand. Audiol. **25**(1), 3–12 (1996)
5. Noble, W., Byrne, D., Lepage, B.: Effects on sound localization of configuration and type of hearing impaired. J. Acoust. Soc. Am. **95**(2), 992–1005 (1994)

6. Lorenzi, C., Gatehouse, S., Lever, C.: Sound localization in noise in hearing-impaired listeners. J. Acoust. Soc. Am. **105**(6), 3454–3463 (1999)
7. Kuk, F., Korhonen, P.: Localization 101: hearing aid factors in localization. Hear. Rev. **21**(9), 26–33 (2014)
8. Feinkohl, A.: Psychophysical experiments on sound localization in starlings and humans. Carl von Ossietzky Universität Oldenberg)
9. Lesica, N.: Why do hearing aids fail to restore normal auditory perception? Trends Neurosci. **41**(4), 174–185 (2018)
10. Cochlear Implants. https://nidcd.nih.gov/health/cochlear-implants. Accessed 1 June 2020
11. Grieco-Calub, T., Litovsky, R.: Spatial acuity in 2-to-3-year-old children with normal acoustic hearing, unilateral cochlear implants, and bilateral cochlear implants. Ear Hear. **33**(5), 561–572 (2012)
12. Mueller, M., Meisenbacher, K., Lai, W., Dillier, N.: Sound localization with bilateral cochlear implants in noise: how much do head movements contribute to localization? Cochlear Implants Int. **15**(1), 36–42 (2014)
13. Cochlear Implant Cost. www.babyhearing.org/devices/cochlear-implant-cost. Accessed 3 June 2020
14. McPherson, B.: Innovative technology in hearing instruments: matching needs in the developing world. Trends Amplif. **15**(4), 209–214 (2011)
15. Tucker, B.: Deaf culture, cochlear implants, and elective disability. Hastings Cent. Rep. **28**(4), 6–14 (1998)
16. Darcy, K.: Personal Interview, taken on 2019/1/18
17. American Sign Language. https://www.nidcd.nih.gov/health/american-sign-language. Accessed 10 June 2020
18. Mitchell, R., Young, T., Bachleda, B., Karchmer, M.: How many people use ASL in the United States? Why estimates need updating. Sign Lang. Stud. **6**(3), 306–335 (2006)
19. Assistive Devices for People with Hearing, Voice, Speech, or Language Disorders. https://www.nidcd.nih.gov/health/assistive-devices-people-hearing-voice-speech-or-language-disorders. Accessed 4 June 2020
20. Matthias vom Stein, A., Günthner, W.: Work-by-Inclusion - Inclusive information system for picking using smart glasses. ZWF Magazine for Economical Factory Operation, vol. 112, no. 10, pp. 670–674 (2017)
21. Ho-Ching, F., Mankoff, J., Landay, A.: Can you see what I hear? The design and evaluation of peripheral sound display for the deaf. In: SIGCHI Conference on Human Factors in Computing Systems, pp. 161–168. Association for Computing Machinery, New York (2003)
22. Jain, D., et al.: Head-mounted display visualizations to support sound awareness for the deaf and hard of hearing. In: 33rd Annual ACM Conference on Human Factors in Computing Systems (CHI 2015), pp. 241–250. Association for Computing machinery, New York (2015)

Web Accessibility in Portuguese Museums: Potential Constraints on Interaction for People with Disabilities

Pedro Teixeira[1], Diana Lemos[1], Maria João Carneiro[2], Celeste Eusébio[2], and Leonor Teixeira[3](✉)

[1] Department of Economics, Management, Industrial Engineering and Tourism, University of Aveiro, 3010-193 Aveiro, Portugal
{pmiguel,dianalemos}@ua.pt

[2] Governance, Competitiveness and Public Policies, Department of Economics, Management, Industrial Engineering and Tourism, University of Aveiro, 3010-193 Aveiro, Portugal
{mjcarneiro,celeste.eusebio}@ua.pt

[3] Institute of Electronics and Informatics Engineering of Aveiro, Department of Economics, Management, Industrial Engineering and Tourism, University of Aveiro, 3010-193 Aveiro, Portugal
lteixeira@ua.pt

Abstract. Museums play a major role as tourism attractions worldwide. Nevertheless, and despite the increasing awareness of the need to improve accessibility for people with disabilities in tourism, museum websites are still identified by this group as a major constraint for visiting and having pleasurable experiences in museums. Despite the existence of constraints in this scope, empirical research that examines the accessibility of museums websites is very scarce with only one study being known in this field. Even this study only considers a small set of museums in one region of the United States and adopts a non-automatic, and thus subjective procedure, not enabling great conclusions about the accessibility of these museum web platforms. The present paper aims to fill some of the previous gaps by assessing the accessibility of websites of museums located in Portugal. To achieve this aim, a total of 575 websites of museums located across different regions were assessed using two automated tools based on the Web Content Accessibility Guidelines: AccessMonitor and *Test de Accesibilidad Web*. Results reveal that although websites of museums present higher levels of accessibility than those of other tourism supply agents, they still have several accessibility problems that must be solved. Findings also show that there is a higher prevalence of failures related to the 'perceivable' and 'robust' principles, and that the accessibility level differs among the NUTS II regions where museums are located. The paper ends by identifying the main conclusions and the major implications for designers or managers of these websites.

Keywords: Accessible tourism · Web accessibility · Museums

C. Stephanidis et al. (Eds.): HCII 2020, LNCS 12426, pp. 371–386, 2020.
https://doi.org/10.1007/978-3-030-60149-2_29

1 Introduction

The growing concern with accessibility and the elimination of barriers in tourism, not only at the physical and attitudinal levels but also in terms of information, is becoming one of the main research problems across different sectors. The Internet has become a vehicle for delivering information, communication, leisure, and work that replaces or complements conventional forms of disclosure or provision of a service [1]. However, there are still great barriers to web accessibility for people with disabilities (PwD) [2]. To increase the participation of PwD in tourism activities, it is of utmost relevance to overcome web accessibility barriers in all components of the tourism industry (e.g. accommodation, transport, tour operators, travel agents and tourism attractions such as museums) [3–7]. This kind of accessibility is essential to ensure that PwD are not excluded from tourism activities, since the greater the accessibility requirements, the greater is the need for providing detailed information in an accessible way [8].

Currently, the Internet is one of the main sources of information used by visitors, including visitors with disabilities [9, 10]. Sharing information online is very important in order to transmit more security and confidence to visitors with disabilities during the decision-making process [2]. However, there are still many barriers which result in difficulties in using websites [11]. Therefore, there is a need for recommendations and legislation to guide website creators. Mineiro [12] explained, in a good practices guide, that website content should be easily located and that there must be indications about this, as well as having text alternatives to non-text content, and that listening and viewing main elements should be highlighted on the page presented. The elimination of barriers will allow people with disabilities, who often travel accompanied [13] in the hope of overcoming these barriers, to feel more confident in traveling. To increase the websites' accessibility levels, and to help designers and developers to create websites which are more accessible to PwD, the Web Content Accessibility Guidelines (WCAG) were developed by the World Wide Web Consortium [14]. These guidelines are taken as a reference at a worldwide level, as they are becoming a reference for increasing website accessibility for PwD.

This work intends to explore web accessibility in museums, which are important cultural tourism attractions for a great number of visitors. In this context, the museums' websites are important for PwD in planning their tourism trips [15, 16]. Although there are many countries where the legislation establishes the minimum requirements to ensure the accessibility of public spaces, information about museum accessibility is often neglected, and has become one of the barriers that many PwD face when they intend to visit museums. Despite the recognized importance of digital accessibility in museology [18–20], only a few studies are known that assess the level of accessibility of museum websites [17–20]. Moreover, researchers only consider a very small set of museums, and adopt a non-automatic, and thus subjective, procedure. The lack of research is even greater when considering the Portuguese case, where no study of this type is known. With the aim of increasing knowledge in this area, this study aims to analyze the level of accessibility of museum websites in Portugal, based on the WCAG 2.0 [14] using two web diagnostic tools: AccessMonitor and TAW (*Test de Accesibilidad Web*). The study also intends to ascertain if there are differences in the level of accessibility of museum websites according to their location in the Portuguese national territory (NUTS

II). Based on the results obtained in this study, the accessibility barriers that PwD face when interacting with the websites of Portuguese museums are identified and discussed.

The present paper is structured in five sections. In this introduction the relevance and the aims of the paper are highlighted. Next, there is a discussion on human-computer interaction and usability in tourism, on web accessibility and, specifically, on web accessibility of museums, based on a literature review. Then, the methodology of the empirical paper is described, and the results of the study are presented and discussed. Finally, there is an identification of the main conclusions and implications of the paper for designing and developing websites, and suggestions for further research are provided.

2 Literature Review

2.1 Human-Computer Interaction, Usability, and Accessibility in Tourism

In the field of human-computer interaction (HCI), the concepts of usability and accessibility have gained importance over recent years, due to the increase in the number of interactive applications, and particularly the growth of the Internet. While the term usability is a substitute for the terms 'user friendliness' and 'ease of use' [21], accessibility is a broader term and refers to the way in which products, devices, services, or environments are designed so as to be usable by people with disabilities [6].

In the tourism sector, these terms have become increasingly important, since the most immediate process for finding tourism products and solutions is an Internet search. When a visitor intends to gather information about a tourism offer, they usually search on different platforms, such as websites. These tasks are related to inserting inputs in search engines, understanding and clicking through the results, evaluating the results, reformulating the search, and then clicking on the intended information [22]. As described by Wang, Hawk, and Tenopir [23], information search processes for visitors can be illustrated as an interaction between three parties: the visitor, the interface (the platform that interacts with the visitor), and the tourism information space. The interface and subsequently interaction of tourism platforms are directly related to HCI in tourism and have been explored as a major challenge to the flow of information across different sectors [24]. As expected, PwD have greater requirements for information, as well as special needs during the information search process, for planning their trips, and feel highly constrained when this information is inexistent or when it is difficult to access [25, 26].

HCI and a good interaction experience can be considered as major factors for PwD to truly make the most of a tourism product. For example, access to culture, where museums play an important role, should be facilitated with that interaction, allowing usability to visitors with disabilities. Engaging visitors in museums by using different technologies, such as web platforms, is a great challenge [27], especially regarding information flow, as visitors intend to gather more knowledge about the architectural conditions [15]. There is thus a growing concern with the interaction and usability of tourism-related web platforms for PwD. Despite this, the accessible tourism market is very heterogeneous [28], as visitors with disabilities have different demands and information requirements [29]. In this line of thought, the concept of web accessibility makes it urgent to overcome these potential constraints and ensure successful interaction between visitors with disabilities and web platforms.

2.2 Web Accessibility

Although the lack of physical and attitudinal barriers are considered as grave impediments for PwD [13], the presence of information and the way it is communicated often constitute the main obstacle in the field of accessible tourism [30]. With web platforms taking the central stage in sharing information across diverse sectors, web accessibility is becoming a crucial matter. Web accessibility can be expressed as the degree to which a website allows access to the greatest possible number of people, including PwD [31]. It was in this sense that guidelines and legislation [4] were created for greater and better accessibility on the web, with the Guidelines for Accessibility for Web Content, developed by the World Wide Web Consortium, also known as W3C, being one of the most important. The W3C is an international organization dedicated to standardizing the World Wide Web and making content more accessible [32]. Despite the fact that there exist different versions, the WCAG 2.0 launched in 2008 is the most widely used today, since it became an ISO standard: ISO/IEC 40500 [33]. This version is divided into four principles of web accessibility, according to the World Wide Web Consortium website [34]: (i) perceivable—the information and user interface components must be presented to users in a way that they can perceive; (ii) operable—user interface and navigation components must be operable and navigable; (iii) understandable—the information and operation of the user interface must be understandable; and (iv) robust—the content must be robust enough to be able to be reliably interpreted by different types of users, including assistive technologies. Within these four principles, there are thirteen accessibility guidelines or success criteria that can be tested and evaluated according to three levels of compliance: A (the lowest), AA, and AAA (the highest) [35]. Currently, different tools use WCAG 2.0 as a standard for performing web accessibility evaluations [36].

2.3 Web Accessibility in Museums

PwD find it very important to have useful information on the website regarding accessibility conditions, in order to be able to plan better and avoid possible barriers [15, 16]. Due to this group of people's high need for information, it is essential to analyze websites to ensure that the type of information conveyed and the level of accessibility when accessing information is appropriate. To this end, legislation is crucial. However, Michopoulu, and Buhalis [30] claim that although there are many countries where legislation establishes minimum requirements to ensure the accessibility of public spaces, information about museum accessibility is often neglected. It is extremely important to provide this same ease of access to information for museums in a reliable and detailed way in order to meet market needs [30, 37]. In the case of Portugal, regarding accessibility in information, Portuguese law, more precisely Decree-Law No. 83/2018 (2018), defines the guidelines for the web accessibility of the websites of public bodies.

Only one study was found that evaluated web accessibility in museums. Furthermore, it did not use automatic evaluation tools. This makes it difficult to draw conclusions on the current state of web accessibility in museums. However, in a survey undertaken by Argyropoulos and Kanari [20] on museum accessibility, website accessibility was one of the most critical factors identified. Also, this lack of accessibility worked as motivation for Luccio and Beltrame [19] to develop a WIX website that, despite all content limitations, obtained a good web accessibility evaluation from potential users. Another study by Mangani and Bassi [18] tried to ascertain if the museums in Tuscany (Italy) have online information for PwD, and only a restricted group of those museums analyzed took information needs for visitors with disabilities into consideration. Finally, only one study, undertaken by Langa et al. [17], examined the accessibility levels of websites belonging to a small set of museums (less than 15) of the Mid-Atlantic region of the United States, based on the guidelines for accessible web design of the United States Rehabilitation Act, using a non-automatic evaluation tool. Websites were revealed to be lacking in several areas regarding web accessibility features. As web accessibility in tourism is a crucial matter, the present study intends to provide significant contributions by exploring the particular case of the web accessibility state of Portuguese museums.

3 Methodology

3.1 Data Collection

The evaluation of the museum websites' accessibility levels was conducted using a multiphase method. First, to find the museum websites, two platforms were consulted: (i) *Museus de Portugal* (available at http://museusportugal.org/) and (ii) *Direção Geral do Património Cultural* (available at http://www.patrimoniocultural.gov.pt/en/). Next a search on the Google platform was also carried out to complement the information obtained on the two abovementioned platforms. Finally, the websites of city councils were also analyzed to identify some museum websites that are managed by these organizations. With the results obtained in this search, a database with the name of the museum, the website link and the location of the museum was created. This database includes 681 museums across the country, but only 575 (83.92%) had a working website.

3.2 Data Analysis Methods

To examine the web accessibility of the Portuguese museums, two automatic tools were used: (i) AccessMonitor and TAW (*Test de Accesibilidad Web*). These tools provided the necessary features to carry out a study of this type and they have already proved to be very useful for studies in tourism measuring web accessibility. AccessMonitor is a software application that was developed by the Portuguese Foundation for Science and Technology and that analyzes websites according to the accessibility guidelines for the web (WCAG 2.0). The website link is inserted on the AccessMonitor page and the accessibility index is automatically generated, with the errors found on the website being presented by degree of compliance (A, AA, and AAA). Moreover, this tool provides an AccessMonitor global index. This index ranges from 1 (very poor web accessibility practice) to 10 (excellent web accessibility practice). This tool has been used to examine the accessibility level of tourism activities in Portugal [38–40].

TAW is also an automatic online tool which has been referenced in some studies. It verifies the level of accessibility of websites taking into account the WCAG 2.0 guidelines, but the results are presented in 3 levels, namely "problems" (corrections are needed), "warnings" (points out the need for a technical review) and "unverified" (not reviewed). However, given that almost the same values were obtained on all analyzed websites, the "not reviewed" data were not examined in this study. Like AccessMonitor, TAW has often been used to analyze the web accessibility of tourism supply agents [3, 7, 31, 41–43].

Analysis of the websites and data collected from both tools was carried out during July and August 2019. Quantitative analysis was performed with SPSS – Software Package for the Social Sciences. Descriptive statistics were used to characterize the sample and the level of web accessibility in the Portuguese museums analyzed. Moreover, to check if there are differences in the level of accessibility of museum websites according to their geographic location, bivariate statistical techniques were used, namely the *Kruskal-Wallis* test, as the assumptions of the ANOVA test were not met in most cases.

4 Results and Discussion

4.1 Sample Profile

Of the 682 museums that were identified in this research as existing in Portugal, 575 have a website (84.3%), and 107 museums do not (15.7%). Therefore, 575 websites were analyzed with the tools AccessMonitor and TAW. Figure 1 presents the location of the museums analyzed in terms of NUTS II. The Central region of Portugal is the region with the largest number of museums analyzed (29.9%) followed by the Metropolitan Area of Lisbon (23.1%) and the North region (19.8%).

4.2 Website Accessibility Analysis

Results Obtained with AccessMonitor. The first analysis was conducted with AccessMonitor, as the results of the global access index and the total errors were collected. Table 1 illustrates the values for the global index. The average of the global accessibility index of museum websites is 5.80. However, the Algarve region and the Metropolitan Area of Lisbon stand out with 6.62 and 6.03 respectively, with better accessibility than the average in Portugal. The minimum value was recorded in the Autonomous Region of Madeira (4.13).

In terms of errors found by the level of compliance (A, AA, and AAA), the results presented in Table 2 reveal that, on average, 7.51 errors were detected on each website analyzed, with compliance level A (the lowest compliance level) showing the highest average number of errors per website (4.98). As for AA compliance errors, websites have an average of 1 error and the AAA level has an average of 1.6 errors per website. Moreover, differences in the number of errors identified according to the location of the museum were observed. The websites belonging to museums located in the Autonomous Region of Madeira and the Alentejo show a much higher number of errors than the national average, while the websites of museums located in the Algarve and the Metropolitan Area of Lisbon have a number of errors which is much lower than the national average.

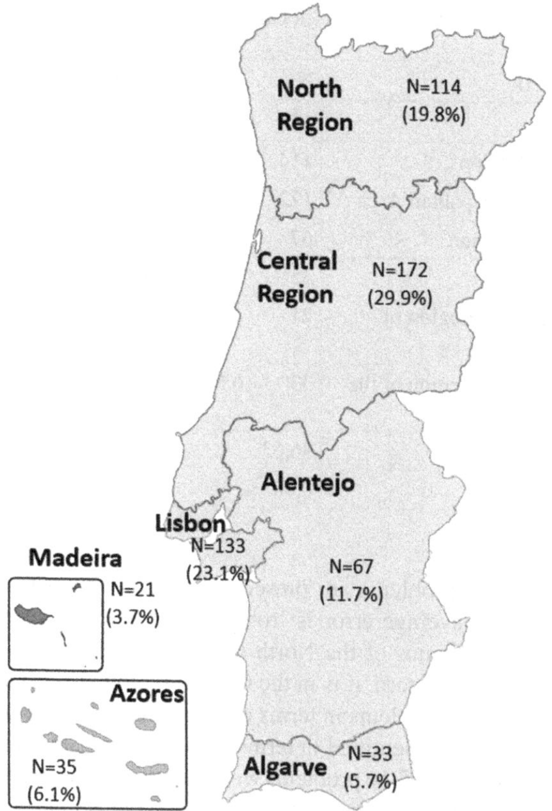

Fig. 1. Location of the museums analyzed

A deeper analysis of the type A errors highlights that the websites of museums located in the Autonomous Region of Madeira have the highest average of errors, while the websites of museums located in the Algarve have the lowest average of errors. In turn, in terms of type AA errors, museums located in Madeira also have the highest average of this type of error, while museums located in the Azores have the lowest average of errors. Finally, in terms of type AAA errors, the museums located in the Alentejo have the highest average of errors and those located in the North are the ones that have fewer accessibility problems of this type. These results clearly reveal that apart from problems existing in terms of the accessibility of the museums websites, there is also heterogeneity across the country concerning this issue.

Results of Analysis with TAW. Analysis of web accessibility with the TAW tool allows identification of problems, warnings, and situations which the tool cannot verify (not reviewed). As explained in the methodology section, "not reviewed" was not analyzed in this paper, since results were not significantly different in the websites analyzed.

Table 1. AccessMonitor global index of museum websites

NUTS II	N	Mean	Standard deviation
North	133	6.03	1.91
Central Region	114	5.84	2.04
Lisbon Metropolitan Area	172	5.68	1.61
Alentejo Region	67	5.81	1.96
Algarve	35	5.57	0.97
Autonomous Region of Madeira	21	4.13	1.11
Autonomous Region of the Azores	33	6.62	1.54
Kruskal-Wallis	36.63		
p value	0.00		

The results regarding problems are presented in Table 3. Of the four principles, the one with the highest average error is 'robust', with the highest average of problems belonging on the websites of the North region (33.20), followed by the Lisbon Metropolitan Area (26.97). In turn, it is in the Central region (16.34) and in the Azores (16.46), that the average of problems in terms of robustness on websites is the lowest.

Concerning the problems identified in terms of the 'perceivable' principle, on average, in each website analyzed, 17.16 problems were identified, and the standard deviation was 30.01. It is also noted that the highest average of problems in terms of website visibility is clearly on the websites of the Autonomous Region of Madeira (50.33) followed by the Alentejo (24.30). In turn, it is in the Central region (10.74) and the Algarve (11.73) that the average of problems in terms of perceptibility on websites is lowest. Regarding the results obtained in terms of the 'Operability' principle, on average, each website analyzed presented 15.18 problems. It is also noted that the lowest average number of problems in terms of website operability is registered on the websites of the Autonomous Region of Madeira (9.05) followed by the Autonomous Region of the Azores (9.54). In turn, it is in the Metropolitan Area of Lisbon (18.56) and in the Central region (16.44) where the average of problems in terms of operability on the websites is highest. Regarding 'understandable' problems, the greatest average of problems in terms of understanding the website, is clearly on the websites of museums in the North (2.76) followed by the Azores (2.31). In turn, it is on the websites of the Algarve (0.85) and the Alentejo (1.04) that the average of problems in terms of understanding on the websites is lowest.

In summary, it can be observed that the biggest problems of the websites analyzed are found in terms of robustness and perceptibility. These results corroborate other studies that were carried out in the area [7, 40, 42]. Moreover, the results obtained with the *Kruskal-Wallis* test revealed statistically significant differences in the type of problems identified concerning the location of the museum.

Table 2. AccessMonitor errors in web accessibility of museum websites

NUTS II	A			AA			AAA			Total (A + AA + AAA)		
	N	Mean	Standard deviation	N	Mean	Standard deviation	N	Mean	Standard deviation	N	Mean	Standard deviation
North	133	4.56	3.22	133	0.94	0.92	133	1.43	0.81	133	6.92	4.139
Central Region	114	5.09	3.76	114	0.91	0.95	114	1.39	0.83	114	7.39	4.48
Lisbon Metropolitan Area	172	4.93	2.98	172	1.03	1.03	171	1.54	0.74	171	7.49	3.80
Alentejo Region	67	5.13	4.08	67	1.03	0.738	67	2.03	0.72	67	8.19	4.67
Algarve	35	5.20	2.18	35	0.71	0.79	35	1.83	0.69	35	7.74	2.661
Autonomous Region of Madeira	21	10.14	3.62	21	1.24	0.44	21	1.62	0.81	21	13.00	3.950
Autonomous Region of Azores	33	2.82	1.91	33	0.97	0.98	33	1.45	0.56	33	5.24	2.53
Total	575	4.98	3.46	575	0.97	0.93	574	1.56	0.78	574	7.51	4.190
Kruskal Wallis	45.39			9.84			39.22			40.76		
p value	0.00			0.13			0.00			0.00		

Table 3. Problems identified with TAW

NUT II	N	Identified Problems							
		Perceivable		Operable		Understandable		Robust	
		Mean	Standard deviation	Mean	Standard deviation	Mean	Standard deviation	Mean	Standard deviation
North	132	15.81	25.89	18.56	33.61	2.24	4.16	26.97	54.37
Central Region	114	20.55	42.92	15.06	24.40	2.76	6.77	33.20	48.90
Lisbon Metropolitan Area	172	10.74	9.31	16.44	37.84	1.82	2.13	16.34	32.57
Alentejo Region	67	24.30	36.11	10.61	23.59	1.04	1.76	22.55	36.88
Algarve	35	14.29	11.85	9.54	7.05	2.31	2.47	16.47	21.75
Autonomous Region of Azores	33	11.73	21.77	14.61	21.15	0.85	0.94	30.39	36.21
Autonomous Region of Madeira	21	50.33	56.00	9.05	36.88	1.57	0.81	25.19	36.46
Total	574	17.16	30.01	15.18	30.85	1.98	3.93	24.00	42.58
Kruskal-Wallis		37.67		22.90		34.95		21.51	
p-value		0.000		0.001		0.000		0.001	

The results obtained in terms of warnings (Table 4), pointed out the existence of possible problems, requiring human review to resolve them. Notably, the number of warnings exceeds the problems identified by a considerable margin. However, as in the case of the problems, the highest number of warmings are related to the 'perceivable' and 'robust' principles. The 'perceivable' principle has the highest average of notices (113.89) with the museums located in the Autonomous Region of Madeira having the highest average of warnings in the websites (247.38). In contrast, the museums located in the Algarve region reveal the lowest average of warnings related to the 'perceivable' principle (94.06).

In turn, the 'understandable' guideline presents a much lower average of errors than the other principles, with a value in the order of 6.81. Regarding this guideline, the websites of museums located in the Autonomous Region of Madeira have the lowest average errors (5.43), and North region has the highest number of warnings in this principle (19.97). The situation is quite similar in the 'robust' principle, with once again the North (116.32) being the region with the least accessible museums and the Azores (40.52) having the museums with fewest warnings. Finally, some similarities exist in the 'operable' principle, with the North region (64.37) being once again the least accessible region, but the Algarve (18.34) being the most accessible.

Table 4. Warnings identified with TAW

NUT II	N	Identified warnings							
		Perceivable		Operable		Understandable		Robust	
		Mean	Standard deviation	Mean	Standard deviation	Mean	Standard deviation	Mean	Standard deviation
North	114	94.62	101.42	54.93	101.56	6.51	6.56	89.01	197.84
Central Region	172	107.00	139.06	40.56	50.49	5.70	4.09	44.15	109.67
Lisbon Metropolitan Area	133	107.24	114.20	64.37	72.64	8.83	19.97	116.32	210.87
Alentejo Region	67	148.88	129.52	45.33	48.78	6.64	5.69	69.72	143.00
Algarve	33	94.06	148.79	42.06	28.50	7.21	4.47	40.52	142.19
Autonomous Region of Azores	35	107.34	240.35	18.34	16.48	6.34	4.10	70.74	73.32
Autonomous Region of Madeira	21	247.38	118.48	22.81	49.54	5.43	3,23	41.38	167.19
Total	575	113.89	137.03	47.56	67.76	6.81	10.62	74.02	164.68
Kruskal-Wallis		34.75		32.74		5.22		35.10	
p-value		0.000		0.000		0.517		0.001	

4.3 Discussion

Concerning the evaluation results reported by AccessMonitor, it was possible to conclude that accessibility of museum websites in Portugal follows "regular practice", with a mean of 5.80 on the global index, and a mean of 7.51 problems per website. When comparing the results to other types of tourism supply agents, such as hotels [39] and travel agencies [44], which also used AccessMonitor to evaluate the websites, the museum website results indicate a better performance.

The evaluation performed with TAW revealed a higher average of identified incidents in the principles 'perceivable' and 'robust', with 'understandable' being the principle with the lowest average of identified errors. These results are in line with those presented in the study conducted by Dominguez Vila, González, and Darcy [3], who analyzed official tourism websites, demonstrating that the 'perceptible' and robust' principles were the most critical in terms of recorded incidents. Other studies concerning official tourism websites [7, 31, 41, 43] also share some common agreements with the results found, since the analyzed websites failed in at least one WCAG criterion, which consequently may constitute a difficulty in accessing and navigating through websites for users with some type of disability or need. However, it should be noted that the average of detected errors is lower in the case of museums, compared to the official tourism websites.

The better results in the evaluation of the state of web accessibility in museums could be related to the fact that they are public entities, and in Portugal, legislation already exists concerning web accessibility guidelines (Decree-Law No. 83/2018). Nonetheless, the failures in some of the WCAG 2.0 guidelines, could mean that legislation alone is not enough, as the low results found may have a negative impact on the interaction process between PwD and web platforms. A closer look at the 'perceivable' principle allows us to understand that the failures in this guideline may prevent the flow of information, since it cannot be perceived. Specifically, issues are pointed out in the user interface, which cause problems by preventing the user from interacting completely with the platform. The same can be interpreted in the 'robust' principle, as the errors in its guidelines influence the use of assistive technologies, preventing the interaction of the assistive technology with the content on the web platform. Also, even though the 'understandable' and 'operable' principles are less affected, failures in the guidelines associated with them may bring up problems of interaction, regarding navigation interfaces and control functionalities.

Finally, another fact that was verified during the evaluation of the websites and which should be taken into account when designing websites is the statistical difference between the websites of different regions in Portugal. It could be seen that the North region displayed lower levels of web accessibility, while the Autonomous Region of the Azores and the Algarve achieved better web accessibility levels. This may indicate cultural differences by region with an impact on the type of consumption of tourism products and consequently on the adaptation of those products to different user needs. Even though the Algarve is a well-known destination for tourism in Portugal, the Azores have been experiencing a considerable increase in tourism demand in recent years. These differences mark a need for designing websites in such a way that everyone can access them. Therefore, in order to promote better practices and overcome barriers in HCI on museum websites and to make them more accessible to differently able people, a more universal design following the WCAG 2.0 accessibility guidelines should be applied by web developers.

5 Conclusion and Implications

The study evaluated the website accessibility of 575 museums located across different regions of Portugal using two automated tools, AccessMonitor and TAW, which are both based on WCAG 2.0. AccessMonitor allowed the identification of website components that should be improved, and TAW identified major problems and warnings according to the success criteria in WCAG 2.0. From the sample analyzed, it was possible to draw three main conclusions. First, the study revealed that the web accessibility level of the museums analyzed is medium, which is better than other tourism supply agents analyzed. Second, the 'perceivable' and 'robust' principles are the most critical, as they displayed the highest mean value of problems and warnings identified, hampering correct interaction between visitors with disabilities and museum web platforms. Third, the results reveal that, in most cases, there are statistically significant differences in web accessibility levels according to the region where the museums are located, meaning that interaction and usability of museums web platforms are not homogeneous across the Portuguese territory.

The flaws detected in web accessibility prevent visitors with disabilities from gaining full access to the available information through websites. AccessMonitor displayed a medium level of web accessibility for the museums, as the global index indicated a level of 5.80 (on a scale of 1 to 10). Even though this reveals a slightly better result than that obtained in other analyzed supply agents' websites, the errors found still are a source of major concern. The main failures detected with TAW indicate that the most affected principles are 'perceivable' and 'robust'. The problems affect the presentation of information in an accessible way and mainly influence the components of the user interface, which has direct implications in the interaction of visitors with disabilities with museum websites. The findings previously discussed point to the need to assess the accessibility of museum websites due to failures detected in the web platforms analyzed. They also suggest that the managers of the museums' websites must make special efforts to improve performance concerning the 'perceivable' and 'robust' principles.

It can also be concluded that there are differences in the level of accessibility of the museum websites according to their location in the national territory, namely in terms of NUTS II. In fact, these results reveal that many of the websites do not fully meet the basic requirements of web accessibility, thus constituting or increasing an impediment to the use of websites by PwD. These differences in the various regions indicate that there is no homogeneity regarding interaction and usability across Portugal in the case of museum websites. These results highlight that different efforts are required to increase the accessibility of websites belonging to museums located in different regions, with more efforts being required in some NUTS II.

Even though the study contributed to the diagnosis of web accessibility of museum websites and identification of possible requirements, some limitations can be found. The use of automatic evaluation tools only allows a narrow vision of problems, which might affect a correct interaction between visitors with disabilities and museums' web platforms. Since the accessible tourism market is very diverse, it is essential to examine the perception of people who experience some disability in their interaction with this type of web platforms. It is also crucial to mark the importance of accessible design while these types of platforms are being conceptualized. A more universal design, combined with correct adoption of the WCAG 2.0 guidelines, is a necessary step to ensure the success of human-computer interaction in the field of accessible tourism.

Acknowledgements. This work was developed in the scope of the research project ACTION - POCI-01-0145-FEDER-030376, funded by FEDER through COMPETE2020 – Programa Operacional Competitividade e Internacionalização (POCI), and by national funds (OE), through FCT/MCTES.

References

1. Abascal, J., Arrue, M., Fajardo, I., Garay, N., Tomás, J.: The use of guidelines to automatically verify web accessibility. Univ. Access Inf. Soc. (2004). https://doi.org/10.1007/s10209-003-0069-3
2. Evcil, A.N.: Barriers and preferences to leisure activities for wheelchair users in historic places. Tour. Geogr. (2018). https://doi.org/10.1080/14616688.2017.1293721
3. Domínguez Vila, T., Alén González, E., Darcy, S.: Accessible tourism online resources: a Northern European perspective. Scand. J. Hosp. Tour. **19**, 1–17 (2018). https://doi.org/10.1080/15022250.2018.1478325

4. Kuzma, J., Yen, D., Oestreicher, K.: Global e-government Web Accessibility: An Empirical Examination of EU, Asian and African Sites Joanne M. Kuzma Faculty of Computing, University of Worcester, UK Dorothy Yen Faculty of Business, University of Worcester, UK Klaus Oestreicher Faculty. Policy, pp. 1–6 (2009)
5. Mills, J.E., Han, J.-H., Clay, J.M.: Accessibility of hospitality and tourism websites. Cornell Hosp. Q. (2008). https://doi.org/10.1177/1938965507311499
6. Akgul, Y., Vatansever, K.: Web accessibility evaluation of government websites for people with disabilities in Turkey. J. Adv. Manag. Sci. **4**, 201–210 (2016). https://doi.org/10.12720/joams.4.3.201-210
7. Shi, Y.: The accessibility of Queensland visitor information centres' websites. Tour. Manag. **27**, 829–841 (2006). https://doi.org/10.1016/j.tourman.2005.05.012
8. Buhalis, D., Eichhorn, V., Michopoulou, E., Miller, G.: Accessibility Market and Stakeholder Analysis. OSSATE Access. Mark. Stakehold. Anal (2005)
9. Papadimitriou, N., Plati, M., Markou, E., Catapoti, D.: Identifying accessibility barriers in heritage museums: conceptual challenges in a period of change. Mus. Int. (2016). https://doi.org/10.1111/muse.12134
10. Walsh, D., Hall, M.M., Clough, P., Foster, J.: Characterising online museum users: a study of the national museums liverpool museum website. Int. J. Digit. Libr. **21**(1), 75–87 (2018). https://doi.org/10.1007/s00799-018-0248-8
11. Schmutz, S., Sonderegger, A., Sauer, J.: Implementing recommendations from web accessibility guidelines. Hum. Factors **58**, 611–629 (2016). https://doi.org/10.1177/0018720816640962
12. Mineiro, C., Garcia, A., Neves, J.: Comunicação Inclusiva em Monumentos, Palácios e Museus, p. 104 (2017)
13. Yau, M.K., McKercher, B., Packer, T.L.: Traveling with a disability - more than an Access Issue. Ann. Tour. Res. (2004). https://doi.org/10.1016/j.annals.2004.03.007
14. W3C: How to Meet WCAG 2 (Quick Reference). https://www.w3.org/WAI/WCAG21/quickref/
15. Handa, K., Dairoku, H., Toriyama, Y.: Investigation of priority needs in terms of museum service accessibility for visually impaired visitors. Br. J. Vis. Impair. (2010). https://doi.org/10.1177/0264619610374680
16. Poria, Y., Reichel, A., Brandt, Y.: People with disabilities visit art museums: An exploratory study of obstacles and difficulties. J. Herit. Tour. (2009). https://doi.org/10.1080/17438730802366508
17. Langa, L., et al.: Museum web accessibility: a pilot assessment of Mid-Atlantic museums. Int. J. Incl. Museum. (2012). https://doi.org/10.18848/1835-2014/CGP/v04i01/44360
18. Mangani, A., Bassi, L.: Web information, accessibility and museum ownership. Int. J. Tour. Policy **9**, 265–281 (2019). https://doi.org/10.1504/IJTP.2019.105486
19. Luccio, F.L., Beltrame, L.: Accessible tourism for users with hearing loss. In: ACM International Conference Proceeding Series, pp. 243–248 (2018). https://doi.org/10.1145/3284869.3284909
20. Argyropoulos, V.S., Kanari, C.: Re-imagining the museum through "touch": reflections of individuals with visual disability on their experience of museum-visiting in Greece. Alter. **9**, 130–143 (2015). https://doi.org/10.1016/j.alter.2014.12.005
21. Shneiderman, B.: Designing the user interface strategies for effective human-computer interaction. ACM SIGBIO Newsl. (1987). https://doi.org/10.1145/25065.950626
22. Pan, B., Fesenmaier, D.R.: Semantics of online tourism and travel information search on the internet: a preliminary study. In: Information and Communication Technologies in Tourism 2002 (2002)

23. Wang, P., Hawk, W.B., Tenopir, C.: Users' interaction with world wide web resources: an exploratory study using a holistic approach. Inf. Process. Manag. (2000). https://doi.org/10.1016/S0306-4573(99)00059-X
24. Cipolla Ficarra, F.V.: Human-computer interaction, tourism and cultural heritage. In: Cipolla Ficarra, F.V., de Castro Lozano, C., Nicol, E., Kratky, A., Cipolla-Ficarra, M. (eds.) HCITOCH 2010. LNCS, vol. 6529, pp. 39–50. Springer, Heidelberg (2011). https://doi.org/10.1007/978-3-642-18348-5_5
25. Daniels, M.J., Drogin Rodgers, E.B., Wiggins, B.P.: "Travel tales": an interpretive analysis of constraints and negotiations to pleasure travel as experienced by persons with physical disabilities. Tour. Manag. **26**, 919–930 (2005). https://doi.org/10.1016/j.tourman.2004.06.010
26. Devile, E., Kastenholz, E.: Accessible tourism experiences: the voice of people with visual disabilities. J. Policy Res. Tour. Leis. Events. (2018). https://doi.org/10.1080/19407963.2018.1470183
27. Othman, M.K., Petrie, H., Power, C.: Engaging visitors in museums with technology: scales for the measurement of visitor and multimedia guide experience. In: Campos, P., Graham, N., Jorge, J., Nunes, N., Palanque, P., Winckler, M. (eds.) INTERACT 2011. LNCS, vol. 6949, pp. 92–99. Springer, Heidelberg (2011). https://doi.org/10.1007/978-3-642-23768-3_8
28. Buhalis, D., Michopoulou, E.: Information-enabled tourism destination marketing: addressing the accessibility market. Curr. Issues Tour. **14**, 145–168 (2011). https://doi.org/10.1080/13683501003653361
29. Figueiredo, E., Eusébio, C., Kastenholz, E.: How diverse are tourists with disabilities? A pilot study on accessible leisure tourism experiences in portugal. Int. J. Tour. Res. (2012). https://doi.org/10.1002/jtr.1913
30. Michopoulou, E., Buhalis, D.: Information provision for challenging markets: The case of the accessibility requiring market in the context of tourism. Inf. Manag. **50**, 229–239 (2013). https://doi.org/10.1016/j.im.2013.04.001
31. AkgÜL, Y., Vatansever, K.: Web accessibility evaluation of government websites for people with disabilities in Turkey. J. Adv. Manag. Sci. (2016). https://doi.org/10.12720/joams.4.3.201-210
32. W3C: Web Content Accessibility Guidelines (WCAG) 2.1
33. Lisney, E., Bowen, J.P., Hearn, K., Zedda, M.: Museums and technology: being inclusive helps accessibility for all. Curator Mus. J. **56**, 353–361 (2013). https://doi.org/10.1111/cura.12034
34. W3C: Techniques for WCAG 2.0. https://www.w3.org/TR/WCAG-TECHS/
35. W3C: Understanding WCAG 2.0. https://www.w3.org/TR/UNDERSTANDING-WCAG20/
36. W3C: Web Accessibility Evaluation Tools List. https://www.w3.org/WAI/ER/tools/
37. Pühretmair, F., Buhalis, D.: Accessible tourism introduction to the special thematic session. In: Miesenberger, K., Klaus, J., Zagler, W., Karshmer, A. (eds.) ICCHP 2008. LNCS, vol. 5105, pp. 969–972. Springer, Heidelberg (2008). https://doi.org/10.1007/978-3-540-70540-6_145
38. Borges, I., Silva, F., Costa, E., Pinto, A.S., Abreu, A.: Infoaccessibility on the websites of inbound markets of Portugal destination. Advances in Tourism, Technology and Smart Systems. SIST, vol. 171, pp. 105–117. Springer, Singapore (2020). https://doi.org/10.1007/978-981-15-2024-2_10
39. Macedo, C.F., Sousa, B.M.: A acessibilidade no etourism: um estudo na ótica das pessoas portadoras de necessidades especiais. PASOS. Rev. Tur. y Patrim. Cult. **17**, 709–723 (2019). https://doi.org/10.25145/j.pasos.2019.17.050
40. Teixeira, L., Eusebio, C., Silveiro, A.: Website accessibility of Portuguese travel agents: a view using web diagnostic tools. In: Iberian Conference on Information Systems and Technologies, CISTI (2019)

41. Akgül, Y.: Web content accessibility of municipal web sites in Turkey. In: Proceedings of the European Conference on e-Government, ECEG (2015)
42. Domínguez Vila, T., Alén González, E., Darcy, S.: Accessibility of tourism websites: the level of countries' commitment. Univ. Access Inf. Soc. **19**(2), 331–346 (2019). https://doi.org/10.1007/s10209-019-00643-4
43. Vila, T.D., Brea, J.A.F.: A new challenge: The content and the accessibility on the Spanish tourist web [Un nuevo desafío: El contenido y la accesibilidad al contenido de las web turísticas españolas]. Rev. Galega Econ. (2009)
44. Silveiro, A., Eusébio, C., Teixeira, L.: Heterogeneity in accessibility of travel agency websites: a study in the central Portugal region. RISTI - Rev. Iber. Sist. e Tecnol. Inf. (2019). https://doi.org/10.17013/risti.35.18-34

A Context Driven Indoor Localization Framework for Assisted Living in Smart Homes

Nirmalya Thakur(✉) and Chia Y. Han

Department of Electrical Engineering and Computer Science, University of Cincinnati, Cincinnati, OH 45221-0030, USA
thakurna@mail.uc.edu, han@ucmail.uc.edu

Abstract. The proposed Context Driven Indoor Localization Framework aims to implement a standard for indoor localization to address the multiple needs in different indoor environments with a specific focus to contribute towards Ambient Assisted Living (AAL) in the Future of Smart Homes for healthy aging of the rapidly increasing elderly population. This framework has multiple functionalities. First, it presents the methodology to analyze any given IoT-based environment, in terms of spatial information, to classify it into specific zones or functional areas based on the activities performed by users with different environment parameters in those respective zones. Second, it discusses the approach to analyze the macro and micro level user interactions with context parameters for any user in the given IoT environment. Finally, it possesses the methodology to track user interactions, analyze and access the Big Data associated with these interactions and map the user to a specific zone or area in the given IoT-based environment using a learning model. To evaluate the efficacy of this framework, it has been implemented on a dataset related to performing different activities in IoT-based settings. The results presented and discussed uphold the relevance and potential for real-time implementation of this framework for addressing multiple needs associated with aging in smart homes as well as for various other applications of indoor localization in different environments and contexts.

Keywords: Indoor localization · Big Data · Assisted Living · Smart Homes

1 Introduction

The means of navigation, travelling and tracking both people and landmarks have been significantly transformed by Global Positioning System (GPS) and Global Navigation Satellite Systems (GNSSs). However, in the context of indoor navigation as part of our daily living activities, GPS and GNSS are still ineffective [1]. There has been an increasing need for developing systems and applications for indoor navigation and localization in different environments which involve human-human, human-robot and human-computer interactions for instance – smart homes, schools, multi-storied buildings, shopping malls, healthcare facilities and nursing homes. As there are multiple needs in myriad of environments, only one area of interest, in the context of healthy aging of

C. Stephanidis et al. (Eds.): HCII 2020, LNCS 12426, pp. 387–400, 2020.
https://doi.org/10.1007/978-3-030-60149-2_30

older adults in the future of technology-laden living spaces of smart homes and smart cities, will be addressed here.

At present there are around 962 million elderly people [2] across the world. A recent study [3] has predicted that by the year 2050 the population of elderly people will become around 1.6 billion globally and will end up outnumbering the population of younger people worldwide. Elderly people have several needs and requirements due to physical disabilities, cognitive issues, weakened memory and disorganized behavior, that they face with increasing age. Thus, there is an increasing need to develop a Personal Care System (PCS) – which involves care anywhere, care networking and care customization for this sector of society. A PCS would be able to contribute towards fostering the biological, psychological, behavioral, physical, mental, and emotional well-being of older adults in smart homes in multiple ways. Many situations can be readily identified and the requirement for indoor localization becomes relevant. For instance, (1) detection of the exact location of an elderly fall and providing this location to emergency responders; (2) assisting elderly people with various forms of Cognitive Impairments (CI) to perform their daily routine tasks through conversational agents that can detect their exact locations in real-time; (3) helping older adults with visual impairments to navigate to specific objects of their interest for performing an activity – based on their instantaneous location with respect to those objects; and (4) development of assistive robots that can track the position of the elderly and navigate to their location to address any needs.

The intersection of indoor localization with Activity-Centric Computing in an Internet of Things (IoT)-based environment has the potential to address these global challenges. Leveraging this potential to develop a long-term, robust, feasible, easily implementable, sustainable, and economic solution serves as the main motivation for the proposed multifunctional indoor localization framework. This paper is organized as follows. We present an overview of the related works in this field in Sect. 2. The proposed framework is introduced and explained in Sect. 3. Section 4 discusses the results and performance characteristics of this framework. It is followed by Sect. 5 where conclusion and scope for future work are outlined.

2 Literature Review

This section outlines the recent works in the fields of Activity Centric Computing, IoT in Smart Homes and Indoor Localization. To broadly summarize the works related to Activity Centric Computing, IoT in Smart Homes, based on the methodologies and approaches proposed and implemented, they fall into two broad categories – knowledge-specific and data-specific. Knowledge-specific approaches work based on using ontologies to reason and recognize activities. Data-specific approaches primarily rely on the characteristics of the data in order to apply different learning models and computational methods to infer about the activity. Azkune et al. [4] developed a framework based on wireless sensor data acquisition and semantic analysis to perform activity recognition. Riboni et al. [5] developed a model that utilized ontologies to study, understand and reason about activities. Another example of a knowledge-specific approach is the work done by Nevatia et al. [6], where image data and video data were used for activity recognition and understanding. Kasteren et al. [7] used a data-specific approach based on

Hidden Markov Models to analyze raw sensor data for activity recognition. An image recognition and video content analysis-based activity recognition model was proposed by Cheng et al. [8] for tracking activities both at an individual level and a group level. An Artificial Neural Network driven activity recognition approach was developed by Skocir et al. [9] specifically for detection of certain events, like entering and exiting a room, in an IoT laden environment. Several approaches for activity recognition and its related applications have also been developed by Thakur et al. [10–18]. An indoor navigation system that was QR code driven was proposed by Idrees et al. [19]. The system consisted of multiple QR codes set up in the environment and based on the specific QR code being scanned by the user the location was determined. Chaccour [20] used a host of cameras to track a user in a given indoor space. The cameras were mounted at strategic locations in the given environment which tracked users by mapping markers which were fixed on the heads of the users. A similar work based on tracing by cameras was done by Sun et al. [21], however instead of markers they had an indoor map and their system used a background subtraction approach to locate the users. A wireless sensor driven indoor localization system was developed by Desai et al. [22] where the time difference of arrival method was used with video data obtained from cameras to detect a person's location. A combination of RSSI and video data was used by Grzechca et al. [23] to develop an indoor location tracking system. An inertial sensor powered computer vision-based framework for indoor location detection was proposed by Rituerto et al. [24] and an LSD-SLAM based indoor localization framework was developed by Endo et al. [25].

Despite several works in these fields, there are a number of limitations in the existing systems – (1) most of these systems are built specific to lab environments and their implementation in a real-time context is difficult because of the required infrastructures; (2) it is costly to implement these systems in the actual IoT-based living spaces, which are larger as compared to lab environments; (3) some of these systems are based on wearable data and quite often users are hesitant to put on an wearable device all the time; (4) specific indoor environments were modelled in the labs so there is lack of training data that can be used to train a model that works in any indoor environment; (5) the tracking of distances by depth cameras from reflective and untextured surfaces is not very accurate; and (6) cameras and wireless sensors have limitations in terms of the range they can track. Thus, there still exists the need to develop a standard for indoor location detection in the daily functioning and living environments of users. This work aims to explore the intersection of multiple disciplines with a specific focus on the intersection of Activity Centric Computing and Internet of Things to establish a standard for indoor localization.

3 Proposed Framework

This section presents the architecture of the proposed framework. The contextual intelligence of our framework is developed based on one of the existing works in this field [26]. The purpose of developing contextual intelligence in our framework is to analyze user interactions associated with any activity in terms of its tasks, actions, environmental parameters, spatial and temporal features. The following are the steps to develop the contextual intelligence in this proposed framework:

i. Develop the methodology [26] to analyze a complex activity in terms of atomic activities and its associated context attributes
ii. Assign weights to these atomic activities and context attributes based on probabilistic reasoning
iii. Identify the atomic activities and their associated context attributes that are responsible for the start and end of the given complex activity
iv. Identity the core atomic activities and core context attributes – these atomic activities and context attributes receive the highest weights and are crucial for successful completion of the given complex activity
v. Identify the most important context attribute [18] and its associated atomic activity
vi. Track and record the spatial features of the most important context attribute
vii. Track and record the temporal characteristics of the atomic activity performed on the most important context attribute
viii. Calculate the total weight of the complex activity and the threshold function. The threshold function represents the condition for successful activity completion
ix. Track the sequence in which the atomic activities are performed on the respective context attributes and analyze these relationships to define the complex activity based on its temporal and spatial features.

In this context, atomic activities refer to the small actions and tasks associated with an activity. The environment variables or parameters on which these tasks are performed are known as the context attributes. The complex activity is a collection of the atomic activities and context attributes along with their characteristics [26]. This is further elaborated in Fig. 1 and Fig. 2 describes a few atomic activities and complex activities in a typical environment.

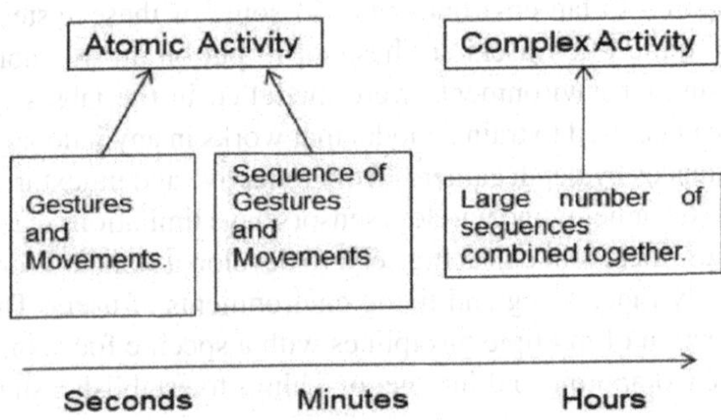

Fig. 1. Analysis of atomic activities and complex activities in terms of tasks and actions [29]

Upon development of this contextual intelligence in our framework, we developed the characteristics for contextual mapping of a given indoor Internet of Things (IoT)-based environment, based on the multiple features of complex activities performed in that environment. The following are the characteristics for contextual mapping of the given IoT-based indoor environment:

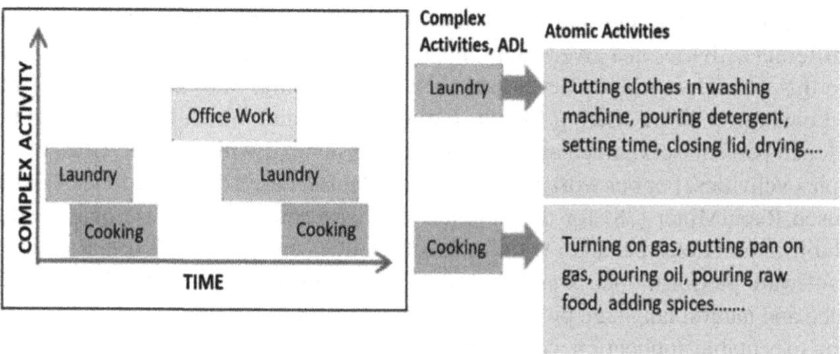

Fig. 2. Analysis of typical complex activities in terms of the associated atomic activities [29]

i. Every IoT-based environment consists of a set of context parameters that are typically associated with one complex activity, in some cases with more than one complex activity.
ii. The most important context attribute for a given complex activity is uniquely associated with that complex activity and can never be associated with any other complex activities
iii. The interaction patterns in terms of atomic activities performed on the most important context attribute determine the success or failure of performing that complex activity
iv. The most important context attribute for a given complex activity has specific spatial and temporal characteristics that are obtained upon studying the definition of the complex activity in terms of its atomic activities, context attributes including their spatial and temporal features
v. The spatial and temporal characteristics associated with each most important context attribute is unique for that given environment
vi. These spatial features can be studied to map the given environment in terms of most important context attributes and their associated location information
vii. Mapping the given IoT-environment in terms of the most important context attributes and their associated location information allows spatial mapping of the environment into specific 'zones' that are uniquely associated with specific activities
viii. This spatial mapping is specific to a given environment and stays consistent for that environment unless the most important context attributes are removed from that environment or their spatial features undergo a change
ix. These 'zones' do not overlap with each other and uniquely characterize a complex activity in that given IoT environment

For implementation of these contextual mapping characteristics, in a given environment, a learning model may be developed for classifying that environment into specific zones. We developed a dataset based on [27], for development of such a learning model as outlined in Sect. 4. This dataset was developed by Ordóñez et al. [27] where a host of wireless and wearable sensors were used to collect data in the context of users performing different activities in a given environment. The specific activities that were recorded while this dataset was being developed include - Sleeping, Showering, Eating Breakfast, Leaving for Work, Eating Lunch, Eating Snacks and Watching TV. The authors developed two datasets named as OrdonezA and OrdonezB with characteristics of these complex activities. For our work we developed a dataset based on the OrdonezA dataset. We used RapidMiner [28] for development of this framework because of its features and built-in functions that align with the functionalities our framework has. RapidMiner is a software platform, that is used specifically for developing machine learning, data science and natural language processing models as well as for integrating these models into an executable application, called 'process' in RapidMiner. We used the free version of RapidMiner for development of this framework.

4 Results and Discussion

This section outlines the results obtained from the framework as outlined in Sect. 3. We first analyzed the different characteristics of the various complex activities that were present on this dataset. Figure 3 shows all the complex activities analyzed with respect to their temporal characteristics and Figs. 4, 5, 6, 7, 8 and 9 represent the individual mapping of some of these complex activities as per their temporal features. In all these features the X-axis denoted the time and the values 0 and 1 on the Y-axis denote unsuccessful and successful attempts of the complex activities, respectively.

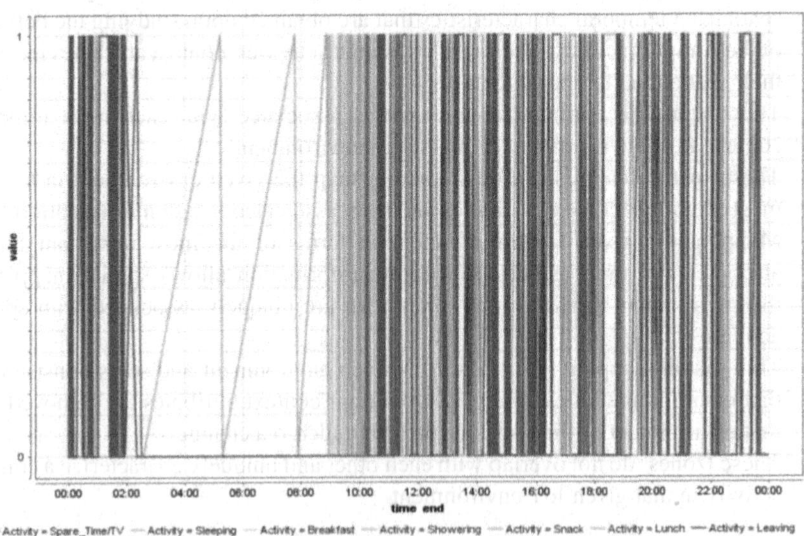

Fig. 3. Multiple instances of the complex activities of Sleeping, Showering, Eating Breakfast, Leaving for work, Eating Lunch, Eating Snacks and Watching TV analyzed over a 24-h time period [29]

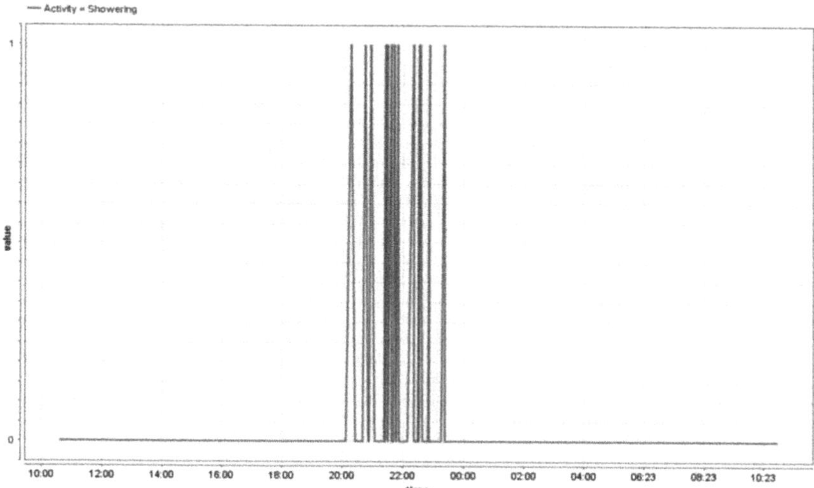

Fig. 4. Multiple instances of the complex activity of Showering analyzed over a 24-h period [29]

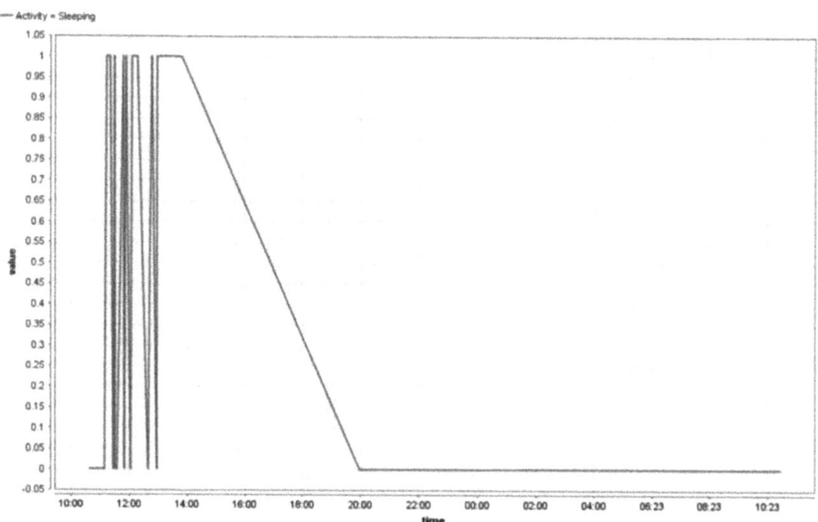

Fig. 5. Multiple instances of the complex activity of Sleeping analyzed over a 24-h period [29]

Fig. 6. Multiple instances of the complex activity of Watching TV analyzed over a 24-h period [29]

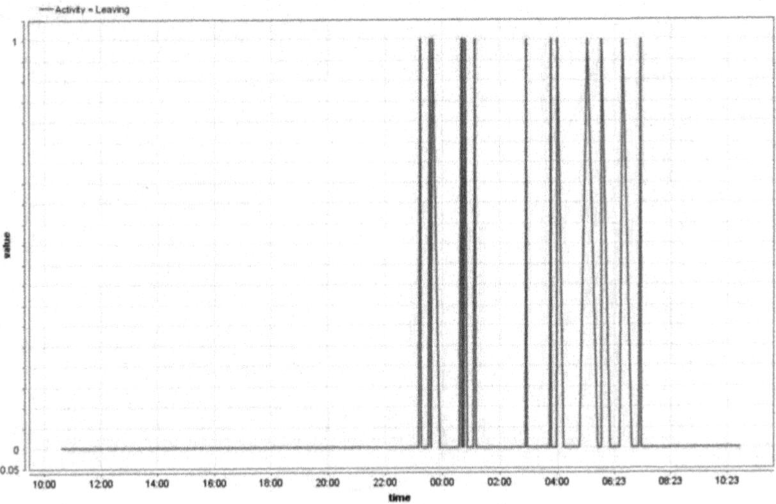

Fig. 7. Multiple instances of the complex activity of Leaving for Work analyzed over a 24-h period [29]

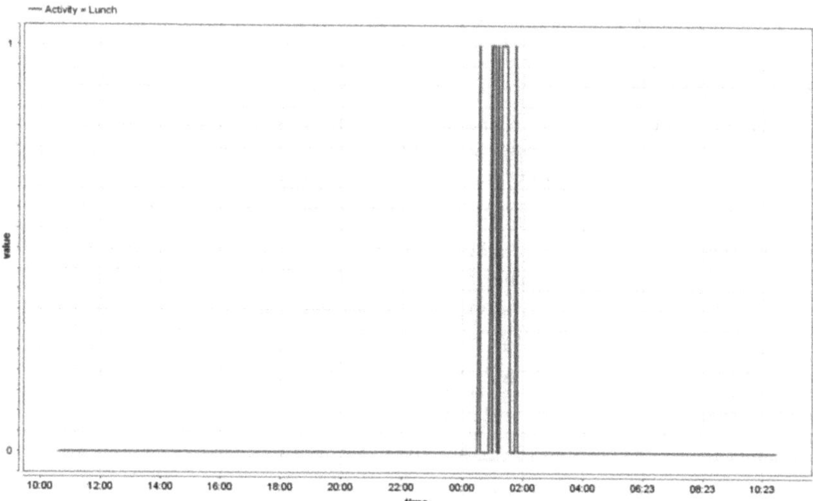

Fig. 8. Multiple instances of the complex activity of Eating Lunch analyzed over a 24-h period [29]

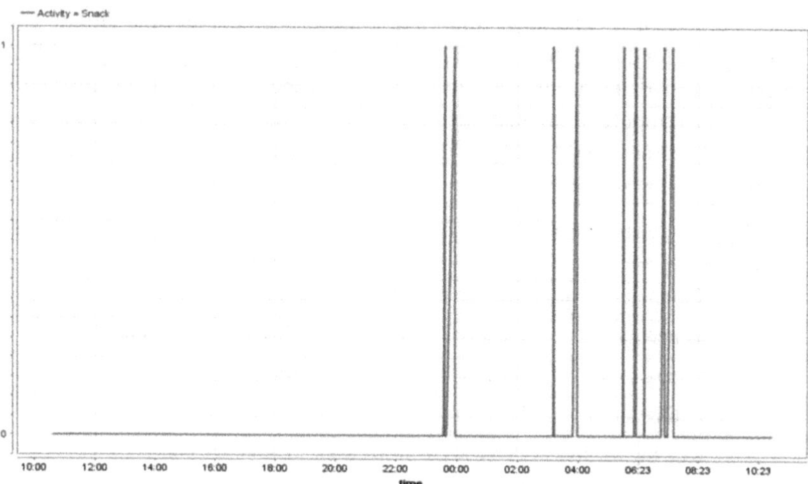

Fig. 9. Multiple instances of the complex activity of Eating Snacks analyzed over a 24-h period [29]

Next, the characteristics of all these complex activities in terms of atomic activities, context attributes and their associated features were analyzed. We present the analysis of one of these complex activities in Table 1.

Table 1. Analysis of the complex activity of watching TV

Complex activity of watching TV	
Atomic activities, Ati	At1: Standing (0,15), At2: Walking towards TV (0.15), At3: Turning on the TV (0.25), At4: Fetching the remote control (0.15), At5: Sitting down (0.08), At6: Tuning Proper Channel (0.12), At7: Adjusting display and audio (0,10)
Context attributes, Cti	Ct1: Lights on (0.15), Ct2: Entertainment Arua (0.15), Ct3: Presence of TV (0.25), Ct4: Remote control available (0.15), Ct5: Sitting Area (0.08), Ct6: Channel Present (0.12), Ct7: Settings working (0.10)
Core Ati and Cti	At1, At2, At3, At4, At5 and Ctl1, Ct2, Ct3, Ct4 and Ct5
Start Ati and Cti	At1, At2 and Ct1, Ct2
End Ati and Cti	At5, At6, At7 and Ct5, Ct6, Ct7
Most important Ati and Cti	At3: Turning on the TV (0.25) and Ct3: Presence of the TV (0.25)

Similarly, the analysis of other complex activities was performed, and their characteristics were studied. The most important context attribute and the atomic activity associated with it for each complex activity were recorded to study their spatial features for mapping the given environment into respective 'zones' as per the spatial characteristics of the most important context attributes. Table 2 lists the most important context attributes and the associated 'zones' of all the complex activities from this dataset.

Table 2. Most important context attributes associated with the complex activities from this dataset

Complex activity	Most important Cti	Associated zone
Watching TV	Presence of the TV	Entertainment zone
Eating snacks	Snacks	Refreshment zone
Eating lunch	Lunch food	Dining zone
Leaving for work	Presence of work-dress	Dressing zone
Eating breakfast	Breakfast food	Relaxation zone
Showering	Working shower	Bathroom
Sleeping	Bed	Sleeping zone

As can be observed from Table 2 – these complex activities which occur on the dataset can be mapped into unique spatial zones associated with them, which are - Entertainment Zone, Refreshment Zone, Dining Zone, Dressing Zone, Relaxation Zone, Bathroom and Sleeping Zone. These respective zones are indicative of the specific location of a person while they are performing these activities. For instance, while performing the complex activity of 'Watching TV' – the person would always be present in the Entertainment

Zone and the presence of the person in any of the other zones is not possible. Using these characteristics, we developed a 'process' in RapidMiner that would detect a person's location in terms of the zone they are present in during different time instants. These findings of the most important context attributes and the respective zones were added to the dataset and we developed a learning model in RapidMiner using the Random Forest approach. This is shown in Fig. 10.

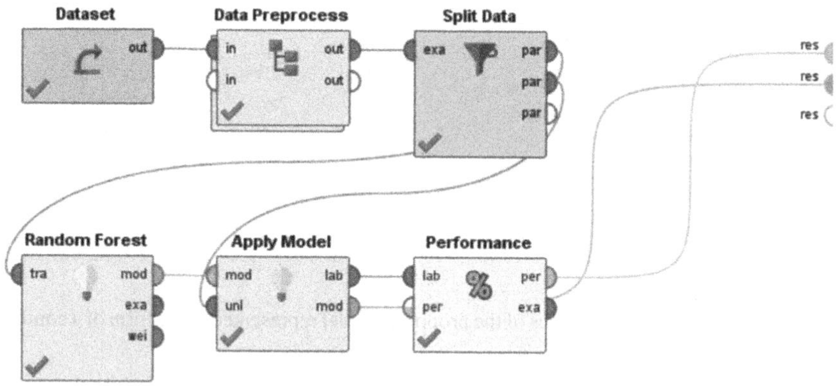

Fig. 10. The proposed model with all its functionalities as developed in RapidMiner

The 'Data Preprocess' operator was used to pre-process the data and study the relationships of the various characteristic features of these complex activities. The 'Split Data' operator was used to split the data into training set and test set. We used 70% of the data for training the model and 30% of the data for testing the model. The 'Random Forest' operator was used to implement the random forest learning approach. The 'Apply Model' operator was used to test the performance of the learning model on the test dataset. The 'Performance' operator was used to analyze the performance characteristics of the learning model and we performed this analysis in the form of a confusion matrix. This is shown in Figs. 11 and 12 where the tabular view and plot view of the confusion matrix are represented, respectively.

accuracy: 74.17%

	true Sleeping Z...	true Dressing ...	true Entertain...	true Refreshm...	true Bathroom	true Dining Zone	true Relaxation...	class precision
pred. Sleeping ...	11	0	0	0	0	0	2	84.62%
pred. Dressing...	0	15	0	0	0	1	0	93.75%
pred. Entertain...	2	7	52	3	3	6	6	65.82%
pred. Refresh...	0	0	1	7	0	0	0	87.50%
pred. Bathroom	3	0	0	0	11	0	0	78.57%
pred. Dining Z...	0	2	0	0	0	4	1	57.14%
pred. Relaxatio...	0	1	0	0	0	1	12	85.71%
class recall	68.75%	60.00%	98.11%	70.00%	78.57%	33.33%	57.14%	

Fig. 11. Performance characteristics of the proposed model represented in the form of a confusion matrix (tabular view)

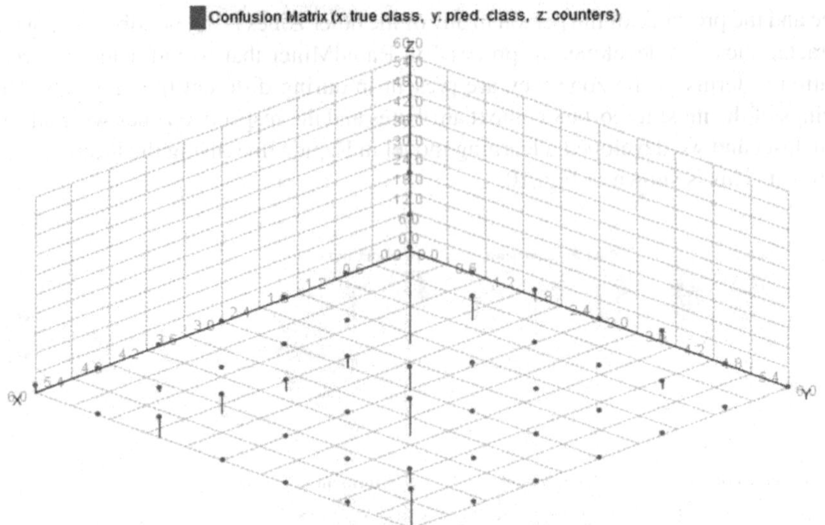

Fig. 12. Performance characteristics of the proposed model represented in the form of a confusion matrix (plot view)

As can be observed from Figs. 11 and 12, the overall performance accuracy of this learning model is 74.17%. The class precision values for the different zones - Entertainment Zone, Refreshment Zone, Dining Zone, Dressing Zone, Relaxation Zone, Bathroom and Sleeping Zone are 65.82%, 87.50%, 57.14%, 93.75%, 85.71%, 78.57% and 84.62%, respectively.

5 Conclusion

There is a need for development of a standard for indoor localization in the future of technology-based living and functional environments which would involve human-human, human-robot and human-computer interactions, for instance in smart homes, schools, multi-storied buildings, shopping malls, healthcare facilities and nursing homes. Indoor localization has multiple application domains. In the context of the constantly increasing elderly population with their associated diverse needs and requirements, a standard for tracking the location of older adults has the potential to address their needs and contribute towards AAL of elderly in the future of Smart Homes. A multifunctional framework at the intersection of Activity Centric Computing, Internet of Things, Assistive Technology, Human Computer Interaction, Machine Learning and their related application domains is proposed in this work with the aim to develop a standard for indoor location tracking to improve the quality of life and contribute towards healthy aging of the elderly population in the future of Smart Homes. Multiple functionalities of this framework are presented and discussed. First, the framework allows mapping a given IoT-based environment into specific zones or functional areas based on the activities performed in those zones. It discusses an approach to analyze the Big Data associated with activities performed in the given IoT environment. It also presents a methodology that is primarily a learning model developed using the Random Forest approach that can locate a user in a specific zone based on the Big Data and multiple characteristics of user interactions associated with the activities. The Random Forest approach achieves an overall performance accuracy of 74.17% when tested on a dataset of activities performed in an IoT-based environment. To the best knowledge of the authors, no similar work has been done yet. Future work along these lines would involve setting up an IoT-based Smart Home environment using a host of wearables and wireless sensors for real-time implementation of this framework.

References

1. Langlois, C., Tiku, S., Pasricha, S.: Indoor localization with smartphones. IEEE Consum. Electron. Mag. (2017)
2. United Nations: 2020 Report on Ageing (2020). http://www.un.org/en/sections/issuesdepth/ageing/
3. He, W., Goodkind, D., Kowal, P.: An aging world: 2015. International Population Reports, by United States Census Bureau (2016)
4. Azkune, G., Almeida, A., López-de-Ipiña, D., Liming, C.: Extending knowledge driven activity models through data-driven learning techniques. Expert Syst. Appl.: Int. J. **42**(6) (2016)
5. Riboni, D., Bettini, C.: Context-aware activity recognition through a combination of ontological and statistical reasoning. In: Zhang, D., Portmann, M., Tan, A.-H., Indulska, J. (eds.) UIC 2009. LNCS, vol. 5585, pp. 39–53. Springer, Heidelberg (2009). https://doi.org/10.1007/978-3-642-02830-4_5
6. Nevatia, R., Hobbs, J., Bolles, B.: An ontology for video event representation. In: CVPRW 2004: Proceedings of the 2004 Conference on Computer Vision and Pattern Recognition Workshop, vol. 7, p. 119. IEEE Computer Society, Washington, DC (2004)
7. van Kasteren, T., Noulas, A., Englebienne, G., Kröse, B.: Accurate activity recognition in a home setting. In: UbiComp 2008: Proceedings of the 10th International Conference on Ubiquitous Computing, pp. 1–9. ACM, Seoul (2008)
8. Cheng, Z., Qin, L., Huang, Q., Jiang, S., Yan, S., Tian, Q.: Human group activity analysis with fusion of motion and appearance information. In: Proceedings of the 19th ACM International Conference on Multimedia, Scottsdale, Arizona, USA, pp. 1401–1404 (2011)
9. Skocir, P., Krivic, P., Tomeljak, M., Kusek, M., Jezic, G.: Activity detection in smart home environment. In: Proceedings of the 20th International Conference on Knowledge Based and Intelligent Information and Engineering Systems (2016)
10. Thakur, N., Han, C.Y.: An improved approach for complex activity recognition in smart homes. In: Peng, X., Ampatzoglou, A., Bhowmik, T. (eds.) ICSR 2019. LNCS, vol. 11602, pp. 220–231. Springer, Cham (2019). https://doi.org/10.1007/978-3-030-22888-0_15
11. Thakur, N., Han, C.Y.: Framework for a personalized intelligent assistant to elderly people for activities of daily living. Int. J. Recent Trends Hum. Comput. Interact. (IJHCI) **9**(1), 1–22 (2019)
12. Thakur, N., Han, C.Y.: Framework for an intelligent affect aware smart home environment for elderly people. Int. J. Recent Trends Hum. Comput. Interact. (IJHCI) **9**(1), 23–43 (2019)
13. Thakur, N., Han, C.Y.: A context-driven complex activity framework for smart home. In: Proceedings of the 9th Annual Information Technology, Electronics and Mobile Communication Conference (IEMCON), Vancouver, Canada (2018)

14. Thakur, N., Han, C.Y.: A hierarchical model for analyzing user experiences in affect aware systems. In: Proceedings of the 9th Annual Information Technology, Electronics and Mobile Communication Conference (IEMCON), Vancouver, Canada (2018)
15. Thakur, N., Han, C.Y.: An approach to analyze the social acceptance of virtual assistants by elderly people. In: Proceedings of the 8th International Conference on the Internet of Things (IoT), Santa Barbara, California (2018)
16. Thakur, N., Han, C.Y.: Methodology for forecasting user experience for smart and assisted living in affect aware systems. In: Proceedings of the 8th International Conference on the Internet of Things (IoT), Santa Barbara, California (2018)
17. Thakur, N., Han, C.Y.: An activity analysis model for enhancing user experiences in affect aware systems. In: Proceedings of the IEEE 5G World Forum Conference (IEEE 5GWF 2018), Santa Clara, California (2018)
18. Thakur, N., Han, C.Y.: A complex activity based emotion recognition algorithm for affect aware systems. In: Proceedings of IEEE 8th Annual Computing and Communication Workshop and Conference (IEEE CCWC), Las Vegas (2018)
19. Idrees, A., Iqbal, Z., Ishfaq, M.: An efficient indoor navigation technique to find optimal route for blinds using QRcodes. In: Proceedings of the 2015 IEEE 10th Conference on Industrial Electronics and Applications (ICIEA), Auckland, New Zealand (2015)
20. Chaccour, K., Badr, G.: Computer vision guidance system for indoor navigation of visually impaired people. In: Proceedings of the 8th IEEE International Conference on Intelligent Systems, Sofia, Bulgaria (2016)
21. Sun, Y., Zhao, K., Wang, J., Li, W., Bai, G., Zhang, N.: Device-free human localization using panoramic camera and indoor map. In: Proceedings of the 2016 IEEE International Conference on Consumer Electronics-China (ICCE-China), Guangzhou, China (2016)
22. Desai, P., Rattan, K.S.: Indoor localization and surveillance using wireless sensor network and Pan/Tilt camera. In: Proceedings of the IEEE 2009 National Aerospace & Electronics Conference (NAECON), Dayton, OH, USA (2009)
23. Grzechca, D., Wróbel, T., Bielecki, P.: Indoor location and identification of objects with video surveillance system and WiFi module. In: Proceedings of the 2014 International Conference on Mathematics and Computers in Sciences and in Industry, Varna, Bulgaria (2014)
24. Rituerto, A., Fusco, G., Coughlan, J.M.: Towards a sign-based indoor navigation system for people with visual impairments. In: Proceedings of the 18th International ACM SIGACCESS Conference on Computers and Accessibility (ASSETS 2016), Reno, NV, USA (2016)
25. Endo, Y., Sato, K., Yamashita, A., Matsubayashi, K.: Indoor positioning and obstacle detection for visually impaired navigation system based on LSD-SLAM. In: Proceedings of the 2017 International Conference on Biometrics and Kansei Engineering (ICBAKE) (2017)
26. Saguna, S., Zaslavsky, A., Chakraborty, D.: Complex activity recognition using context-driven activity theory and activity signatures. ACM Trans. Comput. Hum. Interact. **20**(6), Article 32 (2013)
27. Ordóñez, F.J., de Toledo, P., Sanchis, A.: Activity recognition using hybrid generative/discriminative models on home environments using binary sensors. Sensors **2013**(13), 5460–5477 (2013)
28. Ritthoff, O., Klinkenberg, R., Fischer, S., Mierswa, I., Felske, S.: YALE: yet another learning environment (2001). https://doi.org/10.17877/de290r-15309
29. Thakur, N.: Framework for a context aware adaptive intelligent assistant for activities of daily living. M.S. thesis, University of Cincinnati (2019)

Social Intervention Strategy of Augmented Reality Combined with Theater-Based Games to Improve the Performance of Autistic Children in Symbolic Play and Social Skills

Wei-Zhen Wang and I-Jui Lee(✉)

Department of Industrial Design, National Taipei University of Technology, Taipei, Taiwan
t107588006@ntut.org.tw, ericlee@ntut.edu.tw

Abstract. The main congenital defects in autism spectrum disorder (ASD) are social communication barriers and behavior defects in social reciprocity, of which the common defects include impaired social interaction, oral communication ability and expression barriers, lack of empathy and imagination, and other ability defects. Therefore, the appropriate application of teaching media is quite important. Related literature has confirmed that autistic children are highly interested in interactive media, with the positive effect of augmented reality (AR) on social training. Therefore, this study used AR as a social training tool for autistic children, combined with the social intervention strategy of theatre-based games, to enable autistic children to pretend to be the protagonist of the classic fairy tale "The Wizard of OZ" through role-play.

In the process, children learn symbolic play, so as to improve their imagination and empathy. In the experiment, a case study on a 6-year-old high-function autistic child was conducted to record his social behaviors in theater with three non-autistic children of the same age, the theater framework enables the autistic children to interact with different characters (such as Cowardly Lion, Scarecrow, etc.) through role-play, thereby helping them to understand the symbolic and actual meanings of different roles and various social situations. As a result, they can make appropriate social action feedback, which can enhance the imagination and social skills of autistic children.

Keywords: Augmented reality · Autism · Micro-behavior for video coding · Pretend play · Symbolic play · Theater-based game · The wizard of OZ

1 Introduction

1.1 Congenital Social Defects of Autistic Children

Children with ASD face many difficulties in social aspects, whose main core characteristics include the lack of interpersonal interactions, communication and understanding of verbal and non-verbal cues, and imagination [1]. In the process of social interaction, ASD lacks the ability of theory of mind (ToM), which makes it difficult for these children

C. Stephanidis et al. (Eds.): HCII 2020, LNCS 12426, pp. 401–411, 2020.
https://doi.org/10.1007/978-3-030-60149-2_31

to understand the meaning of actions and eye contact of others, as well as emotional performance and potential psychological feelings of themselves and others [2]. In addition, due to the lack of proper social greeting behavior, autistic children are hindered in their social interaction with their peers [3], which makes it difficult for them to understand the symbolic language meaning of their peers and develop deep social relationships with their peers. As they grow up, the degree of interaction between social network and people will become more complex and the problems more obvious. Thy will have a negative impact on their social development process.

1.2 Defective Capability of Autistic Children in Symbolic Play

Symbolic play is usually related to the emotional and social development of children, so it is also considered as one of the most important social foundations [4]. However, autistic children usually do not exhibit the behavior of symbolic play [2]. Baron Cohen pointed out that compared with typical developed children, autistic children lack the ability of theory of mind (ToM), which results in their inability to understand the views and mental states of others; thus, they cannot conduct pretend play through imagination and speculation. Such problems are related to their imagination defects [5]. Many studies have pointed out that it is difficult for autistic children to introduce symbolic meaning into abstract things, or convert these meaningful symbols into other substitutes or objects without literal meaning [6]. In other words, as it is difficult for them to engage in pretend play, it will negatively affect their social skills performance; the lack of this ability is considered to be one of the main reasons for the executive dysfunction of social cognition [7]. In addition, autistic children have poor ability to link abstract symbols with symbolic meanings, which makes it difficult for them to carry out reciprocal interactions with their peers in social situations, which affects their future life and learning development. Therefore, researchers generally believe that such ability defects must be improved through social intervention training, and that appropriate social intervention training can help autistic children to better understand the ideas of others and enhance their empathy and social cognitive relationships.

2 Related Work

2.1 Common Social Training Strategies for Autistic Children

According to the literature, it is difficult for autistic children to establish in-depth social relations with others due to their inability to master appropriate social reciprocity skills [8]. In the past, researchers usually used different social training strategies for intervention; the most common social training strategy was Social Stories™ [9], aiming to enable autistic children to learn social concepts and skills from a series of designed events and stories [10]. Social Stories™ has been proven to effectively reduce the frequency of problem behavior for autistic children as well as to effectively improve their social reciprocity [11].

2.2 Developmental Defects of Autistic Children in Symbolic Play

The difficulty autistic children experience in trying to understand the meaning of symbolic symbols leads to their inability to perform pretend play. In the past, the literature divided pretend play into traditional imaginative play and symbolic play [12]. Pretend play can be regarded as the performance to develop and practice various social and communication behaviors for children so that they learn how to regulate their behaviors and emotions. Some studies have pointed out that it is difficult for autistic children to spontaneously develop pretend play behavior [13, 14]. In fact, the lack of pretend play behavior is one of the common typical defects of autistic children, and indirectly affects their social cognition and social behavior development [15, 16]. Hobson proposed that the participation or sharing of social game relationships between autistic children and children with typical development would help to trigger the development of their pretend play behavior [16]. In addition, it has been confirmed that intervention training based on pretend play has significant benefits for the early intervention of autistic children [17]. As role-play is based on pretend play, the approach using both will help to improve the social reciprocity skills of autistic children.

2.3 Application of AR Technology in Social Skills Training of Autistic Children

AR technology can superimpose virtual imaging on real scenes and arouse the high attraction and interest of autistic children [18]. While it is difficult for autistic children to engage in pretend play on their own, fortunately, it has been proven that AR can effectively improve the performance of pretend play for autistic children, and promote the transformation and understanding of abstract social concepts for them [19]. Many studies have shown that when AR is used in social intervention, it can train the behavior skills, emotional and social cognition of autistic children [20], make them more focused on learning materials, and make the process more interesting. The 3D interactive mode presented by AR technology can complement the social situation of autistic children, due to the lack of imagination, through visual cues and presentation [21].

2.4 Theater-Based Training Can Help Autistic Children Build Empathy and Social Cognition

Based on the theater-based training mode, the experiential teaching strategy is emphasized. Such a training mode enables participants to integrate theatre and role-play games through role-play. These game processes will help participants improve their mastery of this ability and knowledge [22]. Therefore, the use of theater-based training methods combined with the concept of pretend play can enable autistic children to perform role-play in specific situations, aiming to enable autistic children to gain the ability of social integration as well as social development [23].

A theatre-based approach provides a potential interactive platform for autistic children to learn how to master the ability to socialize with others [24]. Theater-based social training strategies have also proven to be effective in improving the social behaviors and reciprocal skills of autistic children [25]. Through the game concept of social stories, autistic children are integrated into the theater environment, led to develop social interaction, with the performance of social reciprocal ability promoted by means of scenario promotion and implementation of training objectives.

Through the intervention measures of theater-based training, autistic children can understand the cognitive differences from different perspectives, and learn the ability of empathy and empathy from different roles [23], and to master different emotional representations and social behavior performance, which is also a widely used learning method of theater-based games combined with role-play in many early treatment training programs. Such a teaching method can provide a safe and effective training environment, so that autistic children can carry out exercises simulating real life situations, experience more diverse social situations, and establish social cognitive concepts of empathy and symbols.

2.5 Summary

The literature points out that the intervention of theater-based training can effectively improve the social skills of autistic children, and develop their basic social reciprocity. Therefore, this study starts from the pretend play behaviors that autistic children lack, and provide visual cues for autistic children in the understanding of symbolic symbols through the assistance of AR technology, in an attempt to improve the observation ability of autistic children in regard to understanding abstract symbols through symbolic AR 3D animation, and through the game development of theater-based stories. The social story is written into the theater context, and the autistic children are allowed to practice role-play in the theater, to promote their further understanding of abstract things, body and emotional expression.

3 Methods

3.1 Participants

In this study, 4 children were recruited to participate in AR social game training based on theater; one 6-year-old high-function autistic child and three ordinary children with the same age (non-autistic) were included. During the experiment, a total of five social training courses were carried out. Each training involved four children in theater activities, accompanied by the assisted teaching of therapists and observation of social interaction between autistic children and their peers.

3.2 The Purpose of Social Intervention Training of AR Combined with Theater-Based Games

According to the social theory put forward by Aldabas in 2019 [24], peer intervention training will help improve the social behavior and communication skills of ASD children. Therefore, ordinary children and autistic child were taught in this study through the theater-based AR social game training system. The teaching content was adapted from the social stories and character situations in the story of "The Wizard of OZ" to provide social training for autistic children and their peers. During the training process, they were combined with theater-based storybooks (Fig. 1) to guide the game, and integrate the situational props of the theater and other characters to perform together.

Fig. 1. Theater-based social storybook

In the course of training, children gain basic concepts and understanding of the development and role of "The Wizard of OZ" story through theater-based storybook, and interact with different role-players (peers, 3 children with the same age). The purpose is to help autistic children understand abstract social stories and social situations, and then through role-play and AR social game system to promote autistic children in pretend play, and guide them to have simple social interaction.

3.3 Design and Development of a "Theater-Based AR Social Game Training System"

The system of this study mainly uses theater-based storybooks, and combines AR app and interactive props as the main social training tools. The social situational characters and scenario scripts in the theater-based storybook are adapted from the original story of "The Wizard of OZ", compiled after discussion with the therapist. Theatrical storybooks were made into entity storybooks by Adobe Illustrator, which makes storybooks easy to teach autistic children to read. The supporting AR social game system was developed by using a Unity game engine and Vuforia engine suite; the 3D symbolic animation modeled by Maya was added. Finally, the AR symbolic symbol card was made into AR Marker to provide the interaction of autistic children in theater situations, and cards also became part of the role-play of children and scene props. After the completion of the system design, it was handed over to the therapist for related delivery and training evaluation, to ensure that the autistic children would not feel discomfort and panic in its use.

3.4 Teaching Implementation and Progress

Stage 1: Building social correspondence between characters and situational stories. After the completion of the theater-based AR social game training system, we conducted teaching and training through two-stage courses. The first stage was to establish the social correspondence between characters and situational stories, and letting the therapist accompany autistic children trying to understand the social relations and social events described in the situational story by reading the theater-based storybook (script) preview. The theater-based storybook is based on theater concepts, like actors previewing a script, enabling autistic children to connect all the social situations encountered in the storybook naturally and logically through the script, and establish the social relationship between the story characters through these social situations and story scripts (Fig. 2).

Fig. 2. Autistic child and other participants read theater-based social storybooks and build character relationships

Stage 2: Social script rehearsal and actual performance with an AR social game training system.

The second stage was script rehearsal and actual performance with an AR social game training system. After the first stage established a structured concept and understanding of the social plot of the storybook, it allowed the autistic and ordinary children to wear corresponding role clothing, and according to the written story script, figure out the dialogue and emotional correspondence of each role. This stage mainly made the autistic children practice active speech, maintain continuous dialogue, describe situations, etc. In the process of role-play, we linked different symbolic object cards through different scenario scripts (the cards were accompanied by AR animation to attract the autistic children to pay attention to these symbolic objects and the concepts and abstract symbols behind them) (as shown in Table 1), teach the autistic children to learn the corresponding abstract symbols, and increase the opportunity of social interaction with peers by understanding these symbols, while observing the social actions and dialogues of the characters (Fig. 3).

3.5 Evaluation Tool

During the experiment, 5 social training courses were conducted, guided by the therapist to assist the autistic children to perform role-play independently. After each training,

Table 1. Abstract symbolic actions and the corresponding relationship between animation and entity symbols

Entities + action	Symbolic animation	Corresponding symbolic meaning
Given book	Bright head	Wisdom
Given axe	Strong arms	Courage
Given crown	Shiny heart	Self-confidence

Fig. 3. The participants wear role clothings for role playing

we recorded the participation of the autistic cases, and evaluated their behaviors in the process of social activities and role-play through MBV Quantification [26]; this assessment method can help quantify the behavioral performance of autistic children. After 5 training sessions, the researchers could observe whether autistic children have improved in five behavioral indicators: mutual attention, proximity, responds, meaningful conversation and after sharing. From the scores of these 5 behavioral indicators, we could know whether autistic children can: (1) participate in the training courses continuously and attentively, (2) interpret the scenario with their peers after having memory of the structure of the story script, (3) understand and respond to the symbolic symbols of others when asked by their peers, (4) engage in pretend play independently in the training process, and (5) understand the meaning of the story and respond to the questions of therapists and researchers. By using this assessment method, we could judge whether the "theater-based AR social game training system" developed in this study can improve the understanding of social symbols and show sufficient positive and positive behaviors of autistic children.

4 Results

In this study, we conducted 5 play experiments and observations with a special education teacher and a therapist on an autistic child, and recorded the whole training process. During the whole training, we cooperated with three other ordinary children in peer cooperation to understand whether the theater-based AR social game training system and the AR social game under the teaching strategy can help autistic children to more easily carry out role-play, promote the disguised game, and improve their social ability such as empathy.

Through the statistical analysis of video coding by MBV, we used 0–5 points to evaluate whether autistic cases could master the abstract social cognition, symbolic symbols and peer interaction of theater design. (0 indicates the lack of this capability; 5 indicates that the capability pointer has been fully demonstrated). After 5 times of play experiment and observation, the social training performance of the autistic was discussed with the therapist, and the scores were as follows: (a) the training strategy for the attention ability of autistic children got 4.2 points (0 for no attention, 5 for enough attention). (b) The ability to actively participate in the training course got 3.4 points (0 represents difficulty in responding, 5 represents active involvement). (c) The response ability of role-play scored 3.4 points (0 for difficult response, 5 for smooth response). (d) The ability of communication and expression was scored 4 points (0 for difficult communication with peers, 5 for smooth communication with peers). (e) The ability to share events scored 3.2 points (0 for difficult to describe sharing, 5 for active description sharing). From the above scores, we can see that the theater-based AR social game training system and teaching strategies led to positive social cognitive improvement for autistic children, and improved their degree of focus and use interest.

In general, after 5 times of play experiments and observation (Fig. 4), the therapist pointed out that autistic children and general children showed active participation, which confirmed that the theater-based AR social game training system and teaching strategies had a considerable attraction for autistic cases, and again proved that the learning effect of AR for autistic children was positive and positive. In addition, the scores of autism cases in five ability indicators are good. Although the autistic case needs the guidance of the therapist when it actively starts the dialogue, it can also perform well in the subsequent dialogue with peers and body deduction interaction, understand the meaning of abstract symbols and make oral response from the sentences before and after the dialogue. The above results also reflect that the autistic case can master the social relationship under the theater-based AR social game training Context content, which helps autistic cases integrate into more real social situations.

Fig. 4. Participants make full use of an AR system in social training courses

5 Discussion and Conclusion

Based on the above, it can be proven that the use of a theater-based AR social game training system and teaching strategies can greatly help autistic children to improve their social skills. For autistic children, the understanding of abstract symbols and transposition thinking, and even simple behavior reciprocity improved. We attribute the success of training to the following points:

5.1 Theatre-Based Teaching Structure and Training Strategies Help Autistic Children Understand the Social Situation Framework

The traditional teaching mode is to read a general storybook. Although it provides a simple story content for autistic children, there is no clear social structure and social situation script designed for autistic children. In contrast, through the designed theater-based storybook and AR system, just like reading a script, we can copy a previously understood social situation, and in the actual rehearsal, through the interaction with ordinary children and the guidance of the therapist, we can organize and realize the social framework constructed in the story into the real social interaction, enabling autistic children to initiate and maintain the conversation in a gradual way.

5.2 Theatre-Based Games Combined with AR Provide Autistic Children with Increased Attention and Interactivity to the Symbol

The biggest advantage of theater-based games is to provide autistic children with an environment close to the real world for social speculation and imitation in different situations. In role-play with ordinary child participants, the 3D dynamic symbols (bright heart or strong arm 3D animation) on the screen will attract the attention of autistic children after scanning the picture card through the tablet computer. By displaying 3D dynamic symbols, autistic children can understand and pay attention to the symbolic meanings behind abstract concepts, and help therapists and teachers to explain social cognitive ability in a direct and simple way, and even further guide and explain other social reciprocal behaviors. Compared with simple role-play games, theater-based games combine AR, so that autistic children and ordinary child participants can use the content generated by AR to increase their attention and interaction to the symbol, and master different social symbol content through arranged situational scripts.

5.3 Cooperative Strategies with Peers Help Autistic Children to Pretend Play in Theatre-Based Games

Through the training process, it was found that autistic children began to talk according to the script at the beginning, and then to ask and respond to each other. Autistic children would observe and start to imitate the tone and action of their peers. After the guidance of researchers and therapists, they would slowly practice the dialogue with symbols. For example, autistic children will ask for the meaning of "courage" in abstract words, and finally bring it into the dialogue. When the other person asks, "do you want to help me find my lost courage?", autistic children bring the axe through understanding the situation of the story, a symbol of courage, to other role-play participants, and successfully carry out role-play and pretend play. The training process can effectively help autistic children to maintain dialogue and bring in abstract symbolic meaning through the peer cooperation strategy and theater game structure.

5.4 Future Work

The theater-based AR social game training system and teaching strategies designed in this study are aimed at improving the transformation and understanding of social cognitive abstract symbols of autistic children, as well as their social reciprocity skills. Observing the use of this training by autistic and ordinary child participants reveals that it can promote their social adaptation and oral expression. We also found that theater-based games can maintain autistic focus and interest in learning tasks when combined with the structured strategies of AR app. In addition to autistic children, we observe that the behavior of ordinary children participating in the experiment can be improved. Therefore, the curriculum design of this training system is also applicable to ordinary children and even older groups. In addition, the researchers also collected the statistical data and considered adding different theater-based story scripts to help improve the theater-based AR social game training system and teaching strategies, so that more experimental data can be further studied in the future.

Acknowledgments. We are grateful to the Executive Yuan and Ministry of Science and Technology for funding under project No. MOST 107-2218-E-027 -013 -MY2.

References

1. Hooper, S.R., Poon, K.K., Marcus, L., Fine, C.: Neuropsychological characteristics of school-age children with high-functioning autism: performance on the NEPSY. Child Neuropsychol. **12**(4–5), 299–305 (2006)
2. Baron-Cohen, S., Leslie, A.M., Frith, U.: Does the autistic child have a "theory of mind". Cognition **21**(1), 37–46 (1985)
3. Fodstad, J.C., Matson, J.L., Hess, J., Neal, D.: Social and communication behaviours in infants and toddlers with autism and pervasive developmental disorder-not otherwise specified. Dev. Neurorehabil. **12**(3), 152–157 (2009)
4. McCune, L.: Developing symbolic abilities. In: Wagoner, B. (ed.) Symbolic Transformation: The Mind in Movement Through Culture and Society, pp. 173–192. Routledge, London (2010)
5. Honey, E., Leekam, S., Turner, M., McConachie, H.: Repetitive behaviour and play in typically developing children and children with autism spectrum disorders. J. Autism Dev. Disord. **37**(6), 1107–1115 (2007)
6. Rutherford, M.D., Rogers, S.J.: Cognitive underpinnings of pretend play in autism. J. Autism Dev. Disord. **33**(3), 289–302 (2003)
7. Mundy, P., Sigman, M., Ungerer, J., Sherman, T.: Nonverbal communication and play correlates of language development in autistic children. J. Autism Dev. Disord. **17**(3), 349–364 (1987)

8. Kovshoff, H., Grindle, C.F., Hastings, R.P.: A psychological perspective. Child and Adolescent Psychopathology: Theoretical and Clinical Implications, p. 246 (2006)
9. Gray, C.A., Garand, J.D.: Social stories: Improving responses of students with autism with accurate social information. Focus Autistic Behav. **8**(1), 1–10 (1993)
10. More, C.: Digital stories targeting social skills for children with disabilities: multidimensional learning. Interv. Sch. Clin. **43**(3), 168–177 (2008)
11. Hutchins, T.L., Prelock, P.A.: The social validity of Social Stories™ for supporting the behavioural and communicative functioning of children with autism spectrum disorder. Int. J. Speech Lang. Pathol. **15**(4), 383–395 (2013)
12. Stagnitti, K., Unsworth, C., Rodger, S.: Development of an assessment to identify play behaviours that discriminate between the play of typical preschoolers and preschoolers with pre-academic problems. Can. J. Occup. Ther. **67**(5), 291–303 (2000)
13. Charman, T., Swettenham, J., Baron-Cohen, S., Cox, A., Baird, G., Drew, A.: Infants with autism: an investigation of empathy, pretend play, joint attention, and imitation. Dev. Psychol. **33**(5), 781 (1997)
14. Jarrold, C., Boucher, J., Smith, P.: Symbolic play in autism: a review. J. Autism Dev. Disord. **23**(2), 281–307 (1993)
15. Manning, M.M., Wainwright, L.D.: The role of high level play as a predictor social functioning in autism. J. Autism Dev. Disord. **40**(5), 523–533 (2010)
16. Hobson, J.A., Hobson, R.P., Malik, S., Bargiota, K., Caló, S.: The relation between social engagement and pretend play in autism. Br. J. Dev. Psychol. **31**(1), 114–127 (2013)
17. Campbell, S.B., Mahoney, A.S., Northrup, J., Moore, E.L., Leezenbaum, N.B., Brownell, C.A.: Developmental changes in pretend play from 22-to 34-months in younger siblings of children with autism spectrum disorder. J. Abnorm. Child Psychol. **46**(3), 639–654 (2018)
18. Bai, Z., Blackwell, A.F., Coulouris, G.: Through the looking glass: Pretend play for children with autism. In: 2013 IEEE International Symposium on Mixed and Augmented Reality (ISMAR), pp. 49–58. IEEE (2013)
19. Bai, Z., Blackwell, A.F., Coulouris, G.: Using augmented reality to elicit pretend play for children with autism. IEEE Trans. Visual Comput. Graphics **21**(5), 598–610 (2014)
20. Lee, I.J.: Augmented reality coloring book: an interactive strategy for teaching children with autism to focus on specific nonverbal social cues to promote their social skills. Interact. Stud. **20**(2), 256–274 (2019)
21. Tang, T.Y., Xu, J., Winoto, P.: An augmented reality-based word-learning mobile application for children with autism to support learning anywhere and anytime: object recognition based on deep learning. In: Antona, M., Stephanidis, C. (eds.) HCII 2019. LNCS, vol. 11573, pp. 182–192. Springer, Cham (2019). https://doi.org/10.1007/978-3-030-23563-5_16
22. Bappa, S., Etherton, M.: Popular theatre: Voice of the oppressed. Commonwealth **25**(4), 126–130 (1983)
23. Reading, S., Reading, J., Padgett, R. J., Reading, S., Pryor, P.: The use of theatre to develop social and communication behaviors for students with autism. J. Speech Pathol. Therapy **1**(1) (2015)
24. Kim, A.J., Stembridge, S., Lawrence, C., Torres, V., Miodrag, N., Lee, J., Boynes, D.: Neurodiversity on the stage: the effects of inclusive theatre on youth with autism. Int. J. Educ. Soc. Sci. **2**(9), 27–39 (2015)
25. Pomeroy, R.: Improv for autism: using theatre to teach social communication skills to children and youth with autism (2016)
26. Albo-Canals, J., et al.: A pilot study of the KIBO robot in children with severe ASD. Int. J. Soc. Robot. **10**(3), 371–383 (2018)

Optimized User Experience Design for Augmentative and Alternative Communication via Mobile Technology: Using Gamification to Enhance Access and Learning for Users with Severe Autism

Oliver Wendt[1(✉)], Natalie E. Allen[2], Olivia Z. Ejde[2], Sylvia C. Nees[2], Megan N. Phillips[2], and Daniella Lopez[1]

[1] Research Lab on Augmentative and Alternative Communication in Autism, School of Communication Sciences and Disorders, University of Central Florida, Orlando, FL, USA
oliver.wendt@ucf.edu

[2] Department of Computer Science and Engineering, Rose-Hulman Institute of Technology, Terre Haute, IN, USA

Abstract. One of the most significant disabilities in autism spectrum disorder (ASD) includes a delay in, or total lack of, the development of spoken language. Approximately half of those on the autism spectrum are functionally non-verbal or minimally verbal and will not develop sufficient natural speech or writing to meet their daily communication needs. These individuals receive intervention in the area of augmentative and alternative communication (AAC) using mobile technologies. AAC services ideally should be provided starting at an early age but many young learners experience some degree of difficulty in gross and fine motor functioning that prevents accessing and benefitting from mobile AAC applications.

A suite of evidence-based iPhone® applications, SPEAKall! Lite© and SPEAKplay!©, was developed to help learners with ASD (a) acquire initial speech and language skills, and (b) train critical gestures needed to fully access mobile touch screen devices. SPEAKplay! trains the performance of gestures including Directed and Sustained Touch, Drag and Drop, and Vertical and Horizontal Swipe through a gamification approach. Serious game design principles guided the creation of three arcade-style games including *Pop the Bubbles*, *Fly the Rocket*, and *Feed the Dino.* Initial usability testing with experienced AAC practitioners indicated SPEAKplay! to be a potentially viable intervention tool.

Keywords: Autism spectrum disorder · Mobile technology · Augmentative and alternative communication · Gamification · Serious game design · Motor access

1 Technology-Based Intervention in Autism Spectrum Disorder

1.1 Learners with Minimally-Verbal Autism and Their Needs

Individuals with autism spectrum disorder (ASD) experience a severe delay or atypical development in the areas of language and communication (American Psychiatric

C. Stephanidis et al. (Eds.): HCII 2020, LNCS 12426, pp. 412–428, 2020.
https://doi.org/10.1007/978-3-030-60149-2_32

Association 2013). Worldwide, 1 in 160 children is estimated to have ASD (Elsabbagh et al. 2012), and it has been estimated that between 30% and 50% of children with ASD are non-verbal or minimally verbal (Tager-Flusberg and Kasari 2013). Students with ASD who are nonverbal, or minimally verbal can face significant challenges to academic growth because speaking and listening are key components of literacy measures in K-12 education that require developmentally appropriate and socially expected levels of proficiency in all four literacy modalities across several content areas. Limited communication skills also pose repercussions beyond the academic setting by predisposing these students to increased risks of depression, lowered sense of well-being, lack of autonomy and self-determination in the workplace, and in society at large (Taylor et al. 2015; Scott et al. 2018; Kirby et al. 2016; Henninger and Taylor 2012; Chiang et al. 2011; Hotulainen et al. 2010; and Friedman et al. 2019).

The legal and social impetus for providing evidence-based practices to help this student population succeed is clear. However, very few studies have examined "the progress or lack thereof for minimally verbal children with ASD" in response to interventions (Bak et al. 2017). This area of research has been intriguing legislators, educators, clinicians, and researchers since Kanner's identification of autism in 1943. Improving educational results for children with disabilities, including minimally verbal children with ASD, is an essential component of policies across national boundaries and jurisdictions since an ever growing corpus of research shows that educational attainment is linked to improved chances for equity of opportunity, full participation in society, independent living, and economic self-sufficiency for individuals with disabilities (World Health Organization 2014a, 2014b; American Speech Language Hearing Association 2016; U.S. Department of Education 2004). Clinical interventions to improve educational outcomes for minimally verbal children with ASD are critical for meeting these goals.

1.2 Intervention Through Augmentative and Alternative Communication

In clinical and educational practice, the most immediate need for learners with severe, minimally verbal autism is to establish functional communication to meet basic wants and needs and to participate in daily life. Augmentative and Alternative Communication (AAC) interventions have been developed and implemented to address this most pressing need. AAC approaches range from low-technology paper-based communication boards (Ratusnik and Ratusnik 1974) to the more current and widely used high-technology strategies including speech generating devices (SGDs) and tablets such as the iPad with corresponding tablet applications (Wendt et al. 2019a, 2019b; Waddington et al. 2014).

The growing ubiquity of smartphone and tablet usage in society at large has prompted much interest in the deployment of this convenient and affordable technology due to its social validity. This normalization of usage fosters potential for increased therapeutic applications to enhance communication and to also ideally increase the natural speech production of minimally verbal children (McNaughton and Light 2013; Schäfer et al. 2016).

1.3 New Opportunities and Challenges Through Mobile Technologies

The introduction of the Apple iPad in 2010 had a significant impact on the range of tools available for AAC intervention. Established dedicated devices, that had a rather high price point and were limited to communication purposes, lost their appeal as the go-to solution for minimally verbal children with autism. The iPad provided a more flexible platform to run a variety of AAC apps to go beyond the functions that most SGDs were able to supply. iPad-based AAC interventions helped to save costs while increasing motivation and social appeal (Wendt 2014).

This affinity for technology has been further explored in the systematic literature review conducted by Valencia et al. (2019). The authors point to a growing body of research documenting benefits of technology-based interventions in educational settings, with about 25% of included studies targeting communication and language skills as primary learning outcomes.

The literature on technology usage to teach students with ASD suggests the need for future research into user experience and effects of gamification on learning to validate this mode of intervention (Valencia et al. 2019). The need for further validation of, and research in, technology-based interventions is also highlighted in the meta-analysis by Watkins and colleagues (2019), examining best practices for students with ASD in inclusive educational settings. Nonverbal, or minimally verbal students with ASD in particular are an underrepresented population in the intervention literature, for example composing only 4% of included participants in the meta-analysis by Watkins et al. (2019).

1.4 SPEAKall! for AAC Intervention in Autism Spectrum Disorder

To create an autism-specific AAC solution that directly targets critical speech and language milestones while being sensitive to the cognitive and sensory processing characteristics of learners with autism, the UCF Research Lab on AAC in Autism developed a suite of mobile AAC applications including SPEAKall!® and SPEAKall! Lite®.

The original SPEAKall! application was designed for the iPad® platform to target AAC intervention outcomes such as functional communication skills, natural speech production, and social-pragmatic behaviors. SPEAKall! creates a very intuitive user experience for the non-verbal learner (see Fig. 1). A selection portion at the top of the screen provides graphic symbols and photographs which can be moved via drag and drop to a storyboarding strip at the bottom to construct sentences. The drag and drop gesture can be substituted by a simple touch gesture for learners with motor control difficulties. Caretakers can take their own photos to extend the existing bank of symbols and to create relevant and recognizable content that reflects the user's everyday life. Once a user combines the symbols into a sentence, the activation of the "Speak All" icon will speak the sentence out loud. Voice-output is provided via pre-recorded speech from caretakers or by using Apple's synthetic Siri voice.

To explore the full functionality of iOS-based platforms and to fill the gap on feasible AAC apps for smaller screen devices, the research lab developed an iPhone/iPod-based version, SPEAKall! Lite (see Fig. 2). The purpose of SPEAKall! Lite is to provide a

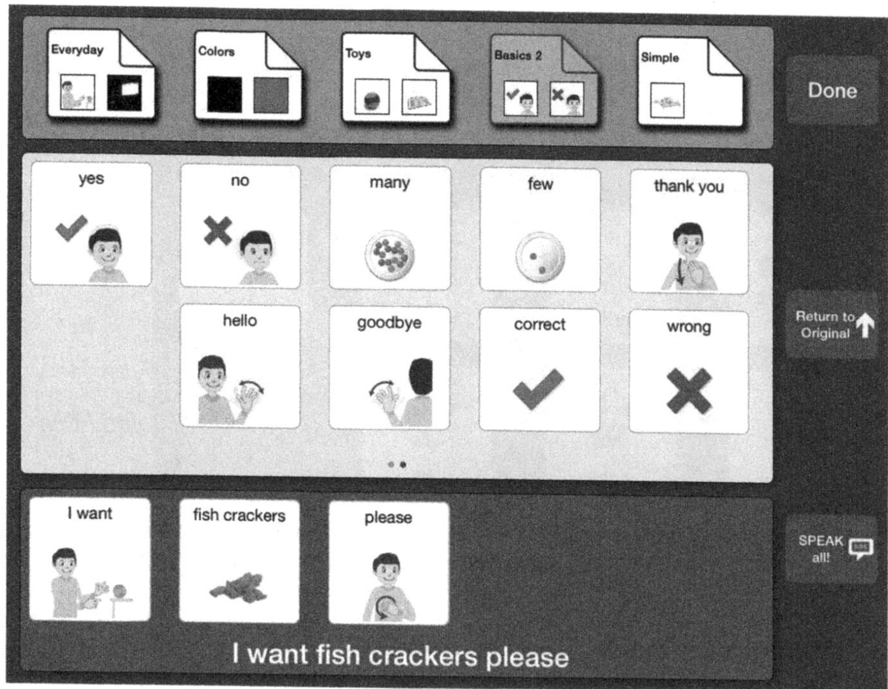

Fig. 1. An example for a communication display on the SPEAKall! application to teach functional communication skills. (Courtesy of the UCF Research Lab on AAC in Autism).

readily available communication tool for individuals and their caretakers. Because many families affected by autism or developmental disability may not have immediate access to an iPad, but may already possess an iPhone, SPEAKall! Lite has the potential to be an instantly available solution that practitioners and caretakers can use to establish basic but crucial communication skills and assess whether or not the learner may benefit from a mobile technology solution.

From an early intervention perspective, AAC experiences should be provided to learners with severe speech and language delay as early as 2 years of age (Davidoff 2017). At such a young age, however, many young infants, especially when affected by developmental delay or disorders, do not possess fully developed fine motor skills to operate mobile devices with strong proficiency. Particularly for learners with autism, it has been well documented that about 80% are affected by some difficulty in fine or gross motor function (Hilton et al. 2012; Isenhower et al. 2012). Often times, additional training becomes necessary to teach the proper motor access strategies for the user to properly operate applications on mobile devices.

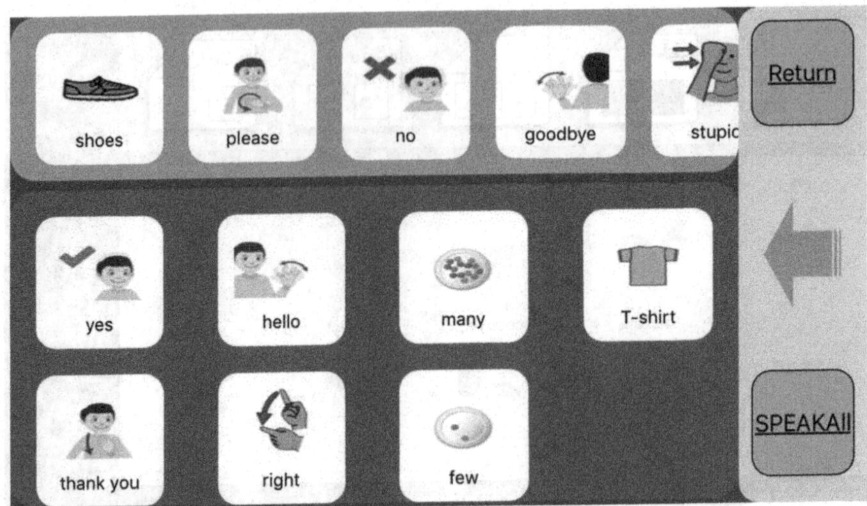

Fig. 2. An example for a communication display to teach basic wants and needs with the iPhone application "SPEAKall! Lite©". (Courtesy of the UCF Research Lab on AAC in Autism).

1.5 Gamification to Enhance Learner Experience

Gamification is a design approach for optimized human computer interaction that holds great promise to facilitate skill acquisition on mobile devices used in ASD.

Originally, gamification was defined as the "application of game-like accelerated user interface design to make electronic transactions both fast and enjoyable" (Marczewski 2015). The approach has grown in popularity because it enables skill development and retention. By providing incentives to users and motivating them to strive towards rewards throughout their user experience, users tend to spend more time interacting with the technology. Essentially, gamification uses the most prominent elements of games and combines these elements with nongame components and contexts to motivate users to increase target behaviors (Goethe 2019). It enhances the level of user engagement and leads users to make the most out of their natural desires including learning, socializing, achievement, mastery, and status. Training skills and behaviors that originally appeared hard, tedious, and boring can become a fun and motivating exercise (Hamari 2017).

Of particular interest for computer based ASD intervention is the idea of 'serious game design', an approach to boost the effect of these interventions, facilitate acquisition and generalization of targeted skills to everyday environments (Whyte et al. 2015). Serious games incorporate pedagogical principles and motivational aspects of game design to optimize the process of skill acquisition while also exploring the benefits of motivational design components to create the best possible learning experiences for the user. Serious games have shown promise in enhancing the skill repertoire related to emotion recognition in youth with ASD (Tang et al. 2018) and the potential to improve a variety of ASD interventions (Boucenna et al. 2014; Grossard et al. 2017).

1.6 Project Goals

Our project goals were to use the approach of serious game design to develop a series of gesture-based games that directly target the difficulties in learning complex and multi-step motor skills to access content on mobile AAC devices. The envisioned outcome of engaging with these games was to enhance motor functioning of the young child or first time AAC user to maximize operational competence in navigating touchscreen-based content. With better gesture and operating skills, children can get started earlier on mobile devices and benefit from SPEAKall! and similar AAC applications to the full extent. The purpose for the resulting application was to train users in major iOS gestures through a gaming experience that is engaging, rewarding, and motivating while targeting fine motor control skills.

2 Design and Development Process

2.1 General Requirements for SPEAKplay!

The design and development process was a collaborative effort between a senior design team in software engineering at Rose-Hulman Institute of Technology and the AAC and Autism Research Lab at the University of Central Florida. The larger project team decided to label the new application "SPEAKplay!". An initial needs assessment revealed the following critical user aspects to address:

1. Children with special needs, in this case with severe communication disorders, have difficulty performing the motor tasks necessary to use touch screen devices. This prevents them from accessing and using learning and therapeutic applications to their full extent.
2. Games should be intuitive.
3. Games should be engaging and motivating.
4. Games should be challenging without causing frustration.
5. Current games are not child friendly.
6. Current games take too long to play.
7. Current games do not offer an option to pause.
8. Existing applications do not take into account that children do not have the ability to configure the application to fit their needs in terms of cognitive, motor, and sensory abilities and characteristics.

Subsequently, the larger project team identified the general design requirements for the SPEAKplay! application:

A. SPEAKplay! will train motor capabilities for operating AAC apps on mobile devices; the training will focus on the critical gestures of (i) Directed and Sustained Touch, (ii) Drag and Drop, and (iii) Vertical and Horizontal Swipe.
B. Different levels of difficulty are desirable to gradually enhance learner performance.
C. The skills should be taught through gamification elements that keep the learner engaged and motivated. This can be accomplished through a series of brief "arcade-style" games.

D. The games include "Pop the Bubbles" (for targeted touch), "Fly the Rocket" (for targeted and sustained touch), and "Feed the Dino" (for horizontal and vertical swipes as well as drag and drop).

2.2 General Design and Visualization Process

The general design and visualization process focused on the goal of helping children learn and practice the motor skills necessary to use other applications in the SPEAK*** suite. Game design was the priority, with an admin mode serving as a lightweight method of enhancing basic games on a per user basis. To get started, the UCF research team created some initial game idea sketches. These pen and paper sketches focused on capturing a cohesive theme for each game, defining the gesture skill to practice, and creating a simple, yet engaging, layout and play style to teach the target skill (see Fig. 3).

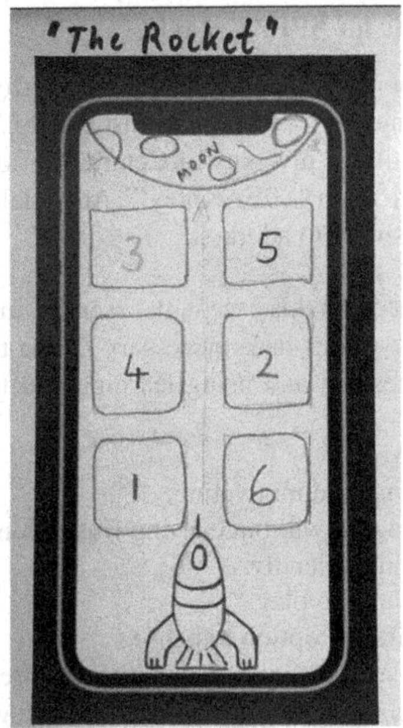

Fig. 3. An initial sketch of the Rocket Game. (Courtesy of the UCF Research Lab on AAC in Autism).

Afterwards, the Rose-Hulman team created prototypes for the entire application using Figma ©, v 76.4.0 (Field 2019), a collaborative interface design tool (see Fig. 4). Over several weeks of discussion, the team utilized Figma to quickly and easily make app design changes, from overall screen flow to color, sizing, and animation choices.

Figma's demo features allow the prototype to be downloaded to a mobile phone and capture the "feel" of clicking through the app (see Fig. 5).

A variety of graphic images were incorporated to enhance visual appeal. Most icons came from Flaticon (Freepik Company 2019), a source for thousands of free to use

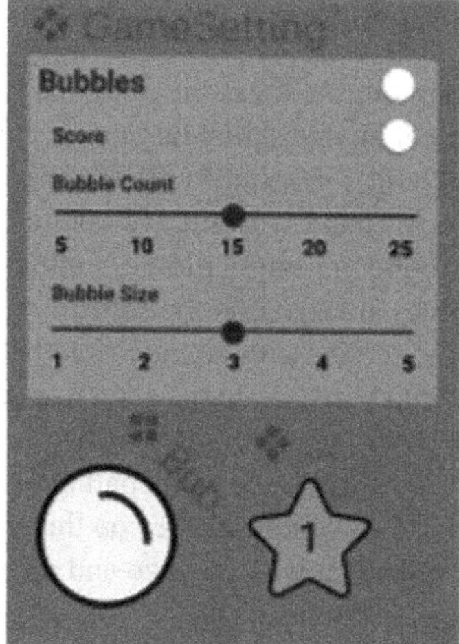

Fig. 4. Reusable Figma components. (Courtesy of Rose-Hulman Institute of Technology).

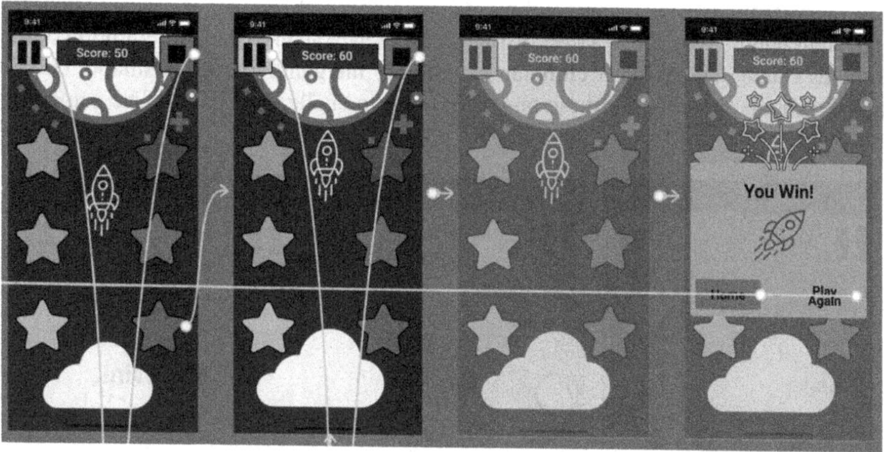

Fig. 5. Various screens of the Rocket Game linked to allow application playthrough. (Courtesy of the UCF Research Lab on AAC in Autism).

images. The prototype design process resulted in the decision to create a home page with a list of games and a button to access the administrative mode. Games can be launched directly from the home screen and can be paused and stopped during gameplay. The administrative mode was kept minimal, allowing a few settings for each game to be changed on a per user basis. One such setting option per game, is the ability to hide it from the home page's game list. Once the prototypes were finalized, the team created views of the application using the storyboard on the development environment Xcode, v.11.5 (Apple Inc. 2020). Because iPhone screen sizes vary across device versions, the team programmatically positioned the same icons used in the prototypes to ensure uniform display across iPhone devices.

2.3 Gamification Element "Bubbles"

While the Bubbles Game looks simple, it has the potential to train children to learn two of the most essential touchscreen motor skills: targeted touch as well as touch and hold (a.k.a "press" and "press and hold"; Wrobleski 2010). When the user opens the game, they are faced with a blue background with the silhouette of a bathtub on the bottom. Placed upon this blue background are multicolored bubbles serving as the main touch targets in the game. The bubbles are fixed on the screen, but when tapped or "popped" by the user, disappear from the screen with an auditory "bubble pop" cue. When all of the bubbles are "popped", a "You win!" dialogue screen appears informing the user that they have completed the Bubbles Game and giving them the chance to return home or play again. Upon pressing "Play again", the same bathtub background is displayed but with different randomized locations of the bubbles on the screen.

This game is highly customizable, with the size and number of bubbles available to modify through the application's settings page. The fixed screen size can accommodate more small bubbles onscreen than large bubbles. For this reason, the maximum number of bubbles onscreen ultimately depends on the set size of the screen. In terms of difficulty levels, a Bubbles Game set up with a low number of onscreen bubbles and large bubble size is substantially easier than a Bubbles Game with a high number of onscreen bubbles and small bubble size. Once a user displays proficiency at an easier configuration of the Bubbles Game, the parent or clinician can modify the game to display smaller bubble targets and a larger count of these targets in order to challenge the user. The game also

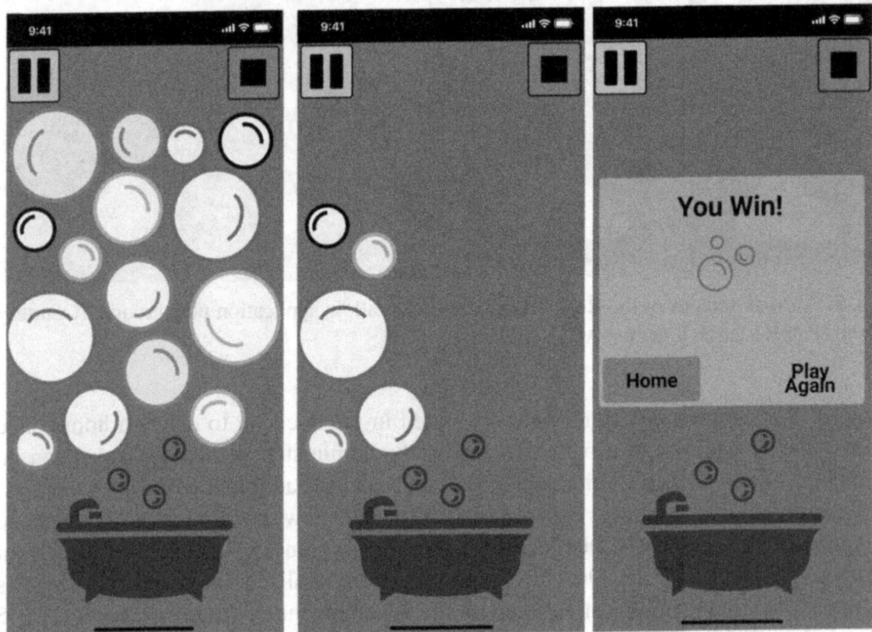

Fig. 6. The Bubbles Game sequence of events, from start to finish. (Courtesy of the UCF Research Lab on AAC in Autism).

includes pause, stop, and start functionality. At any point in the game, the user can press the pause button in the upper left corner of the screen to pause the game. The game will freeze and a pop-up will display with a "Resume" button allowing the user to resume the game upon clicking. The stop button is located in the upper right corner of the game. A button press will trigger a pop-up window providing "Restart Game" and "Return to Home" options. Selecting the "Restart Game" option will restart the game with a new randomized set of bubbles. Selecting the "Return to Home" option will bring the user back to the application's home screen (Fig. 6).

2.4 Gamification Element "Rocket"

The purpose of the Rocket Game is to provide additional training for targeted touch using a different scenario that mimics a sequence of button presses typically found on mobile AAC applications. The Rocket Game teaches its users to respond to a visual stimulus, the movements of the stars. The stars either pulse, shake or flash. When pulsing, stars repeatedly expand and contract. Shaking consists of the star moving slightly from side to side repeatedly. Flashing means that the star becomes transparent across a gradient and then returns to opaque. Each movement type lasts between 1.3 and 1.6 s, pauses for two seconds, and then repeats the animation until the user selects that star. When the activated star is pressed, the star stops animating, then a new star becomes activated and animates. The rocket icon advances towards the moon. On the last turn, the rocket reaches the moon, and the user wins the game. A popup with an explosion of animated

Fig. 7. Images of each star configuration in the Rocket Game. (Courtesy of the UCF Research Lab on AAC in Autism).

stars appears, with the words "You won!" There is an option to return to the home screen or to repeat the game.

The Rocket Game has three levels of difficulty; four, six, or eight stars (see Fig. 7). Activated stars and animations are always random. Thus, the user will not be forced to continue tapping in the same spot each time and must move to a different one. Randomization of the sequence also makes the game different and unpredictable each time. Each difficulty level places the stars at slightly different places on the screen in order to properly accommodate the varying number of stars. For graphics, as in the Figma mocks, icons from Flaticon were used for the rocket, moon and stars. Star colors were chosen to be distinctive from one another and eye-catching, without being excessive.

2.5 Gamification Element "Dino"

The last game in SPEAKplay! is the Dino Game. This game aims to provide practice dragging elements on a phone to on-screen targets. It serves as a precursor to the "Drag & Drop" mode for building sentences within the SPEAKall! application. The user learns to press and hold onto a dinosaur and move it around to food and bones scattered around the screen. To reward and encourage the user to keep playing, the dinosaur dances for a moment as bones are collected before continuing. Once all the food and bones are collected, the user drags the dinosaur to its home to complete the game and reach the win screen. From there, the player returns to the home screen or plays again. When replaying, the food and bones are placed in new locations on the screen to provide a fresh game for the user.

The game has two modes, one with a free moving dino in Fig. 8 and one with a path following dino shown in Fig. 9. For the "free moving dino" mode, food and bones are placed all over the screen and the player moves the dinosaur anywhere on the screen. This mode allows the user to freely test dragging on a touch screen. To increase the difficulty of this mode, there is a setting to increase the amount of food and bones. For the path

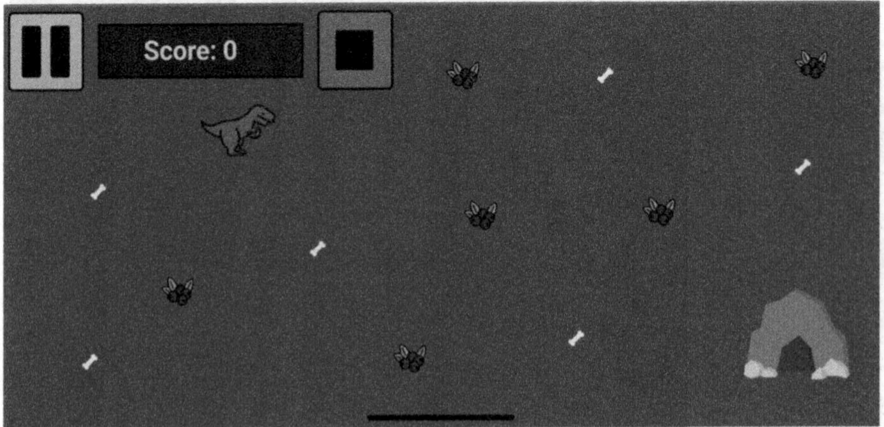

Fig. 8. The Dino Game: "Free Moving" Mode. (Courtesy of the UCF Research Lab on AAC in Autism).

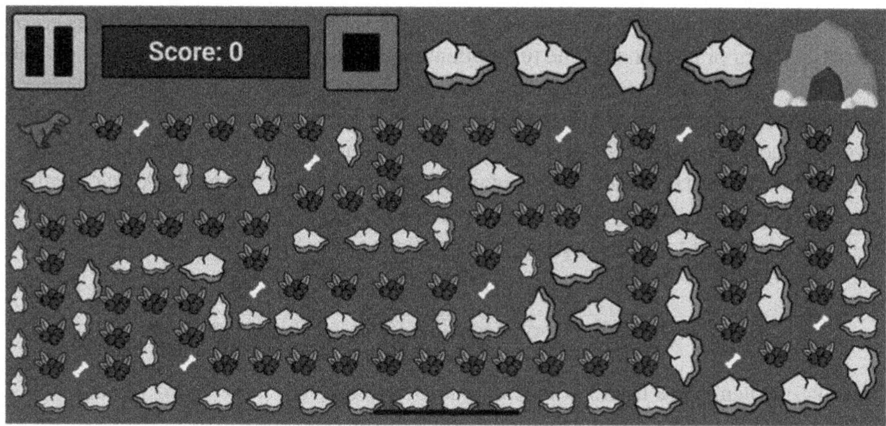

Fig. 9. The Dino Game: "Path" Mode. (Courtesy of the UCF Research Lab on AAC in Autism).

following dino, the game displays a pathway that leads to the dinosaur's home. The food and bones are restricted to the path and the user is only able to move the dinosaur along the path. This mode helps the user learn to target a specific direction if they had trouble targeting food and bones in the first mode. The settings include an option to make the path in this mode longer or shorter to adjust the difficulty of the game to the user's needs.

3 Future Directions and Conclusion

3.1 Clinical Evaluation of SPEAKplay!

Current research efforts in the UCF Research Lab on AAC in Autism aim to generate proof-of-concept for the SPEAKplay! application by generating behavioral data as well as usability data. Behavioral data can be obtained by examining the effects of SPEAKplay! training on enhancing fine motor skills in the context of a single-case experimental design. Single-case research designs are one of the most rigorous methods to examining treatment efficacy and are ranked equally to quasi-experimental group designs in evidence hierarchies for AAC (Schlosser and Raghavendra 2004). These designs are typically examining pre-treatment versus post-treatment performance within a small sample of participants (Kennedy 2005).

Usability data can be generated by asking clinicians and caretakers to provide feedback on the user interface design and gamification elements by quantitative and qualitative survey. For this purpose, the UCF research team designed an initial usability survey containing eleven items. Nine questions required a Likert Scale response of 1 (Strongly Disagree) to 5 (Strongly Agree). Additionally, two open-ended questions were asked regarding needed improvements and desirable new features. The format was loosely based on the Treatment Acceptability Rating Form (TARF) by Reimers and Wacker (1988).

The survey was conducted after respondents had evaluated the SPEAKplay! application through a hands-on test of the latest Beta version with particular instruction to engage with the gamification elements. A total of twelve evaluations were returned by the participating practitioners. The respondents were primarily speech-language pathologists ($n = 7, 58\%$; one person was also certified as an Assistive Technology Provider); the remainder included graduate students in speech-language pathology ($n = 3, 25\%$), university faculty ($n = 1, 8\%$) and a general education teacher ($n = 1, 8\%$).

Results of the Likert Scale items indicate a predominantly "Strongly Agree" evaluation of the application as shown in Table 1. Comments generated through the open-ended questions were used to inform future development (see below).

Table 1. Summary of usability survey – SPEAKplay!

Questionnaire item (rated from 1 = lowest value to 5 = highest value)	User rating mean ($n = 12$)
1. I found the various functions in the SPEAKplay! app were well presented and integrated	4.5 ("strongly agree")
2. I would imagine that most clients and their caretakers would learn to use the SPEAKplay! app quickly	4.8 ("strongly agree")
3. Once I learned to set up SPEAKplay! and used it with my client, I felt confident using it as an intervention tool	4.4 ("agree")
4. The amount of time needed to learn, understand, modify, or develop a specific function of the SPEAKplay! app was appropriate	4.9 ("strongly agree")
5. The look and feel of the SPEAKplay! interface is comparable to other AAC/educational game apps	4.4 ("agree")
6. The three game activities in the SPEAKplay! app offer a fun and motivating experience for my client(s)	4.8 ("strongly agree")
7. The SPEAKplay! app offers meaningful training to work on the motor access skills (e.g., targeted and sustained touch, swiping, dragging, etc.) for my client to better operate a mobile platform	4.8 ("strongly agree")
8. The SPEAKplay! app would be appropriately used with a variety of language development difficulties (e.g., autism, developmental language disorder, general language delay, etc.)	4.8 ("strongly agree")
9. I would recommend the SPEAKplay! app for use as a tool to support the clinical AAC intervention of a client	4.8 ("strongly agree")
10. Which current element of the SPEAKplay! app needs most revision?	"_____"
11. What other features would you like to see incorporated into the application?	"_____"

Note. Questionnaire based on the Treatment Acceptability Rating Form (TARF) by Reimers and Wacker (1988)

3.2 Future Development

During initial usability testing, respondents were asked to indicate elements for improvement of the existing SPEAKplay! application and suggest any additional features that might improve future versions. This input will guide future development efforts. The majority of the respondents' comments focused on three primary issues:

1. Fine-tuning of the motion abilities for the "dino" icon: Responses indicated a need to modify the sensitivity to detect user movement on the screen to better resemble a Drag and Drop gesture. Future work may focus on creating different maze scenarios with varying levels of difficulty. Potential activities may include further exercises to drag the "dino" icon to specific screen locations to train a variety of slide gestures.
2. Incorporating progress tracking and scoreboard options: Respondents articulated a need to monitor users'skill development. Such progress tracking will allow to better align the difficulty level for the various games with the current capabilities of the user. Adding on scoreboard and progress tracking options within the games can help users to stay engaged and motivated.
3. Expanding the tutorial within the application: This will help practitioners to quickly learn how to set up user profiles and program games within the application. Future tutorials may also include "best practice" lesson plans and ideas for seamlessly incorporating SPEAKplay! into clinical activities.

In addition, the SPEAKplay! interface can be replicated across a variety of mobile devices and platforms beyond the iPhone. This will allow to extend the motor skills training onto those devices that prospective AAC candidates ultimately end up using. Currently, SPEAKplay! supports a limited range of critical gestures (i.e., Directed and Sustained Touch, Drag and Drop, and Vertical/Horizontal Swipe). Future versions may add training for further gestures such as Free Rotate, Pinch, Spread and Flick that are commonly used in mobile applications designed for young children (Abdul-Aziz 2013). Accompanying research will refine the current SPEAKplay! design and validate its effectiveness to enhance motor access skills and operational competence for mobile touch screen technologies.

3.3 Potential for Gamification to Improve Clinical Practice

In sum, the results from the initial usability testing suggest that SPEAKplay! meets an important clinical need and has the potential to enhance the fine motor skills repertoire needed to access and operate mobile touch-screen devices. Training these motor skills in isolation would be a daunting and difficult to accomplish task. Adopting the principles of 'serious game design' into the SPEAKplay! interface creates an experience that has the potential to be more motivating and engaging for young users or beginning communicators who are making their first steps on mobile devices.

When designing this application, the UCF and Rose-Hulman research teams tried to adhere to the five serious game principles conceptualized by Whyte et al. (2015): 1) embed learning experiences into a motivating storyline (e.g., "feed the dino"), (2) create short term and long term goals that lead up to the targeted skills (e.g., "pop all these bubbles for a reward"), (3) have consistent rewards and feedback to mold behavior and provide guidance through difficult game levels (e.g., "aim for the winning screen"), (4) allow for individualized levels of difficulty that match the activity to the users current capabilities (e.g., "tap four, six, or eight stars to fire the rocket"), and (5) offer the user different choices to support autonomy (e.g., "chose between Bubble, Rocket, or Dino Games"). The utility of this framework goes beyond targeting motor skills in AAC users with severe autism and can easily be extended to other target skills and other target populations within severe communication disorders.

Serious game design holds a lot of promise to benefit acquisition and generalization of emerging expressive and receptive language skills for AAC users. Oftentimes, AAC intervention sessions are focused on repetitive, basic tasks such as choice making, labeling items, and producing short two- or three-term utterances, all of which could be enhanced through a motivating and engaging gamification experience. Inclusive design practices that are focused on seeking direct input from users and related stakeholders (e.g., Frauenberger et al. 2011, 2013) can help to identify those AAC scenarios and activities most appropriate for a gamification approach. Future research in this direction will help to understand the utility of serious game design in enriching mobile technology AAC interventions.

References

Abdul-Aziz, N.A.B.: Childrens interactions with tablet applications: gestures and interface design. Int. J. Comput. Inf. Technol. **2**(3), 447–450 (2013)

American Psychiatric Association: Diagnostic and Statistical Manual of Mental Disorders (DSM-V), 5th edn. American Psychiatric Association, Washington, D. C. (2013)

American Speech-Language-Hearing Association: Scope of practice in speech-language pathology [Scope of Practice]. (2016). www.asha.org/policy/

Apple Inc.: Xcode (Version 11.5) [Computer Software]. https://developer.apple.com/documentation/xcode. Accessed 10 June 2020

Bak, M.Y.S., Plavnick, J.B., Byrne, S.M.: Vocalizations of minimally verbal children with autism spectrum disorder across the school year. Autism **23**(2), 371–382 (2017)

Boucenna, S., Narzisi, A., Tilmont, E., Muratori, F., Pioggia, G., Cohen, D., et al.: Interative technologies for autistic children: a review. Cognit. Comput. **6**(4), 722–740 (2014)

Chiang, H.-M., Cheung, Y.K., Hickson, L., Xiang, R., Tsai, L.Y.: Predictive factors of participation in postsecondary education for high school leavers with autism. J. Autism Dev. Disord. **42**(5), 685–696 (2011). https://doi.org/10.1007/s10803-011-1297-7

Davidoff, B.: AAC with energy – earlier. ASHA Lead. **22**(1), 50–53 (2017)

Elsabbagh, M., et al.: Global prevalence of autism and other pervasive developmental disorders. Autism Res. **5**(3), 160–179 (2012)

Field, D.: Figma Desktop App (Version 76.4.0) [Computer Software]. https://www.figma.com/design/. Accessed 28 Oct 2019

Frauenberger, C., Good, J., Alcorn, A., Pain, H.: Conversing through and about technologies: design critique as an opportunity to engage children with autism and broaden research(er) perspectives. Int. J. Child Comput. Interact. **1**(2), 38–49 (2013)

Frauenberger, C., Good, J., Keay-Bright, W.: Designing technology for children with special needs: bridging perspectives through participatory design. CoDesign **7**(1), 1–28 (2011)

Freepik Company S.L.: 2010–2020. Flaticon [Web Database]. https://www.flaticon.com/. Accessed 28 Oct 2019

Friedman, L., Sterling, A., Dawalt, L.S., Mailick, M.R.: Conversational language is a predictor of vocational independence and friendships in adults with ASD. J. Autism Dev. Disord. **49**(10), 4294–4305 (2019)

Goethe, O.: Gamification Mindset. HIS. Springer, Cham (2019). https://doi.org/10.1007/978-3-030-11078-9

Grossard, C., Grynspan, O., Serret, S., Jouen, A.-L., Bailly, K., Cohen, D.: Serious games to teach social interactions and emotions to individuals with autism spectrum disorders (ASD). Comput. Educ. **113**(Supplement C), 195–211 (2017)

Hamari, J.: Do badges increase user activity? A field experiment on effects of gamification. Comput. Hum. Behav. **71**, 469–478 (2017)

Henninger, N.A., Taylor, J.L.: Outcomes in adults with autism spectrum disorders: a historical perspective. Autism **17**(1), 103–116 (2012)

Hilton, C.L., Zhang, Y., White, M.R., Klohr, C.L., Constantino, J.: Motor impairment in sibling pairs concordant and discordant for autism spectrum disorders. Autism **16**, 430–441 (2012)

Hotulainen, R., Lappalainen, K., Ruoho, K., Savolainen, H.: Pre-school verbo-sensory motor status as a predictor of educational life-courses and self-perceptions of young adults. Int. J. Disabil. Dev. Educ. **57**(3), 299–314 (2010)

Isenhower, R.W., Marsh, K.L., Richardson, M.J., Helt, M., Schmidt, R.C., Fein, D.: Rhythmic bimanual coordination is impaired in young children with autism spectrum disorder. Res. Autism Spect. Disord. **6**, 25–31 (2012)

Kennedy, C.H. (ed.): Single-Case Designs for Educational Research. Pearson Education, Boston (2005)

Kirby, A.V., Baranek, G.T., Fox, L.: Longitudinal predictors of outcomes for adults with autism spectrum disorder. OTJR Occup. Particip. Health **36**(2), 55–64 (2016)

Marczewski, A.: Even Ninja Monkeys Like to Play: Gamification, Game Thinking, and Motivational Design, 1st edn. Gamified UK, UK (2015)

McNaughton, D., Light, J.C.: The iPad and mobile technology revolution: benefits and challenges for individuals who require augmentative and alternative communication. Augment. Altern. Commun. **29**, 107–116 (2013)

Reimers, T.M., Wacker, D.P.: Parents' ratings of the acceptability of behavioral treatment recommendations made in an outpatient clinic: a preliminary analysis of the influence of treatment effectiveness. Behav. Disord. **14**(1), 7–15 (1988)

Ratusnik, C.M., Ratusnik, D.L.: A comprehensive communication approach for a ten year-old nonverbal autistic child. Am. J. Orthopsychiatry **44**(3), 396–403 (1974)

Schäfer, M.C.M., et al.: Research note: attitudes of teachers and undergraduate students regarding three augmentative and alternative communication modalities. Augment. Altern. Commun. **32**(4), 312–319 (2016)

Schlosser, R.W., Raghavendra, P.: Evidence-based practice in augmentative and alternative communication. Augment. Altern. Commun. **20**, 1–21 (2004)

Scott, M., et al.: Factors impacting employment for people with autism spectrum disorder: a scoping review. Autism **23**(4), 869–901 (2018)

Tager-Flusberg, H., Kasari, C.: Minimally verbal school-aged children with autism spectrum disorder: the neglected end of the spectrum. Autism Res. **6**, 468–478 (2013)

Tang, J.S.Y., Falkmer, M., Chen, N.T.M., Bölte, S., Girdler, S.: Designing a serious game for youth with ASD: perspectives from end-users and professionals. J. Autism Dev. Disord. **49**(3), 978–995 (2018)

Taylor, J.L., Henninger, N.A., Mailick, M.R.: Longitudinal patterns of employment and post-secondary education for adults with autism and average-range IQ. Autism **19**(7), 785–793 (2015)

U.S. Department of Education: Building the legacy: IDEA (2004). http://idea.ed.gov

Valencia, K., Rusu, C., Quiñones, D., Jamet, E.: The impact of technology on people with autism spectrum disorder: a systematic literature review. Sensors **19**(20), 4485 (2019)

Waddington, H., et al.: Three children with autism spectrum disorder learn to perform a three-step communication sequence using an iPad®-based speech-generating device. Int. J. Dev. Neurosci. **39**, 59–67 (2014)

Watkins, L., Ledbetter-Cho, K., O'Reilly, M., Barnard-Brak, L., Garcia-Grau, P.: Interventions for students with autism in inclusive settings: a best-evidence synthesis and meta-analysis. Psychol. Bull. **145**(5), 490–507 (2019)

Wendt, O.: Experimental evaluation of SPEAKall! an evidence-based AAC app for individuals with severe autism. Commun. Matters **28**, 26–28 (2014)

Wendt, O., Bishop, G., Thakar, A.: Design and evaluation of mobile applications for augmentative and alternative communication in minimally-verbal learners with severe autism. In: Antona, M., Stephanidis, C. (eds.) HCII 2019. LNCS, vol. 11573, pp. 193–205. Springer, Cham (2019a). https://doi.org/10.1007/978-3-030-23563-5_17

Wendt, O., Hsu, N., Dienhart, A., Cain, L.: Effects of an iPad-based speech generating device infused into instruction with the Picture Exchange Communication System (PECS) for young adolescents and adults with severe autism. Behav. Modif. **43**, 898–932 (2019b). Special Issue on Communicative Interventions

Whyte, E.M., Smyth, J.M., Scherf, K.S.: Designing serious game interventions for individuals with autism. J. Autism Dev. Disord. **45**(12), 3820–3831 (2015)

World Health Organization: "WHA67/2014/REC/1 - Comprehensive and Coordinated Efforts for the Management of Autism Spectrum Disorders." World Health Organization (2014a). www.who.int/mental_health/maternal-child/WHA67.8_resolution_autism.pdf

World Health Organization: International Classification of Functioning, Disability and Health. Geneva, Switzerland (2014b). www.who.int/classifications/icf/en/

Wrobleski, L.: Design for mobile: what gestures do people use? https://www.lukew.com/ff/entry.asp?1197. 22 Sept 2010

A Head Mouse Alternative Solution Proposal for People with Motor Impairments: Design and Usability Assessment Study

Hasan A. Zengin[1], Arsénio Reis[2](✉), João Barroso[2], and Tânia Rocha[2]

[1] Architecture and Engineering Faculty, Burdur Mehmet Akif Ersoy University, Burdur, Turkey
hasalp38@gmail.com

[2] INESC TEC and University of Trás-os-Montes and Alto Douro, Vila Real, Portugal
{ars,jbarroso,trocha}@utad.pt

Abstract. Accessibility is important to include people with disabilities in public life. People with disabilities experience problems in their lives due to products which aren't designed for them. Addressing these problems is the responsibility of all humanity and the search for solutions should increase. Improving disabled persons' lives is only possible by applying some rules to product design, such as, improving use-case scenarios. Software solutions must be considered as products in this case. Developing special software programs and upgrading existing solutions to improve the user experience for disabled persons is the obligation of all software developers. Even though the mouse is one of the most important tools, required to access webpages and many other software programs, using it can be a huge problem for people with disabilities, such as, paralysis patients. Therefore, throughout history, different types of methods have been presented as solution. Most of them are not suitable, due to various reasons, like, economic feasibility, mechanic stability and bad designs. In this work, a new method, with more in-built modern and simple technologies, is presented as an alternative to others. To outclass the good economic advantage of its competitors, a limit was set on a low budget webcam and low-tier computer specifications. The Camera tracks the user's head movements and reacts according to it, using as measurement some metrics about the physiology of human body. Machine learning is used to extract face features and learn the user's face to determine mouse movements. Machine learning was kept as simple as possible, in order to cope with the low system specification limitations. The main topic of the work is the design and development experience. The solution was tested with a small group of participants and their feedbacks were taken to plan for future improvements. In generally, the users' comments were good, although some features, such as sensitivity, should be improved. The result of this work will be used to improve the software solution and hopefully will touch the life of people with disabilities.

Keywords: Accessibility · Mouse · Head-tracking · Computer vision · OpenCV

C. Stephanidis et al. (Eds.): HCII 2020, LNCS 12426, pp. 429–436, 2020.
https://doi.org/10.1007/978-3-030-60149-2_33

1 Introduction

Spinal cord functions outlined in the spine and spinal cord anatomy page may be lost for various reasons. For the spinal cord to lose its function, it must be pressurized due to illness or trauma. Areas that are damaged as a result of this pressure become unable to function. In other words, the contact between the organs and the brain is lost in the damaged areas and below.

1. Diseases
   a. Tumors
   b. Infections
   c. Soft Tissue Diseases
2. Traumas
   a. Traffic Accidents
   b. High Falls
   c. Sportive Injuries
   d. Firearm Injuries
   e. Work Accidents
   f. Natural Disasters

Spinal cord damages have 3 general types:

- Tetraplegia: Disability of arms, body, legs.
- Paraplegy: Disability of body that under neck.
- Low Paraplegia: Disability of Legs.

Persons with spinal injury are classified in 6 different degrees according to their ability to sit and move. These degrees depend on the level of injury, other illness or damage, age, gender, physical structure, motivation and environment. For the person with the spinal cord injury to accept and to best cope with this reality, it is of great importance that the person's family, friends and health workers are encouraging and supportive.

In this work, computer usability tries to improve the life of patients who have spinal cord injuries, especially the tetraplegia and paraplegy type, with head movements to control the mouse device. These patients can't control mouse because today's mouse technologies use arm movements for control, which is not suitable for people unable to move the arms.

2 State of Art Review

To solve this problem, we need to discard the arm movements to control the mouse and a new approach should be implemented to control the computer. Voice recognition technologies are useful, but different applications are not compatible with this method and applications should be adapted to this change. Some devices are available to determine eye movements according to screen position, but this method needs expensive devices and doesn't always work very well [1].

As a different approach, Argyros and Lourakis implemented a hand gesture controller [2], but this method is not suitable for people that can't use their hands. Gratzel et al. [3] has another solution to use computer mouse during the surgery for the doctors but this approach needs movement ability to control it. The most effective method came from Betke et al. [4]. They used computer vision to read head's features and control the mouse, but they had to use advanced camera for this purpose.

With the development of cameras and computer vision methods, it became feasible to apply this approach. A simple algorithm can be the solution for this problem and this paper will present an implementation case.

3 Technology Presentation

The Head Mouse project has a simple algorithm to determine the user's head movements and features. OpenCV is used for the implementation in Python language. The software modules are presented in Table 1, with their descriptions.

Table 1. Head mouse project modules

No	Module	
	Module name	Description
1	cv2	OpenCV is a library of programming functions mainly aimed at real-time computer vision
2	Dlib	Dlib is a general-purpose cross-platform software library. It contains networking, threads, gui, data structures, linear algebra, machine learning, image processing, data mining, text parsing components
3	numpy	Numpy adds support for large, multi-dimensional arrays and matrices, along with a large collection of high-level mathematical functions to operate
4	pyautogui	Cross-platform GUI automation library. Generally using to control mouse and keyboard
5	Imutils	A series of convenience functions to make basic image processing functions such as translation, rotation, resizing, skeletonization, displaying Matplotlib images, sorting contours, detecting edges etc.
6	Time	Vanilla python module to handle time-related tasks
7	face_utils	Imutils's sub-module has facial image operations

Dlib module has a shape_predictor method to use the trained machine learning model "shape_predictor_68_face_landmarks.dat" and returns a predictor method. This file has the weights of the pre-trained model.

Face_utils has statistic validation to extract the features of the faces, such as, left_eye, right_eye, mouth and nose, of the imported image. In this project, 4 point are used to determine the face position.

The face images are identified with OpenCV and different camera angles are used so there's a variety of images. The algorithm for the extracting of face features is described in Algorithm 1.

```
Take frame from camera source
Flip frame vertically
Resize frame
Change frame color to GRAY Scale
Run face detector with that image
if face detected:
  get first detected face
else:
  pass to next frame
  Run face feature predictor and get predict
  nose = features[nose_start: nose_end]
  if process == false:
    l_eye = features[l_eye_start: l_eye_end]
    r_eye = features[r_eye_start: r_eye_end]
    if eyes are inside the rectangle:
      counter += 1
      if (counter/10)>10:
        guide cross = nose
        process = true

    else:
      counter = 0
  else:
    mouth = features[mouth_start: mouth_end]
    draw guide cross, treshold rectangle and nose circle
    show frame
    if nose[0] > guide_cross+threshold:
      move mouse left
    elif nose[0] < guide_cross-threshold:
      move mouse right
    if nose[1] > guide_cross+threshold:
      move mouse bottom
    elif nose[1] < guide_cross-threshold:
      move mouse top
    if isMouthOpen(mouth):
      clickevent(mouse.x, mouse.y)
```

This algorithm runs in one thread, so it is easy to run other applications while this one is working on the background. The IsMouthOpen function calculates the distance between the top and bottom lips. Figure 1 shows the visualization of the calculation made by the isMouthOpen function.

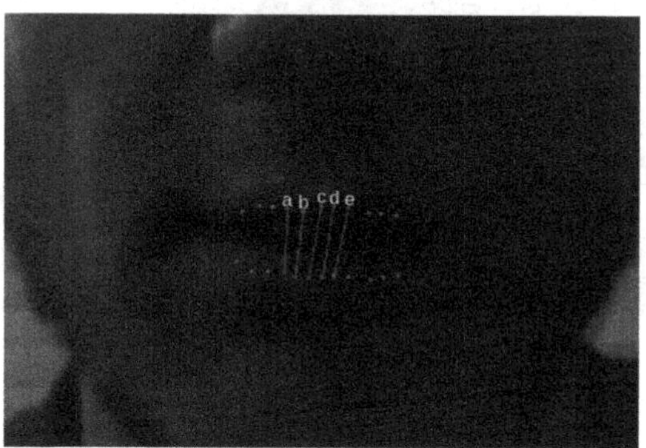

Fig. 1. Visualization of the mouth open function.

To create a reference point, the person must keep the head between the guide points. After that operation, the program defines a reference point to calculate the head position. The Fig. 2 and Fig. 3, show the before and after the guide point detection.

Fig. 2. Before the guide point operation

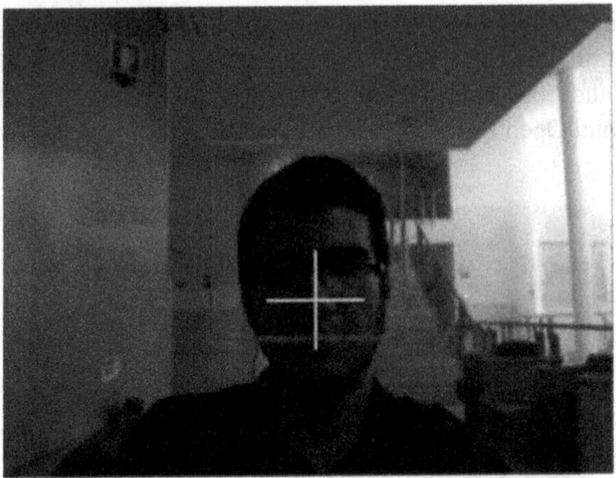

Fig. 3. With the guide point.

The program detects the eyes to determine if the face is inside of the rectangle. After the guide point has been set, the program determines the head's position using the nose feature. When the user rotates his head, it affects the nose's position, so when the nose is moved to the other side of the guide point, the program moves the mouse in that orientation, for each second. The guide point has a threshold to detect movement, so if the user doesn't want to move the mouse, just holding the nose on the middle is enough. After that operation, the user can open the mouth to apply a mouse click event.

4 Testing

Tests were made by 4 people and 4 computers. The computers had different software systems, including different windows, linux and mac operating systems. Table 2 shows the test subjects, by age, ethnicity, gender and system.

Table 2. Test subjects

Name	Gender	Age	Ethnicity	OS
Hasan Alp Zengin	Male	22	Turkey	Linux
Ahmet Burak Tektaş	Male	21	Turkey	Linux
Fikret Onur Özdil	Male	22	Turkey	Mac
Marcin Podlovski	Male	19	Poland	Windows
Serdar Ilhan	Male	20	Turkey	Windows

Some test images of Ahmet Burak Tektaş and Fikret Onur Özdil are presented in Fig. 4.

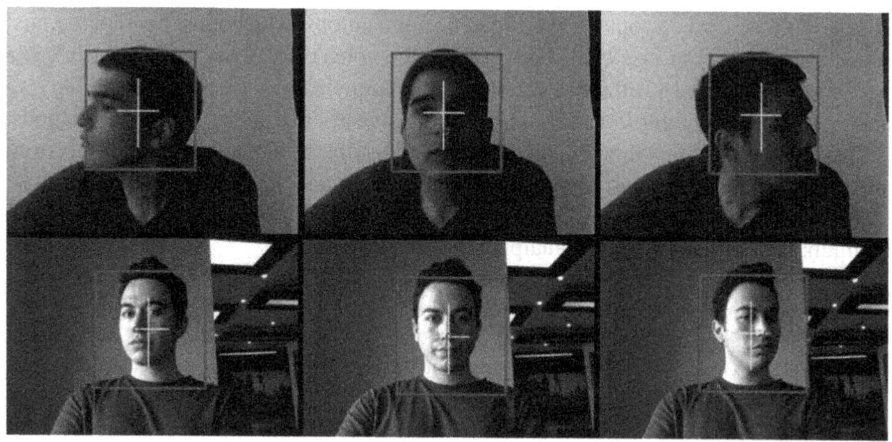

Fig. 4. Top: Ahmet Burak Tektaş, Bottom: Fikret Onur Özdil.

5 Testing Results

As result it was registered the comments from the test participants, which are presented in Table 3.

Table 3. Test results

Name	Comment
Ahmet Burak Tektaş	It was good and cheap option to control mouse with just head. Sensitivity can be better because it takes too much to moving mouse between the edges
Fikret Onur Özdil	I love that program's simplicity. It was easy to getting used to do it. I was comfortable while using it
Marcin Podlovski	This program can be a solution for mentioned problem but it may need some configuration because moving mouse cursor is little bit slow
Serdar İlhan	Nice, easy, simply and satisfying

6 Conclusion

This project tried to implement a simple mouse controlling application according to the accessibility concept. The main objective is to improve the quality of life of disabled people, unable to use the arms. The work is particularly focused on patients with spinal cord injury.

The current existent solutions don't fully solve the problem of mouse control. Some solutions require good quality cameras or specific cameras, which have high costs.

Others, which use voice control, need specific applications, which must be implemented to use voice control or else can't benefit from the voice control system. Our work is a more simple, modern and effective solution. Computer vision is still a new technology, so using it to solve problems like this can be as effective as other more expensive methods.

Test results show that this project has got good feedback, but it can be more improved and advanced. Some test participants mentioned that mouse speed is slow, which can be fixed by applying a gradient descent approach. The source code of project can be found in github: https://github.com/hasanalpzengin/Head-Mouse.

Acknowledgements. This work is a result of the project INOV@UTAD, NORTE-01-0246-FEDER-000039, supported by Norte Portugal Regional Operational Programme (NORTE 2020), under the PORTUGAL 2020 Partnership Agreement, through the European Regional Development Fund (ERDF).

References

1. Tsai, M., Hou, H., Lai, M., Liu, W., Yang, F.: Visual attention for solving multiple-choice science problem: an eye-tracking analysis. Comput. Educ. **58**, 375–385 (2012)
2. Argyros, A.A., Lourakis, M.I.A.: Vision-based interpretation of hand gestures for remote control of a computer mouse. In: Huang, T.S., et al. (eds.) ECCV 2006. LNCS, vol. 3979, pp. 40–51. Springer, Heidelberg (2006). https://doi.org/10.1007/11754336_5
3. Gratzel, C., Fong, T., Grange, S., Baur, C.: A non-contact mouse for surgeon-computer interaction. Technol. Health Care **12**(3), 245–257 (2004)
4. Betke, M., Gips, J., Fleming, P.: The camera mouse: visual tracking of body features to provide computer access for people with severe disabilities. IEEE Trans. Neural Syst. Rehab. Eng. **10**(1), 1–10 (2002). https://doi.org/10.1109/tnsre.2002.1021581

Design for Aging

Assisted Caretaking System for Geriatric Home Care

Isabel Barroso[1], Salviano Soares[2,3], Vitor Rodrigues[1,4](✉), Sérgio Silva[2,5], Maria João Monteiro[1,6], Conceição Rainho[1,4], Diogo Duarte[3], and António Valente[2,7]

[1] School of Health, University of Trás-os-Montes and Alto Douro, Vila Real, Portugal
vmcpr@utad.pt
[2] School of Science and Technology, University of Trás-os-Montes and Alto Douro, Vila Real, Portugal
[3] Institute of Electronics and Telematics Engineering, University of Aveiro, Aveiro, Portugal
[4] Research Center in Sports Sciences, Health Sciences and Human Development, CIDESD, University of Trás-os-Montes and Alto Douro, Vila Real, Portugal
[5] Globaltronic, Águeda, Portugal
[6] Center for Health Technology and Services Research, University of Porto, Porto, Portugal
[7] Institute for Systems and Computer Engineering - Technology and Science, Porto, Portugal

Abstract. This project is being developed to access elder dependent people, inspired by a geriatric care management@home. According to the project's main assessment, three stages have been completed and now, in the fourth stage, we are implementing a bio-network with several sensors that assists the caregiver in applying the therapeutic plan. At this point, we have collected data regarding the level of dependency of the elderly, and the risk of development of pressure ulcers, so that we can adapt the sensors according to their need. For example, sensors installed in a bed can warn the caregiver that it is time to change the position of the elderly patient. As such, after testing a prototype in laboratory, we installed the system in two homes where we are currently collecting data.

Keywords: Bio-network · RFID sensors · Elderly · Fall detection · Caregivers

1 Introduction

Many elderly people who are in home care carried out by informal caregivers, have difficulties in locomotion and are often immobilized in bed. Immobility produces musculoskeletal pathophysiological changes that cause deformities and postural alterations, promoting the appearance of pressure lesions. If there is no regular care and dedicated interventions, these changes will affect the quality of life of the elderly and predispose the elderly to diseases [1]. Pressure ulcers are defined as localized damage to the underlying skin and/or soft tissue, striking regions of bone prominence or in regions of prolonged contact with equipment or devices that cause prolonged or intense pressure, combined,

C. Stephanidis et al. (Eds.): HCII 2020, LNCS 12426, pp. 439–449, 2020.
https://doi.org/10.1007/978-3-030-60149-2_34

or not, with friction. The pressure on bone prominence affects blood circulation promoting cell death and consequent appearance of these lesions in places of greater risk, such as in the occipital, scapular, elbow, sacral, malleolus and calcaneal regions [2].

Pressure ulcers, according to the Portuguese Direction of Health [3], are a public health problem and an indicator of the quality of the care provided. They cause suffering and decreased quality of life to both patients and caregivers and can lead to death. They are a recurring problem in Portugal. About 95% of pressure ulcers are estimated to be preventable by early identification of the degree of risk. Patients with pressure ulcers have a larger number of hospitalization days and re-admissions translating into a greater financial burden for the National Health Service.

The elderly, when bedridden, even with the alternated pressure mattresses and frequent change of bed position, can still develop ulcers. Therefore, we intend to develop a mattress that, not only maintains the alternation of pressure, but can also detect, through sensors placed in the mattress, if any bone prominence exceeds the pressure that leads to ulcers, if the standard time between change of position is not exceeded.

This problem has become more and more important since the legal publication of the informal caregiver's status. It establishes and states the rights and duties of the caregiver and the patient. The Portuguese law [4] states that a caregiver is anyone who receives financial reward to care for the elder person. The care giver can have direct relation, or not, to the patient or can be a Health Professional.

The burden, associated with the therapeutic plan can be very stressful and sometimes is not correctly follow by the caregiver, especially due to the number of new tasks and the tight schedules involved in trying to avoid the emergence of pressure ulcers. Even when the elder is able to move around the house, the risk of falling increases and consequently increases the stress of the caregiver. Therefore, over the last years several fall detection systems have been developed in order to minimize the fear of falling and the subsequent negative impact of falls. Certainly, one of the most serious consequences of falling is the "long-lie" condition [5], where the elder is unable to get up and remains on the ground for several hours until the caregiver notices or it is medication time. Several problems can occur directly related to falls, from muscle damage, pressure ulcers, dehydration and hypothermia, [6]. There are several advances in low power wearable devices to detect falls that minimizes the risk of the "long-lie" condition [7] suggesting the use of a wearable device with an estimated battery life of 664.9 days and with high sensitivity and specificity in its test data set (93% and 87.3%, respectively). Other approaches use cameras to detect falls and other events simultaneously [6], but they are more intrusive in terms of data privacy, therefore, people are more reluctant to accept them.

In our system we use a fall-detection system based on a wearable device issuing an alert to the caregiver in case of a fall. The global purpose of the implemented system is to release the pressure from the caregiver, also improving their overall quality of life. After the research team completed all the three initial tasks [8], the next sections present all the implementation made on the projected system [3, 9].

2 The Geriatric Home Care System

The implemented system is based on a proprietary Gateway, powered by an (Single Board Computer) SBC that besides Ethernet connection, it also has 4G, since the major part of the elder population is situated in the interior and many do not have Internet connection. This gateway then connects to the sensors via RF, which makes the system set up easier.

The system consists in three parts:

i) Medication and SOS. The medication is monitored using a pair of RGB luminaries and button, in which the schedule of when to take the medication is keyed in the gateway, that sends an alarm in form of the luminary turning on with a specific, which can then be deactivated with a press of a button. In parallel, there is also an SOS button which will send an emergency alarm through the system, and alert the caretaker that something might have happened.
ii) Fall Detection. A small embedded system was developed which will send an alarm to the gateway when it detects that the target patient has fallen.
iii) Bed Sensors. Some passive RFID sensors are installed in a bed to, in one hand, detect the presence of the patient, and on the other hand, monitor humidity and temperature values. When some of these values exceed a certain threshold, an alarm is sent to the gateway.

Special care is given to data management, as it is recorded in a protected data base with remote access according the General Data Protection Regulation (GDPR), the Data Protection Law Enforcement Directive and other laws regarding personal data protection [10].

3 System Implementation

Figure 1 shows the system implementation in a floor plan of a house.

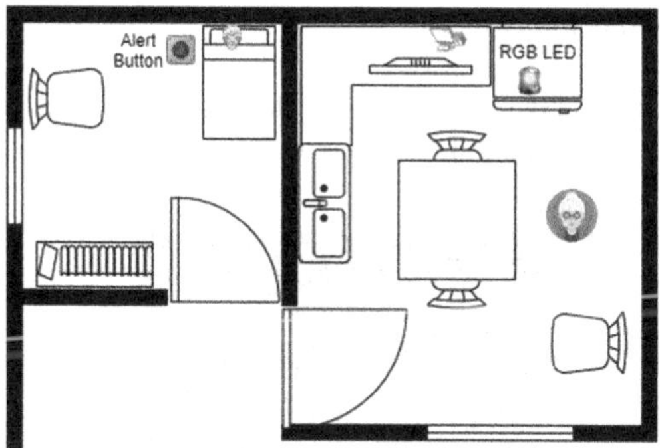

Fig. 1. System implementation in a floor plan.

An alarm button was set beside the bed in case the elderly needs assistance, under the sheets some passive RFID temperature and humidity sensors were installed in order to check abnormal conditions, and possibly prevent the problem of pressure ulcers.

A confirmation button was also placed near the elder's bed in order to reset the current alarm. In the kitchen the gateway was installed and the alerts were set according to the therapeutic plan, as can be seen in Fig. 2.

Gateway

Analisar

Definições

Histórico

Cama	Nome	Tipo	Horas	Período (Horas)	Cor	Estado
Cama1	Medicação [P1]	Medicação	08:00	24		✓
Cama1	Medicação [P1]	Medicação	19:00	24		✓
Cama1	Medicação [P1]	Medicação	15:30	24		✓
Cama1	Medicação [P1]	Medicação	06:30	24		✓
Cama1	Medicação [P2]	Medicação	12:00	24		✓
Cama1	Medicação [P2]	Medicação	19:00	24		✓
Cama1	Medicação [P2]	Medicação	08:00	24		✓
Cama1	Medicação [P3]	Medicação	19:00	24		✓
Cama1	Medicação [P3]	Medicação	08:00	24		✓
Cama1	Mudar Posição [1]	Mudar Posição	09:00	24		✓
Cama1	Mudar Posição [2]	Mudar Posição	12:00	24		✓
Cama1	Mudar Posição [3]	Mudar Posição	16:00	24		✓
Cama1	Mudar Posição [4]	Mudar Posição	21:00	24		✓

Total: 13 Linhas 25 Primeiro Anterior 1 Próximo Último

2019 Globaltronic S.A.

Fig. 2. Gateway's configuration page.

The above colors will be displayed in the RGB LED, indicating the caregiver which action is to be taken, from the following:

- Giving a certain medicine,
- Changing the elder from current position (in order to avoid the appearance of the skin ulcers),
- Alarm messages from the SOS button or the fall detection device,
- Humidity and/or temperature alarms.

The medicine plan can take into account different medicines at different times since the system is using a color medicine box, per elder, as the one displayed in Fig. 3.

Fig. 3. Medicine box used.

The use of the color medicine box together with the system can help a new caregiver to better apply the therapeutic plan [5].

4 System Components

4.1 Proprietary Gateway

An important part of the system is the Gateway, implemented using Linux embedded system [11] (Fig. 4).

Fig. 4. The Gateway

The Gateway is equipped with Real Time Clock and Calendar enabling the therapeutic plan to be processed even when there is no internet connection. Nevertheless, a 3G/4G connection was also implemented allowing remote secure access to the data by using a username and password. The implementation of the system is also possible under limited network connection, as the gateway supports external 3G antennas in order to successfully be access.

4.2 Fall Detection

The fall detection device is composed of a triple axis accelerometer, the LSM303C, and a RF radio. The LSM303C is a 6 degrees of freedom (6DOF) inertial measurement unit (IMU) in a single package, housing the accelerometer and a magnetometer. Figure 5 shows the board used.

Fig. 5. Board used for fall detection.

The LSM303C communicates over SPI with a PIC32 processor and has interruptions enabled, in particular, the free-fall interruption from the accelerometer allowing the system to wake-up whenever there is a possible fall detection enabling the system to be in low power mode with a current consumption of 6 μA. Because the movement of elderly people is normally slow, the acceleration change will not be very high during the walking motions. The most pronounced acceleration is a 3-g spike in Y (and the vector sum) at the instant of sitting down. On the other hand, the accelerations during falling is completely different and can be detailed in 3 different parts:

The start of the fall. This is the part that the Interrupt vector of the LSM303C will detect. A weightlessness will occur which in general will become more and more significant during free fall, and therefore, the vector sum of the acceleration will tend toward 0 g, been in general substantially less than 1 gas in usually conditions.

The Impact. After the fall, the human body will impact the ground or onto an object and the acceleration curve will show this as a large shock. This shock is detected by the ACTIVITY interrupt from the LSM303c.

The Long-lie. After falling and impact, the elder cannot rise immediately; rather he/she will remain in a motionless position for a short period (or longer as a possible sign of unconsciousness), to the LSM303C this is detected by the INACTIVITY interrupt.

The combination of these qualifications forms the entire fall-detection algorithm, which, can cause the system to raise an appropriate alert that a fall has occurred and the RGB LED is lit under the color RED indicating the caregiver assistance must be provided. To implement the LSM303C we have used the following schematic in Fig. 6.

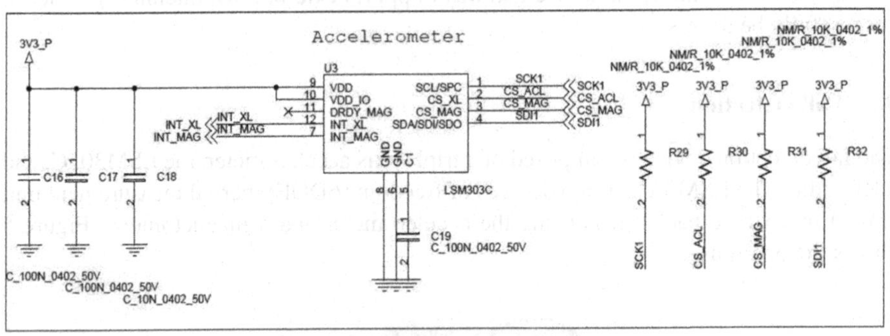

Fig. 6. LSM303C schematic implementation.

PIN 12 of the LSM303C is connected to PIN 34 of the PIC32 allowing the Interrupt functions to detect the fall. Another implementation in the fall board was the buzzer. The system can emit a high pitch sound in order to allow the caregiver to easily identify the location of the fall.

Figure 7 displays the schematic implementation of the buzzer. The buzzer is directly controlled by a PWM PIN of PIC32 allowing us to define the tone pitch that is projected whenever the buzzer is activated.

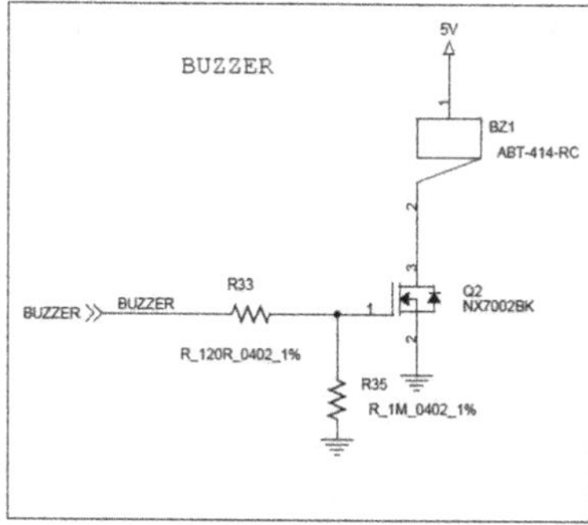

Fig. 7. Buzzer schematic implementation.

4.3 RFID Bed Sensors

The RFID temperature and humidity sensors use the technology call the Chameleon. Proprietary of ON Semiconductor's, the Chameleon technology is powered by the Magnus-S integrated circuit (IC). The IC automatically adjusts the input impedance to optimally tune the tag every time it is accessed.

The Magnus-S IC uses a bank of capacitors with 32 capacitance states represented by a 5-bit sensor code that is the tuning setting. The sensor code provides a measure of the tag antenna impedance and therefore a direct indication that the impedance as impedance change between readings of the tag. Figure 8 illustrates the Magnus-S Die concept.

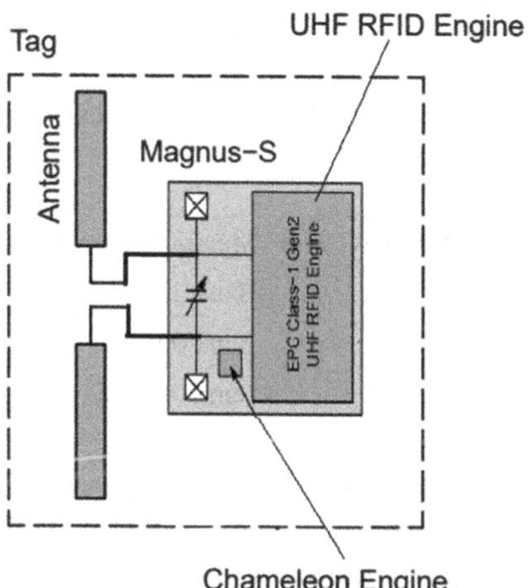

Fig. 8. Magnus-S die RFID engine and Chameleon adaptive engine

The capacitor bank in the middle changes its value in order to achieve the maximum power delivery to the RFID engine. The sensor code can be read using a standard Gen2 READ command. If the sensor tag is wet the values read will be between 0 to 15 while if the tag is dry the values will be between 25 to 31. The above illustration explains how we can use this passive battery-less sensor to measure humidity in order to alert the caregiver to the necessity to verify the elderly that is bedridden. Figure 9 illustrates the humidity sensor.

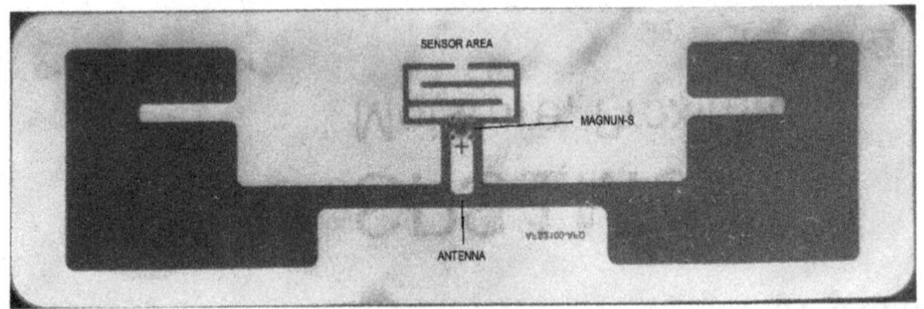

Fig. 9. A capacitance-based battery free wireless moisture sensor

As explain before, variations in the capacity change sensor code therefore, if humidity or water get in contact with sensor area a change in the sensor codes will be displayed and the system can trigger an alert to the caregiver. The resolution of the system is 5 bits, since the Magnus-S engine can only set change its frequency between one of the 32 available capacitances.

The other tags used are temperature tags, unlike the simple system explained for measuring humidity, temperature sensor tags also provide the user with a temperature Code stored at three different word addresses in the sensor tag memory. As all words in the sensor tag memory are two bytes wide, if the Tag Model Number is not known in advance, it can be determined by reading word 1h in the memory bank 2h using a standard UHF Read command. The following table displays the 3 most significant values from the read word and the memory bank and word address where the Sensor Code will be situated according to the model:

Tag model number starts with	Memory bank	Word address
401h	Bank 3h	Bh
402h	Bank 0h	Bh
403h	Bank 0h	Ch

One other important consideration, according to the Model read, is the number of bits of the sensor code. If the Tag Model Number Starts with 401h or 402h then the Sensor Code uses 5 bits else it will use 9 bits (The remaining bits of the word are 0).

To read the Temperature Sensor Code so that it can be translated to a value in degrees there is the need to make a two-step process requiring standard UHF Select and Read command. First send a standard Select command using the memory Bank 3h with pointer Bit address E0h, follow by a standard Read command to retrieve the Temperature Code from the sensor tag memory Bank 0h and word address Eh. Note that the response of the Temperature Code occupies the least-significant 12 bits of the word; the other bits are 0. In order to ensure a proper reading, the reader must not power down at any time between the Select and Read commands ensuring at least 2 ms between the select and the read commands. This will allow the Temperature sensor the time for reading. As all the Temperature-enabled MagnusS3 ICs come with a calibration data pre-loaded in the last four words of the User memory bank (words 8h, 9h, Ah, and Bh). These four words – 64 bits – are organized into six data fields that describe a 2-point linear calibration. Using the calibration data, it is possible to convert an arbitrary Temperature Code C into a calibrated value in degrees Celsius, applying the formula below, where all values are in decimal.

$$Temperature\ in\ {}^{\circ}C = \frac{1}{10}.\left[\left(\frac{TEMP2 - TEMP1}{CODE2 - CODE1}.(C - CODE1)\right) + TEMP1 - 800\right]$$

As an example, suppose that the words 8h, 9h, Ah, and Bh in the User memory bank are read to be BD9Fh, 88A7h, E147h, and 7900h, respectively. Figure 10 illustrates the unpacking process necessary to obtained the CODE1 = 88Ah, TEMP1 = 3F0h, CODE2 = A3Bh, TEMP2 = 640h, and VER = 0h.

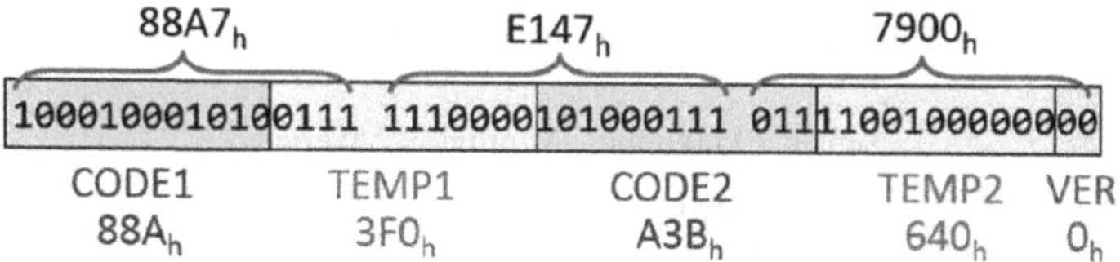

Fig. 10. Unpacking calibration words into fields

If the Temperature Code reported was 2315 in decimal, this value applied with rest of the values in the above formula gives a temperature of 38.44 °C.

5 Preliminary Results

The system is currently installed and data is being collected to address usability, response time, temperature sensing and data extracting from temperature measurements, number of alerts given out by the fall system, number of false alerts issued by the fall system and number of humidity alerts.

The two main criteria used to select the houses were:

1. The geographical proximity with the University of Trás-os-Montes and Alto Douro,
2. The availability and willingness of the caregivers to participate in the project, the system has been installed in two houses, since February of 2020:

- The first house has 1 elderly and 1 caretaker, with 3 scheduled alarms a day.
- The second house has 3 elderly and 1 caretaker, with 13 scheduled alarms a day.

Table 1. Testing table.

House	Mean (Minutes)	Standard deviation (Minutes)
1	143	506
2	23	37

In this initial test, we have been able to obtain the values in Table 1 in terms of the response time of the alert, in minutes, per house, that is, the difference between the alert being sent to the system, and it is being turn off.

In terms of fall detection, the system has not yet detect any falls, which, according to the caregivers, is true in the two weeks of the experiment.

Finally, the RFID bed sensors are still in a developing phase, but we have already able been to install the sensors in a bed and extract the values that are presented in Table 2. In this installation, two Temperature RFID sensors were positioned in a bed, side by side, with an approximate distance of 30 cm.

Table 2. Results from RFID temperature sensors.

Sensor	Maximun	Minimum	Average
Sensor A	35,06	22,76	27,46
Sensor B	33,91	21,85	25,15

6 Conclusion

The proposed geriatric home care system will help the caregiver with his/her daily therapeutic plan, issuing warnings for medicine times and other daily responsibilities that usually overwork the caregiver. The system has been installed and is expected to gather data that can be used to improve the therapeutic plan. A fall alert, which warns the caregiver in case of elderly fall, has also been developed and installed. Finally, a passive RFID sensor system has been installed and data is being collected to enhance the system.

As our forthcoming work, we are driving on the robustness of the system, continuing its update with the caregivers' feedback, as well as trying to integrate other sensors, such as breathing and heart rate sensors.

Finally, the next two stages, following the project assessment, consist on evaluating, through normalized medical statistics, the impact of the therapeutic plan assistance and vigilance program, on promoting the elderly person's health and on assisting the caregiver.

Acknowledgments. This work was supported by the project "IPAVPSI - Impact of an aid program and surveillance of the therapeutic plan supported by a sensor network, in promoting the health of the dependent elderly in their homes", referenced as: NORTE- 01-0145-FEDER-023428, financed by the Foundation for Science and Technology and co-financed by the Regional Development European Fund (FEDER), through the North Regional Operational Program (NORTE2020).

References

1. de Assis, V.I.F., de Castro Vidal, A.P., Dias, F.M.V.: Avaliação postural e de deformidades em idosos acamados de uma instituição de longa permanência. Revista Brasileira de Ciências do Envelhecimento Humano **12**(2) (2015). https://doi.org/10.5335/rbceh.v12i2.4926
2. da Silva, J.R.T., dos Santos, C.T., Zoche, D.A., Argenta, C., Ascari, R.A.: Diagnósticos e cuidados de enfermagem para pacientes com risco de lesão por pressão: relato de experiência. Braz. J. Surg. Clin. Res. **20**(1), 98–103 (2017)
3. Rodrigues, V., et al.: The use of a sensor network in the promotion of the health of the dependent elderly at home. In: International Science and Technology Conference - Proceedings Book of International Science and Technology Conference (ISTEC Europe & America), pp. 252–256 (2019)
4. Lei n.º 100/2019, September 2019. https://dre.pt/home/-/dre/124500714/details/maximized
5. Gama, O., et al.: A platform with combined environmental and physiological wireless data acquisition for all applications. In: ISAmI 2010 (2010)
6. Taramasco, C., et al.: A novel monitoring system for fall detection in older people. IEEE Access **6**, 43563–43574 (2018). https://doi.org/10.1109/access.2018.2861331
7. Wang, C., et al.: Low-power fall detector using triaxial accelerometry and barometric pressure sensing. IEEE Trans. Ind. Inform. **12**(6), 2302–2311 (2016). https://doi.org/10.1109/TII.2016.2587761
8. Monteiro, M.J., Barroso, I., Rodrigues, V., Soares, S., Barroso, J., Reis, A.: Designing and evaluating technology for the dependent elderly in their homes. In: Antona, M., Stephanidis, C. (eds.) HCII 2019. LNCS, vol. 11573, pp. 506–510. Springer, Cham (2019). https://doi.org/10.1007/978-3-030-23563-5_40
9. Rodrigues, V., et al.: Development of help and surveillance technologies for dependent elderly people at home. Eur. J. Public Health **29**(Supplement), 2 (2019). https://doi.org/10.1093/eurpub/ckz096.006
10. Data protection rules as a trust-enabler in the eu and beyond – taking stock, September 2019. https://ec.europa.eu/info/law/law-topic/data-protectionen
11. Globatronic: Gateway FE - narrowband IoT gateway (2020). http://www.globaltronic.pt/en/product/gateway-fe/

UCD in AAL: Status Quo and Perceived Fit

Silas Barth[1,2(✉)], Rebecca Weichelt[1], Stephan Schlögl[1], and Felix Piazolo[2]

[1] MCI – The Entrepreneurial School, Innsbruck, Austria
silas.barth@web.de
[2] University of Innsbruck,Innsbruck, Austria
https://www.mci.edu
https://www.uibk.ac.at/

Abstract. The development of Active Assisted Living (AAL) technologies requires a clear understanding of the distinct needs and challenges faced by senior citizens. Yet, these relevant insights are often missing, which makes the application of User-Centered Design (UCD) approaches an even more important factor significantly influencing the success of these envisioned solutions. The goal of the work presented in this paper was therefore to identify UCD approaches commonly used with AAL projects, and to evaluate their compatibility with the elderly target group. A mixed-methods approach composed of an online survey targeted at European AAL Projects, and a guided interview study with experts, revealed that AAL projects often apply techniques which are popular and well-known in the design and development community, but not specific to UCD. Furthermore, we found that many UCD techniques are unknown, even to experts, or simply too complicated to be used with elderly users.

Keywords: User-Centered Design · Active Assisted Living · Design techniques · Elderly users

1 Introduction

Throughout the second half of the 20th century, we have been seeing a continuous demographic shift, pointing to a significant reduction of citizens aged 64 and younger (i.e., people of working age) and a noticeable increase of those aged above (for Europe cf. [7]). With this consequent ageing of the population, the burden on national health and social care systems is increasingly rising, for older adults have a stronger demand for health and social services than younger people [12]. Solutions based on modern Information and Communication Technology (ICT) have shown to contribute to a better healthcare provision and thus help relieve some of this financial pressure resting on public providers. Active Assisted Living (AAL) technologies, which fall under the above-mentioned ICT solutions, are emerging and have been receiving public funding and support for

C. Stephanidis et al. (Eds.): HCII 2020, LNCS 12426, pp. 450–469, 2020.
https://doi.org/10.1007/978-3-030-60149-2_35

several years. Yet, while research in the field of ICT for elderly is thriving and backed by political support and funding programs, the widespread adoption and respective market success of such products is still to be seen [13,26]. To this end, it has been shown that User-Centered Design (UCD) approaches support the design and development of technologies, fostering usability and furthermore increasing user acceptance. However, these approaches are not generally applicable and may need alteration when utilized during the design and development of AAL solutions. The work presented in this paper thus aimed at a better understanding of the type of UCD methods that are currently employed when working with elderly user groups. To this end, our analysis was guided by the following research question:

To what extend and how expedient are User-Centered Design approaches applied in the development of elderly focused Active Assisted Living technologies?

2 Related Work

There is a prevailing viewpoint within the field of AAL that UCD approaches are essential for achieving a high level of product usability, product safety and product acceptance. The importance of this subject has also been taken up by the AAL Joined Programme (JP) which made the inclusion of UCD approaches a general requirement to be applied in projects[1]. So far, there has been only little research on whether this shift towards implementing UCD in AAL actually took place. For projects participating in the first phase of the AAL JP (i.e., between 2008 and 2013) previous analyses have shown an uptake of user representation in the design and development processes, but a lack of sufficient user integration and user contribution [5]. A systematic literature review on the status quo by Queirós and colleagues [23] detected only a small number of articles concerning the involvement of end users into the development, evaluation and validation phases of AAL projects. Adding to this, Calvaresi et al. [2] conducted a systematic literature review on papers in the domain of AAL focusing particularly on Germany. Also they did not find any evidence as to whether existing AAL developments meet the actual end user needs and thus proposed an increase in efforts put into understanding these needs and preferences. A study conducted with AAL projects in Austria did point to some success in integrating users, yet it also showed that projects utilized methods which did not specifically relate to UCD [14]. Consequently, the use and dissemination of more advanced UCD approaches was endorsed. Finally, conducting a qualitative study including participants with extensive experience in AAL, Hallewell-Haslwanter and Fitzpatrick further revealed a general lack of knowledge regarding the correct application of UCD methods in AAL, and the non-existence of UCD techniques specifically geared towards engaging elderly users [11].

[1] http://www.aal-europe.eu/wp-content/uploads/2017/02/AAL-Call-Text-2017-15022017.pdf.

3 Methodology

Based on this previous work and driven by the earlier outlined research question, our goal was to explore UCD methods in AAL projects, and investigate their involvement of elderly and/or old-adult participants in the development process. As elderly we considered people between 60 and 75 years of age, as old-adults those aged above 75 [1,9,17,20]. Doing this, we followed a mixed-methods approach. First, an online survey gave insights into the use of UCD methods in currently ongoing as well as already completed AAL projects participating in the AAL JP. It furthermore asked participants to rate the suitability and perceived efficiency of different UCD techniques in light of their specific projects. A subsequently conducted interview study asked open-ended questions to experts so as to obtain a more in-depth understanding of the appropriateness of UCD methods when used with elderly participants, and the respective challenges which need to be tackled in such contexts.

3.1 Online Survey

The online survey was available for the duration of 6 weeks during April and May 2019 and targeted directly at members of AAL JP projects who had sufficient information on the therein applied procedures. Questions were organized in three sections. The first section, asked participants to provide relevant information on the year and duration of their AAL project, its test regions/countries, and the area the respective AAL product was situated in.

In the second section, participants were confronted with five categories of UCD methods, which held a total of 46 different UCD techniques found in the literature (cf. Tables 1 and 2). This list was created in a multi-stage process in which we used the listings of Still and Crane [29], Maguire [19], Shneiderman et al. [24], Glende [10], Dwivedi et al. [6], Spinsante et al. [27], and Czaja et al. [3] to select techniques and respective categories, aiming to include all common UCD techniques without being too excessive. For each category, participants were then asked to select those UCD techniques that were utilized in their AAL project. At the end of each category, the respondents were furthermore asked to state, if they were familiar with the techniques they did not select. Next they were asked to state for each technique they did apply in their project, the phase of the product development in which this application happened. In a next step, participants were then asked to evaluate these specific UCD techniques according to their preparatory effort (e.g., procurement of working materials, training of moderators, selection of representative test participants), their financial effort (i.e., level of financial effort/resources required for the use of the specific UCD technique), their conduction effort (i.e., the need for technical equipment, premises, moderators or assistants), their evaluation effort (i.e., the perceived effort attached to the evaluation of the results produced by the selected UCD technique), their feasibility in terms of validity (i.e., the degree to which the technique did measure what it claimed to measure), their scalability (i.e., the perceived effort required to include more participants), their 'fun factor', and to

Table 1. Categories and types of User-Centered Design techniques (part I)

Creativity methods	Analysis methods	Evaluation methods
• Brainstorming	• Kano model	• Idea-evaluation-matrix
• SIL method	• Contextual inquiry	• Argumentative balance
• 6-3-5 method	• Focus group discussion	• Benefit analysis
• Gallery method	• Observation	• Simple point scoring
• Walt-Disney-method	• Written survey	• Selection list
• Six thinking hats	• Interview	• Systems-usability-scale
• Bisociation	• Critical-incident-technique	• Quantitative
• Morphological box	• NAUA	• ISO 9241 questionnaire
• Osborn check-list		
• Synectics		
• Idea contest		
• TRIZ		
• Stop-technique		
• Identification method		
• Attribute listing		
• Crowdsourcing		

Table 2. Categories and types of User-Centered Design techniques (part II)

Test methods	Support methods
• Field test	• Offering map
• Remote-usability-test	• Thinking aloud
• Out-of-the-box test	• Audio/video recording
• Multip. user simult. testing	• Personas
• Tree test	• Eye tracking
• User experience test	
• Card sorting test	
• RITE method	
• Click stream analysis	

what degree participants would recommend them. All parameters were assessed on a 5-point Likert scale (Low: 1.0–1.4; Moderately Low: 1.5–2.4; Moderate: 2.5–3.4; Moderately High: 3.5–4.4; High: 4.5–5.0)

Finally, in the third section, participants were asked to describe the developed solution in some more detail and to rate the level of success they think their solution has attained.

3.2 Interview Study

For the follow-up interview study we directly contacted UCD/AAL experts through phone or Skype calls. Targeted participants had to have either extensive practical experience in conducting UCD within AAL projects, or had to be dedicated experts in specific UCD techniques. To this end, potential interview partners were considered as qualified either based on their academic credentials or based on recommendations. Those who agreed to participate came from research institutions in either Austria or Germany, had extensive experience with research and development in the field of AAL and are still active in the AAL, HCI and/or UCD area. The guiding questions we asked participants during these interviews aimed at elaborating on the suitability of different UCD techniques when used in AAL projects.

4 Results

A total of 27 European AAL projects responded to our survey request and completed the entire survey. More than 80% of the projects were conducted in the past five years. With this data set we particularly looked at the frequency of application and the level of familiarity the different UCD techniques held. With respect to the follow-up interview study, we were able to conduct 5 guided interviews (EP1–EP5), all of which lasted between 40 and 60 min. In order to analyze the data, we used a content analysis method based on a combination of deductively and inductively generated codes. We followed the coding method proposed by Lazar and colleagues [16], where the responses to the open-ended questions were assigned to types of UCD methods (i.e., deductive codes) and additional concepts evolving from the data (i.e., inductive codes). We employed magnitude coding so as to evaluate the frequency of feedback and consequently its relevance and informative value [16].

4.1 Creativity Methods

With respect to creativity methods, our results show that brainstorming is the most often applied technique (70%), while all other techniques are hardly considered, even though techniques like crowd-sourcing (44%), Six Thinking Hats (41%) and the Walt-Disney-Method (41%) were familiar to over 40% of the participants (cf. Fig. 1).

Focusing on the brainstorming technique, Table 3 illustrates that the preparatory effort (mean 2.47) and the financial effort (mean 1.95) were assessed as moderately low, while the conduction effort (mean 2.72) as well as the evaluation effort (mean 3.42) were both rated as moderate. The feasibility received a moderately high mean of 3.63 and the scalability was rated as moderate (mean 3.00). Further on, participants considered the fun factor as moderately high (mean 3.53) and likewise the recommendation of brainstorming received a moderately high score (mean 3.89).

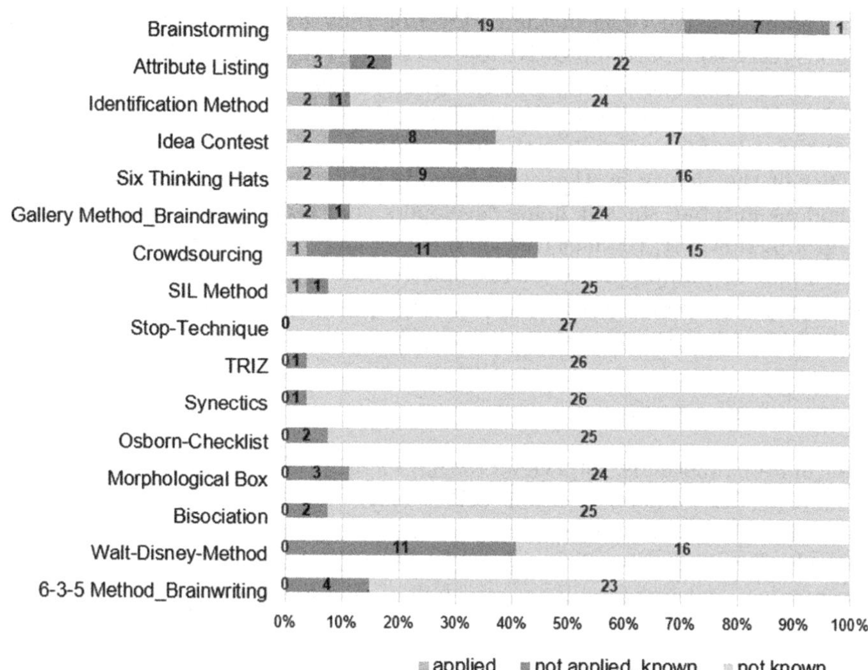

Fig. 1. Application and knowledge of creativity methods

Table 3. Characteristics brainstorming technique

Brainstorming	n	Mean	Median	Mode	SD
Preparatory effort	19	2.47	2	1	1.35
Financial effort	19	1.95	2	1	0.85
Conduction effort	18	2.72	3	3	0.77
Evaluation effort	19	3.42	3	3	0.96
Feasibility	19	3.63	4	3	0.94
Scalability	19	3.00	3	4	0.84
Fun factor	19	3.53	4	4	0.94
Recommendation	19	3.89	4	4	1.35

To expand upon these results, the open-ended questions posed to experts revealed that brainstorming is often not applied as UCD method with elderly participants, but rather with project members or external professionals (EP1, EP4 and EP5). To this end, EP5 argues that brainstorming is not suitable for older adults, as they could be confused or over-strained by the unstructured characteristic of the technique. In contrast, EP2 remarked that in their project brainstorming was not applied as a standalone technique but as part of other more comprehensive UCD methods. Overall, only 5 of the 16 listed creativity methods received a partial positive assessment by the experts. EP3, for example, deems the 6-3-5 brainwriting and the gallery braindrawing technique as very applicable for the target group, while EP4 experienced good results with utilizing the Osborn-checklist as well as the idea contest, as long as it is adapted to the specifics of the elderly participants. Finally, EP2 emphasized the identification method as suitable, since it helps developers gain a deep understanding of the user group. However, the fact that all of these methods were also often rated as too complex or inappropriate for the elderly user group, points to a great level of disagreement among experts. Other techniques were either not known or not at all addressed as being used.

4.2 Analysis Methods

As for analysis methods, interviews (96%), focus group discussions (89%), written surveys (70%) and observations (67%) achieved notable high application and familiarity ratings. In contrast, the NAUA method and the Kano Model were not applied at all and barely known. The contextual inquiry technique revealed a discrepancy as it was familiar to over half of all participants (56%) but applied by only 26% (cf. Fig. 2).

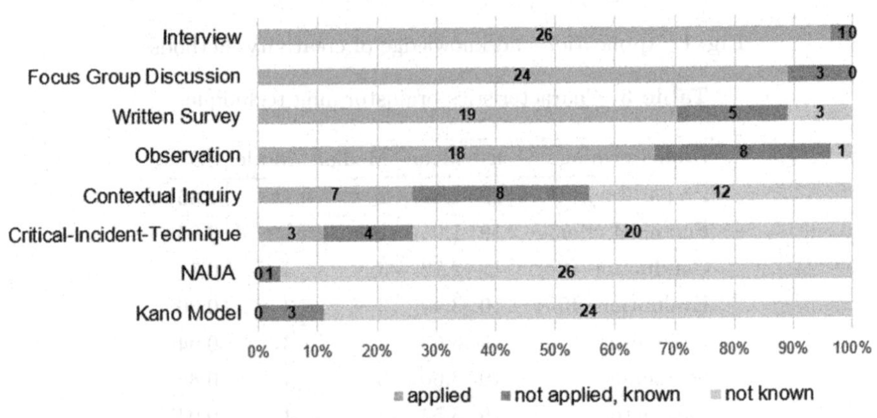

Fig. 2. Application and knowledge of analysis methods

Table 4 shows that interviews received a moderately high score for the preparatory effort (mean 3.62), the conduction effort (mean 3.96) and the evaluation effort (mean 4.31), while the financial effort (mean 2.73) was perceived as moderate. Focus groups received similar ratings for these parameters (cf. Table 5). In terms of feasibility, both techniques were rated as moderately high, with interviews (mean 4.04) receiving a higher score as focus group discussions (3.63). The scores for scalability, fun factor and the degree of recommendation for both methods were also similar. Here, the focus group discussions received a higher rating with respect to the fun factor (mean 3.46) whereas interviews seem to be more recommended (mean 3.96).

Table 4. Characteristics interview technique

Interview	n	Mean	Median	Mode	SD
Preparatory effort	26	3.62	4	4	0.90
Financial effort	26	2.73	2.5	2	1.25
Conduction effort	26	3.96	4	4	0.82
Evaluation effort	26	4.31	4	4	0.68
Feasibility	26	4.04	4	4	0.53
Scalability	26	3.04	3	3	0.87
Fun factor	26	3.12	3	3	0.86
Recommendation	26	3.96	4	4	0.66

Table 5. Characteristics focus group technique

Focus group	n	Mean	Median	Mode	SD
Preparatory effort	24	3.42	4	4	0.97
Financial effort	24	2.50	3	3	0.93
Conduction effort	24	3.50	3.5	3	0.66
Evaluation effort	24	4.00	4	4	0.78
Feasibility	24	3.63	4	4	0.65
Scalability	24	2.79	3	3	1.06
Fun factor	24	3.46	4	4	0.98
Recommendation	24	3.88	4	3	0.80

In Table 6 it can be seen that preparatory effort for written surveys was perceived similar to interviews (mean 3.63 vs. mean 3.62). In contrast, observations received a lower score with a mean of 2.89 (cf. Table 7). Moreover, written surveys and observations showed similarities in terms of a moderate financial effort, a moderate conduction effort and a moderately high level of feasibility. The evaluation effort for the written survey was rated as moderate (mean 3.42) and for the observation as moderately high (mean 3.78), although both scores are rather close. A greater variation can be observed for scalability, which was rated as moderately high for the written survey (mean 4.05) and as moderate for the observation (2.78). Both methods received a moderately high level of recommendation, whereas the score for observations shows an upwards tendency (mean 4.06).

Table 6. Characteristics written survey technique

Written survey	n	Mean	Median	Mode	SD
Preparatory effort	19	3.63	4	4	1.21
Financial effort	19	2.58	3	3	1.35
Conduction effort	19	2.79	3	4	1.32
Evaluation effort	19	3.42	3	3	1.07
Feasibility	19	3.79	4	4	1.03
Scalability	19	4.05	4	5	1.18
Fun factor	19	2.32	2	1	1.29
Recommendation	19	3.53	4	4	0.70

Table 7. Characteristics observation technique

Observation	n	Mean	Median	Mode	SD
Preparatory effort	18	2.89	3	3	1.23
Financial effort	18	2.56	2.5	2	0.92
Conduction effort	18	3.11	3	3	1.02
Evaluation effort	18	3.78	4	4	1.00
Feasibility	18	3.89	4	4	0.83
Scalability	18	2.78	3	3	1.00
Fun factor	18	2.94	3	2	1.11
Recommendation	18	4.06	4	5	0.87

From the experts' point of view, EP1 and EP2 emphasized the suitability of using interviews with older adults. The involving nature of interviews makes older adults feel valued and leads to more comprehensive answers. With respect to focus groups, four of the five experts stated that they had successfully used this method with elderly participants and that it had provided valuable and extensive insights, although the preparatory and evaluation efforts were considered high. EP1 and EP5 further highlighted the enjoyment older adults felt when interacting with other participants, while EP3 noted that, due to the group dynamics which may evolve, the method could over-strain participants. As for the written surveys, replies were rather controversial. That is, EP1 reported that often relatives or professional caregivers completed the surveys and EP3 added that elderly participants were often overwhelmed with the technical complexity of AAL questionnaires. In contrast, EP 2 and EP 4 reported that written surveys were deemed a successful method and well applicable with elderly participants. Also the contextual inquiry method was identified as suitable and expedient in the context of AAL technology development (4 out of 5 experts). EP2, for example, emphasized the importance of this technique for receiving usability insights, and EP5 accentuated that this method may be particularly useful in cases where the product developers are not that familiar with the actual area of application. Finally, observations were considered an integral part of the contextual inquiry and as useful to gain insights on a specific problem.

4.3 Evaluation Methods

Investigating different evaluation methods, Fig. 3 shows that only the System-Usability-Scale (44%) and the Benefit Analysis (33%) were applied by more than one third of the participating projects, although Quantitative UX (User Experience) Surveys (33%) as well as Simple Point Scoring (30%) and the ISO 9241 Questionnaire (30%) were known by at least 8 of the respondents.

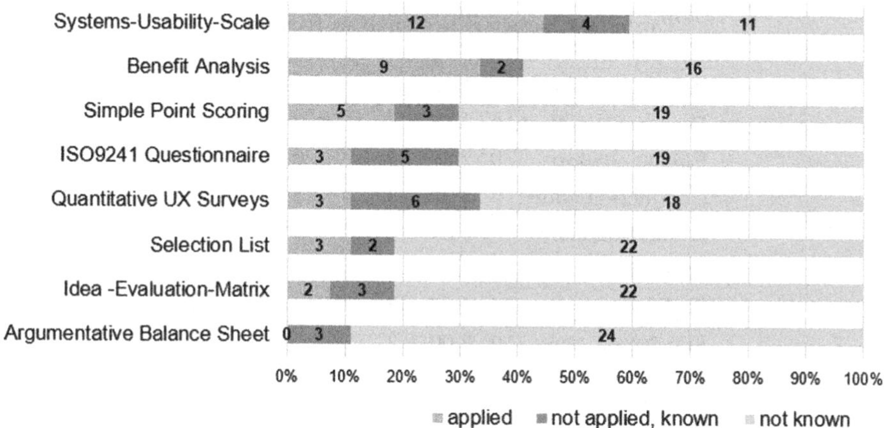

Fig. 3. Application and knowledge of evaluation methods

Table 8 and Table 9 illustrate that the overall perceived efforts for the System-Usability-Scale (SUS) were lower than for the Benefit Analysis. Notable differences can also be found for the preparatory effort, which was rated as moderately low for the SUS (mean 1.92), and as moderate for the Benefit Analysis (mean 3.33). Moreover, for the evaluation effort the moderately low mean score for the SUS and the moderately high mean score for the Benefit Analysis differed by over 1.5 points. In turn, the Benefit Analysis was rated as more feasible (mean 4.11) and received a higher degree of recommendation (mean 4.11). The fun factor was perceived as moderately low for the SUS and as moderate for the Benefit Analysis. Both methods received a similar, moderately high, score for their scalability.

The interviews with the experts revealed similar results as the online survey. From the eight listed techniques, four were either not applied or not addressed. Thereby, EP4 considered the ISO 9241 Questionnaire as too general and therefore as inappr opriate to be used in the context of AAL, yet he/she stated that the Benefit Analysis and the Simple Point Scoring were successfully applied in

Table 8. Characteristics system-usability-scale technique

SUS	n	Mean	Median	Mode	SD
Preparatory effort	12	1.92	2	1	1.00
Financial effort	12	1.58	1.5	1	0.67
Conduction effort	12	2.17	2	1	1.11
Evaluation effort	12	2.33	2	1	1.37
Feasibility	12	3.25	3.5	4	1.36
Scalability	12	3.75	4	5	1.42
Fun factor	12	2.17	2	1	1.19
Recommendation	12	3.25	3.5	4	1.14

Table 9. Characteristics analysis technique

Benefit analysis	n	Mean	Median	Mode	SD
Preparatory effort	9	3.33	3	3	1.32
Financial effort	9	2.67	2	2	1.12
Conduction effort	9	3.22	3	2	1.09
Evaluation effort	9	3.89	4	4	1.05
Feasibility	9	4.11	4	4	0.78
Scalability	9	3.67	4	4	0.87
Fun factor	9	3.00	3	3	1.22
Recommendation	9	4.11	4	5	0.93

previous AAL development projects (note: none of the other experts addressed or applied these methods). The most extensive feedback was received for the Systems-Usability-Scale and the Quantitative UX Surveys. While EP1 stated that the SUS had been used successfully with elderly participants and provided valuable results, EP4 and EP5 questioned its suitability. EP4 particularly criticized the general manner of the questions and the low informative value of the outcome, while EP5 deemed the SUS as too complex to be used with older adults. As for the Quantitative UX Survey, EP2 reported good applicability and emphasized the capability of the tool as a means to assess the emotional level of participants. EP5, on the other hand, deemed the method as too complicated for the elderly user group, while the other experts did not consider this method at all. Finally, EP3 noted that standardized questionnaires or worksheets cannot capture the complexity and different parameters which are often present in AAL projects.

4.4 Test Methods

With respect to test methods, Field Tests (74%) and User Experience (UX) Tests (59%) were the most often applied techniques in this category and also received the highest familiarity ratings (cf. Fig. 4). Notable in this section is that the Card Sorting technique was known to 17 participants but only applied by one.

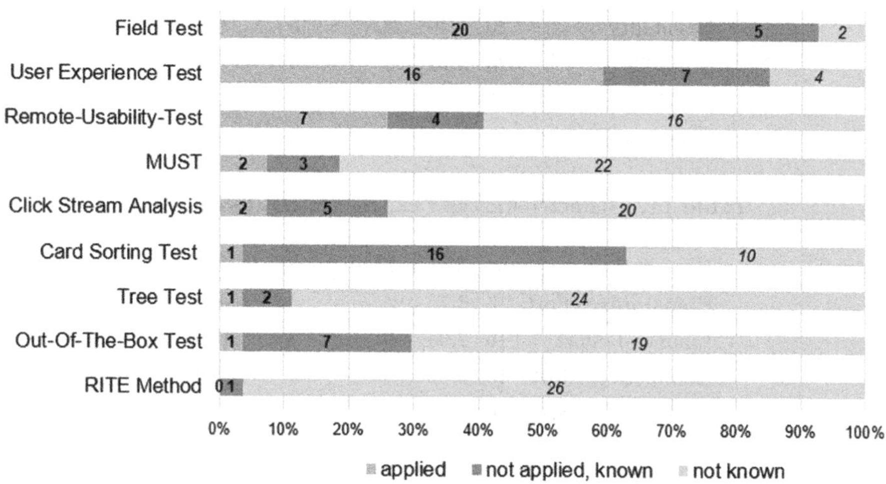

Fig. 4. Application and knowledge of test methods

Tables 10 and 11 illustrate that the preparatory effort, the conduction effort and the evaluation effort were rated as moderately high for both the Field Test and the UX test. A clear difference between both techniques can be found, however, in the financial effort, which was perceived as moderately high for the Field Test (mean 4.10) and as moderate for the UX Test (mean 2.94). The feasibility, the fun factor and the degree of recommendation for the Field Test and the UX Test were all rated as moderately high, whereas the scalability for the UX test was rated with a moderate score compared to the moderately high score for the Field Test. To this end, it should further be noted that the Field Test shows a mode of 5 for the parameters preparatory effort, financial effort, conduction effort, feasibility and degree of recommendation.

From an experts' point of view, Field Test were assigned a good level of applicability in AAL projects. EP2 and EP3, in particular, considered the method as essential for developing AAL technologies according to the needs and preferences of the target group. EP1 further added that Field Tests would provide valuable suggestions for improving the functionalities of respective products. However, the experts mentioned certain requirements so that Field Tests are efficient. That is, EP2 suggested that Lab Tests should be applied as a preceding measure, while EP5 remarked that successful Field Tests demand a well-functioning, robust and self-explanatory prototype for a valid and fruitful testing. Furthermore, EP3

Table 10. Characteristics field test technique

Field test	n	Mean	Median	Mode	SD
Preparatory effort	20	4.25	5	5	1.25
Financial effort	20	4.10	4.5	5	1.25
Conduction effort	20	4.45	4.5	5	0.60
Evaluation effort	20	4.15	4	4	0.75
Feasibility	20	4.40	4.5	5	0.68
Scalability	20	3.70	4	4	0.86
Fun factor	20	3.75	4	4	0.97
Recommendation	20	4.45	5	5	0.69

Table 11. Characteristics user experience test technique

UX test	n	Mean	Median	Mode	SD
Preparatory effort	16	3.75	4	4	1.13
Financial effort	16	2.94	3	3	1.06
Conduction effort	16	3.69	4	3	1.08
Evaluation effort	16	4.00	4	4	0.73
Feasibility	16	3.94	4	4	0.68
Scalability	16	3.13	3	3	1.02
Fun factor	16	3.50	3.5	3	0.89
Recommendation	16	4.06	4	4	0.68

noted that Field Tests should not exclusively focus on assessing the usability, as thereby further influence factors on the users' product acceptance and application would be neglected. In addition, three of the five experts deemed the User Experience Test as suitable for the AAL field and stated a good applicability with elderly participants. EP4 reported that the technique delivers useful information on how well the functionalities of the developed technologies are accepted. EP5, however, remarked that the User Experience Test was more successful for products with a specific purpose and short-term application, as opposed to products that aim at changing a user's complete lifestyle and/or behaviour. The Out-of-the-Box test (EP4 and EP5), the Tree Test technique (EP1 and EP4) as well as the Click Stream Analysis (EP1 and EP4) were also thought applicable to AAL projects, while Card Sorting only received one positive feedback (EP4).

4.5 Support Methods

Finally, looking at support methods, Fig. 5 shows that the Personas technique (67%), the Thinking Aloud technique (63%) and Audio/Video recording (33%) were applied by at least one third of the projects. The familiarity ratings showed furthermore that, except for Offering Maps, most of the support methods were familiar to participants.

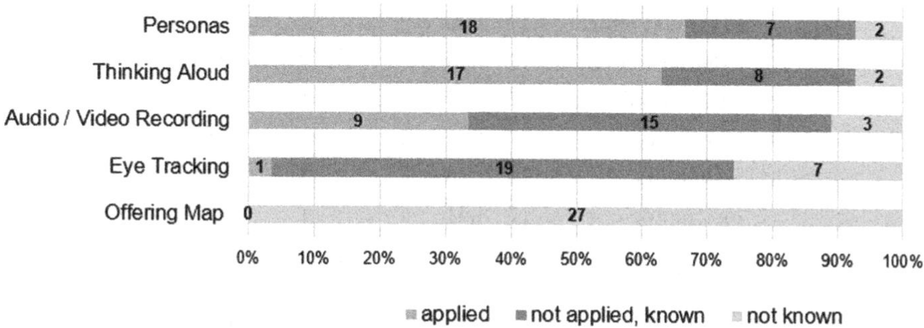

Fig. 5. Application and knowledge of support methods

Comparing the results listed in Tables 12, 13 and 14, it can be seen that the preparatory effort for Personas and Audio/Video recordings was perceived as moderate, while Thinking Aloud was rated with a moderately low level of preparatory effort. Regarding the financial effort, both the Personas technique (mean 1.72) and the Thinking Aloud technique (mean 2.00) received moderately low scores, while Audio/Video recording was perceived as moderate (mean 3.00). A further notable difference can be seen for the evaluation effort, which was rated high for Audio/Video recording, moderately high for Thinking Aloud and moderate for Personas. As for the fun factor, both the Personas technique with a mean score of 2.50 and the Audio/Video recording with a mean score of 2.44 achieved lower ratings than the Thinking Aloud technique with a mean rating of 3.41. All three techniques received similar recommendation ratings.

Table 12. Characteristics personas technique

Personas	n	Mean	Median	Mode	SD
Preparatory effort	18	3.39	3.5	3	1.29
Financial effort	18	1.72	1.5	1	0.89
Conduction effort	18	2.89	3	3	1.08
Evaluation effort	18	3.11	3	3	1.08
Feasibility	18	3.06	3	3	1.11
Scalability	18	2.83	3	2	1.10
Fun factor	18	2.50	3	1	1.29
Recommendation	18	3.50	3.5	3	1.04

Table 13. Characteristics thinking aloud technique

Thinking aloud	n	Mean	Median	Mode	SD
Preparatory effort	17	2.12	2	2	0.93
Financial effort	17	2.00	2	2	1.06
Conduction effort	17	3.18	3	4	1.24
Evaluation effort	17	3.82	4	4	0.88
Feasibility	17	3.24	3	3	0.83
Scalability	17	2.76	3	3	0.83
Fun factor	17	3.41	4	4	0.80
Recommendation	17	3.82	4	4	0.73

Table 14. Characteristics audio/video recording technique

Audio/Video	n	Mean	Median	Mode	SD
Preparatory effort	9	3.11	3	2	1.05
Financial effort	9	3.00	3	3	1.22
Conduction effort	9	2.89	2	2	1.45
Evaluation effort	9	4.67	5	5	0.50
Feasibility	9	3.89	4	4	1.05
Scalability	9	2.22	2	2	0.97
Fun factor	9	2.44	2	2	1.13
Recommendation	9	3.56	4	4	0.88

All experts explained that in their projects Personas were utilized to create a common conception of the potential end users. To this end, EP3 emphasized that Personas should always be based on scientifically substantiated data so as to avoid invalid assumptions. However, none of the experts reported that the Personas were evaluated with real end users, which would be reasonable according to EP5. Also the Thinking Aloud technique was attested good applicability for the use with older adults (EP4 and EP5), although EP2 reported that participants may be uncomfortable with the method. For the Audio/Video recording, EP2, EP4 and EP5 stated consistently that older adults often refuse to be recorded, which raises additional ethical questions.

4.6 Some General Feedback on UCD in AAL

During the final part of the interview study, experts had the possibility to state concluding remarks regarding UCD in AAL and the application of UCD methods with elderly users, allowing for the identification of challenges and barriers. Both EP1 and EP3 mentioned that limited financial and time resources in AAL development projects often hinder the application of several suitable UCD methods.

Also, the physical and mental conditions of elderly participants complicate the use of some UCD techniques. EP3 added that the application of UCD methods within the development of AAL technologies often demands a higher sensitivity from the developers as it is the case for technologies that do not touch upon personal privacy or the health state of users. Consequently, the utilization of UCD techniques in the AAL field is often more labour-intensive and time consuming. A further barrier identified by EP3 concerns the often varying interpretation and application of UCD methods by different professional disciplines, which leads to inconsistencies. In this context, EP1 recommends a better identification and listing of suitable UCD methods to be used in AAL so as to provide an overview of existing methods and information on their correct application. EP3 gave warning that such a list should not aim at being generally applicable as so far there is still no commonly accepted understanding of the scope AAL and AAL technologies should cover.

EP1 further noted the necessity of adapting the selected UCD techniques to the elderly participants and suggested to apply the techniques in an informal atmosphere so as to not overwhelm the participants with the specifics of the respective technique. As a concluding remark, EP2 suggested to move from UCD to Human-Centered Design as this methodology places an even greater emphasize on the special needs and preferences of the users and thus would better comply with the requirements inherent to the AAL field.

5 Discussion

Overall, our study results show that the AAL field uses many rather generic UCD techniques such as interviews, focus group discussions, field tests or observations. Yet, as all of them require direct interaction and collaboration with elderly participants, it was also shown that the commitment to include potential end users during the development processes is present in the AAL community. A surprising result of our study is the rather low familiarity with more specific UCD methods. This applies especially to those techniques which were emphasized by the experts but not considered by the participating AAL projects. However, techniques highlighted by single experts have to be treated with caution, as for most cases they may only be applied in specific settings and for specific AAL technologies, which makes their generalizability difficult. Furthermore, we have seen that techniques which advise a very strict procedure are difficult to adhere to, for they often do not suit the specific application area or user profile of the respective AAL technology. This is in accordance with Newell et al. [21], who criticise the strict adherence to standard procedures while developing and designing with older adults. Generally, less standardized guidelines and more flexibility seems to be more suitable for the AAL field, and would furthermore support the underlying concept of UCD. Also, it may prevent some of the 'tick-box attitudes' present in other design and development communities [18].

Generally, several experts concluded that grounding the complete design and development process in user-centered or human-centered methodologies and incorporating these core concepts is more important than applying and adhering to specific techniques. Hallewell-Haslwanter et al. [14] detected a similar attitude within their study and reported of other European research projects having received similar comments.

In line with Eisma et al. [8] and Newell et al. [22], several experts stressed the need to adapt the traditional UCD approaches and techniques to better support the interaction with older people. In particular, it was deemed important that designers and developers empathize with potential end users, which includes the understanding of peoples' emotional states, their specific life situation and their surrounding environment. Compatible with this viewpoint, Still and Crane [29] consider the emotional assessment during the user's interaction with the product as crucial and therefore recommend emotion heuristics or enjoyability surveys as further complementary techniques.

Yet, even with appropriate UCD methods and techniques for the AAL field being available, the resources are often limited, which may bring all UCD efforts to an abrupt ending. Several experts we talked to reported resource scarcity on both the developer as well as the participant side.

Damodaran [4] as well as Stenmark et al. [28] identified limited resources as a general barrier for the involvement of users into product design and development processes. Thus experts reported the application of those UCD techniques that are the most cost-effective or the least labour-intensive, and not those that are the most suitable.

Another difficulty highlighted by our results concerns the physical and mental strains caused by certain techniques, which may inhibit analyses. Hallewell-Haslwanter [14] and Fitzpatrick [13] noted similar findings in their studies.

In summary, while these results are based on only 27 AAL projects and 5 expert opinions they do cover a big part of the current work conducted in this field and its implementation of UCD techniques. Further it may be argued that the sample size equals those of previous investigations, such as Hallewell-Haslwanter et al. [14] or Hornung-Prähauser et al. [15]. Consequently, we consider these results to show a robust trend supporting previous work.

6 Conclusion and Future Outlook

The aim of this study was to investigate to what extent UCD is applied within the development of elderly focused AAL technologies and how expedient this implementation is perceived. Results show that AAL projects primarily apply techniques which are popular and well-known in the design and development community but not specific to UCD. While the evaluation of these techniques (e.g., interviews, focus group discussions, field tests, observations) underlined their applicability and appropriateness for the AAL field, several experts recommended the use of some of the more UCD specific techniques, indicating a need for better dissemination. A distinct conceptualisation of UCD techniques that are generally applicable for the development of AAL technologies was, however, considered unrealistic, given the multifaceted characteristics of both the AAL technologies and the end users. Nonetheless, investigating the suitability of distinct UCD techniques for the development of a certain category of AAL technology and a thoroughly selected user group, should be considered an important piece of future work. If applied to a diverse set of technologies and user groups, this could eventually lead to a toolkit providing developers and designers with information on which UCD techniques are appropriate for which specific product and/or user group. Furthermore research should include alternative end users as well as relatives. In this whole context, the cultural and country-related peculiarities as, for example, the specifics of the different European health and social systems, the family and care situations, or the public support given to product developments in the field of AAL, need to be considered.

Our results also revealed the need for a certain compliance with the core values of the UCD or HCD methodology, noting that they are considered more important than adhering to predefined techniques. This would allow AAL developers to work user-centered and achieve valuable outcomes independently from specific techniques and procedures. In order to further distribute and endorse such approaches, activities on a regional or national level, comparable to for instance the efforts the European Union puts into the support of education and training for researchers in the field of Gerontechnology [25], would definitely benefit the development of AAL technologies.

Overall, we believe the results presented in this paper provide a general overview of the status quo regarding the use of UCD techniques in AAL, yet further studies with a similar focus are recommended. Those could for exampled gain additional insights by investigating UCD approaches of developers which operate outside the radar of the AAL JP community. Therefore, a detailed market analysis, which should go beyond what is currently happening in this field in Europe, is necessary. Global initiatives like the WHO funded Global Cooperation on Assistive Technology (GATE), which also provides the Priority Assistive Products List (APL), could serve as a reference point.

Also, gathering information on the use of UCD from those solution providers, that were able to develop successful products without the support of funding programs or other public initiatives, would be interesting. Considering the approaching end of the AAL JP in 2020, this could produce valuable insights with respect to the future development of European AAL technologies.

It is likely that the barriers for introducing AAL technologies will decrease, as modern technology becomes ever more established in our daily lives - even in those of the elderly. However, if we want for these solutions to serve the needs of the actual end users, the design and development processes have to be altered so as to better integrate the feedback of this distinct target population.

References

1. Astell, A.: Technology and fun for a happy old age. In: Sixsmith, A., Gutman, G. (eds.) Technologies for Active Aging. International Perspectives on Aging, vol. 9, pp. 169–187. Springer, Boston (2013). https://doi.org/10.1007/978-1-4419-8348-0_10

2. Calvaresi, D., Cesarini, D., Sernani, P., Marinoni, M., Dragoni, A.F., Sturm, A.: Exploring the ambient assisted living domain: a systematic review. J. Ambient Intell. Hum. Comput. **8**(2), 239–257 (2017). https://doi.org/10.1007/s12652-016-0374-3
3. Czaja, S.J., Boot, W.R., Charness, N., Rogers, W.A.: Designing for Olderadults: Principles and Creative Human Factors Approaches. CRC Press (2019)
4. Damodaran, L.: User involvement in the systems design process-a practical guide for users. Behav. Inf. Technol. **15**(6), 363–377 (1996)
5. Dózsa, C., Mollenkopf, H., Uusikylä, P.: Final evaluation of the ambient assisted living joint programme (2013)
6. Dwivedi, S.K.D., Upadhyay, S., Tripathi, A.: A working framework for the user-centered design approach and a survey of the available methods. Int. J. Sci. Res. Publ. **2**(4), 12–19 (2012)
7. ECFIN, ECD: The 2018 ageing report: economic and budgetary projections for the 28 EU member states (2016–2070) (2015)
8. Eisma, R., Dickinson, A., Goodman, J., Syme, A., Tiwari, L., Newell, A.F.: Early user involvement in the development of information technology-related products for older people. Univ. Access Inf. Soc. **3**(2), 131–140 (2004). https://doi.org/10.1007/s10209-004-0092-z
9. Fisk, D., Rogers, W., Charness, N., Czaja, S., Sharit, J.: Principles and creative human factors approaches (2009)
10. Glende, S.: Entwicklung eines Konzepts zur nutzergerechten Produktentwicklung mit Fokus auf die Generation Plus. Ph.D. thesis, Technische Universität Berlin (2010)
11. Hallewell Haslwanter, J.D., Fitzpatrick, G.: The development of assistive systems to support older people: issues that affect success in practice. Technologies **6**(1), 2 (2018)
12. Hamblin, K.A.: Active Ageing in the European Union: Policy Convergence and Divergence. Palgrave Macmillan, London (2013). https://doi.org/10.1057/9781137303141
13. Haslwanter, J.D.H., Fitzpatrick, G.: Why do few assistive technology systems make it to market? The case of the *HandyHelper* project. Univ. Access Inf. Soc. **16**(3), 755–773 (2017). https://doi.org/10.1007/s10209-016-0499-3
14. Hallewell Haslwanter, J.D., Neureiter, K., Garschall, M.: User-centered design in AAL. Univ. Access Inf. Soc. **19**(1), 57–67 (2018). https://doi.org/10.1007/s10209-018-0626-4
15. Hornung-Prähauser, V., Wieden-Bischof, D., Willner, V., Selhofer, H.: Methoden zur geschäftsmodell-entwicklung für aal-lösungen durch einbeziehung der endanwenderinnen (2015)
16. Lazar, J., Feng, J.H., Hochheiser, H.: Research Methods in Human-Computer Interaction. Morgan Kaufmann (2017)
17. Leist, A., Ferring, D.: Technology and aging: inhibiting and facilitating factors in ICT use. In: Wichert, R., Van Laerhoven, K., Gelissen, J. (eds.) AmI 2011. CCIS, vol. 277, pp. 166–169. Springer, Heidelberg (2012). https://doi.org/10.1007/978-3-642-31479-7_26
18. Lindsay, S., Jackson, D., Schofield, G., Olivier, P.: Engaging older people using participatory design. In: Proceedings of the SIGCHI Conference on Human Factors in Computing Systems, pp. 1199–1208 (2012)
19. Maguire, M.: Methods to support human-centered design. Int. J. Hum.-Comput. Stud. **55**(4), 587–634 (2001)

20. Neves, B.B., Vetere, F.: Ageing and emerging digital technologies. In: Neves, B.B., Vetere, F. (eds.) Ageing and Digital Technology, pp. 1–14. Springer, Singapore (2019). https://doi.org/10.1007/978-981-13-3693-5_1
21. Newell, A., Arnott, J., Carmichael, A., Morgan, M.: Methodologies for involving older adults in the design process. In: Stephanidis, C. (ed.) UAHCI 2007. LNCS, vol. 4554, pp. 982–989. Springer, Heidelberg (2007). https://doi.org/10.1007/978-3-540-73279-2_110
22. Newell, A.F., Carmichael, A., Gregor, P., Alm, N., Waller, A.: Information technology for cognitive support. In: Human-Computer Interaction, pp. 69–86. CRC Press (2009)
23. Queirós, A., Santos, M., Dias, A., da Rocha, N.P.: Ambient assisted living: systems characterization. In: Queirós, A., Rocha, N.P. (eds.) Usability, Accessibility and Ambient Assisted Living. HIS, pp. 49–58. Springer, Cham (2018). https://doi.org/10.1007/978-3-319-91226-4_3
24. Shneiderman, B., Plaisant, C., Cohen, M., Jacobs, S., Elmqvist, N., Diakopoulos, N.: Designing the User Interface: Strategies for Effective Human-Computer Interaction. Pearson (2016)
25. Sixsmith, A.: Technology and the challenge of aging. In: Sixsmith, A., Gutman, G. (eds.) Technologies for Active Aging. International Perspectives on Aging, vol. 9, pp. 7–25. Springer, Boston (2013). https://doi.org/10.1007/978-1-4419-8348-0_2
26. Sixsmith, A., Mihailidis, A., Simeonov, D.: Aging and technology: taking the research into the real world. Public Policy Aging Rep. **27**(2), 74–78 (2017)
27. Spinsante, S., et al.: The human factor in the design of successful ambient assisted living technologies. In: Ambient Assisted Living and Enhanced Living Environments, pp. 61–89. Elsevier (2017)
28. Stenmark, P., Tinnsten, M., Wiklund, H.: Customer involvement in product development: experiences from Scandinavian outdoor companies. Procedia Eng. **13**, 538–543 (2011)
29. Still, B., Crane, K.: Fundamentals of User-Centered Design: A Practical Approach. CRC Press (2017)

Defining Digital Joy-of-Use Criteria for Seniors: An Applied Design Approach to Build Motivational User Experiences for Older Generations

Michel Bauer[1], Bruno M. C. Silva[1,2(✉)], and Carlos Rosa[1,3]

[1] Universidade Europeia, IADE, Av. Dom Carlos i 4, 1200-649 Lisbon, Portugal
bruno.silva@universidadeeuropeia.pt

[2] Instituto de Telecomunicações, Universidade da Beira Interior, R. Marquês de Ávila e Bolama, 6201-001 Covilhã, Portugal

[3] UNIDCOM/IADE - Unidade de Investigação em Design e Comunicação, Av. Dom Carlos i 4, 1200-649 Lisbon, Portugal

Abstract. The recent increase of aging population across Europe and the rest of the globe represents one of the most radical demographic changes in the history of humankind. The increase of ageing society will have a vast impact on governments, families, individuals and companies. Humans getting older has deeply modified societies, making it possible that three or more generations live together within the same environment. Due to the advent of digital environments, it is important that the needs of older generations are adequately taken into account when it comes to modern communication. In recent years, there has been a lot of research on necessary usability standards within website development for the aged generation, however a functioning usability is not the only point to consider for a successful realization of a digital product. Therefore, the main objective of this work is to study and describe which criteria in terms of Joy-of-Use can help to motivate older people to use digital applications. The underlying research in this paper is divided in two parts, in the first part experts in the field of ageing society have been interviewed using non-structured interview guidelines, to get a better understanding and validate the findings within the literature review. In the second part of the study, people over the age of 60 years have been interviewed, to understand which criteria of Joy-of-Use motivates them to use digital applications. The results of this research will provide recommendations for the development of digital projects for senior generation.

Keywords: Joy-of-Use · Ageing society · User-experience

1 Introduction

Many people experience loneliness and depression in old age, either as a result of living alone or due to lack of close family ties and reduced connections with their culture

C. Stephanidis et al. (Eds.): HCII 2020, LNCS 12426, pp. 470–481, 2020.
https://doi.org/10.1007/978-3-030-60149-2_36

of origin. A study carried out by the industrial psychiatry journal [1], proves a significant correlation between depression and loneliness. Especially as the intergenerational exchange in everyday life became very rare. A huge part of today's human communication is based on digitalization. In particular the interaction between younger and older generations suffers from it and also leads to an extinction of cultural knowledge. In a study [2] conducted by the Nielsen and Norman Group and written by Kane, older people were surveyed about their perception of digital content. The researchers found that seniors often feel that websites and applications are not designed with consideration for their needs and interests. One senior participant said that he felt left out of the online world because it was created with someone very different in mind, another senior observed:

"You look at things that are on the internet and it's skewed towards not my demographic. The younger people, this is their medium. People my age did not grow up with it. People my age are not in charge of it." [2]

This view is certainly a bit radical, nevertheless older generations are often not sufficiently considered when creating digital applications. Literature on web design for the elders is heavily focused on readability and simple usability. In fact, a simple and ergonomically considered usability is especially relevant when developing for seniors, however other aspects of a qualitative user experience should not be ignored. The focus of this paper is Joy-of-Use; therefore, it will be investigated how Joy-of-Use can be achieved when older people use digital applications. Never-too-old is a web application, accompanying this work and providing the elderly a concept through which they can promote and offer workshops. This gives them the opportunity to connect with younger people and pass on their knowledge gained throughout their lives. In addition, there is a marketplace within the concept of the application, where older people can sell their own handcrafted products. Within this paper older people are referred to as the primary user group of the application Never-too-Old. The project should serve as a practical research reference for the paper, in chapter 4.2.2. the application is described in more depth. The present study aims to answer the following question:

Which criteria for achieving Joy-of-Use must be considered when developing digital applications for older people?

The remainder of this paper is organized as follows. The next section identifies some work that is related to the research question proposed in this article. Following the thermology Joy-of-Use is being defined and usability guidelines for the development for the elders are being described. The following section describes the research and presets the results of the study. The final part of this paper presents the conclusions as well as some suggestions for future work.

2 Related Work

2.1 Joy-of-Use According to Jordan

According to Jordan [3], users are no longer happily surprised when a product is simple to use but are at most unpleasantly surprised when it is difficult to use. Jordan sees usability as more than a problem-solving discipline and favors a more holistic usability approach, a so-called pleasure-based approach, in which the products offer more than usability. This is intended to increase the market value of a product positively. Jordan describes that it is important to define all the essential factors, that need to be fulfilled before thinking about creating pleasure or Joy-of-Use.

Within his book "Designing Pleasurable Products" [3] Jordan describes that unlimited usability and utility is required for a Joy-of-Use. With his "Hierarchy of Consumer Needs", the functionality, also known as utility, must first be fulfilled, followed by usability and finally "pleasure" can be achieved. To visualize that thought, Jordan developed a diagram, similar to Maslow's pyramid of needs [4]. As with Maslow, the need for a higher level only arises when the underlying need is satisfied. This paper supports the idea of Jordan that especially with older people a certain quality of usability is necessary to create Joy-of-Use. Therefore, it is essential to describe the necessary usability actions to create a user-friendly application for the respective target group. However, before this term can be analyzed in more detail, the generally known criteria for achieving Joy-of-Use must be described.

2.2 Joy-of-Use Criteria

The criteria for Joy-of-Use described by the various literature [3, 5–7] for a Joy-of-Use product are often similar and the criteria partly merge. Individualization, challenging the user and enabling social interaction are particularly often described. The following criteria are especially relevant and will form the basis for the measurability of Joy-of-Use in the course of this paper:

- individualization
- reasonable challenges
- arousal of curiosity
- social interaction
- identification with the product
- stimulation of the intellect
- control of the application as the basis for Joy-of-Use

Creating an experience for the user is of particular importance. It is emotions and positive experiences with the product, that makes the user experience Joy-of-Use. Usability as a basic requirement for Joy-of-Use is described by literature as indispensable. The user can only experience Joy-of-Use if the system is absolutely usable. If the user cannot do his job satisfactorily, it is unlikely that he will also have a Joy-of-Use experience that will encourage him to continue using it. If, for example, the links lead the user to a dead end or if the white writing on the yellow background is difficult to read, negative emotions are created before Joy-of-Use can be elicited. The user does not have to be aware of these sensations, but they do influence their impression about the interactive product and their willingness to use it again.

2.3 Usability Guidelines

In order to be able to create Joy-of-Use, it is essential to research the information required for a suitable usability for the respective user group. According to literature review, the following guidelines should be considered when developing for older people. Nevertheless, the perception of software or a product is very contextual or person dependent, why these guidelines should only be considered as an approach to better usability before testing with respective users.

Guidelines for Readability. The term that occurs most frequently with regard to usability for older people is readability. Within the Nielsen & Norman research [2], one respondent describes that the internet is unfriendly to people with bad eyesight. This fact refers in particular to two factors, which will be examined in more detail in the following.

Font Type: Within the development guidelines of Apple [8], it is described, that if the application doesn't necessarily need a custom font such as for branding or to create an impressive user experience, it's usually best to use the system fonts. If a custom font is used, it is important to make sure it is readable even at small sizes. Furthermore, it is described that italics and all capital letters for long text passages shall be avoided since it makes the text difficult to read.

Font Size: One point not mentioned within Apple's guidelines [8] is the minimum size for developing digital solutions for older people. Of course, this can vary depending on the device and especially the contrast of the colors used. Nevertheless, it is important to set a minimum font size for development. In a study by Kenji Kurakata [9], it was found that the minimum size for the legibility of text for seniors should be at least 12 points. Converted to digital pixels this means at least a font size of 16px.

Color Contrast: Another point besides the appropriate font selection is the choice of the right colors and contrasts. The development Guidelines of Apple [8] suggest using strongly contrasting colors to improve readability. By increasing the color contrast of visual elements like text, glyphs and controls, the content used can be interpreted by more people. To find out if the developed UI meets minimum acceptable levels of contrast regarding readability, an online color calculator based on the Web Content Accessibility Guidelines (WCAG) should be used in the early development stages of the project.

Guidelines for Interaction. Controls that are too small can be frustratingly difficult for elderly users to hit. This statement is also confirmed by the research of the Nielsen and Norman Group [2], in which the frustration of the target group is expressed. They describe that older users make more mistakes than younger users do. Their study participants often commented on errors, saying "I fat-fingered that one". It's a classic finding in usability research [2] that users blame themselves, although it should actually be the task of the designer and the developer to minimize these obstacles.

Interactive Elements: To make the interaction as barrier-free as possible for the older user, the right size of the hit zones is therefore an important point. Hit zones describe the clickable area surrounding an interaction element. The development guidelines of Apple

[8] suggest a minimum hit zone for all controls and interactive elements that measures at least 44pt × 44pt. To facilitate the interaction regarding the navigation through the application it is important to mark the buttons accordingly. Apple describes that it is important to have a consistent style hierarchy to communicate the relative importance of buttons. By using a consistent hierarchy of button styles, elderly people can grasp the importance of buttons based on their appearance.

3 Expert Interview Study

Within the following description of qualitative research, experts in the field of the ageing society industry have been interviewed. This phase should help to identify the relevant aspects of the application in terms of functionality, usability and branding. This phase can be seen as a preparation phase for the testing with the primary user group.

By using non-standardized interviews, selected experts on the topic were interviewed for this paper. The word expert is to be understood in the sense of people who have special knowledge in working together with elderly people. Expert interviews are especially relevant in the exploratory phase of a project. Talking to experts can serve to shorten time-consuming data gathering within the literature review of a research as well as in the development phase of a project. Besides the time-saving aspects of talking to experts, it can also be used to get insider knowledge, which would not be accessible otherwise. For this investigation, the interviews were partly carried out in person and partly by phone (skype). For the present work it was important to examine the topic from different perspectives. Therefore, a diverse group of experts has been interviewed, which are listed in the following:

Ana João Sepúlveda leads the 40+ Lab in Lisbon, Portugal. The consultancy is focusing to transform Portugal into an age-friendly country. Ana is an expert in the field of Ageing Society and understands the needs and benefits in working together with elderly people.

Elena Parras is the founder of 55mais. The start-up provides a platform where elderly people can offer their services in different areas. Elena Parras brings a lot of experience in building a digital business for older people. At the same time, she is in contact with a lot of organizations and individual seniors.

Klaudia Bachinger is the founder of Wisr, Wisr is a start-up company founded in Vienna, which mediates older people with companies. Klaudia Bachinger is an expert in building networks in the field of ageing society and has a lot of knowledge in building user friendly websites for the respective user group.

3.1 Results (Expert Interviews)

A suitable qualitative evaluation method must be selected to match the qualitative survey method of the non-standardized interviews. Since interviews with experts lead to intensive discussions, not all information is relevant to the underlying work. For this reason, the method of qualitative content analysis was chosen. Qualitative content analysis allows to reduce and structure the mass of information systematically to the relevant parts for the investigation. [10] The aim is to create a compact corpus that reflects the selected material, namely an abstract and linguistically simplified summary of the analytically relevant communication content. In this way the material is gradually generalized and the amount of material is reduced. [11] The data presented from the expert interviews has therefore been systematized for a better overview. The extracted data of the interviews was thus assigned to the following categories. Based on the findings, the following conclusions can be drawn for the research study:

(1) The digital skills of older generations cannot be compared to that of generations as for example millennials. It is important to use as little complexity as possible. It is important to focus on relevant content and try to minimize the unnecessary.
(2) A fully inclusive design is difficult to achieve. It is important to convince people in the target group with a good digital competence. They can then act as mentors for other people in the same age group.
(3) One of the biggest challenges is the description of the target group. The terms "old" or "elderly" can be understood as discriminating.
(4) Social interaction is a key motivational factor in using a digital tool for the respective target group.

Concluding, it can be said that the interviews with the experts confirmed the findings from the literature review concerning usability. In the following section, the survey of the primary target group will be discussed. The findings from the literature review as well as the qualitative pilot study will serve as a foundation for the research design applied.

4 Primary User Group Testing

Within the following testing with the primary user group, the main objective is to find out which criteria can contribute to an increase in Joy-of-Use for digital applications. First and foremost, it is important to create empirical data in order to provide recommendations for third parties.

4.1 Selection of Test Persons

The selection of suitable test persons should be representative of the later user group. However, with few test persons it can be difficult to consider all relevant groups. According to Sarodnick & Brau [12], actual later users should be selected if possible. After consultation with the experts, it has been decided to target primarily +60-year old persons with a certain level of digital skills. The expert interviews showed that digitally inexperienced persons could distort the test results. It was therefore recommended to start with digitally experienced persons first, as they usually act as mentors for digitally weaker persons in the same age group. According to Nielsen [13] already 5 persons are sufficient to uncover up to 75% of usability problems. However, since usability can be tested more specifically, five people are not sufficient for a valid result within this generative research. By looking at other generative testings, usually 10–20 test persons are cited for a valid result. In a study conducted by Thomas Tullis and Larry Wood

[14] the minimum number of participants needed for a card-sorting study was assessed. They found out that from a number of 12 test users on, the correlation was already only at a value of about 0.85. Since the number of concept possibilities to be discussed in this thesis is limited to only 6, it is assumed that 12 users are sufficient for a valid test result. After evaluating the expert interviews, it became clear that there is a difference in behavior between older men and older women. In order to make the expected differences between the sexes visible, the same number of women and men was chosen for this study.

Due to the outbreak of the Corona Pandemic and the subsequent restrictions, the execution of the testing had to be reconsidered and adapted. After consultation with the test persons, it was decided to arrange the interviews via the digital services Zoom and Skype. Therefore, it had to be made sure in advance that each participant had a computer at home, which would allow a problem-free screen transmission.

4.2 Execution of the Testing

The interviews have been estimated to last in total between 30 and 45 min in total. Before starting the tests, the test persons were asked whether sound recording was permitted during the tests to be performed. Furthermore, the test persons have been assured that the results will be used anonymously and that they can stop the test at any time. Before the start of the test, a personal introduction round was carried out. This is important in order to create a pleasant atmosphere. The more harmoniously the atmosphere, the more valuable the generated data becomes. The execution of the test interviews was divided into the following two survey elements general questionnaire and concept validation.

Survey Element 1 - General Questionnaire. The first part of the survey was based on a general questionnaire, which served to get a better understanding about the user group and their motivational factors behind general website usage. Within this questionnaire the demographic information about the person as well as the user behavior of digital services has been questioned. The focus was primarily on the validation of the importance regarding Joy-of-Use and usability factors identified in the previous chapters. As described above, 12 people took part in the survey. Of these, six were male and six females with an average age of 65.6 years. Nine of the 12 people described were already retired. Six of the respondents were British, three were Portuguese and three German. The professions of the test subjects involved three former teachers, three former business consultants, a former police dog handler, a former secretary, a former medical doctor, a former accountant, a former gardener and a former university professor. In total, the participants rated their digital competence with 6.83 out of 10 points. The most favorite tools among the participants are Google (9 mentions), Facebook (6 mentions), Zoom (6 mentions), Skype (5 mentions), WhatsApp (4 mentions) and Instagram (2 mentions). Additionally, applications in the area of news and banking were mentioned. The most relevant question regarding the importance of the analyzed Joy-of-Use criteria in the use of digital applications is visible in the following Fig. 1 represents "not important", 2 represents "less important", 3 represents "moderately important", 4 represents "important" and 5 represents "very important".

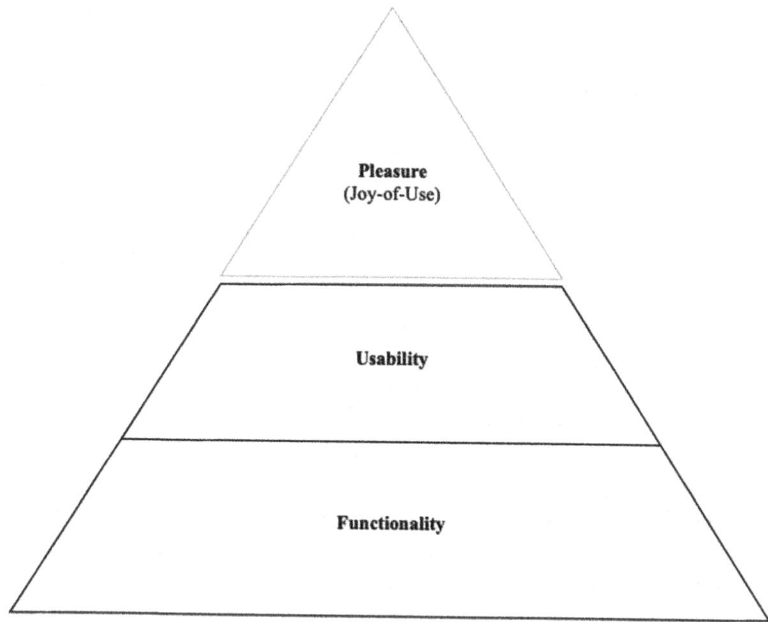

Fig. 1. Pyramid of pleasure according to Jordan

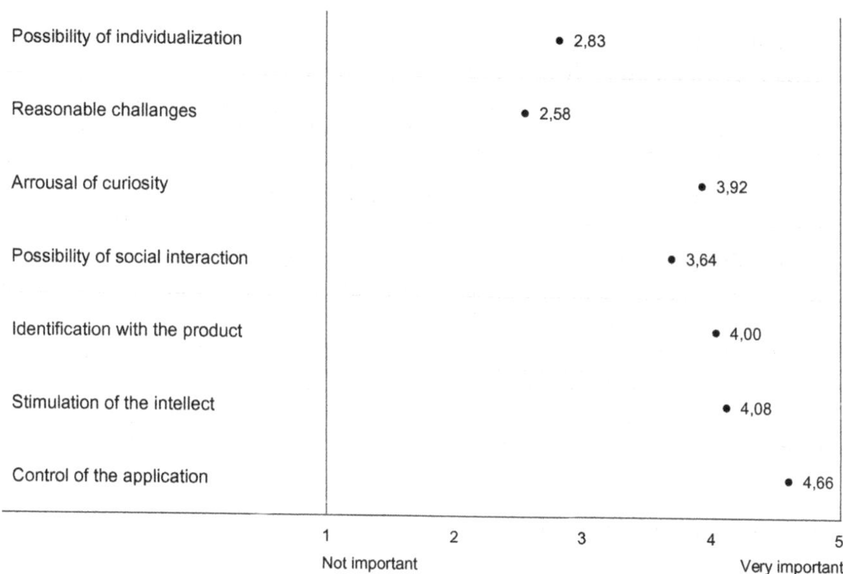

Fig. 2. How important are the following criteria in using a website/software for you?

The elderly answered that individualization and reasonable challenges are rated between less important to moderately important. The possibility of social interaction was rated between moderately important and important, with a stronger tendency towards important. Curiosity, identification with the project, and stimulation of the intellect were evaluated as important criteria when using a website. Having control over an application in the form of understandable usability for example was rated as very important within the target group. The complete questionnaire document can be found in the appendix of this paper.

Survey Element 2 – Concept Validation (SE2). Concept validation is a method of showing design, concepts, screens or ideas to potential users to find out, whether the users feel a specific need or interest in the described object. (Slack, 2020) It is important to involve customers in the conceptual design phase to understand user needs, expectation, satisfaction and the motivation for using a specific application. The main part of this survey element was to find out which concept extensions could help to increase joy when using the application. A concept extension is understood within this thesis as an additional element, which extends the core functionality (in this case the presentation and booking of the workshops) by elements to potentially increase Joy-of-Use. The six concepts extensions were created with regard to the quality criteria developed in chapter 2.4.5. (Joy-of-Use Criteria). In the following, the six concepts and the included Joy-of-Use criteria will be explained briefly.

(1) **Reviews**: Within this section, potential users have the opportunity to view comments and ratings on their offered workshops. Based on Joy-of-Use criteria "social interaction" and "curiosity".
(2) **Trophies**: This section offers users the opportunity to collect trophies by completing certain tasks. Based on Joy-of-Use criterion "challenge".
(3) **Leaderboard**: In this area users can see how they compete against others in terms of workshops held based on a point system. Based on Joy-of-Use criterion "challenge".
(4) **Trends**: Here users can view current trends in the form of a news feed created by younger generations. Based on Joy-of-Use criteria "stimulation of the intellect" and "curiosity".
(5) **Personalization:** This area offers the possibility to personalize the user's profile by, for example, adding a profile picture. Based on Joy-of-Use criteria "identification with the product" and "individualization".
(6) **Control Center:** The control center offers users the possibility of transparency. Current statistics can be viewed as well as a calendar to determine when the next appointment will take place. Based on Joy-of-Use criteria "control over the application".

5 Discussion and Open Issues

At the end of the concept validation, the test persons were asked to sort the six concepts by popularity in a sequence from 1 to 6 (1 - most important to 6 - least important) Later, the individual results were matched with points from 6 to 1. For example, if a concept was put on 1, 6 points were added to the concept. If a concept was put on 2, 5 points were added and so on. This system should contribute to the overall analysis. Table 1 shows the results after interviewing 12 people.

Table 1. Results concept validation

	Concept name	Joy-of-use criterion	Total points
1	Reviews	Social interaction & curiosity	57 points
2	Trends	Stimulation of intellect & curiosity	52 points
2	Personalization	Identification & individualization	52 points
4	Control center	Control of the application	43 points
5	Leaderboard	Challenge	26 points
6	Trophies	Challenge	22 points

According to the data, the concepts trophies and leaderboard have been rated as being of least relevance. Of particular interest is the clarity of the results. Trophies were ranked last or second to last by 10 of the 12 respondents. For Leaderboard this applies to 9 of the 12 answers. The Control Center was perceived by the test persons as much more popular then Leaderboard and Trophies, but on average it was ranked only on fourth position. The concept Trends and Personalization have been rated as popular on average. While personalization was taken for granted by many test persons, many test persons found the trends especially exciting. In total, the reviews were rated as the most popular concept extension. In general, there were no significant differences between the sexes.

5.1 Recommendations for Actions Regarding Joy-of-Use

This section aims to translate the findings of the study into recommendations for designers that develop for the respective target group. The question to be answered within this paper is:

> *Which criteria for achieving Joy-of-Use must be considered when developing digital applications for older people?*

(1) The usability is indeed the foundation for a successful increase of Joy-of-Use. Designers should orientate themselves on existing literature.
(2) The results show that especially the criteria stimulation of the intellect, identification with the product and arousal of curiosity play an important role within the analyzed target group. Since these three criteria are particularly relevant for generating Joy-of-Use in the respective user group, it is important to take them into account in the creation of the content strategy.
(3) Another important finding that designers should consider is the importance of the terminology used when communicating with older target groups. An incorrect use of terms can lead to frustration within the target group which can have a significant negative impact on the identification with the product. It is advisable for the communication strategy to work closely with the target group and focus on user-centered development.

(4) The integration of challenges should be verified carefully with the target group, as the results of the study indicate that this criterion seems to be of less necessity.
(5) Furthermore, it became apparent that stimulating elements such as trends or news adapted to the target group were considered particularly important. Especially the integration of social components as well as the integration of elements that stimulate the intellect can serve as a mediator for increasing curiosity within aged generation. The outcomes are particularly interesting for designers who develop for the senior population, the implications can help to increase user satisfaction and further motivational user experience.

5.2 Open Issues

This work also identified related open issues which will be discussed below and create space for further research. One limitation was the fact that the studies had to be conducted via digital channels due to the corona pandemic. Therefore, the observation possibilities of the researcher via Skype and Zoom were limited. As the topic of Joy-of-Use is a very emotional one, the direct analysis of emotions by testing in the same room would have been more complete. Another limitation is the fact that the average age of 65 is relatively young for a general picture of the "older generation". Within the conversations with the 12 test persons, some of them perceived major differences in digital competence and interests. Also, regarding the level of education, not all relevant groups within the study could be considered. Therefore, the results of this study can only be considered as a tendency. A deeper insight can only be achieved by enlarging the test group.

Another constraint is the fact that the application was tested at a very early stage of development. A complete validation of a functioning usability can therefore not be made at this stage. Nevertheless, the results serve as a first assessment for the successful further development of an application.

6 Conclusion

Comparing the statement of the questionnaire (Fig. 2) and the results of the sorting (Table 1) it becomes apparent that those statements are confirmed by the concept validation. The results of this paper show that not all of the quality criteria for Joy-of-Use found in the literature research are of high relevance for the respective target group. Above all, it can be stated that the quality criterion challenge is of minor relevance. This became apparent not only from the general questionnaire but also from the concept validation research. The criterion identification with the product could be analyzed as an important aspect in developing for the respective user group. Another important criterion is the identification with the product or a website. Stimulation of the intellect can be evaluated as the most important criterion after a functioning usability.

Regarding usability, it is important to follow existing research. Especially the readability of the content and the interaction with this application are essential elements, that need to be considered, in the development. The readability can be achieved by the correct choice of font, the size of the font and a contrast check regarding the color values. At the same time, it is important to ensure that as little content as possible is presented per screen view. In order to guarantee the best possible interaction, it is important to keep a minimum size of buttons and to design the hit zones for interaction with those buttons accordingly large.

Acknowledgements. The study was supported by UNIDCOM under a grant from the Fundação para a Ciência e Tecnologia (FCT) No. UIDB/00711/2020 attributed to UNIDCOM – Unidade de Investigação em Design e Comunicação, Lisbon, Portugal. This work was also partially supported by Instituto de Telecomunicações and funded by FCT/MCTES through national funds and when applicable co-funded EU funds under the project UIDB/EEA/50008/2020.

References

1. Singh, A., Misra, N.: A loneliness, depression and sociability in old age. Ind. Psychiatry J. **18**, 51–55 (2009)
2. Nielsen & Norman Group Homepage. https://www.nngroup.com/articles/usability-for-senior-citizens/. Accessed 01 May 2020
3. Jordan, P.W.: Designing Pleasurable Product. Routledge, Abingdon (2002)
4. Csikszentmihalyi, M.: Flow: The Psychology of Optimal Experience. Harper Perennial, New York (2003)
5. Blythe, M., Overbeeke, K.: Funology: From Usability to Enjoyment. Springer, Netherlands (2008)
6. Naumann, I.: Joy-of-Use: Ästhetik, Emotion und User Experience für interaktive Produkte. AV Akademikerverlag, Germany (2012)
7. Tiger, L.: The Pursuit of Pleasure. Routledge, London (2002)
8. Apple Developer Website. https://developer.apple.com/design/human-interface-guidelines/accessibility/overview/best-practices/. Accessed 19 Feb 2020
9. Kurakata, K.: Estimation of legible font size for elderly people (2013). https://www.researchgate.net/publication/269750946_Estimation_of_legible_font_size_for_elderly_people
10. Gläser, J., Laudel, G.: Experteninterviews und qualitative Inhaltsanalyse: Als Instrumente rekonstruierender Untersuchungen (5. Aufl.). VS Verlag für Sozialwissenschaften Springer, Frankfurt (2020)
11. Mayring, P.: Einführung in die qualitative Sozialforschung. Beltz, Germany (2016)
12. Sarodnick, F., Brau, H.: Methoden der Usability Evaluation: Wissenschaftliche Grundlagen und praktische Anwendung (2011)
13. Nielsen, N.: https://www.nngroup.com/articles/why-you-only-need-to-test-with-5-users/. Accessed 22 Mar 2020
14. Tullis, T., Wood, L.: How Many Users Are Enough for a Card-Sorting Study? (2014)

Study on Acceptance of Social Robots by Aging Adults Living Alone

Na Chen, Xiaoyu Liu, and Yue Sun(✉)

Beijing University of Chemical Technology, Beijing 100029, China
chenn4@163.com, ytlxy@126.com, y_sun_kyu@outlook.com

Abstract. Social robots have become an important way to alleviate the impact of aging on society and families. This study aims to explore the influence of the living state of the elderly on robot acceptance. Based on Unified Theory of Acceptance and Use of Technology (UTAUT) questionnaire, this study conducted a questionnaire survey for the elderly. The results show that performance expectancy, social influence, facilitating conditions have significant positive effects on robot acceptance of the elderly. In addition, the gender of aging adults moderates the influence of performance expectancy on robot acceptance, the experience of using intelligent products for the elderly moderates the impact of social influence on robot acceptance, and the living state of the elderly moderates the significant influence of facilitating conditions on robot acceptance. Intelligent robots can improve the lives of aging adults living alone, and the higher the convenience of robots, the stronger the usage intention of aging adults living alone to use robots. The results of this study can help relevant researchers to better understand the psychological needs of the elderly, provide ideas for the design of robot products, and provide references for the establishment of social pension system.

Keywords: Aging adults living alone · Social robot · Acceptance · UTAUT

1 Introduction

The problem of aging in Chinese society is becoming increasingly prominent. The growth rate of the elderly population continues to rise rapidly, putting great pressure on social and family resources. Robots with artificial intelligence are an important way to alleviate the shortage on pension resources. With the increase of age, the daily activities of the elderly are restricted, and social activities change significantly, these have caused the elderly to lack sufficient family and social mental support and face serious mental health problems. This requires robots to provide both life help and some psychological comfort. Social robots can provide informal help and support for the elderly, including assessing and managing symptoms, using medication and providing personal care [1, 2]. Social robots improve the feasibility of home care [3], then reducing the cost of home care [4, 5]. Some intelligent robot products with simple accompanying function have already entered the market. For example, Paro, a seal-like robot from the institute of intelligent systems in Japan, offers solace to the elderly by responding to touch, hugging, remembering faces

C. Stephanidis et al. (Eds.): HCII 2020, LNCS 12426, pp. 482–494, 2020.
https://doi.org/10.1007/978-3-030-60149-2_37

and learning to act in ways that produce favorable responses. Research proved that social robotics products can to some extent alleviate the elderly's loneliness, depression and other psychological problems, and improve their mental health. However, the existing research hasn't study enough on the acceptance of social robots in the elderly. Studying the acceptance of robots by the elderly can help society and families better understand the psychological needs of the elderly, provide ideas for the design of robot products, and provide reference for the establishment of a social pension system.

The UTAUT model is a technology acceptance model that has been widely adopted in recent years. Venkatesh et al. [6] integrated technology acceptance models such as Technology Acceptance Model (TAM), Theory of Reasoned Action (TRA), Theory of Planned Behavior (TPB), Social Cognitive Theory (SCT), aimed at exploring the influencing factors of user awareness, put forward Unified Theory of Acceptance and Use of Technology (UTAUT). The UTAUT model believes that behaviors and behavioral intentions are affected by performance expectancy, effort expectance, social influence, and facilitating conditions. At the same time, these effects are adjusted by four factors: gender, age, experience, and usage intention. Studies show that although it includes more factors at the expense of parsimony, the UTAUT model can account for as much as 70 percent of the usage intention. Among them, performance expectancy refers to the extent to which individuals believe that using the system can help them achieve job performance. effort expectance refers to the ease of using the system. social influence refers to the extent to which important social relationships influence the individual's use of the system. facilitating conditions refers to the extent to which the organization and infrastructure support the use of the system. More previous studies used the TAM to study the robot acceptance of the elderly, and less research used the UTAUT [7]. This study explores the acceptance of robots among elderly on the basis of the UTAUT.

Studies show that aging adults living alone without caregivers face more adverse physical and psychosocial health issues [8]. aging adults living alone face greater challenges in terms of physical, social, emotional and survival needs [9], They need more assistance in their daily activities, but have less access to services and comfort [10, 11]. aging adults living alone are more likely to feel lonely, frustrated, and unable to move [12]. Functional and cognitive impairments, chronic illnesses, reduced social relationships, and low levels of physical activity pose challenges to the lives of aging adults living alone [13–15]. Technology may provide them with some solutions. Therefore, this study included the living status of the elderly as a factor in the UTAUT model to explore the effect of the elderly's living status on their robot acceptance.

Based on the UTAUT model, this study aims to explore the influence of the living state of the elderly on their robot acceptance, which will help to better understand the psychological needs of the elderly, provide ideas for social robot product design, and provide references for the establishment of social pension system.

2 Model and Hypotheses

Based on the UTAUT model, this study believes that the use of social robots by elderly can help them improve their quality of life, how easy it is for elderly to use robots, how social relationships around elderly affect their use of robots, and the infrastructure required to use a robot will affect its robot acceptance. In addition, both gender and age of the elderly moderate the effects of performance expectancy, effort expectancy and social influence on robot acceptance. Therefore, this study proposes the following seven hypotheses. The model framework is shown in Fig. 1.

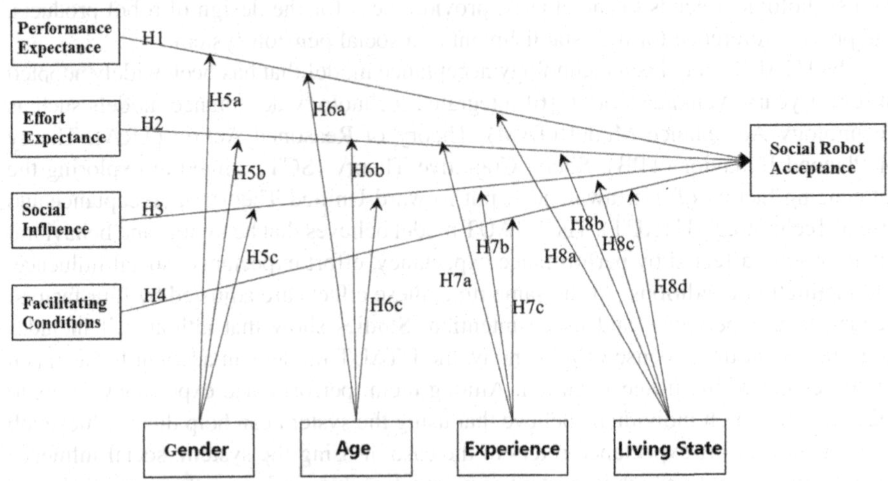

Fig. 1. Framework of the elderly's acceptance of social robots

H1: Performance expectancy has a significant effect on acceptance of social robots of the elderly.
H2: Effort expectance has a significant effect on acceptance of social robots of the elderly.
H3: Social influence has a significant effect on acceptance of social robots of the elderly.
H4: Facilitating conditions have a significant effect on acceptance of social robots of the elderly.
H5a: Gender moderates the effect of performance expectance on acceptance of the elderly.
H5b: Gender moderates the effect of effort expectance on acceptance of the elderly.
H5c: Gender moderates the effect of social influence on acceptance of the elderly.
H6a: Age moderates the effect of performance expectance on acceptance of the elderly.
H6b: Age moderates the effect of effort expectance on acceptance of the elderly.
H6c: Age moderates the effect of social influence on acceptance of the elderly.
H7a: Experience moderates the effect of effort expectance on acceptance of the elderly.
H7b: Experience moderates the effect of social influence on acceptance of the elderly.
H7c: Experience moderates the effect of facilitating conditions on acceptance of the elderly.

In addition, the living state of the elderly affects the social support they can get, and aging adults living alone receive less psychological comfort and life help, so the acceptance and expectation of using social robots may be different from that of non-solitary elderly people. Therefore, this study proposes the hypothesis that the living state of the elderly moderates the effect of performance expectance, effort expectance, and social influence on robot acceptance.

H8a: Living state moderates the effect of performance expectance on acceptance of the elderly.
H8b: Living state moderates the effect of effort expectance on acceptance of the elderly.
H8c: Living state moderates the effect of social influence on acceptance of the elderly.
H8d: Living state moderates the effect of facilitating conditions on acceptance of the elderly.

3 Methodology

3.1 Participants

In this study, seven communities and senior universities in Beijing were selected to distributed questionnaires. A total of 492 questionnaires were distributed and 386 questionnaires were collected, including 274 valid questionnaires, with an effective recovery rate of 55.69%. Among the valid questionnaires, 146 are male, accounting for 53.28%, and 128 are female, accounting for 46.72%. The age range is 63 to 85 years, with an average age of 69.69 years. Living state includes 81 people living alone, accounting for 29.56%, and the remaining 193 people living with a partner or other family members, accounting for 70.44%.

3.2 Questionnaire Design

The questionnaire in this study contains three parts: demography related questions (moderator variables), acceptance influencing factors, and acceptance questions. the demographics section includes four factors, which measure participants' gender, age, living state, and experience with intelligent products. experience was measured by Likert 5-point scale (1 = inexperienced, 5 = experienced). The results show that the experience of these participants in using intelligent products is 1.92, which is relatively low.

The McColl and Nejat [16] scale was appropriately modified to obtain the acceptance factors scale and acceptance scale. The acceptance factor section contains four sub-scales, which are performance expectance, effort expectance, social influence, and facilitating conditions. The acceptance section includes a sub-scale, that is, usage intention. Each of these sub-scales contains three items. Therefore, this study questionnaire modifies some items to better fit the research context. For the performance expectance sub-scale, this study selects three typical use scenarios to measure whether older people think that social robots can play a role in these situations. These scenarios include companionship and care (i.e. tea and chat), and management of daily matters (i.e. reminding you to take medicine, etc.) and supporting remote collaboration (i.e. getting in touch with people and medical staff). For the social influence sub-scale, the study measures the effects of children, brand promotion, and national policies on the elderly. These items are measured by a Likert 5-point scale (1 = strongly disagree, 5 = strongly agree).

4 Data Analysis

4.1 Reliability and Validity Analysis

The factor load of each item in the sub-scale is greater than 0.665, indicating that the items in the measure scale all reflect the same construct. Cronbach's Alpha is 0.668, which indicates that the questionnaire of this study has high reliability, and the items of each subscale can be combined into the same factor for subsequent analysis. The KMO value of each subscale is greater than 0.585, and the scale has good structural validity. The CR value of each subscale is greater than 0.821, and the scale has good construction reliability. The square root of the AVE value of each subscale is greater than its correlation coefficient, and the scale has high convergence validity. Cronbach's Alpha, CR and AVE values of the subscales are shown in Table 1.

Table 1. Reliability and validity analysis results of the questionnaire.

Factor	M	SD	Cronbach's Alpha	CR	AVE	AVE square root
Usage intention	2.51	0.77	0.777	0.871	0.692	0.83
Performance expectance	2.36	0.37	0.692	0.828	0.620	0.79
Effort expectance	2.42	0.63	0.720	0.843	0.642	0.80
Social influence	2.61	0.59	0.668	0.821	0.608	0.78
Facilitating conditions	2.62	0.63	0.763	0.864	0.679	0.82
Gender	0.53	0.50				
Age	69.60	3.17				
Experience	1.92	0.83				
Living state	0.30	0.46				

According to the correlation analysis, in addition to the non-significant correlation between the effort expectance and the usage intention ($p > 0.05$), there is a correlation between the other variables, and the correlation coefficients are less than 0.6 (the highest is 0.233), It can be considered that the collinearity degree of the data is within the acceptable range in this paper. At the same time, the square root of AVE of each variable is greater than the correlation coefficient between the variables, indicating that there is a good discriminative validity between the variables. correlation coefficients between variables are shown in Table 2.

4.2 Model Test

Perform a regression test on the variables. The test results are shown in Table 3. In model 1, the effort expectance is not significant, therefore, H2 is not verified. Remove effort expectance from the model. According to the results of model 2 and model 3, there is a positive correlation between performance expectance, social influence, facilitating

Table 2. Correlation coefficient matrix.

Factor	Performance expectance	Effort expectance	Social influence	Facilitating conditions	Gender	Age	Experience	Usage intention
Effort expectance	0.193**							
Social influence	0.163**	0.094						
Facilitating conditions	0.164**	0.130*	0.105					
Gender	0.120*	−0.011	−0.010	0.067				
Age	−0.105	−0.046	−0.096	0.072	0.022			
Experience	0.009	−0.209**	−0.048	0.016	0.055	0.086		
Living state	−0.056	−0.034	0.116	0.037	−0.019	−0.024	0.046	
Usage intention	0.198**	0.048	0.233**	0.196**	−0.060	−0.004	0.172**	0.502**

conditions and the elderly's acceptance of social robots ($\beta = 0.108, p < 0.05; \beta = 0.149, p < 0.01; \beta = 0.117, p < 0.05$). H1, H3, H4 are verified. The regression coefficient between performance expectance and gender is −0.074, which is significant at the 0.05 level. H5 is partially verified. The regression coefficient of social influence and experience is −0.101, which is significant at the level of 0.01. H7 is partially verified. The regression coefficient of facilitating conditions and living state is −0.133, which is significant at the level of 0.001. H8 is partially verified.

Table 3. Regression analysis results (standardize coefficients).

Variable		Robot acceptance		
		Model 1	Model 2	Model 3
Independent	Performance expectance	0.111*	0.108*	0.174***
	Effort expectance	−0.014	–	–
	Social influence	0.150**	0.149**	0.049
	Facilitating conditions	0.119**	0.117*	0.046
Moderator	Gender			−0.065*
	Age			−0.005
	Experience			0.129***
	Living state			0.440***
Moderator effect	Performance expectance × gender			−0.074*
	Performance expectance × age			0.057
	Performance expectance × living state			0.031
	Social influence × gender			0.022
	Social influence × age			−0.027
	Social influence × experience			−0.101**
	Social influence × living state			−0.004
	Facilitating conditions × experience			−0.017
	Facilitating conditions × living state			−0.133***
	R2	0.103	0.103	0.575
	Adjusted R2	0.090	0.093	0.548
	F	7.753***	10.340***	21.906***

In order to more intuitively describe the moderating effects of gender, experience and living state on the acceptance of the elderly, this paper draws interactive graphs between variables to illustrate. It can be seen from Fig. 2 that the slope of the solid line (male elderly) is greater than that of the dashed line (female elderly). Gender has a significant moderating effect between performance expectance and elderly acceptance. For male and female elderly, the higher the performance expectance, the higher their acceptance of robots (male: $t = 2.221$, $p = 0.028$; female: $t = 5.709$, $p < 0.001$), but the female elderly's acceptance is more affected. It can be seen from Fig. 3 that the slope of the dashed line (low intelligent device experience) is greater than that of the solid line (high smart device experience), and there is a significant moderating effect between the social influence and the acceptance of the elderly. For the elderly with less experience in using intelligent devices, the higher the experience, the higher the acceptance of the robot ($t = 2.350$, $p = 0.021$). For the elderly with more experience in using intelligent devices, experience has no significant effect on their acceptance ($t = -1.520$, $p = 0.137$). It can be seen from Fig. 4 that the slope of the solid line (non-solitary living) is negative, and the slope of the dashed line (solitary living) is positive. There is a significant moderating effect between the facilitating conditions and the acceptance of the elderly. For solitary elderly people, the higher the facilitating conditions, the higher their acceptance of the robot. For non-solitary elderly people, the lower the facilitating conditions, the higher their acceptance of robots.

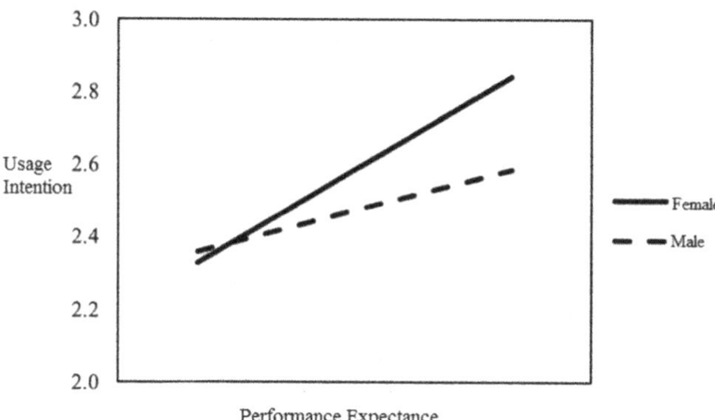

Fig. 2. The moderating effect of gender between performance expectance and usage intention.

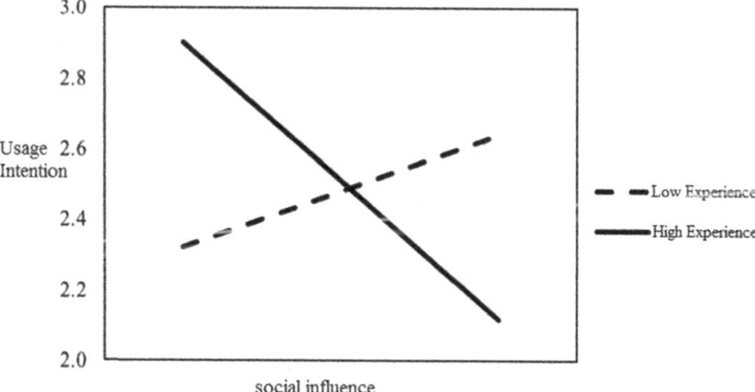

Fig. 3. The moderating effect of experience between social influence and usage intention.

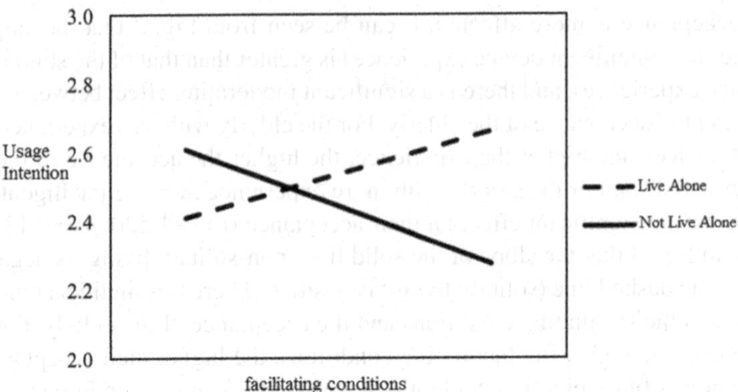

Fig. 4. The moderating effect of living state between facilitating conditions and usage intention.

The hypothesis verification status of this study can be summarized as shown in Table 4.

Table 4. Hypothesis verification.

Number	Hypothesis	Verification
H1	Performance expectancy has a significant effect on acceptance of social robots of the elderly	Verified
H2	Effort expectance has a significant effect on acceptance of social robots of the elderly	Unverified
H3	Social influence has a significant effect on acceptance of social robots of the elderly	Verified
H4	Facilitating conditions have a significant effect on acceptance of social robots of the elderly	Verified
H5a	Gender moderates the effect of performance expectance on acceptance of the elderly	Verified
H5b	Gender moderates the effect of effort expectance on acceptance of the elderly	Unverified
H5c	Gender moderates the effect of social influence on acceptance of the elderly	Unverified
H6a	Age moderates the effect of performance expectance on acceptance of the elderly	Unverified
H6b	Age moderates the effect of effort expectance on acceptance of the elderly	Unverified
H6c	Age moderates the effect of social influence on acceptance of the elderly	Unverified

(*continued*)

Table 4. (*continued*)

Number	Hypothesis	Verification
H7a	Experience moderates the effect of effort expectance on acceptance of the elderly	Unverified
H7b	Experience moderates the effect of social influence on acceptance of the elderly	Verified
H7c	Experience moderates the effect of facilitating conditions on acceptance of the elderly	Unverified
H8a	Living state moderates the effect of performance expectance on acceptance of the elderly	Unverified
H8b	Living state moderates the effect of effort expectance on acceptance of the elderly	Unverified
H8c	Living state moderates the effect of social influence on acceptance of the elderly	Unverified
H8d	Living state moderates the effect of facilitating conditions on acceptance of the elderly	Verified

5 Result and Discussion

This study explores the impact of the living state of the elderly on their robot acceptance. The results show that the living state moderates the impact of facilitating conditions on the acceptance of the elderly, and the standardization coefficient of the living state is very high.

Further illustrates that the impact of facilitating conditions on the acceptance have bigger difference between solitary people and non- solitary people. Robots can help the elderly live better independently [17]. For aging adults living alone and not living alone, there may be differences in the impact of facilitating conditions on their lives. For aging adults living alone, the better the facilitating conditions, the better the maintenance of the robot can be guaranteed, and the more likely it is to use an intelligent robot. For aging adults who are not living alone, the better the facilitating conditions, the more life support they receive from the outside world, and the less their motivation for using intelligent robots.

This study did not find a significant effect of effort expectance on the acceptance of the elderly, which is somewhat different from previous studies [18, 19]. This difference may be due to the influence of the technology acceptance model over time. Although UTAUT is powerful and robust, technology acceptance may fluctuate over time [20–22]. The influence of certain factors in the technology acceptance model is different before the technology is implemented (when the technology is not used) and after the technology is implemented (when the user has used and experienced the technology) [23, 24]. The conclusion of this study is significant for the current stage when intelligent robots have not entered the consumer goods market. However, when intelligent products are widely used by the elderly, the conclusion of this study needs to be further discussed and adjusted. In addition, Although the questionnaire in this research emphasizes intelligent robot products, the elderly still has very little experience in using intelligent products, which may make it difficult for the elderly to imagine what kind of effort is required to use the robot, causing the effect of effort expectance on acceptance is not significant.

Based on the UTAUT model, the results of this study show that performance expectance, social influence and facilitating conditions have significant effect on the acceptance of the elderly. However, there are also literatures argue that the acceptance model ignores the basic determinants [25–27]. Such as specific biophysical factors associated with aging (e.g., cognitive and physical decline), and psychosocial factors (e.g., social isolation, fear of disease, etc.) [28]. In addition, the cost (price) of technology is also ignored in many studies [28]. Therefore, more research is needed to better understand the acceptance of the elderly. Based on the acceptance model, another paper explores the impact of robot prices on the acceptance of the elderly.

The results of this study showed that gender moderates the influence of performance expectance on the acceptance of the elderly, and that for female elderly, performance expectance have a greater impact on acceptance, and that female elderly are more acceptable, which is somewhat different from the previous research results. More previous studies have shown that men are more receptive and willing to use robots [29, 30]. However, the subjects of these studies were non-elderly, while the subjects of this study were elderly Chinese. Therefore, for different age groups, the influence of user gender on the acceptance of intelligent robot products may be different, which needs further exploration.

6 Conclusion

The application of intelligent robots to alleviate the increasingly severe problem of aging in Chinese society has become a hot topic in industry and academia, and the acceptance of the elderly is a fundamental issue in the development of the intelligent robot industry. This study uses an acceptance study method and uses a questionnaire to explore the acceptance of robots of the elderly in China. The results of data analysis show that performance expectance, social influence and convenience have significant positive effects on acceptance, while effort expectations have no significant effects on acceptance.

This study explores the effects of performance expectance, effort expectance, social influence, and facilitating conditions on the acceptance of the elderly, and explores the moderate effects of gender, age, experience with intelligent products, and living state. A total of 386 valid questionnaires were collected. The results of data analysis show that performance expectance, social influence and facilitating conditions have significant positive effects on acceptance, while effort expectance have no significant effects on acceptance. In addition, the gender of aging adults moderates the influence of performance expectancy on robot acceptance, the experience of using intelligent products for the elderly moderates the impact of social influence on robot acceptance, and the living state of the elderly moderates the significant influence of facilitating conditions on robot acceptance.

The results of this study show that the living state of the elderly affects their robot acceptance. Intelligent robots can improve the lives of the elderly living alone, and the higher the facilitating conditions of the robot, the stronger the willingness of the elderly living alone to use the robot.

In addition, elderly women have a higher acceptance of robots, and their acceptance of robots to improve their lives is more significantly affected than that of elderly men. Experience with intelligent products will increase the acceptance of older people. Therefore, this study suggests that intelligent robot products and functions should be developed more specifically for the lifestyle and psychological state of the elderly living alone, so as to provide more convenient service conditions and environment and improve the quality of life and mental health of the elderly living alone. In addition, different intelligent robot services are provided for female and male senior citizens to provide them with differentiated services. This study also recommends that older people should be provided with a wider range of easy-to-understand recommendations for intelligent products to improve their understanding and acceptance.

The results of this study can help relevant researchers to better understand the psychological needs of the elderly, provide ideas for the design of robot products, and provide references for the establishment of social pension system.

Acknowledgement. This study was funded by a Ministry of Education of Humanities and Social Science project 19YJC840002, a Beijing Social Science Fund 17SRC021 and a Beijing Natural Science Foundation 9184029.

References

1. Funk, L., Stajduhar, K., Toye, C., Aoun, S., Grande, G., Todd, C.: Home-based family caregiving at the end of life: a comprehensive review of published qualitative research (1998–2008). Palliat. Med. **24**, 594–607 (2010)
2. Stajduhar, K., Funk, L., Toye, C., Grande, G., Aoun, S., Todd, C.: Home-based family caregiving at the end of life: a comprehensive review of published quantitative research (1998–2008). Palliat. Med. **24**, 573–593 (2010)
3. Hudson, P.: Applying the lessons of high risk industries to health care. BMJ Qual. Saf. **12**(Suppl. 1), i7–i12 (2003)
4. Aoun, S., Kristjanson, L., Currow, D., Hudson, P.: Caring for the terminally ill: at what cost? Palliat. Med. **19**, 551–555 (2005)
5. Rolls, L., Seymour, J.E., Froggatt, K.A., Hanratty, B.: Older people living alone at the end of life in the UK: research and policy challenges. Palliat. Med. **25**(6), 650–657 (2011)
6. Venkatesh, V., Morris, M.G., Davis, G.B., Davis, F.D.: User acceptance of information technology: toward a unified view. MIS Q. **27**, 425–478 (2003)
7. Peek, S.T., Wouters, E.J., Van Hoof, J., Luijkx, K.G., Boeije, H.R., Vrijhoef, H.J.: Factors influencing acceptance of technology for aging in place: a systematic review. Int. J. Med. Inform. **83**(4), 235–248 (2014)
8. Aoun, S.M., Breen, L.J., Howting, D.: The support needs of terminally ill people living alone at home: a narrative review. Health Psychol. Behav. Med. **2**, 951–969 (2014)
9. Aoun, S., Kristjanson, L.J., Oldham, L., Currow, D.: A qualitative investigation of the palliative care needs of terminally ill people who live alone. Collegian **15**(1), 3–9 (2008)
10. Aoun, S., Kristjanson, L.J., Currow, D., Skett, K., Oldham, L., Yates, P.: Terminally ill people living alone without a caregiver: an Australian national scoping study of palliative care needs. Palliat. Med. **21**, 29–34 (2007)

11. Currow, D.C., Christou, T., Smith, J., Carmody, S., Lewin, G., Aoun, S., et al.: Do terminally ill people who live alone miss out on home oxygen treatment? An hypothesis generating study. J. Palliat. Med. **11**, 1015–1022 (2008)
12. Aday, R.H., Kehoe, G.C., Farney, L.A.: Impact of senior center friendships on aging women who live alone. J. Women Aging **18**(1), 57–73 (2006)
13. Gaugler, J.E., Duval, S., Anderson, K.A., Kane, R.L.: Predicting nursing home admission in the US: a meta-analysis. BMC Geriatr. **7**(1), 13 (2007)
14. Luppa, M., Luck, T., Weyerer, S., König, H.H., Brähler, E., Riedel-Heller, S.G.: Prediction of institutionalization in the elderly. A systematic review. Age Ageing **39**(1), 31–38 (2009)
15. Perissinotto, C.M., Cenzer, I.S., Covinsky, K.E.: Loneliness in older persons: a predictor of functional decline and death. Arch. Internal Med. **172**(14), 1078–1084 (2012)
16. McColl, D., Nejat, G.: Meal-time with a socially assistive robot and older adults at a long-term care facility. J. Hum.-Robot Interact. **2**(1), 152–171 (2013)
17. Góngora Alonso, S., Hamrioui, S., de la Torre Díez, I., Motta Cruz, E., López-Coronado, M., Franco, M.: Social robots for people with aging and dementia: a systematic review of literature. Telemedicine e-Health **25**(7), 533–540 (2019)
18. Heerink, M.: Exploring the influence of age, gender, education and computer experience on robot acceptance by older adults. In: Proceedings of the 6th International Conference on Human-Robot Interaction, pp. 147–148. ACM, New York City (2011)
19. Heerink, M., Kröse, B., Evers, V., Wielinga, B.: The influence of social presence on acceptance of a companion robot by older people. J. Phys. Agents **2**(2), 33–40 (2008)
20. Liao, C., Palvia, P., Chen, J.L.: Information technology adoption behavior life cycle: toward a technology continuance theory (TCT). Int. J. Inf. Manag. **29**(4), 309–320 (2009)
21. Venkatesh, V., Davis, F., Morris, M.G.: Dead or alive? The development, trajectory and future of technology adoption research. J. Assoc. Inf. Syst. **8**(4), 267–286 (2007)
22. Zheng, K., Padman, R., Johnson, M.P., Diamond, H.S.: Evaluation of healthcare IT applications: the user acceptance perspective. Soc. Psychol. **65**, 49–78 (2007)
23. Bhattacherjee, A., Premkumar, G.: Understanding changes in belief and attitude toward information technology usage: a theoretical model and longitudinal test. MIS Q. **28**, 229–254 (2004)
24. Karahanna, E., Straub, D.W., Chervany, N.L.: Information technology adoption across time: a cross-sectional comparison of pre-adoption and post-adoption beliefs. MIS Q. **23**, 183–213 (1999)
25. Bagozzi, R.P.: The legacy of the technology acceptance model and a proposal for a paradigm shift. J. Assoc. Inf. Syst. **8**(4), 244–254 (2007)
26. Bouwhuis, D.G., Meesters, L.M.J., Sponselee, A.A.M.: Models for the acceptance of tele-care solutions: intention vs behaviour. Gerontechnology **11**, 45–55 (2012)
27. Yousafzai, S.Y., Foxall, G.R., Pallister, J.G.: Technology acceptance: a meta-analysis of the TAM: part 2. J. Model. Manag. **2**(3), 281–304 (2007)
28. Chen, K., Chan, A.H.S.: A review of technology acceptance by older adults. Gerontechnology **10**, 1–12 (2011)
29. Kuo, I.H., et al.: Age and gender factors in user acceptance of healthcare robots. In: Proceedings of the 18th IEEE International Symposium on Robot and Human Interactive Communication, Hawaii, pp. 214–219. IEEE (2009)
30. McDermott, H., Choudhury, N., Lewin-Runacres, M., Aemn, I., Moss, E.: Gender differences in understanding and acceptance of robot-assisted surgery. J. Robot. Surg. **14**(1), 227–232 (2019). https://doi.org/10.1007/s11701-019-00960-z

Designing for Experiences in Blended Reality Environments for People with Dementia

Shital Desai[1(✉)], Deborah Fels[2], and Arlene Astell[3,4]

[1] SaTS Lab, York University, Toronto, ON M3J 1P3, Canada
desais@yorku.ca
[2] Inclusive Media and Design Centre, Ryerson University, Toronto, ON M5B 2K3, Canada
[3] Rehabilitation Sciences Institute, Faculty of Medicine, University of Toronto, Toronto, Canada
[4] Toronto Rehabilitation Institute, University Health Network, Toronto, Canada

Abstract. Blended Reality environments have the potential to provide scalable solutions that are affordable, adaptable and easily deployable to support people with dementia. Use of these technologies is associated with experience of presence which is an experience with technologically mediated perceptions that generates a feeling of being there and the illusion of non-mediation. Our study examines what constitutes an experience of presence for people with dementia when they interact with MRTs.

An observational study with ten participants (MoCA = 18 to 23, Age = 63 to 88 years) played a game of Tangram on Osmo. Six of these participants also played Young Conker on HoloLens. The experiences of the participants in the digital space, the physical space, and their attention crossover between the two spaces were coded in Noldus Observer XT 14.1.

The study found four main themes that have an impact on the experience of presence in PwD – correspondences, effortless access to physical and digital content, awareness of reality and emergence. Correspondences between physical and digital spaces require PwD to have constant information about the state and nature of physical and digital content. The transitions between physical and digital should be seamless. PwD demonstrated positive experiences with Osmo, an augmented Virtuality technology while their experience with HoloLens, augmented reality technology was negative. The factors impacting experience of presence were prominent in Osmo while they were mostly absent in HoloLens throughout the game play. The outcomes of this study have resulted in a set of recommendations and guidelines for designers to design correspondences for experience of presence. We are currently working on developing prototypes using these guidelines for evaluations with PwD.

Keywords: Blended reality · Mixed reality · Presence · People with dementia · Assistive technology

1 Introduction

People with dementia (PwD) struggle to participate in Activities of Daily Living (ADL) such as cooking and laundry as they have difficulty in sequencing tasks in an activity.

C. Stephanidis et al. (Eds.): HCII 2020, LNCS 12426, pp. 495–509, 2020.
https://doi.org/10.1007/978-3-030-60149-2_38

Blended environments such as Mixed reality technologies (MRTs) could present opportunities for older adults with dementia to carry out ADL independently with little or no help from care givers. Intelligent prompting systems have been developed and evaluated with people with dementia (Mihailidis et al. 2008; Pigot et al. 2003). Orpwood et al. (2008) created a smart apartment equipped with passive sensors and light controls, bed occupancy monitor, tap and cooker monitors and voice prompting devices. Although these developments have been promising, they lack scalability in terms of adapting to different places and activities in the house. Blended environments could offer affordable, adaptable solutions that can be easily adopted and deployed.

Use of MRTs as intelligent devices have been explored with Microsoft Kinect (Chang et al. 2013), augmented reality (AR) HoloLens (Aruanno and Garzotto 2019) and projection based systems (Ro et al. 2019). Kinect-based prompting system improved task completion in two participants, one with early onset dementia and one with an acquired brain injury. AR HoloLens was used to develop a game-based memory assessment tool for early Alzheimers diagnosis. Garzotto et al. (2019) developed three holographic activities using HoloLens in cooperation with neurologists to stimulate memory functions affected by Alzheimers disease, with the goal of delaying the cognitive decline. A projection based MRT with 360° of space was evaluated with PwD for applications such as therapy, entertainment, spatial art and mental care aids. Although the technologies were successful in meeting the functional needs of people with dementia, there is a need to understand experience and engagement of people with dementia with blended environments and mixed reality technologies. This study thus has investigated engagement and experiences of PwD with MRTs through the concept of presence in blended environments proposed by (Benyon et al. 2014; Hoshi and Waterworth 2009). The study explores two types of MRTs – Augmented reality and Augmented virtuality to understand the experience of presence in these technologies and how can designers develop these technologies for people with dementia to engage with the content and medium presented by MRTs.

2 Background

A blended environment such as MRTs consists of a physical and digital space which have been brought together to create opportunities for new experiences. Each of these spaces are defined by elements to interact with, people and the relationship between them. Examples of physical elements are objects and artefacts that build these spaces, while examples of digital elements are buttons, images, animations, information architecture, etc. According to Benyon et al. (2014), volatility of the space to change is also a characteristic of these spaces. Mixed reality is a combination of physical and digital spaces and it comes in different forms depending on how the physical and digital worlds are integrated (Desai et al. 2016). It spans physical-digital reality spectrum (Fig. 1) proposed by Milgram and Kishino (1994), from physical spaces augmented by digital elements (augmented reality) to digital spaces augmented by physical spaces (augmented virtuality).

An example of augmented reality (AR) technology is HoloLens from Microsoft with overlapped physical and digital spaces. Digital holograms are overlaid in the physical

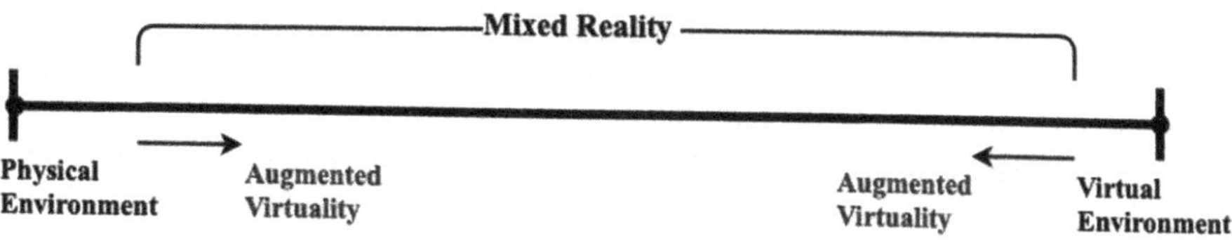

Fig. 1. Mixed reality on a physical-digital continuum, (from Milgram and Kishino (1994))

world. An example of augmented virtuality (AV) is Kinect Xbox from Microsoft where digital elements are manipulated by elements in the physical world. The middle section of the continuum represents various combination of physical and digital objects and spaces, ranging from spaces with sensors and QR codes, to augmented reality overlays in physical space, seen through a smartphone.

Blended theory provides a theoretical framework for research into mixed reality technologies for people with dementia, specifically with the focus on their experiences with physical and digital worlds and the transition between them. The concept of a presence articulated through blended spaces gives us a way of designing for people with dementia. Fauconnier and Turner (2008) discussed blending as a process of generating new insights by blending four mental spaces into new ideas. Two input spaces that have something in common to a generic space are blended into a new space that has partial structures from the two input spaces but has its own emergent structure. Our past experience and knowledge influenced by our cultural and cognitive models allow the new mental space to be experienced in a different way. The new experiences and logic could then result in new insights and ideas. Benyon et al. (2014) applied conceptual blending to conceptualise a blend of physical and digital spaces (Fig. 2). Spaces are associated with properties of oncology, topology, volatility and agents, which define the generic space. Designing blended spaces involves developing physical and digital spaces such that people can observe and interact with them and can also experience the transition between them. In other words, correspondences between physical and digital spaces should be developed for an experience of presence. This study thus discusses the experience of PwD with MRTs using blending theory.

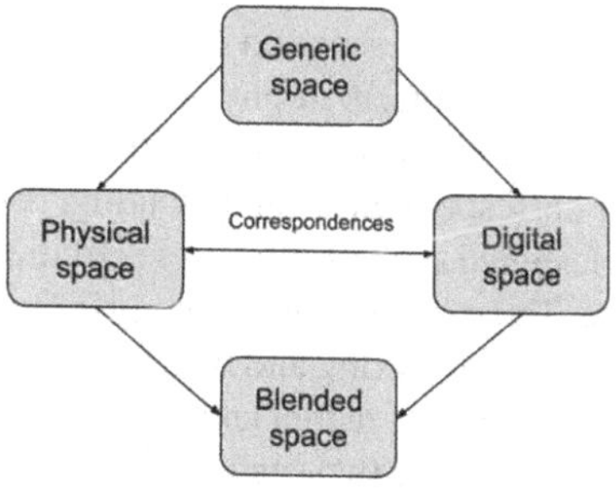

Fig. 2. Conceptual blending of physical and digital spaces (Benyon et al. 2014)

Blended spaces present challenges to people in terms of engagement with each of the spaces and making a smooth and natural transition between the two spaces. These spaces should be designed for people's interactions, such that they are able to understand the concepts and the design elements. Rather than focusing on technological innovations in blended reality, the design focus should be on innovations in interaction modalities and experiences with them. Research such as Astell et al. (2019) have shown that PwD engage with digital interfaces on tablets and smartphones. Recent works by Aruanno et al. (2018), Desai et al. (2020), Garzotto et al. (2019) have explored the use of mixed reality technologies with PwD for cognitive assessment and rehabilitation. Desai et al. (2020) studied interactions of PwD with off the shelf technologies. They found that PwD could complete continuous perception action loops of interactions with appropriate audio and visual prompts presented by the MRT.

This study investigates experience of presence in PwD by understanding their experience in physical and digital spaces and how they navigate the transitions between them. The success with which physical and digital entities are observed and detected by people with dementia, referred to as presence in blended spaces (Benyon 2012; Floridi 2005), affects experience and engagement of people with MRTs. This will help us design engaging experiences with blended spaces for PwD. This is essential for designing assistive support systems for PwD.

2.1 Tangible Presence

Engagement with a technology is possible if we feel present in the medium and do not notice the mediating technology (Benyon 2012). Lombard and Ditton (1997) defined presence as a feeling of 'illusion of non-mediation'. Witmer and Singer (1998) referred to presence as 'the subjective experience of being in one place or environment even when one is physically situated in another'. Both the definitions, developed in the context of virtual reality environments, suggest that the digital world should remain ubiquitous to us when we interact with it from the physical world. Floridi (2005) rejects this idea of presence and suggests that successful observation and detection of all the entities in the environment, both in physical and digital constitutes experience of presence. Benford et al. (2005), Benyon (2012), Wagner et al. (2009) and others have further emphasised that blended environments are not just about creating illusions of being in a certain environment. Tangible presence in blended reality spaces involve people moving through experiences with objects in physical and digital worlds, such that the actions on the objects flow naturally and there is direct access to information (Hoshi and Waterworth 2009). The correspondences and blending between physical and digital spaces should be carefully designed such that the user activities flow seamlessly between the physical digital interface. The mediating technology disappears from the perception. Hoshi (2011) differentiates between mixing and blending of physical and digital spaces. Mixing refers to distribution of objects, media and content between physical and digital spaces. However, blending between the two spaces requires careful design and planning for continuous flow of information between the two spaces. The objects in the physical space for example could offer prompts that direct the user to perceive the feedback from the digital space. Hoshi (2011) refers to this as blending of the spaces and suggests that

MRTs for the vulnerable, the elderly and the socially handicapped should be designed through blending rather than mixing.

PwD respond differently to various types of objects and content in the physical and digital spaces due to their impairment (Desai et al. 2020). Thus, their experience of presence with blended reality spaces could also be different. This study will study experience of presence in PwD with blended reality spaces. Thus, the concept of presence could be used to develop design guidelines for engaging user experiences with blended reality for PwD. Although experience of presence has been discussed in literature, mostly from the context of virtual reality environments, there is lack of study that investigates factors that influence presence in blended environments such as MRTs for PwD. The research question for this study thus was: What aspects does blended environments such as MRTs contribute to the experience of presence in PwD?

3 Research Design

This research was an observational study conducted at Memory and Company, a memory health club for seniors with dementia. Game play using MRTs - Osmo and HoloLens was introduced to Memory and Company clients in their daily day programs. Only participants who consent to participate in the study were recorded playing games on MRTs. The study was approved by Ontario shores centre for mental health hospital research ethics board. Informed written consent was obtained from all participants and their care givers.

Ten people in early stages of dementia and low cognitive impairment (MoCA = 18 to 24, Age = 63 to 88 years) participated in the study. The Montreal Cognitive Assessment (MoCA) is a rapid screening tool to detect cognitive dysfunction for early diagnosis of Alzheimers disease. It consists of 30 questions targeting attention, concentration, executive functions, memory, language, visuo-constructional skills, conceptual thinking, calculations, and orientation. Each question is scored as per the MoCA scoring guidelines. The total possible score is 30 points. A score of 26 or above means that there is no cognitive impairment. As the score gets lower, the level of impairment increases.

We used two MRTs – HoloLens from Microsoft and Osmo from Tangible Play in the study. These two technologies represented AR (HoloLens) and AV (Osmo) types of MRT and were easily available for the study off the shelf. Participants played Tangram on Osmo and Young Conker on HoloLens. These games were chosen after exploring several games available on these technologies and in consultation with the staff at Memory and Company. The primary criteria for the selection was that the games should be easily introduced in the day program of the participants and should also be known to be usable in general masses which we assessed through user ratings and reviews. Pilot studies with 2 older adults in their early stages of dementia (MoCA = 18 and 22) were carried out before the actual study to determine the suitability of the technologies and games for the study.

We will describe the technologies using blending theory shown in Fig. 2 to understand the physical and digital spaces in these technologies and the correspondences between them.

3.1 Osmo and Tangram

Osmo, AV technology, with distinct physical and digital environments to interact with separately, allows physical play with a digital environment on a tablet. It comes with a reflector, a stand to place the tablet on, and games (Fig. 3). The camera on the tablet captures any physical activity performed in front of the tablet. The captured information is fed back into the digital world on the tablet and integrated with added digital elements in an app.

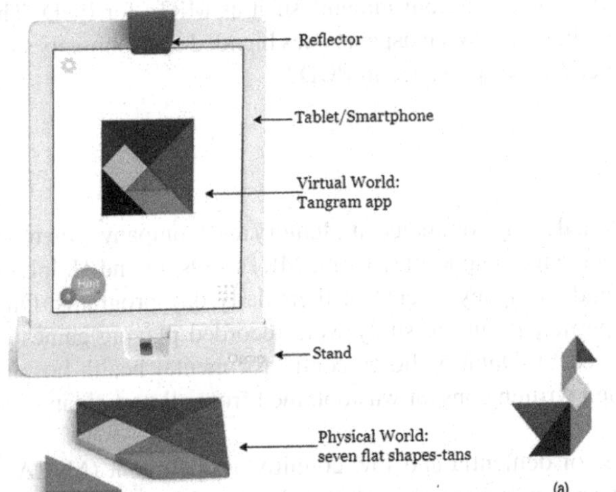

Fig. 3. Osmo setup and Tangram

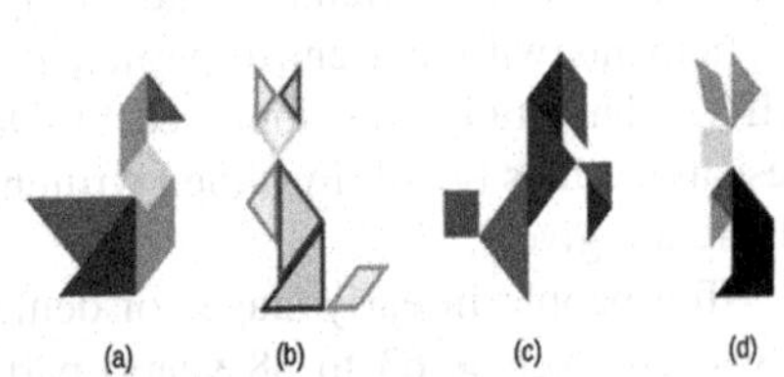

Fig. 4. Tangram pieces arranged in shapes. (a) Seven tans arranged in the shape of a swan. (b) Easy level shape presented in the app (digital world) consists of shape and colour information. (c) Medium level shape presented in the app (digital world) consists of shape and colour tone information. (d) Hard level shape presented in the app (digital world) consists of partial shape information

Physical space consists of seven flat shapes, called tans, which are put together to form shapes (Fig. 4). The objective of the game is to form a specific shape using all seven pieces, without overlapping each other. A shape is presented to the player on the tablet screen through the Tangram app. The player is expected to arrange the seven flat shapes in physical space to match the shape on the tablet. When the correct flat shape is placed in the right place in the physical space, the corresponding flat shape in the app on the screen is filled with the corresponding colour. This is an indication that the placement of the shape in the physical space is correct.

Digital space consists of a Tangram app on a tablet or smartphone, which presents puzzles and prompts to the player to solve the puzzle. Depending on the level of the game chosen (Easy, Medium and Hard), the puzzles are presented with promots that range from colour and shape information to only shape information (see Fig. 4). Prompts such as blinking shapes, animations of next steps and audio prompts are presented to the player through the app.

Correspondences between the two spaces is implemented through image capture of manipulations of tans in the physical space through a camera in the digital space. This means that every manipulation in the physical space is tracked and reflected in the app in the digital space, which in turn informs generation of prompts for the player.

3.2 Hololens and Young Conker

HoloLens, AR technology with overlapped physical and digital spaces is a holographic computer in the form of a headset (Fig. 5). HoloLens uses the physical world to overlay holograms for the user (who wears the headset) to interact with them, see and hear them within their environment.

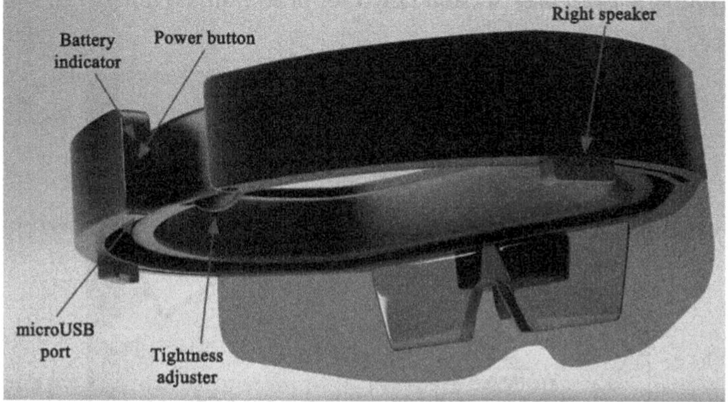

Fig. 5. HoloLens - AR technology

Digital space consists of a game app 'Young Conker' that can be installed in HoloLens from Windows app store. The app transforms existing real-world setting such as a living room into a platform to go on a mystery adventure. The game starts with a scan of the physical space to detect walls and other objects. The game consists of different levels referred in the game as missions. Each mission involves looking for generated holograms in the space. A holographic squirrel character, Conker interacts with the user through speech. The player is required to guide Conker through their gaze movements to the holograms in each mission. The game prompts the player through visual texts, graphics, animations and Conker's voice to accomplish a set mission in the game.

Physical space is the place or the environment where the game is being played. The player performs embodied actions such as walking around in the room, looking for prompts in the digital space and performing gestures required to complete the mission requirements in the game.

Correspondences between the two spaces is made possible through a headset equipped with a range of sensors that tracks gestures of the player in front of the headset and the eye gaze of the player to inform decisions made within the Young Conker app in the digital space.

3.3 Data Collection

Ten participants consented for the study who played Tangram on Osmo. Of these, six also played Young Conker on HoloLens. Four participants did not show up for the play session with HoloLens.

The study was conducted in three sessions on three different days of the day program. Cognitive impairment of the participant was recorded using MoCA assessment tool in the first session followed by game play with Osmo and HoloLens in each of the next two sessions. On the day of the game play with MRT, participants were explained how each technology works and how to play the games on the MRT. Participants were prompted by the researcher when they were unable to proceed with the game play or/and when they asked for help. Each play session lasted for maximum 60 min (Figs. 6 and 7).

Fig. 6. Participant P1_2000 playing a game of Tangram on Osmo

At the end of each of the game plays, the participants were asked to describe their experience with the technologies, how did they feel about it and if they would like to play again. This was also audio and video recorded for analysis.

3.4 Data Analysis

The video data of game play in HoloLens and Osmo was coded in Observer XT from Noldus using thematic analysis techniques of Braun and Clarke (2006), Fereday and Muir-Cochrane (2006) and Tuckett (2005). Inductive coding process was used where themes and sub-themes that were seen to be impacting experience of presence in the interactions of PwD with the MRTs were coded, see Fig. 8 (a) and (b).

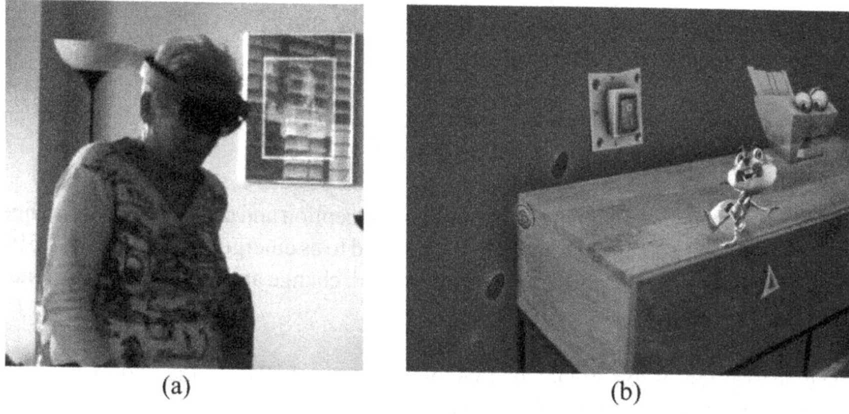

(a) (b)

Fig. 7. Participant P9_2009 playing a game of Young Conker on HoloLens (a) using gaze to move young Conker, the squirrel from one place to another in the game (b) screen capture of what participant sees through the headset

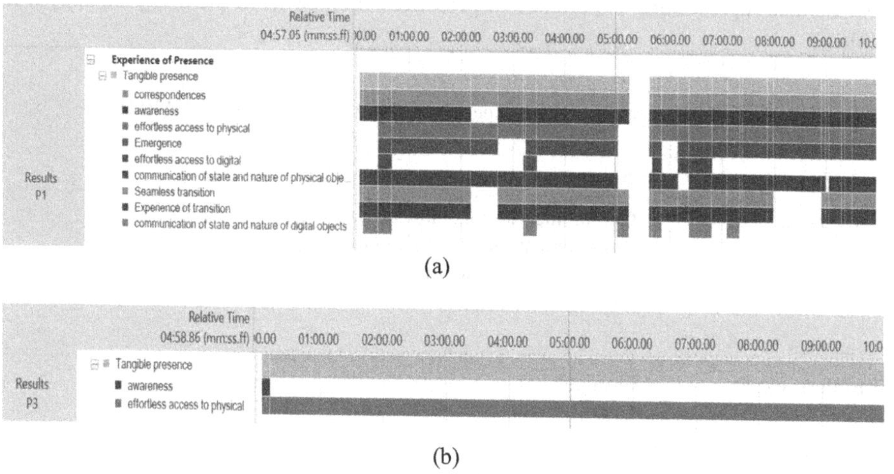

(a)

(b)

Fig. 8. Visualisation of experience of presence with factors impacting it in PwD with (a) Augmented Virtuality - Osmo (b) Augmented Reality - HoloLens

The heuristics used for coding presence in the data were:

- Awareness of the state and nature of objects in each space for them to make appropriate decisions (Riva et al. 2007)
- Experience the movement across the physical and digital spaces.
- Awareness of self, blended environment and the existence of the digital content
  - Extension of themselves through mediated technology
- Access to the content in physical and digital spaces is effortless

– Direct interaction with the content in each of the spaces
– Effortless action and perception

For example, input from the user and environment in physical world and feedback/notifications from the digital world

- Changes in the environment due to continuous perception and action results in changes to the subsequent perceptions and actions, referred to as emergence (Desai et al. 2019). This is possible if the user has opportunities to add, change and manipulate the content in physical or digital space or both.

The description of experience of PwD with the two MRTs at the end of the game was coded inductively for type of experience.

4 Results and Findings

Four themes representing experience of presence emerged from the analysis, shown in Table 1.

Table 1. Factors impacting experience of presence in PwD with MRTs

Themes	Sub-themes
Correspondences	– Communication of state and nature of physical objects – Communication of state and nature of digital objects – Experience of transition – Seamless transition
Awareness	
Effortless access -	– Physical – Digital
Emergence	

Correspondences between the physical and digital spaces represent the physical and cognitive coupling between the physical and digital content. The coupling is achieved through technology (sensors and computing resources) and the media content that prompts PwD to transition between the two spaces. Physical coupling represents the movements of PwD through interactions such as gestures and gaze. Technologies facilitate physical coupling in both the technologies – Osmo and HoloLens through sensors and computing resources as discussed above in Sects. 3.1 and 3.2. However, effective correspondences also require cognitive coupling achieved through appropriate prompting in the physical and digital spaces that steer PwD between the two worlds. At the same time, the prompts should also ensure that PwD are aware of the transition made into another world and the transition is smooth and seamless. Thus, the effectiveness of the correspondences depends on the communication of state and nature of physical and digital objects to PwD, experience of transition (the user should be aware of their movement from one space to another) and seamless transition. Contrary to the requirement of an experience of illusion in Virtual reality, Blended environments such as MRTs require PwD to be aware of the reality of the space that they are in at any given instant during their interactions with the technology. The theme of effortless access to physical and digital content in the two spaces covers interaction modalities that PwD are comfortable with in the perception action loops of interactions. Emergence, term introduced by Desai et al. (2019) in interaction design, defines the ability of the technology to afford change in the environment (physical or digital or both) brought about the user (PwD in this study). The factors impacting presence in PwD interacting with apps - Tangram in Osmo and Young conker in HoloLens are shown in a visualisation along time scale (Fig. 8).

5 Discussion

Experience of presence, in the true definition in the context of blended environments, is important for engagement of PwD with MRTs as assistive technologies to support in their everyday activities. This study aimed to understand factors that contribute to experience of presence in PwD, found four main factors – correspondences between physical and digital, awareness of the reality, effortless access to the spaces and emergence. The objective of the study was not to compare the two types of augmentations, but to develop a better understanding of the factors contributing to presence in both augmentations. We used two off the shelf technologies as case studies to understand experience of PwD with the technologies.

5.1 Presence in Augmented Virtuality – Osmo

PwD were comfortable interacting with Osmo, they described their experience with the technology as fun and easy. Participant P1_2001 continued playing the game of Tangram beyond the time limit of 60 min and said,

> *"I play lot of puzzles on my phone. But this is different. I enjoyed it, the hard level was difficult, but I like a challenge. It was nice to see that I could solve it."*

The participant added that she would like to play the game again and collected information about Osmo and where to buy from. Figure 8 (a) shows that the factors affecting experience of presence in PwD were consistently valid for the entire game play with Osmo.

Manipulation with physical objects, tans, in the physical space provided avenues for communication of the state and nature of the physical objects. The direct interaction with the objects ensured that PwD have effortless access to the space. PwD used touch interactions with tans to receive spatial and visual feedback in return, making perception action loops continuous and effortless. The sub-theme, *Communication of state and nature of physical objects*, part of the theme, *correspondences* was predominantly valid throughout the game play. The direct interaction with the physical objects contributed to the consistently valid theme '*effortless access to the physical*'.

On the other hand, PwD had problems understanding the meaning of some digital objects such as coloured circles representing easy, medium and hard levels of the game. They also could not understand technical language used in a text prompt, 'flip', meaning to turn over the tan. When PwD were prompted with an intervention from the researcher to 'turn over', they immediately understood the meaning. Some prompts such as music tones to represent popping of a prompt or successful placement of the correct tan in the right place in the given puzzle, went un-noticed. This explains consistent absence of the sub-theme, *Communication of state and nature of digital objects*, part of the theme, Correspondences, throughout the game play.

PwD transitioned between physical and digital spaces most often without any issues. They were most often aware that they are moving from one space to another. Some PwD got engrossed in solving the puzzle with the objects in the physical space and completely forgot to check the prompts in the digital space. They were able to solve the puzzle only through physical manipulations and did not look into the digital space for prompts. The participant had to be prompted to check for the prompts by the researcher. This affected their movement from physical to digital space. This explains the gap in the sub-themes of the theme '*correspondences*' - '*seamless transition*' and '*experience of transition*' in Fig. 8 (a).

The material, spatial and visual properties of the physical objects contrinuted to the realization in PwD that they are interacting with the physical world. PwD associated the screen-based interaction on the Ipad to the digital world. Thus, the physical properties (materiality, spatiality and visual features) of the physical objects and the materiality of Ipad contributed to the consistent theme '*awareness*' throughout the game play. The small gap in the theme is because the '*seamless transition*' to digital world and '*experience of transition*' was lost at the same time.

Emergence which represents dynamic nature of the system, was consistently valid for the entire game play. The effortless manipulations of the physical objects resulted in changes in the physical and digital world. The new setup means new perceptions and actions. Emergence ensures continuous engaging perception and action loops. The period when emergence was absent in Fig. 8 (a) remains unexplained.

Pwd had positive engaging experience interacting with Osmo and the factors affecting experience of presence in PwD were present throughout the game play. However, the ineffectiveness of prompts in the digital space in facilitating effortless perception, transitions and communication of the information to PwD impacted the experience of presence and engagement to some extent.

5.2 Presence in Augmented Reality – HoloLens

Most PwD were very excited to use a new emerging technology, HoloLens, however lacked confidence to use it correctly. Almost all PwD described their experience with HoloLens as confusing and difficult. Participant P3_2003 said,

> *"This is new for me. Sorry, I am not good at this. I could not understand what that animal [conker] was saying. I could not understand what was happening. Is it [HoloLens] spoilt?"*

The participant said that she would not play the game again. Participants felt that either they were doing something wrong or there was some malfunction in the technology. Figure 8 (b) shows that all factors affecting experience of presence in PwD were consistently absent for the entire game play with HoloLens except for one theme, '*effortless access to physical*'. PwD were found to be interacting with the physical space through gestures and movements across the room. However, they could not understand the prompts presented to them through the digital space. For example, arrows pointing in the direction of the prompt, suggesting that the user should look in that direction could not be mapped into appropriate gaze and head movements. The voice of the conker was not clear to PwD. Although, audio prompts are more effective in successful perception in PwD (Desai et al. 2020), clear human voice is preferred. Graphic icons such as tap icon were also difficult to understand. Thus, the theme '*effortless access to digital*' was absent throughout the game play.

'*Awareness*' of physical and digital spaces was seen very briefly at the start of the game play. PwD for most of the game play thought that they were interacting with a computer mounted on their head. The reality that they are present in both the spaces at any given time is lost after that initial period. We think this is partly because of the lack of effortless access to the digital content. '*Emergence*' was not possible in the game play as perception action loops were not possible.

The '*correspondences*' between physical and digital spaces in HoloLens were completely missing from the entire game play. PwD could not get any information about the state and nature of the physical and digital objects in the two spaces. PwD were often seen blindly using 'air tap' gesture in the hope that something will happen. Transitions between the physical and digital spaces was not seamless and most often the transition was not experienced by PwD. This is due to lack of awareness of the reality in which PwD are interacting at a given instant.

The experience of PwD with HoloLens was not positive, although they are keen to use the technology but not in the current state. They could not engage with the 'Young conker' app and HoloLens due to lack of experience of presence. Designing correspondences for seamless transition experience and clear communication channels that provide information about the content in the two spaces to PwD. This requires appropriate design of prompts in the digital space for PwD.

5.3 Design Recommendations

It is evident from the two case studies with Osmo and HoloLens that careful approach is required to design correspondences between physical and digital spaces. We recommend following guidelines:

- The prompts in the digital spaces should be designed for effortless perception in PwD resulting in actions that PwD are comfortable with. Successful perception ensures that PwD have constant information about the state and nature of the digital content and elements.
- Interactions with the physical content should be embodied through the sensory systems of PwD.

- Interactions with the physical and digital content should be direct through the use of physical affordances of the content. Use of metaphors or symbolic processing should be avoided as much as possible.
- Prompts to direct PwD to experience seamless transitions between physical and digital spaces should be incorporated. For example, use of verbal narratives to steer people between the two worlds.

Other than correspondences, awareness of the reality of space is possible through sensory feedback from each of the spaces. Well-designed correspondences ensure successful perception action loops, resulting in emergence which could add to the engagement with the technology.

6 Conclusion

There is a need to design assistive technologies to support PwD in their everyday activities using human centred methods. Blended environments such as MRTs could provide scalable and deployable options to support PwD. However, it is important to understand experiences and interactions of PwD with these emerging technologies. Ongoing adoption and use of these technologies require PwD to engage with the technology. For this, PwD should experience presence in their interactions with MRTs. This study thus aimed at understanding the factors that impact experience of presence in PwD.

The study found that it is critical to design correspondences between physical and digital spaces such that PwD have access to information about the state and nature of the physical and digital objects. PwD should experience seamless transitions between the two spaces. Experience of presence requires awareness of the reality of the space in which PwD are interacting at any given instant. This is done through appropriate digital prompts and sensory feedback from the physical space. The findings from this study have resulted in recommendations and guidelines for designing experience of presence in MRTs for PwD. We are working on translating these encouraging outcomes into prototypes for evaluation with PwD.

References

Aruanno, B., Garzotto, F.: MemHolo: mixed reality experiences for subjects with Alzheimer's disease. Multimed. Tools Appl. **78**(10), 13517–13537 (2019). https://doi.org/10.1007/s11042-018-7089-8

Aruanno, B., Garzotto, F., Torelli, E., Vona, F.: Holo learn: wearable mixed reality for people with neurodevelopmental disorders (NDD). In: ASSETS 2018 - Proceedings of the 20th International ACM SIGACCESS Conference on Computers and Accessibility, no. 1, pp. 40–51 (2018). https://doi.org/10.1145/3234695.3236351

Astell, A., Smith, S., Joddrell, P.: Using Technology in Dementia Care: A Guide to Technology Solutions for Everyday Living. Jessica Kingsley Publishers, London (2019)

Benford, S., Magerkurth, C., Ljungstrand, P.: Bridging the physical and digital in pervasive gaming. Commun. ACM **48**(3), 54–57 (2005). https://doi.org/10.1145/1047671.1047704

Benyon, D.: Presence in blended spaces. Interact. Comput. **24**(4), 219–226 (2012). https://doi.org/10.1016/j.intcom.2012.04.005

Benyon, D., Mival, O., Ayan, S.: Designing blended spaces. Int. J. Arch. Spatial Environ. Des. **7**(2), 1–12 (2014). https://doi.org/10.18848/2325-1662/cgp/v07i02/38363

Braun, V., Clarke, V.: Using thematic analysis in psychology. Qual. Res. Psychol. **3**(2), 77–101 (2006). https://doi.org/10.1191/1478088706qp063oa

Chang, Y.-J., Chou, L.-D., Wang, F.T.-Y., Chen, S.-F.: A kinect-based vocational task prompting system for individuals with cognitive impairments. Pers. Ubiquit. Comput. **17**(2), 351–358 (2013)

Desai, S., Blackler, A., Fels, D., Astell, A.: Supporting people with dementia-understanding their interactions with mixed reality technologies. In: DRS 2020, Brisbane (2020)

Desai, S., Blackler, A., Popovic, V.: Intuitive interaction in a mixed reality system. In: DRS 2016: Future-Focused Thinking, vol. 8 (2016). https://doi.org/10.21606/drs.2016.369

Desai, S., Blackler, A., Popovic, V.: Children's embodied intuitive interaction–design aspects of embodiment. Int. J. Child-Comput. Interact. **21**, 89–103 (2019)

Fauconnier, G., Turner, M.: The Way We Think: Conceptual Blending and the Mind's Hidden Complexities. Basic Books, New York (2008)

Fereday, J., Muir-Cochrane, E.: Demonstrating rigor using thematic analysis: a hybrid approach of inductive and deductive coding and theme development. Int. J. Qual. Methods **5**(1), 80–92 (2006)

Floridi, L.: The philosophy of presence: from epistemic failure to successful observation. Presence: Teleoper. Virtual Environ. **14**(6), 656–667 (2005)

Garzotto, F., Torelli, E., Vona, F., Aruanno, B.: HoloLearn: learning through mixed reality for people with cognitive disability. In: Proceedings - 2018 IEEE International Conference on Artificial Intelligence and Virtual Reality, AIVR 2018, pp. 189–190 (2019). https://doi.org/10.1109/AIVR.2018.00042

Hoshi, K., Öhberg, F., Nyberg, A.: Designing blended reality space: conceptual foundations and applications. In: Proceedings of HCI 2011 - 25th BCS Conference on Human Computer Interaction, pp. 217–226 (2011). https://doi.org/10.14236/ewic/hci2011.50

Hoshi, K., Waterworth, J.A.: Tangible presence in blended reality space. In: The 12th Annual International Workshop on Presence, pp. 1–10 (2009). http://umu.diva-portal.org/smash/get/diva2:311021/FULLTEXT01.pdf

Lombard, M., Ditton, T.: At the heart of it all: the concept of presence. J. Comput.-Med. Commun. **3**(2) (1997). para. 30

Mihailidis, A., Boger, J.N., Craig, T., Hoey, J.: The COACH prompting system to assist older adults with dementia through handwashing: an efficacy study. BMC Geriatr. **8**(1), 28 (2008)

Milgram, P., Kishino, F.: A taxonomy of mixed reality visual displays. IEICE Trans. Inf. Syst. **77**(12), 1321–1329 (1994)

Orpwood, R., Adlam, T., Evans, N., Chadd, J., Self, D.: Evaluation of an assisted-living smart home for someone with dementia. J. Assist. Technol. **2**(2), 13–21 (2008)

Pigot, H., Mayers, A., Giroux, S.: The intelligent habitat and everyday life activity support. In: Proceedings of the 5th International Conference on Simulations in Biomedicine, 2–4 April (2003)

Riva, G., et al.: Affective interactions using virtual reality: the link between presence and emotions. CyberPsychol. Behav. **10**(1), 45–56 (2007)

Ro, H., Park, Y.J., Han, T.-D.: A projection-based augmented reality for elderly people with dementia (2019). http://arxiv.org/abs/1908.06046

Tuckett, A.G.: Applying thematic analysis theory to practice: a researcher's experience. Contemp. Nurse **19**(1–2), 75–87 (2005)

Wagner, I., et al.: On the role of presence in mixed reality. Presence: Teleoper. Virtual Environ. **18**(4), 249–276 (2009)

Witmer, B.G., Singer, M.J.: Measuring presence in virtual environments: a presence questionnaire. Presence **7**(3), 225–240 (1998)

Exploring the Contextual Relationship of Narrating Life Stories by Elderly People

KuangYi Fan[1] and PeiFen Wu[2](✉)

[1] The Graduate Institute of Animation and Multimedia Design, National University of Tainan, Tainan, Taiwan

[2] Department of Information Management and Master Program in Digital Content Technology and Management, National Changhua University of Education, Changhua City, Taiwan

pfwu@cc.ncue.edu.tw

Abstract. Global aging is an important issue for global development. Elderly people should not be the burden of individual families, but the assets of the entire society. With the help of life stories or past events that elderly people often repeat, we can better understand the importance of certain things. Therefore, life review is a normal and necessary process that can help the elderly to review past experience with a rational attitude, help them to find the meaning of life, and see the essence of their life. The interviews in this study used Nvivo qualitative software to record and analyze the life stories of 4 elderly people in southern Taiwan, in order to understand the important memories and emotions in their lives, discover the background factors of elderly people recalling their life, and maintain precious human stories for families and society via recording and saving. Guiding the elderly to review their lives through nostalgic narrative has the function of storied therapy, and its values include: personal self-identification, rebuilding the integrity of life through memories, and helping the elderly to reposition themselves in a lonely life through their past experience.

Keywords: Storied therapy · Narrative gerontology · Elderly · Life narrative · Autobiographical memory

1 Introduction

In June 2019, the United Nations pointed out three major trends: the number of new births has decreased, the number of elderly people has grown rapidly, and more countries are facing population decline. The well-being of the aging population is a current and growing concern. In Taiwan, the proportion of the elderly population over the age of 65 has reached 14.05%, meaning one in seven people is an elderly person, which represents a significant number, and Taiwan has entered an "aged society". An elderly society, which is already an important global development issue, has huge impacts on the elderly themselves, their families, and on society and country.

It is a physiological phenomenon of aging and a self-rescue method to repair the unresponsive brain of the elderly to help them remember their past and talk about the

C. Stephanidis et al. (Eds.): HCII 2020, LNCS 12426, pp. 510–523, 2020.
https://doi.org/10.1007/978-3-030-60149-2_39

past. The memory ability in old age is related to the health status of each individual, and has influence on social ability. It is pointed out that recall in old age is more frequent, and this spontaneous process can help the elderly think more clearly and regain confidence. The retrospective "storytelling" process involves complex cognitive processes, including imagination, organizational skills, and narrative skills. The benefits of storytelling are enhanced relationships and communication, and storytelling and restorying are important ways for individuals to build a complete and interconnected relationship with society. Restorying is one of the important channels of experience inheritance. When people look back on life, they will have a reminiscence bump, and the stage of a reminiscence bump can cause more intense and positive reactions. The elderly often play a story-telling role in real life, but the stories are not recorded and kept. Many of their experiences are worth exploring, and more records and preservation can be provided by the popularization of modern digital audio and video equipment.

This is a pilot study for a future study on VR nostalgia situations, which is used in the reminiscence therapy of the elderly to allow them to tell their stories with a more specific direction of audiovisual content, and helps the elderly to further stimulate their memories. Therefore, at this research stage, we hope to video record the stories of the elderly, extract their narrative concepts, and understand the narratives of their life experiences. The topics discussed in the study are: 1) What is the relationship between the elderly in Taiwan and their background of local life? 2) What factors affect the life concept and thinking of the elderly? 3) Are there specific background factors that affect the social function and psychological significance of the elderly? The early development of Taiwan was from south to north, thus, the development of the southern region of Taiwan has great significance. Therefore, this study was aimed at elderly people in southern Taiwan, used their oral narratives to express stories, and recorded and analyzed the context of elderly people's memory stories. This study explored the life course of elderly people by recording their stories, in order to leave their precious human story assets for families and society. The follow-up research will further sort out the narrative structure of elderly people's storytelling, and develop it into story contents worthy of preservation.

2 Literature Review

2.1 Life Story

Sobol et al. (2004) mentioned that storytelling is a basic human ability and an element of human nature. Storytelling is a basic medium that plays a fundamental role, maintains human culture, and enables elements of humanity. Storytelling is a very important part of the human pursuit of the meaning of life, it is a way for humans to inherit culture and wisdom, and is an experience inheritance activity in fact. Randall and McKim (2004, 2008) mentioned that understanding the meaning of life through life stories more fully reflects the meaning of "aesthetics", because life is like a storyline, and the storyline is like life, thus, the more you listen to the story, the more you can experience poetic aging, and then, understand the meaning of life.

Dempsey et al. (2014) mentioned that life review is a process that occurs at different stages and involves recalling the interactions between early life events and individuals, and there is very little difference between a life story and a life history. The difference between a life story and an oral history is usually emphasis and scope. An oral history most often focuses on a specific aspect of a person's life, which most often focuses on the community or what someone remembers about a specific event, issue, time, or place, thus, it is usually referred to as a life story or a life history. A life story is a fairly complete narration of one's entire life experience as a whole, and highlights the most important aspects (Atkinson 1998). Kenyon (2002) emphasized that storytelling and restorying are important for individuals to build a complete and interconnected relationship with society, and to find the meaning and value of life through stories.

Autobiographical Memory is the experience and memory related to an individual's past experience or events. Brockmeier and Carbaugh (2001) pointed out that autobiographical memory is a conscious feature of humans. Autobiographical memory consists of two components: semantic memory and episodic memory. Semantic memory is a link to a specific event at a specific time; episodic memory is an event at a specific time and place. Autobiographical memory allows you to define yourself and construct meaningful life stories (El Haj et al. 2016). Therefore, the elderly' experiences, deeds, and achievements, and missing relatives, friends, and hometowns can be explored through autobiographical memory for their thinking and narrative context. This study hoped to show the impact of life stories on the elderly via their participation in the storytelling process of their life stories, as well as their perception of the review, narration, organizational and narrative abilities, and to reaffirm their lives' value through the recognition of storytelling.

2.2 The Benefit of Storied Therapy

White and Epston (1990) mentioned that narrative plays a central role in therapy. Storied therapy tells a person's lived experience, invites a reflexive posture, and encourages a sense of authorship and reauthorship of one's experiences and relationships in the telling and retelling of one's story. By telling stories, the elderly have the opportunity to reflect on their past life experiences, obtain a sense of self-satisfaction and joy, and increase their self-esteem, while simultaneously building healthy relationships with others in the process of sharing. It can even awaken past successful experiences of coping with sadness through the process of happy memories at the psychological level, and assist in coping with stress (Kovach 1991). Telling one's own life experience has the possibilities of self-healing, self-reflecting, and liberating functions, and helps to demonstrate their inner positioning. If experience is narrated as a story, life can have meaning and continuity, and people will feel that life is meaningful; however, most life experience is not expressed as stories, but left in its original place, without organization (White and Epston 1990). Therefore, if a story can be expressed, it will guide the elderly to review their past life and re-experience fragments of their past life, which will further be indirectly converted into psychological therapy through storied therapy, assist the elderly to understand themselves, reduce feelings of loss, increase self-esteem, and promote socialization (Taylor-Price 1995).

Guillemot and Urien (2010) mentioned six intrinsic motivations for the elderly to love narrating past things: flattering the ego, mending the ego, being remembered, sharing, transmitting, and bearing witness, and their views illustrate the establishment of self-confidence. Elderly people have the wisdom to accept themselves, unify the past, and think that their life course is meaningful (Erikson et al. 1994). Nostalgic narrative uses past events, feelings, and thoughts to guide the elderly to review their life and re-experience fragments of their life, and it contains important values: 1) personal self-identification; 2) rebuilding the integrity of life through memories; 3) affirming oneself through the past.

Pan et al. (2018) mentioned that storytelling is a form of active reminiscing that compiles the personal information told by an individual into a chronicle of their life, and presents it by oneself. In actual life, while the elderly often play a role of storyteller, their stories have not been recorded or preserved. Restorying is one of the important channels of experience inheritance. The elderly can tell their story more clearly by recording their story. This study focuses on exploring the experience of participatory storytelling, which is achieved through direct participant involvement in the production of the narrative.

3 Method

In this study, the content of autobiographical memory was analyzed in the context of elderly narratology, and qualitative research was performed using NVIVO qualitative analysis software to explore the coherence, correspondence, and correlation analysis of patients' narrative content.

3.1 Research Questions

By remembering stories, elders can provide researchers with information about the social reality existing outside the story; a story can define an individual's place in the social order of things and explain or confirm the experience through the moral, ethical, or social context of a given situation (Atkinson 1998). Therefore, this research explores the background factors that affect the life thinking of elderly people living in southern Taiwan. The research questions are mainly to understand the relationship between Taiwan's elderly people and the local living background. What influences their life concepts and thinking? Are they influenced by specific background factors?

3.2 Data Processing and Analysis

This research is based on qualitative research for data processing, and the process is shown in Fig. 1:

Fig. 1. Qualitative research data processing flow

3.3 Interview Process

The research tools used in this research are mainly qualitative interviews. In order to understand the life growth stories of elderly people in Taiwan, the researchers used the interview outlines, as developed by themselves, to collect and understand the changes in the subjects and analyze them.

The research subjects were elderly people. Considering the physical and mental conditions at the time of the interview, there was no limit on the length of the interview, and it was subject to the elders. In order to reduce the feelings of strangeness, the interviewers were the elderly's family members. The content of the interviews began with their own related feelings and ideas, as based on the defined research questions. First, 3 interview principles were set, such as: The happiest thing that occurred in their life? The saddest thing that occurred in their life? What is the thing that impressed them the most?, etc.

When the interview was conducted, the researcher recorded the entire interview process with DV and a mobile phone, and wrote a verbatim draft after the interview for analysis.

3.4 Participants

Purposive sampling was adopted for the respondents in this study. There were a total of 4 males and 3 females, aged between 69–87 years, with an average age of 80.5 years, all living in southern Taiwan, and having the ability to express themselves in Taiwanese. There was no time limit for storytelling, thus, the total time was 92 min and 14 s, with an average time of about 23 min per person (Table 1). The choice of venues was to avoid unfamiliarity affecting their emotions, and the venues were all familiar living spaces. During the interview, the elderly were encouraged to tell their own stories and share their past experiences. After the interviews, the data were converted verbatim, and the analysis tool was the Nvivo 12 plus version software, which assists in the qualitative study of case analysis and classifies the context of the homogeneous story for visualization analysis in qualitative research. Opening code data was initially coded with NVivo 12, and then, exported to and analyzed by NVivo 12, which was conducted between September 2019 and January 2020. The history of the guided life review has unified all segments of life in the analysis of audiovisual and textual records, making it meaningful.

Table 1. Basic information of participants

Participant	Age	Gender	Place of birth	Educational background	Interview duration
E1	69	Male	Tainan	Junior High School	18′11″
E2	87	Female	Chiayi	Junior High School	50′56″
E3	86	Female	Tainan	Senior High School	9′21″
E4	80	Female	Tainan	Elementary School	13′46″
Average	80.5				23 min 3 s

3.5 Data Processing

The research data was coded, and organized to form categories and topics and to seek interpretation, and finally, it was analyzed and discussed. NVivo was used to administer data and literature, and to code the variety of sources used. In this study interview transcripts are used to capture, organize, and analyze. (1) Transcribing verbatim text: The audio content and transcripts, as produced during the interviews, were transcribed as verbatim text, and oral and non-verbal speech were added. (2) Coding: Nodes and memos of the original data, as collected during the research process, were produced to facilitate interpretation and analysis of subsequent research. (3) Analysis and discussion: organization and visualization.

4 Result and Discussion

4.1 Respondents' Environmental Background

Taiwan was under Japanese colonial rule for 50 years (1895–1945), which was an important life experience for the elderly who were born before the war and received Japanese education. Such elderly people are now over 80 years old and are gradually dying

4.2 Analysis of Respondents' Node Content

This research focused on the interview contents of 4 respondents (Table 2) to understand the impact of the context of their growing age through their life stories. According to the verbatim version of the interviews, it was classified into three parts: personal information, group relationship, and time and society (Fig. 2–Fig. 3):

Table 2. Shows the codes of 4 respondents.

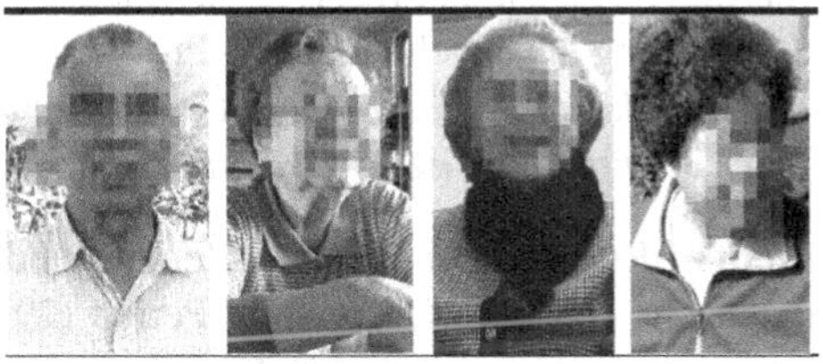

E1	E2	E3	E4

The number of nodes for the four respondents in the three parts after analysis of the verbatim contents is shown in Table 3.

Analysis of Node Content of Respondent E1. E1 is male, and the discussion focus was: N-08: outlook on life (41.5%), N-02: Republic of China education (21.8%), N-13: Taiwanese social status (16.5%), and N-09: personal relationship (14.8%) (Fig. 4). Men usually have more subjective judgments regarding their outlook on life or values.

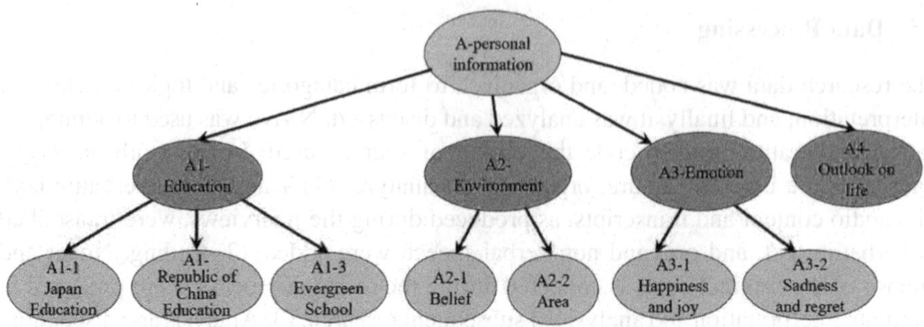

Fig. 2. Interview verbatim classification

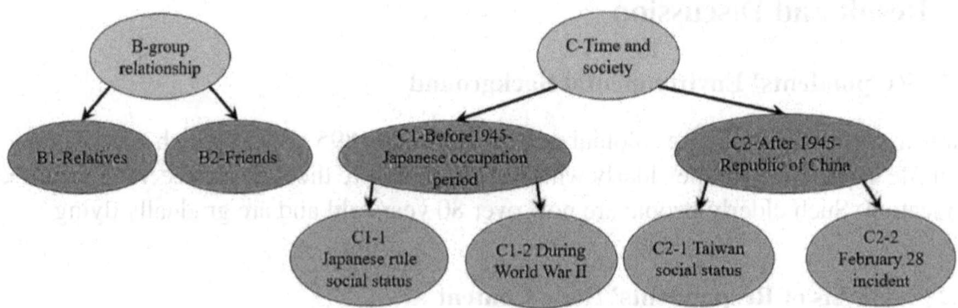

Fig. 3. Interview verbatim classification

E1: *When children notice that adults have something, they learn to be like the adults after they grow up, so adults' influence on children is to teach by personal example...*

Elderly likes to talk about social status and educational perspectives.

E1: *Life was hard in the past, but it was actually a bit concrete.*

E1 was born after the war, so he had not received any Japanese education; however, there was profound talk regarding the development of Taiwan as a whole after the war.

E1: *All of us, cramming education ..., Taiwanese teachers always said: You are stupid, it is useless to teach a stupid kid, useless! We are tired of teaching ...*

Analysis of Node Content of Respondent E2. E2 is female, and the discussion focus was: N-11: social status during Japanese Occupation Period (29.4%), N-09: relatives (18.5%), N-01: Japanese education (13.4%), and N-13: Taiwanese social status (10.7%) (Fig. 5).

She was 86 years old, and had received Japanese and Taiwanese education after the war. She was deeply impressed with the social state during the period of Japanese rule, and had good memories.

E2: *Japanese seem to have better quality ... it was not so good just after liberation, it was messy.*

E2 was part of a big family, and their economic conditions during the Japanese rule were better than that of ordinary Taiwanese people.

Table 3. Number of nodes for verbatim categories of respondents

Category	Sub Content Item	3rd. Sub. Content Item	Code	E1	E2	E3	E4	Node No.
A-Personal Information	A1-Education	A1-1 Japan Education	N-01		■	■		2
		A1-2 Republic of China Education	N-02	■	■	■		3
		A1-3 Evergreen School	N-03		■		■	2
	A2-Environment	A2-1 Area	N-04	■	■	■		3
		A2-1 Belief	N-05			■		1
	A3-Emotion	A3-1 Happiness and joy	N-06	■	■	■	■	4
		A3-2 Sadness and regret	N-07	■	■	■	■	4
	A4-Outlook on life		N-08	■	■	■	■	4
B-group relationship	B1-Relatives		N-09	■	■	■	■	4
	B2-Friends		N-10	■		■		2
C-Time and society	C1-Before1945-Japanese occupation period	C1-1 Japanese rule social status	N-11		■			1
		C1-2 During World War II	N-12		■	■	■	3
	C2-After 1945-Republic of China	C2-1 Taiwan social status	N-13	■	■	■		3
		C2-2 February 28 incident	N-14		■			1
			Total	8	12	11	6	

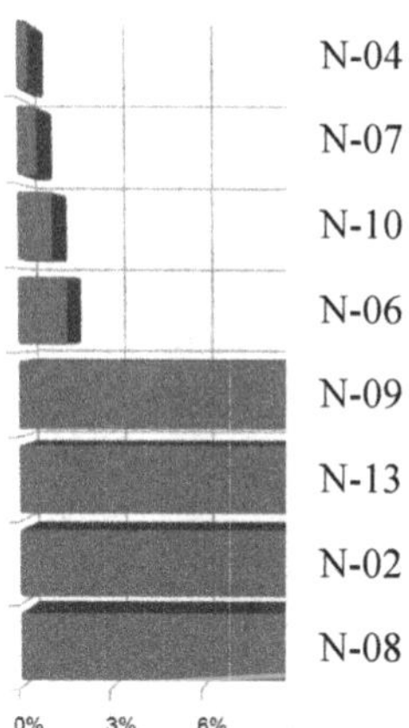

Fig. 4. Respondent's node content distribution

E2: *My family used to run a rice factory, so there was no problem having rice to eat* ...

She continued to finish her studies in junior high school, which can be regarded as a good education in an agricultural society. Comparing society under Japanese rule and Taiwanese society after the war, she naturally put forward corresponding views and comments.

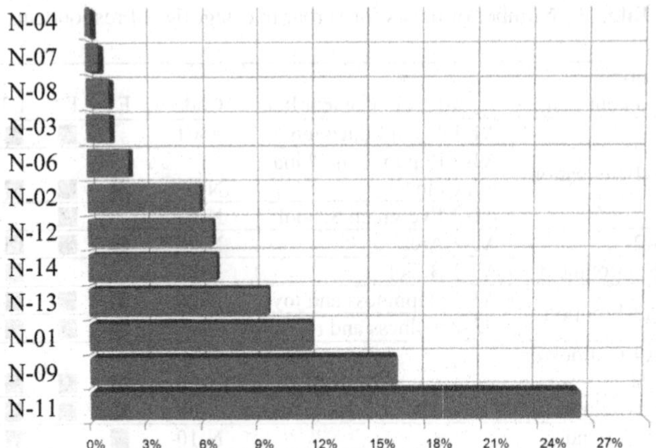

Fig. 5. Respondent's node content distribution

Analysis of Node Content of Respondent E3. E3 is a female, and the discussion focus was: N-05: belief (25.6%), N-06: happiness and joy (19.9%), N-01: Japanese education (8.6%), N-02: Republic of China education (8.3%) (Fig. 6).

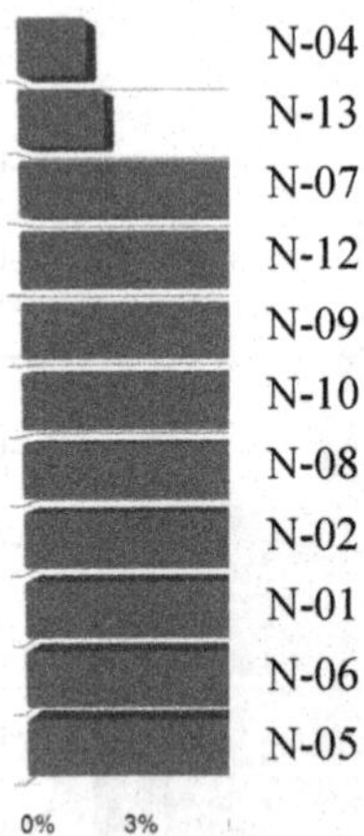

Fig. 6. Respondent's node content distribution

At the age of 85, she had the highest education among the 4 respondents and graduated from senior high school. Faith is her focus.

E3: I am a very devout Christian … I go to church diligently, attend a choir, youth fellowship, and go to church every time.

Her devout faith affected her concept of marriage in girlhood and her focus in old age. She had clear expressions of both happy and sad things that occurred in her life.

E3: *The happiest was when I went abroad in my 60s, I felt free! I was all by myself then; the most painful was when I first married, because my family was better-off, while my husband's family was poor.*

She received Japanese education until the fourth grade of elementary school, and completed her 5th and 6th grades in elementary school and middle school education after the war. In addition to religious and emotional matters, there was a brief and clear expression of each stage of education.

E3: *I continued to study in elementary school after two years of war, and then, it was six years of middle school. This was my girlhood.*

Analysis of Node Content of Respondent E4. E4 is female, and her discussion focus was: N-09: relatives (58.0%), N-07: sadness and regret (23.6%), N-03: the Evergreen Seniors' School (9.9%), N-06: happiness and joy (5.2%) (Fig. 7).

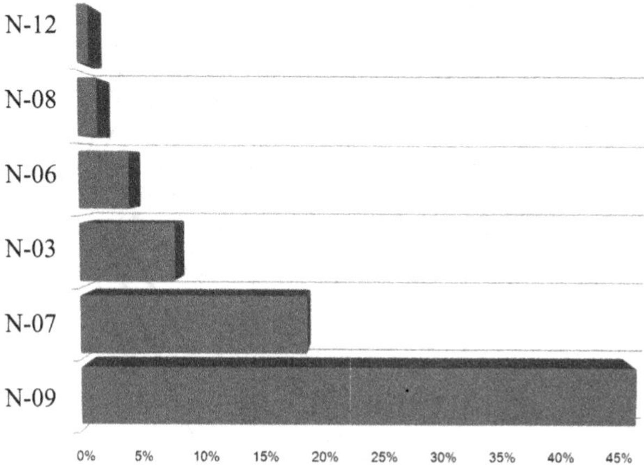

Fig. 7. Respondent's node content distribution

Her growth and life were relatively simple and hardworking, and she has strong affection for her family. She affirmed her son's honesty and hard work during the conversation.

E4: *Your father, your uncle, your aunt, the second aunt, they are all good and don't need me to worry about them ... your dad and your uncle are kind and excellent.*

She paid a lot of attention to the life status of her loved ones. The death of her loved ones made her feel sad.

E4: *My sister and my brother-in-law were on good terms with him, but they both passed away, and my aunt is also dead, and my third sister-in-law is dead, my third aunt is blind now ...*

Her simple life is also shown in the focus of talking about relatives and fewer nodes.

4.3 Comparative Analysis of Relevant Factors Affecting Respondents

Figure 8 shows a comparison of the related factors of two elderly respondents: E2 and E3. They were 86 and 85 years old, respectively, and with senior high school education. They both received Japanese education in elementary school, and the impact is far-reaching. E2 has a clear view of the different societies before and after the war, and talked more about loved ones. E3 is obviously affected by religion, and talked more about the process of studying.

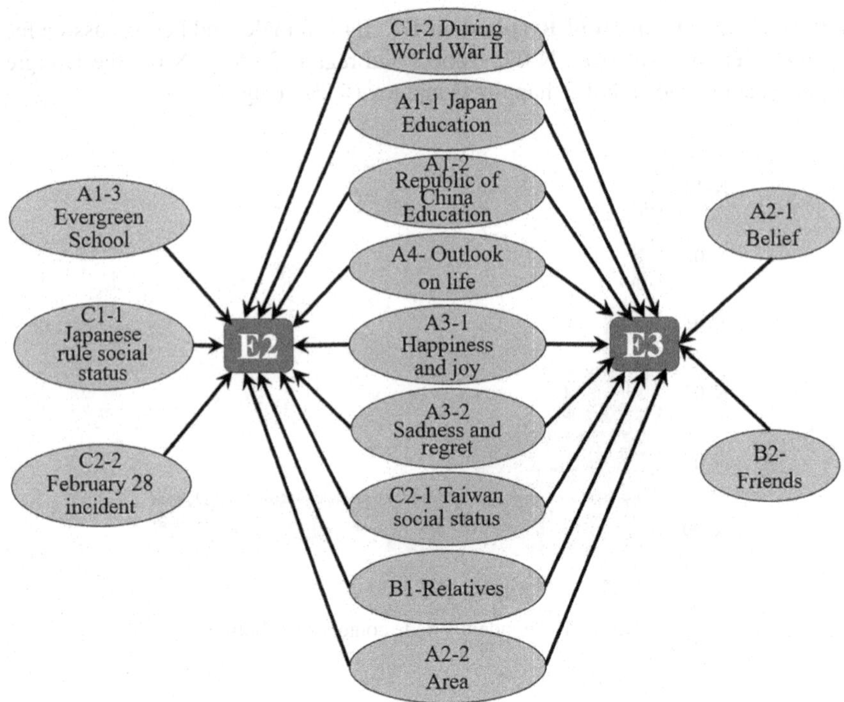

Fig. 8. Comparison of related factors between elderly respondants E2 and E3

E3: *When I was in elementary school, the Chang Jung Senior High School was near the elementary school. Every morning, I would hear beautiful poems from there, so I would say then that I want to study in this middle school in the future.*

The two shared life memories of avoiding air raids during World War II.

E2: *When the United States came to bomb Taiwan, I was still in school and I ran to the air-raid shelter.*

E3: *All were running away from air raids one after another, but I am not very good at speaking Japanese, as Japanese was only taught until the 4th grade, and we were all busy hiding from the air-raids at that time.*

Better family economic conditions tend to lead to higher education level. Both E2 and E3 had a good family background, thus, their educational backgrounds are junior high school and senior high school, respectively. Most Taiwanese seniors of the same generation only finished elementary school, while some received no education! A good growth environment is also reflected in the value of experience in life. The number of nodes represents the diversity of life experience; the number of nodes for respondents E1 is 8, E2 is 12, E3 is 11, and E4 is 6. The number of nodes for E2 and E3 are the largest, and the life stories are richer and more diverse. The life experiences of these two seniors validates Atkinson's (1998) theory: The individual ego can be strong only through a mutual guarantee of strength given to and received by all whose life-cycles intertwine. Whatever chance man may have to transcend the limitations of his ego seems to depend on his prior ability, in his one and only life cycle, to be fully engaged in the sequence of generations.

4.4 Analysis of Influencing Factors of Storied Therapy

Narrating one's life experience can have the functions of self-healing, reflection, and liberation. Narratives can provide the possibility and opportunity to liberate oneself and reflect, and help one show his or her inner positioning.

E3: *When I were 65 years old, I traveled abroad with my church members because my husband had died. I went to China 3 times, Japan 4 times, and visited Indonesia, the Philippines, Korea, Canada, the United States, and other countries.*

She stated that these were her happiest memories, because she had freedom.

While the birth environment cannot be selected, the opportunities for education in Taiwan are relatively equal, thus, striving for higher education is still a very important condition for future development in life.

E1: *I don't think my education is high. If my child wants to be competitive in society, he must be given a good education.*

Regardless of their situation, expecting the next generation to be better is a common wish of the elderly.

E1: *I think we should now be thinking of advancing the country, and if we make more efforts, our next generation will be better than us.*

It is not necessary to make a lot of money, so they can be more in line with social norms when it comes to dealing with people.

E4: *I don't want my children to be a borough chief or other official, it is fine as long as they go the right way.*

Nostalgia can maintain personal self-identity. Nostalgia is often caused by insecurity due to anxiety or uncertainty. The elderly can maintain stable psychological emotion through nostalgia, thus avoiding perplexity and helplessness.

E4: *The hardest thing was that my husband went out to gamble, then I couldn't sleep all night, and I had to help her husband plow the field …*

5 Conclusion

Life stories and personal narratives are increasingly being used in a wide range of disciplines. Through different particular topics or questions, when learning more about the elderly' lives and society in general from one person's perspective, life stories serve as an excellent means for understanding how people see their experiences, their lives, and their interactions with others. In particular, it is possible to continue to explore the influence of the connection between the elderly and the local culture.

The process of life review can usually be viewed from a rational and objective point of view. The importance of certain things can also be understood from the life stories or past events that elderly people often repeat, and the elderly will often find their own importance in such narration. Through nostalgic narratives, we can guide elderly people to review their lives, in order that they can have opportunities for self-reflection, emancipation, and showing their self-positioning, which is the function of storied therapy. The values include: personal self-identification, rebuilding the integrity of life through memories, and self-affirmation from reviewing the past. Storied therapy will help the elderly reposition themselves in their life.

This study provides further insights into the storytelling experiences of elderly lives to evaluate the impact of active reminiscing. The prospective impact of this study is to create a process for people to narrate their life to gain potential personal and family benefits. The results of this study provide further references for the future development of VR narrative scripts for the elderly in Taiwan.

References

Atkinson, R.: The Life Story Interview. SAGE Publications, Thousand Oaks (1998)

Brockmeier, J., Carbaugh, D. (eds.): Narrative and Identity: Studies in Autobiography, Self and Culture, vol. 1. John Benjamins Publishing, Amsterdam (2001)

Dempsey, L., et al.: Reminiscence in dementia: a concept analysis. Dementia **13**(2), 176–192 (2014)

El Haj, M., Antoine, P., Nandrino, J.L., Kapogiannis, D.: Autobiographical memory decline in Alzheimer's disease, a theoretical and clinical overview. Ageing Res. Rev. **27**, 15 (2016)

Erikson, E.H., Erikson, J.M., Kivnick, H.Q.: Vital Involvement in Old Age. W. W. Norton & Company, New York (1994)

Guillemot, S., Urien, B.: Legacy writing among the elderly: conceptual bases, dimensioning and a proposed scale for measuring motivations. Recherche et Applications en Marketing (English Edition) **25**(4), 25–43 (2010)

Kenyon, G.M.: Guided autobiography: in search of ordinary wisdom. In: Rowles, G.D., Schoenberg, N.E. (eds.) Qualitative Gerontology: A Contemporary Perspective, 2nd edn, pp. 37–50. Springer, New York (2002)

Kovach, C.R.: Content analysis of reminiscences of elderly women. Res. Nurs. Health **14**, 287–295 (1991). https://doi.org/10.1002/nur.4770140407

Pan, Y., Simonian, N., Beleno, R., Liu, L., Kaufman, D., Astell, A.: Impact of digital storytelling experience among people living with dementia. Gerontechnology **17**(Suppl), 72s (2018). https://doi.org/10.4017/gt.2018.17.s.072.00

Randall, W.L., McKim, A.E.: Reading Our Lives: The Poetics of Growing Old. Oxford University Press, New York (2008)

Randall, W.L., McKim, A.E.: Toward a poetics of aging: the links between literature and life. Narrative Inquire **14**(2), 235–260 (2004)

Sobol, J., Qentile, J., Sunwolf: Storytelling, self, society: an interdisciplinary journal of storytelling studies. Storytelling Self Soc. **1**(1), 1–7 (2004). https://doi.org/10.1080/15505340409490254

Taylor-Price, C.: The efficacy of structured reminiscence group psychotherapy as an intervention to decrease depression and increase psychological well-being in female nursing home residents. Unpublished doctoral dissertation, Faculty of Mississippi State University (1995)

UN: The 2019 Revision of World Population Prospects. https://population.un.org/wpp/. Accessed 2 Mar 2020

White, M., Epston, D.: Narrative Means to Therapeutic Ends. W. W. Norton & Company, New York (1990)

Designing Digital Technologies and Safeguards for Improving Activities and Well-Being for Aging in Place

Helene Fournier[1](✉), Irina Kondratova[2], and Heather Molyneaux[2]

[1] National Research Council Canada, 50 de la Francophonie Street, Moncton, NB E1A 7R1, Canada
helene.fournier@nrc-cnrc.gc.ca
[2] National Research Council Canada, 46 Dineen Drive, Fredericton, NB E3B 9W4, Canada
{irina.kondratova,heathermolyneaux}@nrc-cnrc.gc.ca

Abstract. Older adults (65+) are becoming primary users of technologies, including IoTs, wearables and emerging smart systems, especially for aging in place and in daily living activities related to better health and wellness. Research demonstrates some critical features in home health care and wearable technology adoption by older adults such as wearability, device appearance, display and interaction, the modeling and technical aspects of data measurement and presentation, with more sophisticated, personalized interaction systems and data analysis expected over time. The design and development of home health care technologies are often led by the requirements of their social and caregiving environments rather than the needs and preferences of older adult users. The mismatch between functionalities, intrinsic motivations and expected benefits has a detrimental impact on user acceptance. User acceptance is critical for technology to be integrated within daily living especially in areas such as IoTs and wearables. Cybersecurity is an essential part of a safe, effective and reliable healthcare delivery system. Security and privacy challenges can be overcome by implementing best practices to safeguard systems and devices. There are significant privacy risks associated with wearables and home IoTs. The literature review has identified emerging issues that underscore the need to develop a set of guidelines for conducting HCI and human factors research based on an understanding of older adults' perceptions and preferences about data privacy and security. Additionally, directions for current and future research are discussed in the paper, including late breaking research on virtual care and support vulnerable seniors during the COVID 19 pandemic.

Keywords: Human computer interaction · Human factors · IoT · Wearables · Privacy · Aging in place

1 Introduction

Older adults (65+) are becoming primary users of technologies, including IoTs, wearables and emerging smart systems, especially for aging in place, in daily living activities

C. Stephanidis et al. (Eds.): HCII 2020, LNCS 12426, pp. 524–537, 2020.
https://doi.org/10.1007/978-3-030-60149-2_40

related to better health and wellness [1–3]. However, such technologies are often not designed for older users and can pose serious privacy and security concerns due to their novelty, complexity, and propensity to collect vast amounts of sensitive information [4–7].

Research indicates that isolation from significant relationships and support services is one of the most significant factors undermining the quality of life and longevity of seniors [8, 9]. The COVID-19 pandemic is causing untold fear and suffering for older people across the world [10]. The literature also points out that with the right tools, seniors of all ages can create unique solutions to enhance the quality of their life and stay connected. For example, many older adults use wearables, such as electronic monitoring devices, that enable them to track and monitor their health-related physical fitness metrics including steps taken, level of activity, walking distance, heart rate, and sleep patterns to improve their health and wellbeing. These devices are also used for treatment to collect certain information (e.g., steps, heart rate, and sleep) to better manage functional status assessment and provide support in the clinical setting and for aging at home. Wearables have potential as an intervention tool to increase activity levels for older adults through self-monitoring in the short term, however there is a need to evaluate the long-term impacts of these devices [1]. Wearables are useful for motivating older adults through personal goal setting, self-monitoring and for social connectivity. Both wearables and IoTs are critical parts of the Personal Informatics (PI) systems, "those that help people collect personally relevant information for the purpose of self-reflection and gaining self-knowledge" [12].

Research demonstrates some critical features in wearable technology adoption by older adults such as wearability, device appearance, display and interaction, the modeling and technical aspects of data measurement and presentation, with more sophisticated, personalized interaction systems and data analysis expected over time [11]. Users over age 50 with chronic illnesses and older adults would benefit from cheaper and more compatible devices, and user acceptance may be improved by addressing barriers during deployment, such as by providing tutorials on challenging features and communicating the device's usefulness. There are, however, some privacy risks associated with wearables and IoTs. In contrast to medical health wearables and IoTs, where electronic records are created and managed by healthcare providers, users of consumer health wearables and IoTs create and manage their own personal health information without the help of a physician [13]. While data collected by healthcare wearables and IoT devices are subject to various legal protections [14], the same protections are not provided for in consumer wearables. Researchers [15] have identified a number of privacy risks for consumer wearables including user context privacy, bystander privacy during data collection, and external data sharing privacy.

The current pandemic has created challenges for healthcare in both hospital and in home care settings with an increased need for virtual care and online consultations for vulnerable populations; seniors living alone and in fair or poor health are considered vulnerable and at-risk for health-related complications. Dr. Paul Hebert, Special Advisor to the Canadian Red Cross expressed that "these are not new challenges for isolated older adults, especially those with chronic health concerns. The pandemic simply underscores them" [16]. The pandemic has also increased the proliferation of technological solutions around digital health. Older adults in particular could be the main benefactors from this shift, and, as a result, become primary users of technologies for aging in place, including IoTs, wearables and emerging smart systems, for daily living activities related to better health and wellness. The next section will look at the emerging issues from the literature on HCI and health technologies related to technology acceptance, privacy and security challenges for aging in place.

2 Literature Review

Recent HCI research addresses the major societal concern of an aging population in the developed world. Currently most websites, apps, and digital devices are used by diverse populations, thus they should not be design with a 'one size fits all' approach [17]. The 50+ age group is the fastest growing demographic online and according to Home Care Magazine, 46% of baby boomers use a cell phone, 65% are active on social media, and a whopping 75% are digital buyers [18]. Research has shown that ability and motivation to use new technologies are strongly determined by work experience and education, and the difficulties people experience around the use of technology are related to past performance rather than age-related factors [19].

The rapid development of digital proficiency in an aging population has accelerated research and development in areas of gerontechnolgy, which merges the study of aging with the study of technology, and includes the following five aspects: enhancement, prevention, compensation, care and research [20]. With over 10,000 people turning 65 every day in America, this is a market about to explode, and building technology for an aging population is at a critical tipping point [18].

The HCI literature points to important issues related to user acceptance factors in health applications aimed at an aging population [3]. Researchers argue that the purpose and functionalities of gerontechnologies are often led by the requirements of their social and caregiving environments [21] rather than the needs and preferences of older adult users resulting in a mismatch between functionalities, basic motivations and expected benefits which in turn has a negative impact on user acceptance [21], which is critical for technologies to be integrated as part of daily living [22].

The literature around technology acceptance highlights the connection between technologies that support self-determination as having a positive impact on acceptance. That is, older adults are 'intrinsically motivated' by technology that promotes autonomy [23]. Acceptance and perceptions around assistive technologies can also be influenced by individual factors such as gender, previous experience, attitude towards technology, and education. Environmental factors such as accessibility and the availability of assistance, support and guidance from immediate family or their social network can either positively or negatively affect acceptance and perceptions around assistive technologies and their integration as part of daily living [23]. Age-related factors such as biological age, perceived age and attitudes towards aging are considered relevant parameters for technology acceptance [24], and part of the ever changing demographics to consider in an aging population. Capturing the daily life of older adults has become a major task for researchers and service providers alike. A thorough understanding of the expectations of older adults, their likes and dislikes, and the nature of their social relationships is essential in designing meaningful tools and devices they will actually accept and integrate as part of their daily living.

One type of health technology for use in the home is wearable technology, which refers to any electronic device with sensors, typically worn on the body, that is used to collect and deliver information about health and fitness related activities. Wearable devices (such as smart watch, smart ring, smart band, smart clothing, etc.) are used widely by the general population to track exercise and health [25]. Originally designed to support medical needs, modern consumer wearables have sensors that monitor and record not only sensitive patient health information (such as heart rate, respiratory rate, oxygen saturation, blood pressure, temperature, ECG, etc.), but also record physical activity (e.g., steps taken, distance traveled, sleep patterns, exercise activity, falls, etc.). Consumer wearables also serve a function of ancillary healthcare, when medical attention is triggered by a wearable device that detects a life threatening event (heart attack, stroke, fall, etc.). Widespread use of wearables has allowed researchers [26] to use data from wearables for tracking influenza-like illness in real time using temperature, heart rate and activity data, including location. In other studies of activity trackers, comfort issues related to continuous wearing, design comparability considering older adult's mental and physical constraints, and utility of historical activity data were identified as major usability issues [27]. Historical data without any interpretation display in the tracker or associated apps may not be useful for older adults. The data needs to be more informative and deliver more meaningful and empowering directions for long-term use [27].

Cybersecurity is an essential part of a safe, effective and reliable healthcare delivery system [28]. Researchers note that privacy and security challenges can be overcome by implementing best practices to safeguard systems and devices [29]. The context of use is also important: devices operating in the home, such as wearable technology are more exposed to unauthorized access than those in more controlled environments, such as nursing homes and hospitals [30]. Despite the widespread proliferation of wearables, there are many privacy issues and risks associated with consumer wearables that have yet to be resolved by industry and law makers [13]. In contrast to medical health wearables for professional usage, where electronic records are created and managed by healthcare providers, users of consumer health wearables create and manage their own personal health information without the help of physicians [14]. While data collected by healthcare wearables are subject to various legal protections [15], the same protections are not available for consumer wearables.

Data generated by consumer wearables are extremely personal and considered to be even more sensitive and vulnerable than user's financial data. If accessed by a hacker, health data and activity data from a wearable (including location data) could easily be used against the individual. Researchers [13] have identified a number of privacy risks for consumer wearables including user context privacy, bystander privacy during data collection, and external data sharing privacy, and proposed technology solutions to mitigate the risks. Typically, wearable data is stored on the server of a company-provider, therefore, the user's data is never immune to a breach by hackers and there is no guarantee of permanent data deletion even if the user wants to delete their own account data [13]. The literature indicates that users are frequently not aware of the degree of anonymization of their data on the provider's server, they have concerns about the improper access to their data, and have concerns about the privacy complacency of companies in particular [31]. Thus, along with privacy by design technology solutions for wearables, privacy laws and regulations need to be updated to include wearables, and new ways to improve clear notice and consent from users need to be developed.

The concept of privacy by design by Dr. Ann Cavoukian states that the principles of Fair Information Practice (FIPs) need to be built into systems [21]. Home healthcare technologies need to be built with cybersecurity in mind; however, such systems also have to consider human needs and perceptions of security in order to ensure successful use [31]. Research has shown that older populations are very aware of privacy issues [33, 34] and that privacy considerations are key factors in the adoption of assistive technologies. Privacy seems to be more of an issue for technologies designed for aging in place, especially as older populations with health issues must learn to manage their personal health data [35]. Older people are faced with having to navigate a complex relationship between loss of privacy and increased freedom for users and caregivers to collect data and opening up the home environment to calls, checks, and visits.

Additionally, systems perceived as intrusive can impact user acceptance – a fact that many researchers overlook [33]. Applications of technological solutions still suffer from sociocultural misunderstandings of group differences, and poor acceptability of technology for patients and caregivers [33]. Researchers emphasize that older adult users should be included in the design of remote home monitoring technologies and in gathering privacy requirements for such technologies [34, 36]. Care technologies in the home environment require different contextual considerations whereby privacy issues are key. From a data privacy perspective, devices operating in the home are more exposed to unauthorized access than those in more controlled environments, such as nursing homes and hospitals [30]. Additionally, devices in the home also invade the personal space of the user, and their friends and family.

The literature points to barriers such as the concern for privacy, followed by issues of trust when adopting technologies for use by older adults [32]; however there is a willingness to give up some privacy for the benefit of staying in their home [37]. Older adults view personal data as only one important dimension of privacy concerning home healthcare technologies: they also have other privacy concerns related to aspects of personal privacy such as intrusiveness and feelings of surveillance—this has an impact on technology acceptance [38, 39]. Technological solutions for home healthcare still suffer from sociocultural misunderstanding of group differences, and poor acceptability of technology from patients, caregivers and clinicians [38]. Researchers emphasize that older adults as end-users should be included in the design process as well as in gathering privacy requirements for such technologies [34, 36]. Privacy concerns should be considered when designing health technologies for in home use, and not just the privacy of personal data [34]. All levels of users should be consulted, including the end user (older adults), secondary users (caregivers) and tertiary users (clinicians). An overarching theme that warrants further exploration is the trade-off between privacy (data and information privacy), the sense of surveillance and the invasion of personal space and the freedom of safely living independently at home [39, 40]. End-user perspectives and the need for autonomy and control must be balanced with privacy, security and trust in systems and devices [40].

2.1 User Acceptance and Satisfaction

While there is a large swath of literature on heath related IoTs and wearables for older adults, most current publications on technological solutions for aging in place do not report on user acceptance and satisfaction [29]. Research demonstrates that the following conditions are necessary for persuasive technology to promote a behavior: motivation, physical ability, and an effective trigger [41]. Additionally, persuasive fitness technologies are attractive because they "automate" behavior change [42]. Persuasive technologies should offer convenient data collection, analysis, and storage over long periods of time with immediate automated feedback. There are few studies of user needs and user acceptance of wearables and IoTs by older adults. For example, as shown by face-to-face interviews with senior citizens [43], older people see the future of wearable devices in the healthcare sector by indicating the need for stakeholders to get involved in promoting physical activity trackers to patients as a possible way to improve their health. In fact, most of the interviewed older adults wished the devices were available in pharmacies, and that they could learn about the devices from someone in health care, such as pharmacists, similarly to what is done with other health-monitoring systems (e.g., blood glucose meters, blood pressure meters), with the standard health-related tax exemptions or credits [43]. Older adults who were interviewed also indicated that they were also interested in doctors or other health care professionals potentially taking advantage of the data provided by the devices [43]. The functionality of IoT/wearables data sharing with health professionals would be particularly useful in a pandemic lock out situation.

Older adults often feel that modern consumer wearables are "not built with us in mind," that they are created "for someone younger," and that devices needed a more "tech-savvy" user. The design and development of home healthcare technologies are often led by the requirements of their social and caregiving environments rather than the needs and preferences of older adult users resulting in a mismatch between functionalities, intrinsic motivations and expected benefits which in turn has a detrimental impact on user acceptance [21]. User acceptance is critical for technology to be integrated within daily living [22] especially in areas such as IoTs and wearables. Another issue brought up was that there were no instruction manuals, which prevent them from feeling comfortable with the various devices [43]. Long-term use was significantly associated with wearing the device every day, being female, exercising more frequently, having higher education, not engaging in step count competition, and not having chronic conditions [44]. Older adults may not always accept and use wearables, even if they have initially accepted the technology. Acceptance of this technology may be improved by addressing barriers during deployment, such as providing tutorials on challenging features and communicating the device's usefulness. Users over age 50 with chronic illnesses would benefit from cheaper and more compatible devices, and more comprehensive set-up assistance.

Wearable activity trackers (WAT) are electronic monitoring devices that enable users to track and monitor their health-related physical fitness metrics including steps taken, level of activity, walking distance, heart rate, sleep patterns, etc. [11]. WAT are useful for motivating patients through personal goal setting, self- monitoring and the devices' social connectivity enhancements. Users have mixed feelings after having disengaged with their device, ranging from relief and freedom to feelings of frustration and guilt about having abandoned it. The most commonly cited deterrent to smart wearables is privacy concerns. According research, privacy and security are the foremost concerns of consumers regarding the use of smart wearables [45]. Research on consumer abandonment of smart wearable devices revealed privacy considerations as the most prevalent reason for desertion [46]. The study found that 45.2% of the time privacy concerns were cited as driving consumer decisions to abandon smart wearables. The concerns were multi-faceted, including users being uncomfortable with location tracking that revealed their movements to others and objected to selling their information to third parties for advertising purposes. In recent years, advancements in smart wearables have allowed the integration of biotechnology to collect consumer health data. "In the age of the Fitbit, strapping technology onto your body to track and monitor yourself is not only doable, but desirable. Bio-sensing wearables meld together passive and active data collection, often offering round the clock and personal self-surveillance, knowledge, and control. In other words, wearable technologies that have come into fashion are making the line between creepy vs. cool much fuzzier." [47]. Without adequate assurances and practices in place to protect highly personal biotechnology data and information, consumers will remain hesitant to participate in the ecosystem of IoT. Robust privacy legislation is a necessary ingredient for an effective ecosystem of IoT and wearables. While it is users who opt into data sharing, how the data will be shared is deeply affected by designers, "who have the power to enable and constrain certain action possibilities through their design choices" [48].

Currently, the lack of standards around user privacy and security issues can be a potential regulatory hurdle for adoption of wearables and IoTs by older adults, as well as data sharing issues due to low integration between public and private healthcare systems [49].

2.2 Design Guidelines

The current literature review has identified emerging issues that underscore the need to develop a set of guidelines for conducting HCI and human factors research that builds an in-depth understanding of older adults' perceptions and preferences about data privacy and security for these technologies. Research studies on older adults' use of wearable trackers demonstrate that the successful design of an all-purpose, universal device is unreasonable and that design concepts and data models should align with the personal preferences of various groups of users [11]. More research needs to be carried out to fully understand the best practices for designing wearables for older adults. Current recommendations and suggestions include the following (see Table 1):

Table 1. Design and user experience recommendations for wearable trackers for older adults.

Recommendations and suggestions for wearable trackers for older adults	References
Make devices available in pharmacies, with the standard health-related tax exemptions or credits	[43]
Provide an option to learn about the devices from someone in health care, such as pharmacists, similarly to what is done with other health-monitoring systems (e.g., blood glucose meters, blood pressure meters)	[43]
Include a simple paper-based instruction manual that clearly addresses set up, how to use the device, and basic problem solving	[43]
Allowing access to device on both a computer and a mobile app would allow older adults to access data in a more familiar way, in terms of comfort with technology and by allowing them to view results on a bigger screen	[43]
Displays for wearables should consider using large, high-contrast text with large light-on-dark letters and numbers to allow for easier viewing	[43]
Waterproof design decreases worry about the fragility of the device if it is forgotten, and accidentally damaged by doing dishes or the laundry, and also allows older adults to use it in the water-based activities that are commonly recommended by health care providers as part of a low-impact way to increase physical activity	[43]
Older adults use wearable trackers longer if they use a wider variety of functions to track health and activity levels (calories burned, distance, heart rate, mood, sleep time, steps, blood oxygen saturation, etc.)	[44]
Wearable trackers targeting patients with chronic illness should focus on mHealth, integrating programs that designed for specific patient populations, using a customized regimen and specific levels of physical activities	[11]
Users over age 50 with chronic illnesses would benefit from cheaper and more compatible devices, and more comprehensive set-up assistance	[11]
Critical features for adoption include wearability, device appearance, display and interaction, as well as the modeling and technical aspects of data measurement and presentation	[11]
To stay engaged with the device, users expect a more sophisticated, personalized interaction system and data analysis over time	[11]
Technology providers should increase the reliability of their products, by limiting technology errors, malfunctioning devices, improving connectivity, and enhancing the analytics for better healthcare delivery and treatments	[49]
There is an ethical issue around the inclusion that needs to be resolved, especially in insurance-defined wearable-based new products, of people with specific conditions (e.g., subjects in a wheelchair), which, in programs based solely on physical activity evaluation, may be disadvantaged by earning a lower amount of points/discounts compared to normal subjects owing to their conditions	[49]

There is also the need to implement cybersecurity safeguards with design considerations for enhancing privacy and security for sharing health information, including designing interfaces not only for single users but with the ability to add others as medical conditions change; either temporarily, during times of surgery or illness recovery or more permanently, during cognitive decline. An in-depth case study of adults with mild cognitive impairments and their caregivers highlighted the importance of shared decision making-user interfaces to improve joint decision making practices [50]. A study of residents in senior care facilities identified the design implications to support communication for older adult related to privacy and sharing of health information. The design consideration presented in Table 2 are based on privacy and health information sharing concerns derived from semi-structured interviews with a dozen residents from senior care facilities [51].

Table 2. Design consideration for privacy and health information sharing

Category of decision making	Recommendation
Choosing recipients	Should be based on information relevance
Levels of communication	Should be based on urgency, relevance and individual attitudes
Content and information	Should be based on information relevance and characteristics of recipient
Choice of delivery method	Should be based on urgency and established communication style

The literature on mHealth and new technologies for home care highlights the importance of autonomy, self-management and control as part of the efforts around aging in place, along with the need for user centered, collaborative, interdisciplinary research and development [52]. The next section highlights research and development efforts currently underway as part of the National Research Council of Canada pandemic challenge program with vulnerable seniors.

3 Current Research and Development

Work is underway to advance the design and implementation of an early prototype help system for tablet devices to support older adults as they interact with unfamiliar interfaces and new technologies for aging in place. This work will explore the design of contextual support for vulnerable seniors as many current interfaces such as mobile (i.e., tablet) devices often do not incorporate elements that align with older adults' models of use: explicit help menus, user manuals, and navigational cues and affordances.

The current pandemic will require remote usability testing with end-users from their home, using online tools that help to identify navigational and usability issues. Usability testing will help to identify important elements of interface and navigational cues to manage health information, including preferences for digital or tactile help buttons, and which elements would be more effective in supporting older adults as they interact with new interfaces in the context of managing their own health and wellness, particularly for a range of seniors who are no longer absolute novices. This work aims to provide useful recommendations for designers of mobile interfaces, who seek to implement effective help and support systems for vulnerable seniors.

A survey on home health care services is also being launched across the USA and Canada. This project will use convenience sampling to collect primary data through online surveys. The online surveys will target persons who are concerned about the well-being and care of aging adults and personnel who work in a clinical or administrative capacity in home health care services. The end-user survey will be distributed widely across the USA and Canada using internet sites like Quora, LinkedIn, Reddit, or other panels of interested people. Publicly available information and lists provided by industry associations will be used along with an e-mail invitation to professionals with the request to fill out an online survey. A targeted sample size of 300 respondents is expected. The knowledge from survey results will help to identify opportunities to improve adoption experiences for innovative health services for vulnerable seniors. This research is especially important in the face of the current pandemic where seniors would have benefited greatly from remote care technology when face-to-face interaction was restricted. There are currently gaps in knowledge around the level of technology use and integration in home health care services as well as senior's level of technology adoption and acceptance for managing their health and wellness. It is expected that the survey data will provide insights into the current state of home health care services and help to inform future phases of the research on assistive technologies for aging in place.

4 Conclusions and Discussion

A review of the literature in the area of HCI and human factors has pointed out important issues related to user acceptance factors in health applications and important challenges related to privacy, security, trust, and technology acceptance among older adult users. The protection of personal data is an area of concerned expressed by older adults, along with concerns about the improper access and use of their data, and especially concerns about the privacy complacency of companies. It is important to consider privacy concerns when designing health technologies for in home use especially. More research needs to be carried out to fully understand the best practices for designing wearables for older adults, along with robust privacy legislation as a necessary ingredient for an effective ecosystem of IoT and wearables. While it is users who opt into data sharing, how the data will be shared is deeply affected by designers, "who have the power to enable and constrain certain action possibilities through their design choices". Currently, the lack of standards around user privacy and security issues can be a potential regulatory hurdle for the adoption of wearables and IoTs by older adults. Older adults should be included as co-creators in the research and development of technologies that meet their needs and support them in living a quality of life now and in the long-term. Future research directions will focus on user friendly and secure technologies for home healthcare, including wearables for self-monitoring, and technologies for caregivers and home healthcare professionals. Further research is required to improve the design of new technologies for health and wellbeing, while empowering older adults to make informed decisions, to maintain their dignity and control over their personal data through HCI and more transparent safety and security mechanisms. Ongoing research is needed to address societal changes of an aging population and to advance research and development in digital technologies in the context of aging in place.

References

1. Azimi, I., Rahmani, A.M., Liljeberg, P., Tenhunen, H.: Internet of Things for remote elderly monitoring: a study from user-centered perspective. J. Ambient Intell. Humanized Comput. **8**, 273–289 (2017). https://doi.org/10.1007/s12652-016-0387-y. Accessed 20 Apr 2020
2. Takahashi, Y., Hishida, Y., Kitamura, K., Mizoguchi, H.: Handrail IoT sensor for precision healthcare of elderly people in smart homes. In: 2017 IEEE International Symposium on Robotics and Intelligent Sensors (IRIS) (2017). https://doi.org/10.1109/iris.2017.8250149. https://www.researchgate.net/publication/322416543_Handrail_IoT_sensor_for_precision_healthcare_of_elderly_people_in_smart_homes. Accessed 25 Apr 2020
3. Pan, A., Zhao, F.: User acceptance factors for mHealth. In: Kurosu, M. (ed.) HCI 2018. LNCS, vol. 10902, pp. 173–184. Springer, Cham (2018). https://doi.org/10.1007/978-3-319-91244-8_14
4. Boyd, D., Crawford, K.: Critical questions for big data. Inf. Commun. Soc. **15**(5), 662–679 (2012). https://doi.org/10.1080/1369118X.2012.678878
5. Cavoukian, A., Jonas, J.: Privacy by design in the age of big data (2012). https://jeffjonas.typepad.com/Privacy-by-Design-in-the-Era-of-Big-Data.pdf. Accessed 13 May 2020
6. Cormack, A.: A data protection framework for learning analytics. *Community.jisc.acuk* (2015). http://bit.ly/1OdIIKZ. Accessed 20 Mar 2020
7. Fenwick, T.: Professional responsibility in a future of data analytics. In: Williamson, B. (ed.) Coding/Learning, Software and Digital Data in Education. University of Stirling, Stirling (2015)
8. Chopik, W.J.: The benefits of social technology use among older adults are medicated by reduced loneliness. Cyberpsychol. Behav. Soc. Netw. **19**(9), 551–556 (2016). https://www.liebertpub.com/doi/full/10.1089/cyber.2016.0151. Accessed 20 Mar 2020
9. Zamir, S., Hagan Hennessy, C., Taylor, A.H., Jones, R.B.: Video-calls to reduce loneliness and social isolation within care environments for older people: an implementation study using collaboration action research. BMC Geriatr. **18**(62) (2018). https://doi.org/10.1186/s12877-018-0746-y. Accessed 12 Jun 2020
10. Guterres, A.: United Nations COVID-19 Response (2020). https://www.un.org/en/coronavirus/our-response-covid-19-must-respect-rights-and-dignity-older-people. Accessed 6 Jun 2020
11. Shin, G., et al.: Wearable activity trackers, accuracy, adoption, acceptance and health impact: a systematic literature review. J. Biomed. Inform. **93**, 103153 (2019). https://doi.org/10.1016/j.jbi.2019.103153. Accessed 20 Apr 2019
12. Li, I., Froehlich, J., Grevet, C., Ramirez, E., Larsen, J.E.: Personal informatics in the wild: hacking habits for health & happiness. In: Conference on Human Factors in Computing Systems - Proceedings, 2013-April, pp. 3179–3182 (2013). https://doi.org/10.1145/2468356.2479641. Accessed 15 Jun 2020
13. Becker, M., Widjaja, T., Matt, C., Hess, T.: Understanding privacy risk perceptions of consumer health wearables – an empirical taxonomy. In: ICIS 2017: Transforming Society with Digital Innovation, pp. 0–21 (2018)
14. Banerjee, S., Hemphill, T., Longstreet, P.: Wearable devices and healthcare: data sharing and privacy. Inf. Soc. **34**(1), 49–57 (2018). https://www.tandfonline.com/doi/full/10.1080/01972243.2017.1391912. Access 15 Jun 2020

15. Perez, A.J., Zeadally, S.: Privacy issues and solutions for consumer wearables. IT Prof. **20**(4), 46–56 (2018). https://doi.org/10.1109/MITP.2017.265105905. Accessed 10 Jun 2020
16. Canadian Red Cross: Pandemic Study reaffirms Red Cross concern for vulerable seniors (2020), https://www.redcross.ca/about-us/media-news/news-releases/pandemic-study-reaffirms-red-cross-concern-for-vulnerable-seniors. Accessed 20 Jun 2020
17. Johnson, J.A.: Designing technology for an aging population. In: CHI 2018. https://dl.acm.org/ft_gateway.cfm?id=3170641&type=pdf. Accessed 20 Jun 2020
18. Burkhardt, W.: The next hottest thing in silicon valley: Gerontechnology (2016). https://www.forbes.com/sites/vinettaproject/2016/09/20/the-next-hottest-thing-in-silicon-valley-gerontechnology/#5b8b70763abe. Accessed 20 May 2020
19. Tacken, M., Marcellini, F., Mollenkopf, H., Ruoppila, I., Széman, Z.: Use and acceptance of new technology by older people. findings of the international MOBILATE survey: enhancing mobility in later life. Gerontechnology **3**(3), 128–137 (2005), http://citeseerx.ist.psu.edu/viewdoc/download?doi=10.1.1.474.3979&rep=rep1&type=pdf. Accessed 15 Jun 2020
20. Jansson, T., Kupiainen, T.: Aged people's experiences of gerontechnology used at home. a narrative literature review. Final Thesis. Helsinki Metropolia University of Applied Sciences (2017). https://www.theseus.fi/bitstream/handle/10024/129279/Jansson_Kupiainen_ONT_21.4.17.pdf?sequence=1. Accessed 05 Apr 2020
21. Cavoukian, A., Fisher, A., Killen, S., Hoffman, D.A.: Remote home health care technologies: how to ensure privacy? Build it Privacy by Design. IDIS **3**(363), 363–378 (2010). https://doi.org/10.1007/s12394-010-0054-y
22. Chen, K., Chan, A.H.S.: A review of technology acceptance by older adults. Gerontechnology **10**, 1–12 (2011)
23. Cahill, J., McLoughlin, S., O'Connor, M., Stolberg, M., Wetherall, S.: Addressing issues of need, adaptability, user acceptability and ethics in the participatory design of new technology enabling wellness, independence and dignity for seniors living in residential homes. In: Zhou, J., Salvendy, G. (eds.) ITAP 2017. LNCS, vol. 10297, pp. 90–109. Springer, Cham (2017). https://doi.org/10.1007/978-3-319-58530-7_7
24. Offermann-van Heek, J., Gohr, S., Himmel, S., Ziefle, M.: Influence of age on trade-offs between benefits and barriers of AAL technology usage. In: Zhou, J., Salvendy, G. (eds.) HCII 2019. LNCS, vol. 11592, pp. 250–266. Springer, Cham (2019). https://doi.org/10.1007/978-3-030-22012-9_19
25. Radin, J.M., Wineinger, N.E., Topol, E.J., Steinhubl, S.R.: Harnessing wearable device data to improve state-level real-time surveillance of influenza-like illness in the USA: a population-based study. Lancet Digit. Health **7500**(19), 1–9 (2020). https://doi.org/10.1016/S2589-7500(19)30222. Accessed 19 Mar 2020
26. Lee, B.C., Ajisafe, Toyin D., Vo, T.V.T., Xie, J.: Understanding long-term adoption and usability of wearable activity trackers among active older adults. In: Zhou, J., Salvendy, G. (eds.) HCII 2019. LNCS, vol. 11592, pp. 238–249. Springer, Cham (2019). https://doi.org/10.1007/978-3-030-22012-9_18
27. Nash, E.J.: Notice and consent: a healthy balance between privacy and innovation for wearables. BYU J. Pub. L. **33**(2), 197–226 (2018)
28. Jalali, M.S., Razak, S., Gordon, W., Perakslis, E., Madnick, S.: Health care and cybersecurity: bibliometric analysis of the literature. J. Med. Internet Res. **21**, 2 (2019)
29. Maresova, P., et al.: Technological solutions for older people with Alzheimer's disease: review. Current Alzeimer Res. **15**, 975–983 (2018)
30. Henriksen, E., Burkow, T.M., Johnsen, E., Vognild, L.K.: Privacy and information security risks in a technology platform for home-based chronic disease rehabilitation and education. BMC Med. Inform. Decis. Mak. **13**, 85 (2013). https://doi.org/10.1186/1472-6947-13-85

31. Dodd, C., Athauda, R., Adam, M.P.: Designing user interfaces for the elderly: a systematic literature review. In: Australasian Conference on Information Systems, Hobart, Australia (2017). https://www.acis2017.org/wp-content/uploads/2017/11/ACIS2017_paper_146_FULL.pdf
32. Peek, S.T.M., Wouters, E.J.M., van Hoof, J., Luijkx, K.G., Boeije, H.R., Vrijhoef, J.M.: Factors influencing acceptance of technology for aging in place: a systematic review. Int. J. Med. Inform. **83**(4), 235–248 (2014). https://doi.org/10.1016/j.ijmedinf.2014.01.004
33. Al-Shaqi, R., Mourshed, M., Rezgui, Y.: Progress in ambient assisted systems for independent living by the elderly. SpringerPlus **5**, 624 (2016). https://doi.org/10.1186/s40064-016-2272-8
34. McNeill, A.R., Coventry, L., Pywell, J., Briggs, P.: Privacy considerations when designing social network systems to support successful ageing. In: CHI 2017: Proceedings of the 2017 CHI Conference on Human Factors in Computing Systems, pp. 6425–6437 (2017). https://doi.org/10.1145/3025453.3025861. Accessed 28 May 2020
35. Kolkowska, E., Kajtazi, M.: Privacy dimensions in design of smart home systems for elderly people. In: WISP 2015 Proceedings, vol. 17 (2015)
36. Yusif, S., Soar, J., Halfeez-Baig, A.: Older people, assistive technologies, and the barriers to adoption: a systematic review. Int. J. Med. Inform. **94**, 112–116 (2016). https://doi.org/10.1016/j.ijmedinf.2016.07.004. Accessed 20 May 2020
37. Jaschinski, C., Ben Allouch, S.: Listening to the ones who care: exploring the perceptions of informal caregivers towards ambient assisted living applications. J. Ambient Intell. Humaniz. Comput. **10**(2), 761–778 (2018). https://doi.org/10.1007/s12652-018-0856-6
38. Tsertsidid, A., Kolkowka, E., Hedstrom, K.: Factors influencing seniors' acceptance of technology for ageing in place in the post-implementation stage: A literature review. Int. J. Med. Inform. **129**, 324–333 (2019), https://doi.org/10.1016/j.ijmedinf.2019.06.027. Accessed 15 May 2020
39. Mortenson, W.B., Sixsmith, A., Beringer, R.: No place like home? Surveillance and what home means in old age. Can. J. Aging **35**(1), 103–114 (2016). https://doi.org/10.1017/S0714980815000549
40. Schomakers, E.-M., Ziefle, M.: Privacy perceptions in ambient assisted living. In: Proceedings of the 5th International Conference on Information and Communication Technologies for Ageing Well and e-Health (ICT4AWE 2019), pp. 205–212 https://doi.org/10.5220/0007719802050212
41. Dasgupta, K., Rosenberg, E., Daskalopoulou, S.S.: Step Monitoring to improve ARTERial health (SMARTER) through step count prescription in type 2 diabetes and hypertension: trial design and methods. Cardiovasc. Diabetol. **13**(1), 7 (2014)
42. Fogg, B.J.: A behavior model for persuasive design. In: Proceedings of the 4th International Conference on Persuasive Technology, pp. 1–7 (2009)
43. Mercer, K., Giangregorio, L., Schneider, E., Chilana, P., Li, M., Grindrod, K.: Acceptance of commercially available wearable activity trackers among adults aged over 50 and with chronic illness: a mixed-methods evaluation. JMIR MHealth UHealth **4**(1), e7 (2016), https://doi.org/10.2196/mhealth.4225. Accessed 20 Apr 2020
44. Li, L., Peng, W., Kononova, A., Bowen, M., Cotten, S.R.: Factors associated with older adults' long-term use of wearable activity trackers. Telemed. E-Health **26**, 769–775 (2019)
45. Kerr, D., Butler-Henderson, K., Sahama, T.: Security, privacy, and ownership issues with the use of wearable health technologies. In: Cyber Law, Privacy, and Security: Concepts, Methodologies, Tools, and Applications, pp. 1629–1644. IGI Global (2019)
46. Epstein, D.A., Caraway, M., Johnston, C., Ping, A., Fogarty, J., Munson, S.A.: Beyond abandonment to next steps: understanding and designing for life after personal informatics tool use. In: Proceedings of the 2016 CHI Conference on Human Factors in Computing Systems, pp. 1109–1113 (2016)
47. Wissinger, E.: Blood, sweat, and tears: navigating creepy versus cool in wearable biotech. Inf. Commun. Soc. **21**(5), 779–785 (2018)

48. Bucher, T., Helmond, A., et al.: The affordances of social media platforms. In: Burgess, J., Marwick, A., Poell, T. (eds.) The SAGE Handbook of Social Media, pp. 223–253. Sage, Newcastle upon Tyne (2017)
49. Tedesco, S., Barton, J., O'Flynn, B.: A review of activity trackers for senior citizens: research perspectives, commercial landscape and the role of the insurance industry. Sensors (Switzerland) **17**, 1277 (2017). https://doi.org/10.3390/s17061277
50. Trendafilova, Z.K.: Discussing Cybersecurity Safeguards Between Older Adults with Mild Cognitive Impairement and their Caregivers. University of Maryland, Baltimore County, p. 22615443. ProQuest Dissertations Publishing, Ann Arbor (2019)
51. Nurgalieva, L., Frik, A., Ceschel, F., Egalman, S., Marchese, M.: Information design in an aged care context: views of older adults on information sharing in a care triad. In: PervasiveHealth 2019: Proceedings of the 13th EAI International Conference on Pervasive Computing Technologies for Healthcare May 2019, pp. 101–110 (2019). https://doi.org/10.1145/3329189.3329211
52. Matthew-Maich, N., et al.: Designing, implementing, and evaluating mobile health technologies for managing chronic conditions in older adults: a scoping review. JMIR Mhealth Uhealth **4**(2), e29 (2016)

Digital Health Engineering and Entrepreneurial Innovation – Education for the Development of ICT for Older Adults

Andrea Greven[1], Peter Rasche[2(✉)], Cara Droege[1], and Alexander Mertens[2]

[1] Innovation and Entrepreneurship Group (WIN) – TIME Research Area, RWTH Aachen University, Kackertstrasse 7, 52062 Aachen, Germany
{digitalhealth,cara.droege}@time.rwth-aachen.de

[2] Chair and Institute for Industrial Engineering and Ergonomics, RWTH Aachen University, Bergdriesch 27, 52062 Aachen, Germany
P.Rasche@iaw.rwth-aachen.de

Abstract. Considering that more than 20% of Europe's population is above 65 years old (Eurostat, 2017) and the increasing nature of this figure, this one-semester block course was created. Students from various disciplines are introduced to the current challenges of home health care for older adults, learn the fundamentals of entrepreneurship and combine this knowledge to develop and implement digital health app solutions for improving the health of older adults within interdisciplinary teams. The focus of this course is to teach the hard and soft skills necessary to found a start-up and implement a first click-prototype. Methods used in this course include an age-simulation suit, the method of lean startup, design thinking, personas and participative user-centered design to generate and ethically validate ideas. Implementation of the click-prototype is done within MIT AppInventor. Besides this students are trained on how to pitch and present ideas to potential investors. Within this article, the initial development process of this course and results from accompanying scientific evaluation are presented.

Keywords: Education · Older adults · Digital health

1 Introduction

1.1 Motivation

Healthy aging is one of the core concerns in industrialized societies due to demographic change [1]. Closely linked to this goal is the desire of many older adults to live independently at home on a long-term basis. This desire requires that a growing number of traditional health care processes are brought into the home environment [2]. This process yields many challenges, as younger and older people differ in the use and acceptance of digital products, especially in the very sensitive area of health care. Poorly developed products might overtax older users or are not accepted or even used by them [2]. Within the course, learners are sensitized to these problems and given targeted methods and tools to develop excellent participatory digital health products in the complex environment of home health care.

C. Stephanidis et al. (Eds.): HCII 2020, LNCS 12426, pp. 538–548, 2020.
https://doi.org/10.1007/978-3-030-60149-2_41

1.2 Aim of the Course

The aim is to develop and evaluate a transdisciplinary block course, in which interested learners from various disciplines are developing home health care solutions for older adults (65+ years) in interdisciplinary teams. Triggered by an interactive experience of aging using an age simulation suit, learners are expected to develop digital solutions to tackle older adults' problems in healthcare and everyday life. To achieve this the course consists of interactive teaching modules focusing on entrepreneurship, user-centered design as well as ethically oriented product development. Additionally, this course should address the need for interdisciplinary specialists in the future field of digital medicine. Specialists in this field require a shared, human-oriented understanding of the product development process, which is based on ethical, social and legal norms. Hereby, cost efficiency and patient welfare are the key objectives. This course is designed to provide learners with the necessary tools to develop and deepen these skills and competences.

2 Design of the Course

RWTH's Entrepreneurship and Innovation Group (WIN) and the Chair and Institute of Industrial Engineering and Ergonomics (IAW) collaborated in order to offer this course. The WIN Chair focuses on the entrepreneurship aspects of this course while the IAW Chair specializes in the more technological parts of course content. This way both chairs are able to focus on their expertise generating an interdisciplinary course on the supply side.

The starting point for the course is that it can be completed without previous knowledge in the areas of health care, entrepreneurship or app development. The students should be introduced rudimentarily to these three topics during the course, so that they can develop their own ideas and implement them in the form of a simple click prototype. The basis for the development and the design are the learning outcomes as shown below.

Learning Outcomes of the designed Course:

- Learn the application of entrepreneurial methods to generate ideas
- Train to transform ideas into valuable products
- Interactively experience aging by simulation
- Gain knowledge about age-related ICT product design
- Learn the application of user-centered development methods
- Design and implement a click prototype
- Strengthen presentation skills
- Learn to perform valuable peer review
- Gain insights from entrepreneurs and experts of the field by various guest lectures

A review of the learning outcomes illustrates the practical nature of this course. The students should be able to develop their own idea and implement it, including a business plan and a click prototype [3]. Accordingly, a project report was defined as the examination performance, which on the one hand consists of a business plan and on the other hand describes the app developed comprehensively. Furthermore, presentation deliverables were defined, since the presentation of one's own idea is an important skill of entrepreneurs.

Based on the planned learning outcomes and the examination modalities, the next step was to define the course format. Due to the mostly practical part of the course, a block seminar is the most suitable format. This has the further advantage that the theoretical input can be given very intensively and compactly and at the same time, the students should have completed the course before the typical examination time at the RWTH.

The course is designed iteratively according to classical software development methods such as SCRUM and contains two specific phases [4, 5]. Starting point is a first lecture block focusing on theory, introducing the current challenges of healthcare and allowing the participants to experience what it means to age using an age simulation suit. Based on these inputs learners are be trained in idea generation and idea creation using design thinking and the method of lean startup. Additionally, students learn about participative design process as well as age-related app design. Until the second lecture block, participants are asked to generate and validate ideas for digitally supported healthcare solution for older adults in interdisciplinary teams. To document their efforts participants prepare a pitch of their idea including first results regarding the business potential of this idea. This presentation takes place at the mid of the semester in front of a board of experts. Based in this presentation teams receive feedback regarding their idea. With the help of this feedback, the participants work on their Business Model Canvas to develop a profound business model [6, 7]. Additionally, external input by keynote speakers is offered at this stage. Classroom trainings on ethics, entrepreneurial finance and an introduction into MIT AppInventor (Massachusetts Institute of Technology, Boston, USA) for turning their ideas into working prototypes conclude this block [8]. Based on this input, the students further develop their idea and validate a meaningful business plan as well as implement a first click prototype for their digital health solution. Following this self-working phase, the student teams present their business plan and click prototypes in a sales pitch to the board of experts in a final presentation at the end of the course. Figure 1 shows the time schedule of the course.

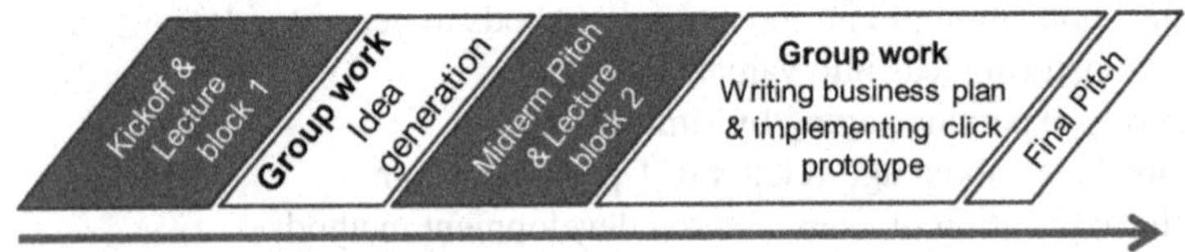

Fig. 1. Time schedule of the course.

Since interdisciplinary group work is the foundation of this course, special attention was paid to the question of the composition of the groups during the conception of the course. A specific questionnaire was developed for the task in which the students could evaluate their previous knowledge and experience in the three focus areas of health care, entrepreneurship and app implementation on a 5-point Likert scale in addition to their field of study. Based on this profile, balanced interdisciplinary teams are then put together, in terms of both expertise and gender.

3 Method of Scientific Evaluation

The presented course is a new construct. The evaluation and further development of the course are accordingly important. Three different evaluation methods were chosen for this purpose. The Teaching Analysis Poll is used during the semester and enables short-term follow-up control with regard to weak points in the course concept. Two other methods, "Teaching Evaluation Survey at the RWTH" and self-evaluation essays of the students, were used for the summative evaluation after completion of the course.

3.1 Teaching Analysis Poll

At the mid of semester participants participated in a Teaching Analysis Poll (TAP) during the semester conducted by the "Excellent Academic Teaching" Team of RWTH Aachen University. A Teaching Analysis Poll is a qualitative form of mid-term evaluation [9, 10]. The evaluation consists of a 30-min discussion between the Excellent Academic Teaching Team and the students. The date of the evaluation is deliberately chosen as the middle of the term so that the results of the TAP can be used to improve the course.

Key Questions of the Teaching Analysis Poll are:

1. How did you learn best in this course?
2. What makes your learning in this course more difficult?
3. What suggestions do you have for removing the obstacles to your learning process in this course?

3.2 General Course Evaluation According RWTH Aachen Regulations

At the end of semester this course was evaluated using the EvaSys System (Electric Paper Evaluationssysteme GmbH, Lüneburg, Germany) at RWTH Aachen University. Applying this system enables an anonymous evaluation based on a paper-based questionnaire. The questionnaire contains 35 questions on seven different topic blocks (Demographics, Seminar Concept, Supervision during Lecture and Elaboration, Presentation and Discussion, Organization and Implementation, Personal Summary and further comments) spread over two pages. The questions are always evaluated on a 5-Likert scale (1 = strongly agree to 5 = strongly disagree). All courses at RWTH Aachen University are evaluated by this standardized questionnaire.

3.3 Self-evaluation Reports of Students

Third, participants were asked to write a self-assessment essay in the length of three pages reflecting their own performance as well as the performance of the team during the entire course. To gain further insights on the design of the course and potential to improve, students were asked to document their ideas, questions, problems, and solutions during the course as well. Besides the scientific aspect of the analysis of the self-assessments, a second point was that this way students become mature learners as they reflect their performance during the course.

Key Questions for the Self-assessment Essay are:

- What role did you play in the team?
- What challenges and pitfalls did you and your team face during this project?
- What is your personal take-away for future project work?

4 Results

The course was conducted the first time in the summer semester of 2019. The course was offered by the Faculties of Mechanical Engineering and Business Administration, allowing students of these disciplines to earn 5 ECTS points by participating in this course.

4.1 Participants

In total 24 students (9 female) grouped in six interdisciplinary teams completed this course during the summer term of 2019. All students were within their first year of master program. 21 out of the 24 students were enrolled in the department of business administration. Remaining students were enrolled within the mechanical engineering department.

4.2 Teaching Analysis Poll

The Teaching Analysis Poll was conducted by the Excellence Academic Teaching team of RWTH Aachen University at the mid of the second lecture block. The qualitative evaluation took 30 min and was performed by means of a group discussion.

Results are shown in Fig. 2 according to the questions asked during the Teaching Analysis Poll.

4.3 General Course Evaluation According to RWTH Aachen Regulations

General course evaluation applying the standardized questionnaire of RWTH Aachen University was performed after the course was completed. In total 20 students handed in their feedback. 40% of these were female.

Students rated this course with an average of 1.6 (standard deviation = 0.7) on a 5 point Likert scale (1 = strongly agree to 5 = strongly disagree). The concept itself was rated on average 1.9 (SD = 1) on named 5 point Likert-Scale. Regarding the question whether the learning goals of the course are experienced as clearly defined, participants answered 1.9 (SD = 0.9) on average. Similar results were given for the structure of the course (mean 1.9; SD = 0.8). The relevance of the course topic was rated 1.7 (SD = 0.8). Regarding the question whether participants think, they have the required basic knowledge to participate in this course average rating was 2 (SD = 1.1) on mentioned 5 point Likert-Scale. Overall, participants evaluated the concept of the course as good (see Fig. 3).

What makes you learn the most in this event?

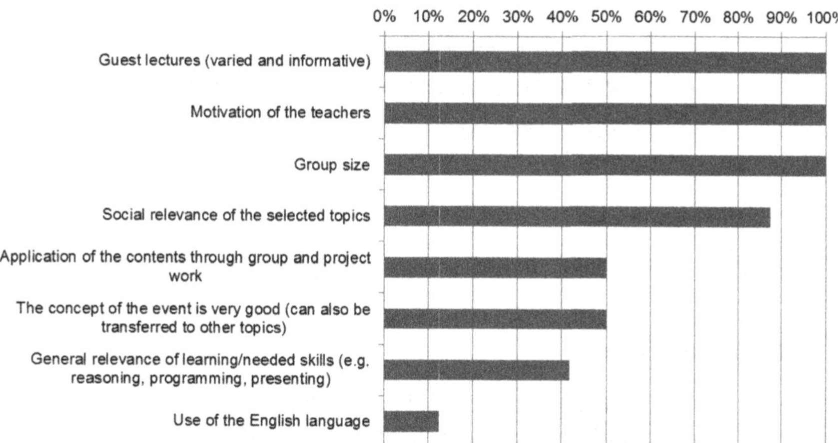

What makes your learning in this event more difficult?

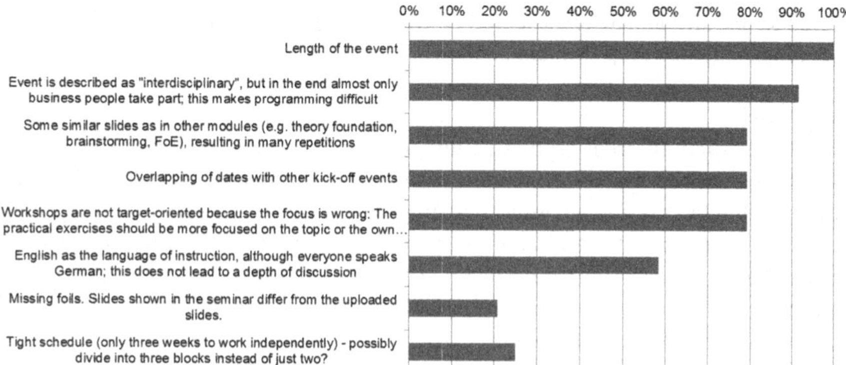

Which suggestions for improvement do you have for the obstructive points for this event?

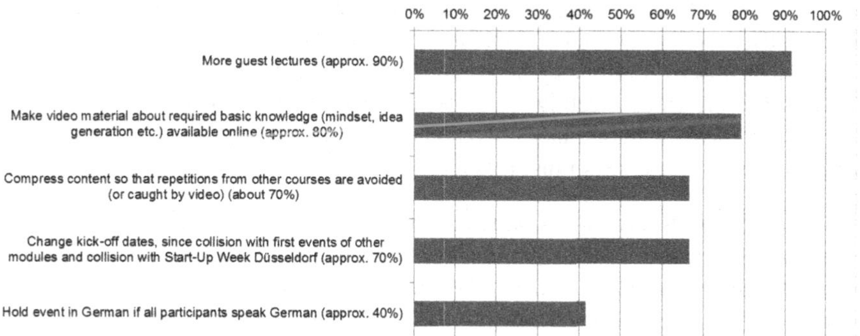

Fig. 2. Results of the teaching analysis poll

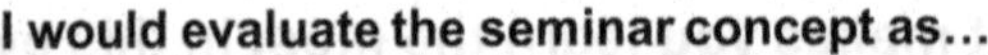

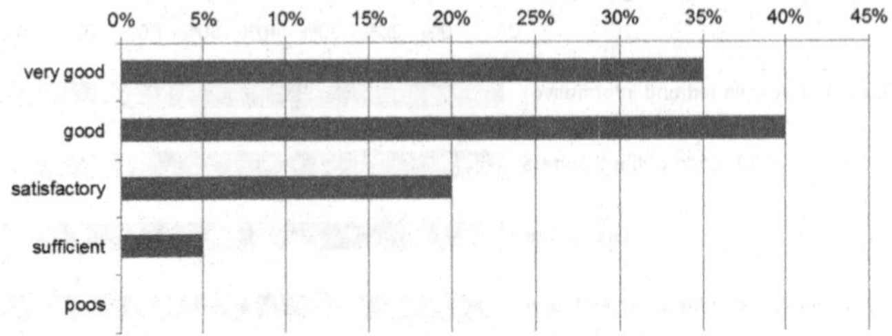

Fig. 3. Results regarding evaluation of the seminar concept (N = 20).

4.4 Self-evaluation Essays

A total of 24 self-evaluation essays were collected. These were qualitatively analyzed and coded by two independent researchers. Based on this analysis two main topics were identified. The first topic addresses group work and deals with best practices and aspects that have positively influenced group work. The second topic covers students' personal knowledge growth and will be presented by the three key topics of the course (Healthcare, Entrepreneurship and App Implementation).

Group Work

Students identified different aspects as important to facilitate good group work. Most frequently mentioned was the demand to distribute tasks equally. 18 out of 24 students reflected within their self-evaluation essay this aspect. Due to the very tightly scheduled time in this course, an effective and transparent division of tasks within the team was considered a particularly important factor. This partly led to a division of labor within the groups, where one part of the group took care of the app and another part of the group took care of the business plan.

Closely related to this aspect is also the second aspect mentioned in connection with good group work. 17 of the 24 students indicated that they felt that regular, structured team meetings were very important and positive for the successful solution of the task. It was emphasized that it is helpful to set an agenda for the meetings in order to discuss purposefully, as well as to resolve discussions with a compromise considering the limited in order to be able to continue in the group work.

Related to the group meetings is the aspect that 14 out of 24 students in their self-evaluation stressed the importance of common deadlines within the team. The following quote from one of the essays illustrates this.

> *"While all of the team members have done their job conscientiously and well, some of my team members were faster than the others. So sometimes you had to ask after the self-imposed deadline or ask if the task is done. I would wish for future group work, that the team members also jointly set and keep deadlines together."*

Another aspect of good group work, also emphasized by over half of the students, is the discussion and feedback culture within the group. 13 out of 24 students described the discussion and feedback culture as an important aspect, as this is the core of interdisciplinary cooperation. The following quote from one of the essays points this out.

"A lot of opinions can and will improve the result and it will get better and better until it is quite close to optimal in the end."

Based on the discussion and feedback culture, the students also highly favored a "Decide early and often" mentality. Due to the high time pressure within the course, the time for the discussion of ideas and possible background research was very limited. Accordingly, 9 out of 24 students stress that it is more important to make a decision than to make the 'correct' decision:

"The biggest pitfall at team level was certainly investing a lot of time in selecting the idea. This extra time could have been used towards the end of the project."

In connection with this, 9 out of 24 students found it helpful that the course had a strict time schedule and thus a corresponding time pressure. The opinion was that time is only a problem if the group as such does not harmonize and does not organize itself efficiently. The following quotation illustrates this fact very impressively:

"A strong team does not need a lot of time."

Finally, it can be stated that the circumstance of interdisciplinary cooperation are displayed throughout all self-evaluations submitted by a group. However, this fact was not directly mentioned by any student.

Individual Knowledge Evolvement

The individuals increase in knowledge is regularly spread over all three key topics. 10 out of 24 students stated that they had improved their knowledge of entrepreneurship through this course. Also, 10 students indicated that their knowledge of the German healthcare system had improved. 9 students explicitly stated that their ability to create a business plan had improved through participation in this course. A further 7 out of 24 students stated that they had expanded their knowledge of app implementation. Overall, there were no students who stated that they had not gained any knowledge through this course.

5 Discussion

This study presents the concept of an interdisciplinary block course, in which master students without previous knowledge independently develop a digital health solution together with a suitable business plan with the aim of founding a start-up. In accordance with current methods of the Scholarship of Teaching movement, the course was scientifically evaluated both during and after completion.

The results of the evaluation show that the students rate the concept of this course as very good on average. Both the relevance of the topic and the implementation of the individual modules were rated as very good to good according to the General Evaluation of Courses at the RWTH. This is a pleasing result, since it shows that the combination of two disciplines (Business Administration and Mechanical Engineering/Industrial Engineering) was successful. Even though the two disciplines were handled with precision in the modules and also in the implementation, they still form an interdisciplinary unit which is perceived by the students as a uniform concept.

Furthermore, the detailed evaluation in the self-evaluation papers showed that there are interesting parallels between the group work reported by the students and common concepts in software development like Scrum. Scrum is an agile process framework which enables agile and goal-oriented software development. It is designed for small teams. When implementing Scrum the ultimate goal is broken down into several smaller ones which can be completed within time-limited phases, so called sprints [5]. These phases should not be longer than one month and are in most cases two weeks long. Sprints are organized in an iterative manner. At the end of each sprint the team evaluates the results, best practices and pitfalls. Based on this analysis the next sprint is planned and completed. By each sprint a piece of the puzzle towards the ultimate goal is delivered.

If one compares these characteristics and framework conditions of the Scrum method to the self-evaluations of the students, different parallels can be recognized. The aspect of limiting the available time is noticeable. The students reported how beneficial the time pressure and the clear definition of deadlines by the course concept were. It forced the teams to make decisions, similar to the idea of using the Scrum framework. Furthermore, common task sharing and the importance of common deadlines by the students were discussed. Both are aspects that can also be found in Scrum. It is common for all tasks planned for the sprint to be posted on a board that is accessible to all team members. This ensures transparency about the current work status and tasks can be selected according to individual capacities, whereby the completion of the work phase is defined by the end of the sprint and not by the completion of the individual tasks. A corresponding procedure was also considered important by the teams with regard to successful group work. A conclusion related to the independent and transparent processing of tasks, which the students have drawn as experiences from their group work, is the necessity of a pronounced discussion and feedback culture in the team. Corresponding aspects can also be found in methods such as Scrum. Respect is a core value of the agile way of working. Furthermore, Scrum method asks for daily meetings so called stand-ups, which provide space for structured discussion and incorporation of feedback. Furthermore, each sprint is evaluated retrospectively in order to draw conclusions and learnings for further cooperation and to improve future cooperation.

Overall, it can be said that the self-evaluation reports of the students provided interesting insights into group work and participation in the course. It turned out that best practices, as exemplified by agile project management methods, were also recognized as such during this course, even though project management was not the core topic of the course.

6 Conclusion and Lessons Learned

The fusion of two independent disciplines into one module has proven to be a good solution for designing and introducing an application-oriented course in an interdisciplinary field such as digital health care. Based on the collected data it could be shown that this concept reaches acceptance by the students and is suitable for the further development of the individual abilities in the area of certain disciplines, such as entrepreneurship, health care or app development, as well as the topic complex as such.

The strong time pressure in the course paired with a clearly defined but nevertheless high workload turned out to be an advantage and led to the fact that the students gained various insights into project management and group work.

For future courses this concept has to be further developed and further disciplines and student groups should be integrated. Medical students in particular would certainly benefit from and contribute to this course, as they have a much broader knowledge of the hurdles and challenges in healthcare, which in turn is the breeding ground for good ideas and exciting business ideas. The practical relevance should also be strengthened through guest lectures by entrepreneurs from the field of digital health. The relevance of the course contents, the knowledge and methods imparted are once again made clear to the students by the sharing of first-hand experiences and thus motivates a more intensive examination of the course contents.

The evaluation of the course for the winter semester 2019 is still pending at the time of writing. It therefore remains to be seen whether the results obtained can be confirmed and thus be traced back to the concept or whether the results presented are primarily based on the students' characteristics and the group composition created.

References

1. Batini, N.: The Global Impact of Demographic Change. s.l.: International Monetary Fund (2006)
2. Devine, M., Hasler, R., Kaye, R., Rogers, W., Turieo, M.: Human factors considerations in the migration of medical devices from clinical to homecare settings. In: Proceedings of the Human Factors and Ergonomics Society Annual Meeting, vol. 48, pp. 1685–1689 (2004). https://doi.org/10.1177/154193120404801512
3. Brettel, M., Heinemann, F., Sander, T., Spieker, M., Strigel, M., Weiß, K.: Erfolgreiche Unternehmerteams: Teamstruktur - Zusammenarbeit – Praxisbeispiele, 1st edn. Gabler Verlag/GWV Fachverlage GmbH Wiesbaden, Wiesbaden (2009)
4. Gloger, B.: Scrum. Informatik Spektrum **33**, 195–200 (2010). https://doi.org/10.1007/s00287-010-0426-6
5. Rising, L., Janoff, N.S.: The scrum software development process for small teams. IEEE Softw. **17**, 26–32 (2000). https://doi.org/10.1109/52.854065
6. Joyce, A., Paquin, R.L.: The triple layered business model canvas: a tool to design more sustainable business models. J. Clean. Prod. **135**, 1474–1486 (2016). https://doi.org/10.1016/j.jclepro.2016.06.067
7. Muhtaroglu, F.C.P., Demir, S., Obali, M., Girgin, C.: Business model canvas perspective on big data applications. In: 2013 IEEE International Conference on Big Data; Silicon Valley, CA, USA, 06.10.2013–09.10.2013, pp. 32–37. IEEE (2013). https://doi.org/10.1109/bigdata.2013.6691684

8. Pokress, S.C., Veiga, J.J.D.: MIT App Inventor: Enabling Personal Mobile Computing (2013)
9. Schmohr, M., Müller, K., Philipp, J. (eds.): Gelingende Lehre: erkennen, entwickeln, etablieren: Beiträge der Jahrestagung der Deutschen Gesellschaft für Hochschuldidaktik (dghd) 2016, 1st edn. wbv Publikation, Bielefeld (2018)
10. Hochschulen AEuQBuB. QM-Systeme in Entwicklung: Change (or) Management?: Tagungsband der 15. Jahrestagung des Arbeitskreises Evaluation und Qualitätssicherung der Berliner und Brandenburger Hochschulen am 2./3. März 2015. Freie Universität Berlin, Berlin, Februar 2017

Practical Implementation of an Innovative Design Aimed at Increasing Enthusiasm for Exercise Among the Elderly

Hui-Jiun Hu[1](✉) and Li-Shu Lu[2]

[1] Department of Visual Arts, National Chiayi University, Chiayi, Taiwan
momo@mail.ncyu.edu.tw

[2] Department and Graduate School of Digital Media Design, National Yunlin University of Science and Technology, Yunlin, Taiwan

Abstract. The experience of old age differs greatly from individual to individual. Some people are able to maintain active social lives and travel widely, while others may be confined to their beds for long periods with no one to talk to. During the aging process, muscle loss occurs at a faster rate compared to the decline of other organ functions, and without adequate muscle strength, the bone joints will be subjected to more stress, leading to the frequent occurrence of inexplicable back pain and, eventually, sarcopenia. For elderly individuals, this decline in muscle strength will bring inconveniences; affect their health, mobility, and quality of life; and increase their risk of falling. However, research has shown that sarcopenia is reversible and that exercise can halt muscle loss. Furthermore, it is also possible to regain one's muscle mass through training. Given these findings, our study utilized a user-oriented design and the scenario method to develop a course structure based around problem-based learning and the topical objective of increasing enthusiasm for exercise among elderly individuals. Students were guided to adopt a user perspective in developing potential innovative designs for the future, and scenario-based simulations were performed to analyze the interactional relationships between people and products, assess adherence to design themes. The study revealed that the empathy mapping allowed the students to think from other perspectives that facilitated their understanding of the elderly's pain points and needs, and that the visual scenario method was effective in promoting consensus among team members and expanding the diversity of ideas, leading to the quick development of innovative designs.

Keywords: Innovative design · User-centered design · Sarcopenia

1 Introduction

As the saying goes "One must move in order to live." This is often easier said than done, however. According to a 2014 survey conducted by the Health Promotion Administration, almost 60% of elderly Taiwanese aged above 65 years are usually not very willing to go outdoors. They prefer to stay at home and maintain a mundane lifestyle,

C. Stephanidis et al. (Eds.): HCII 2020, LNCS 12426, pp. 549–563, 2020.
https://doi.org/10.1007/978-3-030-60149-2_42

which reduces their vitality (Administration 2014). In addition, they are susceptible to sarcopenia, which causes low muscle mass and, consequently, increased strain on the bones and joints and frequent bouts of back pain and aches. Those with severe cases are even unable to stand up. Clinical studies have shown that the onset of muscle loss begins around the age of 30 with a 3–8% decrease occurring every 10 years. Muscle loss often accelerates with age, as elderly groups aged above 70 years will experience a 15% decrease every 10 years (Melton et al. 2000). Muscle loss not only causes inconvenience, but also affects the health, mobility, and quality of life of the elderly, as well as increasing their risks of fall and fractures, which, in turn, impedes their ability to live independently. Falls have become the leading cause of death among the elderly (NCOA 2014). However, evidence-based studies have revealed the reversible nature of sarcopenia, more specifically, exercise can alleviate muscle loss and increase muscle mass through training. Raguso (2006) investigated the effects of physical exercise on the prevention of sarcopenia and fat accumulation among the elderly (Raguso et al. 2006). In a report published in Neurology, Dr. Kirk Erickson (2010) suggested that regular exercise can indeed mitigate decreased cognitive and memory functions caused by white matter changes. He suggested a thrice-weekly exercise routine in which each session involves more than 40 min of walking, so as to reduce the risk of cognitive impairment (Erickson et al. 2010).

Physical activity not only helps the elderly to maintain the strength they need to carry out their daily routines, as evidence has shown that it also prevents dementia and other chronic diseases. In addition, physical activity can improve social interactions among the elderly, which is beneficial for their physical and mental health. Even though it is often perceived that sarcopenia only happens to the elderly, the lack of physical activity, imbalanced nutrition intakes, and weight loss measures have also resulted in low muscle mass among the younger generations, which puts them at risk of premature osteoporosis. In particular, as women have lower testosterone levels, they often have lower muscle mass than men. They also tend to devote themselves to work and chores during their younger years, and thus, neglect the importance of the physical activity. An article published by top1 health.com reported that, in 2018, the employment rate among married and employed women between the age of 15–64 years was 57.24%. As mothers have to balance between their jobs and chores, they often felt stressed and experienced back pain and aches, headaches, and insomnia. The also faced psychological issues such as depression and mood swings (top1health 2018). Therefore, everyone should engage in strength training and regular exercise regardless of their age. Families should participate in daily exercise sessions lasting 20 to 30 min and encourage one another along the way. This will allows family members to train their muscles together, such that they become capable of taking care of themselves and their loved ones. In the study utilized a user-oriented design, students focused on practical issues, with empathetic observation and team communication being used to facilitate brainstorming, inductive analysis, critical thinking, teamwork, and ultimately, the creation of innovative designs jointly developed by team members. In the study utilized a user-oriented design, students focused on practical issues, with empathetic observation and team communication being used to facilitate brainstorming, inductive analysis, critical thinking, teamwork, and ultimately, the creation of innovative designs jointly developed by team members.

2 Literature Review

2.1 User-Centered Design

Design is regarded as a means of solving problems as well as a process of discovery (Kimbell 2011). In the past, many traditional systemized designs emphasize the designer and aim to create functional designs by uncovering the relationships between objects. This approach neglects the differences between the problems and needs perceived by the designer and the user (Hu and Yen 2010; Tang et al. 2005). The concept of user-centered design (UCD) was initially introduced by Norman (1983). UCD emphasizes the collaboration between design teams and users to produce easy-to-use products based on user experience. From the initial stages of design, the focus must be placed on the users and the objectives of use and design procedures must include continuous testing and revising processes (Norman 1983). Norman (1988) discussed that engineers and designers possess ample technical knowledge but lack knowledge on how people live their lives and the activities that people participate in, resulting in designs that are induced frustration among users or are disconnected from users. According to Brown (2010), genuinely good designs should not only elaborate on the appearance or aesthetics of a product, but must also emphasize precise insight, observation, and empathy, so as to discover models in complex places, identify noteworthy elements in seemingly meaningless fragments, and convert problems into opportunities. Therefore, user-centered designs should factor in social issues, as research involving user-centered methods is the key to creating innovative designs.

2.2 Generating Fun Through Technology

We need to maintain our health by maintaining healthy habits. The introduction of technology may improve one's condition. Rapid advancements in technology have changed the lifestyles of many elderly Taiwanese. In Taiwan, nearly 50% of elderly individuals aged above 65 years own a smartphone. The elderly also enjoy social media. Over 90% of them are users of LINE, a social networking app, and almost 60% of them are Facebook users (Chinatimes.com 2017). According to Lu (2012), technology can produce factors that contribute to happiness. The author implemented a series of hedonic experiential designs that allow users to feel the four senses of happiness – a sense of personal value, a sense of well-being, a sense of security, and a sense of serenity. In recent years, geriatric technology has emerged as a novel field that assists the elderly to live independently and enhances their quality of life. Therefore, technology is no longer limited to assisting frail elderly individuals in their daily lives or alleviating their disease. Vilans, the National Center of Expertise for Long-term Care in the Netherlands has proactively applied technology to innovative projects developed for the elderly. They proposed the notion of using technology to support independent living among the elderly and enhance their vitality (Global 2019). Lu and Liou (2018) also revealed that empowerment through gamification can allow elders to maintain a regular life and a certain level of motivation, as well as beginning a post-retirement life with optimism and dignity. Yet, in the past, many elders engaged in residential rehabilitation, in which a lack of motivation and professional guidance often results in incorrect postures and irregular exercise schedules and intensities. As such, it is difficult to elders to carry out their rehabilitation exercises at home according to their guidebooks (Lloréns et al. 2015). Moreover, the elderly often find traditional rehabilitation exercises to be boring and tedious. According to flow theory (Csikszentmihalyi 2000), one will become bored when they exit the "flow channel." Therefore, patients often give up rehabilitation, thus letting their health deteriorate (Syu and Bo 2018). Conversely, Zimmerli (2012) revealed that when rehabilitation exercises are transformed into interactive rehabilitation games that are more interactive and entertaining, patients will focus more on participating in these games and, thus, less on the agony and dullness of rehabilitation exercises (Zimmerli et al. 2012).

Fun is progressive and gives us a breath of fresh air and a sense of accomplishment. It not only achieves initial expectations and fulfills one's desires or needs, but also generates unimagined or unplanned feelings. For instance, the full attention given by children as they learn a new skill best describes the discovery of fun (Csikszentmihalyi 2008). Volkswagen utilized the fun theory to change the behaviors of city dwellers (Voslkswagen 2009). As shown in Fig. 1, designers and engineers collaborated to transform the staircase of a subway station into a giant piano, which played notes when people walked over them. This design enabled people to enjoy taking the stairs while concurrently exercising and contributing to energy conservation, to the extent that the escalators became less frequently used than the stairs.

Fig. 1. Piano stairs, Odenplan Metro Station, Stockholm, Sweden (source: http://thefuntheory.com/).

3 Research Method

Design teams in IDEO, a design company, emphasize design thinking, that is, seeking innovative solutions for various issues by prioritizing the needs of humans while opening up more possibilities for creation. Throughout the process of design, each step is constantly and repeatedly assessed and revised, so as to achieve a balance between desirability, feasibility, and viability (Brown 2010). In other words, innovative approaches are used to solve problems, and innovation must meet user requirements while achieving commercial and technical feasibility. Therefore, designers must listen carefully to and understand the opinions of users before designing a product. Various solutions can be created by combining various forms of communication with the observations and insights of designers. With over 20 years of experience in research on geriatric technology, e-health teams in the Netherlands stress that users are their best partners, and when technology is introduced into the field of long-term elderly care, innovation will only be relevant if human-centered concepts are be incorporated (Global 2019).

In the scenario approach, designers to put themselves in virtual scenarios that enable them to unleash their creativity and focus their attention on user needs and product systems. Concurrently, the approach also allows designers to stay rooted in reality, such that they are able to assess the feasibility of their product designs, vividly experience the usage environment of these products, and thereby better understand the preferences and needs of users (Liang 2000) The scenario design procedure consisted of four steps, which were observation, characters, scenario, and invention (Verplank et al. 1993).

Given these findings, our study utilized a user-oriented design and the scenario method to develop a course structure based around problem-based learning and the topical objective of increasing enthusiasm for exercise among elderly individuals. Students were guided to adopt a user perspective in developing potential innovative designs for the future, and scenario-based simulations were performed to analyze the interactional relationships between people and products, assess adherence to design themes, and assess whether the design concepts in question meet the needs of the elderly. This study was implemented through five phases as shown in Fig. 2, i.e. observe and understand, explore empathy, define points of view, ideate concepts, and learning reflection assessment.

(1) Observe and understand: In this phase, one aimed to understand the relationship between the needs of humans, the environment, and all things. By spreading points of view, he or she should get to know and comprehensively understand the backgrounds of learners, as well as making an inventory of "a known" and "unknown" knowledge and discovering problems and issues. According to Brown (2008), the first step in design is to directly observe and understand the work, living, and community environments of consumers, users, and customers to uncover the needs that they may be unable to describe. Design must be person-centric and must consider people's behaviors, needs, and preferences, as well as the feasibility of the technology and business. Such comprehensive thinking is necessary to match innovative concepts to people's needs and ideas and, thus, create value.
(2) Explore empathy: Innovative designs should be centered on humans. Empathy is the ability to recognize and understand the opinions, feelings, motivations, and personal traits of others. To empathize is to not judge by one's standards and worldview and experience the world through the eyes of another person, so as to uncover the potential needs of target users.
(3) Define points of view: During this phase, one aimed to establish a common knowledge base, in which acquired knowledge is classified, restructured, omitted, and deepened. Points of view that encompass all aspects were used to construct problems that need to be solved immediately, define relevant points of view, and deduce key questions that denote user requirements.

(4) Ideate concepts: Scenario-based approaches were introduced and high quantities of brainstorming activities were utilized to simulate scenarios involving the use of services in the future, as well as creating various possible solutions.
(5) Learning reflection: The course on the innovative design was designed according to the concepts of problem-based learning. A questionnaire assessing the students' core competencies was administered before and after the implementation of the course, so as to validate the students' learning outcomes after they had engaged in the course.

4 Results and Analysis

In this study, students focused on practical issues, with empathetic observation and team communication being used to facilitate brainstorming, inductive analysis, critical thinking, teamwork, and ultimately, the creation of innovative designs jointly developed by team members. The course content included the following (presented in order of implementation): understanding the target group, empathy mapping, future trend analysis, main concept derivation, application of scenario-based thinking, role setting, scenario-based story crafting, concept design and development, technical feasibility assessment, and learning reflection assessment.

4.1 Observe and Understand

The students collected relevant information pertaining to the elderly participants, including their health, lives, economic status, use of technology, and environments. Next, the nonparticipant observation approach was adopted to understand the target population (i.e. the elderly), such as their daily routines and physical activities. Nine elderly participants (four men and five women) participated in this study. Their mean age was 79.2 years. The participants received guidance during the interview process, which was recorded and covered the five dimensions A (activities); E (environments); I (interactions); O (objects); and U (users), as shown in Fig. 2. The participants described their daily physical condition and problems in a stress-free environment. Participant n01 was unable to farm due to having a stroke. He also experienced difficulties in walking due to muscle atrophy in the left hand and leg. Even though he did not expect his condition to improve, he felt happy when he was able to move and converse, as well as when his children returned home. Participant n02 enjoyed hiking with her family members. As she had waist pain which required her to be supported or to use an umbrella when walking, she enjoyed exercising with her family, even though she had to rest frequently. Participant n05 often dozed off while watching television. She claimed that she was unable to fall asleep on her bed when asked to do so. Participant n08 used to exercise regularly. However, she preferred to stay at home after her husband had passed away. She felt happy during family gatherings, and enjoyed walking outdoors with the company of others. Due to her old age, participant n09 had developed the degenerative joint disease, which reduced her willingness to go outdoors. In this phase, we found that the participants had gradually lost their motivation to engage in exercise after their bodily functions deteriorated. Their long-term lack of exercise resulted in muscle loss, making them susceptible to injury and emotional trauma.

Subject：家庭日出遊 Place：郊外爬山 Time：2018.03.14.
Description
Subject：阿嬤常常看電視度估 Place：客廳沙發 Time：2018.04.11 下午
Description

Fig. 2. Observation record (left) participant n02 (right) participant n05.

4.2 Empathy Exploration

In this phase, the participants' reasons for engaging and not engaging in routine exercise, as well as their needs, problems, and the feasibility of implementing technology-based interactions were uncovered through approaches such as empathy, visualization, classification, and summarization of associations. Then, the students observed the information gathered through the interviews and wrote their ideas on sticky notes (each sticky note contained one idea) according to four aspects – see, hear, say and do, and think and feel. Each note was stuck onto their corresponding area on a whiteboard and was later repositioned and classified. The rate of appearance of each idea, as well as its corresponding aspect (ideas that belonged to none of the four aspects were placed separately), were then discussed according to their relevance and contradiction. In the end, two new aspects, pain and gain, were identified as shown in Fig. 3.

Fig. 3. Empathy map.

(1) See: would rather watch TV than exercise, Laziness doesn't want to move, feel uncomfortable all over, feel unable to keep up with the child, only exercise together when meeting old friends…
(2) Hear: pray for the children, can't hear what others say, murmured, cycling is slow…
(3) Say & do: like to go to the market, participate in activities for the elderly community, watering flowers, foot pain can't move, cook three meals every day, love grandson, walk to buy food, complaining about life being boring, flash to the waist, forgot to take the medicine, dull taste.
(4) Think & feel: like sweet things, often give grandson money, remember a lot of young things…
(5) Pain: inconvenient to move and not want to exercise, need to rest after walking a few steps, knee pain in older age, hypertension can't sleep well, poor physical strength, at home alone, lonely
(6) Gain: like to hug, like to chat with family, hope to be with family, like family travel, children praise his sports behavior, need life goals, make big money ……

4.3 Define Point of View

The third phase involved the integration of the participants' needs and a value analysis. Points of view were defined through a 360-° perspective. Then followed two steps: (1) analysis of information and construction of problems, and (2) deepening of various questions in the problems and construction of key questions.

(1) Analysis of information and construction: First, we utilized a macroscopic perspective to deduce future trends and current statuses of points of view pertaining to the fields of society, economy, and technology, regardless of the positive or negative nature of the points of view. The students then brainstormed to consolidate the top ten points of view that are most needed or most likely to be needed by the participants. The points of view were also ranked by their importance, as shown in Fig. 4. These choices were mostly generated from the students' recognition toward the participants' needs in the first phase (observe and understand).

We determined that the major problems faced by the elderly at present are as follows:

- Social problems: Solitary elderly, long-term care, medical resources and emotional adjustment and support.
- Economic problems: Sport centers for the elderly, quality of medical treatment, family care.
- Technological problems: Empowerment-promoting games, wearable technology, transportation for the elderly, home surveillance system.

(2) Deepening of various questions in the problems and construction of key questions: With regard to the top ten problems in the aforementioned fields, we noted problems that received the most attention or resonated the most among the students. After converging and consolidating these problems, we constructed the following key questions: "What are the ways we can allow the participants to engage in

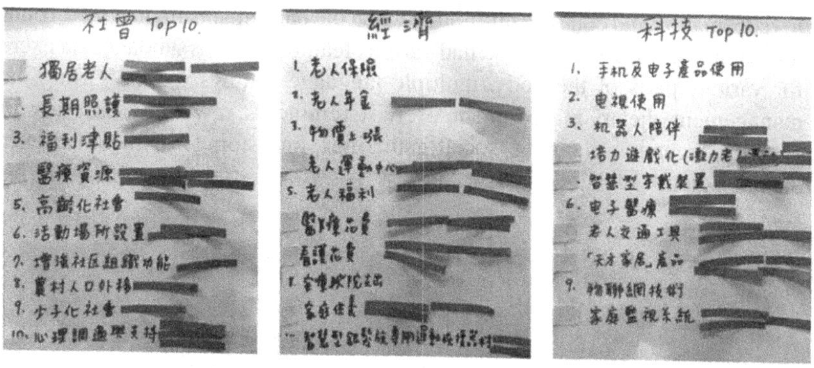

Fig. 4. Top ten points of view in the fields of society, economy, and technology.

daily exercise?"; "How can we enhance their motivation to engage in exercise?; How can we maintain their persistence and sense of accomplishment in relation to maintaining their exercise habits?"; and "How can we enable the participants to go outdoors?" Afterward, the students brainstormed to extend existing concepts, and then from the large pool of concepts, they voted to select the top eight concepts that were most likely to be accepted by the participants. These concepts were ranked by their importance and would serve as subsequent targets of development. Subsequent scenario-based approaches will be centered on the selected direction.

- One-day excursions: Encouraging the elderly to go outdoors and raising their physical, mental, and spiritual satisfaction.
- Group exercises: Building friendships and inviting family and friends to exercise together.
- VR exercises at home: Through the use of virtual reality (VR) technology, the elderly get to immerse themselves in various sceneries while exercising at home.

4.4 Conceptual Ideate

The fourth phase involved the utilization of scenario-based approaches and brainstorming to simulate future scenarios and involving the use of services in the future, as well as creating various possible solutions.

(1) Key idea generation
Students used mind maps to develop creative ideas. Based on the point of view of "What are the ways we can use to help the participants complete their daily exercise?", the team members completed a mind map of systematic concepts, as shown in Fig. 5. Then, we proposed a user-friendly social networking platform called "the Gray Hair Paradise App", in which the elderly exercise and physiological data were recorded into a sports bracelet and deliver to a cloud database (see Fig. 6). The objective of the app was to enhance the participants' level of fun through virtual point accumulation when they engaged in exercise. The points could then be used

to redeem gifts and could be multiplied when the participants invited their friends to join their exercise. The app also had various features such as guidance on exercises for various parts of the body, multiple language settings, points gifting, health management, dietary management, exercise reminders, rewards at different levels, one-day excursion planning, social gatherings, and storage of recorded exercise data in a cloud database.

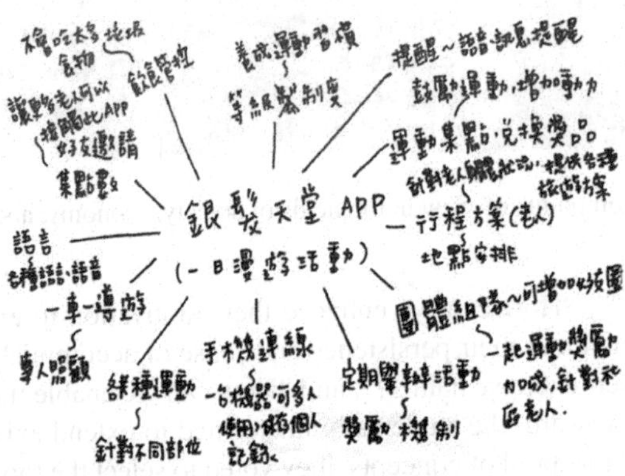

Fig. 5. Mind map of systematic concepts.

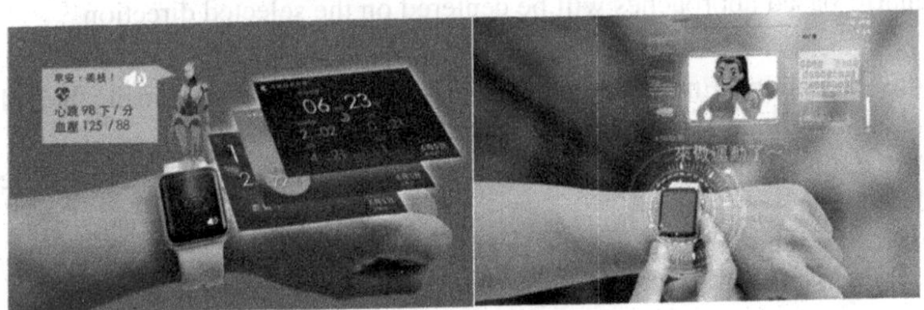

Fig. 6. Simulation of a sports bracelet.

(2) Character Mapping and Scenario
A persona is a virtual character created through user-centered design. It primarily represents the scenarios or experiences of a specific group of target users (Cooper 1999). The use of a persona can eliminate designer-centered problems, enable the complex needs and preferences of users to be explored, and allow for the replacement of users who are unable to make observations or access at any time (Pruitt and Adlin 2006). Furthermore, it also helps a research team to strike a chord with its target users. Figure 7 shows the character mapping and depiction of a persona named Lin Mei-Chih, who is 69 years old; has completed her primary education; is literate, mainly converses in Taiwanese; has lived on her own for a long time; requires a walking stick when walking; is able to take care of her own daily routine; has a conservative personality; usually chit chats with her neighbors; is visited by her family once every month; has a moderate acceptance toward high-tech products,

and knows how to use a smartphone. Ever since her friend Pao-Lien introduced her to the Gray Hair Paradise app, she started to enjoy hand-swinging exercises, as she was able to redeem gifts through point accumulation. Every day, she would walk to the park using her walking stick, which improved her spirits. Pao-Lien even used the Gray Hair Paradise app to help Mei-Chih celebrate her 70th birthday. Her neighbors and friends joined her on a one-day excursion, during which Mei-Chih discovered the beauty and fresh air of the countryside that can help improve her vitality and physical strength.

Fig. 7. Character mapping (left), persona depiction (center), and scenario creation (right).

(3) Simulation of conceptual design
The design of the app's interface is shown in Fig. 8. The interface was designed to be simple and straightforward, so that the participants were able to learn without feeling any stress. The concept was to encourage the participants to engage in daily exercise through a point accumulation incentive, which reduced the boredom of exercise. The points could be used for gift redemption or discounts, so as to enhance their persistence in exercising. The participants could also engage in group exercise with their friends, thus enabling them to encourage and interact with one another. The app also featured a cloud-based exercise data management system that allowed family members to know the physical condition of the participants. The voice reminders and time management features increased the efficiency and convenience of exercise, while the one-day excursion scheduling function encouraged the participants to go outdoors and live an active elderly life.

4.5 Learning Reflection

In this study, the Interdisciplinary Integration-Based Core Competencies Scale (IIBCCS) developed by Chen et al. (2017) served as a reference in the formulation of a 12-item questionnaire used to assess the core competencies of the students before and after the implementation of the course. Six indicators of core competencies were extracted, namely domain knowledge, professional ethics, team communication, cooperative reflection,

Fig. 8. The simulation of APP interface design.

innovative practice, and technological value. Table 1 compares the pre-test and post-test core competencies. As this study introduced design thinking and scenario-based approaches, the students experience positive growth in each of the six core competencies (Fig. 9 is a holistic analysis of the pre-test and post-test). The problem-based learning course design enabled the students to learn by doing and experience the need for communication, reflection, and implementation in teamwork while acquiring domain knowledge. Furthermore, the students were able to conform to a professional code of ethics while making good use of technological skills to increase the possibility of implementing an innovative design.

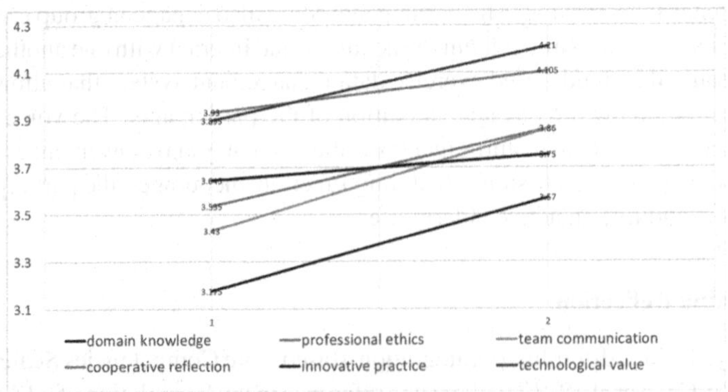

Fig. 9. Holistic analysis of the pre-test and post-test.

Table 1. Compares the pre-test and post-test core competencies.

Core	No	Item	Pre-test		Post-test		Gain scores
			Mean	SD	Mean	SD	
Domain knowledge	1	I understand the needs of actual target users and expertise in the field	3.21	0.77	3.57	0.73	0.36
	2	I can notice the status and trends of the global aging society	3.14	0.74	3.57	0.73	0.43
Professional ethics	3	I can understand the importance of ethics in the elderly technology industry	3.57	0.62	3.86	0.83	0.29
	4	I can understand personal assets and human rights protection practices in elderly research	3.5	0.63	3.86	0.83	0.36
Team communication	5	When discussing with team members, I can listen to the opinions of different members	3.29	0.7	3.86	0.83	0.57
	6	I can use effective communication tools to promote communication among team members	3.57	0.62	3.86	0.83	0.29
Cooperative reflection	7	I can reflect and generate new ideas in the process of interacting with team members	4	0.53	4.14	0.35	0.14
	8	When working with my classmates to complete tasks, I was able to clarify the problems I have encountered and actively seek out possible solutions	3.86	0.64	4.07	0.46	0.21
Innovative practice	9	I can propose practical solutions to the problems found during the teamwork	3.29	0.8	3.43	0.49	0.14
	10	After working with team members to complete tasks, I was able to evaluate the performance of the group's overall work	4	0.53	4.07	0.59	0.07
Technological value	11	I think the interaction with technology is interesting	3.86	0.64	4.29	0.45	0.43
	12	I think that the proper introduction of technology can help solve problems encountered in life	3.93	0.7	4.13	0.53	0.2

5 Conclusions

This study introduced the concept of user-centered design to assist students to understand the behavioral models, needs, and expectations of users, as well as to develop their empathy. A 360-° perspective approach was used to identify key questions and opportunities. One has the opportunity to implement innovation and service design only when the direction of a question is correct. This study yielded the following results (1) Based on problem-based learning can guide students' insight and observation training; (2) the empathy mapping allowed the students to think from other perspectives that facilitated their understanding of the elderly's pain points and needs, (3) the visual scenario method was effective in promoting consensus among team members and expanding the diversity of ideas, leading to the quick development of innovative designs. (4) The user-centered instructional design involved repeated exploration, creation, implementation, and reflection, which enabled innovative ideas to become more user-centric. (5) Finally, with regard to assessing their learning reflections, the students experienced a positive growth based on a comparison of the pre-test and post-test results, indicating that the designed instructional approach was beneficial toward the students. The study led to the development of the Gray Hair Paradise APP. This is an application that allows its users to create social groups in which enthusiasm toward team sports is promoted and members can influence each other. Furthermore, users can also wear bracelets to track the reward points earned from walking and participation in sports and competitions. These reward points can be converted into virtual currency that is used to obtain rewards such as gift redemptions and shopping discounts, so as to give elderly individuals a sense of accomplishment and encourage them to maintain their exercise habits.

Due to time constraints relating to the course implemented in this study, subsequent research on innovative design should include expert assessment and recommendations based on the three principles of conceptual design - desirability, feasibility, and viability. Furthermore, prototype designs should be created and revised according to the experiences and feedbacks of target users, so as to enhance the implementation of innovative user-centered design.

Acknowledgments. The researchers of the present study would like to extend their gratitude to the Ministry of Science and Technology (MOST), for their grant (Program No. 108-2410-H-415-010-).

References

Administration, H.P.: 2014 National Health Agency Annual Report (2014). http://health99.hpa.gov.tw/educzone/edu_detail.aspx?CatId=21770

Brown, T.: Design Thinking (2008). https://hbr.org/2008/06/design-thinking

Brown, T.: Change by Design: How Design Thinking Transforms Organizations and Inspires Innovation. Linking Publishing, Taipei (2010). (Translated by L. J. Wu)

Chen, L.-C., Wang, T.-H., Chiu, F.-Y., Shen, S.-Y., Zeng, M.: Developing the interdisciplinary integration-based core competencies scale: a case study of maternal-infant services curriculum. J. Sci. Educ. **25**(2), 143–168 (2017)

Chinatimes.com: More than 90% of elders like to use LINE (2017). https://www.chinatimes.com/newspapers/20170816000150-260204?chdtv

Cooper, A.: The Inmates Are Running the Asylum: Why High Tech Products Drive Us Crazy and How to Restore the Sanity. Sams, Indianapolis (1999)

Csikszentmihalyi, M.: Beyond Boredom and Anxiety. Jossey-Bass, San Francisco (2000)

Csikszentmihalyi, M.: Flow: The Psychology of Optimal Experience. HarperCollins, New York (2008)

Global, S.L.: When technology meets aging innovation (2019). https://blog.silverliningsglobal.com/%E5%9C%8B%E9%9A%9B%E8%A6%96%E8%A7%92-%E7%95%B6%E7%A7%91%E6%8A%80%E9%81%87%E4%B8%8A%E9%AB%98%E9%BD%A1%E5%89%B5%E6%96%B0-%E8%8D%B7%E8%98%AD%E9%95%B7%E7%85%A7%E6%99%BA%E5%BA%ABvilans%E7%9A%84ehealth%E5%AF%A6%E8%B8%90%E4%B9%8B%E8%B7%AF-8b4ddaaaf942

Hu, H.J., Yen, J.: Eliciting and describing design models of website construction. Japn. Soc. Sci. Des. **56**(5), 55–64 (2010)

Erickson, K.I., et al.: Physical activity predicts gray matter volume in late adulthood: the cardiovascular health study. Neurology **75**(16), 1415–1422 (2010)

Kimbell, L.: Designing for service as one way of designing services. Int. J. Des. **5**(2), 41–52 (2011)

Liang, Y.J.: Seven Principles of Innovative Design (2000)

Lloréns, R., Noé, E., Colomer, C., Alcañiz, M.: Effectiveness, usability, and cost-benefit of a virtual reality–based telerehabilitation program for balance recovery after stroke: a randomized controlled trial. Arch. Phys. Med. Rehab. **96**(3), 418–425 (2015)

Lu, S.P.: Does technology can produce factors that contribute to happiness? (2012). https://solomo.xinmedia.com/globaltourismvision/128308

Lu, G.M., Liou, F.R.: The empowerment games activate the silver-haired. Sci. Dev. **548**, 16–19 (2018)

Melton, L.J., Khosla, S., Crowson, C.S., O'Connor, M.K., O'Fallon, W.M., Riggs, B.L.: Epidemiology of sarcopenia. J. Am. Geriatr. Soc. **48**(6), 625–630 (2000)

NCOA: Fall is the main cause of death among older people (2014). https://www.epochtimes.com/b5/14/6/23/n4184608.htm

Norman, D.A.: Some Observation on Mental Model. Lawrence Erlbaum, Mahwah (1983)

Norman, D.A.: The Design of Everyday Things. Doubleday, New York (1988)

Pruitt, J., Adlin, T.: The Persona Lifecycle: Keeping People in Mind Throughout Product Design. Morgan Kaufman, San Francisco (2006)

Raguso, C.A., et al.: A 3-year longitudinal study on body composition changes in the elderly: role of physical exercise. Clin. Nutr. **25**(4), 573–580 (2006)

Syu, Y.L., Bo, L.: Prospects for the application of smart technology in the life and care of the elderly. J. Gerontechnol. Serv. Manag. **6**(3), 307–320 (2018)

Tang, H.H., Kao, S.A., Lin, R.T.: A study of frustration of using mobile phone for elderly users-a mental model approach. J. Ergon. Study **7**(1), 63–71 (2005)

top1health: Take care of your family and start loving yourself for 30 minutes every day (2018). https://www.top1health.com/Article/64654

Verplank, B., Fulton, J., Black, A., Moggridge, B.: Observation and invention: use of scenarios in interaction design. Paper presented at the Tutorial at INTERCHI 1993, Amsterdam (1993)

Voslkswagen: The Fun Theory (2009). http://www.thefuntheory.com/

Zimmerli, L., Krewer, C., Gassert, R., Müller, F., Riener, R., Lünenburger, L.: Validation of a mechanism to balance exercise difficulty in robot-assisted upper-extremity rehabilitation after stroke. J. Neuroeng. Rehab. **9**(1), 6 (2012). https://doi.org/10.1186/1743-0003-9-6

Research on GP-GC Intergeneration Affective Interaction Product Design: Analysis from Chinese Social Perspective to Value Proposition

Kuo-Liang Huang[1(✉)] and Hsuan Lin[2]

[1] Department of Industrial Design, Design Academy, Sichuan Fine Arts Institute, Chongqing, China
shashi@scfai.edu.cn

[2] Department of Product Design, Tainan University of Technology, Tainan, Taiwan R.O.C.
te0038@mail.tut.edu.tw

Abstract. Aging and baby bust are the problems that many countries are facing. Estranged intergenerational relationship has generally weakened family functions. How does grandparents-grandchildren intergenerational emotions interact and how to build sustainable relationships between grandparents and grandchildren have aroused great scientific interest in recent years. With the purpose of providing references for product design in promoting Intergenerational GP/GC relations, this paper, from the perspective of Chinese social thinking, extracted the needs and value propositions of GP/GC affective interaction that accords with China's national conditions through literature review and user study on Chinese Intergenerational GP/GC relations. Research findings showed that design requirements and propositions can be defined as: activities that increase GP/GC physical contacts or interesting joint tasks that require manual operations by both generations, providing opportunities that give play to creativity, meeting demands of intergenerational outdoor leisure activities and family trips, and creating memories of the younger generation's growth and happy time spent together.

Keywords: Intergenerational grandparent-grandchild (GP-GC) relations · Affective interaction · Value proposition

1 Introduction

China has undergone various changes over the past few decades along with scientific and technological, medical and economic development. For example, the development trends of aging and baby bust have changed family structure, which resulted in increased dual-earner families and larger differences among generations (Song and Fan 2016). In today's family, Grandparent-grandchild (GP-GC) intergenerational affective interaction is often restricted by geographical distance, family values difference, physical and structural factors (Yang and Li 2009). Widened intergenerational gap and estranged GP-GC

C. Stephanidis et al. (Eds.): HCII 2020, LNCS 12426, pp. 564–573, 2020.
https://doi.org/10.1007/978-3-030-60149-2_43

relations make the two generations emotionally detached from each other that the young fails to communicate well with the elderly and the elderly finds no shared topics with the younger. In order to fulfill intergenerational interaction requirements, traditional family functions are not adequate any more, but it calls for more psychological functions of the family.

Intergenerational relationships established between grandparents and grandchildren have aroused great scientific interest in recent years. However, few researches on promoting intergenerational relationship through product design is found. With the purpose of providing references for product design in promoting Intergenerational GP/GC relations, this paper, from the perspective of Chinese social thinking, extracted the needs and value propositions of GP/GC affective interaction that accords with China's national conditions through literature review and user study on Chinese Intergenerational GP/GC relations. Under the topic of Chinese Intergenerational GP/GC relations at the childhood stage, we studied on the following issues: (1) Which minor trends would be developed with the development of Chinese society? (2) What is the family profile of typical Chinese GP/GC generations? (3) What are the overall situation of Intergenerational GP/GC relationship and current family status? (4) what are the design requirements and value propositions in designing products that promote Intergenerational GP/GC affection?

2 Literature Review

2.1 GP-GC Relations and Emotions

"Intergenerational relationship" refers to interpersonal relationship between different generations, which include parenthood of more than two generations, such as parents-children relations and grandparents-parents-grandchildren relations (Yuesheng 2008). The two-way relationship between grandparents and grandchildren is referred to as GP-GC intergenerational relation. Affective communication, financial support and life caring are regarded as three main aspects of intergenerational relations within family (Hoff 2007; Yuesheng 2008). Chinese nation's fine tradition to respect the aged and take good care of the young is at the core of Chinese family ethic; it's also the basic value proposition of Chinese social morality and the sign of national civilization development. Establishment of satisfying and enduring GP-GC interactions of high-quality is essential to the maintenance of emotional bondage and family harmony (Mansson et al. 2017, 2010). Particularly, in Chinese society that upholds intergenerational transition, close interactions and affective communications between parents and children can contribute not only to the health of family members, but also to the harmony and stability of families and society. Moreover, establishment of emotional bond between grandparents and grandchildren is of the utmost importance to grandchildren's development (Mansson et al. 2017).

2.2 Influence Aspects of GP-GC Intergenerational Interaction

For grandparents, passing on positive knowledge, skills and emotions to the younger generations through increased GP-GC intergenerational interactions will add to the life meaning and value of the older generation, contribute to their ability to adjust to family life and society after retirement and help them to postpone senility. For grandchildren, GP-GC interactions will influence their attitude to aging, learning and marriage (Brussoni and Boon 1998; Harwood 2007; Kalpana and Rosaline 2018). In most cases, grandparents in the eyes of children are more than just playmates, but who will provide appropriate supports when they have relevant necessities and give assistance when they encounter troubles. And participating in grandchildren's growth process could inject more vitality into grandparents and make them feel the value of life in old age (Huang et al. 2015).

The GP-GC intergenerational interaction is deemed as helpful for grandparents to improve self-confidence and build positive attitudes, and grandchildren to improve the sense of self-value and happiness, etc. (Becker and Steinbach 2012; de Souza and Grundy 2007). Joint learning activities on intergenerational GP-GC relations help two generations to interact with each other, which not only fill an important gap in the lives of many children, but also help break down the stereotypes held by young and old; they encourage mutual understanding between generations and also give grandchildren positive role models (Hopkins 2000; Kalpana and Rosaline 2018). Besides, two generations participating together in family life, learning activities and leisure spots has clear positive impact to both grandparents and grandchildren, it's also helpful to the establishment of good GP-GC relations, the cohesion among family members and the harmony and stability of the society (Song and Fan 2016).

2.3 Intergenerational Interaction Orientation

Intergenerational interaction is conducted on the premise that increased contact or interaction could promote intergenerational communication and understanding. Factors affecting intergenerational contact and communication were discussed, as well as how to promote meaningful intergenerational social interactions, eliminate disagreement and develop friendship between generations through favorable change in environment and increased dialogue (Fox and Giles 1993). Affective interaction, as an adaptive behavior, is an evolutionary force of human survival and fertility. While the differences between generations in terms of age, self-respect, life purpose, socio-economic class, fear of aging, social regulation, social distance and view on vitality of generations, etc. will impact communication quality and change the attitude in current contact and behaviors in future contact (Kalpana and Rosaline 2018). Fox and Giles (1993) paid more attention to the factors of contact process, environment and situation, behaviors and communication exchanges in intergenerational interactions.

3 Method

Focused on Chinese GP-GC intergenerational relations at the childhood stage, this study aims at extracting GP-GC intergenerational affective interaction needs and value propositions that accords with China's national conditions. Study object is set to be families that have grandparents of 60–75 years old and children of 4–12 years old. Research process and methods adopted are illustrated in Fig. 1.

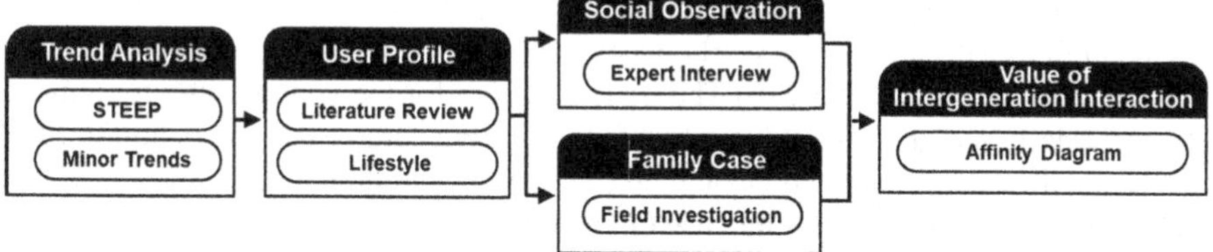

Fig. 1. Research process and methods

Firstly, STEEP trend analysis approach was adopted to sort out minor trends of intergenerational interaction through analyzing society, technology, economics, ecology, and politics-oriented literatures on aging and baby bust. Secondly, user profile of typical Chinese GP-GC generations were obtained through study of statistics and materials published by public authorities and literature review. Thirdly, in order to achieve a complete view of intergenerational interaction observation and analysis, social topics of discussion from the perspective of Chinese society were formed according to the literature review results; seven scholars and social workers in the field of GP-GC relations were invited to an expert interview to discuss observations in daily life and give advices on improvement of intergenerational relations; family cases of GP-GC relations were collected, and field investigation was conducted on six voluntary families of typical user characteristics. After that, expert interview transcript and field investigation video were sorted out to conclude findings. Fourthly, a discussion group was formed in terms of the common point between intergenerational interaction issues and phenomenon scenarios, group members adopted affinity diagram approach and design thinking viewpoint to figure out design clues/triggers, wrote them down on sticky notes (each idea on one page), and took turns to explain each observation point. Lastly, observation points were gathered within the group, differences in GP/GC generations' Wants and Needs (W&Ns) and their physical/mental characteristics were sorted out by adopting structured method; intergenerational interaction needs and affective images were analyzed; and value propositions of intergenerational interaction product were summarized.

4 Results

4.1 Minor Trends of GP-GC Intergenerational Interaction Groups

Considering possible future change of target group's lifestyle and values through development trends of STEEP five fields, we could foresee possible user concerns and hidden requirements in developing intergenerational interactive products. Minor trends were analyzed as follows:

(1) **Widening age gap between grandparents and children.**
Under the general trend of aging and baby bust, there derive minor tendencies such as late marriage and late childbearing. Age gap between grandparents and children is widening, which might bring following issues and derivational problems: (a) Difference in ideas and perceptions. In this case, how should they interact? What

problems will it cause? What are the derived demands? (b) Change of external conditions will cause difference between GP-GC generations. How is this difference related to generation gap? (b) The issue of caring for the young. After retirement, the elderly prefer to enjoy his own life than taking care of the grandchildren. But for dual-earner family, who would take care of the children then?

(2) **Solve the problem of taking care of each other.**
In the need of taking care of each other, following family forms might be derived: (a) (young/old) live in one community but not the same building; (b) live in one building but not on the same floor; (c) live within 5–10 min' walking distance (the distance of a bowl of steaming soup); (d) live within 15–20 min' car drive distance; (e) as long as family members live close, they can look after each other and provide support in emergency.

(3) **Family restructuring.**
Under the tendency of family member relationship diversification, new family types such as split households, holiday parents, commuter marriage and other false-single parent households are formed.

4.2 User Profile

Through study of statistics and materials published by public authorities and literature review, it was found that Chinese family structures are mainly nuclear family and three-generation family; dual-earner family with one child is typical city family pattern in modern China.

4.3 Social Observation Analysis and Family Case Study

Findings of expert interview transcript and field investigation video were sorted out and key points and discussion topics/phenomena were concluded as follows:

(1) **Except for grandparents and grandchildren generations, children's parents should also be included as a target in the GP-GC intergeneration interaction.**
According to experiences shared by numerous participants, however close the GP-GC relation is, the issue of children's education should still be taken charge of by their parents, as grandparents' tough educational mode could conflict with that of parents'. Thus, do not overlook parents' family role when thinking about GP-GC interactive relations.

(2) **In GP-GC interaction, grandparents and grandchildren are companions instead of superior-subordinate relations.**
An equal relationship of companion, as well as an interesting way of interaction, is essential to generations interacting easily, longer and fore more times.

(3) **Joint tasks for grandparents and grandchildren or activities that require manual operation which is interesting for both generations.**
Interaction activities/products must be interesting to both generations in order to make GP-GC interactions more natural and frequent. Besides, activities that require manual operation would be more attracting and yield more happiness when accomplished.

(4) **Activities that encourages more physical contact between grandparents and grandchildren.**
Because of limited time of getting together, grandparents would call for more close contact, hug or kiss, with their grandchildren through interaction. Thus if the activities/facilities could promote physical contact, the willingness of grandparents to join/use would be increase greatly. Also, grandchildren can feel more sense of closeness and trust from physical contacts.

(5) **Produce moderate user viscosity and provide opportunities for grandchildren to develop creativity.**
A well-designed activity/product will give play to grandchildren's creativity but bring them no extra stress. Also, attention must be paid to the physical strength and safety issues of the grandparents, and activities/products should be easy for them to use. Stimulated by new learning and based on daily life situations, grandchildren may raise questions full of imagination. The pattern of "children keeping asking questions" and "grandparents sharing rich life experiences" could bring more happiness to both generations (Table 1).

Table 1. Social observation and family case study result

Topic/ phenomena	Content
Serve the desire of expressing oneself	Grandchildren's desire for teaching and being a teacher
	Grandchildren are easily affected by the education of caregivers
	Grandparents' old knowledge may undermine children's creativity
	Grandchildren adopt jump thinking in learning
	Grandchildren love to be "little pickets"
	Perform grown up's rights of education, personality
	Grandchildren's performance desire, feeling of honor
	Should adopt heuristic teaching and guided learning
	Preschool education and guidance
	Return to the nature of being human-oriented
Share and interact for knowledge	Who in the family loves to share knowledge?
	Who in the family loves to acquire knowledge?
	Will it provide stimulations for children to raise questions?
	Is it a must to answer children's questions with the "correct answer"? How about searching answers together?
Experience mutual understanding	Have shared experience and memory
	Listening is important

(*continued*)

Table 1. (*continued*)

Topic/ phenomena	Content
	What approaches can bring two parities closer through other than interaction?
	Discover similarities and differences between individuals
	Break boundaries
Can bring two generations heart to heart	Intergenerational GP/GC interaction layout
	Respect characteristics of different ages
	Solve the recognition difference between grandparents and grandchildren
	Grandparents and grandchildren are connected through something they have in common
	Promote mutual understand through role exchange
	Participate in joint activities, create memory and enjoy learning achievements
	Grandchildren should learn to care about others, instead of regarding himself as the center of the world
	Emotional connection
	Individuals are born different
	GP-GC co-learning
	GPs generation is less willing to invest in playing games
Product nature should be user-oriented	Avoid to be too commoditize to consider interpersonal emotional interaction
	Product design should be humanized and user-oriented, and should follow the principle of product meeting user needs rather than the opposite
	Avoid making users too addicted but ignoring interpersonal interactions
	Intergenerational interaction calls for common prosperity, joint operation and shared fun for both generations
	User is subject to product
	Contribute to GP-GC interaction
	Joint operation of both parties
Should embody diversification and be attractive for longer time	Increase time for fun and adhesive force. Limited time but repeated contact
	Product should develop along with age line
Develop diversified life for the grandparents	Second life
	New life after retirement
	The elderly lives healthy and fulfilling life; be accepted and achieves self-fulfillment
	Narrowed daily life circle of the elderly (explore new areas and broaden horizon)

(*continued*)

Table 1. (*continued*)

Topic/ phenomena	Content
	The elderly's life after retirement will be affected by taking care of the young
Experience inheritance	Rich experience; knowledgeable
	Children is full of imagination
	Grandchildren like to ask questions, some of which are very difficult to answer
	Grandparents give play to their strong points of mentoring and teaching
	Grandparents relearn new knowledge & experience
	To pass on the stories and personal experiences of grandparents to younger generations
	Grandparents actually like the feeling of freshness and are actually curious about new knowledge
	Give play to grandparents' strong points and give them feeling of achievements
Can promote recognition of both generations	Promote affective communication through shared experience
	Promote sense of mutual trust
	Build environment to stay together which is comfortable to both generations

Source: Collation of this study

4.4 Motivation, Wants and Needs and Interaction Value

Through a series of user study process, differences of GP/GC generations' Wants and Needs (W&Ns) and their physical/mental characteristics were sorted out, and relevant intergenerational interaction values are summarized through Affinity Diagram approach as Fig. 2. Searching for the source, we found that "having fun together" is a catalyst that directly promotes close relationships and happiness for the two generations.

In terms of participation motivation and benefits, grandparents and grandchildren both pay greater attention to experience pattern than to interestingness while learning is at the last. In terms of two generations' W&Ns, there is much in common that both expect attentions from others and like the feeling of being needed. In terms of personal ability and self-confidence, degree of individual importance can be promoted through mutual help between generations. In terms of requirements and value, product design should: embody activities that promote GP/GC physical contacts or interesting joint tasks that require manual operation of both generations; provide opportunities for the young to give play to their creativity; meet the requirement of outdoor leisure activities and family trips; and keep record of the growth process and happy time spent together.

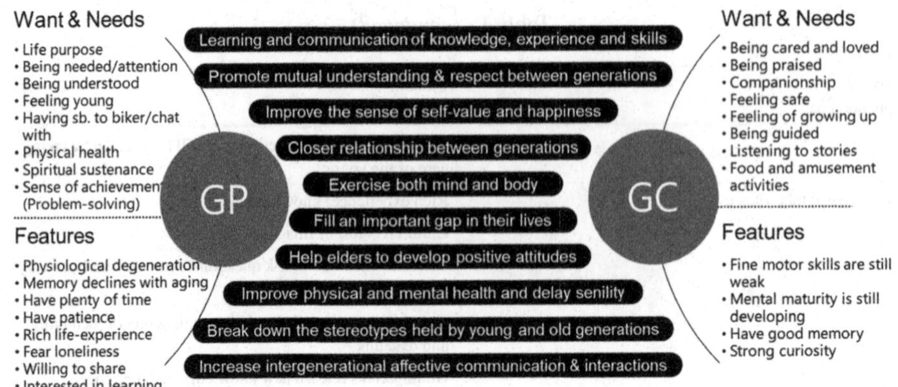

Fig. 2. Value relations of GP-GC intergenerational interaction

5 Conclusions and Suggestions

Out of empathy, parents of the post-baby boom generation tend to prevent the next generation from bearing heavy family burdens like them did. Mostly, they relieved children's family responsibilities by not requiring them to look after or live with the old, nor to bear the burden of household expenses. While on the other hand, some of the elderly tend to get rid of the bond and stay away from traditional family responsibilities of looking after grandchildren, but prefer to travel around the nation and the world. It is possible that traditional concepts of grandparents taking care of the grandchildren, bring up sons to support parents in their old age and carrying on the family line could be abandoned in the next generation.

Based on explorations of GP-GC intergenerational affective interaction product design, we analyzed research data from Chinese society observation and user study and extracted following features of emotional images that should be embodied in intergenerational interaction products as: being happy, funny and memory-related. Therefore, design of GP-GC intergenerational interacting products should meet following requirements: (1) activity time of 30–50 min; (2) sufficient room for grandparents and grandchildren to excise physically; (3) plenty stimulations for both generations to participate in; (4) being experience-required; grandparents can give guidance to grandchildren through personal knowledge, experience and skills; (5) creating happy and funny emotional images that promotes development tendency of grandparents and grandchildren having fun together.

"Value proposition" refers to the benefits that target users can expect to receive from created products or services. Based on above discussions, we can conclude that GP-GC intergenerational relation is everlasting; any physical or emotional support should be based on living needs or spiritual sustenance. Thus the value proposition of intergenerational interaction products should be "Take a step forward, create shared happiness".

Acknowledgments. Supported by the Science and Technology Research Program of Chongqing Municipal Education Commission (Grant No. KJZD-K201901001) and the Sichuan Province Academy of Fine Arts PhD Major Project Cultivation Project (Project Number: 19BSPY010).

References

Becker, O.A., Steinbach, A.: Relations between grandparents and grandchildren in the context of the family system. Comp. Popul. Stud. **37**(3–4) (2012)

Brussoni, M.J., Boon, S.D.: Grandparental impact in young adults' relationships with their closest grandparents: the role of relationship strength and emotional closeness. Int. J. Aging Hum. Dev. **46**(4), 267–286 (1998)

de Souza, E.M., Grundy, E.: Intergenerational interaction, social capital and health: results from a randomised controlled trial in Brazil. Soc. Sci. Med. **65**(7), 1397–1409 (2007)

Fox, S., Giles, H.: Accommodating intergenerational contact: a critique and theoretical model. J. Aging Stud. **7**(4), 423–451 (1993)

Harwood, J.: Understanding Communication and Aging: Developing Knowledge and Awareness. Sage, Thousand Oaks (2007)

Hoff, A.: Patterns of intergenerational support in grandparent-grandchild and parent-child relationships in Germany. Ageing Soc. **27**(5), 643–665 (2007)

Hopkins, G.R.: How important are intergenerational programs in today's schools? Phi Delta Kappan **82**(4), 317–319 (2000)

Huang, K.-L., Yuan, N.-C., Tai, W.-Y.: A user study of intergenerational interaction product: from sociological analysis to value proposition. Paper presented at the 2015 International Conference on Kansei Engineering: Sensibility and Rationality Chang Gung University, Taiwan (2015)

Kalpana, D., Rosaline, D.Z.: Intergenerational relationship between grandchildren and grandparents – an overview. Res. Rev. Int. J. Multidiscip. **3**(7), 169–171 (2018)

Mansson, D.H., Floyd, K., Soliz, J.: Affectionate communication is associated with emotional and relational resources in the grandparent-grandchild relationship. J. Intergenerational Relationsh. **15**(2), 85–103 (2017)

Mansson, D.H., Myers, S.A., Turner, L.H.: Relational maintenance behaviors in the grandchild–grandparent relationship. Commun. Res. Rep. **27**(1), 68–79 (2010)

Yuesheng, W.: Theoretical analysis of intergenerational relations in Chinese family. Popul. Res. **2008**(4), 13–21 (2008)

Song, J., Fan, W.: Emotional relation between generations in Chinese urban families-an empirical study in the perspective of the only Chind's life course. South China Popul. **31**(2), 26–35 (2016)

Yang, J., Li, L.: Intergenerational dynamics and family solidarity: a comparative study of mainland China, Japan, Korea and Taiwan. Soc. Stud. (3), 26–53 (2009)

Discriminative Model for Identifying Motion Primitives Based on Virtual Reality-Based IADL

Yasuhiro Iwashita[1(✉)], Takehiko Yamaguchi[1], Tania Giovannetti[2], Maiko Sakamoto[3], and Hayato Ohwada[4]

[1] Suwa University of Science, 5000-1 Toyohira, Chino, Nagano, Japan
s316012@ed.sus.ac.jp, tk-ymgch@rs.sus.ac.jp

[2] Temple University, Philadelphia, PA 19122, USA
tgio@temple.edu

[3] Saga University, 5-1-1 Nabeshima Saga, Saga, Japan
masaka@cc.saga-u.ac.jp

[4] Tokyo University of Science, 2641 Yamazaki, Noda, Chiba, Japan

Abstract. Although the number of patients with dementia has been increasing with the aging of society, no efficient treatment for advanced dementia forms has been proposed yet. Therefore, it is important to detect mild cognitive impairment (MCI) to prevent dementia from further progressing. According to a recent study, people with MCI tend to perform more inefficiently compared with healthy older adults during performance-based tests on instrumental activities of daily living (IADL). In this research, we aim to develop a discriminative model to identify motion primitives based on virtual reality-based IADL. In the experiment, finger movement was measured through the Lunchbox Task simulating meal preparation using a touch panel and a three-dimensional motion sensor. The time series velocity was estimated from the obtained position data, and segmentation was conducted based on the property of the reaching motion between two points. Considering the data of each segment interval, feature extraction and coding were performed according to the predefined motion primitives, and modeling based on machine learning was implemented. As a result, the identification accuracy of motion primitives was 97.1%. Sensitivity by category was 99% for stationary actions, 93% for pointing, 97% for drag, and 93% for click or release. These results indicate that hand movements during VR-IADL can be classified into four categories based on their behavioral characteristics. On this basis, the automatic identification of the motion primitive in VR-IADL is deemed realizable.

Keywords: Mild cognitive impairment · Instrumental activities of daily living · Virtual reality.

1 Introduction

An important problem presented in an aging society is an increase in the number of dementia patients. As of 2018, it has been estimated that the number of people suffering from dementia worldwide would increase from 50 million to 82 million by 2030 and to

C. Stephanidis et al. (Eds.): HCII 2020, LNCS 12426, pp. 574–585, 2020.
https://doi.org/10.1007/978-3-030-60149-2_44

152 million by 2050 [1]. In Japan, it has been estimated that the number of people with dementia would increase to about 4.62 million in 2012 and 7 million in 2025 [2]. The disease type of dementia is generally classified as Alzheimer's disease (AD) and vascular dementia. People with dementia of AD-type constitute from 40% to 60% of the total number of patients. The cause of the onset of this disease has not been clarified yet, and efficient treatment methods have not been discovered. Therefore, at present, it is possible to focus only on the deceleration of the disease progression. Several related studies have focused on mild cognitive impairment (MCI), which is a precursor of dementia. MCI corresponds to an intermediate stage between the normal state and dementia, and it is reported that approximately 50% of MCI patients progress to dementia within five years [3]. However, it is suggested that MCI may be reversed to the normal cognitive status owing to appropriate rehabilitation [4]. Therefore, early detection and treatment of MCI is an essential issue to prevent dementia.

To perform early MCI detection, it is necessary to perform early screening. Current screening methods for dementia include brain imaging using functional magnetic resonance imaging (fMRI) and cognitive function tests, such as mini-mental state examination (MMSE), revised Hasegawa dementia scale (HDR-S), Montreal cognitive assessment, and clinical dementia rating (CDR) [5, 6]. These tests are conducted in a face-to-face manner and are intended to evaluate the subject's memory, awareness, executive function, etc. However, the discrimination accuracy of MMSE corresponding to the severe disability stage is approximately 100% at the stage of moderate dementia and approximately 50% at the stage of mild dementia, and that of the MCI stage is only about 30%. As a result, it is considered that it is difficult to distinguish the difference between healthy conditions and a slight symptom, as the timing, which can be used to identify a pathological dysfunction in the process of healthy aging, is not clarified. In addition, there is a problem that the corresponding examination requires time and labor. Therefore, it is necessary to develop a new screening method capable of mitigating these issues.

1.1 Previous Study

Recently, research focused on instrumental activities of daily living (IADL) has advanced considerably. IADL refers to everyday activities such as shopping, preparing meals, managing money, and traveling using transportation. Compared with necessary activities of daily living such as moving, bathing, eating, and dressing, IADL movements are more complex and require more careful consideration [7, 8].

Therefore, in the previous study, the naturalistic action test (NAT) was developed to evaluate the performance of IADL [9]. NAT is a task that reproduces IADL on a table. We evaluated the IADL performance based on the difference in the frequency of human errors caused by a functional decline. It was assumed that analyzing human errors can help in distinguishing MCI patients from healthy people.

However, establishing an IADL task environment in a real space, such as NAT, requires a considerable amount of time. Moreover, it was not suitable for mass screening because of the large number of objects required for tasks. To solve the problem of IADL tasks in the real space, we proposed the virtual kitchen challenge (VKC) using the virtual reality (VR) technology [10, 11]. VKC is a task that simplifies NAT and reproduces it in a virtual space. IADL in VKC (VR-IADL) is space-saving, and the required measurement time is shorter compared with that in NAT.

An attempt to evaluate the IADL performance using the proposed VR-IADL approach is underway. Specifically, the research on operation frequency was conducted to perform the clustering of a healthy subject and an MCI patient based on the generation frequency of the motion primitives, which were considered the smallest units of motion in VR-IADL. By applying LDA (Latent Semantic Analysis) model to motion frequency data such as touching and dragging objects, clustering was carried out. According to the estimation results, the proportion of healthy university students fitting Topic 3 was high, and the proportion of MCI patients fitting Topic 2 was also high. The topic was not confirmed only concerning healthy older adults, and therefore, the corresponding proportion was divided among Topics 2 and 3. These results indicated that there was a difference in the methods of performing movements during VKC between healthy university students and MCI patients. It was confirmed that the healthy elderly represented the features of both healthy university students and MCI patients. However, in the previous study, the determination of motion primitives was performed only by analyzing video materials. Therefore, the subjective view of the observer might have affected the results. Moreover, there was a problem that only movements on the screen, such as touch and drag, could be registered in the action during the task. Consequently, it is necessary to formulate the index for objectively evaluating the action primitive. In the present study, we aimed to develop a discriminative model of motion primitives based on VR-based IADL by measuring and recording the movement of a fingertip of a subject during VR-IADL and analyzing the obtained time series and video data.

2 Method

2.1 Lunchbox Task

VKC allows the execution of two tasks: a Toast-and-Coffee Task and a Lunchbox Task. Each task is supposed to reproduce the breakfast and lunch preparation behaviors, respectively. These tasks consist of several main tasks and a number of subtasks and can be evaluated according to the degree of completion of a task. The Lunchbox Task considered in this experiment includes three main tasks: preparing sandwiches and cookies, filling in water bottles, and putting sandwiches, cookies and water bottles in the lunch box. Each process is implemented by considering 16 subtasks in total.

The Sandwich Task consists of eight subtasks: (1) place a piece of bread on a paper towel, (2) open a jar of blueberry jam, (3) spread the blueberry jam on the bread, (4) open a jar of peanut butter, (5) spread the peanut butter on the bread, (6) close with another piece of bread and make a sandwich, (7) wrap the sandwich in aluminum foil, and (8) place the wrapped sandwich in a lunch box.

The Cookie Task consists of three subtasks: (1) placing all three cookies on a paper towel, (2) wrapping three cookies together with aluminum foil, and (3) placing the wrapped cookies in a lunch box.

The Water Bottle Task consists of five subtasks: (1) open the lid of the juice, (2) pour the juice into the water bottle, (3) close the inner lid of the water bottle, (4) close the outer lid of the water bottle, and (5) put the water bottle into the lunch box.

After completing the three main tasks, the final task is to close the lunch box lid and then to press the quit button in the upper right of the screen to finish. These tasks can be performed in any order according to the preferences of a subject. If the quit button is pressed before all of the tasks are completed, it is regarded as finished. The experiment was conducted after the training and studying the procedure description, and the subtasks were performed once before the start of the experiment. After these preparation steps, it was confirmed that an examinee could understand the test procedure. Figure 1 shows the Lunchbox Task established in VKC.

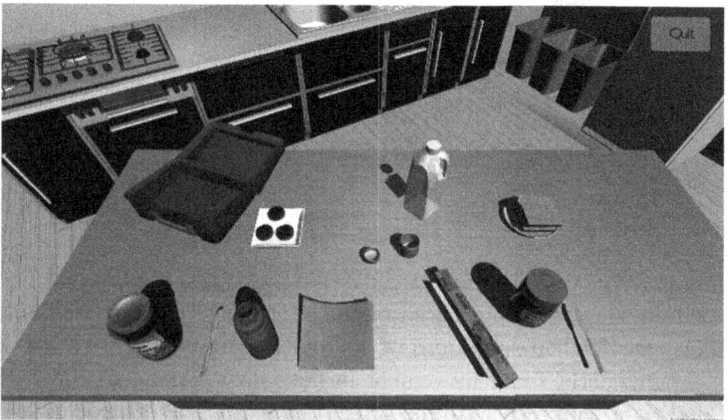

Fig. 1. Screen of the lunchbox task

In this experiment, a 24-in monitor (Dell P 2418 HT) with a touch panel, which was laid on a desk, was used. Subjects were asked to sit down in front of the monitor and manipulate the objects on the screen using only the right-hand index finger. The experiment was recorded using a web camera attached to the top of the monitor. For the measurement of the finger movement during the experiment, the position data were obtained using the reflection marker placed on the fingertip composed of OptiTrack of Acuity Co., which is a high-precision three-dimensional motion sensor. The sampling rate during the measurement was 120 Hz, and the video was shot at 60 fps. Figure 2 outlines the experimental environment.

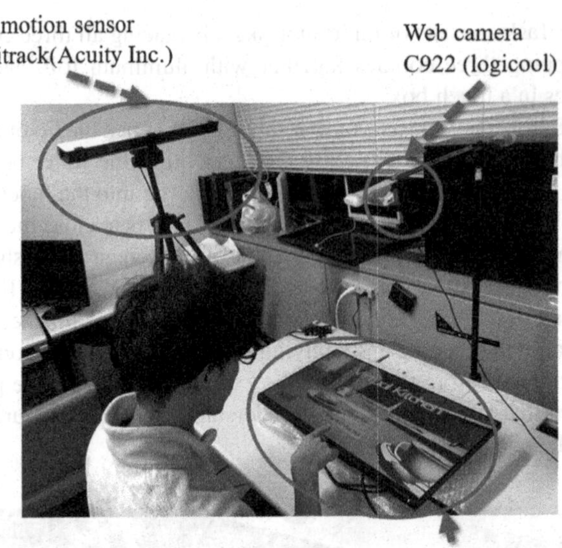

Fig. 2. Experimental environment

2.2 Motion Primitive

In the present study, motion primitives are classified into four categories (static, pointing, dragging, and clicking/releasing) based on the video materials recorded during tasks. Figure 3 shows the detailed definitions of the four categories. Here, a static action was defined as a particularly small movement in the x-axis and z-axis directions (front, back, left, and right with respect to the screen), pointing was considered a significant movement in the x-axis and z-axis directions or a movement in the y-axis direction (vertical direction of the screen) not equal to 0, dragging was defined as a significant movement in the x-axis and z-axis directions or a movement in the y-axis of 0, and finally, clicking or releasing was considered a small movement in the x-axis and z-axis directions and a movement in the y-axis direction crossing 0 (height of the finger at the edge of the screen).

All movements observed during VR-IADL were considered to be explained by combinations of these movements, and motion analysis was performed accordingly.

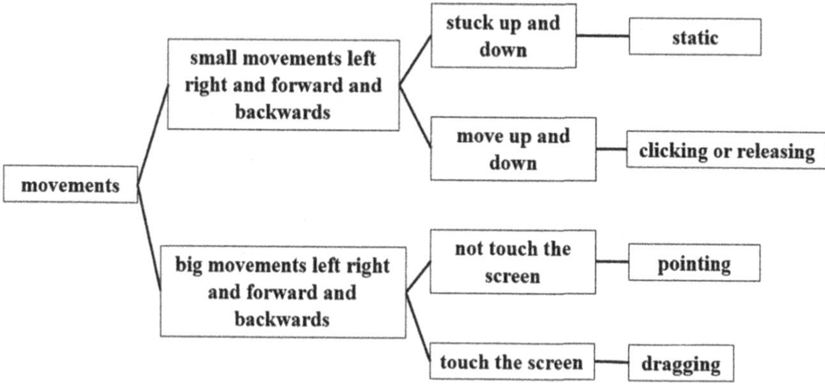

Fig. 3. Definition of motion primitives

2.3 Time Series Segmentation

The time series data on the speed were obtained by calculating the speed from the position data provided by a three-dimensional motion sensor. We considered using these data to identify the motion primitives. To do so, it was necessary to segment the time series data according to motion primitives. Then, the motion observed during the task was segmented by considering the continuation of the reaching motion between two points in which it was considered that the velocity and acceleration became 0 in the starting point and the reaching point of the motion. The segmentation was conducted concerning the zero intersection of the acceleration. Equation (1) represents the formula used to calculate the segmentation. To estimate the direction of an acceleration vector to obtain a zero-crossing point at an arrival point, Eq. (2) represents the sign of acceleration as 1 or 0. Here, the zero intersection was obtained from the multiplication of a certain acceleration point and the preceding acceleration point according to Eq. (3).

$$Segment(t) = \begin{cases} zerocross(step(a)) = 1 \\ zerocross(step(a)) = 0 \end{cases}, \tag{1}$$

$$\because step(a) = \begin{cases} 1(a \geq 0) \\ 0(a < 0) \end{cases}, \tag{2}$$

$$\because zerocross(a) = \begin{cases} 1 if\,(a_i * a_{i-1}) \\ 0 if\,(a_i * a_{i-1}) \end{cases}. \tag{3}$$

However, in actual motion, segment points can be excessively detected for local speed changes so that unnatural segmentation may occur in the middle of motion, as shown in Fig. 4.

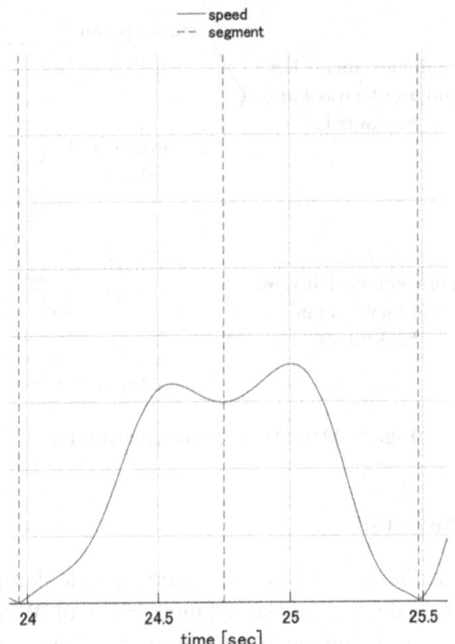

Fig. 4. Segmentation error

In the present study, we applied machine learning to identify the criteria for segmentation. Specifically, for each segment point obtained from the zero intersection of acceleration, it was analyzed whether a segmentation result was correct or not, and the processing to eliminate erroneous segmentation was performed. Figure 5 shows the corresponding algorithm formulated to implement this step.

First, we calculated and coded the feature values corresponding to segment points and constructed the training dataset. Second, the model used to correct the segmentation results by applying machine learning to the target dataset was formulated, and the accuracy was evaluated accordingly. Then, the motion primitive was identified based on the finally obtained segment point. The feature quantity for each segment interval was extracted according to the definition of the action primitive. Furthermore, a label column of the data used for coding was established based on each action primitive obtained from the video data to save the results as a CSV file. The model used to distinguish actions in the task into four categories (static, pointing, dragging, and clicking/releasing) was formulated based on machine learning applied to the dataset, and the accuracy was evaluated accordingly.

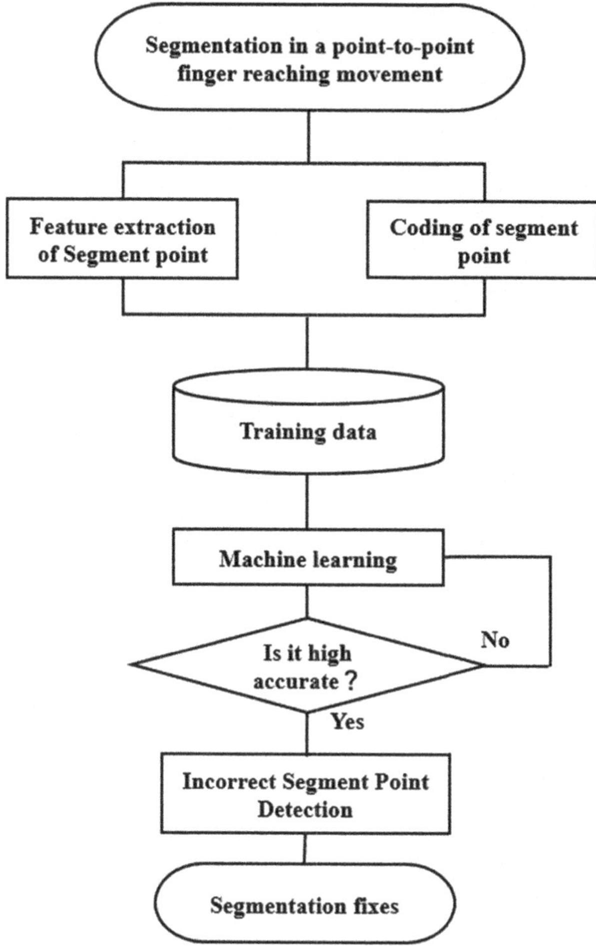

Fig. 5. Segmentation algorithm

3 Results and Discussion

3.1 Discriminative Model of Segmentation

For a group of six healthy subjects (Mean = 22.0, Standard Deviation = 0.63), the difference between the position data of the time series obtained using the three-dimensional motion sensor was calculated as the speed, and the difference between the speed values was calculated as the acceleration. At first, the segmentation was conducted at a point in which the acceleration switched from negative to positive, and then, calculation and coding of the feature quantity of each segment point were performed. The dataset was constructed by considering the four features: velocity at the segment, temporal velocity decrease, velocity increase calculated from the peak values before and after the segment, and the presence or absence of a zero intersection at the y coordinate. The total size of the dataset was 1,157 points for each feature. Figure 6 outlines the results of modeling using

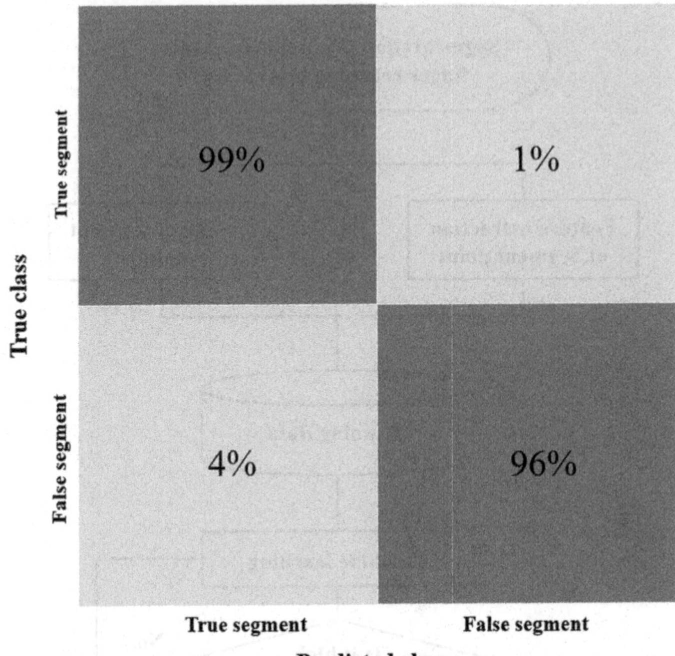

Fig. 6. Confusion matrix of the error detection result using a classification learner

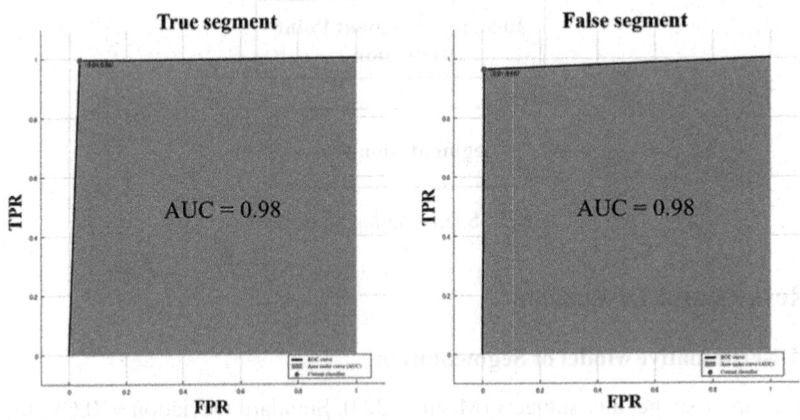

Fig. 7. ROC curve

the decision tree applied to the constructed dataset, and Fig. 7 depicts the corresponding ROC curve.

As a result, it was possible to implement the model with a high accuracy of 99.4%. Sensitivity by category was 99% for the correct segments and 96% for the incorrect segments that is segmented during a point to point motion. As this result, it is considered that it was possible to carry out the right and wrong decision of the high-precise segmentation. Based on this model, we conclude that it is possible to obtain partial time series data of a motion primitive unit.

3.2 Discriminative Model of Motion Primitives

For a group of healthy subjects, including 30 persons (Mean = 22.4, Standard Deviation = 2.67), Lunchbox task was conducted. The segmentation was performed based on the time series data of the speed and the y coordinate of the operation of a finger in the task, and then, the operation primitive was coded for every segment interval. Figure 8 shows an example of the correspondence between the segmented time series data and a corresponding action primitive. Next, basic statistics such as an average and a variance of velocity, an average of the y coordinate, and the existence of zero crossings of the y coordinate were calculated for each segmented interval, and a dataset was constructed as a feature quantity of each segment interval.

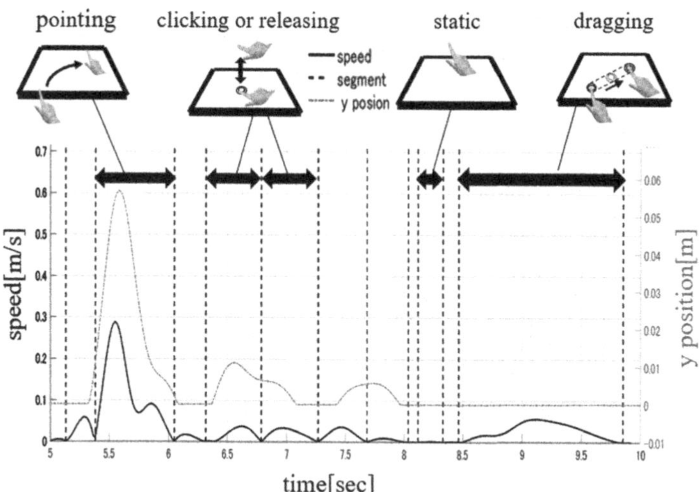

Fig. 8. Example of the correspondence between the time series data and motion primitives

The total number of points in the dataset was 6224 for each feature. At this time, 156 data points that did not fit the predefined four categories were considered out of the category and excluded. Figure 9 shows the result of modeling using ensemble learning based on this dataset, and Fig. 10 shows the ROC curves for each category.

As a result, it was possible to formulate a model with a high discrimination accuracy of 97.1%. Sensitivity by category was 99% for static actions, 93% for pointing, 97% for dragging, and 93% for clicking or releasing. It was suggested that finger movements during the VR-IADL tasks could be classified according to the four categories depending on their behavioral characteristics: rest, pointing, dragging, and clicking or releasing. Therefore, it is considered that automatic identification of motion primitives in VR-IADL is deemed realizable.

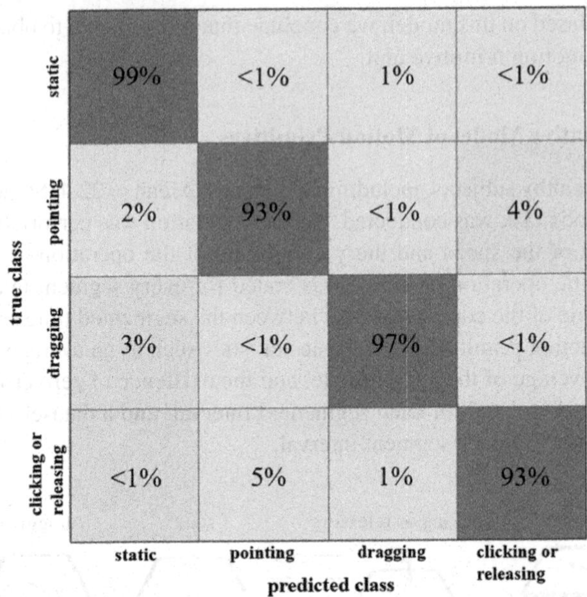

Fig. 9. Confusion matrix of the identification result using a classification learner

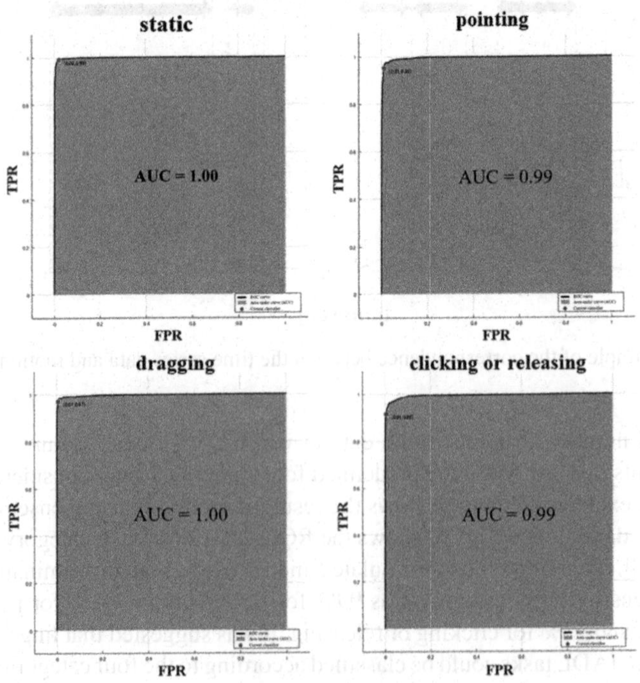

Fig. 10. ROC curve

4 Conclusion

In the present study, we developed a model to identify motion primitives in VR-IADL tasks by analyzing the time series and video data obtained by measuring and recording fingertip movements during VR-IADL. It is suggested that the time series velocity data can be divided into four categories corresponding to motion primitives. As a future study, considering that the object of the conducted experiment has only been young healthy subjects, comparison and examination of the discrimination accuracy of the model concerning healthy older adults and MCI patients will be conducted to avoid bias corresponding to the examinee. Moreover, it is necessary to verify whether there is a difference in the clustering results obtained for the healthy subject and MCI patients by analyzing the operating frequency and concerning the difference between the operation primitive defined in the present paper and those of the previous research work.

References

1. World Alzheimer Report 2018: The Global Impact of Dementia, p. 34 (2018)
2. Comprehensive Promotion of Measures for Dementia - Ministry of Health, Labour and Welfare (2019). https://www.mhlw.go.jp/content/12300000/000519620.pdf
3. Yasuji, Y.: Current topics about mild cognitive impairment (MCI). Psychiatria et Neurologia Jponica **113**(6), 584–592 (2011)
4. Malek-Ahmadi, M.: Reversion from mild cognitive impairment to normal cognition: a meta-analysis. Alzheimer Dis. Assoc. Disord. **30**(4), 324–330 (2016)
5. Shojei, K., Yuta, S., Akiko, K., Toshiaki, K., Hidenori, I., Akira, H.: A preliminary study of speech peosody-based. Trans. Jpn. Soc. Artif. Intell. **26**(2), 347–352 (2011)
6. Fujiwara, Y., et al.: Brief screening tool for mild cognitive impairment in older Japanese: validation of the Japanese version of the montreal cognitive assessment. Geriatr. Gerontol. Int. **10**(3), 225–232 (2010)
7. Wadley, V.G., Okonkwo, O., Crowe, M., Ross-Meadows, L.A.: Mild cognitive impairment and everyday function: evidence of reduced speed in performing instrumental activities of daily living. Am. J. Geriatr. Psychiatry **16**(5), 416–424 (2008)
8. Schmitter-Edgecombe, M., McAlister, C., Weakley, A.: Naturalistic assessment of everyday functioning in individuals with mild cognitive impairment: the day-out task. Neuropsychology **26**(5), 631–641 (2012)
9. Schwartz, M.F., Segal, M.E., Veramonti, T., Ferraro, M.K., Buxbaum, L.J.: The naturalistic action test: a standardised assessment for everyday action impairment. Neuropsychological **12**(4), 311–339 (2002)
10. Yamaguchi, T., Foloppe, D.A., Richard, P., Richard, E., Allain, P.: A dual-modal virtual reality kitchen for (re) learning of everyday cooking activities in Alzheimer's disease. Presence Teleoperators Virtual Environ. **21**(1), 43–57 (2012)
11. Giovannetti, T., et al.: The virtual kitchen challenge: preliminary data from a novel virtual reality test of mild difficulties in everyday functioning. Neuropsychological **26**(6), 823–841 (2019)
12. Shirotori, A., et al.: Topic Model-based Clustering for IADL Motion Primitives (2019)

The Relationship Between the Seniors' Appraisal of Cognitive-Training Games and Game-Related Stress Is Complex: A Mixed-Methods Study

Najmeh Khalili-Mahani[1,2,3](✉), Bob de Schutter[4], and Kim Sawchuk[3,5]

[1] PERFORM Centre, Concordia University, Montreal, QC, Canada
najmeh.khalili-mahani@concordia.ca
[2] McGill Centre for Integrative Neuroscience, McGill University, Montreal, QC, Canada
[3] engAGE Centre for Studies in Aging, Concordia University, Montreal, QC, Canada
kim.sawchuk@concordia.ca
[4] Armstrong Institute for Interactive Media Studies, Miami University, Oxford, OH, USA
b@bobdeschutter.be
[5] Department of Communication Studies, Concordia University, Montreal, QC, Canada

Abstract. In this paper, we deploy and evaluate the potential of the Affective Game Planning for Health Applications (AGPHA) framework, that draws on Lazarus' Appraisal Theory of Stress and Coping for evaluation of reflexive and reflexive response to a brain training game. Fourty two older adults (70.5 ± 4.5 years of age) took an electronic survey about attitude towards digital play. A smaller sample of this sample (n = 19) volunteered to participate in an experiment to play a simple brain training game (*Simple MindGames*) in a laboratory setting (PERFORM Centre, Montreal, Canada). The study was framed in a quantitative context and involved repeated measurements of physiological stress metrics (salivary cortisol, galvanic skin conductance, and heart rate). We found that those who participated in the experiment were less likely to consider digital games too hard to learn, age-inappropriate, or disruptive to real life. Physiological measures were correlated with some of game experience factors, namely perceived visual intensity of the games was correlated with cortisol levels (Spearman's $rho = 0.61$, $p < .01$), and disliking the game was correlated with heart rate ($rho = 0.47$, $p < .05$) and EDA ($rho = 0.53$, $p < .05$). These physiological measures were indirectly linked to pre-playing assumptions about digital games being *too hard to learn* and *disruptive to real life*; and to the post-game assessment of the game as *useless*. Our findings underline the importance of appraisal factors that can make the experience of game playing stressful or enjoyable for older adults. Monitoring the primary appraisal factors, and iterative evaluation of secondary appraisal in different stages of game learning are important both in designing, and in clinical evaluation of games with expected health-related outcomes.

Keywords: Cognitive games · Theory of stress · Mixed methods · Interindividual differences · Serious games · Older adults · Human computer interface · Cognitive and emotional arousal · Physiological monitoring · Cortisol

C. Stephanidis et al. (Eds.): HCII 2020, LNCS 12426, pp. 586–607, 2020.
https://doi.org/10.1007/978-3-030-60149-2_45

1 Introduction

In recent years, the rapid growth of smart-computing and interactive communication technologies has opened important frontiers in the design and development of digital health strategies at the level of screening, prevention and importantly, intervention and rehabilitation. The potential for providing assistive care to older adults through these strategies is tremendous, once we overcome the existing and well-documented challenges with acceptability and accessibility of these technologies [1, 2], and when we have developed a standard system of evaluation of the efficacy of health-games [3].

To address these needs, we have proposed a theoretical model that describes the relationship between player's stress (reflective and reflexive), which can be empirically and iteratively tested using psychophysiological assessment methods from stress research [4], and the likelihood of adopting the game.

Our proposed model, Affective Game Planning for Health Applications (AGPHA) [4], builds on an evidence-based Appraisal Theory of Stress by Lazarus [5], which has articulated the relationships between the neurobiology of adaptation and behavioral strategies for learning to overcome challenges (Fig. 1A).

Within neurobiology, research indicates that emotional experiences manifest immediate and quantifiable variations in physiological states [6] and cause reflexive embodied experiences such as changes in heart and breathing rate, galvanic skin response, pupil dilation, facial reflex, movement reflex, gut reflex, etc. These signals have been considered as 'biomarkers' of cognitive and emotional arousal that guide attention, and are often used to study physiological responses to film [7–10] or video-gaming [11] experiences. These physiological reflexes can be altered with distressing or joyful and challenging stimuli, and represent the body's non-specific (but controlled) physiological and endocrinological response to what challenges the body's metabolic homeostasis. Because the stress response represents the sum-total of an increased demand on the metabolic resources of the body, which are needed to restore it to baseline [12], the dynamics of adaptation differ between individuals, based on the resources that are available to them.

Evaluating the physiological stress response to digital games, which are marketed as beneficial to the health and well-being of older adults, is important for several reasons. First, because many seniors are not familiar with them and research indicates that novelty, unpredictability and uncontrollability are generally stressful conditions [13]. Second, because the implied importance of cognitive abilities in game performance might challenge the self-esteem or self efficacy of seniors who may be concerned about their cognitive decline, thus make the game itself into a detrimental stressor [14]. Third, and most importantly, because games should provide a ludic and pleasurable experience for players, thus they can function as de-stressors, especially to distract from pain, to provide behavioral therapies for affective disorders, or to make rehabilitational therapies more enjoyable. All of this is, of course, dependent on a variety of factors specific to an individual, including physical abilities as well as personality and life experience [15]. We argue that methods from stress research can help us quantify the striking balance between the levels of good stress (caused by willingness to engage in a meaningful challenge) and bad stress (caused by the physical or psychological discomfort of the game's mechanics, dynamics or even aesthetics).

Figure 1A summarizes the transactional model of stress appraisal and coping, proposed by Folkman and Lazarus [16]. This model emphasises individual differences in iterative evaluation of, and adaptive coping with, any new challenge. Briefly, when confronted with a challenging encounter, individuals engage in a primary appraisal process in order to categorize the challenge's as irrelevant, benign-positive, or 'stressful,' depending on what implications it could have for their well-being [16]. If a person has no investment in the outcome of the challenge, then they will have no need for it and will not commit to engaging with it. On the other hand, if they perceive immediate or potential benefits, they will experience a positive affective response to increased their

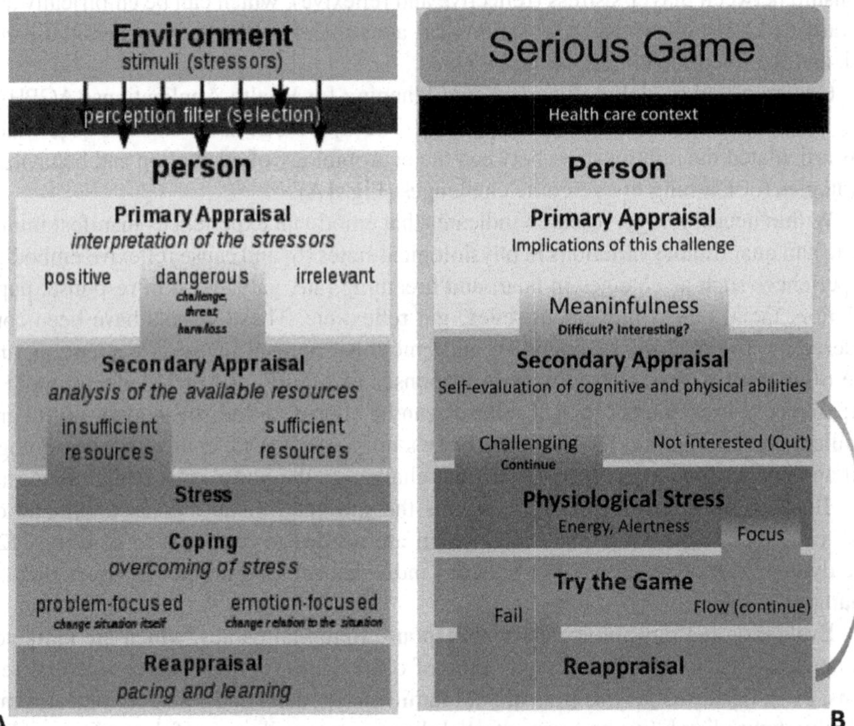

Fig. 1. (A): A diagram of the Lazarus' transactional model (Source: Wikipedia, by Pilipp Guttmann, based on Folkman and Lazarus [16], Stress, Appraisal and Coping. New York: Springer). (B) An adapted experimental model that we can test in the AGPHA framework. When presented with a conceptual game, the primary appraisal of the game is dependent on beliefs about the meaning and value of the game, and the users' perception of the challenge of the game and potential threats to social or physical self. In our adapted model, a positive primary attitude leads to increased cognitive arousal, which helps learning, performing, and feeling more motivated to replay. In contrast, if the primary appraisal is negative, the stress levels are initially high, in order to help the user cope with stress. If this coping produced positive outcome, then the user learns and recovers from initial stress. If the outcome is not successful, then the player becomes more distracted, will fail more and discontinue. The secondary appraisal stage is recursive, and constituted the process of behavioral adaptation.

motivation to overcome the challenge. It is also possible that they are uncertain about its benefits, in which case case, whether an individual will persevere when confronted with a challenge may depend on the secondary appraisal process whereby the individual evaluates a situation (*"I don't like this challenge."*) and then poses a second question like: "*Should I do something about it*?".

At the secondary stage of appraisal, the physical and cognitive abilities and past experiences of an individual can play a significant role. If the challenge is feasible, then the player may experience what is termed as 'Flow.' In this case, the appraisal typically becomes positive and the individual may continue playing to increase the sensation of pleasure and well-being. If it is not, then the challenge itself may be experienced as benign, or 'stressful.'

The secondary appraisal, as well as personality, and other resources (metabolic or social) available to the individual will determine the coping process, broadly defined as 1) the ability to deal with functional demands, 2) creating motivations to meet those demands, and 3) maintaining a state of equilibrium that would allow a player to transfer their skills and energy towards the demands that are posed within the structure of an activity, such as a digital game (p. 149) [16].

1.1 Study Objectives

The objective of the study is to deploy the AGPHA framework to test the validity of our adapted model of serious game stress (Fig. 1B) in the context of older adults playing cognitively 'beneficial' games. Note that, in the context of Canada and the United States, our definition of 'older adult' is players who are 65 years of age and older.

We considered the following hypothetical scenario: A senior person is introduced to a competitive digital game that they have never played before. If this person has a positive attitude towards games in general (e.g., as source of entertainment, healthy life style or social connection), then the choice to play or not will depend on their choice of whether or not it is worth their time (primary appraisal). After playing the game, the player will enter the secondary stage of appraisal: if the game is perceived to be stimulating and cognitively beneficial, this will frame the experience.

Having initially accepted the game as a potentially beneficial activity, if the player enjoys the game, it is likely that they will feel stimulated by the game, pay attention to the gameplay, try to learn it and improve their scores. If this perseverance results in improvements and the gameplay becomes rewarding, it is probable that the player will continue to play, particularly if they experience a state of game flow. If positive results are not produced – there is no learning or improvement, no meaningful connections forged to their personality or cultural context - then there is a chance that the player will become frustrated and stressed. At this stage, the likelihood of continuing with the gameplay depends on the degree to which the player has first appraised the game as potentially beneficial and positive.

Conversely, having accepted the game as a potentially meaningful and health-beneficial activity, if the player perceives the game negatively (e.g. it is too difficult to learn and execute, or meaningless, uninteresting or aesthetically unappealing, etc.) then the experience of an unwinnable challenge and game difficulty will exacerbate their level of stress and lead to the discontinuation of gameplay. If this state of frustration is not overcome, the player will abandon the game and seek alternatives.

In the adapted model (Fig. 1B), we hypothesize that the secondary appraisal of the game can modify the primary appraisal, and will influence whether or not the player will engage with the game beyond this first encounter and initial appraisal.

The aim of this study is to deploy the theoretical model and methods proposed in the AGPHA framework to investigate the following questions:

1. To what extent does the primary appraisal of the game (in terms of the relevance and meaning of the activity and beliefs about its accessibility) predict measurable differences in reflective (post-game experience of stress, enjoyment, stimulation, value, etv) and reflexive (post-game physiological change) response to games as stressful?
2. What are the central primary and secondary appraisal factors (i.e. pre- or post-game evaluations, respectively), or physiological markers, that can predict the desire to play again?

2 Materials and Methods

2.1 Recruitment

After receiving approval from our institutional review board to conduct this study, we targeted a general mailing list of the PERFORM Centre, which consists of individuals who have expressed interest in participating in preventative health studies. The email invited individuals 65 years of age and older to participate in a study entitled *"Finding Better Games for Older Adults: an objective assessment of interactions between appraisal, arousal and cognitive benefits of electronic playing."* The recruitment period was about two months. Participation was voluntary and not financially remunerated.

2.2 Experimental Design and Data Collection

Experimental design and data collection are summarized in Fig. 2. To implement the AGPHA framework we proposed the following steps:

Screening the Participants' Primary Appraisal. To determine who would join the study, we administered an online 'recruitment' survey to assess the general attitudes and digital gaming experiences of the responders within this age cohort (Fig. 3).

Repeated Measures Design. In this report, we present partial results from the first session of a three-session game interventions study involving brain training games, a car racing game and an exergame (for details see JMH Preprint) [24]. In the first session, participants were shown five games on an iPad: *Solitaire* (v1.5.6, Brainium Studios LLC), *Dots* (v 2.3.5, Playdots, Inc.)–a block match puzzle, and three tasks from a brain training game (*Simple MindGames*; v2.5, by Tom Lake). In the demo session, they received instructions on how to play each of the games. After a short delay following a simple memory test, they were asked to play *Reaction* (speed and accuracy of detecting a red dot appearing among a matrix of green dots), *Match* (a short term memory, recall test, to pick the shape if it looks like the shape seen immediately before–irrespective of color) and *Pattern* (another short term memory test, asking to replicate the pattern of dots seen on a 5 × 5 matrix, by removing them in a full matrix), 3 min each. They were given a sheet and asked to mark their scores and rate whether they had fun or found each game difficult (rate 0–10).

Subjective Gaming Experience (Secondary Appraisal). After the first mandatory play session, we performed other cognitive tests and then gave participants 15 min to relax and pick any of the five games that they wished to replay. The preferences were documented. At the end of the session, we administered an exit survey loosely based on the intrinsic motivation inventory (IMI), which tapped into the following: Enjoyment (*The experience was enjoyable, The experience was interesting*); Competence (*The game was difficult*); Tension (*The experience was stressful; I found this to be a frustrating experience; These games are visually intense*); Choice (*I would like to play this game that I just played, again; I will play this game again; I did not like this experiment*); Value (*This game helps improve my mental wellness; I think this game is useless; These games are cognitively stimulating*). Instead of rating the questions on a 7-point Likert scale, we provided a limited option to agree (somewhat or definitely) or disagree (somewhat or definitely). The reason for this forced choice and omission was because we wanted to push participants to indicate where their interests tended to lie. Because the questionnaires were on paper, we encouraged them to comment next to a question if they did not agree with the provided response choices (Fig. 4).

Physiological Measurements. The AGPHA framework includes physiological assessments in order to create a body of data that would allow us to assess the relation between physiology and gameplay experience in the short and long term. For this purpose, we used a light wristband device E4 (Empatica, Inc), which is equipped with sensors to monitor various ambulatory signals, such as galvanic skin conductance or electrodermal activity (EDA) and heart rate (HR) variability, which have long been used in human-computer interface and games studies [17–23]. For simplicity, and also to encourage replication studies, here we report electrodermal activity and heart rate values as they were computed by the device software and recorded by our assistants at the beginning and end of each activity interval. We compute the percentage of change in signal by the end of playing activity, with respect to the onset of activity, in order to asses activity-dependent autonomic response to the activity. We also computed the cumulative average of the signal over the course of the experiment as proxy for general states of physiological activity. In addition, we acquired 4 saliva samples, roughly at 20 min intervals, to assess the unbound salivary cortisol which is often used as biomarker of psychological stress. Details of these measurements and validation process are presented elsewhere [24].

Qualitative Evaluations. We performed semi-structured interviews at the beginning and the end of the experiment to capture more nuances in the relevance and valence of our study as they relate to the lives of our participants. Specifically, we asked everyone about their familiarity with digital technologies (comfort with technology, their employment history, their experience with games); the potential or actual meaning and value of digital play in their lives or the lives of other seniors, and their preferences and suggestions about what kinds of games would be hypothetically useful to them. We also asked them to elaborate why they would or would not play the games we presented to them as well. Details of these analyses are presented elsewhere [25]. For the purpose of this report, we present case studies of individuals who had negative primary appriasals, and transcribe the summary of their statements with regards to three reflective factors: their familiarity with digital play, the meaningfullness and value of digital play in their life, and their preferences.

Controlling for Interindividual Stress Sensitivity. We gathered data about participants' characteristics such as general self-efficacy (10-item scale) [26], UCLA loneliness scale [27], and perceived stress (9-item scale [28]) to assess whether these scores explained variations in reflective (primary, secondary and qualitative assessments), or reflexive (EDA, HR, Cortisol).

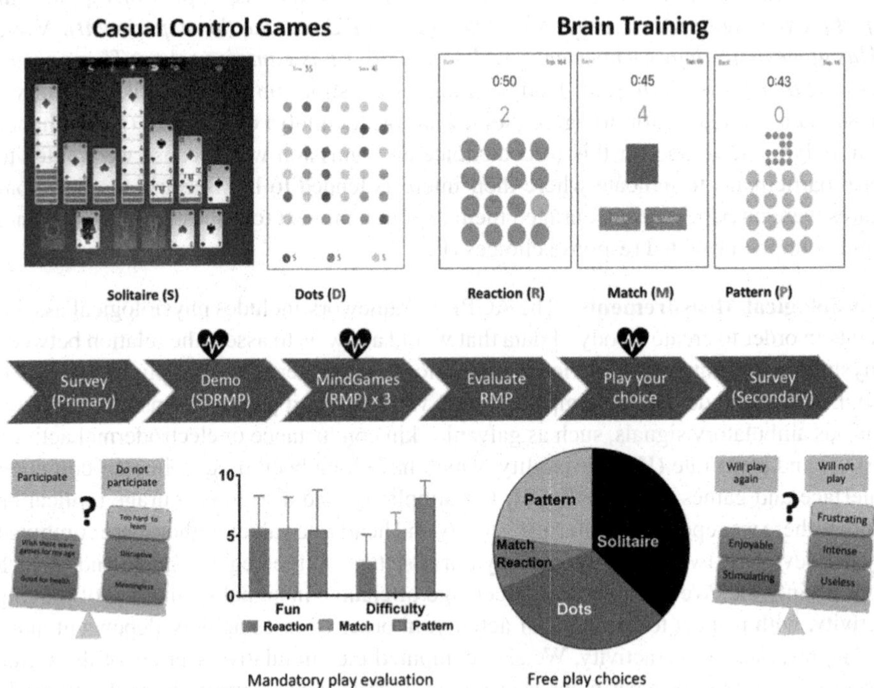

Fig. 2. Summary of experimental design. The primary appraisal was done at the screening stage, where participants were given the choice to join further studies or not. The experimental session included a demo session where two casual and three brain training games were introduced. After that, players were asked to play each of the *MindGames* three times and to evaluate them on how fun and how difficult they were (Likert 1–10, where 10 was most fun and most difficult). At the end, participants were given the option to play any of the five games they saw in the demo. The secondary appraisal was done at the end, with administration of a modified version of IMI, to assess whether games were stressful or enjoyable, and whether those predicted an interest in replay. The physiological signals (EDA and HR) were monitored continuously, but for the purpose of this work, we computed the average as well as the start-to-end values computed over Demo, mandatory play and free play sessions.

2.3 Statistical Analysis

Due to the small sample size, all statistical analyses have used non-parametric methods. Spearman's-*rho* test was used to measure the rank of correlations between variables of interest. Mann-Whitney U-test was used for between-group comparisons of the ranked frequency of response to survey questions. Statistical measures that are reported are rounded up to the third digit. All statistical analyses were performed using SPSS 21 (IBM, Inc.) for MAC OS. Graphs were generated with Prism 7.0 (Graphpad, Inc.)

3 Results

3.1 Demographic and Psychometric Characteristics of Participants and Non-Participants

In total, 42 adults meeting the age criteria (>65) responded to the survey, 19 of which volunteered to enroll in the experimental study. Only one participant dropped out of the experimental phase after the first visit, due to extreme physical discomfort which forced her to eat and drink (thus invalidating the cortisol sampling). Differences in participant characteristics are presented in Table 1. No significant demographic or psychometric group differences were observed (all $p's > 0.5$). What is noteworthy is that in the non-participating group, 9 participants skipped answering questions about mental health, perceived stress, loneliness and general self-efficacy. These observations must be considered as the backdrop of all the following discussions.

Table 1. Sample characteristics

Characteristics	Volunteered for full study	Dropped out after survey
Gender(M/F)	6/13	10/13
Mental health (good/could be better/no answer)	17/2/0	13/2/9
Physical health (good/could be better/no answer)	14/5/0	10/5/9
Age (mean, std)	70.47, 4.49	69.70, 4.20
Years of education (mean, std)	16.26, 3.68	16.22, 2.58
Generalized self efficacy* (mean, std) [max 40]	33.79, 2.80	32.42, 4.77
Perceived stress scale* (mean, std) [max 40]	17.78, 3.83	18.46, 3.83
Loneliness index* (mean, std) [max 80]	11.21, 11.36	18.8, 15.54

* 9 of participants (who only did the survey) did not respond to the psychometric questionnaires, but completed the game appraisal questionnaire

3.2 Differences in Primary Appraisal Between Study Participants and Nonparticipants

Figure 3 shows the response frequency to the primary appraisal survey.

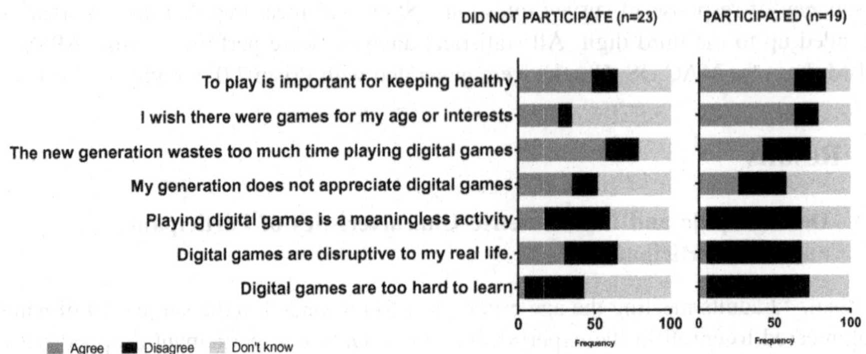

Fig. 3. Differences in response frequencies to primary appraisal of digital games, between those who responded to the online survey and joined the quantitative study, and those who responded but did not join the quantitative study.

The Mann-Whitney U test shows significant differences between the attitudes of those who participated in the quantitative study, compared to those who opted out after pre-study survey, especially in "*digital games are too hard to learn*" (*p* = .*02*) and "*I wish there were more games for my generation*" (p = .04). We also found a trend in those who did not participate for finding "*digital games are too disruptive to real life*" and "*to play digital games is a meaningless activity*" (*p's* < .*09*). This indicates that from the onset, participants who did not appraise digital gaming in a positive light were self-excluded from the challenge of learning new games. Therefore, we did not expect to measure significant stress responses in the remaining sample.

3.3 Secondary Appraisal (Game Experience)

Figure 4 summarizes the player's subjective evaluation of the brain training games after trying them (secondary appraisal).

The majority of participants had a positive experience with the gaming session. We found significant correlations between liking the game experience and finding it useful (*rho* = .*623, p* = .*004*). As well, we found an inverse correlation between disliking the session and "*I would like to play this game again*" (*rho* =− .*613, p* = .*005*), "*These games are cognitively stimulating*" (*rho* = −.*547, p* = .*01*) or "*The experience was enjoyable*" (*rho* = −.*50, p* = .*029*). The strongest correlation was observed between scores of "*These games will help improve my mental wellness*" and "*I think this game is useless*" (*rho* =− .*857, p* < .*001*) and "*I would like to play this game that I just played, again*" (*rho* = −.*838, p* < .*001*), suggesting that mental wellness was a strong predictor of perceiving the game as useful, and wishing to replay it. We observed only a trend for correlations between finding the game *difficult* and the experience *frustrating* (*rho* =

.397, p = .092), or *stressful* (*rho = .450, p = .053*). It is plausible that individuals with high scores of general self-efficacy, and low scored of perceived stress, did not find the *Simple MindGames* very challenging. In fact, the only correlation between personality factors and appraisal factors was a mild inverse correlation between perceived stress scale and finding the experience interesting (*rho =− .466, p = .040*).

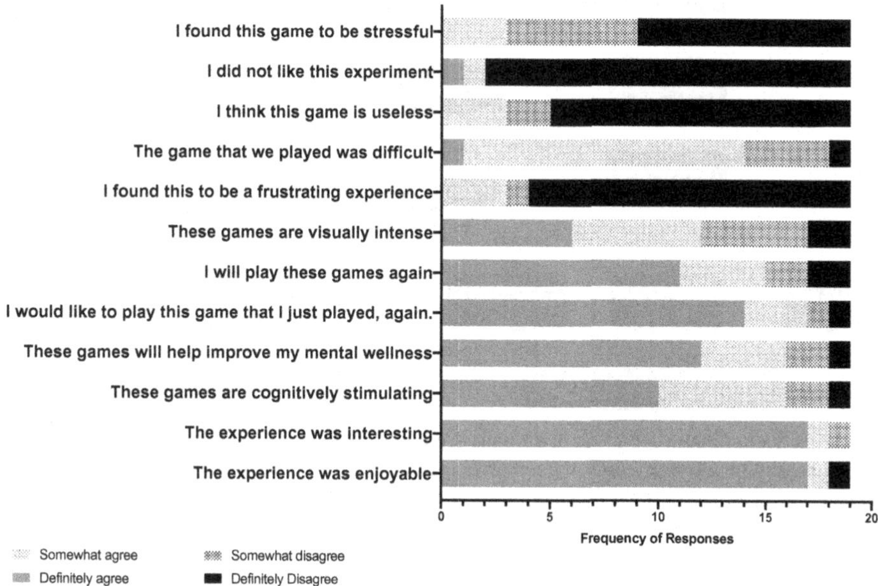

Fig. 4. Response frequencies to the secondary appraisal questions after the game play session.

3.4 Appraisal and Physiological Factors

Given the small size of our sample, and the large number of variables, we are not able to perform linear regression or mediation analysis. However, as this is a proof-of-concept application of the AGPHA framework, correlations between study factors are worth reporting. Figure 5 summarizes all pairwise correlations between the primary and secondary appraisal variables, as well as average physiological measures.

The Most Central Primary Appraisal Questions. While considering the entire sample (N = 42), the primary appraisal factors "*digital games are too hard to learn*" seems to be the most central factor, as it correlates with four other factors (disruptive, meaningless, young waste too much time, and I wish there were more games for my age group). In the subsample that went on to trying the game and the secondary stage of appraisal, the correlations, between finding fames too hard to learn, and meaningless, wasteful, and age-inappropriate were no longer significant. However, the negative correlation between "*to play is important for keeping healthy*" and the "*young waste too much time playing digital games*" (*rho =− .33, p = .029, n = 42*), became even stronger in the subsample

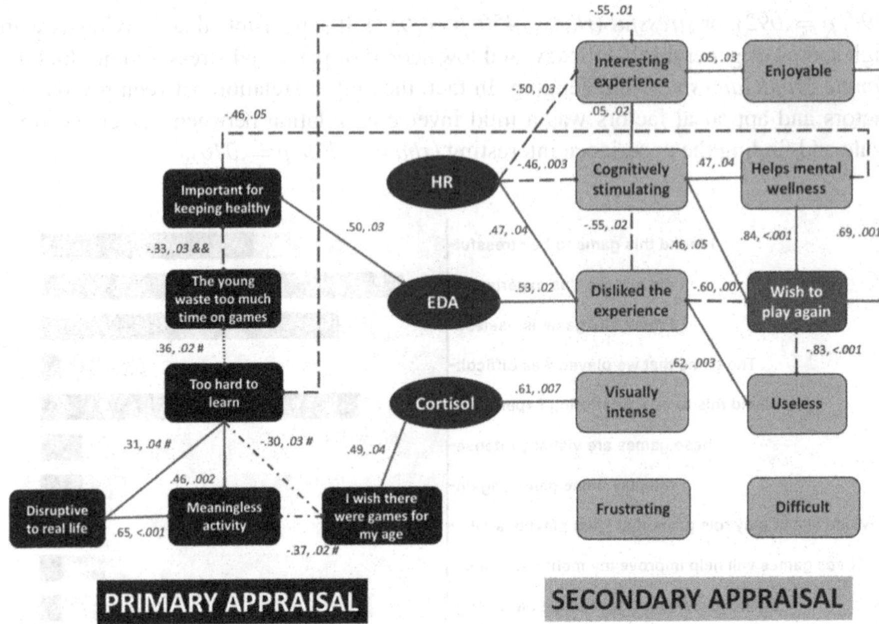

Fig. 5. A diagrammatic depiction of all pairwise nonparametric correlations without controlling for collinearity between variables. Green links indicate positive correlations and dashed red lines indicate negative correlations. "#" denotes correlations that were no longer significant for the primary appraisal of the test sample (N = 42). "&&" denotes correlations that became even stronger (larger correlation coefficients) in the test sample (n = 19).

who participated in the experiment (*rho* =− .53, *p* = 0.018, *n* = 19). Also, the correlation between finding digital games "*too hard to learn*" and "*disruptive to real life*" increased from (*rho* = .31, *p* = .043, *n* = 42) to (*rho* = .47, *p* = .043, *n* = 19). The correlation between disruptiveness and meaninglessness also became stronger (from *rho* = .65, *p* < .001, *n* = 42 to *rho* = .70, *p* < .001, *n* = 19).

The Most Central Secondary Appraisal Questions. Among the secondary appraisal questions, "*These games are cognitively stimulating*" and "*I did not like this experiment*" were most centrally correlated with other factors (and with each other, inversely).

Interestingly, we found no correlations between: "*The game was difficult*", "*I found the experience to be frustrating*" or "*I found this game to be stressful*", and any other variables, suggesting that an explicit question about the challenge of the play would not necessarily reflect a quantifiable appraisal.

In contrast, we did find correlations between the questions "*I did not like this experience*" and "*I think this game is useless*" and other secondary appraisal factors. Here, we found the strongest correlations between answers to "*I wish to play this game again*" and "*These games will help improve my mental wellness" (rho = .84, p < .001),* which was inversely correlated with "*I think this game is useless*" (*rho* =− .83, *p* < .001). The *wish to play again* was also correlated with "*The experience was enjoyable (rho = .69, p = .001*) and inversely correlated with "*I did not like this experience*" (*rho* =− .59,

$p = .007$). Weaker, but still significant correlation was observed between "*I wish to play this game again*" and "*These games are cognitively stimulating*" ($rho = .46, p = .047$). These observations confirm that enjoyment and the potential for mental wellness are the most likely predictors of the wish to replay.

Correlations Between Primary and Secondary Appraisal Questions. In terms of the relationship between the pre-play stage (primary) and post-play stage (secondary) appraisals, we found a negative correlation between "*digital games are too hard to learn*" and "*The experience was interesting*" ($rho =- .46, p = .047$), suggesting that those who perceived games to be difficult to learn also found the experience less interesting (but did not rate the experiment as difficult or stressful in the second stage). Also, we observed a negative correlation between "*To play is important to keep healthy*" (Primary) and "*This game will help my mental wellness*" ($rho =- .55, p = .014$) (Secondary), suggesting a dissociation between the stages of appraisal of the game benefits.

Physiological Factors Role in Mediating the Relationship Between Primary and Secondary Appraisal. We hypothesized that if the primary appraisal of games would be negative, then it will increase autonomic and stress responses in order to help the player with metabolic demands to help them overcome the challenge. We therefore expected to find a correlation between primary appraisal "*digital games are too heard to learn*" and physiological responses. This was not the case. Instead, we found a significant positive correlation between average EDA measured over the course of the experiment, and response to question, "*To play is important for keeping healthy*" ($rho = .499, p = .03$). We also found a positive correlation between cortisol levels and "*I wish there were more games for my age or interest*" ($rho = .49, p = .04$). These observations point to heightened state of vigilance related to higher basal cortisol [29, 30], or electrodermal and cardiac activity. Given a lack of precise experiment, we refrain from interpretation of psychobiological meaning of the observations, and suffice to point that these variables are important for monitoring baseline physiological states that would determine an individual's resilience to coping with cognitive challenges like games.

Relationship Between Secondary Game Appraisal and Physiological Response. According to the model in Fig. 1, we hypothesized that negative primary appraisal of the game would be associated with increased stress (higher cortisol and higher EDA/HR). We also expected that higher cognitive arousal and effort would be associated with playing difficulty and with increased physiological response. We found a positive correlation between cortisol levels and rating the games as visually intense ($rho = .61, p = .007$). Disliking the experience was also correlated with both higher EDA ($rho = .53, p = .02$) and higher HR ($rho = .46, p = .04$). By contrast, finding the games to be *cognitively stimulating* and the *experience interesting* were negatively correlated with HR ($rho =- .64, p = .003$; and $rho =- .50, p = 0.03$; respectively). Other correlations were not statistically significant. Notably, we found no correlations between finding the games *difficult* or the experience *frustrating*, and any other physiological or appraisal variables. It should also be noted that we did not find any correlations between activity-dependent changes in physiology and any of the appraisal variables, again confirming that the physiological correlations related to higher degree of vigilance and emotional arousal in the participant–thus satisfying the appraisal model that primary expectations of a stimulus as challenging would be associated with increased physiological responses to meet the metabolic demands of the challenge.

3.5 Appraisal and the Willingness to Play Again

We examined the responses to primary and secondary appraisal questions in relation to how players responded to the question of "*I will play the games again.*"

Based on our observations in Fig. 5, we examined the response to the primary appraisal questions "*I find digital games too hard to play*" and "*Digital games too disruptive to one's real life*", or "*I find playing digital games to be a meaningless activity.*" We also examined responses to secondary appraisal questions: "*The experience was frustrating* or *stressful,*" and the "*I think these games are useless*" or "*I did not like the experience*". Figure 6 summarizes the results.

In general, more men (4/6) had a negative primary attitude towards games compared to women (3/16); but 3/4 of these men changed their views. Of course, it should be noted that at the stage of free play, the casual games *Dots* and *Solitaire* were proportionately more popular than *Pattern*, which was rated as more difficult than the rest of the brain training games, yet it had most replays. (Please see Fig. 2).

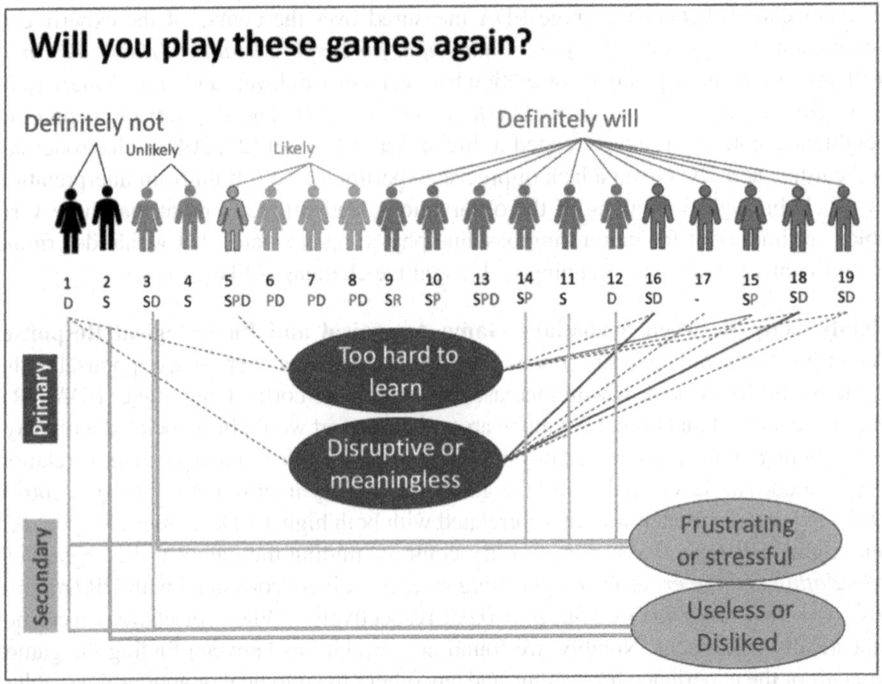

Fig. 6. A diagrammatic representation of individuals who had a negative primary appraisal of digital games, in relation to how likely they were to pledge to playing the game again.

3.6 Qualitative Case Studies

To examine the relation between primary and secondary appraisal qualitatively, we present the statements of individuals who had a negative primary appraisal. The subject numbers correspond to the numbers in Fig. 5.

Case 1: Ambivalent primary appraisal, negative secondary appraisal, won't play again.
Female, 66 yrs old (#1), was uncertain about difficulty to learn and disruptiveness of digital games. After the experiment, she stated that she will not play the Simple Mind Games again.

Familiarity: A technology user, but prefers to play *Solitaire* with cards than with computers.

Meaning and value: The reason why she joined the study was to see what we are doing and what is happening. With a history of dementia in the family, if someone told her that *Solitaire* is beneficial to preventing dementia, then she would play it.

Preferences: She prefers the touch of materials like paper over digital surfaces. She is competitive but found all the brain training games to lack fun–either too boring or too difficult.

Reflexive response: The range of EDA during the playing session was .33–1.6 muS (low arousal). The range of her heart rate was between 78–80 bpm. At the end of the obligatory gameplay, her EDA increased by 41% and her heart rate increased by 4.7%, compared to the start.

Reflective response: In terms of post-game experience, this individual found the game somewhat stressful, frustrating, difficult. She did not find the game visually intense, or interesting. She did not know whether the game was useless or of benefit to mental wellness. She strongly disagreed with statements of finding the session enjoyable, disliked the game, and did not wish to play it again.

Case 2: Positive primary appraisal, negative secondary appraisal, won't play again.
Male, 74 yrs old (#2), does not find games too hard to learn nor disruptive. After the experiment, he stated that she will not play the *Simple Mind Games* again.

Familiarity: He is a highly active and life-long learner. He used to work in tech and played *Solitaire* up to two years prior.

Meaning and value: He finds digital playing an activity that he would do with his grandchildren. He finds games may be useful for older people who are in worse physical or cognitive shape than he is in.

Preferences: For cognitive stimulation or mental health, he prefers to read or write books, or engage in conversations with researchers like us.

Reflexive response: The range of EDA during the playing session was 6.3–8.8 muS (high emotional arousal). His range of heart rate was between 79–82 bpm. At the end of the obligatory gameplay, his EDA decreased by 28% and his heart rate increased by 1.9%, compared to the start.

Reflective response: In terms of post-game experience, this individual did not find the game stressful, or frustrating, and not too difficult. He found the game to be very visually intense, and very interesting. He stated that the game was somewhat useless and strongly disagreed with the statement that it was of benefit to mental wellness. He strongly agreed with statements of finding the session enjoyable, but disliked the game somewhat, and somewhat wished to play it again.

Case 3: Negative primary appraisal, positive secondary appraisal, will play again. Female, 76 yrs old (#15), finds games too hard to learn, uncertain about disruptiveness, After the experiment, he stated that she will not play the Simple Mind Games again.

Familiarity: She used to playing *Solitaire* before going to bed, although not regularly.

Meaning and value: She has memory concerns and has questions about benefits of brain games.

Preferences: She takes fitness classes and plays guitar. Seeing the screen is not easy for her and she finds the games too fast. Although she indicated that she will play the brain game again, when given the option of free play, she chose to play *Solitaire*.

Reflexive response: Her range of EDA during the playing session was 1.1–3.9 muS (medium arousal). Her range of heart rate was between 79–106 bpm. At the end of the obligatory gameplay, her EDA decreased by 69% and her heart rate increased by 11%, compared to the start.

Reflective response: In terms of post-game experience, this individual did not find the game stressful, frustrating, nor particularly difficult. She found the game to be very visually intense, and very interesting. She strongly disagreed that game was useless and strongly agreed that it was of benefit to mental wellness. She strongly agreed with statements of finding the game enjoyable, liked the game, and wished to play it again.

Case 4: Negative primary appraisal, ambivalent secondary appraisal, will play again. Male, 68 yrs old (#18), was uncertain about difficulty to learn but was certain that digital games are disruptive. However, after playing the Simple Mind Games, he stated that he will play the game again.

Familiarity: He is not an electronic game player and finds that technology is not generally helpful. He knows technology is important, but it is pointless to him. He finds the problem with technology to be a lack of proper 'how to,' which causes him waste too much time to find the information that he needs. The terminology and acronyms frustrate him.

Meaning and value: He lamented that these days, instead of having social interactions, people are just watching texts on their phones. He plays *Solitaire* when waiting for something, but is not interested in such mindless activity in general.

Preferences: He did not find brain games as fun; for fun he would pick *Solitaire*. But they were challenging, so he would pick them up to play again for the challenge.

Reflexive response: His range of EDA during the playing session was .28–.74 muS (low arousal). His range of heart rate was between 52–99 bpm. At the end of the obligatory gameplay, his EDA increased by 15% and his heart rate increased by 31%, compared to the start.

Reflective response: In terms of post-game experience, this individual did not find the game stressful, frustrating, but somewhat difficult. He found the game to be very visually intense, and very interesting. He strongly disagreed that game was useless and strongly agreed that it was of benefit to mental wellness. She strongly agreed with statements of finding the game enjoyable, liked the game, and wished to play it again.

Case 5: Ambivalent primary appraisal, positive secondary appraisal, will play again. Male, 76 yrs old (#19), was uncertain about difficulty to learn and uncertain about disruptiveness, but stated that he will play the *Simple Mind Game* again.

Familiarity: Technology-savvy an avid digital-player, he has been playing digital games with his family since youth.

Meaning and value: Playing needs to serve a purpose for him, either to make or to facilitate relationships, or to help physical fitness.

Preferences: He prefers the cerebral challenges of a game (like *Tetris*).

Reflexive response: His range of EDA during the playing session was .18–.71 muS (low arousal). His range of heart rate was between 57–120 bpm. At the end of the obligatory gameplay, his EDA increased by 33% and his heart rate decreased by 14%, compared to the start.

Reflective response: In terms of post-game experience, this individual did not find the game very stressful, frustrating, but somewhat difficult. He found the game to be not very intense visually, but very interesting. He strongly disagreed that game was useless and strongly agreed that it was of benefit to mental wellness. He strongly agreed with statements of finding the session enjoyable, liked the game, and wished to play it again.

4 Discussion

4.1 Principle Findings

The aim of this proof-of-principle study was to test the model and methods proposed in the AGPHA framework to investigate the relation between the primary or first stage appraisal of a digital games, and the secondary, or second stage appraisal, and psychophysiological stress response to a simple brain training game (*Simple MindGame*) in a older adults.

We considered the following scenario: A senior person is introduced to a competitive digital game that they have never played before. If this person has a positive attitude towards games in general (e.g., as source of entertainment, healthy life style or social connection), then the choice to play or not will depend on their choice of whether or not it is worth their time (primary appraisal).

Indeed, we showed that those participated in our quantitative study had a generally more positive attitude towards digital game playing, compared to those who did not.

Of course there were individuals who did not have a positive attitude towards the game, but joined the study. We hypothesized that after playing the game, these individuals will enter the secondary stage of appraisal: if they perceive the game to be stimulating and cognitively beneficial, then they will replay, otherwise quit.

As hypothesized, we found that in the secondary appraisal stage, to have found the game cognitively stimulating and enjoyable were central characteristic of the secondary appraisal, which were linked both to physiological response (HR) as well as desire to play the game again (Fig. 5).

We also found evidence for the hypothesis that if the game experience was enjoyable and meaningful, even if the game wass perceived as too difficult, the players would increase attention and effort to engage with it (e.g. cases, 15, 16, 19 and 18), otherwise discontinue (e.g. cases 1 and 2).

The most important finding of this study is to illustrate the complex relationship between reflective and reflexive variables that mark stress, especially in finding incongruencies in the direction of change of physiological and subjective measures. These observations highlight the necessity of taking a player-centred approach to game customization, and employing quantitative methodologies that enable us to capture a comprehensive profile of an individual, and the dynamics of their adaptation to a game challenge.

4.2 Evaluating Games for Serious Application

Previously, it is argued that pleasurable and enjoyable experiences are sufficient to justify why computer gaming is 'good' for older adults [32–36]. However, it seems that the potential cognitive or health-related benefits are important motivations for playing computer games [37–41]. Our study confirms this, indicating that the greatest variations in the *wish to play the game again* is explained by *it will help improve mental wellness* (72% of variation), *not being useless* (69%) and by it being an *enjoyable experience* (48%).

While biomarkers such as cortisol levels and ambulatory signals were not as powerful in predicting the likelihood of game replay, these factors were linked to secondary appraisal scores of enjoyment, challenge and the value of games in mental wellness. We found increased HR with disliking the game experience, and decreased HR with finding the experience cognitively stimulating and interesting–indicating that our method were sensitive to detect the link between reflexive and reflective game stress. We also found a positive correlation between EDA and dislikeing the game, but also a positive correlation between EDA and the expectation that to play is important for keeping healthy, suggesting that the pre- and post-game appraisal factors affected the levels of cognitive or emotional arousal.

It should be mentioned that in our sample, Cortisol, HR and EDA variables were not colinear. This is not suprising because changes in EDA relate to sympathetic activity while heart rate (HR) is predominantly controlled by the parasympathetic nervous system, and cortisol to the neuroendocrine stress system. These systems do interact, but the timecourse of response and their tonic activity is under different control mechanisms, whose discussion is outside the scope of this report. Nevertheless, as Lazarus' empirical model indicates, all these adaptive responses are modulated an individual's perceptual and coping strategies [4, 16]. Our case studies illustrate the importance of including qualitative data in disambiguating the objective measures.

For example, in Cases 1 and 4, where the primary and secondary appraisals were both negative or ambivalent, then both EDA and HR increased during the mandatory game play. This finding is consistent with previous reports that increased EDA and HR are positively correlated with negative affect caused by game experience [31].

In contrast, in cases 2 and 5, who had a negative or ambivalent primary appraisal of digital games, but positive secondary appraisal (judged by their stated interest to play the *MindGames* again), EDA and HR responses were dichotomous. It is plausible to interpret the dichotomous direction of change in EDA, and HR in relation to individual differences in perceptual and coping processes. For instance, variations in game tension and competence (Which are shown by [31] to be correlated with HR but not with EDA). Therefore, differences in effort, tension and experience of flow may contribute to such variations.

While the small sample of this study does not warrant strong conclusions, these results show that physiological measurements are sensitive to game-playing experience, and thus important to include, not only in the stage of design and evaluation of user affect, but also in clinical evaluations of serious games designed for healthcare interventions such as cognitive and physical rehabilitation.

4.3 Towards a Unifying Framework

If games are made for health related interventions, they need to be first acceptable and appealing to their users, and then tested in large scale clinical trials to illustrate their efficacy. To address these needs, we proposed the AGPHA framework [4] to unify how game designers and clinicians can work together to qualify and quantify the efficacy of any particular gamified health interventions for older adults.

AGPHA builds on the appraisal theory of stress [16] that encompasses two dominant game-design theories, Self Determination Theory (SDT) [42] and Flow Theory (FT) [43, 44].

According to SDT, humans have a need for autonomy, and a desire to develop the competencies and relationships that help them fulfill their goals for growth and self-actualization.

According to FT, a successful game must counterbalance a user's experience of challenge and difficulty: if the level of challenge is too high and the player abilities are not commensurate, it will likely lead to anxiety and discontinuation. If the level of challenge is lower than the abilities of the player, it will likely lead to boredom and discontinuation.

Whereas SDT underlines the reflective component of playing motivation (competence, relatedness, autonomy), Flow Theory underlines the reflexive aspect (arousal, pleasure, frustration, success).

This proof-of-concept study illustrates that intricate motivational components give rise to individual differences in perception of, and coping with, the potential game stress, which are also linked to quantifiable physiological responses. Elsewhere [24], we have shown that these relationships are not simple, and vary not only with perceptions but also cognitive reserves of individuals. Thus, larger data points are needed to detect patterns that will help us design adaptive and personalized games that deliver their expected *serious* outcome. The need for such data adds to the incentive for using a unifying framework that maps adaptive behavioral changes through different stages of re-appraisal and learning, in the process of game design and game adoption.

5 Conclusions, Limitations and Future Work

5.1 Conclusions

This pilot study provides preliminary data to support the applicability and validity of the AGPHA framework to potentially address the need for standardized methods to evaluate the effectiveness of serious games for seniors. Our study underlines the importance of monitoring perceptual and game appraisal differences that arise at the stage of recruitment, which may bias the conclusions of a study. It emphasizes the importance of combing multifactorial qualitative and quantitative methods to document the processes through which discordances between first stage and second stage appraisals of a game experience. It also illustrates that although the relationship between game playing and stress is complex and variant between individuals, it can be quantitatively documented.

5.2 Limitations

Given the small sample size, we acknowledge that our findings are not fully immune to the problem of multiple comparisons - the possibility for finding spurious correlations increases with the number of test variables. These preliminary results only serve to illustrate the application of the model proposed in Fig. 1B.

We emphasize that our data and analyses do not warrant a generalized interpretation of the EDA, HR or Cortisol results. Both the autonomic and the neuroendocrine systems that modulate the physiological responses are under control of a complex neural control system. For example, EDA and HR can be modulated by musculoskeletal tone, by hypothalamic thermoregulation, by amygdalar emotional processing, or by prefrontal cognitive attention (pp. 217–243) [45], none of which we have measured or controlled for.

We have also not carefully considered subtle differences arising from tonic or phases changes in EDA, which could explain the absense of activity-dependent correlations between physiology and primary or secondary appraisal. Another important factor, which we have not considered is variations that can arise from health states and medications of our participants, but these are all important questions than can be tested with our model.

5.3 Future Work

In future work, we will test the applicability of this model by comparing *MindGames* to other forms of cognitively stimulating games, that the participants in the current study experienced [24].

While limited by the small sample size, our preliminary results illustrate the importance of multifactorial data collection. Increasingly, digital games lend themselves to massive online neuropsychological data collection [46, 47]. Hypothetically speaking, structural equation modeling with a large number of variables (Fig. 5) is possible, and in fact, with growing availability of wearable biosensors and pervasive computing technologies, such complex and multivariate modeling approaches, are advised in human-computer interface design [48]. To add these evaluative steps to the process of serious game design will hopefully help us disambiguate inconsistencies in evaluation of the efficacy of such interventions in seniors' healthcare.

Finally, *Brain Training* games offer relatively isolated cognitive challenges that lend themselves to experiments that investigate their relation to biomarkers of stress. However, prior research [33, 34] has indicated that the large groups of younger but already actively playing generations of older adults (50+) have a different relationship to digital games than the older sample of this study. While brain training games may be appealing to the majority of participants of this health-related study, future work should evaluate similar measures with games that promise other, non-cognitive gratifications to older adults as well.

Acknowledgements. This paper is part of an empirical investigation of Finding Better Games for Older Adults supported by the seed funding from Concordia University's office of research and PERFORM Centre. We thank the following research assistants who were involved in data collection: Atousa Assadi, Mahsa Mirgholami, Kate Li and Anna Smirnova. Logistic support from McGill Centre for Integrative Neuroscience (mcin-cnim.ca), the Ageing + Communication + Technologies (ACT) network (http://actproject.ca/), and Technoculture, Arts and Games (TAG) Centre (tag.hexagram.ca) is acknowledged. We thank Ms Chloe Smith for proof-reading the manuscript.

References

1. Marston, H.R., et al.: A scoping review of digital gaming research involving older adults aged 85 and older. Games Health J. **5**(3), 157–174 (2016)
2. Marston, H.R., Smith, S.T.: Interactive videogame technologies to support independence in the elderly: a narrative review. Games Health J. **1**(2), 139–152 (2012)
3. Loos, E., Kaufman, D.: Positive impact of exergaming on older adults' mental and social well-being: in search of evidence. In: Zhou, J., Salvendy, G. (eds.) ITAP 2018. LNCS, vol. 10927, pp. 101–112. Springer, Cham (2018). https://doi.org/10.1007/978-3-319-92037-5_9
4. Khalili-Mahani, N., De Schutter, B.: Affective game planning for health applications: quantitative extension of gerontoludic design based on the appraisal theory of stress and coping. JMIR Serious Games **7**(2), e13303 (2019)
5. Folkman, S., Lazarus, R.S.: The relationship between coping and emotion: implications for theory and research. Soc. Sci. Med. **26**(3), 309–317 (1988)
6. Cannon, W.B.: The Wisdom of the Body. W.W. Norton & Company, New York (1932). (xv p., 1 l., 19–312 p.)
7. Hubert, W., de Jong-Meyer, R.: Autonomic, neuroendocrine, and subjective responses to emotion-inducing film stimuli. Int. J. Psychophysiol. **11**(2), 131–140 (1991)
8. Maguire, G.P., Maclean, A.W., Aitken, R.C.: Adaptation on repeated exposure to film-induced stress. Biol. Psychol. **1**(1), 43–51 (1973)
9. Adamson, J.D., et al.: Physiological responses to sexual and unpleasant film stimuli. J. Psychosom. Res. **16**(3), 153–162 (1972)
10. Goldstein, M.J., et al.: Coping style as a factor in psychophysiological response to a tension-arousing film. J. Pers. Soc. Psychol. **1**, 290–302 (1965)
11. Carroll, D., et al.: Temporal consistency of individual differences in cardiac response to a video game. Biol. Psychol. **19**(2), 81–93 (1984)
12. Selye, H.: Stress and distress. Compr. Ther. **1**(8), 9–13 (1975)

13. Mason, J.W.: A review of psychoendocrine research on the pituitary-adrenal cortical system. Psychosom. Med. **30**(5), 576–607 (1968). (Suppl)
14. Dickerson, S.S., Kemeny, M.E.: Acute stressors and cortisol responses: a theoretical integration and synthesis of laboratory research. Psychol. Bull. **130**(3), 355–391 (2004)
15. Lazarus, R.S.: Emotions and interpersonal relationships: toward a person-centered conceptualization of emotions and coping. J. Pers. **74**(1), 9–46 (2006)
16. Lazarus, R.S., Folkman, S.: Stress, Appraisal, and Coping, vol xiii, 445 p. Springer, New York (1984)
17. Larradet, F., Barresi, G., Mattos, L.S.: Effects of galvanic skin response feedback on user experience in gaze-controlled gaming: a pilot study. Conf. Proc. IEEE Eng. Med. Biol. Soc. **2017**, 2458–2461 (2017)
18. Ortiz-Vigon Uriarte Ide, L., Garcia-Zapirain, B., Garcia-Chimeno, Y.: Game design to measure reflexes and attention based on biofeedback multi-sensor interaction. Sensors (Basel) **15**(3), 6520–6548 (2015)
19. Mandryk, R.L., Inkpen, K.M., Calvert, T.W.: Using psychophysiological techniques to measure user experience with entertainment technologies. Behav. Inf. Technol. **25**(2), 141–158 (2006)
20. Poels, K., et al.: Pleasure to play, arousal to stay: the effect of player emotions on digital game preferences and playing time. Cyberpsychol. Behav. Soc. Netw. **15**(1), 1–6 (2012)
21. van Reekum, C., et al.: Psychophysiological responses to appraisal dimensions in a computer game. Cogn. Emotion **18**(5), 663–688 (2004)
22. Mandryk, R.L., Atkins, M.S.: A fuzzy physiological approach for continuously modeling emotion during interaction with play technologies. Int. J. Hum.-Comput. Stud. **65**(4), 329–347 (2007)
23. Hébert, S., et al.: Physiological stress response to video-game playing: the contribution of built-in music. Life Sci. **76**(20), 2371–2380 (2005)
24. Khalili-Mahani, N., et al.: Reflective and reflexive stress responses of older Adults to three gaming experiences in relation to their cognitive abilities: a mixed methods study. JMIR Ment. Health **7**(3), e12388 (2020). https://doi.org/10.2196/12388
25. Khalili-Mahani, N., et al.: For whom the games toll: a qualitative and intergenerational evaluation of what is serious in games for older adults. Computer Games (Special Issue: Intergenerational Games) (2020, submitted)
26. Schwarzer, R., Jerusalem, M.: Generalized self-efficacy scale, in measures in health psychology: a user's portfolio. Causal Control Beliefs, pp. 35–37. NFER-NELSON: Windsor, England (1995)
27. Russell, D., Peplau, L.A., Ferguson, M.L.: Developing a measure of loneliness. J. Pers. Assess. **42**(3), 290–294 (1978)
28. Hong, G.R., et al.: Reliability and validity of the Korean version of the perceived stress scale-10 (K-PSS-10) in older adults. Res. Gerontol. Nurs. **9**(1), 45–51 (2016)
29. Khalili-Mahani, N., et al.: Hippocampal activation during a cognitive task is associated with subsequent neuroendocrine and cognitive responses to psychological stress. Hippocampus **20**(2), 323–334 (2010)
30. Henckens, M.J., et al.: Interindividual differences in stress sensitivity: basal and stress-induced cortisol levels differentially predict neural vigilance processing under stress. Soc. Cogn. Affect Neurosci. **11**(4), 663–673 (2016)
31. Drachen, A., et al.: Correlation between heart rate, electrodermal activity and player experience in first-person shooter games. In: Proceedings of the 5th ACM SIGGRAPH Symposium on Video Games - Sandbox 2010, pp. 49–54 (2010)
32. Kaufman, D., et al.: Older adults' digital gameplay: patterns, benefits, and challenges. Simul. Gaming **47**(4), 465–489 (2016)

33. De Schutter, B.: Never too old to play: the appeal of digital games to an older audience. Games Cult. **6**(2), 155–170 (2011)
34. De Schutter, B., Malliet, S.: The older player of digital games: a classification based on perceived need satisfaction. Commun.-Eur. J. Commun. Res. **39**(1), 67–87 (2014)
35. De Schutter, B., Brown, J.A.: Digital games as a source of enjoyment in later life. Games Cult. **11**(1–2), 28–52 (2016)
36. Narme, P.: Benefits of game-based leisure activities in normal aging and dementia. Geriatr. Psychol. Neuropsychiatr. Vieil. **14**(4), 420–428 (2016)
37. De Schutter, B., Abeele, V.V.: Towards a gerontoludic manifesto. Anthropol. Aging **36**(2), 112 (2015)
38. Whitcomb, G.R.: Computer games for the elderly. SIGCAS Comput. Soc. **20**(3), 112–115 (1990)
39. Allaire, J.C., et al.: Successful aging through digital games: socioemotional differences between older adult gamers and non-gamers. Comput. Hum. Behav. **29**(4), 1302–1306 (2013)
40. Whitlock, L.A., et al.: Older adults' perception of the benefits associated with intervention-based video game play. Gerontologist **51**, 40 (2011)
41. Boot, Walter R., Souders, D., Charness, N., Blocker, K., Roque, N., Vitale, T.: The gamification of cognitive training: older adults' perceptions of and attitudes toward digital game-based interventions. In: Zhou, J., Salvendy, G. (eds.) ITAP 2016. LNCS, vol. 9754, pp. 290–300. Springer, Cham (2016). https://doi.org/10.1007/978-3-319-39943-0_28
42. Deci, E.L., Ryan, R.M.: Intrinsic Motivation and Self-determination in Human Behavior, vol. xv, 371 p. Plenum, New York (1985)
43. Csikszentmihalyi, M.: Beyond Boredom and Anxiety: (The Experience of Play in Work and Games), vol. xviii, 231 p. Jossey-Bass, San Francisco, London (1975)
44. Csikszentmihalyi, M.: Flow: The Psychology of Optimal Experience, p. 1. HarperCollins e-books, Pymble, NSW, New York (1990). (online resource)
45. Cacioppo, J.T., Tassinary, L.G., Berntson, G.G.: Handbook of Psychophysiology. Cambridge Handbooks in Psychology, 4th edn, vol. xvi, 715 p. Cambridge University Press, Cambridge (2017)
46. Coughlan, G., et al.: Toward personalized cognitive diagnostics of at-genetic-risk Alzheimer's disease. Proc. Natl. Acad. Sci. U.S.A. **116**(19), 9285–9292 (2019)
47. Mandryk, R.L., Birk, M.V.: The potential of game-based digital biomarkers for modeling mental health. JMIR Ment. Health **6**(4), e13485 (2019)
48. Gonzalez-Sanchez, J., et al.: Affect measurement: a roadmap through approaches, technologies, and data analysis. In: Emotions and Affect in Human Factors and Human-Computer Interaction, pp. 255–288 (2017)

Application of Game Therapy in the Health of Future Elderly: An Experience Design Perspective

Yuqi Liu[1](✉) and Ryoichi Tamura[2]

[1] School of Design, Kyushu University, Fukuoka, Japan
lyqeven@hotmail.com
[2] Faculty of Design, Kyushu University, Fukuoka, Japan
tamura@design.kyushu-u.ac.jp

Abstract. Gameplay maintains a deep part of human nature, and there is no difference between young people and elderly group. With the unprecedent advance of Cloud Computing, The Internet of Things, Artificial Intelligence and sensing technology, different forms of digital games could benefit older adults in a variety of fields, including physical exercise, rehabilitation drill, entertainment, social interaction, emotional adjustment, knowledge and skills acquisition, etc. This study starts from the development trend and future market prospects of digital game for the elderly, analyzes the attributes and characteristics of older adults which may influence the game therapy developing process. Then, taking the characteristics analysis result into consideration, the essay divides the types of game therapy into four types, physical game therapy, psychological game therapy, cognitive game therapy and comprehensive game therapy. Furthermore, all the typical functions of these game therapy types have been clarified from the perspective of the elderly needs. What's more, five levels hierarchy of how to construct elderly game therapy experience has been proposed, including strategy level, scope level, structure level, skeleton level and surface level. Last but not least, the paper has put forward six principles which should be followed during the development process of game therapy for older adults. This research provides new insights and creative solutions for the elderly healthcare industry, and explores how to use game therapy to improve their quality of life and wellbeing in old stage. It has deep impacts both for the game industry and pension industry.

Keywords: Game therapy · Experience design · User needs · Future · The elderly · Healthcare · Pension industry

1 Introduction

With the great development of medical technology, human longevity has been gradually and continuously extended. The proportion of elderly people all of the world keeps growing, and the phenomenon of aging society both in developed and developing countries turns out to be increasingly serious. According to the prediction of the United Nations,

C. Stephanidis et al. (Eds.): HCII 2020, LNCS 12426, pp. 608–625, 2020.
https://doi.org/10.1007/978-3-030-60149-2_46

by 2020, Chinese people aged 65 and over will reach 167 million, accounting for about 24% of the world's elderly population. It is estimated that by 2050, the number of China's elderly population will expand to 300–400 million, and the proportion of Chinese elderly aged 65 and over in the total population will reach around 21.7%, making the country with the largest aging population in the world [1]. The "silver-wave" in China and all of the world has brought tremendous pressure and burden to the whole human society in all aspects. Therefore, the concepts of healthy aging and active aging are bound to be on the agenda [2]. Gameplay is a behavior following certain rules within a certain time and space to pursue the satisfaction of spiritual needs based on the material fulfillment. It is also an attractive way to reduce psychological pressure and pursue happiness for people of all ages [3]. For elderly group, the functions of gameplay are far more beyond the entertainment aspect, but also could play an important role in meeting their physical, psychological and social needs [4]. Game therapy is an intervention method that uses game as an indispensable element in the healthy treatment process. It was first used in the rehabilitation of children's psychological problems [5]. But nowadays, how to apply it on dealing with the health problems of older adults also raises profound and meaningful concerns both in commercial and academic fields. This study explores the application and all-around possibility of game therapy in the field of elderly healthcare. Based on the insight into the characteristics and needs of older adults, the market potential, game types, and functions of game therapy for the elderly group are analyzed. Moreover, how to use game therapy in the prevention, treatment and rehabilitation of physical, psychological and cognitive diseases of elderly people has been systematically discussed. Last but not least, the essay puts forward five layers and six principles of game therapy development for older adults from an experience design perspective which provides insightful and creative solutions for the combination of game and pension industry.

2 Literature Review

Game therapy refers to a medical intervention method that uses games as a therapeutic medium or carrier to conduct treatment with human health problems based on the theory of plasticity and sufficient function of the human brain, with entertainment therapy as its main purpose [6]. It originated from psychoanalysis, Sigmund Freud is a well-known Austrian psychologist and the pioneer of the psychoanalytic school. He pioneered the use of games to treat children's mental illness [7]. Nowadays, game therapy is widely used in the treatment of childhood depression, which has laid the corresponding theoretical foundation for game therapy of elderly diseases. Game therapy for the elderly is mostly used in scientific brain training, recognitive training, and the prevention of negative psychology. At present, many world-renowned universities have set up topics on games and psychotherapy, such as Carnegie Mellon University, which offers courses to help student acquire knowledge of game culture and the psychology of the middle-aged and elderly people. Stanford University also opened a research project on healthcare game design. Jason Allaire of the Game Lab at North Carolina State University in the United States believes that: "Games can promote positive influence, especially on psychology. In order to fully understand the role of games in human psychology, researchers need to specialize in some topics like the impact of game on cognition and learning, such as the effects of games on individual memory, attention, flexibility, thinking and reaction" [8]. Mark Griffith, a professor of game research at the Nottingham Trent University, claims that game can successfully transfer patients 'pain and can be used to assist patients in physical therapy or to help strengthen patients' physical strength, thereby, speeding up the process of rehabilitation treatment [9]. "Archives of neurology" published a research report that, game can delay or even avoid the development of Alzheimer's disease, and can also improve player memory ability. The process of playing game can help to stimulate the player's brain and cognitive functions [10]. It is obvious that scientists in different fields have already paid attention to solving health issues for the aging group through game therapy. But few of them has discussed the game therapy for elderly group in a systematical way and puts forward the structure and insights of how to do game therapy development from an experience design perspective to deliver good and pleasure therapy experience for the elderly.

3 The Development Trend and Market Prospects for the Elderly Digital Game

In the future, with the rapid development of advanced science and technology, including Artificial Intelligent, Big Date, The Internet of Things, Virtual Reality, Augmented Reality, Mixed Reality, identification technology, etc., digital games will present trends include the combination of virtual and reality, closer social interaction between players, multidimensional sensory response, multi-functional control terminals and diversified control behaviors, etc. [11]. Numerous novel forms of games will emerge and be more and more popular, such as virtual reality games, somatosensory games, etc. Digital games will not only exist on mobile phones, tablets and computers, but also in virtual helmets, wearable devices, home theater, spatial projection, and other innovative ways, creating an immersive experience for gamers [12]. The game control terminal will not only work by the cooperation of the eyes, hands and brain, but also mobilize all the multi-sensory control of player's bodies [13], which will lay the technology foundation for the full-scale application of game therapy in the field of elderly health in the future. The elderly industry is a collective term for industries that provide various products and services for older adults. The elderly industry stays undeveloped in China since the country has not walked into the aging society very long time, but its aging process runs very fast [14]. According to a survey, the current elderly industry demand in the Chinese market is about 600 billion yuan per year, and the products and services provided are less than one sixth of the demand [15]. With the provision of material living standards, the elderly's consumer demand has begun to be diversified. Unlike the conservative consumer image in our impression, contemporary elderly people value the quality of products and services increasingly seriously and are also willing to accept fresh things [16]. As an emerging industry, elderly games are still in their infancy in China. However, with the upgrading of people's consumption levels and the generations affected by the Internet and born in the Internet era will gradually enter the aging stage in the coming future, the aging population will increase dramatically and the elderly game therapy market will become huge and flourish.

4 The Attributes and Characteristics of the Elderly

With the increase of the age of the elderly, their physical and social functions will unavoidably decline and decay. Table 1 is about the aging age of the main organs of the human body, which is compiled and summarized by the author based on literature and materials reading. From the table, we can see the human body aging laws and regulations, which could provide support for the characteristics analysis of the elderly.

Table 1. Main human organs aging age.

Human organs aging age								
Brain	Lung	Skin	Muscle	Breast	Bone	Fertility	Heart	Eyes
20	20	25	30	35	35	35	40	40
Teeth	Prostate	Kidney	Hearing	Intestine	Taste & Smell	Bladder	Sound Gland	Liver
40	50	50	55	55	60	65	65	70

Based on the table above, the following will analyze and summarize the characteristics of the elderly group from physical, psychological and cognitive aspects.

4.1 Physical Characteristics

Human body is composed of the following nine major systems: motor system, nervous system, endocrine system, circulatory system, respiratory system, digestive system, urinary system, reproductive system, and immune system [17]. From the perspective of game experience, the author summarizes the system degradation of the elderly that may have a major impact on game therapy design.

Degeneration of Sensory System. Degeneration of the nervous system could directly leads to the degradation of the elderly's sensory system, which is mainly reflected in the aspects of vision, hearing, taste, smell, and touch, and will affect external stimuli and information acceptance, manifested as unresponsiveness, especially hearing and vision. It can lead to serious life disorders.

Degeneration of Skeletal and Muscle System. For elderly group, the decrease of calcium in bone and bone density may easily multiple fractures. Muscle tissue of ordinary human body begins to decrease from about 50 years old, and the process accelerates greatly after 60 years of age, which leading to muscle relaxation and may turn into amyotrophic lateral sclerosis (ALS) in severe cases. It could greatly affect the daily life of older adults, such as being unable to perform high-intensity exercise. And if the situation getting worse, it may bring walking obstacle in a daily life.

Degeneration of Cardiopulmonary System. Because of the decline of endocrine system, female ovaries or testes begin to reduce the quantity of hormones which will directly affect the nervous system works. During this period, people often experience chest tightness, shortness of breath, palpitations, shortness of breath, dizziness, tinnitus, irregular heart rate, and even cardiovascular and cerebrovascular diseases. Deterioration of the heart and lungs could cause respiratory and circulatory problems, like heart disease, hypertension and hyperglycemia, which are very common in the elderly group.

High Incidence of Chronic Disease. Chronic diseases are closely related to the individual's lifestyle. Multiple stress from work and life in middle age and former life is one of the important reasons leading to the high incidence of chronic diseases for the elderly. Being lack of exercise, unhealthy eating habits could also be the causes. Over time, unhealthy lifestyle will cause declines of the body's immune system, eventually leading to the occurrence of various chronic diseases.

4.2 Psychological Characteristics

In China, after retirement, the social scope of seniors is usually limited to the family and surrounding communities. At the same time, the majority of their children are busy with their own works and live away in another city, so that they could not give enough companionship and concerns to their parents. This situation may easily cause some psychological diseases which being ignored by their children even themselves. Moreover, physical function declines and chronic diseases of the elderly could also bring older adults different degree of psychological changes, over time, it may lead to serious psychological diseases and affect the physical health.

Loneliness and Depression. The majority of elderly people in China live a busy life before retirement, moving between work and family all day long. It is hard for them feel lonely because of the strong spiritual pursuit of career success and value realization. However, after retirement, they are easy to lose the life goals and future plan. Some seniors could easily get depression. As time goes by, such negative feelings of loneliness and depression will lead to poor mental state of the elderly and invoke suspicious and anxious emotions. For instance, the phenomenon of "empty nest elderly" is a serious problem in China. There are no family members accompany with them, which will lead their sense of security to drop and loneliness to rise.

Inferiority and Frustration. Due to the decline of physical and cognitive functions of the elderly, many inconveniences and mistakes could appear in life, such as improper handling of things, difficulty in accepting new things, the pain of illness, etc. These situations are very likely to bring negative emotions of inferiority and self-criticism to seniors, they will be more sensitive and easily get frustrated because of their powerless to reality and aging.

Degeneration of Cardiopulmonary System. The secretion quantity of hormones will be reduced with the aging process of endocrine system including ovaries and testes, which will directly affect the nervous system. During this period, people often experience chest tightness, shortness of breath, palpitations, shortness of breath, dizziness, tinnitus, irregular heart rate, and even cardiovascular and cerebrovascular diseases. Deterioration of the heart and lungs has caused respiratory and circulatory problems in older people. Diseases such as respiratory diseases and heart disease, as well as hypertension and hyperglycemia are very common in the elderly.

Menopause Symptoms. After entering menopause, both men and women's physical and psychological state will change significantly. Poor mood, irritability, nervousness, anxiety, insomnia, and sentimentality are often presented. Elderly people are eager for receiving attention and respect in old age and reducing the psychological gap resulting from retirement. Therefore, it is extremely important to pay attention to the mental health of retired elderly, enrich their spiritual and cultural life, and help them to expand their social circles.

4.3 Cognitive Characteristics

With the aging process, brain cells begin to decrease, nervous system begins to shrink, information delivery and nerve conduction efficiency will greatly be slowed down compared to young people. The recognitive characteristics of the elderly are mainly reflected in recognition aging and recognition impairment.

Cognition Aging. The characteristics of recognition aging are mainly manifested in slower motion and central nervous processing speed, reduced working memory, decreased ability to suppress the effects of irrelevant stimuli, and increased physical disharmony. It includes intelligence decline, thinking ability decline, memory decline, responsiveness decline, learning and operating ability decline. Because of these, most older people have a weaker ability to perceive and accept new things, which make they spend more time than young group to learn a new operation or master a new skill.

Recognition Impairment. Recognition impairment could be divided into mild degree and serious degree. Studies have shown that there is a great chance of mild cognitive impairment could turn into Alzheimer's disease [18]. Alzheimer's disease is a neurological degenerative disorder with a more insidious, progressive development [19]. Cognitive impairment, memory impairment, visual impairment, speech loss, executive disability, and personality change, are all its clinical symptoms [20]. The etiology has not been identified so far. Professor Reidrey of the Alzheimer's Research Fund Committee in the UK said: "Researchers believe that the hidden dangers of Alzheimer's disease begin in middle age. Maintaining an active and healthy lifestyle, such as keeping good diet and doing regular examination of blood pressure and cholesterol can significantly reduce the prevalence of Alzheimer's disease [21]. According to the characteristics of the elderly's being discussed above, the author draws Fig. 1.

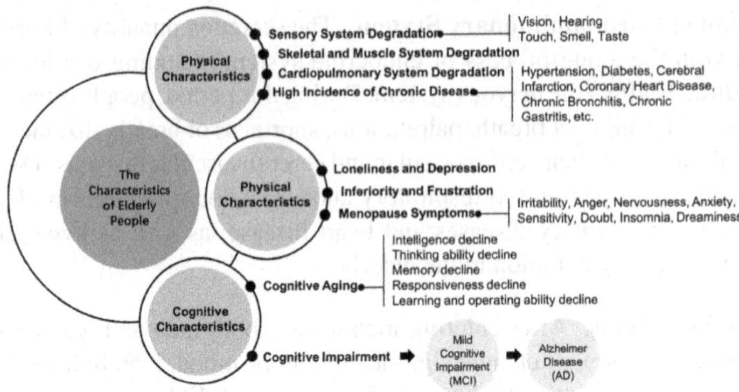

Fig. 1. The characteristics of the elderly

5 The Types and Functions of Game Therapy for the Elderly

According to the characteristics of the elderly summarized in the previous article, the author classifies the digital game therapy for the elderly into four categories: physical game therapy, psychological game therapy, cognitive game therapy, and comprehensive game therapy. The roles and functions of each game therapy are explained in Table 2 and will be discussed in detail in the following content.

5.1 Physical Game Therapy

Physical game therapy focuses on the prevention, treatment and rehabilitation of physical disease of the elderly, including sensory movements, hand and foot exercises, muscle exercises, cardiopulmonary exercises, joint exercises, strength, balance, and tolerance training. It has the following functions.

Stimulate and Train the Sensory System. In the future, with the development of advanced Artificial Intelligence and sensing technology, such as 4D, 5D, and 6D technologies, VR, AR, MR, and XR, game could stimulate players' senses from multiple dimensions, including vision, hearing, smell, touch, and even taste. This provides an all-around possibility for the stimulation and drill of elderly people sensory system.

Improve the Function of Motion System. Using gameplay to improve the physical function is beneficial to the circulatory, nervous, immune, digestive and musculoskeletal systems, and will help to expand the range and amount of activities for the elderly. It can also be combined with sports and fitness equipment to provide the drill of strength, balance, and tolerance ability to train and intervene the elderly's locomotor system. For example, a study showed that VR intervention treatment reduced the elderly's chance of falling by 42% [22].

Treat and Relieve Chronic Diseases. This function means to establish regular exercise habits to train the body's skeletal muscles and cardiopulmonary functions, which can help treat and alleviate the degree of chronic diseases. For example, the combination of

Table 2. Types of game therapy for the elderly.

Type	Definition	Functions	Content
1	Games that prevent, treat, or rehabilitate physical diseases	Stimulate and train the sensory system; Improve the function of motion system Treat and relieve chronic diseases Rehabilitation training, etc.	Sports, music, dance, racing, shooting, etc.
2	Games that prevent, treat, or rehabilitate mental illness	Build positive emotions Expand and promote social interaction Find virtual meaning and belongings Develop a sense of meaning Gain a sense of achievement, etc.	Role-playing, adventure, social, tactical competition, leisure, entertainment, etc.
3	Games that prevent, treat, or rehabilitate cognitive impairment or barrier	Improve cognitive ability Master knowledge and skills Prevent cognitive impairment and Alzheimer Disease, etc.	Education, strategy, puzzle, board and card, etc.
4	Games that integrate above two or three	Integration of above two or three functions	Integration of different content

Note: 1 = Physical game therapy; 2 = Psychological game therapy; 3 = Cognitive game therapy; 4 = Comprehensive game therapy.

running games and treadmills, cycling games and bicycles, all could help the elderly to establish a regular activity mode in a positive and pleasure way to do physical fitness. Now there are many exercise equipment combining with AR, VR technology and somatosensory games. For example, Japanese taiko games, taking the traditional Japanese taiko culture as the carrier, using two-handed sticks to perform different actions according to the notes displayed on the electronic screen and beat the drum head with the intensity according to the music rhythm. The speed and difficulty of the music are adjustable, which has a good exercise effect for the player.

Rehabilitation Training. For the elderly who have already gotten illness or experienced surgery, gameplay can also be used for reasonable intensity rehabilitation training. The method and training intensity depend on the disease type and physical condition of the old people. For example, studies in patients with chordal injuries have shown that patients' participation in recreational activities and exercise, can help redefine themselves and achieve higher life satisfaction, which is really helpful to promote active aging [23].

5.2 Psychological Game Therapy

Psychological game therapy mainly refers to games for the prevention, treatment or rehabilitation of mental illness. For older people, psychological problems sometimes are far more serious than physicals, and will always accelerate the appearance of physical diseases which could dramatically affect the seniors' physical health. The author summarizes the psychological effects of game therapy into the following categories.

Build Positive Emotions. Game therapy can help to optimize participants' moods and remove emotional disorders to help them build positive emotions [24]. According to some studies, games, like music, dance, painting, and literature, are the main forms of positive art therapy for the elderly [25]. Recreational games can help the elderly to find their interests and suitable leisure methods more easily, and get positive emotions including love, hope, optimism, contentment, happiness, excitement, as well as getting rid of the common depression. Some creative entertainment games also have the effect of relieving the stresses and pains.

Expand and Promote Social Communication. Older adults often share some common characteristics because of retirement, such as reduced social interaction, more leisure time, narrower interpersonal communication, and weaken information acquisition ability. Some studies have shown that the function of games is very effective in treating children with autism [26]. And so do the elderly group. Today's computer games and digital entertainment are often inconvenient for intergenerational family interactions. According to a survey in Japan, a high percentage of older people have video or computer games, but they rarely play with their family members [27]. This is a positive sign that more and more older people are participating in the digital gaming field. But if they can actively interact with young family members through games, it will be even more beneficial. For example, they can interact and entertain with their grandchildren through games, or even use game to conduct educational activities. In addition, not only with family, gameplay can also strengthen communication and interaction with their friends, and even strangers. It is an effective and efficiency way to expand the socialization circle of the elderly.

Find Virtual Meaning and Belongings. Gameplay could help older people try a plenty of fresh things that they have never tried in their former lives. For example, Role-playing games could make the elderly to do things that they want to but impossible in real life, like to do their favorite jobs and become their favorite person, to join the virtual community and meet people sharing the same interests and goals with them. The shaping and experience of virtual meaning and substitution could help them solve an amount of psychological problems.

Develop a Sense of Achievement. Game can help seniors to gain competence and sense of success which is one of the typical characteristics of gameplay. It is an experience that overcomes difficulties and gain encouragements and awards as feedback. Erikson, a representative of the new psychoanalytic school, he not only emphases that games can not only reduce the sense of anxiety and depression, but also highlight the role of games in self-development [28]. In the future, game therapy could open up a field to cultivate players' co-creation ability in the game environment, which means that following the basic guidance and regulations of game, the elderly could do creative and innovative activities freely by themselves in the virtual environment to enhance their sense of achievement. Also, how to use gameplay to dig out the value of the elderly group and help them gain respect and competence could be another meaningful and interesting topic.

5.3 Cognitive Game Therapy

Cognitive game therapy mainly refers to games that prevent, treat and rehabilitate the elderly's cognitive problems. Their effects mainly include the following two aspects.

Improve Cognitive Ability of the Elderly and Master Knowledge and Skills. With the increase of age, the aging and degradation of the elderly's intelligence, thinking, memory, reaction, learning and operating ability are inevitable, but regular training can improve and delay the time of cognitive aging and relieve its extent. Game therapy can help with these training in a much more pleasure way. And it can also let players to participate in certain social or leisure entertainment activities, which could benefit their cognitive ability, social and communication skills [29].

Prevent and Relieve the Recognitive Impairment and Stay Away from Alzheimer Disease. Active cognitive exercise and thinking training can delay recognition aging and avoid the occurrence of mild cognitive impairment. However, if cognitive impairment unfortunately occurs, game therapy could also help with rehabilitation training and recovery. While mind cognitive impairment goes worse, Alzheimer's disease may appear. It is one of the most common cognitive dysfunction disorders in elderly group. Patients will gradually lose their short-term memory and control of emotions, fall into depression, mania and delusion, and bring a lot of pain and burden to themselves and the people around them. Game therapy can assist with finding and diagnosing Alzheimer's disease, and help with proper recovery training. At the same time, it could help researchers collect a large amount of behavioral data, and use artificial intelligence to analyze and grasp the pathogen, so that to create a better living environment for Alzheimer's patients. For example, in 2016, Deutsche Telekom, game developer Glitchers, and several european universities launched a study on the diagnosis of Alzheimer's disease, they used a game called Sea Hero Quest to help predict the probability and risk of having Alzheimer's diseases for the players [30].

5.4 Comprehensive Game Therapy

The Comprehensive game therapy refers to games that have more than two curative effects being discussed above. It has the blending effect of physical, psychological or cognitive therapy for the elderly.

6 Hierarchy and Strategies of Game Therapy Experience Design for the Elderly

Don Norman, one of the most influential designers of this century, coined the term "user experience" in the 1990s, saying that "user experience includes all aspects of user interaction with companies, services, and their products." [31]. In short, UX design relates to all the elements that affects the user's interaction with the product. Its branches include interaction design, information architecture, visual design, usability, and human-computer interaction, etc. Experience design thinking could standardize the design and development process of game therapy to shape the perfect gaming therapeutic experience for the elderly. The American designer, Garrett. JJ, puts forward the elements and five layers of user-centered Experience design for website development. They are surface layer, skeleton layer, structure layer, scope layer and strategy layer [32]. The author inspires from that, define and analyze the design of game therapy for the elderly from those five layers based on the analysis of the characteristics and needs of the elderly players, and form a cross matrix between the five layers and the four types of game therapy, as shown in Fig. 2.

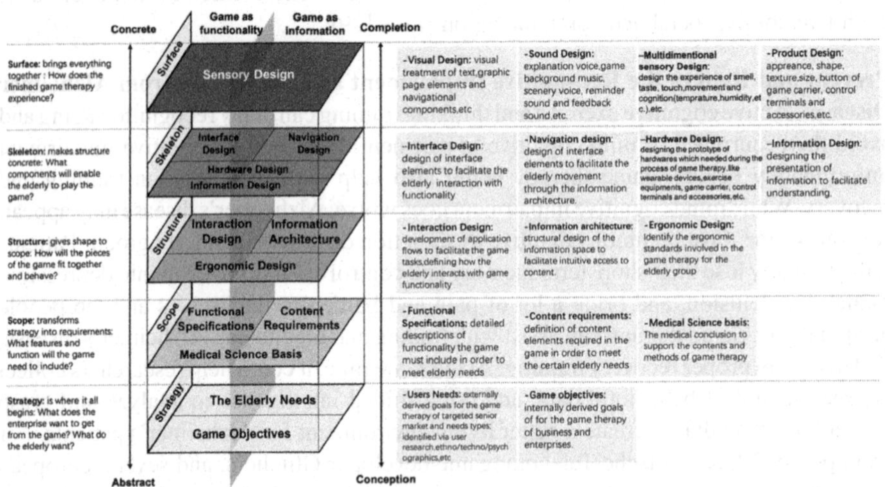

Fig. 2. The layers of game therapy experience design for the elderly

6.1 Strategy Layer

The design of the strategy layer is reflected in two aspects: one is to clarify the core needs of users and their pain points, another one is to set business goals of the game development. A successful product should not only meet the goals and interests of the business, but also deliver good experiences to meet or exceed the user expectations. For the strategic layer of game therapy design for the elderly, the core appeal of elderly users is to pursue physical, psychological and cognitive health and to prevent, treat and rehabilitate various elderly's diseases in a pleasant way. Also, for therapy enterprises, they undoubtedly need to expand the targeted customers group through business goals, brand image, strategic planning, etc., to maximize business benefits and profits. This layer is the core and bottom layer of the whole product and service system.

6.2 Scope Layer

The pain points of the users and the company's goals were found at the strategic level, while the scope level needed to figure out effective solutions. Through strategic thinking, the general functions and contents of the product were clearly identified. This layer needs the "functions combination" and "content requirements" of the product in detailed description. It can also be analyzed from the perspective of both company goals and the user needs. On the user side, the target group needs to be subdivided, and specific usage scenarios should be constructed. The process of scenario analysis could help to find certain methods to solve the pain points. For the company, at the scope level, it is necessary to consider how to produce a welcome product, build a recognizable brand and gain quantity of customers to maximize the market share and profits. For game design, this step can further subdivide the specific scenarios used for elderly users and game therapy, streamline game functions and content, determine the priority of content information presentation and column setting levels; organize related text, pictures, audio and video materials; add, retain, and remove tasks based on the needs of older users.

6.3 Structure Layer

If the scope layer provides a solution to the problem, then the structure layer is the detailed decomposition of these methods into various steps and organized the conduction according to a certain logic from the perspective of users. In this step, we need to focus on functional logic, including two aspects: connection logic between different functions, and connection logic between different elements of the same function. For the first aspect, it is necessary to make every effort to make the distinction between different functions to let them be easily identified. So that when users use a certain function, they can find the corresponding elements at a glance. For the second aspect, to make the different elements of a function integrate with each other well, each step must comply with the basic operating logic. For the design of game therapy for the elderly, this layer mainly includes functional interaction design and information architecture construction. The fundamental purpose is to rationally arrange game content elements to promote the understanding of game information for the elderly, reduce user understanding costs, improve game system operation efficiency, usability and ease of use. Hence, they can reach a certain interface quickly and accurately, and complete a game therapy task easily.

6.4 Skeleton Layer

If the structure layer is the information architecture and interaction logic of the game therapy, focusing on how users can complete the jump between different interface perfectly, the skeleton layer is more inclined to the concrete layout design of elements in a game page and give functional guidance. It defines the arrangement and combination of various elements on interface navigation, while the structure layer just determines the specific locations of different types of elements. Specifically, when a new user opens a game, he can successfully complete a task without prompts in accordance with previous cognition and operation habits. When combining the skeleton and surface layer, it belongs to the prototype stage, including the placement of interface elements and the design of navigation information. In game therapy for the elderly, the task how to properly design elements well and maximize the best conditions of the combination of all the elements belongs to skeleton layer, so that elderly users can operate it smoothly without any barriers.

6.5 Surface Layer

The main purpose of the surface layer is to create complete therapy experience of the final product for the elderly. It is the final effect of the above four layers. It involves the game experience design of all senses, vision, hearing, touch and motion, etc. If the skeleton layer focuses on the concrete guidance of an interface or function, which is specifically reflected in the layout of the interface and the placement, then the surface layer focuses on the realization details and specific components treatment, like videos, pictures, the shape, color, size, duration, etc., are all the focus of this layer. The surface layer of game therapy design for the elderly, including visual design, audio design and tangible product design. In visual design, users see the combination of interface, roles, objects, environment, videos, pictures, and text. In audio design, users hear the background music and scene sounds of the game. In terms of product design, it is the carrier part of game therapy, including terminals and auxiliary equipment, like public medical facilities, home theater, wearable devices, gamepads, etc., depending on the specific therapy goals and contents.

7 Principals for the Development of Game Therapy for the Elderly

The following is the summarized principles that should be followed in the development of game therapy products for the elderly.

7.1 Taking the Elderly Needs as Start Point

The game therapy development for the elderly should give the first priority of user-centered design principle and develop game products based on the characteristics and needs of the elderly. Only in this way, can we combine the pain points of the elderly with game design that meet both the business goals and user expectations. For example, a plenty of elderly people want to travel and see the world, but the places they could go are very limited due to their physical declines and aging, take this pain point into consideration, some business could provide virtual traveling, like VR games, to satisfy their desire and curiosity about the outside world and help them stay in good recognition and emotion level. What's more, older adults are the group most concerned about health status, many diseases can be prevented and controlled by the elderly themselves without going to hospitals and seeing doctors at the initial stage. For this insight, we can add healthcare knowledge and content into gameplay process and help them form a healthy lifestyle.

7.2 Considering from the Perspective of Prevention, Treatment and Rehabilitation of Health Problems

All the diseases curing process includes three stages, prevention, treatment and rehabilitation. According to this insight, all types of game therapy development can start from these three perspectives. Among them, disease prevention should be the first focus of game development, and it is also an area where game therapy can exert its profound impact. When diseases occur, games can help to figure out the causes and evaluate the serious degree, especially psychological and cognitive diseases, and assisting with the treatment. After the completion of treatment, game could be effective in another way against aging diseases, that's rehabilitation training. These three aspects are very important game therapy goals for elderly group.

7.3 Making Parameters Setting Comply with the Elderly Ergonomic Standards

Game therapy development for seniors should pay close attention to ergonomic considerations and the physical indicators and behavioral capacity of the elderly, mainly including the followings.

Parameter Adjustable. The diversified parameters of game therapy system should be adjustable. For example, the graphics and text should be designed according to the recognition and cognitive ability of the elderly, and the size should be adjustable, so do the volume, music speed and intensity and difficulty of the game level, etc. These could make the game suitable for older adults with different physical, psychological and cognitive conditions.

Moderate Function. For the elderly, game functions should be simple and complicated settings should be avoided. Unnecessary and redundant functions should be deleted and take the ease of use into consideration according to intellectual differences of older adults.

Simple Operation. The control way and operation of games for seniors should be as simple as possible. We can use advanced technologies such as eye capture, video, and voice to make the elderly as convenient as they can. For games such as traditional tablet and those in mobile platform, the user interface and information meaning is best seen at a glance, avoiding redundant and complex layers. If the game controllers are carried with advanced technology and the types are quite new, such as motion sensing games, we should take the elderly's duration into consideration, and pay attention to the fact that their athletic ability, focus, and response time will be relatively delayed as game time goes by.

Suitable Content. The elderly usually suffer from diverse chronic cardiovascular diseases, their sympathetic nervous system is relatively excited and the adrenaline secretion level in the body is high, which resulting in high neuro-sensitivity and reduced tolerance to external stimuli. Therefore, special attention should be paid to the materials and content used in games, and check if it is in line with the preferences of the elderly. Also, during the game therapy process, taking care of dignity of the elderly group is necessary, aging discrimination contents and behaviors should be totally forbidden in the game therapy process.

7.4 Increasing Social Interaction in Games

The core needs of older group, besides health, is social interaction. The state of interpersonal relationships will affect the emotion and psychological state of the elderly, and then have an effect to their healthy status. Therefore, in game therapy development process, developers could consider adding interaction functions to promote the communication of older people with others. For example, many Chinese elderly helps to take care of their grandchildren after retirement, and they want to know how to get along with their grandchildren and do the education activities. According to this insight, developers can design games for old people and their grandchildren and make them complete certain tasks together, so that they could cooperate and understand each other better. It is also an effective way of promoting intergenerational communication and interaction.

7.5 Ensuring Safe and Healthy Game Environment

The development of game therapy for the elderly should ensure a healthy and safe game environment and avoid any potential dangers, accidents and unhealthy settings during the game therapy process, such as falls, sedentary, high blood pressure, shortness of breath, etc., There should be some corresponding protection settings and auxiliary equipment, such as seat belts, waist protection, bowl protection, etc., to protect the players. Moreover, preventing game addiction measures are also necessary to guarantee their healthy playing behaviors.

7.6 Providing Modular and Personalized Customization Services

The healthy status and needs of the elderly in different age stages are different, and they change very quickly with the growth of age. Hence, detail classification of the aging group's characteristics and needs are necessary. At the same time, users' demands and game expectations have individual differences. Considering these two aspects, game therapy development could consider inserting various modular functions meet their preferences and provide them distinguished experience. It could also reserve space for personalized customization to satisfy some individuals' certain needs.

8 Discussion and Conclusion

This study practices the interdisciplinary innovation of digital game and informatic health from an experience perspective, aims to propose the method of digital game therapy to provide good prevention, treatment and rehabilitation for future older adults' healthcare. Based on the analysis of characteristics and pain points of the elderly group, the author divides the elderly game therapy into four types, physical game therapy, psychological game therapy, recognitive game therapy, and comprehensive game therapy, and explains the functions and effects of each therapy category in detail. At the same time, the study proposes five layers and related strategies of game therapy experience design for the elderly. Moreover, six principles during the game developing process are clarified. With the generations who influenced and born in Internet era entering the middle-aged and old stage, digital game market and healthcare market for the elderly will have a continuously rapid development. Older adults game therapy industry, as an important part of entertainment and healthcare market, is supposed to maintain huge business potential in the coming future. It is of great social, economic and practical significance to exert its effects for future elders and help them respond to health issues in a more active and pleasure way.

Acknowledgments. The present work should give special acknowledgment to China Scholarship Council (CSC) for providing the funding support.

References

1. World population ageing 1950–2050. United Nations, New York (2002)
2. Briggs, A., et al.: Musculoskeletal health conditions represent a global threat to healthy aging: a report for the 2015 world health organization world report on ageing and health. Gerontologist **56**, S243–S255 (2016)
3. Warburton, D., et al.: The health benefits of interactive video game exercise. Appl. Physiol. Nutr. Metab. **32**, 655–663 (2007)
4. Wilkinson, N., Ang, R., Goh, D.: Online video game therapy for mental health concerns: a review. Int. J. Soc. Psychiatry **54**, 370–382 (2008)
5. Bhatt, S., De Leon, N., Al-Jumaily, A.: Augmented reality game therapy for children with autism spectrum disorder. Int. J. Smart Sens. Intell. Syst. **7**, 519–536 (2014)
6. Mader, S., Natkin, S., Levieux, G.: How to analyse therapeutic games: the player/game/therapy model. In: Herrlich, M., Malaka, R., Masuch, M. (eds.) ICEC 2012. LNCS, vol. 7522, pp. 193–206. Springer, Heidelberg (2012). https://doi.org/10.1007/978-3-642-33542-6_17
7. Leblanc, M., Ritchie, M.: A meta-analysis of play therapy outcomes. Couns. Psychol. Q. **14**, 149–163 (2001)
8. Allaire, J., McLaughlin, A., Trujillo, A., Whitlock, L., LaPorte, L., Gandy, M.: Successful aging through digital games: socioemotional differences between older adult gamers and Non-gamers. Comput. Hum. Behav. **29**, 1302–1306 (2013)
9. Griffiths, M., Meredith, A.: Videogame addiction and its treatment. J. Contemp. Psychother. **39**, 247–253 (2009)
10. Anchisi, D., Borroni, B., Franceschi, M., et al.: Heterogeneity of brain glucose metabolism in mild cognitive impairment and clinical progression to Alzheimer disease. Arch. Neurol. **62**, 1728 (2005)

11. Rizzo, A., Lange, B., Suma, E., Bolas, M.: Virtual reality and interactive digital game technology: new tools to address obesity and diabetes. J. Diabetes Sci. Technol. **5**, 256–264 (2011)
12. Chang, C., Hwang, G.: Trends in digital game-based learning in the mobile era: a systematic review of journal publications from 2007 to 2016. Int. J. Mob. Learn. Organ. **13**, 68 (2019)
13. Bianchi-Berthouze, N., Kim, W.W., Patel, D.: Does body movement engage you more in digital game play? and why? In: Paiva, A.C.R., Prada, R., Picard, R.W. (eds.) ACII 2007. LNCS, vol. 4738, pp. 102–113. Springer, Heidelberg (2007). https://doi.org/10.1007/978-3-540-74889-2_10
14. Dong, B., Ding, Q.: Aging in China: a challenge or an opportunity? J. Am. Med. Directors Assoc. **10**, 456–458 (2009)
15. Chenghui, A.L.: Big market for the aging Chinese society. J. Beijing Polytechnic Univ. **25**, 68–71 (1999)
16. Zhan, H.J., Liu, G., Guan, X.: Willingness and availability: explaining new attitudes toward institutional elder care among Chinese elderly parents and their adult children. J. Aging Stud. **20**, 279–290 (2006)
17. Forbes, G.B.: Human Body Composition: Growth, Aging, Nutrition and Activity. Springer, New York (1987). https://doi.org/10.1007/978-1-4612-4654-1
18. Peterson, R.C.: Mild cognitive impairment: Transition from aging to Alzheimer's disease. Neurobiol. Aging **21**, 1 (2000)
19. Reitz, C., Brayne, C., Mayeux, R.: Epidemiology of Alzheimer disease. Nat. Rev. Neurol. **7**, 137 (2011)
20. Reisberg, B., Borenstein, J., Salob, S.P., Ferris, S.H.: Behavioral symptoms in Alzheimer's disease: phenomenology and treatment. J. Clin. Psychiatry **48**, 9–15 (1987)
21. Ridley, R.M., Baker, H.F., Crow, T.J.: Transmissible and non-transmissible neurodegenerative disease: similarities in age of onset and genetics in relation to aetiology. Psychol. Med. **16**, 199–207 (1986)
22. Rendon, A.A., Lohman, E.B., Thorpe, D., Johnson, E.G., Medina, E., Bradley, B.: The effect of virtual reality gaming on dynamic balance in older adults. Age Ageing **41**, 549–552 (2012)
23. Cahow, C., et al.: Relationship of therapeutic recreation inpatient rehabilitation interventions and patient characteristics to outcomes following spinal cord injury: the SCIRehab project. J. Spinal Cord Med. **35**, 547–564 (2012)
24. Fagundo, A.B., Santamaría, J.J., Forcano, L., et al.: Video game therapy for emotional regulation and impulsivity control in a series of treated cases with bulimia nervosa. Eur. Eating Disord. Rev. **21**, 493–499 (2013)
25. Snyder, B.A.: Expressive art therapy techniques: healing the soul through creativity. J. Humanist. Educ. Dev. **36**, 74–82 (1997)
26. Malinverni, L., Mora-Guiard, J., Padillo, V., Valero, L., Hervás, A., Pares, N.: An inclusive design approach for developing video games for children with autism spectrum disorder. Comput. Hum. Behav. **71**, 535–549 (2017)
27. Pyae, A., Liukkonen, T.N., Saarenpää, T., Luimula, M., Granholm, P., Smed, J.: When Japanese elderly people play a Finnish physical exercise game: a usability study. J. Usability Stud. **11**, 131–152 (2016)
28. Erikson, E.H.: Elements of a psychoanalytic theory of psychosocial development. Course Life: Psychoanal. Contrib. Toward Underst. Pers. Dev. **1**, 11–61 (1980)
29. Gamberini, L., Raya, M.A., Barresi, G., Fabregat, M., Ibanez, F., Prontu, L.: Cognition, technology and games for the elderly: an introduction to ELDERGAMES Project. PsychNology J. **4**, 285–308 (2006)
30. Aškić, L., Mimica, N., Šimić, G., Mimica, N., Huić, T., Dajčić, T.: «Sea Hero Quest» -with videogame to scientific advancement in the understanding of dementia. Neurologia Croatica. Supplement. **65**, 93 (2016)

31. McCarthy, J., Wright, P.: Technology as experience. Interactions **11**, 42–43 (2004)
32. Garrett, J.J.: The Elements of User Experience: User-Centered Design for the Web and Beyond. New Riders, Berkeley (2011)

Construction and Evaluation of Situational System for Introducing Interactive Technology into Ecotourism of Active Aging Group

Li-Shu Lu[1(✉)], PeiFen Wu[2], and Guan-Yuan Huan[1]

[1] Department and Graduate School of Digital Media Design, National Yunlin University of Science and Technology, Douliu, Taiwan, R.O.C.
luls@gemail.yuntech.edu.tw

[2] Department of Information Management and Master Program in Digital Content Technology and Management, National Changhua University of Education, Changhua, Taiwan, R.O.C.

Abstract. Due to the issue of population aging faced by Taiwan, the government is implementing policies on encouraging the elderly to engage in social activities in their life after retirement, so as to enable them to enjoy a contented and happy retirement life and further forget their ages. In the population aging society, the elderly have an increasingly greater demand for ecotourism. Therefore, in this study, by taking ecotourism as an example, a research on the engagement of the elderly in technology enhanced interactive scenarios of ecotourism was conducted. Purpose of this study was mainly to propose the design system of technology enhanced interactive scenarios suitable for experience of the elderly. In this study, experience demands of the elderly were understood through relevant literature review, preliminary survey and field survey. Subsequently, design concepts of interactive scenarios were proposed through Scenario Approach and a prototype of interactive scenario was designed through Rapid Prototyping Method. Research results: a total of 8 concepts of interactive scenarios were proposed in this study through demand investigation, including provision of experience information, voice guide experience, enhancement of experience fun, trigger of experience scenario, enhancement of intellectual fun, basic knowledge query, enhancement of sensory experience, and sharing and memory. At last, the prototype of "i-Travel" interactive experience scenario was proposed through Prototyping Method. The interactive system consists of 8 interactive scenario concepts, experience contents and navigation design, design of scenario navigation APP, etc. Results of this study will be applied for subsequent assessment and validation of scenario experience awareness of this system.

Keywords: Active aging group · Ecotourism · Interactive technology · Interactive situation design

1 Introduction

At present, the world is facing an aging population. According to the estimation of National Development Council (2016), Taiwan's population over 65 years old will reach

C. Stephanidis et al. (Eds.): HCII 2020, LNCS 12426, pp. 626–642, 2020.
https://doi.org/10.1007/978-3-030-60149-2_47

20.9% of the total population in 2025, and Taiwan will officially become a super-aging society. The White Paper on Population Policy revised by the Taiwan Government mentions that the policy of encouraging the elderly to participate in leisure activities in society will help adjust their emotions and strengthen their physique, slow down the decline of physical functions and improve the quality of life. In particular, eco-tourism that allows the elderly to experiences nature can not only promote tourists' five-sense experience, but deepen impression of senior citizens. It also helps senior citizens to interact with each other, so as to extend interpersonal relation (Shimizu 2010). In this way, they may have a better quality of life, and live long, live well, and live with dignity. The most important thing is to live happily and forget their age. Just like the concept of "senior citizens". The word "senior citizens" derives from Singapore's respect for the elderly (Minister of Education 2009). It refers to the elderly whose age is between 45 and 65 years old, and who are about to retire or are planning to retire (Chang 2013), and are in good physical condition, and regard leisure as an important part after retirement (Chen and Wu 2009). Through participating in eco-tourism, they can obtain different leisure experiences, acquire ecological knowledge, appreciate natural scenery, and understand local cultural characteristics, etc. Therefore, this study defined senior citizens as people with the age between 45 and 64 years old, who have retired or are planning to retire and have good physical function. In recent years, the tourism of senior citizens has also changed significantly, from traditional outdoor and shopping trips to in-depth experience contents such as culture and ecology. Its tourism mode has changed from traditional leisure tourism to more in-depth and learning experience tourism (Bauer 2012). Among the natural ecological contents, culture and contact learning are very popular with the elderly (Yu and Hsiao 2012). Therefore, appropriate use of science and technology can increase the experience and learning of eco-tourism and further achieve the goal of happy learning for senior citizens. In addition, it is also possible to enhance the sense of identity and belonging by increasing interactive experience in tourism (Blanco 2011).

According to the above, the demand of the elderly for eco-tourism has become a trend in recent years, enabling the elderly to acquire leisure relaxation and ecological knowledge from the process of eco-tourism, and allow them to learn happily and forget their age. Therefore, according to the theories of interactive science and technology development and leisure in recent years, this paper collected and analyzed the needs of the senior citizens and related cases in the past, put forward an interactive situational system that conforms to the participation of senior citizens in ecotourism, and then invited senior citizens to experience and evaluate the interactive situational system. Finally, it proposed amendments to make it more in line with the experience fun of senior citizens in ecotourism. The purpose of this study is: 1. Put forward the concept of interactive situation design in line with senior citizen eco-tourism. 2. Explore the experience and feelings of senior citizens after participating in eco-tourism interactive situations. 3. Design the prototype of eco-tourism interactive situation and put forward suggestions for modification of the prototype.

2 Literature Review

The term eco-tourism was derived from the eco-tourism proposed by Hetzer in 1965. Also, he proposed 4 criteria of eco-tourism: minimum impact on the natural environment, minimum impact on the culture of the tourist destination, maximum benefit based on the local cultural characteristics, and maximum recreation satisfaction for participating tourists, which are the original intention of eco-tourism, and contribution to the protection and improvement of the natural environment through tourism (1989).

Context-aware technology-assisted tour guide is also becoming a trend (Lee and Lee 2015). If tourists can find deeper information, knowledge or spontaneous experience activities in the process of traveling, their experience of tourism can be enhanced (2007). Mobile device-assisted tour guide has the characteristics of no time and space limitation, low cost, real-time and easy use. For tourists, mobile device-assisted tour guide can be used at any time and place to improve tourist satisfaction (2005). Technology-assisted action tour guide not only solves the shortage of eco-tourism tour guide personnel, but improves tourists' satisfaction with knowledge acquisition and experience (2013). In the design process of context awareness, it is important to participate in the user-centered design process (2006). Attention should be paid to factors such as users' age, gender and use experience (Wang et al. 2012). Due to the aging of physical functions and the degeneration of the central nervous system, the mental skills of the elderly will degenerate (2002). The health status of the elderly will also worsen with the increase of age. All these phenomena will affect the learning situation of the elderly (2010). Experience design in eco-tourism must also consider the current local characteristics. The survey and planning of the situation should be used to enhance experience interaction, and the situation design should be carried out through the scenario approach. The scenario approach originates from the human-computer interaction design and is a design method that connects personnel, time, place, articles and other event segments in chronological order (1992) Tang and Lin (2011). Through vision, script or scenario, efforts are made to describe how the product assists users in their design and research methods, and helps designers to imagine the use situation of products to meet the needs of consumers (2000), and use the rapid prototype method to build the prototype in future life. This method is a model that emerged in the early 1980s. It develops the system prototype in a short period of time in the most economical and fast way to carry out experiments or verify unclear system requirements as soon as possible (Chi and Kuo 1995). Also, it can quickly build and continuously revise the system, which can effectively improve satisfaction of participants (Chou and Li 2009). John F. jeff Kelley first proposed Oz Paradigm in 1980. It mainly guides participants to think that they are interacting with the system. The Paradigm was actually for a researcher to interact with participants in the behind-the-scenes operating system. This method enables users to experience the products or interfaces in the design before investing in the prototype, providing an evaluation of participants' acceptance of the new method (Kelley 1984)

In order to effectively put forward eco-tourism situational awareness assessment projects that are suitable for senior citizens, this study explored the results of meeting senior citizens' needs and improving their physical and mental state according to literature, and integrated the aspects of senior citizens' participation in eco-tourism interaction. They are situational content: that is, whether the interactive situational content meets the needs of senior citizens in eco-tourism; leisure attitude: whether senior citizens are pleasant and positive in the use process in interactive situational prototype of ecotourism; system value: whether the prototype of the whole situation has achieved positive experience and high satisfaction of eco-tourism. In order to understand the feelings of senior citizens after experiencing interactive situations and provide suggestions for correction through literature induction, this study sorted out the interactive situation experience evaluation constructs suitable for this study, and subdivided such constructs into the following indicators. Each evaluation content is described in Table 1, and 26 indicators (see Fig. 1) are subdivided as the basis for designing the questionnaire content through the above-mentioned constructs.

Table 1. Content of evaluation.

Level 1	Level 2	Description of evaluation contents
Leisure attitude	Leisure emotion	Explore users' post-experience feelings of interactive experience situations
	Leisure cognition	Explore the benefits brought by users to leisure activities
	Leisure behavior	Explore the degree of behavioral activities when participating in leisure activities
Contextual content	Information design	Explore whether the knowledge content is correctly and clearly transmitted to users
	Tour guide design	Explore whether the tour guide will help guide users to experience different situations in the field
	Visual design	Discuss whether the field design and picture are attractive to users
System value	Perceived usefulness	Explore whether users think context-aware services and designs are complete experiences
	Satisfaction	Explore users' feelings in the process of using situational awareness services and situational experience
	Continuous use	Explore whether users' experience after experiencing the prototype of interactive situation affects their willingness to use the same type of services and goods again

Nowadays, the aging of the population is an inevitable trend, accompanied by changes in physical function, spiritual level and social status. By participating in recreational activities of eco-tourism, senior citizens can understand different ecological knowledge and cultural characteristics, provide secondary learning opportunities, satisfy their bodies and minds, and make them become who can conduct lifelong learning and forget their age. Therefore, if the experience mode of combining field construction and smart mobile phones is adopted, senior citizens will be able to experience the interpretation service by themselves, learn things easier and more convenient, and have an eco-tourism full of knowledge learning and leisure.

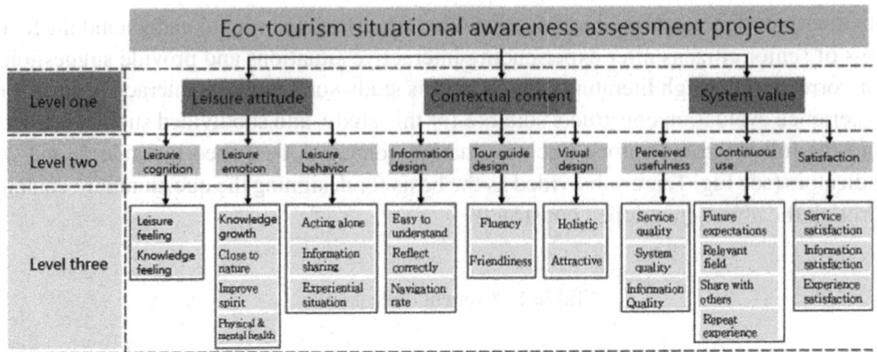

Fig. 1. Subdivided as the basis for designing the questionnaire content.

3 Methods

This study took the interactive situational experience survey of senior citizens participating in the introduction of science and technology into eco-tourism as the subject, and the research was divided into two stages: design and construction (pre-survey integration, prototype design and construction), and evaluation and verification (verification tool establishment, perceptual measurement and evaluation). The research subjects were 32 senior citizens. Non-participatory observation method was used to record the use of experience interactive situational system by senior citizens, and the data were collected and analyzed. Finally, suggestions for revising the interactive system were put forward. Research processes are shown in Fig. 2.

3.1 Construction of Interactive Situational Prototype Design

The research team believed that the survey of eco-tourism needs of senior citizens and the guidance of context-aware technology enable senior citizens to have a pleasant eco-tourism experience, bring in life-like information to resonate with the past life of senior citizens, and increase the pleasant feeling of ecological knowledge and experience (2015; 2016).

In order to enhance the possibility of implementing interactive situations in the future, this study, based on the five-sense experience and scientific and technological guidance, designed the concept of interactive situation prototype experience situation through the scenario approach proposed by Robinson et al. (1991), and designed interactive situation system from five aspects: activity, environment, interaction, subject and user. Interactive situational experience system and content planning, including story script design, ecological interactive tour guide point design, as well as interactive situational tour guide App production, situational awareness technology, use iBeacon's active trigger as the main interactive mode. When it detects that the user is within 2 m, it will actively push and broadcast the knowledge content of the place. The content source is mainly the ecological commentary of volunteers with many years of actual tour guide experience, and it is also written into colloquial commentary content. When the user wants to know

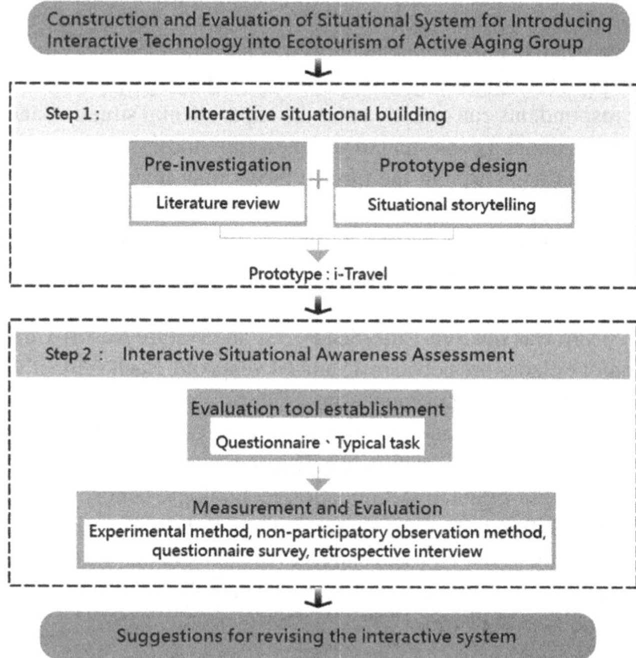

Fig. 2. Research methods and processes.

more about information, the system provides App to let senior citizens browse all kinds of information, and makes up for the deficiency of voice tour guide content (see Fig. 3).

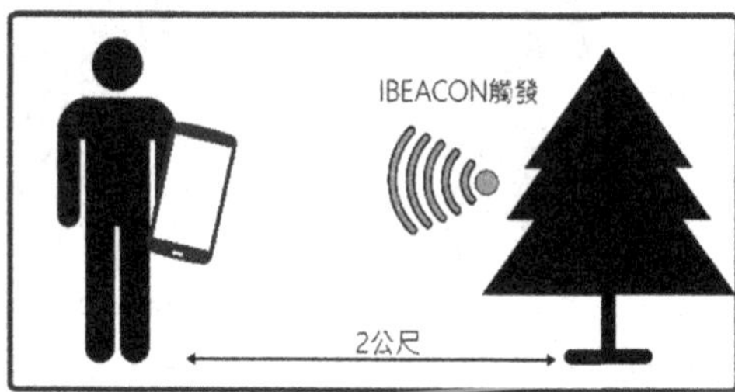

Fig. 3. The concept of interactive situation

3.2 Interactive Context Awareness Assessment and Verification

In this study, the questionnaire was tested by inviting senior citizens to experience the interactive situation prototype. The Likert scale was used to allow the senior citizens to design a questionnaire in a ticked manner to carry out interactive situation prototype measurement. To further gain senior citizens' suggestions for amending the interactive situation prototype, open-ended questions were designed at the end of the questionnaire, and the retrospective interview method was used to let senior citizens personally describe their experience to make up for the shortcomings of the questionnaire. In order to ensure that the respondents can quickly enter the experimental situation and make evaluation measurements under a consistent experience, this study shot simulation videos and formulated typical tasks. Through the film, subjects may understand the experimental content and follow the task to gradually complete the experience task. Questionnaires were made and interviews were carried out upon completion of the task. Finally, based on the experimental results, the interactive situation experience results and correction suggestions were proposed.

The research site was the Sun-Link-Sea Forest and Nature Resort-Chuanlin Trail in Taiwan. The senior citizens are between 45 and 64 years old. Each subject's experimental time is at least 80 min. The experimental program first invited senior citizens to watch situational simulation movies, and then performed the typical tasks set by the research with actual interactive situational experience. Due to time and manpower constraints, this study used Oz Paradigm interactive simulation technology, connects to senior citizens through the Bluetooth function of the researcher's mobile phone, and iBeacon's active push and broadcast mode, so that users can receive the feedback from the system. In the process, the experience of senior citizens is observed and recorded by non-participatory observation method (see Fig. 4).

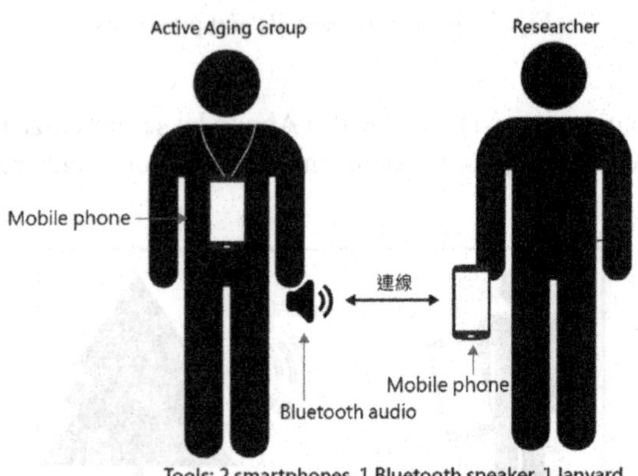

Fig. 4. Oz Paradigm interactive simulation technology

Then, according to the collected data, the basic data, reliability and validity of the questionnaire, the overall perception scale and the content cognition degree of each tour guide point were analyzed respectively. Among them, the overall perception scale was divided into three items: leisure attitude, situational content and system value for discussion. Finally, through interviews, senior citizens were asked to describe their own experiences and feelings to supplement the information that the questionnaire could not obtain. The data analysis invited the two researchers to use content analysis to code the verbatim transcripts of the interviews and classify them into piles (see Fig. 5).

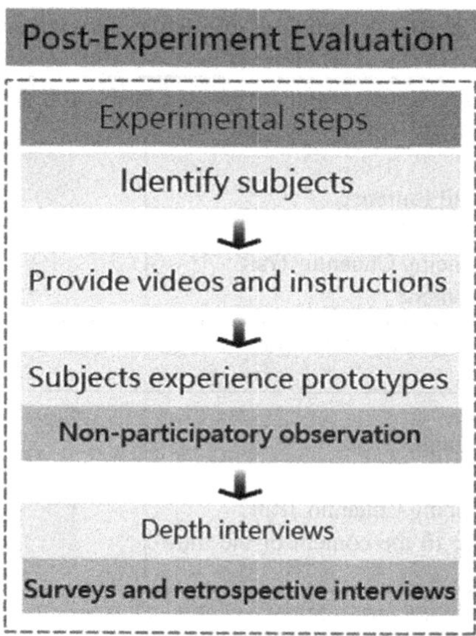

Fig. 5. Post-experiment evaluation process.

4 Result and Discussion

4.1 Construction of Interactive Situation Building System

According to the definition of activity, environment, interaction, object and user in the interactive situation concept table, and the current situation of the environment field, 8 concepts of eco-tourism tour guide for senior citizens were developed, such as Table 2. After summarizing and sorting out the ecological contents of Sun-Link-Sea Chuanlin Trail guide volunteers, 18 ecological interactive guide points were selected for system introduction, trail introduction, plant introduction and information provision respectively. System Introduction: Explain the usage of App used in the eco-tourism process and inform users of the matters needing attention after the tour, including: introducing App service and informing users of the end of the tour. Trail Introduction: Introduce the historical knowledge and contents of various scenic spots in Chuanlin Trail, including: Chuanlin Trail Introduction, Trail Introduction, Random Stop Entrance, Five Sense Experience Area, Fairy Terrace Route Notice, Jiazouliao Creek Introduction, Plant-Red Juniper Tree Head, Qingshui Ping Route Notice, Hydrophilic Ping Introduction, and Three-story Ridge. Plant introduction includes ginkgo tree, Taiwan green pod leaf, butterfly on pearl flower, hongwai tree head. Information provision: When walking in Chuanlin Trail, senior citizens will provide environmental knowledge such as temperature, humidity and altitude of the current location. As to the 18 ecological interactive tour guide points in this study, Google Map was used to draw maps to understand the distribution of each point, such as Fig. 6.

This study proposed “i-Travel” interactive situational experience. The single-ear Bluetooth headset provides the most comfortable tour guide mode. Senior citizens can hear the sound in the environment to avoid danger. They wear the mobile phone around

Table 2. The definition of interactive situation concept

Concept 1. Experience information: Introduce the tour guide App and guide senior citizens to experience ecology through the App.	
User: senior citizens Environment: Chuanlin Trail Entrance Object: Chuanlin Trail Billboard Interaction: Before experiencing Chuanlin Trail Activity: Introduce App Content	
Concept 2. Voice-guided experience: Provide ecological experience information mainly with voice to reduce reading	
User: senior citizens Environment: All over Chuanlin Trail Object: Mobile App Interaction: When experiencing Chuanlin Trail Activity: Design according to the content of the introduced object	
Concept 3. Enhance experience fun: Introduce ecological experience with virtual characters to improve experience fun	
User: Virtual ecological guide-Shan Shan Environment: All over Chuanlin Trail Object: Mobile App Interaction: Introduce in a lively tone Activity: Introduce interactive situational content	
Concept 4. Trigger experience situation: iBeacon micro-positioning is used as the trigger medium to actively provide information.	
User: senior citizens Environment: All over Chuanlin Trail Object: Mobile App Interaction: Location close to iBeacon settings Activity: Provide relative knowledge based on the setting position	
Concept 5. Increase the fun of knowledge: Connect knowledge and life with stories to strengthen experience.	
User: Anthropomorphism of animals and plants Environment: Introduction to birds Object: Mobile App Interaction: Introduce in a lively tone Activity: Provide relative knowledge based on the setting position	
Concept 6. Basic Knowledge Query:If the introduction is insufficient, the App content will be more abundant. 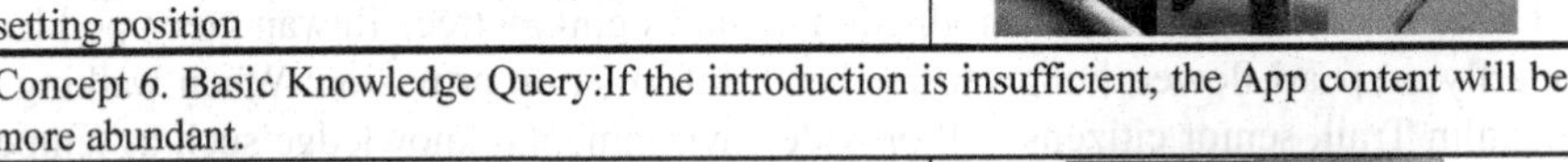	
User: senior citizens Environment: All over Chuanlin Trail Object: Mobile App Interaction: senior citizens may search information on the mobile phone Activity: Rich introduction to animals, plants and environment	

(*continued*)

Table 2. (*continued*)

Concept 7. Increase Sensory Experience: Integrate 5 sensory experiences to deepen experience impression	
User: senior citizens Environment: Random Stop, Fairy Terrace, Medicine Garden Object: Mobile App, Commentary board Interaction: On the way to experience Activity: Guide experience with sensory theme	
Concept 8. Sharing and Memories: Complete the experience and provide small gifts that can be shared with relatives and friends.	
User: senior citizens Environment: Medicine garden Object: Mobile App, Service personnel Interaction: Check App for service personnel Activity: Provide five-sensory gifts	

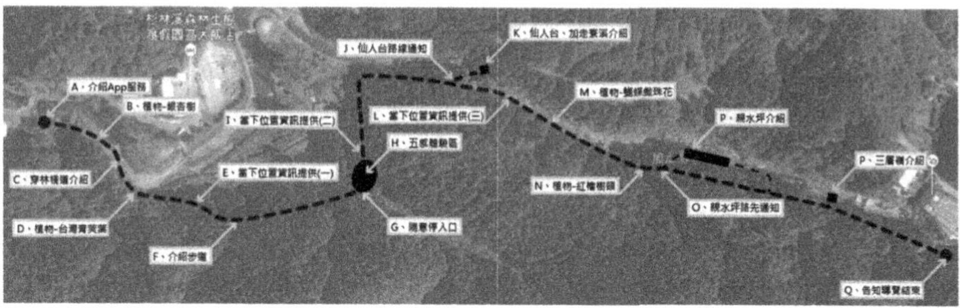

Fig. 6. Actual field location distribution map.

the neck with a hanging rope to free their hands, and can fully experience eco-tourism. They can download the "Chuanlin Trail-Travel" mobile phone App through an intelligent mobile device and open it, and then start to experience interactive situations. When the distance between the mobile phone and iBeaco is within 2 m to 5 m, the device will be triggered, and the knowledge content of the location will be actively pushed and broadcast (see Fig. 7).

Finally, this study adopted the methods of questionnaire and retrospective interview, divided the questionnaire into 3 parts: situational content, leisure attitude and system value, and designed the topic according to the 26 indexes proposed by the literature discussion, so as to understand the experience status of senior citizens' interactive situational prototype of eco-tourism. The questionnaire content is shown in Table 3. The questionnaire was tested by inviting senior citizens to experience the interactive situation prototype. The Likert scale was used to carry out interactive situation prototype measurement.

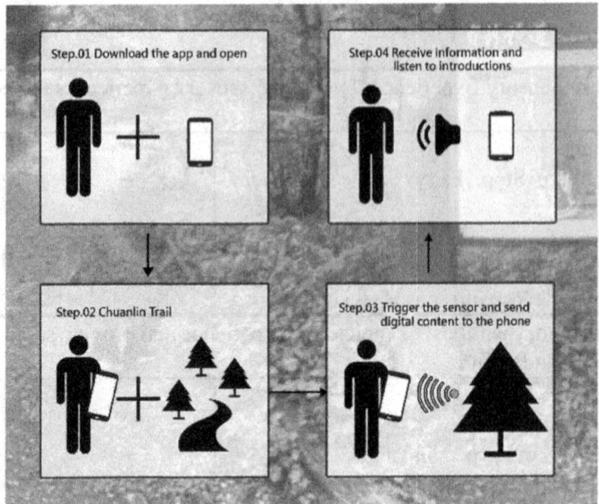

Fig. 7. The procedure of interactive situational experience.

4.2 Interactive Context Awareness Assessment and Verification Results

Reliability and Validity Analysis of Questionnaire. Interactive situation prototype assessment measurement is mainly divided into 3 aspects: leisure attitude, situation content and system value. Cronbach Alpha value is calculated to judge the reliability of the questionnaire. When Alpha > 0.9, it indicates that the reliability is better. When 0.7 < Alpha < 0.9, it indicates that the reliability is acceptable. When 0.5 < Alpha < 0.7, it indicates that the reliability is low. When Alpha < 0.5, it indicates that no object has been raised against the reliability is no objection. The reliability analysis results of the questionnaire are shown in Table 4. The Cronbach Alpha values of leisure attitude, situational content and system value and content degree were 0.797, 0.832, 0.870 and 0.867 respectively, indicating that the questionnaire is credible.

In the validity part, Kaiser-Meyer-Olkin sampling suitability quantity was used to analyze the validity with Barlett spherical test. KMO value is between 0 and 1. KMO > 0.8 indicates good (Meritorious); KMO > 0.7 means medium (Mediocre), KMO > 0.6 means normal, and when KMO < 0.5 means unacceptable. The results of validity analysis of the questionnaire in this study are shown in Table 5. KMO value in leisure attitude, situational content, system value and cognitive degree of each point content are 0.604, 0.690, 0.791 and 0.644 respectively, all of which are above ordinary performance, and the significance of Bartlett ball test is 0.000, which is less than the significance standard value of 0.5. From these two parts we can know that the validity of the questionnaire is valid, as shown in Table 5.

Table 3. Level 3 indicators and questionnaire content description

Level 2	Level 3	Questionnaire content
Leisure emotion	Leisure perception	i-Travel helps me relax
	Knowledge perception	i-Travel helps me get a sense of accomplishment in my knowledge
Leisure cognition	Smart growth	i-Travel helps me understand the things around me during the tour guide
	Be close to nature	i-Travel helps me absorb new knowledge during the tour guide
	Enhance spirit	i-Travel's tour guide helps me enrich myself
	Physical and mental health care	i-Travel can keep me in a good mood during the tour guide
Leisure behavior	Act alone	After i-Travel's tour guide, I can enjoy it even if I experience it alone
	Peer sharing	After i-Travel's tour guide, I would like to share it with my peers in real time
	Experience situation	After i-Travel's tour guide, I can fully experience the system
Information design	Easy to understand	i-Travel makes it easy for me to understand the content of the information provided
	Correct response	i-Travel provides the information I need in the right place
	Tour guide rate	i-Travel guides the entire experience with gentle sound rates
Tour guide design	Fluency	I feel fluent about the i-Travel tour guide
	Degree of friendliness	I feel friendly about i-Travel's tour guide
Visual design	Integrity	The design of mobile phone APP, signs and five-sense small gifts is consistent
	Attraction	The design of mobile phone APP, signs and five-sense small gifts is attractive

(continued)

Table 3. (*continued*)

Level 2	Level 3	Questionnaire content
Perceived usefulness	Service quality	I think i-Travel's service can replace the tour guide to help me experience Chuanlin Trail
	System quality	I think i-Travel's knowledge content can be correct
	Information quality	I think i-Travel's tour guide service can help me stably experience the entire Chuanlin Trail
Satisfaction	Future expectations	If Shanlin Creek launches i-Travel in the future, I will be very looking forward to it
	Correlation fields	If I go to other eco-tourism sites, I also expect to have an i-Travel system
	Share with others	If others want to experience i-Travel, I will give a positive response
	Repeated experience	On the whole, I would like to experience i-Travel again
Continuous use	Service satisfaction	I am satisfied with i-Travel's guided experience service
	Information satisfaction	I am satisfied with the knowledge content of i-Travel
	Experience satisfaction	I am satisfied with the stability of i-Travel's guiding experience

Table 4. Reliability analysis of interactive situational i-Travel measurement

Content	Cronbach's alpha value	Cronbach alpha value based on Standardized Items	Number of items
Leisure attitude	.797	.809	9
Contextual content	.832	.847	7
System value	.870	.878	10
Cognitive degree of each content	.867	.864	18

Table 5. Validity analysis results of interactive situational "i-Travel" measurement

Content	Kaiser-Meyer-Olkin measurement sampling suitability	Bartlett spherical verification significance
Leisure attitude	.604	.000
Contextual content	.690	.000
System value	.791	.000
Cognitive degree of each content	.644	.000

Perception Scale Analysis. The conclusions of this study are respectively explained in the form of interactive situation design suggestions and interactive situation interaction:

1. Suggestion of Interactive Situation Design

- Presentation of real-life pictures of billboards: It is suggested to use actual scenery pictures in the graphic aspect to increase the speed and degree of plant identification.
- Mobile phone synchronization data display content: It is suggested that the mobile phone must synchronously display the introduction content of this point. For example, when passing through ginkgo trees, one can start the information synchronously by picking up his mobile phone.
- Add the "Skip Tour guide" button: When users are not interested in tour guide, they can freely choose to skip tour guide and increase flexibility in use.
- Advance the next attraction function: It is suggested to add a simple advance notice description of the next tour location.
- Add background music: Not the whole experience journey is introduced during the tour guide. It is suggested that background music can be added as a companion.
- Multilingual version: Since not all senior citizens can understand Mandarin, it is suggested to add Taiwanese and other languages, such as Japanese and English.
- Expansion of knowledge content category: It is suggested that plants, animals and natural landscape content can be added.
- Seasonal selection of knowledge content: The content can be corrected in real time according to the actual seasonal climate. As Shanlin Creek belongs to alpine climate and its seasonal changes are very obvious, the plants displayed in different seasons are quite different in content design, such as peony season March - April and hydrangea flower September - November.

2. The type of Interactive Situation

- Auditory interaction: Mainly lead the subjects to experience Chuanlin Trail in an auditory way, and cooperate with mobile device audio, Bluetooth audio, headphones and other equipment, so that senior citizens can concentrate on the things in front of

them and avoid the danger caused by spending too much attention and time on the intelligent mobile device.
- Voice tour guide prompt: Voice tour guide is recorded according to its content and plays specific content in coordination with iBeacon set in the venue. It is recommended that a prompt tone can appear about 2 to 3 s before providing voice tour guide message to reduce sudden sound interference.
- Voice tour guide function: It is recommended to have repeated playback, playback, pause…and other functions.
- Willingness to participate in eco-tourism: Through the "i-Travel" tour guide mode, the participation in tour guide can be increased, which can not only enable senior citizens to understand the knowledge in the field, but effectively promote the field service.
- Replace the traditional tour guide: Most senior citizens think that "i-Travel" can replace the tour guide, but suggest that they can communicate with users or increase the function of users asking questions.
- Ecological tour guide interaction points: It is suggested to increase the number of scenic spots for ecological interaction tour guide so as to have a more comprehensive understanding of the ecological information of the park.

4.3 Discussion on Evaluation Results

1. Leisure attitude of 「i-Travel」

Leisure attitude is defined as when an individual holds a positive attitude towards leisure activities, the more likely he is to participate in the activities. According to the research results, the introduction of science and technology into eco-tourism can really increase senior citizens' experience of eco-tourism, enhance the richness of eco-tourism, increase their interest in eco-tourism, enhance their willingness to explore on their own, and give them the experience of learning again after retirement. However, the current situational technology still needs to use intelligent mobile devices as interactive media, hoping that more advanced technologies will be available in the future to free senior citizens' hands to experience nature.

2. Situational content of 「i-Travel」

Situational content is defined as providing service information due to environmental factors or users' requirements. When service information can effectively and appropriately transmit easily understood knowledge content to users, users may have higher satisfaction with the system. According to the research results, it is known that understanding various ecological knowledge and sensory experiences through sound guidance can really increase the attraction of senior citizens to ecological knowledge and achieve the purpose of knowledge acquisition. At present, the content of voice guidance is still mainly static, such as the introduction of the plank road, the plants along the road, and the dynamic features (birds, fish) etc. When senior citizens raise questions, the system is still unable to do explanation in real time. This part hopes to have a faster way to do the inquiry in the future.

3. System value of 「i-Travel」

System value is defined as whether the whole situation design achieves the positive experience and satisfaction of eco-tourism. According to research, after experiencing i-Travel interactive situational experience, most senior citizens show positive experience and high satisfaction. i-Travel interactive scenarios are indeed able to operate without a navigator. Senior citizens may also acquire ecological knowledge, and adjust at their own pace to improve their satisfaction with eco-tourism. They also willing to use services related to similar services again or share with relatives and friends, which is indirectly helpful to the publicity of the industry. However, the content of interactive situation only focuses on the "ecological" aspect in this study. If interactive situation is extended to different aspects (such as humanities, history, etc.), there may be different conclusions and suggestions. It is expected that the following related research will continue to discuss.

5 Conclusion

<u>Design with the user as the center to enhance the feeling of self-experience fun.</u>
In the process of interactive situation design, if the needs of senior citizens can be met, the experience brought by eco-tourism can be strengthened, and the impression of eco-tourism can be deepened through various sensory experiences.

<u>Appropriate development of ecotourism experience guided by new types of science and technology</u>
Experiments prove that interactive situational awareness can guide senior citizens to participate in eco-tourism experience, which allows them to experience eco-tourism without pressure and easily, and correctly absorbs ecological knowledge, thus achieving the goal of happy learning and forgetting age.

<u>Overall design of introducing science and technology into ecotourism</u>
The guidance of interactive situation system design should be based on intuition, with hearing as the main guidance, so that senior citizens can understand the explanation content in the first place, reduce visual pressure, and focus on the natural ecology instead of the intelligent mobile device in their hands. The strengthening of personalized design will deepen their experience of eco-tourism.

Acknowledgment. This research is partially supported by the "108 A Study on the Interactive Integration Design and Evaluation of the Application of Somatosensory Technology into Thematic Display Education of Museums" of National Yunlin University of Science and Technology (College of Design), sponsored by the Ministry of Science and Technology, Taiwan, R.O.C under Grant no. MOST 108-2410-H-224-018-MY2.

References

Blanco, J.: World Tourism Organization (UNWTO) Affiliate Members AM-reports –Technology in Tourism, vol. 1, p. 10 (2011)

Campbell, R.L.: Will the real scenario please stand up? ACM SIGCHI Bull. **24**(2), 6–8 (1992)

Chen, C., Wu, C.C.: How motivations, constraints, and demographic factors predict seniors' overseas travel propensity. Asia Pac. Manage. Rev. **14**(3), 301–312 (2009)

Engardio, P., Matlack, C.: Global aging. Bus. Week **31**, 42–51 (2005)

Häkkilä, J., Mäntyjärvi, J.: Developing design guidelines for context-aware mobile Applications. In: Proceedings of the 3rd International Conference on Mobile Technology, Applications & Systems, p. 24. ACM (2006)

Hetzer, N.D.: Environment, tourism, culture. Links **1**(3) (1965)

Kelley, J.F.: An iterative design methodology for user-friendly natural language office information applications. ACM Trans. Inf. Syst. (TOIS) **2**(1), 26–41 (1984)

Kjeldskov, J., et al.: Evaluating the usability of a mobile guide: the influence of location, participants and resources. Behav. Inf. Technol. **24**, 51–65 (2005)

Myerson, J.: Masters of Innovation. Laurence King Publishing, New York (2000)

Tussyadiah, I.P., Fesenmaier, D.R.: Interpreting tourist experiences from first-person stories: a foundation for mobile guides. In: ECIS, pp. 2259–2270 (2007)

Whitbourne, S.K., Whitbourne, S.B.: Adult Development and Aging: Biopsychosocial Perspectives. Wiley, New York (2010)

Wijesuriya, M.U.E., et al.: Interactive mobile based tour guide. In: Proceedings of SAITM Research Symposium on Engineering Advancements (RSEA), pp. 53–56 (2013)

Ziffer, K.A.: Ecotourism: The Uneasy Allian, Working Papers Series. Conservation international, Washington, DC (1989)

Zimprich, D., Martin, M.: Can longitudinal changes in processing speed explain longitudinal age changes in fluid intelligence? Psychol. Aging **17**(4), 690–695 (2002)

Yu, P., Hsiao, C.L.: Wellness learning travel interests and perceived importance of lodging related services for older adults. J. Tour. Leisur. Stud. **18**(2), 111–134 (2012)

Lee, W.T., Lee, C.F.: Context awareness applied to mobile guide in ecological field for active aging elderly. J. Gerontechnol. Serv. Manage. **3**(4), 421–436 (2015)

Tang, H.H., Lin, Y.C.: The Influence and Problems of Scenario Design Approach on Multidisciplinary Collaboration Design (2011)

National Development Council. Population Estimation of the Republic of China (2014 to 2061). https://goo.gl/g0a9qv. Accessed 14 July 2016

Shimizu, M.: Moved by Nature, Universal Design for Sightseeing, Akiyama Tetsuo et al. (co-author), pp. 116–119. Gakugei Publishing, Tokyo (2010)

Ministry of Education. Final Report of the Elderly Education Campaign Counseling Group (2009)

Chang, C.L.: Starting from the Elderly to Make "Social Enterprises" Blossom. Social Enterprise Insights (2013). https://goo.gl/GWPGdU. Accessed 22 July 2016

An Age-Friendly System Design for Smart Home: Findings from Heuristic Evaluation

Adriana Marques da Silva[1], Hande Ayanoglu[1,2], and Bruno M. C. Silva[1,3](✉)

[1] Universidade Europeia, IADE. Av. D. Carlos I, 4, 1200-649 Lisbon, Portugal
adrianampms@gmail.com,
{hande.ayanoglu,bruno.silva}@universidadeeuropeia.pt

[2] UNIDCOM/IADE, Av. D. Carlos I, 4, 1200-649 Lisbon, Portugal

[3] Instituto de Telecomunicações, Departamento de Informática, Universidade da Beira Interior, Rua Marquês d'Ávila e Bolama, 6201-001 Covilhã, Portugal

Abstract. The age group of 65 years has been described as the fastest growing demographic in the world. As life expectancy increases, older adults prefer to remain independent at home. Smart Home systems and Assistive Technologies have been developed to enable older adults to live in their own homes as they age, enhancing safety, independence and quality of life. Although considerable Smart Home mobile applications exist focused on older adult's wellbeing, they still face considerable challenges in usability, feasibility and accessibility regarding design of interfaces. There is a gap in recent research on evaluation of User Interface (UI) designed or adapted to address older adults needs and abilities. The main objective of the paper is to show findings of a Heuristic Evaluation (Nielsen's 10 Heuristics) of an age-friendly smart home application which is a part of an ongoing project. Experts identified the potential usability problems through task analysis that could impact the experience of older adults as they interact with the UIs. Afterwards, the experts identified violated heuristics and estimated severity rating for each violation. The results showed that 80 usability problems found, 8 out of 10 heuristics were violated, and 78 violations were encountered. However, only 3% of the problems were considered catastrophic and it must be a high priority to fix them. It is concluded that findings should be supported with more experts and target user testing to provide insights to designers and developers to create more usable interfaces to address the needs and abilities of the older adults.

Keywords: Smart home · Age-friendly design · User interface design · Heuristic evaluation

1 Introduction

This paper presents the user evaluation (Heuristics) stage from an on-going project aiming to develop an age-friendly system design for smart homes that increases independence of older adults by enabling them to age in their own homes. The ongoing project will propose a system design that explores daily activities by monitoring, predicting and reminding functionalities, aiming for comfort and independent living for

C. Stephanidis et al. (Eds.): HCII 2020, LNCS 12426, pp. 643–659, 2020.
https://doi.org/10.1007/978-3-030-60149-2_48

older adults ageing at home. The system is based on pressure, motion, temperature and air quality sensors that monitor the daily activities of the user and send the information to the system hub. The collected data will set alarms and reminders to assist older adults and their caregivers in predicting, preventing or providing emergency support. The project aims to take into consideration age-friendly design guidelines of a mobile application to address older adults' users [1]. The proposed system is composed of three interactive interfaces: Smart TV app, home hub tablet and smartphone app, to work as a personal assistant at home. In this paper, the smartphone application interfaces were evaluated to apply the findings on the other system interfaces.

In 2019, as reported by the United Nations [2], the range of 65 years of age was identified as the world fastest-growing population. Therefore, by 2050, is projected that the share of older adults population will reach 28.7% of the total population in the European Union [3]. As life expectancy increase, most of older adults prefer to remain independently in their own places [4]. The concept of ageing at home enable older adults to live in their own homes as they age despite health and mobility changes [5]. As life expectancy grows, in many countries the older adults' population is retiring later in life [6]. Therefore, it is important not to stereotype the ageing population based on common perceptions and assumptions when developing comprehensive and accessible solutions. This outdated stereotypes for older adults' lifestyle and behavior limits the comprehension of their problems and the development of innovative opportunities for the ageing population needs [7]. A new perspective should be taken into consideration for the future ageing population. This emphasizes the importance of ageing research, especially innovative solutions (i.e., smart home systems and assistive technologies) that have significant potential to empower older adults to remain independent, safe and comfortable at home. The smart home concept can be defined as a lifestyle support that represents a house installed with sensors and control devices connected through a communication network [8]. It empowers the users to remotely control household appliances and it can provide comfort, security, convenience and energy efficiency. A smart home environment aims to assist and support residents to feel more comfortable, safe and independent at their home, using monitoring, warning and remote controlling integrated systems [9]. Smart and assistive technologies can provide older adults self-care, relieve caregivers support and also supply new opportunities for personalized healthcare monitoring [7]. Moreover, it can offer constant health and safety management enhancing their convenience and comfort in their daily activities [8]. This innovative technology can have a great impact to improve quality of life and encourage independent living at home so older adults can achieve long and healthy life [10].

Smart home systems have been highly increased to facilitate assisted living and health monitoring so older adults can live independently in their home, and also improve the relationship and proximity with their families and caregivers [11]. Currently, a large number of existing mobile applications are focused on health monitoring and assistive living; though, most of the existing systems have not been developed or adapted enough to older adults needs and abilities [12]. In this sense, the older adults still face considerable challenges in usability, feasibility and accessibility among User Interfaces (UIs), such as small fonts, low color contrasts and complex interactions [12]. It is essential to take into consideration the natural ageing declines that can potentially impact their experience with the technology and provide them accessible age-friendly products and services [12, 13]. Technologies, tools and devices, when properly designed to address older adults' abilities, needs and preferences, can empower their sense of wellness and independence. Once they are introduced to the basic functions, they feel included to the technology, and interested in and curious about smart devices that can enhance their daily activities [12]. Although, when they can't adapt or understand those tools and devices it can cause the sense of frustration and isolation [14, Ch. 21].

There are significant studies [1, 15, 16] about the natural ageing, cognitive, sensitive and motoric declines and how it affects the older adults learning process and experience when navigating on the web or using mobile applications. Some cognitive abilities, such as vocabulary, can be resilient to an aging brain and sometimes even improve with age. However, other abilities, such as conceptual reasoning, memory, and processing speed, decline gradually over the years. On the other hand, some activities can be associated with high cognitive function in older adults, such as intellectual engaging activities (e.g., doing puzzles, reading, using a computer, playing musical instruments), physical activities and social engagement [17]. Ageing behavior process can be hard to generalize. It always depends on the context living of the older adult. Although, to assist the development of age-friendly products and services, there is a slightly gap on recent research on usability heuristics for UIs to address older adults needs, abilities and limitations [18]. Age-friendly design aims to help older adults read, notice, scan and understand the information displayed on the interface. Age-friendly guidelines would not only help older adults, but would also be more user friendly for all users [1]. Developing an age friendly system design, to a complex smart home and health monitoring system, enables the opportunity to increase the adoption of assistive technologies by older adults. As the older adult's population increases, they turn to be potential beneficiaries of digital products. The age-friendly design should go further off accessibility, it should also make the technology attractive, powerful, easy and enjoyable to use [1].

Usability is a key aspect of the multidisciplinary field of Human Computer Interaction (HCI) to ensure the ease of use of a system, tool or device. When designing and building interactive systems the user should be first priority. It is about to understand human capabilities and limitations [19]. In many UI designs, with low contrast colors, small fonts, small targets, it can make it difficult for older adults easily use and accept mobile technologies and other smart devices [1]. Among current studies of heuristic evaluation of mobile applications to support older adults' users, Silva et al. [20] identified a research gap of appropriate heuristics to evaluate smartphone applications to be suitable and inclusive for such user groups. In this sense, this paper shows results of a heuristic evaluation that identified potentially usability problems which could be faced by older adults when interacting with a smartphone app for Smart Home.

2 Methodology

The expert-based method developed by Nielsen [21] is applied to evaluate the usability problems of a smart home and health monitoring prototype supporting older adults. The objective of the heuristic evaluation is to evaluate the UI usability characteristics according to the principles and guidelines. The 10 Heuristics are as follows: "Consistency and

Standards" (H1), "Visibility of the system" (H2), "Match between the system and the real world" (H3), "User control and freedom" (H4), "Error prevention" (H5), "Recognition rather than recall" (H6), "Flexibility and efficiency to use" (H7), "Aesthetic and minimalist design" (H8), "Help users recognize, diagnose, and recover from errors" (H9) and "Help and documentation" (10).

According to Rogers et al. [22], if heuristic evaluation is conducted on a functioning product or a conceptual prototype, the experts need to have some specific user tasks in mind to focus the inspection. Therefore, representative user tasks were defined for the experts.

2.1 Participants

Three experts with high expertise in user experience were selected to participate in the study. The user experience experts have also relevant expertise in performing heuristic evaluation in digital products.

2.2 Procedure

The procedure was published online. Each evaluator received by email the heuristic evaluation sheet with the instructions and list of tasks with a link for the interactive prototype. These tasks were selected due to their representation of the main functions of the system related to health and home features. The procedure was done in three stages:

(i) Briefing Stage. This stage entailed giving the evaluators the description and objective of the project with the information in detail about the goals and procedure of the heuristic evaluation.
(ii) Task Analysis. In this stage, the evaluators performed tasks analysis to find usability problems they face within each interface of each given task. The flow of each task was shown in Fig. 1, 2, 3, 4, 5, 6, 7, 8 and 9.
(iii) Evaluation Stage. In this stage, the evaluators conducted the evaluation (Nielsen's 10 Heuristics) on the usability problems that they found in the interactive prototype and prioritize them according to Nielsen's five-point Severity Ranking scaled from 0–4, where 0- indicates no problem, 1- cosmetic problem, 2- Minor problem, 3- Major problem, and 4- catastrophic [23]. During the evaluation, evaluators also compiled a document where they reported the usability problems, the descriptions of the problems, place of occurrence on the UIs, and related to the violated heuristics and the severity ratings applied.

3 Results and Discussion

The data were reported both quantitatively and qualitatively. Quantitatively, after receiving the heuristics severity ratings by each evaluator, the results were combined. Qualitatively, the evaluators performed task analysis to identify the problems and, also, sent a report by compiling their feedback regarding the problems.

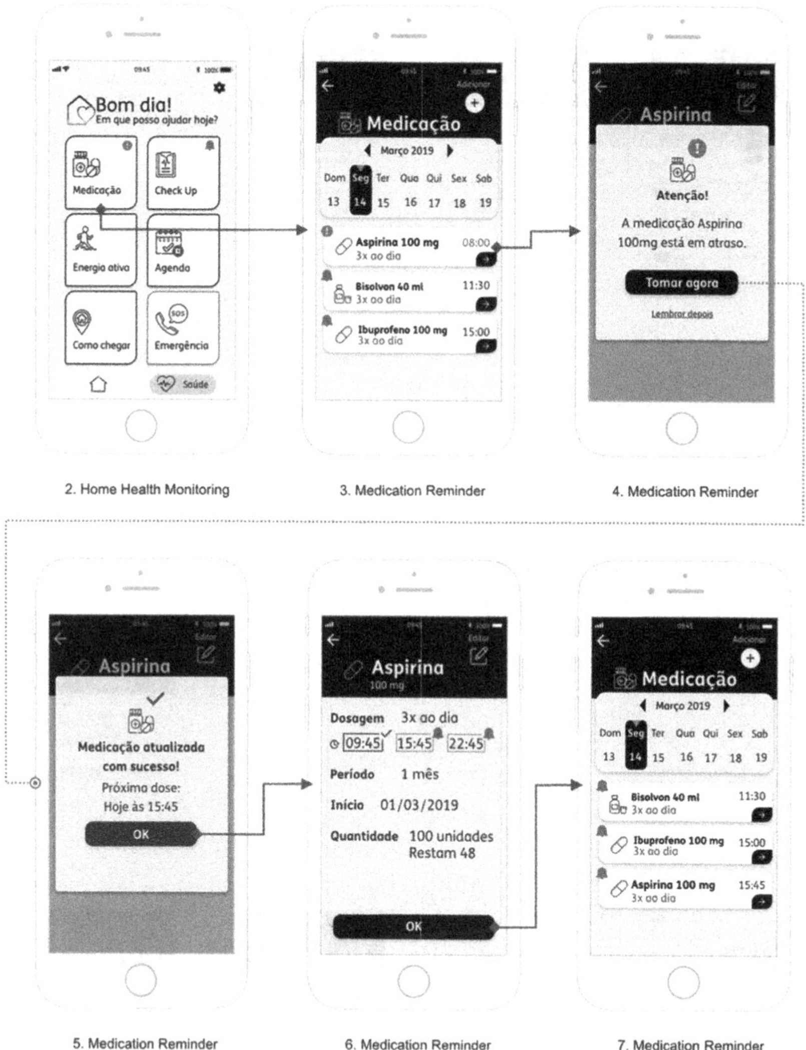

Fig. 1. User flow of Task 1 "You should take "Aspirina" 3 times a day. Check if you are taking it correctly".

a) **Task analysis and heuristic evaluation**

The UI compliance to Nielsen's heuristics was inspected while the experts performed the representative tasks. Evaluators were asked to highlight and describe each usability problem while they were performing each task. The problems were sorted in 6 categories: labelling, visual hierarchy, visual consistency, terminology, feedback and interaction. The most common usability problems found in the task analysis is reported in Table 1.

Fig. 2. User flow of Task 2: You should take 2 pills of "Dipirona" per day, starting at 10 a.m. for one week. Add "Dipirona" to your medicine reminder list.

In total, there were 80 usability problems found, 8 out of 10 heuristics were violated, and 78 violations were encountered. For each usability problem one or more heuristics violations could be assigned. "Consistency and Standards" (H1), "Match between the

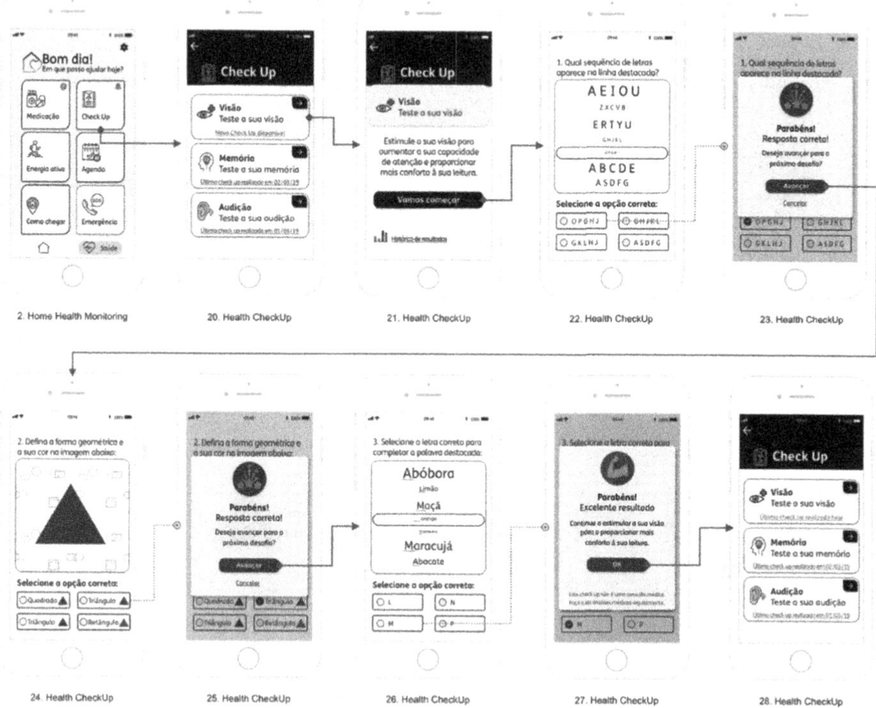

Fig. 3. User flow of Task 3: New check-ups become available from time to time. Check if you are missing any available health checkup.

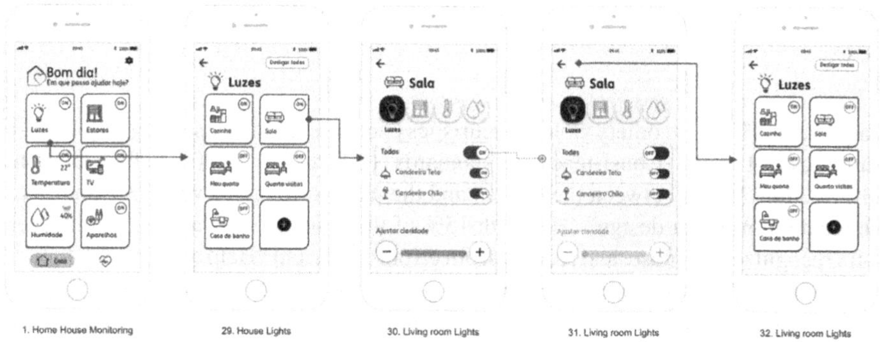

Fig. 4. User flow of Task 4: You remembered that you left the living room lights on and you are in your bedroom, reading a book. Turn off the lights in the living room.

system and the real world" (H3) and "Aesthetic and minimalist design" (H8) were the most violated heuristic, encountered in 66 usability problems, equivalent to 68% of the overall problems. "Visibility of the system" (H2), "Error prevention" (H5), "Flexibility and efficiency to use" (H7), "User control and freedom" (H4) and "Recognition rather

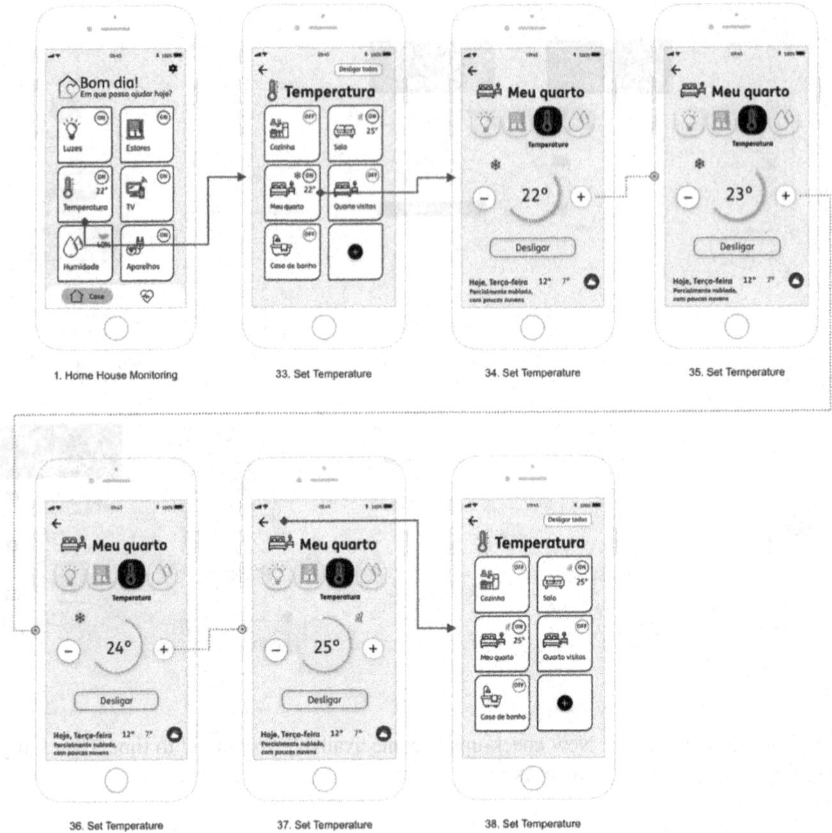

Fig. 5. User flow of Task 5: You are feeling cold in your bedroom. Increase the temperature to 25 °C.

than recall" (H6) were others violated heuristics encountered in 31 usability problems. In heuristics violations, "Consistency and standards" (H1) represents 30% of the violations, followed by "Match between the system and the real world" (H3) with 23% and "Aesthetic and minimalist design" (H8) with 15% of the heuristics violations. While "Help users recognize, diagnose, and recover from errors" (H9) and "Help and documentation" (10) had no violations identified. Heuristics violations percentages are shown in Fig. 10.

Experts estimated the severity rating for each Heuristics. The severity mean analysis showed that 3% of the problems were considered catastrophic (mean > 3,5) and it must be a high priority to fix them [23]. 13% were considered major usability problems (3,5 > severity rating <=2,5), according to Nielsen [21] that have the potential for confusing users and making them use the system erroneously. While 81% were minor usability problems (2,5 > severity rating >=1,5), that might slow down the interactions or cause some unnecessary inconveniences for the users [21]. Finally, 6% were considered cosmetic problems. Figure 11 illustrates the average severity rating given among Heuristics.

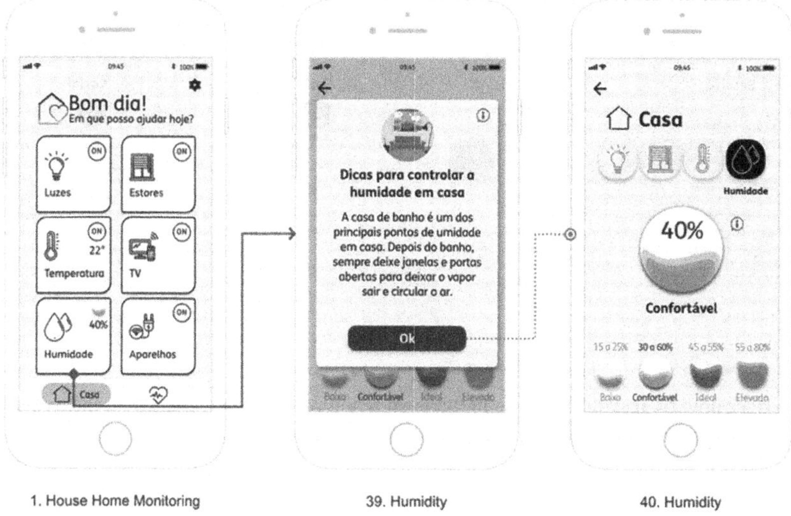

Fig. 6. User flow of Task 6: It's raining a lot lately and it causes humidity problems at home. Check the humidity of the house.

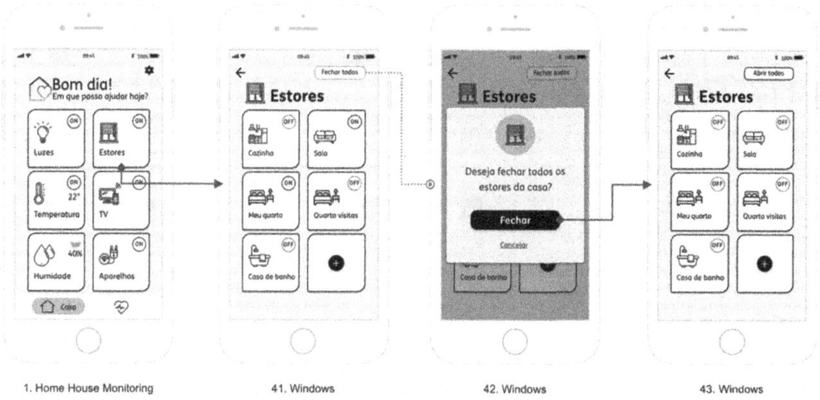

Fig. 7. User flow of Task 7: You are arriving at the supermarket and it just started to rain. Check if you left your windows open.

On the overall, the experts found eight major and two catastrophic usability problems (Table 2). At the main screens related to health (saúde) and home (casa) features, the experts found the majority of major usability problems and two catastrophic. On the tab navigation bar, the experts considered as catastrophic the unlabeled icons even when the screen is not displayed. This problem can confuse the user and impact the main features of the system. Confusing and technical language was also reported as catastrophic when using terms that might not be familiar for the older users and in generic feedback messages. As the project developed in Portuguese language, the experts recommended to avoid using English terms, highlighting that it is a more familiar language for young

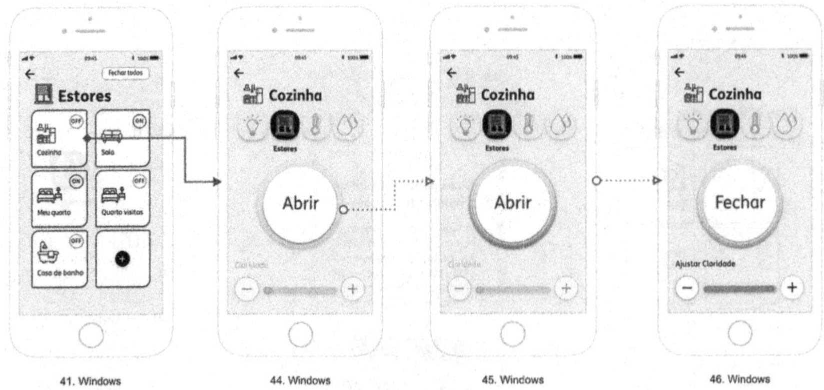

Fig. 8. User flow of Task 8: A cake is in the oven while you are watching TV in the living room. You decided to open the kitchen window to release the heat. Check if the kitchen window is open.

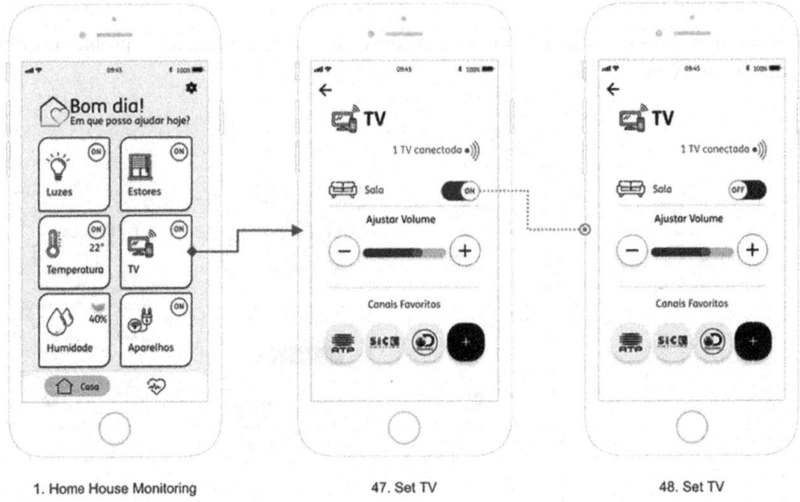

Fig. 9. User flow of Task 9: You are not at home and you wonder if you left your TV on. Check if the TV in the living room is on.

users than and for the older ones. As the main page of the system, these catastrophic problems can compromise the system comprehension, consequently they are urgent to be fixed. Major usability problems were encountered on medication features. The experts reported that there is too much complex information on medication details that can make it difficult for users to read and it can highly compromise the user comprehension of this important feature for the user's health. Notifications and status of the system were also reported as major problems as experts reported that is insufficient visual identification and it can be almost unnoticed for the user.

Table 1. Common usability problems identified

Task description	Place of occurrence	Problem Category
Task 1: You should take "Aspirina" 3 times a day. Check if you are taking it correctly.	4, 5. Medication reminder; 6. Medication reminder	Interaction
	2. Home Health Monitoring; 4, 5. Medication reminder; 6. Medication reminder	Feedback
	1. Home House Monitoring; 4, 5. Medication reminder; 6. Medication reminder	Labelling
	6. Medication reminder	Visual consistency
	2. Home Health Monitoring; 6. Medication reminder	Visual hierarchy
Task 2: You should take 2 pills of "Dipirona" per day, starting at 10 a.m for one week. Add "Dipirona" to your medicine reminder list.	13, 14, 15, 16, 17, 18. Add new medication	Interaction
	13. Add new medication	Feedback
	14, 15, 16, 17. Add new medication	Labelling Terminology Visual hierarchy
	9, 10, 14, 15, 16, 17. Add new medication	Visual consistency
Task 3: New check-ups become available from time to time. Check if you are missing any available health checkup.	20, 28. Health Checkup	Labelling
	22, 23, 24, 25, 26, 27. Health Checkup	Interaction
	2. Home Health Monitoring; 20, 21, 28. Health Checkup	Terminology
	20, 22, 23, 24, 25, 26, 27, 28. Health Checkup	Visual consistency
Task 4: You remembered that you left the living room lights on and you are in your bedroom, reading a book. Turn off the lights in the living room.	1. Home House Monitoring; 29. House Lights; 30, 31, 32. Living room Lights	Terminology
	1. Home House Monitoring; 29, 32. House Lights;	Visual consistency
Task 5: You are feeling cold in your bedroom. Increase the temperature to 25°C.	34, 35, 36, 37. Set Temperature	Terminology Interaction
	1. Home House Monitoring; 33, 34, 35, 36, 37, 38. Set Temperature	Visual consistency
Task 6: It's raining a lot lately and it causes hu-	39. Humidity	Terminology

(*continued*)

Table 1. (*continued*)

midity problems at home. Check the humidity of the house.	39, 40. Humidity	Visual consistency
Task 7: You are arriving at the supermarket and it just started to rain. Check if you left your windows open.	41, 42, 43. Windows 1. Home House Monitoring; 41, 42, 43. Windows	Interaction Terminology Visual consistency
Task 8: A cake is in the oven while you are watching TV in the living room. You decided to open the kitchen window to release the heat. Check if the kitchen window is open.	44, 45, 46. Windows 41, 44, 45, 46. Windows	Visual consistency Interaction Terminology
Task 9: You are not at home and you wonder if you left your TV on. Check if the TV in the living room is on.	47, 48 Set TV	Labelling Terminology Visual consistency

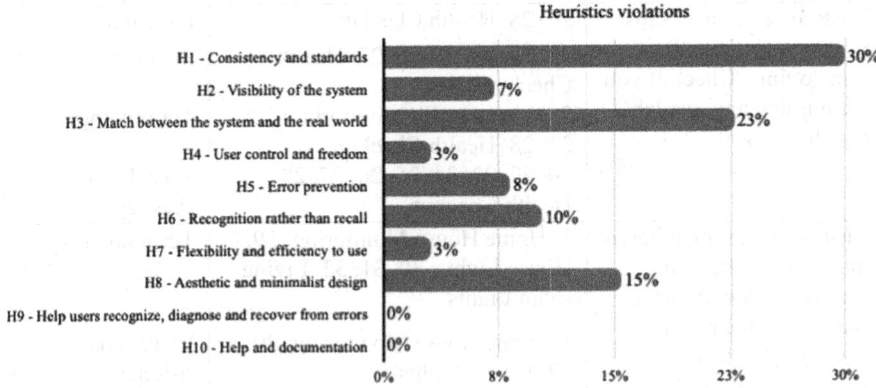

Fig. 10. Percentages per each Heuristics

The severity given by heuristics showed that the catastrophic problems were identified in "Match between the real world and the system" (H3) and "Aesthetic and minimalist design" (H8). However, on the mean severity analysis, no catastrophic problem was encountered. Most major usability problems were considered into "Recognition rather than recall" (H6). While minor usability problems were considered mostly into "Consistency and standards" (H1) followed by "Match between the system and the real

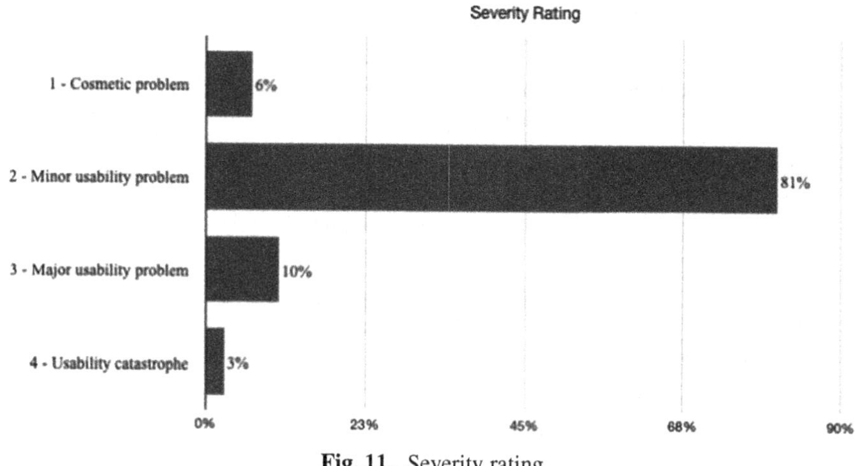

Fig. 11. Severity rating

world" (H3) and "Aesthetic and minimalist design" (H8). The distribution of severity rating is shown in Fig. 12.

b) **Experts recommendations**

Overall, the health monitoring features were considered to be more important for the users than the smart home features. Therefore, experts recommended that the health monitoring screen should be displayed as a homepage by default, instead of house monitoring features.

The usage of plain, obvious and natural language is recommended to improve error prevention and ease of use of a complex system, avoiding technical and English terms, even that it seems to be a common use in other systems.

Minimalist design is also recommended to clarify and visually reinforce important information for the user. They suggested removing unnecessary visual elements (e.g., underlined text, icons with no context of actions, unnecessary pop ups) to keep relevant graphics (e.g., graphics should provide relevant and simple information for the user) and visual consistency so don't distract the user from important information. And create an effective visual language to maintain the visual consistency of the system.

They were concerned that using only Nielsen heuristics on a design process would not improve the interface considerably and provide a granularity of findings on the performed user tasks, according to the identification discovery protocol, identifying as violated heuristics and severity level. Combining these findings with real user testing will provide a return of more discoveries which could be more valuable to improve the interface and the overall experience.

Through the heuristic evaluation method, experts identified potential usability problems that would probably impact older adults' experience. This study showed that applying Nielsen´s broad usability rules with evaluators with high expertise in user experience can provide relevance and knowledge to improve usability and experience

Table 2. Catastrophic and major usability problems

Place of occurrence	Problem category	Problem description	Heuristic Violated
6. Medication reminder	Visual consistency	- Too much and complex information related with medications routines. - Unaligned text.	H8
2. Home Health monitoring; 1. Home House Monitoring	Labelling	- Missing labels on the homepage icon.	H6
2. Home Health monitoring; 6. Medication reminder; 13. Add new medication	Feedback	- No medication labels on feedback messages.	H6
2. Home Health monitoring	Feedback	- No visual notification to show that a medicine was not taken.	H2
14, 15, 16, 17. Add new medication	Visual hierarchy	- Too much complex information to add new medication details. - Many small inputs to fill and understand.	H8
14, 15, 16, 17. Add new medication	Labelling	- Difficult to understand the "Dosage" (Dosagem) label associated with the context of taking pills.	H5
14, 15, 16, 17. Add new medication	Interaction	- Too much complex information to interact. - No automatic filling in all the fields in the form with the medical prescription. - Small input controllers.	H7
2. Home Health monitoring; 20, 28. Health Checkup; 29. House Lights; 30, 31, 32. Living room Lights; 33, 38. Set Temperature; 41, 43. Windows 47, 48. Set TV	Terminology	- Wrong use of term "Check-up" as well as not appropriate to use the term for Portuguese users. - Subtle way of using the English labels "ON" and "OFF".	H3
34, 35, 36, 36. Set Temperature	Terminology	- Creation of confusion with the term "Desligar" (Turn off).	H1

(continued)

Table 2. (*continued*)

1. Home House Monitoring; 41, 42, 43, 44, 45, 46. Windows	Terminology	- Incorrect use of Curtains (Estores) instead of Windows (Janelas).	H3

Note. "Consistency and Standards" (H1), "Visibility of the system" (H2), "Match between the system and the real world" (H3), "User control and freedom" (H4), "Error prevention" (H5), "Recognition rather than recall" (H6), "Flexibility and efficiency to use" (H7), "Aesthetic and minimalist design" (H8), "Help users recognize, diagnose, and recover from errors" (H9) and "Help and documentation" (10).

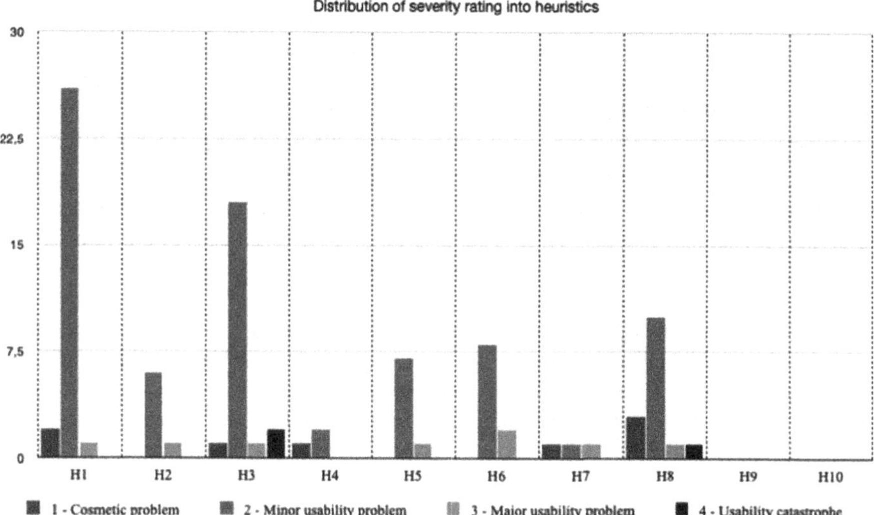

Fig. 12. Distribution of severity rating into heuristics

in age-friendly design. However, more specific existing heuristics for mobile applications (SMASH) [18] and for elderly users [24] could be explored to inspect age-friendly design guidelines.

4 Conclusions and Future Work

This paper presents the user evaluation (Heuristics) stage from an on-going project aiming to develop an age-friendly interface design for older adults to enable them age in their own homes while increasing their independence. The objective of the paper is to report the findings of a heuristic evaluation that identified potentially usability problems which could be faced by older adults when interacting with a smartphone app for Smart Home.

Through the heuristic evaluation method, experts identified potential usability problems that would probably impact older adults' experience. This study showed that applying Nielsen´s broad usability rules with evaluators with high expertise in user experience can provide relevance and knowledge to improve usability and experience in age-friendly design. It can be noticed that Nielsen's heuristics are broadly generic to evaluate age-friendly design guidelines. However, it is still relevant to provide substantial and important findings in the evaluation process.

In an iterative design process, these usability issues can be fixed so the smart home system can evolve into a more usable application for older adults. Despite the valuable expert's evaluation, it is important to say that this methodology doesn't overpass the importance of user testing studies with the real end users of the product. It is concluded that findings should be supported with more expert's evaluation and target user testing to provide insights for designers and developers and create design guidelines for more usable interfaces to address the needs and abilities of the fast-growing population.

As a future work, besides more expert's evaluation, the design review of the interactive prototype will be applied to individual usability tests to assess its usability and to obtain more detailed users' feedback. The same tasks in Heuristics will be applied to the target users to evaluate the relevance and acceptance of the smart home mobile application. Furthermore, the rest of the smart home system (i.e., Smart TV app and home hub tablet) besides smart phone appl will be designed which will follow the same guidelines for an age-friendly system design. This iterative process could improve the acceptance and usefulness of assistive systems among older adults.

Acknowledgement. The study was supported by UNIDCOM under a grant from the Fundação para a Ciência e Tecnologia (FCT) No. UIDB/00711/2020 attributed to UNIDCOM – Unidade de Investigação em Design e Comunicação, Lisbon, Portugal. The study was also partially supported by the Instituto de Telecomunicações and funded by FCT/MCTES through national funds and when applicable co-funded EU funds under the project UIDB/EEA/50008/2020.

References

1. Johnson, J.: Designing User Interfaces for an Aging Population. Elsevier, Amsterdam (2017)
2. United Nations, World Population Prospects 2019: Highlights, no. (ST/ESA/SER.A/423) (2019)
3. Eurostat, "Ageing Europe," Luxembourg (2019)
4. Xu, L., Fritz, H.A., Shi, W.: User centric design for aging population: early experiences and lessons. In: Proceedings - 2016 IEEE 1st International Conference on Connected Health: Applications, Systems and Engineering Technologies CHASE 2016, pp. 338–339 (2016)
5. Carnemolla, P.: Ageing in place and the internet of things – how smart home technologies, the built environment and caregiving intersect. Vis. Eng. **6**(1), 7 (2018)
6. Nielsen, J.: Usability for Senior Citizens: Improved, But Still Lacking (2013). https://www.nngroup.com/articles/usability-seniors-improvements/. Accessed 03 Oct 2019
7. World report on Ageing And Health Summary (2015)
8. Marikyan, D., Papagiannidis, S., Alamanos, E.: A systematic review of the smart home literature: a user perspective. Technol. Forecast. Soc. Change **138**(November 2017), 139–154 (2019)

9. Liu, L., Stroulia, E., Nikolaidis, I., Miguel-Cruz, A., Rios Rincon, A.: Smart homes and home health monitoring technologies for older adults: a systematic review. Int. J. Med. Inform. **91**, 44–59 (2016)
10. Alaa, M., Zaidan, A.A., Zaidan, B.B., Talal, M., Kiah, M.L.M.: A review of smart home applications based on internet of things. J. Netw. Comput. Appl. **97**, 47–65 (2017)
11. Alsinglawi, B., Nguyen, Q.V., Gunawardana, U., Maeder, A., Simoff, S.: RFID systems in healthcare settings and activity of daily living in smart homes: a review. E-Health Telecommun. Syst. Networks **06**(01), 1–17 (2017)
12. Kalimullah, K., Sushmitha, D.: Influence of design elements in mobile applications on user experience of elderly people. Procedia Comput. Sci. **113**, 352–359 (2017)
13. Petrovčič, A., Rogelj, A., Dolničar, V.: Smart but not adapted enough: heuristic evaluation of smartphone launchers with an adapted interface and assistive technologies for older adults. Comput. Hum. Behav. **79**, 123–136 (2018)
14. Barney, K.F., Perkinson, M.A.: Occupational Therapy With Aging Adults. Elsevier Inc., St. Louis (2016)
15. Pericu, S.: Designing for an ageing society: products and services. Des. J. **20**(sup1), S2178–S2189 (2017)
16. Czaja, S.J., Boot, W.R., Charness, N., Rogers, W.A., Arthur, D.F.: Designing for Older Adults Principles and Creative Human Factors Approaches, 2nd edn. CRC Press, Boca Raton (2009)
17. Harada, C.N., Natelson Love, M.C., Triebel, K.L.: Normal cognitive aging. Clin. Geriatr. Med. **29**(4), 737–752 (2013)
18. Salman, H.M., Wan Ahmad, W.F., Sulaiman, S.: Usability evaluation of the smartphone user interface in supporting elderly users from experts' perspective. IEEE Access **6**, 22578–22591 (2018)
19. Dix, A., Finlay, J., Abowd, G.D., Beale, R.: Human Computer Interaction-Lab, 3rd edn. Pearson Education, London (2004)
20. Silva, P.A., Holden, K., Jordan, P.: Towards a list of heuristics to evaluate smartphone apps targeted at older adults: a study with apps that aim at promoting health and well-being. In: Proceedings of Annual Hawaii International Conference on System Science, vol. 2015-March, no. May, pp. 3237–3246 (2015)
21. Nielsen, J.: Finding Usability Problems Through Heuristic Evaluation (1992)
22. Rogers, Y., Preece, J., Sharp, H.: Interaction design - beyond human-computer interaction. In: Interaction Computing New Paradigm, pp. 227–254 (2002)
23. Nielsen, J.: Severity Ratings for Usability Problems: Article by Jakob Nielsen (1994). https://www.nngroup.com/articles/how-to-rate-the-severity-of-usability-problems/. Accessed 05 May 2020
24. Al-Razgan, M.S., Al-Khalifa, H.S., Al-Shahrani, M.D.: Heuristics for evaluating the usability of mobile launchers for elderly people. In: Marcus, A. (ed.) DUXU 2014. LNCS, vol. 8517, pp. 415–424. Springer, Cham (2014). https://doi.org/10.1007/978-3-319-07668-3_40

Mobile Application to Record Daily Life for Seniors Based on Experience Sampling Method (ESM)

Takahiro Miura[1(✉)], Masafumi Arata[2], Yasushi Sukenari[3], Rinpei Miura[4], Akiko Nishino[5], Toshio Otsuki[6], Kazuhiko Nishide[5], and Junichiro Okata[5]

[1] Human Augmentation Research Center (HARC), National Institute of Advanced Industrial Science and Technology (AIST), c/o Kashiwa II Campus, The University of Tokyo, 6-2-3 Kashiwanoha, Kashiwa, Chiba 277-0882, Japan
miura-t@aist.go.jp

[2] Faculty of Sociology, Toyo University, 5-28-20, Hakusan, Bunkyo-ku, Tokyo 112-8606, Japan

[3] Graduate School of Humanities and Sociology, The University of Tokyo, 7-3-1 Hongo, Bunkyo-ku, Tokyo 113-8656, Japan

[4] Graduate School of Urban Innovation (IUI), Yokohama National University, 79-5 Tokiwadai, Hodogaya-ku, Yokohama 240-8501, Japan

[5] Institute of Gerontology, The University of Tokyo, 7-3-1 Hongo, Bunkyo-ku, Tokyo 113-8656, Japan

[6] Graduate School of Engineering, The University of Tokyo, 7-3-1 Hongo, Bunkyo-ku, Tokyo 113-8656, Japan

Abstract. Many countries, including Japan, face the hyper-aged society and consolidate the nursing homes for seniors, such as the housing for the elderly with home-care services provided as well as "Aging in Place" support such as improvement of services in local environments and communities. However, it is challenging to comprehend the diversified needs of a wide variety of seniors about their livelihood supports. Also, to establish new living supports, we should clarify seniors' current situation, including everyday life and service usages in spheres of daily life. Nevertheless, the useful measure to investigate the situation remained unconsidered. In this study, our objective is to develop an application to collect seniors' impressions on various locations at a different time and to investigate the characteristics of seniors individuals and local services by using our system. Mainly, we implemented the application named HabitLet that is based on the experience sampling method (ESM) on a smartphone and then asked twenty seniors to input their situations when the alarm of HabitLet rang. The results indicated that the HabitLet could reveal their lifestyles and the impressions in their life sphere.

Keywords: Experience sampling method (ESM) · Seniors · Smartphones

C. Stephanidis et al. (Eds.): HCII 2020, LNCS 12426, pp. 660–669, 2020.
https://doi.org/10.1007/978-3-030-60149-2_49

1 Introduction

The remarkable population aging all over the world, especially in the US, countries in the EU, and East Asia, has caused the increasing costs of social security and medical care and reducing domestic productivity. In Japan, which entered the hyper-aged society in 2007, the population ratio of over 65 years and under 15 years were 27.5% and 12.4% in 2017, respectively [1,3]. These rate has been estimated to be as high as 40.5% and 8.4% by 2055 [9,18]. The ratio of social security benefits to national income increased from 5.8% in 1970 to 29.4% in 2009, reaching the highest level ever [9]. Also, the ratio of the number of young people to the number of older adults was 2.81 in 2009, but it is predicted to be 1.26 in 2055 [22]. Since there are similar situations in the countries in the EU and East Asian region [2,5], issues about a sustainable social security system for the elderly gave rise to worldwide discussion. Specifically, for realizing age-friendly society and community, governments of various nations have developed infrastructure of the community-based long-term care system such as the continuing care retirement community (CCRC) and small-scale special elderly nursing homes [20,23]. However, because it is challenging to grasp the livelihood needs of various seniors with wide diversely about their life support, the compatible achievement of enriching care services with reducing the cost and ensuring human dignity and quality of life (QoL) becomes a central issue for sustaining societies.

On the other hand, rapid progress in mobile technologies, including the development of smartphones, has provided highly functional applications that were hitherto available only on personal computers [25]. Mobile devices currently contain numerous sensors, including acceleration/gyro sensors and location sensors based on global positioning systems (GPS), and some mobile applications make interesting use of these sensors. Particularly, these mobile applications can execute measurement functions with or without external sensors, e.g., measurement functions for the user's activity and physical condition, and support software designed for workouts, including aerobic exercises and progressive resistance training. For example, Hammerl et al. have proposed a semi-automatic personal digital diary [15] in order to improve the efficiency of various Diary studies [6,10,16]. On the motor function side, Brajdic et al. developed a walking detection technique using acceleration sensors, and Miura et al. developed a smartphone-based gait measurement application using the GPS for older adults [8,21]. Miura et al. also reported that their application could help motivate seniors to walk more regularly and improve their walking ability. Some of them became interested in participating in social activities and using new technologies as a consequence [21].

However, despite the progress of lifelog recording method using mobile technologies, there are little mobile services for seniors that based on the knowledge of diary and monitoring studies. For implementing new services for older adults in the specific local area, it is necessary to consider their daily life and current usage of local public and private services, which can realize by using the data measured with mobile technologies. Nevertheless, acquiring older adults' impressions of their behavior and their living sphere, as well as the actual conditions of their life, is challenging. For this purpose, we should not only implement the mobile application to collect their impressions in the living conditions, measure and evaluate by various older adults, and then ensure the feasibility of the methodology.

Thus, in this paper, our final goal is to develop and evaluate the mobile application that can investigate the impression of seniors in their living sphere. First, we focused on the experience sampling method (ESM) proposed by Csikszentmihalyi et al. [13,17]. We then developed the ESM-based mobile application for the seniors named HabitLet to record impression data at a specific place and time. After that, we asked the seniors in a local district to use our application to record their impressions of their daily life. We analyzed their registered data and then discuss their conditions of emotion, behavior at any place.

2 Our Application: HabitLet

2.1 Overview

We developed the HabitLet, a smartphone application of experience sampling that can decrease the input burden for seniors. In the implementation of this application, we referred to implementation guides of the experience sampling method described by Consolvo et al. and Baxter et al. [7,12], and designed based on the participatory design approach [11].

2.2 Overview of Experience Sampling Method (ESM)

Experience sampling method (ESM) proposed by Csikszentmihalyi et al. [13,17] is a survey technique for asking the survey participants to report their present states in specific fixed or random time in the daily life for several days to several weeks a day. Originally, when the participants notice an alarm of a distributed mobile device such as a pocket pager, they recorded their state to a paper-based format by a pen. In recent times, with the development of mobile technology, participants were asked to bring a smartphone or a feature phone and to input the data on the survey screen on the device every time an alarm rang by the trigger of SMS, e-mail, or other notification methods. The advantages of this method include the acquirability of the daily experience of participants in detail, such as the effect of time fluctuations and event-related variations.

2.3 Interface

The interface of this system is shown in Fig. 1. This application consists of (A) top view, and (B) questionnaire view for input. We employed Xcode 8.1–9.2.0 (OS: Mac OS X 10.11.6–macOS 10.13.4) and Objective-C as an integrated development environment and programming language, respectively. This application was available on iOS devices such as the iPhone and iPad (OS: iOS 9.0–12.3). These views, including the button and font sizes, were designed and developed by referring to the Apple iOS Human Interface Guidelines and a guideline for seniors proposed by Kobayashi et al. [4,19]. Also, we designed the application,

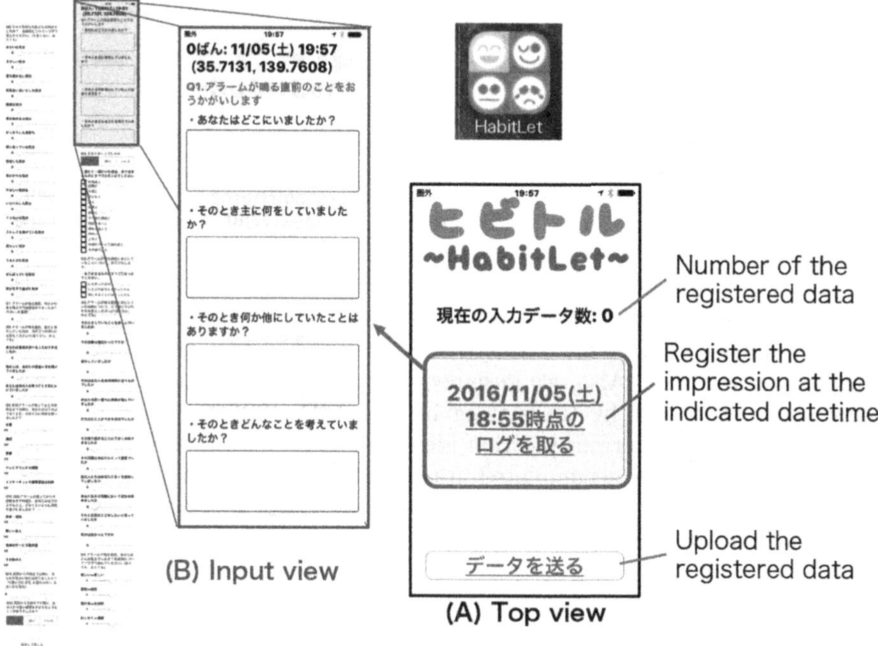

Fig. 1. User interface of our smartphone application for registering user's current status

based on the procedure of the ESM, to notify the user side to open the application and answer the present condition on the questionnaire screen at various times. For realizing senior-friendly operations, the screen was set to jump to the top screen (A) when tapping the notification window on the iPhone, based on the brief result of the cyclic evaluations by seniors.

The top view (A) is the screen that appears when the user launches the application. It shows the number of registered data as well as the datetime that the system requested the user to input data. This datetime would be fixed until the update of the datetime to input the next data entry. When a new notification arrives, the users read a page where they can register new information at the next time slot.

We designed this application to support the local notification and the push notification, which are iOS functions, for displaying the notifications to input the data. The former generates a notification trigger in a local smartphone, and the latter generates a trigger from a server. In the evaluation experiment described in the next section, we employed the former one.

In the questionnaire view (B), the users can register and edit the data of the user associated with the place. The questionnaire includes the following items:

- What was done at the alarming time of the notification
- What was on the mind

- Who was with them
- What was felt about their acts
- Users' psychological state
- The states of their pain
- The changes in their mood since the last notification.

We selected the questionnaire items from the studies of experience sampling conducted by Csikszentmihalyi and Schneider [14,24]. This view has the forms to input by the text, the sliders to answer as 5-scale or 7-scale of subjective evaluation and as minutes unit of what they did, and the checkboxes to tap the items that applied. Though this application could record photos and sounds, we turned off these functions in consideration of the feedback by the ethical review board of our institute. Also, we designed this application to turn the question items appeared or not by the setting interface. The input by the users was associated with their current position identified based on the GPS coordinates. The registered data are accumulated in the SQLite database in the smartphone and can be converted to other formats such as JSON and XML. Note that this application does not record any personally identifiable information, such as name.

The application allows users to upload their registered information on the smartphone to a specific server. The server application is coded in PHP 5.6.0 and the Google Maps JavaScript API v3 that has a MySQL database and runs on Ubuntu Linux 16.04. This web application enables users to check their registered history hovered as a marker on a map.

3 Evaluation

We asked seniors living in a specific housing complex to record their actions, feelings, and durations about what they would do by using the application described in the previous section. This evaluation was approved by the Research Ethics Committee at the Graduate School of Engineering, the University of Tokyo.

3.1 Participants

Seventeen seniors living independently (Average age: 6.9 ± 75.6 years) participated in this evaluation. Five of them (Average age: 70.0 ± 6.6 years) were males and twelve (Average age: 78.0 ± 5.4 years) were females. Twelve of them lived in the housing complex, and others lived outside the housing complex but had previously lived in the complex.

3.2 Procedure

Before the evaluation, we set the alarm to sound five times in a day (8–20 o'clock) on the developed application. The alarm was set to sound once each in the morning (8:00–9:00), AM (10:00–11:00), noon (12:30–13:30), afternoon (15:30–16:30) and evening (18:00–20:00).

Table 1. The number of inputs by the participants at whether they were at home or not and whether they were alone or not. The left and right tables are the inputs by the female and male participants, respectively.

Female	Place to input	
	Home	Others
Alone	200 (54%)	91 (25%)
With others	35 (9%)	43 (12%)

Male	Place to input	
	Home	Others
Alone	74 (37%)	71 (36%)
With others	43 (22%)	12 (6%)

In the evaluation, we first gave the participants the smartphones (Apple iPhone 5s (OS: iOS 10.1.1)) with our application installed, and then gave instructions on how to use them and the precautions about the evaluation. After this instruction, they practiced registering the data on the application. At that time, the participants who insisted on the difficulty of operating the application were informed that they could answer on the paper-based form after ranging the alarm of the smartphone application. In total, eight participants selected to fill out the paper-based form, and we instructed them that the smartphone was only a notification device. At that time, we also told them that they could input the answer on the smartphone application if they temporarily wanted to answer on the smartphone even if they chose the paper-based format. The rest of the people (9 participants) continued to use our application.

Then, they were asked to bring the smartphone continuously for a week. At that time, after they noticed the alarm sounding or the presence of the notification, they registered the behavior and psychological state at the time of the notification on the application or the paper-based form before they received the next notification. We also asked them to charge the smartphones as much as possible at times other than 8 to 21 o'clock.

Besides, at the end of the evaluation, we asked them to answer a paper-based questionnaire survey. The overview of the questionnaire is as follows:

- The individual characteristics of the participants: age, gender, and ICT experience.
- Family relationship, the circle of friends, social and personal activities including work, exercise, volunteering, and other activities.
- Living places and outgoing places/frequency.
- Good points and usability of our smartphone application.

4 Results and Discussion

4.1 Inputs to Our Smartphone Application

In this article, we state the result of the preliminary examination. This paper describes the feasibility to clarify the participants' living conditions by our application.

First, 6 out of 9 participants responded to all of the notifications (35 times) from smartphones. Their age range was 68–88 years, and there was no significant difference in age with the remaining 3 participants (Age range: 73–81) whose number of inputs was less than 10 (Welch's test, $p = .43 > .10$). Not age but other factors may be strong in the continuous use of the application.

Table 1 shows the number of inputs by the female and male participants. About half of the inputs were done at participants' homes, and most of the inputs were conducted when participants were alone in these two. The female participants tended to be alone when they were at home while they were not alone when they were not at home. On the other hand, the male participants tended to input more when they were at the outside of their home alone and the inside of their home with other people. Thus, the result indicated that male and female elderly participant groups could generally have different lifestyles.

Based on the registered data, the places excluding their own home include local public facilities such as neighborhood community centers and housing complex meeting places, commercial facilities such as shopping malls and department stores, and medical facilities, including hospitals and nursing homes. In these places, some of them participated in the disaster prevention course in the regional cultural facilities, the circle activity at the nearby elementary school, the volunteer activity in the nursing home for the elderly with frailty. Thus, the result indicated that the application could acquire their various activities that experience sampling method was implemented. Further analysis of what they felt and thought will be the future work.

4.2 What to Spend in the Older Adults

Figure 2 shows what to spend between notifications in the male and female participants. These results indicated that male participants might be likely to affect the place and with whom they were. Particularly in the male, the time for working, hobbies and housework significantly increase when they were with other people while the duration to watch TV and listen to the radio significantly increase when they were alone. However, in female participants, there were generally no significant differences among the places and whether they were alone. Also, female participants spent more time doing housework. Since the number of participants was small, we could confirm that the individual difference of the elderly in the hyper-aged society in Japan, though there may be a bias in this data. Though the representativeness of this data should be analyzed further in the future, the result also suggested that elderly males are significantly activated by other people's encouragement or, in some cases, the fact that other people are in the same place.

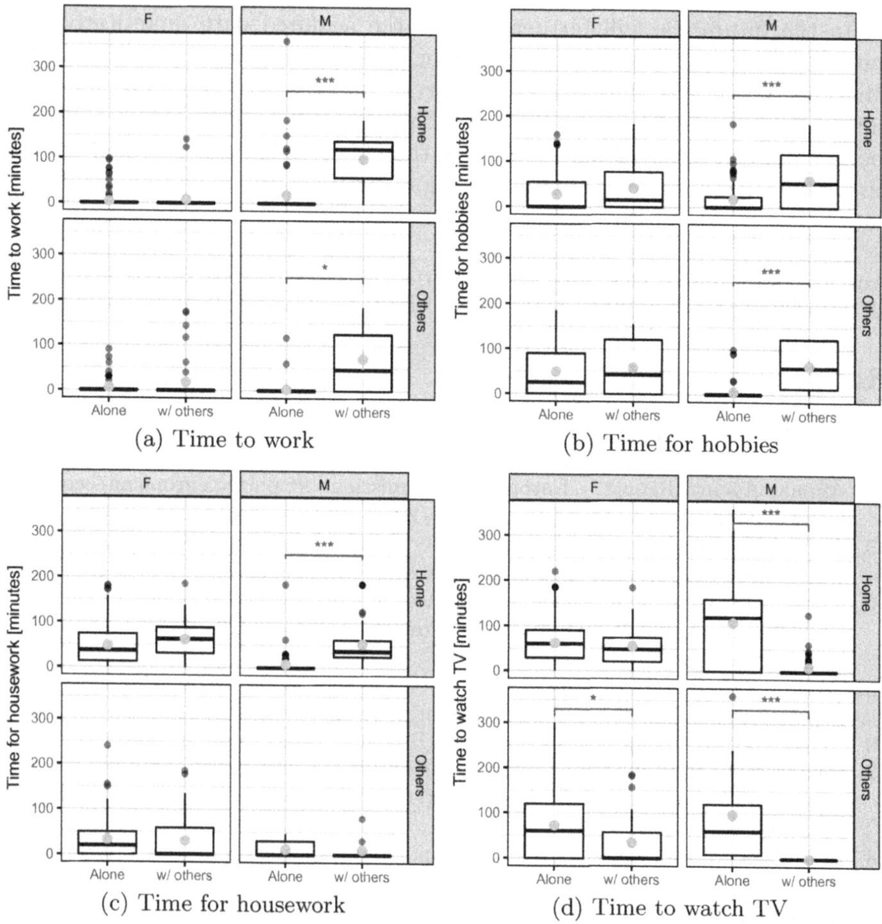

Fig. 2. Durations of what was done between notifications when they were alone or not and with whom they were in male and female participants. red points and error bars represent mean and standard errors, respectively. Blue annotations with *** and * represent $p < .001$ and $p < .05$ based on the multiple comparison test with the aligned rank transform (ART) [26], respectively.

5 Conclusion

In this article, we first developed a smartphone application named *Habitlet* to investigate actual life conditions in seniors and usages of the local services based on the experience sampling method (ESM). Then, this paper roughly describes the preliminary analysis of the data obtained by this application and the behavior difference in male and female seniors in Japan. Based on the data, our application could be useful to investigate rough life trends and usage situations of regional services.

In the future, we will further analyze the acquired data quantitatively in more detail to clarify the relationship among individual characteristics, including emotional conditions, what to do and service usages, where they are and going out tendency, and with whom they are. Then, we will consider the arrangement methodology of the regional service for the elderly based on the analysis and discussion of the combined data of seniors participants' conditions and GPS data.

Acknowledgement. This work was supported by JSPS KAKENHI Grant Numbers JP15H02282 and JP18K18445, and the SECOM Science and Technology Foundation.

References

1. A 2016 Declining Birthrate White Paper. http://www8.cao.go.jp/shoushi/shoushika/whitepaper/measures/english/w-2016/
2. Annual Ageing Report - European Commission. http://ec.europa.eu/economy_finance/publications/european_economy/2014/ee8_en.htm
3. Annual Report on the Aging Society 2017. http://www8.cao.go.jp/kourei/whitepaper/w-2017/zenbun/29pdf_index.html. (in Japanese)
4. Apple iOS Human Interface Guidelines. https://developer.apple.com/library/ios/#documentation/UserExperience/Conceptual/MobileHIG/Introduction/Introduction.html
5. World Population Ageing 2013. http://www.un.org/en/development/desa/population/publications/pdf/ageing/WorldPopulationAgeing2013.pdf
6. Alaszewski, A.: Using Diaries for Social Research. Sage, London (2006)
7. Baxter, R.J., Hunton, J.E.: Capturing affect via the experience sampling method: prospects for accounting information systems researchers. Int. J. Account. Inf. Syst. **12**(2), 90–98 (2011)
8. Brajdic, A., Harle, R.: Walk detection and step counting on unconstrained smartphones. In: Proceedings of the 2013 ACM International Joint Conference on Pervasive and Ubiquitous Computing, pp. 225–234. ACM (2013)
9. CabinetOffice: Annual Report on the Aging Society 2013. http://www8.cao.go.jp/kourei/whitepaper/w-2013/gaiyou/s1_1.html. (in Japanese)
10. Carter, S., Mankoff, J.: When participants do the capturing: the role of media in diary studies. In: Proceedings of the SIGCHI conference on Human Factors in Computing Systems, pp. 899–908. ACM (2005)
11. COlEmaN, R., ClaRkSON, J., Cassim, J.: Design for Inclusivity: A Practical Guide to Accessible, Innovative and User-centred Design. CRC Press, Boca Raton (2016)
12. Consolvo, S., Walker, M.: Using the experience sampling method to evaluate ubicomp applications. IEEE Pervasive Comput. **2**(2), 24–31 (2003)
13. Csikszentmihalyi, M., Larson, R.: Validity and reliability of the experience-sampling method. In: Flow and the Foundations of Positive Psychology, pp. 35–54. Springer, Dordrecht (2014). https://doi.org/10.1007/978-94-017-9088-8_3
14. Csikszentmihalyi, M., Schneider, B.: Becoming Adult: How Teenagers Prepare for the World of Work. Basic Books, New York (2001)
15. Hammerl, S., Hermann, T., Ritter, H.: Towards a semi-automatic personal digital diary: detecting daily activities from smartphone sensors. In: Proceedings of the 5th International Conference on PErvasive Technologies Related to Assistive Environments, PETRA 2012, New York, NY, USA, pp. 24:1–24:8. ACM (2012). http://doi.acm.org/10.1145/2413097.2413128

16. Hayashi, E., Hong, J.: A diary study of password usage in daily life. In: Proceedings of the SIGCHI Conference on Human Factors in Computing Systems, pp. 2627–2630. ACM (2011)
17. Hektner, J.M., Schmidt, J.A., Csikszentmihalyi, M.: Experience Sampling Method: Measuring the Quality of Everyday Life. Sage, London (2007)
18. Kaneko, R., et al.: Population projections for Japan: 2006–2055 outline of results, methods, and assumptions. Jpn. J. Popul. **6**(1), 76–114 (2008)
19. Kobayashi, M., Hiyama, A., Miura, T., Asakawa, C., Hirose, M., Ifukube, T.: Elderly user evaluation of mobile touchscreen interactions. In: Campos, P., Graham, N., Jorge, J., Nunes, N., Palanque, P., Winckler, M. (eds.) INTERACT 2011. LNCS, vol. 6946, pp. 83–99. Springer, Heidelberg (2011). https://doi.org/10.1007/978-3-642-23774-4_9
20. Krout, J.A., Moen, P., Holmes, H.H., Oggins, J., Bowen, N.: Reasons for relocation to a continuing care retirement community. J. Appl. Gerontol. **21**(2), 236–256 (2002)
21. Miura, T., Yabu, K., Hiyama, A., Inamura, N., Hirose, M., Ifukube, T.: Smartphone-based gait measurement application for exercise and its effects on the lifestyle of senior citizens. In: Abascal, J., Barbosa, S., Fetter, M., Gross, T., Palanque, P., Winckler, M. (eds.) INTERACT 2015. LNCS, vol. 9298, pp. 80–98. Springer, Cham (2015). https://doi.org/10.1007/978-3-319-22698-9_7
22. Muramatsu, N., Akiyama, H.: Japan: super-aging society preparing for the future. Gerontol. **51**(4), 425–432 (2011)
23. Nakanishi, M., Hattori, K., Nakashima, T., Sawamura, K.: Health care and personal care needs among residents in nursing homes, group homes, and congregate housing in Japan: Why does transition occur, and where can the frail elderly establish a permanent residence? J. Am. Med. Dir. Assoc. **15**(1), 76–e1 (2014)
24. Schneider, B.E., Waite, L.J.: Being Together, Working Apart: Dual-career Families and the Work-life Balance. Cambridge University Press, Cambridge (2005)
25. Siewiorek, D.: Generation smartphone. IEEE Spectr. **49**(9), 54–58 (2012)
26. Wobbrock, J.O., Findlater, L., Gergle, D., Higgins, J.J.: The aligned rank transform for nonparametric factorial analyses using only ANOVA procedures. In: Proceedings of the SIGCHI Conference on Human Factors in Computing Systems, pp. 143–146 (2011)

A Preliminary Study on Reaching Position Estimation Model for the Subtle Action Disruption

Yoshinobu Miya[1(✉)], Takehiko Yamaguchi[1], Tania Giovannetti[2], Maiko Sakamoto[3], and Hayato Ohwada[4]

[1] Suwa University of Science, 5000-1 Toyohira, Chino, Nagano, Japan
7420528@ed.tus.ac.jp, tk-ymgch@rs.sus.ac.jp
[2] Temple University, Philadelphia, PA 19122, USA
tgio@temple.edu
[3] Saga University, 5-1-1 Nabeshima, Saga, Saga, Japan
[4] Tokyo University of Science, 2641 Yamazaki, Noda, Chiba, Japan

Abstract. In neuropsychological impairment, micro-error (ME) defines the slight stagnation of movement in reaching actions when the patient is presented with an interference stimulus satisfying the condition around the target stimulus of the reached object. After passing the interfering stimulus, the reaching orbit at the ME-generation point is corrected to the direction of the target stimulus. To identify the interfering stimuli that cause ME, we developed a model that estimates the arrival position in the initial motion time. The reaching position is estimated from the momentum features by a Gaussian-process regression model during two time periods: the time of the velocity waveform peak and the time of the acceleration peak. The coefficients of determination in the acceleration and velocity models were 0.98 respectively, in both the x and z directions. Given the information up to the peak velocity time, the arrival position was estimated to within ± 1 cm.

Keywords: Dementia · Mild cognitive impairment · Micro-error · Instrumental activities of daily living · Gaussian process regression · Machine learning

1 Introduction

Early detection of mild cognitive impairment (MCI) and the prevention of progression to dementia are important challenges. The number of dementia patients was 46.8 million in 2015, and is projected to reach 82 million by 2030 and 152 million by 2050 [1]. In Japan, the number of dementia sufferers is estimated to increase from approximately 4.62 million in 2012 to 10.16 million in 2050 [2]. The prevalence and disease rate of dementia increase remarkably with age, and 70% of dementias are reported as Alzheimer's dementia. Although the progression of dementia can be slowed, neither the cause nor the treatment of dementia-causing diseases is known. Therefore, detecting the early prodromal stage of dementia is essential for preventing dementia onset. The present study focuses on MCI, a precursor stage of dementia. Fifty percent of patients diagnosed with

C. Stephanidis et al. (Eds.): HCII 2020, LNCS 12426, pp. 670–678, 2020.
https://doi.org/10.1007/978-3-030-60149-2_50

MCI, which is intermediate between the normal mental state and dementia, will develop dementia within 5 years if the condition remains untreated. On the other hand, MCI patients have recovered in some cases [3]. Previous studies have demonstrated behavioral dysfunction by MCI patients in the Instrumental Activities of Daily Living (IADL) test. MCI can be identified by errors made in the Naturalistic Action Test, a standardization of the IADL. Here, we assess the behavioral characteristics of MCI patients by the micro-error (ME) index, which models the stagnation of reaching movements in the neuropsychological field. Recently, the authors of [3] clarified a significant difference in the ME-generation frequencies of healthy subjects and MCI patients, and developed an approach that distinguishes MCI by the generation frequency of MEs. The incidence of ME increases dramatically with increasing average difficulty level of the subtasks, defined as the small actions that constitute IADL tasks [3]. The nature of IADL tasks can be simplified to reaching and selection tasks.

The authors of [4] estimated the occurrence probability of ME in a model based on the difficulty of reaching objects with similar colors and shapes. They reported high ME-generation frequency when the interference stimulus was very similar to the target stimulus [4]. However, this study assumes that the interfering stimuli are known because of independent variables. Identifying the interfering stimuli at the onset of ME, which is essential for quantifying their effects, has not been attempted in previous studies. To this end, we predict a characteristic of ME called the reaching orbit. ME patients typically reach linearly toward the interfering stimulus, then reach linearly toward the target stimulus. The trajectory and velocity waveforms of ME reaching actions are shown in Fig. 1.

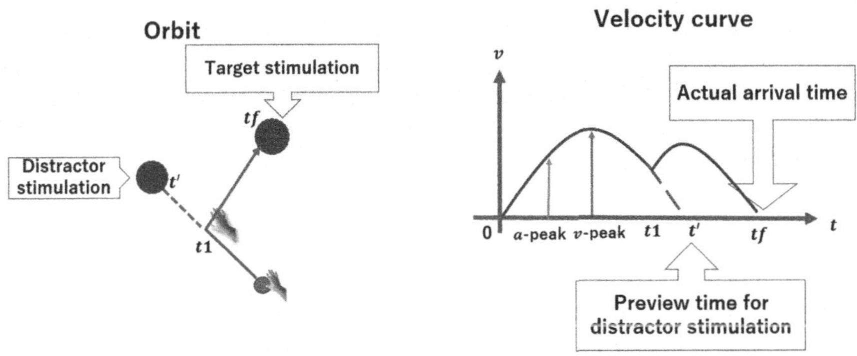

Fig. 1. Reaching operations by ME patients

In the present study, the reaching action was predicted at the initial time of a two-point reaching motion, in which the subject linearly pointed to the first point and then to the second point. In [5], the two-point reaching motion of the hand was modeled by Jerk's minimum model:

$$C_j = \frac{1}{2}\int_0^{t_f}\left(\frac{d^3x(t)}{dt^3} + \frac{d^3y(t)}{dt^3} + \frac{d^3z(t)}{dt^3}\right)^2 dt. \tag{1}$$

The orbit is found by minimizing the function C_j. The arrival position is represented by a polynomial in time, and the velocity and acceleration at the start and end of the two-point arrival motions are assumed as 0. The acceleration and time of the motion are respectively given by

$$x(\tau) = x_0 + \left(x_f - x_0\right)\left(6\tau^5 - 15\tau^4 + 10\tau^3\right), \tag{2}$$

$$\tau = \frac{t}{t_f}. \tag{3}$$

The acceleration [2] is obtained by differentiating the equation three times, so the acceleration is calculated as follows:

$$\begin{cases} \tau_1 \approx 0.21 \\ \tau_2 \approx 0.79 \end{cases}. \tag{4}$$

The inflection point of the acceleration, that is, the time τ_1 at the peak of the acceleration, is known to be approximately 21% of the arrival time. Therefore, the arrival position can be estimated from the acceleration peak. Substituting τ_1 into Eq. (2) and solving for x_f, the arrival position of the terminal point is found as

$$x_f = \frac{4x(\tau_1) - \left(2 + \sqrt{3}\right)x_0}{2 - \sqrt{3}} \tag{5}$$

from which the position of the terminal point can be obtained.

In this model, the velocity waveform of the finger is assumed to follow an ideal bell curve, obtained by differentiating Eq. (2). However, in actual finger-reaching operations, the subject adjusts the reaching position within a finite time, so the velocity waveform is distorted from the ideal bell curve [6]. A typical bell-shaped velocity waveform in this experiment is shown in Fig. 2.

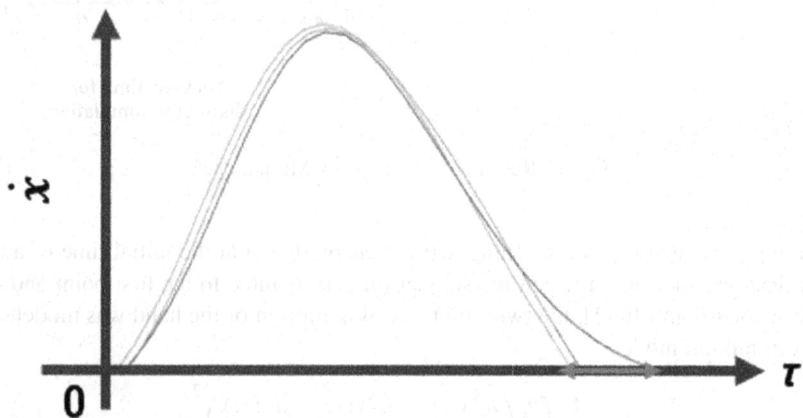

Fig. 2. Speed waveforms, showing the distortion of the velocity in the experimental reaching task from the ideal bell curve

The adjustment time depends on the location of the reached object and the peculiarities of individual subjects, and cannot be included in the model. Excluding the adjustment time introduces a large error in certain types of reaching operation. To avoid this problem, we seek a new model that estimates the positions of the finger at the acceleration and velocity peaks of the reaching motion.

2 Methods

2.1 Gaussian Regression

The Gaussian regression model is a learning model that estimates the probability distribution of a dependent variable with noise.

In this paper, the noise is sourced from the adjustment time in the velocity waveform. When constructing the machine learning model, the independent variable was assigned as the feature quantity during the initial action time of the reaching, and the dependent variable was the final reaching position.

2.2 Virtual Kitchen Challenge System

Previously, we developed the Virtual Kitchen Challenge (VKC) system that measures the reaching performance in virtual reality (VR) IADL by configuring the IADL task environment (VR-IADL) on a tablet device using VR technology. The real-space IADL task environment was found to be unsuitable for mass screening, as constructing the task environment was time-intensive and the task results were not reproducible. The VKC based on VR technology was proposed to alleviate this problem. In real-world IADL tests, objects must be selected and then grasped and moved, but in the Lunchbox Task of VKC, these actions are mapped to interactions such as touching and dragging the tablet screen. The Lunchbox Task consists of three main reaching tasks related to lunch: a sandwich and a cookie made from bread spread with jam and peanut butter and wrapped in aluminum foil, a container of juice, and a covered water bottle. The subjects must work around interference stimuli, items that are not environmentally necessary. Figure 3 shows the Lunchbox Task in VKC. Previous studies have clarified a correlation between the number of ME occurrences in VKC and real-space IADL tasks [3].

2.3 Task for Measuring the Reaching Movement Between Two Points

As VKC mimics an IADL task, it is affected by the planning of operating procedures and the immediately preceding action. To control for these effects, we subdivided the main task into subtasks and developed independent trial tasks simplified as reaching actions. Here, the releasing task was the action of releasing the finger from the target stimulus at the action start point on the task screen. The target stimulus of the reaching task was marked with a plus-symbol (+), and the touch range was defined by a 2-cm radius from the target. 20 male university students (Mean = 21.87 Standard Deviation = 0.73) performed reaching movements between two points. To measure the reaching movements at different distances in different directions, the target stimuli were randomly

Fig. 3. The Virtual Kitchen Challenge (VKC) system based on virtual reality technology

displayed at eight distances ranging from 7.5 cm to 20 cm at 2.5-cm intervals, and in 12 directions ranging from 0° to 180° in 22.5° intervals. The measurements were acquired by optical motion capture (Opti Track). The display was a 24-in touch display and the sampling rate was 120 Hz. As the screen size was limited, the tasks of displaying the Home Position on the screen and at the bottom of the screen were performed in sequence. To offset the order effect, the order of the tasks was counterbalanced. In Figs. 4 and 5, the plus-symbol is displayed on the lower and upper side of the screen, respectively.

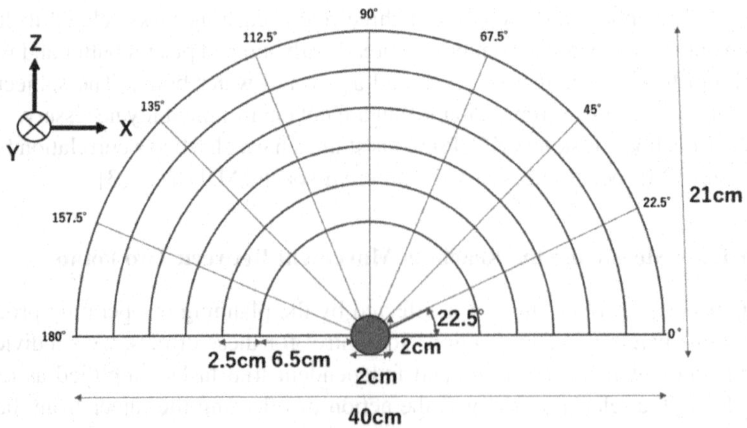

Fig. 4. Task screen 1

The task was a pattern of 192 consecutive reaching trials. The subjects performed four reaching operations at each distance in each direction. The tasks were interspersed

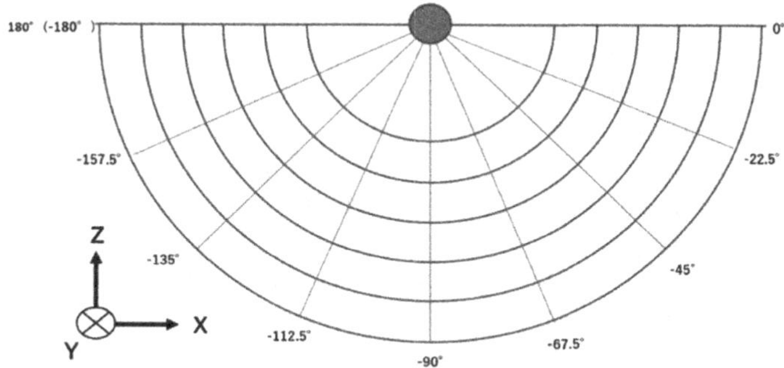

Fig. 5. Task screen 2

with breaks to reduce the effects of arm fatigue. The measurement scene is shown in Fig. 6.

Fig. 6. Measurement environment of the reaching experiments

2.4 Building a Learning Model

To estimate the arrival position, the information up to the time of maximum velocity and acceleration was set as the explanatory variable, and the position coordinates of the arrival point were set as the response variables. To ensure directional independence in the learning process, we adopted the Gaussian regression model and chose an exponential kernel function. The feature quantities at the acceleration peak were the position at the motion start, position at the acceleration peak, the velocity, acceleration, and direction vector of the position from the motion start, the direction vector of the velocity, direction vector of the acceleration, and that time. In the model at the velocity peak, the feature quantities were those at the acceleration peak, plus the positions at the velocity peak, the velocity, acceleration, and direction vector of the position from the motion start, the direction vector of the velocity, the direction vector of the acceleration, and the arrival time (number of data n = 5190). The feature quantities of failed trials with incorrect reaching actions were excluded. The model was evaluated by five-fold cross-validation.

3 Results

3.1 Reaching-Position Model at the Acceleration Peak

The coefficient of determination of the learning model, determined by the five-fold cross-validation, was 0.98 in both the x-axis and z-axis directions. The root-mean-square errors (RMSEs) were 0.011 and 0.012 in the x-axis and z-axis directions, respectively. The RMSE between the arrival position predicted by the model and the actual arrival position at each arrival point is plotted on a heatmap in Fig. 7. The darker the color, the higher is the RMSE.

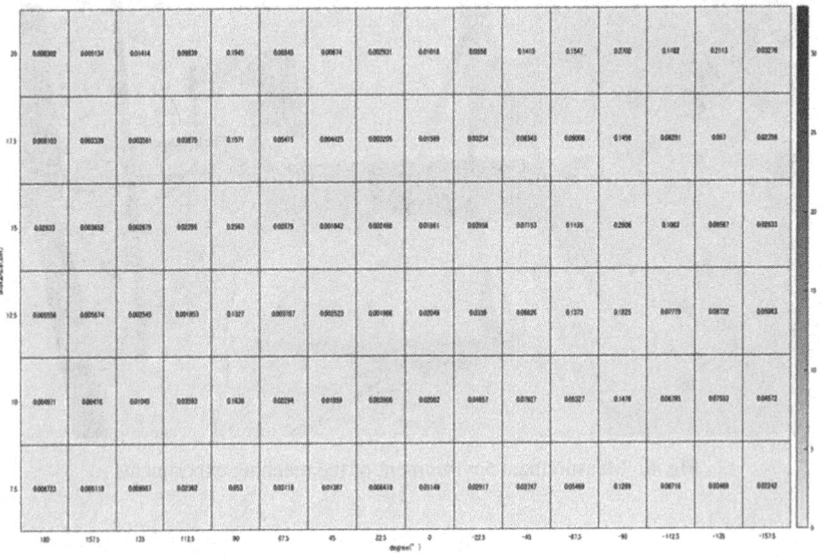

Fig. 7. Heatmap of the RMSE between the predicted and actual arrival positions at each point in the acceleration model

Reaching-Position Model at the Velocity Peak. The coefficient of determination of the learning model at the velocity peak, determined by the five-fold cross-validation, was 0.99 in both the x-axis and z-axis directions. The RMSEs were 0.007 and 0.004 in the x-axis and z-axis directions, respectively. Figure 8 is a heatmap of the RMSE between the arrival position predicted by the model and the actual arrival position at each arrival point.

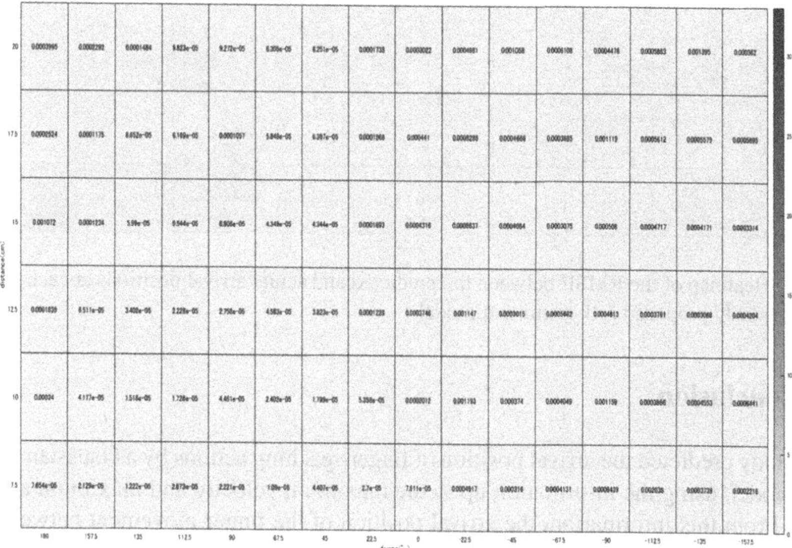

Fig. 8. Heatmap of the RMSE between the predicted and actual arrival positions at each point in the velocity model

4 Discussion

4.1 Reaching-Position Model at the Acceleration Peak

Figure 9 shows the estimated arrival positions in the previous study, namely, the Jerk minimum model.

This result confirms the superior accuracy of the proposed model over the conventional technique.

4.2 Reaching-Position Model at Peak Speed

The RMSEs were smaller in the velocity model than in the acceleration model, suggesting that the velocity feature significantly influenced the position estimation. Moreover, the arrival position was estimated with high precision (error ± 1 cm or smaller) when the information up to the peak speed was available.

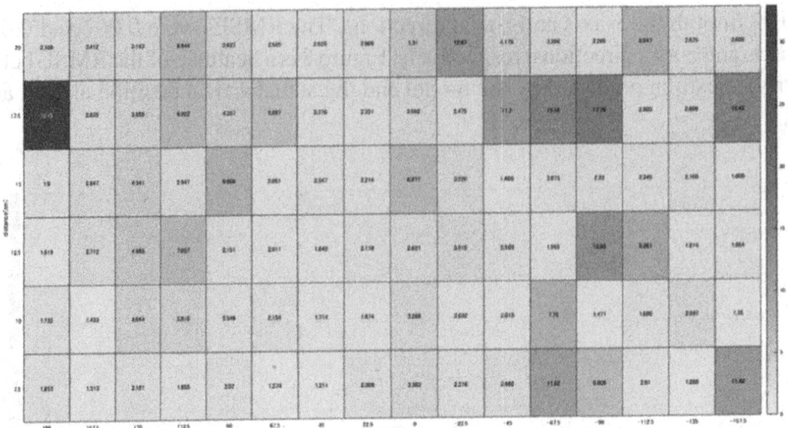

Fig. 9. Heatmap of the RMSE between the predicted and actual arrival positions at each point in the previously proposed Jerk minimum model

5 Conclusion

This study predicted the arrival position of finger-reaching actions by a Gaussian regression model, using the information up to the maximum velocity and maximum acceleration. From this information, the arrival position of the finger movement between two points could be estimated in real time, and the interference stimulation could be specified. In future work, we hope to construct a system that discriminates ME and non-ME cases by comparing the model-predicted positions with the actual arrival positions.

Acknowledgement. This research was supported by Grants-in-Aid for Science Research (C) 18k12118.

References

1. World Alzheimer Report 2018: The state of art of dementia research: New frontiers, p. 7 (2018)
2. Current status and future estimation of dementia. https://www.tr.mufg.jp/shisan/mamori/dementia/02.html
3. Seligman, S.C., Giovannetti, T., Sestito, J., Libon, D.J.: A new approach to the characterization of subtle errors in everyday action: implications for mild cognitive impairment. Clin. Neuropsychologist **28**(1), 97–115 (2014)
4. Gyoji, H., et al.: Statistical analysis of micro-error occurrence probability for the Fitts' law-based pointing task. In: Yamamoto, S., Mori, H. (eds.) HCII 2019. LNCS, vol. 11569, pp. 317–329. Springer, Cham (2019). https://doi.org/10.1007/978-3-030-22660-2_22
5. Flash, T., Hogan, N.: The coordination of arm movements. J. Neuroscience **5**, 1688–1703 (1985)
6. Takashima, K.: Osaka University Knowledge Archive. http://hdl.handle.net/11094/1520

Approaching Behavior Analysis for Improving a Mobile Communication Robot in a Nursing Home

Misato Nihei[1,2,3(✉)], Mio Nakamura[1,2,3], Kohei Ikeda[1,2,3], Kazuki Kawamura[1,2,3], Hiroki Yamashita[1,2,3], and Minoru Kamata[1,2,3]

[1] Department of Human and Engineered Environmental Studies, The University of Tokyo, Chiba, Japan
{mnihei,nakamura.mio,ikeda.kohei,mkamata}@atl.k.u-tokyo.ac.jp
[2] Institute of Gerontology, The University of Tokyo, Chiba, Japan
[3] Softbank Robotics Co. Ltd, Tokyo, Japan
{kazuki01.kawamura,hiroki.yamashita04}@g.softbank.co.jp

Abstract. This paper reports a study of a mobile communication robot in a nursing home. The objective of this study was to clarify how seniors living in a nursing home react to a teleoperated robot approaching to start a conversation. To this end, we observed a series of robot and human behaviors while approaching and initiating conversation and referred to it as "approaching behavior" with the caregivers to the residents in a nursing home. We then analyzed contributory factors. Based on the findings of the analysis, we designed an approaching behavior of a robot. An experiment was conducted with four residents in a nursing home to evaluate our approach behavior design. The subjects reacted positively to the approaching teleoperated robot without exhibiting fear of the robot. Furthermore, they responded positively when the robot talked to them. On the other hand, a unique reaction of the subjects was found when the subjects approached and made eye contact for themselves while the robot approaching them.

Keywords: Older adult · Moving robot · Remote control · Assistive robotics

1 Introduction

As a society, Japan has achieved the longest life expectancy in the world with seniors among 28.4% of the population, while facing social problems such as the increasing number of seniors requiring care and the shortage of the caregivers. At the same time, the government proposed the idea of Society 5.0 in the 5th Science and Technology Basic Plan, which means in a human-centered society the economy is developed by combining cyber space and real space technologies to solve social problems [1]. In, they thought of the possibility of robotic deployment solving the social problem of caring for the elderly. The deployment of communication robots have shown positive effects, such as the improvement on the quality of life (QOL) of seniors by promoting conversation and maintaining cognitive functions [2, 3]. A trial study reported that when numbers

C. Stephanidis et al. (Eds.): HCII 2020, LNCS 12426, pp. 679–688, 2020.
https://doi.org/10.1007/978-3-030-60149-2_51

of communication robots were introduced in nursing homes, improvement on the QOL was reported with one third of the participants [4]. However, most of the communication robots used in nursing homes are placed in a certain positions, for example, in the corner of a shared room, that has led to a declining use of the robots because the seniors have become bored with and stopped approaching the robots [5].

To maintain the frequent use, in this study, we propose to design communication robots that have the mobility to approach and initiate conversation with seniors. A study shows that a robot with mobility has a more positive impression than a robot without mobility [6]. Another study reports that the Mobile Robotic Telepresence, a robot with mobility for talking to people on its screen, promotes the social interaction of older people with dementia [7]. However, introducing mobile robots in care facilities brings a risk of the residents' colliding with the robot or falling because of their diminishing mental and physical functions or the use of a wheelchair or mobility aids [8]. Such a risk should be considered when robots approach seniors.

The focus of this study is therefore to find a method for a communication robot with mobility to approach older people in an older adult care situation and start conversation with no risk of danger. To that end, we have clarified the reaction and the response of older people when a robot was approaching them.

2 Method

The safety distance to a subject must be kept, and an intent to start a conversation must be evident in a teleoperated robot approaching and starting conversation with seniors. A series of behaviors of a robot or a human approaching and initiating conversation with a certain person are called "Approach Behavior" in the work of Satake et al. [9]. They proposed a set of design requirements for a mobile communication robot to improve the success rate of initiating conversation by conducting an experiment in a commercial building with unspecified walkers as subjects.

However, the decline of auditory, visual, walking, and cognitive functions are yet to be considered. Moreover, places such as a shared space in nursing homes have different characteristics from places in commercial buildings. Care faculties have residents and caregivers with various means and speeds of moving. Moreover, such places have a small space for a robot to move around. Thus, another approaching behavior that takes the characteristics of seniors into account is needed. In this paper, we refer to this as "Approaching Behavior (APB)".

We first observed the APB of caregivers for the residents in a nursing home to clarify the intention of each behavior in their APB and found the design requirements of APB for promoting conversation with older people. An experiment was conducted with the residents in a nursing home. A mobile teleoperated communication robot, following an APB method based on the findings of the observation, approached the participants, while their reactions were analyzed.

2.1 Communication Robot Named "Pepper"

A teleoperated communication robot, Pepper, shown in Fig. 1, was used in this study. Residents and caregivers could easily notice the presence and approach of Pepper with a height of 121 cm that was close to a child's height. Figure 2 shows the controller for the teleoperation of mobility. Teleoperated conversation was also available. In addition to teleoperated mobility, Pepper has an obstacle detection system, so the risk of collision and falling of the residents in a small space in a nursing home could be lowered. Silly conversation could be avoided by a teleoperated conversation system which meets the situation and responds reasonably. Table 1 shows the specifications of Pepper's hardware, and Table 2 shows the detailed information on the mobility.

Fig. 1. Communication robot "Pepper"

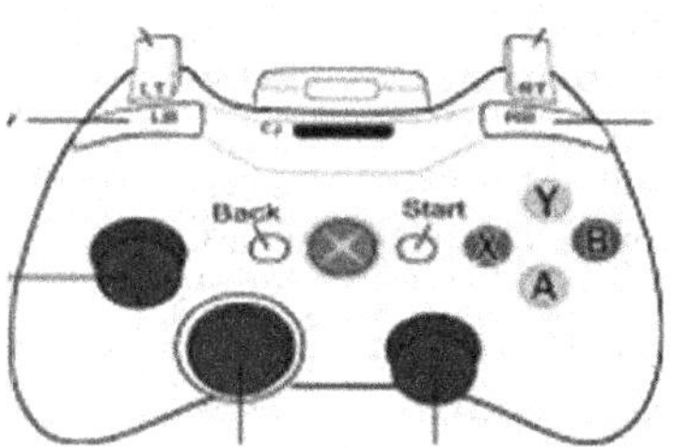

Fig. 2. Remote controller for Pepper

Table 1. Technical specifications

	Specifications
Size	Height: 120 cm, width 42,50 cm, length: 48,50 cm
Weight	28 kg
Degree of freedom of the joints	Head: 2, shoulder: 2, elbow: 2, wrist: 1, hands (5 fingers): 1, waist: 2, knees: 1, base: 3
Motion sensors	One 3D camera behind the eyes for depth and detection of movements and obstacles, In the legs: 2 sonar, 6 lasers, one gyro sensor
Interaction sensors	4 microphones, 2 RGB HD cameras (mouth and forehead), 5 tactile sensors (3 in the head and 2 on the hands), touch screen on the breast
Speaker	2 Head speakers
Display	Écran tactile de 10,1 pouces
Drive mode	3 Motor driven omni wheel
Maximum speed	2 km/h

Table 2. Move function of pepper

	Moving specifications
Moving speed	0.3 km/h
Degree of freedom of move	Forward, reverse, left/ right turn, left/ right parallel movement
Safety function	If an obstacle is detected within 30 cm, it will stop safely at a higher priority than remote control
Remote control	Operate using the controller shown in Fig. 2. The state of the image of the robot's head camera is transferred to the personal computer
Connectivity	Bluetooth®

2.2 Approach Behavior of the Caregivers for Residents Using the Way of Participant Observation

Participants. Six caregivers working in a nursing home and twenty-five residents in that nursing home agreed to participate.

Method for Participant Observation. Approaches and the content of conversation between the caregivers and the residents in daily life were observed and recorded by an experimenter. Two floors in the nursing home were selected. Observation was conducted for twenty-four hours on two different days (9:30–16:30, 16:30–9:30).

Analysis and Ethics. The record of the conversation was classified by the situation. For each group, the approaching path, behaviors while approaching, distance and the angle while talking, and behaviors while talking were collected. With these, design requirements appropriate for seniors were extracted. The Ethical Committee of University of Tokyo (19-332) granted ethics approval.

Result of the Participant observation. Approach behaviors were observed in five situations: 1) Calling out when caregiver served meals, 2) Calling out of resident wandering around the ward, 3) Call for encouragement of activities for resident, 4) Dialogue between caregiver and resident after the nurse call and 5) Daily conversation between caregiver and resident. These approach behaviors were classified into three groups as shown in Table 3.

In situations of group 1, caregivers approached residents at a quick pace with calling out the name of the resident loudly and stating the business in brief words, like "Mr./Ms. Xx, meal is ready". In situations of group 2, caregivers approached residents in the same way as group 1, but they called out in a quiet voice because in these situations, the residents requested the visit of caregivers by a nurse call, so there was no need for caregivers to show their intention to talk. In group 3, caregivers approached residents with or without calling out the name of the resident and the caregivers did not directly notify the residents of their approach. With these results, caregivers were found to notify residents of their approach by calling out the name of the resident loudly.

In daily conversation, a consent of both people to initiate conversation was required. However, in the situations of group 1 or 2, such consent was not required because group 1 was a unilateral talk of caregivers rather than conversation, and in the group 2 situation, the residents required conversation that the caregivers responded to. In group 3, caregivers showed their intention to initiate conversation by making eye contact with the residents. At the same time, residents were observed to talk face to face with more words spoken than without face to face.

As a result, the APB of caregivers for residents included the following four characteristics: 1) Calling out loudly, 2) Calling the name, 3) Matching eye contact, and 4) Talking face to face. The APB of caregivers are shown in Table 4.

Table 3. Approaching behavior for each conversation situation at nursing home

Group 1: Caregiver initiates dialogue and does not require consent of Resident	
1)	Calling out when caregiver serving meals
2)	Calling out of resident wandering around the ward
3)	Call for encouragement of activities for resident
Group 2: Resident requests a dialogue and caregiver has already agreed	
4)	Dialogue between caregiver and resident after nurse call
Group 3: Caregiver initiates dialogue and requires resident consent	
5)	Daily conversation between caregiver and resident

Table 4. Approaching behavior for caregivers

Action	Aim
· Call out loudly to residents · Call his/her name	Inform the caregiver of their approach at public distances
· Match eyes with residents	Communicating the caregiver's own dialogue in a personal space
· Talk face to face with residents	Make it easier to interact with residents

2.3 Design Requirement of Approaching Behavior

Based on the result of the participant observation, the following two design requirements of the APB of a robot were derived: 1) robot called the name of the resident out loudly, 2) robot matched eyes in approaching, then started conversation face to face.

With these requirements and the limitations of the robot, an APB of the robot for residents was designed as shown in Table 5. Pepper, following this APB method, was used in an experiment with residents in a nursing home as participants.

Table 5. Approaching Behavior Parameters for Seniors

Approach route	Approaching while making eye contact
Approach speed	0.3 km/h
Final approach distance	30 cm
Final approach angle	Less than 90°
Conversation during approach	Call out loudly

2.4 Measurement of Approach Behavior

Participants. Four residents in a nursing home were recruited and agreed to participate. They were made of 4 women and 1 man, aged between 81 and 91. The profile of the participants are shown in Table 6.

Table 6. Profile of participants

Participant	Age	Gender	MMSE (Max 30 points)	Mobility aids	Hearing
A	98	Male	26 Points	Walker	Hearing aids used
B	81	Female	24 Points	Walker	Hearing aids used
C	81	Female	27 Points	Wheelchair	Hearing aids used
D	90	Female	27 Points	Wheelchair	Hearing aids used

Method. The experiment was conducted in a shared dining room in a nursing home where the participants lived. Figure 3 shows the layout of the dining room.

A Pepper was teleoperated to approach each participant following the APB when they came to the room at any time during the experiment. The words spoken by the robot were shown on the 10.1-in. display on the robot. The experiment period was for two days, three hours in total (13:00–14:30 for each day). Video recording was made by two cameras placed in the room.

Analysis and Ethics. For each participant, the approaching path of the robot, the talk distance and angle, and the reaction of approach were extracted and put together. The characteristics of the APB of a robot for a human were analyzed.

Ethics approval was granted by the Ethical Committee of University of Tokyo (19-332).

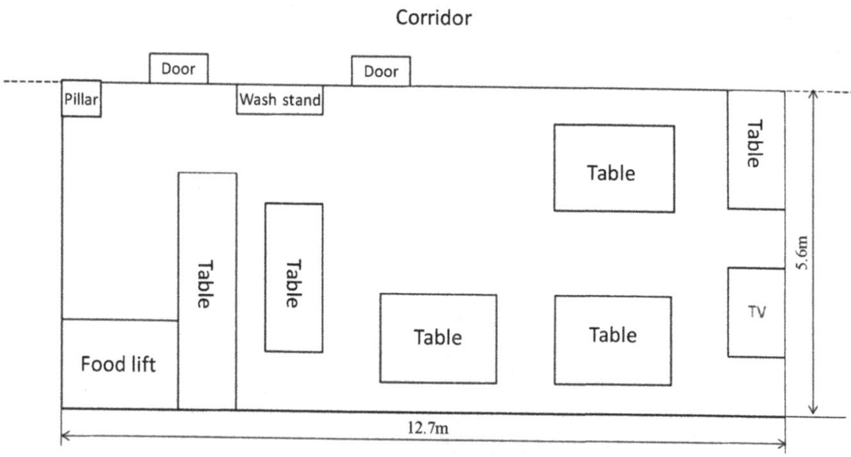

Fig. 3. Dining room layout

Result. The results are s shown in Table 7. Every participant responded positively to the approaching robot and enjoyed the conversation with it. No sign of fear or unpleasantness was observed though the robot approached within 30 cm at the closest.

Participant A had hearing difficulties and failed to respond to the call of the robot though it was in sight of participant A. He leaned forward to the robot and read the words on the display mounted at the robot's chest. The participant then responded to the words of the robot. In this case, we were not able to let him know the approach of the robot by only the call.

Participant B noticed the approach of the robot and respond to the call. She talked face to face with the robot by twisting herself at the waist.

Table 7. Results of approaching behavior between resident and robot

ID	Approach route	Final approach distance [cm]	Final approach angle [deg]	Reaction to calling
A	In sight	50	45	No
	In sight	80	0	No
B	In sight	30	90	Yes
	In sight	30	0	No calling
C	In sight	30	90	Yes
	Out of sight	50	45	Yes
D	Out of sight	30	90	Yes
	Out of sight	50	45	Yes

Participant C and D responded to the robot approaching from behind them by first looking backward, then turned their wheelchair back and faced the robot. From these results, we found that the robot's call from behind caused them to turn backward. Furthermore, they adjusted the talk distance and talk angle for themselves when they are not comforted with it (Fig. 4).

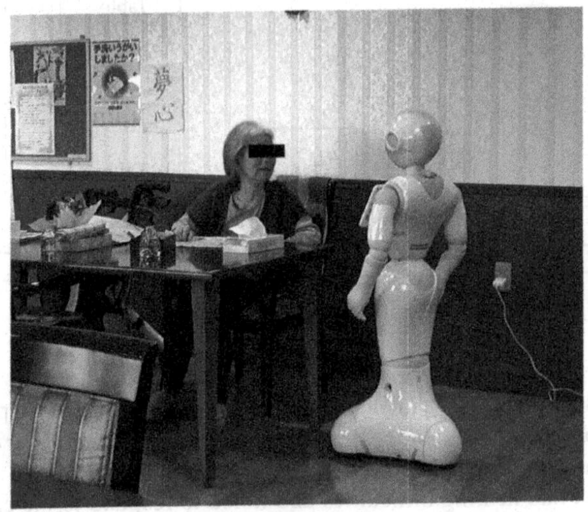

Fig. 4. Experiment situation of Case B

3 Discussion

3.1 APB of the Communication Robot in the Nursing Home

We observed the APB of caregivers for the residents in a nursing home to clarify the intention of each behavior in their APB. As a result, the design requirements such as calling the name out loudly, making eye contact when close to the residents, and face to face conversation were extracted with these requirements, a teleoperated communication robot, following an APB method based on these findings, approached a resident in a nursing home.

The results show that every participant responded positively to the approaching robot and talked cheerfully with it, while no sign of fear was observed. On the other hand, the difference of the approaching path, the talking distance, and angle caused the participants to turn back to and approach the robot by themselves. These kinds of responses were not observed in the APB of caregivers during the participant observation. Kanda reported that people reacted to a robot differently than to a human even when the robot and the human behaved similarly [10]. It is suggested that there is an unspoken behavior sharing rule between caregivers and residents that when a caregiver approaches a resident, the resident stops and waits for the caregiver to arrive. However, the participants recognized the robot not as a caregiver, but as a new intervenor. For this reason, the participants moved and adjusted the angle in favor of the approaching robot. This peculiar behavior by the participants to the robot clarified the points to be improved in the APB of the robot.

3.2 Improving Requirements of APB for Residents

From the result of the experiment with the robot, the following three behaviors were learned: 1) It was difficult to notify the approach of a robot only by calling, 2) Calling from behind the residents caused him/her to turn back, 3) residents would approach for themselves in response to the approach of a robot.

With age-related hearing difficulties prevalent in seniors. In this experiment, we chose the robot's auditory function of calling as an appealing means to notify the approach of the robot. When a participant failed to recognize the call, their response was to read the words on the display. Therefore, we learned that appealing to visual function, such as moving of the hands, was desired in addition with calling.

It was observed that the participants with wheelchairs turned back and faced the robot in response to the robot's call from behind. A wheelchair has a turning radius of 75 to 85 cm [11], so there is a risk of hitting the robot, which could come within 30 cm at the closest. Such a risk could be reduced by calling in sight of the resident and by the robot's words controlling the resident not to move.

The robot was not able to adjust the distance to the resident easily with its functional limitations. The participants adjusted their talk distance themselves by moving their wheelchairs appropriately, which could increase the risk of colliding with the robot. Therefore, the talk distance and angle need adjusting with the functional limitations of the robot being considered.

4 Conclusion

In this research we conducted observation of participants in a nursing home and learned the requirements of the APB of caregivers for residents, with a purpose of clarifying how residents in nursing homes react to the approach of a teleoperated robot. An experiment was made with four participants and a communication robot following an APB method based on the requirements obtained in the participant observation. As a result, the participants responded positively and talked cheerfully with the approaching teleoperated robot with no sign of fear or being afraid. On the other hand, the participants were observed to move for themselves and try to make eye contact with the robot when they were talked to. The results of the observation of the residents with caregivers compared to with a robot suggest that the robot would not be a substitute for a caregiver but a new intervenor.

This research has shown the need to take in account the peculiar reactions between a senior and a robot that is not observed between humans when designing an APB of a robot for older people.

Acknowledgements. We would like to thank Unimat Retirement Community Co., Ltd. and the participants of the experiments for their cooperation in this study. This research was supported by AMED under Grant Number JP19he2002016.

References

1. Ministry of Economy, Trade and Industry: Japan's Robot Strategy 2015 (2015)
2. Nihei, M., et al.: Change in the Relationship between the elderly and information support robot system living together. In: HCI International 2017 (2017)
3. Igarashi, T., Nihei, M., Nakamura, M., Obayashi, K., Masuyama, S., Kamata, M.: Socially assistive robots influence for elderly with cognitive impairment living in nursing facilities: micro observation and analysis. In: 15th AAATE Conference (2019)
4. Japan Agency for Medical Research and Development: Project to Promote the Development and Introduction of Robotic Devices for Nursing Care (2017)
5. Nakamura, M., Kato, N., Kondo, E., Inoue, T.: Verification of effectiveness of introducing communication robots in residential facilities for the elderly. In: The 11th Conference on Rehabilitation Engineering and Assistive Technology Society of Korea 2017 (2017)
6. Nakano, H., Ishida, J., Hanashima, N., Ymashita, M., Hikita, H.: Impression evaluation on interaction with a communication robot with mobility. In: Proceedings of the 2008 JSME Conference on Robotics and Mechatronics (2008)
7. Moyle, W., Jones, C., Dwan, T., Ownsworth, T., Sung, B.: Using telepresence for social connection: view of older people with dementia, families, and health professionals from a mixed methods pilot study. Aging Mental Health **12**(23), 1643–1650 (2018)
8. Moyle, W., Jones, C.M., O'Dwyer, S., Sung, B., Drummond, S.: Social robots helping people with dementia: assessing efficacy of social robots in the nursing home environment. In: IEEE 2013 Proceedings (2013)
9. Satake, S., Kanda, T., Glass, F.D., Imai, M., Ishiguro, H., Hagita, N.: J. Rob. Soc. Jpn. **28**(3), 327–337 (2010). (in Japanese)
10. Kanda, T.: Distance between communication robot and human. Inf. Process. **49**(1) (2008)
11. Ministry of Land, Infrastructure, Transport and Tourism: An architectural design standard that considers the smooth movement of the elderly and the disabled, Chap. 4.2 (2017)

User-centered Implementation of Rehabilitation Exercising on an Assistive Robotic Platform

Xanthi S. Papageorgiou[1](✉), George Tsampounaris[1], Alexandra Karavasili[2], Eleni Efthimiou[1], Stavroula-Evita Fotinea[1], Anna Vacalopoulou[1], Panagiotis Karioris[1], Fotini Koureta[2], Despina Alexopoulou[2], and Dimitris Dimou[2]

[1] Institute for Language and Speech Processing/ATHENA RC, Athens, Greece
{xpapag,eleni_e,evita,avacalop,pkarior}@athenarc.gr, g.tsampounaris@di.uoa.gr

[2] DIAPLASIS Rehabilitation Center, Kalamata, Greece
akaravasili@gmail.com, fwteini.kou@gmail.com, dalexopoulou@diaplasis.eu, dimou.ergo@gmail.com

Abstract. The paper focuses on the method and steps implementing a suite of rehabilitation exercises on an assistive robotic platform. The suite is based on extensive user needs identification procedures and consultation with medical and rehabilitation experts. For the design of the human-robot interaction (HRI) component of the platform, the user centered approach was adopted, which in this case employed a range of multimodal interaction facilities including a free user-robot dialogue, visual and speech signals.

Keywords: Human-robot interaction · Multimodal HRI design · User-centered design · Assistive HRI · User group recruitment methodology · Rehabilitation strategy

1 Introduction

A direct consequence of the rapid change in demographic data associated with the aging of populations in modern developed societies is the increase of the population percentage that faces different degrees of mobility and cognitive problems apart from those caused by chronic related diseases and/or accidents [1, 2]. Under this perspective, the need to improve the quality of daily living by supporting mobility and vitality and to enhance independent living of individuals with motor limitations [3] has inspired technological solutions towards developing intelligent active mobility assistance robots for indoor environments, which should provide user-centered, context-adaptive and natural support [4–6].

The role of personal care robots is multiple, covering physical, sensorial and cognitive assistance, health and behavior monitoring, and companionship. The necessity for robotic assistants that could help with elderly mobility and rehabilitation is clear. Almost twenty years have passed since the first robotic rollators [7–12], as well as sensorial and cognitive assistance devices for the elderly [13] emerged. However, most

C. Stephanidis et al. (Eds.): HCII 2020, LNCS 12426, pp. 689–698, 2020.
https://doi.org/10.1007/978-3-030-60149-2_52

intelligent assistive platform designs aim to solve only specific problems, while considerable research effort has focused on analysing anthropometric data from various sensors for assessing human state and, eventually, control a robotic platform.

The i-Walk project aims at developing and testing a new pioneering robotic system that will provide a range of mobility and cognitive support functions for the targeted population groups. To do so, it builds upon the experience gained from research in the framework of the previously accomplished MOBOT[1] project [14], targeting the development of a flexible platform of robotic technologies adapted on a rollator walker, which will provide active assistance, incorporating the ability to acquire knowledge and adapt to the environment, personalized to each individual user, in order to support mobility and enhance health and vitality. To achieve this goal, several methodologies are currently being developed, which are foreseen to be synergistically utilized. These include:

- Processing of multi-sensory and physiological signals and identification of actions for the monitoring, analysis and prediction of human gait and other actions of the user.
- Behavioral and user-adaptive robot control and autonomous robot navigation for the dynamic approach of the user and the interactive co-occurrence combined also with voice guidance
- Human-robot communication, including speech synthesis and recognition technologies and a virtual assistant (avatar) to enhance the naturalness of communication.

The i-Walk project is researching the enhancement of these technologies and their application to meet major social needs. One of the project's major characteristics is the synergy of the technological achievements with medical services that concern rehabilitation, aiming at interacting with target audiences (i.e. patients) to design and integrate systems based on the needs of potential users.

Overall, the i-Walk project aims to support elderly people and patients with mobility and/or cognitive inabilities, by achieving:

- More effective patient mobilization in the clinical environment of a rehabilitation centre, reducing the burden on clinical staff and increasing the efficiency of rehabilitation programs, and
- Continuous support at home through technologies monitoring patients' progress, but also their mobilization through interfaces of cognitive and physical support, increasing their degree of independence and improving their quality of life (Fig. 1).

Here, we focus on the user-centered characteristics of the platform, which serve rehabilitation purposes. Emphasis is placed on the design and implementation of the human-robot interaction component, which derives from extensive research on defining end-user needs.

[1] http://www.mobot-project.eu/.

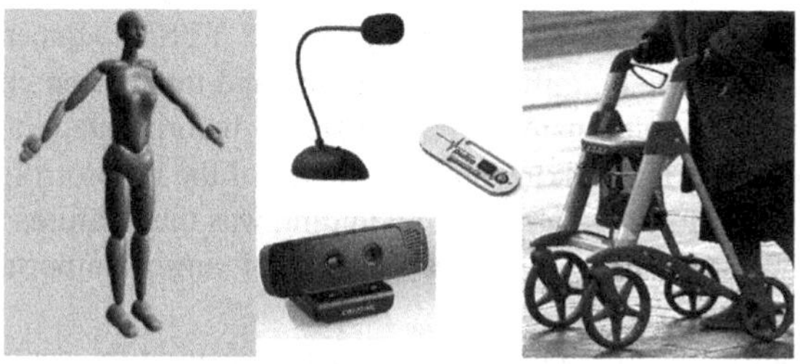

Fig. 1. The i-Walk concept components

2 Definition of User Group and System Specifications

The investigation of user needs followed standard procedures which were developed in two stages. During the first stage, user needs were collected by means of organizing workshops with potential users and rehabilitation experts, which involved interviews as well as questionnaires.

At the second stage, the target group was defined as entailing people with a functional impairment in movement due to a neurological condition (e.g. Parkinson's Disease or Multiple Sclerosis) and/or elderly people and/or people with cognitive impairment. The state of cognitive and motor ability of the users were the two main inclusion criteria to the project target group.

The data collection took place at Diaplasis Rehabilitation Center in Kalamata, Greece, where participants were patients attending rehabilitation sessions either as in-patients or as out patients.

After the evaluation of the medical files by clinical experts, 21 patients were selected, based on their medical history, to participate in the required tests and provide feedback during the design and implementation stages, evaluate the system's components and, finally, use the robotic walking device experimentally. All participants were informed about the research stages and their voluntary participation by the clinical experts. Subsequently, their cognitive status was imprinted and they were subjected to functional tests to evaluate their mobility, mainly in terms of balance and gait. Patients who met the inclusion criteria (Table 1) conducted tests with the robotic i-Walk platform according to scheduled appointments. The process began with the written consent of the participants and the provision of specific information about the i-Walk research program for the collection and processing of personal data.

Table 1. Inclusion criteria to data collection and platform evaluation user group

Inclusion criteria
Mini Mental State Examination-MMSE ≥ 17
4M Gait Speed Test, $u < 0.6$ m/s
Five-time chair sit-to-stand test (5-STS), $t > 16.7$ s.

User Specifications were based on user input on 18 YES/NO questions and free discussion, which targeted the definition of functional and interaction characteristics of a robotic rollator that users anticipated to be necessarily incorporated in such a device. As expected, basic features of a walking support device of the rollator type were prevalent among user priorities. However, a surprising finding was that features such as the availability of rehabilitation exercises have proven to be of similar importance according to user preferences.

User specifications were completed through consultation sessions with expert groups, where similar procedures (free discussion and questionnaires) completed the picture of the features users felt were necessary to incorporate in system functional and interaction design.

Furthermore, this work also resulted in the definition of the use case scenarios, which form the testbed for the platform functionality and interaction characteristics. The adopted scenarios involve:

- *Walking with a rollator*. This scenario covers basic rehabilitation needs of supporting patients with ambulation problems.
- *Rehabilitation Exercises*. The users are instructed to perform a suite of rehabilitation exercises in seated and standing position including hand raises, torso turns, sit-to-stand transfers, etc.
- *Use of the elevator*. This scenario targets the support of patients' independent living.
- *Transfer to bathroom*. This scenario covers needs of patients with mobility problems in basic activities of daily life.

The user group which provided the initial input on the i-Walk HRI design, consisted of 13 adults (6 female and 7 male subjects) from 50 to 86 years of age, also including one adult of 25 years old. All subjects experienced comparable functional impairments deriving from different pathologies such as Parkinson's disease, multiple sclerosis, stroke, hip fracture and rheumatologic disorders. All subjects have been users of walking aids such as walker, cane, quad cane and rollator [15, 16]. The screening process followed to extract the participants group made use of several evaluation scales including the MMSE scale for mental status evaluation, the BERG [17] and TUG scales for balance, dynamic balance and mobility evaluation, as well as the TINETTI POMA scale for gait and balance evaluation. It also made use of two tests: (i) the Chair-Stand Test, which evaluates lower limb and corps strength [18], and (ii) the Gait-Speed Test [19], also used for evaluating mobility. This complex screening method, on the one hand, allowed for mapping the targeted user population and, on the other hand, enabled collection of data well fitted within this population spectrum (Figs. 2 and 3).

3 Design and Implementation of the Rehabilitation Exercising Suites

The i-Walk platform has been designed to fill a range of user needs, by combining multisensory streams to perform a multitask understanding of human behavior, including speech intention recognition, generalized human activity recognition, and mobility

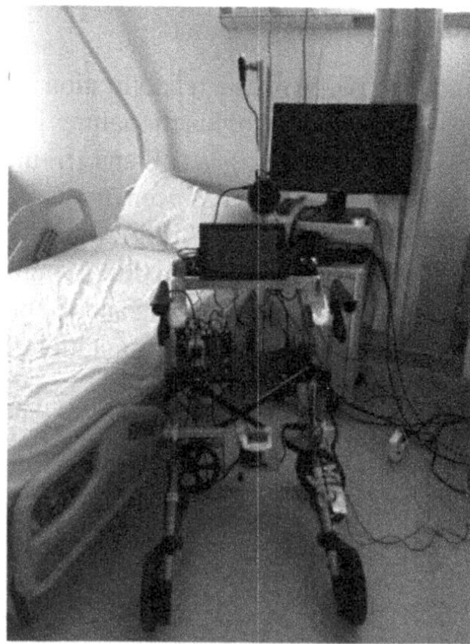

Fig. 2. The i-Walk passive rollator used for initial testing of HRI design

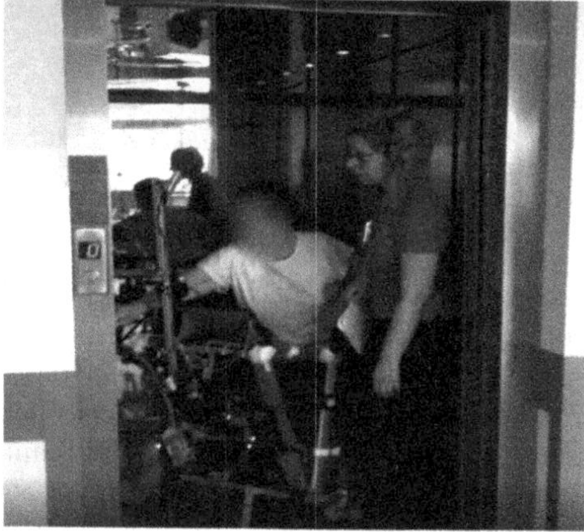

Fig. 3. Trials of the preliminary edition of the i-walk aiming at user needs definition

analysis. The multimodal interaction framework of i-Walk [20] aims to provide natural communication but also essential feedback to the user and the medical expert regarding the progress of an applied rehabilitation program, in a way close to that of a personal carer.

Furthermore, the i-Walk communication ecosystem incorporates a set of multimodal interaction options, which intent to raise user trust and engagement, as a result of the user-centered approach followed in designing the user-platform interaction environment.

3.1 HRI Design Based on User Needs

Since the platform is designed to perform as a rehabilitation aid to patients with motion problems, focus has been placed on two major functionalities incorporated in the platform interaction design. That is (i) the walking assistant, and (ii) the rehabilitation exercises instructor. The design of both these modules has been driven by user needs, as identified and prioritized via the procedures described in Sect. 2.

When designing the rehabilitation exercises module, a number of parameters had to be taken into account, which led to exercise grouping and the building of the multimodal interaction dialogue system accompanying their presentation (Fig. 4).

Fig. 4. Execution of rehabilitation program, aided by audio-visual instructions

Furthermore, after consultation with the team of experts, issues relating to the appearance and performance of the virtual instructor, as well as its placement in the most appropriate virtual environment, should also be dealt with, since these have been elements significant for the perception of the message sent to the user. Under this perspective, avatars of manga or transformer type have been excluded. Similarly, virtual environments incorporating various sound or visual effects and/or decorative elements have been considered inappropriate.

3.2 Virtual Instructor Implementation

The principal technologies that have been utilized for the implementation of the virtual instructor are motion capture and real-time rendering. We have followed a motion capture pipeline process that is similar to the ones that we meet for the implementation of animated characters in video games and films. It is important to mention that the rendered output is done in Unreal game engine that in combination with a high-end graphics card and CPU allows renderings of Full High Definition (1080p) and high frequency of frames per second to be completed in minutes instead of hours that usually happen in 3D softwares. The series of processes that contribute to the pre-mentioned implementation are mentioned below and are schematically depicted in Fig. 5:

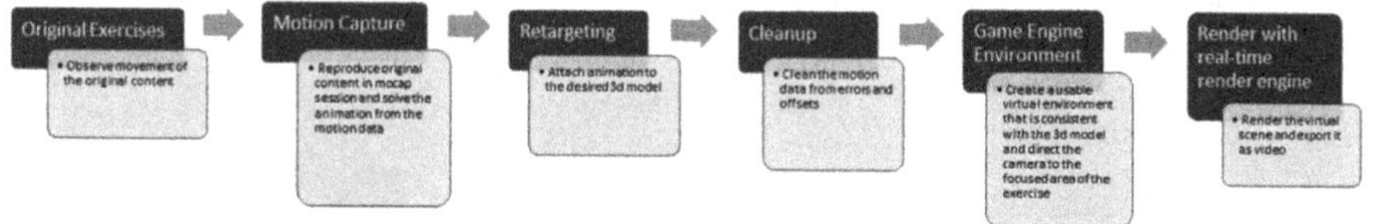

Fig. 5. Pipeline of processes resulting to the virtual instructor performance

Original Content: With the guidance of rehabilitation experts, we captured in video the actual exercises that need to be presented to the patient. These have been used as reference for the motion capture session.

Motion Capture: We setup a markerless optical motion capture system consisting of two Kinect V2 devices, each of which was connected to a computer in a local network, where the first one acted as a "master" and the second one as a "slave" computer. A rehabilitation expert reproduced the exercises having as reference the pre-recorded videos mentioned in the previous step. Both Kinect V2 devices captured the movement of the subject and the slave computer provided the master computer with motion data. The combination of these two camera outputs was fused to a virtual skeleton that was constructed accordingly. The two Kinect V2 devices were set up against each other in order to capture data about the entire body of the subject and avoid data errors or offsets due to occlusion of body parts. This is the point where a virtual skeleton animation was constructed, while its motion data was still uncleaned; this means that there would be possible offsets in the animated movement, for instance, an arm would visually clash with the main body.

Retargeting: We chose a rigged and skinned 3D model representing a user-friendly virtual instructor and we attached the movement onto it so as to execute the animation. In order to do this, we ensured that the 3D model mesh corresponded to the needs of our use scenarios. In addition, since the mesh itself is not movable, it was mandatory to attach a rig into it. A rig represents a hierarchy of virtual bones that correspond to the standard body-type of a human. Thus, the skinning method is the procedure of attaching the 3D mesh into the rig. The weights of the skins are configured to each body part, and they correspond to how much the body part can bend. Finally, it is important to clarify that the bone hierarchy of the 3D model's rig is the same or similar with the virtual skeleton of the animation in order to have a successful retargeting.

Cleanup: This is the stage where the virtual skeleton is imported into a 3D software in order to edit the motion data that is problematic. A control rig is created in order to have access to the Inverse Kinematics/Forward Kinematics (IK/FK) of the virtual skeleton, and thus to edit its movement data more efficiently through positional and rotational curves. An fbx format, the most compatible one for inter-platform utilization, is exported (Fig. 6).

Environment in Game Engine: The animated 3D avatar is imported to the Game Engine, where a virtual scene is constructed that is consistent to the usability scenario. In our case, we developed a well-lit, minimal room that allows the user to focus exclusively

Fig. 6. Virtual instructor implementation following user specifications; avatar viewing options enable disambiguation of the movements to be im

to the virtual character and, at the same time, feel that they are in an exercise room. For each exercise, the camera is focused and moves accordingly to the dedicated area of the body that is exercised.

Rendering: The fact that this scene is implemented in a game engine indicates that it runs as a real-time application and, following specific actions, it executes the corresponding animation of exercise at that moment. However, for the time being, we decided to have pre-rendered animations reproduced according to the needs of the patients. Since the visualization can be reproduced in real time, in high quality and in fps format, rendering to a video format can be completed within minutes instead of hours for an output of FHD or 2K quality and 60 fps or 120 fps.itated by end users.

4 Conclusion

Cognitive and robotic architectures may be able to provide advanced interactive capabilities with humans and influence the usability and functionality of a resulting system, thus, contributing to its quality of services. Such systems may not only integrate multiple advanced cognitive abilities, but also employ methods that are extendible to various other robotic and non-robotic applications required in assisting humans with mobility limitations [21]. Since systems aiming to address the requirement of high user trust [22] and acceptance seem to fail in respect to user engagement, user-centered system design incorporating "natural", "intelligent" ways of human-machine communication is becoming obligatory.

The current goal is to bring HRI modeling further by: (i) fully exploiting information derived from patients' everyday routines as regards the range of both physical and mental functionalities available and tasks to be accomplished, and (ii) augmenting the device's communication capabilities, based on the actual linguistic and embodied interaction patterns used by the targeted user group in real use environments.

Beyond any short- and mid-term goals, the long term goal should be set towards increasing user engagement with a given assistive device for a longer period, which is also the perspective underlying the i-Walk services design. In this line, extensive evaluation with end users has been planned for all components of the i-Walk platform. Subjective and objective user evaluation results will be reported as soon as related data analysis is available.

Acknowledgements. This research has been co-financed by the European Union and Greek national funds through the Operational Program Competitiveness, Entrepreneurship and Innovation, under the call RESEARCH – CREATE – INNOVATE (project code: T1EDK- 01248/MIS: 5030856), as well as POLYTROPON project (KRIPIS-GSRT, MIS: 448306).

References

1. OECD/EU. Health at a Glance: Europe 2018: State of Health in the EU Cycle, OECD Publishing, Paris (2019). https://doi.org/10.1787/health_glance_eur-2018-en
2. EUROSTAT. Disability statistics. Statistics Explained. Online publication, ISSN 2443-8219. Accessed Sep 2019. https://ec.europa.eu/eurostat/statistics-explained/index.php?title=Disability_statistics
3. Hirvensalo, M., Rantanen, T., Heikkinen, M.: Mobility difficulties and physical activity as predictors of mortality and loss of independence in the community-living older population. J. Am. Geriatr. Soc. **48**, 493–498 (2005). https://www.ncbi.nlm.nih.gov/pubmed/10811541
4. Chuy, O.J., Hirata, Y., Wang, Z., Kosuge, K.: Approach in assisting a sit-to-stand movement using robotic walking support system. In: 2006 IEEE/RSJ Int'l Conference on Intelligent Robots and Systems, Beijing, pp. 4343–4348 (2006). https://doi.org/10.1109/iros.2006.282007
5. Chugo, D., Asawa, T., Kitamura, T., Jia, S., Takase, K.: A rehabilitation walker with standing and walking assistance. In: 2008 IEE/RSJ Int'l Conf. on Intelligent Robots and Systems, Nice, pp. 260–265 (2008). https://doi.org/10.1109/iros.2008.4650845
6. Hirata, Y., Komatsuda, S., Kosuge, K.: Fall prevention control of passive intelligent walker based on human model. In: 2008 IEE/RSJ Int'l Conference on Intelligent Robots and Systems, Nice, pp. 1222–1228 (2008). https://doi.org/10.1109/iros.2008.4651173
7. Morris, A., Donamukkala, R., et al.: A robotic walker that provides guidance. In: ICRA 2003 (2003)
8. Dubowsky, S., et al.: Pamm - a robotic aid to the elderly for mobility assistance and monitoring: a 'helping-hand' for the elderly. In: IEEE Int'l Conf. on Robotics and Automation, pp. 570–576 (2000)
9. Graf, B., Hans, M., Schraft, R.D.: Mobile robot assistants. IEEE Rob. Autom. Mag. **11**(2), 67–77 (2004)
10. Rodriguez-Losada, D., Matia, F., Jimenez, A., Galan, R., Lacey, G.: Implementing map based navigation in guido, the robotic smartwalker. In: Proceedings of the 2005 IEEE International Conference on Robotics and Automation, pp. 3390–3395, April 2005
11. Kulyukin, V., Kutiyanawala, A., LoPresti, E., Matthews, J., Simpson, R.: iwalker: toward a rollator-mounted wayfinding system for the elderly. In: 2008 IEEE International Conference on RFID, pp. 303–311, April 2008
12. Ohnuma, T., et al.: Particle filter based lower limb prediction and motion control for JAIST active robotic walker. In: 2014 RO-MAN (2014)
13. Jenkins, S., et al.: Care, monitoring, and companionship: Views on care robots from older people and their carers. Int. J. Soc. Robot. **7**, 673–683 (2015)

14. Efthimiou, E., et al.: The MOBOT rollator human-robot interaction model and user evaluation process. In: Proceedings of the IEEE SSCI Conference, 6–9 December 2016, Athens, pp. 1–8 (2016). https://doi.org/10.1109/ssci.2016.7850061
15. Härdi, I., Bridenbaugh, S.A., Gschwind, Y.J., Kressig, R.W.: The effect of three different types of walking aids on spatio-temporal gait parameters in community-dwelling older adults. Aging Clin. Exp. Res. **26**(2), 221–228 (2014). https://doi.org/10.1007/s40520-014-0204-4
16. Applebaum, E.V., et al.: Modified 30-second sit to stand test predicts falls in a cohort of institutionalized older veterans. PLoS ONE **12**(5), e0176946 (2017). https://doi.org/10.1371/journal.pone.0176946
17. Berg, K., Wood-Dauphinee, S., Williams, J.I.: The balance scale: reliability assessment with elderly residents and patients with an acute stroke. Scand. J. Rehabil. Med. **27**, 27–36 (1995). https://www.ncbi.nlm.nih.gov/pubmed/7792547
18. Bateni, H., Maki, B.E.: Assistive devices for balance and mobility: benefits, demands, and adverse consequences. Arch. Phys. Med. Rehabil. **86**(1), 134–145 (2005). https://doi.org/10.1016/j.apmr.2004.04.023
19. Donoghue, O., Savva, G., Cronin, H., Kenny, R.A., Horgan, F.: Using timed up and go and usual gait speed to predict incident disability in daily activities among community-dwelling adults aged 65 and older. Arch. Phys. Med. Rehabil. **95**(10), 1954–1961 (2014). https://doi.org/10.1016/j.apmr.2014.06.008
20. Efthimiou, E., Fotinea, S.-E., Vacalopoulou, A., Papageorgiou, X., Karavasili, A., Goulas, T.: User centered design in practice: adapting HRI to real user needs. In: PETRA 2019 Proceedings of the 12th ACM International Conference on PErvasive Technologies Related to Assistive Environments. Rhodes, Greece—05–07 June 2019, pp. 425–429. ACM, New York (2019). https://doi.org/10.1145/3316782.3322778
21. Kötteritzsch, A., Weyers, B.: Assistive technologies for older adults in urban areas: a literature review. Cogn. Comput. **8**(2), 299–317 (2016). https://doi.org/10.1007/s12559-015-9355-7
22. Stuck, R.E., Rogers, W.A.: Understanding older adult's perceptions of factors that support trust in human and robot care providers. In: 10th Int'l Conference on PErvasive Technologies Related to Assistive Environments (PETRA 2017), Rhodes, 21–23 June 2017, pp. 372–377. ACM New York (2017). ISBN: 978-1-4503-5227-7. https://doi.org/10.1145/3056540.3076186

"The Terms and Conditions Came Back to Bite": Plain Language and Online Financial Content for Older Adults

Alessandra Rossetti(✉), Patrick Cadwell, and Sharon O'Brien

Dublin City University, Glasnevin, Dublin 9, Ireland
alessandra.rossetti8@gmail.com,
{patrick.cadwell,sharon.obrien}@dcu.ie

Abstract. With financial institutions increasingly transferring products and services online, the interaction of older adults with the web has received some attention. However, research on the accessibility and usability of the language of online financial content for older adults is lacking. Furthermore, evidence on the potential benefits of plain language is needed. We conducted a two-part study to fill these research gaps. First, we conducted a focus group with four older adults to find out: (i) if participants had concerns about the accessibility of online financial texts; and (ii) which types of texts might have benefited from plain language editing in their experience. We observed that older adults regarded Terms and Conditions as difficult to read. In a second stage, we examined the usability of Terms and Conditions through an experiment with 25 older adults. We tested the impact of plain language on different usability components, namely satisfaction ratings, reading comprehension, perceived comprehensibility, and reading behaviour for Terms and Conditions related to direct debits provided by a bank and an insurance company. We found no benefits of plain language on the usability components under investigation. However, despite a general tendency to skim through or read only parts of Terms and Conditions, we also observed that reading behaviour was more varied—including repeated readings, section skipping, and reading abandonment—with texts that had not undergone plain language editing. Furthermore, aspects other than language (such as visual components) were valued by older adults. Conclusions and implications are outlined.

Keywords: Older adults · Plain language · Terms and Conditions

1 Introduction

Longer life expectancy and declining fertility rates have been leading to population ageing [30]. Despite some disagreement on when old age starts [25, 27], researchers, practitioners, and policymakers agree on the importance of considering the specific needs and challenges that ageing entails for all aspects of life and in all sectors of society, including the financial sector [5].

Information and communication technologies can play a role in ensuring that older people are not left behind and have access to products, services, and information [38]. In particular, the web has the potential to reach users (including older adults) regardless of

C. Stephanidis et al. (Eds.): HCII 2020, LNCS 12426, pp. 699–711, 2020.
https://doi.org/10.1007/978-3-030-60149-2_53

their skills, abilities, and demographics [4]. Unsurprisingly then, financial institutions such as banks and insurance companies have been increasingly transferring their services and communications online [28, 42]. Despite obvious benefits, use of the web can also raise issues related to the user's abilities. In particular, older users might be at a disadvantage when accessing financial services and information online as a result of: a decline in financial literacy [20]; reduced cognitive abilities that might impact on their comprehension of texts [15]; or a general lack of familiarity with computers and/or the web [13].

The accessibility and usability of the language of online textual content for older people has received little attention, particularly as far as Terms and Conditions provided by financial institutions are concerned. Plain language—defined as communication that is comprehended the first time it is encountered, and that relies on textual features such as active voice and common terms [39]—is frequently advocated, but empirical evidence on its necessity and impact for older people in the online financial domain is lacking. This research gap is surprising when considering that "[u]sing the clearest and simplest language possible" is listed among the principles set forth by the Web Accessibility Initiative (WAI) [40].

Against this background, this article describes an exploratory study that answered the following research questions (RQs):

RQ1. How accessible (i.e. comprehensible) are online financial texts according to older people?
RQ2. Does plain language increase the usability of online financial texts for older people?

This article is organised as follows. After this introduction, we review related work. Subsequently, we report on the methodology that we adopted to answer our RQs. We then present the results, which are summarised and discussed in the conclusions.

2 Related Work

2.1 Accessibility and Usability

(Web) accessibility and (web) usability are related and partially overlapping notions, but their relationship is unclear [41]. A recent analysis of 50 definitions of web accessibility conducted by Petrie, Savva, and Power [33] led to the development of a unified definition in which web accessibility seems to coincide with usability. The same overlap between accessibility and usability is contained in ISO 9241-171 [23].

When referring to textual content, however, accessibility and usability have often been regarded as separate concepts. Accessibility is used as a synonym of readability or comprehensibility, particularly when referring to content written in plain language [2, 6]. Usability, on the other hand, is traditionally measured along the dimensions of effectiveness, efficiency, and satisfaction when conducting tasks with specific textual content [12].

Since the focus of our study was on online textual content, we also treated accessibility and usability as separate, but only partially. Specifically, by *accessibility*, we referred to how difficult online financial texts were to comprehend; and by *usability*, we referred to how satisfied and effective older people were with online financial texts that had been written in plain language. We measured effectiveness in terms of various measures related to comprehension, hence the partial overlap with accessibility. We did not include efficiency in our assessment of usability.

2.2 (Web) Accessibility and Older People

There is a dearth of studies on the need for accessible language among older people using the web to deal with financial institutions. However, interactions of older people with the web for other purposes have been investigated in terms of accessibility and cognitive problems [10]. For instance, Sayago et al. [36] observed that difficulty in remembering steps and in comprehending computer jargon were accessibility barriers with strong impact.

Several web design guidelines and resources have been developed to make websites and applications accessible. In particular, the Web Content Accessibility Guidelines 2.0 are widely adopted in both research and practice [11], but they were developed having in mind users with disabilities, rather than older people [36], and they have been shown to have shortcomings [31]. Abou-Zahra et al. [1] describe the WAI-AGE project, whose goal is to address some of the limitations of the web accessibility guidelines in relation to the needs of older people.

2.3 (Web) Usability and Older People

Usability in itself is a complex and multifaceted concept [16, 35]. Despite different definitions, there seems to be some agreement that the ability to conduct a task (with as little effort as possible) when using a product (including a text) is as important as the satisfaction experienced when using it [16]. A widely adopted definition of usability that encompasses these aspects is reported in ISO 9241-11 [24], paragraph 3.1.1: "extent to which a system, product or service can be used by specified users to achieve specified goals with effectiveness, efficiency and satisfaction in a specified context of use". For the purpose of our study, and drawing upon previous research on textual content, we also adopted this definition.

Research on the usability of online financial texts (and on the impact of plain language) is lacking. However, the usability of websites and other information and communication technologies for older adults has received some attention [17, 32]. Furthermore, Rodrigues et al. [34] identified several usability and accessibility issues on frequently accessed websites, such as information overload and unclear terminology.

2.4 Terms and Conditions

Terms and Conditions play a key role in informing the signatory of a contract of their rights and obligations. Gaining informed consent to a contract should therefore require a thorough understanding of its Terms and Conditions [29]. However, customers have been found to misunderstand the specific conditions of their contracts or the extent of their rights [26]. Additionally, Terms and Conditions are rarely read (in their entirety) because of the effort required to understand contract terms [3]. Length, lack of time, and trust in the fairness of terms are also likely to discourage readers [22].

The language and readability of Terms and Conditions has received little attention [29]. Kvalnes [26] points out that drafting these documents in plain language can result in "a better ethical climate", while Van Boom et al. [37] found that increased readability of insurance contract terms boosts consumers' expectations of receiving cover. The application of plain language guidelines to Terms and Conditions can be beneficial, but might not lead to the desired level of usability and comprehensibility [9], possibly because contract terms can be simplified only up to a certain extent [19]. To the best of our knowledge, the main focus so far has been on the legal (rather than on the financial content) of Terms and Conditions. Moreover, the impact of plain language on the usability of this type of content for older people seems to be an under-researched area.

3 Methodology

Answering RQ1 (How accessible (i.e. comprehensible) are online financial texts according to older people?) represented a preliminary step, which was needed to find out: (i) if participants had concerns about the accessibility of online financial texts; and (ii) which types of texts they thought might have benefited from text simplification (i.e. plain language editing). To answer RQ1, we conducted a small focus group.

The data gathered through the focus group informed the set-up of the experiment conducted to answer RQ2 (Does plain language increase the usability of online financial texts for older people?). Specifically, after identifying concerns about the accessibility of online financial content (in particular, Terms and Conditions), we investigated the potential benefits of plain language on a set of usability components.

Details on the focus group and on the experimental study are provided separately in the two sections below. For the purpose of our study, we focused on participants aged 54 and older.

3.1 Focus Group

The focus group, which lasted about 80 min, was run at the researchers' institution in April 2019, and was audio recorded. Four older people agreed to participate. The authors of this paper had prepared a list of topics to guide the focus group discussion. However, spontaneous topics were also encouraged during the focus group. One of the researchers acted as the moderator, while another took notes.

The coding and analysis of the transcribed interview data was conducted using a thematic analytical strategy described in Braun and Clarke [8], and was carried out with the NVivo software. Six themes were identified in the focus group discussion, namely: (i) communications from financial institutions; (ii) personal experiences with financial institutions; (iii) reading behaviour with financial information; (iv) trust in financial institutions; (v) response to change; and (vi) Terms and Conditions.

The focus group showed that participants had concerns about the accessibility of online financial content and found it difficult to comprehend at times. In addition, findings from the focus group showed that Terms and Conditions should be the object of plain language editing. Below we report an extract from the theme Terms and Conditions to back up this point:

P03: The day-to-day things seem to be kind of straightforward and easy to understand. I… For me, I think, it's when you get into the terms and conditions, and particularly with regard to insurance policies, or opening accounts, or whatever… It's the language that's used there, and it's the interpretation of that language that's sometimes… Whether it's online or paper-based, that's where it can become difficult.

Informed by the findings of the focus group, we selected Terms and Conditions from a bank and an insurance company as the texts to be used for our experimental study aimed to test the impact of simplification (or plain language editing) on text usability.

3.2 Experimental Study

Operationalisation of Variables. As already specified, by usability, we referred to how satisfied and effective older people were with online financial texts.

Satisfaction. We defined satisfaction as older people's opinions of: (i) the informativeness and helpfulness of the content; (ii) the understandability of the language; and (iii) the understandability of the content. Participants were asked to rate these aspects on a scale from 1 (lowest satisfaction) to 4 (highest satisfaction). Questions on satisfaction were taken from Castilho and Guerberof [12].

Effectiveness. Regarding effectiveness, ISO 9241-11 [24], paragraph 3.1.12, defines it as "the accuracy and completeness with which users achieve certain goals". For the purpose of this study, we defined effectiveness as older people's ability to reach goals related to comprehension. To this end, we develop our own questions to measure their reading comprehension, perceived comprehensibility, and reading behaviour with simplified Terms and Conditions (written in plain language) and non-simplified Terms and Conditions:

- Reading comprehension was measured through multiple-choice questions. Specifically, each text was followed by four multiple-choice questions;
- Perceived comprehensibility was measured by asking participants to indicate which text (between the simplified and the non-simplified) they found easier to read. Participants were also asked to indicate the reasons for their preference;
- Reading behaviour was assessed by asking participants to report whether, with each text presented to them, they would: (i) read it in its entirety; (ii) read some parts of it; (iii) skim through it; (iv) skip it altogether; (v) or other.

Experimental Design and Procedure. Twenty-five older people agreed to be involved in the experiment. Each participant took part in the experiment individually at the researchers' institution. We adopted a within-subjects design whereby each participant was asked to read and answer usability questions on two financial texts.

Participants were randomly assigned to either a treatment (N = 13) or a control group (N = 12). In the treatment group, each participant read a simplified text written in plain language and a non-simplified text. The difference in readability between the two texts, as determined by the Flesch Kincaid Grade Level formula, represented our independent variable and is reported in Fig. 1 below. Specifically, the simplified text had a lower Flesch Kincaid Grade Level (indicating higher readability), while the non-simplified text had a higher Flesch Kincaid Grade Level (indicating lower readability). The order of text presentation (simplified vs. non-simplified) was counterbalanced. Participants were also blinded to the design. In the control group, the two texts presented to each participant had a similar level of readability as determined by the Flesch Kincaid Grade Level formula (Fig. 1).

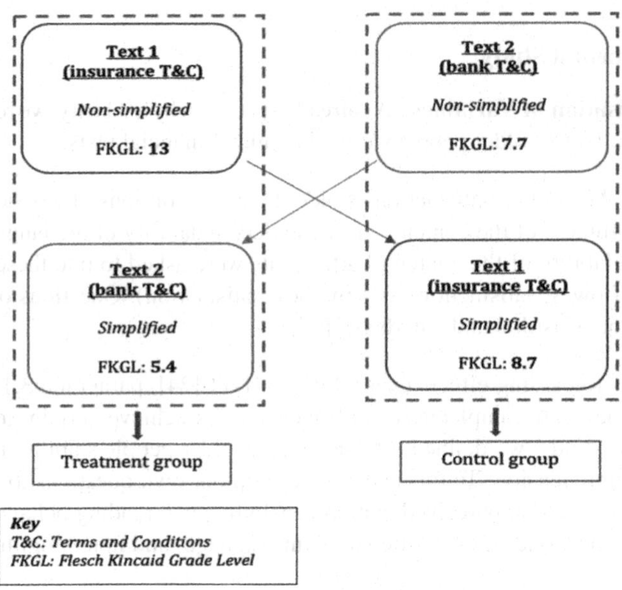

Fig. 1. Texts and experimental groups

Participants also completed a background questionnaire and took part in a warm-up reading task. In addition, participants rated their familiarity with direct debits, since this was the topic of the texts used. All participants conducted the experimental tasks (reading and answering questions) using a computer. Only one participant did not feel comfortable using the keyboard, so he read the texts on the computer screen but then dictated the answers to one of the researchers, who typed them.

Texts. We selected extracts of Terms and Conditions provided by a bank and an insurance company on their websites, and dealing with the topic of direct debits, which are a common method of payment. The texts were in English and contained between 280 and 369 words. The specific terms and conditions set forth in the texts were different so as to avoid a learning effect. However, the same general topic of direct debit was selected to prevent topic knowledge from acting as a confounding variable.

After selecting the two online texts, one of the researchers manually checked them against the WAI [40] plain language guidelines and revised them accordingly. These guidelines address a broad range of readability issues, such as sentence/word length and structure, terminology, consistency, and cohesion. Figure 1 shows readability scores (as per Flesch Kincaid Grade Level readability formula) before and after the implementation of plain language guidelines. It also displays how texts were matched for the treatment and the control group. We maintained the original formatting of the texts (e.g. in terms of font and layout) as displayed on the websites from which they were extracted.

4 Results

4.1 Background Characteristics of Experimental Participants

Our participants were aged between 58 and 84 years of age. The mean age of the participants in the treatment (N = 13) and in the control group (N = 12) was similar (mean = 67 in the treatment group, and mean = 69 in the control group). Participants varied in terms of highest education level, with most of them having either a secondary or a third-level education degree. As far as gender distribution is concerned, there were 11 female participants and two male participants in the treatment group, while the control group included seven male participants and five female participants. All participants held a bank account, and the vast majority of them were used to reading financial information online (either online alone or in combination with printed information) (Fig. 2).

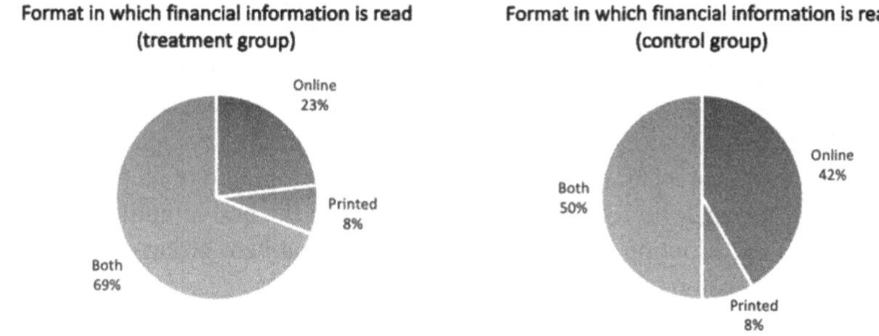

Fig. 2. Format in which financial information is read

In both the treatment and the control group, most participants reported reading information from their banks either always or often. There was more variability in terms of the frequency with which financial information from insurance companies was read. Most participants in both the treatment and the control group stated that they had an average level of financial knowledge. Regarding familiarity with computers, the majority of participants in both groups reported being either comfortable or very comfortable with them. As far as tablets and/or smart phones are concerned, fewer participants stated that they were very comfortable with them. Finally, participants in both the treatment and the control group were quite familiar with the topic of direct debits.

4.2 Satisfaction

We measured satisfaction by asking participants how strongly they agreed or disagreed with the three statements in Table 1 (first column), on a 4-point scale. We report the mode scores. In the treatment group, despite the fact that the simplified text had been revised substantially for plain language (Fig. 1), the mode values show that the satisfaction ratings provided by the majority of older participants on the simplified and non-simplified text were similar. Slight differences between the two texts were also observed in the control group.

Table 1. Satisfaction ratings from the treatment group

Measures (on a scale from 1 to 4)	Simplified text	Non-simplified text
Informativeness and helpfulness of the text	Mode = 2	Mode = 3
Perceived understandability of the language	Mode = 2	Mode = 2 and 3
Perceived understandability of the content	Mode = 2	Mode = 2

4.3 Effectiveness

Effectiveness was defined in terms of achieved reading comprehension, perceived comprehensibility, and reading behaviour. Regarding reading comprehension, we assigned a score of 1 to the multiple-choice answers that participants answered correctly, and a score of 0 to wrong answers. There were no missing answers. Subsequently, we added up the scores to obtain a total score per participant, for each of the two texts read. Then we calculated the mean total score of all participants in each group, for each of the two texts read. Table 2 reports the mean scores (and standard deviation, SD) of all the participants in the treatment group, who read the simplified text and the non-simplified one. It can be observed that the adoption of plain language in the treatment group did not result in improved comprehension among our older participants.

Table 2. Treatment group's comprehension scores

Text	Comprehension scores
Simplified	Mean = 3.08, SD = 0.76
Non-simplified	Mean = 3.08, SD = 0.64

As far as perceived comprehensibility is concerned, we asked participants to indicate which of the two texts they found easier to read, and why. We observed that a slightly higher number of people in the treatment group selected the simplified text. However, a similar slight preference for one text over another was also observed in the control group

(Fig. 3), suggesting that this slight preference for a text over another might not be due (exclusively) to decreased language difficulty. Specifically, in both the treatment and the control group, participants showed a preference for Text 2—it should be remembered that, while Text 2 was considerably more readable in the treatment group, in the control group its readability level was very similar to that of Text 1 (Fig. 1). Therefore, the results in Fig. 3 seem to indicate that some features of Text 2 (different from the readability level) might have acted as a confounding variable.

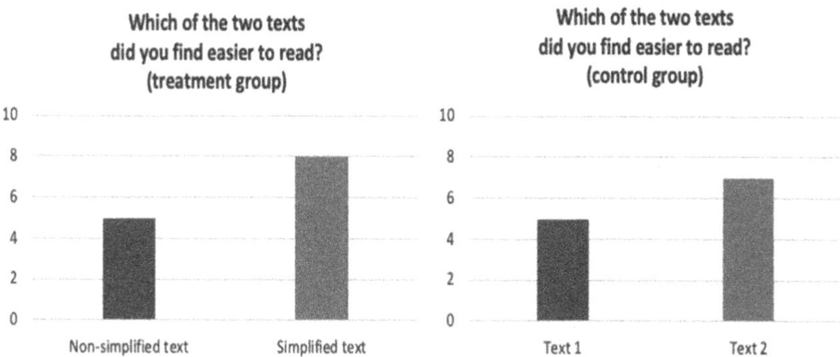

Fig. 3. Results on perceived comprehensibility

This claim that older people's preference for one text is not the result of language only seems to be supported by their answers regarding the reasons behind their preferences. More precisely, when asked why they found a text easier to read than the other, older participants did not mention only plain language, but also the intention of the text and visual aspects, such as layout and colour. Below we report one extract from their short answers:

P05: I prefer the manner on which it was set out, the text was better divided up and the matter more accessible that [sic] a large block of words.

With regard to reading behaviour, for each text, older participants were asked to indicate what they would do if they were presented with it. They could select an option (ranging from Reading it in its entirety to Skip it altogether) or add another option. When looking at the number of selections per each option in the treatment group, we observed a widespread tendency to read only parts of the Terms and Conditions or to skim through them, regardless of whether they were written in plain language or not. However, in the case of non-simplified Terms and Conditions, reading behaviour seemed more varied, with one participant mentioning she would have to read them several times, and others stating that they would skip reading altogether, try reading but then give up, or abandon what they were doing (Fig. 4). In the control group, reading behaviour between texts was quite similar (Fig. 5), suggesting that it was plain language (and absence thereof) in the treatment group that influenced the reading behaviour of some participants:

Interestingly, reading behaviour with Terms and Conditions was also a theme in the focus group data, as shown in the extracts below:

P01: I don't read them. I scroll down through them, and I tick the box 'I have read the terms and conditions' and I feel... Great...

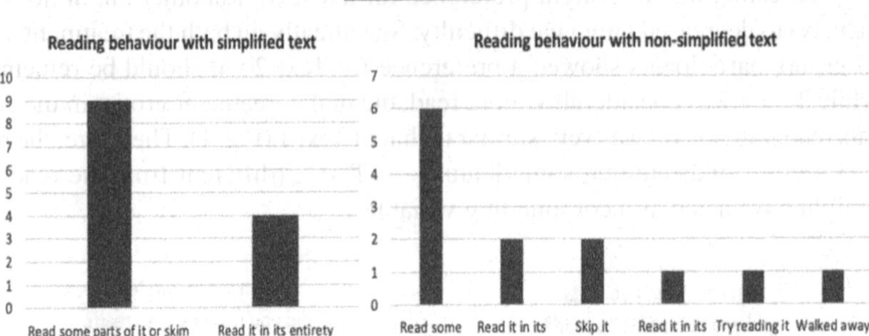

Fig. 4. Reading behaviour in the treatment group

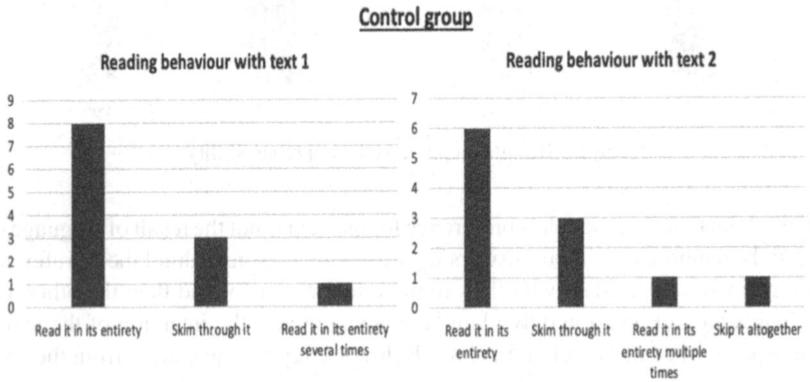

Fig. 5. Reading behaviour in the control group

P03: If it's something to do with terms and conditions, [...] I sometimes ask for those on hard copies because sometimes you need to read them, and then you need to re-read them, and then you need to re-read them...

5 Conclusions

We conducted an exploratory investigation on the need for and impact of plain language among older adults reading online financial information. We observed that these were two under-researched aspects in the broader areas of web accessibility and web usability.

We found that applying plain language guidelines to Terms and Conditions extracted from the websites of financial institutions did not lead to improved reading comprehension, as assessed through multiple-choice questions. Furthermore, simplifying Terms and Conditions using plain language editing did not increase older people's perceptions of comprehensibility, nor their ratings of informativeness/helpfulness, understandability of language, and understandability of content. Bearing in mind that the benefits of plain language have been extensively discussed [21], results from our study might be due to the reduced number of participants, and to the fact that they were already familiar with the topic of direct debits. Further investigations with larger groups and more complex/unfamiliar texts are likely to highlight the benefits of plain language.

Qualitative data obtained through follow-up questions showed that language was not the only aspect valued by older people, as they also focused on visual aspects, such as layout and colour. The importance of visual aspects for older people (and users with disabilities) also emerged in Curran et al. [14]. The interplay between language and the non-linguistic aspects of texts should also be the object of follow-up research.

As far as reading behaviour is concerned, we found that, regardless of whether online Terms and Conditions were simplified or not, the general tendency among older people was to read some parts of them or just skim through them, depending on their needs. Similar findings are reported in Bakos et al. [3]. We also observed higher variability in terms of reading behaviour with non-simplified Terms and Conditions. Specifically, when presented with difficult texts, some older people seemed to either read them several times in order to understand them, or avoid reading them altogether. This result seems to indicate that plain language might have an impact on reading behaviour.

The importance of Terms and Conditions in financial agreements cannot be overstated, as these texts represent the basis of rational decisions and consumer protection [18]. While (older) people might be inclined to avoid reading Terms and Conditions, or skimming through them, this reading behaviour would result in them providing uninformed acceptance of agreements and, in turn, would leave them in a vulnerable position, at the mercy of financial institutions [26]. Our study highlighted the need for creating engaging and visually appealing Terms and Conditions/financial content to counteract what is known as *rational apathy*, which emerges when consumers believe that the costs of monitoring (reading) outweigh the expected benefits [7].

Acknowledgments. This research has been funded by Science Foundation Ireland through the SFI Research Centres Programme and is co-funded under the European Regional Development Fund through Grant n. 13/RC/2106.

References

1. Abou-Zahra, S., Brewer, J., Arch, A.: Towards bridging the accessibility needs of people with disabilities and the ageing community. In: Proceedings of the 2008 International Cross-Disciplinary Conference on Web Accessibility, pp. 83–86. Association for Computing Machinery, New York (2008)
2. Aluísio, S.M., Gasperin, C.: Fostering digital inclusion and accessibility: the PorSimples project for simplification of Portuguese texts. In: Proceedings of the NAACL HLT 2010 Young Investigators Workshop on Computational Approaches to Languages of the Americas, pp. 46–53. Association for Computational Linguistics, Stroudsburg (2010)
3. Bakos, Y., Marotta-Wurgler, F., Trossen, D.R.: Does anyone read the fine print? consumer attention to standard-form contracts. J. Legal Stud. **43**(1), 1–35 (2014)
4. Berners-Lee, T.: The future of the World Wide Web. http://dig.csail.mit.edu/2007/03/01-ushouse-future-of-the-web.html. Accessed 12 May 2020

5. Bloom, D.E., et al.: Macroeconomic implications of population ageing and selected policy responses. Lancet **385**(14), 649–657 (2015)
6. Boldyreff, C., Burd, E., Donkin, J., Marshall, S.: The case for the use of plain English to increase Web accessibility. In: Proceedings of the Third International Workshop on Web Site Evolution, pp. 42–48. Institute of Electrical and Electronics Engineers, Piscataway (2001)
7. Bolodeoku, I.O.: Corporate governance in the new information and communication age: an interrogation of the rational apathy theory. J. Corpor. Law Stud. **7**(1), 109–141 (2007)
8. Braun, V., Clarke, V.: Thematic analysis. In: Cooper, H., Camic, P.M., Long, D.L., Panter, A.T., Rindskopf, D., Sher. K.J. (eds.) APA Handbook of Research Methods in Psychology, Research Designs, vol. 2, pp. 57–71. American Psychological Association, Washington (2012)
9. Burger, J.M.: The Effect of Iteratively Applying Plain Language Techniques in Forms and Their Terms and Conditions. Dissertation, Stellenbosch University (2018)
10. Burmeister, O.K.: Websites for seniors: cognitive accessibility. Aust. J. Emerg. Technol. Soc. **8**(2), 99–113 (2010)
11. Caldwell, B., Cooper, M., Guarino Reid, L., Vanderheiden, G.: Web Content Accessibility Guidelines (WCAG) 2.0. https://www.w3.org/TR/WCAG20/. Accessed 12 May 2020
12. Castilho, S., Guerberof, A.: Reading comprehension of machine translation output: What makes for a better read? In: Proceedings of the 21st Annual Conference of the European Association for Machine Translation, pp. 79–88. http://eamt2018.dlsi.ua.es/proceedings-eamt2018.pdf. Accessed 12 May 2020
13. Chang, J., McAllister, C., McCaslin, R.: Correlates of, and barriers to, Internet use among older adults. J. Gerontolog. Soc. Work **58**(1), 66–85 (2015)
14. Curran, K., Walters, N., Robinson, D.: Investigating the problems faced by older adults and people with disabilities in online environments. Behav. Inf. Technol. **26**(6), 447–453 (2007)
15. De Beni, R., Borella, E., Carretti, B.: Reading comprehension in aging: the role of working memory and metacomprehension. Aging Neuropsychol. Cogn. **14**(2), 189–212 (2007)
16. Dix, A., Finlay, J., Abowd, G.D., Beale, R.: Human-Computer Interaction, 3rd edn. Pearson, Harlow (2004)
17. Doménech, S., Rivero, J., Coll-Planas, L., Sainz, F.J., Reissner, A., Miralles, F.: Involving older people in the design of an innovative information and communication technologies system promoting active aging: the SAAPHO project. J. Access. Des. All **3**(1), 13–27 (2013)
18. Faure, M.G., Luth, H.A.: Behavioural economics in unfair contract terms. J. Consum. Pol. **34**(3), 337–358 (2011)
19. Felici, A., Griebel, C.: The challenge of multilingual 'plain language' in translation-mediated Swiss administrative communication. Transl. Spaces **8**(1), 167–191 (2019)
20. Finke, M.S., Howe, J.S., Huston, S.J.: Old age and the decline in financial literacy. Manage. Sci. **63**(1), 213–230 (2017)
21. Garwood, K.: Plain but not simple: Plain language research with readers, writers, and texts. Ph.D thesis, University of Waterloo, Canada (2014)
22. Hillman, R.A.: On-line consumer standard-form contracting practices: a survey and discussion of legal implications. Cornell Legal Studies Research Paper Series. https://scholarship.law.cornell.edu/lsrp_papers/29/. Accessed 12 May 2020
23. ISO 9241-171:2008: Ergonomics of Human-System Interaction—Part 171: Guidance on Software Accessibility. https://www.iso.org/obp/ui/#iso:std:iso:9241:-171:ed-1:v1:en. Accessed 12 May 2020
24. ISO 9241-11:2018: Ergonomics of Human-System Interaction—Part 11: Usability: Definitions and Concepts. https://www.iso.org/obp/ui/#iso:std:iso:9241:-11:ed-2:v1:en. Accessed 12 May 2020

25. Klimova, B., Simonova, I., Poulova, P., Truhlarova, Z., Kuca, K.: Older people and their attitude to the use of information and communication technologies – a review study with special focus on the Czech Republic (older people and their attitude to ICT). Educ. Gerontol. **42**(5), 361–369 (2016)
26. Kvalnes, Ø.: Blurred promises: ethical consequences of fine print policies in insurance. J. Bus. Ethics **103**(1), 77–86 (2011)
27. de Lara, S.M.A., Fortes, R.P.M., Russo, C.M., Freire, A.P.: A study on the acceptance of website interaction aids by older adults. Univ. Access Inf. Soc. **15**(3), 445–460 (2015)
28. Lee, K.W., Tsai, M.T., Lanting, M.C.: From marketplace to marketspace: Investigating the consumer switch to online banking. Electron. Commer. Res. Appl. **10**, 115–125 (2011)
29. Luger, E., Moran, S., Rodden, T.: Consent for all: revealing the hidden complexity of terms and conditions. In: Proceedings of the SIGCHI Conference on Human Factors in Computing Systems, pp. 2687–2696. Association for Computing Machinery, New York (2013)
30. Lutz, W., Sanderson, W., Scherbov, S.: The coming acceleration of global population ageing. Nature **451**, 716–719 (2008)
31. Milne, S., Dickinson, A., Carmichael, A., Sloan, D., Eisma, R., Gregor, P.: Are guidelines enough? An introduction to designing web sites accessible to older people. IBM Syst. J. **44**(3), 557–571 (2005)
32. Page, T.: Touchscreen mobile devices and older adults: a usability study. Int. J. Hum. Fact. Ergon. **3**(1), 65–85 (2014)
33. Petrie, H., Savva, A., Power, C.: Towards a unified definition of web accessibility. In: Proceedings of the 12th web for all conference, pp. 1–13. Association for Computing Machinery, New York (2015)
34. Rodrigues, S.S., Scuracchio, P.E., De Mattos Fortes, R.P.: A support to evaluate web accessibility and usability issues for older adults. In: Proceedings of the Eight International Conference on Software Development and Technologies for Enhancing Accessibility and Fighting Info-Exclusion, pp. 97–103. Association for Computing Machinery, New York (2018)
35. Rubin, J., Chisnell, D.: Handbook of Usability Testing: How to Plan, Design and Conduct Effective Tests, 2nd edn. Wiley Publishing Inc., Indianapolis (2008)
36. Sayago, S., Camacho, L., Blat, J.: Evaluation of techniques defined in WCAG 2.0 with older people. In: Proceedings of the 2009 International Cross-Disciplinary Conference on Web Accessibility, pp. 79–82. Association for Computing Machinery, New York (2009)
37. Van Boom, W.H., Desmet, P., Van Dam, M.: "If it's easy to read, it's easy to claim"—The effect of the readability of insurance contracts on consumer expectations and conflict behaviour. J. Consum. Pol. **39**(2), 187–197 (2016)
38. Warburton, J., Cowan, S., Winterton, R., Hodgkins, S.: Building social inclusion for rural older people using information and communication technologies: Perspectives of rural practitioners. Aust. Soc. Work **67**(4), 479–494 (2014)
39. Warde, F., Papadakos, J., Papadakos, T., Rodin, D., Salhia, M., Giuliani, M.: Plain language communication as a priority competency for medical professionals in a globalized world. Can. Med. Educ. J. **9**(2), e52–e59 (2018)
40. Web Accessibility Initiative: Accessibility Principles. https://www.w3.org/WAI/fundamentals/accessibility-principles/. Accessed 12 May 2020
41. Yesilada, Y., Brajnik, G., Vigo, M., Harper, S.: Understanding web accessibility and its drivers. In: Proceedings of the International Cross-Disciplinary Conference on Web Accessibility. Association for Computing Machinery, New York (2012)
42. Yi, Y.J.: Web accessibility of healthcare Web sites of Korean government and public agencies: a user test for persons with visual impairment. Univ. Access Inf. Soc. **19**, 41–56 (2018)

Security, Privacy and Trust for a Crowd-Sourced Semantic Accessibility Database for Public Transport

Daniel Tabellion, Moritz Wolf, Jochen Britz, Maurice Rekrut, and Jan Alexandersson(✉)

DFKI GmbH, Saarbrücken, Germany
{daniel.tabellion,moritz.wolf,jochen.britz,maurice.rekrut, jan.alexandersson}@dfki.de
http://www.dfki.de

Abstract. With the growing popularity of wearable devices and smartphones, mobile crowdsourcing applications (MCNs) have prevailed as a standard for collectively gathering geo-spatial information. This can be very valuable, especially in the public transport section where the associated challenge consists of acquiring area-wide accessibilty information for points of interest. The aim of this work is to describe the implementation of a mobile crowdsourcing platform for the secure recording of accessibility information: mobisaarWORLD. We analyse and discuss which approach is best for its implementation with a focus on ensuring security, privacy and trust. We examine in detail the state-of-the-art in the field, taxonomies of crowdsourcing platforms and the associated security, privacy and trust requirements, issues and countermeasures. In order to measure the effectiveness of the applied countermeasures and the resulting security properties, the platform is then compared to OpenStreetMap. We show that the mobisaarWORLD is able to provide a simple, but effective verification mechanism to ensure data trust and that it can provide personal information privacy, in particular location privacy for its workers.

Keywords: Crowd sourcing · Public transport · Accessibility · AAL

1 Introduction

One of the most fundamental human rights is the freedom to act and decide for oneself. Therefore, a mandatory requirement for the design and implementation of Ambient Assisted Living (AAL) solutions is perceiving people who interact with the solution as subjects rather than objects. Subjects are liberated to act as they like, so the AAL system should allow them to choose how to interact with the system based on their momentary desire and constitution. Since 8 years, we are engaged in research and development of a socio-technical system mobiSAAR (formerly mobia) [14,15]. This system allows—in principle—*everyone* to use public transport in the German state Saarland. The core is a

C. Stephanidis et al. (Eds.): HCII 2020, LNCS 12426, pp. 712–727, 2020.
https://doi.org/10.1007/978-3-030-60149-2_54

human-based door2door service, where so-called Mobility Pilots (MPs) assist a passenger in using public transport. This also requires a technical infrastructure i.e. a central coordination system and mobile apps for travellers and MPs to interact with it In order for passengers to be in control of the decision as to whether (s)he needs assistance a particular day, given e.g., subjective fitness etc., the passenger needs information about the current situation of all aspects of the route, including weather condition, delays, Points of Interest (POI, e.g. bus stops), conditions etc.

Previous approaches to compile accessibility relevant information[1] are very technically oriented and target technical systems that compute accessible routes. However, the BAIM/ BAIMPlus information style is not always comprehensible for passengers which is why (s)he is reduced to a system's objects. Passengers profit from easily digestible information like pictures and/or videos, which are not part of the BAIM/BAIMPlus catalogue. Changes in routes and POIs demand a highly dynamic and reliable database that can serve individuals with mobility issues. Our approach is based on crowdsourcing [8,12].

In order for the crowd to work properly, we need good answers to at least the following two issues:

- Which crowdsourcing approach is suitable in terms of feasibility and security?
- How can security, privacy and trust be ensured?

This paper is about how to design such a security-privacy-trust-preserving crowdsourcing approach for a semantic database that contains all possible static and dynamic relevant accessibility information for public transport thus allowing a traveller to decide as to whether (s)he momentarily needs assistance or not. Its main content is bus/tram stops and their properties.

2 Background

In this section we examine crowdsourcing platforms' different attributes and explain which consequences various configuration options can have on such a platform. In order to later on evaluate the security of the mobisaarWORLD, we then take a detailed look on requirements of a secure, privacy-preserving and reliable crowdsourcing service whilst also discussing possible countermeasures.

2.1 Crowdsourcing Taxonomies

In order to argue about security requirements and properties of crowdsourcing platforms it is important to understand the platforms' various differences in architecture and configuration. Following [7], crowdsourcing platforms are in general composed of four entities: the Crowd (consisting of crowd workers), the Crowdsourcer (or End User), the Task and the Platform. Moreover, these four

[1] See the German projects BAIM/BAIMPlus, e.g., http://ftb-esv.de/baimplus.html.

parties have several interlinked attributes, which ideally need to be defined during the design process of the platform. Importantly, each party plays a distinct role in the system, again shaped by their attributes.

The general method of the data gathering chain of a crowdsourcing application consists of multiple steps: First, the Crowdsourcers commit the Tasks that they want the Crowd to solve to the Platform. The Platform then divides these Tasks into smaller, so called Micro-Tasks, and assigns them to a group of crowd workers. Workers can report their solution via the platform. Once all micro-tasks have been aggregated and marked as resolved, in a next step, a platform-internal verification algorithm checks the veracity of the end results. Having passed this, the data is made accessible to the Crowdsourcer.

In the following, we will describe the previously mentioned four parties and define the various attributes that are relevant for designing mobisaarWORLD as a platform.

The Crowd. The crowd is the collection of people who are willing to take part in a crowdsourcing activity and deliberately share their knowledge with the Crowdsourcer.

- In addition to physiological diversity, such as age and gender diversity, the crowd's ***diversity*** also refers to different levels of expertise and spatial diversity. Age and gender influence the intrinsic motivation to solve a specific task whereas the expertise of participants can have a big impact on the correctness of solved tasks.
- ***Largeness*** refers to the crowd's size—number of participants—but also to the comprehensiveness. A too large crowd can be hard to manage, but a too small or not comprehensive enough crowd can yield unreliable results.
- ***Suitability*** in this context means the crowd is suiting a given purpose, occasion or condition to be able to solve their tasks reliably and correctly.
- ***Anonymity*** of the crowd means that the crowd may be unknown to the Crowdsourcer or vice versa. Obviously this attribute is directly linked to privacy aspects of the platform itself.

The Crowdsourcer. This entity may be a single person, a for-profit or a non-profit organization which seeks the collective knowledge of a crowd for a certain predefined task.

- ***Ethical Provisions*** are some ethical requirements the Crowdsourcer should assure towards the crowd. Firstly, there should be an opt-out procedure to assure that workers can leave as soon as they do not feel comfortable completing the task anymore. Secondly, there should be some feedback about completed tasks towards the crowd by the Crowdsourcer. This can enhance the motivation of workers, since they notice possible positive changes. Lastly, the crowd should not be harmed during task completion. This is especially important for spatial crowdsourcing, where participants are requested to gather information about a specific location (which could potentially be dangerous).

- ***Privacy Provision*** means, that the privacy of a worker should not be harmed in any way. This is one of the fundamental conditions the Crowdsourcer should be able to assure for the workers.

The Task. This is the activity the crowd is willing to participate in. It is determined by the crowdsourcer and is often divided into so called microtasks which are smaller and easier-to-solve problems that, put together, form a solution to the given general task.

Modularity of a task specifies whether the task is an atomic one or if it can and should be broken down into microtasks, which are easier to solve small tasks that contribute to the bigger picture when put together. This is for the implementation of the platform, since the correct conjunction of these microtasks can be rather complex and could lead to verification issues. The ***automation characteristics*** of task refer to the level of automation possible within the task and highly depends on its ***complexity***.

The Platform. This is the system given by the service provider within which crowdsourcing tasks are performed and end results assembled. The specification and implementation of the platform is fundamental for a reliable and secure crowdsourcing application, since it is responsible for enforcing security goals like anonymity, privacy, authentication, verification, integrity of reports and many more. Due to the flexibility and openness of the definition of crowdsourcing, the following list is not exhaustive, but tries to cover most interactions and facilities important for mobisaarWORLD between the platform and the crowd, the crowdsourcer, tasks and the platform itself.

Crowd-related interactions for the sake of security should contain an ***enrollment*** mechanism and an ***authentication mechanism***, which form the basis for arguing about other security requirements.

The core of the task-related facilities is the ***aggregation mechanism***, which is responsible for correctly assembling any incoming micro-tasks to the end result. This ensures that a minimally required quality or quantity of tasks is met before aggregating into the bigger picture. Furthermore, it might be critical for the platform to be able to ***hide results*** of one participant from another to ensure the ethical privacy provision towards the crowd. Keeping ***history*** of task results is also crucial. Besides ensuring correct behaviour in certain situations, history can provide a basis for statistical analysis of completed tasks. This can for instance provide insights about the origins of bad results or improve future tasks. Also in case of privacy related violations, a detailed history could resolve legal disputes.

2.2 Security Requirements

Especially in mobile crowdsourcing platforms privacy, trust and many other security related attributes, like verification, location privacy, confidentiality/integrity, authenticity, worker trust and data trust are essential for building a not only reliable but also trustworthy and secure platform for the workers. In order to secure a system against potential misuse and attacks, we will first have to explore which requirements a secure platform should bring. The extensive review by [4] analyzes over a hundred publications about general security in crowdsourcing applications and as a result summarizes potential security threats in a crowdsourcing setting and sets up a detailed threat model for such platforms. The resulting mandatory requirements and potential countermeasures for crowdsourcing applications in this context are also examined in detail.

Extracting the most important security requirements for mobisaarWORLD gives an overview on how to design and importantly also secure the platform against a broad spectrum of security flaws.

Confidentiality and Integrity (C/I) are the two basic principles every secure system should aim for. This does not mean that they are simple to realize, but achieving confidentiality and integrity opens further possibilities for other security-related improvements. Confidentiality on the one hand means that information is protected from disclosure to unauthorized parties. In the context of an MCN, specific tasks may only be seen by selected people: solutions and tasks from one worker should be protected from other workers' sight. Integrity on the other hand means that data cannot be altered by other entities than the originator himself. Together, these two attributes should protect against eavesdropping, corruption and leakage of any data in any unintended form.

Authenticity is another basic security requirement, which ensures that any sender of data, claiming to be a certain entity, actually is the claimed entity. In MCNs this means that data coming from a certain worker can be verified to actually originate from that worker and no other worker is able to impersonate the originator. This is crucial for further promises like for instance non-repudiation, access control and revocation.

Trust can be split into *worker trust*, *data trust*, and *personal information trust*. ***Worker Trust***(WT) as defined in [4]:

> "[...] represents the confidence on a worker with regard to its dependability, abilities (computing abilities, communication abilities, sensor abundance, etc.), reliability, worker preference, worker expertise, and availability of sensors, reputation, worker honesty and loyalty".

Due to their direct impact on the quality of output data, workers with high trust are crucial for a well-working crowdsourcing service.

Data Trust (DT) means that the platform is able to verify the veracity of collected data and to exclude low quality data from results. Not only low quality data by benign workers, but also cloaked or fake data may be generated by selfish or malicious workers, who, if not filtered, may manipulate output results to a great extent.

Personal information trust (PT) ensures that workers' personal information is validated by the platform. This information is important to ensure that the Platform allocates Tasks to the correct workers depending on their skill level and general suitability.

Privacy as well plays an important role in the security aspects of a crowdsourcing platform. Preserving ***task privacy*** (TP), ***collected data privacy*** (DP) and ***personal information privacy*** (PP), which includes the workers identity privacy, is of direct interest. If not protected correctly, adversaries could extract relevant information about the workers identity, location, trajectory, his preferences and abilities/disabilities or other personal information about the Crowdsourcer. Personal information privacy is also an important factor for third parties, who are indirectly influenced by the platform and its uploaded information. Uploaded pictures for example may contain sensible personal information of non-involved people.

After inspecting potential weaknesses and resulting requirements and countermeasures of crowdsourcing services, we have a first look on how to conceptualize the mobisaarWORLD, such that misuse is minimized and privacy retains.

3 mobisaarWORLD

This section is aimed towards presenting the core concept behind the Mobisaar project, why mobisaarWORLD is a necessary addition to the Mobisaar project, and how it is conceptualized in order to prevent misuse and other security-related attacks.

3.1 Concept and Architecture

The Mobisaar service has been started first and foremost to enable public transport for everyone, especially for individuals with reduced mobility. By offering a door to door service and supplying travellers with trained pilots that help with transportation between public transport facilities and with other difficulties regarding mobility, this platform enables users to travel more freely. Currently, this service is only available in some regions of the state Saarland in Germany. The overall goal beyond that is to offer personalized routes based on the abilities or disabilities of each individual user and to boost autonomy in public transport. Therefore, we need accessibility information of points of interest along the route.

Another important component for achieving this, besides the supply of verified accessibility tags, is the inclusion of pictures for various Points of Interest (POIs), like bus stops, elevators, construction sites and so on. Pictures might act as a basis for deciding whether to travel alone or not, since they can unfold valuable and individually differing information of accessibility of a POI, that otherwise might not have been captured by the crowd yet. Without all this information, computing personalized barrier-free routes and allowing the user to choose which route to take without the help of a pilot is not possible. Therefore, mobisaarWORLD, intended as an easy and secure solution to this problem, is designed to collect primarily accessibility info about POIs in form of an Mobile Crowdsourcing Network (MCN) (Fig. 1).

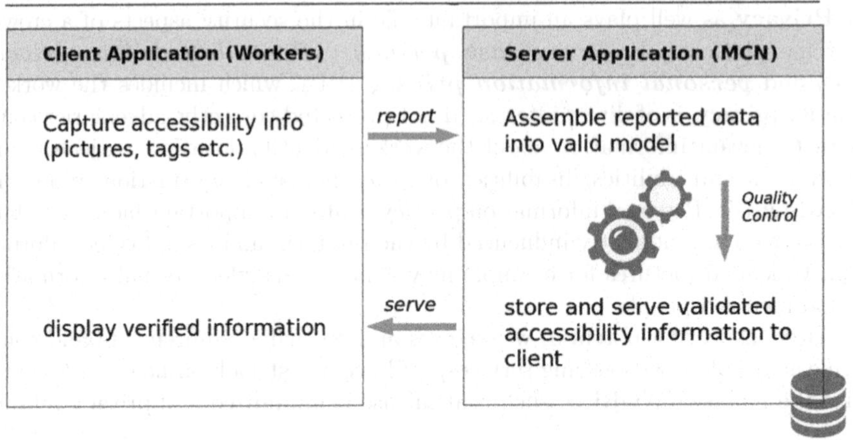

Fig. 1. The client-server architecture of mobisaarWORLD and its processes.

3.2 The Platform

mobisaarWORLD platform consists of two parts, a server and a client application:

The Server is responsible for answering requests and managing, amongst other things, POI attributes, pictures and crowd workers' meta information. Updates can either come from commits by client users or by draining updates from the OSM database, if there are no according entries deposited in mobisaarWORLD already. The overall idea is to pull verified data from OSM and enrich them with accessibility information collected within mobisaarWORLD. Additional responsibility lies in the correct assembly of incoming reports, such that the veracity of the delivered information of the POIs and their attributes to the client can be ensured. It is therefore also important to maintain a history of incoming changes, as well as versioning the state of the POIs, not only for correctly assembling incoming reports, but also for logging and statistical purposes, to be able to trace bad behaviour of users and to mitigate misconduct.

The Client Application is used to lookup public transport routes and booking pilots for these routes. Since Mobisaar is a project that aims to support accessibility, the client is also screen reader friendly for visually impaired people and to some extend configurable in its UI settings, like the icon size on the map. It also provides information about a POI's accessibility features. The other main feature of the client application is to provide an interface for reporting accessibility information about POIs. Authenticated users that are willing to contribute can commit changes to existing POIs, add missing POIs or upload Pictures to certain POIs (see Sect. 3.3).

3.3 Verification Mechanism

In order to provide these benefits to the users, the Mobisaar client offers an interactive user interface that represents mobisaarWORLD's reporting mechanism. This mechanism is allows users to commit new tasks to mobisaarWORLD by adding new attributes to POIs, updating attributes of an already existing POI in various ways and verifying tasks uploaded by other users. An overview of the verification mechanism and the Microtask Lifecycle can be seen in Fig. 2.

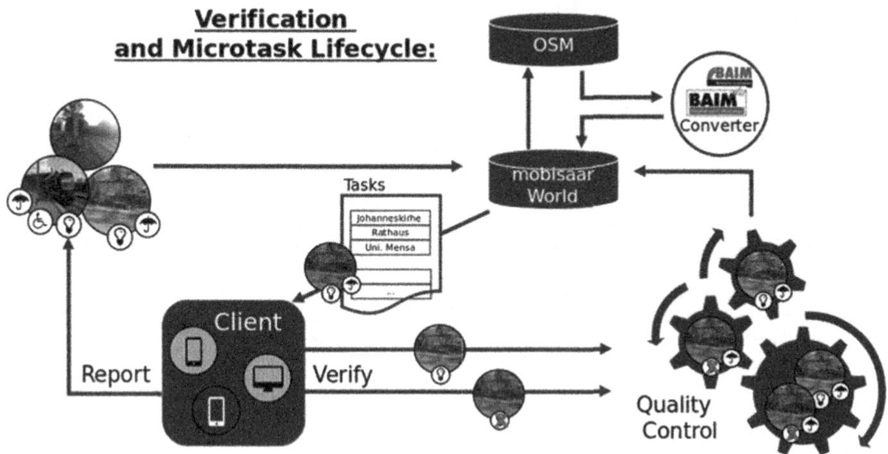

Fig. 2. The verification and microtask lifecycle

To grasp the reporting mechanism as a whole, the underlying server side Microtask Lifecycle and its directly linked quality control mechanism have to be discussed first. mobisaarWORLD is a MCN that supports worker selected task mode, called pull-mode, meaning that registered workers can choose which open tasks they wish to solve. If a user reports new information about a POI, this information will be sent to the the server and are published as new micro-tasks for the corresponding POI. When changes in attributes of a POI are being reported, and thus being adopted as one or more micro-tasks by the server, the resulting micro-tasks are at first in an unverified state. There can only be one instance of an, as we call it, "staged change" per attribute per POI. If other users now report similar results about the same POI they improve the veracity of the corresponding staged change by implicitly voting for it. When several different clients, including the initial reporting client, voted for the same staged change its attribute is being resolved as either correct or invalid depending on how many of those verifiers committed approving or rejecting results. At a certain threshold the task is then either accepted or declined. If verified, the task is changed accordingly in the final list of POIs and their linked attributes. All POIs and their according verified accessibility features are then depicted in the OSM map of the clients user interface (see Fig. 3).

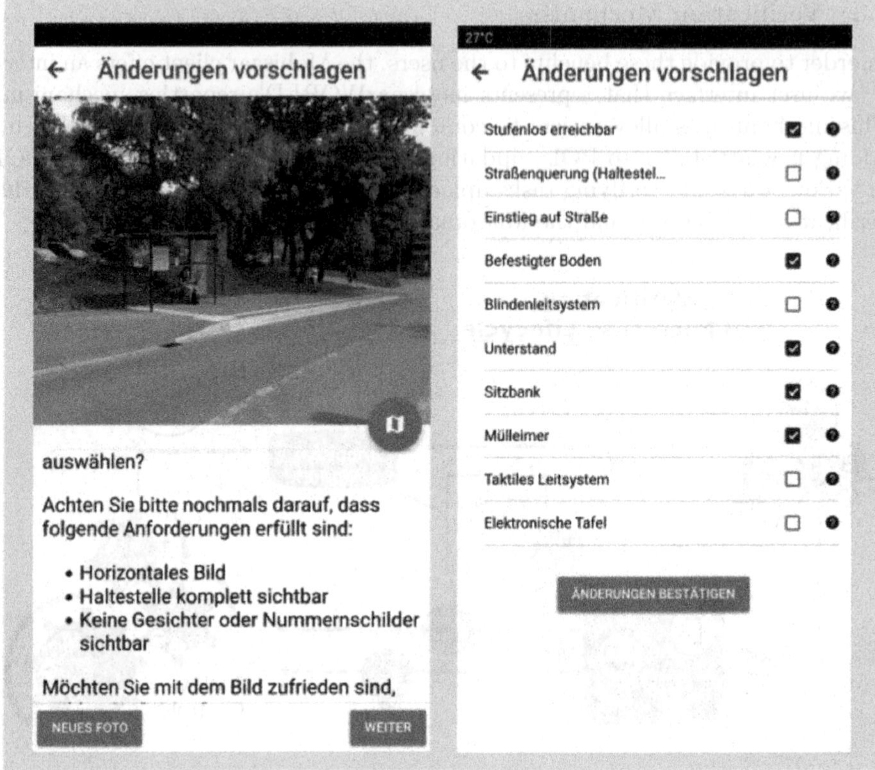

Fig. 3. Verified picture and attributes of a POI displayed by the client application.

The verification process, which in many ways is an important feature of any crowdsourcing platform, tries to undermine users' malicious or selfish behaviour and other fraud attempts, while first and foremost ensuring a certain level of veracity of the resulting data collection. But, as stated, not only verification and data trust is of interest for a secure crowdsourcing service, but also confidentiality/integrity, privacy, authentication, revocation, access control, non-repudiation and availability.

3.4 Other Security Measures

In order to utilize the service users have to register either via the app itself or by calling the Mobisaar Hotline. In the former case, the phone number is verified via an SMS verification code to reduce the risk of fake accounts. The authentication itself is handled by a dedicated backend server, which, amongst other things, is responsible for managing user data and computing route suggestions depending on the user's status. Since a third party is responsible for authentication, neither credentials nor personal information of any user are required to be stored directly in mobisaarWORLD. Only the username from the originator of a report is stored, so that users cannot commit changes to a micro-task twice.

mobisaarWORLD is configured in pull-mode for task assignment. Therefore, in order to support location privacy, additional countermeasures have to be adopted during the reporting phase. Else, computing the trajectory of any user would be possible due to the link of solved micro-tasks (and their publicly known location) to the user. As a countermeasure, names are pseudonymized with a cryptographically secure hash function, utilized in a signed JSON Web Token (JWT). This hash function is per default set to SHA-256 with elliptic curve cryptography ("ES256"), but can be changed according to the specification of the JWT [10]. Hence, instead of exposing the username directly during reports, the JWT only includes a hash of the username of the authenticated user. In this way, mobisaarWORLD never sees any actual username, but only a unique hash, which enables the server to track which users have edited which micro-tasks. This separation, often referred to as compartmentalization, is a common technique for enabling the different entities to focus on the level of their operation and thus better enforce specific security countermeasures. Additionally, this makes it easier for mobisaarWORLD to focus on and solve the crowdsourcing-related security problems rather than user database-related problems.

Finally, since mobisaarWORLD keeps history of submitted changes, workers submitting a lot of wrong changes can potentially be detected and ultimatively excluded from the service.

4 Evaluation

In this section we will evaluate security properties of mobisaarWORLD, resulting from the applied countermeasures. We also compare the effectiveness of our crowdsourcing approach to OpenStreetMap's. In order to evaluate the effectiveness of countermeasures implemented in mobisaarWORLD, we previously looked at security related threats and the resulting requirements for a secure, privacy-preserving and trustworthy crowdsourcing service. We discussed how to be able to comply with these requirements and some potential security measures in Sect. 3.4. Here, we will further analyze the security measures implemented in mobisaarWORLD. Special attention will lie on the verification process and the trust management in general and the users privacy, especially location privacy. After that the overall effectiveness of mobisaarWORLD in providing accessibility information for POIs while preserving privacy and data trust will be briefly compared to the widely spread volunteered geographic information (VGI) platform OpenStreetMap.

4.1 Evaluation of Security Mechanisms

In the previous sections we learned, that the overall security of a crowdsourcing platform heavily relies on its architecture and configuration. Accordingly, several countermeasures should be adopted in order to fulfill its various security requirements. In this section we will list configuration-dependent required security goals and work through the corresponding mitigation techniques and countermeasures.

Confidentiality/Integrity and Overall Security. The basis of any secure service is the confidentiality and integrity of its communication channels. Without encrypted transmission of data, which ensures C/I, non of the other security requirements can be guaranteed. For accepting requests over HTTPS, mobisaarWORLD is hosted with a certificate issued by Let's Encrypt.

Furthermore, one of the most prominent attacks in the web consists of injecting client-side scripts, called Cross-Site Scripting (XSS), which is here, to the most part, prohibited by the utilized angular framework and its use of templates and their interpolation feature, see [1]. Templates are created on the client side only, and its input data sanitized by using the interpolation feature. In this way, markup cannot be interpreted as code. Since XSS attacks trigger at the client side exclusively by rendering markup as code, the application should be secure against such kind of attacks. Moreover, to be sure that no data leak out of the database, due to some NoSQL injection, user input is always sanitized on the database level.

Together, these countermeasures build the basic security needed in terms of mobisaarWORLD's overall integrity.

Authenticity. As already briefly touched on in the introduction to mobisaarWORLD, a trusted third party service is utilized for authentication. This third party server manages any user related data for the Mobisaar Project and is responsible for letting users receive an authentication token after successfully logging in. This JSON Web Token is then appended to any subsequent request to mobisaarWORLD and contains relevant information for tracking reports and ensuring that the corresponding user has been authenticated successfully. It acts as a server signed, client side stored contract that may contain arbitrary claims about the client.

This widely used approach has many advantages over traditional token based authentication schemes. The most prominent advantage is that JWTs are stateless and thus information about an ongoing session does not have to be stored on the server side. The state is self-contained in the JWT and secured through encrypting the appended claims with the private key of the server (signed by the server). No database needs to be managed and cached. Consequently, there probably exist less unwanted sideffects and possible ways to manipulate a session without owning it. One major drawback of any token-basked authentication scheme is that tokens are stored and sent via cookies and thus are prone to Cross-Site Request Forgery (CSRF).

Important for the personal information privacy of mobisaarWORLD users is that the JWT does not contain any private data but only a unique hash of the username. By receiving a token, which has to be kept privately by the client in order to prevent impersonation attacks, the crowdsourcing server does not know from which user the request comes, but can trust its validity. Furthermore, this hash can be stored in a per-task history and then checked whether the same pseudonymized user already reported changes for this task. This history is crucial for trust management and is additionally handy for several statistical analyses.

Overall this mechanism ensures authentication of users and builds the foundation for computing workers' trust, whilst also preserving their privacy. Since any client action in the server is authenticated via a token, non-repudiation for those actions is given as well. By additionally appending a worker's role according to the systems access control policy, such a policy can be enforced as well.

Access Control. Since there exist different types of users in the Mobisaar project, like mobility pilots and passengers, those can be mapped one to one into mobisaarWORLD and its access control policy.

Passengers, or reporters in the context of mobisaarWORLD's access control policy, are able to carry out most actions that include reporting and verifying micro-tasks regarding a POI's attributes. The only exceptions here are tags about wheelchair accessibility, since from our experience most non-wheelchair passengers lack the knowledge about various specific things, like varying width for different types of wheelchairs or the maximum size of gaps that can be handled, to correctly estimate a a POI's wheelchair accessibility very well. Similarly, blind people should add information related to blind passengers. Since workers of mobisaarWORLD are mostly users of the Mobisaar service, the target group should provide eligible people for these kinds of tasks. Moreover, measuring tasks that require tools, like a meter, or prior specific knowledge about a certain circumstance, which might not be easily solvable by the average passenger, should only be reported and verified by people with profound knowledge.

Currently, this strict policy is only enforced on the client side. In the long run, this is not ideal since requests that do not originate from the client do not underlie an access control policy. A server side enforced policy would be a preferred solution, which would require additional knowledge on the role of the user in the JWT of the request. But this might complicate the overall authentication scheme and as a result reduce the privacy promises regarding personal information privacy and potentially location privacy of the platforms users.

In addition to the access control policy so far, some workers might be trusted more than others, reflected by their worker trust estimation. Thus, it is possible to give these workers higher privileges or a higher weighting in their verification and reporting skills. With the current system each worker has exactly one vote per micro-task, but it might be wise to put more trust in the top performing reporters, since the distribution of VGI contributors usually follow the 90-9-1 rule [2]. This rule states that approximately only 1% of active workers of a system contribute most of the data, whereas 9% contribute occasionally and the remaining 90% only once or twice.

Trust. Besides estimating a workers trust, the platform is mainly required to hold a certain level of data trust in order to provide a reliable service. Ensuring a certain level of worker trust overall and excluding underperforming workers has an impact on the veracity of output data, but a dedicated verification mechanism is crucial for ultimately controlling the trustworthiness of data. A minimal quality control mechanism is enough to exclude such constantly underperforming workers and to yield similar results for data trust in comparison to other complicated, and sometimes computationally costly, quality control mechanisms, see [9].

mobisaarWORLD's verification mechanism relies on other participants verifying the initially reported data. By aggregating a large number of overlapping information related to the same environment, the corresponding data gets more trustworthy. This phenomenon is called *Linus' Law.* However, this law often only partially applies to VGI, due to variance in the prominence, interest, visibility and timeliness of data to be collected and varying local knowledge of their collectors, see [6]. So for this to be a valid strategy for verifying information about POIs, the information to be verified need to be publicly accessible, visible and static in some sense. Otherwise collected data would be incomplete, inaccurate and outdated. Since, in the context of mobisaarWORLD, we are talking about POIs, and mainly bus, tram and train stations, these requirements hold true. They are publicly accessible, obviously visible and most of the time don't change. And if POIs move or change attributes, they are still regularly visited due to public transport and thus are captured by reporters frequently. Also, since mobisaarWORLD is a dedicated VGI for collecting accessibility information and there is no monetary award at all, the intrinsic interest of its workers should be present. Furthermore, in order to sustain correct data with this strategy, reporters should have local knowledge of the tasks they perform. For mobisaarWORLD, this means that reporters should have an idea about a POI's geographic circumstances whilst also possessing the required knowledge for correctly completing the POI's accessibility tags. The current access control policy tries to ensure this by only letting workers with the required knowledge answer micro-task they are eligible for. Also, since the mobisaarWORLD workers are mostly pilots or users of the Mobisaar service, we assume that local knowledge is given due to the fact that reported POIs are visited on the fly. Even if this is not the case, a combination of pictures of POIs, tooltips and descriptions for a specific task can provide the required knowledge and form a good basis for correctly verifying given tasks.

This, together with the fact that mobisaarWORLD is a specialized VGI which requires some specific knowledge about accessibility from its workers, should make clear that the concerns about Linus' Law with VGI do not apply in our case. The original quote of the Linus' Law "Given a large enough beta-tester and co-developer base, almost every problem will be characterized quickly and the fix obvious to someone." [16] states exactly this: The more contributors, that have specific knowledge about a topic, the better the result.

Important to note is that the quality of data rises with the number of participants and that rural areas oftentimes suffer from not having enough participants, which influences the completeness of data in such areas.

Privacy. Regarding privacy, there exist virtually no private data of any user present in mobisaarWORLD at any time, not even their username, only a unique hash and the corresponding access control role. This has various positive consequences for the workers' privacy, in particular for their location privacy. Since reports only contain an author's pseudonym, their trajectory cannot be inferred and mapped to by the server from a history of completed tasks and their implicit location information. The only knowledge the server has, is that a user of a certain role completed a number of tasks, which is not back-traceable to a specific user. Together with the fact that mobisaarWORLD operates in pull-mode, and thus clients do not have to disclose their location information or any other private information during task assignment, location privacy overall is assured. The ability of filtering tasks for nearby location, home location or booked routes on the way does not weaken these promises, since filtering happens client side, so again the server never sees the actual location or booked routes.

There is one possible threat to privacy of workers and potentially non-involved persons though: pictures and videos. These might contain private data about the visual appearance of the worker itself, the specifications of the workers device or the appearance of other non-involved persons. Together with a timestamp of a picture, which is often implicitly included in picture's files, it could be possible to infer spatio-temporal information about depicted individuals. Currently, this is mitigated by educating the reporters, that no persons or number plates should be identifiable on uploaded pictures. This is also part of the terms of use for mobisaarWORLD, which have to be accepted before being able to contribute.

Regarding privacy in the EU, there are only publicly available tasks about accessibility and other publicly accessible information about POIs, thus there seems to be no privacy concern of disclosed private information from tasks. Despite the fact that some tasks are hidden for some users by the access control mechanism, it does not mean that this information should be private. This measure is merely applied due to data trust management reasons, see above.

4.2 Comparison

While it would be perfectly possible to solely rely on Open Street Map (OSM) as a crowdsourcing platform, several problems regarding security, privacy and trust would come up when collecting accessibility information of POIs. Many of the problems regarding privacy and trust discussed in the previous sections are not being addressed by OSM. Even though OSM applies quality control mechanisms, which have been examined by many researchers and seem to work well in terms of completeness, positional accuracy and attribute accuracy [2,3,11], there is no profound, built in effort in preserving the privacy of its users. Users, that wish to contribute to OSM cannot report anonymously but have to authenticate and, according to the terms of use of OSM, sent reports implicitly containing user information and meta data of the originator [5]. Also the full history of changes, including any assigned meta data, is publicly available. This might disclose personal information, like interests and even location information of specific users if analyzed. Therefore, from a security standpoint this makes transparent that using OSM as a basis for crowdsourcing accessibility information would have an impact on the privacy of active contributors.

Furthermore several core principles and useful functionalities embedded in mobisaarWORLD, would not be available via the OSM API. Uploading pictures for specific POIs for example is not possible in OSM. This could potentially prevent our main users to travel autonomously—one of the major goals of the Mobisaar project. Additionally, the machine learning approach for automatically detecting information about attributes, like bins, shelter, seating and stop signs in pictures, would not be possible with OSM out of the box. Even though there exist several approaches for automatically detecting attributes for OSM, they are not tailored to the mobisaarWORLD usecase [13]. Utilizing the OSM crowdsourcing mechanisms instead of implementing a dedicated VGI would additionally mean, that each user of mobisaarWORLD first had to register for OSM in order to report changes. This is obviously a further obstacle to the willingness of reporters to sign up to the service. The alternative of using one central OSM account for the whole mobisaarWORLD crowd would lead to a loss of information in the history of reported tasks, which again would lead to several problems regarding data trust and worker trust. There is also no access control scheme implemented in the OSM crowdsourcing infrastructure that would satisfy the usecase of mobisaarWORLD and its purpose of managing the collection of accessibility attributes by its users. This might lead to wrong information published by users who have no or little adequate knowledge for resolving specific tasks.

One potential major drawback of mobisaarWORLD is, that its user base has to be built from scratch in contrast to the already established eco-system of OSM. This can be also seen as an advantage over OSM, since the new set up user base is a dedicated one, localized and educated for the specific task. As we have seen before, these are two essential prerequisites for the application of Linus' Law in VGI and results in better data trust.

5 Conclusion

We have described an approach for crowdsourcing accessibility information for public transport by means of a methodology that respects security, privacy and trust of participating workers. We are currently monitoring the progress in terms of number of workers and growth and size of the database. Future Work includes introducing audio and video into the database. We will also distinguish workers' reputation based on correlation between reported and accepted database entries.

References

1. Angular Security. https://angular.io/guide/security/. Accessed 22 Nov 2019
2. Arsanjani, J.J., Barron, C., Bakillah, M., Helbich, M.: Assessing the quality of OpenStreetMap contributors together with their contributions. In: Proceedings of the AGILE, pp. 14–17 (2013)
3. Campelo, C., Elízio, C., Bertolotto, M., Corcoran, P.: Volunteered Geographic Information and the Future of Geospatial Data. IGI Global (2017)
4. Feng, W., Yan, Z., Zhang, H., Zeng, K., Xiao, Y., Hou, Y.T.: A survey on security, privacy, and trust in mobile crowdsourcing. IEEE Internet Things J. **5**(4), 2971–2992 (2017)
5. OpenStreetMap Foundation: Privacy policy – OpenStreetMap foundation (2019). https://wiki.osmfoundation.org/wiki/Privacy_Policy. Accessed 31 Oct 2019
6. Goodchild, M.F., Li, L.: Assuring the quality of volunteered geographic information. Spatial Stat. **1**, 110–120 (2012)
7. Hosseini, M., Phalp, K., Taylor, J., Ali, R.: The four pillars of crowdsourcing: a reference model. In: 2014 IEEE Eighth International Conference on Research Challenges in Information Science (RCIS), pp. 1–12. IEEE (2014)
8. Howe, J.: The rise of crowdsourcing. Wired Mag. **14**(6), 1–4 (2006)
9. Krause, M., Afzali, F.M., Caton, S., Hall, M.: Is quality control pointless? In: Proceedings of the 52nd Hawaii International Conference on System Sciences (2019)
10. Jones, M., Bradley, J., Sakimura, N.: Json Web Token Specification (2015). https://tools.ietf.org/html/rfc7519/. Accessed 03 Nov 2019
11. Meier, J.C.: An analysis of quality for volunteered geographic information. Thesis and Dissertations (Comprehensive) (2015)
12. OpenStreetMap contributors: OpenStreetMap. https://www.openstreetmap.org/. Accessed 16 Oct 2019
13. OpenStreetMapWiki: Quality assurance – openstreetmap wiki (2020). https://wiki.openstreetmap.org/w/index.php?title=Quality_assurance&oldid=1952028. Accessed 23 Oct 2019
14. Rekrut, M., Tröger, J., Alexandersson, J., Bieber, D., Schwarz, K.: Is co-creation superior to user centred design? preliminary results from user interface design for inclusive public transport. In: Zhou, J., Salvendy, G. (eds.) ITAP 2018. LNCS, vol. 10926, pp. 355–365. Springer, Cham (2018). https://doi.org/10.1007/978-3-319-92034-4_27
15. Tröger, J., Alexandersson, J., Britz, J., Rekrut, M., Bieber, D., Schwarz, K.: Board games and regulars' tables — extending user centred design in the mobia project. In: Zhou, J., Salvendy, G. (eds.) ITAP 2016. LNCS, vol. 9754, pp. 129–140. Springer, Cham (2016). https://doi.org/10.1007/978-3-319-39943-0_13
16. Wikipedia contributors: Linus's law – Wikipedia, the free encyclopedia (2020). https://en.wikipedia.org/wiki/Linus'_law/. Accessed 31 Oct 2019

Design Education Regarding Products for Use by Elderly People

Takamitsu Tanaka[1(✉)], Kun Xue[2], Yunan Wang[3], YongJian Huang[2], and Yen-Yu Kang[4]

[1] Iwate University, Morioka, Japan
taktak@iwate-u.ac.jp
[2] Shandong University of Art and Design, Jinan, China
13954179079@139.com, 1009468845@qq.com
[3] Zaozhuang University, Zaozhuang, China
yunan90812@163.com
[4] Kaohsiung Normal University, Kaohsiung, Taiwan
yenyu@nknu.edu.tw

Abstract. This study considers an example of university product design education practices targeted at elderly people, whose numbers will be increasing in China in the near future. For the purposes of this paper, from January 4–8, 2019, a workshop was held at China's Shandong University of Art & Design. University students studying design in order to serve society attended the workshop, which was to give them the opportunity to think about elderly people. Twenty-nine second- and third-year students from the department participated in the workshop. The students split up into groups of four to five, and following brainstorming sessions, created idea sketches. Then, after a field trip to an actual facility for elderly people, individual students drew up final design proposals and gave presentations. Tanaka, a coauthor of this work responsible for teaching students, evaluated the presentations. Subsequently, university instructors teaching product design in China and Taiwan also performed evaluations. This paper discusses the workshop based mainly on these evaluations.

Keywords: Elderly people · Design education

1 Introduction

It is projected that people over the age of sixty-five will comprise more than 14% of the Chinese population in 2028. This paper defines "elderly people" as those aged sixty-five or over, the definition used by most countries. Further, the proportion of elderly people will rise to more than 23% of the population by 2050. Considering Chinese population figures, 318 million people will be sixty-five years of age or older in 2050. Japan, which neighbors China, had a population of approximately 127 million in 2018, including 35,570,000 people aged sixty-five or older. In other words, elderly people comprise 28% of the population of Japan. In recent years, Japanese nursing homes and facilities for the

C. Stephanidis et al. (Eds.): HCII 2020, LNCS 12426, pp. 728–736, 2020.
https://doi.org/10.1007/978-3-030-60149-2_55

elderly have begun to make improvements; however, there is a great disparity between nursing homes and facilities for the elderly in urban and rural areas. In rural areas, there is a tendency for many young people to move to urban areas for work, leaving these areas populated by the elderly only. Additionally, savings are required to use facilities for elderly people. Facilities for elderly people are also in shortage. Further, elderly people who need nursing care, such as those who have difficulty walking, receive priority for admission to facilities. Thus, in daily life, there is a demand for design that considers ease of living. Due to the above-described issue of the rise in China's elderly population, the present study carried out a workshop on design considering the elderly, which is different from the regular courses of Shandong University of Art & Design and not part of its curriculum. The university students who participated were studying product design and had reached the level of being able to express concepts and design proposals they devised through sketches and so on. Additionally, most of the students who participated had grandparents, meaning they lived near elderly people and interacted with them in the course of daily life. The workshop proceeded in the following sequence: explanation of the course, discussion among students (brainstorming), idea sketches, field trip to facility for elderly people, design proposals, and evaluations. This paper discusses mainly the above process.

2 Related Studies and the Present Study's Role

This section will discuss studies related to the process of the workshop described in this paper. Osborn's brainstorming method [1], which this paper employed on a trial basis, is a means of supporting generation of ideas used in a wide range of fields. We will also discuss examples of previous studies relating to generation of ideas for/thinking about highly innovative products. An interest in human generation of ideas/thinking developed in the 1950s, and training methods for generating ideas through analogy and association, such as Gordon's Synectics [2], have been developed. Well-known means of generating ideas from the 1960s include the KJ method of Kawakita [3] and the NM method of Nakayama [4], which developed from cultural anthropology research methods. Additionally, Ichikawa's theory of equivalent exchange is an attempt to generalize the process of human idea generation [5]. Additionally, Ueno et al. developed Robert P's attribute listing method into a method with an awareness of the fact that narrowing down the topics at hand makes it easier to generate ideas [6]. Additionally, as a means of supporting divergent thinking in design, a cross inference model study by Noguchi [7] taught neural networks multiple models for learning rule-like information between concepts and forms, then used these in alternation to perform extrapolative deduction in an attempt to support the generation of highly novel ideas. Noguchi's study suggests that forced inference is necessary in order to increase abstraction of thought and broaden the investigative space and that at such time an ability to carry out inference with goals that are to some extent predetermined rather than randomly divergent thought is necessary. However, this does not refer to the convergence stage proceeding to the divergence stage. Additionally, Tanaka proposes a design methodology using negative expression as a method of divergent thinking [8]. Furthermore, Nagai et al. research human creativity and thought based on cognitive science, analyzing the characteristics of creative thinking processes and putting forth a process for generating new concepts [9]. Based on previous studies, we believe this workshop can present hypothetical ideal methods for arts and design education regarding idea generation/thinking and generation of concepts for highly novel products we conceive of as situated at the upper reaches of idea generation. Some studies in the design field focusing on elderly people have pointed out problems with facilities for elderly people themselves. Such studies in the fields of interior design and architecture have focused on the theme of livable spaces for elderly people. However, there are studies such as Yamada et al., which examines the burden on caregivers at facilities for elderly people, and Kim et al., which examines the nursing care services provided by two facilities, a small scale many functions type home care establishment and a local coherence type place care establishment. Additionally, some studies have researched implements used by elderly people, such as chairs, from the perspective of ergonomics [10, 11]. Furthermore, few Chinese studies in the field of design have focused on elderly people, and most of those that have are surveys of conditions at current facilities for elderly people. Very few Chinese design education studies have taken up the theme of elderly people or focused upon them. By generating divergent ideas through brainstorming and taking a field trip to an actual facility for elderly people, we believe that the present study would help students understand the difference between hypothesis and reality and thus generate design ideas in a convergent fashion and propose furniture for use by elderly people.

3 Explanation to Students

The lead instructor lectured on the above-described issues of elderly people and explained the design process and schedule. Furthermore, as elderly people face differing social conditions in Japan, where the lead instructor is from, than in China, Kun XUE, Yunan WANG, and Yong Jian HUANG, coauthors of this paper, gave additional explanations. As most of the students were studying furniture design, the theme of the workshop was the design of furniture for use by elderly people.

4 Discussion Among Students (Brainstorming)

Brainstorming is a process for proposing ideas. Processes for generating ideas can be roughly separated into divergent and convergent processes. Divergent processes involve expansive generation of ideas with no limitation on the investigative space of thought. However, convergent processes involve restricting the investigate space of idea generation obtained through divergent processes with reference to design and planning restrictions, bearing in mind consistency with goals. It is believed that divergent processes and convergent processes proceed in a mutually complementary fashion. Convergent processes are indispensable in extracting ideas with practical applications to product design, but divergent processes are critical in obtaining highly novel ideas because the more ideas exceed established concepts in divergent processes, the higher the likelihood of obtaining creative results in convergent processes. Thus, groups of four to five students were assembled, brainstorming was carried out, and sketches were created as needed. Figure 1 shows the brainstorming process, and Fig. 2 shows the presentation of ideas obtained through brainstorming. Representatives of each group gave presentations on processes confirming the ideas and keywords obtained through brainstorming.

Fig. 1. Brainstorming

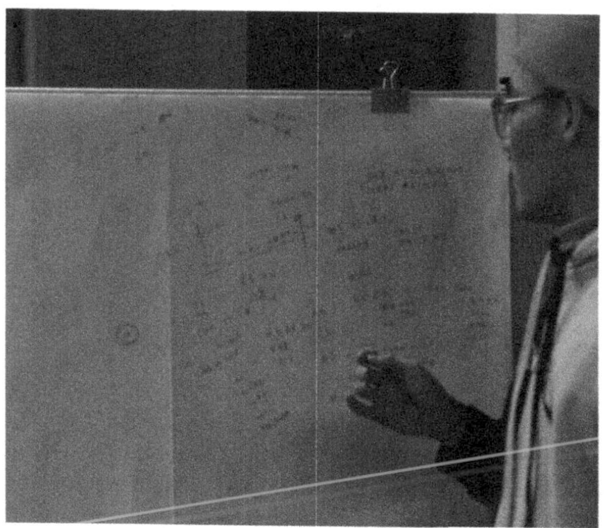

Fig. 2. Presentation of ideas

Additionally, because different groups often presented similar ideas, groups were allowed to exchange views among each other. Figure 3 shows an example of the results of brainstorming. (Because the actual text is in Chinese, the authors added the English text in red.) Based on keywords focusing on elderly people, multiple challenges in everyday life were discussed. These included, for instance, "Designs smoothing out angles for safety considerations", "The necessity of assistive tools for showers", and "Proposals for lighting devices due to the difficulty of walking in dark indoor areas at night". Many students live around elderly people; however, because it is unclear which actual challenges they face, it seems that most students used their imaginations and posited hypotheses during the brainstorming sessions. In Fig. 3, we see divergent thinking within a narrowed range of ideas; one student went on to perform further divergent thinking after proposing problems.

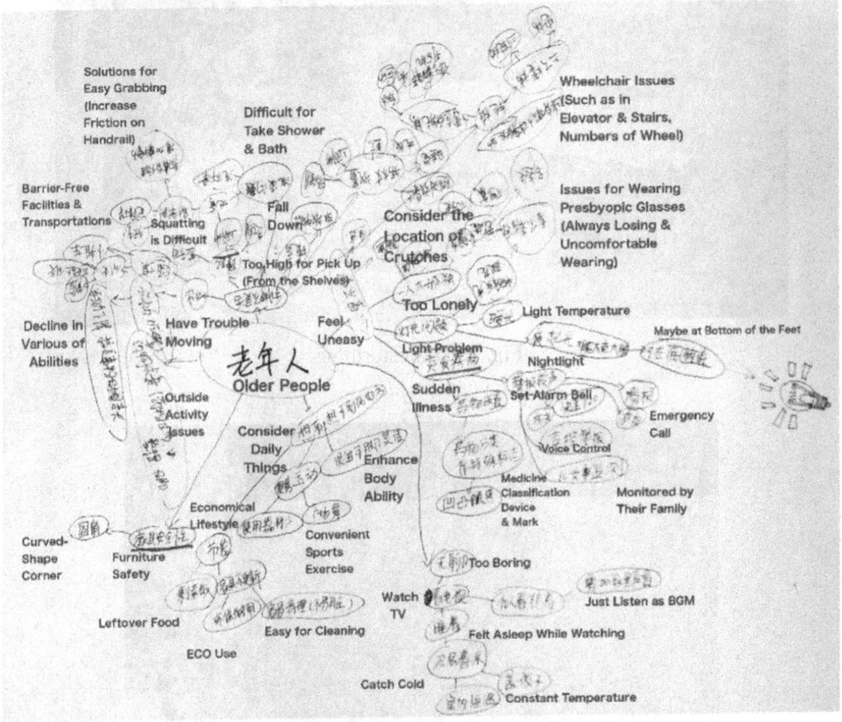

Fig. 3. Divergent thinking (Color figure online)

We conjecture that this is similar to the mind map model Tony Buzan advocates; thus, it seems that thinking developed in a radiant fashion [12]. The theme is written in the center, similar everyday keywords that come to mind are positioned at the outer circumference, and specific things and events felt to be dissatisfactory or puzzling are in turn positioned at the outer circumference of these. The descriptions of a thinking process in which reference was made to the outermost circumferential areas to generate subsequent concepts also seem to indicate that divergent thinking was used in brainstorming. Additionally, because the increase in the Chinese elderly population is a challenge that will be faced in the near future, the process by which students proposed problems in a divergent fashion and discussed their solutions itself seems to be valuable in design education.

5 Idea Sketches

In this process, individual students sketched the ideas obtained through brainstorming. Most students presented their final ideas using computer graphics; therefore, their idea sketches were extremely rough. As most of the brainstorming was done using language, students were instructed to remove ideas that could not be put into tangible form. Figure 4 is an example of a brainstorming idea sketch. Everyone at the workshop reviewed the ideas of all the students. The ideas were characterized by a focus on everyday life, such as "A functional design allowing elderly people to easily lie down in bed" and "A scheme allowing legs to be stretched out in a chair". In both cases, these ideas took shape as the imaginings of students prior to the field trip to the facility for elderly people, the subsequent step. Additionally, numerous ideas were redesigns improving upon social welfare products actually sold on the market.

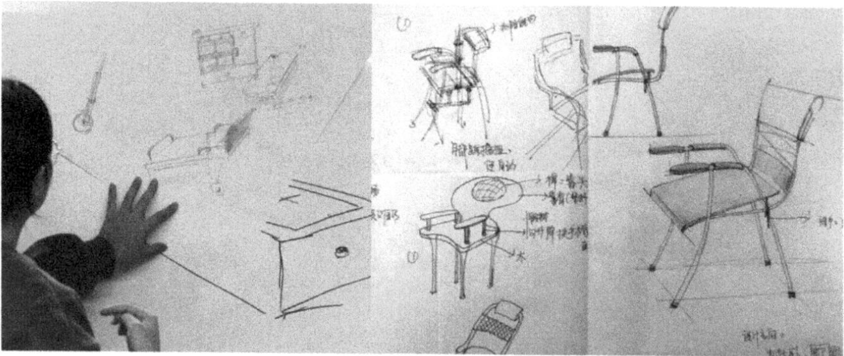

Fig. 4. An example of a brainstorming idea sketch

6 Field Trip to a Facility for Elderly People

The university received permission from the facility, and the students were taken on a field trip. This was the first such experience for most of the students, and it proved highly educational for them. Following the field trip, the students expressed opinions such as, "The elderly people I know in everyday life are members of my family, and I thought they had only minor difficulties relative to healthy people, but actually many of these elderly people had difficulty walking", and "I never imagined their living spaces would be so dirty. I felt sorry for them". On the field trip, most students made unexpected discoveries, experiencing a gap between their initial ideas and reality.

7 Creating Designs

The students ultimately produced one to two design proposals using methods such as computer graphics and summarized them on a presentation board. Figure 5 is design that widens the angle of a chair back, designed by a student after visiting the facility for elderly people and observing that many of the elderly people had back trouble. There is also a proposal for another chair matching this one allowing the elderly to stretch out their legs, demonstrating a consistent sense of design. Figure 6 is a stool installed next to a bed with a design allowing elderly people to take things out easily. Figure 7 is a design intended to avoid injury in the event that an elderly person bumps into the corner of a piece of furniture, employing a corner with a large curved surface. Figure 8 is a design for a massage chair proposed by a student after asking the residents of the facility for elderly people which features they desired.

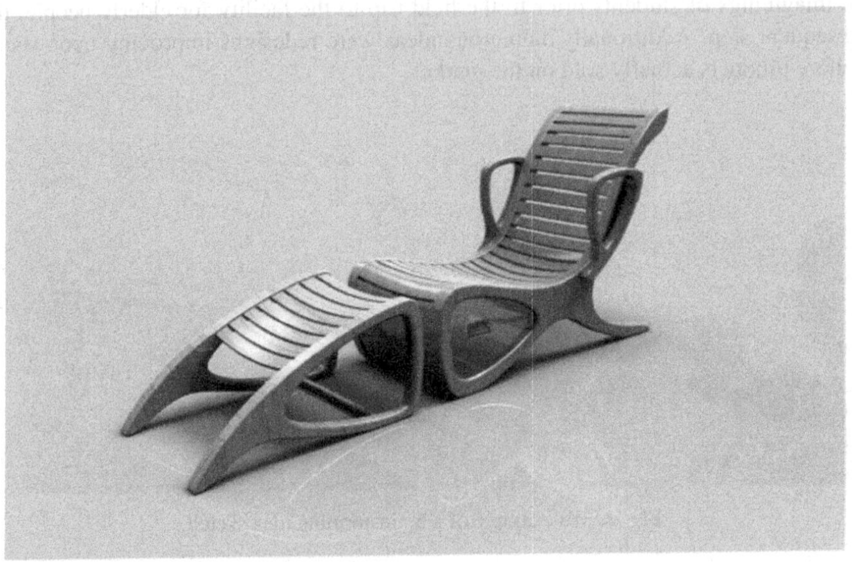

Fig. 5. Design that widens the angle of a chair back

Fig. 6. A stool design

Fig. 7. Table design

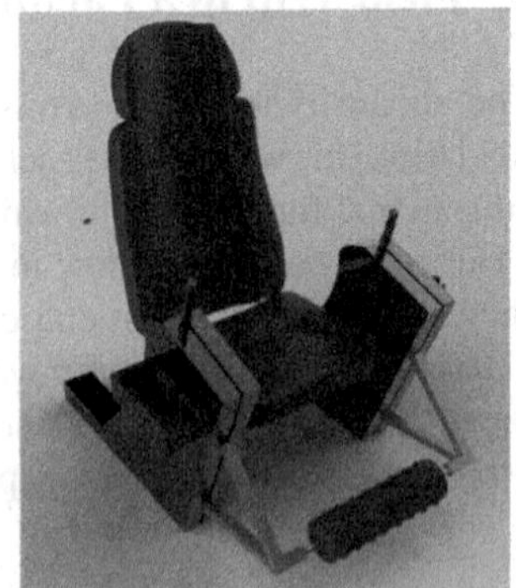

Fig. 8. Design for a massage chair

8 Evaluations

Evaluations were performed at the workshop, and at a later date, four product design experts performed additional evaluations. The experts were design instructors at Japanese, Chinese, and Taiwanese universities. The evaluations assigned one of five grades to the design proposals of twenty-nine students. It was determined that the most outstanding 10% of designs would receive an A, 20% would receive a B, 40% would receive a C, 20% would receive a D, and 10% would receive an E. The proposed designs were submitted as a PowerPoint file containing the final design resulting from the processes described in this paper, including brainstorming and the field trip to the facility for elderly people. These processes were reviewed, and an overall grade was assigned. The overall grade differed depending on which process received additional points; however, all four evaluators agreed that Fig. 9 is an excellent design. It solves a problem of elderly people and proposes a design for final form and function.

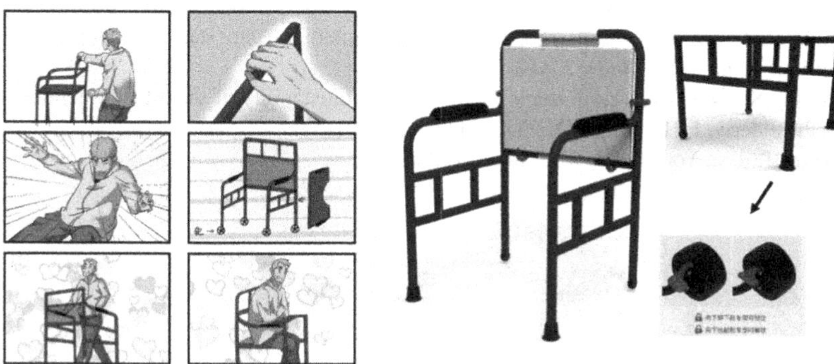

Fig. 9. An excellent design of example

9 Conclusion

We expect that in China, products for elderly people will begin to be developed in earnest. We believe that the workshop this paper discusses will prove useful in encouraging awareness of elderly people among the next generation of designers. However, in Japan, where the population is aging, real social problems are already becoming apparent, and national facilities and support systems are being instituted. Awareness at the national level is important in China as well; however, it is crucial to incorporate such ideas into education. Additionally, for students' evaluations, it is necessary to determine criteria that differ from those of design proposals in ordinary classes. Particularly, it became clear through this workshop that it is important to make students aware of the contrasts between the hypotheses generated through brainstorming and the realities they became aware of through the field trip to the facility for the elderly.

Acknowledgements. We received support from Dr. Peng JIANG.

References

1. Osborn, A.F.: Your Creative Power. Charles Scribner's Sons, New York (1953)
2. Gordon, W.J.J.: Synectics, Harper & Brothers Publishers Inc. (1961)
3. Kawakita, J.: Idea Method, Chukoshinsho (1967). (in Japanese)
4. Nakayama, M.: Everything about the NM method-Theory and practical method of idea generation (1980). (in Japanese)
5. Ichikawa, K.: Science of Creaitivity. NHK Publishing, Inc. (1970)
6. Crawford, R.P.: Techniques of Creative Thinking (1964)
7. Noguchi, H.: How do material constrains affect design creativity? In: Proceedings on 3rd Creativity & Cognition Conference, Loughborough, pp. 82–87 (1999)
8. Tanaka, T., Noguchi, H.: Study on creative design concept consideration for design concept through a denial expression method and case studies. In: Proceedings of International Design Congress-IASDE 2005, International Association of Societies of Design Research (2005)
9. Nagai, Y., Noguchi, H.: Proceedings of the 4th Conference on Creativity & Cognition, Loughborough, United Kingdom, 13–16 October 2002, pp. 118–125 (2002)
10. Kim, J., Takakubo, Y., Wada, K., Hatakeyama, Y.: A characteristic of the space use and the action of the care staff, the user judging from the ratio of the care staff in small senior citizen facilities. Bull. JSSD **66**(2), 2_1–2_8 (2019)
11. Takeshi, S., Watanabe, Y.: A study on design and adjustability of the tilt and reclining chair for the elderly. J. Hum. Life Des. (13), 437–450 (2018)
12. Buzan, T.: Use Your Head. BBC Books (1995)

A Framework for Monitoring Indoor Navigational Hazards and Safety of Elderly

Nirmalya Thakur(✉) and Chia Y. Han

Department of Electrical Engineering and Computer Science, University of Cincinnati, Cincinnati, OH 45221-0030, USA
thakurna@mail.uc.edu, han@ucmail.uc.edu

Abstract. Providing environmental and navigational safety to occupants in workplace, public venues, home and other environments is of a critical concern and has multiple applications for various end users. A framework, for monitoring movement, pose and behavior of elderly people for safe navigation in indoor environments is presented in this work. This framework, at the intersection of different disciplines has multiple functionalities. First, it provides a definition of human behavior in terms of joint point movements associated with Activities of Daily Living (ADL), while discussing two most common forms of human motions during stair navigation – upstairs and downstairs; second, it presents a two-fold approach – context-based and motion-based for accurate detection of these movements amongst other human motions associated with ADL; third, it consists of a methodology to study the Big Data associated with these movements and finally it also includes a rather comprehensive case study where the performance of multiple learning models are evaluated to identify the best learning model for development of this framework.

Keywords: Big Data · Behavior monitoring · Elderly falls · Smart homes

1 Introduction

At present there are around 962 million elderly people in the world [1] and their population is anticipated to reach upto 1 billion and even more by 2030 [2]. Elderly people face several issues like vision impairments, physical disabilities, cognitive issues, weakened memory and disorganized behavior with increasing age which limit their abilities to perform ADL. ADL may be defined as activities related to Personal Hygiene, Dressing, Eating, Maintaining Continence and Mobility, which are essential for one's sustenance. Falls while navigating environmental hazards are common in elderly people in the context of ADL. As per [3], the rate of falls in elderly has increased by 30% from 2007 to 2016 and is expected to further increase. Every 11 s, an elderly person who has experienced a fall needs to be rushed to the emergency room and in every 19 min, an elderly person dies after having experienced a fall. Annually, there are 800,000 hospitalizations, 2.8 million cases of emergency and more than 27,000 deaths in elderly from falls. In 2015 the total cost incurred to the healthcare industry for treating fall related injuries was $50 billion and this is expected to reach around $70 billion by the end of 2020 [3].

C. Stephanidis et al. (Eds.): HCII 2020, LNCS 12426, pp. 737–748, 2020.
https://doi.org/10.1007/978-3-030-60149-2_56

The causes of a fall may be broadly categorized as external and internal [4]. In this context, external relates to the environment or context parameters such as a slippery surface, stairs etc. and internal refers to factors pertaining to the individual such as low vision, cramps, chronic disorders etc. Falls have a range of impacts [4]. The effects of a fall could range from minor to major injuries and can even lead to death. These may be individual – injuries, bruises, blood clot; social life – reduced mobility leading to loneliness and social isolation; cognitive or mental – fear of moving around, loss of confidence in carrying out ADL and financial – cost of medical treatments and caregivers. In the context of falls, a "long lie" is defined as a person involuntarily lying on the ground for an hour or more after the fall [5]. "Long lie" can cause significant damage to the person's body and morale. It could also cause various medical complications, like internal bleeding, dehydration, pressure sores, rhabdomyolysis and could even lead to death. Around half of the people who have experienced a "long lie" have been found to die within the next six months [6]. According to a recent study [7], thirty percent of fallers experience a "long lie"; therefore, it represents a great threat to the long-term health of older adults.

There are many architectural features within any building [8] that may provide challenges to people with limited physical abilities. One example is stairs, which are considered the most common environmental hazard responsible for elderly falls [9] that could lead to "long lie's", so the challenge in this field is to track and monitor the movements of older adults during stair navigations so that any abnormalities in their behavior, for instance a fall, could be detected and analyzed and immediate help in the form of contacting emergency responders, caregivers, medical practitioners or through assistive robots can be provided. There have been several researches conducted in this field to monitor human behavior during navigation in living environments. However there are a number of challenges which exist in these systems which include – (1) Most of these systems are built specific to lab environments and their implementation in a real-time context is difficult because of the required infrastructures; (2) it is costly to implement these systems in the actual IoT-based living spaces, which are larger as compared to lab environments; (3) some of these systems are based on the acceleration data collected from a mobile-phone's accelerometer, which implies that a user has to carry a phone all the time; (4) a number of these systems are based on tracking human gait positions and movements which could be different for different people based on user diversity and (5) very few of the existing works have investigated the effects of indoor navigational hazards which could lead to falls during ADL. Thus, there still exists the requirement of developing a standard for human behavior monitoring in the context of indoor navigational hazards for older adults. Addressing this challenge to contribute towards Ambient Assisted Living (AAL) of elderly in the future of Internet of Things (IoT)-based living spaces serves as the main motivation for this work. This paper is organized as follows. We present an overview of the related works in this field in Sect. 2. The proposed framework is introduced and explained in Sect. 3. Section 4 discusses the results and performance characteristics of this framework. It is followed by Sect. 5 where conclusion and scope for future work are outlined.

2 Literature Review

Dai et al. [10] proposed a fall detection system which primarily used an android phone's data to detect falls. Tomkun et al. [11] developed a wearable device that could detect a fall based on motion data. This device also interfaced with a computer or a mobile phone to make emergency calls when a fall occurred. In [12], Li et al. developed a framework that could recognize various kinds of static postures as well as dynamic movements, in the context of detecting a fall. This framework was driven by accelerometer and gyroscope data collected from wearables which were then analyzed by the framework. Sabelman et al. [13] proposed Wearable Accelerometric Motion Analysis System (WAMAS) which used accelerometer data collected from wearables to perform analysis of the gait of the user. These sensors were placed on a glass to be worn by the user as well as they were placed on the waist of the user. In [14], Degen et al. developed a wearable device, SPEEDY which resembled the appearance of a watch and could be worn by a person on their wrist. This device was primarily accelerometer data driven. It also had a calling feature to make emergency calls during a fall. In [15], Chen et al. used a wireless sensor data-driven architecture to develop a fall detection system. In the work by Pister et al. [16], MEMS accelerometers were used to detect falls. The system also had the functionality to detect the location of the person using RF signals. In [17], the authors developed a health status tracking system using Zigbee technology for activity monitoring with an aim to analyze falls during different activities. Huang et al. [18] developed a wearable device built inside a fabric belt that consisted of a sensor to track the physiological health indicators of the user for detecting falls. In [19] the authors developed a fall detection system that was human behavior driven. It tracked the behavior of the user at different times and was able to detect falls which were considered as anomalies from normal behavior. Toreyin et al. [20] developed a framework that recorded and analyzed video and audio data using Hidden Markov Models to study human behavior and perform fall detection. Similarly, there have other related works in this field in the domain of human behavior analysis [21–29]. Despite the preliminary success of all these works, there exist several limitations in these systems as outlined in Sect. 1 and that is precisely why none of these works have gone on to become a standard for human behavior analysis in the context of indoor navigational hazards for detection of any anomalies, such as a fall.

3 Proposed Work

This section outlines the multiple functionalities of this framework. First, we discuss the approach based on one of our previous works [30] to model human behavior in the form of skeletal tracking and movement of joint points. The methodology to define human behavior using skeletal tracking in the form of joint point characteristics extends one of the previous works [31] in this field. It consists of the following steps:

i. Identify the atomic activities associated with the given complex activity
ii. Identify the context attributes on which these atomic activities need to be performed for successful completion of the activity
iii. Track the user's behavior to study when the complex activity started and when it ended – this includes tracking

a. when the user successfully reached the goal and
b. when it was a false start

iv. Record the most important context attribute [29] and the action or actions performed by the user on it
v. Study the user's behavior associated with performing each of the atomic activities while interacting with the context attributes:

a. Develop a methodology to represent the skeletal tracking of the user using Microsoft Kinect Sensors
b. Identify specific feature points on the skeletal tracking
c. Define these feature points according to their locations and functions
d. Analyze characteristics of these feature points – which include joint distance, joint movements, joint angle and joint rotation speed
e. Record the sequence in which the characteristics of these feature points change or influence one another

vi. Compile the sequence of the characteristics of human behavior and how they change for the complex activity.

In this context, atomic activities refer to the small actions and tasks associated with an activity. The environment variables or parameters on which these tasks are performed are known as the context attributes. The complex activity is a collection of the atomic activities and context attributes along with their characteristics [31]. Microsoft Kinect Sensors provide real-time skeletal tracking of any user and upto 20 joint points on the skeletal [32]. For defining these joint points as per the associated movements and functions, we review [32]. This definition is presented below (Fig. 1).

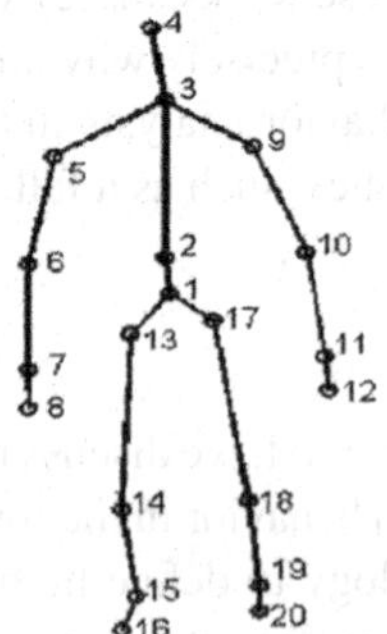

Joint	Definition	Joint	Definition
1	Center of Hip	11	Right Wrist
2	Spine	12	Right Hand
3	Center of Shoulder	13	Left Hip
4	Head	14	Left Knee
5	Left Shoulder	15	Left Ankle
6	Left Elbow	16	Left Foot
7	Left Wrist	17	Right Hip
8	Left Hand	18	Right Knee
9	Right Shoulder	19	Right Ankle
10	Right Elbow	20	Right Foot

Fig. 1. Definition of joints points on the skeletal tracking from Kinect Sensor

Prior to implementation of this framework for analyzing a complex activity, we present an example to study a specific macro-level task. For instance, if the user has to answer the phone, then in this context the most important context attribute is the phone. The behavior associated with interacting with the phone would involve bringing the phone close to the ear – this involves the distance between joint point pairs (6,4), (7,4), (8,4), (6,3), (7,3), (8,3) or (10,4), (11,4), (12,4), (10,3), (11,3), (12,3) getting less.

Such a definition is aimed at studying human motions at a fine-grain level especially during navigation in indoor environments in the context of any environmental hazards, for instance stairs, so that any anomalies in the motion, which could be caused due to a fall, can be tracked and detected for providing immediate assistance and reducing its impacts. Next, we implemented the functionality of our framework for analysis of behavioral patterns during different ADL based on this methodology to define human behavior. This consists of the following steps:

i. Develop a database consisting of definitions of different activities in the given IoT-based environment
ii. From each of these definitions – track the environment parameters that the user interfaces with
iii. Compile a list of the actions or behavioral patterns associated with interacting with these environment parameters
iv. For each environment parameter

    a. If the associated action is upstairs – study the user behavior for detection of any anomalies, for instance, a fall, from the definition of human behavior for upstairs movement
    b. If the associated action is downstairs – study the user behavior for detection of any anomalies, for instance, a fall, from the definition of human behavior for downstairs movement

v. Develop a learning model to analyze these characteristics of user interactions and user behavior during stair navigation
vi. Implement multiple learning approaches to deduce the learning approach best suited for development of this framework by analyzing their performance characteristics.

For implementing this multifunctional framework, we used an existing dataset [33] which consisted of multiple human behavioral patterns performed in an IoT environment. We developed the system consisting of all these functionalities in RapidMiner [34]. RapidMiner is a software tool that provides a framework for implementation of various kinds of learning models and data science approaches as an integrated application. An advantage of RapidMiner over other software development tools is that it provides a range of built-in functions known as 'operators' which could be customized conveniently as per the specific problem needs and integrated into an application, called 'process' in RapidMiner. For development of this framework, the free version of RapidMiner was used. We used 70% of the data as the training data and the remaining 30% was used as test data.

4 Results and Discussion

This section outlines the results obtained upon development of the framework as outlined in Sect. 3. First, we present the results for defining human behavior in the context of complex activities. Multiple complex activities from the dataset [35] were studied and a definition for each of those was developed to create a knowledgebase of human behaviors during complex activities. This definition for one of the activities 'Eating Lunch' is shown in Table 1.

Table 1. Definition for the activity 'Eating Lunch' in the form of joint-point characteristics

Atomic Activities	Context Attributes	Joint Points pairs that experience change
At1: Standing (0.08)	**Ct1**: Lights on (0.08)	No change
At2: Walking towards dining table (0.20)	**Ct2**: Dining Area (0.20)	(13,17), (14,18), (15,19), (16,20)
At3: Serving food on a plate (0.25)	**Ct3**: Food present (0.25)	(7, 11), (8,12)
At4: Washing Hand/Using Hand Sanitizer (0.20)	**Ct4**: Plate present (0.20)	(7, 11), (8,12)
At5: Sitting down (0.08)	**Ct5**: Sitting options available (0.08)	No change
At6: Starting to eat (0.19)	**Ct6**: Food quality and taste (0.19)	(6,3), (7,3), (8,3), (6,4), (7,4), (8,4) or (10,3), (11,3), (12,3), (10,4), (11,4), (12,4)

Next we developed the framework in RapidMiner using the dataset [33] as outlined in Sect. 3. This dataset consists of multiple forms of human behavior – walking, sitting, standing, laying, walking upstairs and walking downstairs during different activities performed in an IoT-based environment. These activities were performed by a total of 30 individuals in the age group of 19 to 48 years. As we are specifically interested in detecting movement related to stairs which are primarily upstairs and downstairs so while performing data preprocessing, we labelled all the other activities - walking, sitting, standing and laying as 'other motion'. Also, this dataset consisted of multiple data attributes related to the user interaction data, in the context of these motions, but as we are interested in analyzing human behavioral patterns so we selected the attributes tBodyAcc-mean()-X, tBodyAcc-mean()-Y and tBodyAcc-mean()-Z, which refer to mean of the total body acceleration in the X, Y and Z directions respectively. The system as developed in RapidMiner is shown in Fig. 2. We used the free version of RapidMiner for development of this work. Due to the limitations of the free version of RapidMiner and the steps involved for preprocessing the data, we selected a subset from this dataset for development of our framework. This subset consisted of 500 rows and in terms of the activity labels there were 153 instances of 'downstairs', 145 instances of 'upstairs' and 201 instances of 'other motion' in this subset.

The data preprocess 'operator' was used to perform the above-mentioned operations on the dataset so these various characteristics of human behavior could be studied to detect movements related to stairs. This 'operator' was also used to study the relationships of each of these attributes to the 3 activity labels – 'upstairs', 'downstairs' and 'other

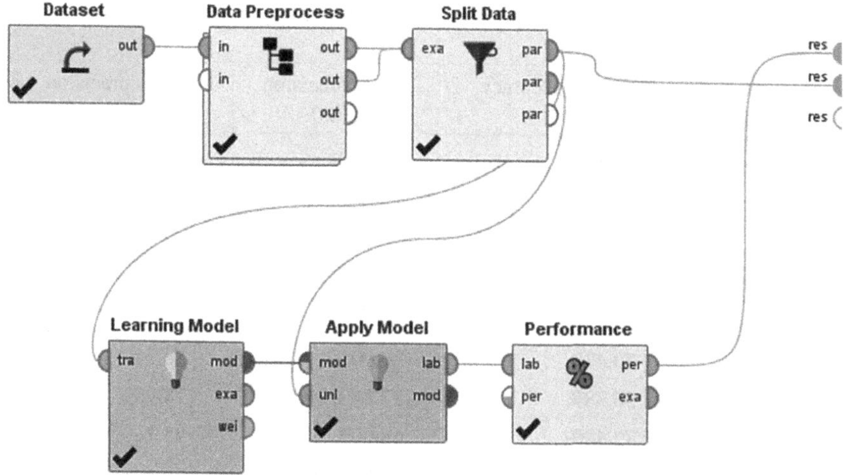

Fig. 2. The proposed framework developed in RapidMiner

motion'. This is represented in Fig. 3 in the form of a heat map. The split data 'operator' was used to split the data into training set and test set. The learning model 'operator' was used to develop a general architecture that would allow implementation of a range of learning models to conduct a study to deduce the learning model best suited for development of this framework. We implemented a range of learning models and this included - Artificial Neural Network, Decision Tree Learning, Gradient Boosted Trees, Random Forest, Naïve Bayes, KNN Classifier and Support Vector Machine. The apply model 'operator' was used to test the learning model on the test dataset and the performance 'operator' was used to evaluate the performance characteristics of the learning model in the form a confusion matrix. The performance accuracies of these learning models as studied from confusion matrices for each of the associated RapidMiner 'processes' is represented in Table 2.

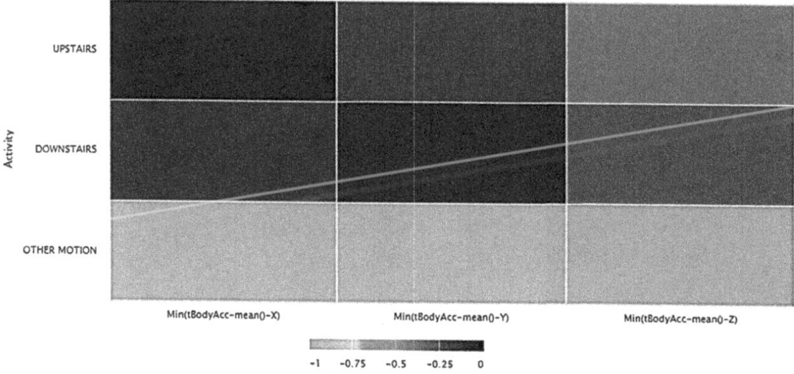

Fig. 3. Heatmap representing the variation of different data attribute values (aggregate by minimum) for the different activity labels in this dataset

Table 2. Performance accuracies of different learning methods

Learning model	Overall accuracy	Class precision (Upstairs)	Class precision (Downstairs)
Artificial Neural Network	59.73%	42.50%	52.35%
Decision Tree Learning	59.73%	50.00%	50.00%
Gradient Boosted Trees	77.85%	79.55%	90.62%
Random Forest	70.47%	80.00%	88.24%
Naïve Bayes	56.38%	37.84%	78.95%
KNN Classifier	72.48%	68.00%	85.71%
Support Vector Machine	42.95%	16.67%	41.30%

As can be observed from Table 2, Gradient Boosted Trees achieves the highest performance accuracy with overall accuracy being 77.85% with the class precision values for upstairs and downstairs being 79.55% and 90.62% respectively. Figure 4 shows the RapidMiner process that implements Gradient Boosted Trees. The performance accuracy of this process is shown in Figs. 5 and 6 via the tabular form and plot view of the confusion matrix respectively.

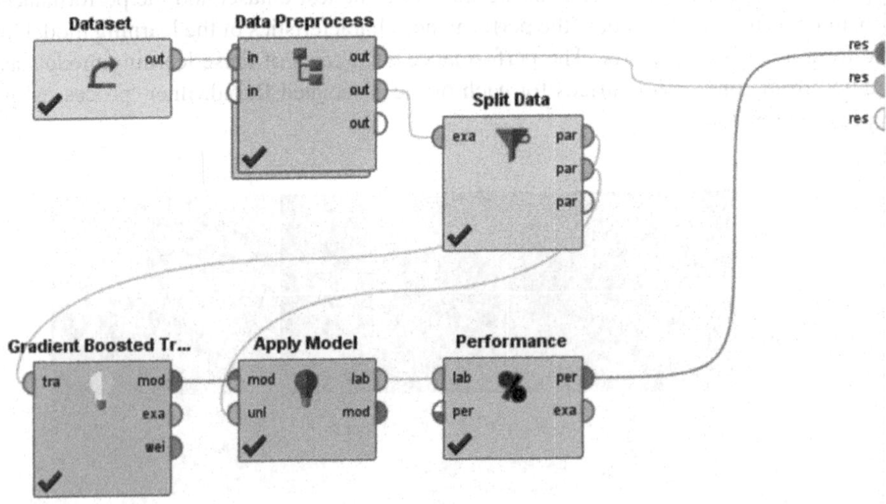

Fig. 4. The proposed framework as a RapidMiner process by using the Gradient Boosted Trees learning approach

accuracy: 77.85%

	true OTHER MOTION	true UPSTAIRS	true DOWNSTAIRS	class precision
pred. OTHER MOTION	52	7	14	71.23%
pred. UPSTAIRS	6	35	3	79.55%
pred. DOWNSTAIRS	2	1	29	90.62%
class recall	86.67%	81.40%	63.04%	

Fig. 5. Performance accuracy as a confusion matrix (tabular view) of the proposed framework as a RapidMiner process by using the Gradient Boosted Trees learning approach

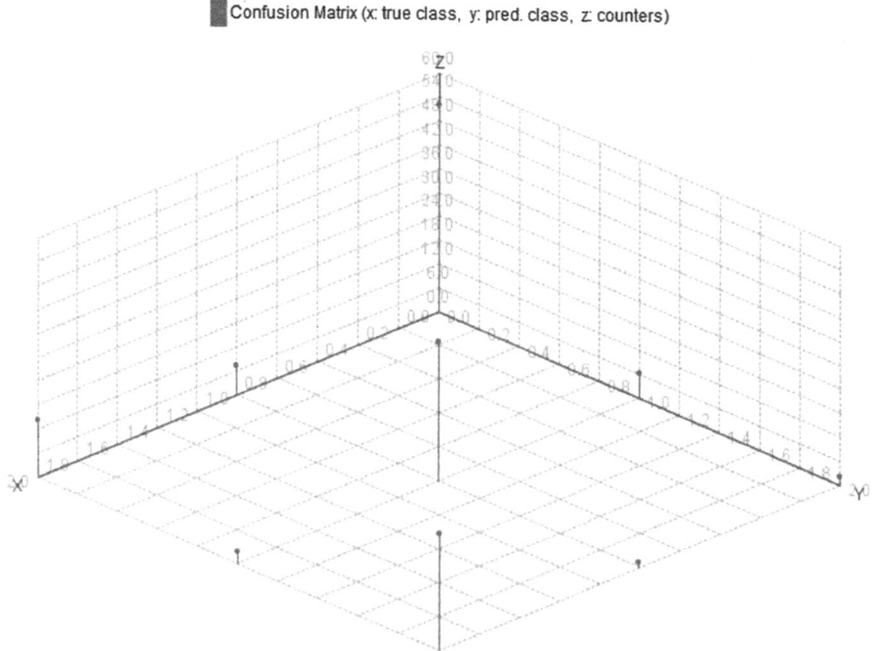

Fig. 6. Performance accuracy as a confusion matrix (plot view) of the proposed framework as a RapidMiner process by using the Gradient Boosted Trees learning approach

5 Conclusion

Falls in the context of indoor navigational hazards are very common in the elderly population. In addition to injuries and wounds, falls can also affect the personal, social, emotional and cognitive well-being of an individual which in turn affects their health, quality of life and independence in the context of carrying out ADL - which are essential for one's sustenance. Providing safety in navigation in the context of daily routine tasks is crucial for healthy aging and assisted living of the elderly population. In this paper, we propose a framework at the intersection of Activity Centric Computing, Big Data,

Machine Learning, Human Behavior Analysis and their interrelated disciplines with the aim to monitor elderly behavior during stair navigation – specifically upstairs and downstairs, as stairs are the most common form of indoor hazards that are responsible for elderly falls [9]. This framework has been tested on a dataset related to human behavior during stair navigation associated with ADL and the results are presented and discussed. A case study is also presented in the context of development of this framework where we implement different learning methods - Artificial Neural Network, Decision Tree Learning, Gradient Boosted Trees, Random Forest, Naïve Bayes, KNN Classifier and Support Vector Machine and compare their performance characteristics. After this study we arrive at the conclusion that Gradient Boosted Trees are best suited for development of this framework as they achieve an overall performance accuracy of 77.85% with the class precision values for upstairs and downstairs being 79.55% and 90.62% respectively. To the best knowledge of the authors no similar work has been done in this field yet. Future work would involve setting up an IoT-based environment and using a host of wireless and wearables to implement this framework in a real-time setting.

References

1. United Nations: 2020 Report on Ageing (2020). http://www.un.org/en/sections/issuesdepth/ageing/
2. He, W., Goodkind, D., Kowal, P.: An Aging World: 2015. International Population Reports, by United States Census Bureau (2016)
3. National Council on Aging Report.: Fall Prevention Facts. https://www.ncoa.org/news/resources-for-reporters/get-the-facts/falls-prevention-facts/
4. El-Bendary, N., Tan, Q., Pivot, F., Lam, A.: Fall detection and prevention for the elderly: a review of trends and challenges. Int. J. Smart Sens. Intell. Syst. **6**, 1230–1266 (2013)
5. Lord, S.R., Sherrington, C., Menz, H.B.: Falls in Older People: Risk Factors and Strategies for Prevention. Cambridge Univ. Press, Cambridge (2001)
6. Wild, D., Nayak, U.S., Isaacs, B.: How dangerous are falls in old people at home? Br. Med. J. (Clin. Res. Ed.) **282**, 266 (1981)
7. Jane, F., Carol, B.: Inability to get up after falling, subsequent time on floor, and summoning help: prospective cohort study in people over 90. BMJ **337**, a2227 (2008)
8. Dzambazova, T., Krygiel, E., Demchak, G.: Introducing Revit Architecture 2010 BIM for Beginners. Wiley Publishing Inc., Indianapolis (2009). ISBN: 978-0-470-47355-9
9. La Grow, S.J., Robertson, M.C., Campbell, A.J., Clarke, G.A., Kerse, N.M.: Reducing hazard related falls in people 75 years and older with significant visual impairment: how did a successful program work? Inj. Prevent. **12**(5), 296–301 (2006)
10. Dai, J., Bai, X., Yang, Z., Shen, Z., Xuan, D.: PerFallD: a pervasive fall detection system using mobile phones. In: Proceedings of the 8th IEEE International Conference on Pervasive Computing and Communications Workshops (PERCOM Workshops), Germany, pp. 292–297 (2010)
11. Tomkun, J., Nguyen, B.: Design of a fall detection and prevention system for the elderly. In: EE 4BI6 Electrical Engineering Biomedical Capstones, Department of Electrical and Computer Engineering, McMaster University, Hamilton, Ontario, Canada (2010)
12. Li, Q., Stankovic, J.A., Hanson, M.A., Barth, A.T., Lach, J., Zhou, G.: Accurate, fast fall detection using gyroscopes and accelerometer derived posture information. In: Proceedings of the 6th International Workshop on Wearable and Implantable Body Sensor Networks, (BSN 2009), Berkeley, CA, USA, pp. 138–143 (2009)

13. Sabelman, E.E., Schwandt, D., Jaffe, D.L.: The WAMAS wearable accelerometric motion analysis system: combining technology development and research in human mobility. In: Proceedings of the Conference on Intellectual Property in the VA: Changes, Challenges and Collaborations, Arlington, VA, United States (2001)
14. Degen, T., Jaeckel, H.: SPEEDY: a fall detector in a WristWatch. In: Proceedings of the 7th IEEE International Symposium on Wearable Computing (ISWC 2003), White Plains, NY, USA, pp. 184–189 (2003)
15. Chen, J., Kwong, K., Chang, D., Luk, J., Bajcsy, R.: Wearable sensors for reliable fall detection. In: Proceedings of the 27th Annual International Conference of the Engineering in Medicine and Biology Society (IEEE-EMBS 2005), pp. 3551–3554 (2005)
16. Pister, K., Hohlt, B., Jeong, J., Doherty, L., Vainio, J.P.: Ivy - A Sensor Network Infrastructure for the Berkeley College of Engineering. University of California (2003)
17. Suryadevara, N.K., Gaddam, A., Rayudu, R.K., Mukhopadhyay, S.C.: Wireless sensors network based safe home to care elderly people: behaviour detection. In: Proceedings of Eurosensors XXV, Elsevier Procedia Engineering, vol. 25, pp. 96–99 (2011)
18. Huang, Y.M., Hsieh, M.Y., Chao, H.C., Hung, S.H., Park, J.H: Pervasive, secure access to a hierarchical sensor-based healthcare monitoring architecture in wireless heterogeneous networks. IEEE J. Sel. Areas Commun. **27**(4), 400–411 (2009)
19. Lai, C.F., Huang, Y.M., Park, J.H., Chao, H.C.: Adaptive body posture analysis for elderly-falling detection with multisensors. IEEE Intell. Syst. **25**(2), 20–30 (2010)
20. Toreyin, B.U., Dedeoglu, Y., Cetin, A.E.: HMM based falling person detection using both audio and video. In: Proceedings of the 14th IEEE Signal Processing and Communications Applications, Antalya, Turkey, pp. 1–4 (2006)
21. Thakur, N., Han, Chia Y.: An improved approach for complex activity recognition in smart homes. In: Peng, X., Ampatzoglou, A., Bhowmik, T. (eds.) ICSR 2019. LNCS, vol. 11602, pp. 220–231. Springer, Cham (2019). https://doi.org/10.1007/978-3-030-22888-0_15
22. Thakur, N., Han, C.Y.: Framework for a personalized intelligent assistant to elderly people for activities of daily living. Int. J. Recent Trends Hum. Comput. Interact. (IJHCI) **9**(1), 1–22 (2019)
23. Thakur, N., Han, C.Y.: Framework for an intelligent affect aware smart home environment for elderly people. Int. J. Recent Trends Hum. Comput. Interact. (IJHCI) **9**(1), 23–43 (2019)
24. Thakur, N., Han, C.Y.: A context-driven complex activity framework for smart home. In: Proceedings of the 9th Annual Information Technology, Electronics and Mobile Communication Conference (IEMCON), Vancouver, Canada (2018)
25. Thakur, N., Han, C.Y.: A hierarchical model for analyzing user experiences in affect aware systems. In: Proceedings of the 9th Annual Information Technology, Electronics and Mobile Communication Conference (IEMCON), Vancouver, Canada (2018)
26. Thakur, N., Han, C.Y.: An approach to analyze the social acceptance of virtual assistants by elderly people. In: Proceedings of the 8th International Conference on the Internet of Things (IoT), Santa Barbara, California (2018)
27. Thakur, N., Han, C.Y.: Methodology for forecasting user experience for smart and assisted living in affect aware systems. In: Proceedings of the 8th International Conference on the Internet of Things (IoT), Santa Barbara, California (2018)
28. Thakur, N., Han, C.Y.: An activity analysis model for enhancing user experiences in affect aware systems. In: Proceedings of the IEEE 5G World Forum Conference (IEEE 5GWF) 2018, Santa Clara, California (2018)
29. Thakur, N., Han, C.Y.: A complex activity based emotion recognition algorithm for affect aware systems. In: Proceedings of IEEE 8th Annual Computing and Communication Workshop and Conference (IEEE CCWC), Las Vegas (2018)

30. Thakur, N., Han, C.Y.: Towards a language for defining human behavior for complex activities. In: Proceedings of the 3rd International Conference on Human Interaction and Emerging Technologies (IHIET 2020), Paris, France (2020)
31. Saguna, S., Zaslavsky, A., Chakraborty, D.: Complex activity recognition using context-driven activity theory and activity signatures. ACM Trans. Comput. Hum. Interact. **20**(6) (2013). Article 32
32. Chakraborty, C., Han, C.Y., Zhou, X., Wee, W.G.: A context driven human activity recognition framework. In: Proceedings of the International Conference on Health Informatics and Medical Systems, pp. 96–102 (2016)
33. Anguita, D., Ghio, A., Oneto, L., Parra, X., Reyes-Ortiz, J. L.: A public domain dataset for human activity recognition using smartphones. In: 21st European Symposium on Artificial Neural Networks, Computational Intelligence and Machine Learning, ESANN 2013, Bruges, Belgium (2013)
34. Ritthoff, O., Klinkenberg, R., Fischer, S., Mierswa, I., Felske, S.: YALE: Yet Another Learning Environment (2001). https://doi.org/10.17877/de290r-15309
35. Ordóñez, F.J., de Toledo, P., Sanchis, A.: Activity recognition using hybrid generative/discriminative models on home environments using binary sensors. Sensors **13**, 5460–5477 (2013)

Perceived Self-efficacy in Parkinson's Disease Through Mobile Health Monitoring

Sabine Theis[1(✉)], Dajana Schäfer[2], Christina Haubrich[3], Christopher Brandl[1], Matthias Wille[1], Sonja A. Kotz[2], Verena Nitsch[1], and Alexander Mertens[1]

[1] Chair and Institute of Industrial Engineering and Ergonomics, RWTH Aachen University, Eilfschornsteistraße 18, 52062 Aachen, Germany
s.theis@iaw.rwth-aachen.de

[2] Faculty of Psychology and Neuroscience, Maastricht University, Universiteitssingel 40, 6229 Maastricht, The Netherlands

[3] Center for Translational and Clinical Research Aachen (CTC-A), Uniklinik RWTH Aachen, Pauwelsstraße 30, 52074 Aachen, Germany

Abstract. Parkinson's disease (PD) is one of the most common neurodegenerative diseases. The non-specific symptoms lead to a diagnosis years after the actual onset of the disease. However, the earlier a diagnosis can be made, the more effective therapies are. Here we present and evaluate a smartphone app prototype supporting an early diagnosis with patients ($N = 20$). Since self-efficacy is decisive for the patient's handling of the disease, the mobile diagnostic app should optimally support a patients' self-efficacy. In this regard, a mixed-methods study revealed significant negative relationships of depression (BDI-FS) and technical competence belief ($\rho = 0.46$, $p < 0.05$) and technical commitment ($\rho = 0.48$, $p < 0.05$). Qualitative results revealed that PD patients confirm a PD diagnosis app as enriching their daily lives and imagined that the app could have an impact on their self-efficacy. Patients believed that the awareness and knowledge about the disease enhances their self-efficacy and reduce emotionally charged uncertainty as well as to let them regain a sense of control through active self-management.

Keywords: Parkinson's disease · Self-efficacy · eHealth · Health-app · Mixed methods · Affective states

1 Introduction

Parkinson's disease (PD) is the second most common neurodegenerative disease after Alzheimer's disease with around 6.1 million people suffering from it [15]. At the time of diagnosis, most patients are around 60 years old, while in five to ten percent of patients, the disease is already noticeable between 20 and 40 years of age but often unrecognized. Many early symptoms are not necessarily associated with PD. Therefore, a definitive diagnosis tends to occur relatively late in the neurodegenerative disease process. In fact, PD actually starts many years before cardinal symptoms occur. Cardinal symptoms include slowed movement (bradykinesia), resting tremor, muscle stiffness (rigor), immobility (akinesia), and postural instability [33]. Despite the validated diagnostic criteria,

C. Stephanidis et al. (Eds.): HCII 2020, LNCS 12426, pp. 749–762, 2020.
https://doi.org/10.1007/978-3-030-60149-2_57

patients are often misdiagnosed [37]. Consequently, the main aim of the PCompanion project was to develop a mobile, patient-oriented screening and monitoring system for the early diagnosis and management of PD. Such a tool should benefit the reliability of the diagnosis, the treatment quality, the prognosis, and above all the PD patients' quality of life. User-centered development processes ensure the best possible use of a mobile monitoring app for patients. Here, the mechanisms of action between humans and technical systems are examined and harmonized early and iteratively.

An important human factor in dealing with serious neurodegenerative diseases such as Parkinson's disease is the so-called *self-efficacy*. People who believe that they can cope with new or difficult situations based on their own abilities are highly self-efficient. They expect to act successfully in order to reach desired goals [1]. The psychologist Albert Bandura first described the concept of self-efficacy in 1977. He explained that at the core of self-efficacy lies in the expectations people have of their own control and handling of situations and how they can influence them. These expectations affect both the kick-off and persistence of their coping behavior [1, 2]. This means dependent on how strong people believe in their own abilities, they deal differently with a difficult situation. They either show approaching or avoiding behavior [24, 32]. According to Bandura there are four main sources that shape a persons' self-efficacy: (1) Enactive mastery experiences as the most influential source. They describe situations in which people successfully handle obstacles or achieve a goal. (2) Vicarious experiences, which are experiences in which people observe role models that they identify with and then transfer, observed success to their own probability of success. (3) Verbal persuasion, which stands for encouragement and feedback from other people. (4) Physiological and affective states as the assessment of one's own capability also depends on sensations. Another source of influence is thus the assessment of physiological and emotional states in challenging situations [2].

Self-efficacy also shows strong positive relationships with other psychological constructs such as self-esteem, neuroticism, and control [20]. Of further note are significant negative relationships with mental illnesses such as depression and anxiety [4, 31]. Additionally, related measures such as affective states and health-related quality of life (HRQoL) seem to relate to self-efficacy [9]. Thus, not surprisingly, self-efficacy has been considered in the context of several chronic diseases such as cancer, cardiovascular disease or PD, which we here focus on [4, 6, 18, 22, 29]. The effect of self-efficacy has been shown to play a relevant role in the self-management of Parkinson's disease and the quality of care [10, 12, 34]. Researchers such as Mulligan et al. (2011) have already approached the topic of self-management in PD. They describe that PD patients regardself-management programs such as seminars as enhancing self-efficacy and a useful intervention to improve their everyday life. In a recent review Linares-del Rey et al. (2019) reported and evaluates several studies on the use of health-apps for PD patients. Although the authors considered many apps as useful, methodological limitations made it questionable whether the apps truly offer any benefits [23]. Therefore, the focus on an iterative process to determine the user requirements as well as considering their evaluation and experience working with the health-app is very important. Furthermore, emphasizing on how improved self-efficacy could result in better HRQoL by rebuilding patients' belief that they handle their disease better is important. Therefore, the aim of the here presented project was to tackle these issues by means of a prototype of a newly developed mobile health-app named Parkinson Companion (PCompanion). Patients of German Parkinson self-help organizations, physicians, and caregivers took part in the iterative process of the PCompanion development. Central to the current study were patient-meetings to evaluate the first prototype of the Parkinson monitoring app. More specifically, the present study aimed to develop general implications and design recommendations with special regard to self-efficacy for managing PD. To understand how the application might benefit PD patients' self-efficacy, one first needs to consider influential variables such as technical commitment. Even more older adults use mobile technology [25, 35] there is still a fraction that does not use this technology. On the one hand, not using mobile technology may result from not accepting them as useful or too complicated to use [11]. On the other hand, non-use may also result from low technically-related self-efficacy or lack of experience in dealing with this technology [14]. Furthermore, differences in age, gender, level of education, and affective and depressive states have to be taken into account when investigating and developing health-related technical devices [9, 13]. On basis of these facts the central research questions (RQ) of this study were:

RQ 1: How do PD patients feel about the app's prototype, the properties of the app, and what would have to be developed to achieve positive influence on self-efficacy?
RQ 2: What are the relationships between self-efficacy and other factors such as depression, affect, and technical commitment?

2 Method

2.1 Monitoring System

The monitoring system consists of a smartphone diary app, a sensor device, and a web-platform. An electronic health file system based on the Elektronische Fallakte (EFA), stores diary and sensor data to later train machine-learning algorithms that identify REM-sleep behavior disorder (RBD) and predict diagnostic probabilities. The EFA ensures German data protection requirements. The clickable prototype of the smartphone diary app was created using the Software Balsamiq Mockups 3. Figure 1 illustrates the four main sections of the app and their underlying functions. In addition to the diary app, the optional sensor system as shown in Fig. 2 records sleep and vegetative functions. A ten-channel device monitors respiratory pressure, snoring, blood oxygen (SpO^2), pulse rate, body posture, activity (sleep/wake determination), continuous positive airway pressure, bi-level positive airway, pressure, periodic limb movement, electrocardiography, electroencephalography, electrooculography, and electromyography. Bluetooth then transfers data in real time to the web platform.

2.2 Questionnaires

A self-constructed sociodemographic and health-related questionnaire based on Hoffmeyer-Zlotnik and Warner's sociodemographic questionnaire modules for comparative social surveys was used [19]. Typical variables are gender, age, and education

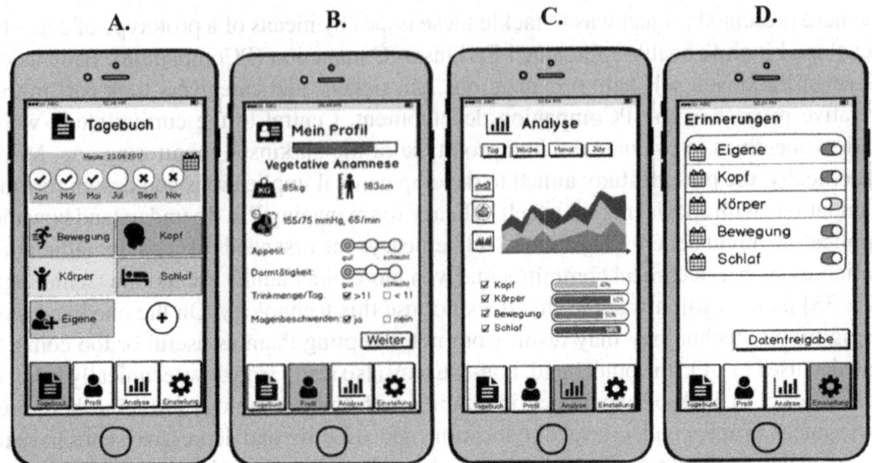

Fig. 1. **A.** Diary function to fill in medical questionnaires based on the four main symptoms of PD. **B.** Profile function to offer the user insight into relevant personal health information that is stored in their electronic case file. **C.** Analysis function to inform the user about the symptom progression over different periods derived from the diary entries. **D.** Setting function to allow the user to set reminders for filling in the diary or taking medication and to adjust data sharing with their MDs.

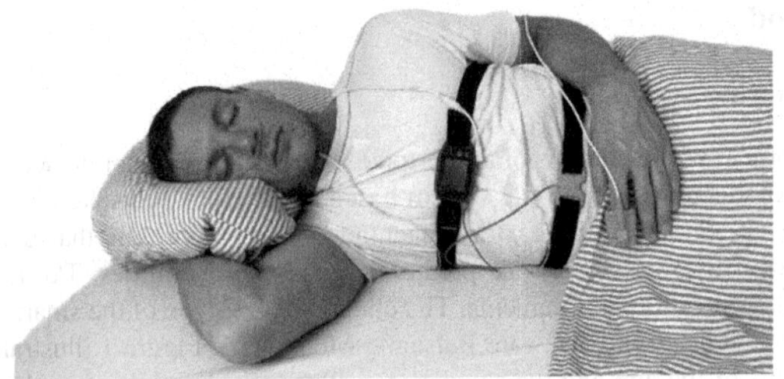

Fig. 2. Sleep and vegetative sensors.

but also health-related variables such as disease duration and medication intake. This questionnaire supports better classification of the qualitative data.

The PANAS measures both transient positive affective (PA) and negative affective (NA) states [8, 36]. The questionnaire consists of 20 adjectives that describe different sensations and feelings. Each of these 20 items can be answered on a 5-step Likert scale where one indicates "not at all" and 5 "extremely". For each affect dimension (PA and NA) a mean value is calculated. Higher scores for PA or NA represent a greater degree of positive or negative affect at the time of measurement, respectively. This test checks for possible influences of the affective state on the results.

The BDI-FS is a short version of the Beck Depression Inventory II, which screens for depression [5, 21]. The questionnaire consists of seven items with answers of four statements that best describes both the patients' current situation as well as that of two weeks ago. Total scores of 0-3 indicate minimal depression, scores of 4-6 mild depression, scores of 7-9 moderate depression, and scores of 10-21 severe depression. Given that there is a relationship between depression and self-efficacy, we included this test to check for possible influences.

The SES6G is the German version of the self-efficacy scale to manage chronic disease [17, 30]. The scale consists of six items with a 10-step Likert scale ranging from one ("not at all confident") to 10 ("totally confident"). A higher mean value of given answers represents higher self-efficacy in dealing with chronic disease. This scale is included to test the patients' self-efficacy in dealing with their disease.

Technology Commitment (T-Comm) is a short scale measuring someone's readiness to use technology [28]. The scale consists of 12 items with a 5-step Likert scale where one means "not true at all" and 5 "completely true". The scale is composed of three different facets of technology commitment. These include technology acceptance (T-A), technology competence belief (T-Comp), and technology control belief (T-Con). A total score is the sum of all item values but also for one scale or dimension. This scale was included to check whether there are any age differences or relationships to other outcomes.

2.3 Participants

Advertisement in clinics, visits of the local Parkinson sports group, as well as e-mails distributed by the local Parkinson self-help group leaders or advertisements in hospitals facilitated the recruitment of participants. A sample of 20 participants (14 females, 6 males) was included in the analysis (see Table 1). The mean age of the sample was 64 years, the youngest participant was 37 and the oldest 82 years old (SD = 12.1). The average duration of PD was 6.75 years with a minimum of one year and a maximum of 20 years (SD = 5.3). The majority of the participants had vocational training (35%). Only two participants had a lower secondary school education (10%) and three a secondary school education (15%). Four participants had a high school diploma (20%) and another four a university degree (20%). Furthermore, the majority of the participants already used a computer (85%), a smartphone (65%), and/or a tablet PC (60%).

2.4 Procedure

The participants had a choice whether they wanted to use university facilities or do the study at home. Before starting the testing procedure, the participants had to read an information letter and sign an informed consent form. The four-step test procedure lasted approximately one and a half hours. First, the participants filled in questionnaires. Second, the interviewer presented the PCompanion application explaining all attributes and functions. The interviewer answered questions on behalf of the participants. Then the participant interacted with the prototype before the semi-structured interview conducted with the help of an interview outline (see Table 2). Interviews were in German and recorded by a dictation machine, lasting 45 min on average. After filling in the remaining

Table 1. Participant profiles

ID	Age	Gender	Education	Time since diagnosis
01	69	Female	Secondary school	13 yr.
02	79	Male	Vocational training	5 yr.
03	61	Female	Vocational training	10 yr.
04	71	Female	Secondary school	18 yr.
05	82	Female	Lower secondary school	20 yr.
06	75	Female	Secondary school	5 yr.
07	67	Female	University	2 yr.
08	48	Male	High school	4 yr.
09	65	Female	University	2 yr.
10	79	Female	Vocational training	8 yr.
11	76	Male	Lower secondary school	4 yr.
12	67	Female	Vocational training	10 yr.
13	53	Male	University	6 yr.
14	37	Female	High school	2 yr.
15	51	Female	High school	5 yr.
16	55	Female	University	3 yr.
17	74	Male	High school	6 yr.
18	52	Female	Vocational training	1 yr.
19	55	Female	Vocational training	2 yr.
20	64	Male	Vocational training	9 yr.

questionnaires, participants received a monetary compensation of 20 euros. The Ethics Commission at the Medical Faculty of the RWTH Aachen approved the study with the internal file number "EK 042/18".

Table 2. Questions of the semi-structured questionnaire

No.	Question
1	How would you rate the app as a potential enrichment for your everyday life?
2	Do you think that the app could give you the feeling of having more influence on your personal situation and more confidence to manage it? How so?
3	What do you think are influential factors that would make a patient use an app like this?
4	What does quality of life mean to you? How would you define it?

2.5 Data Analysis

Theoretical thematic analysis inspired by Braun and Clarke's 6-step recursive process analyzed the qualitative interview data. The main advantages of thematic analysis lie in its flexibility, usefulness in working within a user-centered research design, quick learnability, and easy access to researchers who are new to qualitative research [7]. Transcripts were analyzed thematically. The thematic analysis is characterized by an essentialist, analyst-driven and semantic approach, which means that the process of coding was done in relation to the research questions, pre-researched concepts of self-efficacy and thus with regard to particular areas of interest. A progression from a semantic level to a level of interpretation gave rise to broader meanings and implications. MAXQDA software coded and analyzed the data. IBM SPSS V25 served the quantitative data analysis. Initially, the Shapiro-Wilk test checked all variables derived from the questionnaires for normal distribution. Bivariate correlation analysis then followed a descriptive one. Spearman's rho addressed the normally distributed variables while Pearson's correlation coefficient targeted not-normally distributed data [16].

3 Results

The order of the results corresponds to the order of the two research questions. Part 1 reports the participants' impression of the PCompanion app and their thoughts on how its use might have an influence on their self-efficacy. Part 2 reveals the quantitative results of the bivariate correlation analysis between questionnaire data.

3.1 Relation Between Self-efficacy and App Usage

The majority of the sample showed a positive reaction to the app's prototype and categorized it as a possible enrichment to their lives. The rest of the participants were either not sure about it or did not currently see an enrichment in it (see Fig. 3). With regard to self-efficacy and the app's potential of having a positive influence on it, three main themes were generated from the interview data which are as follows: 1. Limited potential, 2. Knowledge enhancement, and 3. Influence, structure & decision support.

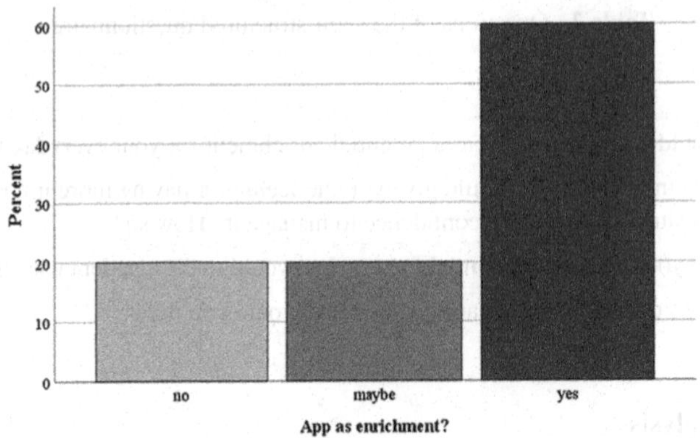

Fig. 3. Participants' considering the PCompanion app an enrichment for their daily lives.

4 Limited Potential

Although some participants rated the app as an enrichment for their daily lives, they were insecure about how much it would influence their self-efficacy. One reason for this was the hypothetical character of a click-prototype:

> *"I cannot say that. I would have to try that."* (ID04)

> *"Yes, you would have to try that out, so to what extent anything changes at all."* (ID06)

Others simply did not see any or only a limited potential either because the app would only be a nice add-on to their current way of disease management or because they could not imagine any direct influence of app use on self-efficacy:

> *"It wouldn't affect me. It would affect me somewhere... I would simply say, in my own data collection of information, which would at best support me."* (ID11)

> *"That's basically when I get something right back, then I can say that helped. However, assuming that it is so distant that you have evaluated it, and then you have taken the right action, a lot of time has passed. [...] And what did it do? Nothing. Because there is no direct answer."* (ID13)

Some participants even saw a danger in the use of it, because they thought it was likely that one would get too involved with the disease:

> *"The danger of being too busy with it and being a little preoccupied. [...] The patients see what's on the scale and think, 'oh, it's gotten so bad already. It used to be like that and now it is like that'."* (ID01)

5 Knowledge Enhancement

Benefit. One argument was that the app's potential to enhance the management of PD and one's own influence, would only be possible if the use of the app also fulfilled an added value:

> *"If I had the feeling it made sense what I was doing. In addition, it makes sense to me if I can make it out of a social aspect or if I personally derive benefit from it. [...] I have to find some benefit in it. This means that the analysis results should offer me some-thing that I would not have come up with myself. If I recognized it then [...] it would probably be that way that you get a little bit of the feeling that you are still managing something here."* (ID08)

Overview of Symptoms & the Course of PD. Many participants found it particularly helpful to gain an insight or an overview of the course of symptoms, as it could improve their understanding of their disease and possible influences:

> *"[...] always at 11 o'clock I feel bad or always in the night at 2 o'clock I am awake. So, you can check it very well over a few days or weeks and then you can show it to the doctor."* (ID18)

> *"I think it's good that you can see the course, a bit like how that works. And then I can judge that better myself and maybe you can even see for yourself what has done you some good."* (ID15)

Visual expressiveness & reflection. Several participants considered it helpful that the app and the insight into their health data would offer them more transparency and thus a clearer estimation of their health status.

> *"[...] and if I now have such an idea of 'oh look, that's black on white', that has a different power than what creeps around in my head. If you see that, then of course it can unfold a completely different power. So, I imagine it to be very helpful."* (ID16)

In addition, some participants saw that the app could motivate them to take time for reflection at the end of the day and thus maybe offer them some relief:

> *"Yes, simply that when I have typed it in, I have it somehow off my chest [...] I find it important that I have documented it and can also show it to the doctor."* (ID19)

5.1 Influence, Structure and Decision Support

Some participants also reported that they believed that the app could strengthen their influence on disease management.

> *"I just feel good when I think I just did my part of the job."* (ID15)

In addition, the use of the app could also add more structure to the everyday life of the participants.

> *"I work in a very structured way and I need that, and I think that's very important."* (ID07)

Finally, a better understanding of the data could help them make better decisions and support them in their actions.

> *"The overview is there... that if I also have a doctor who works together with me in this direction, that you can really approach it in a structured way and say: 'we have to intervene a bit more at the right spots'."*(ID18)

Influence on Self-Efficacy

Bivariate correlation analysis revealed several significant relationships between questionnaire data (see Table 3). Significant negative relationships were found between depression score (BDI-FS) and self-efficacy for managing a chronic disease (SES6G), $\rho = 0.68$, $p < 0.01$, between BDI-FS and technical competence belief, $\rho = 0.46$, $p < 0.05$, between BDI-FS and technical commitment (T-Comm), $\rho = 0.48$, $p < 0.05$, and as expected between BDI-FS and positive affect, $\rho = 0.48$, $p < 0.05$. Moreover, there was a significant positive relationship between SES6G and positive affect, $\rho = 0.45$, $p < 0.05$. In addition, we also found a significant positive relationship between education and technical acceptance (T-A), $\rho = 0.49$, $p < 0.05$, and between education and technical commitment, $\rho = 0.46$, $p < 0.05$. Interestingly, we did not find any significant relationship between age or gender and the other questionnaire outcomes (technical commitment, PANAS, etc.). However, there were significant relationships between age and other sociodemographic variables such as education (see Table 3. for more detail).

Table 3. Correlations Spearman's rho

	1.	2.	3.	4.	5.	6.	7.	8.	9.	10.
1. Age	–									
2. Gender	0.06	–								
3. Education	0.58^{**}	0.07	–							
4. Duration	0.48^{*}	0.03	0.51^{*}	–						
5. BDI-FS	0.02	0.07	0.17	0.24	–					
6. T-A	0.21	0.19	0.49^{*}	0.01	0.35	–				
7. T-Comp	0.33	0.05	0.28	0.03	0.46^{*}	0.63^{**}	–			
8. T-Con	0.11	0.19	0.16	0.07	0.28	0.57^{**}	0.23	–		
9. T-Comm	0.25	0.07	0.46^{*}	0.03	0.48^{*}	0.90^{**}	0.85^{**}	0.56^{**}	–	
10. SES6G	0.14	0.35	0.14	0.19	0.68^{**}	0.19	0.24	0.21	0.27	–
11. PA	0.16	0.40	0.02	0.04	0.48^{*}	0.24	0.22	0.04	0.23	0.45^{*}

6 Discussion

The current study investigated self-efficacy in Parkinson's patients and the possible influence of PCompanion Health app use on it. In addition, factors such as depression, technical commitment, and age that were previously reported to show relationships with self-efficacy and app-use were considered.

Concerning RQ 1, the majority of the participants reported a positive impression of the current prototype. Most participants believed that using the app would enrich their daily lives and that they were interested in trying out the final product as soon as it is available. Furthermore, we established three main themes that describe the participants' view on the PCompanion prototype and its' potential to have an enhancing effect on self-efficacy. In general, relatively few statements concerned this matter. This is most likely due to the hypothetical nature of the question itself. Still, some participants immediately expressed that they cannot imagine that the app has the potential to enhance self-efficacy. Even if this argument related to health-apps in general. Moreover, some participants also worried that one might get too preoccupied with PD. Altogether, participants suggested that although for some the PCompanion might be an enrichment, this would not necessarily be due to an increase in self-efficacy but rather due to simple increase in knowledge. Interestingly, the matter of knowledge enhancement was the top argument for most participants that considered PCompanion-use as a potential self-efficacy enhancement. More precisely, they thought that this could be achieved through better insight into their personal health-status and course through the analysis function. Thus, it would improve their awareness and estimation of their illness and thereby reduce uncertainty and emotional stress. This is consistent with the findings of Mulligan et al. (2011) where PD patients emphasized that knowledge about their disease is empowering them and allows for better decision making. In addition to knowledge enhancement, some participants also considered the PCompanion's visualization of personal health data as another attribute to relieve stress as it defuses possible upsetting health-related imaginations. Altogether, this implies that the use of the PCompanion could have a positive effect on the participants' affective states that appears. Finally, entering the information into the app through the diary function could also give some participants a stronger sense of actively managing the disease than just being a passive part of it. Furthermore, some participants also stated that they would feel more at eye-to-eye with their MD through continuous access to wh health information. These two arguments support the fact that the PCompanion-use might also affect participants' sense of enactive mastery experience as it regains their control behavior and thereby enhances self-efficacy.

With regard to RQ 2, several significant relationships appeared that again support the importance of affective states in relation to self-efficacy. Namely, there were significant relationships between depression and self-efficacy for managing a chronic disease, between depression and technical self-efficacy (technical competence belief), and between depression and positive affect. This is supported by the socio-cognitive theory of Bandura [2, 3] and consistent with previous literature highlighting the impact of depression in PD [26]. Additionally, these relationships showed that depression affects self-efficacy across different domains, not only in clinical settings but also in the technology domain. Furthermore, depression also revealed to have a significant relationship with technical commitment. This implies that negative affective states might hinder the

PCompanion-use from the start. However, several participants that scored high on depression still expressed a positive attitude towards the PCompanion and even supported the potential self-efficacy enhancing effect. Hence, the connection between depression and technical commitment might be a very general one and maybe exclude PCompanion-use.

In conclusion, both the quantitative and the qualitative results underline the impact of affective states including depression, anxiety, and uncertainty on self-efficacy and thus on participants' self-management and well-being. However, while interpreting the results, several limitations need to be considered. One being that the majority of participants were also participants or members of a self-help group and frequently took part in group-sport activities. This could mean that the participants were particularly motivated and committed participants and thus individuals that might already have a higher self-efficacy than the average PD patient. Furthermore, it is likely that there are individual differences in the comprehension of interview questions as self-efficacy is a subjective topic but also because there were sometimes minor inconsistencies in the interviewer's formulation of the questions. Moreover, only one researcher carried out the analysis. Finally, only long-term use of the PCompanion app can truly offer benefits for self-efficacy can only be said after participants used the app for a longer period. The current study only worked with hypothetical questions regarding this topic, thus providing little information about the actual effect of app use. As a result, further longitudinal studies with the final product are needed to examine this question. Despite these drawbacks, the results of this study enabled us to gain in-depth understanding of PD patients' self-efficacy and in what way PD influenced this construct. Self-efficacy in turn influenced how PD patients feel, think, motivate, and behave and is thus a very important topic for the self-management of PD and the development of technical devices such as the PCompanion to support self-management.

References

1. Bandura, A.: Self-efficacy: toward a unifying theory of behavioral change. Psychol. Rev. **84**(2), 191–215 (1977)
2. Bandura, A.: Self-efficacy: The Exercise of Control. W H Freeman/Times Books/Henry Holt & Co, New York (1997)
3. Bandura, A.: On functional properties of perceived self-efficacy revisited. J. Manage. **38**(1), 9–44 (2012)
4. Banik, A., Schwarzer, R., Knoll, N., Czekierda, K., Luszczynska, A.: Self-efficacy and quality of life among people with cardiovascular diseases: a meta-analysis. Rehabil. Psychol. **63**(2), 295–312 (2018)
5. Beck, A.T., Steer, R.A., Brown, G.K.: BDI-fast Screen for Medical Patients: Manual. Psychological Corporation, San Antonio (1996)
6. Bodenheimer, T., Lorig, K., Holman, H., Grumback, K.: Patient self-management of chronic disease in primary care. JAMA **288**(19), 2469–2475 (2002)
7. Braun, V., Clarke, V.: Using thematic analysis in psychology. Qual. Res. Psychol. **3**(2), 77–101 (2006)
8. Breyer, B., Bluemke, M.: Deutsche Version der Positive and Negative Affect Schedule PANAS (GESIS Panel). Zusammenstellung sozialwissenschaftlicher Items und Skalen (2016)

9. Calandri, E., Graziano, F., Borghi, M., Bonino, S.: Depression, positive and negative affect, optimism and health-related quality of life in recently diagnosed multiple sclerosis patients: the role of identity, sense of coherence, and self-efficacy. J. Happiness Stud. Interdisc. Forum Subject. Well Being **19**(1), 277–295 (2018)
10. Charlton, G.S., Barrow, C.J.: Coping and self-help group membership in Parkinson's disease: an exploratory qualitative study. Health Soc. Care **10**(6), 472–478 (2002)
11. Chen, K., Chan, A.H.S.: A review of technology acceptance by older adults. Gerontechnology **10**(1), 1–12 (2011)
12. Chenoweth, L., Gallagher, R., Sheriff, J.N., Donoghue, J., Stein-Parbury, J.: Factors Supporting Self-Management in Parkinson's Disease: Implications for Nursing Practice, pp. 187–193. Blackwell Publishing, Malden (2008)
13. Chiu, C., Liu, C.: Understanding older adult's technology adoption and withdrawal for elderly care and education: mixed method analysis from national survey. J. Med. Internet Res. **19**(11), 374 (2017)
14. Czaja, S.J.: Factors predicting the use of technology: findings from the center for research and education on aging and technology enhancement (CREATE). Psychol. Aging **21**(2), 333–352 (2006)
15. Dorsey, E., et al.: Projected number of people with Parkinson disease in the most populous nations, 2005 through 2030. Neurology **68**(5), 384–386 (2007)
16. Field, A.: Discovering Statistics Using SPSS, 3rd edn. SAGE Publications Ltd., London (2009)
17. Freund, T., Gensichen, J., Goetz, K., Szecsenyi, J., Mahler, C.: Evaluating self-efficacy for managing chronic disease: psychometric properties of the six-item self efficacy scale in Germany. J. Eval. Clin. Pract. **19**(1), 39–43 (2013)
18. Gallagher, R., Donoghue, J., Chenoweth, L., Stein-Parbury, J.: Self-management in older patients with chronic illness. Int. J. Nurs. Pract. **14**(373), 382 (2008)
19. Hoffmeyer-Zlotnik, J.H.P., Warner, U.: Sociodemographic Questionnaire Modules for Comparative Social Surveys. SPS. Springer, Cham (2018). https://doi.org/10.1007/978-3-319-90209-8
20. Judge, T.A., Erez, A., Bono, J.E., Thoresen, C.J.: Are measures of self-esteem, neuroticism, locus of control, and generalized self-efficacy indicators of a common core construct? J. Pers. Soc. Psychol. **83**(3), 693–710 (2002)
21. Kliem, S., Mößle, T., Zenger, M., Bräher, E.: Reliability and validity of the beck depression inventory-fast screen for medical patients in the general German population. J. Affect. Disord. **156**, 236–239 (2014)
22. Kristofferzon, M., Lindqvist, R., Nilsson, A.: Relationship between coping, coping resources and quality of life in patients with chronic illness: a pilot study. Scand. J. Caring Sci. **25**, 476–483 (2010)
23. Linares-del Rey, M., Vela-Desojo, L., Cano-de la Cuerda, R.: Mobile phone applications in Parkinson's disease: a systematic review. Neurología **34**(1), 38–54 (2019)
24. Luszczynska, A., Gutiérrez-Doña, B., Schwarzer, R.: General self-efficacy in various domains of human functioning: evidence from five countries. Int. J. Psychol. **40**(2), 80–89 (2005)
25. Mertens, A., Rasche, P., Theis, S., Bröhl, C., Wille, M. Use of information and communication technology in healthcare context by older adults in Germany: initial results of the Tech4Age long-term study. i-com **16**(2) 165–180 (2017)
26. Mhyre, T.M., Boyd, J.T., Hamil, R.W., Maguire-Zeiss, K.A.: Parkinson's disease. Subcell. Biochem. **65**, 389–455 (2012)
27. Mulligan, H.F., Arps, G., Bancroft, N., Mountfort, R., Polkinghorne, A.: 'Living Well with Parkinson's': evaluation of a programme to promote self-management. J. Nurs. Healthcare Chron. Illness Banner **3**(3), 222–233 (2011)

28. Neyer, F., Felber, J., Gebhardt, C.: Entwicklung und Validierung einer Kurzskala zur Erfassung von Technikbereitschaft. Diagnostica **58**, 87–99 (2012)
29. Nilsson, M.H., Hagell, P., Iwarsson, S.: Psychometric properties of the general self efficacy scale in Parkinson's disease. Acta Neurol. Scand. **132**, 89–96 (2015)
30. Ritter, P.L., Lorig, K.: The english and spanish self-efficacy to manage chronic disease scale measures were validated using multiple studies. J. Clin. Epidemiol. **67**(11), 1265–1273 (2014)
31. Tahamassian, K., Moghadam, N.J.: Relationship between self-efficacy and symptoms of anxiety, depression, worry and social avoidance in a normal sample of students. Iran J. Psychiatry Behav. Sci. **5**(2), 91–98 (2011)
32. Theis, S., et al.: What do you need to know to stay healthy? – health information needs and seeking behaviour of older adults in Germany. In: Bagnara, S., Tartaglia, R., Albolino, S., Alexander, T., Fujita, Y. (eds.) IEA 2018. AISC, vol. 822, pp. 516–525. Springer, Cham (2019). https://doi.org/10.1007/978-3-319-96077-7_55
33. Thümler, R.: Morbus Parkinson: Ein Leitfaden für Klinik und Praxis. Springer, Heidelberg (2013). https://doi.org/10.1007/978-3-642-56392-8
34. Van der Eijk, M., Faber, M.J., Al Shamma, S., Munneke, M., Bloem, B.R.: Moving towards patient-centered healthcare for patients with Parkinson's disease. Parkinsonism Related Disord. **17**, 360–364 (2011). https://doi.org/10.1016/j.parkreldis.2011.02.012
35. Vaportzis, E., Clausen, M.G., Gow, A.J.: Older adults perceptions of technology and barriers to interacting with tablet computers: a focus group study. Front Pschol. **8**, 1687 (2017)
36. Watson, D., Clark, L.A., Tellegen, A.: Development and validation of brief measures of positive and negative affect: the PANAS scales. J. Personal. Soc. Psychol. **54**, 1063–1070 (1988)
37. Wolf, E.: Fehldiagnose Morbus Parkinson. Psychopraxis **15**(4), 19–22 (2012)

Research on Cognitive Training of Digital Application System Introducing Reminiscence Therapy for the Experience of People with Dementia

PeiFen Wu[1](✉), Hui-Jiun Hu[2], WenFu Wang[3], KuangYi Fan[4], and ChunWe Huang[1]

[1] Department of Information Management and Master Program in Digital Content Technology and Management, National Changhua University of Education, Changhua City, Taiwan
pfwu@cc.ncue.edu.tw

[2] Department of Visual Arts, National Chiayi University, Chiayi, Taiwan

[3] Department of Neurology, Changhua Christian Hospital, Changhua, Taiwan

[4] The Graduate Institute of Animation and Multimedia Design, National University of Tainan, Tainan, Taiwan

Abstract. Dementia is a very common disease among the elderly, and its main symptom is cognitive dysfunction. Relevant research suggests that the course of dementia can be delayed through non-pharmacological intervention. Therefore, the purpose of this research is to develop a cognitive training system with the aid of digital technology to help people with dementia strengthen their brain and slow their cognitive function degradation. This research cooperates with the Changhua Christian Hospital in Taiwan, and the research subjects are a total of 16 mild dementia patients with an average age of 79.6 years old, who are divided into a traditional group and a digital group. The experimental tool is the "Recall" digital cognitive application system, as developed by this research, which includes sharing nostalgic storytelling and the introduction of technology for cognitive training. There are five types of systematic cognitive training questions: quiz questions, calculation questions, puzzle questions, weight questions, and silhouette questions, which mainly train memory, logic, and concentration. After treatment, the subjects are investigated via behavior observation, questionnaires, and interviews to learn their perceptions of the usability and experience of digital cognitive application systems for patients with dementia, and the Pearson correlation coefficient is used to analyze the relevance of the four factors of the experience, namely, feel, sense, relate, and think. The results show that the experience of using this system is significantly related in the factors of sense, relate, and think. On the whole, the application system developed in this research should have benefit in the introduction of technology into reminiscence therapy for patients with mild dementia via cognitive training through games.

Keywords: Dementia · Cognitive training · Cognitive stimulation · Reminiscence therapy · User experience

C. Stephanidis et al. (Eds.): HCII 2020, LNCS 12426, pp. 763–777, 2020.
https://doi.org/10.1007/978-3-030-60149-2_58

1 Introduction

In order to delay the aging rate and activate the brain, many scholars are committed to studying the issue of dementia. Non-pharmacological therapy can delay the cognitive function decline caused by dementia. It is pointed out that cognitive functional training or external memory aids can be used in cognition and memory training to improve forgetful behavior (Beigl 2000; DeVaul and Corey 2003; Levinson 1997). Takeda et al. (2012) mentioned non-pharmacological therapy methods for mental symptoms, including cognitive training, cognitive rehabilitation, cognitive stimulation therapy, multisensory stimulation, reminiscence therapy, music therapy, etc. Reminiscence therapy is a treatment activity often used for the care of dementia patients, as it emphasizes the process of reminiscence as a pleasant experience. Re-experience through familiar activities can link with past life events, increase socialization, and produce self-confidence and pleasure effects (McDougall et al. 1997; Watt and Cappeliez 2000). Rubin et al. (1998) mentioned that reminiscence bumps occur when people look back at life, and the reminiscence trigger phase can cause a strong and positive response (Hepper et al. 2012).

Most studies show that proper technology introduction can effectively delay the degradation of the elderly. The game developed by Hall and Marston (2014) allows seniors to learn knowledge while playing to improve their quality of life; Foo et al. (2017) developed a guessing game "Guess it" to help caregivers analyze the patient's cognitive status. Zheng et al. (2017) used game intervention to treat patient coordination, which improved both cognitive function and mental state. Related technology-assisted design emphasizes that cognitive function stimulation can help brain activation and reduce the risk of dementia. However, in addition to considering the daily activities, behavioral safety, and psychological symptoms of patients with dementia, technology-assisted design may also focus on companionship to increase patients' interest in life, give appropriate sensory stimulation, and allow patients to continue using their brain.

In addition to reducing the burden on caregivers, improving the mood of dementia patients is a major research direction for the assistive technology for dementia. At present, system development in terms of the emotional factor is still relatively lacking, thus, there are still research and development issues to be explored. Patients with dementia can no longer judge or resolve things at the later stage, thus, if their cognitive function can be promoted at the early stage, in order to stabilize their current function and delay the progression of the disease, early treatment will provide the opportunity to prevent and slow the degradation. Therefore, the purpose of this research is to introduce a digital cognitive application system in the early stage of decline for patients with mild dementia. This study first performed application system prototype development, and then, conducted user experience evaluation surveys to achieve the benefit of delaying cognitive degradation.

2 Literature Review

2.1 Non-pharmacological Therapy for Dementia: Cognitive Stimulation

General cognitive functions include various functions, such as attention, memory, language ability, spatial orientation, decision-making, and execution, and dementia is an irreversible symptom that produces cognitive impairment. While clinical drugs related to dementia have been continuously developed, there are no exact drugs that can cure dementia, thus, seeking non-pharmacological therapy has become an important method for the treatment of dementia. Takeda et al. (2012) pointed out that non-pharmacological therapy has an improvement effect on cognitive function, the activities of daily living (ADL), and the behavioral and psychological symptoms of dementia (BPSD). Orrell et al. (2012) believed that cognitive stimulation aimed at memory and thinking capacity can improve the quality of life of patients with dementia and improve their communication and interaction skills.

Cognitive Stimulation Therapy (CST) is a non-pharmacological therapy proposed by Spector et al. (2003) and his research team. Cognitive stimulation training is divided into compensatory and restorative. The purpose of the compensatory strategy is to classify and organize the received information through internal and external training; the restorative strategy is to allow the subject to practice reminiscence of past things, such as reminiscence therapy and repeated memory training (Sitzer et al. 2006). The contents of such therapy cover a variety of different areas, including childhood, food, other types of memories, word spelling, and puzzle games, and are designed to improve patients' brain activity and increase sensory stimuli, which is helpful to people with mild cognitive impairment and patients with moderate dementia (Craig 2018).

2.2 Reminiscence Therapy

Reminiscence therapy is a psychological intervention therapy widely used for dementia. This process involves discussions of past events and experiences, and specific prompts and props are used to evoke the patient's memory or dialogue. Woods (1996) pointed out that reminiscence therapy is to recall profound past life experiences through the process of reminiscence, and then, increase the interactions between the elderly and others, thus, it is suitable for patients with dementia. This approach can improve patients' psychological state (O'Philbin et al. 2018). Reminiscence can maintain personal self-identity and a stable psychological mood, which helps patients to be free from frustration and feelings of helplessness. Therefore, reminiscence therapy, which can effectively promote the cognitive function of dementia patients, is regarded as one of the important strategies for psychotherapy activities (Ball and Haight 2005; Hope 1998).

The operation methods of reminiscence therapy are divided into individual therapy and group therapy. Compared with individual therapy, group therapy is a better choice when the staff and material resources for long-term care are limited (Syed Elias et al. 2015). The main advantages of group reminiscence therapy are to share experiences with each other, let individuals learn how to communicate with a group, and increase the ability to interact with society (Burnside and Haight 1994), thus, group reminiscence therapy will improve the elderly's cohesion to and communication with the group and the parent-child relationship (Bender et al. 1998).

2.3 Technology-Assisted Care Therapy Applications

Technology is an indispensable part of modern people's life with a wide range of uses, including safety, navigation, social networking, etc., and is used in many environments, such as medical or care systems (van der Roest et al. 2017). Researchers have begun to introduce technology into the deferral and treatment of dementia patients, and have developed many applications to train cognitive impairment. Lazar et al. (2018) believed that the introduction coverage of Information and Communication Technology (ICT) includes hardware, content, applications, and navigation. Compared with traditional nursing staffs, the introduction of technology on a tablet or computer can improve the patient's self-confidence and sense of achievement. As mobile devices facilitate higher mobility, patients can conduct their own training at home, and even simple training will help patients improve their cognitive function and increase their interactions with their families (Kueider et al. 2014).

Doniger et al. (2018) introduced technology into their experiment to prevent dementia, where participants were middle-aged with a history of dementia in their families. They used virtual reality in combination with exercise to train, and the results showed that the risks for developing dementia were low for those who had participated in the experiment, which confirmed that the introduction of technology to delay dementia treatment has positive benefits. Linda, Adi, and Eric developed technology for dementia patients to introduce adjuvant therapy, which can improve the quality of life of dementia patients and their families. Therefore, there is still much room for improvement in the field of technology.

There are many application systems developed for people with dementia to perform non-pharmacological therapy in an entertaining manner. The < Sea Hero Quest > , as jointly developed by the Alzheimer's Research Centre in the UK and Deutsche Telekom, trains sense and reactivity through games to help scientists study dementia and understand how the brain works to find more effective treatments and prevention methods (Rigg 2017). The extensive use of intelligent technology is an important strategy for contemporary non-pharmacological therapy to meet dementia patients' needs for life and health care. Technical assistance brings new opportunities for the care and treatment of dementia, which can reduce the burden of care, improve the participation of non-pharmacological therapy, slow down degradation, control dementia behaviors and psychological symptoms, and assist in determining the degree of dementia.

2.4 User Experience

"Experience" can be obtained through activities, sensory and psychological feelings, and learning, and be simultaneously stimulated by physical sceneries and sounds in the context, as well as intangible services and experiences (Baker and Kennedy 1994; Tynan and McKechnie 2009). Regarding the user experience, Schmitt (1999) proposed Strategic Experiential Modules (SEMs), which divides the experience behavior into 5 factors, including the experiences of sense, think, feel, act, and relate, thus, a variety of experiences can be created through individual or multiple experience methods. These factors are described according to the needs of this research, as follows:

1. Sense: Create the perception of experience, which consists of sight, hearing, touch, taste, and smell, to achieve the purpose of experiencing through sensory stimulation, and explore what elements can trigger interest.

2. Think: Stimulate users to actively participate in solving tasks, trigger thinking in new and interesting ways in the process, and create a cognitive and problem-solving experience for users.
3. Feel: Feelings can be mild, tender, and positive feelings that can lead to joy, pride, and even strong emotions of excitement. It mainly explores which design will make users recall the past, and which will cause emotional changes and integrate into nostalgic situations.
4. Act: Through personal experience and interaction, it will affect life styles and behaviors, and change the original cognitive attitude, generate new life styles and interaction modes, and explore whether users will increase their willingness to participate in similar experience activities after experiencing the interactive technology.
5. Relate: Combine the above four experience modes to explore the correlation between the user and other users.

Referring to the strategy experience module, this research divided the experience behavior into 5 factors. Among them, the experience of act is an analysis factor that has been previously used, thus, this research mainly analyzed the situation of users in system usage, and the act experience was not included in this research analysis, meaning analysis was based on the experience factors of sense, think, feel, and relate.

3 Research Method

A digital cognitive system designed in the Taiwanese nostalgic style was developed for patients with dementia by this research, which combined photo story sharing and cognitive training questions, in order to analyze the benefits of a digital cognitive system for reminiscence therapy, and explore the experience of use by patients with dementia.

3.1 Research Method and Implementation

Application System Prototype Development Phase. The initial period of this research was system design, which focused on nostalgic image investigation, interface design for the elderly, evaluation, and prototype design of dementia care units. System prototype design and revision were carried out with the literature research method, questionnaire survey method, expert in-depth interviews, and other methods.

(1) Preliminary prototype design of the application system: This digital *reminiscence* system was named "Recall", with "playing together, reminisce, longing for more" as the core. The nostalgic elements collected in the system design reference were the design style and cognitive question bank. The nostalgic old songs familiar to people with dementia were used as the background music to enable them to be in a nostalgic atmosphere. The number of participants was 2–4 each time, which allowed participants and accompanying persons to enter the nostalgic situation and play together to achieve the purpose of interacting with people.

(2) A total of 4 medical experts and interactive technology design experts were invited to conduct system evaluation. The opinions of the experts were obtained via semi-structured interviews to revise the cognitive question bank, in order to better meet the cognitive training needs of dementia patients.
(3) In order to come up with operational suggestions, such as the system and experimental procedures, pre-tests were performed after the system prototype was completed. A total of 5 non-dementia patients over 65 years of age were recruited in the pre-test experimental stage, and all of them had used smartphones for an average of 7 years or more. Observation and interview methods were used to give them operational tasks to understand their technology use behaviors.
(4) System modification: Corrections were made based on the above survey results.

Usability Experience Analysis. In order to explore the experience of patients with dementia when using digital cognitive systems, observations, interviews, and questionnaires were used for investigation. The study subjects were 16 patients with mild dementia in the Dementia Service Base (Deyiyuan) of the Changhua Christian Hospital's Chinese District, with an average age of 79.6 years. The experimental tool used is the digital cognitive system, as constructed in this research, for group reminiscence therapy. The entire experiment was recorded with a camera for subsequent research and analysis. During the experiment, researchers observed the behavior of the subjects and recorded them on paper, and after the experiment, the records were used in combination with the questionnaires to investigate the users' experience.

In order to understand the differences in the use of traditional and digital cognitive training in patients with dementia, this experiment was divided into two groups, the traditional group and the digital group. The subjects' faces are blocked or blurred to protect the privacy and meet the requirements of academic ethics.

3.2 The Research Hypotheses

The purpose of this research was to investigate the differences in usability and experience between patients with dementia in the digital group and the traditional group. The research hypotheses are, as follows:

H1: The traditional group has significant positive correlation in the use of cognitive training.
H2: The digital group has significant positive correlation in the use of cognitive training.
H3: The traditional group has significant impact on the experience of patients with dementia.
H4: The digital group has significant impact on the experience of patients with dementia.
H5: Compared with the traditional group, the digital group can significantly affect the experience of patients with dementia.

3.3 Digital Cognitive Application System

System Development. This research developed the system based on the literature review and field visit data, and consulted relevant medical experts. After several tests and corrections, a tool for this research experiment was produced. The content of this research question bank is shown in Fig. 1.

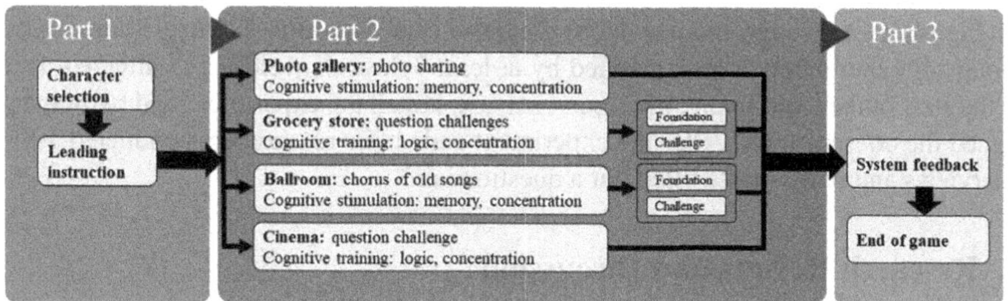

Fig. 1. System architecture diagram

System Interface. Due to the participants' lack of scientific and technological operation experience, system operation was performed by touch, in order to reduce the operating burden. This system's operation process starts from the homepage with character selection and teaching guidance in order. After entering the nostalgic old street, users can freely choose any level (Fig. 2). Among them, simple questions must be answered in the grocery store and leather-silhouette show be conducted before one can challenge the questions to receive a reward.

Fig. 2. System interface

3.4 Experimental Process

Experimental Design. This research arranged a pre-test experiment 2 weeks before the formal experiment to simulate the possible problems in the formal experiment, and a total of 5 elderly people were recruited as the pre-test subjects.

In this research, in cooperation with Changhua Christian Hospital, the experiment was conducted in a place familiar to the subjects. The formal experiment was divided into the experimental group (digital group) and the control group (traditional group).

The formal experimental test was performed once a week for two weeks. The subjects were all patients with mild dementia, as diagnosed by the hospital, and two or three patients were tested in one group. Two experiments were performed in each group, and the total time of each experiment was about 90 min. In order to prevent the subjects having prior knowledge and considering the subjects' forgetful characteristics, the two groups of experiments were separated by at least 7 days to avoid being affected. Prior to the start of the experiment, the researchers explained the experiment and participants signed the consent form. After the experiment ended, the researchers conducted 1-to-1 interviews and participants filled out a questionnaire.

4 Research Results and Discussion

4.1 Analysis of Subject's Basic Data

A total of 16 subjects were recruited in this research, with an average age of 79.5 years, a maximum age of 94 years, and a minimum age of 65 years; 7 subjects received the clinical dementia CDR score of 0.5, and 9 received the score of 1. The educational level for most subjects was from elementary school to middle school; nearly half of the subjects had never used any interactive technology.

4.2 Questionnaire Reliability and Validity Analysis

A total of 16 valid questionnaires were collected in this research experiment. After reliability analysis, the Cronbach's Alpha value of the questionnaire of the traditional group was 0.887 and higher than 0.7, and the Cronbach's Alpha of the questionnaire of the experimental group was 0.850 and higher than 0.7, indicating that the questions have reliability. The traditional group questionnaire data was orthogonally rotated using the maximum variation method of the main axis method. A total of 10 factors were extracted, which could explain a total of 94.376% of the amount of variation; a total of 9 factors were extracted for the digital group, which could explain a total of 90.300% of the variation, showing that the scale has construct validity.

4.3 Correlation Coefficient Analysis of Usability Factors

In order to understand the correlation between the various factors of the questionnaire and the topic, the Pearson correlation analysis method was used for analysis. The analysis results show that the usability of traditional cognitive training had significant positive correlation with efficiency of the r value $(14) = .615$, $p = .011$, efficacy of $r(14) = .892$, $p < .001$, task of $r(14) = .957$, $p < .001$, and learning of $r(14) = .901$, $p < .001$, while the usability and satisfaction of $r(14) = .105$ and $p = .70$ had no significant correlation (as shown in Table 1).

The usability of digital cognitive training had significant positive correlation with efficiency of the r value $(14) = .666$, $p = .005$, efficacy of $r(14) = .808$, $p < .001$, task of $r(14) = .872$, $p < .001$, and cognitive use of $r(14) = .617$, $p < .011$, while usability was not significantly correlated to the learning of $r(14) = .470$, $p = .066$ or the satisfaction of $r(14) = .286$, $p = .284$ (Table 2).

Table 1. Usability correlation matrix for traditional group

	Usability	Effectiveness	Efficacy	Task	Learning	Satisfaction
Usability	–					
Effectiveness	.615*	–				
Efficacy	.892**	.532*	–			
Task	.957**	.488	.801**	–		
Learning	.901**	.552*	.838**	.760**	–	
Satisfaction	.105	.103	−.118	.034	.155	–

*p < .05, **p < .01

Table 2. Usability correlation matrix for digital group

	Usability	Effectiveness	Efficacy	Task	Learning	Cognitive use	Satisfaction
Usability	–						
Effectiveness	.666**	–					
Efficacy	.808**	.594*	–				
Task	.872**	.496	.643**	–			
Learning	.470	.226	.408	.112	–		
Cognitive use	.617*	.285	.397	.485	.113	–	
Satisfaction	.286	.293	.119	.140	.293	−.062	–

*p < .05, **p < .01

4.4 Experience Correlation Analysis of Traditional Group

The experience of traditional cognitive training was significantly positively correlated in feel $r(14) = .781$, $p < .001$, relate $r(14) = .778$, $p < .001$, and think $r(14) = .765$, $p = .001$, and negatively correlated in the factor of sense $r(14) = -.068$, $p = .804$ (Table 3).

Table 3. Experience correlation matrix of traditional group

	Experience	Feel	Sense	Relate	Think
Experience	–				
Feel	.781**	–			
Sense	−.068	−.339	–		
Relate	.778**	.525*	−.333	–	
Think	.765**	.475	−.011	.349	–

*p < .05, **p < .01

According to the results of the traditional group questionnaire analysis, it was found that the experience factors of feel, relate, and think were more influential (Fig. 3) in the experiment, and the subject would think of his or her own memories through the nostalgic elements of traditional cognitive training materials, and thus, extend more relevant memories.

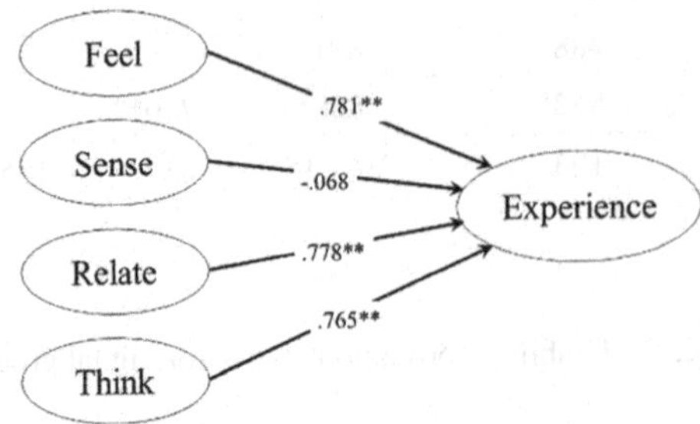

Fig. 3. Link diagram of experience correlation of traditional group

4.5 Experience Correlation Analysis of Experimental Group

Digital cognitive training had significant positive correlations with sense of the r value (14) = .730, p = .001, relate of r (14) = .807, p < .001, and think of r (14) = .580, p = .019, but had no significant correction with the factor of the feel of r (14) = .385, p = .14 (Table 4).

Table 4. Digital group experience correlation rotation component matrix

	Experience	Feel	Sense	Relate	Think
Experience	–				
Feel	.385	–			
Sense	.730**	.707**	–		
Relate	.807**	.050	.274	–	
Think	.580*	−.334	.212	.393	–

*p < .05, **p < .01

According to the analysis results of the digital group, it was known that sense, relate, and think had greater impact on user experience (Fig. 4). The subjects were happy in the experiment due to the sound effects of the digital cognitive system. When sharing photos or answering cognitive training questions, there was discussions with each other, and they also recalled the past through the nostalgic elements in the system and further shared their experiences. The sense of experience of the digital group was significantly related to the factors of sense, relate, and think.

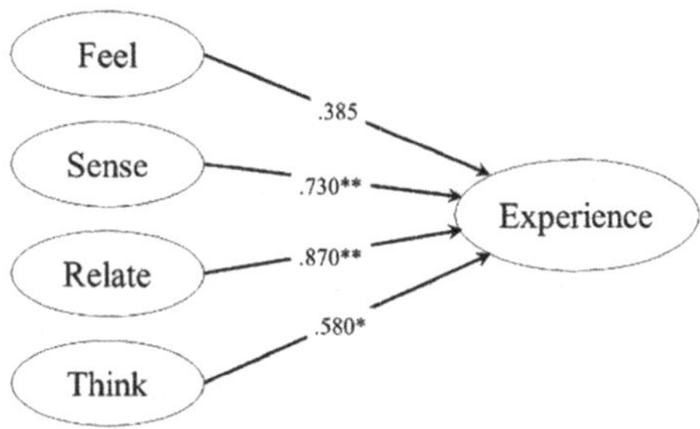

Fig. 4. Link diagram of digital group experience

4.6 Analysis of Differences in Experience Between Two Groups

In order to explore the differences between the subjects in the digital and traditional experience, the questionnaire was used for t testing of the dependent samples for each factor and the overall experience. The traditional group and the digital group had significant differences in the related factors and overall experience. The results are shown in Table 5:

Table 5. T-Test results of difference between experience of two groups

Factor	Mean (standard deviation)		Degrees of freedom	T value	P value
	Digital group	Traditional group			
Feel	4.59 (.27)	4.37 (.42)	15	1.710	.108
Sense	4.40 (.62)	4.08 (.49)	15	1.505	.153
Relate	4.22 (.85)	3.53 (.76)	15	5.129	.000*
Think	4.33 (.78)	4.06 (.79)	15	.980	.343
Experience	4.41 (.38)	4.05 (.38)	15	3.661	.002*

$*p < .05$

The analysis of the above hypotheses is integrated into Table 6:

Table 6. Analysis results research hypotheses

Hypotheses	Result
H1: The traditional group has significant positive correlation in the use of cognitive training	Partially accepted
H2: The digital group has significant positive correlation in the use of cognitive training	Partially accepted

(*continued*)

Table 6. (*continued*)

Hypotheses	Result
H3: The traditional group has significant impact on the experience of patients with dementia	Partially accepted
H4: The digital group has significant impact on the experience of patients with dementia	Partially accepted
H5: Compared with the traditional group, the digital group can significantly affect the experience of patients with dementia	Partially accepted

4.7 Behavior Observation Analysis

The experiences of the two groups were discussed on the basis of the results of behavior observations:

(1) Sense factor: The overall design of the content of this system was based on the visual style of nostalgic elements, the auditory stimulation of old songs, the tactile sensation of physical characters, traditional retro microphones, and intuitive screen touch operations to shape the perception experience and enable the overall nostalgic impression, and the digital group was provided with better sensory pleasure and satisfaction than the traditional group.

(2) Feel factor: The textbook content of this experiment was novel to the subjects, and all of them showed positive emotions during the two-week experiment; however, the textbook of the traditional group could stimulate the nostalgia of the subjects more than the digital group to generate the emotional links of personal memory; the teaching materials of the digital group initially caused tension and psychological rejection for some subjects. Both groups were given feedback and physical rewards, which were also helpful to the subject's emotional encouragement, in order that they could be immersed in the activity and have positive participation, and joyful emotions were even induced. The content design of this topic can provide good stimulation for feelings. Especially regarding some of the subjects that had never been exposed to such systems; they felt very powerful when they suddenly realized that they could also use computers, which gave them a higher sense of accomplishment and identity.

(3) Think factor: The think factor requires intelligence. The thinking training at each level of this experiment can stimulate the subjects' problem-solving ability and motivate their longing for freshness and attempt to try. This shows the difficulty of the design of this experiment can effectively meet the cognitive stimulation of the two groups.

(4) Relate factor: Relevance includes the above three factors (sense, feel, and think), which allowed the subjects to integrate into the group life via this activity, and have a good interactive relationship through this experimental activity. In addition to rational cognitive thinking during the experimental process, the subjects also exchanged their memories and solved problems with each other. The end result

shows that the two groups were significantly different, emotional memory links were generated through system guidance, and self-value was built in the activity.

It was clearly observed in the overall experience that the subjects felt the novelty of using the touch screen, there was a lot of excitement in the activities of the digital group, the interactions between the subjects were obviously more than those of the traditional group, and the group members helped each other to answer questions. In contrast, photos sharing or answers in the traditional group were made by the subjects themselves, and there were fewer opportunities for communication. The digital group was more willing to share photos and past memories, the subjects actively helped other subjects with weaker capacity in cognitive problem solving, and they were more intoxicated by the singing activities than the traditional group. In the interviews after the experiment, some subjects stated that they had less exposure to digital technology in the past. They felt it was refreshing and fun, as the pictures and nostalgic elements in the system could trigger their memories and make them recall the details of their past lives.

5 Conclusion

This research cooperated with Changhua Christian Hospital in Taiwan, took local patients with mild dementia as the research subjects, designed a digital cognitive application system "Recall" for patients with dementia via Non-pharmacological therapy combining cognitive stimulation, cognitive training, reminiscence therapy, etc., and explored the user experience of a digital cognitive application system for patients with dementia through behavior observations, questionnaires, and interviews.

This research conducted a survey of the usability and experience of patients with mild dementia, and found that most patients with mild dementia had no obstacles in the operation of the system, and they highly praised the rewards provided by the system and the feedback of the sound effects. The patients in the digital group were more willing to share memories with others and interacted more frequently with each other. They were also immersed in thinking about the cognitive training questions designed for the digital group, and actively assisted their peers when answering the questions. They happily swayed their bodies with the randomly chosen melodies during music therapy. The experience of patients with dementia in the factor of sense showed happiness, a sense of accomplishment, and pride; in terms of the factor of relate, it could effectively promote their social skills; for the factor of think, it generated resonation and inspired more memories. This system allows patients with mild dementia to be integrated into reminiscence therapy, which can promote cognitive stimulation training for people with mild dementia, be connected to emotions and memories, and help enhance positive emotional factors and promote social interaction.

One part of the cognitive training system developed by this research is nostalgic storytelling and the spontaneous process of reminiscence therapy to recall memories through storytelling, and such cognitive training can help stimulate memory and language skills, promote communication and increase socialization, and generate confidence and pleasure. The other part is cognitive training, which mainly trains memory, logical judgment, and other abilities. Cognitive training can slow the decline of cognitive ability, thus, in addition to helping patients with dementia, it can strengthen the brain and prevent degradation in elderly people without dementia. The introduction of technology will contribute to the application of dementia treatment.

This study has both research and practical value, as it is combined with the hospital's professional dementia medical team, and is a research cooperation integrating design, technology, and medical fields. The integration and use of different professional knowledge, resources, and experience can be implemented in the clinical application of reminiscence therapy and knowledge training in the future, and will directly contribute to dementia patients and their families.

Acknowledgment. This research is based on work supported by the Ministry of Science and Technology of Taiwan, Republic of China, under contract MOST 108-2410-H-018-009-. The authors would like to thank the Changhua Christian Hospital for supporting this research. This study gives special thanks to the experts, participants, and research team; without them this study could not have been completed.

Ethical Statement: The study was approved by the Research Ethics Committee of National Changhua University of Education, ethics board of no. NCUEREC-107-038. In accordance with this approval and informed consent was taken from all the participants.

References

Baker, S.M., Kennedy, P.E.: Death by nostalgia: a diagnosis of context-specific cases. Adv. Consum. Res. **21**, 169–174 (1994)

Ball, J., Haight, B.: Creating a multisensory environment for dementia: the goals of a Snoezelen room. J. Gerontol. Nurs. **31**(10), 4–10 (2005)

Bender, M., Bauckham, P., Norris, A.: The Therapeutic Purposes of Reminiscence. Sage Publications Ltd., Thousand Oaks (1998)

Beigl, M.: Memo clip: a location-based remembrance appliance. Pers. Technol. **4**(4), 230–233 (2000)

Burnside, I., Haight, B.: Reminiscence and life review: therapeutic interventions for older people. Nurse Pract. **19**(4), 55–61 (1994)

Craig, S.: Helpful Daily Activities for Dementia Patients: 50 Expert Tips and Suggestions to Keep Your Loved One Engaged. Clinical Program Innovation Manager (2018). https://www.seniorlink.com/blog/helpful-daily-activities-for-dementia-patients-50-expert-tips-and-suggestions-to-keep-your-loved-one-engaged

DeVaul, R.W., Corey, V.R.: The memory glasses: subliminal vs. overt memory support with imperfect. In: IEEE International Symposium on Wearable Computers (2003)

Doniger, G.M., et al.: Virtual reality-based cognitive-motor training for middle-aged adults at high Alzheimer's disease risk: a randomized controlled trial. Alzheimer's Dement. **4**, 118–129 (2018). https://doi.org/10.1016/j.trci.2018.02.005

Foo, W.Y., Lim, W.N., Lee, C.S.: Drawing guessing game for the elderly. In: TENCON 2017-2017 IEEE Region 10 Conference, pp. 2236–2241. IEEE, November 2017

Hall, A., Marston, H.: Gaming and Older Adults in the Digital Age of Healthcare (2014). https://doi.org/10.1007/978-3-319-01904-8_55-1

Hepper, E.G., Ritchie, T.D., Sedikides, C., Wildschut, T.: Odyssey's end: lay conceptions of nostalgia reflect its original homeric meaning. Emotion **12**(1), 102–117 (2012)

Hope, K.: The effects of multisensory environments on older people with dementia. J. Psychiatr. Ment. Health Nurs. **5**, 377–386 (1998)

Kueider, A., Krystal, B., Rebok, G.: Cognitive training for older adults: what is it and does it work? (Issue Brief October 2014). Center on Ageing, American Institutes for Research, Washington, D.C., October 2014

Lazar, A., Thompson, H.J., Demiris, G.: Design recommendations for recreational systems involving older adults living with dementia. J. Appl. Gerontol. **37**(5), 595–619 (2018)

Levinson, R.: The planning and execution assistant and trainer (PEAT). Head Trauma Rehabil. **12**, 769–775 (1997)

McDougall, G.J., Blixen, C.E., Suen, L.J.: The process and outcome of life review psychotherapy with depressed homebound older adults. Nurs. Res. **46**(5), 277 (1997)

Orrell, M., Woods, B., Spector, A.: Should we use individual cognitive stimulation therapy to improve cognitive function in people with dementia? BMJ **344**, e633 (2012)

O'Philbin, L., Woods, B., Farrell, E.M., Spector, A.E., Orrell, M.: Reminiscence therapy for dementia: an abridged Cochrane systematic review of the evidence from randomized controlled trials. Expert Rev. Neurother. **18**(9), 715–727 (2018)

Rigg, J.: 'Sea Hero Quest' hides dementia research inside a VR game [Online forum comment]. https://www.engadget.com/2017/08/30/sea-hero-quest-vr/. Accessed 30 Aug 2019

Rubin, D.C., Rahhal, T.A., Poon, L.W.: Things learned in early adulthood are remembered best. Mem. Cogn. **26**, 3–19 (1998)

Spector, A., et al.: Efficacy of an evidence-based cognitive stimulation therapy programme for people with dementia: randomised controlled trial. Br. J. Psychiatry **183**(3), 248–254 (2003)

Schmitt, B.: Experiential marketing. J. Mark. Manag. **15**(1–3), 53–67 (1999). https://doi.org/10.1362/026725799784870496

Syed Elias, S.M., Neville, C., Scott, T.: The effectiveness of group reminiscence therapy for loneliness, anxiety and depression in older adults in long-term care: a systematic review. Geriatr. Nurs. **36**(5), 372–380 (2015)

Sitzer, D.I., Twamley, E.W., Jeste, D.V.: Cognitive training in Alzheimer's disease: a meta-analysis of the literature. Acta Psychiatr. Scand. **114**, 75–90 (2006)

Takeda, M., Tanaka, T., Okochi, M., Kazui, H.: Non-pharmacological intervention for dementia patients. Psychiatry Clin. Neurosci. **66**(1), 1–7 (2012)

Tynan, C., McKechnie, S.: Experience marketing: a review and reassessment. J. Mark. Manag. **25**(5–6), 501–517 (2009)

van der Roest, H., Wenborn, J., Pastink, C., Dröes, R.-M., Orrell, M.: Assistive technology for memory support in dementia. Cochrane Database Syst. Rev. **6**, CD009627 (2017). https://doi.org/10.1002/14651858.cd009627.pub2

Watt, L., Cappeliez, P.: Integrative and instrumental reminiscence therapies for depression in older adults: intervention strategies and treatment effectiveness. Aging Mental Health **4**, 166–177 (2000)

Woods, R.T.: Handbook of the Clinical Psychology of Aging. Wiley & Sons, NY (1996)

Zheng, J., Chen, X., Yu, P.: Game-based interventions and their impact on dementia: a narrative review. Australas. Psychiatry **25**(6), 562–565 (2017)

Author Index

Printed in the United States
By Bookmasters